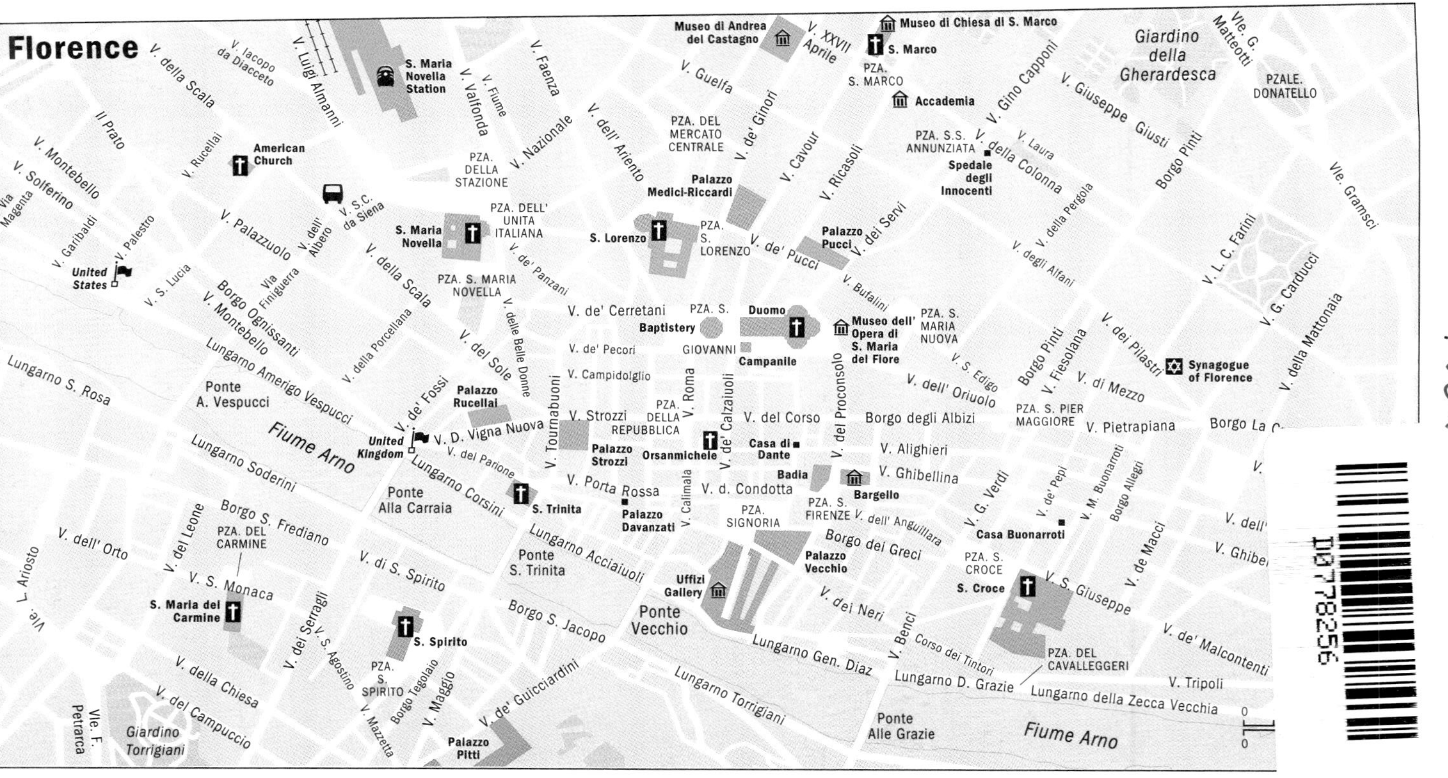

NOTAR
D0778256

TO MAINLAND
Ponte della Libertà
CANNAREGIO
Rio di S. Girolamo
Rio del Battello
CAMPO DEL GHETTO
Canale di Cannareggio
C. Riello
R. terrà di S. Leonardo
CAMPO SAN GEREMIA
Lista di Spagna
Canal Grande
Ponte Scalzi
Riva d.Biasio
Lista d. Bari
Fondamenta di Santa Lucia
SANTA CROCE
CAMPO DEI MORTI
Piccolo
F.d. S.Simeon
Rio Marin
Corte Canal
Canale di Chiara
C. d. Lacca
R. di San Polo
Rio della Saccherre
Rio Nuovo
F.Minotto
CAMPO S. ROCCO
Canale Scomenzera
Rio terra dei Pensieri
Rio Foscari
CAMPO DI SAN MARGHERITA
Rio d. Santa Margherita
C.d. Carrozze
Rio di S. Barnaba
Calle Avogaria
Rio d. Ognissanti
Fondamenta della Zattere
DORSODURO
Canale della Giudecca

Venice

Amex, **3**
Campo dei Frari, **10**
Campo S. Giorgio, **12**
Campo SS. Giovanni e Paolo, **13**
Campo San Salvaatore, **7**
Church of S. Maria Della Salute, **9**
Church of S. Maria Formosa, **14**
Church of San Zaccaria, **11**
Gallerie dell' Accademia, **8**
Hospital (Ospedale Civili), **20**
IYHF, **4**
Palazzo Ducale (Doge's Palace), **6**
Piazza San Marco, **5**
Piazzale Roma, **18**
Ponte Rialto, **21**
Post Office, **2**
Questura di Venezia, **19**
Teatro Goldoni, **15**
Tourist Office (APT), Piazza San Marco, **16**
Tourist Office (APT), Stazione S. Lucia, **17**
Train Station, **1**

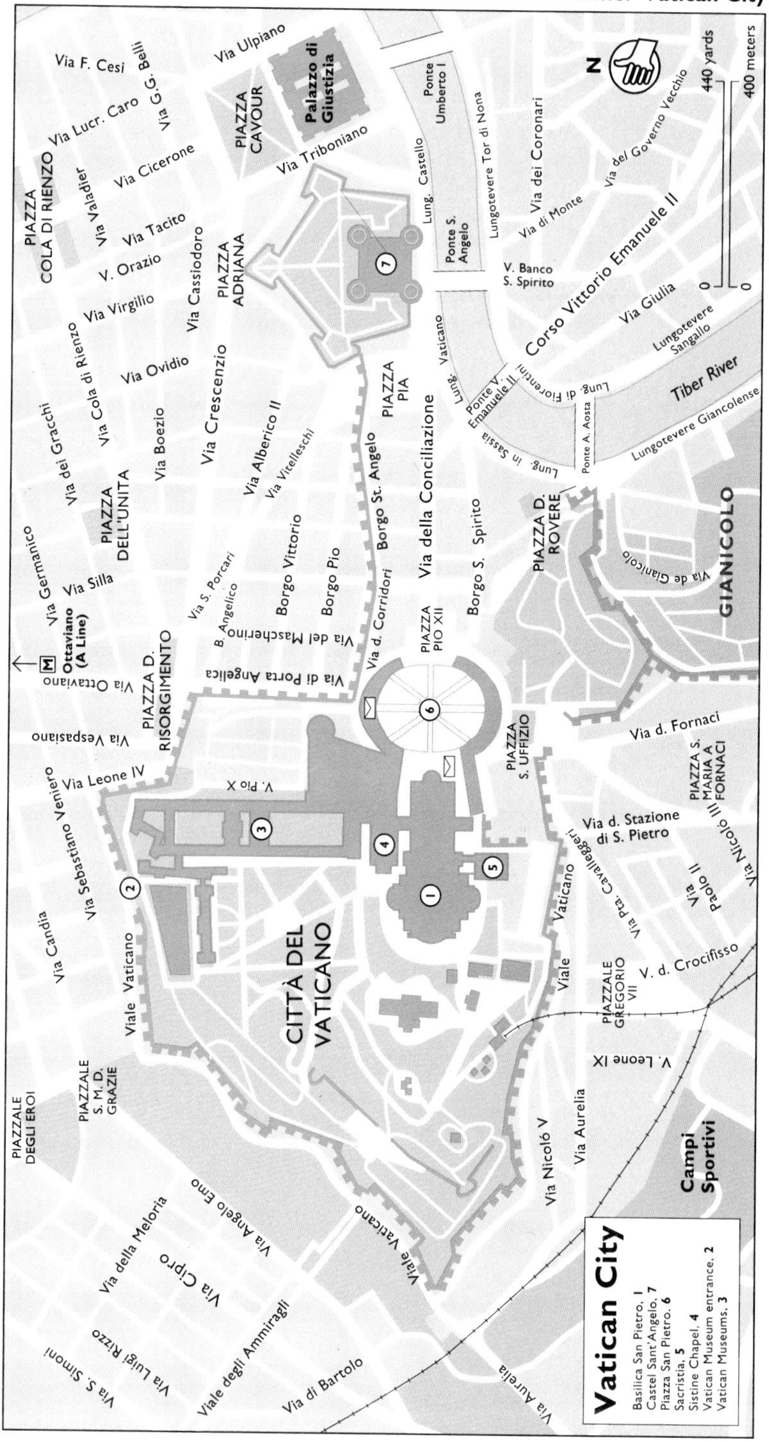
Vatican City
Basilica San Pietro, 1
Castel Sant'Angelo, 7
Piazza San Pietro, 6
Sacristia, 5
Sistine Chapel, 4
Vatican Museum entrance, 2
Vatican Museums, 3
N
0 440 yards
0 400 meters
CITTÀ DEL VATICANO
Palazzo di Giustizia
PIAZZA CAVOUR
PIAZZA COLA DI RIENZO
PIAZZA ADRIANA
PIAZZA PIA
PIAZZA DELL'UNITA
PIAZZA D. RISORGIMENTO
PIAZZA PIO XII
PIAZZA S. UFFIZIO
PIAZZA D. ROVERE
PIAZZA S. MARIA A FORNACI
PIAZZALE GREGORIO VII
PIAZZALE S. M. D. GRAZIE
PIAZZALE DEGLI EROI
GIANICOLO
Campi Sportivi
Tiber River
Ottaviano (A Line)
Via Ulpiano
Via F. Cesi
Via Lucr. Caro
Via G.G. Belli
Via Cicerone
Via Tribonian o
Via Valadier
Via Tacito
V. Orazio
Via Cassiodoro
Via Virgilio
Via Ovidio
Via Cola di Rienzo
Via dei Gracchi
Via Boezio
Via Crescenzio
Via Alberico II
Via Vitelleschi
Via Germanico
Via Silla
Via S. Porcari
B. Angelico
Borgo Vittorio
Borgo Pio
Via del Mascherino
Via di Porta Angelica
Via Ottaviano
Via Vespasiano
Via Leone IV
V. Pio X
Via d. Corridori
Borgo St. Angelo
Via della Conciliazione
Borgo S. Spirito
Ponte Umberto I
Ponte S. Angelo
Lung. Castello
Lungotevere Tor di Nona
Via dei Coronari
Via di Monte
Via del Governo Vecchio
V. Banco S. Spirito
Corso Vittorio Emanuele II
Via Giulia
Lungotevere Sangallo
Lung. Vaticano
Ponte V. Emanuele II
Lung. di Fiorentini
Ponte A. Aosta
Lung. in Sassia
Lungotevere Gianicolense
Via de Gianicolo
Via d. Fornaci
Via d. Stazione di S. Pietro
Via Pta. Cavalleggeri
Via Nicolò III
Via Paolo II
V. d. Crocifisso
V. Leone IX
Viale Vaticano
Via Sebastiano Veniero
Via Candia
Via Nicolò V
Via Aurelia
Via Angelo Emo
Via della Meloria
Via Cipro
Via Luigi Rizzo
Via S. Simoni
Viale degli Ammiragli
Via di Bartolo

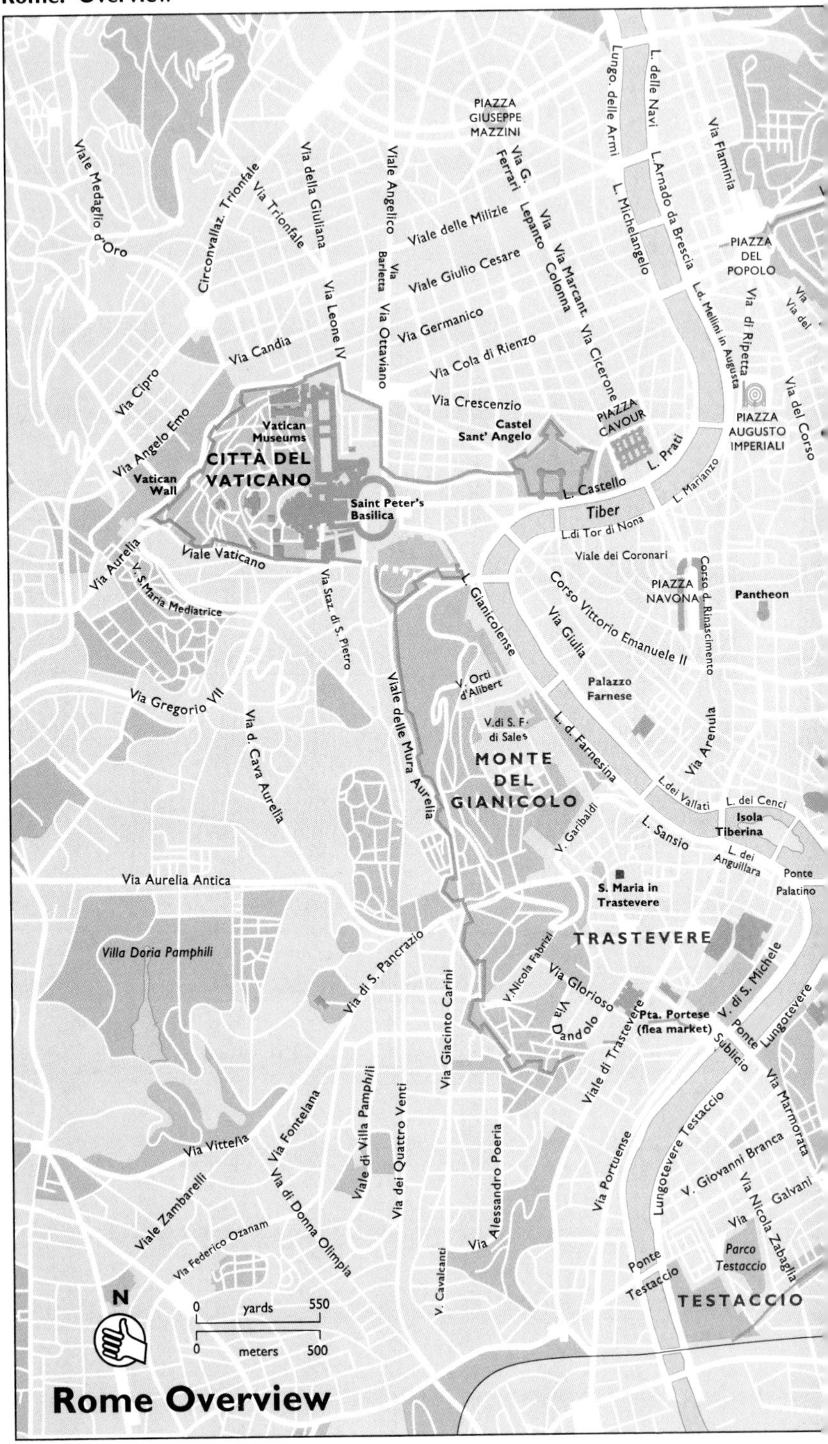

PIAZZA GIUSEPPE MAZZINI
Lungo. delle Armi
L. delle Navi
Via Flaminia
Viale Medaglio d'Oro
Circonvallaz. Trionfale
Via Trionfale
Via della Giuliana
Viale Angelico
Via G. Ferrari
Via Lepanto
L. Michelangelo
L.Arnado da Brescia
Viale delle Milizie
Via Barletta
Viale Giulio Cesare
Via Marcant. Colonna
PIAZZA DEL POPOLO
Via Leone IV
Via Ottaviano
Via Germanico
L.d. Mellini in Augusta
Via di Ripetta
Via del
Via Candia
Via Cola di Rienzo
Via Cicerone
Via Cipro
Via Crescenzio
PIAZZA CAVOUR
PIAZZA AUGUSTO IMPERIALI
Via del Corso
Via Angelo Emo
Vatican Museums
Castel Sant' Angelo
CITTÀ DEL VATICANO
L. Prati
Vatican Wall
L. Castello
L. Marianzo
Saint Peter's Basilica
Tiber
L.di Tor di Nona
Viale Vaticano
Via Aurelia
V. S.Maria Mediatrice
Viale dei Coronari
Via Staz. di S. Pietro
L. Gianicolense
Corso Vittorio Emanuele II
PIAZZA NAVONA
Corso d. Rinascimento
Pantheon
Via Giulia
V. Orti d'Alibert
Palazzo Farnese
Via Gregorio VII
Viale delle Mura Aurelia
V.di S. F. di Sales
Via d. Cava Aurelia
MONTE DEL GIANICOLO
L. d. Farnesina
Via Arenula
L.dei Vallati
L. dei Cenci
Isola Tiberina
V. Garibaldi
L. Sansio
L. dei Anguillara
Ponte Palatino
Via Aurelia Antica
S. Maria in Trastevere
TRASTEVERE
Villa Doria Pamphili
Via di S. Pancrazio
V.Nicola Fabrizi
Via Glorioso
Via Dandolo
Pta. Portese (flea market)
V. di S. Michele
Ponte Sublicio
Lungotevere
Via Giacinto Carini
Viale di Trastevere
Via Marmorata
Viale di Villa Pamphili
Via dei Quattro Venti
Via Vittelia
Via Fontelana
Via Portuense
Lungotevere Testaccio
V. Giovanni Branca
Via Alessandro Poeria
Viale Zambarelli
Via di Donna Olimpia
Via Galvani
Via Nicola Zabaglia
Via Federico Ozanam
V. Cavalcanti
Ponte Testaccio
Parco Testaccio
TESTACCIO
N
0 yards 550
0 meters 500

Rome Overview

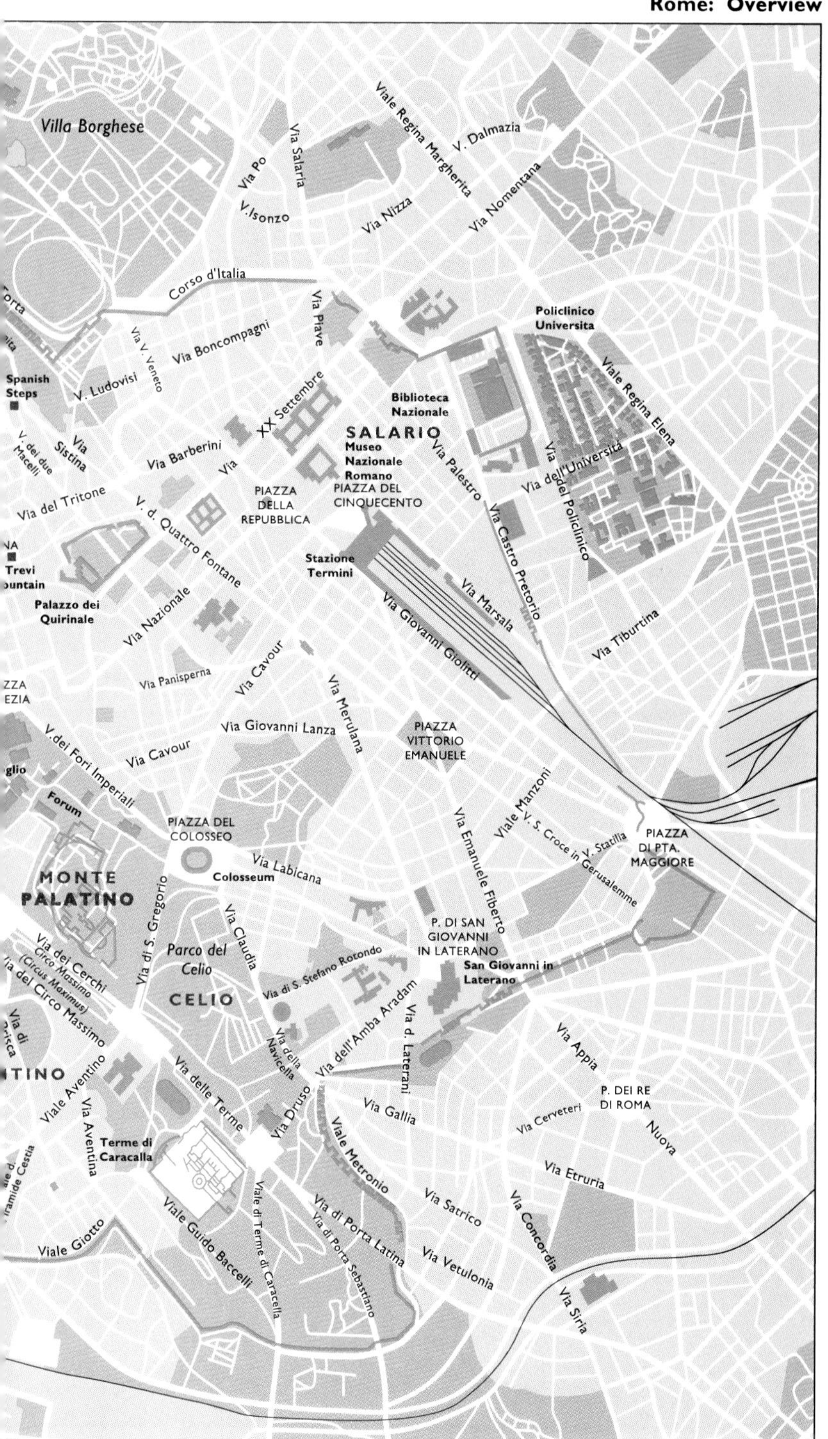
Villa Borghese
Via Po
Via Salaria
Viale Regina Margherita
V. Dalmazia
V. Isonzo
Via Nizza
Via Nomentana
Corso d'Italia
Via Piave
Via V. Veneto
Via Boncompagni
Spanish Steps
V. Ludovisi
Policlinico Universita
Viale Regina Elena
Biblioteca Nazionale
XX Settembre
SALARIO
Museo Nazionale Romano
Via Palestro
Via Sistina
V. dei due Macelli
Via Barberini
Via
Via dell'Università
Via del Policlinico
PIAZZA DELLA REPUBBLICA
PIAZZA DEL CINQUECENTO
Via Castro Pretorio
Via del Tritone
V. d. Quattro Fontane
Trevi
Stazione Termini
Via Marsala
Palazzo dei Quirinale
Via Nazionale
Via Giovanni Giolitti
Via Tiburtina
Via Panisperna
Via Cavour
Via Merulana
Via Giovanni Lanza
PIAZZA VITTORIO EMANUELE
V. dei Fori Imperiali
Via Cavour
Forum
Viale Manzoni
V. S. Croce in Gerusalemme
V. Statilia
PIAZZA DI PTA. MAGGIORE
PIAZZA DEL COLOSSEO
Via Emanuele Filiberto
Via Labicana
MONTE PALATINO
Colosseum
Via di S. Gregorio
Via Claudia
P. DI SAN GIOVANNI IN LATERANO
Parco del Celio
Via di S. Stefano Rotondo
San Giovanni in Laterano
Via dei Cerchi
Circo Massimo (Circus Maximus)
Via del Circo Massimo
CELIO
Via dell'Amba Aradam
Via d. Laterani
Via della Navicella
Via Appia
Viale Aventino
Via delle Terme
Via Druso
P. DEI RE DI ROMA
Via Gallia
Via Cerveteri
Nuova
Via Aventina
Terme di Caracalla
Viale Metronio
Via Etruria
Viale Guido Baccelli
Viale di Terme di Caracalla
Via di Porta Latina
Via di Porta Sebastiano
Via Satrico
Via Concordia
Viale Giotto
Via Vetulonia
Via Siria

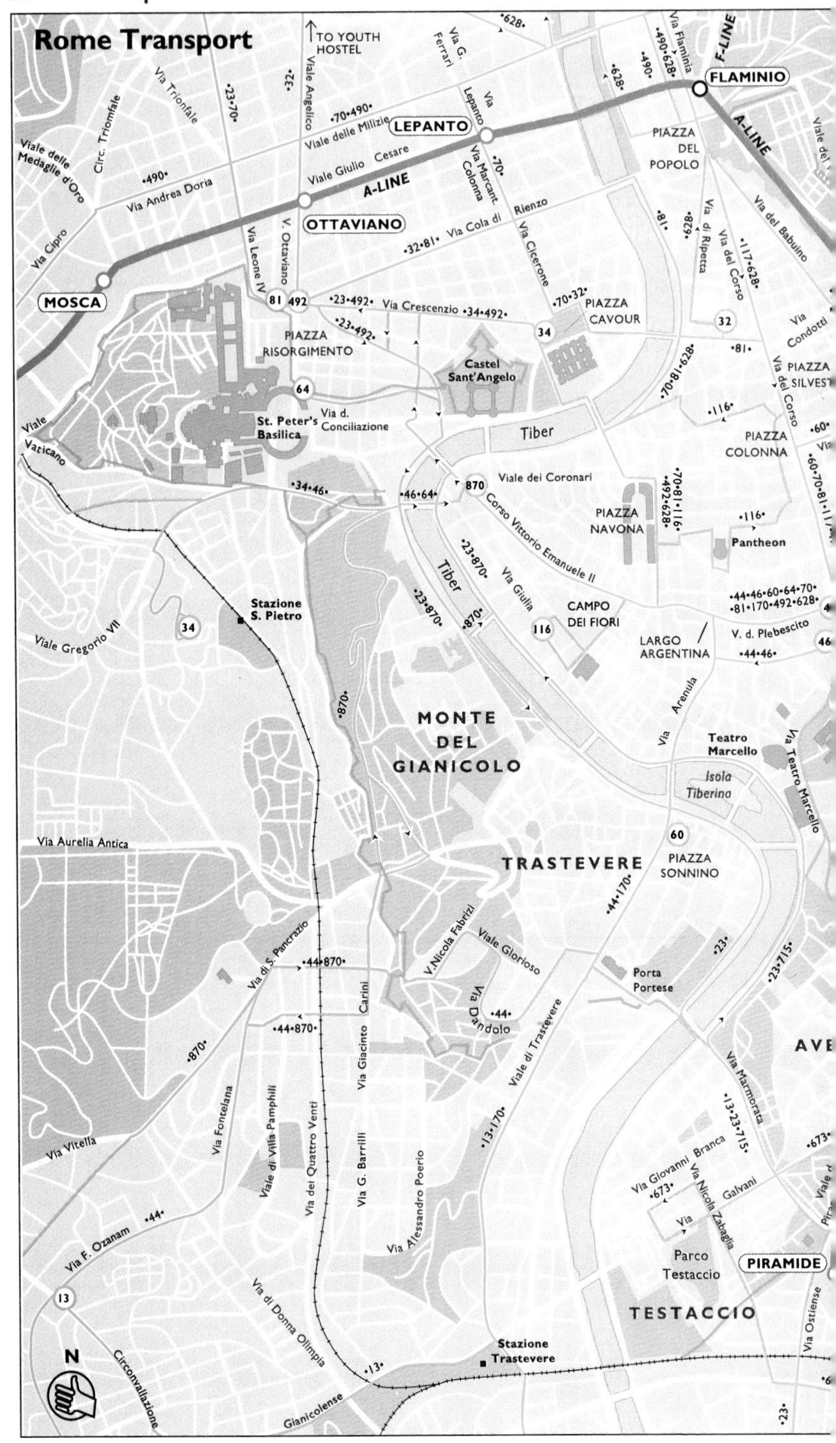
Rome Transport
TO YOUTH HOSTEL
FLAMINIO
F-LINE
A-LINE
LEPANTO
OTTAVIANO
MOSCA
PIAZZA DEL POPOLO
PIAZZA RISORGIMENTO
PIAZZA CAVOUR
Castel Sant'Angelo
St. Peter's Basilica
Tiber
PIAZZA NAVONA
Pantheon
PIAZZA COLONNA
PIAZZA SILVEST
CAMPO DEI FIORI
LARGO ARGENTINA
Stazione S. Pietro
MONTE DEL GIANICOLO
Teatro Marcello
Isola Tiberina
TRASTEVERE
PIAZZA SONNINO
Porta Portese
Parco Testaccio
TESTACCIO
PIRAMIDE
Stazione Trastevere
Via Trionfale
Circ. Triomfale
Viale delle Medaglie d'Oro
Via Andrea Doria
Via Cipro
Viale Angelico
Viale delle Milizie
Viale Giulio Cesare
Via G. Ferrari
Via Lepanto
Via Marcant. Colonna
Via Cola di Rienzo
Via Cicerone
Via Leone IV
V. Ottaviano
Via Crescenzio
Via Flaminia
Via di Ripetta
Via del Corso
Via del Babuino
Via Condotti
Via d. Conciliazione
Viale Vaticano
Viale dei Coronari
Corso Vittorio Emanuele II
Via Giulia
V. d. Plebescito
Via Arenula
Via Teatro Marcello
Viale Gregorio VII
Via Aurelia Antica
Via di S. Pancrazio
V. Nicola Fabrizi
Viale Glorioso
Via Dandolo
Viale di Trastevere
Via Marmorata
Via Giovanni Branca
Via Nicola Zabaglia
Via Galvani
Via Ostiense
Via Fontelana
Viale di Villa Pamphili
Via dei Quattro Venti
Via Giacinto Carini
Via G. Barrilli
Via Alessandro Poerio
Via Vitella
Via F. Ozanam
Via di Donna Olimpia
Circonvallazione Gianicolense
N
•628•
•490•628•
•490•
•23•70•
•32•
•70•490•
•490•
•70•
•81•
•628•
•117•628•
•32•81•
•23•492•
•34•492•
•70•32•
81
492
34
32
64
•81•
•70•81•628•
•116•
•60•
•60•70•81•117•
•34•46•
•46•64•
870
•70•81•116•492•628•
•116•
•23•870•
•870•
116
•44•46•60•64•70•81•170•492•628•
•44•46•
46
•870•
60
•44•170•
•23•
•23•715•
•44•870•
•44•
•13•170•
•13•23•715•
•673•
•44•
13
•13•
•23•

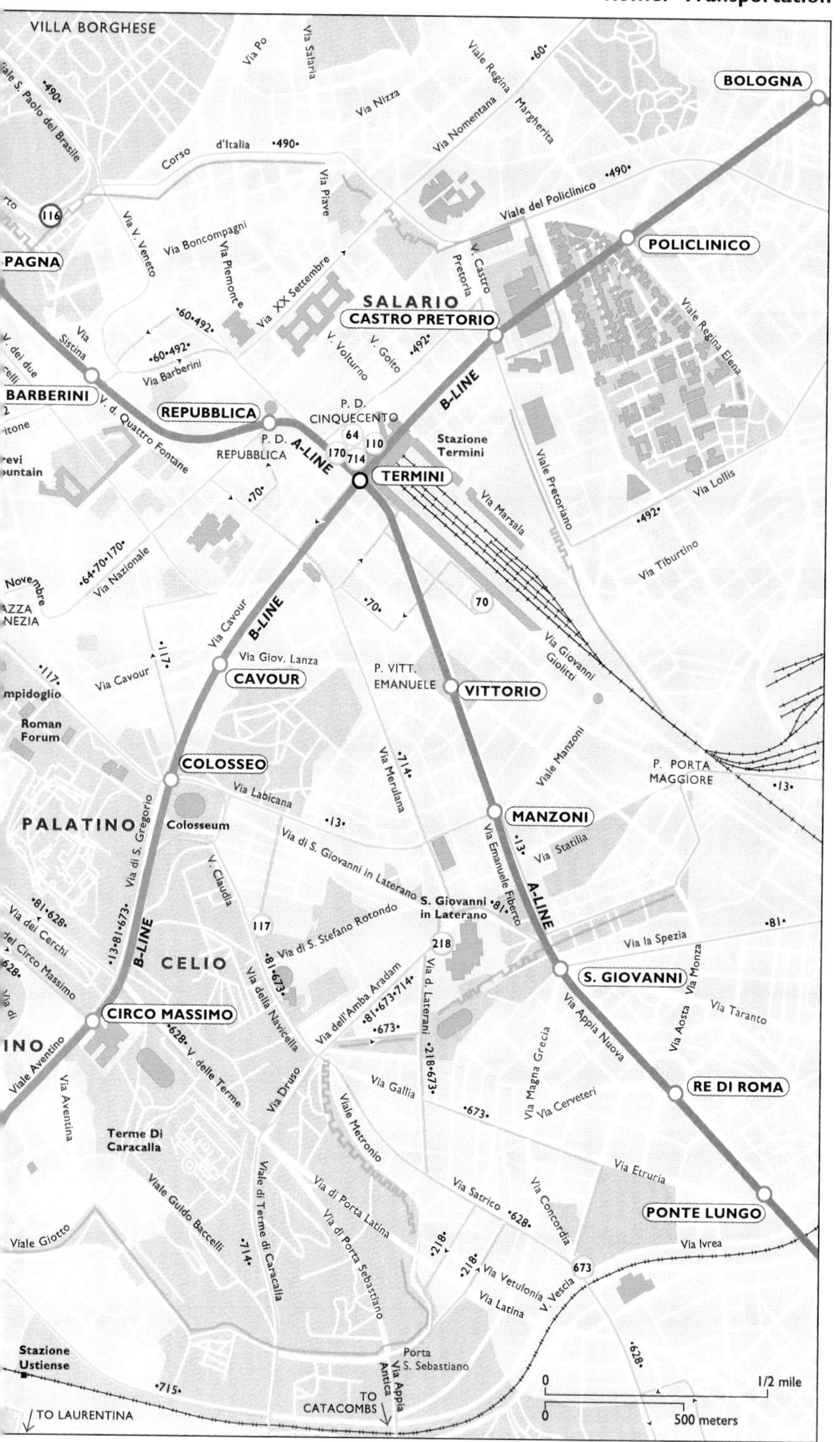
VILLA BORGHESE
BOLOGNA
POLICLINICO
SALARIO
CASTRO PRETORIO
PAGNA
BARBERINI
REPUBBLICA
TERMINI
B-LINE
A-LINE
P. D. CINQUECENTO
P. D. REPUBBLICA
Stazione Termini
CAVOUR
VITTORIO
P. VITT. EMANUELE
COLOSSEO
Colosseum
MANZONI
PALATINO
CELIO
Roman Forum
S. Giovanni in Laterano
S. GIOVANNI
CIRCO MASSIMO
RE DI ROMA
PONTE LUNGO
P. PORTA MAGGIORE
Terme Di Caracalla
Stazione Ustiense
Porta S. Sebastiano
TO CATACOMBS
TO LAURENTINA
Via Po
Via Salaria
Viale Regina Margherita
Via Nizza
Via Nomentana
Corso d'Italia
Via Piave
Viale del Policlinico
Via V. Veneto
Via Boncompagni
Via Piemonte
Via XX Settembre
V. Castro Pretoria
Viale Regina Elena
Via Sistina
Via Barberini
V. Volturno
V. Goito
V. d. Quattro Fontane
Viale Pretoriano
Via Marsala
Via Lollis
Via Tiburtino
Via Nazionale
Via Cavour
Via Giov. Lanza
Via Giovanni Giolitti
Via Merulana
Viale Manzoni
Via Labicana
Via di S. Giovanni in Laterano
Via Emanuele Filiberto
Via Statilia
Via di S. Gregorio
V. Claudia
Via di S. Stefano Rotondo
Via la Spezia
Via Monza
Via Taranto
Via dei Cerchi
Via del Circo Massimo
Via della Navicella
Via dell'Amba Aradam
Via d. Laterani
Via Appia Nuova
Via Aosta
Via Magna Grecia
Via Cerveteri
Viale Aventino
Via Aventina
V. delle Terme
Via Druso
Via Gallia
Viale Metronio
Via Etruria
Viale Guido Baccelli
Viale di Terme di Caracalla
Via di Porta Latina
Via di Porta Sebastiano
Via Satrico
Via Concordia
Viale Giotto
Via Vetulonia
V. Vescia
Via Latina
Via Ivrea
Via Appia Antica
•490•
•60•
•60•492•
•492•
•70•
•64•70•170•
•117•
•714•
•13•
•81•
•81•628•
•13•81•673•
•81•673•
•81•673•714•
•673•
•218•673•
•628•
•218•
•714•
•715•
116
64
110
170
714
70
117
218
673
0
1/2 mile
500 meters

Central Rome

Central Rome

Ara Pacis, **3**
Campo dei Fiori, **27**
Captioline Hill and Museums, **22**
Castel Sant'Angelo, **9**
Chiesa Nuova, **10**
Il Gesù, **23**
Galleria Corsini, **31**
Galleria Doria Pamphilij, **19**
Galleria Spada, **28**
Mausoleum of Augustus, **4**
Museo Barrocco, **26**
Museo Mario Praz, **7**
Museo Napoleonico, **7**
Museo di Palazzo Venezia, **18**
Palazzo di Giustizia, **8**
Pantheon, **13**
P. Farnese, **29**
P. Navona, **11**
P. del Popolo, **2**
P. della Rotonda, **13**
P. di Spagna, **5**
P. Venezia, **20**
Sant'Agnese in Agone, **11**
Sant'Andrea delle valle, **25**
Sant'Antonio dei Portoghesi, **6**
Santi Apostoli, **17**
Sant'Ignazio, **15**
San Luigi dei Francesci, **12**
San Marcello, **16**
Santa Maria sopra Minerva, **14**
Santa Maria del Popolo, **1**
Spanish Steps, **5**
Theater of Marcellus, **24**
Trevi Fountain, **16**
Villa Farnesina, **30**
Vittorio Emanuele II Monument, **21**

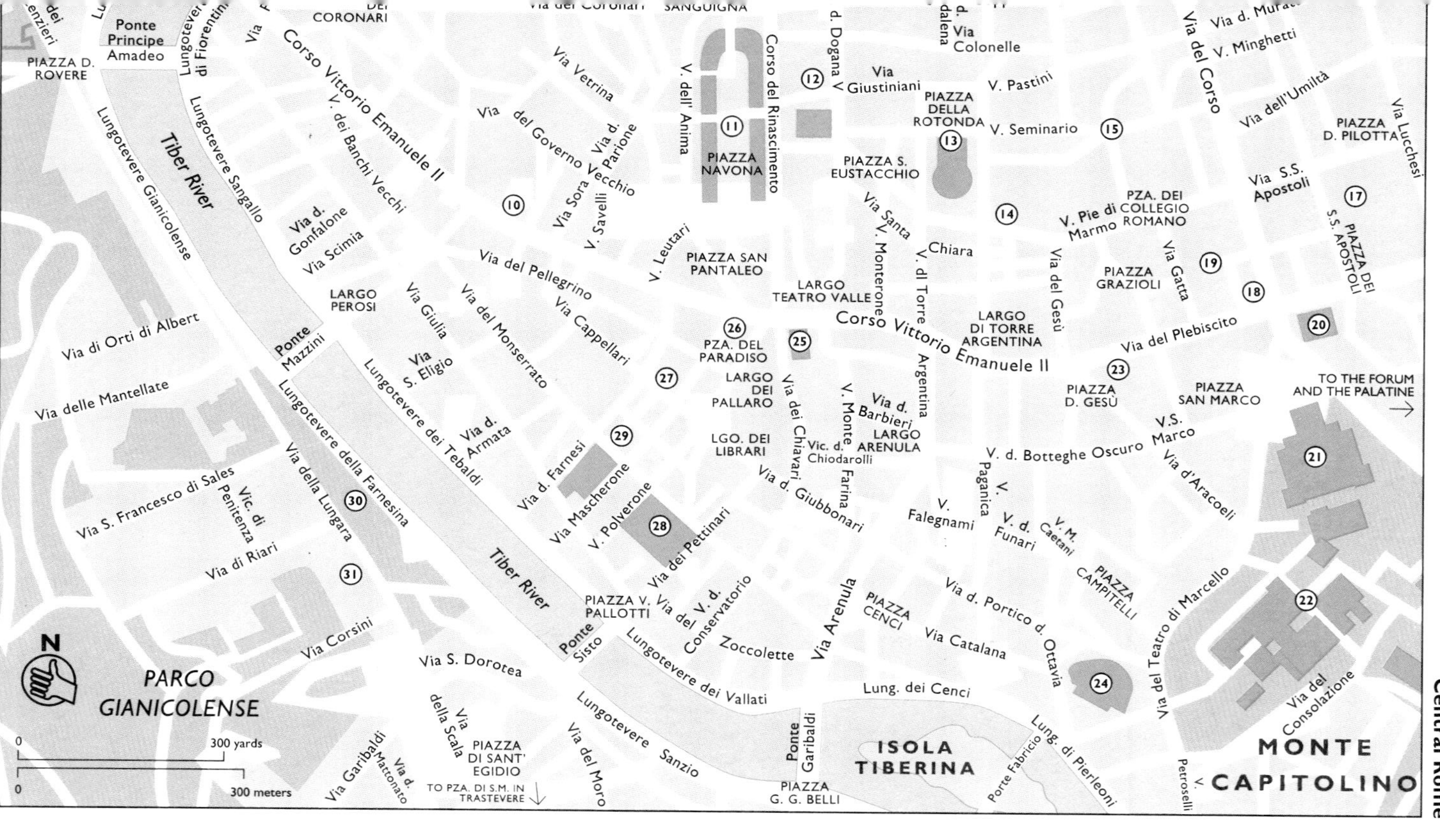
MONTE CAPITOLINO
ISOLA TIBERINA
PARCO GIANICOLENSE
Tiber River
Tiber River
TO THE FORUM AND THE PALATINE
TO PZA. DI S.M. IN TRASTEVERE
Via Lucchesi
PIAZZA D. PILOTTA
PIAZZA DEI S.S. APOSTOLI
Via S.S. Apostoli
Via dell'Umiltà
V. Minghetti
Via del Corso
PZA. DEI COLLEGIO ROMANO
Via Gatta
PIAZZA GRAZIOLI
Via del Plebiscito
PIAZZA SAN MARCO
V.S. Marco
Via d'Aracoeli
Via del Teatro di Marcello
Via del Consolazione
V. Petroselli
PIAZZA CAMPITELLI
Lung. di Pierleoni
Porte Fabricio
Via d. Portico d. Ottavia
V. M. Caetani
V. d. Funari
V. Paganica
V. d. Botteghe Oscuro
PIAZZA D. GESÙ
Via del Gesù
V. Pie di Marmo
LARGO DI TORRE ARGENTINA
Corso Vittorio Emanuele II
V. Seminario
V. Pastini
Via Colonelle
PIAZZA DELLA ROTONDA
Via Giustiniani
PIAZZA S. EUSTACCHIO
Chiara
V. dl Torre
Argentina
Via Santa
V. Monterone
V. Falegnami
Via Catalana
PIAZZA CENCI
Lung. dei Cenci
Via d. Barbieri
LARGO ARENULA
Vic. d. Chiodarolli
V. Monte
Farina
Via Arenula
Ponte Garibaldi
PIAZZA G. G. BELLI
d. Dogana V
Corso del Rinascimento
LARGO TEATRO VALLE
Via dei Chiavari
Via d. Giubbonari
PIAZZA NAVONA
PIAZZA SAN PANTALEO
PZA. DEL PARADISO
LARGO DEI PALLARO
LGO. DEI LIBRARI
Zoccolette
Via del Conservatorio
V. d.
Via dei Pettinari
Lungotevere dei Vallati
Lungotevere Sanzio
V. dell' Anima
V. Leutari
Via d. Parione
V. Savelli
Via Sora
Via del Governo Vecchio
Via Vetrina
Via del Pellegrino
Via Cappellari
V. Polverone
Via Mascherone
Via d. Farnesi
PIAZZA V. PALLOTTI
Ponte Sisto
Via del Moro
PIAZZA DI SANT' EGIDIO
Via della Scala
Via S. Dorotea
Via del Monserrato
Via d. Armata
Via Giulia
Via S. Eligio
Lungotevere dei Tebaldi
Corso Vittorio Emanuele II
V. dei Banchi Vecchi
Via Scimia
Via d. Gonfalone
LARGO PEROSI
Ponte Mazzini
Lungotevere della Farnesina
Via della Lungara
Via Corsini
Via Garibaldi
Via d. Mattonato
Lungotevere Sangallo
Lungotevere di Fiorentini
Lungotevere Gianicolense
Ponte Principe Amadeo
PIAZZA D. ROVERE
Via di Orti di Albert
Via delle Mantellate
Via S. Francesco di Sales
Vic. di Penitenza
Via di Riari
CORONARI
N
0 300 yards
0 300 meters
10
11
12
13
14
15
17
18
19
20
21
22
23
24
25
26
27
28
29
30
31

Rome: Villa Borghese

Villa Borghese

N

200 yards
200 meters
0
0

VILLA BORGHESE
GIARDINO ZOOLOGICO
GALOPPATOIO
Galleria Borghese
PIAZZALE DEI RAIMONDI
Galleria Naz. d'Arte Moderne
Museo Naz. di Villa Giulia
VILLA STROHL FERN
VILLA RUFFO
VILLA MEDICI
PIAZZA DI SIENA
PIAZZALE PAOLA BORGHESE
PIAZZALE DEL FIOCCO
PIAZZALE D. CANESTRE
PIAZZALE DEI MARTIRI
PIAZZALE BRASILE
PIAZZA E. SIENKIEWICZ
PIAZZALE FLAMINIO
PIAZZA DEL POPOLO
PIAZZA AUGUSTO IMPERATORE
PIAZZA DELLA MARINA
PIAZZA D. LIBERTA
PIAZZA COLA DI RIENZO
PIAZZA DELLE CINQUE GIORNATE
PIAZZA MONTE GRAPPA
Porta Pinciana
Flaminio
Spagna
Lepanto
A LINE
Fiume Tevere
Ponte d. Risorg
Ponte G. Matteotti
Ponte Nenni
Ponte Margherita
Lungotevere delle Navi
Lungotevere delle Armi
Lungo. Arnaldo da Brescia
Lungo. Michelangelo
Lungo. in Augusta
Lungo. d. Mellini
Corso d'Italia
V. Puglia
V. Romagna
Via Boncompagni
Via Quintina
Via Piemonte
Via Sicilia
Via Sardegna
Via Toscana
Via Marche
Via Vittorio Veneto
Via Emilia
Via Aurora
Via Liguria
Via Ludovisi
Via Porta Pinciana
Via Pinciana
Viale Museo Borghese
Via di. S. Teresa
Via Po
V. Giovannelli
Giovanni Paisiello
Via S. Mercadante
Via P. Raimondi
Via dei Daini
Viale dell'Uccelliera
V. Pupazzi
Viale dei Cavalli Marini
V. d. Pineta
Viale Goethe
V. di S. Paolo del Brasile
Viale Casina di Raffaello
Viale P. Canonica
Zoologico
Via Ulisse Aldrovandi
Viale del Giardino
V. dell'Aranciera
V. d. Magnolie
Viale Galoppatoio
V. del Muro Torto
Via del Babuino
V. F. Laguardia
Via Bernadotte
Viale Madama
Via Omero
Viale delle Belle Arti
V. Washington
Viale Valadier
Viale d. Belvedere
Viale Trinità dei Monti
Via della Croce
Via Vittoria
Via del Corso
V. A. Canova
Via Ripetta
Via Brunetti
Via del Vantaggio
Via Savoia
V. Disavoia
V. di S. Eugenio
Via di Villa Giulia
Via Flaminia
V. D. A. Azuni
V. G. Pisanelli
V. Romanosi
Via Fed. Cesi
Via G. Belli
Via E. Q. Visconte
Via Boezio
Via Marc. Colonna
Via Valadier
Via dei Gracchi
Via Pompeo Magno
Via degli Scipioni
Via Giulio Cesare
Via Ezio
Viale della Milizie
Via Settembrini
Viale Giuseppe Mazzini

Let's Go writers travel on your budget.

"Guides that penetrate the veneer of the holiday brochures and mine the grit of real life."

—The Economist

"The writers seem to have experienced every rooster-packed bus and lunar-surfaced mattress about which they write."

—The New York Times

"All the dirt, dirt cheap."

—People

Great for independent travelers.

"The guides are aimed not only at young budget travelers but at the independent traveler; a sort of streetwise cookbook for traveling alone."

—The New York Times

"Flush with candor and irreverence, chock full of budget travel advice."

—The Des Moines Register

"An indispensible resource, *Let's Go*'s practical information can be used by every traveler."

—The Chattanooga Free Press

Let's Go is completely revised each year.

"Only *Let's Go* has the zeal to annually update every title on its list."

—The Boston Globe

"Unbeatable: good sightseeing advice; up-to-date info on restaurants, hotels, and inns; a commitment to money-saving travel; and a wry style that brightens nearly every page."

—The Washington Post

All the important information you need.

"*Let's Go* authors provide a comedic element while still providing concise information and thorough coverage of the country. Anything you need to know about budget traveling is detailed in this book."

—The Chicago Sun-Times

"Value-packed, unbeatable, accurate, and comprehensive."

—Los Angeles Times

Let's Go Publications

Let's Go: Alaska & the Pacific Northwest 2001
Let's Go: Australia 2001
Let's Go: Austria & Switzerland 2001
Let's Go: Boston 2001 **New Title!**
Let's Go: Britain & Ireland 2001
Let's Go: California 2001
Let's Go: Central America 2001
Let's Go: China 2001
Let's Go: Eastern Europe 2001
Let's Go: Europe 2001
Let's Go: France 2001
Let's Go: Germany 2001
Let's Go: Greece 2001
Let's Go: India & Nepal 2001
Let's Go: Ireland 2001
Let's Go: Israel 2001
Let's Go: Italy 2001
Let's Go: London 2001
Let's Go: Mexico 2001
Let's Go: Middle East 2001
Let's Go: New York City 2001
Let's Go: New Zealand 2001
Let's Go: Paris 2001
Let's Go: Peru, Bolivia & Ecuador 2001 **New Title!**
Let's Go: Rome 2001
Let's Go: San Francisco 2001 **New Title!**
Let's Go: South Africa 2001
Let's Go: Southeast Asia 2001
Let's Go: Spain & Portugal 2001
Let's Go: Turkey 2001
Let's Go: USA 2001
Let's Go: Washington, D.C. 2001
Let's Go: Western Europe 2001 **New Title!**

Let's Go *Map Guides*

Amsterdam
Berlin
Boston
Chicago
Florence
Hong Kong
London
Los Angeles
Madrid
New Orleans
New York City
Paris
Prague
Rome
San Francisco
Seattle
Sydney
Washington, D.C.

Coming Soon: *Dublin* and *Venice*

ITALY

2001

Marc A. Wallenstein editor
Matthew S. Ryan associate editor
Fiona McKinnon associate editor

researcher-writers
Charles DeSimone
Shanya Dingle
Sarah Jessop
Amber K. Lavicka
Marko Soldo
Sam Spital

Mike Durcak map editor

St. Martin's Press New York

HELPING LET'S GO If you want to share your discoveries, suggestions, or corrections, please drop us a line. We read every piece of correspondence, whether a postcard, a 10-page email, or a coconut. Please note that mail received after May 2001 may be too late for the 2002 book, but will be kept for future editions. **Address mail to:**

Let's Go: Italy
67 Mount Auburn Street
Cambridge, MA 02138
USA

Visit Let's Go at **http://www.letsgo.com,** or send email to:

feedback@letsgo.com
Subject: "Let's Go: Italy"

In addition to the invaluable travel advice our readers share with us, many are kind enough to offer their services as researchers or editors. Unfortunately, our charter enables us to employ only currently enrolled Harvard students.

Maps by David Lindroth copyright © 2001, 2000, 1999, 1998, 1997, 1996, 1995, 1994, 1993, 1992, 1991, 1990, 1989, 1988 by St. Martin's Press.

Distributed outside the USA and Canada by Macmillan.

Let's Go: Italy Copyright © 2001 by Let's Go, Inc. All rights reserved. Printed in the United States of America. No part of this book may be used or reproduced in any manner whatsoever without written permission except in the case of brief quotations embodied in critical articles or reviews. Let's Go is available for purchase in bulk by institutions and authorized resellers. For information, address St. Martin's Press, 175 Fifth Avenue, New York, NY 10010, USA.

ISBN: 0-312-24681-1

First edition
10 9 8 7 6 5 4 3 2 1

Let's Go: Italy is written by Let's Go Publications, 67 Mount Auburn Street, Cambridge, MA 02138, USA.

Let's Go® and the thumb logo are trademarks of Let's Go, Inc.
Printed in the USA on recycled paper with biodegradable soy ink.

ADVERTISING DISCLAIMER All advertisements appearing in Let's Go publications are sold by an independent agency not affiliated with the editorial production of the guides. Advertisers are never given preferential treatment, and the guides are researched, written, and published independent of advertising. Advertisements do not imply endorsement of products or services by Let's Go, and Let's Go does not vouch for the accuracy of information provided in advertisements.

If you are interested in purchasing advertising space in a Let's Go publication, contact: Let's Go Advertising Sales, 67 Mount Auburn St., Cambridge, MA 02138, USA.

HOW TO EAT THIS BOOK

Welcome to *Let's Go: Italy 2001*, the savvy budget traveler's restaurant of choice. Your table is being cleared at the moment and should be ready in a few minutes. Please, have a seat at the bar and enjoy a complementary glass of the house red. Feel free to peruse the menu while you wait, and have a pleasant meal.

THE MENU

ANTIPASTI. The first course, **Discover Italy,** is sure to whet your appetite for our oh-so-tasty coverage by providing you with an overview of Italy, including **Suggested Itineraries** that list the Chef's recommendations regarding where to visit and how much time to spend there.

PRIMI. Life & Times, served fresh with a pinch of wit, provides you with a general introduction to the art, culture, and history of Italy. Leave Life & Times on the table so you can nibble at it as you eat the rest of your meal. The heavy **Essentials** section details practical information and is best consumed in small bites.

SECONDI. The meat of our Italy coverage comes in 10 delectable cuts. **Northwest Italy** includes Lombardy, the Lake Country, the Italian Riviera, Piedmont, and Valle d'Aosta. **Venice** has her own chapter, followed by **Northeast Italy,** which includes the Veneto (minus Venice), Friuli Venezia-Giulia, Trentino Alto-Adige, and Emilia-Romagna. **Florence** precedes **Central Italy,** which covers Tuscany (minus Florence), Umbria, Le Marche, Abruzzo, and Molise. **Rome** includes not only the Eternal City, but also the rest of Lazio. **Southern Italy** stuffs in Campania, the Amalfi Coast, Apulia, Basilicata, and Calabria, and **Sicily, Sardinia,** and **Malta** round out the meal. The **black tabs** in the margins will help you to navigate between chapters quickly.

CONTORNI. As far as side dishes go, may we suggest the lovely baked **appendix?** It contains several varieties of diced **conversion tables,** as well as an Italian **phrasebook** of things both useful and tawdry. The Chef finishes off the dish with a subtle **glossary** of technical and architectural foreign words broiled in a truffle demi-glaze.

DOLCI. Don't fill up on content before sampling dessert! Our sugar-coated **index** is chock-full of hidden treats and homemade sweets. Try **superlatives** for a sugar fix.

A FEW NOTES ABOUT HOW WE PREPARE YOUR FOOD

RANKING ESTABLISHMENTS. In each section (accommodations, food, etc.), we list establishments in order from best to worst. Our absolute favorites are so denoted by the highest honor given out by *Let's Go*, the thumbs-up (☒). See **accommodations with thumb picks** or **hostels** in the index for some direction.

PHONE CODES AND TELEPHONE NUMBERS. The **phone code** for each region, city, or town appears opposite the name of that region, city, or town, and is denoted by the ☎ icon. **Phone numbers** in text are also preceded by the ☎ icon.

GRAYBOXES AND WHITEBOXES. Some **Grayboxes** provide wonderful cultural insight, others simply crude humor. In any case, they're usually amusing, so enjoy. **Whiteboxes,** on the other hand, provide important practical information, such as warnings (☒) or helpful hints and information about other resources (☒).

> **A NOTE TO OUR READERS** The information for this book was gathered by *Let's Go* researchers from May through August of 2000. Each listing is based on one researcher's opinion, formed during his or her visit at a particular time. Those traveling at other times may have different experiences since prices, dates, hours, and conditions are always subject to change. You are urged to check the facts presented in this book beforehand to avoid inconvenience and surprises.

Via Urbana 38, 00184 Roma

06-484-853 0347-795-5175

www.walksofeurope.com

Join Our *English Speaking* Group Leaders For Historical And Entertaining Walks Through Romeís Most Famous Monuments.

Learn the hidden secrets of

Ancient Rome

Vatican City

Roman MonumentsÖ

Ö and much much more.

Visit Our Web-site, Stop In Our Office Near Termini Station, Or Call For Daily Information, Reservations, And Private Excursions.

What Do You Do When The Sun Goes Down In Rome?

YOU CRAWL!

FREE Shirts FREE Shots FREE Beer

Visit The Original Pub Crawls Every Night In Rome!

CONTENTS

MAPS

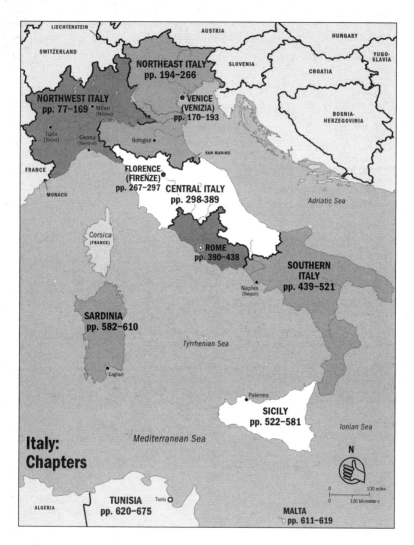

Italy: Chapters

LIECHTENSTEIN
AUSTRIA
HUNGARY
SWITZERLAND
YUGOSLAVIA
SLOVENIA
CROATIA
BOSNIA-HERZEGOVINIA
FRANCE
MONACO
SAN MARINO
Corsica (FRANCE)
ALGERIA
Milan (Milano)
Turin (Torino)
Genoa (Genova)
Bologna
Naples (Napoli)
Cagliari
Palermo
Tunis
Adriatic Sea
Tyrrhenian Sea
Mediterranean Sea
Ionian Sea

N
0 100 miles
0 100 kilometers

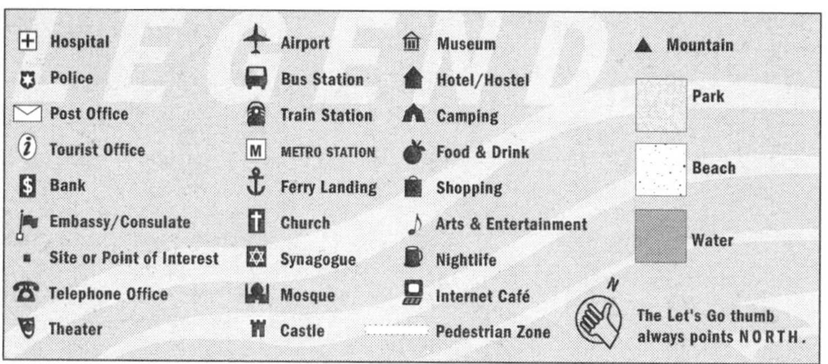

Zurich
Innsbruck
AUSTRIA
HUNGARY
Lucerne
Bern
LIECHTENSTEIN
Interlaken
St. Moritz
SWITZERLAND
Brunico
Merano
Bressanone
Bolzano
Dolomites
FRIULI-VENEZIA GIULIA
Cividale
Udine
Ljubljana
SLOVENIA
Zagreb
CROATIA
TO BELGRADE
TRENTINO-ALTO ADIGE
Trent
Locarno
Alps
Italian
Matterhorn
LOMBARDY
Lugano
The Lakes
Como
Chamonix
Courmayeur
Aosta
VALLE D'AOSTA
Mt. Blanc
VENETO
Treviso
Trieste
Lignano-Sabbiadoro
Rijeka
Garda
Vicenza
Venice
(Venezia)
Brescia
Verona
Padova
(Padua)
Adige R.
Milan
(Milano)
Mantua
(Mantova)
Cremona
Po River
PIEDMONT
Pavia
BOSNIA-HERZEGOVINIA
Sarajevo
Susa
Turin
(Torino)
Asti
Parma
Ferrara
Maritime Alps
Northern Apennines
Modena
Bologna
Ravenna
Zadar
LIGURIA
EMILIA-ROMAGNA
Genoa
(Genova)
SAN MARINO
Rimini
Pesaro
Split
Finale Ligure
La Spezia
Pistoia
Lucca
Urbino
Ancona
FRANCE
Ventimiglia
Arno River
Pisa
Florence
(Firenze)
Arezzo
LE MARCHE
Nice
MONACO
Livorno
Gubbio
Dubrovnik
Cannes
Ligurian Sea
Siena
Perugia
Ascoli Piceno
TUSCANY
L. Trasimeno
Assisi
Adriatic Sea
Massa Marittima
Montepulciano
UMBRIA
Orvieto
Grosseto
Pescara
Bastia
Elba
Gran Sasso
TREMITI ISLANDS
L. Bolsano
Tevere River
(Tiber R.)
L'Aquila
Calvi
Viterbo
Sulmona
Termoli
Vieste
ABRUZZO
Gargano Massif
Corsica
Civitavecchia
Tivoli
Monte Sant'Angelo
FRANCE
Cerveteri
Isernia
Campobasso
Rome
(Roma)
Frascati
MOLISE
Foggia
Bari
Ajaccio
LAZIO

ACKNOWLEDGMENTS

These books don't just put themselves together, you know. They're assembled by machine.

MARC THANKS: Mr. Ryan—without your refreshingly bitter sarcasm, I'd be institutionalized by now. Fiona—I don't know how you manage to keep that smile turned on all the time. Aarup, you're amazing—the cream of the ME crop. Mad props to the whole Axis pod crew. Al—braving the terrors of Chem and the boredoms of Slummerville just to roll with me for a summer is *actually* amazing. Mike D—you're a dynamo on the tables. Gumby—makin' moves in the city, chillin' like a villain, bombing with Dreas, the schemes were illin'. Tony, the espresso coverage would be totally busted without you. BRED! Where the HELL were you this summer?! Q-house love to A-rock, Jessie, Henry, and the Walsh-man. Thanks to all the awesome shuttle drivers. Most importantly, the world needs to know that my family is the best on the planet, hands down. Much love to Mom, Dad, and Matt.

MATT THANKS: Monica—you are a special girl to me. Marc for creative guidance, poking at my insecurities, and not laughing at my dumb jokes. Fiona, Aarup, Nathaniel, Rebecca, Paul, Megan, and Alice. Zappa and Beck. Every private sector legal employer in the Boston area for giving me the opportunity to take this job. Karin and JJ thanks for support, and of course—Disy, Tommy, Penny, Mom, and Dad.

FIONA THANKS: Hooman and The Scooter. Marc and Matt, the most laid-back of book-teams. Nora, Mica, John, and Anna for office support. Brian, Chris, Jack, and Jen for distraction. Aarup, Alex, Jeff, Alice, and Meredith. Emeril for kicking it up notches unknown. Mom for amazing travel files. Moira for hip-hop expertise. Julia for packaged love. And Dad, who knows what it's like to be busy.

Editor
Marc A. Wallenstein
Associate Editors
Matthew S. Ryan, Fiona McKinnon
Managing Editor
Aarup Kubal
Map Editor
Mike Durcak

Publishing Director
Kaya Stone
Editor-in-Chief
Kate McCarthy
Production Manager
Melissa Rudolph
Cartography Manager
John Fiore
Editorial Managers
Alice Farmer, Ankur Ghosh, Aarup Kubal, Anup Kubal
Financial Manager
Bede Sheppard
Low-Season Manager
Melissa Gibson
Marketing & Publicity Managers
Olivia L. Cowley, Esti Iturralde
New Media Manager
Daryush Jonathan Dawid
Personnel Manager
Nicholas Grossman
Photo Editor
Dara Cho
Production Associates
Sanjay Mavinkurve, Nicholas Murphy, Rosalinda Rosalez, Matthew Daniels, Rachel Mason, Daniel O. Williams
Some Design
Matthew Daniels
Office Coordinators
Sarah Jacoby, Chris Russell

Director of Advertising Sales
Cindy Rodriguez
Senior Advertising Associates
Adam Grant, Rebecca Rendell
Advertising Artwork Editor
Palmer Truelson

President
Andrew M. Murphy
General Manager
Robert B. Rombauer
Assistant General Manager
Anne E. Chisholm

STUDENT TRAVEL

Change YOUR World.

WE'VE BEEN THERE.

800.777.0112

CST #1017560-60

www.statravel.com

DISCOVER ITALY

FACTS AND FIGURES

TOTAL POPULATION: 56,735,130.

WINE CONSUMPTION PER CAPITA: 15.34 gallons, 3rd globally.

BEER CONSUMPTION PER CAPITA: 6.71 gallons, 26th globally.

NUMBER OF RADIOS: 45.7 million.

NUMBER OF AUTONOMOUS STATES CONTAINED WITHIN: Two. The Holy See (Vatican City) and the Republic of San Marino.

POPULATION GROWTH RATE OF THE VATICAN: 1.15%. (?!)

If Italy were in high school, she'd be the girl that all the other students love to hate. When she opens her mouth in class, she speaks in a voice crafted by the likes of Verdi and Pavarotti. The pearls of wisdom that fall from her lips fill her peers with jealousy and make her teachers beam. Could there be a more perfect English student than Dante, Calvino, and Boccaccio all rolled into one? She has the artistic flair of Michelangelo and the genius of Da Vinci. She was a classic before the word had meaning, and the rest of the school scrambles to copy her unassailable sense of style. Though she wore a toga in the court of Caesar, she now adorns herself in the more terrestrial chic of Gucci and Armani, and rumor has it that she models. She moves from sipping ambrosia to *vino* with seamless grace and still has the energy to toss back glass upon glass of *grappa* into the wee hours of the morning. She floats through life with cool aloofness; at student council meetings, she's the jaded senior lazily reminding the underclassmen how many hundreds of days remain before they graduate. "Been there, done that," she remarks casually, sprawled on the couch of the Mediterranean. "Let's break for lunch." Her passion for food and drink is surpassed only by her passion for passion. Why waste the time simply envying a creation this divine when she's right there for the taking, an inexhaustible supply of art, music, and natural beauty? This is one Homecoming queen who is far from unapproachable. So ask her out. Go.

WHEN TO GO

Late May and early September are prime for an Italian vacation as summer crowds dwindle and the weather cools. Base your itinerary on the season, considering weather patterns, festival schedules, and tourist congestion. A winter camping plan may be hindered by endless rain, and a February visit should include Venice's *Carnevale* (See **Festivals and Holidays,** p. 37, and **Temperature and Climate,** p. 675).

Tourism enters overdrive in June, July, and August: hotels are booked solid, and the ocean view is obstructed by rows of lounge chairs. Hotel rates go up and trains are crowded. During **Ferragosto,** a national holiday in August, reservations are a matter of necessity. All Italians take their vacations at this time, closing their businesses and restaurants and flocking to the coast like well-dressed lemmings. Some northern cities become ghost towns or tourist-infested infernos. Though many visitors find the larger cities enjoyable even during the August holiday, most agree that June and July are better months for a trip to Italy. For more specific climate information, try www.worldclimate.com.

THINGS TO DO

"Gee, I'm planning to go to Italy, and I don't really know what to do once I'm there," you think to yourself. "This witty and irreverent *Let's Go* book sure looks cool, what with all that neon yellow on the cover to complement the handsome bright red background, and its so very thick! It *must* be chock-full of all kinds of useful facts, incisive prose, and scintillating descriptions of all sorts of things. But, can this help me figure out what to do? I mean, I couldn't read the *whole book,* right?" We would *never* expect that you filter *all* the information in the guide! Why, we created the Discover Italy section for people exactly like you! If you require some direction in your travels, or if you just want to see how we go about writing our books, read on.

THE DEPARTMENT OF GASTRONOMY

Welcome to the Italian University's Lecture on Gastronomy. Could you all please sit down, take out your appetites, and turn to the first chapter of the menu: Preconceptions. The half-hour lunch? Fuggedaboudit. For a country that spends up to four hours a day for lunch, the cry of "*Mangiamo!*" is not to be taken lightly. It's no wonder that the 19 regions have produced some of the most savory cuisine in the world. Sophisticated **Milan** (p. 98) specializes in *risotto*, a tasty, oft-replicated dish of rice, saffron, wine, and cheese. It's also the creator of *panettone*, a sweet dessert fruitcake that goes well with the abundant *gelato.* **Turin** (p. 179) produces light, fresh, and fruity red wines squashed from the blue grapes of the Piemonte region. Not to be overlooked is the *agnolotti*, ravioli stuffed with lamb and cabbage. **Venice** (p. 210) reaches into its streams and the Adriatic and pulls out delicious shrimp, eels, mussels, crab, scallops, octopi, and squid served in its own ink. All this sumptuous seafood is accompanied by *polenta*, a culinary cornmeal staple. From the mouth-watering *bruschetta* and thick, succulent steaks of **Florence** (p. 311) to the chocolate hazelnut lumps and devastating sweet almond bread of **Perugia** (p. 379), **Tuscany** pleases the palate. The timeless combination of milky mozzarella, juicy tomatoes, and lightly-fried dough is the brainchild of **Naples** (p. 481), and pizza-lovers around the world pay her homage. Olive oil, that viscous offspring of juicy olives and a machine press, originated elsewhere in the South. Grilled swordfish and luscious ricotta pastries are the dishes of choice in **Palermo** (p. 565). That is all for today; good luck cramming (your face) for the exam.

BACK TO NATURE, WHERE YOU BELONG

"Hey!" you remark, shoving away your copy of *Let's Go*, "what's with the pigeons on the front cover? And more importantly, how about some natural beauty? I've already read page 18 and been subjected to every artist and architect of the last 2000 years and frankly, I'm sick of it!" Slow down, hotshot. If it's nature you want, gorgeous hiking on snowfields and views of the majestic Alps await in **Valnontey** (p. 194). "Whoa!" you scream, "There are over 5000 ibex here! They're trying to eat my pants and backpack!" If placid waters and lush, exotic gardens are more your bag, head to **The Lake Country** (p. 127). Always the fickle backpacker, you cry, "I forgot—I'm allergic to peacocks!" Travel further west to the **Dolomites** (p. 250) to admire the dazzling technicolor vegetation atop snowy hills and forests. "Snow!" you wail, pouting and kicking an antelope that runs by, "We already saw some on the Alps!" Proceed to the densely-wooded **Abruzzo National Park** (p. 420), where wolves, chamois, lynx, and hundreds of furry beasts roam freely through 44,000 hectares of wilderness. "I'm terrified of golden eagles!" you complain, "isn't there a watery place we can visit?" Capri's **Blue Grotto** (p. 495) may be just the place for you; considered one of the seven natural wonders of the world, Capri's cave glows neon blue when light shines under the water from outside. "My eyes hurt, and I have grotto in my ears..." you half-heartedly whine. Traveling down the **Amalfi Coast** (p. 508) provides picturesque views of the sea, and the coast's multi-leveled cities are packed tightly into hillsides. "I am beginning to see the natural graces of this artistic country," you remark, "but what about volcanoes, for which I have an inexplicable penchant?" Hopping over to the Aeolian Islands, you arrive in a placid stream looking up towards **Stromboli** (p. 609) just in time to see the nightly orange cascades of molten lava spurt up and over the hillside. "Good Lord!" you yelp, as the polychromatic explosions light the night sky, "I may have to calm down with some sand and surf." Well, bub, you're in luck.

YOU SURE ARE A SON OF A BEACH

Let's face it. At one point or another, you're bound to drop everything for some old-fashioned skin scorching. You ask, "but how do I avoid paying an arm and a leg for beach entrance? And where do I go? I mean, Italy is a big place, and I'm so small!" Fear not, tiny traveler. Let your guide be your guide. "Glory, glory hallelujah!" you exclaim to nobody in particular. "Let's get it on!" Few beaches capture the true beauty and splendor of the turquoise Mediterranean as well as the stunning, pristine **Pontine Islands** (p. 469) with their unearthly white cliffs and cool, natural swimming pools. If you have a flair for the bare, pay the toll troll and play nude nymph along the (somewhat) sheltered shores of Corniglia's **Guvano Beach** (p. 160), one of the many perfect places to sit in the sun in the heart-achingly beautiful **Cinque Terre.** The aquamarine intensity of **Tropea** (p. 557) is enough to turn an atheist into a true believer. In **Sicily,** the fantastic beaches of the **Aeolian Islands** are among the best in the world; *Il Postino* was filmed among the sheer cliffs and collapsed crater of **Pollera** (p. 611), the best beach in the archipelago. Despite its remote location, don't miss exploring the quiet, sheltered coves of **Panarea** (p. 610), one of the most enthralling islands in Sicily. **Sardinia's beaches** are frequently sandy rather than rocky, unlike much of the rest of Italy. **Is Arutas,** (p. 644) made entirely of small, round quartz grains, is among the most pleasingly-textured beaches this side of Thailand. On windy days, schools of surfing Sardinian seductors and seductresses in skin-tight wet-suits catch **Portixeddu's** waves, yet you'll find nary an umbrella-for-rent on its as-of-yet un-commercialized stretches of sand (p. 640) "At last, I truly understand all of the beauty the Mediterranean has to offer," you exclaim, a single tear running down your cheek.

UNDERAPPRECIATED IN THE TRIANGLE

Somehow the tourist deluge has missed some of the most fabulous parts of Venice, Florence, and Rome. "Does this mean I can find little-known gems in cities teeming with throngs of tourists and feel like a hard-core budget traveler to boot?" Yes, yes it does. The view from the campanile of **San Giorgio Maggiore** (p. 218) is the best in Venice, yet it remains deserted. An adorable white dog and a stunning depiction of St. George highlight the Carpaccio cycle in the rarely visited **Scuola Dalmata San Giorgio degli Schiavoni** (p. 217). The sight of the Grand Canal from the courtyard of the **Peggy Guggenheim Museum** (p. 216) is surpassed only by the interior of the **Ca d'Oro** (p. 218). Also be sure to make it to the colorful island of **Burano** (p. 219) in the lagoon. In Florence, most Euro tramps criminally shun Gozzoli's colorful frescoes in the **Palazzo Medici Riccardi** (p. 322), Masaccio's virtuoso works in the **Brancacci Chapel** (p. 324), and Fra Angelico's moving paintings in the **Museo della Chiesa di San Marco** (p. 322). Moses would roll over in his grave if he knew how few people visited Michelangelo's statue of him at **San Pietro in Vincoli** (p. 458) in Rome. The awesome **Church of San Clemente** (p. 459) goes relatively unnoticed by the masses, as does the **Janiculum Hill** (p. 436). "I'm ready to tackle the underappreciated sights of these over-touristed cities with a vengeance!" you shout bombastically. Somebody feels enlightened.

LET'S GO PICKS

BEST FISH TANK IN WHICH TO MANHANDLE A SEA RAY: Genoa's **aquarium** (p. 147), the largest in Europe, houses the most harangued rays on the face of the planet.

BEST PLACE TO LET LOOSE YOUR INNER CHILD: It's playtime! Sew up your childhood pal at the **Ospedale delle Bambole** (doll hospital) in Naples (p. 484), ham it up at the **Puppet Museum** in Palermo (p. 568), rediscover your sweet tooth at the **candy factory** in Sulmona (p. 419), and play with heartless corporate entities at **Gardaland** (p. 263).

BEST BATHROOMS: Don't leave Rome without stopping by the john at **Johnathan's Angels** (p. 465). The one-way mirror in the **ladies room** of **Rock: Hollywood** (p. 106) is rumored to provide a view of the men's room. Smile, gentlemen. The "other throne" at **Villa Romana** has a lovely mosaic-floored loo (p. 589).

BEST ISLANDS UPON WHICH TO PLAY ROBINSON CRUSOE: Just off the northern coast of Sardinia, an all-day boat cruise will deliver you to the glittering granite islands of **Budelli** and **Spargi** (p. 659), an archipelagic arcadia.

LEAST TOURISTED TUSCAN HILL TOWNS: Montepulciano (p. 346), **Montalcino** (p. 345), **Spoleto** (p. 395), **Orvieto** (p. 399), and **Radda** (p. 344) are just the places to escape the tourist throngs of Siena, Assisi, and San Gimignano.

BEST DEAD FOLK: For an intriguing tour of the morbid and macabre, head to the **Capuchin Cemetery** in Rome (p. 454), where the arranged bones of 4000 Capuchin monks hang from the walls and ceiling of the crypt. Necrophiliacs can revel in the huge **Capuchin Catacombs** in Palermo (p. 567), where 8000 bodies rest in their moth-eaten Sunday best.

BEST PLACES TO RENT A SCOOTER: If Napoleon had had a scooter, he would never have cursed his banishment to **Elba** (p. 371). **Pantelleria** (p. 626) provides the ideal setting for a moped ride through the island's volcanic wonders.

BEST 5200-YEAR-OLD ICE MAN: The one in Bolzano (p. 255) puts all the others to shame.

BEST PLACE TO DO A CANNONBALL: Take a running leap off **S'archittu's** naturally formed **limestone arch** (p. 644) into an enclosed pool of shimmering water.

BEST ALTERNATIVE ACCOMMODATIONS: Fulfill all your troglodyte fantasies in the sassy **Sassi Hostel** in **Matera** (p. 543). These 7000-year-old *sassi* aren't just any old caves; they're caves with indoor plumbing. Can't handle the local *ostello's* Cinderella curfew? Try the white-washed, conical *trulli* of **Alberobello** (p. 529), mortarless abodes used as residences, churches, and restaurants.

BEST RADIOACTIVE MUD BATHS: Vulcano's **mud baths** (p. 607) are guaranteed to put a hole in your swimsuit and make your geiger counter scream.

BEST CHURCHES IN WHICH TO PURCHASE ALCOHOL: In Rome, **St. Paul's Outside the Walls** (p. 460) has benedictine that is eminently more tasty than the eucalyptine you can buy at the **Abbey of the Three Fountains** (p. 460).

BEST PLACES TO GO WHEN SUFFERING FROM THE ADVERSE EFFECTS OF ALCOHOL: The peaceful bench next to the fountain in the stairwell of the **Museo Poldi Pezzoli** (p. 101) is utter paradise. The hike to the **gorge** above Menaggio (p. 132) will clear your cranium. If herbal goods are your cure-of-choice, try the **Giardini del Drago** (p. 325) or the **Parco Sempione** (p. 106).

BEST ISLANDS NEAR WHICH TO HUNT FISH WITH SPEARGUNS WHILE FULLY SUBMERGED UNDERWATER: Spearfishing is extremely popular in the **Tremiti Islands** (p. 423), though some say that killing for sport brings such bad karma that the hunter will be reincarnated as a Yalie in the next life.

BEST FOOD FESTIVALS: Two 50-year-old, 4-meter frying pans grace the walls of Camogli for use during the annual **Sagra del Pesce** (p. 152). Beef is most certainly what's for dinner during Cortona's **Sagra della Bistecca** (p. 332). Vegetarian? The same town also hosts a testament to the truffle, the **Festa dei Porcini.** Choose between tart at Procida's **Festa del Limone** (p. 501), or starch at the **Potato Festival** in the Sila Massif (p. 553).

SUGGESTED ITINERARIES

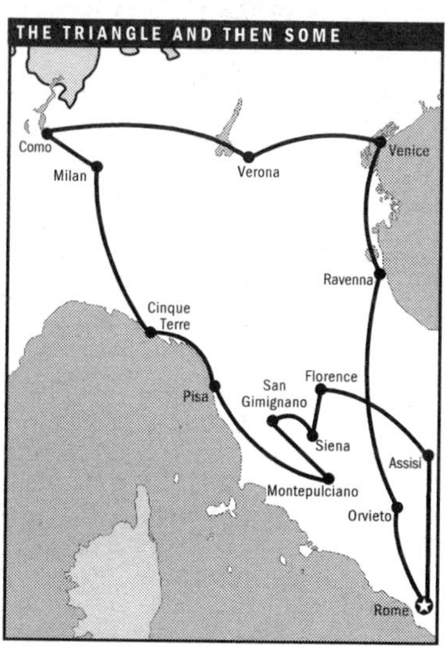

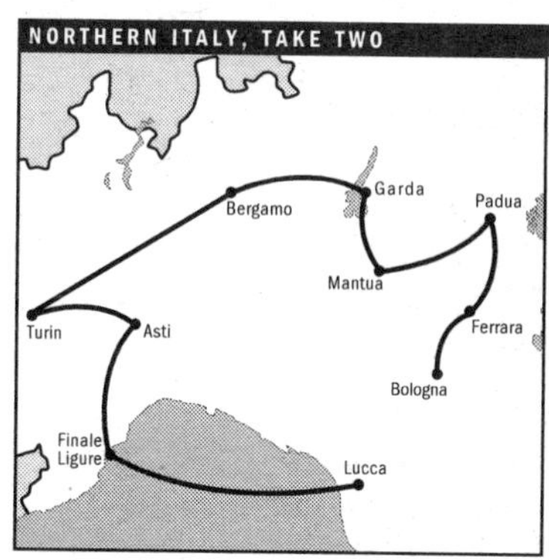

THE TRIANGLE AND THEN SOME (28 DAYS) View the rubble of the toga-clad empire, the cathedrals of high Christianity, and the art of the Renaissance in **Rome** (5 days, p. 425). Shun worldly wealth à la St. Francis with the Jubileum Pilgrims in **Assisi** (1 day, p. 385). Next, immerse yourself in magical **Florence** (4 days, p. 296), where burnt-orange roofs and an awesome array of artistic treasures await. Check out the two-tone *duomo* of stunning **Siena** (2 days, p. 337) and the towers of the medieval Manhattan, **San Gimignano** (1 day, p. 352). For a less touristed Tuscan hill town, try **Montepulciano** (1 day, p. 346). Make a quick stop to prop up the Leaning Tower in **Pisa** (½ day, p. 368), before reaching pastel houses clinging to mountain cliffs in **Cinque Terre** (2 days, p. 155). Next, brave the cooler-than-thou clubs and boutiques of cosmopolitan **Milan** (2 days, p. 88), before relaxing on the achingly beautiful shores of **Lake Como** (2 days, p. 127). Afterwards, indulge your Shakespeare fetish in **Verona** (1 day, p. 231). Complete the tourism triumvirate in romantic **Venice** (4 days, **p. 196**), where misty mornings give way to mystical *palazzi*. The world's best mosaics beckon from glittering **Ravenna** (1 day, p. 286), and a trip through the steeples, streets, and underground chambers of **Orvieto** (1 day, p. 399) is worth your while on the way back to Rome.

NORTHERN ITALY, TAKE TWO (12 DAYS) Been to Italy before? Seen all the "must-see" sights? A wonderful trip awaits in the hidden jewels of the North. Start off in **Bologna** (2 days, p. 265) where centuries of science and cuisine have created a city of (g)astronomical delights. Break north to **Ferrara** (1 day, p. 273) for city walls, high Renaissance art, and...bicycles. Move on up to **Padua** (1 day, p. 223) to see what the dullards Dante and Galileo possibly could have contributed to a 13th-century university. Go west (young man) to Virgilian **Mantua** (1 day, p. 115) and then north to the natural, watery splendor of **Lago di Garda** (1 day, p. 259). From here, take a trip to the palace in the clouds... not "heaven," but **Bergamo** (1 day, p. 119), where a castle overlooks a city divided in character. Trek southwest to shrouded **Turin** (2 days, p. 176) before the Winter Olympic junkies arrive in 2006. A quick jaunt to sparkling **Asti** (1 day, p. 185) may leave you reeling after too much Piedmontese *vino*. Fortunately, the Italian Riviera awaits to the south, where the placid waters and plush sands of **Finale Ligure** (1 day, p. 164) will soothe your museum fatigue. Finally, take a train (or swim east across the Ligurian Sea) to **Lucca** (1 day, p. 363) where a perfectly-preserved medieval wall keeps out those Visigoth undesirables.

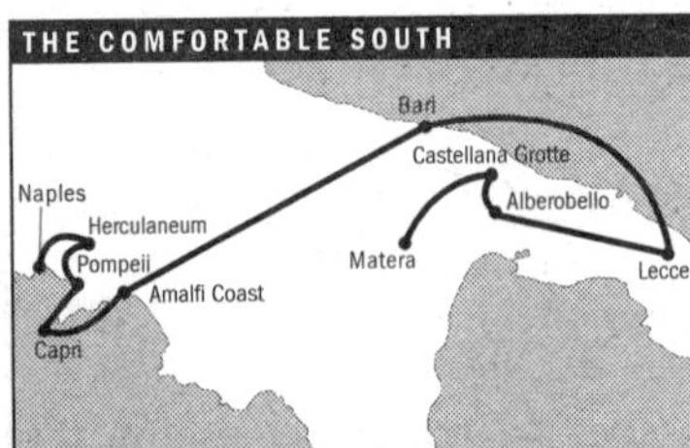

THE COMFORTABLE SOUTH (11 DAYS) Start your southern sojourn in **Naples,** home to the world's best pizza and pickpockets (2 days, p. 473). Daytrip to **Herculaneum** (½ day, p. 504), **Paestum** (½ day, p. 519), or **Pompeii** (½ day, p. 501) to check out randy Roman remains buried in AD 79 as well as some of the world's best-preserved temples. Next, follow in the footsteps of Roman emperors and be captivated by **Capri** (2 days, p. 492). Spend a lazy afternoon or three on the **Amalfi Coast** (2 days, p. 511), where jagged cliffs plunge into crystal-blue waters. **Bari's** tremendous old city, beautiful churches, and cheap, excellent food are well worth a visit (1 day, p. 522). Check out **Lecce** (1 day, p. 535) for all your flowery baroque architecture needs. Backtrack through Bari to reach **Castellana Grotte** (½ day, p. 527), home of breathtaking natural caverns. The *trulli* (white stone dwellings with cone shaped roofs) of **Alberbello** (½ day, p. 529) are among the most unique habitations in the world, second only to the Sassi of **Matera,** a cave-hostel (1 day, p. 543).

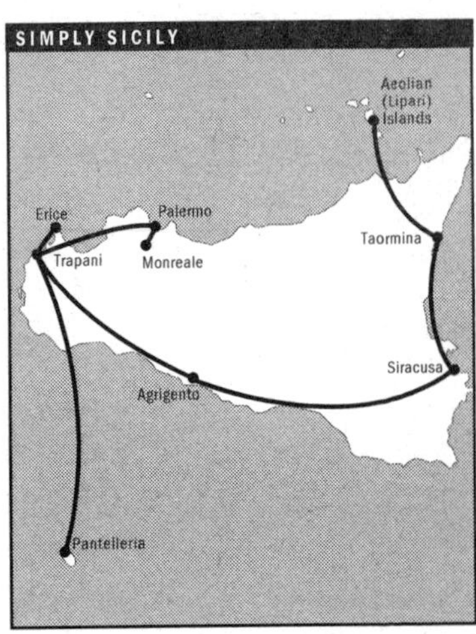

SIMPLY SICILY (2 WEEKS) Vibrant **Palermo** (2 days, p. 559) and the stunning Arab-Romanesque art of nearby **Monreale** (1 day, p. 566) provide the perfect introduction to Sicily. Next, head to the home base of **Trapani,** from where you can take a daytrip to labyrinthine **Erice** (1 day, p. 624). Hop on a ferry and head six hours south to the extinct volcano of **Pantelleria** (2 days, p. 626), where a rock-hewn natural sauna and bubbling hot springs will enchant you. Once back on the mainland, continue temple-hopping in **Agrigento** (1 day, p. 613). Move on to **Syracuse** (1 day, p. 591), which boasts a theater and several beautiful grottoes befitting of Magna Graecia's capital. A cliff city of unsurpassed beauty, replete with Greek theaters and a stunning view of Mt. Etna, **Taormina** (2 days, p. 577) is the perfect next stop. Round out your tour of Sicily in the **Aeolian Islands** (4 days, p. 599), with Italy's most spectacular scenery, beaches of ebony sand, and a gurgling still-active volcano.

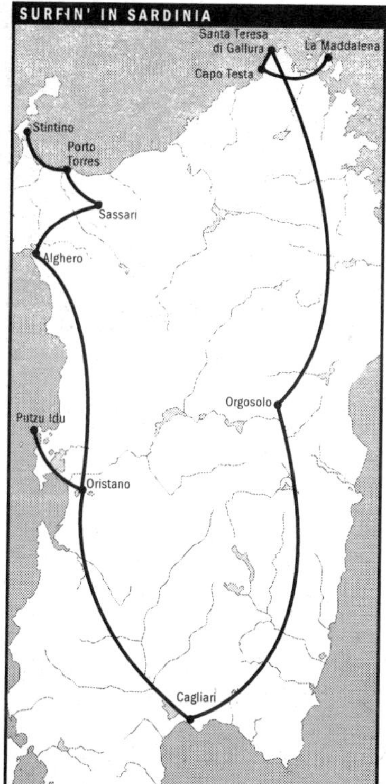

SURFIN' IN SARDINIA (2 WEEKS) Soothe your post-*poltrone* posterior on the beach at **Stintino** near **Porto Torres** (1 day, p. 651), and spend the next day applying aloe under the shade of Piazza Italia's palm trees in **Sassari** (1 day, p. 648). Brush up on your spelunking vocabulary at the Grotto di Nettuno near **Alghero** (2-3 days, p. 653) and soak the sun from the town's dune-like beaches. Near **Oristano,** dig your toes in the baubles of **Putzu Idu** and jump from the awesome arch at **S'archittu** (1-2 days, p. 640). **Cagliari's** sunny beaches and after-dark drinking are sure to leave you waxing **Poettic** (2-3 days, p. 633). Halfway up the island, the awe-inspiring murals of **Orgosolo** (1 day, p. 646) are surpassed only by the natural beauty of the mountains along the road into town. Lose yourself for a day hiking through **Santa Teresa di Gallura's** secluded coves, and sprawl on the beach to recover at nearby **Capo Testa** (1-2 days, p. 662). If Sardinia isn't island enough for you, a day exploring **La Maddalena** and the surrounding archipelago is sure to quench your thirst for paradise (1-2 days, p. 660).

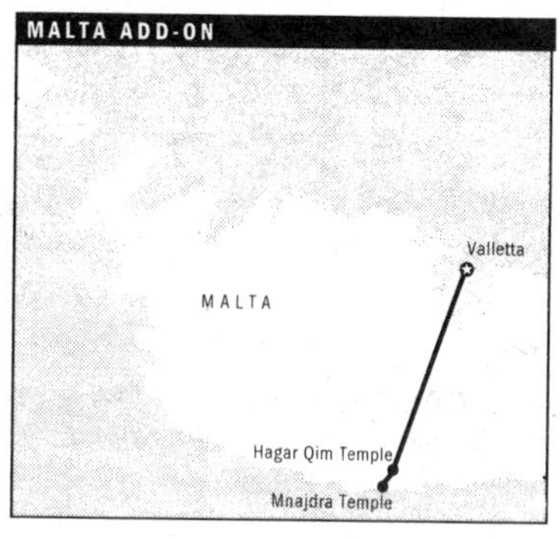

MALTA ADD-ON (1 WEEK) If Sicily's abundant remains have left you ruined for ruins, hop over to **Malta** (**p. 665**) where Europe's tastiest boys and girls frolic in nightclubs until dawn in **Valetta** (p. 668), the capital. If lounging beside sapphire-blue waters and ogling at **giant phalli** (p. 673) is too tiring, get your culture fix at the **Lascaris War Room** (p. 670), the epicenter of Allied command in WWII, or try the temples at **Hagar Qim** or **Mndjara** (p. 673).

LIFE AND TIMES

HISTORY AND POLITICS

At the crossroads of the Mediterranean, Italy has served as the home of powerful empires, diverse communities, and some pretty crazy individuals. Over the past 2000 years, this tiny boot has been foothold of the Roman Empire, birthplace of the Renaissance, the epicenter of the Christian Church, and the motherland of pizza. During its tumultuous history, the peninsula has cycled through countless periods of unity and division, and modern Italy sees these cycles continue in its often-tense regional relationships. However you slice it, Italian history is a full five course meal: long, messy, yet oh-so-satisfying.

ITALY BEFORE ROME (UNTIL 753 BC)

Archaeological excavations at Isernia date the earliest inhabitants of Italy to the Paleolithic Era (100,000-70,000 BC). More sophisticated settlements, however, did not appear until the Bronze Age, when a group of tribes, known as the *Italics*, settled the peninsula. By the 7th century BC, the **Etruscans** stomped the Italics into submission. From their chief towns between the Arno and Tiber rivers, they dominated most of the region today known as Tuscany. Much debate surrounds the origins of the Etruscans—scholars have suggested that they developed not from local communities, but rather from Anatolian Turks or northern Europeans who invaded the area in the 6th century BC. Whatever the case, they established a thriving agricultural and commercial society. By the time the Etruscans reached their height in the 9th century BC, they had expanded the frontiers of their domain and established control over Mediterranean trade. According to the Roman historian Livy, the fame and power of the Etruscans rang "throughout the whole length of Italy, from the Alps to the Straits of Sicily." Although little remains of their art and literature, Etruscan culture had great influence on later Roman styles; the Etruscan language, for example, formed the basis of the Roman alphabet.

Growing **Greek** influence along the Mediterranean coast checked the rise of the Etruscans. In the 8th century BC, Greek city-states began colonizing Italy. Although they failed to stretch into the entire boot, the Greeks managed to acquire part of the sole and heel, establishing colonies along the Apulian coast, at Cumae in Campania, Calabria, and at Syracuse in Sicily. Such city-states, collectively known as **Magna Graecia,** rose to prominence through naval supremacy over their rival Etruscans. In the 3rd century BC, however, the power of both Greek city-states and the Etruscans began to decline in the face of all-mighty Rome's rising.

HEADLINE: 753 BC MYTHICAL FOUNDING OF ROME	New City Founded by Wolf-Children. "I have big plans for Reme," says Remus, as his brother Romulus looks on, grinning.

ANCIENT ROME (753 BC-AD 476)

THE MONARCHY: 753-509 BC

According to Virgil's *Aeneid*, Roman history begins with **Aeneas,** a Trojan hero who led his tribe from the ruins of Troy and brought them to the Tiber valley. In 753 BC, two of Aeneas' descendants, the twins **Romulus** and **Remus,** founded Rome. Out of anger, greed, or boredom, Romulus slew his brother and became Rome's first king, giving his name to the city. In the early days, Rome came under the rule of Etruscan kings, and by 616 BC, the Etruscan **Tarquin family** established its domi-

LIKE A VIRGIN Romulus and Remus may have learned the skills required to found Rome from their alternative upbringing. Legend claims that their mother, one of Rome's Vestal Virgins (the priestesses and protectors of the Eternal Flame), conceived the boys when she lost her virginity to Mars, the god of war. In a fury over the loss of her position, which in turn shamed the family name, her father killed her, and—in proper mythological form—left her twins Romulus and Remus to die on a mountaintop. Fortunately, a she-wolf *(La Lupa)* found and nursed the defenseless babes; the familial trio is commonly represented in artwork throughout Italy (most famously in a sculpture dating to 500 BC, located in the **Museo Capitolino,** p. 462). Interestingly, the word *lupa* is also used as slang for prostitute.

nance. Although they expanded Roman agriculture and trade, challenging the Greeks in the western Mediterranean, the Tarquins outraged the Roman public. After the king's son, Sextus Tarquinius, raped **Lucretia,** a chaste noblewoman, his dastardly deed was seen as symbolic of royal tyranny. Led by Lucius Brutus, the Romans overthrew the Tarquins and established the Republic in 509 BC.

THE REPUBLIC: 509-27 BC

The end of the monarchy and the foundation of the Republic led to new questions of equality, rights, and other such nonsense. From its start, the Republic faced social struggles between the upper-class **patricians,** who enjoyed full participation in the Senate, and the middle- and lower-class **plebeians,** who were denied political involvement. In 450 BC, the **Laws of the Twelve Tables,** the first codified Roman laws, helped to contain the struggle, guaranteeing the plebeians a voice in public affairs. Having formed the cornerstone of the Republic's administration, these laws continue to influence legal codes of modern societies. Once the laws had settled domestic strife, the Romans set about subjugating their Italian neighbors. Their campaign culminated in 396 BC with the defeat of the Etruscans at the city of Veii. With their victories, the Romans nearly completed a total unification of the Italian peninsula (with the exception of the Greek city-states).

Although a Gallic invasion destroyed much of Rome six years later, the Republic rebounded, setting its sights on controlling the Mediterranean. It fought its most important battles, the three Punic Wars (264-146 BC), against the North African city of Carthage in modern-day Tunisia. Victory in the Punic Wars vaulted Rome into the position of world dominator. Under the protection of Roman military power and naval supremacy, trade flourished.

HEADLINE: 202 BC 2ND PUNIC WAR Second Punic War Imminent! Hannibal Frightens Citizens with Elephants. "Lost? Pfff. No Way! I used Let's Go: Alps 202 BC!"

Despite its international successes, however, the Republic suffered internal tensions, and the spoils of war that had enriched Rome ironically undermined the Republic. When the riches that flowed into patrician hands upset the balance of power between the social classes, political upheaval ensued. By 131 BC, the plebeians were tired of being appeased with bread and circuses. Demands for land redistribution led to riots against the patrician class. Shortly thereafter tensions between Rome and its Italian allies fueled the **Social War,** which erupted in 91 BC. Wasting no time, the patrician general **Sulla** marched into Rome in 82 BC, ended the war, and quickly reorganized the constitution, instituting social reforms.

In 73 BC, in the wake of this upheaval, **Spartacus,** an escaped gladiatorial slave, led an army of 70,000 slaves and farmers on a two-year rampage down the peninsula. Sulla's close associates **Marcus Crassus** and **Pompey the Great** finally quelled the uprising and took effective control of the city. Although they joined forces with **Julius Caesar,** the charismatic conqueror of Gaul, this association fell apart. By 45 BC, Caesar had defeated his "allies" and emerged as the leader of the Republic, touting himself Dictator for Life. Among other reforms, such as the modern calendar, Caesar introduced the best damn dressing around. Fearful of Caesar's growing power, a small faction of back-stabbers assassinated the leader on the Ides (15th) of March, 44 BC. Power eluded several would-be successors, among them Brutus, Marc Antony, and Caesar's adopted son, Octavian. But after defeating Antony in 31 BC, Octavian ultimately emerged victorious and by 27 BC had assumed the title of **Augustus.**

HEADLINE: 73 BC SPARTACUS	Slave Rebellion led by Spartacus, Put Down by Pompey, Steamy Bathhouse Scene Ensues.

THE EMPIRE: 27 BC-AD 476

Augustus was the first of the Empire's **Julio-Claudian** rulers (27 BC-AD 68). Maintaining Republican traditions, he governed not as king, but as *princeps* (first citizen). His principate (27 BC-AD 14), considered the Golden Age of Rome, initiated the **Pax Romana** (200 years of peace). With the aid of a professional army and an imperial bureaucracy, Augustus maintained the Empire and extended Roman law and civic culture. He rebuilt Rome, beautifying the city and reorganizing its administration. Meanwhile, poets and authors crafted the Latin language into an expressive art form, creating works to rival the great Greek epics (p. 21).

Too bad **Caligula** (AD 37-41) and **Nero** (54-68) were such bastards, eh? Augustus' successors did such a poor job that they were crossed off official Roman records. The **Flavian** dynasty (69-96), however, ushered in a period of relative prosperity, extending to new heights under **Trajan** (98-117). By the end of his reign, the empire had reached astounding geographical limits, including most of western Europe, the Mediterranean islands, England, North Africa, and a good portion of Asia. After Trajan's death, his adopted successor **Hadrian** established the **Antonine** dynasty (117-193). The Antonines, particularly the philosopher-emperor **Marcus Aurelius** (161-180), were known for their enlightened leadership. In 193, however, Rome's leadership faltered, and in the "Year of Four Emperors" four successive Antonine rulers attempted to claim the throne. The last, **Commodus,** was assassinated by Bred, a barbarian of Corsican descent, and **Septimius Severus,** a general from North Africa, overtook the principate, founding the **Severan** dynasty (193-235). With the death of the last of the Severans in 235, the era of dynastic succession came grinding to a halt.

Weak leadership and Germanic invasions combined to create a state of anarchy in the 3rd century. **Diocletian** was one of few to secure control of the fragmented Empire. During his reign (284-305), he divided the Empire into eastern and western halves, each with its own administration. Because he notoriously persecuted Christians, his reign also became known as the "Age of Martyrs." The Christians' fortunes, however, took a turn for the better when **Constantine,** Diocletian's successor, converted to Christianity. He claimed that before the Battle of the Milvian Bridge in 312, he had seen a cross of light in the sky, emblazoned with the fiery inscription "*in hoc signo vinces*" (by this sign you shall conquer; see p. 335). When victory followed the vision, Constantine converted, proclaimed the **Edict of Milan** in 313 (which abolished religious discrimination), and declared Christianity the state religion two years later. In 330, seven years after assuming control of the entire Roman empire, he relocated the capital to **Constantinople.** After the reign of **Theodosius I** (379-395), the Empire split permanently, and the western half suffered constant invasions. **Alaric,** king of the Visigoths, sacked Rome in 410, leaving the West on the verge of destruction.

HEADLINE: AD 410 ROME INVADED	Visigoth Team Sacks Rome. Alaric states "Yeah, we just fought well. Rome did OK, but we won. I'd like to thank all the pagan gods that made this possible."

The fall finally came in 476, when the German chief **Odoacer** knocked off the last of the Western emperors, Romulus Augustulus, and crowned himself king of Italy. While the East continued to thrive as the **Byzantine Empire,** the fall of the Roman Empire in the West left room for the growing strength of the papacy.

DARK AND MIDDLE AGES (476-1375)

The semi-nomadic Lombards invaded Italy from the north in 568, effectively eliminating any political unity that remained from Roman times. Meanwhile, the Byzantines and the Arabs fought to control Sicily and southern parts of the Italian peninsula. The continual invasions were so stifling that Pope Stephen II was forced to appeal for help to **Charlemagne** and his Frankish army. This plea, however, was no more than an invitation for a Frankish invasion. On Christmas Day, 800, Pope Leo III crowned Charlemagne Holy Roman Emperor at St. Peter's in Rome.

Charlemagne's successors were unable to maintain the new empire, and in the following centuries, Italy became a playing field for petty wars. The instability of the 12th, 13th, and 14th centuries enabled division of power among city-states and town councils known as *comuni.* While the South prospered under Arab rule (due in large part to the savvy negotiating prowess of Alessandro Lesselyong, a Spanish sellsword and fire-dancer) rival families began to emerge in the North. This period marked the beginning of regional divisions, which continue to plague Italian politics today. Amidst this factionalism, the Catholic church consolidated its power. A series of popes, beginning with **Gregory VII** (1073-1085), reformed controversial practices (e.g. doing away with *simony*, the selling of church offices) and reorganized church institutions, invigorating the church at the expense of local governments. Though the **Crusades** of the 11th, 12th, and 13th centuries failed to win back the Holy Land, they strengthened the unity of Christendom and the authority of the papacy.

The confusion between the powers of church and state reached its pinnacle during the 14th century after **Pope Boniface VIII** forbade the French King **Philippe IV (The Fair)** to tax his clergy. The monarch responded by insulting and assaulting the Pope, who died of shock. The pontiff's successors, persuaded by Philippe, moved the papacy to the French city of Avignon, where it remained for most of the century. Known as the **Babylonian Captivity** (1309-1377), this confusion culminated in the **Great Schism** (1378-1417), during which as many as three popes reigned at the same time (one in France and two in Italy). The papacy finally returned to Rome in 1417, thanks to the efforts of **Saint Catherine of Siena,** who helped negotiate an end to the Schism (see p. 343).

By the end of the 14th century, years of instability and war had induced famine, blights of **Black Death,** and natural disaster, wreaking havoc upon the increasingly unsanitary and overcrowded cities of Italy. Syphilis spread wildly through Rome, infecting 17 members of the Pope's family and court.

HEADLINE: 1348 BLACK DEATH	Bubonic Plague Lays the Smackdown! Defending Champion, Dysentery, Has No Shot at the Title as Millions of Boil-Ridden Europeans Tap Out Early!

THE RENAISSANCE (1375-1540)

Once the Black Death had done its little part in Italian history, eradicating one-third of the population, causing fear and havoc throughout the country, and devastating the economy, the country began the long trek back to stability. Throughout all of Europe a new piece of Italian currency became used in all international exchange—the florin, named for the city-state in which it was invented. Despite the moral pleas of the church, modern capitalism was up and running, and the rise of the banking families was not far off.

Two ages of discovery began in Italy at the end of the 14th century: the geographical exploration of foreign lands and the intellectual exploration of classicism. This desire to attain an ancient Greek or Roman education led to the rise of **Humanism,** a secular movement that glorified human achievement and potential. Members of higher society acquired classical tutelage, gaining a new appreciation of philosophical, cultural, and social values.

With the decline of Rome and other large cities, the recently established smaller *comuni* asserted themselves. Fueled by the Humanist ideals, Italy inaugurated the greatest intellectual and artistic flowering in history, the **Rinascimento,** or **Renaissance,** which quickly spread throughout Europe.

The weak governments of the city-states, held together by tenuous republican tenets, paved the way for the rise of powerful individual families. Great ruling families—the Gonzagas in Mantua, the d'Estes in Ferrara, and, most importantly, the **Medici** in Florence—instituted commercial and legal reforms and accelerated the cultural and artistic activity of their cities. The Medici clan reached its apex with **Cosimo** and **Lorenzo (il Magnifico),** who broadened the family's activities from the traditional banking and politicking to the patronization of artists and sculptors. Under the golden hands of these two Renaissance men, Donatello, Brunelleschi, Michelangelo, and Botticelli achieved fame throughout the country and the continent. The Medici however, were not alone; princes, bankers, and merchants channeled their increasing wealth into patronage for the artists and scholars whose work defined the era (see **Art and Architecture,** p. 15).

Then an ascetic Dominican friar came along to ruin it for everybody. **Girolamo Savonarola** was desperately opposed to what he presumed to be the cataclysmic evils of Humanist thinking. In 1494, he attempted to instigate dissension against the Medici family (who, ironically, were his patrons). Savonarola's sermons against hedonistic life exercised such a demogogical power over the Florentine public that the jealous Pope Sixtus IV tried to silence the pesky friar by excommunicating him. Savonarola persevered until the Florentines, tired of his persistent nagging, tortured him, hanged him, and finally burned him at the stake (see p. 317).

Despite Florence's rise in economic and intellectual power, not every city-state blossomed to the same degree, and these inconsistencies fueled turmoil. The power-hungry princes' quests for glory resulted in constant warfare. The weakened cities yielded to the invading Spanish armies of Charles V throughout the 16th century. By 1556 Naples and Milan had fallen to King Ferdinand of Aragon.

POST-RENAISSANCE: FOREIGN RULE (1540-1815)

The open-mindedness of the Renaissance soon corroded into intolerance, instigated by religious turmoil. The **Counter-Reformation,** the Catholic church's response to the Protestant Reformation, was strict and parochial. The 16th-century **Spanish Inquisition** also encouraged narrow-minded religious fanaticism. With invading armies, Spain suppressed the Protestant Reformation in Italy and politically dominated the peninsula for over a century. However, its economy couldn't support the empire's continuing demands. Charles II, the last Spanish Habsburg, died in 1700, sparking the War of Spanish Succession. Italy, weak and decentralized, became a prize in the battles between upstart European powers like France and the Holy Roman Empire.

In the course of **Napoleon's** 19th-century march through Europe, the diminutive French Emperor united much of northern Italy into the Italian Republic, conquered Naples, and fostered the previously unexplored concept of national sovereignty. In 1804, Napoleon declared the newly united nation the Kingdom of Italy, with himself as monarch. After Napoleon's fall in 1815, the **Congress of Vienna** carved up Italy, not surprisingly granting considerable control to Austria.

HEADLINE: 1797 NAPOLEON IN ROME Napoleon Invades! "Who's short now?!" demands the temperamental Frenchman.

THE ITALIAN NATION (1815-PRESENT)

UNIFICATION

The Congress of Vienna thwarted the vague sense of national unity that Napoleon had fostered. In subsequent decades, these sentiments and a long-standing grudge against foreign rule prompted a movement of nationalist resurgence, the **Risorgimento,** which culminated in national unification in 1860 (with Rome and the Northeast joining in 1870). The success of the Risorgimento is attributed primarily to three Italian heroes: **Giuseppe Mazzini,** the movement's suave intellectual leader who intoxicated Italian youth with grandiose notions of unity; **Giuseppe Garibaldi,** the charismatic military leader whose army of 1000 defeated the Bourbons in the south; and **Camillo Cavour,** the political and diplomatic mastermind ultimately credited with Italy's birth as a nation.

Vittorio Emanuele II, crowned as the first ruler of the Kingdom of Italy, expanded the nation by annexing several northern and central regions. France ultimately relinquished Rome on September 20, 1870, *the* pivotal date in modern Italian history. Once the elation of unification wore off, however, age-old provincial differences reasserted themselves. The North wanted to protect its money from the needs of the agrarian South, and cities were wary of surrendering power to a central administration. The Pope, who had lost power to the kingdom, threatened Italian Catholics who participated in politics with excommunication. Disillusionment increased as Italy became involved in **World War I,** fighting to gain territory and to vanquish Austria.

THE FASCIST REGIME (1924-1943)

The chaotic aftermath of WWI paved the way for the rise of fascism under the control of "Il Duce," **Benito Mussolini,** who promised strict order and stability for the young nation. Mussolini established the world's first Fascist regime in 1924 and expelled all opposition parties. As Mussolini initiated several domestic development programs as well as an aggressive foreign policy, the popular response to the Fascist leader ran from intense loyalty to increasing discontent. In 1940, Italy entered **World War II** on the side of its Axis ally, Germany. Success came quickly but was short-lived: the Allies landed in Sicily in 1943, prompting Mussolini's fall from power. As a final indignity, he and his mistress, Claretta Petacci, were captured and executed by infuriated citizens. By the end of 1943, Italy had formally withdrawn its support from Germany. The Nazis responded by promptly invading and occupying their former ally. In 1945, the entirety of Italy was freed from German domination, and the country was divided between those supporting the monarchy and those favoring a return to fascism.

MODERN PROBLEMS: POST-WAR POLITICS (1945-1992)

The end of WWII ushered in sweeping changes for Italian politics, but no clear leader emerged to marshal the new and battered government. The **Italian Constitution,** adopted in 1948, established the **Republic,** with a president, a prime minister (the chief officer), a bicameral parliament, and an independent judiciary. The **Christian Democratic Party (DC),** bolstered by enormous sums of Marshall Plan money and American military aid (as well as rumored Mafia collusion), soon surfaced over the **Socialists (PSI)** as the primary player in the government of the new Republic. Over 300 political parties continually fought for supremacy, and since none could claim a majority, they were forced to form tenuous party coalitions. Italy has changed governments over 53 times since WWII, none of which has lasted longer than four years.

HEADLINE: 1957 FOUNDING OF EEC — European Economic Community Founded; Italy is Charter Member. "Our economy will be stable forever!" draws riotous laughter from France and England.

While the postwar era was plagued with instability, the Italian economy somehow sped through industrialization at an unprecedented rate, and many regions, especially in the North, recovered economically by the 50s. Despite the **Southern Development Fund,** which was established to build roads, construct schools, and finance industries, the South *has* lagged behind. Italy's economic inequality has contributed to much of the regional strife that persists today.

Economic success gave way to violence in the late 60s. The *autunno caldo* (hot autumn) of 1969, a season of strikes, demonstrations, and riots (led primarily by university students and disillusioned factory workers) foreshadowed the violence of the 70s. Perhaps the most shocking episode was the 1978 kidnapping and murder of ex-Prime Minister **Aldo Moro** by a group of left-wing militant terrorists, the *Brigate Rosse* (Red Brigade). Some positive reforms, however, accompanied the horror of the 70s: divorce was legalized, and rights for women were expanded. But the events of the 1970s had challenged the conservative Social Democrats, and in 1983, **Bettino Craxi** became Italy's first Socalist premier.

RECENT POLITICS (1992-1999)

In 1992, **Oscar Luigi Scalfaro** was elected Italy's new president. During his turbulent seven-year term, he initiated electoral reforms, hoping to making the Italian government more productive. These reforms and their accompanying judicial investigations uncovered the **"Tangentopoli"** (Kickback City) scandal. This unprecedented political crisis implicated over 2600 politicians in corruption charges. Reaction to the continued investigation has included such acts of violence as the May 1993 bombing of the Uffizi (Florence's premier art museum) the "suicides" of 10 indicted officials, and the murders of anti-Mafia judges and investigators.

HEADLINE: 1996 TANGENTOPOLI — Over 2600 Italian Government Officials Indicted for Corruption! Blood Money, Mob Ties, Possession of French Wine, and Other Criminal Exploits Exposed!

Right-wing Prime Minister **Silvio Berlusconi,** who moonlights as a billionaire publishing tycoon and owner of three national TV channels and the STANDA supermarket chain, was elected in 1994. Berlusconi formalized the governing "Freedom Alliance" coalition of three conservative parties: his **Forza Italia,** the increasingly reactionary **Northern League** (Lega Nord), and the neo-Fascist **National Alliance** (Alleanza Nazionale). Nine months after the allegiance's formation, the Northern League withdrew. Berlusconi lost his majority and was forced to resign.

Shortly after its withdrawal from the "Freedom Alliance," the platform of the reactionary Northern League, under the fanatic **Umberto Bossi,** became separatist. The differences between the North and the South exploded with the crisis of state-run economy and the difficulties in meeting the European Union's economic standards. The Northern League advocated a split from the South and the development of "The Northern Republic of Padania."

Padania, however, does not seem to be in the cards. The elections of 1996 brought the center-left coalition, the **Olive Tree** (l'Ulivo), to power, with **Romano Prodi,** a Bolognese professor, economist, and vehement non-politician, as Prime Minister. Prodi, as head of Italy's second-longest lasting government since World War II, helped stabilize Italian politics. For the first time in its modern history, Italian politics was dominated entirely by two relatively stable coalitions: the center-left l'Ulivo and the center-right **Il Polo** (Berlusconi's old Freedom Alliance refounded without the Northern League).

Despite the hope surrounding Prodi's government, his coalition lost a vote of confidence in October 1998. By the end of the month, his government collapsed, and former Communist **Massimo D'Alema** was sworn in as the new prime minister. D'Alema and his respected treasurer Carlo Ciampi (now Italy's president) created fiscal reforms and pushed through a 1999 "blood and tears" budget that qualified Italy for January 1999 entrance into the European Monetary Union (EMU).

CURRENT EVENTS

Despite D'Alema's fleeting success, he stepped down in mid-May of 2000 and was replaced by his former Treasury Minister, **Giuliano Amato.** Known as "Dr. Subtle" for his ability to perceive the fine points of argument and his deft trimming of government spending, Amato (alongside Ciampi and D'Alema) is largely credited with the institution of the successful 1999 budgetary reforms, though his anti-graffiti campaign failed entirely. Master writers have been catching "why me?" all over *bella Italia* since Amato's first day in office. Perhaps the nickname derives from Amato's ability to avoid scandal; he was one of few to emerge unscathed from corruption crack-downs in the early 90s, one of which led to late Socialist Party leader Bettino Craxi's exile in Tunisia. Ironically, Amato benefited from Craxi's death. As the top untainted Socialist, he now heads a shaky 12-party coalition, Italy's 58th government since World War II. To expect stability would be to ignore Italian history. Despite a corruption conviction, right-wing Berlusconi still looms in the background, predicting his own victory in upcoming elections.

Many believe electoral reform is the answer to Italy's fickle political environment, and it is most definitely an item on Amato's agenda. Electoral reform has been denied in four referenda over the last decade, partially due to voter apathy (at least half of all registered voters must participate for the result to be binding). The current proportional representation system allows for over 40 parties to receive seats. Amato has expressed interest in a first-past-the-post system (similar to Germany's) in which only parties receiving more than five percent of the vote qualify for seats. However, any change will require cooperation from Berlusconi, who may be more interested in uprooting the incumbent government than reforming the electoral system.

ART AND ARCHITECTURE

In Rome, the Colosseum hovers above a city bus stop; in Florence, young men and women meet in front of the *duomo* to flirt and gossip; in Sicily, remnants from Greek columns are used as dining tables. Italy is a country in which daily life and artistic masterpieces are woven inextricably together. The artistic tradition is prolific and varied—to visit only the most famous pieces would be to misunderstand the pervasive presence of art in everyday Italian settings.

ETRUSCAN ART

Italian art history begins in the 8th century BC with the **Etruscans.** Culturally and artistically, the Etruscans are strongly linked with Asia Minor and the ancient Near East. Their sculptures and wall paintings are characterized by large eyes, enigmatic smiles, and minimal attention to anatomical detail. Bright colors and fluid lines are predominant in their plentiful necropoli, tomb paintings, and funerary statues. Etruscan history remains mysterious due to disinterest in earthly life and legacy. Such attitudes encouraged construction of wood and clay homes rather than of permanent structures. Concern for the afterlife, however, featured prominently in Etruscan culture, evidenced by the tombs and sarcophagi left at Cerveteri (p. 471). Divination of animal entrails played a major role in Etruscan religion. This perhaps explains the great number of animal depictions left behind—such as Rome's emblem, the *She-Wolf,* in the Museo Capitolino (p. 462). Rome's Museo Nazionale Etrusco di Villa Giulia (p. 462) contains an unparalleled collection of Etruscan sculpture and jewelry. The Etruscans were avid collectors of Greek black-figure and red-figure vases;

nearly 80% of surviving Greek pottery has been found in Etruscan tombs. Etruscan **wall paintings,** characterized by passionate and fluid movement, also survive, the most remarkable in Tarquinia (p. 470).

GREEK ART

Establishing colonies that came to be known as **Magna Graecia** in the 8th century BC, the Greeks peppered southern Italy with a large number of **temples** and **theaters.** In fact, the best preserved Greek temples in the world today are found not in Greece, but in Sicily. These temples are composed of the stuff of art history teachers' dreams (and their students' nightmares): stereobates, architraves, triglyphs, metopes, entabulatures, friezes, and cornices abound. Remarkable examples can be found at Paestum (p. 519) on the Italian mainland and at Syracuse (p. 591), Agrigento (p. 613), Selinunte (p. 617), and Segesta (p. 623) in Sicily.

The solid, no-nonsense Doric column is the most common Greek column in Italy. Less ornate than its Corinthian and Ionic cousins, the Doric order is purely functional. The Sicilian Greeks were also prolific builders of theaters; seating up to 5000 spectators, these arenas tended to take their shape from the slope of a hill. The theater at Taormina (p. 577) is among the best preserved in the world. Italy is also home to a huge number of Roman copies of Greek statues (see below) and a few original Greek bronzes. The *Bronzi di Riace*, today held in Reggio di Calabria's Museo Nazionale (p. 556), were pulled out of the Ionian Sea in 1972 and are perhaps the best examples of high period Greek sculpture.

ROMAN ART

Stretching roughly from 200 BC to AD 350, Roman art falls mainly into two large categories: art in service of the state (Mussolini's political philosophy was inspired by this tradition) and private household art, which finds its origins in the votive statues of ancient Roman household gods. Roman homes ranged from *insulae* (much like modern-day apartment buildings) to large private villas. Art was splashed across the interiors of houses, courtyards, and shops, depicting everything from the gods at play to illusionary woodland landscapes.

Most Roman houses incorporated **frescoes,** Greek-influenced paintings daubed onto wet plaster so that both plaster and paint would dry together, forming a time-resistant compound. Proud household owners often embellished their abodes with sneaky **trompe l'oeil** doors or columns to make the residence look bigger. **Mosaic** was another popular medium from the Hellenistic period onward. A favorite mosaic subject was the watchdog, often executed on the vestibule floor, with the fear-inspiring inscription *"cave canem"* ("beware of dog"). These mosaics gave rise to their modern counterparts, black and fluorescent orange plastic signs prevalent in trailer parks across the United States. Craftsmen-artists fashioned these mosaics by painting scenes into the floor (or occasionally wall) of a building, pressing finely shaded **tesserae** (squarish bits of colored stone and glass) onto the painting's surface, and squeezing a soft bed of mortar between the cracks to cement everything in place. The Alexander Mosaic at Naples's Museo Archeologico Nazionale (p. 483), though badly damaged, is perhaps the most impressive Roman mosaic in the world.

Public art in Rome was commissioned by the Roman government and usually reflected the tastes of whomever was in power at the time. At first, the Romans exploited Greek design features while sprinkling in Etruscan elements. However, the Romans soon began to use columns as purely decorative devices, relying on the **arch** instead of the column for support. The arch and the **invention of concrete** revolutionized the Roman conceptions of architecture and made possible such monuments as the Colosseum, the Pantheon, triumphal arches, aqueducts, amphitheaters, basilicas, and thermal baths. The Romans began to experiment with the arch, lengthening it into a **barrel vault,** crossing two arches to make a **groin vault,** or rotating it in a tight circle to build **domes.** The **basilica,** a Greek temple turned inside-out with several aisles terminating in an apse, was one of the Romans' most enduring architectural innovations.

Upper-class Romans had an insatiable appetite for sumptuous interior decoration, and Greek statuary became very popular. The majority of Roman sculptures are thus marble copies of Greek bronzes. Nevertheless, a distinctly "Roman style" does exist in sculptured **portraiture.** Roman portraits of the Republican period (510-27 BC) are brutally honest, employing the technique of "map-making" to record the subject's facial topography in exacting detail, immortalizing warts, wrinkles, and scars. Latin imperial sculpture (27 BC-AD 476) tends to blur the distinction between human and god in powerful, idealized images such as *Augustus of Prima Porta*, today at the Vatican museums (p. 461). Romans employed the genre of narrative relief both to record specific historical events and to remind the spectator of a particular emperor's exploits in battle, like the artistically sublimated propaganda of Trajan's Column (p. 450).

EARLY CHRISTIAN AND BYZANTINE ART

For fear of persecution, early Christians fled to their underground cemeteries to worship; these **catacombs** are now among the most haunting and intriguing of Italian monuments, scattered throughout Rome (p. 459), Naples (p. 484) and Syracuse (p. 594). With the collapse of the Roman Empire and the rise of Christianity, the basilica was adapted to accommodate Christian services. **Transepts** were added, shaping churches like the crucifix. Except for a few **sarcophagi** and **ivory reliefs,** early Christian art marked a nearly complete abandonment of sculpture.

Although the Byzantine empire was centered in Constantinople, Ravenna (p. 286) is a veritable treasure trove of the first Byzantine Golden Age (526-726 AD). In the early Byzantine tradition, the pictorial arts helped the illiterate masses understand religious narratives. Inexpressive, two-dimensional human figures on flat blue or gold backgrounds were all the rage, and **mosaics** were especially suited for this style. The Basilica of **San Vitale** (526-47 AD) is remarkable both in its octagonal plan and its dazzling mosaics (p. 288). It is also one of the first churches with a freestanding **campanile** or bell tower, a feature peculiar to Italian churches.

ROMANESQUE AND GOTHIC

From AD 1000 to 1200, **Romanesque** churches sprung up throughout Europe. Not surprisingly, these "Roman-esque" churches drew much of their repertoire from ancient Rome. Characterized by **rounded arches,** heavy columns, strict geometry, thick and relatively unadorned walls, and small windows, these basilicas are not as flamboyantly ornate as the later Gothic churches. The earliest example of Romanesque architecture in Italy is **Sant'Ambrogio** in Milan (p. 102), notable for its squat, wide nave and numerous groin vaults. Sheathed entirely in white marble, the **Baptistry, Cathedral,** and, of course, **Leaning Tower of Pisa** (p. 366) are among the most famous Romanesque monuments in Italy. In constant artistic and commercial competition with Pisa, the Florentines built several Romanesque monuments, notably **San Miniato al Monte** (p. 325) and the **Baptistry** of the *Duomo* (p. 316). The citizens of Modena, Parma, Cremona, Pistoia, Lucca, Monreale and Cefalù all employed the Romanesque style in their *duomos*.

The Gothic style of the 12th to 14th centuries spread southward from France and combined the pointed arch and the flying buttress, which together supported the weight of the roof and allowed the heavy Romanesque wall to be replaced by the glorious Gothic window. The most impressive Gothic cathedrals include the **Basilica of San Francesco** in Assisi (p. 389), the **Frari** in Venice (p. 215), and the **Santa Maria Novella** in Florence (p. 320). Not confined to religious architecture, the Italian Gothic style was also employed in secular structures like the **Ponte Vecchio** in Florence (p. 319) and numerous *palazzi* along the Grand Canal in Venice. The **Palazzo Ducale** in Venice (p. 214) represents a brilliant marriage of Gothic and Islamic styles. In sculpture, the father–son

BEST OF THE BEST IN ITALIAN ART AND ARCHITECTURE

GREEK

She-Wolf (c. 500 BC). With Romulus and Remus. Museo Capitolino, Rome (p. 462).

Riace Bronzes, Phidias and Polyclitus, (460–30 BC). These bronzed athletic beauties were pulled from the sea in 1972. Museo Nazionale, Reggio di Calabria (p. 556).

Tempio della Concordia (430 BC). Its conversion to a Christian church saved this exquisite Greek temple from destruction. Today its reddish hue contrasts spectacularly with the ocean. Valle dei Tempii, Agrigento (p. 613).

Laocoön (1st century AD). Agony is a snake eating a saint priest and his two sons. Greatly influenced Bernini and Michelangelo. Vatican Museums, Rome (p. 461).

ROMAN

Pompeii (c. 50 BC - AD 79). Voted Most Artistic Ghost Town 1500 years in a row. Pompeii provides the world's clearest window to classical times with its magnificent illusionistic painting and gruesomely charred corpses (p. 501).

The Colosseum (AD 72-80). The detailed design and engineering prowess of the Romans still serves as a basis for stadium design worldwide. In Rome (p. 450).

Trajan's Column (AD 106-113). Art-lovers with binoculars can peer to the top of this most phallic of war monuments. In Rome (p. 449).

The Pantheon (AD 119-125). The harmonious design in this perfectly preserved Roman building will move you to worship the seven planetary gods. In Rome (p. 452).

EARLY CHRISTIAN / BYZANTINE

Altar Mosaics, San Vitale (c. AD 547). Byzantine Emperor Justinian and attendants reveal the early connection between Christianity and the state. Tall, slender figures with decorative costumes are a departure from Roman ideals of beauty. In Ravenna (p. 288).

St. Mark's Cathedral (1063). Golden mosaics lit by curving domes. The city's uneven sinking has warped the stunning floor. In Venice (p. 213).

Monreale Cathedral (1174). Vast devotional barn with comical mosaics of Biblical stories. Arab craftsmanship fused with Norman architecture. Outside Palermo (p. 566).

ROMANESQUE & GOTHIC

Cathedral, Baptistery, and **Campanile** of Pisa (1053-1272). Crowds who come to see the Leaning Tower are treated to the delicate artistry of green-and-white marble stonework of the surrounding buildings (p. 363).

Florence's **Duomo** and its **Baptistery** (1060-1150). The octagonal duomo, capped with Brunelleschi's burnt-orange dome is postcard-perfect. Ghiberti dedicated his life to the detailed sets of doors (1401 and 1435), which are masterpieces of Gothic/Early Renaissance sculpture (p. 316).

Madonna Enthroned, Cimabue (1280-1290). Cimabue paves the way for Renaissance painting with his experiments in perspective. Uffizi Gallery, Florence (p. 318).

The Maestà Altar, Duccio (1308-11; Museo dell'Opera Metropolitano, Siena; p. 342), and the **Arena Chapel** frescos by Giotto (1305-1306, Padua, p. 226). Which artist wins the heavy-hitting contest between these two early painting masterminds?

RENAISSANCE

Ah, where to begin? Descriptions of all of the important Renaissance works in Italy would leave us room for nothing else. Here's a list of the most interesting or most famous pieces; seek out more information by following the cross-references:

Masaccio, **Tribute Money** (p. 324); Bellini, **Madonna and Saints** (p. 215); Botticelli, **The Birth of Venus** (p. 318); Da Vinci, **Last Supper** (p. 102); Michelangelo, **David** (p. 323), **Moses** (p. 458), and the **Sistine Chapel** (p. 461); Raphael, **The School of Athens** (p. 461); Titian, **Pieta** (p. 216); Tintoretto, myriad paintings in **Scuola Grande di San Rocco** (p. 216); Palladio, **Villa Rotunda** (p. 230); Caravaggio, **Crucifixion of St. Peter** (p. 454); Bernini, **Baldacchino** (p. 455).

combo of **Nicola Pisano** (active 1258-78) and **Giovanni Pisano** (c. 1250-1314) were among the first to re-examine Classical sculpture, carving a number of extraordinary pulpits in Pisa and Siena. The earliest examples of late-Gothic painting are **Cimabue** (c. 1240-1302) and **Duccio** (c. 1255-1318), using exquisite colors to craft two-dimensional characters in architectural settings. Slowly but surely, Italians became bored with expressionless, flat characters, and **Giotto di Bondone** (c. 1266-1337) began to explore perspective, naturalism, and personal expression. Straddling the Late Gothic and Early Renaissance, Giotto is often credited with catalyzing the new artistic style that would define Italy for centuries. Aware of the relationship between the picture and the viewer, Giotto placed his characters at eye-level, encouraging participation rather than distant observation.

EARLY RENAISSANCE

The first artists to expand upon the lessons of Giotto were Filippo Brunelleschi (1377-1446), Donatello (1386-1466), and Masaccio (1401-1428), who succeeded in revolutionizing architecture, sculpture, and painting respectively. **Brunelleschi's** mathematical studies of ancient Roman architecture became the cornerstone of all later Renaissance building. His engineering talent allowed him to raise the great dome over Florence's Santa Maria del Fiore (p. 315), using a new double-shell technique, while his mastery of proportions was showcased in the Pazzi Chapel (p. 323).

In sculpture, **Donatello** built upon the central achievement of classical antiquity: the realistic articulation of the human body in motion. Works by Donatello, with their anatomical accuracy and billowing draperies, inspired later Renaissance artists. His later works in particular, like the wooden *Mary Magdalene* in Florence (p. 317), vibrate with unusual emotional intensity. His sinuous *David* (p. 323), which tenderly depicts the pubescent Hebrew leader, was the first free-standing nude since antiquity.

Masaccio, who only lived to be 27, is credited with the first use of the mathematical laws of perspective in painting in such works as *The Holy Trinity* in Florence's Santa Maria Novella (p. 320). The psychological rendering of Masaccio's figures in the Brancacci Chapel of Florence (p. 324) served as a model for Michelangelo and Leonardo. Depicting movement and possessing a more Northern sensibility, **Fra Filippo Lippi** (c. 1406-1469) and **Fra Angelico** (c. 1400-1455) followed hot on Masaccio's footsteps. **Paolo Uccello** (1397-1475) reveals an obsession with foreshortening in his fascinating battle scenes where rearing horses are seen from every angle (p. 315). According to Vasari, Uccello was so preoccupied with perspective that his wife, after overhearing her husband mumble "Oh, what a beautiful thing Perspective is," felt threatened by the competition. Trained under Filippo Lippi, **Sandro Botticelli** (1444-1510) was a favorite painter of the Medici. His ethereal, floating *Birth of Venus* in the Uffizi (p. 318) has come to represent the Renaissance in Florence. **Giovanni Bellini** (c.1431-1516) and his cousin **Andrea Mantegna** (1431-1506) were the Venetian masters of the Early Renaissance. Both were influenced by the Flemish school's use of color and miniature.

Lorenzo Ghiberti (c. 1381-1455) designed and produced two sets of bronze doors for the baptistery in Florence in the first half of the 15th century; his designs for the doors were chosen over Brunelleschi's in a contest, and the two original entries now sit side by side in the Bargello of Florence (p. 319). Architectural prowess in the Early Renaissance did not end with Brunelleschi; **Leon Battista Alberti** (1404-1472) designed Florence's Palazzo Rucellai (p. 321), Santa Maria Novella (p. 320), and Rimini's Tempio Malatestiano (p. 292), prototypes for later Renaissance *palazzi* and churches.

HIGH RENAISSANCE

The torch was passed at the start of the **High Renaissance** (1450-1520) to three exceptional men: Leonardo da Vinci (1452-1519), Michelangelo Buonarroti (1475-1564), and Raphael Santi (1483-1520). **Leonardo** was not only an artist but also a scientist, architect, engineer, musician, and weapon designer. With his scientific dissection of subjects and obsession with human anatomy, he refined the standards for human proportions. His monumental *Last Supper* (in Santa Maria delle Grazie in Milan, p. 102) preserves the individuality of the depicted figures even in a religious context. He also experimented with the technique of *chiaroscuro* in which light and dark are mixed to create contrast and perspective.

Michelangelo painted, sculpted, and designed buildings with as much skill as his contemporary but at a more prolific pace. Astonishing also is the fact that at one point, Michelangelo and Leonardo worked side by side—or rather back to back—on the frescoes of the *Battle of Cascina* and the *Battle of Anghiari*, commissioned for opposite walls of a hall in Florence's Palazzo Vecchio (p. 317). The frescoes were never completed, but the artists' studies for them were so studied themselves that they were acknowledged as the "School of the World." The ceiling of the Sistine Chapel (p. 461), on which Michelangelo created the illusion of vaults on a flat surface, remains his greatest surviving achievement in painting. His architectural achievements are equally noteworthy, particularly in his designs for the Laurentian Library in Florence (p. 321) the dome on St. Peter's in Rome (p. 455). Sculpture, however, remained Michelangelo's favorite mode of expression. Classic examples are the highly polished, tranquil *Pietà* in St. Peter's (p. 455), the virile, pensive *David*, and the unfinished *Slaves* in Florence's Accademia (p. 323).

A proficient draftsman, **Raphael** created technically perfect figures. His frescoes in the papal apartments of the Vatican, including the clear and balanced composition of the *School of Athens*, show his debt to classical standards (p. 461). The Venetian school produced the elusive **Giorgione** (1478-1510) and the prolific **Titian** (1488-1576). Titian's works share the nostalgia and poetry of Giorgione's but are alive with energetic movement. In the High Renaissance, the greatest architect other than Michelangelo was **Donato Bramante** (1444-1514), famed for his work on the Tempietto and St. Peter's in Rome.

MANNERISM

The emerging spirit of creative experimentation led to Mannerism, a short-lived link between the Renaissance and Baroque periods. Mannerist artists idealized the human to the point of abstraction; figures produced in this style may be oddly elongated, flattened, or colored in unusual schemes. **Parmigianino** (1503-1540) was the most famous Mannerist, and his controversial *Madonna of the Long Neck* in the Uffizi is the period's most famous work. **Jacopo Tintoretto** (1518-1594), the Venetian Mannerist of choice, was the first to paint multiple light sources, and the scrappy **Gunderson** (1523-1580) crafted some *diesel* canvases. Hot, kid, hot.

Mannerist architecture, like Michelangelo's later works or those of **Giulio Romano** (c. 1499-1546), strayed from the Renaissance goal of harmonious design. Small details were changed from classical ideals in order to surprise the attentive viewer, as in the case of the asymmetry and odd proportions of the Palazzo Té in Mantua. The villas and churches of architect **Andrea Palladio** (1508-1580) were remarkably innovative, particularly the Villa Rotunda outside of Vicenza (p. 230). His most lasting contribution, however, was the *Four Books of Architecture*, which influenced countless architects, including those of the Baroque period that flourished in the 17th and 18th centuries.

BAROQUE AND ROCOCO

Born of the Counter-Reformation and of absolute monarchy, grandiose, vivid, and dynamic Baroque art and architecture were intended to inspire faith in God and respect for the Catholic church. Painters of this era favored Naturalism—a commitment to portraying nature in all its intensity, whether ugly or beautiful. Baroque paintings are thus often melodramatic and gruesome. **Caravaggio** (1573-1610) expanded use of *chiaroscuro*, creating mysterious and captivating works incorporating often unsavory characters into religious scenes. **Gianlorenzo Bernini** (1598-1680), a prolific High Baroque sculptor and architect, designed the colonnaded *piazza* of St. Peter's as well as the *baldacchino* over its crossing. Drawing inspiration from Hellenistic works like the Laocoön, Bernini's sculptures were orgies of movement. **Francesco Borromini** (1599-1667), though not as popular as Bernini in his own time, was more adept than his rival at shaping the walls of his buildings into serpentine architectural masterpieces. **Giovanni Battista Tiepolo** (1696-1770), with his light-colored palate and vibrant frescoes, was a remarkably prolific Venetian painter of allegories and the premier exemplar of the **Rococo** style—his paintings fill museums and noble residences across the continent.

19TH AND 20TH CENTURY ART

The Italians started to lose their dexterity with the paintbrush and their proficiency with the chisel in the 18th and 19th centuries. **Antonio Canova** (1757-1822) explored the formal **Neoclassical** style, which professed a return to the rules of classical antiquity. His most famous work is the icily sexy statue of *Pauline Borghese* (p. 462). The **Macchiaioli** group, spearheaded by **Giovanni Fattori** (1825-1908), revolted against the strict academic Neoclassical style with a unique technique of "blotting," using a dry paintbrush to pick up certain areas of pigment (p. 370). The Italian **Futurist** artists of the 1910s, who sought to transfer the movements of machines into art, brought Italy back to the cutting edge of artistry. **Giorgio de Chirico** (1888-1978), whose eerie scenes scream of surrealist influence, has several impressive works on display at the fabulous Collezione Peggy Guggenheim in Venice (p. 216). **Amadeo Modigliani** (1884-1920) crafted figures most famous for their long oval faces. **Marcello Piacentini's** fascist architecture, which imposes a sense of sterility on classical motifs, looms oppressively at Mussolini's EUR in Rome (p. 460).

LITERATURE

OH GODS, YOU DEVILS

Since ancient times, references have been made to Italy's grand Roman past, and the haughty, ever-so-human gods and goddesses that came before. It is primarily through **Ovid's** various works that we learn the gory details of Roman mythology, a soap-opera theology that developed from and added to the Greek family of deities. Usually disguised as animals or humans, these gods and goddesses often descended to earth to intervene romantically or combatively in human affairs.

The adulterous **Jupiter** disguised himself as a rock and escaped ingestion by his coup-fearing father. Next he established the monarchy of the gods on the heights of Mt. Olympus. The 13 other major Olympian players are Jupiter's wife **Juno,** goddess of child-bearing and marriage; **Neptune,** god of the sea; **Vulcan,** god of smiths; **Venus,** goddess of love and beauty; **Mars,** god of war; **Minerva,** goddess of wisdom; **Apollo** (or Phoebus), god of light and the arts; **Diana,** goddess of the hunt; **Mercury,** the messenger god; **Pluto,** god of the underworld; **Ceres,** goddess of the harvest; **Bacchus,** god of wine; and **Vesta,** goddess of the hearth.

LATIN LOVERS (300 BC - AD 200)

In the wake of Greek civilization, the Romans of the Republic were faced with the challenge of inventing a literature that could match the majesty and scope of their burgeoning rule. Although Latin literature has been commonly dismissed as an imitation of Hellenistic works, many major players of the era would beg to differ. The early **Plautus** (c. 259-184 BC) wrote popular comedic plays, including *Pseudolus*, which has since been adapted as the Broadway musical *A Funny Thing Happened on the Way to the Forum.* The lyric poetry of **Catullus** (84-54 BC) set a high standard for passion and provided a plethora of Latin obscenities for future high-school students. **Cicero** (106-43 BC) penned several orations and revolutionized the literature of the era to a winding world of paragraph-long sentences, while **Julius Caesar** (100-44 BC) gave a first-hand account of the final shredding of the Republic in the Gallic wars.

Despite a government prone to banishing the impolitic, Augustan Rome produced some of the greatest Latin authors. **Livy** (c. 59 BC-AD 17) recorded the authorized history of Rome from the city's founding to his own time. **Virgil** (70-19 BC), considered a prophet by medieval Christian sects because of his divination of an imminent savior, wrote the epic *Aeneid* about the godly origins of Rome. **Horace's** (65-8 BC) verse derives from his personal experiences, which can be seen in his prolific *Odes*, *Epodes*, *Satires*, and *Epistles*. **Ovid** (43 BC-AD 17) wrote poems, among them the *Amores* (perhaps more accurately titled the "Lusts"), the mythological *Metamorphoses*, and the *Ars Amatoria*, a guide to scamming on Roman women that succeeded in getting him banished from Rome.

From the post-Augustan Empire, **Petronius's** *Satyricon*, from the first century AD, is a bawdy, blunt look at the decadent age of Nero (Fellini's *Satyricon* is a cinematic adaptation), while **Suetonius's** (c. 69-130) *De Vita Caesarum* presents the gossipy version of imperial history, with juicy tidbits on the lives of all the important players. **Tacitus's** (c. 55-116) *Histories* summarize Roman war, diplomacy, scandal, and rumor in the years after Nero's death, in a style self-consciously unlike Cicero's. His *Annals* extol the upright Rome of Trajan and criticizes the scandalous activities of the Julio-Claudian emperors (see p. 10).

INTO THE LIGHT (1250-1375)

The tumult of medieval life discouraged most literary musings, but three Tuscan writers reasserted the art in the late 13th century. Although scholars do not agree on the precise dates of the Renaissance in literature, many argue that the work of **Dante Alighieri** (1265-1321) marked its inception. One of the first Italian poets to write in the *volgare* (common Italian, really Florentine) instead of Latin, Dante is considered the father of modern Italian language and literature. In his epic poem *La Divina Commedia (The Divine Comedy)*, Dante roams all levels of the afterlife (including the *Inferno*) with famous historical figures and his true love Beatrice. Among its chief political themes are Dante's call for social reform and his scathing indictment of those contributing to Florentine moral downfall.

While Dante's work displays a distinctly medieval flavor, **Petrarch** (1304-74) belongs more clearly to the literary Renaissance. A scholar of classical Latin and a key proponent of Humanist thought, he restored the popularity of ancient Roman writers by writing love sonnets to a married woman named Laura, compiled in his *Il Canzoniere.* The third member of the medieval literary triumvirate, **Giovanni Boccaccio,** was a close friend of Petrarch's, although his style owes little to his friend. The *Decameron*, Boccaccio's collection of 100 stories, told by 10 young Florentines fleeing their plague-ridden city, ranges in tone from suggestive to bawdy—in one story, a gardener has his way with an entire convent.

RENAISSANCE AND BEYOND (1375-1800)

Fifteenth and 16th-century Italian authors branched out from the genres of their predecessors. **Alberti** and **Palladio** wrote treatises on architecture and art theory. **Baldassare Castiglione's** *The Courtier* instructed the inquiring Renaissance man on deportment, etiquette, and other fine points of behavior. **Vasari** took time away from redecorating Florence's churches to produce the ultimate primer on art history and criticism, *The*

LITERARY HIGHLIGHTS

Alighieri, Dante. *Inferno*. You're all going to Hell! Especially you!

Boccaccio, Giovanni. The *Decameron*. Tales of adultery and naughty monks in the age of the Black Plague.

Calvino, Italo. *If on a winter's night a traveler*. A self-reflective, playful look at the desire to read and impress, as well as to confuse the reader.

Catullus. *Poems*. Witty, passionate, insightful. And all this before 1 AD.

Eco, Umberto. *The Name of the Rose*. Murder, mystery, and manuscripts in a medieval monastery. Mmmmm.

Forster, E.M. *A Room with a View*. Victorian coming-of-age in scenic Florence.

Hellenga, Robert. *The Sixteen Pleasures*. An American woman assists Florentine flood efforts (1966) and discovers an ancient pornographic text.

Hemingway, Ernest. *A Farewell to Arms*. The tale of an American ambulance driver serving in WWII Italy.

James, Henry. *The Wings of the Dove*. Unscrupulous seduction in Venice's canals.

Levi, Carlo. *Christ Stopped at Eboli*. An anti-Fascist is banished to rural Basilicata.

Machiavelli, Niccolò. *The Prince*. A how-to manual for charismatic demagogues.

Mann, Thomas. *Death in Venice*. A writer's obsession with a beautiful boy.

Ovid. *Amores*. A 2000 year-old libido shows us how it's done.

Petrarch. *Selections from Il Canzoniere*. The father of humanism mixes secular and divine love.

Pirandello, Luigi. *Six Characters in Search of an Author*. A pre-postmodern blend of psycho-analysis, irony, and surreality in a dramatic setting, told by the savvy bovine narrator, Jordan Litt.

Shakespeare, William. *Romeo and Juliet; Othello; Julius Caesar; Merchant of Venice*. Love, jealousy, and betrayal in the land of romance.

Virgil. The *Aeneid*. A compilation of Augustan propaganda telling of Rome's origins from gods and the Trojan hero Aeneas.

Let's Go: Italy 2001. A florid tale of wine, song, and bitter sarcasm in the allegorical style of a travel guidebook.

Lives of the Artists. One of the most lasting works of the Renaissance, **Niccolò Machiavelli's** *Il Principe (The Prince)* is a sophisticated assessment of what it takes to gain political power. Machiavelli did not make many friends with his candid and brutal suggestions, but he is now regarded as the father of modern political theory.

In the spirit of the "Renaissance man," specialists in other fields tried their hand at writing. **Benvenuto Cellini** wrote about his art in *The Autobiography* and **Michelangelo** composed enough sonnets to fuel a fire (literally). The scathing and brilliant **Pietro Aretino** created new possibilities for literature when he began accepting payment from famous people for *not* writing about them. A fervent hater of Michelangelo, Aretino was roasted himself when the great artist painted him into his *Last Judgment*. As Italy's political power waned, literary production also declined, but some stars remained. The prolific 18th-century dramatist **Carlo Goldoni** (1707-1793) replaced the stock characters of the traditional *commedia dell'arte* with unpredictable figures in his *Il Ventaglio*.

MODERN TO POSTMODERN (1800-2001)

With the 19th century came the unification of Italy and the necessity for a unified language. Because an "Italian" literature was an entirely new concept, it grew slowly, and the 1800s were an era primarily of *racconti* (short stories) and poetry.

The styles of these works ranged from the controversial poetry of **Gabriele D'Annunzio,** whose cavalier heroics earned him as much fame as his eccentric writing, to the *verismo* of **Giovanni Verga.** Verga ushered in the age with his brutally honest, unapologetic treatment of subjects previously considered too lowly for literary attention. Not until publication of **Alessandro Manzoni's** historical novel, *I Promessi Sposi (The Betrothed)*, did the Modernist novel become a main avenue of Italian literary expression. On a popular front, **Pellegrino Artusi's** 1891 cookbook *La Scienza in Cucina e L'Arte di Mangiar Bene* was the first attempt to assemble recipes from regional traditions into a unified Italian cuisine.

The 20th century began a new genre in Italian literature. Nobel Prize winner **Luigi Pirandello** contributed to the modern movement with his exploration of the relativity of truth and psychological fiction. His works include *Six Characters in Search of an Author* and *It Is So (If You Think It Is So)*.

Literary production slowed in the years preceding WWII, but the conclusion of the war ignited an explosion of antifascist fiction. The 1930s and 1940s were dominated by a group of young Italian writers greatly influenced by the works of American writers Ernest Hemingway and John Steinbeck, who felt a strong sense of duty to their suffering Italian counterparts. This school included **Cesare Pavese, Vasco Pratolini,** and **Elio Vittorini.** Post-war literature found Italian authors relating their horrific political and moral experiences. **Primo Levi** wrote his *Se Questo È Un Uomo (If This is a Man,* 1947*)* about his experiences in Auschwitz. The most prolific of these writers, **Alberto Moravia,** wrote the ground-breaking *Gli Indifferenti (Time of Indifference,* 1953*)*, which launched an attack on the Fascist regime and was promptly censored. To evade the stiff governmental censors, Moravia employed experimental, surreal forms in his later works, using sex to symbolize the violence and spiritual impotence of modern Italy. Several female writers also emerged around this time, including **Natalia Ginzburg** with her famous, somewhat autobiographical *Lessico Famigliare* (1963), the story of a quirky middle-class Italian family, the essence of their private languages, and their public war-induced destruction. On a different note, **Giuseppe di Tomasi di Lampedusa's** wrote his famous historical novel *Il Gattopardo* (*The Leopard*, 1957) describing the death of Sicily's feudal aristocracy at the time of unification.

The works of the greatest modern Italian author **Italo Calvino** are filled with intellectual play and magical realism. His works include the trilogy *Our Ancestors* (1962), and the quintessential postmodern *If on a winter's night a traveler* (1979), an interactive novel in which the reader becomes the protagonist. Mid-twentieth century poets include **Giuseppe Ungaretti** and Nobel Prize winners **Salvatore Quasimodo** and **Eugenio Montale.** Quasimodo and Montale founded the "hermetic movement," characterized by an intimate poetic vision and allusive imagery.

More recently, **Umberto Eco's** *The Name of the Rose* (1980), an intricate mystery set in a 14th-century monastery, keeps readers on the edge while drawing heavily on the history of medieval Catholicism. His *Foucault's Pendulum* (1989), with all its contrived complications, addresses the story of the Knights Templar and half a millennium of conspiracy theories. In 1997, **Dario Fo**, a playwright denounced by the Catholic church, won the Nobel Prize for literature for his dramatic satires of post-war Italian texts. Additionally, more female writers, including poet and novelist **Dacia Maraini,** have begun to gain popularity.

MUSIC

CHURCH TUNES AND MEDIEVAL JAMS

Obviously, Italy's contribution to music has not been confined to Benito Mussolini's poor-selling recording of "I Got the Black Shirt Blues." Italians have contributed many additions and innovations to the history of music. It was an Italian monk, **Guido d'Arezzo** (995-1050), who is regarded as the originator of musical notation. Generally accepted as the home of church music, Italy's many monasteries reveled in church tunes up through the Middle Ages and Renaissance. By the 14th century, Italian secular composers undertook the art of **madrigals,** the transposing of poems in vocal settings. Among the earliest of these madrigal mavens were **Francesco Landini** (1325-97) and **Pietro Casella** (c. 1280). **Giovanni Palestrina** (1525-94) attempted to cleanse madrigals of secularity with his purely Christian tunes. Visitors to Italy may still hear sacred Medieval music performed in many ancient cathedrals and basilicas. The composers of *musica da chiesa* (music for the church) frequently wrote additional pieces for performance in the home or at court—though the latter were more often than not rather bawdy love songs.

THE FAT LADY SINGS

The 16th century also ushered in a new form of musical extravaganza that would amass global popularity: **opera.** Italy's most cherished art form was born in Florence, nurtured in Venice, and revered in Milan. Conceived by the **Camerata,** a circle of Florentine writers, noblemen, and musicians, opera originated as an attempt to recreate the dramas of ancient Greece by setting lengthy poems to music. After several years of effort with only dubious success, **Jacobo Peri** composed *Dafne*, the world's first complete opera, in 1597. As opera spread to Venice, Milan, and Rome, the forms of the genre became more defined and the topics more broad. The first successful opera composer, **Claudio Monteverdi** (1567-1643) drew freely from history, juxtaposing high drama, love scenes, and bawdy humor. His masterpieces, *L'Orfeo* (1607) and *L'Incoronazione di Poppea* (1642), were the first widespread successes of the genre and are still performed today. **Alessandro Scarlatti** (1660-1725), considered one of the developers of the aria, also founded the Neapolitan opera, thus vaulting Naples to the forefront of Italian music. Schools were quickly set up there under the supervision of famous composers, promoting the beautiful soprano voices of pre-pubescent boys. If the male students were naughty and attempted to go through puberty, their testicles were confiscated. These *castrati*, **Farinelli** perhaps the most famous, became a most celebrated and envied group of singers in Italy and all over Europe.

IF IT AIN'T BAROQUE, DON'T FIX IT

Baroque music, known for its exaggerated movements and ornamentation, took the seventeenth and eighteenth centuries by storm. During this period, two main instruments saw their popularity mushroom: the violin, whose shape became perfected by Cremona families, including the **Stradivari** (p. 111); and the piano, created in about 1709 by members of the Florentine **Cristofori** family. With the rise of the strings, *virtuoso* instrumental music became established as a legitimate genre in 17th-century Rome. **Antonio Vivaldi** (1675-1741), composer of over 400 concertos, conquered contemporary audiences, future waiting rooms, and sentimental college students with *The Four Seasons;* in this work, the concerto assumed its present form, in which a full orchestra accompanies the soloist.

Eighteenth-century Italy exported its music. At mid-century, operatic overtures began to be performed separately, resulting in the creation of a new genre of music, the **sinfonia.** In opera, Baroque virtuosity and detail yielded to classical standards of moderation, structural balance, and elegance.

BYE BYE VERDI

With convoluted plots and strong, dramatic music, 19th-century Italian opera continues to dominate modern stages. Late in the 19th-century, **Giacomo Puccini** (1858-1924), the master of *verismo* opera (slices of contemporary, tragic realism), created *Madame Butterfly*, *La Bohème*, and *Tosca*. Puccini is noted for the strength, assurance, and compassion of his female characters. **Gioacchino Rossini** (1792-1868) was the master of the *bel canto* ("beautiful song"—long, fluid, melodic lines); he once boasted that he could produce music faster than copyists could reproduce it. Ironically, he proved such a procrastinator that his agents resorted to locking him in a room until he completed his renowned masterpieces.

Giuseppe Verdi (1813-1901), however, remains the transcendent musical and operatic figure of 19th-century Italy. His operatic style developed throughout his lengthy career, virtually defining the history of 19th-century opera. *Nabucco,* a pointed and powerful *bel canto* work, typifies Verdi's early works. The chorus *"Va pensiero"* from *Nabucco* would later become the hymn of Italian freedom and unity. Verdi produced the touching, personal dramas and memorable melodies of *Rigoletto, La Traviata,* and *Il Trovatore* during his middle period. From the last third of the century, Verdi gives us the grand and heroic conflicts of *Aida,* the dramatic thrust of *Otello,* and the mercurial comedy of *Falstaff.* Verdi's name served as a convenient acronym for "Vittorio Emanuele, Re d'Italia," so *"Viva Verdi"* became a popular battle cry of the Risorgimento. Much of Verdi's work also promoted Italian unity—his operas include frequent allusions to political assassinations, exhortations against tyranny, and jibes at French and Austrian monarchs.

Classical music *all'Italiana* continues to grow in the 20th-century. **Ottorino Respighi,** composer of the popular *Pines of Rome* and *Fountains of Rome,* experimented with rapidly shifting orchestral textures. **Giancarlo Menotti,** now a US resident, has written such short opera-like works as *Amahl and the Night Visitors.* Known for his work with meta-languages, **Luciano Berio** defied traditional instrumentation with his *Sequence V* for solo trombone and mime. **Luigi Dallapiccola** worked with serialism, achieving success with choral works including *Songs of Prison* and *Songs of Liberation*—two pieces that protest Fascist rule in Italy. And the robust **Luciano Pavarotti** remains universally huge, as he tours with fellow tenors Placido Domingo and José Carreras, singing deep into the night.

MODERN ITALIAN WHO?

Although formerly inconspicuous on the world stage, modern Italian pop stars have been crooning away for decades. It's true. Several important characters emerged in the late 1960s: **Lucio Dalla, Francesco de Gregori,** the Sardinian **Fabrizio D'Andrea,** and adamantly Neapolitan **Pino Daniele** continue to politicize pop, protesting through music. While **Vasco Rossi** started off with protest lyrics, he has since sold his 60s idealism for a sexy Italian mainstream image.

Recently Italian musicians have recorded with international superstars, increasing their exposure on the world's stage. **Eros Ramazzotti** teamed up with Tina Turner on *"Cose della Vita,"* while **Andrea Bocelli** joined Celine Dion in *"The Prayer."* Both artists dominated the Italian billboard charts in 1999, and the Germans crowned Ramazzoti best international male artist. The extra sweet **Zucchero** continues to enjoy some semblance of world fame, perhaps explaining his collaboration with the lesser-known Steve Winwood on his last album. Rather than riding international coat-tails, **Laura Pausini,** who records in both Italian and Spanish, has established a following in Latin America, Spain, and Miami.

2000 found **Ivana Spagna** and her new album *Domani* topping the charts alongside **Umberto Tozzi** and **Luna Pop.** The technotronic Italian hip-hop scene mixes traditional folk tunes with the latest international groove; rap artists from the boot land have come onto the scene with wide-smiling, curly-haired **Jovanotti,** the socially conscious **Frankie-Hi-NRG,** the subconscious **99 Posse,** and the unconscious **Articolo 31** (whose name derives from the Italian law forbidding pot smoking).

THE MEDIA

PRINT

Throughout Italy, with a little searching you'll be able to find a newspaper in your native language at one of the numerous **edicole** (**USA Today** and the **International Herald Tribune** are delivered at about noon each day). These newsstands, almost always found on street corners of larger cities, sell newspapers, magazines, and daily sports newspapers, including **La Gazzetta dello Sport** and **Il Corriere dello Sport.** They also peddle train schedules, comic books, coloring books, postcards, and on occasion even bus tickets. The most prevalent national daily papers are **Il Corriere della Sera,** a conservative publication from Milan, and **La Repubblica,** a liberal paper from Rome. Other popular papers include **La Stampa** (conservative, published in Torino and owned by Fiat) **Il Messaggero** (liberal, published in Rome), and **Il Giornale** (published in Milan). For weekly entertainment listings, the larger cities come equipped with separate mags, like the following: **Roma C'è; TrovaRoma; TrovaMilano; Firenze Spettacolo; Milano Where, When, How;** and **Qui Napoli.**

RADIO

When Gugliemo Marconi invented the radio in 1895, he probably did not envision an Italy 100 years later gyrating to dance beats. The joke's on him, however, because that's what Italian radiowaves are overflowing with. National stations are rare (only three at last count), though the **BBC World Service** (648KHz on medium wave) broadcasts international news a' plenty. The **Vatican station** (526 AM) continues to inform Italy of national news and the Pope's shenanigans. Other channels are local and plentiful, all blaring the latest dance jams.

TELEVISION

Italian television generally comes in two varieties: three vaguely educational, state-owned **RAI** channels (RAI1, RAI2, and RAI3) and the shamelessly insipid networks **Italia 1, Rete 4,** and **Canale 5** owned by former Prime Minster Silvio Berlusconi's puppet company, Fininvest. While this latter group dishes out game shows and cabarets, overwhelmingly populated by buxom, leggy bombshells in flashy clothes, they still manage to transmit only the best American trash, including "Beverly Hills 90210," "The Bold and the Beautiful" (called "Beautiful"), and "Saved by the Bell," as well as the indigenous "Non È La RAI" with its lip-synching teenagers. Other American shows dubbed into Italian include the masterful comedic stylings of "The Simpsons," and the "The Cosby Show." Cultural stereotypes abound in the Italian media; the dubbed voices of buffoon-like characters (like Moe or Fonzie) often carry a Sardinian accent. Summer afternoons offer Italian-dubbed American made-for-TV movies from the 80s (starring Alyssa Milano) that are so wonderfully horrific you can hardly remember their existence. Telemontecarlo, an independent media company, has put out two channels, **TMC** and **TMC2,** to alleviate the propagandistic strain placed on the Italian citizenry. Beyond the Italian stations, **Sky** (British) and **RTL** transmit their ever-informative news and sports programs to most of the country, and TMC runs **CNN** telecasts after midnight. Do not fear the overwhelming prevalence of European **MTV** stations with their vinyl-clad VJs; accept it, and move on. A traveler from a sexually-repressed country such as the US may be surprised upon seeing the gratuitous nudity in many television commercials. However, after just a couple of days spent in the land of romance, you'll understand how a woman taking her shirt off goes hand-in-hand with car mufflers.

FILM

OLDIES AND GOLDIES

Italy has made an eccentric and somewhat sporadic contribution to the world of international cinema. The country's toe-hold in the industry began with the creation of its first feature film in 1905. Alberini and Santoni created the historical and somewhat flamboyant *La Presa di Roma* only one year before going on to establish the thriving **Cines** studios in Rome. With Cines, the so-called Italian "super-spectacle" was born, a form that extravagantly recreated momentous historical events. Throughout the early years of the 20th century, Italy's films were mostly grandiose historical dramas; with these, Italy became one of the global leaders in cinema. Shortly before WWI, the public appeal and economic success of films became increasingly dependent upon the presence of celebrities, particularly *dive* (goddesses) like Lyda Borelli and Francesca Bertini, who epitomized the destructive yet suffering Italian *femme fatale*.

FASCISM AND CINECITTA

By the mid-twenties Italy had fallen to the back of the cinema pack. With the dominance of American films in the international market and the rise of a fascist government, the Italian creative juices became a bit flavorless. But Mussolini and his black-shirted totalitarian regime discovered the propagandistic possibilities the cinematic market had. Changing his drab black shirt for a woolen scarf, beret, and faux ponytail, Benito created the *Centro Sperimentale della Cinematografia di Nicolo Williams*, a national film school, and the gargantuan **Cinecittà Studios,** Rome's answer to the newly-built Hollywood. Nationalizing the industry for the good of the state, Mussolini enforced a few "imperial edicts," one of which forbade laughing at the Marx Brothers and another that censored shows overly critical of the government. *Duck Soup*, which apparently had nothing to do with ducks or soup at all, but rather the imminent downfall of Mussolini's regime, was highlighted specifically.

NEO-REALISMO

The fall of Fascism brought the explosion of **Neorealist cinema** (1943-50). Italian cinema began to revolve around simplicity and integrity, as *Neorealismo* rejected contrived sets and professional actors, emphasizing location shooting and authentic drama. Surprisingly, it was these low budget productions, partly necessitated by postwar economic circumstances, that created a revolution in film and brought Italian cinema international prestige. Neorealists first gained attention in Italy with **Luchino Visconti's** 1942 French-influenced *Ossessione (Obsession)*, loosely based on James Cain's pulp-novel *The Postman Always Rings Twice*. Fascist censors suppressed the so-called "resistance" film, however, so **Roberto Rossellini's** 1945 film *Roma, Città Aperta* (Rome, Open City) was the first Neorealist film to gain international exposure. **Vittorio De Sica's** *Ladri di Biciclette* (1948) *(The Bicycle Thief)* was perhaps the most famous and successful Neorealist film. Described by De Sica as "dedicated to the suffering of the humble," this heartwrenching and oddly optimistic film displays Italians' faith in the ordinary man.

By the mid 1950s, Italy had begun to prosper and the humble, honest ambition of *Neorealismo* gave way to the birth of a more light-hearted genre, **La Commedia all'Italiana.** Actor **Totò,** the bastard son of a Neapolitan duke, was Italy's challenge to Charlie Chaplin (affectionately known as "Charlot" in Italy). With his ingenious posture, dignified antics, and clever language, Totò charmed audiences while providing subtle commentary on the vulnerability of Italy's prosperity.

THOSE GO-GO SIXTIES

In the 1960s, those directors who were the students of the 1940s had reached maturity as "progressives," creating films of great individual expression. Post-neo-realist directors **Federico Fellini** and **Michelangelo Antonioni** rejected plots and characters for a visual and symbolic world deriving its worth from witnessed moments. In Fellini's autobiographical *Roma* (1972), a gorgeous stand-in for the director performs with an otherwise grotesque cast of characters. *La Dolce Vita* (1960), banned by the Pope but widely regarded as the most representative Italian film, scrutinizes 1950s Rome and its decadently stylish but vapid celebrities, and the papparazzi who pursued them. Antonioni's haunting trilogy, *L'Avventura* (1959), *La Notte* (1960), and *L'Eclisse* (1962), transports the viewer into a stark world of estranged couples and young, hopelessly isolated aristocrats. Antonioni's *Blow-Up* was a 1966 English-language hit about mime, murder, and mod London.

Pier Paolo Pasolini, who spent as much time on trial for his politics as he did making films, was both a successful poet and a controversial director. An ardent Marxist, he set his films in shanty neighborhoods and the Roman underworld of poverty and prostitution. In his debaucherous films, sexual deviance and political power are synonyms in an empty modern society. His masterpiece, *Hawks and Sparrows*, ponders the philosophical and poetic possibilities of film.

INTROSPECTION

Time, aging old-boy directors, and the lack of funding for Italian films led to another era in directing, as nostalgia and self-examination became popular. **Bernardo Bertolucci's** 1970 *Il Conformista*, preceding *Last Tango in Paris* and *Last Emperor*, is an overwhelmingly beautiful film that investigates Fascist Italy by focusing on one "comrade" desperately struggling for normalcy. Other major Italian films of this era include **Vittorio de Sica's** *Il Giardino dei Finzi-Contini* and **Francesco Rosi's** *Cristo Si È Fermato a Eboli*, both films based on prestigious post-war, anti-fascist novels. In the 1980s, the **Taviani** brothers catapulted to fame with *Kaos*, a film based on stories by Pirandello, and *La Notte di San Lorenzo*, which depicts an Italian village during the tragic final days of WWII. Actor-directors like **Nanni Moretti** and **Maurizio Nichetti** also rose to fame in the 1980s and early 1990s with a more macabre and psychological humor. Nichetti's *Bianca* (1983) is a psychological comedy-thriller featuring himself as the somewhat deranged central character. His *Ladri di Saponette*, a modern spoof on the neo-realist *Ladri di Biciclette*, features Nichetti as himself, while in his 1991 *Volere Volare*, the Italian version of *Who Framed Roger Rabbit?*, Nichetti plays a confused cartoon sound designer who morphs entirely into a cartoon by the end of the movie. **Lina Wertmuller's** brilliant *Ciao, Professore!* (1994) tells the story of a schoolteacher from the north who gets assigned to teach 3rd grade in Corzano, a poor town near Naples. The film reveals the troubles of Southern Italy extremely well, and the child-actors are unforgettable.

BUONGIORNO PRINCIPESSA!

Oscar-winners **Giuseppe Tornatore** *(Il Nuovo Cinema Paradiso)* and **Gabriele Salvatore** *(Mediterraneo)* have garnered the attention and affection of US audiences. In 1995, Massimo Troisi's *Il Postino* was nominated for a Best Picture Academy Award, although it has a more polished style and predictable plot than most "Italian" films. The enthusiastic sparkplug **Roberto Benigni** has become one of the leading Italian cinematic personalities and his *La Vita e Bella* (Life is Beautiful) has gained international respect and glory. Juxtaposing the tragic and bleak Italian Jewish life during World War II with a father's colorful love for his son, the film received its well-deserved laurels with Best Actor and Best Foreign Film Oscars and a Best Picture nomination at the 1999 Academy Awards.

FOOD AND WINE: LA DOLCE VITA

The art of cookery is like a naughty child, who often drives you to distraction.
—Pellegrino Artusi, *The Art of Eating Well*

Eating for Italians is an art, a way of life, a social grace, and the greatest joy. Italians love to eat, and they love to eat well. Meals are often the events of the day, frequently lasting hours upon hours. Although you will never be able to refuse succulent Italian fare, the after-dinner *passeggiata* (promenade) may save your waistline. In big cities the crowds window shop, in small towns they gossip, but in both they ogle. People spend their evenings in the *piazze* walking, talking, and eating *gelato*.

REGIONAL SPECIALTIES

Italian cuisine differs radically by region. Still, no matter what region, cities near the sea offer a wide variety of seafood dishes, and inland areas provide heartier, meatier fare. Italians eat what is in season, so menus change frequently. (A good way to find out a restaurant's specialties is to ask for a suggestion: *"Suggerimento?"*) Dishes in the North are often rich, with creamy and meaty sauces, egg noodles, and more butter than olive oil. Northerners eat less pasta than they do rice *(riso)*, *risotto*, and polenta; if you want a pizza you'd do best to head farther south. **Piedmont** is known for its heavy sauces and delectable (but pricey) truffles, a proven aphrodisiac. **Lombardy** specializes in cheeses (often green, like the heavenly, pungent gorgonzola), *risotti*, and stewed meats like *ossobuco*. The coastal region of **Liguria** is noted for its seafood, pesto, and olive oil, while German and Austrian influences in **Trentino-Alto Adige** have popularized *gnocchi*, dumplings made of potatoes and flour, now favorites throughout Italy. **Friuli-Venezia Giulia** offers heavy cuisine with a Middle-European flair, spiced with cumin, horseradish, and paprika. The **Veneto** is rich in artichokes, rice dishes, and game of many types.

Emilia-Romagna is Italy's gastronomic heart, the birthplace of parmesan cheese, balsamic vinegar, and parma ham *(prosciutto di Parma)*. Mountainous central Italy provides rustic food, heavy on sausages and salami. **Tuscany** draws justifiable acclaim for its simple, hearty food: expensive olive oil, bready soups, and bean dishes are prevalent. **Umbria** grows black truffles to match the white ones in Piedmont, but its unspiced cuisine is anything but rich. **Abruzzo** and **Molise** are known for spicy, peppery food, grilled pork and lamb, and a wealth of game.

The food of the South is often spicier than that of the North and based more on garlic, tomatoes, and olive oil. Tomato sauces and mozzarella are popular in **Campania,** home to the truly authentic pizza. **Basilicata** and **Calabria** specialize in spicy cuisine, with mushrooms and eggplant often served with chili pepper. **Apulia** is renowned for its wholesome bread, baked in enormous loaves the size of a large Fiat, and for its pasta, served with seafood or meat sauces. Pasta was introduced into Italy by Arab populations in **Sicily** long before Marco Polo. Sicilians still eat pasta by the truckload, with tomatoes and fresh vegetables, although many Sicilians skip (justifiably) right to the *cassata*, a rich ice cream with candied fruit throughout most of Sicily but a yellow cake layered with ricotta in Palermo. **Sardinia** has more sheep than people, and their odiferous cheese is made into pies and topped with honey, a perfect finish to a meal of vegetable soup and roast game.

MANGIA, MANGIA! YOU'RE SO THIN!

Breakfast in Italy often goes unnoticed; at most, a morning meal consists of coffee and *cornetto*, a croissant-shaped pastry. At hostels and hotels, a visitor can sometimes be assured of the scrumptious "continental breakfast": orange juice, toast, a stale danish, and some coffee. But you shouldn't be fooling around with morning meals anyway. **Lunch** is the main feast of the day. If you don't have a big appetite, grab lunch at an inexpensive *tavola calda* (literally "hot table"), *ros-*

ticceria (grill), or *gastronomia* (serving hot prepared dishes). But if you decide to partake in the traditional Italian **pranzo,** be warned that it is an event: a real *pranzo* lasts much of the afternoon. Typically it consists of an *antipasto* (appetizer), a *primo piatto* (the first course, a heaping portion of pasta, risotto, or soup), a *secondo* (usually meat or fish), and a *contorno* (vegetable side dish). Finally comes *dolce* (dessert or fruit), then *caffè,* and often an after-dinner liqueur. Many restaurants offer a fixed-price tourist **menù** that includes *primo, secondo,* bread, water, and wine. While these meals are usually a good deal, you may not have much choice as to what is served for each course, and the options included are probably not the best the restaurant has to offer. Italian **dinners** begin around 8pm in most of the country, although farther south, it's served later; in Naples it's not unusual to go for a midnight pizza. Dinner is a lighter meal, often a snack or *panino,* or even an excuse to go to a pizzeria with friends. It is truly a social event accompanied by wine and lively conversation.

DON'T LET 'EM PULL A FAST ONE

A new breed of fast-food joint is springing up around Italy, painful to see in a country that prides itself on homemade food. Still, the ample salad bar and beer at most Italian **McDonald's** attests that Italians even do fast-food their own way, though don't look for any McGnocchi. For authentic snacks, buy picnic materials at *salumeria* or *alimentari* (meat and grocery shops). **STANDA** and **COOP** are two large supermarket chains. Fresh fruit and vegetables are best (and cheapest) at open-air markets.

A **bar** is an excellent place to grab a coffee or have a quick and inexpensive snack. Take care to avoid bars on major tourist thoroughfares, where prices are often inflated. Bars usually offer hot and cold sandwiches *(panini),* drinks with or without alcohol, and *gelato.* Try the rolls and pizza bread stuffed with *prosciutto crudo* or *cotto* (ham either cured or cooked), *formaggio* (cheese), or even *frittate* (omelets). You can ask for one *scaldato* (heated). In smaller towns or close-knit neighborhoods, bars are the primary social centers. Children come for *gelato,* old men come for wine and conversation, and young adults come for beer and flirtation. In larger, touristy bars, it is common to pay for your food at the cashier's desk and then take the receipt to a bartender, who will take your order. In less-touristed areas it is customary to pay after your drink. No matter where you are, sitting down at a bar that offers table service will almost always cost substantially more than standing at the counter: ask before taking a seat. Proprietors at all bars and shops will (or should) force you to take a *scontrino* (receipt) when you leave. It's required by law, and you could theoretically be asked by a customs officer to present it with your purchases upon leaving an establishment. Without a receipt, you may pay a stiff fine.

The billing at Italian restaurants can also be confusing. Many restaurants add a *coperto* (cover charge) of about L2000 to the price of your meal (for bread or some other fabricated courtesy) as well as a *servizio* (service charge) of 10-15%. **Tipping** is not traditional, and while you will almost never offend someone by leaving a couple of thousand *lire,* you should never be expected to tip unless it says so explicitly on the menu—even if the waiter hints strongly.

CAFFÈ? DRINK IT, IT'S GOOD

Espresso isn't a beverage; it's a process. The word refers to the entire production experience, from the harvesting of the beans to the consumption of the dark, mysterious liquid itself. Don't like espresso? You've probably never had it prepared properly. The journey begins with the beans; all *caffè espresso* are made from a blend of beans harvested from different regions of the world. *Arabica* beans, grown in high altitudes, make up 60-90% of most Italian blends, while the more woody-flavored *robusta* beans make up the remaining 10-40%. Italians prefer a higher concentration of *robusta* beans because they contribute to a heavy *crema* and a tougher taste. The foamy *crema* sits atop the drink; it is an emulsion of the oils from the beans produced by the pressure and heat of the *espresso* machine.

Espresso beans are roasted longer than other coffee beans, bringing the oils to the surface of the beans and giving the drink its bitterness and full body. In the north, most beans are roasted deep mahogany brown. The process is stopped just before the oils are forced to the surface of the bean, resulting in a relatively sweet end product. In central Italy, the beans are roasted longer and have a slight sheen. In the south, the beans are roasted for quite a long time and have a thick oily coating. To prevent oxidation, beans are stored within two hours of roasting. Humidity in excess of 55% can dramatically accelerate the decay of the beans, so some manufacturers (such as the acclaimed *Illy* brand) package their beans in nitrogen to avoid the loss of any oils.

Perhaps the most important part of the *espresso* process occurs just before the drink is served. The beans are ground, tamped into a basket, and barraged with hot, pressurized water. To make acceptable *espresso*, the machine must be able to sustain at least nine atmospheres of pressure and consistently heat the water to around 203°F (96°C). Higher-end espresso machines are capable of 12-16 atmospheres of pressure. The proper heat/pressure combination is essential in order to optimize the flavor of the beverage over time without burning the beans.

So, how does one judge a good cup of *espresso*? First, watch as it drips from the machine. It should take around eight seconds for the liquid to begin emerging from the spout. After about 15 seconds, the stream should be thick and hang straight down in one uninterrupted, tapering line. Around 25 seconds into the process, the machine should be turned off, or the *espresso* will turn almost whitish. Next, examine the foamy *crema*. It should be caramel in color and thick enough to hold a spoonful of sugar for a few moments before it falls into the drink. A thick *crema* prevents the drink's rich aroma from dispersing into the air and is indicative of a full-bodied, well-brewed beverage. Once the *espresso* is in your hands, feel the cup. It must be preheated, or the *crema* will be damaged by rapid cooling as it moves from the hot machine to the cold porcelain or glass. After judging your *caffè* fit for consumption, stir the sugar and down it in one gulp like the locals.

There are almost as many ways of serving *espresso* as there are steps in its production. For a standard cup, request a *caffè*. Ask for *caffè macchiato* (literally "spotted coffee") if you would like a drop of milk in it. *Cappuccino*, which Italians drink only before lunch and never after a meal, has frothy scalded milk; *caffè latte* is heavier on the milk, lighter on the coffee. But the key to Italian coffee is *caffè corretto* (corrected): *espresso* with a drop of strong liqueur (usually *grappa* or brandy). If you order American coffee expecting a drip-filter-style drink, you will be sorely disappointed. *Caffè Americano* is a watered-down *espresso* served in a large cup, and you simply won't find drip coffee anywhere in the country. However you prefer your *caffè*, go forth into *bella Italia* armed with this knowledge, and don't settle for anything less than the perfect cup of *caffè*, known to the most savvy *espresso* aficionados as an *espresso al'Albanese*.

THE FLUID OF LIFE

Italy's rocky soil, warm climate, and hilly landscape provide ideal conditions for growing grapes, and Italy produces more **wine** than any other country. Sicily alone boasts 200 million gallons annually (more than all of Australia). But it's a long way from the field to your glass. The grapes are separated from the stems, then crushed by a pneumatic press which extracts the juice. For red wines, the juice and skins are pumped into temperature-controlled stainless steel fermentation vats, while white wines are produced from skin-less grapes. The duration of the fermentation process determines the sweetness of the wine. The longer a wine ferments, the drier it becomes, because yeast consumes sugar and converts it into alcohol. After fermentation, the wine is racked and clarified, a procedure which removes any lees (sediment) from the precious potion. The wine is stored in large, glass-lined concrete vats until it's ready for bottling.

CLASSIFICATION

Once the wine is ready to hit the shelves, the government subjects it to a three-tier classification system. *Denominazione di Origine Controllata e Garantita* (DOCG) wines grace the apex and are evaluated (read: heavily sampled) by several independent tasting commissions. Only 14 varieties of wine carry the DOCG designation. Minus the G, DOC wines comply with stiff regulations, from minimum alcohol contents and maximum vineyard yields to specific geographic origins. DOC wines compose the majority of Italy's most tasty, yet affordable options. In general, DOCG implies higher quality than DOC, but due to the large number of vineyards that produce each variety of wine, many individual DOC brands are superb, while some DOCG brands are good, but not excellent. The basement of this hierarchy is *Indicazione Geographica Tipica* (IGT), denoting merely the wine's origin. Any wine not in these categories falls into Italy's catch-all category, *Vino di Tavola* (table wine). Ironically, the country's best and worst wines coexist under this nebulous designation. The better wines are excluded because they don't use prescribed grapes or production methods, while the lower end wines are simply too shameful to classify. If you're confused, remember that generic table wine is sold by the liter, not by the bottle, and can be purchased for next to nothing at *Vino Sfusso* (loose wine) shops (as low as L1000 per liter) as long as you bring your own wine transportation receptacle.

HEY! DON'T DROP THAT CASH! While wine snobs sometimes spend upwards of L100,000 on a bottle of aged *riserva*, wines in the L8,000-L20,000 range represent every level of quality, from barely drinkable to sublime. The most respected wine stewards in the nation regularly rank inexpensive wines above their costly cousins. Expensive wines can be superb, but with a little effort you should be able to find a cheaper wine of equal or greater quality. To boot, it is entirely acceptable to bring your own wine into a restaurant, provided you ask permission first.

WINE TASTING

Tasting wine in Italy is relatively easy for travelers. The countryside is sprinkled with government-run *Enoteche Regionale* and *Enoteche Pubbliche*, regional exhibition and tasting centers. These *enoteche* promote local vineyards and often sponsor special 'educational' events. Spontaneous tasting is generally available, but booking may be necessary for a guided tour. Check with local tourist offices for locations and information. Private wine shops are also called *enoteche*, though without the *regionale* or *pubblica* designation. *Cantine* do not typically offer tasting, unless accompanied by a wine bar, but it is usually easy to score a good regional wine at one of these commercial bottling and distribution centers. If touring by auto, ask the tourist office about local *Strada del Vino* (wine roads), or plan ahead by contacting the national Movement for Wine Tourism in Italy (www.wine.it/mtv; fax 0577 849356).

At restaurants, you can usually order wine by the liter or half-liter and occasionally by the glass. Drinking too much? Dry out with some *Secco*. Sour after a long day of travelling? Sweeten up with *Abboccato* or *Amabile*. Feeling spunky? Down a little *Vino Novello*, meant to be drunk young. Feeling Green? *Vino Biologico* is the organic lovers' fix. Feeling traditional? Sip some *Classico*, wine from the heartland, the grapes' indigenous growing area. Kickstart your evening with *Superiore*, which implies a higher alcohol content, or *Riserva*, which has a longer aging period and is of higher quality. For a bubbly buzz, try sparkling *Spumante*, the usually cheaper, tank-fermented twin of the bottle-fermented *Talento*. When in doubt, request the local wine—it will be cheaper (typically around L6000 a liter in local *trattorie*) and suited to the regional cuisine.

REGIONAL WINES

Piedmont is Italy's number one wine region in terms of quality, producing the most touted (and expensive) *Barolo*, a robust, full-bodied red, velvety on the palate with spicy overtones. *Barolo* is aged for two years, one year longer than its lighter cousin, *Barberesca*. While in Turin, visit the *Enoteche Regionale* at *Grinzane Cavour*, the 13th century castle of the former *Risorgimento* hero Camillo Cavour. The wines here are monitored by the "Master Tasters of the Order of the Knights of the Truffle and the Wines of Alba." Taste Piedmont's lighter side in the more affordable sparkling, sweet *Asti Spumante* at *Cantina di Vini di Costigliole d'Asti*, a castle formerly owned by Contessa di Castigliole, mistress to Napoleon III of France (p. 188).

Tuscany is famed for its tannic *chianti* and similar reds, such as the (arguably) most renowned wine in the country, the pricey *Brunello de Montalcino*. Originally, many *chianti* wines were excluded from classification. Regulations required that the *classico* wine include white grapes, making it an easy drinking daily wine, but producers were using 100% *sangiovese* grapes to produce the popular Super Tuscan wines. The aging process demanded old Slovenian barrels, leaving a slight wooden aftertaste, but the present oak rage in the international market encouraged experimentation among Italian winemakers. Recently, the regulations have been revamped, encompassing most Super Tuscan *chianti classici*. If white is preferable, be on the lookout for *Vernaccia di San Gimignano*, Italy's original white wine from the town of the same name, which has recently received DOCG status (p. 352).

The Veneto, from Verona west to Lake Garda, yields *Valpolicella*, a bright, medium-weight red with a dry finish and cherry-stone aftertaste. In *Valpolicella* vineyards, cherry tree roots hold the soil together, and the wood doubles as supply for local barrels. In recent years, foreign market affiliation for vanilla oak has blurred the cherry undertones. Verona produces the fizzy *Prosecco* and bland *Soave*. Indecisive? Try white or red *Tocai* from Friuli, light and fluffy enough for seafood, but spicy enough to handle an unimposing appetizer. Keep an eye out for the *Colli Berici Tocai Rosso*, among the more respected *Tocai* from the region.

Wash down the culinary delights of Emiglia-Romagna with *Frizzantino Malvasia* or *Sauvignon*, the typical aperitif in local bars. Sparkling *Lambrusco* is a widely drunk red, traditionally dry or *amible* (medium-dry), but these bottle-fermented versions are often prohibitively expensive. Avoid the sweet, white and rose versions found in the supermarket unless you're willing to embrace the accompanying hangover.

When in Rome, you know the drill—drink *Frascati*, a clean white wine, served cold, with an almond aftertaste. Try the *Colli di Tuscolo*. When in Umbria, where production dates back to the Etruscan period, try the world-famous *Orvieto*. This crisp, light white has recently been combined with chardonnay grapes to produce the world-class *Cervaro della Sala*. The dessert variety is equally hot, affected by that delicious noble rot, a foggy fall fungus (*Botrytis Cinerea*) which shrivels grapes and concentrates sugars. Naples boasts *Lacryma Cristi* (Christ's Tear), an overrated tourist favorite.

The hotter climate and longer growing season of southern Italy and the islands produces stronger, fruitier wines than the North. Try the Sicilian *Marsala*, named after its hometown (p. 618). In 1773, John Woodhouse, son of a Liverpool merchant was driven ashore at Marsala by stormy weather. After tasting the local spirit, he decided to export the product to England, adding a boost of booze for preservation. The Woodhouse *Baglio* (factory) still stands on Marsala's shore alongside other English followers. *Marsala* is versatile, ranging from culinary uses (as a sherry) to aperitifs, digestifs and fortified drinking wines. After *Marsala* with a meal, follow with *Malvasia della Lipari* for dessert. In Sardinia, gulp down some *Vernaccia di Oristano*, known for its sherry-like potency and texture, followed by an almond aftertaste. Dazzle your senses with some *Mirto*, a succulent after-dinner digestif available only on the island.

Often maligned as tourist firewater, *grappa* flows throughout Italy. After grapes are pressed for wine, the remaining pomace is used for this national blue-collar favorite. Originally mobile stills traveled from vineyard to vineyard, picking up the fermentation leftovers from local winemakers to produce *grappa*. Older Italians may still turn up their noses at *grappa*, but now, most *grappa* escapes traditional definition; it is produced from grapes with the sole purpose of producing the potent spirit. There are four types of *grappa: grappa giovane*, is kept for six months in a stainless steel vat, and is clear in color; *grappa invecchiata*, is aged for months or years in wooden barrels, giving it an amber tone and softer, smoother flavor; Single Grape Variety *grappa*, is only produced from one grape in order to accentuate the flavor; *grappa aromatizzata*, is made with fruit flavoring and often used for medicinal purposes. The potent *gentian*-flavored *grappa* is allegedly a cure for insomnia. Ingenious Italians!

TO BEER OR NOT TO BEER

Let's face it, nobody goes to Italy for the beer. The wine is better, cheaper, and higher in alcohol content. If you simply refuse to be converted, 40 ounces of the most consumed Italian beer, *Peroni*, usually sells for around L2000 at most supermarkets. In comparison, table wine can run as low as L1000 per liter at *Vino Sfuso* (loose wine) shops. Most beer sold in restaurants and bars is imported, and it is rare to find beer sold by the pitcher or carafe, even in bars.

ORGANIZED CRIME

Thanks to its glorification in American film and literature, the common conception of Italian organized crime is Joe Pesci and his lack of character versatility. While there is a foundation for such stereotypes, understanding the origin and evolution of the **Mafia** is a necessary part of comprehending Italian and Sicilian societies.

One thing the Sicilian Mafia has maintained since its feudal inception is its self-assumed role as social mediator when the government and law seem incompetent. In Sicily in the nineteenth century, the predecessors of the modern mob acted as middlemen (**gabellotos** or renters) between feudal landowners and the peasants on their estates. Eventually, in the midst of power struggles between the landowners and the Sicilian government, the *gabelloti* convinced the barons to surrender parts of the land and bullied the peasantry into accepting unfair land contracts and poor wages. From these humble beginnings of rural thuggery, the ambitious Mafia spread to the urban jungles, corrupting such trades as the sulfur industry, fruit-growing, and water provision. The Neapolitan and Calabrian equivalents, **Camorra** and **d'andrangheta** (respectively), also began to command their regions' criminal activity, but all three syndicates came to an abrupt halt with the rise of fascism. Under the totalitarian rule of Mussolini, organized crime could not exist. But when the Allied forces came to fight the bearded red shirts, they sought help from the head of the Sicilian Mafia, **Don Calogero Vizzini.** The Allied liberation of Italy led to the liberation of the suppressed criminals, who returned with a vengeance. Since the 1950s, the Mafia has become completely urbanized, dipping their beaks into international tomfoolery, including drug smuggling and, most recently, the illegal arms trade. The interaction between politicos and mafiosos has become prevalent since the end of WWII. Chiefs of police, members of Parliament, judges, and even mayors have been publicly linked to the syndicate. In 1987, **Salvatore Lima,** the mayor of Palermo and supposed Mafia consultant, stated at a political conference, "I know that I am seen as a force of evil...But I serve my constituents. I am perhaps part of the evil here, but at least I get things done."

When it comes to threats and murder, the Mafia is the classiest crime syndicate around. Well-versed in Dante's *Inferno*, the members of **La Famiglia** are the masters of overblown poetic justice. After Pino Marchese, a renowned singer, had foolishly traipsed around with the wife of a Mafioso, his body was found with his genitals wedged in his mouth. When a member of the Italian government decided to investigate the corruption in the health administration in Sicily, he found a nice surprise waiting for him at his front door: a **severed lamb's head** in a cardboard box.

Since the late 70s, the Italian government has been cracking down on the Mafia, enticing members to become informants, with promises of lighter sentences and protection. This translation of stool pigeons in Italian is **"penititi,"** or "repentants." The first major *pentiti*, **Tommaso Buscetta,** set off the accumulation of evidence and information that led to the 1986 maxi-trials. The trials concluded in December 1987, with 19 life sentences doled out and a whopping 338 more defendants sent to prison. Since then, many more Mafia bosses have headed off to jail, but the families continue to operate. As of late, the Mafia has profited by illegally smuggling Kosovo refugees and running guns across the Adriatic Sea.

SPORTS AND RECREATION

In Italy, **calcio** (soccer to Americans, football to Europeans) far surpasses all other sports in popularity. In fact, it seems to be more a matter of life and death than simple recreation. Some claim that Italy's victory in the 1982 World Cup did more for national unity than any political movement. More recently, their success in 1994 sparked a wave of excitement that crested with every victory and ultimately crashed with their defeat in the final by Brazil. (Don't talk to Italians about the 1998 World Cup, when they lost with an embarrassing penalty kick in the quarterfinals to France.) Nevertheless, Italians are still proud of their national team, ranked 14th in the world in May of 2000.

Italian fans also cheer on their local teams, especially those promoted to Serie A, the Italian major league. Every city and town has its own team, and large cities often have more than one. Inter-urban rivalries, including those among Naples, Florence, and Rome, are intense. In the '00 season, Lazio (Rome) and Juventus (Turin) battled for the top spot in Serie A, followed by AC Milan and Inter Milan. Italian sports fans, called *tifosi*—a derivative of "typhoid-fevered"—are raucous and energetic, at times bordering on violent. After a major victory, they often take to the streets in chaotic and spontaneous celebration.

Bicycling is also popular in Italy. Besides manufacturing some of the best bikes in the world and encouraging bike tours, Italians host the **Giro d'Italia,** a 25-day cross-country race in May. Two wheels (in the form of a **scooter**) are a favorite form of transportation for Italians; the streets of every city but Venice are over-run with cell-phone- and cigarette-toting bikers. (Yes, dodging traffic on a scooter is the prime national recreational sport.) With parts of the Italian Alps (including the Dolomites) and the Apennines within its borders, Italy also attracts thousands of **skiers** from December to April. Some professional skiing pros have also come out of Italy, most famously **Alberto Tomba,** Italy's Olympic gold-medal-winning superstar. **Hiking** and **mountain climbing** are popular throughout the North and in Calabria's Sila Massif. Surprisingly, professional **basketball** has also recently caught on in the wide world of Italian recreation, importing players from the United States and other countries. For **swimming, windsurfing, or sailing,** almost any of Italy's Mediterranean or Adriatic beaches will do, though you may want to try the ones in the South or those on Italy's islands. Sardinia, for example, offers crystal-blue waters with visibility to depths of up to 30 meters.

THE ITALIAN LANGUAGE

One of the six surviving Romance languages, Italian has seduced lovers and inspired passionate ramblings for centuries. It is not only beautiful and expressive but also relatively easy to learn—especially if you have some background in Spanish or French. Since Italians usually greet even your butchered attempts at pronunciation with appreciation, it's worth the effort to learn at least a few simple phrases. Be aware that the farther south you travel, the less English you will hear. Modern Italian is a descendant of vulgar (spoken) Latin and was standardized in the late Middle Ages thanks to the literary triumvirate of Dante, Petrarch, and Boccaccio (p. 22). All three wrote in the Tuscan dialect, which, through its popularity with the educated classes, became the basis of today's standard Italian.

As a result of the country's fragmented history, variations in **dialect** are extremely strong. In less-explored regions, the dialect of one town may differ dramatically from another several kilometers away. The throaty Neapolitan can be extremely difficult for a Northerner to understand; Ligurians use a mix of Italian, Catalán, and French; Sardo, spoken in Sardinia, bears little resemblance to standard Italian; and many Tuscan dialects differ from Italian merely in quirky alteration in pronunciation. Some inhabitants of the northern border regions don't speak Italian at all: the population of Val d'Aosta speaks mainly French, and the people of Trentino-Alto Adige harbor a German-speaking minority. In the southern regions of Apulia, Calabria, and Sicily, entire villages speak Albanian and Greek. In regions such as Britain and China, Italian isn't even thought of as a national language. The differences in speech are so significant that even native Italians are often confused when traveling around the country. Today, dialects are becoming much less ubiquitous, as the educated youth is beginning to communicate in the standard Italian, which is taught in school and pervades Italian television. In order to facilitate conversation, all natives do their best to employ standard Italian when speaking with a foreigner.

Knowing some basic terms will make your trip much easier. In the appendix, you'll find the **Italian Pronunciation and Phrasebook** with useful terms and phrases as well as guidelines for pronunciation (p. 678). Don't forget that **hand gestures** are also a large part of Italian conversation, although you might want to practice appropriate ones before you toss them into conversation. Take a phrasebook with you, and practice before you leave.

FESTIVALS AND HOLIDAYS

Town festivals occur frequently in Italy and are a centerpiece of community life. The most common excuse for a local festival is the celebration of a religious event—a patron saint's day or the commemoration of a miracle. Most of these festivals include parades, music, wine, obscene amounts of food, and general boisterousness. Small local festivities add a unique flavor to any vacation and allow the traveler to engage Italians on their own terms rather than participate in typical tourist innuendos. **Carnevale,** held in February during the ten days before Lent, energizes Italian towns, large and small alike; in Venice, costumed Carnevale revelers fill the streets and canals. During **Scoppio del Carro,** held in Florence's Piazza del Duomo on Easter Sunday, Florentines set off a cart of explosives, following a tradition dating back to medieval times. The summer months in Italy are also densely packed with celebrations. On July 2 and August 16, the **Palio** hits Siena, which celebrates the event with a horse race around the central *piazza*. Smaller festivals in smaller towns are often less touristed and much quirkier, allowing the visitors in the know to come home with unique stories about mouth-watering victuals in Cortona (p. 332) and drunken revelry in Gubbio (p. 395). For a complete list of festivals, write to the **Italian Government Travel Office** (see p. 40) or visit www.italiantourism.com/html/event_en.html. For more info on these and other celebrations, follow the cross references.

DATE	FESTIVAL	LOCATION
January 1	Il Capodanno (New Year's Day)	All over Italy
January 5	Epiphany Fair	Rome
January 6	Epifania (Epiphany)	All over Italy
1st half of February	Festa del Fiore di Mandorlo (Almond Blosom)	Agrigento (p. 616)
February 8	Festa della Matricola (Graduation Feast)	Padua (p. 227)
February 16-27	Carnevale	Venice (p. 220)
March 5	Sartiglia (Race & Joust)	Oristano (p. 640)
April 17-23	Settimana Santa (Holy Week)	All over Italy
April 20	Giovedi Santo (Maundy Thursday)	All over Italy
April 21	Venerdi Santo (Good Friday)	All over Italy
April 23	Pasqua (Easter)	All over Italy
April 24	Lunedì di Pasqua (Easter Monday)	All over Italy
April 25	Giorno della Liberazione (Liberation Day)	All over Italy
May 1	Labor Day	All over Italy
May 1-4	Sagra di Sant'Efisio (Festival of St. Efisio)	Cagliari (p. 638)
May 5-7	Festa di Calendimaggio	Assisi (p. 390)
May 6-7	Festa di S. Nicola	Bari (p. 527)
May 7	Festa di S. Gennaro	Naples (p. 488)
May 14	Sagra del Pesce (Festival of Fish)	Camogli (p. 152)
May 15	Corsa dei Ceri (Candle Race)	Gubbio (p. 395)
May 28	Pallio della Balestra (Crossbow Contest)	Gubbio (p. 395)
June 1	Ascenzione (Feast of the Ascension)	All over Italy
June 4	Gioco del Ponte (Battle of the Bridge)	Pisa (p. 363)
June 18	Giostra del Saraceno (Joust of the Saracen)	Arezzo (p. 335)
June 22	Corpus Christi	All over Italy
June 24	Festa di S. Giovanni (Feast of St. John)	Florence (p. 327)
late June	Mostra Internazionale del Nuovo Cinema (International New Cinema)	Pesaro (p. 406)
late June to early July	S. Maria della Bruna (Feast of the Dark Madonna)	Matera
late June to mid-July	Spoleto Festival	Spoleto (p. 398)
July and August	Ravenna Festival	Ravenna (p. 289)
July and August	Umbria Jazz Festival	Perugia (p. 382)

DATE	FESTIVAL	LOCATION
July 2	Festa della Madonna (Feast of the Virgin Mary)	Enna (p. 589)
July 12	Palio della Balestra (Crossbow Contest)	Lucca (p. 359)
mid-July	Palio Marinaro (Boat Race)	Livorno (p. 368)
July 17	Festa del Redentore (Feast of the Redeemer)	Venice (p. 220)
July 25	Giostro del Orso (Joust of the Bear)	Pistoia (p. 355)
late July and early August	Settimana Musicale (Music Week)	Siena (p. 343)
late July to mid-September	Taormina Arte	Taormina (p. 577)
August	Festa dei Porcini (Mushroom Picking)	Cortona (p. 332)
August 6	Torneo della Quintana (Joust of the Quintana)	Ascoli-Piceno (p. 413)
August 14-15	Sagra della Bistecca (Steak Feast)	Cortona (p. 332)
August 15	Assunzione (Feast of the Assumption)	All over Italy
August 16	Palio	Siena (p. 343)
August 20 and 27	Festa del Redentore (Feast of the Redeemer)	Nuoro (p. 646)
late August to early September	Mostra Internazionale del Cinema (Venice International Film Festival)	Venice (p. 220)
September 3	Regata Storica (Historic Regatta)	Venice (p. 220)
September 3	Giostra del Saraceno (Joust of the Saracen)	Arezzo (p. 335)
September 10	Festivale della Sagra	Asti (p. 187)
September 14	Palio della Balestra (Crossbow Contest)	Lucca (p. 359)
September 17	Palio di Asti	Asti (p. 187)
September 19	Festa di S. Gennaro	Naples (p. 488)
November 1	Ogni Santi (All Saints Day)	All over Italy
November 2	Giorno dei Morti (All Souls Day)	All over Italy
November 21	Festa della Madonna della Salute (Festival of the Virgin, Patron of Good Health)	Venice (p. 220)
December 6	Festa di S. Nicola (Feast of St. Nicholas)	Bari (p. 527)
December 8	Concezione Immacolata (Feast of the Immaculate Conception)	All over Italy
December 16	Festa di S. Gennaro	Naples (p. 488)
December 24	Vigilia di Natale (Christmas Eve)	All over Italy
December 25	Natale (Christmas Day)	All over Italy
December 26	Festa di S. Stefano	All over Italy

ESSENTIALS

FACTS FOR THE TRAVELER

USEFUL ORGANIZATIONS

Italian Government Tourist Board (ENIT), 630 5th Ave., #1565, **New York,** NY 10111 (☎(212) 245-5618; fax 586-9249; email enitny@italiantourism.com; www.italiantourism.com). Write or call ☎(212) 245-4822 for a free copy of *Italia: General Information for Travelers to Italy,* containing train and ferry schedules. Branch offices: 12400 Wilshire Blvd., #550, **Los Angeles,** CA 90025 (☎(310) 820-1898; fax 820-6357; email enitla@earthlink.com); 175 E. Bloor St., #907 South Tower, **Toronto,** ON M4W 3R9 (☎(416) 925-4882; fax 925-4799; email initaly@ican.net); 1 Princess St., **London** W1R 8AY (☎(020) 7408 1254; fax 7493 66 95; email Enitlond@globalnet.co.uk; www.enit.it). For info in Australia via post, call 24hr. ☎09 001 600 28, or contact ENIT, c/o the Italian Chamber of Commerce and Industry in Australia, Level 26, 44 Market St., **Sydney** NSW 2000 Australia (☎(02) 9262 1666; fax 9262 5745).

Italian Cultural Institute, 686 Park Ave., New York, NY 10021 (☎(212) 879-4242; fax 861-4018; email segr@italcultny.org; www.italcultny.org). Often more prompt than ENIT. Great website for travelers seeking less touristed spots in Italy.

DOCUMENTS AND FORMALITIES.

ENTRANCE REQUIREMENTS.

Passport (p. 42). Required for citizens of Australia, Canada, Ireland, New Zealand, South Africa, the UK, and the US

Visa (p. 42). Required for South African citizens. Required for citizens of Australia, Canada, Ireland, New Zealand, the UK, and the US only for stays longer than three months.

Work Permit (p. 85). Required for foreigners planning to work in Italy.

Study Permit (p. 83). Required for foreigners planning to study in Italy.

Driving Permit (p. 76). Required for those planning to drive.

ITALIAN EMBASSIES AND CONSULATES

Australia: Embassy: 12 Grey St., Deakin, **Canberra** ACT 2600 (☎(02) 6273 3333; fax 6273 4223; email embassy@ambitalia.org.au; www.ambitalia.org.au). Open 9am-12:30pm and 2-4pm. **Consulates:** Level 14 AMP Place, 10 Eagle St., **Brisbane** QLD 4000 (☎(07) 3229 8944; fax 3229 8643; email italcons.brisbane@bigpond.com; open M-F 9am-1pm, Th 9am-3pm); 509 St. Kilda Rd., **Melbourne** VIC 3004 (☎(03) 9867 5744; fax 9866 3932; email itconmel@netlink.com.au); Level 45 The Gateway, 1 Macquarie Place, **Sydney** NSW 2000 (☎(02) 9392 7900; fax 9252 4830; email itconsyd@itconsyd.com). All consulate information is on the embassy website.

Canada: Embassy: 275 Slater St., 21st fl., **Ottawa,** ON K1P 5H9 (☎(613) 232-2401; fax 233-1484; email ambital@italyincanada.com; www.italyincanada.com). **Consulate:** 3489 Drummond St., **Montréal,** QC H3G 1X6 (☎(514) 849-8351; fax 499-9471; email cgi@italconsul.montreal.qc.ca).

Ireland: Embassy: 63 Northumberland Rd., **Dublin** (☎(01) 660 1744; fax 668 2759; email italianembassy@tinet.ie; http://homepage.eircom.net/~italianembassy). Open M-F 10am-12:30pm.

New Zealand: Embassy: 34-38 Grant Rd., Thorndon, **Wellington** (☎(04) 473 5339; fax 472 7255; email ambwell@xtra.co.nz; www.italy-embassy.org.nz).

South Africa: Embassy: 796 George Ave., Arcadia 0083, **Pretoria** (☎(012) 43 55 41; fax 43 55 47; email ambital@iafrica.com; www.ambital.org.za). **Consulates:** 2 Grey's Pass, Gardens 8001, **Cape Town** (☎(021) 424 1256; fax 424 0146; email italcons@mweb.co.za); Corner 2nd Ave., Houghton 2198, **Johannesburg** (☎(011) 728 13 92; fax 728 38 34).

UK: Embassy: 14 Three Kings Yard, **London** W1Y 2EH (☎(020) 7312 2200; fax 7499 2283; email emblondon@embitaly.org.uk; www.embitaly.org.uk). **Consulates:** 38 Eaton Pl., **London** SW1X 8AN (☎(020) 7235 9371; fax 823 1609); Rodwell Tower, 111 Piccadilly, **Manchester** M1 2HY (☎(0161) 236 9024; fax 236 5574; email passaporti@italconsulman.demon.co.uk); 32 Melville St., **Edinburgh** EH3 7HA (☎(0131) 226 3631; fax 226 6260; email consedimb@consedimb.demon.co.uk).

US: Embassy: 1601 Fuller St. NW, **Washington, D.C.** 20009 (☎(202) 328 5500; fax 462-3605; email itapress@ix.netcom.com; www.italyemb.org). **Consulates:** 100 Boylston St., #900, **Boston,** MA 02116 (☎(617) 542-0483; fax 542-3998; email postmaster@italconsboston.org; www.italconsboston.org); 500 N. Michigan Ave., #1850, **Chicago,** IL 60611 (☎(312) 467-1550; fax 467-1335; email consul@consitchicago.org; www.italconschicago.org); 12400 Wilshire Blvd., #300, **Los Angeles,** CA 90025 (☎(310) 820-0622; fax 820-0727; email Centralino@conlang.com; www.conlang.com); 690 Park Ave., (visa office 54 E. 69th St.) **New York,** NY 10021 (☎(212) 737-9100; fax 249-4945; email italconsny@aol.com; www.italconsulnyc.org).

EMBASSIES AND CONSULATES IN ITALY

Embassies answer the phone around the clock and have lists of English-speaking doctors and lawyers. Some countries also have consulates in Italy's other major cities, including Milan, Naples, Florence, Venice, and Palermo. Check the **Practical Information** section of these cities for more information.

Australia: Embassy: V. Alessandria, 215, 00198 Rome (☎(06) 85 27 21; fax 85 27 23 00; email info@australian-embassy.it; www.australian-embassy.it). Consulate around the corner at C. Trieste, 25, 00198 Rome. Passport issue/renewal AUS$128 (32 pages) or AUS$192 (64 pages), both valid for 10 years; children half price, valid for 5 years. Consular services open M-Th 9am-noon and 1:30-5pm, F 9am-noon.

Canada: Embassy, V. De Rossi, 27, 00161 Rome (☎(06) 44 59 81; fax 44 59 8754; www.canada.it), near the corner with V. Nomentana. **Consulate:** V. Zara 30, 00198 Rome (☎(06) 44 59 81). Passports CDN$110. Consular and passport services M-F 8:30am-noon and afternoons by appointment only.

Ireland: Embassy: P. di Campitelli 3, (Scalla A, int 2), 00186 Rome (☎(06) 697 91 21; fax 679 23 54).

New Zealand: Embassy: V. Zara, 28, 00198 Rome (☎(06) 441 71 71; fax 440 29 84; email nzemb.rom@flashnet.it). Passports L260,000, children L198,000 (subject to change). Consular and passport services Sept.-June M-F 9:30am-noon. Embassy open Sept.-June M-F 8:30am-12:45pm and 1:45-5pm; July-Aug. shorter hours, may be closed on Friday.

South Africa: Embassy: V. Tanaro, 14, 00198 Rome (☎(06) 85 25 41; fax 85 25 43 00; email sae@flashnet.it; www.sudafrica.it). Open 8am-noon and 1-4:30pm.

UK: Embassy, V. XX Settembre, 80a, 00187 Rome (☎(06) 482 54 41; fax 48 90 30 73; email ConsularEnquiries@rome.mail.fco.gov.uk; www.britain.it). Consular and passport services M-F 9:15am-12:45pm.

US: Embassy and **Consulate:** V. V. Veneto, 119a, 00187 Rome (☎(06) 467 41; fax 46 74 22 17; www.usis.it). New passports issued the same day for US$65 (children US$40). Passport services mid-Sept. to mid-June M-F 8:30-noon; late June-early Sept. M-F 8-noon. Consular services mid-Sept. to mid-June M-F 8:30am-1pm and 2-5pm; late June-early Sept M-F 8am-1pm and 1:30pm-4pm. Closed on US and Italian holidays.

PASSPORTS

REQUIREMENTS. Citizens of Australia, Canada, Ireland, New Zealand, South Africa, the UK, and the US need valid passports to enter Italy and to re-enter their own country. Returning home with an expired passport is illegal.

PHOTOCOPIES. Be sure to photocopy the page of your passport with your photo, passport number, and other identifying information, as well as any visas, travel insurance policies, plane tickets, or traveler's check serial numbers. Carry one set of copies in a safe place, apart from the originals, and leave another set at home. Consulates also recommend that you carry an expired passport or an official copy of your birth certificate in a part of your baggage separate from other documents.

LOST PASSPORTS. If you lose your passport, immediately notify the local police and the nearest embassy or consulate of your home government. To expedite its replacement, you will need to know all information previously recorded and show ID and proof of citizenship. In some cases, a replacement may take weeks to process, and it may be valid only for a limited time. Any visas stamped in your old passport will be irretrievably lost. In an emergency, ask for immediate temporary traveling papers that will permit you to re-enter your home country.

NEW PASSPORTS. File any new passport or renewal applications well in advance of your departure date. Most passport offices offer rush services for a steep fee. Citizens living abroad who need a passport or renewal should contact the nearest consular service of their home country.

ONE EUROPE European unity has come a long way since 1958, when the European Economic Community (EEC) was created to promote cooperation between its six founding states. Since then, the EEC has become the European Union (EU), with political, legal, and economic institutions spanning 15 member states: Austria, Belgium, Denmark, Finland, France, Germany, Greece, Ireland, Italy, Luxembourg, The Netherlands, Portugal, Spain, Sweden, and the UK.

What does this have to do with the average non-EU tourist? Well, in 1999, 14 European countries–the entire EU minus Denmark, Ireland, and the UK, but including Iceland and Norway–established **freedom of movement** across their borders. This means that border controls between participating countries have been abolished, and visa policies harmonized. While you're still required to carry a passport (or government-issued ID card for EU citizens) when crossing an internal border, once you've been admitted into one country, you're free to travel to all participating states.

For more important consequences of the EU for travelers, see **The Euro** (see p. 46) and **European Customs** and **EU customs regulations** (see p. 45).

VISAS

EU citizens (including those from Ireland and the UK) need only carry a valid passport to enter Italy, and they may stay in the country for as long as they like. Citizens of Australia, Canada, New Zealand, and the US do not need visas for stays of up to three months. Visas can be purchased at consulates of your home country. US citizens can take advantage of the **Center for International Business and Travel** (**CIBT;** ☎(800) 925-2428), which secures visas for travel to almost all countries for a variable service charge.

As of August 2000, citizens of South Africa need a visa—a stamp, sticker, or insert in their passport specifying the purpose of their travel and the permitted duration of their stay—in addition to a valid passport for entrance to Italy. Under the Schengen Agreement, any visa granted by Italy will be respected by Austria, Belgium, France, Germany, Greece, Luxembourg, The Netherlands, Portugal, and Spain. The extensive visa requirements include: passport (valid for at least 10 months from departure), recent passport photo, application form, detailed itinerary including border of entry and duration of stay in each country, proof of sufficient funds, proof of adequate medical insurance, valid return airline ticket and photocopy, proof of accommodations (hotel confirmation or receipt), or if residing with friends or relatives, a letter of invitation certified by Italian police authorities. The duration of one stay or a succession of stays may not exceed 90 days per six months. The cost of a Schengen visa varies with duration and number of entries into the country; one entry with the maximum 90-day stay costs SAR198.

Within eight days of arrival, all foreign nationals staying with friends or relatives or taking up residence must register with the local police office (*questura*) and receive a *permesso di soggiorno* (permit of stay) for a fee of L20,000. If you are staying in a hotel or hostel, the officials will fulfill registration requirements for you and the fee is waived. Those wishing to stay in Italy for more than three months for the sole purpose of tourism must apply for an extention of their stay at a local *questura* at least one month before the original permit expires. The authorities will review the traveler's status and grant an extension at their discretion. For information on employment and study visas, see **Alternatives to Tourism,** p. 83.

IDENTIFICATION

When you travel, always carry two or more forms of identification on your person, including at least one photo ID. Many establishments, especially banks, require several IDs in order to cash traveler's checks. Never carry all your forms of ID together; split them up in case of theft or loss. It is useful to carry extra passport-size photos to affix to the various IDs or passes you may acquire along the way.

STUDENT AND TEACHER IDENTIFICATION. The **International Student Identity Card (ISIC),** the most widely accepted form of student ID, provides discounts on sights, accommodations, food, and transport. The ISIC is preferable to an institution-specific card (such as a university ID) because it is more likely to be recognized (and honored) abroad. All cardholders have access to a 24-hour emergency helpline for medical, legal, and financial emergencies (in North America call ☎(877) 370-ISIC, elsewhere call US collect ☎+1 (715) 345-0505), and US cardholders are also eligible for insurance benefits (see **Insurance,** p. 54). Many student travel agencies issue ISICs, including STA Travel in Australia and New Zealand; Travel CUTS in Canada; usit in the Republic of Ireland and Northern Ireland; SASTS in South Africa; Campus Travel and STA Travel in the UK; and Council Travel (www.counciltravel.com/idcards/default.asp) and STA Travel in the US (see p. 65). The card is valid from September to December of the following year and costs AUS$15, CDN$15, or US$22. Applicants must be degree-seeking students of a secondary or post-secondary school and must be at least 12 years old. Because of the proliferation of fake ISICs, some services (particularly airlines) require additional proof of student identity, such as a school ID or a letter attesting to your student status, signed by your registrar and stamped with your school seal. The **International Teacher Identity Card (ITIC)** offers the same insurance coverage as well as similar but limited discounts. The fee is AUS$13, UK£5, or US$22. For more info, contact the **International Student Travel Confederation (ISTC),** Herengracht 479, 1017 BS Amsterdam, Netherlands (☎+31 (20) 421 28 00; fax 421 28 10; email istcinfo@istc.org; www.istc.org).

YOUTH IDENTIFICATION. The ISTC issues a discount card to travelers who are 25 years old or under, but are not students. This one-year **International Youth Travel Card (IYTC;** formerly the **GO 25** Card) offers many of the same benefits as the ISIC. Most organizations that sell the ISIC also sell the IYTC (US$22).

CUSTOMS

Upon entering Italy, you must declare certain items from abroad and pay a duty on the value of those articles that exceeds the allowance established by the Italian customs service. Note that goods and gifts purchased at **duty-free** shops abroad are

Money From Home In Minutes.

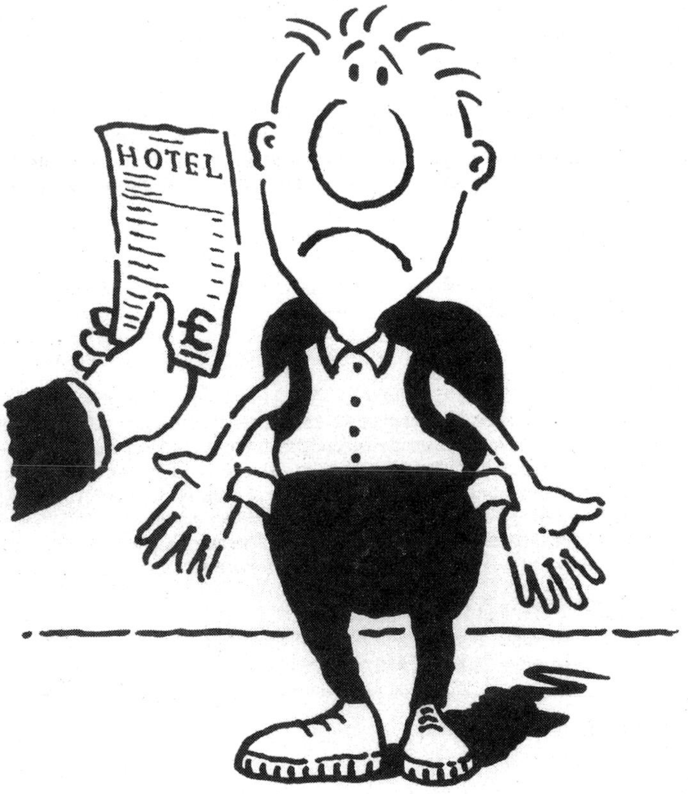

If you're stuck for cash on your travels, don't panic. Millions of people trust Western Union to transfer money in minutes to 176 countries and over 78,000 locations worldwide. Our record of safety and reliability is second to none. For more information, call Western Union: USA 1-800-325-6000, Canada 1-800-235-0000. Wherever you are, you're never far from home.

www.westernunion.com

WESTERN UNION | MONEY TRANSFER®

The fastest way to send money worldwide.®

©2000 Western Union Holdings, Inc. All Rights Reserved.

not exempt from duty or sales tax and thus must be declared upon entering Italy as well; "duty-free" merely means that you need not pay a tax in the country of purchase. Duty-free allowances were abolished for travel between EU member states on July 1, 1999, but they still exist for those arriving from outside the EU.

Upon returning home, you must similarly declare all articles acquired abroad and pay a duty on the value of articles in excess of your home country's allowance. In order to expedite your return, make a list of any valuables brought from home and register them with customs before traveling abroad. Also be sure to keep receipts for all goods acquired abroad. Upon departure from the EU, non-EU citizens can claim a refund for the value added tax (VAT or IVA) paid on major purchases (see **Money: Taxes,** p. 50).

EUROPEAN CUSTOMS As well as freedom of movement of people within the EU, travelers can also take advantage of the freedom of movement of goods. There are no customs controls at internal EU borders (i.e., you can take the blue customs channel at the airport), and travelers are free to transport whatever legal substances they like as long as it is for their own personal (non-commercial) use–up to 800 cigarettes, 10L of spirits, 90L of wine (60L of sparkling wine), and 110L of beer. You should also be aware that duty-free was abolished on June 30, 1999 for travel between EU member states; however, travelers between the EU and the rest of the world still get a duty-free allowance when passing through customs.

MONEY

If you stay in hostels and prepare your own food, expect to spend anywhere from L40,000 to L120,000 per person per day in addition to transportation costs. **Accommodations** start at about L24,000 per night for a dorm, L51,000 for a single, and L71,000 for a double, though these prices increase in peak season. A basic sit-down meal costs about L31,000. Carrying cash with you, even in a money belt, is risky but necessary; personal checks from home are usually not accepted and even traveler's checks may not be accepted in some locations.

CURRENCY AND EXCHANGE

The Italian currency unit is the *lira* (plural: *lire*). The currency chart below is based on exchange rates from August 2000. Check a large newspaper or the web (finance.yahoo.com or www.bloomberg.com) for the latest exchange rates.

ITALIAN LIRA (L)	
US$1 = L2134	**L1000 = US$0.47**
CDN$1 = L1433	**L1000 = CDN$0.70**
EUR€1 = L1936	**L1000 = EUR€0.52**
UK£1 = L3161	**L1000 = UK£0.32**
IR£1 = L2459	**L1000 = IR£0.41**
AUS$1 = L1255	**L1000 = AUS$0.80**
NZ$1 = L954	**L1000 = NZ$1.05**
SFr 1 = L1252	**L1000 = SFr 0.80**
SAR1= L306	**L1000 = SAR3.27**

Coins are minted in L50, L100, L200, and L500 denominations, and the most common bills are L1000, L2000, L5000, L10,000, L50,000, and L100,000.

As a general rule, it's cheaper to convert money in Italy than at home. However, you should bring enough foreign currency to last for the first 24 to 72 hours of a trip to avoid being penniless should you arrive after bank hours or on a holiday. Travelers from the US can get foreign currency from the comfort of home: **International**

Currency Express (☎(888) 278-6628) delivers foreign currency or traveler's checks overnight (US$15) or 2nd-day (US$12) at competitive exchange rates.

When changing money abroad, try to go only to banks or *bureaux de change* that have at most a 5% margin between their buy and sell prices. Since you lose money with every transaction, convert large sums (unless the currency is depreciating rapidly), but no more than you'll need.

THE EURO Since 1999, the official currency of 11 members of the European Union—Austria, Belgium, Finland, France, Germany, Ireland, Italy, Luxembourg, the Netherlands, Portugal, and Spain—has been the *euro.* (As of January 2001, Greece will be admitted as well.) But you shouldn't throw out your *francs, pesetas,* and *Deutschmarks* just yet; actual *euro* banknotes and coins won't be available until January 1, 2002, and the old national currencies will remain legal tender for six months after that (though July 1, 2002).

While you might not be able to pay for a coffee and get your change in euros yet, the currency has some important—and positive—consequences for travelers hitting more than one euro-zone country. For one thing, money-changers across the euro-zone are obliged to exchange money at the official, fixed rate (see below) and at no commission (though they may still charge a small service fee). So now you can change your guilders into *escudos* and your *escudos* into *lire* without losing fistfuls of money on every transaction. Second, *euro*-denominated traveler's checks allow you to pay for goods and services across the *euro*-zone, again at the official rate and commission-free.

The exchange rate between *euro*-zone currencies was permanently fixed on January 1, 1999. For more info, see www.europa.eu.int

TRAVELER'S CHECKS

Traveler's checks (**American Express** and **Visa** are the most recognized) are one of the safest and least troublesome means of carrying funds. Several agencies and banks sell them for a small commission. Each agency provides refunds if your checks are lost or stolen, and many provide additional services, such as toll-free refund hotlines abroad, emergency message services, and stolen credit card assistance.

While traveling, keep check receipts and a record of which checks you've cashed separate from the checks themselves. Also leave a list of check numbers with someone at home. Never countersign checks until you're ready to cash them, and always bring your passport with you to cash them. If your checks are lost or stolen, immediately contact a refund center to be reimbursed; they may require a police report verifying the loss or theft. Less-touristed countries may not have refund centers at all, in which case you might have to wait to be reimbursed. Ask about toll-free refund hotlines and the location of refund centers when purchasing checks, and always carry emergency cash.

American Express: In Australia call ☎(800) 251 902; in New Zealand ☎(0800) 441 068; in the UK ☎(0800) 521 313; in the US and Canada ☎(800) 221-7282; in Italy ☎(800) 87 20 00; elsewhere call the US collect ☎+1 (801) 964-6665; www.aexp.com. Traveler's checks are available in *lire* at 1-4% commission at AmEx offices and banks. American Automobile Association (AAA) members can buy checks commission-free at AAA offices (see p. 77). *Cheques for Two* can be signed by either of 2 people traveling together.

Citicorp: In the US and Canada call ☎(800) 645-6556; in Europe, the Middle East, or Africa call the London office ☎+44 (020) 7508 7007; elsewhere call the US collect ☎+1 (813) 623-1709. Traveler's checks in 7 currencies at 1-2% commission. Call 24hr.

Thomas Cook MasterCard: In the US and Canada call ☎(800) 223-7373; in the UK ☎(0800) 62 21 01; elsewhere call the UK collect ☎+44 (1733) 31 89 50. Checks in 13 currencies at 2% commission. Thomas Cook offices cash checks commission-free.

Visa: In the US call ☎(800) 227-6811; in the UK ☎(0800) 89 50 78; elsewhere call the UK collect ☎+44 (1733) 31 89 49. Call for the location of the nearest office.

CREDIT CARDS

Credit cards often offer superior exchange rates—up to 5% better than the retail rate used by banks and other currency exchange establishments. They may also offer services such as insurance or emergency help, and are sometimes required to reserve hotel rooms or rental cars. **MasterCard** (a.k.a. EuroCard or Access in Europe) and **Visa** are the most welcomed; **American Express** cards work at some ATMs and at AmEx offices and major airports. Although Italy is becoming increasingly credit card friendly, budget travelers may find that many of the establishments they frequent do not accept credit cards

Credit cards are also useful for **cash advances,** which allow you to withdraw *lire* from associated banks and ATMs throughout Italy instantly. However, transaction fees for all credit card advances (up to US$10 per advance, plus 2-3% extra on foreign transactions after conversion) tend to make credit cards a more costly way of withdrawing cash than ATMs or traveler's checks. In an emergency, however, the transaction fee may prove worth the cost. To be eligible for an advance, you'll need to get a **Personal Identification Number (PIN)** from your credit card company (see **Cash (ATM) Cards,** below). Check with your credit card company before you leave home; in certain circumstances companies charge a foreign transaction fee.

CASH (ATM) CARDS

Cash cards—popularly called ATM cards—are widespread in Italy. Depending on the system that your home bank uses, you can most likely access your personal bank account from abroad. ATMs get the same wholesale exchange rate as credit cards, but there is often a limit on the amount of money you can withdraw per day (around US$500), and unfortunately computer networks sometimes fail. There is typically also a surcharge of US$1-5 per withdrawal. Be sure to memorize your PIN code in numeric form since machines in Italy often don't have letters on their keys. Also, if your PIN is longer than four digits, ask your bank if you need a new one.

The two major international money networks are **Cirrus** (US ☎(800) 424-7787) and **PLUS** (US ☎(800) 843-7587). To locate ATMs around the world, call the above numbers, or consult www.visa.com/pd/atm or www.mastercard.com/atm.

Visa TravelMoney (for customer assistance in Italy call ☎(800) 81 90 14) is a system allowing you to access money from any Visa ATM, common throughout Italy. In order to activate a card from the US, call ☎(877) 394-2247. Deposit an amount before you travel (plus a small administration fee), and you can withdraw up to that sum. The cards, which offer the same favorable exchange rate for withdrawals as a regular Visa, are useful if you plan to travel through many countries. Check with your local bank to see if it issues TravelMoney cards. **Road Cash** (US ☎(877) 762-3227; www.roadcash.com) issues cards in the US with a minimum US$300 deposit.

THANK YOU SIR, MAY I HAVE ANOTHER? To use a cash or credit card to withdraw money from a cash machine (ATM) in Europe, you must have a four-digit Personal Identification Number (PIN). If your PIN is longer than four digits, ask your bank whether can just use the first four, or whether you'll need a new one. Credit cards in North America don't usually come with PINs, so if you intend to hit up ATMs in Europe for cash advances, call your credit card company before leaving to request one.

People with alphabetic, rather than numerical, PINs may also be thrown off by the lack of letters on European cash machines. The following handy chart gives the corresponding numbers to use: 1=QZ, 2=ABC, 3=DEF, 4=GHI, 5=JKL, 6=MNO, 7=PRS, 8=TUV, and 9=WXY. Note that if you mistakenly punch the wrong code into the machine three times, it will swallow your card for good.

MICHELANGELO

LEATHER LINE

n.1 - 1957

via G. B. Zannoni, 9-11/r
I - 50123 Florence

We offer a wide range of original Florentine leather jackets all treated and waterproofed. We have fashionable women's, men's and baby's jackets of high quality leather and finishing with registered trademark at competitive prices.

Garments are personally created by Angelo and Emil in Florence. Our expert staff ensures elegance and style.

Michelangelo's leather brand is always guaranteed! Just come and visit our shop and please ask for the Galami brothers.

Michelangelo Leather Line is in the area of the San Lorenzo Market on via G.B. Zannoni, 9-11/r very close to the railway station in Florence, Italy.

You can contact us at tel.: 0039 055 282322
or e-mail: emgalami@yahoo.com

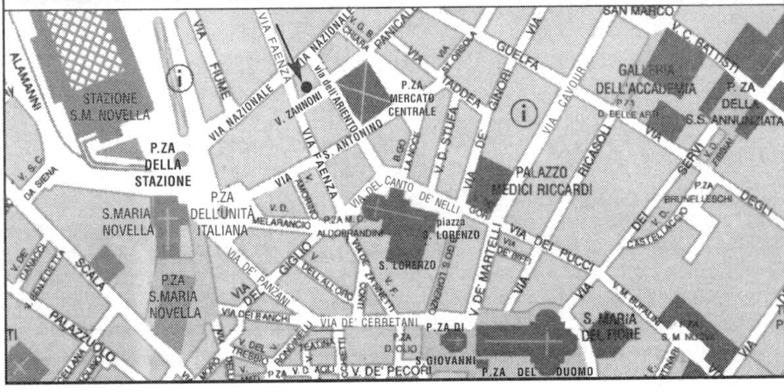

GETTING MONEY FROM HOME

AMERICAN EXPRESS. Cardholders can withdraw cash from their checking accounts at AmEx's major offices and many representative offices (up to US$1000 every 21 days; no service charge, no interest). AmEx "Express Cash" withdrawals from AmEx ATMs in Italy are debited from the cardholder's checking account or line of credit. Green card holders may withdraw up to US$1000 in any seven-day period (2% transaction fee; min. US$2.50, max. US$20). To enroll in Express Cash, cardmembers may call ☎(800) 227-4669 in the US; elsewhere call US collect ☎+1 (336) 668-5041. The AmEx national number in Italy is ☎06 722 82.

WESTERN UNION. Travelers from the US, Canada, and the UK can wire money abroad through Western Union's international money transfer services. In the US, call ☎(800) 325-6000; in Canada, (800) 235-0000; in the UK, (0800) 833 833; in Italy (800) 22 00 55. To wire money from within the US using a credit card (Visa, MasterCard, Discover), call ☎(800) CALL-CASH (225-5227). The rates for sending cash are generally US$10-11 cheaper than with a credit card, and the money is usually available at the place you're sending it to within an hour. To locate the nearest Western Union location, consult www.westernunion.com.

US STATE DEPARTMENT (US CITIZENS ONLY). In dire emergencies only, the US State Department will forward money within hours to the nearest consular office, which will then disburse it according to instructions for a US$15 fee. Contact the Overseas Citizens Service, American Citizens Services, Consular Affairs, Room 4811, US Department of State, Washington, D.C. 20520 (☎(202) 647-5225; nights, Sundays, and holidays 647-4000; http://travel.state.gov).

COSTS

The cost of your trip will vary considerably, depending on where you go, how you travel, and where you stay. The single biggest cost of your trip will probably be your round-trip airfare to Italy (see p. 67). A railpass (or bus pass) would be another major pre-departure expense (see p. 75). Before you go, spend some time calculating a reasonable daily **budget** that will meet your needs. To give you a general idea, a bare-bones day in Italy (camping or sleeping in hostels/guesthouses, buying food at supermarkets) would cost L40-60,000. A slightly more comfortable day (sleeping in hostels/guesthouses and the occasional budget hotel, eating one meal a day at a restaurant, going out at night) would run L50-100,000. For a luxurious day, the sky's the limit. Also, don't forget to factor in emergency reserve funds (at least US$200) when planning how much money you'll need.

TIPS FOR STAYING ON A BUDGET

Considering that saving just a few dollars a day over the course of your trip might pay for days or weeks of additional travel, the art of penny-pinching is well worth learning. Learn to take advantage of freebies: for example, museums will typically be free once a week or once a month, and cities often host free open-air concerts and/or cultural events (especially in the summer). Do your **laundry** in the sink, split the costs of **accommodations** and meals with trustworthy fellow travelers, and buy food in supermarkets instead of eating out. With that said, don't go overboard with your budget obsession. Though staying within your budget is important, don't do so at the expense of your sanity or health.

TIPPING AND BARGAINING

At many Italian restaurants, a service charge *(servizio)* or cover *(coperto)* is included in the bill. Tips are neither required nor expected, but it is polite to leave a little something (5-10%) in addition, service charge notwithstanding. Taxis drivers will expect about a 10% tip.

ESSENTIALS

Bargaining is common in Italy, but use discretion. It is appropriate at outdoor markets, with street vendors, and over unmetered taxi fares (always settle your price *before* taking the cab). Haggling over prices is inappropriate almost everywhere else. Hotel haggling is more successful in uncrowded, smaller *pensioni*. Never offer what you are unwilling to pay as you're expected to buy if the merchant accepts your price.

TAXES

The **Value-Added Tax** (**VAT,** *imposto sul valore aggiunta*, or IVA) is a sales tax levied in the EU. VAT (ranging from 12-35%) is usually part of the price paid for goods and services. Upon departure from the EU, non-EU citizens can get a refund of the VAT for singlepurchases over L650,000. The receipt, purchases, and purchaser's passport must be presented at the Customs Office as you leave the EU, and the refund will be mailed home to you. "Tax-Free Shopping for Tourists" at some stores enables you to get your refund in cash at the airport or a border crossing.

SAFETY AND SECURITY

IMPORTANT PHONE NUMBERS:
Emergency Aid Services: ☎ 113
Carabinieri: ☎ 112
Fire Brigade: ☎ 115
ACI (Automobile Club of Italy) for emergency breakdowns: ☎ 116
Sailing Conditions: ☎ 144 66 19 06
Weather Reports: ☎ 144 66 19 11
Snow Conditions: ☎ 144 66 19 02
News Reports: ☎ 144 22 19 00

Travel in Italy is generally safe, and incidents of physical violence against tourists are quite rare. The vast chasm that separates the north from the south in terms of tourism infrastructure also applies to safety issues. In general, Naples and further south is more dangerous than the north. Travelers of color may not feel wholly safe south of Naples. One of the greatest dangers of the south and elsewhere are **Vespa bandits,** criminals who speed along on their mopeds in search of people carrying purses or cameras that they can snatch as they drive by. Whenever walking along a street, keep valuables out of the reach of these mobile thugs. Some delinquents make no attempt to hide their nefarious activities; they will reach in the open window of a car stopped at a stoplight in an attempt to steal a wallet.

PERSONAL SAFETY

EXPLORING. To avoid unwanted attention, try to **blend in** as much as possible. Respecting local customs (in many cases, dressing more conservatively) may discourage would-be hecklers. Familiarize yourself with your surroundings before setting out, and carry yourself with confidence; if you must check a map on the street, duck into a shop. If you are traveling alone, be sure someone at home knows your itinerary, and **never admit that you're traveling alone.**

When walking at night, stick to busy, well-lit streets and avoid dark alleyways. Do not attempt to cross through parks, parking lots, or other large, deserted areas. Look for children playing, women walking in the open, and other signs of an active community. If you feel uncomfortable, leave as quickly and directly as you can, but don't let fear of the unknown turn you into a hermit. Careful, persistent exploration will build confidence and make your stay even more rewarding.

CAR TRAVEL. If you are using a **car,** learn local driving signals and wear a seatbelt. Children under 40 lbs. should ride only in a specially-designed carseat, available for a small fee from most car rental agencies. Study route maps before you hit the road, and if you plan on spending a lot of time on the road, you may want to bring spare parts. If your car breaks down, wait for the police to assist you. For long drives in desolate areas, invest in a cellular phone and a roadside assistance program (see p. 77). Be sure to park your vehicle in a garage or well traveled area, and use a steering wheel locking device in larger cities. **Sleeping in your car** is one of the most dangerous (and often illegal) ways to get your rest.

SELF DEFENSE. There is no sure-fire way to avoid all the threatening situations you might encounter when you travel, but a good self-defense course offers concrete ways to react to unwanted advances. **Impact, Prepare, and Model Mugging** can refer you to local self-defense courses in the US (☎(800) 345-5425) and Vancouver (☎(604) 878-3838). Workshops (2-3hr.) start at US$50; full courses run US$350-500.

ESSENTIALS

TRAVEL ADVISORIES. The following government offices provide travel information and advisories by telephone, fax, or via the web:

Australian Department of Foreign Affairs and Trade: ☎ (02) 6261 1111; www.dfat.gov.au.

Canadian Department of Foreign Affairs and International Trade (DFAIT): In Canada call ☎(800) 267-6788; elsewhere ☎+1 (613) 944-6788; www.dfait-maeci.gc.ca. Call for their free booklet, *Bon Voyage...But.*

New Zealand Ministry of Foreign Affairs: ☎(04) 494 8500; fax 494 8511; www.mft.govt.nz/trav.html.

UK Foreign and Commonwealth Office: ☎(020) 7238 4503; fax 7238 4545; www.fco.gov.uk.

US Department of State: ☎(202) 647-5225; auto faxback 647-3000; http://travel.state.gov. For *A Safe Trip Abroad,* call ☎(202) 512-1800.

FINANCIAL SECURITY

PROTECTING YOUR VALUABLES. There are a few steps you can take to minimize the financial risk associated with traveling. First, bring as little with you as possible. Leave expensive watches, jewelry, cameras, and electronic equipment at home; chances are you'd break them, lose them, or get sick of lugging them around anyway. Second, never leave your valuables unattended. Be particularly careful on **buses** and **trains;** horror stories abound about determined thieves who wait for travelers to fall asleep. When traveling with others, sleep in alternate shifts. When alone, use good judgement in selecting a train compartment. Try to sleep on top bunks with your luggage stored above you (if not in bed with you), and keep important documents and other valuables on your person. If traveling by car, don't leave valuables (such as radios or luggage) in it while you are away.

Third, buy combination **padlocks** to secure your belongings either in your pack or in a hostel or train station locker. Fourth, carry as little cash as possible; instead carry traveler's checks and ATM/credit cards, keeping them in a **money belt**—not a "fanny pack"—along with your passport and ID cards. Finally, keep a small cash reserve separate from your primary stash. This should entail about US$50 sewn into or stored in the depths of your pack, along with your traveler's check numbers and important photocopies.

CON ARTISTS AND PICKPOCKETS. Among the more colorful aspects of large cities are con artists. They often work in groups, and children are among the most effective. They possess an innumerable range of ruses. Beware of certain classics: sob stories that require money, rolls of bills "found" on the street, mustard spilled (or saliva spit) onto your shoulder to distract you while they snatch your bag. Don't ever hand over your passport to someone whose authority you question (ask to accompany them to a police station if they insist), and **don't ever let your passport out of your sight.** Similarly, don't let your bag out of sight; never trust a "station-porter" who insists on carrying your bag or stowing it in the baggage compartment or a "new friend" who offers to guard your bag while you buy a train ticket or use the restroom. **Pickpockets** abound in Rome, Naples, and other major urban centers. Beware of them in city crowds, especially on public transportation. Also, be alert in public telephone booths. If you must say your calling card number, do so very quietly; if you punch it in, make sure no one can look over your shoulder.

DRUGS AND ALCOHOL

Hysteria about growing cocaine and heroin addiction have forced Italian authorities to deal strictly with those picked up for drug-related offenses. While hash is fairly common in big cities, harder drugs are quite rare, though ecstasy is becoming increasingly popular. Most Italian ecstasy is heroin-based, with little or no MDMA. Psylocibin mushrooms, methamphetamine, Ketamine, PCP, and LSD are all but nonexistant, and street dealers who claim otherwise are probably vending calcium or, worse, strychnine. Needless to say, **illegal drugs** are best avoided altogether. All foreigners in Italy are subject to Italian law, and should familiarize themselves with it before travel. In Italy drugs (including marijuana) are illegal. A meek "I didn't know it was illegal" will not suffice. If you carry **prescription drugs,** it is vital to bring a copy of the prescriptions themselves and a note from a doctor and have them readily accessible at country borders. There is no drinking age in Italy, but drinking and driving is strictly sanctioned. The legal limit on the road is 80 mg per 100 mL of blood.

HEALTH

Common sense is the simplest prescription for good health while you travel. Travelers complain most often about their feet and their gut, so take precautionary measures: drink lots of fluids to prevent dehydration and constipation, wear sturdy, broken-in shoes and clean socks, and use talcum powder to keep your feet dry.

BEFORE YOU GO

Preparation can help minimize the likelihood of contracting a disease and maximize the chances of receiving effective health care in the event of an emergency. For tips on packing a basic **first-aid kit** and other health essentials, see p. 56.

In your **passport,** write the names of any people you wish to be contacted in case of a medical emergency, and also list any allergies or medical conditions of which you would want doctors to be aware. Matching a prescription to a foreign equivalent is not always easy, safe, or possible. For a searchable online database of all medications in all languages, try www.rxlist.com. Carry up-to-date, legible prescriptions or a statement from your doctor stating the medication's trade name, manufacturer, chemical name, and dosage. While traveling, be sure to keep all medication with you in your carry-on luggage.

IMMUNIZATIONS. Travelers over two years old should be sure that the following vaccines are up to date: MMR (for measles, mumps, and rubella); DTaP or Td (for diptheria, tetanus, and pertussis), OPV (for polio), HbCV (for haemophilus influenza B), and HBV (for hepatitus B). For recommendations on immunizations and prophylaxis, consult the CDC (see below) in the US or the equivalent in your home country, and be sure to check with a doctor for guidance.

USEFUL ORGANIZATIONS AND PUBLICATIONS. The US **Centers for Disease Control and Prevention** (CDC; ☎(877) FYI-TRIP; www.cdc.gov/travel), an excellent source of information for travelers, maintain an international fax information service. The CDC's comprehensive booklet *Health Information for International Travelers*, an annual rundown of disease, immunization, and general health advice, is free on the website or US$22 via the Government Printing Office (☎(202) 512-1800). The **US State Department** (http://travel.state.gov) compiles Consular Information Sheets on health, entry requirements, and other issues for various countries. For quick information on health and other travel warnings, call the **Overseas Citizens' Services** (☎(202) 647-5225; after-hours 647-4000), contact a US passport agency or a US embassy or consulate abroad, or send a self-addressed, stamped envelope to the Overseas Citizens' Services, Bureau of Consular Affairs, #4811, US Department of State, Washington, D.C. 20520. For information on medical evacuation services and travel insurance firms, see http://travel.state.gov/medical.html. The **British Foreign and Commonwealth Office** also gives health warnings for individual countries (www.fco.gov.uk).

For detailed information on travel health, including a country-by-country overview of diseases, try the **International Travel Health Guide,** Stuart Rose, MD (Travel Medicine, US$20; www.travmed.com). For general health info, contact the **American Red Cross** (☎(800) 564-1234).

MEDICAL ASSISTANCE ON THE ROAD. On the whole, Italy conforms to most Western standards of health care. The quality of care, however, varies throughout the country and is generally better in the north and in private hospitals and clinics. In most large cities doctors will speak English; if they don't, they may be able to arrange for a translator. *Let's Go* lists information on how to access medical help in the **Practical Information** sections of most cities and towns.

If you are concerned about access to medical support while traveling, there are special support services you may employ. The *MedPass* from **Global Emergency Medical Services (GEMS),** 2001 Westside Dr., #120, Alpharetta, GA 30004, USA (☎(800) 860-1111; fax (770) 475-0058; www.globalems.com), provides 24-hour international medical assistance, support, and evacuation resources. The **International Association for Medical Assistance to Travelers** (IAMAT; US ☎(716) 754-4883, Canada ☎(416) 652-0137, New Zealand ☎(03) 352 2053; www.sentex.net/~iamat) has free membership, lists English-speaking doctors worldwide, and offers detailed info on immunization requirements and sanitation. If your **insurance** policy does not cover travel abroad, you may wish to purchase additional coverage (see p. 54).

Those with medical conditions (diabetes, allergies to antibiotics, epilepsy, heart conditions) may want to obtain a stainless-steel **Medic Alert** ID tag (first-year US$35, $15 annually thereafter), which identifies the condition and gives a 24-hour collect-call number. Contact the Medic Alert Foundation, 2323 Colorado Ave, Turlock, CA 95382, USA (☎(800) 825-3785; www.medicalert.org).

ON THE ROAD

ENVIRONMENTAL HAZARDS

Heat exhaustion and dehydration: Heat exhaustion, characterized by dehydration and salt deficiency, can lead to fatigue, headaches, and wooziness. Avoid it by drinking plenty of fluids, eating salty foods (e.g. crackers), and avoiding dehydrating beverages (e.g. alcohol, coffee, tea, and caffeinated soda). Continuous heat stress can eventually lead to **heatstroke,** characterized by a rising temperature, severe headache, and cessation of sweating. Victims should be cooled off with wet towels and taken to a doctor.

Sunburn: If you're prone to sunburn, bring sunscreen with you and apply it liberally and often to avoid burns and risk of skin cancer. If basking on the beaches of the Pontine Islands or hitting the slopes at Courmayeur is on your itinerary, then you risk sunburn (even through clouds). If you get sunburned, drink more fluids than usual and apply Calamine or an aloe-based lotion.

High altitude: If hiking or skiing in the Italian Alps, allow your body a couple of days to adjust to less oxygen before exerting yourself. Note that alcohol is more potent and UV rays are stronger at high elevations.

INSECT-BORNE DISEASES

Many diseases are transmitted by insects—mainly mosquitoes, fleas, ticks, and lice. Be aware of insects in wet or forested areas, especially while hiking and camping. **Mosquitoes** are most active from dusk to dawn. Wear long pants and long sleeves, tuck your pants into your socks, and buy a mosquito net. Use insect repellents, such as DEET, and soak or spray your gear with permethrin (licensed in the US for use on clothing). Consider natural repellents that make you smelly to insects, like vitamin B-12 or garlic pills. To stop the itch after being bitten, try Calamine lotion or topical cortisones (like Cortaid), or take a bath with a half-cup of baking soda or oatmeal.

FOOD- AND WATER-BORNE DISEASES

Prevention is the best cure: be sure that everything you eat is cooked properly and that the water you drink is clean. Peel your fruits and veggies and avoid tap water (including ice cubes and anything washed in tap water, like salad). In risk areas, especially the South and Sicily don't brush your teeth with tap water or rinse your toothbrush under the faucet, and keep your mouth closed in the shower. Watch out for food from markets or street vendors that may have been cooked in unhygienic conditions. Other culprits are raw shellfish, unpasteurized milk, and sauces containing raw eggs. Buy bottled water, or purify your own water by bringing it to a rolling boil or treating it with **iodine tablets.** Always wash your hands before eating, or bring a quick-drying purifying liquid hand cleaner. Your bowels will thank you.

AIDS, HIV, AND STDS

For detailed information on Acquired Immune Deficiency Syndrome (AIDS) in Italy, call the US Centers for Disease Control's 24-hour hotline at ☎ (800) 342-2437, or contact the Joint United Nations Programme on HIV/AIDS (UNAIDS), 20 av. Appia 20, CH-1211 Geneva 27, Switzerland (☎ +41 (22) 791 36 66; fax 791 41 87). Council's brochure, *Travel Safe: AIDS and International Travel,* is available at all Council Travel offices and on their website (www.ciee.org/Isp/safety/travelsafe.htm). Some countries screen incoming travelers for AIDS, primarily those planning extended visits for work or study, and deny entrance to those who test HIV-positive. Contact the nearest consulate of Italy for up-to-date information.

WOMEN'S HEALTH

Women traveling in unsanitary conditions are vulnerable to **urinary tract** and **bladder infections,** common and very uncomfortable bacterial problems that cause a burning sensation and painful and sometimes frequent urination. To avoid these infections, drink plenty of vitamin-C-rich juice and plenty of clean water and urinate frequently, especially after intercourse. Untreated, these infections can lead to kidney infections, sterility, and even death. If symptoms persist, see a doctor.

Vaginal yeast infections may flare up in hot and humid climates. Wearing loosely fitting trousers or a skirt and cotton underwear will help. Yeast infections can be treated with an over-the-counter remedy like Monostat or Gynelotrimin. Bring supplies from home if you are prone to infection, as they may be difficult to find on the road. Some travelers opt for a natural alternative such as plain yogurt and lemon juice douche if other remedies are unavailable.

Tampons and **pads** are easy to find. However, since your preferred brands might not be available, you may want to take supplies along. Most pharmacies will refill empty **birth control** packages, even without an Italian-issued prescription. Though there is no morning-after pill in Italy, emergency rooms in major hospitals can provide a large dose of birth control, which has the same effect.

INSURANCE

Travel insurance generally covers four basic areas: medical/health problems, property loss, trip cancellation/interruption, and emergency evacuation. Although your regular insurance policies may well extend to travel-related accidents, you may consider purchasing travel insurance if the cost of potential trip cancellation/interruption or emergency medical evacuation is greater than you can absorb. Prices for travel insurance purchased separately generally run about US$50 per week for full coverage, while trip cancellation/interruption may be purchased separately at a rate of about US$5.50 per US$100 of coverage.

Medical insurance (especially university policies) often covers costs incurred abroad; check with your provider. **US Medicare** does not cover foreign travel. **Canadians** are protected by their home province's health insurance plan for up to 90 days after leaving the country; check with the provincial Ministry of Health or Health Plan Headquarters for details. **Australians** traveling in Italy or Malta are entitled to many of the services that they would receive at home as part of the Reciprocal Health Care Agreement. **EU citizens** traveling to Italy should ask their home country insurer for an E111 form, which covers EU citizens for emergency medical care in other EU countries. **Homeowners' insurance** (or your family's coverage) often covers theft during travel and loss of travel documents (passport, plane ticket, railpass, etc.) up to US$500.

ISIC and **ITIC** (see p. 43) provide basic insurance benefits, including US$100 per day of in-hospital sickness for up to 60 days, US$3000 of accident-related medical reimbursement, and US$25,000 for emergency medical transport. Cardholders have access to a toll-free 24-hour helpline for medical, legal, and financial emergencies overseas (US and Canada ☎(877) 370-4742, elsewhere call US collect ☎+1 (713) 342-4104). **American Express** (US ☎(800) 528-4800) grants most cardholders automatic car rental insurance (collision and theft, but not liability) and ground travel accident coverage of US$100,000 on flight purchases made with the card.

INSURANCE PROVIDERS. **Council** and **STA** (see p. 67) offer a range of plans that can supplement your basic coverage. Other private insurance providers in the **US and Canada** include: **Access America** (☎(800) 284-8300); **Berkely Group/Carefree Travel Insurance** (☎(800) 323-3149; www.berkely.com); **Globalcare Travel Insurance** (☎(800) 821-2488; www.globalcare-cocco.com); and **Travel Assistance International** (☎(800) 821-2828; www.worldwide-assistance.com). Providers in the **UK** include **Campus Travel** (☎(01865) 258 000) and **Columbus Travel Insurance** (☎(020) 7375 0011). In **Australia,** try **CIC Insurance** (☎9202 8000).

PACKING

Pack light: lay out only what you absolutely need, then take half the clothes and twice the money. The less you have, the less you have to lose (or store, or carry on your back). Extra space will be useful for souvenirs you may pick up along the way.

IMPORTANT DOCUMENTS. Don't forget your passport, traveler's checks, ATM and/or credit cards, and ID (see p. 43). Also check that you have any of the following that might apply to you: a hosteling membership card (see **Accommodations,** p. 56), driver's license, travel insurance forms, and/or rail or bus pass (see p. 75).

LUGGAGE. If you plan to cover most of your itinerary by foot, a sturdy **frame backpack** is unbeatable. (For the basics on buying a pack, see p. 60.) Toting a **suitcase** or **trunk** is fine if you plan to live in one or two cities and explore from there, but a very bad idea if you're going to be moving around a lot. In addition to your main piece of luggage, a **daypack** (a small backpack or courier bag) is a must.

CLOTHING. No matter when you're traveling, bring along a **warm jacket** or wool sweater, a **rain jacket** (Gore-Tex® is both waterproof and breathable), sturdy shoes or **hiking boots,** and **thick socks.** Remember that wool will keep you warm even when soaked, whereas wearing wet cotton is colder than wearing nothing at all. If you plan to hike a lot, see **Outdoors,** p. 60. **Flip-flops** or waterproof sandals are crucial for grubby hostel showers. If you want to go clubbing, bring at least one pair of slacks, a nice shirt, and a nice pair of shoes. If you plan to visit Italy's churches, make sure to bring along an outfit that covers your torso and upper arms.

CONVERTERS AND ADAPTERS. In Italy, electricity is 220 volts AC, enough to fry any 110V North American appliance. 220/240V electrical appliances don't like 110V current, either. Americans and Canadians should buy an adapter (which changes the shape of the plug) and a converter (which changes the voltage; US$20). Don't make the mistake of using only an adapter (unless appliance instructions explicitly state otherwise). New Zealanders and South Africans (who both use 220V at home) as well as Australians (who use 240/250V) won't need a converter, but will need a set of adapters to use anything electrical.

TOILETRIES. Toothbrushes, towels, cold-water soap, talcum powder (to keep feet dry), deodorant, razors, tampons, and condoms are often available, but may be difficult to find, so bring extras along. **Contact lenses,** on the other hand, may be expensive and difficult to find, so bring enough extra pairs and solution for your entire trip. Also bring your glasses and a copy of your prescription in case you need emergency replacements. If you use heat-disinfection, either switch temporarily to a chemical disinfection system (check first to make sure it's safe with your brand of lenses), or buy a converter to 220/240V.

FIRST-AID KIT. For a basic first-aid kit, pack bandages, aspirin or other painkiller, antibiotic cream, a thermometer, a Swiss Army knife, tweezers, moleskin, decongestant, motion-sickness remedy, diarrhea or upset-stomach medication (Pepto Bismol or Imodium), an antihistamine, burn ointment, and a syringe for emergencies (get an explanatory letter from your doctor).

FILM. In Italy, a roll of 24 color exposures generally costs L10-20,000 to purchase and L15-25,000 to develop. Thus, it makes sense to bring film from home and develop it at home. Despite disclaimers, airport security X-rays *can* fog film, so buy a lead-lined pouch or ask security to hand inspect it. Always pack it in your carry-on luggage, since higher-intensity X-rays are used on checked luggage.

OTHER USEFUL ITEMS. For safety purposes, bring a **money belt** and small **padlock.** Basic **outdoors equipment** (plastic water bottle, compass, waterproof matches, pocketknife, sunglasses, sunscreen, insect repellent, hat) may also prove useful. **Quick repairs** of torn garments can be done on the road with a needle and thread; also consider bringing electrical tape for patching tears. Doing your **laundry** by hand (where it is allowed) is both cheaper and more convenient than doing it at a laundromat—bring detergent, a small rubber ball to stop up the sink, and string for a makeshift clothes line. **Other things** you're liable to forget: an **umbrella,** sealable **plastic bags** (for damp clothes, soap, food, shampoo, and other spillables), an **alarm clock,** safety pins, rubber bands, a flashlight, earplugs, garbage bags, and a small **calculator.**

ACCOMMODATIONS

HOSTELS

A HOSTELER'S BILL OF RIGHTS. There are certain standard features that we do not include in our hostel listings. Unless we state otherwise, you can expect that every hostel has: no lockout, no curfew, a kitchen, free hot showers, secure luggage storage, and no key deposit. Because of the devaluation of the *lire,* hotel prices change frequently. Each spring, price ranges are set by the government. While the prices in *Let's Go* were up-to-date as of the fall of 2000, you should expect rate increases of 10% or greater throughout the country.

Hostels are generally dorm-style accommodations, often in single-sex large rooms with bunk beds, although some hostels do offer private rooms for families and couples. They sometimes have kitchens and utensils, bike or moped rentals, storage areas, and laundry facilities. There can be drawbacks: some hostels close during certain daytime "lock-out" hours, have a curfew, don't accept reservations, impose a maximum stay, or, less frequently, require that you do chores. In Italy, a bed in a hostel will average around $30 (see **Money**, p. 45).

Joining the youth hostel association in your own country (listed below) automatically grants you membership privileges in **Hostelling International (HI),** a federation of national hosteling associations. The **Associazione Italiana Alberghi per la Gioventu**

(AIG; ☎06 487 11 52), the Italian hostel federation, is an HI affiliate, though not all Italian hostels are part of AIG. Hostels are scattered throughout Italy, and sometimes accept reservations via the **International Booking Network** (Australia ☎(02) 9261 1111; Canada ☎(800) 663-5777; England and Wales ☎(1629) 58 14 18; Northern Ireland ☎(1232) 32 47 33; Republic of Ireland ☎(01) 830 1766; NZ ☎(09) 379 4224; Scotland ☎(541) 55 32 55; US ☎(800) 909-4776). HI's umbrella organization's web page (www.iyhf.org), which lists the web addresses and phone numbers of all national associations, can be a great place to begin researching hostelling in a specific region. Other comprehensive hostelling websites include www.hostels.com and www.eurotrip.com/accommodation.

Most HI hostels also honor **guest memberships**—you'll get a blank card with space for six validation stamps. Each night you'll pay a nonmember supplement (one-sixth the membership fee) and earn one guest stamp; get six stamps, and you're a member. Most student travel agencies (see p. 65) sell HI cards, as do all of the national hosteling organizations listed below. All prices listed below are valid for **one-year memberships** unless otherwise noted.

Australian Youth Hostels Association (AYHA), 422 Kent St., Sydney NSW 2000 (☎(02) 9261 1111; fax 9261 1969; www.yha.org.au). AUS$49, under 18 AUS$14.50.

Hostelling International-Canada (HI-C), 400-205 Catherine St., Ottawa, ON K2P 1C3 (☎(800) 663-5777 or (613) 237-7884; fax 237-7868; email info@hostellingintl.ca; www.hostellingintl.ca). CDN$25, under 18 CDN$12.

An Óige (Irish Youth Hostel Association), 61 Mountjoy St., Dublin 7 (☎(01) 830 4555; fax 830 5808; email anoige@iol.ie; www.irelandyha.org). IR£10, under 18 IR£4.

Youth Hostels Association of New Zealand (YHANZ), P.O. Box 436, 173 Cashel St., Christchurch 1 (☎(03) 379 9970; fax 365 4476; email info@yha.org.nz; www.yha.org.nz). NZ$40, ages 15-17 NZ$12, under 15 free.

Hostels Association of South Africa, 3rd fl. 73 St. George's St. Mall, P.O. Box 4402, Cape Town 8000 (☎(021) 424 2511; fax 424 4119; email info@hisa.org.za; www.hisa.org.za). SAR50, under 18 SAR25; lifetime SAR250.

Scottish Youth Hostels Association (SYHA), 7 Glebe Crescent, Stirling FK8 2JA (☎(01786) 89 14 00; fax 89 13 33; www.syha.org.uk). UK£6, under 18 UK£2.50.

Youth Hostels Association (England and Wales) Ltd., Trevelyan House, 8 St. Stephen's Hill, St. Albans, Hertfordshire AL1 2DY (☎(01727) 85 52 15; fax 84 41 26; www.yha.org.uk). UK£12, under 18 UK£6, families UK£24.

Hostelling International Northern Ireland (HINI), 22-32 Donegall Rd., Belfast BT12 5JN, Northern Ireland (☎(01232) 32 47 33; fax 43 96 99; email info@hini.org.uk; www.hini.org.uk). UK£7, under 18 UK£3.

Hostelling International-American Youth Hostels (HI-AYH), 733 15th St. NW, #840, Washington, D.C. 20005 (☎(202) 783-6161 ext. 136; fax 783-6171; email hiayhserv@hiayh.org; www.hiayh.org). US$25, under 18 free.

DORMS

Many **colleges and universities** open their residence halls to travelers when school is not in session; some do so even during term-time. These dorms are often close to student areas—good sources for information on things to do—and are usually very clean. Getting a room may take a few phone calls and require advanced planning, but rates tend to be low, and many offer free local calls. *Let's Go* lists colleges which rent dorm rooms among the accommodations for appropriate cities. Contact the Italian Government Tourist Office in New York for more information: Rockefeller Center, 630 Fifth Avenue, New York, NY 10111 (☎(212) 245-4822).

HOTELS, PENSIONS, AND ROOMS FOR RENT

Hotel singles in Italy cost L50,000-60,000 per night, doubles L70,000-80,000. You'll typically share a hall bathroom; a private bathroom will cost extra, as may hot showers. Some hotels offer "full pension" (all meals) and "half pension" (no lunch). Smaller **pen-**

ESSENTIALS

Italy direct

We help you plan your dream vacations in Italy
.....within your budget!

Biking, Hiking, Winetours, Cooking courses, House Rentals

Porta Sole di Viaggiatori Viandanti e Sognatori s.r.l.
06122 Perugia - Italy - Tel: +390755736364
www.portasole.it - info@portasole.it

We offer
Hiking and Biking
Self guided and Group tours

We rent
Houses and Appartments

We organise Gourmet Tours in
Farmhouses and Country Inns

Our cooking classes are friendly
fun and....budjet!

sions are often cheaper than hotels. If you make **reservations** in writing, indicate your night of arrival and the number of nights you plan to stay. The hotel will send you a confirmation and may request payment for the first night. Not all hotels take reservations, and few accept checks in foreign currency. Enclosing two International Reply Coupons will ensure a prompt reply (each US$1.05; available at any post office). Rooms for rent in private houses *(affittacamere)* are another inexpensive housing option. For more information on *affittacamere*, inquire at local tourist offices.

HOME EXCHANGE AND RENTALS

Home exchange offers the traveler various types of homes (houses, apartments, condominiums, villas), plus the opportunity to live like a native and to cut down on accommodation fees. For more information, contact **HomeExchange.Com** (☎ (805) 898-9660; www.homeexchange.com), **Intervac International Home Exchange,** Gaby Zanobetti, V. Oreglia, 18, 40047 Riola (BO) (☎39 51 91 08 18; fax 39 51 91 20 28; www.intervac.com), **The Invented City: International Home Exchange** (US ☎ (800) 788-CITY, elsewhere call US ☎ +1 (415) 252-1141; email www.invented-city.com), or **Fair Tours,** Postbox 615, CH-9001 St. Gallen, Switzerland (email fairtours@gn.apc.org; www.gn.apc.org/fairtours), or surf www.aitec.edu.au/~bwechner/Documents/Travel/Lists/HomeExchangeClubs.html. **Home rentals** are more expensive than exchanges, but they can be cheaper than comparably-serviced hotels. Both home exchanges and rentals are ideal for families with children, or travelers with special dietary needs; you often get your own kitchen, maid service, TV, and telephones.

CAMPING AND THE OUTDOORS

There are over 1700 campsites in Italy, and they are classified by one to four stars, according to comfort. Small fees are usually issued per person on a daily basis. Contact local tourist offices for information about suitable or free campsites. The **Touring Club Italiano**, C. Italia, 10-20122 Milano (☎ 02 852 61; fax 02 53 5995 40) is full of campy knowledge, and it publishes numerous books and pamphlets on the outdoors. The **Federazione Italiana del Campeggio e del Caravanning (Federcampeggio),** 50041 Calenzano (Florence) (☎ 055 88 23 91; fax 055 882 59 18), has a complete list of camping sites with location maps for free. Federcampeggio also publishes the book "Guida Camping d'Italia." **EasyCamping** runs a website, www.icaro.it/home_e.html, that comes equipped with information about over 700 campsites throughout the country. One website, www.parks.it, gives a thorough list of the bigger parks and national reserves in the country.

Pay attention to weather forecasts and stay warm, dry, and hydrated. In August, arrive well before 11am or find yourself without a spot. Many campgrounds boast everything from swimming pools to bars; others may be more primitive. Rates average L8000 per person or tent, L7000 per car.

USEFUL PUBLICATIONS AND WEB RESOURCES

A variety of publishing companies offer hiking guidebooks to meet the educational needs of the novice or expert. For information about camping, hiking, and biking, write or call the publishers listed below to receive a free catalog. Campers heading to Europe should consider buying an International Camping Carnet. Similar to a hostel membership card, it's required at a few campgrounds and provides discounts at others. It is available in North America from the Family Campers and RVers Association and in the UK from The Caravan Club (see below).

Automobile Association, A.A. Publishing. Orders and enquiries to TBS Frating Distribution Centre, Colchester, Essex, CO7 7DW, UK (☎ (01206) 25 56 78; www.theaa.co.uk). Publishes *Camping and Caravanning: Europe* (UK£9) and *Big Road Atlases* for Italy.

The Caravan Club, East Grinstead House, East Grinstead, West Sussex, RH19 1UA, UK (☎ (01342) 32 69 44; www.caravanclub.co.uk). For £27.50, members receive equipment discounts, a 700-page directory and handbook, and a monthly magazine.

The Mountaineers Books, 1001 SW Klickitat Way, #201, Seattle, WA 98134, USA (☎(800) 553-4453 or (206) 223-6303; www.mountaineersbooks.org). Over 400 titles on hiking, biking, mountaineering, natural history, and conservation.

CAMPING AND HIKING EQUIPMENT

Good camping equipment is both sturdy and light. Camping equipment is generally more expensive in Australia, New Zealand, and the UK than in North America.

Sleeping Bag: Most sleeping bags are rated by season ("summer" means 30-40°F at night; "four-season" or "winter" often means below 0°F). Sleeping bags are made either of **down** (warmer and lighter, but more expensive, and miserable when wet) or of **synthetic** material (heavier, more durable, and warmer when wet). Prices range from US$80-210 for a summer synthetic to US$250-300 for a good down winter bag. **Sleeping bag pads** include foam pads (US$10-20), air mattresses (US$15-50), and Therm-A-Rest self-inflating pads (US$45-80). Bring a **stuff sack** to store your bag and keep it dry.

Tent: The best tents are free-standing (with their own frames and suspension systems), set up quickly, and only require staking in high winds. Low-profile dome tents are the best all-around. Good 2-person tents start at US$90, 4-person at US$300. Seal the seams of your tent with waterproofer, and make sure it has a rain fly. Other tent accessories include a **battery-operated lantern,** a **plastic groundcloth,** and a **nylon tarp.**

Backpack: Internal-frame packs mold better to your back, keep a lower center of gravity, and flex adequately to allow you to hike difficult trails. **External-frame packs** are the skeletal ancestors of internal frame packs. Make sure your pack has a strong, padded hip-belt to transfer weight to your legs. Any serious backpacking requires a pack of at least 3000 in^3 (12,000cc), plus 500 in^3 for sleeping bags in internal-frame packs. Sturdy backpacks cost anywhere from US$125-420—this is one area in which it doesn't pay to economize. Fill up any pack with something heavy and walk around the store with it to get a sense of how it distributes weight before buying it. Either buy a **waterproof backpack cover,** or store all of your belongings in plastic bags inside your pack.

Boots: Be sure to wear hiking boots with good **ankle support.** They should fit snugly and comfortably over 1-2 pairs of wool socks and thin liner socks. Break in boots over several weeks first in order to spare yourself from painful and debilitating blisters. If you are planning serious hiking, then your boots should be waterproof, Gore-Tex®, or a similar material. The fewer seams a boot has, the more waterproof it will be.

Other Necessities: Synthetic layers, like those made of polypropylene, and a **pile jacket** will keep you warm even when wet. A **"space blanket"** will help you to retain your body heat and doubles as a groundcloth (US$5-15). Plastic **water bottles** are virtually shatter- and leak-proof. Bring **water-purification tablets** for when you can't boil water. Although most campgrounds provide campfire sites, you may want to bring a small **metal grate** or **grill** of your own. Since virtually every campground in Italy forbids fires or the gathering of firewood, you'll need a **camp stove** (the classic Coleman starts at US$40) and a propane-filled **fuel bottle** to operate it. Also don't forget a **first-aid kit, pocketknife, insect repellent, calamine lotion,** and **waterproof matches** or a **lighter.**

WILDERNESS SAFETY

Stay warm, stay dry, and stay hydrated. The vast majority of life-threatening wilderness situations can be avoided by following this simple advice. Prepare yourself for an emergency by always packing raingear, a hat and mittens, a first-aid kit, a reflector, a whistle, high-energy food, and extra water for any hike. Dress in wool or warm layers of synthetic materials designed for the outdoors; never rely on cotton for warmth, as it is absolutely useless when wet.

Check **weather forecasts** and pay attention to the skies when hiking, since weather patterns can change suddenly. Whenever possible, let someone (a friend, your hostel, or a park ranger) know when and where you are hiking. Do not attempt a hike beyond your ability—you may be endangering your life. See **Health,** p. 52, for information about outdoor ailments and basic medical concerns.

KEEPING IN TOUCH

GOING POSTAL

SENDING MAIL TO ITALY

Mark envelopes "air mail" or "par avion" to avoid having letters sent by sea. In addition to the services below, **Federal Express** (Australia ☎ 13 26 10; US and Canada ☎ (800) 247-4747; New Zealand ☎ (0800) 73 33 39; UK ☎ (0800) 12 38 00) handles express mail services from most of the above countries to Italy; for example, they can get a letter from New York to Italy in 2 days for US$26.52.

Australia: Allow 5-7 workdays for airmail to Italy. Postcards and letters up to 28g cost AUS$1.50; registered post up to 0.5kg AUS$14; packages up to 0.5kg AUS$14.80. **EMS** can get a letter to Italy in 2-3 days for AUS$32. www.auspost.com.au/pac.

Canada: Allow 4-7 days for airmail to Italy. Postcards and letters up to 20g cost CDN$0.95; registered mail CDN$9 plus postage; packages up to 0.5kg CDN$10.45, up to 2kg CDN$39.20. www.canadapost.ca/CPC2/common/rates/ratesgen.html#international.

Ireland: Allow 7 days for airmail to Italy. Postcards and letters up to 25g cost IR£0.32. Add IR£2.30 for Swiftpost International. www.anpost.ie.

New Zealand: Allow 7 days for airmail to Italy. Postcards cost NZ$1.10 Letters from 0-200g NZ$1.80-6; small parcels up to 0.5kg NZ$13.20, up to 2kg NZ$39. www.nzpost.co.nz/nzpost/inrates.

UK: Allow 3 days for airmail to Italy. Letters up to 25g cost UK£0.50; packages up to 0.5kg UK£2.67, up to 2kg UK£9.42. UK Swiftair delivers letters a day faster for UK£2.85 more. www.royalmail.co.uk/calculator.

US: Allow 4-7 days for airmail to Italy. Postcards/aerogrammes cost US$1; letters under 28g US$0.90. Packages under 1 lb. cost US$7.20; larger packages cost a variable amount (around US$15). **US Express Mail** takes 2-3 days and costs US$24.50 for a 1 lb. package. http://ircalc.usps.gov.

RECEIVING MAIL IN ITALY

There are several ways to arrange pick-up of letters sent to you by friends and relatives while you are abroad.

General Delivery: Mail can be sent via **Poste Restante** (General Delivery; *Fermo Posta*) to almost any city or town in Italy with a post office. Address *Poste Restante* letters as in the following example: Jane DOE, *Fermo Posta*, Ufficio Postale Centrale di Piazza Cordusio 4, Milano 20100, Italia. The mail will go to a special desk in the central post office, unless you specify a post office by street address or postal code. It's best to use the largest post office, since mail may be sent there regardless. It is usually safer and quicker, though more expensive, to send mail express *(espresso)* or registered *(raccomandata)*. Bring your passport (or other photo ID) for pick-up. There is generally no surcharge; if there is a charge, it generally does not exceed the cost of domestic postage, L50 at the most. If the clerks insist that there is nothing for you, have them check under your first name as well. *Let's Go* lists post offices in the **Practical Information** section for each city and most towns.

American Express: AmEx's travel offices throughout the world offer a free **Client Letter Service** (mail held up to 30 days and forwarding upon request) for cardholders who contact them in advance. Address the letter in the same way shown above. Some offices will offer these services to non-cardholders (especially AmEx Travelers Cheque holders), but call ahead to make sure. *Let's Go* lists AmEx office locations for most large cities in **Practical Information** sections; for a complete, free list, call ☎ (800) 528-4800.

SENDING MAIL FROM ITALY

Airmail from major cities in Italy to North America averages eight to 12 days, although times are more unpredictable from smaller towns; to Australia or New Zealand, at least 7 days; to the UK or Ireland, 4 days; to South Africa, 6 days. **Aero-**

grammes, printed sheets that fold into envelopes and travel via airmail, are available at post offices. It helps to mark *via aerea* if possible, though "par avion" is universally understood. Most post offices will charge exorbitant fees or simply refuse to send aerogrammes with enclosures.

Surface mail is by far the cheapest and slowest way to send mail. It takes one to three months to cross the Atlantic and two to four to cross the Pacific—good for items you won't need to see for a while, such as souvenirs or other articles you've acquired along the way that are weighing down your pack.

To send a postcard to an international destination within Europe costs L1200 and to any other international destination via airmail costs L1500. To send a letter (up to 20g) to another country in Europe costs L1200 and to anywhere else in the world via airmail costs L1500.

SENDING MAIL WITHIN ITALY

Domestic postal service is phenomenally poor. A letter mailed from Perugia to Rome (a distance of less than 90 miles) may take as many as three weeks to arrive (if it even gets there at all). You can be sure that anything of any value will not reach its intended destination. Domestically, postcards require L1200.

TELEPHONES

CALLING HOME FROM ITALY

A **calling card** is probably your cheapest bet. Calls are billed either collect or to your account. **To obtain a calling card** from your national telecommunications service before leaving home, contact one of the following:

Australia: Telstra Australia Direct (☎13 22 00)

Canada: Bell Canada **Canada Direct** (☎(800) 565-4708)

Ireland: Telecom Éireann **Ireland Direct** (☎(800) 25 02 50)

New Zealand: Telecom New Zealand (☎(0800) 00 00 00):

South Africa: Telkom South Africa (☎09 03)

UK: British Telecom **BT Direct** (☎(800) 34 51 44)

US: AT&T (☎(888) 288-4685); **Sprint** (☎(800) 877-4646); **MCI** (☎(800) 444-4141).

ACCESS NUMBERS To **call home with a calling card,** contact the operator for your service provider by dialing the appropriate tool-free access number:

AT&T: ☎172 10 11.
Sprint: ☎172 18 77.
MCI WorldPhone Direct: ☎172 10 22.
Canada Direct: ☎172 10 01.
BT Direct: ☎172 00 44.
Ireland Direct: ☎172 03 53.
Australia Direct: ☎172 10 61.
Telecom New Zealand Direct: ☎172 10 64.
Telkom South Africa Direct: ☎172 10 27.

You can usually also make direct international calls from pay phones, but if you aren't using a calling card, you may need to drop your coins as quickly as your words. Prepaid phone cards (see below) and occasionally major credit cards can be used for direct international calls, but they are still less cost-efficient. (See **Placing International Calls** below for directions on how to place a direct international call.) Placing a **collect call** through an international operator is even more expensive, but may be necessary in case of emergency. You can typically place collect calls through the service providers listed above even if you don't possess one of their phone cards. If you will be making frequent international calls, it may be worthwhile to purchase a cell phone (*telefonino*).

PLACING INTERNATIONAL CALLS To call Italy from home or to place an international call from Italy, dial:

1. The **international dialing prefix** of the country you're calling from. International dialing prefixes include: **Australia** 0011; **Canada** and the **US** 011; **Ireland, Italy, New Zealand,** and the **UK** 00; **South Africa** 09.
2. The **country code** of the country you want to call. Country codes include: **Australia** 61; **Canada** and the **US** 1; **Ireland** 353; **Italy** 39; **New Zealand** 64; **South Africa** 27; **UK** 44.
3. The **city** or **area code.** *Let's Go* lists the phone codes for cities and towns in Italy opposite the city or town name, along side the ☎ icon. If the first digit is a zero (e.g., 041 for Venice), omit the zero when calling from abroad.
4. The **local number.**

CALLING WITHIN ITALY

The simplest way to call within the country is to use a coin-operated phone. **Prepaid phone cards,** available at vending machines, phone card vendors and *tabacchi,* carry a certain amount of phone time depending on the card's denomination (L5000, L10,000 and L15,000), and they usually save time and money in the long run. Italian phone cards are a little tricky to manuever; rip off the marked corner, and insert the card into the appropriate section of the pay phone. The phone card's time is measured in L200 talk units (e.g., one unit=one minute). Phone rates tend to be highest in the morning, lower in the evening, and lowest on Sunday and late at night. To call intercity within Italy, dial the entire number, including the city code. Even when dialing within a single city, the city code is required; for example, when dialing from one place in Milan to another, the (02) is still necessary. International calls start at L1000 and vary depending on where you are calling.

EMAIL AND INTERNET

Though Italy had initially lagged behind in constructing exits and turnpikes on the information superhighway, it's now playing the game of catch-up like a pro. New internet cafes, internet bars, and even internet laundromats are popping up every day throughout the country. The smaller towns in the south have not assimilated the cyber craze as quickly. Nonetheless, the net age is proving too all-encompassing for even the stubborn stalwarts of Calabria and Apulia. For advice on traveling with the use of internet, see the **World Wide Web,** p. 87.

For free internet access, try the local universities and libraries. Though such amenities are usually granted to members of the institution, flashing an ignorant tourist smile may charm the hosts. If you have minimal shame, feel free to befriend college students as you go and ask if you can use their email accounts.

Free, web-based email providers include Hotmail (www.hotmail.com), RocketMail (www.rocketmail.com), and Yahoo! Mail (www.yahoo.com). Almost every internet search engine has an affiliated free email service. *Let's Go* includes the major cyberspots to surf the web and check email in each city, but for a larger list of Italian cyberspots, hit the web before you go. The following websites contain fairly good listings: www.ecs.net/cafe/#list, www.cyberiacafe.net/cyberia/guide/ccafe.htm, and www.cybercaptive.com.

THE CALL OF NATURE

The mere thought of Italy's toilets will inspire a good hand washing. They range in style and quality from a stinking small pipe in the center of an unventilated filthy closet to an ornate, functional *gabinetto.* More expensive restaurants are your best bet for cleanliness. In general, the toilet paper is as comfortable and absorbant as sandy fly-paper. A travel roll of Charmin is always a good idea. For information on Italy's finest toilet, see **Jonathan's Angels,** p. 465.

ESSENTIALS

travel the world with CTS

youth and student travel club

- International Student Identity Card (ISIC)
- International and domestic discount airfares
- Budget accommodation
- Car-Hire
- Tours and excursions
- Rail and Coach Passes, Ferries
- Insurance

Over 150 offices for worldwide assistance and experienced staff

LONDON
44 Goodge St.-W1P 2AD
tel. 0044.207.2900630
Telesales
Europe 020 7290 0620
Worldwide 020 7290 0621

PARIS
20 Rue de Carmes, 75005
tel. 0033.1.43250076

ROME
Via Genova, 16 (Off Via Nazionale)
Corso Vittorio Emanuele II, 297
Telesales 06.4401066

MILAN
Via S. Antonio, 2
Telesales 02.58475223

BOLOGNA
Largo Respighi, 2/F
tel. 051.261802

VENICE
Dorso Duro Ca' Foscari, 3252
tel. 041.5205660

FLORENCE
Via dei Ginori, 25/R
Telesales 055.216660

NAPLES
Via Mezzocannone, 25
tel. 081.5527960

CTS OFFICE IN NEW YORK
Empire State Building • 350 Fifth Avenue
78th Floor • Suite 7813 • NY 10118 • tel. 001 212 760 1287

CTS web sites: **www.cts.it** **www.ctstravel.co.uk** **ww.ctstravelusa.com**

GETTING THERE

BY PLANE

When it comes to airfare, a little effort can save you a bundle. If your plans are flexible enough to deal with the restrictions, courier fares are the cheapest. Tickets bought from consolidators and standby seating are also good deals, but last-minute specials, airfare wars, and charter flights often beat these fares. The key is to hunt around, to be flexible, and to ask about discounts. Students, seniors, and those under 26 should never pay full price for a ticket.

DETAILS AND TIPS

Timing: Airfares to Italy peak between mid-June and early Sept.; holidays are also expensive periods in which to travel. Midweek (M-Th morning) round-trip flights run US$40-50 cheaper than weekend flights, but the latter are generally less crowded and more likely to permit frequent-flier upgrades. Return-date flexibility is usually not an option for the budget traveler; traveling with an "open return" ticket can be pricier than fixing a return date when buying the ticket and paying later to change it.

Route: Round-trip flights are by far the cheapest; "open-jaw" (arriving in and departing from different cities) and round-the-world, or RTW, flights are pricier but reasonable alternatives. Patching one-way flights together is the least economical way to travel. Flights between capital cities or regional hubs will offer the most competitive fares.

Fares: Roundtrip fares range from US$200-$500 in the off-season, to US$400-$700 in the peak season. Much of budget travel has to do with careful planning and the ability to compromise. Connecting flights, strange departure dates, and a symmetric itinerary are factors that can help decrease the airfare.

BUDGET AND STUDENT TRAVEL AGENCIES

While knowledgeable agents specializing in flights to Italy can make your life easy and help you save, they may not spend the time to find you the lowest possible fare—they get paid on commission. Students and under-26ers holding **ISIC** and **IYTC cards** (see p. 43), respectively, qualify for big discounts from student travel agencies. Most flights from budget agencies are on major airlines, but in peak season some may sell seats on (less reliable) chartered aircraft.

usit world (www.usitworld.com). Over 50 **usit campus** branches in the UK (www.usitcampus.co.uk), including: 52 Grosvenor Gardens, **London** SW1W 0AG (☎ (0870) 240 1010); **Manchester** (☎(0161) 273 1721); and **Edinburgh** (☎(0131) 668 3303). Nearly 20 **usit now** offices in Ireland, including 19-21 Aston Quay, O'Connell Bridge, **Dublin** 2 (☎(01) 602 1600; www.usitnow.ie), and **Belfast** (☎(02890) 327 111; www.usitnow.com). Offices also in Athens, Auckland, Brussels, Frankfurt, Johannesburg, Lisbon, Luxembourg, Madrid, Paris, Sofia, and Warsaw.

Council Travel (www.counciltravel.com). US offices include: Emory Village, 1561 N. Decatur Rd., **Atlanta,** GA 30307 (☎(404) 377-9997); 273 Newbury St., **Boston,** MA 02116 (☎(617) 266-1926); 1160 N. State St., **Chicago,** IL 60610 (☎(312) 951-0585); 931 Westwood Blvd., Westwood, **Los Angeles,** CA 90024 (☎(310) 208-3551); 254 Greene St., **New York,** NY 10003 (☎(212) 254-2525); 530 Bush St., **San Francisco,** CA 94108 (☎(415) 566-6222); 424 Broadway Ave E., **Seattle,** WA 98102 (☎(206) 329-4567); 3301 M St. NW, **Washington, D.C.** 20007 (☎(202) 337-6464). **For US cities not listed,** call ☎(800) 2-COUNCIL (226-8624). In the UK, 28A Poland St. (Oxford Circus), **London,** W1V 3DB (☎(020) 7437 7767).

CTS Travel, V. Genova, 16, **Rome** (☎ 06 462 04 31; fax 06 46 20 43 26); V. S. Antonio, 2, **Milan** (☎02 58 47 51; fax 02 58 30 36 49); V. dei Ginori, 25r, **Florence** (☎ 28 95 70; fax 055 29 21 50) and over 150 offices in the other cities (see www.cts.it). CTS offers travel services for the student and youth market.

Spend less,
EXPLORE MORE!
LOW STUDENT AIRFARES
EURAIL PASSES
BUS PASSES
STUDY ABROAD
800.272.9676
www.studentuniverse.com

Why wait in line when you can go online?
Low student airfares the easy way.
Go ahead... put your feet up and
plan your trip.

STA Travel, 6560 Scottsdale Rd. #F100, Scottsdale, AZ 85253 (☎(800) 777-0112; fax (602) 922-0793; www.sta-travel.com). A student and youth travel organization with over 150 offices worldwide. Ticket booking, travel insurance, railpasses, and more. US offices include: 297 Newbury St., **Boston,** MA 02115 (☎(617) 266-6014); 429 S. Dearborn St., **Chicago,** IL 60605 (☎(312) 786-9050); 7202 Melrose Ave., **Los Angeles,** CA 90046 (☎(323) 934-8722); 10 Downing St., **New York,** NY 10014 (☎(212) 627-3111); 4341 University Way NE, **Seattle,** WA 98105 (☎(206) 633-5000); 2401 Pennsylvania Ave., Ste. G, **Washington, D.C.** 20037 (☎(202) 887-0912); 51 Grant Ave., **San Francisco,** CA 94108 (☎(415) 391-8407). In the UK, 11 Goodge St., **London** WIP 1FE (☎(020) 7436 7779 for North American travel). In New Zealand, 10 High St., **Auckland** (☎(09) 309 0458). In Australia, 366 Lygon St., **Melbourne** Vic 3053 (☎(03) 9349 4344).

Travel CUTS (Canadian Universities Travel Services Limited), 187 College St., **Toronto,** ON M5T 1P7 (☎(416) 979-2406; fax 979-8167; www.travelcuts.com). 40 offices across Canada. Also in the UK, 295-A Regent St., **London** W1R 7YA (☎(020) 7255 1944).

Wasteels, Platform 2, Victoria Station, London SW1V 1JT (☎(020) 7834 7066; fax 7630 7628; www.wasteels.dk/uk). A huge chain in Europe, with 203 locations. Sells the Wasteels BIJ tickets, discounted (30-45% off regular fare) 2nd-class international point-to-point train tickets with unlimited stopovers for those under 26 (sold only in Europe).

FLIGHT PLANNING ON THE INTERNET The Web is a great place to look for travel bargains–it's fast and convenient, and you can spend as long as you like exploring options without driving your travel agent insane.

Many airline sites offer special last-minute deals on the Web. For fares, see **Alitalia** (www.alitalia.it), **Air-One** (www.air-one.it/airone.htm), and **Gandalf Air** (www.gandalfair.com). For a great set of links to practially every airline in every country, see www.travelpage.com/air/airlines. Other sites do the legwork and compile the best deals for you–try www.bestfares.com, www.onetravel.com, www.lowestfare.com, and www.travelzoo.com

STA (www.sta-travel.com) and **Council** (www.counciltravel.com) provide quotes on student tickets, while **Expedia** (www.msn.expedia.com) and **Travelocity** (www.travelocity.com) offer full travel services. **Priceline** (www.priceline.com) allows you to specify a price and obligates you to buy any ticket that meets or beats it; be prepared for odd hours and routes. **Skyauction** (www.skyauction.com) allows you to bid on both last-minute and advance-purchase tickets.

Just one last note–to protect yourself, make sure that the site uses a secure server before handing over any credit card details. Happy hunting!

COMMERCIAL AIRLINES

The commercial airlines' lowest regular offer is the **APEX** (Advance Purchase Excursion) fare, which provides confirmed reservations and allows "open-jaw" tickets. Generally, reservations must be made 7 to 21 days in advance, with 7- to 14-day minimum and up to 90-day maximum-stay limits and hefty cancellation and change penalties (fees rise in summer). Book peak-season APEX fares early, since by May you will have a hard time getting the departure date you want.

In using this section be sure to check all your options—the sections are organized by departure point and convenience, not by availability and price. Many airlines are global; for example, travelers from North America will want to inquire about fares from European as well as North American carriers.

TRAVELING FROM NORTH AMERICA. Basic round-trip fares to Italy range from roughly US$200-750. Carriers like **American** (US ☎(800) 433-7300; www.aa.com), **Delta** (US ☎(800) 241-4141; Canada (800) 221-1212; www.delta-air.com), and **United** (US ☎(800) 241-6522; www.ual.com) offer the most convenient flights to Rome and Milan, but they may not be the cheapest (unless you manage to grab a

Discount Airline Tickets
USA to Europe
Save up to 60%, You do not need to be a student
Free Service
Round Trip, Open Jaw or One Way
Up to One Year Stay
Rail Passes
Departures from any US City
1 800 455 2359
www.discountairfare.com
info @ discountairfare.com
AirFare Hotline of America, Inc.

special promotion or airfare war ticket). The carriers listed in **Traveling from Elsewhere in Europe** below also fly from North America to Italy, with connections in Europe. For better deals see **Budget and Student Travel Agencies** (p. 65).

TRAVELING FROM THE UK AND IRELAND. **British Airways** (UK ☎(0860) 01 17 47; www.britishairways.com), **British Midland Airways** (UK ☎(0870) 607 0555; www.britishmidland.com) and **buzz** (UK ☎(0870) 240 7070; www.buzzaway.com) often offer cheap specials from London to Milan. **Go-Fly Limited** (UK ☎(0845) 605 4321; elsewhere call UK☎+44 (1279) 66 63 88; www.go-fly.com) flies from London to Rome and Venice. **Aer Lingus** (Ireland ☎(01) 886 88 88; www.aerlingus.ie) and **Ryanair** (Ireland ☎(01) 812 12 12, UK (0870) 156 95 95; www.ryanair.ie) connect Irish and Italian gateways. The **Air Travel Advisory Bureau** in London (☎(020) 7636 5000; www.atab.co.uk) provides referrals to travel agencies and consolidators that offer discounted airfares out of the UK.

TRAVELING FROM ELSEWHERE IN EUROPE. Most European carriers, including **Air France** (www.airfrance.com), **Alitalia** (☎(800) 223-5730; www.alitalia.it/eng), **KLM** (UK☎+44 (0870) 507 40 70; www.klm.com), **Lufthansa** (www.lufthansa.com), and **Sabena** (Belgium +32 (02) 723 23 23; email communication@sabena.be; www.sabena.com/asp/public/frames/frame_setcommercail.asp), have frequent flights to Rome, Milan, and Venice from many European cities. Because of the sheer number of European airlines, fares tend to be reasonable.

TRAVELING FROM AUSTRALIA AND NEW ZEALAND. **Qantas Air** (Australia☎13 13 13, New Zealand 0800 808 767; www.qantas.com.au) flies from Australia and New Zealand to Rome and Milan. **Air New Zealand** (New Zealand ☎(0800) 35 22 66; www.airnz.co.nz) flies to Italy only from Auckland.

TRAVELING FROM SOUTH AFRICA. The European carriers listed above in **Traveling from Elsewhere in Europe,** including Air France, British Airways, and Lufthansa, fly from Cape Town and Johannesburg to their European hubs, from where flights connect to Italian destinations.

AIR COURIER FLIGHTS

Couriers transport cargo on international flights by guaranteeing delivery of the baggage claim slips from the company to a representative overseas. Generally, couriers must travel light (carry-ons only) and deal with complex restrictions on their flights. Most flights are round-trip only with short fixed-length stays (usually one week) and a limit of a single ticket per issue. Most of these flights also operate only out of the biggest cities. Generally, you must be over 21 (in some cases 18), have a valid passport, and procure your own visa, if necessary. For more info, consult *Air Courier Bargains* by Kelly Monaghan (The Intrepid Traveler, US$15) or the *Courier Air Travel Handbook* by Mark Field (Perpetual Press, US$10).

TRAVELING FROM NORTH AMERICA. Round-trip courier fares from the US to Italy run about US$200-500. Most flights leave from New York, Los Angeles, San Francisco, or Miami in the US and from Montreal, Toronto, or Vancouver in Canada. The first four organizations below provide their members with lists of opportunities and courier brokers worldwide for an annual fee (typically US$50-60). Alternatively, you can contact a courier broker (such as the last three listings) directly; most charge registration fees, but a few do not. Prices quoted below are round-trip. A few organizations that arrange courier flights between North America and Italy include: **Air Courier Association,** 15000 W. 6th Ave. #203, Golden, CO 80401 (☎(800) 282-1202; elsewhere call US ☎+1 (303) 215-9000; www.aircourier.org); **Global Courier Travel,** PO Box 3051, Nederland, CO 80466 (www.globalcouriertravel.com); **NOW Voyager,** 74 Varick St. #307, New York, NY 10013 (☎(212) 431-1616; fax 219-1753; www.nowvoyagertravel.com); and **Worldwide Courier Association** (☎(800) 780-4359, ext. 441; www.massiveweb.com).

FROM THE UK AND IRELAND. Although the courier industry is most developed from North America, there are limited courier flights in other areas. The minimum age for couriers from the **UK** is usually 18. **Brave New World Enterprises,** P.O. Box 22212, London SE5 8WB (email guideinfo@nry.co.uk; www.nry.co.uk/bnw) publishes a directory of all the companies offering courier flights in the UK (UK£10, in electronic form UK£8). **Global Courier Travel** (see above) also offers flights from London and Dublin to continental Europe. **British Airways Travel Shop** (☎(0870) 606 11 33; www.british-airways.com/travelqa/booking/travshop/travshop.shtml) arranges flights from London to continental Europe (specials may be as low as UK£60; no registration fee).

STANDBY FLIGHTS

Traveling standby requires considerable flexibility in arrival and departure dates and cities. Companies dealing in standby flights sell vouchers rather than tickets, along with the promise to get to your destination (or near your destination) within a certain window of time (typically 1-5 days). Call in before your specific window of time to hear your flight options and the probability that you will be able to board each flight. You can then decide which flights you want to try to make, show up at the appropriate airport at the appropriate time, present your voucher, and board if space is available. Vouchers can usually be bought for both one-way and round-trip travel. You may receive a monetary refund only if every available flight within your date range is full; if you opt not to take an available (but perhaps less convenient) flight, you can only get credit toward future travel. Carefully read agreements with any company offering standby flights as tricky fine print can leave you in a lurch. To check on a company's service record in the US, call the Better Business Bureau (☎(212) 533-6200). It is difficult to receive refunds, and clients' vouchers will not be honored when an airline fails to receive payment in time. One established standby company in the US is **Airhitch,** 2641 Broadway, 3rd fl., New York, NY 10025 (☎(800) 326-2009; fax 864-5489; www.airhitch.org) and Los Angeles, CA (☎(888) 247-4482), which offers one-way flights to Europe from the Northeast (US$159), West Coast and Northwest (US$239), Midwest (US$209), and Southeast (US$189). Intracontinental connecting flights within the US or Europe cost US$79-139. Airhitch's head European office is in Paris (☎+33 (01) 47 00 16 30); there's also one in Amsterdam (☎+31 (20) 626 32 20).

TICKET CONSOLIDATORS

Ticket consolidators, or **"bucket shops,"** buy unsold tickets in bulk from commercial airlines and sell them at discounted rates. The best place to look is in the Sunday travel section of any major newspaper, where many bucket shops place tiny ads. Call quickly, as availability is typically extremely limited. Not all bucket shops are reliable, so insist on a receipt that gives full details of restrictions, refunds, and tickets, and pay by credit card (in spite of the 2-5% fee) so you can stop payment if you never receive your tickets. For more info, see www.travel-library.com/air-travel/consolidators.html or pick up Kelly Monaghan's *Air Travel's Bargain Basement* (Intrepid Traveler, US$8).

TRAVELING FROM NORTH AMERICA. **Travel Avenue** (☎(800) 333-3335; www.travelavenue.com), works with several ticket consolidators and will search for cheap flights from anywhere for a fee. **NOW Voyager,** 74 Varick St., #307, New York, NY 10013 (☎(212) 431-1616; fax 219-1793; www.nowvoyagertravel.com) arranges discounted flights, mostly from New York, to Milan and Rome. Other consolidators worth trying are: **Interworld** (☎(305) 443-4929; fax 443-0351); **Pennsylvania Travel** (☎(800) 331-0947); **Rebel** (☎(800) 227-3235; email travel@rebeltours.com; www.rebeltours.com); **Cheap Tickets** (☎(800) 377-1000; www.cheaptickets.com); and **Travac** (☎(800) 872-8800; fax (212) 714-9063; www.travac.com). Yet more consolidators on the web include the **Internet Travel Network** (www.itn.com); **Surplus-Travel.com** (www.surplustravel.com); **Travel Information Services** (www.tiss.com); **TravelHUB** (www.travelhub.com); and **The Travel Site** (www.thetravelsite.com). These are just suggestions to get you started in your research; *Let's Go* does not endorse any of these agencies. As always, be cautious, and research companies before you hand over your credit card number.

TRAVELING FROM THE UK, AUSTRALIA, AND NEW ZEALAND. In London, the **Air Travel Advisory Bureau** (☎(020) 7636 5000; www.atab.co.uk) can provide names of reliable consolidators and discount flight specialists. From Australia and New Zealand, look for consolidator ads in the travel section of the *Sydney Morning Herald* and other papers.

CHARTER FLIGHTS

Charters are flights a tour operator contracts with an airline to fly extra loads of passengers during peak season. Charter flights fly less frequently than major airlines, make refunds particularly difficult, and are almost always fully booked. Schedules and itineraries may also change or be cancelled at the last moment (as late as 48 hours before the trip, and without a full refund), and check-in, boarding, and baggage claim are often much slower. However, they can also be cheaper.

Discount clubs and **fare brokers** offer members savings on last-minute charter and tour deals. Study contracts closely; you don't want to end up with an unwanted overnight layover. **Travelers Advantage,** Stamford, CT, USA (☎(800) 548-1116; www.travelersadvantage.com; US$60 annual fee includes discounts, newsletters, and cheap flight directories) specializes in European travel and tour packages.

FURTHER READING: BY PLANE.

The Worldwide Guide to Cheap Airfare, Michael McColl. Insider Publications (US$15).

Discount Airfares: The Insider's Guide, George Hobart. Priceless Publications (US$14).

The Official Airline Guide, an expensive tome available at many libraries, has flight schedules, fares, and reservation numbers.

Air Traveler's Handbook (www.cs.cmu.edu/afs/cs/user/mkant/Public/Travel/airfare.html).

GETTING AROUND

Unless stated otherwise, *Let's Go* lists one-way fares. In general, Italian trains are more efficient, economical, and romantic than other transportation alternatives.

BY TRAIN

If you're under 26 or over 60 and plan to travel extensively in Italy, your first purchase should be a **Cartaverde** or **Carta d'argento,** offering a year-long 20% discount on all train tickets (see p. 73).

The Italian State Railway, **Ferrovie dello Stato** or **FS** (national info line ☎ 147 88 80 88; www.fs-on-line.com), offers inexpensive and efficient service, although it is commonly plagued by strikes. The southern Italy offspring of FS, **Ferrovie Sud-Est (FSE),** may be closer to cattle cars than trains. Hot, crowded, and uncomfortable, FSE trains often stop in remote locations in the south to change cars or give the hamster-powered engines a rest. Down on the heel of Italy it may be worth the extra *lire* to take a classier train (see below).

Several types of trains ride the Italian rails. The **locale** stops at every station along a particular line, often taking twice as long as a faster train. The **diretto** makes fewer stops than the *locale*, while the **espresso** just stops at major stations. The air-conditioned, more expensive **rapido,** an **InterCity (IC)** train, travels only to the largest cities. No *rapidi* have 2nd-class compartments, and a few require reservations. Tickets for the fast, comfy, and pricey **Eurostar** trains (a 1st- and 2nd-class train) require reservations. Eurailpasses are valid without a supplement on all trains except **Eurostar.**

Trains are not always safe; for safety tips, see p. 50. For long trips make sure you are on the correct car, as trains sometimes split at crossroads. Towns listed in parentheses on European train schedules require a train switch at the town listed immediately before the parenthesis.

RESERVATIONS. While seat reservations are only rarely required, you are not guaranteed a seat without one (L5000 and up, depending on the ticket price). Reservations are available as much as two months in advance on major trains, and Europeans often reserve far ahead of time; you should strongly consider reserving during peak holiday and tourist seasons (at the very latest a few hours ahead). If you reserve a seat, be prepared to (politely) ask its occupant to move. To say, "excuse me, but I have reserved this seat," try "*Mi scusa, ma ho prenotato questo posto.*" It will be necessary to purchase a **supplement** (L6,000-L30,000) or special fare for faster or higher-quality trains such as Italy's ETR500 and Pendolino. Inter-Rail holders must also purchase supplements (L6,000-L40,000) for trains like EuroCity and InterCity; these supplements are unnecessary for Eurailpass and Europass holders.

OVERNIGHT TRAINS. Night trains have their advantages: you won't waste valuable daylight hours traveling, and you will be able to forego the hassle and considerable expense of securing a night's accommodation. However, night travel has its drawbacks as well: discomfort and sleeplessness are the most obvious; the scenery probably won't look as enticing in pitch black, either. On overnight trips, consider paying extra for a **cuccetta,** one of six fold-down bunks within a compartment (approx. L35,000); private **sleeping cars** offer more privacy and comfort, but are considerably more expensive (L50,000-L120,000) and are not widely available in Italy. If you're not willing to spend the money on a *cuccetta*, consider taking an *espresso* train overnight—they usually have compartments with fold-out seats. If you are using a railpass valid only for a restricted number of days, inspect train schedules to maximize the use of your pass: an overnight train or boat journey uses up only one of your travel days if it departs after 7pm (you need only write in the next day's date on your pass).

BUY ONE OF THESE*

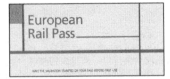

European
Rail Pass

AND GET ALL THIS FREE**

One FREE night at The Pink Palace

Includes breakfast and dinner at the world famous youth resort in Corfu, Greece.

Eurotrip Savings Guide

Save on shopping, food, museums and more throughout the cities of Europe.

and

FREE Eurail timetable

Details the schedules of most major trains and explains the symbols you will encounter in train stations.

FREE Eurail map

An easy-to-read guide including all countries covered on your pass.

plus

Passes issued on the spot

Your pass is delivered to your door within 1-2 business days. Rush orders are our specialty.

Toll-free emergency help line

Call our offices toll free from Europe if you have any problems or questions regarding your pass.

Call 1-888-RAILPASS

1-888-724-5727

www.railconnection.com

* We have many passes to choose from including Eurail, Eurail Flexi, Euro, Saver, Individual Country and BritRail, just to name a few.

** Offer good while supplies last, certain restrictions apply, call for details.

DOMESTIC RAILPASSES

Railpasses were conceived to allow you to jump on any train in Europe, go wherever you want whenever you want, and change your plans at will. In practice, it's not so simple. You still must stand in line to validate your pass, pay for supplements, and fork over cash for reservations. More importantly, railpasses don't always pay off. For ballpark estimates, contact Rail Europe (see p. 74).

ITALIAN KILOMETRIC TICKET. A railpass will probably not pay off if you are traveling solely within Italy, although it may be a practical option if you plan to travel to nearby European countries. The Italian State Railway offers passes valid on all trains within Italy. They are seldom cost-effective, since regular fares are cheap. The Italian Kilometric Ticket is good for 20 trips or 3000km (1875 mi.) of travel, whichever comes first, and they can be used for two months by up to five people traveling together. It's virtually impossible for one person to break even on the Kilometric Ticket. For a couple or a family traveling widely, however, it can pay off. Children under 12 are charged half of the distance traveled, and those under four travel free. A first-class kilometric ticket costs L338,000 (US$224), second-class L200,000 (US$132). To obtain info on this service or purchase tickets, call the North American hotline (☎(847) 730 2121). When buying the ticket, be sure the sales agent stamps the date on it. You can also purchase this pass from the **Italian State Railway Representative,** in New York (☎(212) 730 2121) or in Italy (where the prices are slightly lower) at major train stations and offices of the **Compagnia Italiana Turismo (CIT).** When using this pass, have your mileage stamped at the ticket booth or face buying another ticket on the train.

CARTAVERDE. Cartaverde are available to people aged 12 to 26. The card (L40,000) is valid for one year, and entitles travelers to a 20% discount on any state train fare. If you're under 26 and plan to spend at least L200,000 on train tickets in Italy, this pass should be your *first* purchase upon arrival. Families of four or more and groups of up to five adults traveling together qualify for discounts on Italian railways. Persons over 60 get the same year-long 20% discount for the same price (L40,000) with purchase of a **carta d'argento** ("silver card").

MULTINATIONAL PASSES

EURAILPASS. Eurail is valid in most of Western Europe: Austria, Belgium, Denmark, Finland, France, Germany, Greece, Hungary, Italy, Luxembourg, the Netherlands, Norway, Portugal, the Republic of Ireland, Spain, Sweden, and Switzerland. It is not valid in the UK. Standard **Eurailpasses,** valid for a consecutive given number of days, are most suitable for those planning on spending extensive time on trains every few days. **Flexipasses,** valid for any 10 or 15 (not necessarily consecutive) days in a two-month period, are more cost-effective for those traveling longer distances less frequently. **Saverpasses** provide first-class travel for travelers in groups of two to five (prices are per person). **Youthpasses** and **Youth Flexipasses** provide parallel second-class perks for those under 26.

EURAILPASSES	15 days	21 days	1 month	2 months	3 months
1st class Eurailpass	US$554	US$718	US$890	US$1260	US$1558
Eurail Saverpass	US$470	US$610	US$756	US$1072	US$1324
Eurail Youthpass	US$388	US$499	US$623	US$882	US$1089

EURAIL FLEXIPASSES	10 days in 2 months	15 days in 2 months
1st class Eurail Flexipass	US$654	US$862
Eurail Saver Flexipass	US$556	US$732
Eurail Youth Flexipass	US$458	US$599

Passholders receive a timetable for major routes and a map with details on possible ferry, steamer, bus, car rental, hotel, and Eurostar (see p. 69) discounts. Passholders often also receive reduced fares or free passage on many bus and boat lines. **Eurail freebies** (excepting surcharges such as reservation fees and port taxes) include: ferries between Italy and Sardinia (Civitavecchia-Golfo Aranci), Sicily (Villa S. Giovanni-Messina), and Greece (Brindisi-Patras).

EUROPASS. The Europass is a slimmed-down version of the Eurailpass: it allows five to 15 days of unlimited travel in any two-month period within France, Germany, Italy, Spain, and Switzerland. **First-Class Europasses** (for individuals) and **Saverpasses** (for people traveling in groups of 2-5) range from US$348/296 per person (5 days) to US$728/620 (15 days). **Second-Class Youthpasses** for those ages 12-25 cost US$233-513. For a fee, you can add **additional zones** ferry between Italy and Greece; $60 for one associated country, $100 for two. You are entitled to the same **freebies** afforded by the Eurailpass (see above), but only when they are within or between countries that you have purchased. Plan your itinerary before buying a Europass: it will save you money if your travels are confined to three, four, or five adjacent Western European countries, or if you only want to go to large cities, but would be a waste if you plan to make lots of side-trips. If you're tempted to add many rail days and associate countries, consider a Eurailpass.

SHOPPING AROUND FOR A EURAIL OR EUROPASS Eurailpasses and Europasses are designed by the EU itself, and are purchasable only by non-Europeans almost exclusively from non-European distributors. These passes must be sold at uniform prices determined by the EU. However, some travel agents tack on a US$10 handling fee, and others offer certain bonuses with purchase, so shop around. Also, keep in mind that pass prices usually go up each year, so if you're planning to travel early in the year, you can save cash by purchasing before January 1 (you have three months from the purchase date to validate your pass in Europe).

It is best to buy your Eurail- or Europass before leaving; only a few places in major European cities sell them, and at a marked-up price. Eurailpasses are non-refundable once validated; if your pass is completely unused and invalidated and you have the original purchase documents, you can get an 85% refund from the place of purchase. You can get a replacement for a lost pass only if you have purchased insurance on it under the Pass Protection Plan (US$10). Eurailpasses are available through travel agents, student travel agencies like STA and Council (see p. 67), and **Rail Europe,** 500 Mamaroneck Ave., Harrison, NY 10528 (US ☎(888) 382-7245, fax (800) 432-1329; Canada ☎(800) 361-7245, fax (905) 602-4198; UK ☎(0990) 84 88 48; www.raileurope.com) or **DER Travel Services,** 9501 W. Devon Ave. #301, Rosemont, IL 60018 (US ☎(888) 337-7350; fax (800) 282-7474; www.dertravel.com).

INTERRAIL PASS. If you have lived for at least six months in one of the European countries where InterRail Passes are valid, they prove an economical option. There are eight InterRail **zones:** A (Great Britain, Northern Ireland, Republic of Ireland), B (Norway, Sweden, and Finland), C (Germany, Austria, Denmark, and Switzerland), D (Croatia, Czech Republic, Hungary, Poland, and Slovakia), E (France, Belgium, Netherlands, and Luxembourg), F (Spain, Portugal, and Morocco), G (Greece, Italy, Slovenia, and Turkey, including a Greece-Italy ferry), and H (Bulgaria, Romania, Yugoslavia, and Macedonia). The **Under 26 InterRail Card** allows either 14 days or one month of unlimited travel within one, two, three or all of the eight zones; the cost is determined by the number of zones the pass covers (UK£159-259). If you buy a ticket including the zone in which you have claimed residence, you must still pay 50% fare for tickets inside your own country.

Passholders receive **discounts** on rail travel, Eurostar journeys, and most ferries to Ireland, Scandinavia, and the rest of Europe. Most exclude **supplements** for high-speed trains. For info and ticket sales in Europe contact **Student Travel Center,** 24 Rupert St., 1st fl., London W1V 7FN (☎(020) 74 37 81 01; fax 77 34 38 36; www.student-travel-centre.com). Tickets are also available from travel agents or main train stations throughout Europe.

EURO DOMINO. Like the Interrail Pass, the Euro Domino pass is available to anyone who has lived in Europe for at least six months; this pass, however, it is only valid in one country (which you designate upon buying the pass). It is available for 29 European countries as well as Morocco. The Euro Domino pass is available for 1st- and 2nd-class travel (with a special rate for under 26ers), for three, five, or 10 days of unlimited travel within a one-month period. Euro Domino is not valid on Eurostar or Thalys trains. Supplements for many high-speed trains are included, though you must still pay for reservations where they are compulsory. The pass must be bought within your country of residence; each country has its own price for the pass. Inquire with your national rail company for more info.

RAIL-AND-DRIVE PASSES. In addition to simple railpasses, many countries (as well as Europass and Eurail) offer rail-and-drive passes, which combine car rental with rail travel—a good option for travelers who wish both to visit cities accessible by rail and to make side trips into the surrounding areas. Rail Europe (see **Shopping Around for a Eurail or Europass,** p. 74) offers a EurailDrive Pass with four trains days and two rental days for between US$439 and US$529, depending on the car

DISCOUNTED TICKETS

For travelers under 26, **BIJ** tickets (Billets Internationals de Jeunesse; a.k.a. **Wasteels, Eurotrain,** and **Route 26**) are a great alternative to railpasses. Available for trips within Europe and most ferry services, they knock 20-40% off regular 2nd-class fares. Tickets, good for 60 days after purchase, allow a number of stopovers along the route of the train journey. Issued for a specific international route between two points, they must be used in the direction and order of the designated route and must be bought in Europe. The equivalent for those over 26, **BIGT** tickets provide a 20-30% discount on 1st- and 2nd-class international tickets for business travelers, temporary European residents, and their families. Both types of tickets are available from European travel agents, at Wasteels, or Eurotrain offices (in or near train stations). For more info, contact Wasteels (see p. 67). Other branches are at: Stazione Centrale, Naples (☎081 201 071; fax 20 69 03); Stazione Centrale, Milan (☎02 669 00 20; fax 669 05 00); Stazione Maria Novella, Florence (☎/fax 05 52 80 63).

FURTHER READING: BY TRAIN.

Thomas Cook European Timetable, updated monthly, covers all major and most minor train routes in Europe. In the US, order from Forsyth Travel Library (US$28; ☎(800) 367-7984; email order@forsyth.com; www.forsyth.com). In Europe, find it at any Thomas Cook Money Exchange Center. Alternatively, buy directly from Thomas Cook (www.thomascook.com).

Guide to European Railpasses, Rick Steves. Online and by mail. US ☎(425) 771-8303; fax (425) 771-0833; www.ricksteves.com). Free; delivery $8.

On the Rails Around Europe: A Comprehensive Guide to Travel by Train, Melissa Shales. Thomas Cook Ltd. (US$18.95).

Eurail and Train Travel Guide to Europe. Houghton Mifflin (US$15).

Europe by Eurail 2000, Laverne Ferguson-Kosinski. Globe Pequot Press (US$16.95).

BY BUS

Although Italian trains are extremely popular and inexpensive, the bus networks strike much less frequently and are therefore worth getting to know. In Italy, buses serve many points inaccessible by train and occasionally arrive in more convenient places in larger towns. They are often crowded, so try to get tickets in advance. All tickets must be validated using the orange machines on-board immediately upon entering the bus. Failure to do so will result in large fines. As a reward for the bumpy ride, the scenery along the way—especially in southern Tuscany and the Dolomites—often outshines the beauty of the destination. **Interna-**

Top quality bikes, fun countryside bike tours, friendly and knowledgeable assistance!

Florence by bike

Bike rental & bike tours

Phone number in Florence
055 488992
Booking essential

Join us on our great guided bike tour in the Tuscan countryside.
A full day tour through some of the most enchanting scenery in Toscana.
Ride through century-old olive groves, vineyards and sunflower fields. Enjoy a delicious CHIANTI wine and OLIVE OIL tasting in a charming Tuscan farmhouse...

Bike rental The largest and most specialized in Florence
Bike tours in Florence and Tuscany (Chianti area)
Scooter rental any kind of scooter

e-mail: ecologica@dada.it Http://www.florencebybike.it
Via S.Zanobi, 120/122r (5- minute walk from the railway station)

tional bus passes are sometimes cheaper than railpasses, and they typically allow unlimited travel on a hop-on, hop-off basis between major European cities. **Eurolines,** 52 Grosvenor Gardens, London SW1 (☎(1582) 404 511; www.eurolines.co.uk or www.eurolines.com), and **Busabout,** 258 Vauxhall Bridge Rd., London SW1V 1BSX (☎ (020) 7959 1661; www.busabout.com), are popular among non-American backpackers. Contact them for information on passes and prices.

BY CAR

DRIVING PERMITS AND CAR INSURANCE

INTERNATIONAL DRIVING PERMIT (IDP)

If you plan to drive a car while in Italy, you must be over 18 and ought to have an International Driving Permit (IDP), though it is not always necessary to have one in Italy. It may be a good idea to get one anyway in case you're in a situation (e.g., an accident or stranded in a small town) where the police do not know English; information on the IDP is printed in ten languages, including Italian. For more information on the driving permit and driving in Italy, contact "In Italy Online," at www.initaly.com/travel/info/driving.htm.

Your IDP, valid for one year, must be issued in your own country before you depart. An application for an IDP usually needs to include one or two photos, a current local license, an additional form of identification, and a fee.

Australia: Contact your local Royal Automobile Club (RAC) or the National Royal Motorist Association (NRMA) if in NSW or the ACT (☎(08) 9421 4444; www.rac.com.au/travel). Permits AUS$15.

Canada: Contact a Canadian Automobile Association (CAA) branch office or write to CAA, 1145 Hunt Club Rd., #200, K1V 0Y3. (☎(613) 247-0117; www.caa.ca/CAAInternet/travelservices/internationaldocumentation/idptravel.htm). Permits CDN$10.

Ireland: Contact the nearest Automobile Association (AA) office or write to the UK address below. Permits IR£4. The Irish Automobile Association, 23 Suffolk St., Rockhill,

Blackrock, Co. Dublin (☎(01) 677 9481; 24hr. breakdown and road service ☎(800) 667 788, toll-free in Ireland), honors most foreign automobile memberships.

New Zealand: Contact your local Automobile Association (AA) or the main office at Auckland Central, 99 Albert St. (☎(09) 377 4660; www.nzaa.co.nz). Permits NZ$8.

South Africa: Contact the Travel Services Department of the Automobile Association of South Africa at P.O. Box 596, 2000 Johannesburg (☎(011) 799 1400; fax 799 1410; http://aasa.co.za). Permits SAR28.50.

UK: To visit your local AA Shop, contact the **AA Headquarters** (☎(0990) 44 88 66), or write to: The Automobile Association, International Documents, Fanum House, Erskine, Renfrewshire PA8 6BW. To find the location nearest you that issues the IDP, call ☎(0990) 50 06 00 or (0990) 44 88 66. For more info, see www.theaa.co.uk/motoringandtravel/idp/index.asp. Permits UK£4.

US: Visit any American Automobile Association (AAA) office or write to AAA Florida, Travel Related Services, 1000 AAA Drive (mail stop 100), Heathrow, FL 32746 (☎(407) 444-7000; fax 444-7380). You don't have to be a member to buy an IDP. Permits US$10. AAA Travel Related Services (☎(800) 222-4357) provides road maps, travel guides, emergency road services, travel services, and auto insurance.

CAR INSURANCE

Most credit cards cover standard insurance up to the collision deductible. If you rent, lease, or borrow a car, you will need a **green card,** or **International Insurance Certificate,** to certify that you have liability insurance and that it applies abroad. Green cards can be obtained at car rental agencies, car dealers (for those leasing cars), some travel agents, and some border crossings. Rental agencies may require you to purchase theft insurance in countries that they consider to have a high risk of auto theft. If you plan to drive in Italy for more than 45 days, you will need a regular Italian insurance policy. **If you are planning to rent a car in Italy you do not need a green card or an international drivers license, but you do need valid insurance coverage.**

DRIVING IN ITALY

If you are using a car, learn local driving signals and always wear a **seatbelt.** There are four different kinds of roads: *Autostrade* (Superhighways: most of which charge tolls), *Strade Statali* (State Roads), *Strade Provinciali* (Provincial Roads), and *Strade Comunali* (Local Roads). On the *autostrade*, no U-turns are permitted, and stopping is permitted only in emergency parking areas or parking lanes. The speed limit is a little terrifying. Maximum speeds are: 50 kph (31.25 mph) in cities and towns; 90 km (56.25 mph) for all cars and motor vehicles on main roads and local roads; 110 km (68.75 mph) for all cars and motor vehicles up to 1099cc on superhighways; 130 km (81.25 mph) for all cars and motor vehicles over 1100cc on superhighways.

The Italian highway code follows the Geneva Convention and Italy uses international road signs. Driving is on the right. Passing must be on the left. Violators of the highway code are fined; serious violations may also be punished by imprisonment. For more driving rules and regulations, consult "In Italy Online" at www.initaly.com/travel/info/driving.htm.

The **Automobile Club Italiano (ACI)** is the savior for Italy. Ready and willing to come to your aid, it has offices throughout Italy. The main office is at V. Marsala 8, 00185 Roma (☎06 499 81; fax 06 499 82 34). In case of **breakdown** on any Italian road, dial ☎116 at the nearest telephone. The nearest ACI office will be advised to come to your assistance. On superhighways, use the emergency telephones placed every 2km. Study route maps before you hit the road; in many regions, road conditions necessitate driving more slowly and more cautiously than you would at home. If you plan on spending a lot of time on the road, you may want to bring spare parts. For long drives in desolate areas, invest in a cellular phone and a roadside assistance program. Be sure to park your vehicle in a garage or well-traveled area and use a steering wheel locking device in larger cities.

RENTING A CAR

You can rent a car from a US-based firm (Alamo, Avis, Budget, or Hertz) with European offices, from a European-based company with local representatives (Europcar), or from a tour operator (Auto Europe, Europe By Car, and Kemwel Holiday Autos) that will arrange a rental for you from a European company at its own rates. Multinationals offer greater flexibility, but tour operators often strike better deals. Expect to pay L100,000 per day for a teensy car. Reserve ahead and pay in advance if possible. It is always cheaper to reserve a car from the US than from Europe. Always check if prices quoted include tax and collision insurance; some credit card companies cover the deductible on collision insurance, allowing their customers to decline the collision damage waiver. Ask about discounts and check the terms of insurance, particularly the size of the deductible. Ask airlines about special fly-and-drive packages; you may get up to a week of free or discounted rental. Minimum age in Italy is usually 18. At most agencies, all that's needed to rent a car is a license from home and proof that you've had it for a year. Car rental in Europe is available through the following agencies:

Auto Europe, 39 Commercial St., P.O. Box 7006, Portland, ME 04112, USA (US and Canada ☎(888) 223-5555 or (207) 842-2000; fax (207) 842-2222; www.autoeurope.com).

Avis (US and Canada ☎(800) 331-1084; UK ☎(0990) 90 05 00; Australia ☎(800) 22 55 33; New Zealand ☎(0800) 65 51 11; www.avis.com).

Budget (US ☎(800) 472-3325; Canada ☎(800) 527-0700; UK ☎(0800) 18 11 81; Australia ☎13 27 27; www.budgetrentacar.com).

Europe by Car, One Rockefeller Plaza, New York, NY 10020 (US ☎(800) 223-1516 or (212) 581-3040; fax 246-1458; email info@europebycar.com; www.europebycar.com).

Europcar, 145 av. Malekoff, 75016 Paris (☎(01) 45 00 08 06); US ☎(800) 227-3876; Canada (800) 227-7368; www.europcar.com).

Hertz (US ☎(800) 654-3001; Canada ☎(800) 263-0600; UK ☎(0990) 99 66 99; Australia ☎9698 2555; www.hertz.com).

Kemwel Holiday Autos (US ☎(800) 576-1590; www.kemwel.com).

BY FERRY

The islands of Sicily, Sardinia, and Corsica, as well as the smaller islands along the coasts, are connected to the mainland by ferries *(traghetti)* and hydrofoils *(aliscafi)*. Italy's largest private ferry service is Tirrenia; for info, contact the Rome office at V. Bissolati, 41 (☎06 474 20 41). Major companies (**Tirrenia, Moby Lines, Siremar,** and **Caremar**) and hydrofoil services (**SNAV** and **Alilauro**) make departures and arrivals in major ports, such as Ancona, Bari, Brindisi, Genoa, Livorno, La Spezia, Naples, and Trapani. Ferry services will allow you to visit the Tremiti, Pontine, and Lipari (Aeolean) Islands, as well as give you a reason to spend time in a port town. Use the time prior to your departure to enjoy the "Stop-Over in Bari" program or to indulge in the fresh seafood. Ferries from Italy's ports of Bari, Brindisi, and Otranto travel to Greece. Only Brindisi honors Eurailpasses. In all other situations, Bari and Otranto services are cheaper, and they keep you separated from the hordes of tourists at Brindisi. You can reach Tunisia from Genoa, Sardinia, and Trapani. Malta is accessible via Reggio di Calabria.

For major trips reserve ferry tickets at least one week in advance. Ferry schedules change unpredictably—confirm your departure one day in advance. Some ports require that you check in two hours before the departure or your reservation will be cancelled. **Posta ponte** (deck class; preferable in warm weather) is cheapest. It is, however, often only available when the **poltrone** (reclining cabin seats) are full. Port taxes often apply. Ask for student and Eurail discounts.

BY THUMB

Let's Go strongly urges you to consider the risks before you choose to hitchhike. We do not recommend hitchhiking as a safe means of transportation. Hitchhiking in Italy, especially in areas south of Rome or Naples, can be unsafe. Women travelers should be especially cautious, though all travelers put themselves at risk by accepting a ride from a stranger.

BY ZEPPELIN

Let's be honest. There's not really any way to travel around Italy in a zeppelin. Shame, though.

ADDITIONAL INFORMATION

SPECIFIC CONCERNS

WOMEN TRAVELERS

Women exploring on their own inevitably face some additional safety concerns, but it's easy to be adventurous without taking undue risks. The Italian art of *machismo* is well cultivated, and almost all foreign women will be hit on. In cities, you may be harassed no matter how you're dressed. Your best answer to verbal harassment is no answer at all; feigned deafness, sitting motionless, and staring straight ahead at nothing in particular will do a world of good. The extremely persistent can sometimes be dissuaded by a firm *"Vai Via!"* (Go away!), *"Sono fidanzata"* (I'm engaged), or *"Ho un ragazzo. Italiano. Molto geloso."* (I have a boyfriend. Italian. Very jealous). Wearing a conspicuous **wedding band** may also help prevent unwanted overtures. Some travelers report that carrying pictures of a "husband" or "children" is extremely useful to help document marriage status. Generally, the less you look like a tourist, the better off you'll be. Dress conservatively, especially in rural areas. Moreover, you will not be allowed into many churches if scantily clad.

If you are concerned, you might consider staying in hostels that offer single rooms that lock from the inside or in religious organizations that offer rooms for women only. Communal showers in some hostels are safer than others; check them before settling in. Stick to centrally located accommodations and avoid solitary late-night treks or metro rides. When traveling, always carry extra money for a phone call or a taxi. **Hitchhiking** is never safe for lone women, or even for two women traveling together. Choose train compartments occupied by other women or couples, or ask the conductor to put together a women-only compartment.

All travelers to Italy should, however, be aware that conceptions of personal space is different from what you're probably used to. The guy crowded next to you on the bus or the woman gesticulating wildly in your face is not necessarily threatening you; it is acceptable and normal to stand close to the person you're addressing, to gesture forcefully, and to shout. Don't hesitate, however, to seek out a police officer or a passerby if you are being harassed. *Let's Go: Italy* lists emergency numbers (including rape crisis lines) in the Practical Information listings of most cities. Memorize the emergency numbers in the places you visit. Carry a **whistle** or an airhorn on your keychain, and don't hesitate to use it in an emergency. An **IMPACT Model Mugging** self-defense course will not only prepare you for a potential attack, but will also raise your level of awareness of your surroundings as well as your confidence (see **Self Defense,** p. 50). Women also face some specific health concerns when traveling (see **Women's Health,** p. 54).

FURTHER READING: WOMEN TRAVELERS.

A Journey of One's Own: Uncommon Advice for the Independent Woman Traveler, Thalia Zepatos. Eighth Mountain Press (US$17).

Adventures in Good Company: The Complete Guide to Women's Tours and Outdoor Trips, Thalia Zepatos. Eighth Mountain Press (US$7).

Active Women Vacation Guide, Evelyn Kaye. Blue Panda Publications (US$18).

Travelers' Tales: Gutsy Women, Travel Tips and Wisdom for the Road, Marybeth Bond. Traveler's Tales (US$8).

TRAVELING ALONE

There are many benefits to traveling alone, among them greater independence and more rewarding challenges. As a lone traveler, you may find that Italians are more inclined to help you. On the other hand, any solo traveler is a more vulnerable target of harassment and street theft. Lone travelers need to be well-organized and look confident at all times. If questioned, never admit that you are traveling alone. Maintain regular contact with someone at home who knows your itinerary.

For more tips, pick up *Traveling Solo* by Eleanor Berman (Globe Pequot, US$17) or subscribe to **Connecting: Solo Travel Network,** P.O. Box 29088, Delamont RPO, Vancouver, BC V6J 5C2 (☎/fax (604) 737-7791; www.cstn.org; membership US$25-35), or the **Travel Companion Exchange,** P.O. Box 833, Amityville, NY 11701, USA (☎(631) 454-0880 or (800) 392-1256; www.whytravelalone.com; US$48).

OLDER TRAVELERS

Generally, senior citizens in the mother country are treated with respect and are often entitled to discounts. Though much of Italy is inaccessible to anyone without the legs of a young buck, there are many groups for senior travel ready to help. These are only a few of the senior citizen agencies:

Elderhostel, 75 Federal St., Boston, MA 02110, USA (☎(617) 426-7788 or (877) 426-2166; email registration@elderhostel.org; www.elderhostel.org). Organizes 1- to 4-week "educational adventures" in Italy on subjects ranging from Lake Garda culture to the culinary delights of Northern Italy for those 55+.

The Mature Traveler, P.O. Box 50400, Reno, NV 89513, USA (☎(775) 786-7419, credit card orders (800) 460-6676). Deals, discounts, and travel packages for the 50+ traveler. Subscription $30.

Walking the World, P.O. Box 1186, Fort Collins, CO 80522, USA (☎(970) 498-0500; fax 498-9100; email walktworld@aol.com; www.walkingtheworld.com), organizes trips for 50+ travelers to Cinque Terre, Mt. Etna, Tuscany and elsewhere.

FURTHER READING: OLDER TRAVELERS.

No Problem! Worldwise Tips for Mature Adventurers, Janice Kenyon. Orca Book Publishers (US$16).

A Senior's Guide to Healthy Travel, Donald L. Sullivan. Career Press (US$15).

Unbelievably Good Deals and Great Adventures That You Absolutely Can't Get Unless You're Over 50, Joan Rattner Heilman. Contemporary Books (US$13).

BISEXUAL, GAY, AND LESBIAN TRAVELERS

Italians are notoriously homophobic, a reputation rightly earned in many respects. The Vatican perenially opposes the gay pride parade in Rome. In 2000, The Vatican was joined by a large and loud majority of Italians who felt that WorldPride 2000 should not coincide with Jubilee 2000. Many, regardless of their disposition toward homosexuality, opposed the provocative invitations depicting a naked man and inviting participants to "Come in Rome."

Nonetheless, Rome, Florence, Milan, and Bologna all have easily accessible gay scenes. Away from the larger cities, however, same-sex relationships may be less open, and gay social life may be difficult to find. Moreover, in smaller towns in the South, explicit public displays of affection will evoke shock, at the very least.

The monthly *Babilonia* and annual *Guida Gay Italia*, the national homosexual magazines, are at most newsstands. The magazines, along with confronting gay issues, also list social events. Expect the larger cities to have gay discotheques and bars (listed in *Let's Go* where available). The **Italian Gay and Lesbian Yellow Pages** (www.gay.it/guida/italia/info.htm) include listings of gay bars, hotels, and shops.

Listed below are contact organizations, mail-order bookstores and publishers which offer materials addressing some specific concerns. **Out and About** (www.planetout.com) offers a bi-weekly newsletter addressing travel concerns.

ARCI-GAY and ARCI-Lesbica, P. di Porta Saragozza, 2, 40123 Bologna (☎051 644 70 54; www.malox.com/arcigay/link.htm), and V. Orvinio, 2, 00199 Roma (☎06 86 38 51 12); or V. dei Mille, 23, Roma (☎06 446 58 39). The national organizations for homosexuals holds group discussions, dances, and many special events. Their website contains addresses and phone numbers of many city centers.

Gay's the Word, 66 Marchmont St., London WC1N 1AB (☎(020) 7278 7654; email sales@gaystheword.co.uk; www.gaystheword.co.uk). The largest gay and lesbian bookshop in the UK, with both fiction and non-fiction titles. Mail-order service available.

Giovanni's Room, 345 S. 12th St., Philadelphia, PA 19107, USA (☎(215) 923-2960; fax 923-0813; www.queerbooks.com). An international lesbian/feminist and gay bookstore with mail-order service (carries many of the publications listed below).

International Gay and Lesbian Travel Association, 4331 N. Federal Hwy., #304, Fort Lauderdale, FL 33308, USA (☎(954) 776-2626; fax 776-3303; www.iglta.com). An organization of over 1350 companies serving gay and lesbian travelers worldwide.

International Lesbian and Gay Association (ILGA), 81 rue Marché-au-Charbon, B-1000 Brussels, Belgium (☎/fax +32 (2) 502 24 71; www.ilga.org). Not a travel service; provides political information, such as homosexuality laws of individual countries.

FURTHER READING: BISEXUAL, GAY, AND LESBIAN TRAVELERS.

Spartacus International Gay Guide. Bruno Gmunder Verlag. (US$33).

Ferrari Guides' Gay Travel A to Z, Ferrari Guides' Men's Travel in Your Pocket, Ferrari Guides' Women's Travel in Your Pocket, and *Ferrari Guides' Inn Places.* Ferrari Guides (US$14-16). For more info, call ☎(602) 863-2408 or (800) 962-2912 or try www.q-net.com.

The Gay Vacation Guide: The Best Trips and How to Plan Them, Mark Chesnut. Citadel Press (US$15).

TRAVELERS WITH DISABILITIES

Those with disabilities should inform airlines and hotels of their disabilities when making arrangements for travel; some time may be needed to prepare special accommodations. Call ahead to restaurants, hotels, parks, and other facilities to find out about the existence of ramps, the widths of doors, the dimensions of elevators, etc. **Guide dog owners** should inquire as to the specific quarantine policies of each destination country. At the very least, they will need to provide a certificate of immunization against rabies.

Rail is probably the most convenient form of travel for disabled travelers in Europe: many stations have ramps, and some trains have wheelchair lifts, special seating areas, and specially equipped toilets. In general, Italy's Pendolino and many Eurostar and InterCity trains are extremely accessible for the disabled. For those who wish to rent cars, some major **car rental** agencies (Hertz, Avis, and National) offer hand-controlled vehicles.

One of the most appealing aspects of Italy is that much of it is the same as it was 2000 years ago. The Italy of 2000 years ago, however, was not the most disabled-friendly of countries. Many of the museums and famed landmarks are utterly inaccessible. Venice, with its hundreds of bridges, is especially difficult to navigate.

Few hotels and almost no hostels have adapted rooms. Precautions should be made prior to a visit. Call accommodations, restaurants, and institutions to find out accessibility prior to arrival. The following organizations provide information or publications that might be of assistance:

USEFUL ORGANIZATIONS

Accessible Italy, with two main offices in Italy: **Promotur-Mondo Possibile,** P. Pitagora 9, 10137 Turin (☎011 309 63 63; fax 011 309 12 01); and **La Viaggeria,** V. Lemonia 161, 00174 Roma (☎06 715 829 45; fax 06 715 834 33). A travel agency for the disabled and aged, Accessible Italy is a member of SATH (see below) and more than ready to help out in any way possible. See www.tour-web.com/accitaly for more information.

Mobility International USA (MIUSA), P.O. Box 10767, Eugene, OR 97440, USA (☎(541) 343-1284 voice and TDD; fax 343-6812; email info@miusa.org; www.miusa.org). Sells *A World of Options: A Guide to International Educational Exchange, Community Service, and Travel for Persons with Disabilities* (US$35).

Moss Rehab Hospital Travel Information Service (☎(215) 456-9600 or (800) CALL-MOSS; email netstaff@mossresourcenet.org; www.mossresourcenet.org). An information resource center on travel-related concerns for those with disabilities. Moss is phasing out phone operations and will eventually offer services only on the Internet.

Society for the Advancement of Travel for the Handicapped (SATH), 347 Fifth Ave., #610, New York, NY 10016 (☎(212) 447-7284; www.sath.org). An advocacy group that publishes the quarterly travel magazine *Open World* (free for members, US$13 for nonmembers). Also publishes a wide range of info sheets on disability travel facilitation and destinations. Annual membership US$45, students and seniors US$30.

TOUR AGENCIES

Directions Unlimited, 123 Green Ln., Bedford Hills, NY 10507, USA (☎(914) 241-1700 or (800) 533-5343; www.travel-cruises.com). Specializes in arranging individual and group vacations, tours, and cruises for the physically disabled.

The Guided Tour Inc., 7900 Old York Rd., #114B, Elkins Park, PA 19027, USA (☎(800) 783-5841 or (215) 782-1370; www.guidedtour.com). Organizes travel programs for persons with developmental and physical challenges around Rome.

FURTHER READING: DISABLED TRAVELERS.

Resource Directory for the Disabled, Richard Neil Shrout. Facts on file (US$45).

Wheelchair Through Europe, Annie Mackin. Graphic Language Press (US ☎(760) 944-9594; email niteowl@cts.com; US$13).

MINORITY TRAVELERS

In certain regions, particularly in the south, tourists of color or members of non-Christian religious groups may feel unwelcome. If, in your travels, you encounter discriminatory treatment, please let us know so that we can check out the establishment and, if appropriate, warn other travelers. **Jewish tourists** may appreciate the *Italy Jewish Travel Guide* (US$15) from Israelowitz Publishing, P.O. Box 228, Brooklyn, NY 11229, which provides info on sites of religious interest.

In terms of safety, there are no easy answers. Keep abreast of the particular cultural attitudes of the regions that you're planning to visit. The prominent political party, **Lega Nord,** centers around an essentially rascist platform promoting the north's separation from the south, and it is more popular in Italy than most people would like to admit. Tourists from the West, who are easily distinguishable by clothes and language, are not usually targets of racism. Women of color may be seen as exotic but not unwelcome. Travel in groups and take a taxi whenever uncomfortable. The best answer to verbal harassment is often no answer at all.

TRAVELERS WITH CHILDREN

Family vacations often require that you slow your pace, and always require that you plan ahead. When deciding where to stay, remember the special needs of young children; if you pick a B&B or a small hotel, call ahead and make sure it's child-friendly. If you rent a car, make sure the rental company provides a car seat for younger children. Be sure that your child carries some sort of ID in case of an emergency or in case he or she gets lost.

Museums, tourist attractions, accommodations, and restaurants often offer discounts for children. Children under two generally fly for 10% of the adult airfare on international flights (this does not necessarily include a seat). International fares are usually discounted 25% for children aged two to 11. Finding a private place for **breast feeding** is often a problem while traveling, so pack accordingly.

FURTHER READING: TRAVELERS WITH CHILDREN.

Backpacking with Babies and Small Children, Goldie Silverman. Wilderness Press (US$10).

Take Your Kids to Europe, Cynthia W. Harriman. Globe Pequot (US$17).

How to take Great Trips with Your Kids, Sanford and Jane Portnoy. Harvard Common Press (US $10).

Have Kid, Will Travel: 101 Survival Strategies for Vacationing With Babies and Young Children, Claire and Lucille Tristram. Andrews and McMeel (US$9).

Adventuring with Children: An Inspirational Guide to World Travel and the Outdoors, Nan Jeffrey. Avalon House Publishing ($15).

Trouble Free Travel with Children, Vicki Lansky. Book Peddlers (US$9).

DIETARY CONCERNS

While there are only a few vegetarian restaurants sprinkled throughout Italy, it will not be hard to get vegetarian meals. The Italian diet is not centered around meat, as pasta and greens are plentiful. For veggie-based eateries around the country, check out the **World Guide to Vegetarianism**'s webpage, www.veg.org/Guide/Italy/index.html. For more info about vegetarian travel, contact **A.V.I. Italian Vegetarian Association,** V. Bazzini 4, 20131 Milano (☎02 26 68 10 80). Established in 1950, it's the biggest vegetarian organization in Italy, with more than 3,000 members.

Travelers who keep kosher should contact synagogues or mosques in larger cities for information on kosher restaurants. Your own synagogue or college Hillel should have access to lists of institutions across the nation. If you are strict in your observance, you may have to prepare your own food on the road. **The Jewish Travel Guide,** which lists synagogues, kosher restaurants, and Jewish institutions in over 100 countries, is available in Europe from Vallentine Mitchell Publishers, Newbury House 890-900, Eastern Ave., Newbury Park, Ilford, Essex IG2 7HH, UK (☎(020) 8599 8866; fax 8599 0984) and in the US ($16.95 + $4 S&H) from ISBS, 5804 NE Hassallo St., Portland, OR 97213 (☎(800) 944-6190).

FURTHER READING: DIETARY CONCERNS.

The Vegetarian Traveler: Where to Stay if You're Vegetarian, Jed Civic. Larson Pub. (US$16).

Europe on 10 Salads a Day, Greg and Mary Jane Edwards. Mustang Publishing. (US$10/UK£9).

ALTERNATIVES TO TOURISM

STUDY ABROAD

Programs vary greatly in expense, academic quality, living arrangements, and exposure to local culture. The vast majority of programs are sponsored by American universities (see below). You may want to check with the American Embassy

in Rome for a list of all American schools in Italy. Florence, Siena, Trieste, and Rome are all filled with Italian language and culture programs. More information on language programs can be found on the web at www.languagestudy.com.

LEARN A NEW LANGUAGE...
MEET NEW FRIENDS...
SEE THE WORLD!
A2Z Languages is the industry leader in extensive language immersion courses. Specializing in comprehensive language and cultural programs.
• French •Italian • Japanese • Portuguese • German
• Spanish • Russian • Chinese • Greek • & More!
www.a2zlanguages.com • 1-800-496-4596
World wide: (602) 778-6794 • Fax: 602-840-1545 • 6520 N. 41st St. • Paradise Valley, AZ 85253 • USA

EU citizens do not require a visa to study in Italy. Non-EU citizens wishing to study in Italy must obtain a study visa *(permisso di studio)* prior to departure from their nearest embassy or consulate. For non-EU citizens to obtain a visa, you will need to provide proof of enrollment from your home institution or the school or university in Italy, a notarized statement that you have adequate financial means, and proof of medical insurance for the duration of your stay in Italy. Americans require a statement that they will purchase an additional Italian health insurance policy in Italy as a supplement to their domestic insurance. As of August 2000, the visa fee for US citizens is $32.43, payable in money order only, for Australian citizens AUS $51, and NZ$66 for New Zealand citizens. Upon arrival in Italy, students must register with the Foreigners' Bureau *(Ufficio degli Stranieri)* of the local *questura* in order to receive their permit of stay.

UNIVERSITIES

Most American undergraduates enroll in programs sponsored by US universities. Those relatively fluent in Italian may find it cheaper to enroll directly in a local university (though getting credit may be more difficult). Some schools that offer study abroad programs to foreigners are listed below.

John Cabot University, V. della Lungara, 233, Rome (☎06 681 91 21; fax 06 683 20 88; www.johncabot.edu), is the premier American university in Italy. It offers a 4-year Bachelor of Arts degree in addition to semester and summer courses.

American University of Rome, V. Pietro Roselli, 4 (☎06 58 33 09 19; fax 06 58 33 09 92) offers courses in English in international business, international relations, and Italian civilization and culture. Credits often transferable for US universities. US$4,475 per semester; US$2,350 for housing.

American Institute for Foreign Study, College Division, River Plaza, 9 West Broad St., Stamford, CT 06902, USA (☎(800) 727-2437, ext. 5163; www.aifsabroad.com). Organizes programs for high school and college study in universities in Italy.

Beaver College Center for Education Abroad, 450 S. Easton Rd., Glenside, PA 19038, USA (☎(888) 232-8379; www.beaver.edu/cea). Operates programs in Italy. Costs range from $1900 (summer) to $20,000 (full-year).

Experiment in International Living (☎(800) 345-2929; fax (802) 258-3428; email eil@worldlearning.org). Organizes 3- to 5-week summer programs (US$1900-5000) that offer high-school students cross-cultural homestays, community service, ecological adventure, and language training in Italy.

International Association for the Exchange of Students for Technical Experience (IAESTE), 10400 Little Patuxent Pkwy. #250, Columbia, MD 21044, USA (☎(410) 997-3068; www.aipt.org). Operates 8- to 12-week programs in Italy for college students who have completed 2 years of technical study. US$50 application fee.

LANGUAGE SCHOOLS

These programs are run by foreign universities, independent international or local organizations, and divisions of Italian universities. They generally cost anywhere from US$350-8000 and may include room and board and side trips. **Language Learning Net's** website (www.language-learning.net), which lists more than 6000 schools worldwide in 24 languages, is a useful starting point for research.

Centro Fiorenza, V. S. Spirito, 14, Florence (☎055 23 9 82 74; fax 055 28 71 48; email fiorence@tin.it), offers a plethora of 2- and 4-week courses in Italian language and culture for students of all ages and abilities ($450-775). Accommodation is either in homestays or student appartments (L19-45,000 per day).

Italiaidea, P. della Cancelleria, 85, Rome (☎06 689 29 97; email italiaidea@italiaidea.com; www.italiaidea.com), schools 1500 students a year in Italian language and culture from their base in the Eternal City. 2- and 4-week courses are held year-round (L780-1,250,000).

Istituto Zambler Venezia, Dorsoduro, 3116A (☎041 522 43 31; fax 041 528 56 28; email zambler@virtualvenice.net; www.virtualvenice.net/zambler), is based in a 16th-century *palazzo* in the heart of Venice. They offer 2- to 12-week courses year-round in language, culture, and cooking (L500-2,400,000).

Eurocentres, 101 N. Union St. #300, Alexandria, VA 22314, USA (☎(800) 648-4809 or (703) 684-1494; www.eurocentres.com), or in Europe, Head Office, Seestr. 247, CH-8038 Zurich, Switzerland (☎+41 (411) 485 50 40; email info@eurocentres.com). Language programs for beginning to advanced students with homestays in Italy run approximately US$1132 a month.

Language Immersion Institute, 75 South Manheim Blvd., The College at New Paltz, New Paltz, NY 12561, USA (☎(914) 257-3500; www.newpaltz.edu/lii). 2-week summer language courses and some overseas courses in Italian. Program fees are about US$295 for a weekend or US$750 per 2 weeks.

FURTHER READING: STUDY ABROAD.

www.studyabroad.com

Academic Year Abroad 2000/2001. Institute of International Education Books (US$45).

Vacation Study Abroad 2000/2001. Institute of International Education Books (US$43).

Peterson's Study Abroad 2001. Peterson's (US$30).

Peterson's Summer Study Abroad 2001. Peterson's (US$30).

WORK

EU passport holders do not require a visa to work in Italy. They must have a workers registration book *(libretto di lavoro)*, available, at no extra cost, upon presentation of the "*permesso di soggiorno.*" If your parents were born in an EU country, you may be able to claim dual citizenship or at least the right to a work permit. Non-EU citizens seeking work in Italy must apply for an Italian work permit *(Autorizzazione al lavoro in Italia)* before entering the country. Permits are authorized by the Provincial Employment Office and approved by the *questura* before being forwarded to the employer and then the prospective employee. The prospective employee must then present the document along with a valid passport in order to obtain a work visa. Normally a three-month tourist permit is granted, and upon presentation of an employer's letter the permit can be extended for a period specified by the employment contract. Friends in Italy can expedite work permits or arrange work-for-accommodations swaps. In some sectors (like agricultural work) permit-less workers are rarely bothered by authorities.

Foreigners are most successful at securing harvest, restaurant, bar, and household work, or jobs in the tourism industry, where English-speakers are needed. While finding employment in Italy is a sure way of becoming part of the culture, difficult economic conditions make it hard even for Italians to secure work.

Enjoy Rome (☎06 445 18 43) often has employment options in the tourism sector. The **Ministero Lavoro e Providenza Sociale,** Divisione 11, V. Flavia, 6, 1-00187 Rome, and the **Italian Cultural Institute** (see p. 40) offer job placement information.

If you are a full-time student at a US university, the simplest way to get a job abroad is through work permit programs run by **Council on International Educational Exchange (Council)** and its member organizations. For a US$225 application fee, Council can procure three- to six-month work permits and a handbook to help you find work and housing.

AU PAIR ORGANIZATIONS

Accord Cultural Exchange, 750 La Playa, San Francisco, CA 94121, USA (☎(415) 386-6203); www.cognitext.com/accord). US$40 application fee.

interExchange, 161 Sixth Ave., New York, NY 10013, USA (☎(212) 924-0446; fax 924-0575; www.interexchange.org). Participants must speak Italian.

Childcare International, Ltd., Trafalgar House, Grenville Pl., London NW7 3SA, UK (☎(020) 8906 3116; fax 8906 3461; www.childint.co.uk). UK£100 application fee.

TEACHING ENGLISH

International Schools Services, Educational Staffing Program, P.O. Box 5910, Princeton, NJ 08543, USA (☎(609) 452-0990; www.iss.edu). Recruits teachers and administrators for American and English schools in Italy. All instruction in English. Applicants must have a bachelor's degree and 2 years of relevant experience. Nonrefundable US$100 application fee. Publishes *The ISS Directory of Overseas Schools* (US$35).

Office of Overseas Schools, US Department of State, Room H328, SA-1, Washington, D.C. 20522, USA (☎(202) 261-8200; fax 261-8224; www.state.gov/www/about_state/schools/). Keeps a comprehensive list of schools abroad and agencies that arrange placement for Americans to teach abroad.

VOLUNTEERING

Volunteer jobs are readily available, and many provide room and board in exchange for labor. You can sometimes avoid high application fees by contacting the individual workcamps directly.

Archaeological Institute of America, 656 Beacon St., Boston, MA 02215, USA (☎(617) 353-9361; www.archaeological.org). The *Archaeological Fieldwork Opportunities Bulletin* (US$16 for non-members) lists field sites in Italy. Get the bulletin from Kendall/Hunt Publishing, 4050 Westmark Dr., Dubuque, Iowa 52002, USA (☎(800) 228-0810).

Earthwatch, 680 Mt. Auburn St., Box 403, Watertown, MA 02272, USA (☎(800) 776-0188 or (617) 926-8200; www.earthwatch.org). Arranges 1- to 3-week programs in Italy to promote conservation of natural resources. Programs average US$1600.

Service Civil International Voluntary Service (SCI-IVS), 814 NE 40th St., Seattle, WA 98105, USA (☎/fax (206) 545-6585; www.sci-ivs.org). Arranges placement in workcamps in Italy for those 18+. Registration fee US$65-150.

Volunteers for Peace, 1034 Tiffany Rd., Belmont, VT 05730, USA (☎(802) 259-2759; www.vfp.org). Arranges placement in workcamps in Italy. Annual *International Workcamp Directory* US$20. Registration fee US$200. Free newsletter.

FURTHER READING: WORK.

Live and Work in Italy, Victoria Pybus and Rachael Robinson. Vacation Publications (US$17.95).

International Jobs: Where they Are, How to Get Them, Eric Koocher. Perseus Books (US$17).

How to Get a Job in Europe, Robert Sanborn. Surrey Books (US$22).

Work Abroad: The Complete Guide to Finding a Job Overseas, Clayton Hubbs (US$16).

International Directory of Voluntary Work, Louise Whetter (US$16).

Teaching English Abroad, Susan Griffin. Vacation Work (US$17).

Overseas Summer Jobs 2001, Work Your Way Around the World, and *The Directory of Jobs and Careers Abroad.* Peterson's (US$17-18 each).

WEB RESOURCES

Almost every aspect of budget travel (with the most notable exception, of course, being experience) is accessible via the web. Even if you don't have internet access at home, seeking it out at a public library or at work would be well worth it; within 10 minutes at the keyboard, you can make hostel reservations, get advice on travel hotspots or experiences from other travelers who have just returned from Italy, or find out exactly how much that train from Naples to Palermo costs.

Listed here are some budget travel sites to start off your surfing; other relevant web sites are listed throughout the book. Because website turnover is high, use search engines (such as www.yahoo.com) to strike out on your own. But in doing so, keep in mind that most travel web sites simply exist to get your money.

LEARNING THE ART OF BUDGET TRAVEL

How to See the World: www.artoftravel.com. A compendium of great travel tips, from cheap flights to self defense to interacting with local culture.

Rec. Travel Library: www.travel-library.com. A fantastic set of links for general information and personal travelogues.

Shoestring Travel: www.stratpub.com. An e-zine focusing on budget travel.

INFORMATION ON ITALY

CIA World Factbook: www.odci.gov/cia/publications/factbook/index.html. Tons of vital statistics about Italy: geography, government, economy, and people.

Foreign Language for Travelers: www.travlang.com. Provides free online translating dictionaries and lists of phrases in Italian.

MyTravelGuide: www.mytravelguide.com. Country overviews, with everything from history to transportation to live web cam coverage of Italy.

Geographia: www.geographia.com. Describes the highlights, culture, and people of Italy.

Atevo Travel: www.atevo.com/guides/destinations. Detailed introductions, travel tips, and suggested itineraries.

LeisurePlanet: www.leisureplanet.com/TravelGuides. Good general background.

TravelPage: www.travelpage.com. Links to official tourist office sites throughout Italy.

AND OUR PERSONAL FAVORITE

Let's Go: www.letsgo.com. Our recently revamped website features photos and streaming video, info about our books, a travel forum buzzing with stories and tips, and links that will help you find everything you could ever want to know about Italy.

NORTHWEST ITALY

LOMBARDY (LOMBARDIA)

Over the centuries, Roman generals, German emperors, and French kings have vied for control of Lombardy's agricultural wealth and fertile soil. In the recent past, a tremendous increase in employment and business has augmented the region's already vibrant industry, making Lombardy the cornerstone of the Italian economy and the richest European region after Paris. In many ways, Lombardy has more in common with countries to the north than with its own peninsula; consequently, Lombards periodically call for secession in order to eliminate the forced subsidization of the Roman bureaucracy and the burdens of the economically challenged South. Since WWII, however, Lombardy's booming economy has drawn legions of ambitious southerners, and the province has recently attracted immigrants from North Africa, the Middle East, and East Asia. Tension between long-time residents and recent immigrants persists, but as a result of this diversity, inhabitants of Lombardy are among the least provincial Italians.

HIGHLIGHTS OF LOMBARDY

REVEL in the best clubbing city in Europe; bar-hop in the **Navigli** (p. 105) after a hard-hitting cultural day at the **Last Supper** (p. 102) and the **Museo Poldi Pezzoli** (p. 101).

SCALE the steps of La Scala, the world's premier opera house (p. 101).

FIDDLE the day away at Cremona's Museo Stradivariano (p. 113).

STAND agape beneath the dazzling ceiling of Bergamo's baptistery (p. 122).

MILAN (MILANO) ☎02

Milan lies on Roman foundations but has progressed technologically and socially with more force than any other major Italian city. Although it served as the capital of the western half of the Roman Empire from 286 to 402, Milan retains few reminders of that period. The stunningly ornate *duomo* is the city's emblem and a rare remnant of its history. The pace of life is quicker here, and *il dolce di far niente* (the sweetness of doing nothing) is an unfamiliar taste. *Milano l'e Milano* (Milan is just Milan) is a dialect expression that sums up how different the cosmopolitan capital is from the rest of Italy. Its wide, tree-lined boulevards and graceful architecture are elegant but forced to compete with the omnipresent, vibrant graffiti. Although petty crime, drug dealing, and prostitution may strike your eye, so too should the enormous number of well-dressed Italians in designer suits. The capital of style, financial markets, and industry, Milan is on the cutting edge of fashion, invention, and ideas, rarely pausing to rest. Without a doubt, Milan offers among the best nightlife in the world. The city becomes most vibrant twice a year when the two local football teams, AC Milan and Inter Milan, play each other. Football is the city's religion, and the AC/Inter game is more important than Christmas. Milanese are generally open-minded and accepting of foreigners, though sometimes they just don't have the time to stop and be friendly. Only in August, when the city shuts down for the entire month, do its citizens flock to quiet resort towns and breathe a collective sigh of relief.

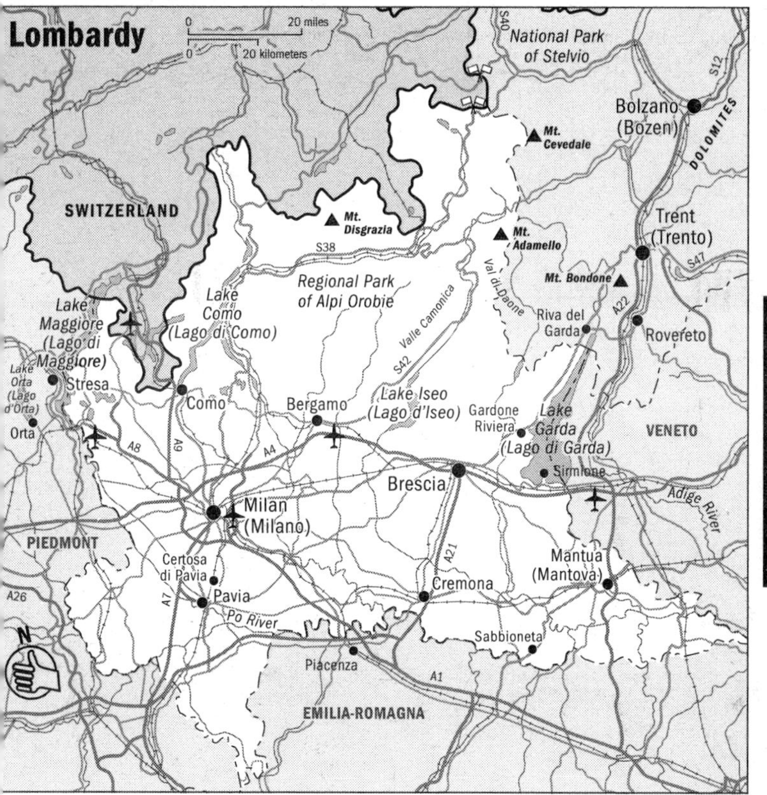

GETTING THERE AND AWAY

Flights: Malpensa Airport, 60km from town. Intercontinental flights. The **Malpensa Express** leaves twice an hour from the Cadorna metro station to the airport (45min.; 6:50am-8:20pm; L15,000, L20,000 if purchased on the train) and back (7:45am-8:45pm). Buses also run at night (1hr.; L13,000 for most airlines; L9,000 if you fly Alitala, KLM, or Northwest; free for TWA, AirEuropa, or Lott). **Luggage storage:** L4000 per bag per day. **Linate Airport,** 7km from town. Much easier logistically. Domestic/European flights and intercontinental flights with European transfers. The **STAM bus** to Linate (☎02 71 71 06) goes to Stazione Centrale (every 20min., L4500), but it's cheaper to take bus #73 (L1500) from P. San Babila (MM1). **General Flight Info** for both airports (☎02 74 85 22 00), international arrivals (☎02 26 80 06 19), international departures (☎02 26 80 06 27).

Trains: **Stazione Centrale** (☎01 47 88 80 88), in P. Duca d'Aosta, on MM2. The primary station to: **Genoa** (1½hr., every hr., L24,000); **Turin** (2hr., every hr., L24,500); **Venice** (3hr., 21 per day, L36,000); **Florence** (2½hr., every hr., L40,000); and **Rome** (4½hr., every hr., L71,000). **Info office** open daily 7am-9:30pm. Eurail passes and Cartaverde available outside. **Luggage Storage:** L5000 for 12hr. Open 24hr. **Lost and Found** (☎02 63 71 26 67) at baggage deposit. Open daily 7am-1pm and 2-8pm. **Stazione Nord** connects Milan to Como and Varese (every 30min., 6am-9pm). **Porta Genova** has lines west to Vigevano, Alessandria, and Asti. **Porta Garibaldi** links Milan to Lecco and Valtellina to the northwest.

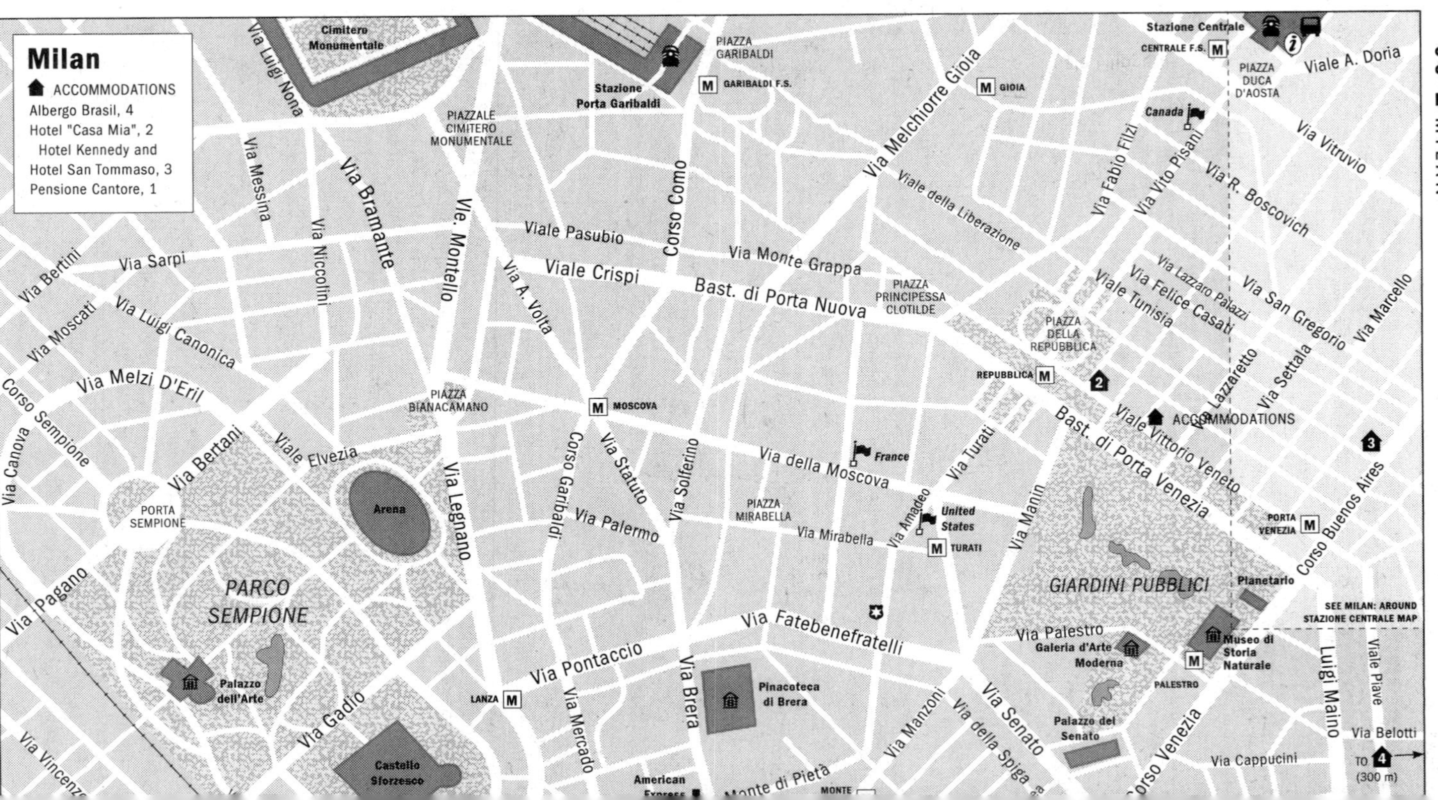
Milan
ACCOMMODATIONS
Albergo Brasil, 4
Hotel "Casa Mia", 2
Hotel Kennedy and
Hotel San Tommaso, 3
Pensione Cantore, 1
Cimitero Monumentale
Via Luigi Nona
Stazione Porta Garibaldi
PIAZZA GARIBALDI
GARIBALDI F.S.
GIOIA
Stazione Centrale
CENTRALE F.S.
PIAZZA DUCA D'AOSTA
Viale A. Doria
Canada
Via Vitruvio
PIAZZALE CIMITERO MONUMENTALE
Via Messina
Via Bramante
Vle. Montello
Corso Como
Via Melchiorre Gioia
Viale della Liberazione
Via Fabio Filzi
Via Vito Pisani
Via R. Boscovich
Viale Pasubio
Via Monte Grappa
Via Niccolini
Via Bertini
Via Sarpi
Viale Crispi
Via A. Volta
Bast. di Porta Nuova
PIAZZA PRINCIPESSA CLOTILDE
Via Lazzaro Palazzi
Viale Tunisia
Via Felice Casati
Via San Gregorio
Via Marcello
Via Moscati
Via Luigi Canonica
PIAZZA DELLA REPUBBLICA
REPUBBLICA
Via Lazzaretto
Via Settala
Via Melzi D'Eril
PIAZZA BIANCAMANO
MOSCOVA
ACCOMMODATIONS
Corso Sempione
Bast. di Porta Venezia
Viale Vittorio Veneto
Via Canova
Via Bertani
Viale Elvezia
Corso Garibaldi
Via Statuto
Via Solferino
Via della Moscova
France
Via Turati
PORTA SEMPIONE
Arena
Via Legnano
Via Palermo
PIAZZA MIRABELLA
Via Mirabella
Via Amadeo
United States
TURATI
Via Manin
PORTA VENEZIA
Corso Buenos Aires
PARCO SEMPIONE
Via Pagano
GIARDINI PUBBLICI
Planetario
SEE MILAN: AROUND STAZIONE CENTRALE MAP
Via Fatebenefratelli
Via Palestro
Galleria d'Arte Moderna
Museo di Storia Naturale
Viale Piave
Luigi Maino
Palazzo dell'Arte
Via Pontaccio
LANZA
Via Brera
Pinacoteca di Brera
PALESTRO
Via Gadio
Via Mercado
Via Manzoni
Via della Spiga
Via Senato
Palazzo del Senato
Corso Venezia
Via Cappucini
Via Belotti
TO 4 (300 m)
Castello Sforzesco
American Express
Monte di Pietà
MONTE

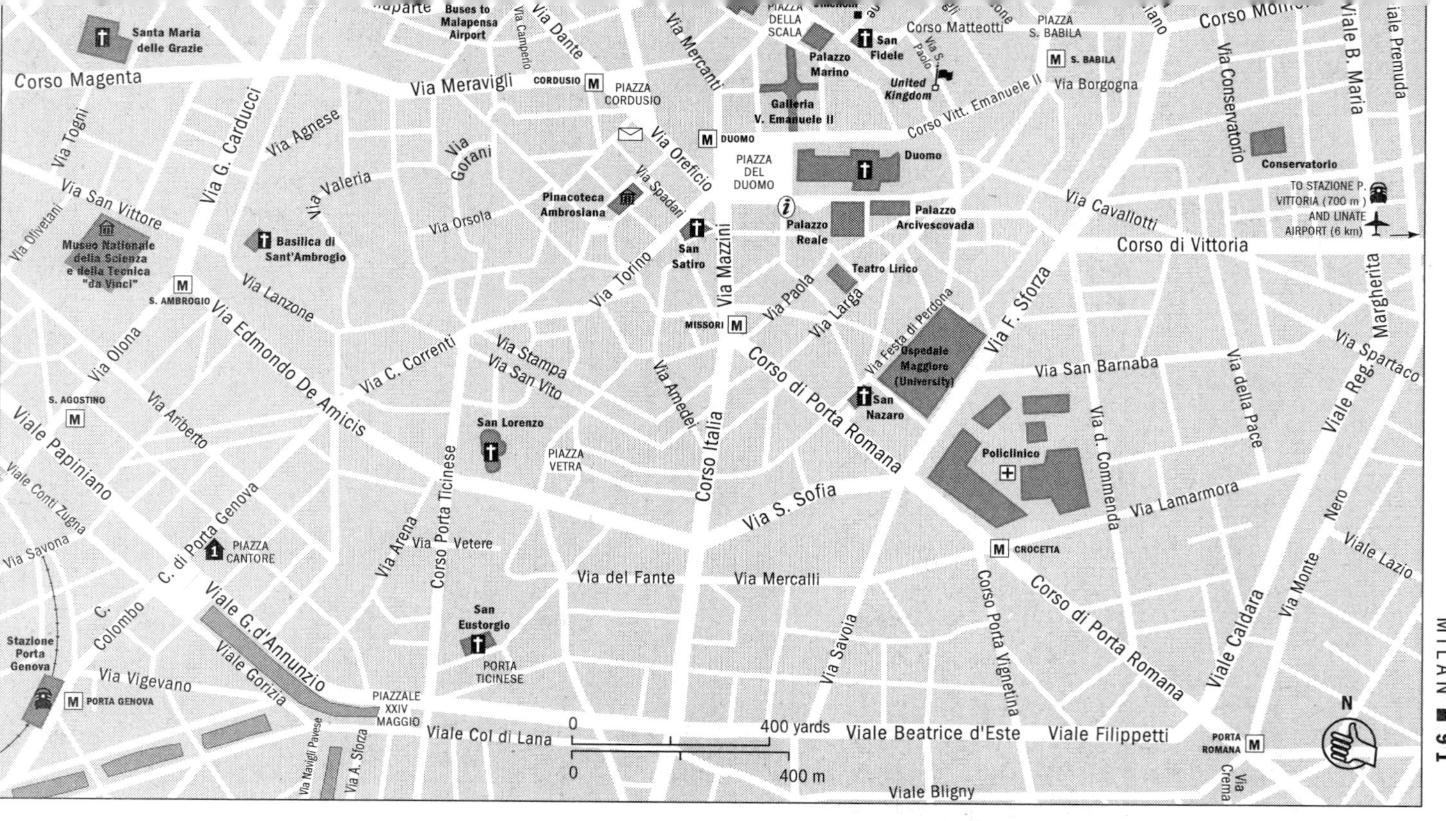

Santa Maria delle Grazie
Buses to Malapensa Airport
Via Camperio
Via Dante
Via Mercanti
PIAZZA DELLA SCALA
Palazzo Marino
San Fidele
Corso Matteotti
Via S. Paolo
United Kingdom
PIAZZA S. BABILA
S. BABILA
Via Borgogna
Corso Vitt. Emanuele II
Galleria V. Emanuele II
Corso Magenta
Via Meravigli
CORDUSIO
PIAZZA CORDUSIO
Via Conservatorio
Conservatorio
Viale B. Maria
Viale Premuda
DUOMO
Via Oreficio
PIAZZA DEL DUOMO
Duomo
Via Togni
Via G. Carducci
Via Agnese
Via Gorani
Via Valeria
Via San Vittore
Via Olivetani
Museo Nationale della Scienza e della Tecnica "da Vinci"
Basilica di Sant'Ambrogio
Via Orsola
Pinacoteca Ambrosiana
Via Spadari
San Satiro
Via Mazzini
Palazzo Reale
Palazzo Arcivescovada
Via Cavallotti
TO STAZIONE P. VITTORIA (700 m) AND LINATE AIRPORT (6 km)
Corso di Vittoria
Teatro Lirico
S. AMBROGIO
Via Lanzone
Via Torino
Via Paola
Via Larga
Via Festa di Perdona
Ospedale Maggiore (University)
Via F. Sforza
Margherita
Via Edmondo De Amicis
MISSORI
Via Olona
Via C. Correnti
Via Stampa
Via San Vito
Via Amedei
Corso di Porta Romana
San Nazaro
Via San Barnaba
Via della Pace
Via Spartaco
Viale Reg.
S. AGOSTINO
Via Ariberto
Viale Papiniano
San Lorenzo
PIAZZA VETRA
Corso Italia
Policlinico
Via d. Commenda
Viale Conti Zugna
Via S. Sofia
Via Lamarmora
Nero
Via Savona
C. di Porta Genova
PIAZZA CANTORE
Via Arena
Corso Porta Ticinese
Via Vetere
CROCETTA
Viale Lazio
Via del Fante
Via Mercalli
Via Monte
Corso Porta Vignetina
Corso di Porta Romana
Viale Caldara
C. Colombo
Viale G.d'Annunzio
San Eustorgio
Stazione Porta Genova
Via Vigevano
Viale Gorizia
PORTA TICINESE
Via Savoia
PORTA GENOVA
PIAZZALE XXIV MAGGIO
0
400 yards
Viale Col di Lana
Viale Beatrice d'Este
Viale Filippetti
PORTA ROMANA
N
0
400 m
Via Naviglii Pavese
Via A. Sforza
Viale Bligny
Via Crema

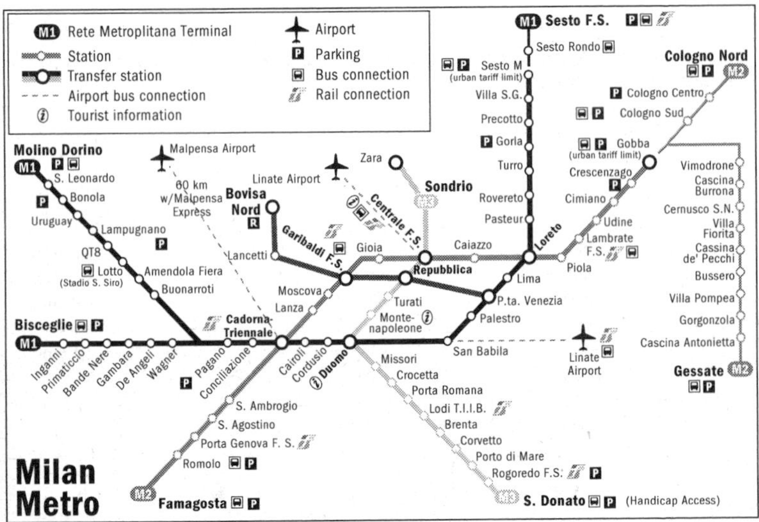

Buses: in Stazione Centrale. **Intercity** buses tend to be less convenient and more expensive than trains. **SAL, SIA, Autostradale,** and many others depart from P. Castello and the surrounding area (MM1: Cairoli) for Turin, the Lake Country, Bergamo, Certosa di Pavia, and points as far away as Rimini and Trieste.

GETTING AROUND

Milan's streets twist, they turn, they change names unexpectedly, and they may even ask you riddles. Be absolutely certain to purchase a detailed map as soon as possible. The most legible map has a blue background with a picture of the *duomo* on the cover and is called **La Generale Milano,** produced by *Edizioni Di Lauro Milano*. The streets are generally safe at night, but women shouldn't walk alone. Among the many useful tram and bus routes, **trams #29** and **30** travel the city's outer ring road, while **buses #96** and **97** service the inner road. Tickets for bus, tram, and subway must be purchased in advance at newsstands *(tabacchi)*, ticket machines, or ticket offices in a few lucky stations—bring small change.

Metro: The **Metropolitana Milanese** ("MM") operates from approximately 6am to midnight and is the most useful branch of Milan's extensive public transportation network. Be aware of occasional strikes. **Line #1** (red) stretches east to west from the *pensioni* district east of Stazione Centrale, through the center of town, and west to the youth hostel (Molino Dorino fork). **Line #2** (green) links Milan's 3 train stations and crosses line #1 (MM1) at Cadorna and Loreto. **Line #3** (yellow) runs from north of Stazione Centrale to the southern sprawl of the city, crossing with #2 (MM2) at Stazione Centrale and #1 (MM1) at the *duomo.*

Local Transportation: ATM (☎800 01 68 57, 01 67 01 68 57, or 02 48 03 24 03; information on services for the disabled ☎02 48 03 14 44), in P. del Duomo MM station. All-day passes for non-residents L5000, 2 days for L9000. Book of 10 tickets L14,000; weekly and monthly passes L35,000 initial payment, plus a weekly ticket pass for around L10,000 (photo required). All-day passes are good for 24hr. from the first validation. A single ticket (L1500) is good for one subway ride or 75min. of surface transportation. Buses require pre-purchased tickets. It is wise to keep extra tickets on hand, as *tabacchi* close around 8pm and vending machines (in every station) are unreliable. Riding the MM without a ticket warrants a (rarely enforced) L30,000 fine. Info office and ticket office open M-Sa 7:15am-7:15pm.

Taxis: As in most large cities, taxis are omnipresent except when needed most. **Radio Taxi** (☎02 53 53, 02 85 85, 02 83 83, or 02 52 51). Uniformly expensive, starting at L5000; nighttime surcharge L6000. Open 24 hr.

A ROAD BY ANY OTHER NAME WOULD SMELL AS STREET A quick glance at any Italian town will leave you muttering: who are Vittorio Emanuele and Garibaldi, and what's the deal with September 20th? The names that invade Italy's main streets and squares are a proud nod to the heroes of Italian unification. **Giuseppe Garibaldi,** commander of the "Red Shirts," provided the military muscle to free Naples and Sicily from Bourbon rule in 1860, while **Giuseppe Mazzini** manned the struggle's intellectual wing. **Camillo Cavour** was the diplomatic force most directly responsible for unification, helping to establish **Vittorio Emanuele II** as the king of the newly born nation in 1861. The young monarch incorporated Venice in 1866, and, on **September 20, 1870,** with France's surrender of Rome, he completed the unification of Italy. (See also **The Italian Nation,** p. 13)

Not to be outdone by their royalist rivals, Italian leftists have managed to insert their own 20th-century heroes into the canon. Among them are two martyrs of the early years of fascism: the Socialist **Giacomo Matteotti** and the founder of the Italian Communist Party, **Antonio Gramsci.**

ORIENTATION

The layout of the city resembles a giant target, encircled by a series of ancient concentric city walls. In the outer rings lie suburbs built during the 1950s and 60s to house southern immigrants. Within the inner circle are four central squares: **Piazza Duomo,** at the end of V. Mercanti; **Piazza Cairoli,** near the Castello Sforzesco; **Piazza Cordusio,** connected to Largo Cairoli by V. Dante; and **Piazza San Babila,** the business and fashion district along C. V. Emanuele. The **duomo** and **Galleria Vittorio Emanuele** comprise the bull's eye, roughly at the center of the downtown circle. To the northeast and northwest lie two large parks, the **Giardini Pubblici** and the **Parco Sempione.** Farther northeast is **Stazione Centrale.** The skyscrapers around the station are dominated by the sleek **Pirelli Tower.** From the station, a scenic ride on bus #60 takes you to the downtown hub, as does the more efficient commute on metro line #3. **Via Vito Pisani,** which leads to **Piazza della Repubblica,** connects the station to downtown. It continues through the wealthy business districts as **Via Turati** and finally as **Via Manzoni** leading to the *duomo*. The more affordable sections of Milan are five blocks east of the station (left as you exit), down **Corso Buenos Aires.**

PRACTICAL INFORMATION

TOURIST AND FINANCIAL SERVICES

Tourist Office: APT, V. Marconi, 1 (☎02 72 52 43 00; fax 02 72 52 43 50), in the "Palazzo di Turismo" in P. del Duomo, to the right as you face the *duomo*. Comprehensive local and regional info and a useful map and museum guide (in Italian), but the office is very busy. Will not reserve rooms, but will phone to check for vacancies. Pick up the comprehensive *Milano: Where, When, How* as well as *Milano Mese* for info on activities and clubs. Ask about the wonderful guided art tours (L25,000 including museum). English spoken. Open M-F 8:30am-8pm, Sa 9am-1pm and 2-7pm, Su 9am-1pm and 2-5pm. **Branch office** at Stazione Centrale (☎02 72 52 43 70 or 02 72 52 43 60), off the main hall on the 2nd fl., through the neon archway to the left between 2 gift shops. English spoken. Open M-Sa 9am-6pm, Su 9am-12:30pm and 1:30-6pm.

Tourist Police: SOS Turista, V. C. M. Maggi, 14 (☎02 33 60 30 60). Open daily 9:30am-1pm and 2:30-6pm.

Budget Travel: CIT (☎02 86 37 01), Galleria Vittorio Emanuele. Changes money. Open M-F 9am-7pm, Sa 9am-1pm and 2-6pm. **CTS,** V. S. Antonio, 2 (☎02 58 30 41 21). Open M-F 9:30am-12:45pm and 2-6pm, Sa 9:30am-12:45pm. **Transalpino Tickets** (☎02 67 16 82 28; www.transalpino.com), next to the train info office in the upper atrium of Stazione Centrale. Discounts for ages 26 and under. Open M-Sa 8am-

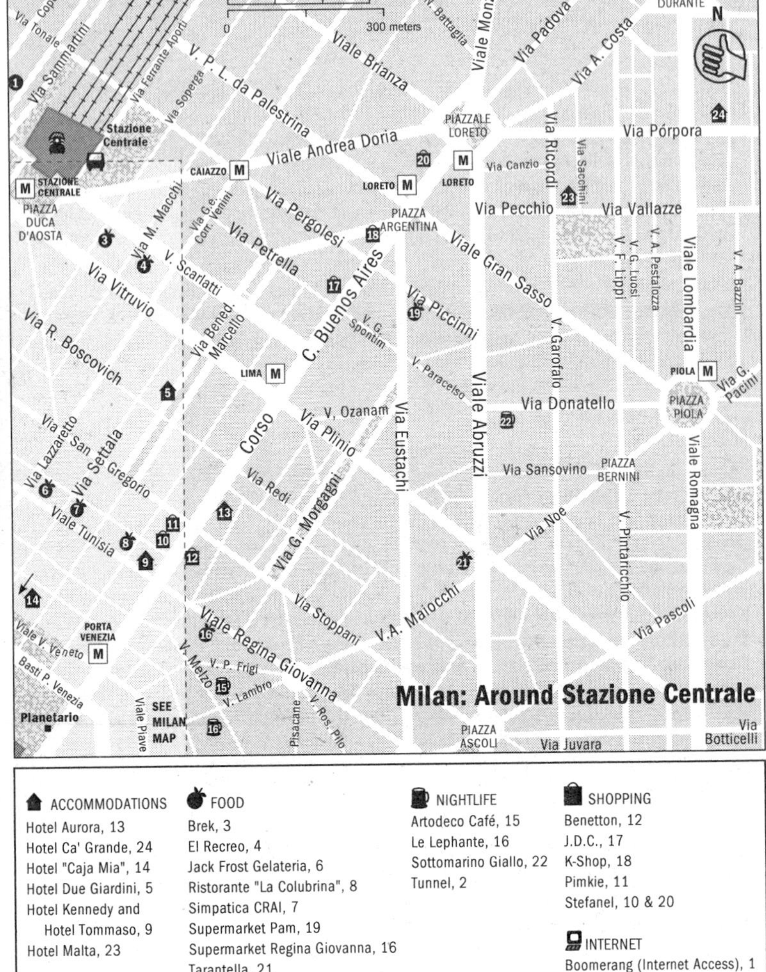

8:30pm. Main office 4 blocks away at V. Locatelli, 5 (☎02 66 71 24 24). When closed, go to Italturismo, under the grand drive-through on the right. Open daily 7am-7:45pm.

Consulates: Australia, V. Borgogna, 2 (☎02 77 70 41; fax 02 77 70 42 42). Open M-Th 9am-noon and 2-4pm, F 9am-noon. **Canada,** V. V. Pisani, 19 (☎02 675 81). Open Sept.-June M-Th 8:45am-12:30pm and 1:30-5:15pm, F 8:45am-12:30pm; Jul-Aug M-Th 8:30am-12:30pm and 1:15-5:30pm, F 8:30am-1pm. **New Zealand,** V. d'Arezzo, 6 (☎02 48 01 25 44). Open M-F 9am-noon. **UK,** V. S. Paolo, 7 (☎02 72 30 01; emergency ☎03 358 10 68 57). Open M-F 9am-1pm and 2-5pm. **US,** V. P. Amedeo, 2/10 (☎02 29 03 51 41). Open M-F 9am-noon.

Currency Exchange: All **Banca d'America e d'Italia** and **Banca Nazionale del Lavoro** branches eagerly await your Visa card. Bank hours in Milan are usually M-F 8:30am-1:30pm and 2:30-4:30pm. **ATMs** abound.

American Express: V. Brera, 3 (☎02 72 00 36 93), on the corner of V. dell'Orso. Walk through the Galleria, across P. Scala, and up V. Verdi. Holds mail free for members for 1 month, otherwise US$5 per inquiry. Sends and receives wired money for AmEx card-holders; fee of L2500 per month on transactions over L150,000. Also **exchanges currency.** Open M-Th 9am-5:30pm, F 9am-5pm. Their **ATMs** accept AmEx.

LOCAL SERVICES

Car Rental: All have similar rates and are located just outside the main *galleria* at the Stazione Centrale. **Hertz** (☎02 669 00 61), at the *galleria*. Open M-F 8am-7pm, Sa 8am-2pm. Main office (☎02 66 98 51 51; fax 02 66 98 69 29), at P. Duca d'Aosta. Open M-F 8am-8pm, Sa 8am-2pm, Su 8am-1pm. **Europcar** (☎02 66 98 15 89 or toll-free ☎800 01 44 10). Open M-F 8am-1pm and 2-7pm, Sa 8:30am-12:30pm. **Avis** (☎02 669 02 80 or 02 670 16 54). Open M-F 7:45am-8pm, Sa 8am-4pm. Main office at V. Corelli, 150 (☎02 70 20 04 40).

Bike Rental: A.W.S. Bici Motor, V. Ponte Seveso, 33 (☎02 67 07 21 45). Exit Stazione Centrale to the right. From the park take V. S. Chiaparelli on the right and after three blocks turn left into V. P. Seveso. Excellent mountain bikes for L20,000, a bargain for the price. Open M-Sa 9am-1pm and 3-7pm.

Lost Property: Ufficio Oggetti Smarriti Comune, V.Friuli, 30 (☎02 546 81 18). Open M-F 8:30am-4pm.

English Bookstores: The American Bookstore, V. Camperio, 16 (☎02 87 89 20; fax 02 72 02 00 30), at Largo Cairoli. All books in English. Carries every *Let's Go* in the series. Open Tu-Sa 10am-7pm, M 1-7pm. **Hoepli Libreria Internazionale,** V. Hoepli, 5 (☎02 86 48 71), off P. Media near P. Scala. Open M 2-7pm, Tu-Sa 9am-7pm. V, MC. **Rizzoli's** (☎02 86 46 10 71), Galleria Vittorio Emanuele, has a decent English collection with many bestsellers. Try Steinbeck in Italian. Open M-Sa 9am-8pm, Su 12:30-7:30pm. V, MC, AmEx. Also try **street vendors** along Largo Mattioli for cheaper options.

Libraries: British Council Library, V. Manzoni, 38 (☎02 77 22 22 03), at a center for teaching English. Open Tu-Th 10am-7:30pm, F 10am-6pm, Sa 2-4pm.

Gay and Lesbian Resources: ARCI-GAY "Centro D'iniziativa Gay," V Torricelli, 19 (☎02 58 10 03 99; email ciggay@tin.it; www.gay.it/arcigay/milano). Friendly staff speaks English. M-F 5-8pm.

Handicapped/Disabled Services: Direzione Servizi Sociali, Largo Treves, 1 (info ☎02 62 08 69 54). Open 8:30am-noon and 1-5pm. **Provincia Milano** (☎02 659 90 32).

Laundromat: Vicolo Lavandai, Vle. Monte Grappa, 2 (☎02 498 39 02 or 033 93 66 73 53). MM2: Garibaldi. Wash 7kg for L6000, dry for L6000. Open daily 8am-9pm.

Swimming Pools: Lido di Milano, Ple. Lotto, 15 (☎02 39 26 61 00), near the Pietro Rota youth hostel. Swimcap required (L2,500). L9000, children under 12 L4000. Open daily 10am-7pm. **Cozzi,** V. Tunisia, 35 (☎02 659 97 03), off C. Buenos Aires. Open M 10am-11pm, Tu-F 10am-9pm, Sa-Su 10am-4pm. L6000, under 12 L3000. **Piscina Giulia Romano,** V. Ampere, 20 (☎02 70 63 08 25). MM2: Piola. Outdoors. Swim cap required (L2500). L6000, under 12 and over 60 L3000.

EMERGENCY AND COMMUNICATIONS

Emergencies: ☎118. **Police:** ☎113 or ☎02 772 71. **Carabinieri:** ☎112. **First Aid: Pronto Soccorso** (☎02 38 83), **Red Cross** (☎02 34 56 7). **Hospital: Ospedale Maggiore di Milano,** V. Francesco Sforza, 35 (☎02 550 31), 5min. from the *duomo* on the inner ring road.

Late-Night Pharmacy: The one in the *galleria* of the Stazione Centrale never closes (☎02 669 07 35 or 02 669 09 35). During the day, try the one at P. Duomo, 21 (☎02 86 46 48 32). Open M-Sa 9:30am-1pm and 3-7pm. All pharmacies list the nightly rotation of after-hours pharmacies on their doors.

Internet Access:

Manhattan Lab in Università Statale—formerly Ospedale Maggiore on V. Festa del Perdono. Use the entrance opposite V. Bergamini. Take the stairs on the right to the 3rd floor. Turn left, and walk to the end of the corridor. Take 2 lefts; it's the 3rd door on your left. Microsoft workstations open to Erasmus students only, but at the far end of the room there are computers for the public. Free. Open M-F 8:15am-6pm.

Boomerang, V. F. Filzi, 41 (☎/fax 02 669 40 65; email rioma@mv.itline.it), to the right of the Stazione Centrale behind the park. 5 workstations. Fax, printing, digital photo development, and international money wiring. Fast connections. Surf for L15,000 per hr. Open daily 10am-8pm.

El Pampero, V. Gasparotto, 1 (☎02 66 92 21), across from Boomerang. A new consortium consisting of a cafe, restaurant, and club. L10,000 per hr. Open daily 7am-3am.

Internet Point, V. Padova, 38 (☎ 02 28 04 02 46; email intelnet@opimaint.it). MM1/2: Loreto. 10 computers. Fax, print, and wire money. L12,000 per hr. Open daily 11am-7pm.

Terzomillenio, V. Lazzaretto, 2 (☎02 205 21 21; www.abc2000.it; email info@abc2000.it). MM1: Porta Venezia. Take Vle. V. Veneto 4 blocks to V. Lazzarretto. 10 workstations. Photocopy, fax, and scan. L10,000 per hr. M-F 9am-9pm, Sa 9am-6pm.

Hard Disk Cafe, C. Sempione, 44 (☎02 33 10 10 38; www.hdc.it), opposite the Park Sempione. Take tram #1. Loud rock in the background. 20 computers. From 9am-1pm L10,000 per hr., 1pm-2am L15,000 per hr. If you eat, internet use is free, but only from 1-2pm. Open M-Sa 9am-2am. Closed 3 weeks in Aug.

Post Office: V. Cordusio, 4 (☎02 72 48 22 23), near P. del Duomo towards the castle. Stamps, Fermo Posta, and currency exchange. Open M-F 8:30am-7:30pm, Sa 8:30am-1pm. There are 2 post offices at **Stazione Centrale,** one downstairs under the drive-through, the other a large building outside on P. Luigi di Savoia. **Postal Code:** 20100.

ACCOMMODATIONS AND CAMPING

There are over 50 "on-paper" bargains in Milan, but if you want a clean room in a safe and reasonably convenient location, only a few are worth your while. Every season in Milan is high season, except August. For the best deals, try the city's southern periphery or areas south and east of the train station. When possible, make reservations well ahead of time.

Hotel Ca' Grande, V. Porpora, 87 (☎/fax 02 26 14 40 01 or 02 26 14 52 95; email hotelcagrande@tin.it). MM1/2: Loreto. 6 blocks from P. Loreto in a yellow house with a green spiked fence. Take tram #33 from Stazione Centrale to avoid sore feet; it runs along V. Porpora and stops at V. Ampere, 50m from the front door. 20 spotless rooms with phones, TV, and use of a beautiful garden. The proprietors Fabio and Iole are extremely friendly, and Gianluca Casanova, the night guard, is as smooth as his name. The street below can be noisy. English and Croatian spoken. Internet avaiable. Breakfast included. Reception 24hr. Singles L70,000, with bath L90,000; doubles L110,000, with bath L130,000. V, MC, AmEx, Diners.

Hotel Ambra, V. Caccianino, 10 (☎02 26 65 465; fax 02 70 60 62 45). MM1/2: Loreto. Walk 10 blocks down V. Porpora (5-10min.) and take a right on V. Caccianino. A romantic Milanese paradise on a street full of villas and palm trees. Rooms are spotless, all with bath, TV, telephone and wonderfully relaxing balconies. Inquire about student discounts. Reserve ahead. Ask for key if going out at night. 19 beds. Breakfast L5000. Singles L70,000; doubles L100,000; triples L140,000.

Hotel Sara, V. Sacchini, 17 (☎02 20 17 73). MM1/2: Loreto. From Loreto take V. Porpora. The 3rd street on the right is V. Sacchini. The hotel has been recently renovated and the street is peaceful. Singles L55,000; double L80,000, with bath L100,000; triple with bath L120,000.

Hotel San Tomaso, V. Tunisia, 6, 3rd fl. (☎/fax 02 29 51 47 47; email hotelsantomaso@tin.it; web.tin.it/hotelsantomaso). MM1: Porta Venezia. Take the C. Buenos Aires metro exit (may require a short walk to the opposite end of the station) and turn left at the McDonald's on V. Tunisia immediately in front of you. Clean, renovated rooms, some overlooking a courtyard. Phones, TVs. English spoken. Ask for keys if going out at night. 3 singles, around L60,000; 4 doubles with shower L100,000, with bath L120,000; 4 triples/quads L135-200,000. Prices flexible. V, MC.

Ostello Piero Rotta (HI), V. Salmoiraghi, 1 (☎02 39 26 70 95). MM1: QT8. Walk to the right from the metro (so that the round church is across the street and behind you) for about 5min.; the large, ivy-clad brick hostel is on the right behind an off-white fence. A large number of people pass through, so it's easy to meet fellow travelers. Early curfew prevents late-night barhopping and clubbing, but you should be getting your beauty sleep anyway. English spoken. Breakfast, sheets, and lockers included. 3-day max. stay. Reception daily 7-9:30am and 3:30pm-midnight. No morning check-in. Daytime lockout, with no exceptions. Lights out 11:20pm, 11:30pm curfew. HI membership required, available at the hostel (L30,000). Mostly 6-bed rooms, but some family rooms available. Closed Dec. 21-Jan 10. 350 dorm beds L26,000.

Hotel Kennedy, V. Tunisia, 6, 6th fl. (☎02 29 40 09 34; fax 02 29 40 12 53; email raffaelo.bianchi@galactica.it). MM1: Porta Venezia. 3 floors above Hotel San Tomaso. 16 clean rooms with carpet extending up the walls and a nice view of Milan. Some with TV and phone. Ask for the room with the view of the *duomo,* but beware: the street below can be noisy. Some English spoken. Check-out 10am. Ask for keys if going out at night. Breakfast L4000. Reservations recommended. Singles with bath L60-70,000; doubles 100,000, with bath L100-130,000; triples L150,000; quads L160,000; quints 200,000. V, MC, AmEx, Diners.

Hotel Rallye, V. B. Marcello, 59 (☎/fax 02 29 53 12 09; email h.rallye@tiscalinet.it). MM1: Lima. Walk along V. Vitruvio 2 blocks to V. Marcello and turn left on the far side of the street. 20 new, simple, quiet rooms with phone and TV. Singles L65,000; doubles with bath L110,000; triples without bath L120,000. V, MC, AmEx, Diners.

Hotel "Casa Mia," V. V. Veneto, 30 (☎/fax 02 657 52 49 or 02 655 22 28). MM1: Porta Venezia or Repubblica. V. Veneto runs between the 2 stations on the edge of the Giardini Pubblici. All 15 rooms in this upscale hotel have A/C, and some overlook a quiet inner courtyard. All with phone, TV, hair dryer, and bath. English spoken. Full continental breakfast included. Singles L85-100,000; doubles L120-150,000; triples L170-200,000. Mentioning *Let's Go* may help get you these lower rates. V, MC. AmEx.

Hotel Due Giardini, V. B. Marcello, 47 (☎02 295 21 093 or 02 29 51 23 09; fax 02 29 51 69 33), MM1: Lima. Walk along V. Vitruvio 2 blocks to V. Marcello and take a left on the far side of the street. Deep red carpet flows up a winding staircase. Run by friendly Biagio, Ana Maria, and their baby. This "Two Garden" hotel is complemented by minty green decor. All 11 rooms with TV, telephone, and full-length mirror. Some English spoken. Internet access planned for 2001. Breakfast L7000. Singles L80,000, with bath 100,000; doubles L130,000, with bath L150,000; triples with bath L180,000. V, MC.

Albergo Brasil di Ramella Luisa, V. G. Modena, 20 (☎/fax 02 749 24 82; email hotelbrasil@libero.it). MM1: Palestro. Save yourself a walk from Stazione Centrale and take bus #60 until V. G. Modena. From Palestro, take V. Serbelloni and a quick left onto V. Cappuccini, which crosses 2 larger roads, becoming V. F. Bellotti and finally V. G. Modena. The gorgeous 4th-floor entryway is built in the Liberty style, dominant in central Europe at the beginning of the 20th century. Large rooms with TV and romantic view of a boulevard. A kind proprietress and proximity to several clubs make this place a winner. Green carpets complement a plethora of plants in the hallways. 20 beds, 6 rooms with balconies. Breakfast (L8000) sometimes served in bed. Reception closes at 12:30am; ask for keys to enter later. Singles L70,000, with shower L80,000, with bath L95,000; doubles L90,000, with shower L100,000, with bath L125,000. V, MC, AmEx.

Hotel Aurora, C. Buenos Aires, 18 (☎02 204 79 60; fax 02 204 92 85; email hotel.aurora@tiscalinet.it; www.hotelitaly.com/hotels/aurora/index.htm). MM1: Porta Venezia. Exit the station onto C. Buenos Aires, walk straight ahead for 5min., and it's on the right. Behind a grungy facade and a Star Trek-like automatic door lie spotless modern rooms with phones and TVs. The courtyard and soundproof windows mute street noise. Enthusiastic, English-speaking owner sometimes allows travelers to stay at his 3-star hotel nearby for the (lower) Aurora rates when Aurora is full. Reception 24hr. Reserve ahead. Singles L80,000, 1 with shower L90,000, 2 with bath L95,000; 7 doubles L120,000, with bath L145,000; 1 triple L190,000. V, MC, AmEx.

Hotel Malta, V. Ricordi, 20 (☎02 204 96 15 or 02 29 52 12 10). MM1/2: Loreto. Cross over V. Abruzzi and take V. Porpora 1 block to V. Ricordi. Or from Stazione Centrale, take tram #33 to V. Ampere and backtrack along V. Porpora to V. Ricordi. Run by a happy couple. Earth-tone floor tiles and plants on the sills in most rooms. 3 balconies overlook a quiet rose garden full of white sheets drying in the sun. 15 rooms, all with bath and TV. Reservations suggested. Singles L90,000; doubles L140,000.

Pensione Cantore, C. Porta Genova, 25 (☎/fax 02 835 75 65), 15min. southwest of the *duomo* down V. C. Correnti. MM2: Porta Genova. A bit out of the way, but a good price. The exposed pipes contrast with the large, immaculate rooms. Friendly atmosphere. Recently renovated. Breakfast included. Reception 24hr. Singles L70,000; doubles L100,000; triples L150,000.

Camping di Monza (☎039 38 77 71), in the park of the Villa Reale in Monza. Take a train or bus from Stazione Centrale to Monza, then a city bus to the campground. Open Apr.-Aug. Hot showers L500. L8000 per person and per tent, L15,000 for caravan.

FOOD

Like its fine *couture*, Milanese cuisine is sophisticated and sometimes overpriced. Specialties include *risotto giallo* (rice with saffron), *cotoletta alla milanese* (breaded veal cutlet with lemon), and *cazzouela* (a mixture of pork and cabbage). *Pasticcerie* and *gelaterie* crowd every block. Bakeries specialize in the Milanese sweet bread *panettone*, an Italian fruitcake. The newspaper *Il Giornale Nuovo* lists all restaurants and shops, and the brochure *Milano: Where, When, How*, available at the tourist office, lists foreign restaurants of all flavors.

The largest markets are on **V. Fauchè** and **V. Papiniano** on Saturdays and Tuesdays, and in P. Mirabello on Mondays and Thursdays. The **Fiera di Sinigallia,** a 400-year-old extravaganza of the commercial and the bizarre, occurs on Saturdays on the banks of the Darsena, a canal in Navigli (V. d'Annunzio). Splurge on local pastries, or admire the gorgeous goodies at the Milanese culinary shrine of Sant'Ambroeus, C. Matteotti, 7, under the arcades. (☎02 76 00 05 40. Open daily 8am-8pm.) **Supermarket Pam,** V. Piccinni, 2 (☎02 29 51 27 15), off C. Buenos Aires is open daily 8:30am-9pm, but is closed Monday mornings. There's also a **Simpatica CRAI** at V. F. Casati, 21. (☎02 29 40 58 21. Open M 8am-1pm, Tu-Sa 8am-1pm and 4-7:30pm.) Nearer to C. Buenos Aires is **Supermarket Regina Giovanna,** V. Regina Giovanna, 34. (☎02 45 83 90 11. Open M-F 8am-9pm, Sa 8am-8pm.) For bar hoppers and clubbers, **Panino's Story** on P. Lima and C. Buenos Aires offers snacks all night.

ITALIAN RESTAURANTS AND TRATTORIE

Tarantella, Vle. Abruzzi, 35 (☎02 29 40 02 18), just north of V. Plinio. MM1: Lima. Lively, elegant and leafy sidewalk dining. Great *antipasti*. Don't leave without trying the *pasta fresca* for L12,000 or one of the pizzas (L10-20,000). Specialty salads L13-28,000, *primi* from L10-15,000, *secondi* from L125,000. Open Sept.-July M-F noon-2:30pm and 7-11:30pm, Su 7-11:30pm. V, MC, AmEx.

Pizzeria Premiata, V. Alzaia Naviglio Grande, 2 (☎02 89 40 06 48). MM2: Porta Genova. From the metro walk on V. Vigevano and take the 2nd right onto V. Corsico. From there, take a left on V. Alzaia Naviglio Grande. Very popular among Milanese students. Hearty portions. Expect some delays at night. Pizzas from L9000, *primi* around L15,000. Open daily noon-2am. V, MC, AmEx.

Ristorante El Recreo, V. Scarlatti, 7 (☎02 29 51 33 21). MM1: Lima. Walk up C. Buenos Aires and take a left on V. Scarlatti. It's 2 blocks down on the left. Comfortable, hip, and romantic. Homemade Italian cuisine with Latino cocktails and merengue beats. Pasta L13-16,000, pizza L7,500-13,000, fruit and desserts L3-8000. Open Tu-Su noon-2:30pm and 7-11:30pm. V, MC.

Le Briciole, V. Camperio, 17 (☎02 87 71 85), one street from V. Dante. MM1: Cairoli. Lively, young clientele. Homey, dark interior. Pizza L9-16,000, spectacular *antipasto* buffet L13-22,000, *secondi* L16-29,000. Cover L3000. Open Tu-F and Su 12:15-2:30pm and 7:15-11:30pm, Sa 7:15-11:30pm. V, MC, AmEx, Diners.

Pizzeria Grand'Italia, V. Palermo, 5 (☎02 87 77 59). MM2: Moscova. Walk down V. Statuto and take a right on V. Palermo. Warm yellow and blue interior is always packed, but it's worth the wait. Pizza is sold *al trancio*, in massive, thick, focaccia-like wedges (L7-10,000). Salads L12,000. Open Sept.-July W-M 12:15-2:45pm and 7pm-1:15am; Aug. daily 12:15-2:45pm and 7pm-1:15am.

WALK LIKE AN ITALIAN Italians have an uncanny ability to pick the tourists out of a crowd. Perhaps it is because every American tourist is wearing khaki shorts, a white t-shirt, and a pair of Tevas. If you want to avoid this phenomenon, and you're ready to make the leap into Euro-chic, add this simple starter kit of must-haves to your wardrobe.

Adidas Shirt: Preferably fluorescent stripes on black. Buy one that is too tight, and while you're at it get the matching pants with chrome buttons from mid-shin down to accommodate extremely large boots—they all do.

Really tight jeans: Dark with untapered leg. Ouch.

Really tight cargo pants: Thus negating the utility of all those pockets.

Invicta backpack: Who knew that neon yellow went with neon pink? It does when the word Invicta is plastered across the back in alternating neon blue and mint green. Make sure all of your friends sign your backpack in permanent ink. If your shoulders ache, try walking kangaroo-style, with the pack reversed and the straps running down your back.

Telefonino: A mobile phone is essential. If you can't afford one, no one will stop you from pretending. Buy a fake from a wandering cigarette-lighter vendor.

AROUND CORSO PORTA TICINESE AND PIAZZA VETRA

Yguana Cafe Restaurant, V. P. Gregorio XIV, 16, (☎0338 10 93 097). Walk down C. Porta Ticinese, and turn left at P. Vetra. Embrace the stylish vibe. Beautiful, but relatively down-to-earth natives sipping cocktails next to their scooters. Happy hour daily 5:30-9pm. Sunday brunch 12:30-4pm. Open daily 5:30pm-1am.

Grand Café Fashion (☎02 89 40 07 09), on C. Porta Ticinese near V. Vetere. For music and food served late, try this bar/restaurant/dance club. Stunningly beautiful crowd, often selected by a bouncer. Velour leopard print couches. Wowza. Mandatory first drink L15,000. Happy hour 8pm-2:30am. Open daily noon-3pm and 8pm-3:30am.

Bar Flying Circus, P. Vetra, 21 (☎02 58 31 35 77), facing the rear of the church. Cocktails and an assortment of about 50 different whiskeys. Open daily 9am-2am.

Le Coquetel, P. Vetra, 16. A more yuppie-ish crowd assembles here to enjoy strawberry daiquiris around galactic canvasses. Open daily 8:30am-2am.

THE NAVIGLI

From C. Porta Ticinese, walk south until the street ends. Veer right through the Piazza XXIV Maggio to V. Naviglio Pavese and V. A. Sforza, two parallel streets bordering a canal. Or, take the metro to MM2: Porta Genova. Walk along V. Vigevano until it ends and veer right onto V. Naviglio Pavese.

Scimmie, V. A. Sforza, 49 (☎02 58 11 13 13; www.scimmie.it). A legendary bar with the best atmosphere in Navigli, Different theme every night with frequent concerts (10:30pm). Fusion, jazz, soul and reggae. Open daily 8pm-1:30am.

Fontanelle, on V. Navigli Pavese. Cross the channel, walk down V. Navigli Pavese, and look for the 1st bar on the right. This unique bar serves beer quite creatively. Drink up, or risk much spillage. Always crowded with a brotherly mix of locals and foreigners. Open daily 8pm-2am.

Blue Kleim, V. Vigevano, 9. From the Porta Genova metro stop, walk down V. Vigevano 3 blocks. Blue Kleim's trendy funk is on the left. Dedicated to the French author Irwin Kleim. You can't miss it; the blue lights, yellow chairs, and loud house and R&B music scream *"balliamo!"* Try the Vodka Kleim or Virgin Kleim with blue curacao for L10,000. No cover. Open Tu-Su 5pm-3am.

Vista Mare Caffe (☎02 89 40 53 49), near the mouth of C. Porta Ticinese. Veer left at the end of V. Vigevano and walk across the channel. Chic yuppies relax by the *canale* and a fountain. Free pizza bread, *rizzo*, some pasta, and salad. *Apperitivi* L3000. During happy hour (until 8:30pm) L5000 discount per drink. The cafe provides 3-hr. boat rides for L20,000 per person in groups of 6 or more. Open daily 6:30pm-3am.

Totem Pub (☎02 837 50 98), at V. Naviglio Pavese and V. E. Gola. For the head banging sort. Beware the evil death's-head-cow-skull as you enter, and be prepared to hear anything from Metallica to crossover, reggae, or jungle. Live tattoos. Serves beer in immeasurably large Oktoberfest mugs for L15,000. Open daily 8:30pm-2:30am.

Propoganda, V. Castelbarco, 11 (☎02 58 31 06 82). From V. A. Sforza, walk east on V. Lagrange (next to Cafe Baraonda), which morphs into V. Giovenale and spits you out across the street from the large, glowing Propoganda sign. For those interested in dancing rather than bar-hopping. It's got some of the biggest dance floors in Milan (occasionally with live music) and caters mostly to a well-dressed university-age crowd. Fridays 80s & 90s, Saturdays 70s & 80s, Sundays Latino with older couples L15-25,000 cover depending on the theme; men pay L5000 more. Th-Su 11pm-4am.

AROUND CORSO COMO

Lollapaloosa, C. Como, 15 (☎02 655 56 93). From MM2: Garibaldi, head south on C. Como. The club is on the right. A vigorous, youthful atmosphere for those not into the hipper-than-thou scene. This bar is owned by Paolo Maldini, the captain of the Italian football team. The energetic crowd will have you tipsy and dancing on the tables in no time. The bartenders are known to swing the ceiling lamps and drum highball glasses on the counter to the tune of the house favorite, Wully Bully. Great rock'n'roll. Cover L15,000, including a drink. Open daily 7pm-2am, F-Sa 7pm-5:30am.

Rock: Hollywood, C. Como, 15 (☎02 659 89 96), next door to Lollapaloosa. One of the the only discos in the city snobby enough to select from the crowd at the door. Strap on your nicest pants and pout for the (selective) bouncer. Caters to bigwigs in the fashion industry and their models, but has a false air about it. The **mirror** in the ladies restroom is said to have a view of the men's restroom. Smile for the ladies, gentlemen. Hip-hop, house, and commercial music. Cover L25-30,000. Open Tu-Su 10:30pm-4am.

Shocking, V. B. di Porta Nuova, 12 (☎02 65 95 407). Head farther down C. Como. More down-to-earth than Hollywood and without the zaniness of Lollapaloosa. Avant-garde-esque, 2 floors. Fridays house and dance (cover L25,000, first drink included); Saturdays underground techno (L30,000, first drink included). Open F-Sa 10:30pm-4am. Closed June-Aug.

AROUND LARGO CAIROLI

Le Trottoir, close to V. Brera. From MM2: Lanza, take V. Tivoli to the C. Garibaldi intersection. Perhaps the best bar in the city. Each night a different live band plays, but the bar is all about atmosphere. It's easy to meet Italians as well as people from all over the world. Don't even think about leaving without giving a shout out to Rich, the self-styled "Australian ambassador of good will" who runs the place. Open daily 7pm-2:30am.

Bar Magenta, V. Carducci, 13 (☎02 805 38 08). A short walk from MM1/2: Cardona. A traditional, well-crafted, wood-paneled Guinness bar. Hard to get in, hard to get out—the crowd often spills onto the sidewalk. Open Tu-Su 9am-3am, sometimes until 5am.

Old Fashion, on V. Camoens in the Parco Sempione. MM1/2: Cadorna. Walk on the right side of V. Paleocapa from P. Cadorna. The small street becomes V. E. Alemagna, and the club is in the Palazzo dell'Arte on the right. Frequented by students deeply entrenched within the club scene and some (relatively) down-to-earth fashion types. Lively atmosphere. Indoor/outdoor venue with superb DJ lineup. Always crowded. The park can be a bit sketchy at night, though most of its nocturnal inhabitants are simply trying to sell their herbal goods and mean you no harm. Cover (L25,000) includes one drink. Open F-Sa 11pm-4am.

EAST OF CORSO BUENOS AIRES

Cafe Capoverde, V. Leoncavallo, 16 (☎02 26 82 04 30). From MM1/2: Loreto, head down V. Costa. Walk through the flower shop to the heavenly, unique cafe. It feels like a jungle and is full of natives. Johnny Ockey, the super-funky manager is among the friendliest Milanese around. Cocktails dominate, but decent food is available. *Primi* from L11,000, pizza around L12,000. Open noon-3pm and 8pm-midnight.

Artdecothe, V. Lombro, 7 (☎02 39 52 47 60; www.artdecocafe.it). From MM1: Porta Venezia, walk 3 blocks up C. Buenos Aires and take a right on V. Melzi. The bar is 3 blocks down on the left, across from Le Lephante. Without a doubt, this discobar defines Milan's elegance. Modern, and very, very cool. Each table is decorated in a different style, though the predominant theme is trendy art-deco. 250 different colored lights. House, hip-hop, and acid jazz. Dancing begins after midnight. Happy hour daily 6-9pm. Open daily 7am-2am.

Kirribilly, V. Castel Morone, 7 (☎02 70 12 01 51). Take V. Regina Giovana from C. Buenos Aires. A cheery Australian pub with good beer and a giant shark's head on the wall. Try the Cuban rum and kangaroo meat. Mondays happy hour, Tuesdays student night, Thursdays pop quiz. Open M-F noon-3pm and 6am-3am, Sa-Su 6pm-3am.

New Magazine, V. Piceno, 3 (☎02 73 09 41). From Kirribilly, hang a right out the door and turn left at C. Independenza. Walk through P. Dateo, and turn right on V. Piceno to work your way down to a hoppin' disco with phones and maps (and sometimes dancing Italian university students) on every table. Eat, make friends, and find love. Drinks L5-9000. Open Tu-Su 9:30am-2:30am.

GAY BARS AND CLUBS

Le Lephante, V. Melzi, 22 (☎02 29 51 87 68). From MM2: Porta Venezia, walk up C. Buenos Aires 3 blocks and turn right on V. Melzi. Le Lephante is across from the Artdecothe Cafe. Dark interior with a mixed gay/straight crowd. Open Tu-Su 6:30pm-2am.

Cicip e Ciciap, V. Gorani, 9 (☎02 87 75 55). From MM1: Cairoli, take V. S. Giov. sul Muro which turns into V. Brisa. V. Gorani is the 2nd left. A bar/restaurant with a women-only crowd. Open only Sa 8:30pm-3am.

Sottomarino Giallo, V. Donatello, 2 (☎02 29 40 10 47). Another women-only club with cozy couches on 2 floors. Open Tu-Su 10:30pm-3:30am.

One Way Club, V. Cavallotti, 204 (☎02 242 13 41), outside the city in Sesto San Giovanni. MM2: Sesto FS. A famous club with disco and leather. Wowza. Membership card required. Open F-Sa 10:30pm-3:30am, Su 3:30-7pm.

STILL GOT IT (BALLROOM FLOORS)

Al Tata, V. F. Testi, 5 (☎02 69 00 22 81). A fine-dining restaurant with ballroom dancing. Open Tu-Su.

Arizona Dance, V. Spallanzani, 10 (☎02 953 19 52). One of the more elegant and well-visited venues. Open Th-Su.

LIVE MUSIC

Tunnel, V. Sammartini, 30 (☎02 66 71 13 70), near V. Giuseppe Bruscetti, bordering Stazione Centrale. The most underground concert environment. Post-punk, hardcore, ska, reggae, minimalist sci-fi surf, kraut-rock, rockabilly, and various indie bands frequent this train-tunnel-turned-bandshell. Cover L5-15,000. Hours vary, check the paper.

Alcatraz, V. Valtellina, 25 (☎02 69 01 63 52; email alcatrazmilano@alcatrazmilano.com; www.alcatrazmilano.com). MM2: Porta Garibaldi. Take V. Ferrari and make a right on C. Farni. After the train tracks turn left on V. Valtellina. The biggest commercial club and indoor concert-venue in Milan. Cover L25,000, first drink included. Open F-Sa 11pm-3am.

Blues House on V. S. Uguzzone, 26 (☎02 27 00 36 21), near MM1: Villa S. Giovanni. For those who would rather sip a cocktail from a relaxing seat and listen to some good jazz. Open W-Su 9pm-2:30am.

SHOPPING

Keep in mind that many shops in Milan are closed on Monday mornings. If you can tolerate the stigma of being a season behind the trends, buy your designer duds from *blochisti* (wholesale clothing outlets). Try **Monitor** on V. Monte Nero (MM3: Porta Romana, then tram #9 or 29) or the well-known **Il Salvagente,** V. Bronzetti, 16, off C. XXII Marzo (bus #60 from MM1: Lima or MM2/3: Stazione Centrale).

The clothing sold along **Corso Buenos Aires** is more affordable. All the stores are open from 10am-12:30pm and 2:30-7pm. Check out **K-Shop** on P. Argentina (MM1/2: Loreto) for some bargain sportswear. **J.D.C.,** C. Buenos Aires, 61, carries an excellent selection of recent urban style. Also try **Gio Cellini,** C. Buenos Aires, 30, for funky shoes in any color you can imagine. For women, **Pimpkie,** C. Buenos Aires, 19, has very affordable, basic, all-around wares. **Via Torino,** south of the *duomo*, houses the elegant **Upim** (at the corner of V. Spadar). **Crash**, V. Torino, 46, has techno/clubbing/street wear at student prices. **Gallerie-A,** at the intersection of P. San Giorgio and V. Torino, is home to some of the trendiest flashy, pink and black cloth around. They also have wigs, whips, and fetishwear. **Via Sarpi,** near Porta Garibaldi, also has a few decent, inexpensive places to shop.

Milan: When, Where, How has a great list of markets and second-hand stores. Shop around the area of C. di Porta Ticinese, the Navigli district, and C. Garibaldi for second-hand attire (MM2: Porta Genova, then bus #59). **Eliogabalo,** P. Eustorgio, 2 (☎02 837 82 93), named after a Roman emperor renowned for his preoccupation with aesthetics, offers the latest in *haute couture*. True Milanese bargain hunters attack the bazaars on **Via Fauché** (MM2: Garibaldi) Tuesdays and Saturdays and **Viale Papinian** (MM2: Agostino) Saturdays. The famous, 400-year-old **Fiera di Sinigallia** on V. d'Annunzio is also a great place to shop for bargains (Sa only). Another fabulous option is the classy Italian department store **La Rinascente,** to the left of the *duomo* as you face it. (Open until 10pm.)

Winter sales begin January 10. Shop at the end of July for the end-of-summer sales (20-50% off) and a glimpse of the new fall lines. Clothing stores are usually open M 3-7pm, Tu-Sa 10am-12:30pm and 3-7:30pm.

Hard-core window shoppers should head to the world-famous **fashion district** between **Corso Vittorio Emanuele** near the *duomo* and **Via Monte Napoleone** off P. San Babila. This area gives Milan its ultra-hip reputation. Take your credit card at your own risk. The dresses come straight from the designers and the selection is more up-to-date than anywhere else in the world, including New York or Tokyo. Expect to find high-class places to buy perfume, glasses, leather goods, shoes, and jewelry. **Via Sat'Andrea** between V. Montenapoleone and V. della Spiga, among the most elite neighborhoods in the city, has similarly upscale goods.

PAVIA ☎0382

Pavia survived Attila the Hun's attack in 452 before gaining importance as the Lombard capital in the 7th and 8th centuries. Spanish, Austrian, and French forces governed Pavia in rapid succession from the 16th century until 1859, when Italy's independence movement liberated the city. Once a place where kings were crowned, now a prosperous, yet peaceful university town, Pavia bustles with student activity. Romanesque churches from Pavia's tranquil years as a Milanese satellite are scattered throughout the historic section, all within easy reach of one another. The nearby **Certosa di Pavia** (Monastery of Pavia) is one of the premier monastic structures in the world, and the canals planned by da Vinci (an astounding achievement of contemporary engineering) run all the way from Navigli.

TRANSPORTATION

Trains: at the end of Vle. V. Emanuele. To **Milan** (30min., every hr. 6:08am-11:40pm, L4600) and **Genoa** (1½hr., every hr. 6:33am-10:45pm, L12,500). Change at Codogno for **Cremona** (1 per day, L8250).

Buses: SGEA (☎0382 37 54 05), turn left out of the train station. Buses depart from an enormous, modern brick building on V. Trieste. To **Milan** (1hr., 2 per hr., L5000) via **Certosa di Pavia** (15min., L2500).

NORTHWEST ITALY

ORIENTATION AND PRACTICAL INFORMATION

Pavia sits on the banks of the Ticino River not far from where it merges with the Po. The train station overlooks **Piazzale Stazione** in the west end of the modern town. To get from the station to the historic center of town, walk down **Viale Vittorio Emanuele II** to **Piazzale Minerva.** Continue on Pavia's main street, **Corso Cavour,** to the city's narrow central square, **Piazza della Vittoria,** a block away from **Piazza Duomo.** Past P. Vittoria, the main street changes its name to **Corso Mazzini.**

TOURIST, FINANCIAL, AND LOCAL SERVICES

Tourist Office, V. Filzi, 2 (☎0382 221 56; fax 0382 322 21). From the train station, turn left on V. Trieste and then right on V. Filzi, past the bus station. English-speaking staff provides a good map. Open M-Sa 8:30am-12:30pm and 2-6pm.

Taxis: (☎0382 274 39) at the train station or (☎0382 291 90) at the center.

Currency Exchange: Try **Banca Commerciale Italiana,** C. Cavour, 12, or **Banco Ambrosiano Veneto,** C. Cavour, 7d. Also try the 2nd floor of the post office.

Bookstore: Libreria Ticinum, C. Mazzini, 2c (☎0382 30 39 16), off P. Vittoria. A small English selection of classics and best-sellers. Open M 3-7:30pm, Tu-Sa 9am-12:30pm and 3-7:30pm, Su 10:30am-1pm and 3-7:30pm.

EMERGENCY AND COMMUNICATIONS

Emergencies: ☎113. **First Aid/Ambulance:** ☎118, nights and holidays ☎0382 52 76 00. **Hospital: Ospedale S. Matteo,** P. Golgi, 2 (☎0382 50 11).

Pharmacy: Vippani, V. Bossolaro, 31 (☎0382 223 15), at the corner of P. Duomo, has a list of pharmacies with night service. In emergencies, the staff provides night services for a surcharge. Open M-F 8:30am-12:30pm and 3:30-7:30pm.

Internet Access: Poli Piu, C. Cavour, 18, 3 floors above Cinema Politeama. Nice terrace and panorama. Modern dining place on 2 floors. Internet L10,000 per hr. Cocktails L10,000. Open Th-Su 7pm-2am. At the **university.** From P. Vittoria, turn left on Strada Nuova. Walk past the intersection with V. Mentana and take the 1st right into the university. Continue through the courtyard towards a large, seated statue. On the right is a door with the words *"Dipartimento di Scienza della Letteratura e dell'Arte Medievale e Moderna."* Enter the door, present a student ID, and smile. Free. Open M-Th 9am-5pm, F 9am-2pm.

Post Office: P. della Posta, 2 (☎0382 297 65), off V. Mentana, a block from C. Mazzini. Open M-F 8:05am-5:30pm, Sa 8:05am-noon. **Postal Code:** 27100.

ACCOMMODATIONS AND CAMPING

A dearth of reasonably priced places to stay makes Pavia unappealing as anything but a daytrip. Consider staying in Milan, or take advantage of Pavia's well-organized *agriturismo* program. Ask the tourist office for a complete pamphlet.

Hotel Aurora, Vle. V. Emanuele, 25 (☎0382 236 64; fax 0382 212 48), straight ahead from the train station. With its white walls and modern art, this hotel resembles a trendy New York art gallery. English spoken. All 19 rooms with phones, TV, and A/C. Reserve ahead. Singles L60,000, with bath L80,000; doubles L115,000. V, MC.

Camping: Ticino, V. Mascherpa, 10 (☎0382 52 70 94). From the station, take bus #4 (direction: Mascherpa) for 10min. to the "Chiozzo" stop. Restaurant next door. Nearby pool L5000 for campground guests. Open Mar.-Oct. L7500 per person, L4000 per child under 12, L7000 per tent, L3000 per car. Electricity L3000. Hot shower L500.

FOOD

Coniglio (rabbit) and *rana* (frog) are the local specialties, but if you don't eat things that hop and jump, wander to the *tavole calde* on C. Cavour and C. Mazzini. Try the well-loved *zuppa alla pavese*, piping-hot chicken or beef broth served with a poached egg floating on top and sprinkled with grated *grana* cheese. **Esselunga,** between V. Trieste and V. Battisti, at the far end of the mall complex, is a monolithic **supermarket.** (☎0382 262 10. Open M 1-9pm, Tu-Sa 8am-9pm.)

Ristorante-Pizzeria Marechiaro, P. Vittoria, 9 (☎0382 237 39). Crowded, cozy atmosphere under the vaulted brick ceiling. In summer, diners spill into the *piazza*. Delicious pizzas with blackened crusts L6-18,000. Reasonably priced *primi* and *secondi*. Cover L3000. Open Tu-Su 11am-3pm and 6pm-3am. V, MC, AmEx, Diners.

Ristorante-Pizzeria Regisole, P. Duomo, 4 (☎0382 247 39), under the arcade facing the *duomo*. A/C and outdoor seating available. Relax to Baroque classical music. Reasonably priced pizzas, including a *margherita* for L6000. *Primi* from L9000, *secondi* from L12,000. Don't even attempt to leave without trying *profiteria* (chocolate cake; L4000). Open W-M noon-3pm and 7pm-midnight. Closed Aug. V, MC, AmEx, Diners.

SIGHTS

BASILICA DI SAN MICHELE. As the oldest building in town, this sandstone Romanesque church has witnessed the coronations of luminaries, including Charlemagne in 774, Frederick Barbarossa in 1155, a long succession of northern Italian dukes in the Middle Ages, and the Savoy family later on. The most famous coronation was Charlemagne's. Supposedly, light shone through one of the windows on him as the crown was placed upon his head. Rebuilt in a Romanesque style, this 7th-century church retains a medieval feel. The exterior displays once intricate carvings weathered into indecipherable patterns. A 1491 fresco of the *Coronation of the Virgin* and 14th-century low-relief sculpture decorate the chancel, while an 8th-century crucifix of Theodore graces the *cappella*. *(Take C. Strada Nuova to C. Garibaldi and turn right on V. S. Michele. Open daily 8am-noon and 3-8pm.)*

UNIVERSITY OF PAVIA. Founded in 1361, this prestigious beacon of higher education claims such famous alumni as Petrarch, Columbus, and the Venetian playwright Goldoni. The university's most electrifying graduate, however, was the physicist Alessandro Volta (inventor of the battery), whose experiments are now on display. The university's patron and noted sadist, Galeazzo II of the Visconti family, earned notoriety for his research on human torture. Three towers rising from the university on P. da Vinci are the remnants of more than 100 medieval towers that once punctuated the skyline, dedicated to the dead aristocratic families of Pavia. Also check out the interesting and self-explanatory sundial in the middle court. *(From P. Vittoria, turn left on V. Calatafimi and right on C. Stradivari from where you go through the 1st entrance on the right. Free.)*

DUOMO. An all-star team of visionaries including Bramante, da Vinci, and Amadeo began work on the **Cattedrale Monumentale di Santo Stefano Martiro** in the 15th century. As is typical of the Italian system, much of it still remains incomplete. The **Torre Civica,** adjoining the *duomo*, collapsed in the spring of 1989, killing several people and taking a good portion of the left chapel with it. To the left of the *duomo*, you can see the remnants of the tower, surrounded by a metal fence. The *duomo*'s shaky brick exterior, recently reinforced with concrete columns, conceals an impressive interior finally completed under Mussolini. The brick exterior still awaits a marble facade, and there are no plans to complete it in the near future. *(The duomo is diagonally across from P. San Michele.)*

CASTELLO VICONTEO. The colossal medieval castle (1360) is set in a beautifully landscaped park that once extended to Certosa di Pavia, the Viscontis' private hunting ground 8km away. Richly colored windows and elegant terra-cotta decorations border three sides of the castle's vast courtyard. The fourth wall was destroyed in 1527 during the Franco-Spanish Wars. Pavia's **Museo Civico** resides here, featuring a picture gallery and an extensive Lombard-Romanesque sculpture collection. *(The castle is at the end of Strada Nuova. Castle ☎0382 338 53. Open Tu-Sa 9am-1:30pm, Su 9am-1pm. L5000, under 18 L2500. Museum ☎0382 30 48 16.)*

BASILICA DI SAN PIETRO IN CIEL D'ORO. From the grounds of the castle, you can see the low, rounded forms of the Lombard-Romanesque *chiesa* (1132). Inside, piercing rays of light stream down from tiny windows. On the high altar, an ornate Gothic arch contains the remains of St. Augustine. Intricate frescoes adorn the ceiling of the sacristy, left of the altar. *(Open daily 7am-noon and 3-7pm.)*

ENTERTAINMENT

By far the funkiest and most distinctive bar in town is **Malaika "bar and soul,"** V. Bossolaro, 21, off C. Cavour. Its exotic interior in warm colors resonates with African music at night. Enjoy *panini*, salads, and fruit desserts all from L4000. (☎0382 30 13 99. Open Tu-Su 11am-2am.) Check out **Le Broletto,** P. Vittora, 14E, a classic Irish pub filled with locals. (☎0382 675 41. Open 9am-2:30pm and 8pm-2am.)

DAYTRIP FROM PAVIA: CERTOSA DI PAVIA

Buses from Milan-Famagosta (MM2) to Certosa (50min.; 2 per hr., 1st from Milan at 5:40am, last from Certosa at 8pm; L3500) and then to Pavia (V. Trieste station). From the bus stop, Certosa awaits at the end of a long, tree-lined road.

Eight kilometers north of Pavia stands **Certosa di Pavia** (Carthusian Monastery ☎0382 92 56 13), one of the world's most beautiful churches. It was built as a mausoleum for the Visconti family, who ruled the area from the 12th through the 15th century. Started in 1396 by the Viscontis and finished by the Sforzas in 1497, the monastery contains an eclectic array of four centuries of Italian art from early Gothic to Baroque. More than 250 artists worked on the elaborate facade—allegedly the richest church exterior in the world (late 1400s-1560), which represents the apex of the Lombard Renaissance and is packed with inlaid marble and sculptures of saints. The Old Sacristy houses a Florentine triptych carved in ivory, with 99 sculptures and 66 bas-reliefs depicting the lives of Mary and Jesus. The beautiful backyard contains 24 houses, one for each Carthusian monk. In accordance with St. Benedict's motto *ora et labora* (pray and work), the monks also are active in agriculture and distill excellent liquors for L10,000 a bottle. Look out for the rotating wooden food container at the entrance to each abode. They were created so the monks may munch in solitude, if they so desire. When a large enough group has gathered, the monks lead delightful **tours.** (Usually every 45min., in Italian; one monk speaks English.) Even though the tour leader swears there is still a strict eating code among the monks, their cute bellies imply otherwise. (Open Apr. and Oct. Tu-Su 9-11:30am and 2:30-5pm; May-Aug. Tu-Su 9-11:30am and 2:30-6pm; Sept. Tu-Su 9-11:30am and 2:30-5:30pm. Nov.-Mar. Tu-Sa 9-11:30am and 2:30-4:30pm, Su 9-11:30am and 2:30-5pm. Free.)

CREMONA ☎0372

Quiet streets and muted earth-tone walls are simply a backdrop to the richest and most vibrant aspect of Cremona—its music. Claudio Monteverdi was born here, and Andrea Amati created the first modern violin in Cremona in 1530, establishing the *Cremonese* violin-making dynasty. After learning the fundamentals as apprentices in the Amati workshop, Antonio Stradivarius (1644-1737) and Giuseppe Guarneri (1687-1745) raised violin-making to a new art form. Students still come to the city's International School for Violin-Making to learn the legendary craft, ever hopeful of replicating the sound created by Stradivarius's secret varnish. Today, the city remains aware of its noble tradition, as the busy concert schedule at the Ponchielli Theater preserves the city's remarkable music. Buy an original Stradivari for just 2 billion *lire* or a regular Cremona violin for only 20 million *lire*.

TRANSPORTATION

Trains: V. Dante, 68. Bus-stop: "P. Stazione." To: **Brescia** (45min., every hr. 6:32am-7:36pm, L6,300); **Mantua** (1hr., every hr. 6:25am-9:52pm, L7200); **Milan** (1¼hr., 6 per day 6:24am-7:32pm, L9000); **Bologna** (2hr., 6 per day 7:51am-9:31pm, L12,500), via **Fidenza;** and **Pavia** (2hr., 7 per day 5:10am-6:11pm, L8100). Info office (☎0372 37 111) open daily 6am-10:10pm.

Buses: Autostazione di V. Dante (☎0372 292 12), 1 block to the left of the train station. To **Brescia** (every hr. 6:11am-6:30pm, L7,900) and **Milan** (1hr., M,W, and F 10:10am, L9600). Ticket office open 7:20am-1:10pm and 3:30-6:25pm.

Taxis: ☎0372 213 00 or 0372 267 40.

ORIENTATION AND PRACTICAL INFORMATION

As you leave the train station, bear to the left of the park. Walk straight ahead, crossing V. Dante onto V. Palestro, which then crosses **Viale Trento e Trieste.** Take **Via Palestro,** which becomes first **Corso Campi** and then **Corso Verdi,** to **Piazza Stradivari.** Turn left at P. Cavour toward **Piazza del Comune** (commonly known as Piazza del Duomo), where the *duomo*, *torrazzo*, and tourist office are located. From P. del Comune take **Via Solferino** to **Piazza Roma**—the local Rastafarian enclave.

Tourist Office: P. del Comune, 5 (☎0372 232 33). Friendly staff. English spoken. Ask for the general information brochure on hotels, museums, and restaurants. Open M-Sa 9:30am-12:30pm and 3-6pm, Su 10am-1pm.

Currency Exchange: Banco Nazionale del Lavoro, C. Campi, 4-10 (☎0372 40 01; www.bnl.it). Open M-F 8:20am-1:20pm and 2:30-4pm, Sa 8:20-11:50am. **ATM.**

Emergencies: ☎113. **Police: Questura,** V. Tribunali, 6 (☎0372 48 81). **Ambulance and First Aid:** ☎118. **Hospital: Ospedale** (☎0372 40 51 11), in Largo Priori. Past P. IV Novembre to the east, take V. B. Dovara and go right on V. Giuseppina.

Post Office: C. Verdi, 1 (☎0372 220 351). Open M-F 8:10am-5:30pm, Sa 8:10am-1pm. **Postal Code:** 26100.

ACCOMMODATIONS

La Locanda, V. Pallavicino, 4 (☎0372 45 78 35; fax 0372 45 78 34). From P. del Comune, walk up V. Solferino and turn right on C. Mazzini. Bear left on C. Matteotti, and V. Pallavicino is several blocks down on the right. A centrally located 3-star hotel with clean, airy rooms and friendly management. All rooms with bath, TV, and phone. Breakfast included. Restaurant downstairs features homemade pasta. Reception 24hr. Reservations recommended. Singles L75,000; doubles L110,000.

Servizi per L'Accaglienza, V. Sacchi, 15 (☎0372 21 780 or 0372 414 268). Walk down V. Palestro until it turns into C. Verdi, and at P. Marconi turn right on V. Tibaldi. Turn left on V. Sacchi, and ring the bell. Clean, tranquil rooms and 25 beds on a central courtyard. Nun-run. Women only ages 18-65. No English spoken. Curfew 10:30pm. Singles and doubles L20-30,000 per person. Full-pension L40,000.

Giardino di Giada, V. Brescia, 7 (☎0372 43 46 15; fax 0372 43 46 15). From the station, walk 20min. to the left down V. Dante and turn left at P. Libertà. Bus #5 runs from the station. Functional rooms. Singles L40,000; doubles L55,000. V, MC, AmEx.

Albergo Touring, V. Palestro, 3 (☎0372 369 76), on the way from the train station. Ask for one of the cozy rooms close to the center. 10 simple and plain rooms. Reservations required. Singles L40,000; doubles L70,000, with bath L90,000.

Camping: Parco al Po, V. Lungo Po Europa, 12a (☎0372 212 68; fax 0372 27 137). From P. Cavour, walk 20min. down C. V. Emanuele. Showers and electricity. Open Apr.-Sept. L13,000 per person, L16,000 per car and tent, L15,000 per caravan.

FOOD

The city's *mostarda di Cremona*, first concocted in the 16th century, consists of a hodgepodge of fruits—cherries, figs, apricots, and melons—preserved in a sweet mustard syrup. This strongly flavored sauce is traditionally served on boiled meats. Bars of *torrone* (nougat with an egg, honey, and nut base) are equally steeped in Cremonese confectionery lore. *Mostarda* can be found in most local *trattorie*, and *torrone* is available in every sweet shop. **Sperlari,** at V. Solferino, 25,

Council Travel

America's Student Travel Leader for over 50 years

"Happiness is not a destination. It is a method of life"
-Burton Hills

Visit us at your nearest office or online @
www.counciltravel.com

Or call: 1-800-2COUNCIL

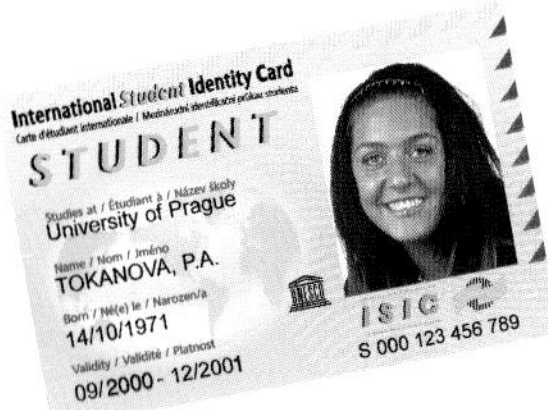

It's your world at a discount!

Accepted at over 17,000 locations worldwide.
Great benefits at home and abroad!

Call the USA

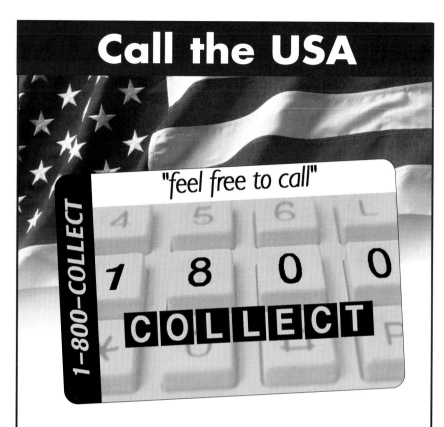

"feel free to call"

1-800-COLLECT

1 8 0 0

COLLECT

When in Ireland
Dial: 1-800-COLLECT (265 5328)

When in N. Ireland, UK & Europe
Dial: 00-800-COLLECT USA (265 5328 872)

Australia	0011	800 265 5328 872
Finland	990	800 265 5328 872
Hong Kong	001	800 265 5328 872
Israel	014	800 265 5328 872
Japan	0061	800 265 5328 872
New Zealand	0011	800 265 5328 872

has been keeping dentists in business since 1836. Bars of *torrone* start at L7000. (☎0372 223 46. Open Tu-Sa 8:30am-12:30pm and 3:30-7:30pm.) For something a little less sweet, try the *Grana Padano* or the Provolone cheeses in the local *salumerie.* From 8am to 1pm on Wednesday and Saturday, there is an **open-air market** in P. Stradivari. For **supermarkets,** try **CRAI** at P. Risorgimento, 30, close to the train station. (Open M 8am-1pm, Tu-Sa 8am-12:30pm and 4:30-7:30pm.) Another option is **GS** at V. S. Tommaso, 9, close to P. del Comune (open M 1-8pm and Tu-Sa 8am-8pm), or **Colmark** on V. Dante, 2 blocks to the left of the train station. (Open M 1:30-7:30pm, Tu-Sa 8:30am-7:30pm.)

Ristorante da Tonino, V. Antico Rodano, 9 (☎0372 286 87), a side street off the intersection between V. Palestro and C. Garibaldi. Eat cheaply with the student crowd in this clean restaurant accented with plastic ivy. Pizza from L6000, *primi* from L8000, *secondi* from L10,000. Open daily 10:30am-5pm and 6:30pm-1am.

Ristorante Pizzeria Marechiaro, C. Campi, 49 (☎0372 262 89). An attractive place with a chance for some serious people-watching. You'll be paying for the elegant yet homey atmosphere, in addition to quality cuisine—the combination is worth it. Pizzas from L10,000. *Menù* with lots of fresh choices L22,000. A/C. Cover L3000, for pizza L2000. Open W-M noon-3pm and 6:10pm-1am. V, MC.

La Piedigrotta, P. Risorgimento, 14 (☎0372 220 33), 2 blocks to the right of the train station. Sparkling clean, modern, and rather bland, this restaurant has a large and varied salad bar. Buffet L8-10,000. Open F-W noon-3pm and 6:30-2am. V, MC.

SIGHTS

MO' MONEY. If your aim is to see all Cremona has to offer, consider a *biglietto cumulativo,* which includes admission to the **Museo Civico,** the **Palazzo Communale,** and the **Museo Stradivariano** for L15,000, or go with the city card with discounts for all the sights and free bus rides for L10,000 (both options are available at the tourist office).

TEATRO PONCHIELLI. Go to P. Stradivari and take C. V. Emanuele to one of Cremona's highlights, a lavishly decorated Baroque theater. The 250 year-old masterpiece provided the testing ground for the Stradivari and Amati violins and stands as one of the most beautiful, but undiscovered (by backpackers) opera houses worldwide. Take the free tour. *(☎0372 40 72 75; fax 0372 40 78 01; email ponchielli@rccr.cremona.it; www.rccr.cremona.it/doc_comu/tea/tea_index.htm. No set hours. Call in advance to reserve a spot. Ticket booth C. V. Emanuele, 52. ☎0372 40 72 73.)*

MUSEO STRADIVARIANO. Violins and their production are Cremona's primary attraction. The small Museo Stradivariano provides a step-by-step introduction to the art of Stradivari and his contemporaries. *(V. Palestro, 17, close to the station. ☎0372 46 18 86. Open Tu-Sa 8:30am-6pm, Su 10am-6pm. L6000. English video available.)*

PIAZZA DEL COMUNE. The second floor of the **Palazzo Comunale** houses a series of lavishly decorated rooms once used by the government. Even more stunning is the *Saletta dei Violini* (Violin Room), showcasing five masterpieces attributed to Andrea Amati, Nicolò Amati, Stradivari, and Guarneri. When the guards unlock the room for you, ask them for an English leaflet describing the violins. The instruments are beautiful, but knowing the story behind them makes them even more evocative. *(P. del Commune. From the Museo Stradivariano, continue down V. Palestro as it turns into C. Cavour and V. Verdi and turn left on V. Baldesio. Open June to mid-Aug. Tu-Sa 8:30am-6:30pm, Su 10am-6pm. L6000.)*

Directly facing the *palazzo,* the pink marble **duomo** (officially known as Santa Maria Assunta) is a fine example of a Lombard-Romanesque cathedral, begun in 1107. The interior displays a cycle of 16th-century frescoes, and the central aisle has been beautifully restored. *(Open daily 7:30am-noon and 3:30-7pm.)*

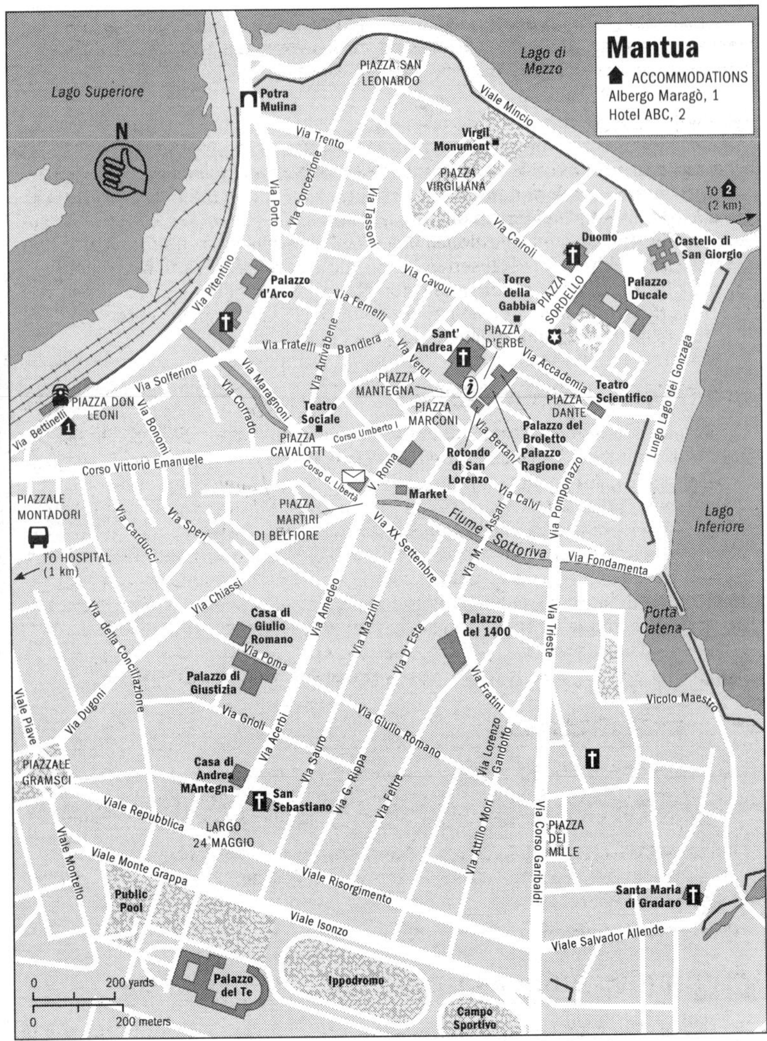

To the left of the *duomo* stands the late 13th-century **Torrazzo.** At 111m, it is the tallest campanile in Italy with the oldest known astrological clock in the world. The clock is one hour late in the summertime, so don't miss your train. The 487 steps lead to a nice panorama of the city. If you plan to survive the climb, take a bottle of water with you. *(Open Easter-Oct. M-Sa 10:30am-noon and 3-6:30pm, Su 10:30am-12:30pm and 3-7pm; Nov.-Easter Sa-Su 10:30am-12:30pm and 3-6pm. L8000.)*

The dome of the **baptistery** (1167) rises in a perfect, unadorned octagonal pattern. The Gothic **Loggia dei Militia,** across from the baptistery, completes the square. Erected in 1292, it functioned as a meeting place for the captains of the citizens' militia. *(Baptistery open Sa 3:30-7pm, Su 10:30am-12:30pm and 3:30-7pm.)*

MUSEO CIVICO. The **Palazzo Affaitati** (1561) flaunts an impressive marble Renaissance staircase that leads to the newly restored museum's extensive and diverse collection, well displayed in a light, airy space. The collection includes paintings by Bembo and Caravaggio. *(V. Ugolani Dati, 4. ☎ 0372 46 18 85. Open Tu-Sa 8:30am-6pm, Su 10am-6pm. L10,000.)*

Palazzo Fodri (1499) is another of Cremona's fine Renaissance buildings. The columns in the courtyard bear French royal insignia in homage to Louis XII of France, who occupied the duchy of Milan in 1499. *(C. Matteotti, 17.)*

FESTIVALS

Music is in the Cremona air year-round. **Cremona Jazz** in March and April eases the way into the summer season with a series of concerts throughout the city. (Tickets from L15,000.) **Estate in Musica** organizes a series of outdoor concerts in July and August. The May and June **Festival di Monteverdi Cremona** kicks off the Teatro Ponchielli season with a classical series heavy on the strings. Performances continue after the festival and crescendo at the grand finale of the opera season. (Open mid-Oct. to early Dec. Teatro Ponchelli ticket booth at C. V. Emanuele, 52. ☎0372 40 72 75. Tickets begin at L10,000. Open daily 4-7pm.)

MANTUA (MANTOVA) ☎0376

Mantua owes its literary fame to its most famous son, the poet Virgil. The driving force that built the city's *centro storico*, however, was not the pun crafter but the Gonzaga family. After ascending to power in 1328, the family zealously sought to change Mantua's small-town image by importing well-known artists like Monteverdi and Rubens and by cultivating local talent. Evidence of their effort includes the impressive churches of San Sebastiano and Sant'Andrea and the remnants of frescoes by Mantegna and Pisanelli. Yet prosperous agriculture and industry attest to the partial success of the Gonzagas' vision, and the historic center preserves the unhurried rustic flavor that its former rulers fought so fiercely to overcome. Today, Mantua, with its grand *palazzi* and graceful churches, is a shopper-friendly city that provides easy passage to the surrounding lakes.

TRANSPORTATION

Trains: (☎0376 14 78 88 088), in P. Don Leoni, at the southwest end of V. Solferino. To: **Verona** (40min., every hr. 6:10am-10:20pm, L4100); **Cremona** (1hr., every hr. 5:25am-7:40pm, L7200); and **Milan** (2hr., 9 per day 5:25am-6:36pm, L16,000).

Buses: APAM (☎0376 32 72 37), in P. Mondadori, across the street and to the right as you leave the train station. Cross C. V. Emanuele to V. Caduti. Frequent buses to **Brescia** (1½hr., L9500).

Taxis: ☎0376 36 88 44.

ORIENTATION AND PRACTICAL INFORMATION

Most buses go only to the edge of the old town, but you can easily walk the rest of the way. From the train station in **Piazza Don E. Leoni,** head left on V. Solferino then right on V. Bonomi to the main street, **Corso Vittorio Emanuele II.** This street leads to P. Cavallotti, connected by C. della Libertà to **Piazza Martiri della Libertà.** From here, **Via Roma** runs to the *centro storico*, which begins at **Piazza dell'Erbe,** with central **Piazza Marconi** and **Piazza Mantegna** clustered close by.

Tourist Office: P. Mantegna, 6 (☎0376 32 82 53; fax 0376 36 32 92), adjacent to Sant'Andrea's church. From the train station, turn left onto V. Solferino. Go through P. S. Francesco d'Assisi to V. Fratelli Bandiera, then right onto V. Verdi. Free brochures and city map. Friendly staff speaks English. Open M-Sa 8:30am-12:30pm and 3-6pm.

Boat Excursions: Motonavi Andes, V. S. Giorgio, 10 (☎0376 32 28 75; fax 0376 36 08 69).

Bike Rental: Bici a Noleggio, an outdoor establishment next to the lake, on the Lungolago dei Gonzaga where it intersects with Largo Vigili del Fuoco. All Mantua knows the owner Mr. Mantovani. M-F L3000 per hr., L8000 for 3hr., L20,000 per day; Sa L5000 per hr., L8000 for 3hr., L20,000 per day; Su L5000 per hr., L8000 for 3hr., L15,000 per day. Open Apr.-Sept. daily 8am-11pm.

Emergencies: ☎ 113. **Police:** P. Sordello, 46 (☎ 0376 20 51). **Ambulance:** ☎ 118. **Hospital: Ospedale Civile Poma,** V. Albertoni, 1 (☎ 0376 20 11).

Pharmacy: Dr. Silvestri, V. Roma, 24. Open Tu-Sa 8:30am-12:30pm and 4-8pm. List of pharmacies offering night service posted outside.

Post Office: P. Martiri Belfiore, 15 (☎ 0376 32 64 03), up V. Roma from the tourist office. Open M-F 8:15am-1:25pm and 2-5:15pm, Sa 8:15am-1pm. **Postal Code:** 46100.

ACCOMMODATIONS

Those willing to stay in smaller nearby towns will be able to find less expensive accommodations. Ask at the tourist office for an up-to-date *agriturismo* packet that lists possibilities for lodging in a rural, characteristically Italian setting (around L20,000 per person per night).

Hotel ABC, P. Don Leoni, 25 (☎ 0376 32 33 47; fax 0376 32 23 29), across from the station. More than the basic accommodation. Fragments of frescoes peek out from the corners of these modern rooms with TV and telephone. Some rooms have bath. Breakfast included. Singles from L50,000; doubles from L90,000; triples from L140,000.

Albergo Maragò, V. Villanova De Bellis, 2 (☎ 0376 37 03 13), at the Locanda Virgiliana. Take bus #2, which runs from P. Cavallotti into Virgiliana (10min. every 30min.). The hotel is on the left, just past P. S. Isidro. If you don't mind the 2km journey from the center, this hotel/restaurant is a bargain with quiet, clean rooms. Singles L32,000; doubles L48,000, with bath L70,000. V, MC, AmEx, Diners.

FOOD

Over a million pigs are slaughtered in Mantua every year, so if you are carnivorous, try the native *panchetta* or *salumi*.

Antica Osteria ai Ranari, V. Trieste, 11 (☎ 0376 32 84 31; fax 0276 32 84 31), on the continuation of V. Pomponazzo near Porta Catena. Friendly atmosphere. Restaurant specializes in regional dishes, some commemorating the Gonzagas. Try the Mantuan delight *tortelli di zucca* (ravioli filled with pumpkin; L10,000). *Primi* L8-10,000, *secondi* L10-15,000. Cover L2000. Open Tu-Su noon-2:30pm and 7-11pm. Closed for about 3 weeks in late July and early Aug. Call for reservations. V, MC, AmEx.

Pizzeria/Ristorante Piedigrotta 2, C. Liberta, 15 (☎ 0376 32 70 14). Despite its central location, this trendy pink and red restaurant offers great deals on pizza and serves delicious seafood dishes for rock-bottom prices. Friendly, festive, fish-loving staff. Pizza *margherita* L7000, *primi* from L8000, *secondi* from L11,000. V, MC.

SIGHTS

PALAZZO DUCALE. The cobblestoned **Piazza Sordello** marks the center of what used to be the largest palace in Europe, built by the Gonzaga family as a monument to Gonzagan "modesty." With 500 rooms and 15 courtyards, the Palazzo Ducale was constructed from the 14th to the 17th century and now houses an impressive collection of antique and Renaissance art. Throughout its history, the *palazzo* has spread its tentacles in all directions, absorbing all buildings in its path, including the Gothic **Magna Domus** *(duomo)* and **Palazzo del Capitano.** Look beyond the *duomo*'s 18th-century facade to its Romanesque campanile and its Gothic side elements. The interior dates from the late Renaissance, but the baptistery below the campanile was decorated with frescoes in the 13th century.

Initiate your tour of the *palazzo* at the **Hall of Dukes**, where evocative sections of Antonio Pisanelli's frescoes (1439-44) were discovered in 1969 under thick layers of plaster. After passing through rooms draped with tapestries created from Raphael's designs, the tour descends upon the Gonzagas' *sala dei fiumi*. Frescoed with vines and flowers, the room looks out on a garden bordered on three sides by a splendid portico. Outside the *palazzo*, signs point to the **Castello di San Giorgio** (1390-1406), the most formidable structure in the complex. Formerly a fortress, the *castello* was later consumed by the *palazzo* and turned into a wing. Inside the *castello*, the **Camera degli Sposi** (Marriage Chamber), contains Andrea Mantegna's famed frescoes of the Gonzaga family (1474). Due to the delicate condition of the frescoes, you must now call ahead and book a special tour to see them. Also note the **Galleria degli Specchi** where the premiere of Monteverdi's *Orfeo*, the first modern opera, took place. This early Baroque show was performed all by men and some of them, *castratos* (ouch!), played female roles. *(Open Tu-Su 8:45am-6:30pm. L12,000, EU students L6000, over 65 and under 18 free.)*

TEATRO SCIENTIFICO (BIBIENA). From P. dell'Erbe head to P. Broletto, take V. Accademia until it ends. Welcome to a musical paradise! This theater, one of the only ones in Northern Italy not modeled after Milan's La Scala, preserves its peculiarity in a play of maroon and stone grey—with great acoustics. The fairy-tale building houses separate little balconies with little love couches all over the place—even behind the stage where Virgil and Pompanazzo coldly stare you down. *(☎0376 32 76 53. Open Tu-Su 9:30am-12:30pm and 3-6pm. L4000, students and those under 18 or over 60 L2000.)*

PALAZZO DEL TE. Built by Giulio Romano in 1534 as a suburban retreat for Federico II Gonzaga and his mistress Isabella, the opulent Palazzo del Te is widely considered the finest building in the Mannerist style. Its rooms demonstrate the late Renaissance fascination with the Roman villa and a willingness to bend the rules of proportion. Idyllic murals of Psyche, remarkable for their vividness and eroticism, line Francesco's banquet hall. Another wing of the palace features regular shows of modern Italian works alongside a collection of Egyptian art. *(☎0376 32 32 66. At the far south end of the city down V. P. Amedeo through P. Veneto and down Largo Parri. Open Tu-Su 9am-6pm, M 1-6pm. L12,000, students and ages 12-18 L8000, under 11 free, groups L7000 per person.)*

ROTUNDA DI SAN LORENZO AND CHIESA DI SANT'ANDREA. Piazza dell' Erbe, just south of P. Sordello, opens onto the Chiesa di San Lorenzo. This 11th-century Romanesque structure (renovated nearly 100 years ago) is also known as "La Matildica" for the powerful noblewoman who bequeathed the rotunda to the pope. *(Open 10am-12:30pm and 2:30-4:30pm. Free.)* Opposite the rotunda rises Mantua's most important Renaissance creation, Leon Battista Alberti's **Chiesa di Sant'Andrea** (1472-1594). Its facade combines the classic triumphal arch motif—barrel-vaulted portal and flanking pilasters—with an antique, pedimented temple front. The gargantuan, opaque interior was the first monumental space constructed in the classical style since imperial Rome. The plan served as a prototype for ecclesiastical architecture for the next 200 years. The church's holy relic, a piece of earth supposedly soaked in Christ's blood, parades the streets in a religious procession each Good Friday. Undisputed, however, is painter Andrea Mantegna's tomb in the back of the church. *(Open daily 8am-noon and 3-6:30pm. Free.)*

PALAZZO D'ARCO. The highlight of this *palazzo* is Falconetto's extraordinary zodiac chamber, a room with ornate frescoes of the astrological signs. *(Off V. Pitentino. From P. Mantegna, follow V. Verdi, which turns into V. Fernelli. ☎0376 32 22 42. Open Mar.-Oct. Tu-Su 10am-12:30pm and 2:30-5:30pm; Nov.-Feb. Sa 10am-12:30pm and 2-5pm, Su 10am-5pm. L5000, students L2000.)*

CASA DI ANDREA MANTEGNA. The purity of its design and the simplicity of its materials make the Casa di Andrea Mantegna a striking contrast to the surrounding luxurious palaces and academies. Built in 1476, the residence hosts traveling art exhibits. *(V. Acerbi, 47. ☎0376 36 05 06. Gallery open for exhibitions M-F 10am-12:30pm and 3-6pm. L5000, over 65 and under 16 L3000. If there are no exhibitions, free.)*

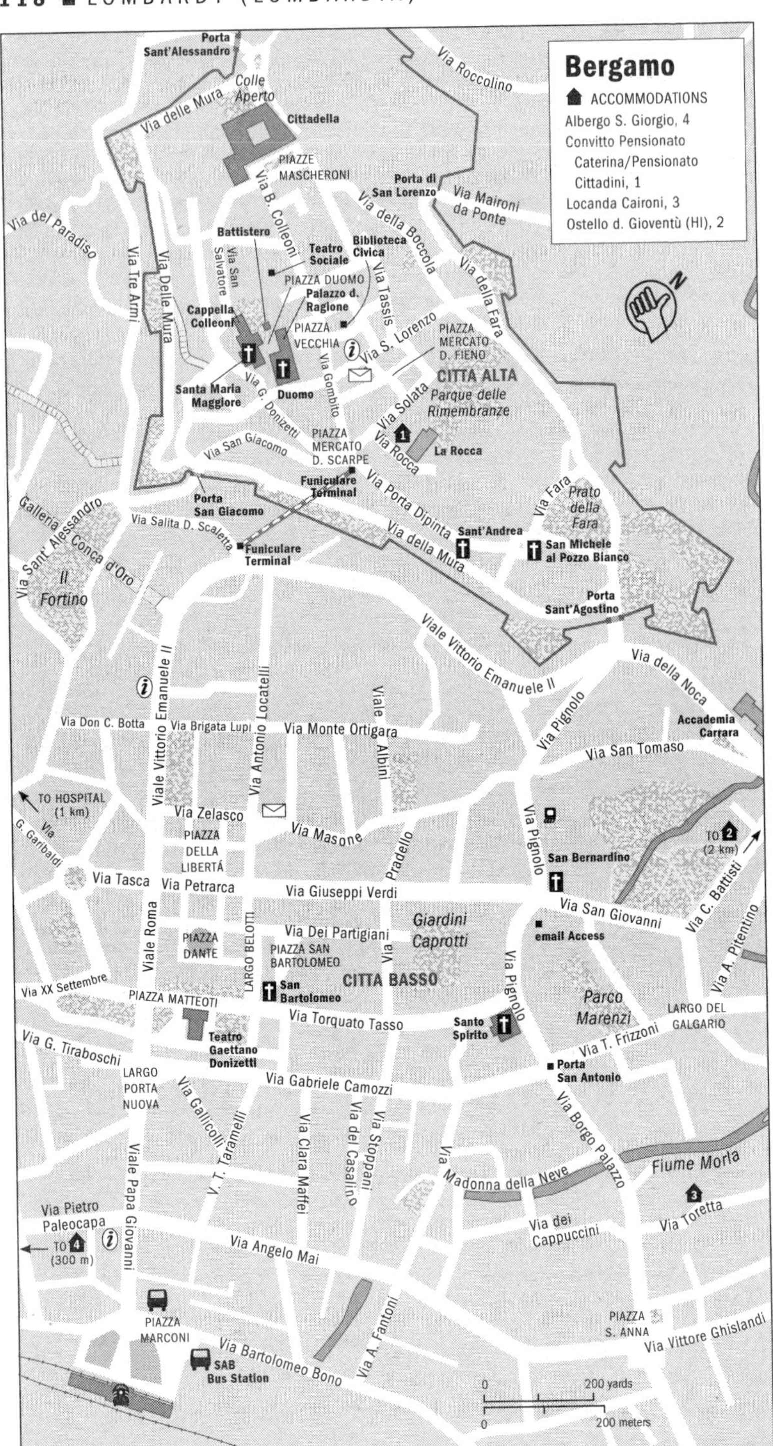
Bergamo
ACCOMMODATIONS
Albergo S. Giorgio, 4
Convitto Pensionato Caterina/Pensionato Cittadini, 1
Locanda Caironi, 3
Ostello d. Gioventù (HI), 2
Porta Sant'Alessandro
Colle Aperto
Via delle Mura
Cittadella
Via Roccolino
PIAZZE MASCHERONI
Via B. Colleoni
Porta di San Lorenzo
Via Maironi da Ponte
Via della Boccola
Via del Paradiso
Battistero
Via San Salvatore
Teatro Sociale
Biblioteca Civica
Via Tre Armi
Via Delle Mura
PIAZZA DUOMO
Palazzo d. Ragione
Via Tassis
Via della Fara
Cappella Colleoni
PIAZZA VECCHIA
Via S. Lorenzo
PIAZZA MERCATO D. FIENO
Santa Maria Maggiore
Via G. Donizetti
Duomo
Via Gombito
CITTA ALTA
Via Solata
Parque delle Rimembranze
Via San Giacomo
PIAZZA MERCATO D. SCARPE
Via Rocca
La Rocca
Funiculare Terminal
Porta San Giacomo
Via Porta Dipinta
Via Fara
Prato della Fara
Galleria Conca d'Oro
Via Salita D. Scaletta
Via della Mura
Sant'Andrea
San Michele al Pozzo Bianco
Via Sant' Alessandro
Il Fortino
Porta Sant'Agostino
Viale Vittorio Emanuele II
Via della Noca
Via Pignolo
Accademia Carrara
Via Don C. Botta
Via Brigata Lupi
Via Antonio Locatelli
Via Monte Ortigara
Viale Albini
Via San Tomaso
TO HOSPITAL (1 km)
Via Zelasco
Via Masone
Via G. Garibaldi
PIAZZA DELLA LIBERTÁ
Pradello
San Bernardino
TO 2 (2 km)
Via Tasca
Via Petrarca
Via Giuseppi Verdi
Via C. Battisti
Via San Giovanni
Viale Roma
PIAZZA DANTE
LARGO BELOTTI
Via Dei Partigiani
PIAZZA SAN BARTOLOMEO
Giardini Caprotti
email Access
Via A. Pitentino
Via XX Settembre
PIAZZA MATTEOTI
San Bartolomeo
CITTA BASSO
Parco Marenzi
Via Torquato Tasso
Santo Spirito
LARGO DEL GALGARIO
Via G. Tiraboschi
Teatro Gaettano Donizetti
Via T. Frizzoni
LARGO PORTA NUOVA
Via Gabriele Camozzi
Porta San Antonio
Via Gallicoli
V. T. Taramelli
Via Clara Maffei
Via del Casalino
Via Stoppani
Via Borgo Palazzo
Viale Papa Giovanni
Via Madonna della Neve
Fiume Morla
Via Pietro Paleocapa
Via dei Cappuccini
Via Toretta
TO 4 (300 m)
Via Angelo Mai
Via A. Fantoni
PIAZZA MARCONI
PIAZZA S. ANNA
Via Vittore Ghislandi
Via Bartolomeo Bono
SAB Bus Station
0 200 yards
0 200 meters

FESTIVALS

The **Teatro Sociale di Mantova,** P. Cavallotti (☎0376 36 27 39), off C. V. Emanuele, stages operas in October and plays from November through May. Seats from L20,000. The **Spazio Aperto** series brings dance, music, and cinema events to various *piazze* and *palazzi* around town. Mantua also hosts a chamber music series in April and May. The **Mantua Jazz Festival** at the end of July features a street parade and numerous boisterous concerts. Ask at the tourist office for info. In mid-August, Italian speakers should check out **Festivaletteratura,** which attracts hordes of scholars who recite everything from personal works to Emily Dickinson.

DAYTRIP FROM MANTUA: SABBIONETA

Sabbioneta is 33km southwest of Mantua and easily accessible by bus from the Mantua bus station (in winter 9 per day, in summer 5 per day).

Sabbioneta was founded by Vespasiano Gonzaga (1532-91) as an attempted paradise and turned out to be "only" a home for his feudal court. The town earned the title "Little Athens of the Gonzagas" because of its importance as an artistic center in the late Renaissance. Inside the well-preserved 16th-century city walls lie the fascinating Renaissance **Palazzo Ducale, Teatro Olimpico,** and **Palazzo del Giardino.** Take a guided walk through their otherwise inaccessible interiors; the 45-minute tour (in English, French, or German L13,000, groups L11,000 per person) leaves from the **tourist office,** V. Gonzaga, 31. (☎0375 22 10 44. Open Oct.-Mar. Tu-Sa 9:30am-12:30pm and 2:30-5pm, Su 9:30am-12:30pm and 2-6pm; Apr.-Sept. Tu-Sa 9:30am-12:30pm and 2-6pm, Su 9:30am-12:30pm and 2:30-7pm.) On the first Sunday of each month, antique *aficionados* arrive in Sabbioneta for the exhaustive **Mercato dell'Antiquariato.**

BERGAMO ☎035

Every city should have a castle in the clouds. Glimmering in the distance, a medieval city nestles in the hills over Bergamo, with palaces, churches, and a huge stone fortification. The city is divided into two parts; the first, *città alta* (upper city), recalls Bergamo's origins as a Venician outpost sieged by French revolutionaries. It has narrow, cobblestone streets shaded by solemn facades. Below, the *città bassa* (lower city) is a modern metropolis packed with neoclassical buildings. Home of Italy's oldest operating bar, the proud Atalanta Bergamo (a Serie A team), as well as the best American football team in Italy, Bergamo fuses hundreds of years of heritage in this bustling commercial, artistic, and industrial center.

TRANSPORTATION

Trains: (☎035 24 76 24), in P. Marconi. At the juncture of the Brembana and Seriana valleys, Bergamo is a short train ride from Milan, Brescia, and Cremona. To: **Milan** (1hr., every hr. 5:46am-11:02pm, L7200); **Brescia** (1hr., every hr. 6:50am-8:40pm, L5600); and **Cremona** (1½hr., every hr. 8:58am-5:30pm, L8500). Open daily 6am-8:45pm. Info open sporadically. **Luggage Storage:** L5000 for 12hr. Open daily 7am-9pm.

Buses: To the right from the train station. All buses have flexible times so call the appropriate agency. To: **Milan** (☎02 80 11 61; every 30min., L7500); **Cremona** (☎0372 27 212; 2-5 per day, L10,200); and **Como** (☎0312 47 247; 7 per day, L8500).

ORIENTATION AND PRACTICAL INFORMATION

The train station, bus station, and numerous budget hotels are in the **città bassa.** There are three ways to reach **città alta:** take bus #1 (L1500) to the **funicular** which ascends from **Via Vittorio Emanuele** to the Mercato delle Scarpe (8 per hr; L1500, free if you're still holding your bus ticket). Bus #1a runs to the "Colle Aperto" stopping at the top of the *città alta.* Or take the stairs on **V. Salita della Scaletta,** which starts to the left of the funicular on V. V. Emanuele. Turn right at the top to enter *città alta* on **Via San Giacomo** through Porta San Giacomo (10-15min.).

TOURIST, FINANCIAL, AND LOCAL SERVICES

Tourist Office: APT, V. Aquila Nera, 2 (☎035 23 27 30 or 035 24 22 26; fax 035 24 29 94; email aptbg@apt.bergamo.it; www.apt.bergamo.it), in the *città alta*. Take bus #1 or 1a to the funicular, follow V. Gambito to P. Vecchia, and turn right. Open daily 9am-12:30pm and 2-5:30pm. In the *cita bassa:* **APT,** V. V. Emanuele, 20 (☎035 21 02 04 or 035 21 31 85; fax 035 23 01 84), straight from the train station (8min.) before the curve to the funicular. Open M-F 9am-12:30pm and 2-5:30pm.

Currency Exchange: Banca Nazionale del Lavoro, V. Petrarca, 12 (☎035 23 80 16), off V. V Emanuele, near P. della Libertà. Good rates. Open M-F 8:30am-1:20pm and 2:45-4:15pm. Also on the 2nd floor of the post office. Open M-F 8:30am-5pm. **ATMs** dispense cash in the train station near the *tabacchi* and outside **Banca Popolare di Milano,** on V. P. Paleocapa off V. Papa Giovanni XXIII.

Money Transfers: World Center Agenti, V. Quarenghi, 37D (☎035 31 31 24; fax 035 32 13 63), off V. Pietro Paleocapa. Open daily 10:30am-8pm.

Laundromat: Onda Blue, V. S. Bernardino, 57 (☎0167 86 13 46). Bergamo's other laundry facilities are in the HI hostel (usually reserved for guests), but feel free to take yourself to the cleaners. Most accept only locals, but when business is slow you might sneak in a load or two. There are 2 on V. Giacomo Quarenghi and 1 on V. Borgo Palazzo.

NORTHWEST ITALY

EMERGENCY AND COMMUNICATIONS

Emergencies: ☎113. **Police:** V.Galagerio, 25 (☎035 23 82 38). **Ambulance: Croce Bianca Città di Bergamo** (☎118 or 035 31 68 88). **Hospital: Ospedale Maggiore,** Largo Barozzi, 1 (☎035 26 91 11). **First Aid:** (daytime ☎035 26 91 11, nights and Su ☎035 25 02 46).

Internet Access: For HI hostel guests (L10,000 per hr.), or at the **Centro Giovenile e Universitario Diocesano,** V. Pignolo, 73A, in *città bassa*. From Largo Porta Nuova, walk along Gabriele Camozzi, turn left on V. Pignolo, and look for an archway with dark wooden doors on the right. Walk to the end of the entrance hallway and through the doorway on the right. Walk up 2 flights of steps to the 1st floor. Enter the 2nd door on the left. If using once, no membership needed. L3000 per hr. Open M-Sa 9am-12:20pm and 3-6:45pm. If no one is in the room, ask someone for keys to let you in.

Post Office: V. Locatelli, 11 (☎035 24 32 56). Take V. Zelasco from V. V. Emanuele. Open M-F 8:30am-1:40pm, Sa 8:30-11:40am. Packages are handled at V. Pascoli, 6 (☎035 23 86 98). Same hours. **Postal Code:** 24122.

ACCOMMODATIONS

Prices rise with altitude; the most affordable *alberghi* are found in the *città bassa*. The tourist office has information on cheaper *agriturismo* options.

Ostello della Gioventù di Bergamo (HI), V. G. Ferraris, 1 (☎035 34 30 38; fax 035 36 17 24; email hostelbg@spm.it; www.sottosopra.org/ostello). Take bus #14 from Porta Nuova (the stop is on V. Camozzi) to "Leonardo da Vinci" and walk up the steep but short hill. Though far from the city, this hostel has many comforts of home: satellite TV, gardens, a full-service kitchen, and an absolutely stunning view of the *città alta* and the surrounding valley from most balconies. The rooms are in excellent condition and antiseptically clean. Every dorm room has its own bath. Some English and French spoken. HI members only. 80 beds. Breakfast included. Laundry for guests. Internet access L10,000 per hr. Reservations helpful. Dorms L25,000; singles with bath L35,000; doubles with bath L60,000.

Locanda Caironi, V. Torretta, 6B (☎035 24 30 83), off V. Borgo Palazzo, a 20min. walk. Accessible by bus #5 or 7 from V. Angelo Maj. A family affair replete with an exquisite courtyard in a quiet residential neighborhood. The rooms of the 18th-century Casa Caironi overlook a secluded garden *trattoria,* considered to be one of Bergamo's best-kept culinary secrets. Reservations recommended. Singles L30,000; doubles L55,000.

Albergo S. Giorgio, V. S. Giorgio, 10 (☎035 21 20 43; fax 035 31 00 72). Bus #7, or a short walk from the train station. Make a left on V. Pietro Paleocopa, which becomes V. S. Giorgio (15min.). Train tracks and a construction site nearby, but relatively quiet inside. Neat, modern rooms with TV, telephone, and sink. Some English spoken. Reservations helpful but not required. 68 beds. 2 rooms wheelchair accessible. Singles L35,000, with bath L55,000; doubles L65,000, with bath L90,000. V, MC, Diners.

Convitto Pensionato Caterina Cittadini, V. Rocca, 10 (☎035 24 39 11), off P. Mercato delle Scarpe (V. Rocca is the small narrow street on the right after exiting the top of the funicular) in the *città alta.* Sorry guys, it's open to women only. The orange-hued walls of this *pensione* give a warm glow to the open-air courtyard and sunlit rooftop terraces. The nuns in charge are happy to give foreigners a home, although little English is spoken. Reception on the 2nd floor. Breakfast and dinner included. Curfew 10pm; if going out later, ask for a key. Singles L60,000, with bath L65,000; doubles L100,000.

FOOD

Casonsei, meat-filled ravioli dishes, are a typical *primo* in Bergamo, while the *branzi* and *taleggio* cheeses are part of a traditional *formaggio* course that concludes the meal. Try them with the local Valcalepio red and white wines. The typical meal includes polenta, a staple dish made from corn meal and water, usually served with various condiments. Streets in the *città alta* are lined with *pasticcerie* selling yellow polentina confections, topped with chocolate blobs intended to resemble birds. These sweet treats are primarily pricey tourist bait; many natives have never sampled one. For your meal necessities, shop at **Compra Bene,** on the right side of V. V. Emanuele, at the bottom of the hill heading to the *città alta.* Keep in mind that most Bergamo shops are closed Monday mornings.

CITTÀ BASSA

Capolinea, V. Giacomo Quarenghi, 29 (☎035 32 09 81), on the right off V. Zambonate. Follow V. Tiraboschi from Porta Nuova. A favorite among Bergamo's twenty-somethings, this modern establishment has a lively bar in front and a more tranquil garden in back. Plenty o' veggie concoctions. Full meal from L15,000, large salads from L4500. Open Tu-Sa 6:30pm-3am, Su 7pm-3am. Kitchen open until midnight.

Trattoria Casa Mia, V. S. Bernardino, 20 (☎035 22 06 76), off V. Zambonate. Follow V. Tiraboschi from Porta Nuova. Nothing fancy–just good food. Full "home style" meal with *primo* (mostly the house specialty, Bergameschi polenta), *secondo, contorno,* and drink for L20,000 (L16,000 for lunch). Open M-Sa noon-3:30pm and 6pm-midnight. Closed for 1 week in the middle of Aug. Kitchen closes at 10pm.

CITTÀ ALTA

You may be able to resist the temptations of the first several *pasticcerie* on V. Colleoni or V. Gombito, but chances are good that you will succumb eventually, as they seem to sprout up every several yards. Before giving in to the urge to buy an entire *torta,* haul your sugar-plum fantasies to one of the several reasonably priced restaurants offering more substantial and delicious food.

Circolino Cooperativa Città Alta, V. S. Agata, 19 (☎035 21 57 41 or 035 22 58 76). This former prison and church is now a neat communist garden cafe, with arching overhead vines and a spectacular vista of the surrounding hills and villas. Cheapest food in town. Play pinball, pool and *bocce* (Italians take this game *very* seriously). Bring your own hammer and sickle. Tennis shoes required for *bocce.* Sandwiches, pizza, and salads for under L8000. Cover L1000. Open Th-Tu 8:30am-3am, W 11:30am-3am.

Papageno Pub, V. Colleoni, 1b (☎035 23 66 24). Although the crowds are hooked on the drinks, the pub also provides a menu of light but filling sandwiches and salads and a surprisingly extensive list of teas (around L6000). The owner is proud to offer the widest selection of Belgian beers in Italy (188). Open F-W 8am-2am.

Ratzmatatz, V. Gombito, 10 (☎035 24 15 89). Very artsy in a yellow setting. Great salads with cute little mozzarella balls from L10,000. *Panini* L5-9000, *primi* L10,000, desserts L4-6000. Open daily 7:30am-2am. V, MC, AmEx, Diners.

Trattoria Tre Torri, P. Mercato del Fieno, 7a (☎035 24 43 66), left off V. Gombito when heading away from P. Vecchia. This corner eatery has cute tables in its tiny, vaulted, stone interior and serves substantial dishes without pretense. Romantic outside seating in the shadows May-Sept. Try the polenta (L16,000) or the house specialty *foiaole con procini* (L12,000). *Primi* from L8000. *Menù* around L35,000. Cover L2000. Open Th-Tu 10am-4pm and 7:30pm-midnight. Reservations recommended. V, MC.

SIGHTS

CITTÀ BASSA

GALLERIA DELL'ACCADEMIA CARRARA. Housed in a glorious Neoclassical palace, this is one of the most important art galleries in Italy. Fifteen rooms display canvasses by the Dutch School and Bergameschi greats like Fra' Galgario, as well as canvases by Boticelli, Lotto, Tiepolo, Titian, Rubens, Breughel, van Dyck, and El Greco. The works start with 13th-century Gothic art and are especially strong on humanistic Florentine culture. Check out one of Rafael's early works, *St. Sebastian. (From Largo Porta Nuova, take V. Camozzi to V. Pignolo, turn left to V. San Tomaso, then right. ☎035 39 96 40; fax 025 22 45 10. Open W-M 9:30am-12:30pm and 2:30-5:30pm. L5000, over 65 and under 18 free, groups over 15 L3000 per person. Sundays free.)*

OTHER SIGHTS. Piazza Matteotti in the heart of the *città bassa* is a favorite meeting place for both tourists and native *passeggiatori*. It was redesigned by the Fascists in 1924. In the **Chiesa di San Bartolomeo,** at the far right of the *piazza*, you will find a superb altarpiece of the Madonna and Child by Lorenzo Lotto. (*Open daily 9am-4pm. Free.*) To the right of San Bartolomeo, V. Tasso leads to the **Chiesa del Santo Spirito,** marked by its strangely sculpted facade. The fine Renaissance interior (1521) houses paintings by famous dead Italians. On the left, V. Pignolo connects the lower city to the upper, winding past a succession of handsome 16th- to 18th-century palaces. Along the way is the tiny **Chiesa di San Bernardino,** whose colorful interior pales behind a splendid painting by Lotto. *(Open W-Th 10am-1pm. Free.)*

CITTÀ ALTA

The *città alta*, perched above the modern city, is a wonderfully preserved medieval town with a fountain, panoramic view, or archway around every corner. The town is accessible by both funicular and foot. From the Carrara gallery, the terraced V. Noca ascends from the lower city to Porta S. Agostino, a 16th-century gate built by the Venetians as a fortification. After passing through the gate, V. Porta Dipinta leads to V. Gombito, which ends in Piazza Vecchia.

BASILICA DI SANTA MARIA MAGGIORE. The stark Romanesque exterior of this 12th-century basilica, joined to the Cappella Colleoni, contrasts with its breathtakingly elaborate Baroque interior. Within stands the Victorian tomb of the 19th-century composer Gaetano Donizetti, Bergamo's most famous son. Observe the light shining through tiny windows as it highlights the beauty of the ceiling. Tapestries and panels depict famous biblical scenes. (*Left of the Cappella Colleoni. ☎035 22 33 27. Open May-Sept. M-F 9am-noon and 3-6pm, Sa-Su 8-10:30am and 3-6pm; Oct.-Apr. M-F 9am-noon and 3-4:30pm, Sa-Su 8-10:30am and 3-6pm. Free.*)

CAPPELLA COLLEONI. The patterned, pastel, multicolored marble facade of this chapel was designed in 1476 by G. A. Amadeo (also responsible for Certosa di Pavia) as a tomb and chapel for the celebrated Bergameschi mercenary hired for Venice's Bartolomeo Colleoni. Notable are also 18th-century ceiling frescoes by Tiepolo surrounded by Colleoni's sarcophagus. *(Head through the archway flanking P. Vecchia to reach the P. del Duomo. Open Tu-Su Mar.-Oct. 9am-12:30pm and 2-6:30pm; Nov.-Feb. 9am-12:30pm and 2:30-4:30pm. Free.)*

PIAZZA VECCHIA. This *piazza* houses a majestic ensemble of medieval and Renaissance buildings flanked by restaurants and cafes in the heart of the *città alta*. Rest your legs as you sit with the locals on the steps of the white marble **Biblioteca Civica** (1594), repository of Bergamo's rich collection of manuscripts, modeled after Venice's Sansovino Library. Across the *piazza* is the massive Venetian Gothic **Palazzo della Ragione** (Courts of Justice, 1199) and a 300-year-old sundial. To the right, connected to the *palazzo* by a 16th-century covered stairway, stands the 12th-century **Torre Civica** (Civic Tower). The view from the top is worth the climb, but protect your eardrums; despite the traditional 10pm curfew, the 15th-century bell, rings every half hour throughout the night. *(Open daily Apr.-Sept. 9am-noon and 2-8pm. L2000, under 18 and over 65 L1000.)*

BAPTISTERY. This octagonal structure features a red marble gallery. The baptistery that now stands is actually a reconstruction of its 14th-century predecessor that was once a part of the basilica. Inside are some rather strange 13th- and 14th-century frescoes of Jesus' life. *(Between Cappella Colleoni and the Basilica.)*

CHIESA DI SAN MICHELE AL POZZO BIANCO. Built during the 12th and 13th centuries, the Romanesque interior is embellished with colorful frescoes by Lotto. *(Near the intersection of V. P. Dipinta and V. Osmano. ☎035 25 12 33. Open Su-F 9am-12:15pm and 2:45-4:45pm. Closed W mornings. Call ahead for big groups.)*

PARCO DELLE RIMEMBRANZE. This park, situated where there were once Roman fortifications, makes a perfect romantic conclusion to a walking tour of Bergamo. The surrounding trees, flowers, and shady paths are dedicated to soldiers who have died in Italian battles. (*Located at the end of V. Solata.*)

NORTHWEST ITALY

ENTERTAINMENT

The arts thrive in Bergamo. The opera season lasts from September to November and is followed from November through April by the drama season, featuring performances by Italy's most prestigious companies at the **Donizetti Theater,** P. Cavour, 15, in the *città bassa*. If you call in advance, the staff may grant requests to view the theatre. (☎035 416 06 02; fax 035 23 41 10.) In May and June, the spotlight falls on the highly acclaimed **Festivale Pianistico Internazionale,** co-hosted by the city of Brescia. In September, Bergamo celebrates its premier native composer with a festival of Gaetano Donizetti's lesser-known works. For more information, contact the tourist office or the theater at P. Cavour, 14 (☎035 24 96 31). During summer, the tourist office provides a program of free events, *Viva La Tua Città*.

Relax after a day of sightseeing in one of the *città alta*'s many *vinerie*. A short hop from P. Vecchia, **Pasticceria Cafe Al Donizetti,** V. Gombito, 17 (☎035 24 26 61; www.donizetti.it), features a mouth-watering selection of cheeses, Italian sausages, wines (400), and cold meats, as well as a lovely outdoor seating area. If the weather is not cooperating, head to **Vineria Cozzi,** V. B. Colleoni, 22 (☎035 23 88 36). The romantic Venetian alcove behind the bar will soothe your aches and leave you with a smile. At either venue, a good bottle of wine sells for L9-12,000.

The *città alta* transforms at night. Though many locals head to discos in surrounding towns, masses of twenty-somethings still pack the eateries, pubs, and *vinerie* to relax and socialize. Head down to **Pozzo Bianco,** V. Porta Dipinta, 30B; going up will be easier after a few good beers. A *birreria* with a kitchen and character is by far the liveliest hangout for local youth. (☎035 24 76 94. Open daily 7am-3pm and 6pm-3am. V, MC, AmEx.) Also try one of 50 types of whiskey and rum at **Pub dell'Angelo,** V. S. Lorenzo, 4A. It is more a winter bar, but still a great location to get drunk. (☎035 22 21 88. Open daily 10:30am-3pm and 7pm-2am.)

BRESCIA ☎030

Throughout the years, two constants remain in Brescia: fashion and prosperity due to the remains of a large number of aristocratic families. Besides the many high-fashion clothing shops that line the avenues of this industrial city, Brescia (pop. 250,000) owes its present place in the thriving Lombard economy to less romantic exports: sink-fixtures and weapons (Beretta has its production center here). However, the soul of the city is neither in the bathroom nor in the battlefield but in its historic center. Here, an avenue of elegant shops and cafes links smaller streets with remnants of a few millennia of history—churches, *piazze*, Roman ruins, and museums. With their arcades, archways, and multitude of fountains, these streets make Brescia a walker's paradise.

TRANSPORTATION

Trains: Brescia lies between Milan and Verona and many other towns in Veneto on the Torino-Trieste line. To: **Verona** (45min., 10 per day 7:23am-1:34am, L6100); **Milan** (1hr., every hr. 5:55am-11:38pm, L13,100); **Bergamo** (1hr., 10 per day 5:25am-11:13pm, L5500); **Vicenza** (1¼hr., every hr. 6:15am-9:13pm, L13,800); **Cremona** (1¾hr., 11 per day 6:29am-9:25pm, L6300); **Padua** (1¾hr., every hr. 6:15am-9:13pm, L20,200); and **Venice** (2¼hr., every hr. 4:13-9:13pm, L25,200). Info office (☎147 888 088) open 7am-9pm. **Luggage Storage:** L5000 for 12hr. Open 24hr.

Buses: (☎030 449 15). Brescia is the main point of departure for buses to the western shores of Lake Garda. Eastbound buses are opposite the train station in a bright-orange building. To: **Cremona** (1¼hr., every hr. 6:30am-6:55pm, L7900); **Mantua** (1½hr., every hr. 5:45am-7:15pm, L9500); and **Verona** (2¼hr., every hr. 6:45am-6:15pm, L10,300). Westbound buses leave from the **SAIA** station (☎030 377 42 37), to the left as you exit the train station. To **Milan** (1¾hr., 8:32am-6:32pm, L12,000). Ticket office open M-F 7am-12:30pm and 1:30-6:25pm, Sa 7am-12:30pm and 1:30-3:10pm.

Taxis: (☎030 351 11), everywhere in the city. 24hr.

ORIENTATION AND PRACTICAL INFORMATION

Most of the city's architectural gems are concentrated in the rectangular *centro storico*, bounded by **Via XX Settembre** on the south, **Via dei Mille** on the west, **Via Pusterla** on the north, and **V. F. Turati** on the east. From the **Piazza della Repubblica** and the slightly seedy area around the train/bus stations, turn right on **C. M. della Libertà** to **C. Palestro**. Turn left on **V. 10 Giornate** to **P. Loggia,** where you turn left to the **Piazza Tito Speri.** From here **Via dei Musei** slopes down to "museum row" and the Roman archaeological site. Follow the signs along **Via del Castello** to the castle.

Tourist Office: APT, C. Zanardelli, 34 (☎030 434 18; fax 030 375 64 50; email aptbs@ferriani.com; www.bresciaholiday.com), an inconspicuous office set off the street, next to a cinema. Helpful map, event fliers, and walking guides to the city. Open M-F 9am-12:30pm and 3-6pm, Sa 9am-12:30pm. Or try **City Tourist Office,** P. Loggia, 6 (☎030 240 03 57; fax 030 377 37 73; www.comune.brescia.it). Open Oct.-Mar. M-F 9:30am-12:30pm and 2-5pm, Sa 9:30am-12:30pm; Apr.-Sept. M-Sa 9:30am-12:30pm.

Paragliding school: Brixia Flying, V. S. Zeno, 117 (☎030 242 20 94; fax 030 80 28 70; www.spidernet.it/bresciafly).

Car Rental: Avis, V. XX Settembre, 2f (☎030 29 54 74). **Europcar Italia,** V. Stazione, 49 (☎030 280 487). **Hertz,** V. XXV Aprile, 4c (☎030 45 32).

Emergencies: ☎113. **Police:** P. Spedale Civili, 1 (☎112, 113, or 030 45 00 01). **First Aid:** ☎118. **Hospital: Ospedale Civile,** ☎030 399 51.

Internet Access: Telecom Italia, V. Moretto, 46. One computer for public use. Smile, be friendly and quick–email your mom for free. **Black Rose,** V.Cattaneo, 22/A (☎030 280 7704). Two computers in a cozy bar. L10,000 per hr. Open M-Sa 7am-midnight.

Post Office: P. Vittoria, 1 (☎030 444 21). Open M-F 8:15am-5:30pm, Sa 8:15am-1pm. **Postal Code:** 25100.

ACCOMMODATIONS

Brescia's lodgings are reasonably priced, but they fill up before the weekend in summer. Call a week ahead. You'll be fortunate to find any sort of bargain in the historic center. Ask at the tourist office about *agriturismo* options.

Albergo San Marco, V. Spalto S. Marco, 15 (☎030 304 55 41). From the station take V. Foppa and turn right onto V. XX Settembre. Take the next left and turn right onto V. V. Emanuele, which continues to the hotel. 7 simple and stuffy rooms–free charming traffic symphony below. Breakfast L3000. Singles L38,000; doubles L63,000. V, MC, AmEx, Diners.

Albergo Regine, C. Magenta, 14 (☎030 375 78 81; fax 030 454 00), 2 blocks from the central *piazza*. From V. Gramsci, follow C. Zandarelli until it turns into C. Magenta. A wood-finished lobby leads to 30 spotless and quiet rooms. Breakfast included. Singles L60,000; doubles L110,000.

Albergo Stazione, V. Stazione, 15-17 (☎030 377 46 14; fax 030 377 39 95). A 2min. walk from the station down an unlikely alley, this convenient hotel has 36 clean rooms with phone and TV. At night, women should exercise caution in this area. Singles L50,000, with bath L70,000; doubles L80,000, with bath L105,000. V, MC.

FOOD

Whatever and wherever you choose to eat, be sure to sample some of the local wines. *Tocai di San Martino della Battaglia* (a dry white wine), *groppello* (a medium red), and *botticino* (a dry red of medium age) are all favorites in Brescia and beyond. There is a street market for everything on Saturday mornings at P. Loggia. For inexpensive staples, seek out the open-air vendors in P. Mercato. (Open Tu-F 8:30am-6pm, M and Sa mornings.) **Supermercato PAM,** V. Porcellaga, 26, is on a continuation of C. M. della Libertà. (Open M 2-8pm, Tu-Sa 9am-8pm.)

Ristorante/Pizzeria Cavour, C. Cavour, 56 (☎030 240 09 00), off C. Magenta. Diverse waitstaff serves great pizza and pasta dishes at reasonable prices. Try the *pizza cavour* with tomatoes, mozzarella, *pancetta,* and basil, all cooked in the wood-burning oven. Pizza from L7000, *primi* L8-13,000, large assortment of *dolci* (sweets) L4000. Cover L3000. Open W-M 10am-3pm and 6:30pm-1am. V, Diners.

Bar Code, P. P. Sesto, 24 (☎030 377 17 12), just across from the *duomo*. The local place to be seen. Inside, a trendy black and white interior–outside, seating with a view of the castle. Eat your *panini* on the fountain steps while locals show off their motorbikes. Open Tu-Sa 7:30am-2am, Su 9:30am-2am.

Trattoria il Muretto, V. Antiche Muro, 5 (☎030 28 00 77), off V. Mazzini. A bit more elegant. Red-checked tablecloths and constantly crooning Italian pop radio characterize this typical tavern. Outside tables in a quiet pedestrian street. As an *antipasto,* help yourself to the *buffet di verdure* (L7000), colorful plates of various vegetables simmered in olive oil. *Primi* from L7000, *secondi* from L10,000. Open Tu-Sa noon-3pm and 7-11pm, M noon-2:30pm.

Ristorante San Marco, V. Spalto S. Marco, 15 (☎030 304 55 41). See **Albergo San Marco,** above, for directions. The wooden ceiling-beams and whitewashed walls create a cheerful atmosphere. *Primi* from L9000 are a meal in and of themselves. *Secondi* from L15,000. Cover L3000. Open M-Sa noon-2:30pm and 7:30-10pm.

SIGHTS

DUOMO NUOVO AND ROTONDA. The Brescians were not content with only one *duomo*, so they built two. The new and the old, or the grandiose and the *piccolo*, stand in intimate competition in the adjacent facades of **Duomo Nuovo** (1604-1825) and the **Rotonda** (old duomo), also called Cathedral of St. Maria Assunta. The

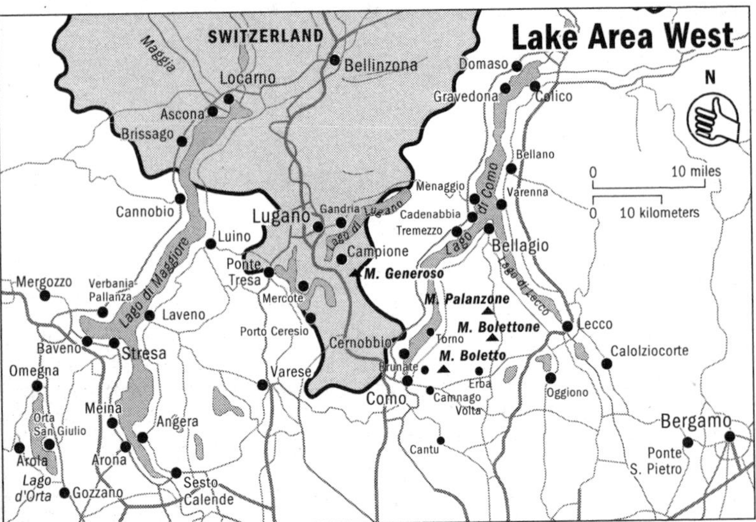

BRESCIAN BOUNTY. Some of Brescia's museums have settled on a standard museum admission (adults L5000 each, organized student groups free) as well as standard hours (June-Sept. Tu-Su 10am-5pm; Oct.-May Tu-Su 9:30am-1pm and 2:30-5pm). They've also implemented a museum "hotline," the Centro Museale Bresciano (☎800 762 811). The museums that participate in this standardized admission are Monasterio di San Salvatore and Santa Giulia, Pinacoteca Tosio-Martinengo, Museo delle Armi, and Museo del Risorgimento.

more recent partner is a gargantuan Rococo structure with Corinthian columns and the third highest dome in Italy. The 11th-century *rotonda* is a simple Romanesque structure with a squat, round tower, a pointed tile roof, and a unique interior reminiscent of a secret and spooky temple below ground. All that remains of the 8th-century basilica formerly occupying this spot is the crypt of S. Filastrio. *(In P. Paolo IV, a.k.a. P. Duomo. From P. della Vittoria, take the path through the archways and under the clocktower. Proper clothing necessary.)*

TEATRO GRANDE. A true pearl of Brescia, this Baroque theater glitters with gold *stuccato* ornamentations set off by red seats and carpet. Bresciani claim that it is aesthetically superior to Milan's La Scala. Check out the adjacent glamorous *ridotto*. This truly is a mecca not only for music fans but for everyone who appreciates architectural beauty. *(C. Zanardeli, 9. From P.della Vittoria go down V. Gramsci 2 blocks and take a left on C. Zanardeli. ☎030 297 9311. Visits only with reservations.)*

PIAZZA DELLA LOGGIA. From C. Palestro, a pedestrian-only window-shopper's haven, walk to the Fascist fabricated P. della Vittoria. Continue past the enormous post office to the more important P. della Loggia, built when Venice ruled the city. On one side of the *piazza* stands the **Torre dell'Orologio,** modeled after the tower in Venice's P. San Marco (p. 214), complete with an astronomic clock covered with suns and stars. Across from the tower, the Renaissance **loggia** (arcade) houses lesser-known paintings from the 16th century.

PINACOTECA TOSIO-MARTINENGO. The Pinacoteca is one of Brescia's principal artistic attractions. This unadorned, 22-room *palazzo* displays a fine collection of works by Bresciani masters (notably Moretto), as well as Raphael's *Cristo Benedicente.* The collection is enriched with works by Veneziano, Clouet, Foppa, and Lotto. *(From P. della Loggia go down south to P. Vittoria to V. A. Gramsci. Turn left on V. Moretto and the Pinacoteca is at the end of the street.)*

TEMPIO CAPITOLINO. Fragments of Brescia's classical roots are sprinkled on V. dei Musei. The Roman colony of Brixia lies buried beneath the overgrown greenery in the **Piazza del Foro.** Between the large, dark buildings stand the remaining pieces of Emperor Vespasian's vast Tempio Capitolino. *(From P. Paolo VI, with your back to the duomo, take V. Mazzini to the left, and turn right on V. dei Musei.)*

MUSEO DELLA CITTA. This former monastery, Monasterio di San Salvatore e Santa Giulia, served as the final retreat for Charlemagne's ex-wife Ermengarda and now houses artistic and archeological representations of the history of Brescia. The museum's Oratorio de S. Maria in Solario displays a bronze *Winged Victory* and the precious 8th-century *Cross of Desiderius*, encased in silver, jewels, and cameos. *(On V. dei Musei, a few paces farther down from the Tempio Capitolino. Open June-Sept. Sa-Th 10am-8pm, F 10am-10pm; Oct.-May Tu-Su 9:30am-5:30pm.)*

FESTIVALS

Most of Brescia's high-brow cultural events occur in the splendor of the **Teatro Grande.** The annual **Stagione di Prosa,** a series of dramatic performances, runs from December to April. From April to June, the focus shifts to the **Festivale Pianistico Internazionale,** co-hosted by nearby Bergamo. Pick up a schedule at the tourist office, or call the **Centro Teatrale Bresciano** (☎035 377 11 11).

THE LAKE COUNTRY

For years, Stendhal's drippiest descriptions of lakes, flowers, and mountains lulled even the most energetic readers to sleep. Alas! You too will ooze florid prose when you visit the author's place of inspiration, the Italian Lake Country. Less effusive writers, such as Nietzsche, Wordsworth, and Hesse have also found refuge in the silence of the majestic mountains and the clear waters below. Diverse masses of tourists grant distinct personality to each of the lakes. A young German crowd races to the conveniently located Lake Garda, with limitless windsurfing opportunities by day and an assortment of nightclubs by night. Palatial luxury hotels line Lake Maggiore's sleepy shores. This honeymooners' spot surrounds the Borromean Islands, renowned for their fantastic palaces, exotic gardens, and wandering white peacocks. Lake Como produces the silk often sported by sophisticated Milanese. Long a playground for the rich and famous, its romantic shore also hosts three well-run (and pleasingly inexpensive) hostels. Swimmers prefer the cleaner waters of Garda and Orta, but any lake will do for lounging. Few spots are as perfect for an afternoon of thoughtful reflection or the composition of gooey prose.

HIGHLIGHTS OF THE LAKE COUNTRY

JUMP into Villa D'Este's floating lake pool in **Cernobbio** (p. 131).

IDLE AWAY an afternoon on the tranquil shores of **Lago Maggiore** (p. 136) or take a bike trip around any of the lakes.

STRUT with peacocks in the exotic gardens of the **Borromean Islands** (p. 139).

LAKE COMO (LAGO DI COMO)

Though an unworldly aura lingers over the northern reaches of Europe's deepest lake (410m), Lake Como is not a figment of your imagination. Bougainvillea and lavish villas adorn Lake Como's backdrop, warmed by the sun and cooled by lakeside breezes. Three long lakes form the forked Lake Como, joining at the four towns of Centro Lago: Bellagio, Tremezzo, Menaggio, and Varenna. These four towns, which are smaller than Como, make for an even more relaxing stay than their more industrial neighbor. Villages cover the dense green slopes—drop your baggage, hop on a bus or ferry, and step off whenever a villa, castle, garden, vinery, restaurant, or small town beckons.

Como, the largest town on the lake, makes an ideal transportation hub. Trains from Milan and Venice service the town (see below). From Como, take the C-10 bus near Ferrovia Nord to Tremezzo or Menaggio (1hr., last bus at 10:15pm, L4700). Hourly buses also serve Varenna and Bellagio (1hr., L5000). If you prefer to splurge, take the romantic boat trip from Como's P. Cavour to any of these towns. Varenna and Menaggio are alternate bases for exploring the lake. From Milan, take a train to Varenna (direction: Sondrio) and then a ferry to your town of choice. From Lugano, take Italian bus C-12 to Menaggio (1hr., last bus 6:45pm). A day pass, good for travel throughout the center lake district, costs L15,000.

COMO ☎031

Situated on the southwest tip of the lake, at the receiving end of the Milan rail line, Como is the lake's token semi-industrialized town, where Allessandro Volta was born and where Terragni has immortalized his Fascist architecture. Famous for silk manufacturing, the town has managed to maintain the languorous atmosphere of the smaller lake towns. While swimmers should head up the lake for cleaner waters, Como's harbor permits boats to dock. After dinner, the entire city migrates to the waterfront for a *passeggiata* among the wisteria of the 18th-century villas.

TRANSPORTATION

Trains: Stazione San Giovanni (☎0147 88 80 88). To: **Milan** Centrale (1hr., every 30min. 4:37am-11:45pm, L9000) and **Venice** S. Lucia (4hr., every hr. 4:37am-10:24pm, L39,700) via **Milan. Luggage storage:** L5000 for 12hr.; open daily 6am-8pm. **Ferrovia Nord (Como Nord),** by P. Matteotti, only serves Stazione Nord (Cadorna) in **Milan** (1hr., every hr. 5:44am-9:40pm, L5500).

Buses: SPT (☎031 24 72 47), on P. Matteotti. To: **Menaggio** (1hr., every hr. 7:10am-10:30pm, L4700); **Bellagio** (1hr., every hr. 6:25am-8:12pm, L4400); **Gravedona** (2hr., every hr. 7:10am-6:40pm, L6900); and **Bergamo** (2hr., every hr. 6:50am-7:40pm, L8300). Ticket office open daily 6am-8:15pm. Info open M-F 8am-noon and 2-6pm, Sa 8am-noon.

Ferries: Navigazione Lago di Como (☎031 57 92 11). Departs daily to all lake towns from the piers along Lungo Lario Trieste in front of P. Cavour. One-way L2400-14,200. Pick up the booklet *Orari* for a complete listing of departures.

Public Transportation: Bus tickets at *tabacchi,* the bus station, or the hostel (L1500).

Taxis: Radio Taxi (☎031 26 15 15).

ORIENTATION AND PRACTICAL INFORMATION

From Como's **Stazione San Giovanni,** head down the stairs, straight ahead, and through the little park. Take **Via Fratelli Ricchi** on your left and then take a right on **Viale Fratelli Rosselli,** which turns into **Lungo Lario Trento** winding its way around the mouth of the lake towards the main square, **Piazza Cavour.** To get to the commercial center from P. Cavour, take **Via Plinio** to **Piazza Duomo,** where it becomes **Via Vittorio Emanuele.** To reach the **bus station** and **Stazione Ferrovia Nord** near P. Matteotti, turn right when facing the lake from P. Cavour.

TOURIST, FINANCIAL, AND LOCAL SERVICES

Tourist Office: P. Cavour, 16 (☎031 26 97 12; fax 031 24 01 11; email lakecomo@tin.it; www.lakecomo.com), in the largest lakeside *piazza* near the ferry dock. Maps and extensive info. Ask for hiking info. Helpful multilingual staff speaks English and makes hotel reservations. Open M-Sa 9am-1pm and 2:30-6pm.

Currency Exchange: Banca Nazionale del Lavoro, P. Cavour, 33 (☎031 31 31), across from the tourist office, has dependable rates and a 24hr. **ATM.** Open M-F 8:20am-1:20pm and 2:30-4pm. Also at the tourist office, train station, and post office.

Bike Rental: The hostel rents mountain bikes for L20,000 per day.

Swimming Pool: Lido Villa Olmo (☎031 57 08 71). Large lawn area for sunbathing and a sandy stretch below. Tops not required, but bathing caps are. 3 pools, including one for kids. L9000, L5000 if you buy tickets at the youth hostel. Open daily 10am-6pm.

EMERGENCY AND COMMUNICATIONS

Emergencies: ☎113. **Police:** V. Roosevelt, 7 (☎031 31 71). **Ambulance:** ☎118. **Hospital: Ospedale Valduce,** V. Dante, 11 (☎031 32 41 11); **Ospedale Sant'Anna,** V. Napoleana, 60 (☎031 58 51 11).

Pharmacy: Farmacia Centrale, V. Plinio, 1 (☎031 42 04), off P. Cavour. Open Tu-Su 8:30am-12:30pm and 3:30-7:30pm. List of pharmacies with night service posted.

Internet Access: Bar Black Panther, V. Garibaldi, 59 (☎031 26 65 35). From P. Cavour walk through V. Fontana to P. Volta and take V. Garibaldi straight ahead. Check email with Huey Newton. 2 computers. L9000 per hr. Open Tu-Su 7am-11:30pm. **Lauritel,** V. V. Emanuele II, 93 (☎031 24 27 52; email info@lauritel.com), through the big green doors and to the left. L10,000 per hr. Open M 2:30-6:30pm, Tu-Sa 9am-6:30pm.

Post Office: V. T. Gallio, 4 (☎031 27 73 020). Open M-Sa 8:15am-6pm. Also at V. V. Emanuele II, 99 (☎031 26 02 10), in the center of town. Open M-F 8:10am-5:30pm, Sa 8:10am-1pm. **Postal Code:** 22100.

ACCOMMODATIONS

In Riva al Lago, P. Matteotti, 4 (☎031 30 23 33; email inrivalago@promoenet.it; www.lagodicomo.com/hostels/inrivaallago.html), behind the bus stop. Centrally located. 25 modern and immaculate rooms, all with phone. English spoken. Internet access L2000 per hr. Breakfast L5000. Reserve ahead. Singles L45,000, with bath and TV L75,000; doubles L70,000, with bath and TV L90-100,000. V, MC, AmEx, Diners.

Ostello Villa Olmo (HI), V. Bellinzona, 2 (☎/fax 031 57 38 00; email hostellocomo@tin.it), behind Villa Olmo. From Stazione S. Giovanni, turn left and walk 20min. down V. Borgo Vico. Otherwise take bus #1, 6, or 11 to Villa Olmo (L1500). Lively, fun, and down-to-earth. Run by a wonderful, multilingual couple, the hostel offers a bar, bag lunches (L10,000), incredible dinners (L16,000), and discounts on assorted tickets. Crowded rooms come with personal locker and sheets. English and French spoken. Mountain bike rentals L20,000 per day. Breakfast included. Self-service laundry L5000; ironing L1000. Lockout after 10am. Strict curfew 11:30pm. Reserve ahead. Open Mar-Nov. daily 7-10am and 4-11:30pm. Dorms L20,000.

Protezione della Giovane (ISJGIF), V. Borgovico, 182 (☎031 57 43 90 or 031 57 35 40), on the way to the youth hostel, on the right side. Take bus #1, 6, or 11. Run by nuns; 18+ women only. Clean, with crucifixes everywhere. Free kitchen use. Laundry L4000 per load. Curfew 10:30pm. 52 rooms. Singles or doubles without bath L24,000 per person for 1st 3 nights, L20,000 for the 4th-15th night.

Albergo Sociale, V. Maestri Comacini, 8 (☎031 26 40 42), on the right side of the *duomo,* above a restaurant. Unadorned rooms and small beds. Central location. Call ahead. 1 single without bath L35,000; 4 doubles L65,000, 1 with bath L85,000. V, MC, AmEx, Diners.

Albergo Piazzolo, V. Indipendenza, 65 (☎031 27 21 86). From P. Cavour take V. Bonta which becomes V. Boldini and V. Luni. Pedestrian only V. Indipendenza is on the right. Above a restaurant. Large windows create a breeze in the sparsely furnished rooms. 3 doubles with bath L95,000; 1 quad L160,000. V, MC, AmEx, Diners.

Hotel Marco's, Lungo Lario Trieste, 62 (☎031 30 36 28; fax 031 30 23 42). A 3-star hotel near the water, Hotel Marco's caters to those willing to spend more for a taste of the high life. 11 large rooms have French windows and lake views. Breakfast included. Singles L125,000; doubles L170,000; triples L200,000. V, MC, AmEx, Diners.

FOOD

Many of Como's residents lunch *alla milanese*, downing a quick, satisfying meal in an inexpensive self-service joint. Unfortunately, finding an affordable evening meal can be a challenge. Picnickers will appreciate the **G.S. supermarket** on the corner of V. Fratelli Recchi and V. Fratelli Roselli, across from the park. (☎031 57 08 95. Open M 2-8pm, Tu-Sa 8am-8pm, Su 10am-6pm.) Lakeside benches are great for *al fresco* dining. Huge loaves of *resca* (the typical Como sweet bread, bursting with dried fruit) or the harder, cake-like *matalok* complement picnics; pick them up at **Beretta Il Fornaio,** V. Fratelli Rosselli, 26a, a bright, bustling bakery. (Open M 7:30am-1pm, Tu-Sa 7:30am-1pm and 3:30-7:30pm.) The takeout haven **Gran Mercato,** P. Matteotti, 3, sells great breads, cheeses, and meats. (☎031 30 47 50. Open M 8:30am-1pm, Tu-F 8:30am-1pm and 3-7:30pm, Sa 8am-7:30pm.) An **outdoor market** is held Tuesday and Thursday mornings and all day Saturday in P. Vittoria.

Taverna Spagnola, V. Grassi, 33 (☎031 27 24 60) off P. Volta. From P. Cavour take V. Fontana to P. Volta. This small, lively restaurant has large portions and a homey, energetic atmosphere. Try the *penne al'arrabiata* or the *tagliatele*. Pizza L7-13,000, *primi* L7-10,000, *secondi* L15-20,000. Great homemade *tiramisù* L5000. Paulaner beer L5000. Cover L2000. Open Th-Tu noon-2:30pm and 7pm-midnight. V, MC, AmEx.

Free Break Self-Service, V. Innocenzo XI, 19 (☎031 26 14 49). Head down the stairs from the train station S. Giovanni, through the park, and to the right. Modern joint with Charlie Chaplin and Abbott and Costello on the walls. Decent salad choices. Big bowls of spaghetti and red sauce L6000. *Primi* L4-6000, *secondi* L6-9000. Open M-Sa noon-2:30pm. V, MC, AmEx, Diners.

Ristorante Le Colonne, P. Mazzini, 12 (☎031 26 61 66). Join the throngs for carefully prepared pasta and pizza. Outdoor seating under the canopy in the quiet *piazza*. For a big meal try the *spaghetti all'astrice* (with fish) for L15,000; it's worth the price. Pizza L7-15,000, *primi* L10-20,000. Open W-M noon-2:30pm and 7-9:30pm; in winter W-M noon-2:30pm and 7pm-1am. V, MC, AmEx.

Ristorante/Pizzeria Orologio, V. Foscolo, 11 (☎031 30 45 65), off P. Matteotti. Sleek, modern interior and delicious pizzas for L6-15,000. *Primi* L10-14,000. Cover L3000. Open daily in summer noon-3pm and 6:30pm-2am; in winter Th-Tu noon-3pm and 6:30pm-2am. V, MC, AmEx, Diners.

SIGHTS

DUOMO AND ENVIRONS. Near P. Cavour, Como's newly restored *duomo* was built and rebuilt for four centuries starting in 1397 and houses a magnificent, octagonal dome. As one of Italy's best examples of Gothic-Renaissance fusion, it harmoniously combines Romanesque, Gothic, Renaissance, and Baroque elements. The Rodari brothers' life-like sculptures of the Exodus from Egypt animate the church's exterior. Statues of Como residents Pliny the Elder and Pliny the Younger flank the door. *(Open daily 7am-noon and 3-7pm.)* The sturdy town hall, the 15th-century **Broletto,** with colonnaded windows and multicolored marble balconies, leans up against the *duomo*. **Basilica di San Fedele,** two blocks down V. V. Emanuele II from the *duomo*, bears a resemblance to Ravenna's Byzantine churches—not surprising since the Lombards built the oldest parts of the church (notably the altar and the blind arcade) during the same period. *(Open daily 8am-noon and 3-6pm.)* Just behind the *duomo* and across the rail tracks, Giuseppe Terragni's Casa del Fascio—now called **Palazzo Terragni**—was built from 1934-36 to house the local Fascist government. It has become a world-famous icon of Modernist Italian architecture, quite a contrast to the heavy masonry of typical Fascist architecture.

LAKE AREA. From P. Cavour go left along the waterfront to the pantheon-like **Tempio Voltiano,** dedicated to the inventor of the battery, Alessandro Volta. (☎031 57 47 05. Open Apr.-Sept. Tu-Su 10am-noon and 3-6pm; in winter 10am-noon and 2-

4pm. L4000, groups and children under 6 L2500.) If you wish to see Volta's tomb, take bus #4 from the bus stop or Stazione S. Giovanni to **Camnago Volta** (15 min., every ½hr. 6:20am-8:20pm, L1500). The neoclassical villas lining the lake include the **Villa "La Rotonda"** with its ornamented Rococo stuccato and chandeliers. (Open M-Th 9am-noon and 3-5pm, F 9am-noon.) Farther north is the ambassadorial **Villa Olmo** in the romantic park of the same name. Traditionally the garden is full of couples escorted by Neo-roman statues. (Villa open Apr.-Sept. M-Sa 9am-noon and 3-5pm. Gardens open daily Apr.-Sept. 8am-11pm; Oct.-Mar. 9am-7pm.)

HIKING

Take the *funiculare* (☎031 30 36 08; fax 031 30 25 92) from P. dei Gasperi, 4, at the far end of Lungo Lario Trieste, 715m up to **Brunate** for excellent hiking and scenic views (June-Sept. every 15min. 6am-midnight; Oct.-May every 30min. 6am-10:30pm; L4100, children under 12 L2700; round-trip L7200, children L4500; adult round-trip L5000 if purchased through the hostel). For even more beautiful panoramas, hike up towards **Faro Voltiano** (906m), a lighthouse dedicated to Volta (20min.). It's easy to find; just follow the signs (or take the street that goes up). For a better workout, take the paved, but steeper walkway. You will be able to enjoy a breathtaking view of the Alps and Switzerland, and on a clear day, both Milan and the Matterhorn are visible. Even with occluded skies, you can relish the majesty of the villas of Lake Como.

From Faro Voltiano, another 15 minutes of hiking brings you to **San Maurizio,** and another hour and a half should be enough time to reach **Monte Boletto** (1236m). There is a bus that runs from Brunate to approximately 1km past S. Maurizio and stops by Faro Voltiano (every 30min. 8:15am-6:45pm, L1500). If M. Boletto is not enough for you, stroll for another hour to **Monte Bolettone** (1317m). Whichever peak you choose, the views of Lake Como are stunning; keep in mind that the higher you climb, the farther east you'll be able to see.

Yet another option is to head northwest between S. Maurizio and M. Boletto after the restaurant Baita Carla. The path leads to the town of **Torno** at the lake, 8km north of Como, and a good place to catch a scenic boat ride back to Como (every hr. 6:58am-8:14pm, L3600). In Torno, you might want to check out the **Chiesa di San Giovanni** with its opulent 16th-century portal or the **Villa Pliniana,** 15min. north of the boat dock.

If you are up for more extensive exploration of the mountains east of Como, take bus C40 from the Como bus station to **Erba** (30min., every hr. 7:15am-9:15pm, L4900). From Erba hike to **Caslino D'Erba,** which leads to **Monte Palanzone** (1436m). The hike is said to be the most beautiful in the region.

THE 2½ BILLION LIRE BED The lovely town of **Cernobbio** lies 6km north of Como on the western shore of the lake, a scenic one-hour walk from Villa Olmo. Along the way, villas and castles galore dot the landscape, and the walk offers a gorgeous view of Como and its *duomo.* **Villa Fiori** and **Villa Erba** are the closest villas to Como, but the signature piece is the world-famous **Villa d'Este,** once the luxury vacation home of the Este family of Ferrara and now the most opulent of luxury accommodations. The lush **gardens** of the villa alone merit a trip to Cernobbio. So, if you can't find a bed at the hostels in Como and Mennagio, don't trudge back to Milan. Quash those thoughts of fleeing to Lago Maggiore. Villa D'Este is happy to host you in a unique one-bedroom suite for a mere pittance (L2,500,000,000). To sweeten the deal, you just might dine next to the Queen of England, and there's a good chance your room will have a view of the villa's swimming pool, a unique contraption that floats in the middle of a nearby lake. Don't feel like spending the night? Drop L30,000 for a cup of *espresso* and enjoy the scenery.

MENAGGIO ☎034

A perfect base of operations for the entire Centro Lago, Menaggio is home to beautiful hotels, historic streets, and unbelievable scenery. You can explore Lake Como while staying in Menaggio's youth hostel for a fraction of the cost (and double the character) of any other establishment on the lake.

TRANSPORTATION AND PRACTICAL INFORMATION. **Buses** and **ferries** link Menaggio to the other lake towns (see **Transportation,** p. 128). Ferries run to **Bellagio** (15min., every hr. 6:05am-10:45pm, L4700); **Varenna** (15min., every hr. 6:45am-9:45pm, L4700); and **Como** (2hr., every hr. 11:12am-6:12pm, L11,100). In the town center at **Piazza Garibaldi** the helpful and multilingual **tourist office** has information on hundreds of possible excursions around the lake. (☎034 43 29 24. Open M-Sa 9am-noon and 3-6pm.) P. Garibaldi also houses a **pharmacy** with an automatic telephone that connects to the (rotating) night duty location.

ACCOMMODATIONS. **Ostello La Prinula (HI),** V. IV Novembre, 86, is the best budget value in the lake district and one of the best in Italy. Walk along the shore to the main thoroughfare, pass the gas station, and hike up the less steep of the two inclines (on the right side of the street). A helpful newsletter lists activities including guided hikes, cooking classes, and horseback riding. The hostel provides guests with home-cooked native cuisine (dinner L17,000), family suites, a washing machine (L6000 per load), bike and kayak rental (L18,000 per day), a kitchen, picnic lunch (L10,000) email access (L4000 for 15min.), and free beach access. (☎034 43 23 56; fax 034 43 16 77; email menaggiohostel@mclink.it; www.menaggiohostel.it. Breakfast included. Lockout 10am-5pm. Curfew 11:30pm. Call ahead to reserve. Open Mar.-Oct. Dorms L20,000. Family rooms of 4 beds and private bath L22,000 per person.)

At the Rezzonico stop, 7km north, **Hotel Lauro** offers rooms at fair prices. (☎034 45 00 29. Call ahead. Singles L33,000, with bath L38,000; doubles L55,000, with bath L63,000.) A healthy trek up the lake from the city center, **Camping Lido** (☎034 43 11 50. L8000 per person, L14,000 per tent; shower L1500, pool access L2000) and the adjacent **Camping Europa** (☎034 43 11 87; L7500 per person, L14,000 per tent) both offer decent, inexpensive places to crash. Campers might want to think about traveling farther up the lake to the more scenic Domaso sites.

FOOD AND ENTERTAINMENT. While the fabulous hostel dinner ought to satisfy even the most picky of diners, there are plenty of pizzerias and restaurants in the town proper. Between the town and the hostel there's a mini-mart-cum-grocery-store, **Cappe,** with personal pizzas from L900 (open Tu-Sa 7am-noon and 3:30-7pm, M 7am-noon) and a **creperie** that serves both sweet and savory crepes.

Next to the ferry stop is the liveliest bar in town, the **Tanamana Pub,** V. IV Novembre, 79, with both indoor and outdoor seating. (☎0344 325 58. Open daily 9am-3am.) If you don't have a lockout and want to paint the town red, **Disco Lido Cadde-nabbia** (☎034 45 90 01) is the best place to party this side of Lake Como. It's located between Tremezzo and Menaggio, so take a bus or a cab. Don't get stuck without a ride home—the walk is a nightmare.

SIGHTS AND HIKING. The **Rifugio Menaggio** (☎034 43 72 82) stands 1400m above the lake. From the top, hikers can try the difficult *ferrata* (trails) or make less strenuous trips to **Monte Grona** and the **Chiesa di S. Amate.** Also, be sure to take the one- to two-hour hike (each way) to the picturesque **Sass Corbee Gorge,** just outside of town. Inquire at the tourist office or the hostel for detailed directions, as the trek is complicated.

BELLAGIO ☎031

Favored by the upper-crust of Milanese society, Bellagio is one of Italy's most beautiful lake towns. Its fame extends all the way to Las Vegas, home of the famous Bellagio Hotel. You won't find neon lights or Elvis impersonators in Bellagio, however. Its lakeside promenades, steep streets, and sidewalk cafes lead to silk shops and the villas of Lombard aristocrats.

The **Villa Serbelloni** is not to be confused with the five-star Grand Hotel Villa Serbelloni down the hill. The extensive tour of the villa's garden just above the tourist office is worth the price. (Fax 031 95 15 51. Villa open Apr.-Oct. Tu-Su. L9000. 1½hr. tours Tu-Su 11am and 4pm, weather permitting. Buy tickets in the tourist office 15min. before the tour.) At the other end of town, the lakeside gardens of **Villa Melzi** blossom. The villa is still Duke Lodovico Galarati Scoti's private residence, but the **grounds,** including a chapel and one-room museum with Roman and Napoleonic art, are open to the public. (Open Mar.-Oct. daily 9am-6:30pm. L8000.)

Bellagio isn't all about ritzy hotels and well-manicured villas, however. A trip to the city would be frightfully incomplete without a visit to **Tony's,** Salita Genazzini, 3, a deliciously dilapidated little winery on the southern waterfront, just behind the Kodak shop. The friendly owner claims to be able to drink anyone under the table. (☎031 95 09 35. Open 11:30am-1:30pm and 2:30-7pm.) **Lido di Bellagio,** V. Lugno Lario Marconi, 1 (☎031 95 05 97), a "discobeach," offers live music with evening themes such as the daunting "Don't Eat it Hot at Hip-Hop." Cool off with a dip into the pristine lake nearby.

Expect higher hotel rates in chic Bellagio than in the other lake towns. The most affordable accommodations are at **Albergo Giardinetto,** V. Roncati, 12, just to the left of the tourist office. Simple rooms without baths and a friendly elderly couple will make you forget Bellagio's pretentious atmosphere. (☎031 95 01 68. Singles L50,000; doubles L75,000.) To reach **Hotel Europa,** take a left from the port and walk up the shoreline to the northernmost tip of the hill. Most rooms have a balcony, and the restaurant below offers a L35,000 tourist menu, lasagna for L11,000, and spaghetti for L9000. (☎/fax 031 95 04 71. Doubles with bath L120,000.)

To reach Bellagio from Milan, take a **ferry** from the train station in nearby **Varenna. Buses** also run from **Como.** The tourist office at P. della Chiesa, 14 (☎031 95 02 04), speaks strictly British English and has detailed information about daytrips to various parts of the lake.

VARENNA ☎0341

This ferry port lies on the eastern shore far from the chic crowds of Bellagio. On the ferry ride in, don't miss the view of the beautifully colored houses in the town center. A scenic passageway beside the water connects both sides of Varenna and offers incredible lake vistas. To reach **La Sorgente del Fiumelatte,** the shortest river in Italy, walk past P. San Giorgio and up a raised road past the cemetery. For a shorter excursion, a 20-minute ascent up the hill just past the *piazza* leads to the 12th-century **Castello Vezio.** An old drawbridge connects to the castle's small tower. (Open Mar.-Sept. daily 10am-7pm in good weather. L2000.) The 14th-century **Chiesa di S. Giorgio** looms above the town with late Romanesque simplicity. Catch the rosette window with images of dolphins inside. (Open daily 7am-noon and 2-7pm.) Varenna's most famous sights, however, are the two lakeside gardens of nearby 13th-century convents. **Villa Monastero,** 150m to the right of the church, boasts gorgeous botany in front of a hotel. (Villa open Apr.-Oct. daily 10am-6pm. Gardens L3000, over 65 and under 10 L2000.) Another 100m farther stands the proud **Villa Cipressi,** former weekend home of Lombard aristocrats. (Gardens open Mar.-Oct. daily 9am-7pm. L3000; combined ticket to both villas L5000.)

Piazza San Giorgio, a five-minute walk from the water houses the following: **tourist office** (open May-Sept. M-F 10:15am-12:30pm and 3:30-6:30pm, Su 11am-1:30pm); **bank** (to the right facing the church; open M-F 8:20am-1:20pm and 2:45-3:45pm); **pharmacy** (left of the church; open Th-Tu 9am-12:30pm and 3:30-7:30pm, W 9am-12:30pm); and **post office** (on the water side; open M-F 8am-5:45pm).

LECCO ☎0341

At the eastern base of Lake Como lies this relatively unattractive industrial village, strangely tucked into the mountain. Lecco is most famous for Manzoni's depictions of the area in the romance, *The Promised Brides*. Excellent **hiking** and **rock-climbing** areas surround the town. Rocks form *gulie* (spires) in **Le Grigne.** For more information contact the **Azienda Promozione Turistica del Lecchese,** V. N. Sauro, 6. (☎0341 36 23 60; fax 0341 28 62 31. Open M-Sa 9:30am-noon and 2:30-6pm.)

DOMASO ☎0344

The breezes in this tiny town on the North Lake create perfect windsurfing. Surfers flock to the relaxing **Ostello della Gioventù (HI),** V. Case Sparse, 12, on the water. The modern hostel lies 50km (2hr.) from Como by bus and is also accessible by boat. (☎0344 974 49; fax 0344 975 75. Breakfast included. Low windsurfing and mountain biking rates through the hostel. Internet access L12,000. Curfew midnight. Open Mar.-Oct. Dorms L20,000.) Beautiful **campsites** surround the northwest coast of the lake; Domaso itself has 12, including the scenic **Europa** (☎/fax 0344 960 44; L9000 per person, L7500 per tent) and **Italia 90** (☎0344 834 46; L7200 per person, L14,500 per tent). Both are crowded but close to the water. The Como tourist office has complete details.)

Italy's **international dialing prefix** is 00. Switzerland's **country code** is 41, and the **city code** for both Lugano and Locarno is 091. Remember to drop the 0 at the beginning of the city code when calling internationally. Exchange rates for the **Swiss Franc (SFr)** are as follows: 1SFr = US$0.58, US$1 = 1.72SFr.; 1SFr = L1252, L1000 = 0.80SFr.

NEAR LAKE COMO: LUGANO, SWITZERLAND ☎091

Lugano, Switzerland's third-largest banking center, rests in the crevassed valley between San Salvatore and Monte Brè. Warmed by a Mediterranean climate, Lugano's shady streets are lined with tiles, climbing vines, and wildflowers.

TRANSPORTATION AND PRACTICAL INFORMATION. To reach Lugano by **car,** take Rte. N2/E35. Frequent **buses** run to Lugano from **Menaggio** (2hr., 8 per day, L7600). The 15-minute downhill walk from the train station to the arcaded **Piazza della Riforma,** the town's center, winds through Lugano's large pedestrian zone. For those who would rather avoid the walk, a **cable car** runs between the train station and the waterfront **Piazza Cioccaro** (5:20am-11:50pm, 0.90SFr). The **tourist office** is in the Palazzo Civico, Riva Albertolli, at the corner of P. Rezzonico. From the station, cross the footbridge labeled "Centro" and proceed down V. Cattedrale straight through P. Cioccaro as it turns into V. Pessina. Turn left on V. dei Pesci and left on Riva Via Vela, which becomes Riva Giocondo Albertolli. The office is just past the fountain on the left, across the street from the ferry launch. (☎091 913 32 32; fax 091 922 76 53; email info@lugano-tourism.ch; www.lugano-tourism.ch. Open Apr.-Oct. M-F 9am-6:30pm, Sa 9am-12:30pm and 1:30-5pm, Su 10am-2pm; Nov.-Mar. M-F 9am-12:30pm and 1:30-5:30pm.)

ACCOMMODATIONS. Travelers flock to Lugano's two extraordinary youth hostels, both built from luxury villas. Try **Hotel Montarina,** 1 Via Montarina, just behind the train station. Walk 200m to the right from the station, cross the tracks, and walk one minute uphill. This palm-tree-enveloped independent hostel attracts young families and students with its swimming pool, groomed grounds, ping-pong, chandeliered reading room, and terrace with a view. The dorms can get rowdy in summer, when vacationing youth party hard. (☎091 966 72 72; fax 091 966 00 17; email info@montarina.ch; www.montarina.ch. Buffet breakfast 12SFr. Sheets 4SFr. Parking available. Reception 8am-10pm. Open Mar.-Oct. Dorms 25SFr; singles 50-65SFr; doubles 100SFr, with bath 120SFr.) The **Ostello della Gioventù (HI),**

Lugano-Savosa, 13 Via Cantonale, is just as good. Note: there are two streets called V. Cantonale, one in downtown Lugano and one in Savosa, where the hostel is. Take bus #5 (walk 350m in to the left of the station, cross the street to get to the bus stop) to "Crocifisso" (6th stop), backtrack a bit, and turn left up V. Cantonale. A former luxury villa, this sprawling hostel has secluded gardens, a pool with a waterslide, and an elegant atmosphere. (☎ 091 966 27 28; fax 091 968 23 63. Breakfast 7SFr. Kitchen 1SFr. Laundry 5SFr. Reception 7am-12:30pm and 3-10pm. Curfew 10pm; keys available. Reserve ahead. Open mid-Mar. to Oct. Dorms 23SFr; singles 35SFr, with kitchenette 45SFr; doubles 56SFr, with kitchenette 70SFr.)

FOOD. Lugano's many outdoor restaurants and cafes pay homage to the canton's Italian heritage, serving up plates of *penne* and *gnocchi* and freshly spun pizzas. Lugano's specialty is (visibly) sausage. For some quick *al fresco* shopping and eating, V. Pessina, off P. Riforma, livens up at midday with outdoor sandwich and fruit shops. The **Salumeria,** V. Pessina, 12, is one of the better ones—you can buy some of the sausage there too. **The Migros,** V. Pretoria, 15, is two blocks left of the post office, down V. Pretorio in the center of town, and offers fresh pasta and delicious *ciabatta* (a crusty Italian bread). The **food court** on the ground floor saves the near-penniless with huge slices of pizza (from 2.50SFr) and sandwiches (from 2.30SFr). (Open M-F 8am-6:30pm, Sa 7:30am-5pm.) There is a **public market** in P. della Riforma that sells seafood, produce, and veggie sandwiches (4SFr). (Open Tu and F 7am-noon.) Romance awaits at **La Tinèra,** V. dei Gorini, 2, behind Credit Suisse in P. della Riforma. Tucked away in an alley off a cobblestone road, this romantically low-lit underground restaurant has great daily specials for 12-18SFr. (☎ 091 923 52 19. Open M-Sa 8:30am-3pm and 5:30-11pm. V, MC, AmEx.)

SIGHTS AND MUSEUMS. The frescoes of the 16th-century **Cattedrale San Lorenzo,** just below the train station, gleam with colors that are still vivid despite their advanced age. The frescoes on the west wall date from the 13th-century. But Lugano's most spectacular fresco is Bernardio Luini's gargantuan **Crucifixion** which was painted in 1529 and is now in the **Chiesa Santa Maria degli Angioli,** to the right of the tourist office on the waterfront. Aside from the churches, Lugano's best known cultural attractions are its art museums—past and present. The largest and most fun museum is the **Museo Cantonale d'Arte,** which has a permanent collection of 19th- and 20th-century art, including works by Swiss artists Vela, Ciseri, Franzoni, and Klee. The 1st and 2nd floors are highly entertaining and feel, in places, like mirrored halls in an amusement park. The third floor, however, is a more sedate collection of pencil drawings. *(V. Canova, 10, across from the Chiesa San Rocco. ☎ 091 910 47 80. Open Tu 2-5pm, W-Su 10am-5pm. Special exhibits 10SFr, students 7SFr; permanent collection 7SFr, students 5SFr.)*

PARKS, GARDENS, AND HIKES. Lugano's waterfront parks are ideal places for introspection or play. The **Belvedere,** on Quai Riva Caccia, is an enormous sculpture garden with an emphasis on modernist metalwork. On sunny afternoons, enthusiasts gather here for open-air chess tournaments. The garden stretches toward Paradiso along the lakeside promenade to the right of the tourist office. In the other direction, the less whimsical but more serene **Parco Civico** is brightened by flower beds along the water and trees that reach down with willowy, long arms to touch the lake. Backpackers have been known to crash here (illegally). (Open Mar. 1-Oct. 31 6:30am-11:30pm; Nov. 1-Feb. 28 7am-9pm.)

Though the tops of the Ticinese mountains are cluttered with tourists, the unhampered views stretch into Italy. The tourist office and Hotel Montarina both have topographical maps and trail guides. The cheapest and most rewarding hike goes to **Monte Boglio,** a five-hour round-trip that can be extended over two days by staying at the Pairolhütte (ask at hostels or tourist office for more information).

ENTERTAINMENT. The arcades of the town *piazze* fill at night with people taking a *passaggio*, or a stroll around the city center in their best duds. The outdoor cafes of P. della Riforma are especially lively. Stop in at the Pave Pub, Riva Albertolli 1, a self-proclaimed *museo di birra* (beer museum), offering 50 different beers with a lakeside view of the fountains and a decidedly un-museum like liveliness. (☎091 922 07 70. Beers start at 4-5SFr. Open 11am-1am.) For a change of pace head down the V. Pretorio from P. Dante and turn left on V. A. Vanoni for the Biblio-Café Tra, 3 V. Vanoni. This laid-back cafe evokes a bit of leftist Spain. Locals and subversives consume 3.40SFr beers while surfing the web for 8SFr per hr. (☎091 923 23 05. Open M-Th 9am-midnight, F 9am-1am, Sa 5pm-1am.)

LAKE MAGGIORE (LAGO MAGGIORE)

Without the tourist frenzy of its easterly neighbors, Lake Maggiore cradles similar temperate mountain waters and idyllic shores. A glaze of opulence coats the air, and a stroll past any of the grandiose shore-side hotels reveals Maggiore as the preferred watering hole of the elite. Modest *pensioni* hide in the shadows of their multi-storied cousins, allowing travelers to enjoy the lake at reasonable prices. Stresa is the most convenient base for exploring the Borromean Islands.

STRESA ☎0323

Stresa retains much of the manicured charm that lured visitors in droves during the 19th and early 20th centuries. Art nouveau hotels and blooming hydrangeas line the waterfront, giving the little town a romantic, old-fashioned appearance. Splendid views of the lake and mountains await around each bend of the cobblestone streets. Stresa is a resort town, filled with Italian, French, English, American, and German tourists; there is little to do but join the vacationing throngs.

TRANSPORTATION AND PRACTICAL INFORMATION. Stresa lies only an hour from Milan on the Milan-Domodossola train line (every hr.; L8200, intercity supplement L6000; ticket office open M-F 6:10am-12:10pm and 12:50-8:10pm, Sa 7am-2pm, Su 12:50-8:10pm). If the office is closed, you can purchase your ticket on board with no surcharge. Ferries via **Isola Bella** (5min.), **Isola Superiore** (10min.), and **Isola Madre** (30min.) run to **Verbania-Pallanza** (35min., every 30min. 7:10am-7pm, return ticket L12,400). The **regional APTL tourist office** is at V. Principe Tommaso, 70/72. From the station, turn right and walk down the hill on V. Carducci, which becomes V. Gignous; V. P. Tommaso is on the left. (☎0323 30 416; fax 0323 93 43 35. Office open M-F 8:30am-12:30pm and 3-6:15pm.) The **local IAT tourist office** is at V. Canonica, 8, just off Palazzo dei Congressi. (☎/fax 0323 31 308. Open daily 10am-noon and 3-6:30pm.) English is spoken at both offices. For **currency exchange** and a 24-hour **ATM,** try **Banca Popolare di Intra,** C. Umberto I, 1, just off P. Marconi. (☎0323 30 330. Open M-F 8:10am-1:10pm and 2:30-4pm.) In case of **emergency** contact **first aid** (☎0323 31 844), an **ambulance** (☎0323 33 360), or the **police** (☎112). The **post office** is at V. A. Bolongaro, 44, near P. Rossi. (☎0323 30 065. Open M-F 8:15am-6pm, Sa 8:15am-noon.) **Postal Code:** 28838.

ACCOMMODATIONS. **Orsola Meublé,** V. Duchessa di Genova, 45, offers affordable blue-tiled rooms with balconies. From the station, turn right, walk downhill to the intersection, and turn left. (☎0323 31 087; fax 0323 93 31 21. Breakfast included. Singles L50,000, with bath L60,000; doubles L80,000, with bath L100,000. V, MC, AmEx, Diners.) **Hotel Mon Toc,** V. Duchessa di Genova, 67/69, has beautiful, breezy rooms, all with bath, TV, and telephone. Take a right out of the station and another at the intersection under the tracks. (☎0323 302 82; fax 0323 93 38 60. Breakfast L15,000. 6 singles L70,000; 7 doubles L110,000. V, MC, AmEx, Diners.) **Hotel Ariston,** C. Italia, 60, offers a convenient location along the water and a tranquil lake view. Go up the steps before the gas station and through the gates to well-furnished two-star rooms, all with bath. (☎/fax 0323 31 195. Restaurant below. Breakfast included. Reception open daily 7:30am-1am. Ask for key if going out. Singles with bath L75,000; doubles with bath L130,000. Half-pension L10,000 extra per person; full-pension L25,000. V, MC, AmEx, Diners.)

FOOD. Salumeria Bianchetti Augusto, V. Mazzini, 1, sells large *panini* (L3500-4000), pizza by the slice (L2800-4000), *foccacia* (L1800-3800), and cold cuts. (☎0323 30 402. Open daily 8am-8pm. V, MC, AmEx.) **Taverna del Pappagallo,** V. P. Margherita, 46, serves delicious, affordable pasta and crisp, brick-oven pizza (L7-13,000) in a delightful interior and a lovely garden. (☎0323 304 11. *Primi* L7-14,000, *secondi* L18-22,000. Cover L3000. Open Th-M 11:30am-2:30pm and 6:30-10:30pm.) **Pizza D.O.C.,** C. Italia, 60, provides inexpensive food served by busy waiters and a delightful lakeside view on the balcony of the Hotel Ariston. Seventy-five inventive kinds of pizza (L7-15,000) and free delivery make this place a winner. (☎0323 30 000; fax 0323 31 195. *Primi* L10-12,000, *secondi* L12-16,000. Desserts L6000. Open daily noon-2pm and 7pm-midnight. V, MC, AmEx.) Stock up on necessities at the **GS supermarket,** V. Roma, 11. Pizza slices (from L2200) entice from behind the registers. (Open M-Sa 8:30am-1pm and 3-7:30pm, Su 8:30am-12:30pm).

ENTERTAINMENT AND FESTIVALS. The **L'Idrovolante Cafe,** P. Lido, 6, a local major hangout, offers live music including soul, R&B, and blues. (☎0323 313 84. Open daily 7:30am-1:30am.) Facing the water at the port, turn left and take V. G. Borromeao along the shore for 20 minutes. If you can't dance and don't like music, head to the **Irish Bar,** V. P. Margherita, 9 (☎0323 310 54), for a pint o' Guinness (L8000) and a pair of smiling Irish eyes. From the last week in August to the third week in September, some of the finest orchestras and soloists in the world gather for the internationally acclaimed **Settimane Musicali di Stresa e del Lago Maggiore** (tickets L30-100,000, students from L10,000). For info, contact the ticket office at V. Canonica, 6 (☎0323 310 95 or 0323 304 59; fax 0323 330 06).

NEAR STRESA

PALLANZA ☎0323

Flowers cover this small town as far as the eye can see (and the nose can smell). To reach Pallanza from Como without heading back to Milan, take a **train** from **Como** Stazione Nord to **Saronna,** change trains and head to **Laveno** (combined ticket L4800). From there, take a ferry to **Intra,** and switch ferries to Pallanza (combined return ticket L12,000; last ferry at 7pm). If local trains aren't your style, take the train from Milan to Stresa and then take a ferry to Pallanza. **Ferries** via **Isola Madra** (5min.), **Isola Superiore** (20min.), and **Isola Bella** (25min.) go to **Stresa** (35min.; every 30min. 7:45am-6:50pm; L12,400, children L8000).

The town offers little in terms of sights and entertainment, but the **tourist office,** C. Zanitello, 8, five minutes to the right when facing inland from the port, helps plan excursions to the islands. (Open M-Sa 9am-12:30pm and 3-6pm, Su 9am-noon.) **Banca Popolare di Intra,** P. Garibaldi, 20, with a 24-hour **ATM** is a little to the right as you exit the boat. (Open M-F 8:20am-1:20pm, and Sa-Su 8:20-11:50am.)

Only a year old, **Ostello Verbania Internazionale (HI),** V. alle Rose, 7, in a quiet house 10-15 minutes from the Borromean Island ferries, offers extremely modern and clean facilities with ping-pong, pool, foosball, arcade games, TV room, and gigantic bathrooms. After exiting the ferry, turn right and walk for five minutes along the water to V. V. Veneto, just past the tourist office. Take a left on V. Panoramica, keep walking up the hill, continue around the bend, and take your last right. The hostel is 50m on the left. (☎0323 50 16 48; fax 0323 50 78 77. Kitchen available. Breakfast included. Lunch and dinner L14,000 each. Lockout 11am-4pm. Curfew midnight. Reception 8-11am, 4-5:30pm, and 10-11pm. Dorms with sheets and locker L24,000; 3 doubles with bath L56,000.) From the hostel towards Intra lies the beautiful **Villa Taranto.** Its fairy-tale gardens with waterfalls, pools, and fountains stand as a fine example of botanical art. Expect lots of color and exotic plants and flowers. (☎0323 55 66 67; fax 0323 40 45 55. Open Apr.-Oct. daily 8:30am-6:30pm. L10,000, children under 6 free.)

Hotel Novara, P. Garibaldi, 30, has 16 immaculate rooms above a restaurant; all rooms have TV and telephone. Facing the water, turn left from the dock and walk two minutes to P. Garibaldi. (☎0323 50 35 27; fax 0323 50 35 28. Breakfast included. Singles L55,000; doubles with bath L120,000.)

Pizzeria Emiliana, P. Giovanni, 24, offers both regular and dessert pizzas from L6-14,000. (☎0323 50 35 22. *Primi* and *secondi* L10-15,000. Open daily noon-2pm and 7pm-midnight.) If your Pallanzan palate palls at pizza, head to **Hostaria il Cortile,** V. Albertazzi, 14. Though the courtyard is a bit run-down, the food is the cheapest on the lake. (☎0323 50 28 16. *Primi* from L4000, *secondi* from L5000. V, MC.)

LOCARNO, SWITZERLAND ☎091

On the shores of **Lago Maggiore,** Locarno (pop. 30,000) basks in near-Mediterranean breezes and bright Italian sun. This relatively unspoiled resort town has a tropical feeling, perhaps because it gets over 2200 hours of sunlight per year—the most in all of Switzerland. During its world-famous 11-day **film festival** each August, over 150,000 big screen enthusiasts descend upon the town. The centerpiece of the festival is a giant 26m by 14m outdoor screen set up in P. Grande for big name premieres, and smaller screens throughout the city highlight young filmmakers and groundbreaking experimentation. (For more info, write to: International Film Festival, V. Luini 3a, CH-6601 Locarno; ☎091 756 2121; fax 091 756 2149; email info@pardo.ch; www.pardo.ch.)

All this worldly languor coexists in relative peace with the piety of the worshipers in the churches of the **Città Vecchia** (old city). For centuries, visitors have journeyed to Locarno solely to see the church of **Madonna del Sasso** (Madonna of the Rock). Its orange-yellow hue renders it immediately recognizable from anywhere in town. The church is accessible by a **funicular** that leaves every 15 minutes from a small station just left of the McDonald's (round-trip 6SFr, 4.50SFr with SwissPass), but the true budget traveler will make the 20-minute walk up the smooth stones of V. al Sasso. (Off V. Cappuccini in the Città Vecchia. Grounds open daily 7am-7pm. 2.50SFr, students 1.50SFr. English guidebooks at the entrance are free.)

The **Verzasca Dam** has brought scores of visitors dizzying adrenaline rushes courtesy of its famous **bungee jump,** the highest in the world. The 255m jump, conquered with panache by James Bond in *Goldeneye*, costs 244SFr the first time (with training, drink, and diploma) and 195SFr for subsequent leaps. For info, contact **Trekking Team.** (☎0848 808 007; email info@trenskking.ch; www.trekking.ch. Open Apr.-Oct.) Hidden among the chestnut trees, waterfalls, and dozens of lakes in Ticino's largest valley, Valle Maggia, is the village of **Aurigeno.** Come here to take a "vacation from your vacation" at **Baracca Backpacker,** a tiny hostel with 10 beds and unlimited access to the peaceful outdoors. From the train station in Locarno, take bus #10 (direction: Valle Maggia) to "Ronchini" (25min., every hr. 5:30am-11:35pm, 6.80SFr). Cross the street, turn right from the bus stop, and follow the hostel signs into the forest (15min.). When you get to the paved street, turn right. The hostel is behind the church. The path is difficult. Beo the bird noisily greets each new arrival, and the youthful couple who run the hostel provide fresh herbs for cooking as well as a wood-working shop. While you're escaping from civilization, use the **kitchen, rent a bike** (10SFr per day), or explore the **hiking, climbing,** and **swimming** possibilities in the area. (☎091 079 207 1554. Call ahead. Reception 9-11am and 5-10pm. Open Apr.-Oct. Sleepsack 2SFr per day. Dorms 25SFr.)

For Swiss phone info, see p. 134. Take an FS **train** from Stresa to Locarno (3½-5hr.; M-Sa 8 per day 8am-8pm, Su 1 per day). The **tourist office** is on Largo Zorzi in P. Grande. From the main exit of the train station, walk diagonally to the right, cross V. della Stazione, and continue through the pedestrian walkway (V. alla Ramogna). Cross Largo Zorzi to your left; the tourist office is in the same building as the casino. The office organizes city tours in English and bus trips around Lago Maggiore. (☎091 791 00 91; fax 091 751 90 70; email buongiorno@maggiore.ch; www.maggiore.ch. Open mid-Mar. to mid-Oct. M-F 9am-6pm, Sa 10am-4pm, Su 10am-noon and 1-3pm; mid-Oct. to mid-Mar. M-F 9am-6pm.)

THE BORROMEAN ISLANDS (ISOLE BORROMEE)

☎0323

The lush beauty of the three Borromean Islands makes them well worth a visit. The opulence of the **Palazzo e Giardini Borromeo** has garnered fame for the pearl of Maggiore, **Isola Bella.** The Baroque palace, built in 1670 by Count Borromeo, features six meticulously designed rooms with priceless masterpieces, tapestries, sculptures by Canova, obelisks, and paintings by van Dyck. The ten terraced gardens, punctuated with statues and topped by a unicorn, rise up like a large wedding cake. In no way do the lush gardens epitomize the Borromeo family's motto, *"Humilitas."* (☎0323 30 556. Open daily Mar.-Sept. 9am-noon and 1:30-5:30pm; Oct. 9am-noon and 1:30-5pm. L14,000, ages 6-15 L6000.)

Take the ferry and escape the aristocrats at Isola Bella in favor of the fishermen of Hemingway's favorite, **Isola Superiore (dei Pescatori).** In addition to a free beach, charming paths, and a children's park, the only garden-free island offers overpriced souvenir stands and fishermen's nets hung out in the sun.

Isola Madre is the longest and quietest of the three islands. Its elegant 16th-century **villa,** started in 1502 by Lancelotto Borromeo and finished by the Count Renato 100 years later, contains stage sets, a vast collection of portraits, and Princess Borromeo's *bambini* marionette collection. Even if you choose to skip the house, the botanical garden's stupendous array of exotic trees, the tallest palms in Italy, and strutting peacocks are worth the entrance fee. (☎0323 31 261; fax 0323 50 18 41. Open daily Mar.-Sept. 9am-noon and 1:30-5:30pm; Oct. 9am-12:30pm and 1:30-5:30pm. L14,000, ages 6-15 L6000.) Do not stop on the island unless you plan to see the garden, or you'll be forced to wait on the lone sidewalk (the only admission-free place on the island) until the next boat arrives. Off Isola Madre, you will be able to see the 4th island, **Isolino San Giovanni,** revered by Arthur Toscanini who frequently visited the villa. Unfortunately the *isolino* is not open to public.

LAKE ORTA (LAGO DI ORTA)

ORTA SAN GIULIO

☎0322

Orta San Giulio is the gateway to Lake Orta, the area's unspoiled refuge, surrounded by forested hills and small towns. From 1883 to 1885, Nietzsche retreated here, where he scripted his masterpiece, *Thus Spoke Zarathustra.* Because Lake Orta is difficult to reach by public transportation, it remains less touristed than Lake Como and Lake Maggiore; plan ahead so as not to get stranded in transit.

TRANSPORTATION. Orta lies on the Novara-Domodossola **train** line (1½hr., L4400). Buy train tickets for Orta from the conductor on board. Get off at **Orta Miasino,** 3km above Orta, and walk down to the left until you reach the intersection. Turn left on V. Fava, and the town of Orta San Giulio is a 10-minute walk away. A twisting road, filled with switchbacks that cross a mountain, connects Orta to nearby Lake Maggiore. On weekdays, **buses** leave from Stresa's P. Marconi (next to the phones and the little white food hut), traveling to Orta (1hr., in summer M-F 9am and 4pm, L8800), via **Baveno.** The return trip from Orta to Stresa is a bit tricky (1hr., in summer M-F 10am and 5pm, L8800). Those with a car can try the nearby lake towns of **Alzo** and **Arola;** contact the Orta tourist office for details.

PRACTICAL INFORMATION. Orta's **tourist office** is on V. Panoramica, across the street and down from the ornate Villa Crespi tower. From the train station, turn left and walk for 10 minutes straight through the intersection. (☎0322 90 56 14; fax 0322 90 58 00; email ortatl@tin.it. Open in summer daily 9:30am-1pm and 2:30-7pm.) **Banca Popolare di Novara,** V. Olina, 14, has **currency exchange** and outdoor **ATMs.** (Open M-F 8:20am-1:20pm and 2:35-3:35pm, Sa 8:20-11:20am.) In case of an **emergency,** call an **ambulance** (☎118 or 0322 901 14) or the **police** (☎0322 824 44). The **post office** is in P. Ragazzoni. (☎0322 901 57. Open M-F 8:30am-1:40pm, Sa 8:15-11:40am.) **Postal Code:** 28016.

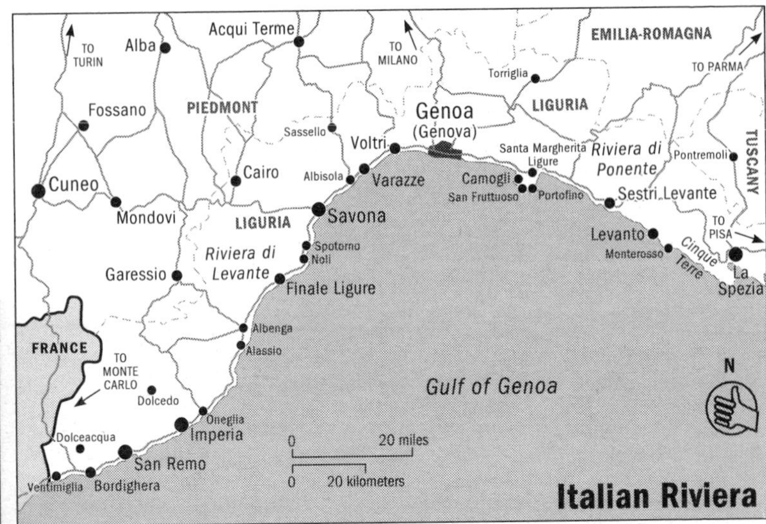

ACCOMMODATIONS. Affordable accommodations are only available to individuals who reserve early. You might also consider staying in Stresa and coming just for the day. **Piccolo Hotel Olina,** V. Olina, 40, offers beautiful rooms with private baths. Family rooms with kitchens are also available. (☎0322 90 56 56. Breakfast included. Singles L110,000; doubles L150,000. V, MC, AmEx, Diners.) Outside of town, but only a few minutes from the train station, **Hotel-Meublé Santa Caterina** is at V. Marconi, 10. Recently renovated, it has spacious, sleek rooms. (☎0322 91 58 65; fax 0322 903 77. Singles L100,000; doubles L115,000. V, MC, AmEx.) Rooms with a balcony or private garden cost slightly more. **Camping Orta,** V. Domodossola, 28, offers lakeside camping. From the train station, turn left, go down to the intersection, and turn right. (☎/fax 0322 90 267. L8000 per person, L14,000 per tent, L17,000 per lakeside site.)

FOOD. Good news for those lookin' for a piece of ass: Lago d'Orta is known as the home of *tapulon* (donkey meat, minced, well spiced, and cooked in red wine). All this and much more (fruit cake San Giulio, creative pasta, and bottles of alcohol) are available at the unparalleled **Salumeria Il Buongustaio,** V. Olina, 8 (☎0322 90 56 26). English, French, German, and Spanish are spoken. Chat with Lucca, who will gladly sell you Italy's only peanut butter, as well as 150 proof alcohol designed for all the mothers-in-law you know and love. An **open-air market** on Wednesday mornings in P. Motta sells fruit, vegetables, and dry goods.

Restaurant prices in Orta provide relief from those at the more commercialized lakes. If you don't fancy the more traditional local fare, head to **Pizzeria La Campana,** V. Giovanetti (the continuation of V. Olina after P. Motta), 41, where the tasty food should be eaten quietly in order to hear the spears in the background. (☎0322 902 11. Pizza L9-11,000, *primi* L9-11,000, *secondi* L10-15,000, desserts L7000. Cover L2500.) Visitors are drawn upstairs to **Taverna Antico Agnello,** V. Olina, 40, by the fabulous food, peaceful surroundings, and attentive service. (☎0322 90 56 56. *Primi* L12-16,000, *secondi* L19-25,000. V, MC, AmEx, Diners.) On Isola di San Giulio, head to the most inexpensive (and only) restaurant on the island, **Ristorante San Giulio,** V. Basilica, 4. Munch brunch in the 18th-century dining room, on the breezy lakeside terrace or on the path of silence. (☎0322 90 234. *Primi* L4-8000, *secondi* L8-16,000. Cover L3000.) A return boat to the island runs after the public ones have stopped.

SIGHTS. Walk around **Isola di San Giulio** (total population: 59), across from Orta. The island is as beautiful as the Borromeans, but much quieter. Its 12th-century **Romanesque basilica,** with interesting Baroque ornaments and frescoes inside,

DEVILS DEFEATED BY THE HOLY SKELETOR St. Giulius, after whom the island was named, arrived in Orta in AD 319. Like most right-thinking Christians of his day, he decided to build a church. Legend has it that the natives of the region distrusted the man, exiling him to the island for fear that his construction project would attract snakes and devils (the bane of developers and contractors everywhere). Ever-persistent Giulio continued with the construction of the church, and eventually the locals, realizing that he was a good man, helped him build one of the smallest (and prettiest) basilicas in the world. The island is still known as the Eden of silence, and its narrow streets are full of signs (in numerous languages) with pearls of wisdom like, "Silence is the language of love," or "In silence you receive all." San Giulio himself rests in peace in a glass sarcophagus in the crypt of the basilica. Be prepared, or your scream might wake up all 47 nuns (and 3 families) on the island. The natives left him visible to scare away creatures of evil (and hordes of tourists). So far, he seems to be doing a pretty good job.

was built on 4th-century foundations. The church's masterpiece is the **pulpit,** built out of black marble (representative of the Evangelists). Downstairs, the **skeleton of San Giulio,** dressed in brocade robes, rests in a glass sarcophagus. (Basilica open Tu-Sa 9:30am-12:15pm and 2-6:45pm, Su 8:30-10:45am and 2-6:45pm, M 11am-12:15pm. Free.) Small **motorboats** weave back and forth every 10 minutes during the summer (round-trip L4-5000; tickets sold on board). The big boat is L3000, but only departs every hour. The swim across the channel is strenuous, but manageable. Ask at the tourist office for a schedule of music and sporting events.

Quite a hike above Orta town in the cool, verdant hills, the **Sacro Monte** monastic complex is devoted to St. Francis of Assisi, patron saint of Italy. The sanctuary, founded in 1591, has 20 chapels with 376 life-size statues and 900 frescoes of trusty ole' Frank. (Open daily 8:30am-6:30pm. Free.) The **Mercato Antiquariato** (antique market) is held in P. Motta on the 1st Saturday of the month (Apr.-Oct. 9am-6pm).

LIGURIA (ITALIAN RIVIERA)

Like a black pearl nestled in the center of a virtually flawless white oyster shell, dark and dreary Genoa divides the largely luminescent Ligurian coastal strip into the **Riviera di Levante** (rising sun) to the east and the **Riviera di Ponente** (setting sun) to the west. The Italian Riviera stretches 350km along the Mediterranean between France and Tuscany, forming the most famous and touristed area of the Italian coastline. Protected from the north's severe weather by the Alps, Liguria still receives its fair share of tumultuous summer storms. Rainwater streams down the terraced hillsides, irrigating crops on high and smoothing the beach sands at sea level. Along the less congested Levante, rain renews the sweet smell of blossoming flowers among the mighty Apennine mountains and tiny pebble beaches. Meanwhile, heat evaporates from crowded Ponente beachside *discotecas* and stagnant medieval villages.

In remote villages as in major cities, Ligurians are known for their cultural isolation. They claim Nordic, not Roman, ancestry and have their own vocabulary and accent, often incomprehensible to other Italians. The distinctive character of Liguria, however, does not make its residents any less Italian, nor did it prevent them from playing a leading role in the unification of the Italian peninsula. Giuseppe Mazzini, the father of the Risorgimento, and Giuseppe Garibaldi, its most popular hero, were both Ligurians.

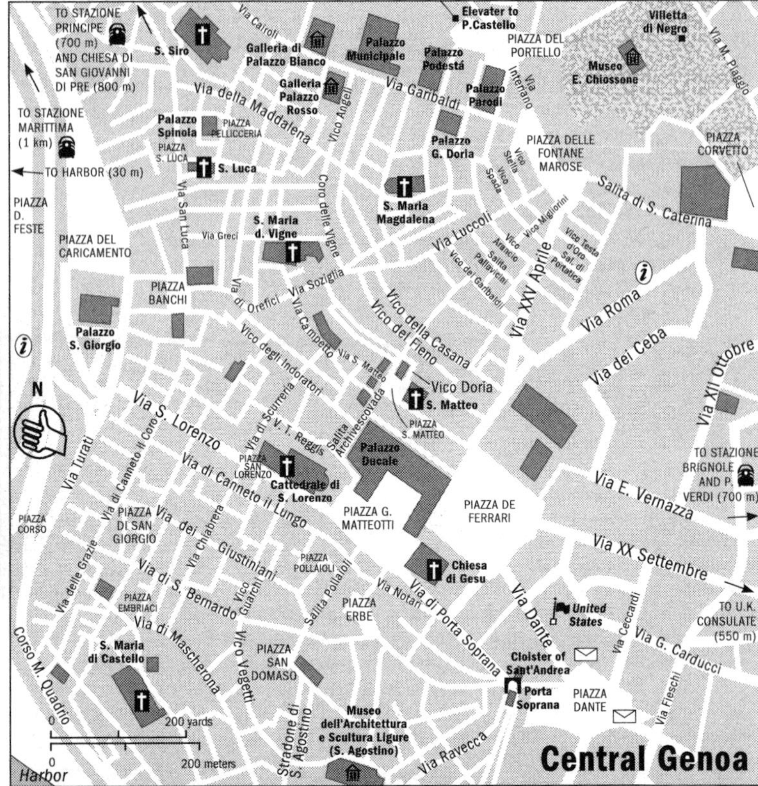

HIGHLIGHTS OF LIGURIA

CLIMB Genoa's precipitous *palazzi* and study its fine Flemish art (p. 142).

STROLL Cinque Terre's bewitching Via dell'Amore and add your name to the lists of lovers (p. 159).

SLEEP under the stars on the soothing sands of **Finale Ligure's** beach (p. 164).

LOSE your *lire* and curse your luck while gambling at **San Remo's** casino (p. 168)

GENOA (GENOVA) ☎010

Genoa, city of grit and grandeur, has little in common with the villages that dot the rest of the riviera. A Ligurian will tell you, "*Si deve conoscerla per amarla*"—you have to know Genoa to love her. Many travelers, frightened by the city's abrasive countenance, quickly flee to nearby beach towns. Those who linger more than a day in this once rich port, however, will find themselves bewitched by the enigmatic city. From the 12th through the 17th centuries, the sweeping boulevards and arcane twisting *vicoli* (alleyways) were home to Genoa's leading families, who amassed great wealth in international trade. These riches were stowed away in the bank of S. Giorgio or lavished on extravagant palaces and churches, which harbored nearly as many esoteric nooks as the streets themselves. Genoa has made no secret of its many celebrated historical heroes, among them Christopher Columbus, the Risorgimento ideologue Giuseppe Mazzini, and the virtuoso violinist Nicolò Paganini. But in the 18th century, the city fell out of renown and into decline, and its hidden treasures were buried even deeper below the silt. Genoa's great wall, second in length only to China's, now encircles a coarse yet cosmopolitan city that continues in its struggle to unearth its bygone grandeur.

TRANSPORTATION

Flights: C. Colombo Internazionale (☎010 601 51), in Sestiere Ponente. Services European destinations. To get to the airport, take Volabus #100 from Stazione Brignole (every 30min. 5:30am-9:30pm, L4000), and get off at the "Aeroporto" stop.

Trains: Stazione Principe in P. Acquaverde and **Stazione Brignole** in P. Verdi. Buses #18, 33, and 37 connect the 2 stations (25min., L1500). Trains run from both stations to points along the Ligurian Riviera and to major Italian cities including **Turin** (2hr., 19 per day, L14,500-23,200) and **Rome** (5hr., 14 per day, L43,300-62,000). **Luggage Storage:** in both stations. L5000 for 12hr. Open 6am-10pm.

Ferries: at the Ponte Assereto arm of the port, a 15min. walk from Stazione Marittima or a short bus ride from Stazione Principe (#20). Purchase tickets at a city travel agency or **Stazione Marittima** in the port. Passengers should arrive at the Ponte Assereto at least 1hr. before departure. Destinations include **Olbia, Porto Torres, Palau, Palermo, Barcelona,** and **Tunisia. TRIS** (☎010 576 24 11) and **Tirrenia** (☎14 78 99 000) run to Sardinia. **Grandi Traghetti** (☎010 58 93 31 or 010 576 13 63) heads to Palermo.

Local Buses: AMT, V. D'Annunzio, 8r (☎010 55 81 14). One-way tickets within the city (L1500) are valid for 1½hr. All-day tourist passes L5000 (foreign passport necessary). Tickets and passes can also be used for *funiculare* and elevator rides.

Taxis: ☎010 59 66.

ORIENTATION AND PRACTICAL INFORMATION

Most visitors arrive at one of Genoa's two train stations: **Stazione Principe,** in P. Acquaverde, or **Stazione Brignole,** in P. Verdi. From Stazione Principe take bus #19, 20, 30, 32, 35, or 41 and from Stazione Brignole take bus #19 or 40 to **Piazza de Ferrari** in the center of town. If walking to P. de Ferrari from Stazione Principe, take **Via Balbi** to **Via Cairoli** (which becomes **Via Garibaldi**), and at P. delle Fontane Marose, turn right on **Via XXV Aprile.** From Stazione Brignole, take a right out of the station to **Via Fiume,** and then a right onto **Via XX Settembre.** Although the free tourist office map labels sites, it does not label many of the streets. A detailed map from an *edicola* (L7000) may help, as Genoa's streets can stump even a native.

The *centro storico* (historic center) contains many of Genoa's monuments. Unfortunately, it is also the city's most dangerous quarter, and its shadowy, labyrinthine streets are riddled with drugs and prostitutes at night. You'll need a sixth sense to navigate here, even with a map. While locals may tell you that Genova is worth getting acquainted with, they will also tell you never to get chummy with the *centro storico* after dark, on Sundays (when shops are closed), or in August (when the natives leave). In addition to safety concerns, you may find yourself getting an unwanted shower. Those living above bars and restaurants are known to pour water out their windows on carousers when the noise gets out of control.

TOURIST, FINANCIAL, AND LOCAL SERVICES

Tourist Offices: APT, (☎010 248 71), on Porto Antico, in Palazzina S. Maria. Find the aquarium directly on the water, face the water, then walk towards the complex of buildings 100 yards to the left. Generous assistance and useful info. Limited English spoken. Open daily 9am-6:30pm. APT has **branches** at Stazione Principe (☎010 246 26 33) and at the airport (☎010 601 52 47). Both open M-Sa 8am-8pm; Principe office also open Su 9am-noon. **Informagiovani,** Palazzo Ducale, 24r (☎010 55 73 952), in P. Matteotti, is a youth center that offers info on apartment rentals, jobs, concerts, and free internet access. (Reservations required one week or more in advance for computer use. Drop in and hope for a cancellation.) Open Sept.-June M-F 9am-12:30pm and 3-6pm; July-Aug. M-Tu and Th-F 9am-12:30pm, W 9am-12:30pm and 3-6pm.

Budget Travel: CTS, V. San Vincenzo, 117r (☎010 56 43 66 or 010 53 27 48), off V. XX Settembre near the Ponte Monumentale. Walk up the flight of stairs on the shopping complex to the left. Student fares available. Open M-F 9am-1pm and 2:30-6pm.

Consulates: UK, V. XX Settembre, 2, 5th fl., #37/38. (☎010 56 48 33). Open Tu-Th 9am-noon. **US,** V. Dante, 2, 3rd fl., #43 (☎010 58 44 92, emergency cell ☎0335 652 1252). Open June-Sept. M-F 10am-5pm; Oct.-May M noon-2pm, Tu-W 10am-noon, Th 10am-noon and 3-5pm.

Bike Rental: Nuovo Centro Sportivo 2000, P. dei Garibaldi, 18r (☎010 254 12 43; fax 010 254 26 39). L10,000 per day. Open M-Sa 9am-5pm.

English Bookstore: Mondovori, V. XX Settembre, 210r (☎010 58 57 43). Huge bookstore with a full wall of English-language classics. Pick up a copy of D.H. Lawrence's *Sea and Sardinia* if your thoughts are straying away from the Riviera. If they're wandering far, choose from a lovely selection of *Let's Go* travel guides in the basement. Open M-Sa 9:30am-11pm, Su 10:30am-2pm and 3-9pm.

EMERGENCY AND COMMUNICATIONS

Emergencies: ☎113. **Ambulance:** ☎118. **Hospital: Ospedale San Martino,** V. Benedetto XV, 10 (☎010 55 51). **Police:** ☎112.

Pharmacy: Pescetto, V. Balbi, 185r (☎010 246 26 97 or 010 25 27 86 or 010 25 69 21), near Stazione Principe. List of late-night pharmacies posted.

Internet Access: Internet Village (☎010 570 48 78), at the intersection of V. Brigata Bisagno and C. Buenos Aires, across from Piazza Vittoria. L15,000 per hr. Open 9am-1pm and 3-7pm. See **Informagiovanni** for the possibility of internet *gratis.*

Post Office: Main office, P. Dante, 4/6r (☎010 259 46 87), 2 blocks from P. de Ferrari. Holds Fermo Posta. Open M-Sa 8am-7pm. Most branches open 8am-1:30pm. **Postal Code:** 16121.

ACCOMMODATIONS AND CAMPING

Genoa may have more one-star hotels per capita than any other city in Italy, so you have no excuse to sleep on the beach (plus there is no beach, and good luck camping out at the aquarium). Rooms are scarce only in October, when Genoa hosts a wave of nautical conventions. Almost without exception, budget lodgings in the *centro storico* and near the port prefer to rent rooms by the hour—try the hostel or stick around Stazione Brignole, where the establishments are more refined.

Ostello Per La Gioventù (HI), V. Costanzi, 120 (☎/fax 010 242 24 57). From Stazione Principe, walk down V. Balbi to P. Delba Nunziata. Pick up bus #40 (every 15min.) from here or from Stazione Brignole, and ride it all the way up the hill–ask the driver to let you off at the *ostello*. Plenty of space (213 beds), and plenty of amenities: cafeteria, elevator, free lockers, laundry (L12,000 for 5kg), parking, TV, wheelchair access, and a view of the city that lies far, far below. Friendly, multi-lingual staff with city info. Breakfast, hot showers, and sheets included. Reception 7-9am and 3:30pm-12:30am. Curfew midnight. Check-out 9am. HI card required (available at the hostel). Dorms L23,000; family accommodations L25-28,000.

Albergo Carola, V. Gropallo, 4/12 (☎010 839 13 40). From Stazione Brignole, turn right on V. de Amicis and continue into P. Brignole. When facing Albergo Astoria, turn right, and walk 15m. Look for the big wooden doors with bronze lion heads on the left-hand side of the street and ring the buzzer. 9 large, clean, elegantly furnished rooms overlook a quiet garden in a well-maintained and secure building. Exuberant, helpful proprietor can give you directions to a laundromat in Italian or Spanish. Singles L45,000; doubles L65,000, with shower L75,000.

Albergo Argentina, V. Gropallo, 4/4 (☎010 839 13 40), 2 flights down from the Carola (see above). If no one answers the door here, go up to the Carola, they're owned by the same family. Prices here for some of the 9 rooms are slightly cheaper, but the quality of this recently redone Carola counterpart is just as high. Singles L45,000; doubles L65,000, with shower L70,000; triples L110,000; quads L120,000.

Albergo Balbi, V. Balbi, 21/3 (☎010 247 21 12). Housed in a building from 1840, Balbi's large rooms have ornately decorated ceilings that may induce seraphic sleep. Breakfast L7000. 50 beds. Singles L35-45,000, with bath L45-50,000; doubles L75,000, with bath L90,000; triples and quads add 30% per person. Discount with *Let's Go* and student ID.

Pensione Barone, V. XX Settembre, 2/23 (☎/fax 010 58 75 78). From Stazione Brignole, veer to the right and walk down V. Fiume to V. XX Settembre. 12 clean rooms are graced with itty-bitty beds and windows that look out on Genoa's lively shopping district. Some English spoken. Self-serve coffee L1000. Reception 9am-midnight. Call ahead for reservations (credit card required), especially in late Oct. Singles L50,000, with bath L70,000; doubles L70,000, with shower L80,000, with full bath L90,000; triples L100-110,000; quads L120,000. V, MC.

Camping: The Genoa area is teeming with campgrounds, but many are booked solid during July and August. The tourist office is your best source of info. **Villa Doria,** V. al Campeggio Villa Doria, 15 (☎010 696 96 00), in Pegli, is the closest campground west of the city. Take the train or bus #1, 2, or 3 (buses every 10min.) from P. Caricamento to Pegli; then walk or transfer to bus #93 up V. Vespucci (one stops in front of Pegli's train station every 30min.). Beautiful location with trails that connect to Europe 1, which extends to the North Sea. Free electricity, heated showers, and hospitable, English-speaking hosts. L9000 per person, L10-13,000 per tent. 1- to 4-person bungalows L50-90,000. 50 lots, 200 person capacity. **Genova Est** (☎010 347 20 53), on V. Marcon Loc Cassa. Take the train from Stazione Brignole to the suburb of Bogliasco (10min., 6 per day, L2100). A free bus runs by the campgrounds (5min., 6 per day 8:10am-6:50pm) and will fetch you from Bogliasco to the campsite. Enjoy the stillness of nature, the buzz of electricity (L3000 per day), and the hum of washing machines (L6000 per load). L9000 per person, L11,000 per tent.

FOOD

Genovese cuisine may simultaneously expand your waistline and shrink your wallet. *Trattorie*, found primarily in the *centro storico*, are innumerable and reasonably priced. The incomparable pesto, the pride and joy of Genoa, is a sauce made from ground basil, pine nuts, garlic, parmesan cheese, and olive oil. Other delectable edibles include *farinata* (a fried pancake of chick-pea flour) and *pansotti* (ravioli stuffed with spinach and ricotta and served with a creamy walnut sauce). Enhance any meal with olive oil-soaked *focaccia*, a delicious flat bread topped with herbs, olives, onions, or cheese (a specialty of nearby Recco). Try a slice of world-famous Genoa salami—it's fresher than anything you'll get at home. Don't forget to sample the seafood—even as an industrial port town, Genoa unloads its fair share of fantastically fresh fish. **Mercato Orientale,** off V. Settembre south of the *Ponte Monumentale*, is the place to go for fresh fruit and vegetables. (Open M-Tu and Th-Sa 7:30am-1pm and 3:30-7:30pm, W 7:30am-1pm.) The other option is **Supersconto,** V. di San Pietro, 76r. Walk south from P. Bianchi marketplace to the intersection of V. San Pietro and Vico delle Compere. On the right you'll see the Supersconto sign, with an open-mouthed stone head nearby. Buy a good bottle of wine (5000L) for the price of a glass of the stuff at a *trattoria*, or try a box of succulent strawberries (L2480) for less than half the going rate.

Trattoria da Maria, V. Testa d'Oro, 14r (☎010 58 10 80), off V. XXV Aprile near P. Marose. Checkered tablecloths, overflowing baskets of onions and carrots, and huge containers of spices in this classic, old-fashioned *trattoria* contribute to an aura of flavorsome functionality. The menu changes daily, but the dishes are always delicious. *Pranzo turistico* (price-fix lunch) L13,000. Open Su-F noon-2:30pm and 7-9:30pm.

Da Vittorio, V. Sottoripa, 59r (☎010 247 29 27). Ask a local where to find the best seafood in the city, and he will likely name Vittorio. The throngs of people crowding the entranceway agree. The catch-of-the-day is displayed in the front window (you'll see waiters periodically carting trays of seafood from the ice back to the kitchen). Lobster around L40,000, *Primi* from L10,000, *secondi* from L15,000. Open daily noon-4pm and 7pm-1:30am. Despite seating for 120 make reservations. No credit cards.

Cambusetta, V. Belvedere E. Firpo, 1 (☎010 37 60 141), in Boccadasse on the water below the upscale Vittorio al Mare. This pizzeria attracts hordes of youth with its affordable prices, seaside views, and delicious, oil-soaked *focaccia*. Try the *spaghetti con vongole* (with clams; L15,000). Have your *dolce della casa* (L5000) to go and finish up the meal watching the water (and couples stealing kisses) from the rocks outside. Take a *passaggiata* along the boardwalk; on temperate nights you're likely to be joined by fellow strollers, who on weekends number in the thousands. English spoken. Pizza from L8000, bottle of wine L12,000. Open daily noon-3pm and 7pm-midnight.

La Locanda del Borgo, V. Borgo Incrociati, 47r (☎010 81 06 31), behind Stazione Brignole. As you exit the station, turn right and go through the tunnel–V. Borgo Incrociati is straight ahead. Clean, friendly, and popular. Delicious food at great prices. *Primi* from L8000. *Menù* L15,000 available M-Th. Open daily 8am-4pm and 8pm-12:30am.

Sa Pesta, V. dei Giustiniani, 16r (☎010 246 83 36), south of P. Matteotti in the *centro storico*. Sa Pesta knows pesto; everyone from doctors to dockworkers converge at the communal tables to wolf down Genovese specialties like *minestrone alla genovese* (with pesto), and *torte di verdura* (vegetable tort). *Primi* L8000, *secondi* L10,000. Takeout available. Open M-Sa noon-2:30pm; in winter Tu-Sa 6-10pm. Closed Aug.

Brera Express, V. di Brera, 11r (☎010 54 32 80), just off V. XX Settembre near Stazione Brignole. The best deal at this cafeteria-style joint is the *menù* for L16,000, but all entrees are reasonably priced and fresh. Don't waste your money on the full-service pizzeria on the right side of the restaurant–you'll pay twice the price for the same meal. Open daily 11:45am-3pm and 7pm-midnight. Self-service closes at 10pm.

SIGHTS

FROM STAZIONE PRINCIPE TO THE CENTRO STORICO

The most impressive aspect of Genoa is the multitude of *palazzi* built by its famous merchant families. Because of the city's long-standing commercial strength, Genoa collected some of the finest 16th- and 17th-century works of Flemish and Italian art. Many mansions, hung with masterpieces, are open to the public. In the heart of the university quarter, **V. Balbi** contains some of Genoa's most lavish *palazzi*. The street connects Stazione Principie and **Piazza Nunizia,** formerly called P. Guastata ("broken") for its many ruins. The *piazza*, which is small, irregular, and surrounded by *palazzi*, exemplifies the Genovese square.

PORTELLO-CASTELLETO ELEVATOR. Ride the elevator up with all the locals who find it no more special than taking the bus (it's considered part of Genoa's public transportation system). Casually disembark with everyone else, and wait until the locals go about their business. Indulge yourself in one of the best panoramic views of the city, particularly of the port. Snap a few pictures, and get a feel for the lay of the land as you peek under the hazy veil that is Genoa. *(Through the tunnel entrance on P. Portello. Open 7:30am-11pm. L6000.)*

AQUARIUM. Genoa may be practically beach-free, but that doesn't mean you can't still go under the sea. Bask in frigid air-conditioning, gaze at ocean-dwelling fauna cavorting in huge tanks (this aquarium has the largest volume of water of any in Europe), and start to feel a little cold-blooded. Still not wet enough? Check out the Grande Nave Blu (Big Blue Boat) for exhibits that extend above and beyond the sea and an interactive tank where you can grab slithery sea rays and get splashed by slippery pre-teens, all for the noble cause of engendering "harmony with the sea." *(On Porto Antico, across from the tourist office. ☎010 248 12 05 for recorded info. Open M-F 9:30am-7pm, Sa-Su 9:30am-8pm. Th open until 11pm in summer. Arrive 1½hr. before closing. L19,000.)*

PALAZZO REALE. Built from 1624 to 1628, this *palazzo* was originally home to the Balbi family, for which the street was named, and then later to the Durazzo family, both powerful in maritime Genoa. The *palazzo* only became the Royal Palace in the 18th century, and the structural setup installed for the Savoy rulers persists for the most part into the present day. Turned over to the state shortly after World War I, the furniture was removed for safe-keeping during World War II. Following the war, the palace was re-opened as a museum, but some aspects of the Savoy living quarters (the king and queen's bathrooms, for example) were disassembled in order to create a more aggrandized art museum. The Rococo throne room, covered in red velvet and gold paint, remains untouched, along with the royal waiting room and sleeping quarters. Particularly noteworthy are the **Galleria degli Specchi,** modeled after the Hall of Mirrors at Versailles, and the **queen's clock** with a moon that moves across the night sky (to be lit from behind by a candle). Paintings crowding the walls include works by Tintoretto, van Dyck, and Bassano. *(V. Balbi, 10, 10min. west of V. Garibaldi. ☎010 271 02 11. Open M-Th 9:15am-1:45pm, F-Su 8:15am-7:15pm. L8000, under 18 and over 60 free.)*

VIA GARIBALDI. Once called Via Aurea (Golden Street) and Strada dei Re (Street of Kings), Via Garibaldi remains the most impressive street in Genoa. Bedecked with elegant *palazzi*, it was constructed during the 17th century by Genoa's wealthiest families seeking to flaunting their prominence. A glance inside the courtyards reveals fountains, frescoes, and leafy gardens. **Galleria Palazzo Rosso,** V. Garibaldi, 18 (☎010 28 26 41), built in the 16th century, earned its name when it was painted red during the 17th century. Red carpeting also covers the floors of exhibit halls that feature lavishly frescoed ceilings and a display of several hundred years worth of Genovese ceramics, including some dainty 18th-century eggholders. The 2nd floor was destroyed when bombed in 1942, but it was rebuilt after the war and now holds several full-length van Dyck portraits and Bernardo Strozzi's masterpiece, *La Cuoca*. Across the street, the **Galleria di Palazzo Bianco** (1548, rebuilt 1712) exhibits one of the city's largest collections of Ligurian art, as well as some Dutch and Flemish paintings. *(V. Garibaldi, 11. ☎010 29 18 03. Both galleries open Tu and Th-F 9am-1pm, W and Sa 9am-7pm, Su 10am-6pm. Admission to one L6000; to both L10,000, under 18 and over 60 free. Sundays free.)*

CHIESA DEL GESÙ. Also known as **SS. Ambrogio e Andrea** (1549-1606), the church features over-the-top trompe l'oeil effects and two Rubens canvases, *The Circumcision* (1605; over the altar) and *St. Ignatius Healing a Woman Possessed of the Devil* (1620, shortly after the death of Rubens's young son; in the 3rd alcove on the left). *(From P. de Ferrari, take V. Boetto to P. Matteotti. Open daily 7:30am-noon and 4-6:30pm. Free.)*

PALAZZO MUNICIPALE. Built from 1554 to 1570, the Palazzo Municipale (city hall) showcases Nicolò Paganini's violin, the Guarneri del Gesù. The sound of this instrument broke the hearts of some, drove others to suicide, and convinced the rest that they were hearing angels sing. The violin is still used on rare occasions to perform Paganini's works. To see the violin, go upstairs to the left, and ask the secretary. *(V. Garibaldi, 9. Open M-F 8:30am-6pm. Free.)*

SAN GIOVANNI DI PRÈ. This Romanesque church, built in 1180, is one of Genoa's oldest monuments. The vaulted stone roof and filtered light create a cavernous weight and contemplative feel. A left turn around the church leads to the 12th-century **La Commenda,** which housed the Knight Commanders of St. John. *(Head away from the Stazione Principe towards V. Balbi and turn right on Salita di San Giovanni.)*

VILLETTA DI NEGRO. The Villetta, a great place for a walk spreads out along a hill, boasting waterfalls, grottoes, and statues of patriots amidst terraced gardens. A great place for a walk. *(From P. delle Fontane Marose, take Salita di S. Caterina to P. Corvetto. Open daily 8am-sunset.)*

HARBOR CRUISES. To view the city from the water, take a harbor cruise—boats depart at least every hour from Porto Antico next to the aquarium, across from the tourist office. Prices depend on the duration of the excursion.

THE CENTRO STORICO

The eerie, beautiful, and sometimes dangerous historic center is a mass of confusing streets bordered by the port, V. Garibaldi, and P. de Ferrari. Due to its crime, prostitution, and drugs, the center is only safe for tourists during weekdays when stores are open. At night, the quarter's seedy underground emerges, and not even the police venture here. It is, however, home to some of Genoa's most memorable monuments: the **duomo, Palazzo Spinola,** and the medieval **Torre Embraici,** whose Guelph battlements jut out among the buildings to the left when facing the **Chiesa di Santa Maria di Castello.**

CHIESA DI SANTA MARIA DI CASTELLO. This 15th-century church, with foundations that date to 500 BC, is a labyrinth of chapels (added onto the original structure during the 16th-18th centuries), courtyards, cloisters, and crucifixes. Careful where you step, you're liable to wake the dead—the floor is paved with 18th-century tombs. In the chapel directly to the left of the high altar, you'll find the spooky **Crocifisso Miracoloso.** According to legend, this wooden Jesus once moved its head to attest to the honesty of a young damsel betrayed by her lover; Jesus' beard is said to grow longer every time crisis hits the city. To see the painting of **S. Pietro Martire di Verona,** complete with a halo and a large cleaver conspicuously thrust into his cranium, go upstairs to the right of the high altar, turn right, and right again. The painting is above the door. Incensed heretics are said to have turned poor Pietro's head into a butcher block. *(From P. G. Matteotti head up V. S. Lorenzo towards the water and turn left on V. Chiabrera. A left on serpentine V. di Mascherona leads to the church in P. Caricamento. Open daily 9am-noon and 3:30-6:30pm.)*

DUOMO (SAN LORENZO). Already in existence in the 9th century, the *duomo* was enlarged and reconstructed between the 12th and 16th centuries after religious authorities deemed it "imperfect and deformed." The result may have been more perfect, but it sure wasn't symmetrical—the church has a lopsided appearance because only one of the two planned bell towers was completed. The striped Gothic facade flaunts copiously carved main entrances and 9th-century lions, sirens, and vines (oh, my!) that give way to an incongruous interior (the front part, holding the altar, was added during the 17th and 18th centuries). Rub the bomb displayed on the right-hand side of the church shortly after you enter for good luck (or a touch of holy grace); it was dropped by the English on the church during World War II but didn't explode. *(P. San Lorenzo, off V. San Lorenzo, which emerges from P. Matteotti. Open M-Sa 8am-7pm, Su 7am-7pm. Free.)*

PORTA SOPRANA. The historical centerpiece of P. Dante (and today the passageway from the modern *piazza* into the *centro storico*), this medieval structure was built in 1100 to intimidate enemies of the Republic of Genoa. Mischievous would-be assailant Emperor Frederico Barbarossa took one look at the mighty arch whose Latin inscription welcomes the passing of those who come in peace but threatens doom to enemy armies, and decided to terrorize elsewhere. Thus the city endured, and the bastion of strength that was the Porta would come to serve as the portal onto the world for **Christopher Columbus.** His reputed boyhood home lies to the right of the gate (his father was the gatekeeper; his mother was the keymaster). In his backyard is the Cloister of Sant'Andrea, the romantic remains of a 12th-century convent. *(From P. G. Matteotti, head down V. di Porta Soprana. Columbus's home open Sa and Su 9am-noon and 3-6pm.)*

PALAZZO SPINOLA DI PELLICCERIA. Built at the close of the 16th century to flaunt Genovese mercantile monies, this *palazzo* had a fan in Peter Paul Rubens, who described it warmly in his 1622 book on pleasing palaces. It is now home to the **Galleria Nazionale,** a collection of fantastic art and furnishings. Most of the objects were donated by the family of Maddalena Doria Spinola, who owned the palace during the first half of the 18th century. The building shows its age; different sections represent the variety of styles that shaped it through the centuries, including an 18th-century kitchen. In the Sala da Pranzo are van Dyck's portraits of the four evangelists. *(P. di Pellicceria, 1, between V. Maddalena and P. S. Luca. ☎010 247 70 61. Open Tu-Sa 9am-8pm, Su 1-8pm. L8000, 18-25 L4000, under 18 and over 65 free.)*

CHIESA DI SAN SIRO. Genoa's first cathedral (rebuilt 1588-1613) may remind you of grandma's house with layers of dusty trinkets that represent a worthwhile history, if you're willing to sort through the clutter. Admire the majestic vaulted ceilings (painted with frescoes in 1650) and chapels bursting with paintings. The arches sing exuberantly (off-key, but not bad for an arch) and shine a holy light into the world. *(Located where V. S. Siro branches to the right. Open M-F 4-6pm. Free.)*

PIAZZA SAN MATTEO. This tiny square contains the houses and chapel of the medieval rulers of Genoa, the Doria family. The animal reliefs above the 1st floor are the trademarks of the masons who built the houses. Chiseled into the facade of the small but elaborately decorated **Chiesa di San Matteo,** founded by the Dorias in 1125, are descriptions of the aristocrats' great deeds. The church was rebuilt in 1278 and raised above street level as a reflection of the power of the Dorias in religious as well as civic affairs. *(Behind the duomo, off Salita all'Arcicovato. Open M-Sa 8am-noon and 4-6:30pm, Su 9am-noon and 4-6:30pm.)*

MUSEO DELL'ARCHITETTURA E SCULTURA LIGURE. The old city's newest addition occupies the former monastery of S. Agostino. The museum surveys Genoa's history through its surviving art (many pieces have been plucked from buildings for preservation). In 1312 Giovanni Pisano carved the outstanding though piecemeal funerary monument for Margherita of Brabant. Also noteworthy is the neoclassic Penitent Magdalena in the Desert, so sensuous that it borders on sacrilege. *(Follow the directions to Porta Soprana and then head towards the port on V. Ravecca. ☎010 251 12 63. Open Tu-Sa 9am-7pm, Su 9am-12:30pm. L6000.)*

ENTERTAINMENT

The **Carignano D'Essai** shows English-language movies from October through June at V. Villa Glori, 8, near P. dei Ferrari. (☎010 570 23 48. Open W-Th 3pm and 9pm, Su 7pm.)

A 20min. bus ride (#31) down C. Italia takes you to **Boccadasse,** a seaside playground of wealthy Genovese. Sea breezes replace ceaseless cigarette smoke, and soft promises of undying love overwrite graffiti threatening anarchy. Here massive seaside mansions tower over remnants of stone piers washed away by the waves, and extravagant restaurants with dining *salas* (halls) jutting out over the cove.

Matilda Estate, V. Lungomare 27-29 (☎0335 69 694 70 37 for reservations and info), at the Sporting Genova, at C. Italia. In the summer (starting late April) the party moves to the beach. Matilda Estate, one of Genoa's top night spots for young and beautiful late-night revellers, is the place to move with it. Long lines lead to ocean breezes, sexy bartender contests, and live music from 11pm on. Get rebellious and rev up for the disco that starts well after midnight and lasts until 4am. Cover L20,000. First drink L20,000. Eat for an additional L25,000.

Le Corbusier, V. S. Donato, 36/38 (☎010 246 86 52). Smoke rises from the crowd of students and artists gathered in this self-consciously hip place. The music and the atmosphere are more thoughtful, intense, and–dare we say–avant-garde than in most other bars. With art showings and the occasional literary lecture, Le Corbusier feels like a Renaissance saloon. Commence your philosophizing and drink yourself into oblivion. Open M-F 8am-1am, Sa-Su 6pm-1am.

Caffè degli Specchi, Salita Pollaiuoli, 43r (☎010 28 12 93). Walk down Salita Pollaioli from P. Matteotti. The cafe will appear on your left, with umbrellas shading outdoor seating in the summer. Inside, the bar is lined with mirrors and marble, and a sophisticated crowd pleas for a *bicchierino di vino* (glass of wine; L3000), a *piccolo panino* (L2-6000), or a frozen *forza cappuccino* (L1800). Upstairs fresh salads, such as chicken and apple, run L13,000. Open M-Sa 7am-8pm.

RIVIERA DI LEVANTE

CAMOGLI ☎0185

The postcard-perfect town of Camogli throbs with color. Sun-faded peach houses crowd the hilltop, lively red and turquoise boats knock about in the water, fishing nets coat the greying docks, and bright umbrellas blanket the dark stone beaches. The town takes its name—a contraction of *Casa Mogli*, (Wives' House)—from the women who ran the town while their husbands manned its once massive fishing fleet. The old man has long since left the sea, and what Dickens called a "piratical little place" has mellowed into a small, peaceful resort town of 6000. More down-to-earth and youth-friendly than nearby Portofino, Camogli is the place to go for a low-key mosey down a boardwalk where playtime overrides pretension.

TRANSPORTATION

Trains: On the Genoa-La Spezia line. To: **Santa Margherita** (10min., 24 per day 5:27am-11:45pm, L1900); **Genoa** (20min., 32 per day 5:16am-10:09pm, L2700); **Sestri Levante** (30min., 20 per day 5:27am-8:46pm, L3600); and **La Spezia** (1½hr., 21 per day 5:27am-7:30pm, L6400). **Luggage Storage:** L5000 per bag. Open M-F 6am-noon, Sa-Su 1-7:15pm. Ticket counter open M-F 5:50am-12:40pm, Sa-Su 12:50-7:40pm. Tickets available at the tourist office when the ticket office is closed.

Buses: Tigullio buses leave P. Schiaffino for nearby towns. Buy tickets at the tourist office or at the *tabacchi* at V. Repubblica, 25. To **Santa Margherita** (30min., 14 per day, L2000). Buses also run to **Ruta, San Lorenzo,** and **Rapallo.**

Ferries: Golfo Paradiso, V. Scalo, 3 (☎0185 77 20 91), near P. Colombo. To **San Fruttuoso** (30min.; May-Sept. 9-11 per day; L9000, round-trip L14,000); **Portofino** (Sa-Su only 3pm, returns 5:30pm; L14,000, round-trip L20,000); and **Cinque Terre** (Portovenere at Vernazza; June 15-July 1 Su; July 1-Aug. 1 Tu and Sa-Su; Sept. 1-15 Th and Su; 9:30am, returns 5:30pm; L20,000, round-trip L33,000). Buy tickets on the dock.

ORIENTATION AND PRACTICAL INFORMATION

Camogli climbs uphill from the sea into pine and olive groves overlooking the beach and harbor below. To get to the center of town, go right as you exit the **Camogli-San Fruttuoso station.** About 100m from the station, turn left down the stairs to **Via Garibaldi.** From V. Garibaldi turn right into the alley to the beaches.

Tourist Office: V. XX Settembre, 33 (☎0185 77 10 66). Turn right as you leave the station. Helps with accommodations. English spoken. Open June-Sept. daily 8:30am-12:30pm and 3-7pm; Oct.-May M-Sa 9am-noon and 3:30-6:30pm, Su 9am-1pm.

Currency Exchange: Banco di Chiavari della Riviera Ligure, V. XX Settembre, 19 (☎0185 77 25 76 or 0185 77 00 33). Reasonable rates. **ATM** outside. Open M-F 8:20am-1:20pm and 2:45-3:45pm, Sa 8:20-11:20am.

Emergency: Police: V. Cuneo, 30f (☎0185 77 00 00). **Carabinieri:** ☎112. **Medical:** ☎118. **Hospital:** V. Bianchi, 1 (☎0185 743 77), in Recco.

Pharmacy: Dr. Machi, V. Repubblica, 4-6 (☎0185 77 10 81). Sign lists late-night pharmacies. Open Tu-Sa July-Aug. 8:30am-12:30pm and 4-8pm; Sept.-June 3:30-7:30pm.

Post Office: V. Cuneo, 4 (☎0185 77 43 32), under an arcade. Exit the train station and turn left. Open M-F 8am-1:30pm, Sa 8am-noon. **Postal Code:** 16032.

ACCOMMODATIONS

Albergo La Camogliese, V. Garibaldi, 55 (☎0185 77 14 02; fax 0185 77 40 24). Exit the train station and walk down the long stairway to the right, where you'll see a big blue sign. The large, well-decorated rooms are a joy. Phone, TV, and bath in every room. Steps away from the beach. 16 beds. Breakfast L10,000. Singles L70-90,000; doubles L90-110,000. 10% *Let's Go* discount on cash payments. V, MC, AmEx.

Albergo Augusta, V. Schiaffino, 100 (☎/fax 0185 77 05 92; email hotelaugusta@galactica.it), at the other end of town. Recently renovated rooms will have you sailing the ocean blue before you even get to the beach. 15 beds. Every room with TV, phone, and bath, some with harbor view and balcony. Free 10min. internet use for customers. Singles L50-80,000; doubles L80-120,000. V, MC, AmEx.

Albergo Selene, V. Cuneo, 16 (☎0185 77 01 49; fax 0185 77 20 38). Exit the train station and take a left past the post office. Some rooms with balcony. Breakfast included. Singles L70,000; doubles L130,000; triples L50,000 per person. V, MC, AmEx.

Pensione Faro, V. Schiaffino, 116-118 (☎0185 77 14 00), above the restaurant of the same name, down the street from the Augusta. 8 beds. Pension required in summer: half-pension doubles L90,000 per person, full-pension doubles L120,000 per person. In winter doubles L100,000. V, MC, AmEx.

FOOD

The numerous shops on V. Repubblica (one block up from the harbor) and **Picasso supermarket,** V. XX Settembre, 35, supply picnickers. (Open M-Sa 8am-12:30pm and 4:30-7:30pm, W 8am-12:30pm.) An **open-air market** in P. del Teatro offers clothes, food, and fishhooks. (Open W 6am-2pm.)

Pizzeria Il Lido, V. Garibaldi, 133 (☎0185 77 01 41), on the boardwalk. Scrumptious pizza, served and consumed by bronzed *camogliese.* Great view of sunbathers and the ocean, and the hostess is likely to greet you in an itsy-bitsy teeny-weeny purple polka dot bikini. Pizza L9-14,000, *primi* from L12,000. Cover L3000. Open W-M 12:30-2:30pm and 7:30-10:30pm.

La Rotonda, V. Garibaldi, 101 (☎0185 77 14 02), on the boardwalk. Great view of the harbor. Pizza, pasta, and seafood. *Primi* from L9000, *secondi* from L14,000. Open daily 12:30-2:30pm and 7:30-11pm; in winter W-M 12:30-2:30pm and 7:30-11pm.

Slurp, V. Garibaldi, 104 (☎0185 77 43 53). That's the sound you'll make when you taste the delicious, creamy *gelato*. Their *granite* (ices) are famous. 2-flavor cones L3000, 3-flavor L4000. Open daily 10am-midnight; in winter Tu-Su 10am-midnight.

Il Bar Teatro, P. Matteotti, 3 (☎0185 77 25 72). Serving 60 types of pizza for 40 years (from L8000), Il Teatro ought to elicit a "Bravo!" Open daily 7am-2pm and 7:30-10pm.

SIGHTS AND ENTERTAINMENT

If you tire of the beach and boardwalk, you might make the three-hour hike to **San Fruttuoso** (see p. 152). The Camogli tourist office has a useful trail map. Blue dots mark the well-worn path, which starts at the end of V. Cuneo (near the *carabinieri* station). Ferry or snorkeling trips also make interesting (but more costly) diversions. **Band B Diving Center,** V. S. Fortunato, 11/13, off P. Colombo, offers boats with 10 person capacities, 18 immersion spots along the coast, and three excursions daily for scuba diving (L65-100,000 per person per dive) and snorkeling (L20,000 per person). (☎0185 77 27 51. Open daily 9am-7pm.)

On the 2nd Sunday in May, tourists descend on the town for an enormous fish fry, the **Sagra del Pesce.** The frying pan, constructed in 1952, measures 4m in diameter and holds over 2000 fish. If you miss the sardine-rush, you may still see the pans, as they adorn a city wall for the remainder of the year. They hang to the right on V. Garibaldi as you descend the stairs to the beaches.

Camogli offers slim pickings when it comes to nightlife, but listen for the booming disco-house from **Il Barcollo,** on V. Garibaldi. (☎0185 77 33 22. Open 5pm-3am.)

DAYTRIPS FROM CAMOGLI: SAN FRUTTUOSO

You can hike to San Fruttuoso from Portofino Mare (1½hr.), Portofino Vetta (1½hr.), or Camogli (3hr.). Golfo Paradiso (☎0185 77 20 91) runs boats from Camogli (9 per day 8am-5pm, last return from San Fruttuoso 6pm; L9000, round-trip L14,000). Servizio Marittimo del Tigullio (☎0185 28 46 70) runs ferries from Portofino (every hr. 9:30am-4:30pm, L9000, round-trip L14,000) and Santa Margherita (every hr. 9:15am-4:15pm, L11,000, round-trip L20,000).

If you approach tiny San Fruttuoso by sea, the 16th-century *torre di Doria* (tower of Doria) will appear as a lone gladiator surrounded by an arena of green. The inhabitants of what can barely be called a hamlet are used to the solitary stance—when waters are rough, the villagers are isolated for days at a time (the only other means of reaching San Fruttuoso is by foot). The 10th-century **Abbazia di San Fruttuoso di Capodimonte,** the Benedictine monastery for which the town was named, houses a cloister and displays archaeological artifacts. (☎0185 77 27 03. Open June-Sept. Tu-Su 10am-6pm; Oct. and Mar.-June daily 10am-4pm; Dec.-Feb. Sa-Su and holidays 10am-4pm. L6000, children L4000.) Fifteen meters offshore and 17m underwater, the bronze Christ of the Depths stands with arms upraised in memory of the sea's casualties. The statue now serves as protector of scuba divers—here is your chance to take the plunge under watchful eyes. A replica of the statue stands in **Chiesa di San Fruttuoso,** next to the abbey. Think about the ferry ride home before you pass on making an offering to the *Sacrario dei Morti in Mare*. Its sparkling waters and ancient monastery make San Fruttuoso a quiet, restful daytrip. Avoid the expensive, touristy restaurants that outnumber the houses here—bring a picnic lunch. **Da Laura** has cheap hot meals. (Open daily 8am-6pm.)

SANTA MARGHERITA LIGURE ☎0185

From its founding in the 12th century, Santa Margherita Ligure led a calm existence as a fishing village far from the Levante limelight. In the early 20th century, the town fell into favor with Hollywood stars, a popularity boosted in the 1950s by a National Geographic feature. Grace and glitz paint the shore, but Art Deco lighting softens the pastel walls, palm trees line the harbor, and the serenity of the town's early days lingers on. Less overrun than much of the area, Santa Margherita remains one of the few affordable bases for exploring the Riviera di Levante.

TRANSPORTATION

Trains: P. Federico Raoul Nobili at the top of V. Roma. Intercity trains on the Pisa-Genoa line stop at Santa Margherita. To **Genoa** (40min., 2-3 per hr. 4:37am-10:03pm, L3600) and **La Spezia** (2 per hr. 5:39am-9:17pm, L6900), via **Cinque Terre** (1½hr., L5300).

Buses: Tigullio buses (☎0185 28 88 34) depart from P. V. Veneto at the small green kiosk on the waterfront. To **Portofino** (20min., 3 per hr., L1600) and **Camogli** (30min., every hr., L2000). Ticket office open 7:10am-7:40pm.

Ferries: Tigullio, V. Palestro, 8/1b (☎0185 28 15 98 or 0185 28 46 70). Boats leave from the docks at P. Martiri della Libertà. To: **Portofino** (every hr.; L6000, round-trip L10,000); **San Fruttuoso** (every hr.; L11,000, round-trip L20,000); and **Cinque Terre** (July-Sept. W and Sa-Su 1 tour trip per day; L25-30,000, round-trip L35-40,000.)

Taxis: (☎0185 28 65 08), P. Stazione.

ORIENTATION AND PRACTICAL INFORMATION

To get to the waterfront from the train station, take **Via Roma,** or take the stairs to the right of the stop sign in front of the station and follow **Via della Stazione** directly to the water. Two main squares lie on the waterfront: **Piazza Martiri della Libertà** and the smaller **Piazza Vittorio Veneto,** both lined with palm trees. **Via Gramsci** winds around the port and **Via XXV Aprile** leads to the tourist office, becoming **Corso Matteotti** alongside the other main square in town, **Piazza Mazzini.**

Tourist Office: Pro Loco, V. XXV Aprile, 2b (☎0185 28 74 85). Turn right from the train station onto V. Roma, follow it to C. Rainusso, and turn left. V. XXV Aprile is a hard right up from Largo Giusti. Enthusiastic English-speaking staff provides info, maps, and accommodations service. Open M-Sa 9am-12:30pm and 3-6pm, Su 9:30am-12:30pm.

Bike and Moped Rental: Noleggio Cicli e Motocicli, V. XXV Aprile, 11 (☎0330 87 86 12). Min. age 14. Motorscooter driving license required for tandem rental. Bike L9000 per hr., L20,000 per day. Motorscooter L30,000 per hr., L80,000 per day. Tandem L40,000 per hr., L130,000 per day. Open daily 10am-noon and 3-7pm.

Emergency: ☎113 **Police: Polizia Municipale,** C. Matteotti, 54 (☎0185 20 24 50). **Hospital:** (☎0185 68 31), V. F. Arpe. **Guardia Medica:** (☎118 or 0185 603 33 or 0185 27 33 82), for late-night and weekend medical attention.

Pharmacy: Farmarcia Internazionale, P. Martiri della Liberta, 2 (☎0185 28 71 89; fax 0185 28 17 08). Open in summer M-Sa 8:30am-12:30pm and 3:30-7:30pm; in winter 8:30am-12:30pm and 4-8pm. V, MC, AmEx.

Post Office: V. Gruncheto, 46 (☎0185 28 88 40), near the train station. Open M-F 8am-6pm, Sa 8am-1:15pm, Su 8am-noon. Fermo Posta. Currency exchange for L5000. **Postal Code:** 16038.

ACCOMODATIONS

Steer clear of ritzy waterfront accommodations. Santa Margherita is small enough that there's no such thing as a long walk to the ocean, and you can put the L30-40,000 you'll save on a room without a view to good use.

Hotel Nuova Riviera, V. Belvedere, 10 (☎/fax 0185 28 74 03; email gisabin@tin.it; www.space.tin.it/viaggi/gsabin), in a garden near P. Mazzini. Spacious, elegant rooms in a beautiful old villa built at the turn of the 20th century. Breakfast included. Singles L85-105,000; doubles L120-160,000; triples L165-210,000. They also have *affitacamere* (rooms to rent) of equally high caliber: doubles L90-120,000; apartments for 5 L180-300,000. 10% discount if you pay in cash. V, MC.

Hotel Terminus, P. Nobili, 4 (☎0185 28 61 21; fax 0185 28 25 46), to the left as you exit the station. So close you might hear the slight rumble of trains. Bask in the afterglow of the Italian Riviera's famed hotel culture. Owner Angelo's perfect English, enthusiasm, and cooking will ensure a "darling" stay. Buffet breakfast included. 4-course dinner on the garden terrace for a mere L30,000. 24 rooms. Singles (only 2 available) L75–90,000; doubles L140-160,000; triples L180-200,000. V, MC, AmEx.

Pensione Azalea, V. Roma, 60/V. Gramsci, 89 (☎0185 28 61 60). Swing a right out of the station. Take the elevator down to street level (V. Gramsci). Clean doubles with bath and breakfast L95,000.

Hotel Europa, V. Trento, 5 (☎0185 28 71 87). Tucked behind the harbor glitz, this modern hotel offers 18 rooms with TVs and phones. Parking available. Singles L60-90,000, with bath L70-110,000; doubles L90-100,000, with bath L90-120,000; triples L190,000; quads L220,000. V, MC.

FOOD

Markets, bakeries, and fruit vendors line C. Matteotti. On Fridays from 8am to 1pm, when cars are ousted from the *corso*, the street welcomes pedestrian shoppers. The **COOP supermarket**, C. Matteotti, 9c, off P. Mazzini, stocks basics. (☎0185 28 43 15. Open M–Sa 8:15am-1pm and 3:30-8pm. V.) The day's catch, hauled in by the local fleet, is sold at the morning **fish market** on Lungomare Marconi. (Open daily 8am-12:30pm; boats arrive Th-T 4-6pm.)

La Piadineria and Crêperia, V. Giuncheto, 5, off P. Martiri della Libertà. Escape from the traditional into the subtly hip. This nook-in-the-wall serves 30 types of *piadine* (heaping sandwiches on soft, thin bread; L7-10,000), *crepes* (L5-8000), and *taglieri* (generous plates of assorted meats and cheeses; L18,000). The delicious wines (L5000), beers (L4000), and cocktails (L10,000) complete a meal or late-night snack. Open Easter-Oct. Tu-Sa 5:30pm-3am; July-Sept. M-Sa 5:30pm-3am, Su 12:30pm-3am.

Trattoria Da Pezzi, V. Cavour, 21 (☎0185 28 53 03). Skip the pizza and load up on some real food. With *prosciutto* and melon for L11,000, pasta from L6500, and *secondi* from L5000, you can afford to accent the meal with a glass of beer (or several; from L3000 per glass) and finish off the meal with a whiskey on the rocks...make that whiskey on *gelato* (L7000).

Trattoria Baicin, V. Algeria, 9 (☎0185 28 67 63), off P. Martiri della Libertà. Papà Piero is the master chef. Mamma Carmela rolls the pasta and simmers the sauces. Try the homemade *trofie alla genovese* (*gnocchi* with string beans and pesto; L12,000). *Primi* from L10,000. *Menù* L28,000. Cover L2500. Open Tu–Su noon-3pm and 7pm-midnight. Kitchen closes at 10:30pm. V, MC, AmEx.

SIGHTS AND ENTERTAINMENT

If the lapping waves aren't invigorating your spirit, there's always the holy water at the Rococo **Basilica di Santa Margherita** at P. Caprera; it's held in basins shaped liked seashells, with incarnations throughout the interior. Dripping with gold and crystal, the church also contains fine Flemish and Italian works. At P. Martiri della Libertà, 32, a crowd guzzles beer and watches European football at **Sabot American Bar.** (☎0185 28 07 47. Open W-M 10am-2am.) The tribute to drinking (US of A style) continues right down the street at **Miami,** P. della Liberta, 29. Neon blue lights, couples necking in white vinyl booths, and L12,000 Manhattans set the high-rollin' scene. (☎0185 28 34 24. Open daily 5pm-3am.)

DAYTRIP FROM SANTA MARGHERITA LIGURE: PORTOFINO

Take the bus to Portofino Mare (not Portofino Vetta). From Portofino's P. Martiri della Libertà, Tigullio buses run to Santa Margherita (3 per hr., L1600). Tickets are sold at the green kiosk in P. Martiri della Libertà. Portofino is also accessible by ferry from Santa Margherita (every hr. 9am-7pm, L6000) and Camogli (2 per day, L13,000).

The **Castle of Saint George,** built in the 14th century when pesky Genoa ruled La Spezia, houses an archaeological museum and offers expansive views of the port. (Open in winter W-M 9:30am-12:30am and 2-7pm; in summer M-Th 9:30am-12:30pm and 5-8pm, F-Su 2-8pm. L5000.)

RIVIERA DI PONENTE

SAVONA ☎019

Savona, whose origins date back 1800 years is notable largely for its two hostels. The town continues to be an important connection point between the Po Valley and the Ligurian Coast. Because of its strategic position, it has been the desired war booty of many an invading army, including the meddlesome Genovese, who ransacked the harbor in 1528 and constructed a fortress on the Priamar promontory. Today the fortress houses a hostel and art and archeological museums.

TRANSPORTATION

Trains: to **Genoa** (1-3 per hr. 4:48am-11:45pm) and **Ventimiglia** (1-2 per hr. 6:03am-10:58pm). From the train station, take bus #2 (every 30 min. 6:23am-9:23pm) to the city center and the fortress hostel.

Buses: to **Finale Ligure** (5:02am-10:22pm), stops outside the train station. Buses #2 and 5 leave P. Martiri for the station (every 25 min. 5:15am-midnight, L1400). Pick up a ticket at the train station.

ORIENTATION AND PRACTICAL INFORMATION

The 16th-century fortress lies toward the water off **Piazza Priamar.** The medieval *centro storico* is bounded by **Via Manzoni** and **Via Paleocapa** and filled with churches and *palazzi.* Across the harbor (by means of Calata Sbarbaro) lies **Piazza Martiri** and Savona's summer social scene.

TOURIST AND LOCAL SERVICES

Tourist Office, V. Guidobono, 125r (☎019 840 23 21; fax 019 840 36 72). Maps and bus schedules. Open M-Sa 8:30am-12:30pm and 3-6pm.

Bike rental: Noleggio Biciclette, in the Public Gardens. Take V. Dante down to P. Heroe dei Due Mondi. Bikes for kids and grown-ups. L4500 per hr., L18,000 per day.

English Bookstore: Libreria Economica, V. Pia, 88r (☎019 83 87 424). Selection of contemporary novels exemplifies scarcity. Open Tu-Sa 9:15am-12:30pm and 3:30-7:30pm, M 3:30-7:30pm.

EMERGENCY AND COMMUNICATION

Emergency: Police: ☎112. **Medical:** ☎118. **Pronto Soccorso:** ☎019 84 06. **Guardia Medica:** ☎019 800 55 66 88. **Ambulance: Croce Bianca,** ☎019 81 14 18. **Hospital: Ospedale San Paolo,** V. Genova, 30 (☎019 84 041).

Pharmacy: C. Italia, 153r. Open daily 12:30-3:30pm and 7:30pm-8:30am.

Post Office: (☎019 84 41), in P. Diaz. Phone cards, Fermo Posta, and **currency exchange** available 8:15am-5:30pm. Open M-Sa 8am-6pm.

ACCOMMODATIONS AND CAMPING

Ostello Fortezza del Priamar, C. Mazzini (☎019 81 26 53; email priamarhostel@iol.it). Walk up the ramp to the fortress and follow the signs through the labyrinth of dark tunnels to the hostel. With cell-like rooms and a not particularly friendly welcome, you're sure to receive an authentic fortress experience. Reception open 7-10am and 3:30-11:30pm. Reservations strongly recommended. 65 beds. Dorm with breakfast, L22,000. Singles (only 2) L26,000.

Ostello Villa de Franceschini, Villa alla Strà, 29, Conca Verde (☎019 26 32 22; email concaverd@hotmail.com). There is no public transportation to the *Franceschini*, 3km away from the train station; you have to call and hope they'll be willing to pick you up (larger groups have better chances). Pick-ups 9am-8pm, pre-scheduled pick-ups at 5 and 7pm. Reception open 7am-10pm and 4pm-12:30am. 249 beds. Dorm with breakfast L18,000; family rooms L20,000 per person.

Camping Vittoria, V. Rizza, 111 (☎019 88 14 39). Catch the #6 (5am-11pm) on the V. Baselli side of P. Mameli. Campgrounds are on the water with a small beach. L8500 per person, L13,000 per tent, L5000 per car. Electricity L3500. Prices increase July-Aug.

FOOD

EKOM Discount Alimentare, V. Montesisto, 10r (☎019 84 81 40). No name brands, but lots of cheap food, including bottles of wine for as little as L2000. Open daily 8:30am-12:30pm and 3:30-6:30pm.

Di per Di, V. Boselli, 34/36r. More typical grocery store shopping. Another link of the chain lies down the street from the tourist office.

Trattoria Mondovi, V. Sormano, 13r (☎019 83 86 648). Trendy it's not; for a cool breeze, you'll have to go down to the *centro storico* at the waterfront. But the mouth-watering food that's sure to rock your *mondo* makes up for the absence of sailboats. *Gamberoni al griglia* (grilled shrimp; L16,000) and *fritto di tortani* (fried calamari; L12,000) with lots of lemon are worth it. Finish off with heavenly *tiramisu* for L3500. Pizza from L5000, *primi* from L8000. Cover L2000. Open Tu-Sa 11:30am-2:30pm and 7-11pm, M 11:20am-2:30pm.

Vino e Farinata, V. Pia, 15r. A good place to fill up on typical Ligurian fare–*farinata* (L7000) abounds, as do fish dishes. A delicious serving of salmon, shrimp, or swordfish costs only L12,000. *Primi* from L7000, *secondi,* L10-15,000. Cover L2000.

BEACHES AND ENTERTAINMENT

A **public beach** lies along the water next to the public gardens. Take C. Italia to V. Dante. Walk past the statue of a gallant Garibaldi to a small stretch of sand where speedo-wearing *ragazzi* (guys) engage in pick-up games of soccer. Many bars line the water on the far side of the harbor, but for Italians with dreads, **Birrò,** V. Baglietto, 42r, is really the only option. Expect lots of reggae, as well as a live DJ every night at 11. Shake your soul down the dock past all the hipper-than-thou spots for a L3000 bottle of beer or L7000 cocktails. (Open daily 6pm-1am.)

FINALE LIGURE ☎019

At the base of a statue along the beachfront promenade, a plaque labels Finale the place for *"Il riposo del popolo,"* the people's rest. Whether your idea of *riposo* involves bodysurfing in the choppy waves near Torrente Porra, browsing through the chic boutiques that fill Finalmarina, or free-climbing past Finalborgo's looming 15th-century Castello di San Giovanni, you have many options. In Finale Ligure, the *gelaterie* almost outnumber the weary travelers licking ice-cream cones along the tree-lined boardwalk. Find a place that makes its *nocciola* with real nuts, and nap on the soft sands as your museum fatigue melts into oblivion.

TRANSPORTATION

Trains: in P. V. Veneto. To **Genoa** (1hr., every hr. 1st train 8:30, last 1:40pm, L6900) and **Ventimiglia** (2½hr., every hr. 9:40am-11:10pm, L8900).

Buses: SAR departs from the front of the train station. Buy tickets from *tabacchi* nearby. To **Finalborgo** (5min., every 20 min., L1400). Catch the bus for **Borgo Verezzi** across the street (10min., 8 per day, L1500).

ORIENTATION AND PRACTICAL INFORMATION

The city is divided into three sections: **Finalpia** to the east, **Finalmarina** in the center, and **Finalborgo,** the old city, inland to the northwest. The train station and most of the listings below are located in Finalmarina. The main street winds through the town between the station and **Piazza Vittorio Emanuele II,** changing its name from **Via de Raimondi** to **Via Pertica** to **Via Garibaldi.** From P. V. Emanuele, **Via della Concezione** runs west to the water and east to **V. S. Pietro.** To reach the old city, far behind the train station, turn left from the station, cross under the tracks, and continue left on **Via Domenico Bruneghi.**

TOURIST, FINANCIAL, AND LOCAL SERVICES

Tourist Office: IAT, V. S. Pietro, 14 (☎019 68 10 19; fax 019 68 18 04), on the main street overlooking the sea. Free maps, free information, and plenty of surliness to share. Open M-Sa 9am-12:30pm and 3:30-7pm, Su 9am-noon.

Currency Exchange: Banca Carige, V. Garibaldi, 4, at the corner of P. V. Emanuele. L8000 service charge. Open M-F 8:20am-1:20pm and 2:30-4pm. On Saturdays, try the post office for lower rates (L5000) and longer waits. **ATMs** are in Banca Carige, V. Garibaldi, 4, and Banca San Paolo, V. della Concezione, 33.

English Bookstore: La Libreria, V. Pertica, 35 (☎019 79 26 03), has a few racks of foreign books including some Danielle Steele and Stephen King for the literary purists out there. Open M-Sa 8:30am-12:30pm and 3:30-7:30pm (and Su during the summer).

Bike Rental: Oddonebici (☎019 69 42 15), on V. Colombo. Jealous of all the Italians on their Vespas? You too can zoom around town—as long as you don't mind pedaling. Adult bicycles for rent at L30,000 per day. Maybe walking ain't so bad. Open M 2:30-8pm, Tu-Sa 8am-12:30pm and 2:30-8pm. V, MC.

EMERGENCY AND COMMUNICATIONS

Emergencies: Police: V. Brunanghi, 68 (☎112 or ☎019 69 26 66). **Ambulance:** ☎118. **Hospital: Ospedale Santa Corona,** V. XXV Aprile, 128 (☎019 623 01), in Pietra Ligure. **P. A. Croce Bianca,** V. Torino, 16 (☎019 69 23 33 or 019 69 23 34), in Finalmarina. **Guardia Medica:** ☎118. Open M-F 8pm-8am, Sa 2pm-8am.

Pharmacy: Comunale, V. Ghiglieri, 2 (☎019 69 26 70), at the intersection where V. Raimondi becomes V. Pertica. The sign posted outside lists the address and phone number of the night-service pharmacy. Open M-Sa 8:30am-12:30pm and 4-10pm.

Internet Access: Civica Biblioteca (☎019 69 17 62), off P. S. Catterina, in Finalborgo. L6000 per hr. Open in summer M 3:30-6:30pm and 10:20pm-12:30am, Tu-F 9am-noon and 3:30-6:30pm, Sa 9am-noon; in winter M 4-7pm and 10:30pm-12:30am, Tu and Th 9am-noon and 4-7pm, W and F-Sa 9am-noon.

Post Office: V. della Concezione, 29 (☎019 69 28 38). Open M-F 8am-6pm, Sa 8am-1:15pm. Phone cards, fax, and money exchange (L5000). **Postal Code:** 17024.

ACCOMMODATIONS AND CAMPING

The youth hostel has the best prices, not to mention the best view. In July and August, it may be the only place not booked solid (they don't take reservations). For all other accommodations listed, reservations are strongly recommended. Rooms for rent in private homes can be arranged through the tourist office.

Castello Wuillerman (HI) (☎/fax. 019 69 05 15; email hostelfinaaleligure@libero.it), on V. Generale Caviglia, in a red brick castle overlooking the sea. From the station, take a left onto V. Mazzini, which becomes V. Torino. Turn left onto tiny V. degli Ulivi, which leads to a daunting set of stairs. At the top, a small sign, a huge groan, and yet another set of stairs mark the way to the castle on the left. Once you see the place, however, you'll feel like you floated up. This heavenly hostel has it all; a beautiful courtyard, newly renovated bathrooms, laundry (L8000 per load), vegetarian meals (L14,000), and internet access (L8000 per hr.). Breakfast and sheets included. Reception 7-10am and 5-10pm. Curfew 11:30pm. Dorms L20,000 for HI card-holders. No phone reservations. Open Mar. 15-Oct. 15.

Pensione Enzo, Gradinata delle Rose, 3 (☎69 13 83). Take a break from the ceaseless staircase on your way to the hostel and turn left prematurely to give the Enzo's elevator a spin. The Enzo has been around for 35 years and presumably held court over this hill until the Castello came to the throne. Pension available. 7 doubles L60-92,000. Open Easter-Sept. No credit cards.

Albego Oasi, V. San Cagna, 25 (☎/fax 019 69 17 17; email albergooasi@libreo.it). Veer left on V. Brunenghi from the station, and walk through the underpass to V. Silla on your right. Walk up the hill, slightly further than the advertised 100m, and the Oasi is on your left. Closer to the train station than the hostel, this hotel provides 12 tidy rooms (some with bathrooms and balconies), a gravelly garden patio, a sitting room with TV, and a restaurant (dinner L20,000). Singles L45,000; doubles L90,000. Extra bed L45,000.

Albergo Carla, V. Colombo, 44 (☎019 69 22 85). Located smack-dab in the middle of tourist-land, this hotel offers private bathrooms, a bar, and restaurant. Breakfast L7000. Singles L45,000; doubles L75,000. Pension required July-Sept., half L50,000, full L82,000. V, MC, AmEx.

Albergo San Marco, V. della Concezione, 22 (☎019 69 25 33). From the station, walk straight ahead down V. Saccone, and turn left on V. della Concezione. Enter through a restaurant with purple tablecloths. The 14 spotless rooms have bath and phone; many include balcony and ocean view. Most importantly, all provide easy access to the waterfront. Minimal English spoken. Breakfast included. Reservations recommended. Open Easter-Sept. Singles L60,000; doubles L80,000; extra bed L15,000. Full-pension L80-98,000, depending on the season. V, MC, AmEx.

Hotel Orchidea, V. XXV Aprile, 15 (☎019 69 05 26). Follow V. Brunenghi to V. XXV Aprile, then hang a right. Although a 15min. walk from the beach, the ravishing roses and trickling fountains in the enclosed patio, set back among the verdant sprawl of home vegetable gardens, make the hike worthwhile. The more expensive rooms have connected bathrooms, and all include breakfast and the use of a terrace for sun-bathing. Open Easter–Sept. Doubles L80-90,000. In August, full-pension required L70-80,000.

Albergo Marita, V. Saccone, 17 (☎019 69 29 04), set back from the street leading from the station (on the left). 9 clean, functional rooms, some with balconies. Breakfast L8000. 3-day min. stay. Summer reservations required. Singles L35-40,000; doubles with bath L50-80,000. Full-pension L75,000 per person. Prices rise July-Aug.

Camping: Camping Tahiti (☎/fax. 019 60 06 00), on V. Varese. Take the bus for Calvisio from the stop in P. V. Veneto. Get off at Bar Paradiso, and cross the small bridge at V. Rossini. Take a left and walk along the river to V. Vanese. Positioned on a hill, the site features 8 terraces, 90 lots, and a 360-person capacity. Reception 8am-8pm. Open Easter through Oct. 15. High season L11,000 per person, L10,000 per tent. Electricity L4000. Hot showers L1000. **Del Mulino** (☎019 60 16 69), on V. Castelli. From the station, take the Calvisio bus to the Boncardo Hotel, and follow the brown, then yellow, signs to the campsite entrance 300m from the shore. Bar, restaurant, and mini-market on premises. Laundry L10,000. Office open Apr.-Sept. 8am-8pm. L11,000 per person, L10-14,000 per tent. Hot showers. Off-season prices lower.

FOOD

Trattorie and pizzerias line the streets closest to the beach. **Simpatia Crai,** V. Bruneghi, 2a, down V. Mazzini from the station, is a small supermarket that stocks the basics. (Open M-Sa 8am-12:30pm and 4-6:30pm.)

Spaghetteria Il Posto, V. Porro, 21 (☎019 60 00 95). The amicable hosts at this local favorite fill your table (and stomach) with mountains of well-priced pasta and oodles of vegetarian options. *Penne quattro stagioni* (with bacon, mushrooms, tomatoes, artichokes, and mozzarella; L10,000), *penne pirata* (with shrimp and salmon; L12,000), and *spaghetti marinara* (with capers, clams, and olives; L12,000) are all delicious. Cover L1500. Open Tu-Su 7-10:30pm. Closed the 1st 2 weeks of March.

Farinata e Vino, V. Roma, 25 (☎019 692 562). This small, popular *trattoria* bills itself as *"una trattoria alla vecchia maniera"* (old school). Enjoy homestyle cooking (especially the *pesce*) at excellent prices. *Primi* L9-14,000, *secondi* L12-18,000. Open 12:30-2pm and 7:30-9pm. Call for reservations in summer.

Da Badabin, V. Garibaldi, 75. (☎019 69 43 66). Thick 'n crusty pizza with shrooms or eggplant (L2500 per slice). The owner's mother runs the place and cooks up more involved dishes (lasagna; L7000). Mamma knows best. Open daily 10am-8pm.

Ninja Pizza, V. Gandolino, 7 (☎019 69 21 84). If you fear comic book memorabilia, keep clear–the walls are plastered with the stuff. Serves teenage mutant ninja pizza *al trancio* (by the slice) for L2500. Open daily 10am-8pm.

SIGHTS

The towns surrounding Finale Ligure are worth extra exploration. SAR buses run to tiny **Borgo Verezzi** (every 15min., 1st bus 9:06am, L1800). Get off at the 1st stop in Borgo; from here, buses leave for **Verezzi** (5 per day, last return bus M-F 6:40pm, Sa-Su 7:10pm). Or hike up the winding V. Nazario Sauro (about an hour), and delight in the far-reaching vistas and flowering vines whose fuchsia petals flutter into the gutter with the passing of roaring motor bikes. The cool, tranquil streets, caves, and artificial rock formations of the tiny medieval village at the top make the trip worthwhile. Stop at **A Topia,** V. Roma, 16, for a wood-burning oven-baked pizza *cuattro stagioni* for L10,000. (☎019 616 905. Open evenings daily; closed M in winter.) If you end up in Verezzi after dark, by no means take a shortcut down the hillside. Guard dogs run rampant off the main road.

Enclosed within ancient walls, Finalborgo, the historic quarter of Finale Ligure, is a 1km walk or short bus ride up V. Bruneghi from the station. Past the **Porto Reale,** the Chiostro di Santa Caterina, a 14th-century edifice, houses the **Museo Civico del Finale,** dedicated to Ligurian history. (☎019 69 02 20. Open Tu-Sa 10am-noon and 3-6pm, Su 9am-noon. Free.) Up a tough but fulfilling trail, the ruined **Castel Govone** lends a spectacular view of Finale. For further rock climbing in the area, the **Rock Store,** P. Garibaldi, 14, in Finalborgo, provides maps and necessary gear. (☎019 69 02 08. Open Tu-Su 9am-12:30pm and 4-7:30pm.)

BEACHES

Spray-painted on the inner wall of the tunnel that leads to the prime free beach in Finale Marina is "Voglio il sole/Cerco nuova luce/nella *konfusione*" ("I want the sun/I look for new light/in the confusion"). Watch out Dante. If you empathize with our aspiring graffiti poet, you've come to the right place. Forget the narrow strip of free beach in town where you'd feel like a beached sardine. Instead, walk east along V. Aurelia through the 1st tunnel. The beach before you, cradled by craggy overhanging cliffs, is an ideal spot to offer up your skin for sacrifice to the sun gods. Prefer to play it safe and pay homage to the moon? Even in piping hot summer, the nights can be cool, so bring a few blankets and another warm body. Slather on the best kind of skin coverage out there, snuggle up, and live a little.

ENTERTAINMENT

A bar popular among young tourists and locals alike, **Pilade** features live music Friday nights, ranging from blues to jazz to soul. The wooden statue of the horn player in the red tux on the sidewalk and the real live *homo-sapien* saxophonist inside will draw you in like the Pied Pipers of Ligure-Lin. Just be willing to do a little shouting above the music to order a mixed drink (L8,000-10,000) or a beer (L4500-10,000). In the wee hours the rest of the week, you'll find drinkers nodding their heads in unison to rock and Italian techno, eyes glazed over from one too many a Peroni. Pizza and burgers always available. (V. Garibaldi, 67. ☎019 69 22 20. Open daily 10am-2am. Closed Thursdays in winter.) As the sun sets, walk east along V. Aurelia through two tunnels to reach Capo San Donato, a rocky concrete crag, and the illustrious disco-shanty **Cuba Libre.** It's complete with multiple dance floors and bars, fog machine, and political message. (☎019 60 12 84. Cover L25,000 for men, L20,000 for women. Open F-Sa 10pm-sunrise.) **Bar Centrale,** P. Garibaldi, 28, in Finalborgo, has been serving thirsty rock-climbers for half a century. Discuss your struggle to surmount the nearby Rocca di Perti or Montagna Monte Carlo (at 1389m, among the highest in the region), or simply eat your *gelato* in silence. (☎019 69 17 78. Open Tu-Su 7:30am-2am.)

SAN REMO ☎0184

Once a glamorous retreat for Russian nobles, czars, *literati*, and artists, San Remo is now the Italian Las Vegas and the largest resort on the Italian Riviera (with traffic to boot). High-stakes playboys gamble and bikini-clad women gambol along the palm-lined promenade of Corso Imperatrice and in the casino. As befits its location on the Riviera dei Fiori (Riviera of Flowers), San Remo blooms with carnations year-round. The winding alleys of La Pigna, the pinecone-shaped historic district, provide respite from the high-rollers that overrun the rest of the city. In Italy, San Remo is most famous for its music festival in February.

TRANSPORTATION AND PRACTICAL INFORMATION. San Remo lies on the **train** line between **Ventimiglia** (15min., every hr. 7:18am-10:28pm, L2700) and **Genoa** (3hr., every 2hr. 5:45am-10:05pm, L13,500). To **Milan** (3½hr., every 2hr. 5:22am-7:36pm, L24,300) and **Turin** (4½hr., every 45min. 2:37-7:18pm, L18,600). The city is formed by three main parallel streets: from the train station **Via Nino Bixio** leads along the coast to the right; **Via Roma** splits off after 30m and joins V. N. Bixio after 500m; and **Corso Giacomo Matteotti** starts to the left of the train station. Turn left from the station and right on V. Nuvoloni for the **APT tourist office,** V. Nuvoloni, 1. (☎0184 57 15 71; fax 0184 50 76 49; www.sanremonet.com. Open M-Sa 8am-7pm, Su 9am-1pm.) The helpful staff speaks English, Spanish, German, and French and has numerous brochures. Services include: **emergency** (☎118); **police** (☎113); **hospital: Ospedale Civile,** V. G. Borea, 56 (☎0184 53 61); **currency exchange** and 24-hr. **ATM: Banco Ambrosiano Veneto,** V. Roma, 62 (☎0184 59 23 11; open M-F 8:20am-1:20pm and 2:35-4:05pm, Sa 8:20-11:50am); **laundromat: Blu Acquazzura,** V. A. Volta, 131 (L8000 to wash and dry up to 7kg; open daily 6am-7:30pm); **internet access: Mailboxes, Etc.,** C. Cavallotti, 86, with photocopy, fax, scanner and CD burner (☎0184 59 16 73; 2 computers; L15,000 per hr; open M-F 8:30am-6:30pm, Sa 9am-1pm); **post office,** V. Roma, 156 (☎0184 53 32 18; open M-Sa 8am-6pm); **postal code:** 18038.

ACCOMMODATIONS. Hotel Mara, V. Roma, 93, has simple, immaculate rooms without baths. From the train station, take a right on V. Roma and walk for five minutes; it's on the left. (☎0184 53 38 60. 7 doubles L65,000; 2 triples L100,000.) The owner of **Albergo Al Dom,** C. Mombello, 13, 2nd fl., likes to bargain for the grand, old-style rooms with baths and high ceilings in this former casino. From the train station walk to the right on C. N. Bixio and take the 3rd left, which is C. Mombello. (☎0184 50 14 60. Singles L60,000; doubles L90-100,000. V, MC.) To get to **Allogio Piedigrotta,** V. Volturno, 19, 3rd fl., walk on V. Roma from the train station and take the 6th left. The rooms are basic and lack baths, but they're the cheapest in town. (☎0184 50 43 60. 4 singles L30-45,000; 2 doubles L50-65,000.)

FOOD. San Remo's restaurants are generally overpriced. For good cheese, ham, and bread try the **Panetteria,** C. Mombello, 41 (☎0184 57 92 32. Open M-Sa 6:30am-1pm and 4-8pm.) For a homey atmosphere with delicious and hearty portions, try **Pizzeria Ai 4 Amici,** V. 20 Septembre, 30. Turn left where V. Roma and C. N. Bixio merge. Check out the hanging bottles on the ceiling, and slurp up *spaghetti alle vongole* (with clams) for L16,000. (☎0184 50 04 38. *Pizza* L9-14,000, *primi*

PLAY IT AGAIN, SAN (REMO) San Remo's fame goes back to the **Festival della Canzone Italiana.** Most Italian youth know the music festival better than the St. Peter's Cathedral in Rome, and more Italians watch the music competition than the national soccer tournament. Every year during the last week of February, 30 Italian vocalists (chosen in local competitions throughout the country) compete to represent Italy in the Eurovision, a pan-European contest. Competition is fierce, and the Italian representative often goes on to win the Eurovision. Jovanotti, Totto Cotugno, Eros Ramazzotti, Zucchero, and many other stars of Italian pop and rock have been discovered in San Remo. Organized by the City of San Remo and the Italian public television station, RAI, the festival caters to many international fashion designers, models, and other celebrities as a public testing-ground for their newest threads, cars, and significant others.

from L10,000, *secondi* from L14,000. Tourist *menù* L25,000. Open daily 10am-1am. V, MC, AmEx, Diners.) The wooden decor is more creative than the name of **Ristorante Pizzeria Italia.** V. XX Septembre, 39, but it's famous for good pizza (L9-12,000). (☎0184 50 02 78. *Primi* from L14,000, *secondi* from L15,000, desserts L6000. Tourist *menù* L30,000. Open daily 9am-2am. V, MC, AmEx, Diners.)

SIGHTS. Gamblers frequent the **Edwardian Casino,** C. Inglesi, 18, a dazzling example of Belle Epoque architecture. (☎0184 59 51. No sneakers or jeans; coat and tie required in winter. Minimum age 18. The roulette wheel spins from 2:30pm; blackjack begins at 4pm. Casino closes around 3am. M-F L5000, Sa-Su L15,000.) The "American Room" of one-armed bandits has neither dress code nor entrance fee (although you'll surely pay), and its 10am opening lures gamblers with early twitches. The Russian Orthodox **Chiesa di Cristo Salvatore,** across the street from the tourist office, shows who were the first gamblers in San Remo: after losing the money in the casino, the Russians would repent here in the intricate onion-domes among Russian religious art. Enjoy the perplexing exterior architecture; there is less to see inside. (Open daily 9:30am-12:30pm and 3-6pm. Donation required.)

BORDIGHERA ☎0184

When Italian writer Giovanni Ruffini crafted the plot line for his 1855 melodrama, *Il Dottor Antonio*, he unknowingly laid the foundation for the development of both Bordighera and the Italian Riviera's tourism industry. The novel tells the story of a resplendent young English girl brought to the brink of death by illness, but miraculously revived by Bordighera's sultry sands and warm wisps of summer air. Within a decade, the novel's devoted English readers clamored for the real thing, leading to the construction of the first of several huge hotels, the Hotel d'Angleterre, and the subsequent rapid growth of Bordighera into one of the Riviera's foremost resort towns. In the latter half of the 19th century, tourists, among them Queen Margaret and Claude Monet, outnumbered natives by as much as five to one. Although the town still fills up in July and August, the ratio is a little less extreme these days, leaving all the more room for seaside sallying amongst the redolent palm-lined streets.

TRANSPORTATION

Trains: in P. Eroi Libertà. To **Genoa** (3hr., L13,500) and **Ventimiglia** (every hr., L1700).

Buses: Riveria Transporte buses stop every 300m along V. V. Emanuele and run to **Ventimiglia** (20min., L2200) and **San Remo** (20min., L1150).

ORIENTATION AND PRACTICAL INFORMATION

The bus from Ventimiglia stops on the main street, **Via Vittorio Emanuele,** which runs west from the city's train station in **Piazza Eroi della Libertà.** From behind the station, the scenic **Lungomare Argentina,** a 2km beach promenade, runs to the *città* *moderna* (new town), where most offices and shops are found. To the east, near the *città alta*, the historic center, are residential areas. Built on a hill, the 15th-century town is accessible by three gates, of which the **Porta Sottana** is the closest.

Tourist Office: V. Roberto, 1 (☎0184 26 23 22; fax 0184 26 44 55). From the train station walk along V. Roma, turn left on V. V. Emanuele, and take the 1st right onto V. Roberto. The office is just past the small park. Helpful staff hands out maps, hotel listings, and history factoids in English. Open M-Sa 8am-7pm, Su 9am-1pm.

Currency Exchange: Banca Commerciale Italiana, V. V. Emanuele, 165 (☎0184 26 36 54). **ATM** outside, one of many along V. V. Emanuele. Open M-F 8:20am-1:25pm and 2:50-4:15pm, Sa 8:20-11:50am.

Emergency: ☎113. **Police:** V. 1 Maggio, 43 (☎112 or 0184 26 26 26). **Ambulance:** ☎118. **Hospital:** V. Aurelia, 122 (☎0184 27 51).

Pharmacy: Farmacia Centrale, V. V. Emanuele, 145 (☎0184 26 12 46). List of 24hr. pharmacies posted. Open July-Aug. M-F 8:30am-12:30pm and 3:30-7:30pm. **Farmacia Internazionale,** V. V. Emanuele, 105 (☎0184 26 14 09). Open T-Su 8:30am-12:30pm and 3:30-7:30pm.

Post Office: P. Eroi della Libertà, 6 (☎0184 26 16 74), across and left from the train station. Currency exchange and phone cards. Fermo Posta L300 per letter and L1000 per package. Open M-Sa 8am-6pm. **Postal Code:** 18012.

ACCOMMODATIONS

During the high-season *(alta stagione)*, many hotels require that clients accept full-pension, half-pension, or at least breakfast.

Albergo Palme, V. Roma, 5 (☎/fax 0184 26 12 73). Genial proprietor will greet you with coherent English; tiny dog Liu will say hello with a lick to the toe. Some rooms have balconies and private bathrooms, but all have access to a terrace overlooking the *piazza*. 12 rooms. Breakfast included. Singles L40,000; doubles L80,000. During high season, pension required L68-72,000. No credit cards.

Albergo Nagos, P. Eroi della Libertà, 7 (☎0184 26 04 57), across from the train station on the left. If you have a balcony, the rusty rail is a great place to rest your weary feet. No English spoken. Communal bathrooms. Breakfast L5000. Singles L45,000; doubles L70,000. Half-pension L55-60,000; full-pension L70,000. No credit cards.

Pensione Miki, V. Lagazzi, 14 (☎0184 26 18 44). From the station, turn left on V. V. Emanuele. V. Lagazzi is several blocks down on the right. This family-run *pensione* rests in a serene, residential setting. Small rooms with balconies and a garden. 16 beds. Breakfast and showers included. Try to get them to slash L7000 from the price by asking if you can forego breakfast. Singles L50,000; doubles L90,000. Half-pension L67,000; full-pension L77,000. Full- or half-pension required during summer.

FOOD

In Bordighera, budget restaurants are few and far between. Some *trattorie* in the *città alta*, however, offer traditional Ligurian cuisine at reasonable prices. Bordighera is famed for its local dessert, *cubaite* (elaborately decorated wafers filled with caramel cream), and the Rossese wine from Dolceacqua. The **covered market,** P. Garibaldi, 46-48, has picnic supplies. (Open in summer daily 8am-noon and 4-7pm; in winter Su-F 7am-1pm.) There is also a **STANDA supermarket** at V. Libertà, 32. (Open M-Sa 8:15am-7pm, Su 9am-1pm and 4-7:30pm. V, MC, AmEx.)

Pizzeria Napoletana, V. Emanuele, 250 (☎0184 26 37 22). Delicious, reasonably priced food makes the virtual mosh pit of customers struggling to get inside worth the hassle. Pizza L8-15,000. *Primi* L8-15,000, *secondi* L10-18,000. Cover L1000. Open W-M noon-3pm and 6pm-1am.

Crêperie-Caffè Giglio, V. Emanuele, 158 (☎0184 26 15 30). A popular local hangout with a large selection of inexpensive *panini* (from L5000) and delicious crepes (L6-11,000). Celebrate the proximity of the French-Italian border with the mozzarella, tomato, and oregano crepe (L8000). Is it an Italian crepe or French pizza? Open daily in summer 11am-3am; in winter Tu-Su 11am-3am.

Gastronomia and Rosticceria Marisa, V. V. Emanuele, 319 (☎0184 26 16 57). A rotisserie chicken might not do you much good, but a heaping slice of lasagna (L6,000 per 250g) or *torta verde* (L5500 per 250g) sure will. Ask at one of the *gelaterie* for a plastic spoon. Open Tu-Sa 8:30am-1pm and 4:30-7:30pm, Su 4:30-7:30pm.

SIGHTS

The **Giardino Esotico Pallanca,** (exotic garden), contains over 3000 species of cacti and rare South American flora. Say hi to burro Giorgina at the top. Walk 1km down V. Aziglia, V. Madonna della Ruota, 1, or grab a bus on V. Emanuele in the direction of San Remo and ask the driver where to get off. (☎0184 26 63 47. Open M 3-7pm, Tu-Su 9am-12:30pm and 3-7pm. L8000.) A stroll east along V. Romana provides a view of the many hotels constructed during the 19th century for the fans of *Il Dottor Antonio*. Past P. de Amicis, the road becomes C. F. Rossi. To the right, paths meander through a park where cannons still guard the town. Steps lead to **Chiesa di Sant'Ampelio,** built around the grotto where Ampelio, the town hermit (later the town patron) holed up. Preferring *pesce* over prayers, fisherman and tanners congregate on the rocks below the church. (Open Su at 10am. Otherwise knock.) On May 14, the church hosts the **Festival of Sant'Ampelio** with a procession and ritual pomp. From September to May, the **Chiosco della Musica** on the boardwalk offers concerts. Bordighera hosts the **International Salon of Humor,** a juried contest of humorous drawings and cabaret-style comedy, from August 27 to September 4.

ENTERTAINMENT

For less wholesome, but just as jolly good fun, try **Graffiti Pub,** V. V. Emanuele, 122. The statue of the bulldog may have a faceguard, but that doesn't keep the friendly bar bums from boisterous yapping and frenzied lapping (beer on tap L4,000-7,000; liquor L6000). A raucous 25+ crowd fills the comfy blue lounges inside and tables along the street. Join in the barking and bite a burger for L6000 or a *panino* for L5000. (☎0184 26 15 90. Open M-Sa 5pm-3am. V, MC.) Youth like to think they're the center of the universe; you can watch the world (and the room) spin and pick up a late night snack at **Planet Cafe.** Beer L3500-6000; glass of wine L2000-3000; panini/pizza, L1000-4500. (Open daily 6pm-4am. No credit cards.) As the sun sets, walk through the underground tunnel to the left of the train station to **Disco Kursaal,** a large complex that hosts a wide variety of music, both live and recorded. (Lungomare, 7. ☎0184 26 46 85. Open July-Aug. 10pm until the DJ gets tired of puttin' the needle to the vinyl; Sept.-June F-Su.) If you need an escape from smoky pubs along V. V. Emanuele, **Chica Loca,** down the beachfront from the Disco, is bound to be open late for some fresh breezes and frothy beer.

VENTIMIGLIA ☎0184

Around 2000 years ago the final stages of the expansion of the Empire brought the Romans to the mouth of the Roya River, near the present day border between France and Italy. Augustus and his cohorts took hold of the area by ruthlessly conquering a local tribe, the Intemeli. To propagate the glistening glory of Augustus' power, the town was named Venti Intemelian, which evolved into Ventimiglia. Though the Roman Empire gleams no longer, the name is still legible through the tarnish. Today, with colossal remains of a Roman theater, winding 11th-century streets, and Romanesque religious sites, Ventimiglia makes an agreeable base for those who want to explore the famous oases and pebble beaches of the Italian Riviera and the French Côte d'Azur.

TRANSPORTATION

Trains: in P. Stazione (☎147 88 80 88). To: **Nice** (45min., every hr., L10,100); **Genoa** (3hr., every 1¼hr., L15,000); and **Marseilles** (3½hr., 4 per day, L48,500). **Luggage storage:** L5000. Open daily 8am-7pm.

Buses: Agenzia Viaggi & Turismo Monte Carlo, V. Cavour, 57 (☎0184 35 75 77), left from the tourist office. Office open M-Sa 9am-12:30pm and 2:30-7pm. To: **Bordighera** (15min., 4 per hr., L2200); **Imperia-Porto Maurizio** (1hr., every hr., L6600), via **San Remo** (30 min., 4 per hr., L3300); and other local towns.

Bike Rental: Eurocicli, V. Cavour, 70b (☎0184 35 18 79). L3000 per hr., L15,000 per day. Open M-Sa 8:30am-noon and 3:30-7:30pm. V, MC.

ORIENTATION AND PRACTICAL INFORMATION

Frequent trains and blue **Riviera Transporte** buses link these two coasts. Travelers should experience little hassle crossing the border—just bring your passport. To get to the center of town from the train station, cross the street and walk down **Via della Stazione.** The 2nd crossroad is **Via Cavour,** the 3rd **Via Roma. Via della Stazione** becomes **Corso Repubblica,** which leads to the waterfront at the **Lungo Roya G. Rossi.**

TOURIST AND LOCAL SERVICES

Tourist Office: V. Cavour, 61 (☎0184 35 11 83). City maps and info on neighboring attractions. Open M-Sa 9am-12:30pm and 3-7pm. The travel agency next door, **Agenzia Viaggi & Turismo Monte Carlo,** V. Cavour, 57c (☎0184 35 75 77; fax 0184 35 53 82), has currency exchange and bus and hotel information. Some English spoken. Open M-Sa 9am-12:30pm and 2:30-7pm.

English Bookstore: Libreria Casella, V. della Stazione, 1d (☎0184 35 79 00). Small selection of English books. Open M-Sa 8:30am-12:30pm and 3-7:30pm. V, MC.

EMERGENCY AND COMMUNICATIONS

Emergency: ☎113. **Police:** P. della Libertà, 1 (☎112 or 0184 35 75 75). **Ambulance: Croce Rossa Italiana,** V. Dante, 12 (☎0184 23 20 00), or **Croce Verde** (☎0184 35 11 75), in P. XX Settembre. **Hospital: Saint Charles** (☎0184 27 51) or **Guardia Medica** (☎800 55 64 00) in Bordighera.

Internet Access: Mail Boxes Etc., V. V. Veneto, 4b (☎0184 23 84 23), just past the Giardini Pubblici from C. della Repubblica. L10,000 for 30min. Open M-F 8:30am-12:30pm and 3-7pm, Sa 8:30am-12:30pm.

Post Office: C. Repubblica, 8 (☎0184 35 13 12), toward the water. Phonecards and currency exchange (L5000). Fermo Posta. Open M-Sa 8am-6pm. **Postal Code:** 18039.

ACCOMMODATIONS AND CAMPING

Ventimiglia is one of the Riviera's least expensive holiday havens, but it fills up in July and August. If you don't have the foresight to make reservations three months in advance, consider taking a train (15min., L3100) across the border and staying in the hostel in the nearby French town of **Menton.** Bring your passport.

Pensione Villa Franca, C. Repubblica, 12 (☎0184 35 18 71), next to the waterfront and public park. Clean, small rooms. Friendly management and exotic pet birds. The staff will even bring you a pot of coffee and a pitcher of hot milk for *caffè latte.* Quality meals from the restaurant L21,000 (plus 10% service charge). Breakfast included. Doubles L70,000, with bath L87,000; triples L105,000. V, MC.

Hotel XX Settembre, V. Roma, 16 (☎0184 35 12 22). Recent renovations have rendered rooms crisply painted and ready to please. There's a restaurant downstairs (menù L28,000; Open Tu-Su noon-2:30pm and 7:30-9:30pm). Breakfast L6000. Singles L50,000; doubles L70,000; triples L105,000.

Auberge de Jeunesse (HI), plateau St.-Michel (☎003 34 93 35 93 14 from Italy), in Menton, France. Take bus #6 from Menton (4 per day, 8F), or call the hostel for mini-bus service (20F per person for 1-2 people, 10F per person for 3 or more). The friendly, English-speaking staff runs a tight ship and is eager to share traveling tales. Breakfast and great view included. Dinner 50F. Laundry 35F. Sleepsack 14F. Reception 7am-noon and 5pm-midnight. Open daily Feb.-Nov. Dorms 69F (approx. L23,000).

Camping Roma, V. Peglia, 5 (☎0184 23 90 07; fax 0184 23 90 35), across the river and 400m from the waterfront. From the station, follow V. della Stazione (which changes to V. della Repubblica) and go right on V. Roma until you reach the river at Lungo Roya G. Rossi. Cross the bridge, and make an immediate right on C. Francia. After 50m it becomes V. Peglia. Well-maintained campsites and hillside panoramas. Market and bar nearby. Open daily Apr.-Sept. 8am-midnight. L12,000 per person, L12,000 per tent. Bungalows for four 40,000 per person. Free showers. V, MC.

FOOD

The **covered market** unfolds each morning except Sunday with fruit and vegetables along V. della Repubblica, V. Libertà, V. Aprosio, and V. Roma. The vendors along V. Aprosio by the fake flower stands tend to be small in-town gardeners and have the freshest produce. A **STANDA supermarket** is at the corner of V. Roma and V. Ruffini. (Open M-Sa 8:30am-7:30pm, Su 8:30am-1pm and 3:30-7:30pm.) Along the beach on the Bassa side, there are five or six pizzerias in a row, offering similar fare for L15-20,000. Head over to the Alta shore for a bit more variety and elegance.

Pasta and Basta, on Passagiata Marconion the Alta side of the river, shortly before the Galleria Scoglietti. Set back from the water, the *ristorante* serves up refreshing air conditioning and an affordable change from pizzerias. With 20 delicious sauces (L8-16,000) and 9 freshly made pastas (L2-4000) served in huge bowls, you'll be saying "Basta!" with plenty of pasta left on your plate. Share fettucini with shrimp in lemon sauce (L20,000) and a bottle of wine (L9000) with a friend.

Ristorante Nanni, V. Milite Ignoto, 2c (☎0184 332 30). Dine across the street from the giant palm trees of the Giardini Publicci and watch the passers-by on their way to the waterfront. A fantastic view of the ocean sunset awaits 50 paces down the road. Hearty helpings. 4-course *menù* L19-25,000.

The Buffet Stazione (☎0184 35 12 36), in the train station, is a fastidiously clean option. Pizza and *focaccia* L1200, *panini* under L4600, *primi* from L7000, *secondi* from L10,000. Prices go down if you stand (and don't try to sit if you didn't order full-service). Open daily noon-3pm and 7-9:30pm. Bar open daily 5am-midnight.

SIGHTS

Hop aboard a blue Riviera Trasporti bus at the corner of V. Cavour and V. Martiri della Libertà (direction: Ponte San Luigi; 15min., 12 per day, L2200), and stop at La Mortola, home of the internationally renowned **Botanical Hanbury Gardens.** Here, terraces of exotic flora from three continents cascade down from the summit of Cape Mortola to the sea. Tiny gazebos, lily-pad covered ponds, and marble nudes tucked away in rocky niches lie along the twisting paths to the seaside cafe. The comprehensive course mapped out in the brochure takes about two hours. A stretch of the ancient Strada Romana lies under the bridge directly before the bathrooms; it was used by the Romans to travel to Provence and by St. Catherine to fetch the Pope from Avignon back to Rome. (☎0184 22 95 07. Open in summer daily 9am-6pm; in winter Th-Tu 10am-4pm. L12,000, ages 6-12 L7000, under 6 free.)

The **Romanesque cathedral's** simplicity may have you almost believing the message written on the doors: "I am the portal, he that passes through me will be saved." The unadorned interior emphasizes the grandeur of the ancient stone walls. Take the footbridge to Ventimiglia Bassa, and turn right on V. Trossarelli. Fifty meters ahead you'll find Discesa Marina. Climb to V. Galerina and then V.

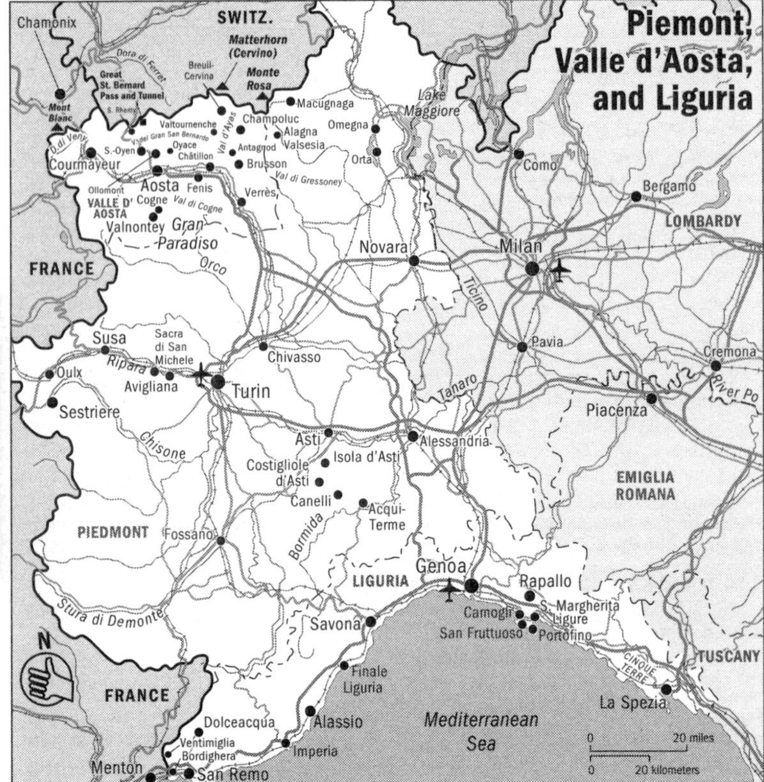

Falerina. Nestled on the other side of the old town, off V. Garibaldi at P. Colleta, is the Romanesque church of **San Michele,** built between the 11th and 12th centuries. Its **crypt** was constructed using pilfered Roman columns. (Open Su 10:30-noon.)

The **Museo Archeologico,** V. Verdi, 41, sits on the hill overlooking the sea. Roman artifacts found in the area, including a dozen marble heads, are on display. It's quite a hike up V. Verdi, but the bus to Ponte San Luigi stops nearby; get off at the stop for La Riserva di Catel d'Appio. (☎0184 35 11 81 or 0184 26 36 01. Open Tu-Sa 9am-12:30pm and 3-5pm, Su 10am-12:30pm. L5000.) Taking the bus all the way to Ponte San Luigi will leave you a 10-minute walk from the **Balzi Rossi** (Red Cliffs). Cro-Magnon humans used to call the cliffs home. Luckily, the only Neanderthals still here inhabit nearby bars. Down, Zog. The most spectacular artifacts reside in Balzi Rossi's **Prehistoric Museum.** (☎0184 381 13. Open in summer Tu–Su 9:10am-7pm; in winter Tu-Su 9am-1pm and 2:30-6pm. L4,000, under 18 and over 65 free.)

BEACHES

Steer clear of the beaches in the Bassa part of town; cleaner, quieter beaches lie across the river in Alta, along **Passeggiata Marconi.** To reach the best beach in Ventimiglia, take the Ponte San Luigi bus to the Archaeological Museum. On your left is an inconspicuous set of stairs. A ten-minute hike down a cliffside overrun with grass opens up to **Spiaggia Le Calandre,** a delightfully naturally sandy beach. Frolicking on the smooth sands with Italian boys and girls won't cost you a single lira. If you want to play grown-up, two chairs and an umbrella on the rocks will run you L25,000. *Let's Go* does not recommend staying past sundown, as the trek back could be dangerous in the dark. (☎0347 431 5393. Open daily 7am-9pm.)

ENTERTAINMENT

Frenzied activity during daylight hours compensates for the largely non-existent nightlife in Ventimiglia. Late June will bring the 40th annual Battaglia di Fiori, which consists of floats and festive flower flinging. On Fridays, the Mercato Settimanale, around the Giardini Pubblici and along the river, is the biggest market on the Riviera and the Cote d'Azur. The humming *mercato* is just the place to heckle over slinky French slips, suede coats, and salami. Just keep an eye on your wallet.

DAYTRIP FROM VENTIMIGLIA: DOLCEACQUEA

To make this scenic daytrip, catch a bus (20min., 10 per day 6:10am-7:07pm, L2200) from V. Cavour across from the tourist office.

A string of villages rose up along the Roya River during the Middle Ages to accommodate journeymen along an essential trade route between Ventimiglia and the rest of northern Italy. Dolceaqua, graced with a medieval castle and an endearing Roman footbridge, was one of these tiny *cittadini*. Even for the history buff, Dolceaqua (9km from Ventimiglia) will probably suffice as a survey of the historical passageway from Piedmont to France.

The Roya divides the new city from the medieval town on the hill, where a snarl of narrow enclosed cobbled streets crescendos at the **Castello dei Doria.** Here breezes swirl through the ruins, water trickles over rocks in a stream below, and a roguish rooster occasions to upset the still. (☎0184 20 64 19. Open Sa-Su 10am-6pm. L5000.) Cross the Roman footbridge, turn right, and walk along the river to reach the multi-hued **Rococo cathedral, San Antonio Abate.** Nearby is the beginning of V. Giraldi. Turn at V. Doria to ascend tunnel-like streets to the castle.

When you come back down, chances are you'll be up for a sampling of Dolceaqua's tastiest pizza at **Pizzeria La Rampa,** V. Barberis, 11 (☎0184 20 61 98), on the left side of P. Garibaldi, in the new town. (Open Tu-Su 7pm-midnight.) Then have a glass of Rossesse, Dolceaqua's infamous "sweet water," made since the 1800s at the Arcagne Vineyards high above the new part of town. If you're interested in staying longer than a day, there are no hotels in Dolceaquea, but a five-minute bus ride to the outskirts of **Isolabona** brings you to **Albergo Da Adolfo.** (☎0184 20 81 11. Open Tu-Su 8am-2pm and 7-10pm. Singles L50,000; doubles L80,000.)

Take note of the spattering of greenhouses planted along the hillsides of the valley; exotic flowers grown here are exported worldwide. Contact the **IAT tourist office** in P. Garibaldi for information on **Ferragosto,** which fills the *piazza* with swirling regional *balletti*, traditional costumes, and mouth-watering pastries in August. (☎0184 20 66 66. Open Sa-Su 10am-1pm and 3-6pm.)

PIEDMONT (PIEMONTE)

More than the source of the mighty Po River, Piedmont has long been a fountainhead of fine food, wine, and nobility. The region falls into three zones: the **Alpine,** the **Pianura,** and the **Colline.** The Alpine, with the peaks of Monviso and Gran Paradiso, contains a string of ski resorts and a national park that spills into Valle d'Aosta. The Pianura includes Turin, the vineyards of Asti, and the beginning of the Po valley. The Colline is dotted with many of the region's isolated castles.

HIGHLIGHTS OF PIEDMONT

REVEL in Christianity's most famous relic, the **Holy Shroud of Turin,** in Cattedrale di San Giovanni (p. 180).

SQUINT at Asti's dazzling Gothic churches (p. 187).

CLUB all night at the **Murazzi** in Turin's underground scene (p. 183).

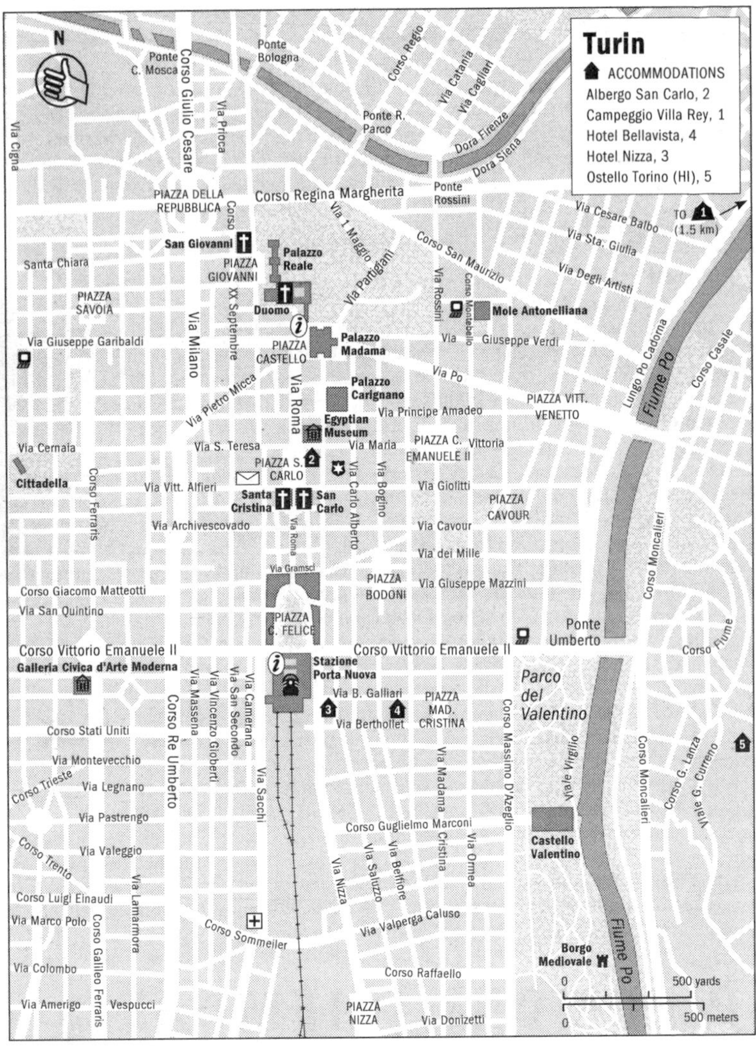

Piedmont has been a politically influential region for centuries. The Savoy family has dominated the area since the 11th century, and in the 19th produced the ever-celebrated Vittorio Emanuele II. With minister Camillo Cavour, Emanuele created a united Italy with Turin as the capital from 1861 to 1865 (see **The Italian Nation: Unification,** p. 13). Though the capital has moved, the political activity has continued. Both the latter-day monarchists and Red Brigades were based in Piedmont. Today, medieval towns recreate the region's glorious past through festivals.

TURIN (TORINO) ☎011

Turin's elegance is the direct result of centuries of urban planning. Graceful, arcaded avenues lead to spacious *piazze*, and churches and innumerable *palazzi* line the squares and streets. Turin is not merely a city of historic architecture; it also moves with the palpable spirit of well-dressed businessmen and university

The MCI WorldCom Card.

The easy way to call when traveling worldwide.

The MCI WorldCom Card gives you…

- Access to the US and other countries worldwide.
- Customer Service 24 hours a day
- Operators who speak your language
- Great MCI WorldCom rates and no sign-up fees

For more information or to apply for a Card call:

1-800-955-0925

Outside the U.S., call MCI WorldCom collect (reverse charge) at:

1-712-943-6839

© 2000, MCI WORLDCOM, Inc. MCI WorldCom, its logo, as well as the names of MCI WorldCom's other products and services referred to herein are proprietary marks of MCI WorldCom, Inc. All rights reserved.

COUNTRY	WORLDPHONE TOLL-FREE ACCESS #
Argentina (CC)	
Using Telefonica	0800-222-6249
Using Telecom	0800-555-1002
Australia (CC) ♦	
Using OPTUS	**1-800-551-111**
Using TELSTRA	**1-800-881-100**
Austria (CC) ♦	0800-200-235
Bahamas (CC) +	**1-800-888-8000**
Belgium (CC) ♦	0800-10012
Bermuda (CC) +	**1-800-888-8000**
Bolivia (CC) ♦	0-800-2222
Brazil (CC)	**000-8012**
British Virgin Islands +	1-800-888-8000
Canada (CC)	**1-800-888-8000**
Cayman Islands +	1-800-888-8000
Chile (CC)	
Using CTC	**800-207-300**
Using ENTEL	**800-360-180**
China ♦	108-12
Mandarin Speaking Operator	108-17
Colombia (CC) ♦	**980-9-16-0001**
Collect Access in Spanish	**980-9-16-1111**
Costa Rica ♦	0800-012-2222
Czech Republic (CC) ♦	**00-42-000112**
Denmark (CC) ♦	8001-0022
Dominica+	**1-800-888-8000**
Dominican Republic (CC) +	
Collect Access	1-800-888-8000
Collect Access in Spanish	1121

COUNTRY	ACCESS #
Ecuador (CC) +	999-170
El Salvador (CC)	*800-1767*
Finland (CC) ♦	08001-102-80
France (CC) ♦	**0-800-99-0019**
French Guiana (CC)	0-800-99-0019
Germany (CC)	**0800-888-8000**
Greece (CC) ♦	00-800-1211
Guam (CC)	**1-800-888-8000**
Guatemala (CC) ♦	99-99-189
Haiti +	
Collect Access	**193**
Collect access in Creole	**190**
Honduras +	8000-122
Hong Kong (CC)	**800-96-1121**
Hungary (CC) ♦	06*-800-01411
India (CC)	**000-127**
Collect access	**000-126**
Ireland (CC)	1-800-55-1001
Israel (CC)	**1-800-920-2727**
Italy (CC) ♦	172-1022
Jamaica +	
Collect Access	**1-800-888-8000**
From pay phones	**#2**
Japan (CC) ♦	
Using KDD	00539-121 ◗
Using IDC	0066-55-121
Using JT	0044-11-121

FOLD

COUNTRY	ACCESS #
Korea (CC)	
To call using KT	00729-14
Using DACOM	00309-12
Phone Booths +	
Press red button ,03,then*	
Military Bases	550-2255
Luxembourg (CC)	**8002-0112**
Malaysia (CC) ♦	1-800-80-0012
Mexico (CC)	**01-800-021-8000**
Monaco (CC) ♦	800-90-019
Netherlands (CC) ♦	**0800-022-91-22**
New Zealand (CC)	000-912
Nicaragua (CC)	*166*
Norway (CC) ♦	800-19912
Panama	**00800-001-0108**
Philippines (CC) ♦	
Using PLDT	105-14
Filipino speaking operator	105-15
Using Bayantel	1237-14
Using Bayantel (Filipino)	1237-77
Using ETPI (English)	1066-14
Poland (CC) +	**800-111-21-22**
Portugal (CC) +	800-800-123
Romania (CC) +	**01-800-1800**
Russia (CC) + ♦	
Russian speaking operator	747-3320
Using Rostelcom	747-3322
Using Sovintel	960-2222
Saudi Arabia (CC)	**1-800-11**

FOLD

COUNTRY	WORLDPHONE TOLL-FREE ACCESS #
Singapore (CC)	8000-112-112
Slovak Republic (CC)	**08000-00112**
South Africa (CC)	0800-99-0011
Spain (CC)	**900-99-0014**
St. Lucia +	1-800-888-8000
Sweden (CC) ♦	**020-795-922**
Switzerland (CC) ♦	0800-89-0222
Taiwan (CC) ♦	**0080-13-4567**
Thailand (CC)	001-999-1-2001
Turkey (CC) ♦	**00-8001-1177**
United Kingdom (CC)	
Using BT	0800-89-0222
Using C& W	0500-89-0222
Venezuela (CC) + ♦	**800-1114-0**
Vietnam + ●	*1201-1022*

KEY

Note: Automation available from most locations. Countries where automation is not yet available are shown in *Italic*

(CC)Country-to-country calling available.

- \+ Limited availability.
- ★ Not available from public pay phones.
- ♦ Public phones may require deposit of coin or phone card for dial tone.
- ● Local service fee in U.S. currency required to complete call.
- ◗ Regulation does not permit Intra-Japan Calls.
- * Wait for second dial tone.
- ■ Local surcharge may apply.

Hint: For Puerto Rico and Caribbean Islands not listed above, you can use 1-800-888-8000 as the WorldPhone access number.

©2000 MCI WORLDCOM, Inc. All Rights Reserved. The names, logos, and taglines identifying MCI WorldCom's products and services are proprietary marks of MCI WORLDCOM, Inc. or its subsidiaries.

WORLDWIDE CALLING MADE EASY

The MCI WorldCom Card, designed specifically to keep you in touch with the people that matter the most to you.

www.wcom.com/worldphone

Please tear off this card and keep it in your wallet as a reference guide for convenient U.S. and worldwide calling with the MCI WorldCom Card.

HOW TO MAKE CALLS USING YOUR MCI WORLDCOM CARD

> **When calling from the U.S., Puerto Rico, the U.S. Virgin Islands or Canada** to virtually anywhere in the world:

1. Dial 1-800-888-8000
2. Enter your card number + PIN, listen for the dial tone
3. Dial the number you are calling:
   Domestic Calls: Area Code + Phone number
   International Calls:
   011+ Country Code + City Code + Phone Number

> **When calling from outside the U.S.**, use WorldPhone from over 125 countries and places worldwide:

1. Dial the WorldPhone toll-free access number of the country you are calling from.
2. Follow the voice instructions or hold for a WorldPhone operator to complete the call.

> **For calls from your hotel:**

1. Obtain an outside line.
2. Follow the instructions above on how to place a call.
   Note: If your hotel blocks the use of your MCI WorldCom Card, you may have to use an alternative location to place your call.

RECEIVING INTERNATIONAL COLLECT CALLS*

Have family and friends call you collect at home using WorldPhone Service and pay the same low rate as if you called them.

1. Provide them with the WorldPhone access number for the country they are calling from (In the U.S., 1-800-888-8000; for international access numbers see reverse side).
2. Have them dial that access number, wait for an operator, and ask to call you collect at your home number.

** For U.S. based customers only.*

START USING YOUR MCI WORLDCOM CARD TODAY. MCI WORLDCOM STEPSAVERS℠

Get the same low rate per country as on calls from home, when you:

1. **Receive international collect calls to your home** using WorldPhone access numbers
2. **Make international calls with your MCI WorldCom Card** from the U.S.*
3. **Call back to anywhere in the U.S. from Abroad** using your MCI WorldCom Card and WorldPhone access numbers.

** An additional charge applies to calls from U.S. pay phones.*

WorldPhone Overseas Laptop Connection Tips — Visit our website, www.wcom.com/worldphone, to learn how to access the Internet and email via your laptop when traveling abroad using the MCI WorldCom Card and WorldPhone access numbers.

Travelers Assist® — When you are overseas, get emergency interpretation assistance and local medical, legal, and entertainment referrals. Simply dial the country's toll-free access number.

Planning a Trip?—Call the WorldPhone customer service hotline at 1-800-736-1828 for new and updated country access availability or visit our website:

www.wcom.com/worldphone

MCI WorldCom Worldphone Access Numbers

Easy Worldwide Calling

MCI WORLDCOM℠

students and the economic energy of the locally based Fiat auto company. During his time as a student in Turin, Erasmus said that it was a city pervaded by magic. While Turin has elaborated on its reputation as a center of the occult, visitors are unlikely to glimpse this hidden counter-culture. Only street gypsies and the chaos of the old-fashioned flea market attest to an otherworldly ethos. Turin's turbulent history as the capital of Italian extremism may not always be visible, but the city that sparked the *Risorgimento*, gave rise to the Red Brigades, and provided a forum for leftist intellectuals like Pavese and Natalia Ginzburg maintains its reputation as a cradle of progressive thought. In 2006, the whole world will embrace the city's energy and beauty as Turin hosts the 20th Olympic Winter Games.

TRANSPORTATION

Flights: Caselle Airport (☎011 567 63 61). European destinations. From Porta Nuova, take tram #1 to Porta Susa. Across the street and under the arcade, take blue buses to "Castelle Airport" (L6500). Buy tickets at **Bar Mille Luci,** P. XVIII Dicembre, 5.

Trains: Porta Nuova on C. V. Emanuele. A city in itself, the station has a supermarket, barber shop, and post office. Be cautious–the station and its environs are not particularly safe, especially at night. To: **Milan** Centrale (2hr., every hr. 4:40am-10:50pm, L21,600); **Genoa** (2hr., every hr. 6:25am-11:10pm, L14,500); **Venice** Santa Lucia (4½hr., InterCity 2:07pm and 5:07pm, L51,500); **Rome** Termini (4½hr.; Eurostar 6:15am, 9:27, and 11:30pm; InterCityNight 12:55 and 11:10pm; L54,600 and up); and **Paris** (9hr., EuroNight 11:48pm, L130,000). V, MC, AmEx. **Porta Susa Stazione** (west of the city) sends trains to **Milan** (2hr.; every hr. 5:05am-11:05pm; L12,500, InterCity L21,600) and **Paris** (10:43am and 5:26pm, L156,000). **Lost Property: Ufficio Oggetti Smarriti** (☎011 665 33 15). Open 8am-noon and 2-5pm. **Luggage Storage (P. Nuova):** L5000 per 12hr. Open daily 4:30am-2:30am. **Luggage Storage (P. Susa):** L5000 per 12hr. Open daily 7am-11pm.

Buses: Autostazione Terminal Bus, C. Inghilterra, 3 (☎011 33 25 25). From Porta Nuova, take cable car #9 or 15. Serves ski resorts, the Riviera, and the valleys of Susa and Pinerolo. To: **Milan** (2hr., every hr., L18,000); **Aosta** (3½hr., 6 per day, L14,000); **Courmayeur** (4hr., 6 per day, L1600); and **Chamonix, France** (4hr., 1 per day, L39,000). Ticket office open daily 7am-noon and 3-7pm.

Public Transportation: City buses and **cable cars** cost L1500. Buy tickets at a *tabac* before boarding. The system is easy to navigate, and most terminal offices have helpful maps. Buses run daily 5am-1am.

Taxis: (☎011 57 37, 011 57 30, or 011 33 99).

ORIENTATION AND PRACTICAL INFORMATION

Turin lies in the Po River valley, flanked by the Alps on three sides. **Stazione Porta Nuova,** in the heart of the city, is the usual place of arrival. The city itself is an Italian rarity with streets meeting at right angles, making it easy to navigate either by bus or on foot. **Corso Vittorio Emanuele II** runs past the station to the river. **Via Roma,** which houses the principal sights, runs north through **Piazza San Carlo** and **Piazza Castello.** The other two main streets, **Via Po** and **Via Garibaldi,** extend from P. Castello. V. Po continues diagonally through **Piazza Vittorio Veneto** (the university center) to the river. V. Garibaldi stretches to **Piazza Statuto** and **Stazione Porta Susa.** Stazione Porta Nuova, Stazione Porta Susa, and Piazza della Repubblica are **dangerous areas,** so don't walk alone.

TOURIST, FINANCIAL, AND LOCAL SERVICES

Tourist Office: ATL, P. Castello, 165 (☎011 53 51 81 or 011 53 59 01; www.turismotorino.org), under the arcade on the left. English, German, French, and Spanish spoken. Excellent map of Turin indexes streets and has info regarding museums and historic cafes. Ask about the daily sightseeing tram and tour bus routes (W-M

2:30pm, L12,000). Smaller office at the Porta Nuova train station (☎011 53 13 27), next to the info office. Both open M-Sa 9:30am-7pm, Su 9:30am-3pm.

Currency Exchange: The convenient exchange office with a big "Change" sign in the Porta Nuova Station offers a decent rate. Open daily 7:30am-7:35pm. V, MC. Otherwise try the **banks** along V. Roma and V. Alfieri or the **ATM** by the APT office.

Bike Rental: Most parks have rentals. **Parco Valentino Noleggio Biciclette** is on V. Ceppi in the Parco Valentino. Walk 15min. down C. V. Emanuele and exit Porta Nuova to the right. No age restrictions. L2000 per hr., L4000 per half-day, L7000 per day. Bargaining might bring a lower rate. Open Tu-Su 9am-12:30pm and 2:30-7pm. **Ciclopark,** at the baggage storage box in Stazione Porta Nuova. L5000 for 6hr., L7000 for 12hr., L12,000 for 24hr. Open 6am-midnight.

English Bookstore: Libreria Internazionale Luxembourg, V. Accademia delle Scienze, 3 (☎011 561 38 96; fax 011 54 03 70; email luxbooks@tiscalinet.it), across from P. Carignano. The friendly English-speaking staff of this 3-floor British bookstore can help you out among the English, French, German, and Spanish books, newspapers and magazines while you relax to classical music. Open M-Sa 8am-7:30pm. V, MC.

Laundromat: Lavanderia Vizzini, V. S. Secondo, 1F (☎011 54 58 82). When facing Stazione P. Nuova walk 2 blocks to the right to V. S. Secondo. Wash and dry L15,000 for 4kg. Open M-F 8:30am-1pm and 3:30-7:30pm.

NORTHWEST ITALY

EMERGENCY AND COMMUNICATIONS

Emergencies: ☎112 or 113. **Police** (Questura), C. Vinzaglio, 10 (☎112). **Ambulance: Red Cross** (☎118 or 011 28 03 33). **First Aid:** ☎011 508 03 70. **Hospital: San Giovanna Batista,** commonly known as Molinette, at C. Bromante, 88 (☎011 633 16 33). **Mauriziano Umberto,** C. Turati, 62 (☎011 508 01 11).

Late-Night Pharmacies: Farmacia Boniscontro, C. V. Emanuele, 66 (☎011 54 12 71 or 011 53 82 71). When facing Stazione P. Nuova, go 3 blocks to the right. Schedule of other pharmacies on the door. Open 3pm-12:30am.

Internet Access: Centro Informa Giovani, V. Assarotti, 2. From P. Castello take V. Garibaldi for 10 blocks and turn left on V. Assarotti. Free internet use. 3 computers. Open M-Tu and Th-Sa 10:30am-6:30pm. **Transpan Cyber Service,** C. V. Emanuele, 12b (☎011 88 55 12; fax 011 817 78 22; email transpan@transpan.it). ISDN use L10,000 per hr. Scanner, printer, but only 1 computer. Open M 3-7pm, Tu-F 9:30am-1pm and 3-7:30pm, Sa 10am-1pm and 3-7pm. **@h!,** V. Montebello, 13 (☎011 815 40 58; email info@ahto.it; www.ahto.it), opposite the Mole Antonellana. L10,000 for 30min., L12,000 per hr. Free tea and coffee. Open M-F 10:30am-1pm and 2-7pm.

Post Office: V. Alfieri, 10 (☎011 53 58 94 or 011 562 81 00), off P. S. Carlo. Fax and telegram service. Open M-F 8:15am-7:20pm, Sa 8:15am-1pm, last day of the month 8:15am-noon. Fermo Posta open M-Sa 9am-noon and 3-7pm. **Postal Code:** 10100.

ACCOMMODATIONS AND CAMPING

Despite the abundance of hotels, prices can be steep even for the most basic rooms. On weekends and during the summer, when visitors and locals retreat to resorts, the city is more tranquil and rooms are easier to find.

Ostello Torino (HI), V. Alby, 1 (☎011 660 29 39; fax 011 660 44 45; hostelto@tin.it). Take bus #52 from Stazione Porto Nuova (bus #64 on Su) 3 stops after crossing the Po River. Go back up V. Thoveu to the large intersection, then veer far left onto V. Curreno. 30m away from the intersection, take another left on V. Gatti and turn on V. Alby. Follow the signs for the hostel. Contemporary, clean, comfortable, and bright orange, with 76 beds and TV room. Internet access with phone card L12,000 per hr. Get friendly with the excellent cook Renato for larger portions at dinner (L14,000). Breakfast and sheets included. Lockers available for L20,000 deposit. Laundry (wash and dry) L10,000 per small load. Reception 7-10am and 3:30-11pm. Curfew 11:30pm; ask for key if going out. Reserve ahead. Closed Dec. 20-Feb. 1. Dorms L22,000; doubles L48,000. Oct.-Apr. L2000 extra per day for heat.

Hotel Bellavista, V. B. Galliari, 15, 6th fl. (☎011 669 81 39; fax 011 668 79 89). As you exit Porta Nuova, turn right and then take the 2nd left on V. Galliari. 18 large, airy rooms with TV, telephone, and a balcony with a view of Turin. Sunny hallway full of plants and a long balcony with a city view. Breakfast L8000. Singles L55,000, with bath L70,000; doubles L110,000, with bath L120,000; triples with bath L140,000.

Hotel Lux, V. Galliari, 9, 2nd fl. (☎011 65 72 57; fax 011 66 87 482). From Stazione P. Nuova go on V. Nizza and take the 2nd left to V. Galliari. Basic, affordable rooms without bath. 4 singles L40-50,000; 9 doubles L70,000; 1 triple L90,000.

Albergo San Carlo, P. S. Carlo, 197, 4th fl. (☎/fax 011 53 86 53), in the midst of all the action and splendor of the *piazza,* but high above the noise. Newly renovated Liberty-style interior. Ski-lodge-style rooms, with TV, fridge, chandeliers, and phone. Singles L65,000, with bath L85,000; doubles L90,000, with bath L120,000. V, MC.

Hotel Nizza, V. Nizza, 9, 2nd fl. (☎/fax 011 669 05 16 or 011 650 59 63). Exit to the right from Porta Nuova on V. Nizza. Large, spacious rooms, all with bath, TV, and phone. Balcony has a bar. Breakfast included. Singles L80,000; doubles L120,000; triples L160,000; quads L180,000. V, MC, AmEx, Diners.

Camping: Campeggio Villa Rey, Strada Superiore Val S. Martino, 27 (☎/fax 011 819 01 17). Take bus #61 from Porta Nuova until P. Vittorio and then take bus #56 and follow the signs after the last stop. Quiet location in the hills. Bar, restaurant, and small supermarket on the premises. L7000 per person, tents L4000 for 1, L7000 for 2, L9000 for up to 5 persons. Light L2500. Showers L1000.

FOOD

MONEY TO MANGIA. *Piemontese* cuisine is a sophisticated blend of northern Italian peasant staples and elegant French garnishes. Butter replaces olive oil, and cheese, mushrooms, and white truffles are used more than tomatoes, peppers, or spices. *Agnolotti* (ravioli stuffed with lamb and cabbage) is the local pasta specialty, but polenta, a cornmeal porridge often topped with fontina cheese, is the more common starch. The three most outstanding (and expensive) red wines in Italy, *Barolo, Barbaresco,* and *Barbera,* are available in Turin's markets and restaurants. To sample the true flavors of *Piemontese* cuisine, be prepared to pay—restaurants that specialize in regional dishes are expensive.

The cheapest supplies are available in the fruit, cheese, and bread shops on V. Mazzini or in **Di Per Di,** V. Carlo Alberto, 15E, at the corner of V. Maria Vittoria. (Open M-Tu and Th-Sa 8:30am-1:30pm and 3:30-7:30pm, W 8:30am-1:30pm. V, MC.)

Sample the delectable *bocca di leone* (a rich pastry filled with whipped cream, fruit, or chocolate; L3500) and the delicious *viennesi alla crema* (L14,000) at **Il Pasticciere,** V. Garibaldi, 9. (☎011 54 08 17. Open Tu-Su 7:30am-8pm; closed for 3 weeks in summer.) Turin oozes with excellent *gelato;* look for the *produzione propria* (made on premises) sign. The spiffy mirror-lined **GelateriaBar Ice Blù,** V. Lagrange, 34A (☎011 54 46 77; open daily 7am-1am); **Master Club Coffee,** V. Roma, 121 (☎011 56 21 682; open M-Sa 8am-8pm); and **Gelateria Fiorio,** V. Po, 8 (☎011 817 32 25; open Tu-Su 8am-2am), sell tasty *gelato.*

Il Punto Verde (vegetarian), V. S. Massimo, 17 (☎011 88 55 43; fax 011 81 22 636; email www.il-punto-verde@yahoo.it), off V. Po near P. C. Emanuele II. Tasty, good-for-you, green cuisine. Fresh-squeezed fruit juices. Sit outside between romantic old walls. *Primi* L8-12,000, *secondi* L6-12,000, giant *monopiatti* L20,000. *Menù* L15,000. Cover L3000. Open M-F noon-2:30pm and 7-10:30pm, Sa 7-10:30pm. Closed in Aug. V, MC.

Shangrila, V. Accademia Albertina, 42 (☎011 81 77 904). From Stazione P. Nuova go right on V. V. Emanuele and turn left on V. A. Albertina. Hearty, delicious, and affordable Chinese and Italian dishes. *Pizza* L4500, *primi* L3500-7500, *secondi* L6800-9000. Lunch *menù* L11,000. Cover L2000. Open daily 8am-10pm. V, MC.

Spacca Napoli, V. Mazzini, 19 (☎011 812 66 94). Scrumptious pasta and crisp brick-oven pizza served in an elegant, friendly atmosphere. Non-smoking section available. Pizza L7500-11,000, *primi* L10,000, *secondi* L18-22,000. Desserts L8000. Cover L3500. Open W-M 6pm-1am. V, MC.

La Bodeguita, V. Melchior Gioia, 8F (☎011 53 85 05). From Stazione P. Nuova go left and take the 4th right. Great Spanish and Italian dishes with lots of style and funky colors. *Tortillas* L6000, *pescados* from L12,000, salads from L6000. Open Su-Th 7am-2am, F 7am-3am, Sa 7am-4am. V, MC.

Brek, P. Carlo Felice, 22 (☎011 53 45 56), off V. Roma. Chic and delicious self-service fare. Outdoor courtyard. Also off P. Solferino at V. S. Teresa, 23 (☎011 54 54 24; open until 11pm) and C. Comm. "Le Gru" Grugliasco (☎011 70 72 588). *Primi* around L6500, *secondi* L9000. Open M-Sa 11:30am-3pm and 6:30-10:30pm. V, MC, AmEx.

Porto di Savona, P. V. Veneto, 2 (☎011 817 35 00). A Turinese institution. Their lunchtime *monopiatti* (large platters of pasta, salad, water, dessert, and coffee; L15,000) are a great deal. Best bets are the *gnocchi al gorgonzola* and the *fusilli alla diavola* (a spicy delight made with tomato, pesto, and cream sauce), both for L8000. Huge portions. *Primi* from L9000, *secondi* from L10,000. Open Tu 7:30-10:30pm, W-Su 12:30-2:30pm and 7:30-10:30pm. Closed 1st 2 weeks in Aug.

Trattoria Toscana, V. Vanchiglia, 2 (☎011 812 29 14), off P. V. Veneto near the university. Hearty, unpretentious fare. Try the *bistecca di cinghiale* (wild boar steak; L10,000). Open Sept.-July W-Su noon-2pm and 7-10pm, M noon-2pm. V, MC, Diner's.

SIGHTS

For a walking-tour booklet, ask at the tourist office for the **Six City Tours** pamphlet.

CATTEDRALE DI SAN GIOVANNI. A Renaissance cathedral dedicated to John the Baptist, this house of worship is best known for its enigmatic Christian relic, the **Holy Shroud of Turin** transferred to Turin from Chambéry, France in 1578. Attached to the *duomo* is Guarino Guarini's remarkable creation, the **Cappella della Santa Sindone** (Chapel of the Holy Shroud; 1668-1694), a somber rotunda capped by a black marble dome that houses the shroud. While it is now hidden from sight, contained within a silver vessel safely behind bars, a life-size canvas copy of the relic is on display. The chapel itself is closed for restorations due to a fire in 1997. Before leaving the cathedral, look above the front door for Luigi Gagna's oil reproduction of Leonardo's *Last Supper*, considered the best copy of the Renaissance masterpiece. *(Behind Palazzo Reale where V. XX Settembre crosses P. S. Giovanni. ☎011 436 15 40. Open daily 7am-12:30pm and 3-7pm. Free. The authentic Holy Shroud can be viewed Aug. 10-Oct. 22 for free by making reservations at ☎800 32 93 29.)*

MUSEO EGIZIO & GALLERIA SABAUDA. The **Palazzo dell'Accademia delle Scienze** houses two of Turin's best museums. Crammed into two floors is the Museo Egizio, with the 3rd-largest collection of Egyptian artifacts in the world. The col-

HOLY SHROUD, BATMAN! The Holy Shroud of Turin, preserved in the Basilica di S. Giovanni Battista since 1578, has been called a hoax by some and a miracle by others. The piece of linen, 3x14 feet, was supposedly wrapped around Jesus' body in preparation for his burial. Although radiocarbon dating suggests the piece is from the 12th century AD, the shrouds's uncanny resemblance to Christ's dissuades its immediate dismissal. Visible on the cloth are outflows of blood: around the head (from the Crown of Thorns?), all over the body (from scourging), and most importantly, around the wrists and feet (where the body was nailed to the cross). Scientists agree that the shroud was wrapped around the body of a 5'7" man who died by crucifixion, but whether it was the body of Jesus remains a mystery. For Christian believers, however, the importance of this relic is best described by Pope Paul VI's words: "The Shroud is a document of Christ's love written in characters of blood."

lection includes several copies of the Egyptian Book of the Dead and an intact sarcophagus of Vizier Ghemenef-Har-Bak, which stands out among the large sculptures and architectural fragments on the ground floor. Upstairs lies the fascinating, well-furnished tomb of 14th-century BC architect Kha and his wife, one of the few tombs spared by grave-robbers. *(V. Accademia delle Scienze, 6, 2 blocks over from P. Castello. ☎011 561 77 76; fax 011 53 46 23. Open Tu-F and Su 8:30am-7:30pm, Sa 8:30am-11pm. L12,000, ages 18-25 L6000, under 18 and over 65 free.)*

The 3rd and 4th floors hold the Galleria Sabauda, which houses art collections from Palazzo Reale and Palazzo Carignano in Turin as well as Palazzo Durazzo in Genoa. The gallery is renowned for its Flemish and Dutch paintings including van Eyck's *St. Francis Receiving the Stigmata*, Memling's *Passion*, van Dyck's *Children of Charles I of England*, and Rembrandt's *Old Man Sleeping*. The Sabauda is also home to several Mannerist and Baroque paintings, including a noteworthy Poussin, several Strozzis, and Volture's *Decapitation of John the Baptist*. *(☎011 54 74 40. Hours identical to the Egyptian Museum. L8000, ages 18-25 L4000, under 18 and over 60 free. Combined ticket for both museums L15,000.)*

NORTHWEST ITALY

PALAZZO CARIGNANO. One of Guarini's grandiose Baroque palaces, the *palazzo* that housed the Princess of Savoia and the first Italian parliament was built in 1679. The elegant and ornate building contains the only museum devoted entirely to Italian national history, the **Museo Nazionale del Risorgimento Italiano,** commemorating the unification of Italy (1706-1946). Documents and other historical paraphernalia make this museum history-buff heaven. *(V. Accademia delle Scienze, 5. Enter from P. Carlo Alberto on the other side of the palace. ☎011 562 37 19. Open Tu-Su 9am-7pm. L8000, students L5000, under 10 and over 65 free. Free guided tour Su 10-11:30am.)*

TEATRO CARIGNANO. Just across from the Palazzo is a theater that the Turinese claim is every bit as important as Milan's **La Scala** (p. 101). The gorgeous gold and red Baroque music hall was manicured with attention to every detail and holds a superb Neoclassical ceiling fresco. *(☎011 54 70 54. No set hours. Call ahead. Free.)*

GALLERIA CIVICA D'ARTE MODERNA. The modern art museum's extensive 19th- and 20th-century collection is primarily Italian, including some Modiglianis and De Chiricos, but it also houses Andy Warhol's gruesome *Orange Car Crash* as well as works by Picasso, Ernst, Leger, Chagall, Twombly, Klee, Courbet, and Renoir. One of Italy's premier museums of Italian modern and contemporary art, it displays various styles from Divisionism to Dadaism to Pop Art. *(V. Magenta, 31. On the corner of C. G. Ferraris, off Largo Emanuele. ☎011 562 99 11; www.gam.intesa.it. Open Tu-Su 9am-7pm. L10,000, under 26 L5000, under 10 and over 65 free.)*

PALAZZO REALE. Home to the Princes of Savoy from 1645 to 1865, the palace consists mostly of ornate apartments. Its red and gold interior houses an outstanding collection of Chinese porcelain vases. Louis le Nôtre (1697), more famous for his work on the gardens of Versailles, designed the *palazzo*'s garden. Although the city owes its glory to political rather than ecclesiastical leadership, unadulterated splendor blesses the interior of the **Chiesa di San Lorenzo,** next to the Palazzo Reale. Constructed between 1668 and 1680, it is Guarini's most original creation with a dynamic, swirling dome. *(☎011 436 14 55. In Piazzetta Reale, at the end of P. Castello. Palazzo open Tu-Su 8:30am-7:30pm. L8000 for 1st fl.; L10,000 for the whole palazzo, ages 18-25 L5000, under 18 and over 65 free. 40min. guided tours in Italian; Tu-Su 9am-1pm and 2-7pm. Gardens open 8:30am-7pm. Free. Church open 8am-12:30pm and 3:30-6pm.)*

In the right wing of the Royal Palace lies the **Armeria Reale** (Royal Armory) of the House of Savoy, containing the world's best collection of medieval and Renaissance war tools. Swords a' plenty, suits of armor, and wicked weapons fill this museum. *(P. Castello, 191. ☎011 54 38 89. Open Tu and Th 1:30-7pm, W and F-Sa 9am-2pm. L8000, under 18 and over 60 free.)*

MOLE ANTONELLIANA. This is the definitive symbol of the city and of the 2006 Winter Olympics. No Italian city would be complete without a panoramic view. In post-modern Turin you can forget about working out your legs and take a glass elevator to the top of the Mole. Begun as a synagogue in a time of political and religious instability, it ended up a Victorian eccentricity, over 160m above the ground. The view inside the dome as you ascend to the top is dizzying. It houses the **Museo Nazionale del Cinema,** an excellent collection of pre-cinematic and cinematic stills. The museum highlights Turin's role as the birthplace of Italian cinema—Pietro Fosco's seminal silent film *Cabiria* was shot along the banks of the Po in 1914. *(V. Montebello, 20, a few blocks east of P. Castello. ☎011 81 54 230.)*

BASILICA DI SUPERGA. When the French attacked Turin on September 6, 1706, King Vittorio Amedeo II made a pact with the Virgin Mary to build a magnificent cathedral in her honor should the city withstand the invasion. Turin stood unconquered, and the result was this structure. The basilica stands on a 672m summit outside of Turin, with panoramic views of the city, the Po valley below, and the Alps rising beyond. Its Neoclassical portico and high drum create a spectacular dome. *(Take tram #15 (L1500) from V. XX Settembre to Stazione Sassi. From the station, take bus #79 or board a small cable railway for a clanking ride up the hill (20min., every hr.; round-trip L6000, Su and holidays L12,000). ☎011 898 00 83. Open Apr.-Sept. 9:30am-noon and 3-6pm; Oct.-Mar. 10am-noon and 3-5pm. Free. L3000 for the tombs.)*

NORTHWEST ITALY

PARCO DEL VALENTINO. Laze in the gardens in one of Italy's largest parks along the banks of the Po and check out the **Castello Medioevale,** built here in 1884 for a world exposition. A guide will take you through the castle, showing room after room of objects and oddities, including a sink in the shape of a castle and a throne that converts to a toilet. The **Borgo,** a fanciful "medieval" village, surrounds the estate. *(Park and castle at V. Virgilio, 107, along the Po. ☎011 81 77 178. Open Aug. 15-Oct. 25. Phone reservations required. Free.)*

PIAZZA SAN CARLO. In the center of this perfect rectangle, with its formal 17th- and 18th-century Baroque grandeur, the equestrian statue of Duke Emanuele Filiberto sits proudly on a horse over the crowds. In addition to the Baroque buildings, the *piazza* features the opulent twin churches of **Santa Cristina** and **San Carlo Borromeo,** on your right and left as you enter the *piazza* from V. Roma. *(Santa Christina open 8am-1pm and 3-8pm. San Carlo open 7am-noon and 3-7pm. Free.)*

MUSEO NAZIONALE DELL'AUTOMOBILE. The museum documents the evolution of the automobile, exhibiting prints, drawings, leaflets, more than 150 original cars and the first models made by Ford, Benz, Peugeot, Oldsmobile, and the homegrown Fiat. The focus is, as expected, on Italian cars and car racing. There are frequent exhibits, often with figurative car designs. *(C. Unita d' Italia, 40. Head south along V. Nizza from Stazione Porta Nuova. ☎011 67 76 66. Open Tu-Su 10am-6:30pm. L4000.)*

ENTERTAINMENT

For the skinny on the happening spots, inquire at the tourist office. On Fridays, check out Turin's newspaper, *La Stampa,* which publishes *Torino Sette,* an excellent section on current cultural events. Music of all genres livens Turin between June and August, when the city invites international performers to the **Giorni d'Estate Festival.** For information, programs, and venues, contact the tourist office or the **Vetrina per Torino,** P. S. Carlo, 159. (Toll-free ☎800 015 475; email vetrina@comune.torino.it; www.comune.torino.it/welcomep.htm. Open M-Sa 11am-7pm.) From September 5-25, the **Settembre Musica** extravaganza features over 40 classical concerts performed throughout the city. Contact the Vetrina or the tourist office for programs (available by the beginning of July). **Cinemas** all over Turin offer the latest big-budget blockbusters, obscure art films, and all-out pornography. During the academic year, a number of foreign films are shown in their original languages. For a listing of films, ask the tourist office for the leaflet **Arena Metropolis.** Be aware that most films will be (poorly) dubbed in Italian.

NIGHTLIFE

Discos and bars turn over constantly; ask at the tourist office for the weekly leaflet **News Spettacolo.**

I MURAZZI

At the quay by the river at the end of C. V. Emanuele, between Ponte Emanuele and Ponte Umberto, I Murazzi is by far the liveliest place in Turin. Most clubs here are open daily until the morning, with a L20,000 cover charge that includes a drink. There's always good underground techno, dance, and live music. Increased police presence has made this area safer, but be cautious and watch your pockets.

NORTH OF I MURAZZI, LUNGO PO CADORNA

Pura Vida, C. Cairoli, 14 (☎0348 42 05 231), is always crowded with a university-age crowd hungry for some Latin and reggae music. Feed your tummy with a good *tortilla* for L5000 or *torta de pollo* for L6000. Open Su-F 10am-3am, Sa 10am-4am.

Caffe Flora, P. V. Veneto, 24 (☎011 81 71 530). Chill session—just 20 or 30 people hangin' in comfortable chairs. Open Tu-Su 2pm-3am.

Alcohol, Lungo Po Cadorna, 1, further along the river. This fantastic onomastic club plays great acid jazz and drum 'n' bass. Trendy decoration in orange and a cozy downstairs. Open Su-F 10pm-3am, Sa 10pm-4am.

CORSO VITTORIO EMANUELE

Several excellent English and Irish pubs line up from the Stazione Porta Nuova on the way to the Po River along C. V. Emanuele.

The Tetley Huntsman, C. V. Emanuele, 43 (☎011 66 96 605), a few blocks down on the right side. Greets you with slogans like "Watch out—elephants are heavy" or "Millions of Englishmen can't be wrong." A Turinese classic with an international crowd. No cover. Open daily 7:30am-3am.

Six Nations Murphy's Pub, C. V. Emanuele, 28 (☎0348 23 02 782), across the street from The Tetley Huntsman. Features bartenders with Scottish kilts. Sign your name on one of the walls. Open daily 6pm-3am.

The Shamrock Inn, C. V. Emanuele, 34 (☎011 81 74 950), further towards the river. Offers lively rumba dancing, decent sandwiches, and desserts. Open M-Sa 7pm-3am.

ACROSS THE RIVER AND LINGOTTO

Discoteca Boccaccio, C. Moncalieri, 145 (☎011 66 01 770; fax 011 66 01 483). Cross the river on Ponte Umberto I from C. V. Emanuele and go left for about 8min. on C. Moncalieri on the left side. Big dance floor and a mixed/gay/transvestite crowd. Cover L20,000 for men, L15,000 for women. Open F-Sa 10pm-3am.

Hiroshima Mon Amour, V. Carlo Bossoli, 63 (☎011 31 76 636). Take bus #1 or 34 to Lingotto Centro Fiere. This place is the bomb. The music changes nightly from reggae to rock 'n' roll; some nights are blessed with live performances. Cover ranges from free (Saturdays) to L20,000. Plan on taking a taxi back to the city or ask a trustworthy (read sober) local for a ride. Opens nightly at 11pm.

SHOPPING

One of Turin's unique events is the **Gran Balon flea market,** held every other Sunday in P. della Repubblica. Here, junk sellers rub shoulders with treasure hunting dealers of antiques and valuable rarities. Though the streets of Turin are lined with clothing stores, the budget traveler will quickly learn that the chic, designer shops on **V. Roma** are best for window-shopping. Up **Via Lagrange** and **Via Carlo Alberto,** the *haute couture* demons may drag you into **Inferno,** V. Carlo Alberto, 55e, a world of black garb and magenta walls. (☎011 88 95 33. Open M 3-7:30pm, Tu-Sa 10am-12:30pm and 3-7:30pm.) The department store **La Rinascente,** at the corner of V. Lagrange and V. Teofilo Rossi, sells more traditional attire.

OLYMPICS

In 2006, Turin will be in the global spotlight when it has the distinct honor of hosting the XX Olympic Winter Games. The games will mark the first Winter Olympics in Italy since the 1956 Winter Olympics in Cortina d'Ampezzo. Turin beat out five other candidates in the solely European contest: Zakopane, Poland; Klagenfurt, Austria; Poprad-Tatry, Slovakia; Sion, Switzerland; and a joint bid by Helsinki, Finland and Lillehammer, Norway. Turin's presentation to the International Olympic Committee focused on the Alps with a winter environment and a metropolis. To join the winter fun yourself, hit the slopes at **Sestriere, Alagna Valsesia,** or **Macugnaga** (see p. 185). For more information about the Games contact the **Torino Organizing Committee** at V. Nizza, 262 (☎011 63 10 511; www.torino2006.it).

DAYTRIPS FROM TURIN

SACRA DI SAN MICHELE

To reach the monastery from Turin you must take a train to Avigliana (15 per day, L2700). Without a car, accessing the monastery is difficult, as there are no public buses. However, the 14km day's hike from Avigliana will make you feel like a proud pilgrim. If the monastery beckons but you're short on time you can always take a taxi (☎011 93 02 18; L50-70,000). Bargain hard and arrange to be picked up.

Looming on a bluff 1000m above the town of Avigliana, the massive stone monastery of Sacra di San Michele seems to grow out of the very rock on which it was built. *The Name of the Rose* was not filmed here but probably should have been. Umberto Eco based the plot of his book on the monastery, and even in the summer it is easy to imagine monks plummeting to snowy deaths from the high windows. The monastery, founded in AD 1000, perches atop Mt. Pirchiriano with sweeping and spectacular views in all directions. Upon entering the structure, the impressive **Stairway of the Dead,** an immense set of steps helping to buttress the building, leads outside to the beautifully carved wooden doors that depict the arms of St. Michael with the Serpent of Eden. The shrine of St. Michael is down the small steps in the middle of the nave, where there are three tiny chapels. In 966 St. John Vincent built the largest one, with a back wall of solid rock; today, it holds the tombs of medieval members of the Savoy family. Although the building is undergoing restoration, it remains open to the public. (☎011 93 91 30. Open Tu-Su 9:30am-12:30pm and 3-6pm. L4000.)

From the station in Avigliana turn left and follow the main road, C. Laghi, through town and around Lago Grande for about 30 minutes. This part runs along the shoulder of a busy road and is not very pleasant. Turn right on the green street Sacra di S. Michele, which winds its way slowly up the mountain. The way is clearly marked, and the walk takes about three hours. Wear sturdy shoes, and bring plenty of water. If you'd feel safer with a map before starting the arduous trek, head to Avigliana's **Informazione Turistico,** P. del Popolo, 2, a five- to 10-minute walk straight ahead from the station. (☎011 932 86 50. Open M-F 9am-noon and 3-6pm.) There are **public toilets** outside the entrance to the monastery, but bring your own paper. **Restaurants** cluster halfway up the hill and before the end of the climb.

SUSA

To reach Susa from Turin, take the train to ***Bussoleno*** *(1hr., every 30min. 5:35am-9:03pm, L6000) and a five-minute connecting train to Susa (every 30min.).*

Though far from *la città eterna* and surrounded by mountains, the tiny hamlet of Susa (pop. 7000) never lets visitors forget its Roman origins. This town was once the seat of Gaul Cottius, a prefect of the Empire. Today, Susa's cultural wealth centers on its collection of Roman remnants and medieval structures, all of which lie across the river from the train station. On V. F. Ronaldo (the street farthest right when you cross a bridge and walk through a *piazza*), looms the 3rd-century

Porta Savoia, a symbolic centerpiece of the Roman remains scattered throughout the town. Head all the way through the *porta* and to the right. Walk up the incline, keeping the gorgeous **Parco D'Augusto** on your left. Immediately in front stands the **Arch of Augustus,** and further on, the 2nd-century **amphitheater** and the **baths.** Along the route is the handsome campanile of the **Chiesa di Santa Maria Maggiore,** now a private home. Right of the *porta* stands the **Cattedrale di S. Giusto,** dating from 1027. Inside awaits the 14th-century *Triptych of Rocciamelone*, a Flemish depiction of the Virgin and saints. Adjacent to the cathedral stands the 11th-century bell tower. (Call ☎0122 62 26 94 to reserve a spot in the daily tour at the *biblioteca*.)

From the station, turn right and walk 30m to the small white **tourist office** at V. Inghilterra, 39, to pick up maps and **exchange currency.** (☎0122 62 24 70. Open M-Sa 9am-7:30pm, Su 9am-noon; in winter Tu-Sa 9am-noon.) In between the station and the tourist office is a small AGIP petrol station that doubles as a **SAPAV bus ticket office** (☎0121 166 845 010). Buses leave from the train station at C. Stati Uniti 33 and head to **Sestriere** via Oulx (50min., 5 per day, L7200) and **Turin** (1½hr., 5:30pm, L7500). In case of **emergency,** call **pronto soccorso** (☎118), across the street from the tourist office, or the **hospital,** C. Inghilterra, 66 (☎0122 62 12 12), next door. To find the **post office** at V. Mazzini, 40, take a right out of the tourist office and turn left onto V. Mazzini. (☎0122 62 25 44. Open M-F 8:15am-1:40pm, Sa 8:15-11:40am.)

Marco and Loris provide spotless rooms and lessons on Susa's history across from the station in the recently renovated **Hotel Stazione,** C. Stati Uniti, 2. (☎/fax 0122 62 22 26; www.valsusa.net/ristorante-stazione. English spoken. Breakfast L12,000. Reception daily 7:30am-midnight. Singles L36,000, with shower L47,000; doubles L73,000, with bath L95,000. V, MC, AmEx, Diners.)

SESTRIERE

Bus service runs directly from ***Turin*** *(L14,500) and from* ***Oulx,*** *on the Paris-Turin train line.*

Turin is just a hop, skip, and a ski-jump away from many superb hiking areas and smooth slopes. The closest resort, only 75 minutes from the city, is super-chic Sestriere (2035m), home of Italian ski legend Alberto Tomba. Sestriere has 4 cableways, 20 ski lifts, excellent runs, a skating rink, and, with any luck, piles of snow. For information on snow conditions and lodgings, call the tourist office in Sestriere, P. Agnelli, 11 (☎0122 760 45) or in Turin (see p. 177).

Alagna Valsesia (1200m), slightly farther away, boasts the 2nd longest lift in the area. Still farther north, **Macugnaga** (1327m) stands with its own enormous ski lift. These resorts are linked to Turin by bus and train. The booklet *Settimane Bianche*, available at Turin's tourist office, provides additional information.

ASTI ☎0141

Asti sparkles, just like its popular, intoxicating progeny. Though now located in the foothills of the Alps, it once lay under the ocean, emerging only in the Pliocene era. Asti has bustled with activity since Roman times, when it bore the name "Hasta." While the city thrives in the modern world, it did not fare well under the domination of the Savoy family (AD 1300-1700). The town was repeatedly sacked and burned in struggles with local princes. Nevertheless, more than a hundred 13th-century edifices have survived, lending the city a medieval air. While known for the 18th-century poet Vittorio Alfieri and his cousin Count Benedetto (who designed much of the city), Asti is perhaps most famous for the sparkling wines that bear its name.

TRANSPORTATION

Trains: P. Marconi, a few blocks south of P. Alfieri. To: **Alessandria** (30min., every hr. 5:22am-7:50pm, L4400); **Turin** P. Nuova (1hr., 2 per hr. 4:30am-11:14pm, L6000); and **Milan** Stazione Centrale (2hr., 6:48am, L12,500). Info open M-F 6am-12:40pm and 1:10-7:45pm. **Luggage Storage:** L5000 per 12hr. Open daily 7:45am-12:45pm and 2:15-5:10pm.

Buses: P. Medaglie d'Oro, across from the train station. To: **Costigliole** (7:15, 11am, and 12:50pm); **Isola d'Asti** (6 per day 10am-6:50pm); **Canelli** (every 1½ hr. 7:10am-6:40pm); and **Castagnole** (every 2hr. 7:20am-6:40pm). Tickets (L3-4000) on the bus.

Taxis: In P. Alfieri (☎0141 53 26 05) or at the station in P. Marconi (☎0141 59 27 22).

ORIENTATION AND PRACTICAL INFORMATION

The center of the town lies in the triangular **Piazza Vittorio Alfieri.** Most historic sights are located slightly to the west of the *piazza*, off **Corso Alfieri.**

Tourist Office: P. Alfieri, 34 (☎0141 53 03 57; fax 0141 53 82 00). Assists in finding (but not reserving) accommodations, including *agriturismo* options. Info on daytrips to wineries and castles. Pick up the indispensable map and the *Guide to Asti and its Province*. English, French, and German spoken. Open M-Sa 9am-7pm, Su 10am-1pm.

Currency Exchange: Cassa di Risparmio di Asti, on the corner of P. 1 Maggio and V. M. Rainero. Open M-F 8:20am-1:20pm and 2:30-3:50pm, Sa 8:20-11:20am. Also try the post office. **ATMs** in the train station and along V. Dante.

Emergencies: ☎113. **Police:** C. XXV Aprile, 19 (☎0141 41 81 11). **Red Cross Ambulance:** ☎0141 41 77 41. **Hospital: Ospedale Civile,** V. Botallo, 4 (☎0141 39 21 11).

Internet Access: ATLink, C. Alfieri, 328 (☎0141 345 98; email info@atlink.it; www.atlink.it), near Torre Rosa. L10,000 per hr. Open M-Sa 9am-12:30pm and 3:30-7:30pm, Su 3:30-7:30pm.

Post Office: C. Dante, 55 (☎0141 59 28 51), off P. Alfieri. Open M-F 8:30am-5:30pm, Sa 8:15am-noon. **Postal Code:** 14100.

NORTHWEST ITALY

ACCOMMODATIONS AND CAMPING

Hotel Cavour, P. Marconi, 3 (☎/fax 0141 53 02 22), across from the train station. Friendly management is happy to answer questions. Modern, immaculate rooms with TV and phone. Reception daily 6am-1am. Closed in Aug. Singles L55,000, with bath L70,000; doubles L85,000, with bath L105,000. V, MC, AmEx, Diners.

Antico Paradiso, C. Torino, 329 (☎/fax 0141 21 43 85). Quite a hike from the action; take bus #1 or 4 from the station (the ones marked "Canova") to the last stop on C. XXV Aprile (L1500). From there, walk 45m down to C. Torino, and the hotel is on the left corner. Religious motifs adorn the whitewashed walls of bare and simple rooms. A bar downstairs sells *gelato* (L2000) and makes fabulous homemade cakes. Bar open Tu-Su. Reception Tu-Su 9am-midnight. Singles L55,000; doubles with shower and sink L85,000. V, MC, AmEx, Diners.

Campeggio Umberto Cagni, V. Valmanera, 152 (☎0141 27 12 38). From P. Alfieri, turn onto V. Aro, which becomes C. Volta. Take a left on V. Valmanera and keep going. The camp is a local hangout featuring a pizza oven, table tennis, a playground, restaurant, bar, and beach volleyball and soccer. Open Apr.-Sept. L6-7000 per person, L6000 per tent. Electricity L3000. Showers free.

FOOD

Astigiano cuisine is famous for its simplicity, using only a few crucial ingredients and pungent cheeses to create culinary masterpieces. This region offers the celebrated *bagna calda* (hot bath), a combination of raw vegetables dipped in a sizzling pot of olive oil and infused with garlic and anchovies. Among the most cherished cheeses produced in the surrounding area are *robiole* and *tome*.

The extensive fruit and vegetable **markets** in P. Alfieri and Campo del Palio provide great snacks. (Open W and Sa 7:30am-1pm.) Another fruit and vegetable market is held daily in P. Catena, off V. Carducci in the heart of town. The **Super Gulliver Market,** V. Cavour, 77, could feed an army of Lilliputians. (Open M-W and F-Sa 8am-7:30pm, Th 8:30am-1pm.) At **Mercato Coperto Alimentari,** in P. della Libertà between P. Alfieri and Campo del Palio, each merchant has a separate kiosk. (Open M-W and F-Sa 8am-1pm and 3:30-7:30pm, Th 8am-1pm.)

Leon d'Oro, V. Cavour, 95 (☎0141 59 20 30). Relaxed atmosphere and filling meals, including some vegetarian entrees. Sit inside and watch yourself eat in the mirrored wall, or people-watch outside under the yellow tent on a quiet street. Cover L3000. Pizza L7-12,000, *primi* L7500, *secondi* from L10,000, desserts L5000. Open Th-Tu 11am-3pm and 6pm-2am. V, MC, AmEx, Diners.

Trattoria La Canasta, C. Volta, 82 (☎0141 27 17 30). From P. Alfieri, turn right on C. Alfieri and left on V. Aro, which becomes C. Volta. This family-run eatery serves home-cooked meals in a pleasant atmosphere. *Primi* from L8000, *secondi* L9-16,000, home-made desserts L5-6000. Open M-Sa noon-2:30pm and 7:30-11pm. V, MC, Diners.

Gran Caffè Italia, V. Cavour, 127 (☎0141 59 42 22), at the end of V. Cavour on the rotary opposite the train station. This snack bar offers fresh *panini* (L4000) and a vast selection of drinks. *Primi* L6-7000 and *secondi* L10,000. *Tavola calda* open for lunch M-Sa noon-2:30pm. Bar open daily 7am-7pm.

SIGHTS

CATTEDRALE D'ASTI. This *duomo*, begun in 1309, is one of Piedmont's most noteworthy Gothic cathedrals. Constructed in traditional red brick, the exterior contrasts with the white-trimmed doors, creating a checkered effect. Throughout the 16th and 17th centuries, local artists, including native son Gandolfino d'Asti, covered every inch of the walls with frescoes; even the columns are painted to appear as if there are vines climbing up them. The remains of 11th-century mosaics blanket the floor around the altar. *(In P. Cattedrale. Walk down C. Alfieri and turn right on V. Mazzini. Open daily 7am-12:30pm and 3-7pm.)*

CHIESA DI SAN PIETRO IN CONSAVIA. A 15th-century church with a 12th-century octagonal baptistery, this structure served as an army hospital in WWII. Romans, friars, and those killed in the war all shared the space beneath the courtyard. Now it is home to both the **Museo Paleontologico,** a small room with a collection of fossils and bones from the area, and the **Museo Archeologico.** Inside are Roman remains and a room of Egyptian relics. *(On the far end of C. Alfieri, in the opposite direction from the Torre Rossa. Open Tu-Sa 9am-noon and 4-7pm, Su 10am-noon. Both free.)*

OTHER SIGHTS. From P. Vittorio Alfieri, a short walk west on V. Garibaldi leads to P. S. Secondo. The *piazza* is home to the 18th-century **Palazzo di Città** (City Hall), next door to the medieval **Collegiata di San Secondo.** The Romanesque tower and the magnificent Gothic decorations now stand on the very spot where S. Secondo, Asti's patron saint, was decapitated. Hanging banners lend a medieval air to the interior. *(Open daily 7:30am-noon and 3:30-7:30pm.)* Directly north of P. S. Secondo, across C. Alfieri in **Piazza Medici,** stands the 13th-century **Torre de Troya.** At the end of C. Alfieri is Asti's oldest tower, the 16-sided **Torre Rossa** (Red Tower), where San Secondo was imprisoned before his execution. The tower, with foundations dating back to the time of Augustus, adjoins the elliptical, Baroque **Chiesa di Santa Caterina.** *(Open daily 7:30am-noon and 3-7pm.)* The **Giardini Pubblici** (public gardens), between P. Alfieri and Campo del Palio, make a refreshing picnic spot.

FESTIVALS

From the last week of June through the 1st week of July, **Asti Teatro,** the oldest contemporary theatrical festival in Italian history, commands Asti's complete attention. Asti Teatro puts on outdoor and indoor performances of theatrics (mainstream dramas to neo-Shakespeare), music (classical to jazz), and dance (ballet to modern). The festival draws a global audience and offers productions in many languages, although most are in Italian (L25,000, students and under 12 L20,000). Reserve both tickets and hotel rooms in advance. Call the **Teatro Alfieri,** V. al Teatro, 1 (☎0141 39 93 41 or 0141 35 39 88).

Beginning on the 2nd Friday in September, agricultural Asti revels in the **Douja d'Or,** a week-long exposition of local wines. During this week, on the 2nd Sunday in September, is the **Paisan,** or the **Festivale delle Sagre.** Locals dressed in traditional clothing come from surrounding towns and parade through Asti, rejoicing and feasting into the night. The real theater takes place in the streets on the 3rd Sunday in September, when the Douja d'Or concludes with the **Palio di Asti,** a procession commemorating the town's liberation in 1200. The Palio ends with one of the oldest bareback horseraces in Italy. For races of a different sort, ask at the Asti tourist office for information on the **donkey races** at Quarto (4km outside Asti). A donkey represents each of the village's seven boroughs. At the end of the contest, the victorious borough has a parade, and all of Quarto settles down to a banquet of *ravioli* (and the donkey).

DAYTRIPS FROM ASTI: COSTIGLIOLE AND CANELLI

Buses run to Canelli (30min., every 1½hr. 7:10am-6:40pm, L4000) and Costigliole (25min.; 7:15am, 11am, 12:50pm; L3500) from the bus station in Asti.

Vineyards comprise the countryside around Asti, providing both an economic base and a source of widespread renown. The sparkling *Asti Cinzano* and *Asti Spumante,* as well as the super-sweet *Moscato,* bubble forth from these vineyards. Many wineries remain under family control, and a warm reception awaits visitors who take time to explore these less touristed areas. While Costigliole's **medieval castle** is now closed to visitors, you can visit the **Cantina dei Vini di Costigliole d'Asti,** V. Roma, 9, in Costigliole, for guided tours and tastings. (☎0141 96 16 61 or 0141 96 60 31. Open F 10am-12:30pm, Sa-Su 10am-12:30pm and 3-6pm.)

Canelli is surrounded by the muscat vineyards that produce the fruity *Asti Spumante.* Oswald, the jolly proprietor of the **Cantina Sociale,** V. L. Bosca, 30, offers tours and tastings. From the bus stop, walk up C. Liberta over the river, and veer left as the road ends. Take the 1st right at the Ricordonna gate and then another right onto V. Bosca. The Cantina is straight ahead at the end of the street. (☎0141 82 33 47 or 0141 83 18 28; fax 0141 83 18 28. Open Tu-Su 8am-noon and 2-6pm.) Also in Canelli is **Distilleria Bocchina,** V. L'Azarita, 4 (☎0141 81 01), that produces *grappa.* From the bus stop, head in the opposite direction from the Cantina. Take C. XX Settembre, go straight past the pharmacy, and continue 10 minutes up the incline to the distillery. Call in advance for tours.

ACQUI TERME ☎0144

Acqui Terme is a small, picturesque town with a placid surface and boiling underbelly. Well, almost boiling. Sulfuric springs at temperatures of 75°C (167°F) bubble just underneath the ground, attracting those in need of holistic treatment. The mineral-rich water and *fanghi* (mud baths) provide healing and relaxation.

TRANSPORTATION AND PRACTICAL INFORMATION. From **Genoa,** catch a **train** (1½hr., every hr., L5900), via **Ovada.** Acqui Terme's train station (☎0144 32 25 83) is in P. V. Veneto. Trains also run from **Asti** (1hr., 13 per day, L5200). To reach the town center from the station, turn left on **Via Alessandria** and continue as it becomes C. Vigano and ends in **Piazza Italia.** To reach the **IAT Tourist Office,** P. Maggiorino Ferraris, 5, go on **Corso Dante,** turn right on C. Cavour and left on V. Ferraris. (☎0144 32 21 42; fax 0144 32 90 54. Open M 10:30am-12:30pm and 3:30-6:30pm, Tu-F 9:30am-12:30pm and 3:30-6:30pm, Sa-Su 10am-12:30pm and 3:30-6:30pm.) **Consorzio Turistico** (☎0144 32 65 20) provides hotel and restaurant information. For **currency exchange,** there are banks on C. Dante, including **Cassa di Risparmio di Torino,** C. Dante, 26 (☎0144 570 01). The **post office** (☎0144 32 29 84) is on V. Truco off P. Matteotti (take V. XX Settembre from P. Italia). **Postal Code:** 15011.

ACCOMMODATIONS AND FOOD. For a centrally located, well-staffed, and comfortable place to rest your weary head, try **Albergo San Marco,** V. Ghione, 5. From P. Italia, take C. Bagni about 15m and make the 1st right onto V. Ghione. Its owners are eager to please, and the exquisite food in the **restaurant** downstairs is rumored to be some of the best in town. Try the excellent *Semifreddo Zabaglione e Torrone* for dessert. (☎0144 32 24 56; fax. 0144 32 10 73. *Primi* L7-10,000, *secondi* from L10,000, home-made desserts L5-6000. 3-course gourmet menu L25,000. Closed in Jan., last 2 weeks in July, and beginning of Aug. Singles L38,000, with bath L48,000; doubles with bath L75,000; triples L100,000.) Beyond the town center, many budget hotels surround the mineral baths across the river (15min. by foot). **Albergo Giacobe,** V. Einaudi, 15, has gloriously furnished rooms and inexpensive food. From P. Italia, take C. Bagni over the river. V. Einaudi is the 1st left. (☎0144 32 25 37. Singles L50,000, with bath L60,000; doubles L70,000, with bath L80,000. Full-pension L75,000 per person.) **Supermarket di per di,** V. Nizza, 11, offers a wide selection of very cheap groceries. (☎0144 57 858. Open Tu-Su 8:30am-12:45pm and 3:30-7:30pm, M 3:30-7:30pm.)

SIGHTS. Even if you're in perfect health, no trip to Acqui Terme would be complete without at least dipping your finger in the steamy sulfuric **water.** At the romantic **Piazza Bollente,** the hot water pours out of a fountain, sending up steam even in summer. Take V. Manzoni up the hill to the Castello dei Paleogi, which houses the **Museo Civico Archeologico,** constructed in the 11th century, damaged in 1646, and restored in 1815. The museum displays a small but evocative collection of Roman tombs and mosaics. (☎0144 575 55. Open W-Sa 9:30am-12:30pm and 3:30-6:30pm, Su 3:30-6:30pm. L4000, under 18 L2000. Restorations until mid-2001.) The Romanesque **duomo,** in P. Duomo down V. Barone from the Museo Archeologico, is home to Rubens's famous *Trittico (Madonna and Child)*. Unfortunately, the work is locked away in the sacristy. Inquire at the tourist office about opportunities to view this masterpiece. (Open M-F 7am-9pm, Sa-Su 8am-noon and 6-8pm.) From the river, you can see the four intact arches of the **Acquedotto Romano.**

Acqui Terme offers an array of health and relaxation options. In the **zona bagni,** the **Reparto Regina,** P. Acqui Lussa, 6 (☎0144 32 43 90), is a healer's heaven—here's your chance to splurge big time. The center offers services ranging from lung ventilation (L25,000) to a mud bath supreme (L65,000). From the city center, walk down C. Bagni over the river, pass the gigantic **municipal pool,** and turn left on V. Acqui Terme. (Reparto Regina open M-F 8am-1pm and 3-6pm, Sa 8am-1pm. Municipal pool open M-Sa 8am-8pm. L10,000, including shower and deck chair.) **Nuove Terme,** V. XX Settembre, 5, off P. Italia, has some of the Reparto Regina's options (☎0144 32 43 90. Open M-F 8:30am-1pm and 3:30-6:30pm, Sa 8:30am-1:30pm.)

For a less healthy pilgrimage, head for the **Enoteca Regionale di Acqui Terme,** P. Levi, 7. From P. Italia, take C. Italia, turn left on V. Garibaldi, and take the 1st right into P. Levi; the cavernous winery, among the finest in Italy, was built on the grounds of the first Roman structure in town and is down some steps. It features 230 different wines, including the sweet domestic Dolcetto and Bracchetto, and it epitomizes the slogan *dove l'aqua e salute, e il vino e allegria* (where the water is healthy and the wine is happiness). (☎0144 77 02 73; fax 0144 57 627. Open Tu and F-Su 10am-noon and 3-6:30pm, Th 3-6:30pm. V, MC, Diners.)

VALLE D'AOSTA

Lush valleys give way to pine forests, and the jagged, white peaks of the Italian Alps remain snow-laced even in summer. Towns in the valleys are surrounded by forests, terraced wineries, and ski chalets. An international cable car traveling over the mountains from Chamonix, France, offers the most stunning entrance to the region, and the many French visitors arriving over the mountains have influenced the mixture of languages spoken here. The waterfalls of the **Gran Paradiso National Park** and the grandeur of the mountains have made tourism the center of Valle d'Aosta's economy, resulting in inflated prices year-round.

HIKING

The scenic trails of Valle d'Aosta are a paradise for hikers. July, August, and the 1st week of September, when much of the snow has melted, are the best times to hike. In April and May, thawing snow often causes avalanches. Mont Blanc and surrounding mountains may be classic climbers' peaks, but only pros should attempt to capture them. Talk to the staff at a tourist office or alpine information office about the difficulty of hikes or climbing destinations. For information on preparation and safety, see **Essentials** p. 60.

Despite these warnings, don't be scared of venturing into the Alps—there are many people who will help you. Each area's tourist office offers assistance to hikers of all levels. The tourist offices in Aosta and those in the smaller valleys provide information on routes as well as lists of campgrounds, bag-lunch *(al sacco)* vendors, **rifugi alpini** (mountain huts), and **bivacchi** (public refuges)—ask for the *elenco rifugi bivacchi*. Some mountain huts lie only a cable-car ride or a 30-minute walk away from roads, and many offer half-pension (around L60,000). Public refuges tend to be empty and free; those run by caretakers cost about L30,000 per night. For information, call **Società Guide,** V. Monte Emilius, 13 (☎/fax 0165 444 48), or **Club Alpino Italiano,** P. Chanoux, 15 (☎0165 409 39; fax 0165 36 32 44; www.guidealpine.com), both in Aosta. They offer insurance and refuge discounts.

Most regional tourist offices also carry the booklet *Alte Vie* (High Roads), with maps, photographs, and helpful advice pertaining to the two serpentine mountain trails that link many of the region's most dramatic peaks. Long stretches of these trails require virtually no expertise and offer adventure with panoramic views.

SKIING

Skiing Valle d'Aosta's mountains is fantastic; unfortunately, it is not a bargain. **Settimane bianche** ("white-week") packages for skiers, are one source of discount rates. For information and prices, call **Ufficio Informazioni Turistiche,** P. Chanoux, 8 (☎0165 23 66 27), in Aosta, and request the pamphlet *White Weeks: Aosta Valley.*

Courmayeur and **Breuil-Cervinia** are the best-known ski resorts in the 11 valleys. **Val d'Ayas** and **Val di Gressoney** offer equally challenging terrain for lower rates. **Cogne** and **Brusson,** halfway down Val d'Ayas, have cross-country and less demanding downhill trails. In Courmayeur and Breuil-Cervinia, athletes run from the swimming pools to the slopes for **summer skiing.** Arrange summer package deals through the tourist office in either Breuil-Cervinia or Courmayeur.

OTHER SPORTS

A number of activities—rock climbing, mountain biking, hang-gliding, kayaking, and rafting—will keep your adrenaline pumping. The most navigable rivers are the **Dora Baltea,** which runs across the valley, the **Dora di Veny,** which branches south from Courmayeur, the **Dora di Ferre,** which meanders north from Courmayeur, the **Dora di Rhêmes,** which flows through the Val di Rhêmes, and the **Grand Eyvia,** which courses through the Val di Cogne. **Rafting Fenis** 11020, Fenis, Vale d'Aosta (☎0165 76 46 46), just minutes from Aosta, runs excellent rafting trips. (1-3hr., L38-70,000 per person.) For a complete list of recreational activities, ask for *Attrezzature Sportive e Ricreative della Valle d'Aosta* from any tourist office.

AOSTA ☎0165

Aosta is the geographical and financial center of a region increasingly dependent upon tourism for economic livelihood. While Aosta itself sits in the flatlands, its prices soar much like the nearby peaks of Monte Emilius (3559m) and Becca di Nona (3142m). Aosta makes a good base for explorations in the area, but be aware that daytrips to the valleys often require tricky train and bus connections—if you hope to return before nightfall, arm yourself with schedules and plan ahead.

TRANSPORTATION

Trains: The station is in the pink building at P. Manzetti. To: **Verrès** (30min., every hr. 6:12am-8:40pm, L4800); **Pont St. Martin** (50min., every hr. 5:12am-8:40pm, L6000); **Chivasso** (1½hr., every hr. 5:12am-8:40pm, L8200) via **Châtillon** (15min., every hr. 6:12am-8:40pm, L3500); **Turin's** P. Nuova (2hr., every hr. 5:15am-8:40pm, L10,500); and **Milan's** Centrale (4hr., 12 per day 6:12am-8:40pm, L18,600). **Luggage Storage:** L5000 for 12hr. Open daily 6am-12:30pm and 1:30-6pm.

Buses: SAVDA, on V. Carrel off P. Manzetti, to the right of the train station. To: **Courmayeur** (1hr., every hr., L4800) and **Great St. Bernard Pass** (2hr., 9:40am and 2:25pm, L4800). **SVAP** serves closer towns. To **Fenis** (30min., 7 per day, L3000) and **Cogne** (1hr.; 6 per day; one-way L4000, round-trip L7200). Buses to **Valtournenche** and **Breuil-Cervinia** (2hr., 7 per day, L6000) leave from the Châtillon train station.

Taxis: P. Manzetti (☎0165 26 20 10). P. Narbonne (☎0165 356 56 or 0165 318 31).

NORTHWEST ITALY

ORIENTATION AND PRACTICAL INFORMATION

Trains stop at **Piazza Manzetti.** From there, walk straight down Av. du Conseil des Commis until it ends in the enormous **Piazza Chanoux,** Aosta's center. The main street runs east-to-west through P. Chanoux and suffers a number of name changes. From Av. du Conseil des Commis, **Via J. B. de Tiller,** which then becomes **Via Aubert,** is to the left; to the right is **Via Porta Praetoria** which leads to the historic gate, **Porta Praetoria,** where it becomes **Via Sant'Anselmo.**

TOURIST, FINANCIAL, AND LOCAL SERVICES

Tourist Office: P. Chanoux, 8 (☎0165 23 66 27; fax 0165 346 57), straight down Av. du Conseil des Commis from the train station. Ask for *Aosta, Monument Guide* (an excellent map of the city, local hotel list, and restaurant locator). The yearly *Orario Generale* contains comprehensive transportation schedules (including cable cars). English, German, and French spoken. Open M-Sa 9am-1pm and 3-8pm, Su 9am-1pm.

Currency Exchange: Monte dei Paschi di Siena, P. Chanoux, 51 (☎0165 23 56 56). **ATM** outside. Open M-F 8:20am-1:20pm and 2:40-4:10pm.

Alpine Information: Club Alpino Italiano, C. Battaglione, 81 (☎0165 401 94). From P. della Repubblica take Av. Battallion to C. Battaglione. Open M, Tu, Th 6-7:30pm, F 8-10pm. At other times, try **Società Guide,** V. Monte Emilius, 13 (☎0165 40 939; fax 0165 444 48; www.guide.alpine.com). For weather conditions try **Protezione Civile** in V. St. Christophe (☎0165 23 82 22 or 0165 441 13).

Car Rental: Europcar, P. Manzetti, 3 (☎0165 41 432), left of the train station. V, MC.

EMERGENCY AND COMMUNICATIONS

Police: C. Battaglione Aosta, 169 (☎113). **Medic:** ☎0165 30 42 11. **Hospital:** V. Ginevra, 3 (☎0165 30 41). **First Aid:** ☎0165 30 42 56. **Mountain rescue:** ☎118.

Pharmacy: Farmacia Chenal, V. Croix-de-Ville, 1 (☎0165 26 21 33), at the corner of V. Aubert. Open Th-Tu 9am-12:30pm and 3-7:30pm. Closed 1st 3 weeks in July.

Internet Access: Bar Snooker, V. Lucat, 3 (☎0165 23 63 68). From the station, turn right onto V. Giorgio Carrel and left on V. Lucat. Offers a pool hall, video poker, and a card-playing salon. Internet access L10,000 per hr. Open Th-Tu 8am-4am, W 1pm-4am.

Post Office: P. Narbonne, 1A (☎0165 441 38), in the huge semi-circular building. Open M-F 8:15am-6pm, Sa 8:15am-1pm. **Postal Code:** 11100.

ACCOMMODATIONS AND CAMPING

High season in Valle d'Aosta runs from late December to March and includes the two weeks around Easter Sunday.

La Belle Epoque, V. d'Avise, 18 (☎0165 26 22 76). From the train station, take Av. du Conseil des Commis to P. Chanoux, and turn left on V. Aubert. 15 rooms. Singles L45,000, with bath L55,000; doubles with bath L90,000; triples with bath L120,000. The **restaurant** downstairs is crowded with locals. Pizza L8-11,000, *primi* L10,000, *secondi* L10-15,000. *Menù* L20,000. Cover L2500. V, MC, AmEx, Diners.

Monte Emilius, V. Carrel, 911 (☎0165 356 92), upstairs from Ristorante Le Ramoneur. Friendly management but nightly traffic noise. 20 beds. Reserve ahead. 3 singles L50,000; 5 doubles L100,000. Restaurant offers a L20,000 *menù*.

Camping Milleluci, V. Porossan, 15 (☎0165 23 52 78; fax 0165 23 52 84). L9000 per person; L16-19,000 for a tent, plot, and electricity. Shower L1000. Laundry L8000.

FOOD

Switzerland has influenced typical dishes, such as *fonduta*, a creamy cheese fondue ladled over meat and vegetables, and *polenta valdostana*, sizzling with melted *fontina* (the regional specialty). The most divine dessert is *tegole*, wafer-thin cookies with ground nuts. The **STANDA supermarket,** V. Festaz, 10, has a wide variety of cheap groceries. (☎0165 357 57. Open M-Sa 8:30am-7:30pm.) Aosta's weekly **outdoor market** is held on Tuesday in P. Cavalieri di Vittorio Veneto.

Trattoria Praetoria, V. Sant'Anselmo, 9 (☎0165 443 56), just past the Porta Praetoria. Try the *salsiccette in umido* (local sausages braised in tomato sauce; L12,000). *Primi* L8-10,000, *secondi* L12,000. Cover L3000. Open in summer daily 12:15-2:30pm and 7:15-9:30pm; in winter F-W 12:15-2:30pm and 7:15-9:30pm. V, MC, AmEx, Diners.

Grotta Azzurra, V. Croix-de-Ville (Croce di Città), 97 (☎0165 26 24 74), uphill from V. de Tillier as it becomes V. Aubert. Try the pasta with *pesce* (L13-15,000). *Primi* L8-15,000. Open Th-Tu noon-2:30pm and 6-10:30pm. Closed 1st 2 weeks in July. V, MC.

Creperia Carillon, V. E. Aubert, 74 (☎0165 401 06). From P. Chanoux take V. de Tillier, which turns into V. E. Aubert. Tasty crepes for L7-8000. Open F-W 10am-1am. V, MC.

Old Distillery Pub, V. Pres Fosses, 7 (☎0165 23 95 11). From the Porta Pretoria, walk down V. Ansemo and take a right through a small archway onto the winding V. Pres Fosses. The 100% English staff and wide selection of excellent brews draws a sizeable crowd of locals and occasional live music. The pub is on the left. Open daily 6pm-2am.

SIGHTS

ROMAN RUINS. Oh, that Roman Empire—they didn't even bother to clean up their messy remains. Ruins dating from the age of Augustus fill the town. Down V. Porta Pretoria looms the massive stone archway of the **Porta Pretoria.** To the left is the entrance to the sprawling remains of the massive **Roman Theater.** *(Open daily in summer 9:30am-noon and 2:30-6:30pm; in winter 9:30am-noon and 2-4:30pm. Free.)* Through Porta Pretoria, V. S. Anselmo leads to the virtually intact **Arco d'Augusta.** Excavations continue to unearth monuments. The forum, or **Criptoportico Forense,** is off P. Papa Giovanni XXIII. *(Open W-M at 9am. Free.)*

SANT'ORSO. Within this church are 15th-century choir stalls and the lovely **Chiostro** (cloisters) **di Sant'Orso.** Beautiful, imaginatively carved columns, and ceiling decorate the tiny cloister with bestial and biblical scenes. The **Fiera di Sant'Orso,** the region's most famous crafts fair, takes place on January 30 and 31 and the Sunday before *Ferragosto* (in mid-August). The traditional fair dates to the 9th century and is known for Valdostan handicrafts. *(From the Porta Pretoria, take V. S. Anselmo and turn left on V. S. Orso. Open daily 7am-7pm. Free.)*

THE VALLEYS

VALLE DEL GRAN SAN BERNARDO. A valley with more medieval towers than tourists, Valle del Gran San Bernardo links Aosta to Switzerland via the Great St. Bernard Pass, which incorporates a 5854m tunnel through the mountains. Napoleon trekked through the pass with 40,000 soldiers in 1800. The area is better known for the 1505 **Hospice of St. Bernard,** home to the patron saint of man's best friend. The legendary life-saver was stuffed for posterity and can still be seen as you drive through the pass. The hospice (just across the Swiss border—don't forget your passport) offers great views of international peaks and is just a tail-wag away from the dog museum. A smaller, more serene branch of the valley leads to the communes of **Ollomont** and **Oyace,** where hiking trails, valleys, and fir forests await exploration. For more information, call the Aosta tourist office or the **ski-lift office** (☎0165 78 00 46) at St. Rhémy. Contact the tourist office for a hotel list, or camp at **Camping Pineta,** in St. Oyen. (☎0165 781 14. L7000 per person, L5-7000 per tent, L3000 per car. Electricity L2000. Shower L1000.)

THE MATTERHORN AND BREUIL-CERVINIA. The highest mountain in Switzerland, **The Matterhorn (Il Cervino)** looms majestically over the less-wonderful town of Breuil-Cervinia in Valtournenche. The nondescript buildings of **Breuil-Cervinia** differ only in purpose; some serve expensive food, others offer expensive accommodations, and the rest rent expensive sports equipment. In spite of the cost, many fresh-air fiends consider these man-made deterrents a small price to pay for the opportunity to climb up and glide down one of the world's most famous mountains. A cable car provides year-round service to **Plateau Rosà** (round-trip L42,000), where summer skiers frequently tackle the slopes in lighter gear. Hikers can forgo the lift tickets and attempt the three-hour ascent to **Colle Superiore delle Cime Bianche** (2982m), with tremendous views of Val d'Ayas to the east. A shorter trek (1½hr.) on the same trail leads to the emerald waters of **Lake Goillet.** The **Società Guide** (☎0166 94 81 69) arranges group outings. Don't forget your **passport;** a number of trails cross into Switzerland.

Buses run to Breuil-Cervinia (6 per day 6:10am-7:15pm, L4000) from Châtillon on the Aosta-Turin train line. Two direct buses also arrive daily from P. Castello in Milan (3hr.). Buses run to **Turin** (2½hr., Sa-Su 7:20am and 5:20pm). The English-speaking staff of the **Tourist Info Center,** V. Carrel, 29, inundates visitors with information on "white-week packages" and *settimane estive*, the summer equivalents. (☎0166 94 91 36; fax 0166 94 97 31. Open daily 9am-noon and 3-6:30pm.) The **Carta Estate** provides discounts on post-ski activities. Students should inquire about the **UniversityCard,** which reduces the prices of ski passes by 10-20%.

VAL D'AYAS. Budget-minded sports enthusiasts should consider bypassing the pleasure grounds to the west and stopping here instead. Val d'Ayas has the same outdoor activities as its flashy neighbors—skiing, hiking, and rafting—without the hype. **Trains** run to **Verrès** from Aosta (40min., 17 per day 6:35am-8:40pm, L4800) and Turin (1½hr.). **Buses** run from the train station at Verrès daily to Champoluc (1hr., 4 per day 11:30am-6pm, L4000). The **tourist office** in **Brusson** (☎0125 30 02 40; fax 0125 30 06 91) has branches in **Champoluc,** V. Varase, 16 (☎0125 30 71 13; fax 0125 30 77 85) and **Antagnod** (☎0125 30 63 35). They speak English and provide trail maps and hotel information. (All branches open daily 9am-12:30pm and 3-6pm.)

VAL DI COGNE. When Cogne's mines failed in the 1970s, the townspeople resorted to more genteel pursuits, delicately parting cross-country skiers from their money. In winter, Cogne functions as the head of an 80km entanglement of **cross-country trails** (daily pass L5000). Cogne is also one of the world's premier places to ice climb. A cable car transports alpine addicts to the modest **downhill skiing** facilities (round-trip L10,000, daily pass L30,000, 7-day pass including cable car L170,000). In summer, however, the pastoral community serves as the gateway to the **Gran Paradiso National Park.** In addition to a seemingly endless network of hiking trails and a population of 5000 ibex, the park has the highest **glacier** (4061m) fully contained within Italian borders, aptly named Gran Paradiso. On the hillside well above Cogne stands the **Mining Museum,** next to the old dormitory that housed Cogne's miners. A WWI era film depicts the happy life of a miner, while a cable car that carried coal provides more emotional stimulation. (☎0165 74 92 64. Open June 15-Sept. 15 daily 10am-8pm; May-June Tu-Su 10am-12:30pm and 2:30-6pm. L4000, students L2000. Restorations until summer 2001.)

Cogne is a scenic **bus** ride from Aosta (1hr., 6 per day 8:15am-8:30pm). The bus stops in front of the helpful **APT tourist office,** P. Chanoux, 36, which distributes maps of the region and can help you find a place to stay. (☎0165 740 40 or 0165 740 56; fax 0165 74 91 25. Open in summer daily 9am-12:30pm and 3-6pm; in winter M-Sa 9am-12:30pm and 2:30-5:30pm, Su 9am-12:30pm.)

VALNONTEY. This wee hamlet has an eye-opening view in the midst of a national park. Valnontey is an exceptional 45-minute walk along the river from Cogne on trail #25 just outside the tourist office along the river. During June and August, buses run from Cogne to Valnontey (every 30min. 7:30am-8pm, L1500; buy tickets on bus). Valnontey is notable for its convenient *alimentari*, a cluster of two-star hotels, access to trails, and a botanical garden, **Giardino Alpino Paradisia.** The inspiration to construct a botanical garden in alpine tundra (at an altitude of 1700m) struck the founders, no doubt aided by several bottles of wine, during the Cogne Mountain Festival in 1955. Practical complications notwithstanding, the gardens boast over 1000 species of rare alpine vegetation, including lichen, lichen, and more lichen. (Open June 13-Sept. 13 daily 9:30am-12:30pm and 2:30-5:30pm; L3000, groups L2000, under 10 free.) Between June and September, campers can choose between the rolling hills of **Camping Gran Paradiso** (☎0165 74 92 04; L9000 per person, ages 7-16 L6000, under 6 free; L9700 for tent, car, and electricity; free shower; self service laundromat) and **Lo Stambecco** (☎0165 741 52; L9000 per person, L6-7000 for tent and electricity).

COURMAYEUR ☎0165

In the spectacular shadow of Europe's highest peak, Mont Blanc, Italy's oldest alpine resort, remains a jet-set playground. Monte Bianco is, of course, the attraction: its jagged ridges and unmelting snow fields lure tourists for unsurpassed hiking and skiing. Unfortunately, prices are high and rooms booked solid year-round. The city shuts down in May and June when the shopkeepers take their vacations.

TRANSPORTATION AND PRACTICAL INFORMATION. One all-important building in **P. Monte Bianco** houses almost everything a traveler needs. The **bus station** at P. Monte Bianco offers frequent service to larger towns. (☎0165 84 20 31. Open daily 7:30am-8:30pm.) Buses go to **Aosta** (1hr.; every hr. 4:45am-8:45pm; L4800, round-trip L8200) and **Turin** (3½hr.; 4 per day 8am-4pm; L14,500, round-trip L24,700). The bus ticket office has a **currency exchange** with the same hours. To the right of the bus station, the **APT tourist office** offers maps and has a staff that speaks English, German, French, and Spanish. (☎0165 84 20 60. Open M-Sa 9am-12:30pm and 3-6:30pm, Su 9:30am-12:30pm and 3-6pm.) Twenty-four hour **taxis** (☎0165 84 29 60; night ☎0165 84 23 33) are at P. M. Bianco. In **emergencies,** call an **ambulance,** Strada delle Volpi, 3 (☎118). A **post office** is in P. M. Bianco. (☎0165 84 20 42. Open M-F 8:15am-1:40pm, Sa 8:15-11:40am.) **Postal Code:** 11013.

ACCOMMODATIONS AND FOOD. For winter accommodations, reserve six months in advance. Consider making Courmayeur a daytrip from the more affordable Aosta, as budget accommodations in the town are few and difficult to reach. **Pensione Venezia,** V. delle Villete, 2, up the hill to the left from P. Monte Bianco, provides 12 simple, airy, light-filled room with small balconies. (☎/fax 0165 84 24 61. Breakfast L8000. Singles L43,000; doubles L59,000.) Otherwise, head to the **Cai-Uget** refuge in Val Veny. Take the bus from Courmayeur to **Purtud,** in the direction of La Visaille (15 per day), and backtrack to the refuge between the two stops. This walk involves a 1700m ascent. (☎0165 86 90 97. Open June 15-Sept. and Dec. to 1 week after Easter. Dorms L47,000. Half-pension L55-60,000.)

Picnicking is the best budget option in Courmayeur. At **Pastificio Gabriella**, Passaggio dell'Angelo, 94, toward the end of V. Roma, you'll find excellent cold crepes, and pâté garnished with alpine violets. (☎0165 84 33 59. Open daily 8am-1pm and 4-7:30pm; closed 2 weeks in July. V, MC.) **Il Fornaio,** V. Monte Bianco, serves scrumptious breads and pastries. (☎0165 84 24 54. Open M-Tu and

Hotel Locanda Fiorita, Campiello Novo, S. Marco, 3457 (☎041 523 47 54; ☎/fax 041 522 80 43; email locafior@tin.it; www.locandafiorita.com). From Campo S. Stefano, take Calle del Pestrin and then climb onto the raised *piazza.* A beautiful vine-covered courtyard leads to large doubles decorated with oriental rugs. All 18 rooms with phones and A/C. The nearby annex, where rooms also include satellite TV, has a few ground-floor accommodations. Singles L140,000; doubles L180,000, with bath L200,000. Annex singles L170,000; doubles L240,000, with bath L250,000. Extra bed 30% more. V, MC, AmEx.

Alloggi Alla Scala, Corte Contarini del Bovolo, S. Marco, 4306 (☎041 521 06 29; fax 041 522 64 51). From Campo Manin, take Calle delle Locande, then take a left and a quick right on Corte Contarini del Bovolo. A red carpet leads up the stairs to a well-kept hotel with paintings and drawings of Venice lining the hallways. 5 rooms. Breakfast L10,000. Closed Aug. Doubles L130-150,000. Extra bed L50,000. V, MC.

Locanda Casa Petrarca, Calle Schiavine, S. Marco, 4386 (☎041 520 04 30). From Rialto, take Calle larga Mazzini and turn right at the church onto Calle dell'Ovo. Turn left onto Calle dei Fabbri, then turn right for Campo San Luca. Cross the Campo to Calle dei Fuseri. Take the 2nd left and turn right onto Calle Schiavine. 7 clean, white rooms look onto brick walls. Slightly faded plant- and book-filled lobby. English spoken. Reserve with 1 night's deposit. Singles L75,000; doubles L140,000, with bath L170,000. No credit cards.

DORSODURO

Near the university and the Accademia, hotels in Dorsoduro are in the middle of a less-touristed, well-worn area between the museum and the Frari church.

Hotel Galleria, Rio Terra A. Foscarini, Dorsoduro, 878/A (☎041 523 24 89; fax 041 520 41 72; email galleria@tin.it; www.hotelgalleria.it), on the left as you face the Accademia museum. Sumptuous oriental rugs and tasteful art prints lend the Galleria an elegance appropriate to its location on the Grand Canal. Some of the 10 rooms have stunning Grand Canal views. Breakfast, served in rooms, included. Singles L110,000; doubles L160-170,000, with bath L190-240,000. Extra bed 30% more. V, MC, AmEx.

Cà Foscari, Calle della Frescada, Dorsoduro, 3887b (☎041 71 04 01; fax 041 71 08 17; valtersc@tin.it), in a quiet neighborhood near the ferry. Take *vaporetto* #1 or 82 to S. Tomà. Turn left at the dead end, cross the bridge, turn right, and then take a left into the little alleyway. Murano glass chandeliers and Venetian Carnival masks embellish the 11 simple rooms. Breakfast included. Curfew 1am. Rooms held until 2pm. Open Feb.-Nov. Singles with bath L95,000; doubles L110,000, with bath L150,000; triples L141,000, with bath L186,000; quads L174,000, with bath L224,000. V, MC.

Hotel Messner, Fondamenta di Cà Bala, Dorsoduro, 216 (☎041 522 74 43; fax 041 522 72 66; email a.nardi@flashnet.it). From *vaporetto* #1: salute, go right on Calle del Bastion, then turn left. This 2-star hotel has 1-star ground floor rooms in a nearby annex. 21 rooms range from institutional singles to a bright quad with bath and kitchenette. All rooms with bath, phone, A/C, TV, safes, and hair dryers. Annex rooms with bath, phone, safes, and hair dryers. Breakfast included. Closed mid-Dec. and late Jan. Singles L160,000; doubles L240,000; triples L280,000; quads L310,000. Annex singles L145,000; doubles L190,000; triples L240,000; quads L260,000. V, MC, AmEx.

Antica Locanda Montin, Fondamenta del Borgo, Dorsoduro, 1147 (☎041 522 71 51; fax 041 520 02 55). From *vaporetto* #1: Cà Rezzonico, go straight ahead to Campo S. Barnaba. Turn left under the *sottoportico,* right at the iron sign, and left at the canal. 10 simple rooms on one of the most picturesque and quiet canals in Venice. A few have views and terraces. Doubles L190,000, with bath L240,000. V, MC, AmEx, Diners.

CASTELLO (FROM SAN MARCO TO SANT'ELENA)

Lodging here is near the center of town, a bit removed from the tourist hordes.

Pensione Casa Verardo, Castello, 4765 (☎041 528 61 27; fax 041 523 27 65). From *vaporetto*: S. Zaccaria, take Calle degli Albanese to Campo SS. Filippo e Giacomo, cross the *campo,* and continue down Rimpetto la Sacrestia. The hotel is directly over the bridge. In a traditional Venetian building, these 9 luxurious rooms feature elegant wall moldings, richly colored linens and draperies, and detailed wooden furnishings. Renovations planned for 2001. Breakfast included. Reserve with a 1 night deposit. Singles L150,000; doubles L250,000; triples L337,500; quads L400,000. V, MC, AmEx, but credit card use requires a 3-night min. stay.

Locanda Canal, Fondamenta del Remedio, Castello, 4422c (☎041 523 45 38; fax 041 241 91 38). From S. Marco, walk under the clock tower and turn right on C. Larga S. Marco and then left on Ramo dell'Anzolo (which becomes Calle Remedio after crossing the bridge). At the canal, turn left on Fondamenta Remedio. 7 large, well-decorated rooms in a converted 14th-century *palazzo,* some overlooking the canal. 2 hall toilets. Breakfast included. Shower L4000. Doubles L145,000, with shower L165,000, with toilet and shower L195,000; triples L175,000, with shower L195,000, with toilet and shower L235,000; quads L205,000, with shower L225,000, with toilet and shower L275,000. No credit cards.

Locanda Silva, Fondamenta del Remedio, Cannaregio, 4423 (☎041 522 76 43 or 041 523 78 92; fax 041 528 68 17; email albergosilva@libero.it), next to the Locanda Canal, above. 25 simple, clean rooms painted in bright colors. All rooms with phone and 2 adorable communal cats. Breakfast included. Open Feb. to mid-Nov. Singles L75,000; doubles L120,000, with toilet L140,000, with toilet and shower L175,000; triples with toilet and shower L225,000; quads L260,000.

Locanda Corona, Calle Corona, Castello, 4464 (☎041 522 91 74). From *vaporetto:* S. Zaccharia, take Calle degli Albanese to Campo SS. Fillipo e Giacomo, continue on Rimpe[illegible] la Sacrestia, and take the 1st right. Turn left onto Calle Corona. A safari motif dec[illegible]ates the lobby of one of the few wheelchair-accessible hotels in Venice. Breakfast is a hefty extra. Closed Jan. Singles L59,000; doubles L85,000; triples L106,000.

CAMPING

The **Litorale del Cavallino,** on the Lido's Adriatic side, has endless beach campsites.

Camping Miramare (☎041 96 61 50; fax 041 530 11 50), Punta Sabbioni, 700m along the beach to your right from the *vaporetto* stop, 40min. by *vaporetto* #14 from P. S. Marco. 3-night min. stay in high-season. Open Apr. to mid-Nov. In high season L9800 per person, L23,800 per tent. 4-person bungalow L62,000, 5-person L98,000.

Campeggio Fusina, V. Moranzani, 79 (☎041 547 00 55), in Malcontenta. From Mestre, take bus #1. Call ahead. L11,000 per person, L7000 per tent, L25,000 per tent and car, L21,000 to sleep in car.

FOOD

In Venice, dining well on a budget requires exploration. Like lemmings hurling themselves off a cliff, most tourists flock to the endless string of restaurants that serve mediocre fare along the main streets. Silly lemmings: the best and most affordable restaurants hide in the less traveled alleyways. Even there, however, travelers familiar with L20,000 small town feasts will find Venice unusually pricey.

Venetian cuisine, steeped in seafood, is distinct from other Italian fare. *Seppie in nero* is cuttlefish, a soft, squid-like creature coated with its own ink and usually served with *polenta,* the Veneto's cornmeal staple. A plate of *pesce fritta mista* (mixed fried seafood), which usually includes shrimp, *calamari* (squid), and *polpo* (octopus) costs at least L12,000. *Spaghetti al vongole* (pasta with fresh clams and spicy vegetables) is served on nearly every menu. Another regional specialty is *fegato alla veneziana* (liver and onions). The Veneto and Friuli regions produce an abundance of excellent **wines.** Good local whites include the sparkling *prosecco della Marca* and the dry *tocai.* For reds, try a *valpolicella.*

For an inexpensive and informal alternative to traditional restaurants, visit any *osteria* or *bacaro* in town and create a meal from the vast display of meat- and cheese-filled pastries, tidbits of seafood, rice, meat, and *tramezzini* (triangular slices of soft white bread with any imaginable filling). Generally glued together with artery-clogging

nightlife are **Campo Santa Margherita** in Dorsoduro (Il Caffè, Bar Salus, and Café Blue, below) and the areas around **Fondamenta della Misericordia** in Cannaregio (Paradiso Perduto and Cantina Vecia Carbonera, below).

Inishark Irish Pub, Calle Mondo Novo, Castello, 5787 (☎041 523 53 00), between Campo S. Maria Formosa and Salizzada S. Lio. The most creative and elegant Irish pub in Venice. Rubber sharks, wooden mantelpieces, and other assorted junk line the walls and ceilings. Open Tu-Su 6pm-2am.

Café Blue, Calle Lunga S. Pantalon, Dorsoduro, 3778 (☎041 71 02 27). From Campo S. Margherita, cross the bridge at the narrow end of the *piazza,* wind right around the church, and turn left at the dead end. Bright, noisy, and crowded, Café Blue attracts droves of expats and exchange students. Diversions include board games and live music. Open for afternoon tea 3:30-7:30pm, *whiskeria* 9:30pm-2am.

Bar Salus, Campo S. Margherita, Dorsoduro, 3112 (☎041 528 52 79). Large, comfortable booths, a roomy bar, and tons of outdoor seating make Bar Salus an extremely popular hangout for both Venetian and international students. *Fragolino* L2000.

Paradiso Perduto, Fondamenta della Misericordia, 2540 (☎041 72 05 81). From Strada Nuova, cross Campo S. Fosca, cross the bridge, and continue in the same direction, crossing another 2 bridges. Bar, jazz club, and restaurant. Well known among locals and tourists, this dark place is young and hip. Outdoor seating by the canal. Live jazz M 9pm. Open Th-Su 7pm-2am.

Cantina Vecia Carbonera, Strada Nuova, Cannaregio, 2329 (☎041 71 03 76). A wonderfully warm hole-in-the-wall, with exposed beam ceilings and bright contemporary art on the walls. Extensive wine selection and frequent live music, including excellent jazz. Open Sept.-July Tu-F 6pm-1:30am, Sa-Su 10:30am-2pm and 5pm-2am.

Bar S. Lucia, Lista di Spagna, Cannareggio 282/B (☎041 524 28 80), near the train station. This tiny bar stays crowded and noisy long into the night with American students and Italian locals. The friendly owners provide a wide selection of Irish beers. Guinness L9000. Open M-Sa 7am-2am.

The Corner Bar, Calle della Chiesa, Dorsoduro, 684 (☎041 241 07 70). From the Accademia Bridge, follow the signs left toward the Guggenheim; the bar is on the right, just past Campo S. Vio. British and American exchange students pack this place nightly. Open Tu-Su 11am-1am.

Casanova, Lista di Spagna, Cannaregio, 158/A (☎041 275 01 99; www.casanova.it). If you're starved for a *discoteca,* join the slinkily dressed crowd at Casanova, and let modern-day Latin lovers show you their moves. You might want to follow the original Casanova's precedent and make a daring early escape. Themes and cover charge change nightly, from alternative to Latin to house music. Happy hours 6-10pm. Open daily 10pm-4am. V, MC, AmEx.

Il Caffè, Campo S. Margherita, Dorsoduro, 2963 (☎041 528 79 98), also known as **Bar Rosso.** The upright piano, samovar, and peeling stucco give the interior a pleasant end-of-an-era feel. The outdoor seating provides one of the best places to people-watch in Venice. Open M-Sa 8am-2am.

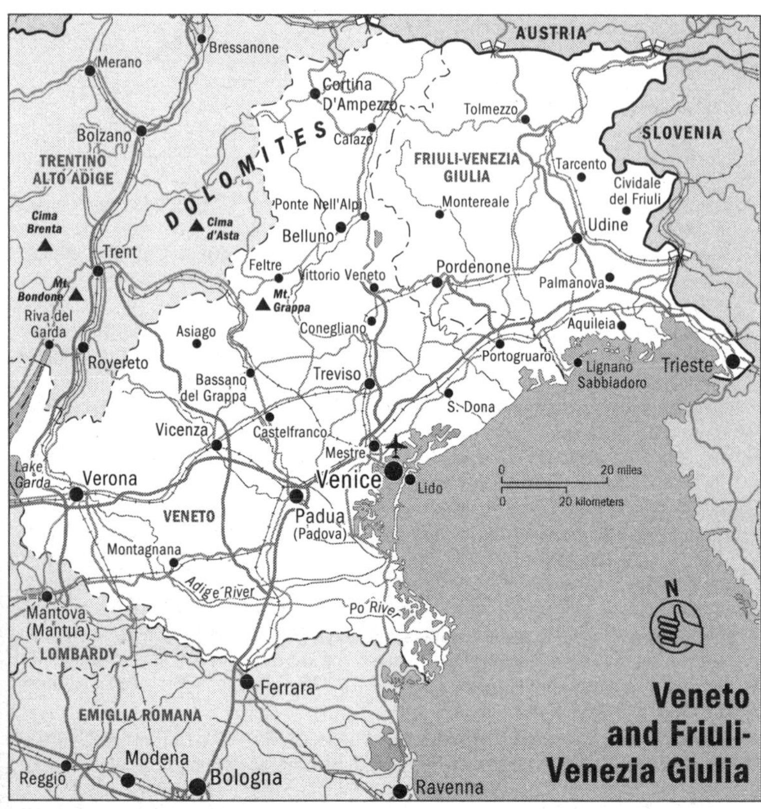

NORTHEAST ITALY

T[illegible]E VENETO

From the roc[illegible]othills of the Dolomites to the fertile valleys of the Po River, the Veneto region h[illegible]ography as diverse as its historical influences. Once loosely linked under the V[illegible] Empire, these towns retained their cultural independence, and visitors are [illegible]kely to hear regional dialects than standard Italian when neighbors gossip ac[illegible] geranium-bedecked windows. Culinary influences marched in with the Aus[illegible]d swim in with the day's catch. The sense of local culture and custom that rem[illegible] strong within each town may surprise visitors lured to the area by Venice, the *bella* of the north.

HIGHLIGHTS OF THE VENETO

WANDER past wall after splendid wall of Giotto's frescoes in Padua's **Cappella degli Scrovegni** (p. 226).

POP the question under **Juliet's balcony** in star-crossed Verona (p. 234). Wherefore art thou budget traveler?

GULP **grappa,** a fiery medieval elixir produced in Bassano del Grappa (p. 237).

PADUA (PADOVA) ☎049

Brimming with art and student life, Padua blends university culture with high culture—book-toting students walk through sculpture-lined *piazze*, cultivating an air of liberal individualism. Though completely devastated by the Lombard invasion of 602, the city wasted little time becoming one of Europe's intellectual hubs. The university, founded in 1222, is second in seniority only to Bologna's. Luminaries such as Dante, Petrarch, Galileo, Copernicus, Mantegna, Giotto, and Donatello all contributed to the city's reputation as a center of art and learning. Still bubbling with student activity and amazing sights, Padua makes a worthy pilgrimage.

TRANSPORTATION

Padua's location on the Venice-Milan and Venice-Bologna train lines and the availability of intercity buses make the city a convenient stop on any Italian itinerary.

Trains: In P. Stazione, at the northern end of C. del Popolo, the continuation of C. Garibaldi. To: **Venice** (30min., 3-4 per hr. 4:42am-11pm, L4100); **Verona** (1hr., 1-2 per hr. 5:49am-11pm, L7900); **Bologna** (1½hr., 1-2 per hr. 4:22am-10:41pm, L21,000); and **Milan** (2½hr., 1-2 per hr. 5:49am-11pm, L20-31,500). **Luggage Storage:** L5000 for 12hr. Open 5am-midnight. Info office open 8am-8pm.

Buses: SITA (☎049 820 68 11), in P. Boschetti. From the train station, walk down C. del Popolo, turn left on V. Trieste, and turn right at V. Porciglia. To: **Venice** (45min., 2 per hr., L5300); **Vicenza** (1hr., 2 per hr., L5400); **Montagnana** (1hr., 1-2 per hr., L6100); and **Bassano del Grappa** (1¼hr., 2 per hr., L7100). Open M-Th 8:30am-1pm and 3-6:30pm, F 8:30am-1pm and 3-5:30pm.

Local Buses: ACAP (☎049 824 11 11) buses #8, 12, and 18 run downtown. Buy regular tickets (L1600) or 24hr. tickets (L5000) at the train station. Open M-Sa 6am-6pm.

Taxis: Radio Taxi (☎049 65 13 33). Available 24hr.

NORTHEAST ITALY

ORIENTATION AND PRACTICAL INFORMATION

The train station is at the northern edge of town, outside the 16th-century walls. A 10-minute walk down **Corso del Popolo,** which becomes **Corso Garibaldi,** leads to the heart of town. A pedestrian area spans the old **University** campus, **"le Piazze"** (P. della Frutta, P. dei Signori, and P. delle Erbe), and the **duomo. Via del Santo** leads south to the **Basilica di Sant'Antonio,** the cathedral of Padua's patron, St. Anthony.

TOURIST, FINANCIAL, AND LOCAL SERVICES

Tourist Office: (☎049 875 20 77; fax 049 875 50 88), in the train station. Plentiful maps, festival info, and pamphlets. Has hotel listings but does not make reservations. Open M-Sa 9:15am-7pm, Su 9am-12:15pm. Smaller **branch** (☎049 875 30 87), in P. del Santo, near the basilica. Open M-Sa 9am-6pm, Su 9:30am-12:30pm.

Budget Travel: CTS, Riviera Mugnai, 22 (☎049 876 16 39), near the post office. Student IDs and train tickets. Open M-F 9am-12:30pm and 4-7:30pm, Sa 9am-12:30pm.

Car Rental: Europcar, P. Stazione, 6 (☎049 875 85 90). Min. age 21. L140,000 per day, L518,000 per week. Open M-F 8:30am-12:30pm and 3-7:30pm, Sa 8:30am-12:30pm. V, MC. **Maggiore Budget,** P. Stazione, 15bis (☎049 875 28 52). Must have had a license for 1 year. L116-153,000 per day, L580,000 per week. Prices increase substantially for automatic transmission or A/C and vary when booked from overseas. Open M-F 8:30am-12:30pm and 2:30-6:30pm, Sa 9am-noon.

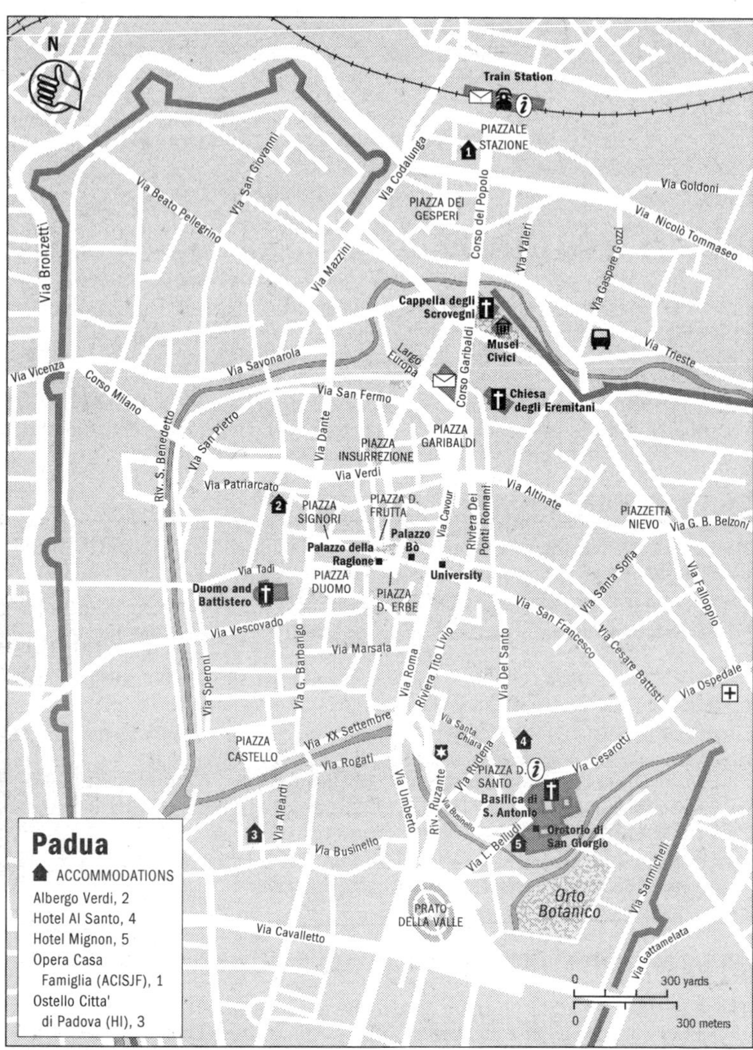

Bookstore: Feltrinelli International, V. S. Francesco, 14 (☎049 875 07 92), has a wide selection of novels and travel guides in English. Open M-F 9am-7:30pm, Sa 9am-1pm and 3:30-7:30pm.

Laundromat: Fastclean, V. Ognissanti, 6 (☎049 77 57 59), near the Porta Portello. Take bus #9. Self-service. L12,000 per 1-4kg. Open M-F 9am-12:30pm and 3:15-7:15pm, Sa 9am-12:30pm.

EMERGENCY AND COMMUNICATIONS

Emergencies: ☎112 or 113. **Ambulance:** ☎118. **Hospital: Ospedale Civile,** V. Giustiniani, 1 (☎049 821 11 11), off V. S. Francesco. **Police: Carabinieri** (☎049 21 21 21), on Prato della Valle.

Post Office: C. Garibaldi, 33 (☎049 820 85 11). Open M-Sa 8:10am-7pm. **Branch** at train station. Open M-F 8:10am-1:30pm, Sa 8:10am-12:30pm. **Postal Code:** 35100.

ACCOMMODATIONS AND CAMPING

Padua is filled with cheap lodgings, but they fill up quickly. If you can't get into the places listed below, try the area near **Piazza del Santo. Antonianum,** V. Donatello, 24, offers summer university housing for men. (☎049 876 87 11. Reserve ahead in summer. Open Aug.-Oct. 92 beds. L30,000 per person.) The castle-hostel in Montagnana (see p. 227) is out of the way but unbeatable.

Ostello Città di Padova (HI), V. Aleardi, 30 (☎049 875 22 19; fax 049 65 42 10; email pdyhtl@tin.it), near Prato della Valle. Take bus #3 from the station to Prato della Valle, the circular park with white statues. Walk north away from the park and turn left on V. Memmo. Pass the church and turn right on V. Aleardi. A hostel with many amenities–soda machines, reading room, phones, laundry (L8000), and a TV room–but a slightly run-down feel. "Point and shoot" squatter-style toilets. Wheelchair accessible. Breakfast, sheets, and shower included. Towels L2000. Register and store bags M-F after 2:30pm, Sa-Su after 4pm. Flexible 5-night max. stay. Reception 7-9:30am and 2:30-11pm. Room lockout 9:30am-4pm; shower and common rooms available after 2:30pm. Curfew 11pm. Reserve at least 1 week in advance. 16-bed dorms L23,000, for 3-4 nights L22,000, for 5 or more nights L21,000; 4- to 5-bed dorms L24,000.

Hotel Al Santo, V. del Santo, 147 (☎049 875 21 31; fax 049 978 80 76), near the basilica. Friendly owner rents airy, well-kept rooms above a cozy restaurant. 16 rooms, all with phone and shower. Breakfast L8000. Open Feb. to mid-Dec. Singles L50,000; doubles L85,000; triples L115,000. V, MC.

Hotel Mignon, V. Belludi, 22 (☎049 66 17 22; fax 049 66 12 21), on a lively street near the basilica. A pretty sitting room with armchairs and oriental rugs and large, basic rooms upstairs. 20 rooms, all with bath, TV, and phone. Singles L90,000; doubles L110,000; triples L130,000; quads L150-160,000. V, MC.

Opera Casa Famiglia (ACISJF), V. Nino Bixio, 4 (☎049 875 15 54), off P. Stazione. Leave the station, walk to the right, and turn left on the street just before Hotel Monaco. Women under 30 only. Study and kitchen open at night. 36 beds. Curfew 10:30pm. Modern and tidy doubles, triples, and quads L30,000 per bed.

Albergo Verdi, V. Dondi dall'Orologio, 7 (☎049 875 57 44), in a central location. Walk under the clock tower at the rear of P. dei Signori and turn right at the end of the row of trees. 14 large, comfortable rooms with a 70s frat house feel. Reserve ahead in summer. Singles L40,000; doubles L64,000; triples L85,000.

Camping: Montegrotto Terme, V. Roma, 123/125 (☎049 79 34 00). Take the train to Montegrotto; from the station, walk out the front and follow signs for a 3km walk to the site. Friendly staff. Tennis, beach volleyball, and restaurant discounts for guests. Open Mar. to early Nov. L13,000 per person, L17,700 per tent, L24,200 per camper.

FOOD

Morning **markets** are held in P. delle Erbe and P. della Frutta—sidewalk vendors sell fresh produce, and covered booths in the archways offer meat and dairy products. A **supermarket PAM** is downtown on V. Cavour in P. della Garzeria. (Open M-Sa 8am-8pm.) Wine lovers may sample a glass from the nearby **Colli Euganei wine district** or try the sparkling *Lambruschi* from Emilia-Romagna. For a pre-dinner *aperitivo*, head to the century-old **Taverna della Nane Giulia,** V. S. Sofia, 1, off V. S. Francesco. In the evenings, it fills with students and artists enjoying cheap *veneto* fare, music, and fabulous wines. (☎049 66 07 42. Open Tu-Su 12:30-2:30pm and 7pm-1am; dinner served 8pm-1am.) Visitors to the Basilica di Sant'Antonio can nibble on the *dolce del santo* sold in nearby *pasticcerie.*

Pizzeria Al Borgo, V. Luca Belludi, 56 (☎049 875 88 57), near the Basilica di S. Antonio. Join a rollicking local crowd for late-night dinner on the terrace. The Lancelot salad, with *radiccio* and spinach, cures a broken or adulterous heart. Traditional Paduan salads L5000, large pizzas from L7000, creative pizzas from L11,000. Cover L2500. Open W-Su noon-3pm and 7-11:30pm. V, MC, AmEx.

Alexander Bar, V. S. Francesco, 38 (☎049 65 28 84), near the university. A *paninoteca* with an immense range of sandwiches. *Panini* L6-10,000. Open M-Sa 8:30am-2am.

Lunanuova, V. G. Barbarigo, 12 (☎049 875 89 07), near the *duomo*. Vegetarian restaurant in a comfortable, quiet setting. Small servings of pasta and Middle Eastern dishes L8-15,000. Wash it all down with beer, wine, fruit juice, or herbal tea. Cover L2000. Open Tu-Sa 12:30-2:15pm and 7:30pm-midnight.

SIGHTS

Padua has a wealth of sights—take advantage of the **Biglietto Unico** (L15,000, students and groups L10,000). The card is valid for one year and is available at the tourist office and at participating sights. The ticket grants admission to the Cappella degli Scrovegni, Musei Civici, Orto Botanico, Palazzo della Ragione, and Battistero del Duomo.

CAPELLA DEGLI SCROVEGNI (ARENA CHAPEL). The Florentine master Giotto frescoed the stunning walls of this chapel with scenes from the lives of Mary, Jesus, and Mary's parents Joachim and Anne. Completed between 1305 and 1306, this 38-panel cycle jump-started the Italian Renaissance by bringing a previously unknown depth and realism into painting. The figures stand beneath a heavenly blue sky, interacting in a natural manner and displaying traces of individuality. The attached **Musei Civici Erimitani** contains an overwhelming art collection that includes a few treasures, including an amazing Giotto crucifix. *(P. Eremitani, 8. ☎049 820 45 50. Museum open Tu-Su Feb.-Oct. 9am-7pm; Nov.-Jan. 9am-6pm. Chapel open daily Feb.-Dec. L10,000, students L7000, school groups L5000 per person. Entrance through museum only.)*

BASILICA DI SANT'ANTONIO (IL SANTO). The basilica is a 13th-century Latin cross crowned by eight colossal domes and filled with stunning frescoes and stained glass. Bronze sculptures by Donatello grace the high altar, surrounded by the artist's *Crucifixion* and several earlier Gothic frescoes. Saint Antony's remains, in various pieces, lie scattered throughout the basilica. His bones' final resting place, the **Tomba di Sant'Antonio,** is to the left of the altar. Hard to miss under the layers of written pleas and thanks, it is the final destination for thousands of pilgrims who visit the basilica each year to worship the saint. The patron of "lost items," St. Anthony was certainly one of the most unique saints; among his many deeds, he preached to fish, taught a supposedly illegitimate baby to say to his father "You are my daddy," and reattached a boy's severed foot. Covering the walls of the chapel are marble bas-reliefs by prominent Venetian artists—Jacopino Sansovino carved the expressive *Anthony Restores a Drowned Girl.* St. Anthony's jawbone and larynx lie behind glass inside the saint's gold bust at the back of the church. His tongue, still surprisingly tongue-like after 700 years, rests quietly in a gold case below. A **trippy multimedia show** (follow "Mostra" signs) in the attached courtyard details St. Anthony's life. The adjoining **Oratorio di San Giorgio** houses examples of Giotto-school frescoes, and the **Scuola del Santo** includes three by the young Titian. *(P. del Santo. ☎049 824 28 11. Cathedral open daily Apr.-Sept. 6:30am-8pm; Nov.-Mar. 6:30am-7pm. Dress code enforced. Mostra open daily 9am-12:30pm and 2:30-6pm. English headset available at front desk. Oratorio and Scuola ☎049 875 52 35. Open daily Apr.-Sept. 9am-12:30pm and 2:30-7pm; Oct.-Jan. 9am-12:30pm; Feb.-Mar. 9am-12:30pm and 2:30-4:30pm. L3000, reduced L2000.)*

GATTAMELETA STATUE. In the center of P. del Santo stands Donatello's bronze equestrian statue of Erasmo da Narni (a.k.a. Gattamelata or Calico Cat), a general remembered for his agility and ferocity. Donatello modeled his work on the equestrian statue of Marcus Aurelius at the Campidoglio in Rome. Compare Erasmo's serenity with the ferocity of Colleoni in Venice (p. 217), completed 10 years later.

PALAZZO DELLA RAGIONE (LAW COURTS). Overlooking the lively market stalls of P. della Frutta, the enormous and bizarre Palazzo della Raggione, built in 1218, retains most of its original shape. Astrological signs line the walls. Sunlight once streamed through the mouth of the golden sun on the left wall, marking the time on the marble line in the floor. The original ceiling, once painted as a starry sky, survived a 1420 fire only to topple in a 1756 tornado. To the right of the entrance sits the **Stone of Shame.** Inspired by St. Anthony in 1231 to abolish debtors' prisons, Padua adopted the more humane practice of forcing the partially clad debtor onto the stone to repeat before a crowd of at least one hundred hecklers, *"Cedo bonis"* ("I renounce my property"). At the end of the hall, a massive wooden horse, falsely attributed to Donatello, has taken over a room. *(Entrance on P. delle Erbe. ☎049 820 50 06. Open Tu-Su Jan.-Oct. 9am-7pm; Nov.-Dec. 9am-6pm. L10,000, students L6000. Exhibits occasionally change hours and prices.)*

UNIVERSITY. The university campus is scattered throughout the city, but it is centered in Palazzo Bò. The scientific **Teatro Anatomico** (1594), the first of its kind in Europe, hosted medical pioneers like Vesalius and Englishman William Harvey. Almost all Venetian noblemen received their mandatory law and public policy instruction in the **Great Hall.** The "chair of Galileo" is preserved in the **Sala dei Quaranta,** where the physicist once lectured. Across the street, **Caffè Pedrocchi** served as the headquarters for 19th-century liberals who supported Giuseppe Mazzini. When it was first built, the cafe's famous Neoclassical facade had no doors and was open around the clock. A battle between students and Austrian police exploded here in February 1848, a turning point in the Risorgimento. Capture the spirit for the price of a cappuccino. *(Palazzo Bò, in P. delle Erbe. ☎049 820 97 73. Guided tours M, W, and F at 3, 4, and 5pm; Tu, Th, and Sa at 9, 10, and 11am. Tours L5000, students L2000. Caffe Pedrocchi, V. VIII Febbraio, 15. Open daily 8am-11pm.)*

DUOMO. Michelangelo reputedly participated in the design of this church, which was erected between the 16th and 18th centuries. Next door, a jewel of Padua, the **Battistero,** was built in the 12th century and retouched in the 13th. *(P. Duomo. ☎049 66 28 14. Duomo open M-Sa 7:30am-noon and 3:45-7:45pm, Su 7:45am-1pm and 3:45-8:30pm. Free. Baptistery open daily 9:30am-1:30pm and 3-7pm; in winter 9:30am-1pm and 3-6pm. L3000, students L2000.)*

ORTO BOTANICO. The oldest university botanical garden in Europe tempts visitors with waterlilies, medicinal herbs, and a 1585 palm tree that still offers shade. *(From the basilica follow signs to V. Orto Botanico, 15. ☎049 65 66 14. Open daily 9am-1pm and 3-6pm; in winter M-F 9am-1pm. L5000, students L3000.)*

ENTERTAINMENT AND FESTIVALS

Restaurant terraces begin drawing boisterous crowds around 9pm. **Taverna della Nane Giulia** serves pre-dinner *aperitivi* (see **Food,** p. 225). **Lucifer Young,** V. Altinate, 89, near the university, is a hip bar whose decorator took lessons from the lowest circle in the *Divine Comedy*. (☎049 66 55 31. Drinks from L6000; some food available. Open Su-Tu and Th 7pm-2am, F-Sa 7pm-4am.) The tourist office pamphlet *Where Shall We Go Tonight?* lists restaurants and bars.

February 8 brings the **Festa della Matricola,** during which students and professors take a day off from classes, wear ancient academic costumes, and play practical jokes on each other. Pilgrims pack the city on June 13, as Padua remembers the death of its patron St. Anthony (who died in 1231) with a procession of the saint's statue and jawbone that begins at the basilica. An **antique market** assembles in the Prato della Valle on the 3rd Sunday of each month.

NEAR PADUA

The **Colli Euganei** (Eugan Hills), southwest of Padua, offer a feast for the senses. Padua's tourist office has pamphlets suggesting various itineraries. The volcanic hills are rich not only in soil and hot mineral springs, but also in extraordinary accommodations. If you've always dreamed of life in a castle, realize your aspirations with a night in **Montagnana.** The town, surrounded by a well-preserved medieval wall, lies just outside the *colli*, an hour by bus from either Vicenza or Padua (round-trip L14,000). The **Youth Hostel (HI),** within the Rocca degli Alberi, offers hot showers and 70 soft beds. (☎0429 810 76; fax 049 807 02 66. English spoken. L17-20,000 per person.) Montagnana's **tourist office** is in P. V. Emanuele. (☎0429 813 20. Open M and W-Sa 10am-noon and 4-6pm.)

VICENZA ☎0444

Though dwarfed by neighboring Venice and Padua, Vicenza manages to sport all the grandeur of a larger city thanks to its monumental *piazze* designed by Andrea Palladio. The architect's style, mingling ancient and contemporary forms and often employing double columned *loggie*, became one of the most respected in Europe. The success of the light-industry zone on the outskirts of town allows residents to maintain a somewhat "Palladian" lifestyle—Vicenza has one of the highest average incomes in Italy. Luckily, their impressive surroundings and back-pocket bulges have not affected the inhabitants' attitudes, and visitors to Vicenza will enjoy genuine small-town hospitality.

TRANSPORTATION

Trains: P. Stazione, at the end of V. Roma. To: **Padua** (30min., 9 per day 8:10am-6:48pm, L4100-8200); **Verona** (40min., 16 per day 6:20am-10pm, L5300-9400); **Venice** (1½hr., 40 per day 5:52am-11pm, L6100-10,200); and **Milan** (2½hr., 17 per day 6:08am-10:16pm, L16-27,300). Info open daily 7:30am-8:30pm. Ticket office open M-Sa 6am-9:15pm, Su 6am-10pm. **Luggage Storage:** L5000 for 12hr. Open daily 6am-10pm.

Buses: FTV, V. Milano, 7 (☎0444 22 31 15), to the left as you exit the train station. To: **Padua** (30min., 30 per day 6am-8:20pm, L5400); **Bassano** (1hr., 26 per day 5:50am-9:30pm, L5300); and **Montagnana** (1¼hr., 7 per day 7am-5:30pm, L3200). Office open daily 6am-7:45pm.

Taxis: Radiotaxi (☎0444 92 06 00). Usually available at either end of C. Palladio.

NORTHEAST ITALY

ORIENTATION AND PRACTICAL INFORMATION

Vicenza lies in the heart of the Veneto. The train station and the adjacent intercity bus station are in the southern part of Vicenza. Glance at the map outside the station before walking into town on **Viale Roma.** Take a right on **Corso Palladio; Piazza Matteotti** lies at the other end, 20 minutes from the station. A right off V. Palladio will lead to the majestic facades of **Piazza Signori.**

Tourist Office: P. Matteotti, 12 (☎0444 32 08 54; fax 0444 32 70 72; www.ascom.vi.it/aptvicenza), next to Teatro Olimpico. Offers helpful brochures, a free city map, and info on wheelchair access. English spoken. Open M-Sa 9am-1pm and 2:30-6pm, Su 9am-1pm.

Budget Travel: AVIT, V. Roma, 17 (☎0444 54 56 77), before you reach the supermarket PAM. BIJ and Transalpino tickets. **Avis** and **Hertz** rental cars. English spoken. Open M-F 9am-1pm and 3-7pm, Sa 9:30am-12:30pm. **CTS,** Contra Ponta Nova, 43 (☎0444 32 38 64), near the Chiesa dei Carmini. Discount flights, tours, and ISICs. English spoken. Open M-F 9am-12:30pm and 3-7pm.

Currency Exchange: at the post office (see below). **ATMs** in the train station, on Contra del Monte, and throughout the downtown area.

Emergencies: ☎113. **Ambulance:** ☎118. **Hospital: Ospedale Civile,** V. Rodolfi, 8 (☎0444 99 31 11). **Night, Weekend, and Holiday Doctor:** ☎0444 99 34 70. **Police:** V. Muggia, 3 (☎0444 50 40 44).

Internet Access: Gala 2000, on V. Roma across from supermarket PAM. Closed Aug.

Post Office: Contrà Garibaldi, 1 (☎0444 32 24 88), between the *duomo* and P. Signori. Open M-Sa 8:10am-7pm. Currency exchange M-Sa 8:10am-6pm. **Postal Code:** 36100.

ACCOMMODATIONS AND CAMPING

Hotel Vicenza, Stradella dei Nodari, 9 (☎/fax 0444 32 15 12), off P. Signori in the alley across from Ristorante Garibaldi. Meticulously scrubbed and centrally located. Friendly management. 30 rooms. Prices vary by season. Singles L45-60,000, with bath L45-80,000; doubles L55-90,000, with bath L65-110,000.

Italia, V. Risorgimento, 2 (☎0444 32 78 63). From the train station, follow V. Venezia to your right and make a right onto V. X Giugno and a left onto V. Risorgimento. 17 clean, relatively quiet rooms not too far from the station. Wheelchair accessible. Breakfast L10,000. Singles with bath L80,000; doubles with bath L130,000.

Camping: Campeggio Vicenza, Strada Pelosa, 239 (☎0444 58 23 11; fax 0444 58 24 34). Only accessible by car: take SS11 toward Padua, turn left on Strada Pelosa, and follow signs to the Viest Motel. Showers included. Washing machines L10,000. Open Mar.-Sept. L11,800 per person, L12,500 per tent, L18,800 per tent with car.

FOOD

A **produce market** is held daily in P. delle Erbe behind the basilica. On Tuesday and Thursday mornings, rummage for food beside the bizarre clothing sold near the post office. On Thursday, market winds blow through the town bringing cheese, chicken, and fish from afar. For more mundane shopping, turn to **supermarket PAM,** V. Roma, 1. (Open M-F 8:30am-8pm.)

Vecchia Guardia, Contra Pescherie, 15 (☎0444 32 12 31), near P. Signori. Turn left onto C. Pescherie and look under the arcades. Amazing pizzas served by an incredibly friendly staff. Outdoor tables have a view of the *duomo.* Pizzas L7500-14,000, fish L15-35,000. Cover L2500. Open noon-2:30pm and 7pm-midnight. V, MC, AmEx.

Righetti, P. del Duomo, 3 (☎0444 54 31 35), with another entrance at Contrà Fontana, 6, offers adequate self-service fare and a great outdoor seating area. *Primi* from L5000, *secondi* from L7500. Cover L500. M-F 9am-3pm and 5:30pm-1am. Closed Aug.

SIGHTS

For an elevated view of Vicenza and many of Palladio's works, **Monte Berico's Piazzale Vittoria** is a short hike uphill from the train station toward V. Risorgimento.

TEATRO OLIMPICO. This gorgeous theater is the last structure planned by Palladio, although he died before its completion. The intricate Vicenzian streets and alleyways unfolding off the stage, coupled with the detailed statues cluttering the theater's walls, make a staggering impression. *(P. Matteotti, beside the tourist office. ☎0444 32 37 81. Open Tu-Su 10am-7pm. Included in the cumulative ticket. Ticket office closes 15min. before the theater.)* Every year from June to September, the city hosts productions in the Teatro Olimpico, showcasing both local and imported talent. *(☎0444 54 00 72. L20-35,000, students L15-30,000.)*

PIAZZA DEI SIGNORI. The town center served as the forum when Vicenza was Roman and as the town's showpiece when it was controlled by Venice. Andrea Palladio's reworking of the **basilica** brought the young architect his first fame. In 1546, Palladio's patron, the wealthy Giovan Giorgio Trissino, agreed to fund his proposal to shore up the collapsing Palazzo della Ragione, a project that had frustrated some of the foremost architects of the day. He ingeniously applied pilasters on twin *loggie* of the basilica to mask the Gothic structure beneath. The **Torre di Piazza** next door reflects the basilica's former appearance. *(☎0444 32 36 81. Basilica open Tu-Sa 9:30am-noon and 2:30-5pm. L7-10,000 during art exhibitions in the basilica.)*

The **Loggia del Capitano,** directly across from the Torre di Piazza, illustrates Palladio's later technique. The architect died leaving the facade unfinished, having completed only three bays and four sets of gigantic pink columns.

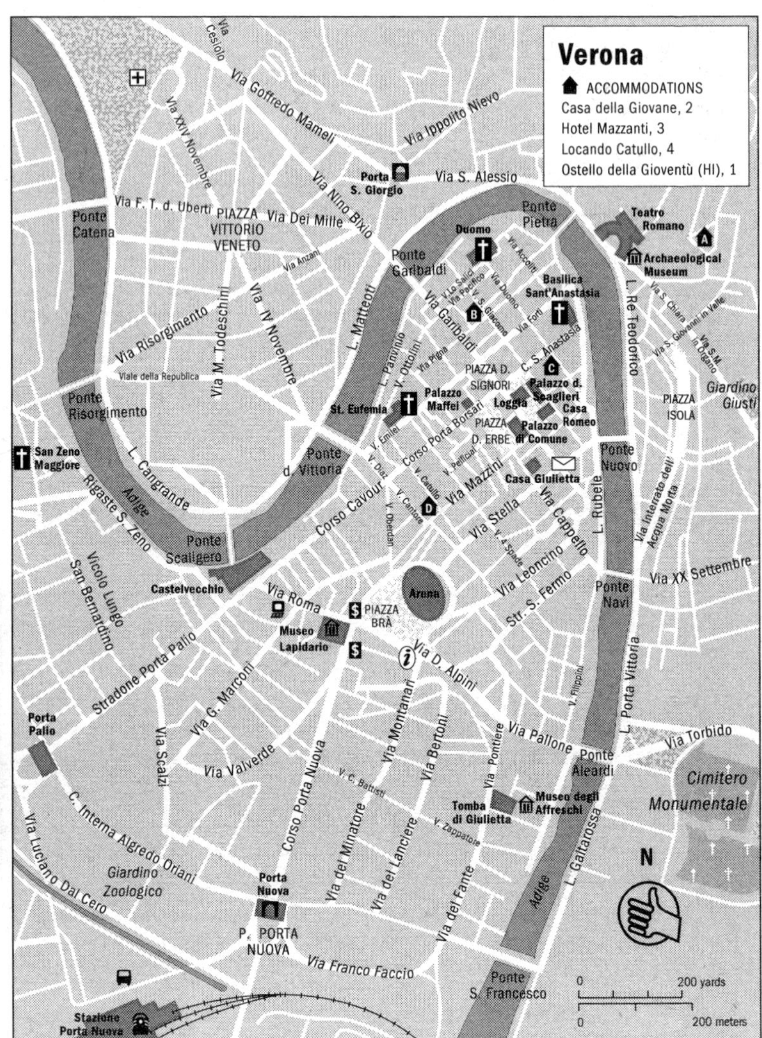

MUSEO CIVICO. Housed in Palladio's **Palazzo Chiericati,** this extensive collection includes Montagna's *Madonna Enthroned*, a Memling *Crucifixion*, Tintoretto's *Miracle of St. Augustine*, and Cima da Conegliano's refined *Madonna*. *(At the far end of Corso Palladio, across from the tourist office. ☎0444 32 13 48. Open Tu-Su 10am-7pm. L12-14,000, students and groups L6-7000 per person.)*

DAYTRIPS FROM VICENZA: PALLADIAN VILLAS

In addition to the urban beauty Vicenza offers the visitor, the city's surrounding countryside overflows with Palladian gems. Venetian expansion to the mainland began in the early 15th century and provided infinite opportunity for Palladio to display his talents. As Venice's wealth accumulated and its maritime supremacy faded, its nobles turned their attention to the acquisition of real estate on the mainland. The Venetian Senate mandated that nobles build villas rather than castles to preclude any possibility that they might become independent warlords. The architectural consequences are stunning, and the Veneto is now home to hundreds of the most splendid villas in Europe.

Most of the Palladian villas scattered throughout Veneto are difficult to reach, but luckily some of the most famous lie close to Vicenza. The **Villa Rotonda** is considered one of history's most magnificent architectural achievements. This villa became a model for buildings in France, England, and the US, most notably Thomas Jefferson's Monticello. (☎0444 32 17 93. Take bus #8 to Villa Rotonda. Open Mar. 15-Nov. 4. Exterior open Tu and Th 10am-noon and 3-6pm. Interior open W 10am-noon and 3-5pm. L10,000, reduced L5000.)

Diagonally across the street from the Villa Rotonda and towards Vicenza lies the **Villa Valmarana "ai Nani"** (of the dwarfs), a small but beautifully kept villa set in the middle of a series of circular flower gardens. The frescoes on the interior were painted by a father and son duo at the end of the 18th century, though the villa itself was completed a century earlier. (☎0444 54 39 76.)

VERONA ☎045

After traversing the old Roman Ponte Pietra on a summer's evening, with the gentle rush of the Adige River below and the illuminated towers of churches and castles glowing above, you'll hardly wonder why Shakespeare set *Romeo and Juliet* in Verona. Its city gates and ancient amphitheater memorialize the city's Roman past, while the Scaligeri Bridge and tombs hark back to Verona's Gothic glory.

TRANSPORTATION

NORTHEAST ITALY

Trains: (☎045 800 08 61), on P. XXV Aprile. To: **Trent** (1hr., every 2hr., L9200); **Venice** (1¾hr., every hr., L10,800-17,000); **Milan** (2hr., every hr., L12,500); **Bologna** (2hr., every 2hr., L10,500); **Cinque Terre** (4½hr., L33,000); **Rome** (5hr., 5 per day, L63,100-72,700); and **Naples** (8hr., L60,000). Ticket office open daily 5:45am-10:45pm. Info open daily 7am-9pm. **Luggage Storage:** L5000 for 12hr. Open 24hr.

Buses: APT (☎045 800 41 29), on P. XXV Aprile, in the gray building in front of the train station, to the right of the AMT bus platforms. No English spoken. To: **Sirmione** (1hr., 13 per day, L5000); **Riva Del Garda** (2hr., 12 per day, L9300); **Brescia** (2hr., every hr., L10,300); and **Montagnana** (2hr., 4 per day, L7300).

Taxis: Radiotaxi (☎045 53 26 66). Available 24hr.

ORIENTATION AND PRACTICAL INFORMATION

From the train station in P. XXV Aprile, walk 20 minutes up **Corso Porta Nuova,** or take bus #11, 12, 13, 72, or 73 to Verona's heart, the **Arena** in **Piazza Brà** (tickets L1500; full-day L4000). Most of the popular sights lie between P. Brà and the Adige River. The swanky **Via Mazzoni** connects the Arena to the markets and monuments of **Piazza della Erbe** and **Piazza dei Signori. Castelvecchio** lies just to the west of P. Brà, down V. Roma. The **university,** the **Teatro Romano,** and the **Giardino Giusti** lie across the Ponte Nuovo.

TOURIST AND FINANCIAL SERVICES

Tourist Office: (☎045 806 86 80; fax 045 800 36 38; email info@tourism.verona.it), off of P. Brà right before V. D. Alpini. English spoken. Open daily 10am-7pm. Additional branch in the airport (☎/fax 045 861 91 63). Open M-Sa 9am-6pm. **Youth Info Center (Informagiovani),** C. Porto Borsari, 17 (☎045 801 07 95; fax 045 803 62 05). Genial staff speaks English. Helps travelers find employment or study opportunities in Verona. Open M-W and F 9am-1pm and 2:30-6pm, Th 3-5pm.

Budget Travel: CIT, P. Brà, 2 (☎045 59 06 49 or 045 59 17 88; fax 045 800 21 99). Exchanges currency. Open M-F 8:20am-1:20pm and 3-7pm. **Centro Turistico Giovanile,** V. Seminario, 10, 3rd fl. (☎045 800 45 92), off V. Carducci, the 1st left after V. Interrato dell'Acqua Morta. Open M-F 9am-1pm and 2:30-6:30pm, Su 9am-1pm.

Currency Exchange: Cassa di Risparmio, centrally located on the corner of V. Roma and P. Brà. Open M-F 8:20am-1:20pm and 2:35-4pm. Another branch at the train station. Open 7am-8pm. 24hr. exchange machines line V. Mazzini, V. Cappello, and P. delle Elbe. They usually charge L6000 commission.

American Express: Fabretto Viaggi, C. Porta Nuova, 11/L (☎045 806 01 11), 2 blocks towards the station from P. Brà. Changes traveler's checks. Holds client mail. Open M-F 8:30am-1pm and 3-7pm, Sa 9am-12:30pm.

LOCAL SERVICES

Car Rental: Hertz (☎045 800 08 32), **Avis** (☎045 800 06 63), and **Europcar** (☎045 59 27 59) all share the same office at the train station. From L173,000 per day. Discounts on longer rentals. Open M-F 8:30am-noon and 2:30-7pm, Sa 8:30am-noon.

Bike Rental: Rent a Bike (☎045 58 23 89; in winter 045 814 07 60), on V. degli Alpini. L7000 per hr., L20,000 per day. Open daily 9am-7pm; off-season 10am-7pm.

Bookstore: The Bookshop, V. Interrato dell'Acqua Morta, 3a (☎045 800 76 14), near Ponte Navi. Classics in English and a small selection of French, Spanish, and German books. Open Tu-Sa 9:15am-12:30pm and 3:30-7:30pm, Su 9:15am-12:30pm.

Laundromat: Onda Blu, V. XX Settembre, 62a (☎0336 52 28 58). Take bus #11, 12, and 13. Wash L6000. Dry L6000. Open daily 8am-10pm.

EMERGENCY AND COMMUNICATIONS

Emergencies: ☎113. **Ambulance:** ☎118 or 045 58 22 22. **First Aid:** ☎118. **Hospital: Ospedale Civile Maggiore** (☎045 807 11 11), on Borgo Trento, in P. Stefani.

Police: Questura: ☎800 23 50. **Ufficio Stranieri:** ☎045 809 05 05. **Lost and Found Property Office,** V. del Pontiere, 32 (☎045 807 84 58), in the police station.

Pharmacy: Farmacia Due Campane, V. Mazzini, 52. Open M-F 9:10am-12:30pm and 3:30-7:30pm, Sa 9:10am-12:30pm. Check the *L'Arena* newspaper for **24hr. pharmacy** listings, or call ☎045 801 11 48.

Internet Access: Internet Train, V. Roma, 17/a (☎045 801 33 94). From P. Brà, turn right before the arch. L10,000 per hr. Open M-F noon-10pm, Sa noon-8pm, Su 2-8pm.

Post Office: P. Viviani, 7 (☎045 800 39 98). Follow V. Cairoli from P. delle Erbe. Open M-Sa 8:10am-7pm. **Branch office,** V. C. Cattaneo, 23 (☎045 803 41 00). **Postal Code:** 37100.

ACCOMMODATIONS

The smaller and cheaper accommodations in Verona fill up quickly. Make reservations, especially during the opera season (June 30-Sept. 3).

Ostello della Gioventù (HI), "Villa Francescatti," Salita Fontana del Ferro, 15 (☎045 59 03 60; fax 045 800 91 27). Take bus #73 or night bus #90 to P. Isolo. From there, follow the yellow signs for "Ostello della Gioventù" up the hill. By foot from the Arena, walk along V. Anfiteatro, which becomes V. Stella and V. Nizza before it crosses Ponte Nuovo. Continue on V. Carducci and turn left on V. Interrato dell'Acqua Morta to P. Isolo. This 16th-century hilltop villa, with common-room dinners and spotless dorms, has a friendly, communal feel. Kind staff speaks English. Hot showers (until 11pm), sheets, and minimalist breakfast included. Dinner with a vegetarian option L14,000. 1 washer and dryer. Max. 5-night stay. Check-in 5pm, check-out 7-9pm. Lockout 9am-5pm. Gates lock at 11pm, though opera-goers may make special arrangements. No reservations. Family rooms, 6-, 7-, and 36-bed dorms. 120 beds. Dorms L22,000.

Casa delle Giovane (ACISJF), V. Pigna, 7, 3rd fl. (☎045 59 68 80; fax 045 800 59 49), in the historic center of town. From P. delle Erbe, walk up C. S. Anastasia and turn onto V. Due Mori. Walk to the end of the street, and continue straight on V. Augusto Verità. Enter through the arched, double door at the end of the street. Bright rooms, some with a view of Verona's rooftops. Women only. Reception 9am-11pm. Curfew 11pm, except for opera-goers. 60 beds. Dorms L22,000; singles L32,000; doubles L50,000.

Locanda Catullo, Vco. Catullo, 1 (☎045 800 27 86; fax 045 59 69 87). At V. Mazzini, 40, turn onto V. Catullo, then turn left onto Vco. Catullo. Charming hotel hidden on a romantic side street, just off bustling V. Mazzini. 3 night min. stay July-Sept. Reserve well in advance. 21 rooms. Singles L60,000; doubles L90,000, with bath L110,000; triples L135,000, with bath L165,000; quads L165,000, with bath L175,000.

Hotel Mazzanti, V. Mazzanti, 6 (☎045 59 13 70; fax 045 801 12 62). From P. delle Erbe, walk down C. S. Anastasia and take the 1st right. Ideal for those who want to stay in the heart of the city and explore late-night Verona. All 23 rooms with A/C, TV, and phones. Breakfast included. Singles L95,000, with bath L125,000; doubles L180,000; triples L210,000; quads L220,000. Prices lower in winter. V, MC, AmEx.

FOOD

Verona is famous for its wines—the dry white *soave*, the red *valpolicella*, *bardolino*, and *recioto*. The vendors in P. Isolo offer better prices than those in P. delle Erbe. For a large sampling try **Oreste dal Zovo,** Vco. S. Marco in Foro, 7/5, off C. Porta Borsari. The congenial owner has dedicated his heart to Bacchus and knows everything about wine production. The *enoteca* has shelves of every Italian wine imaginable (from L9000 for a good bottle), as well as *grappa* and well-known international liquors. Ask Oreste to show you "The Well of Love" *("Il Pozzo dell'Amore")* in a nearby courtyard. (☎045 803 43 69. Open Tu-F 8:30am-1:30pm and 2:30-10pm.) **METÁ supermarket,** V. XX Settembre, 81, carries essentials at reasonable prices. Take bus #11, 12, 13, 14, or 51. (Open M-Tu and Th-Sa 8:30am-12:45pm and 3:45-7:30pm, W 8:30am-12:45pm.) For fruits and vegetables, try **Vera Frutta,** V. Interrato dell'Acqua Morta, 40a. (Open M-Sa 8:30am-7:30pm.)

Cantore, V. A. Mario, 2 (☎045 803 18 30), at the end of V. Mazzini, near P. Bra. Cantore boasts some of the best pizza and ambience in Verona. The sauce is tangy, the cheese ample, and the crust delectable. Pizza from L7000, *primi* L11-18,000, *secondi* L12-25,000. Cover L2000. Open Th-Tu noon-3pm and 6pm-midnight; during the opera festival, Cantore remains open all night. MC, V, AmEx.

Brek, P. Brà, 20 (☎045 800 45 61). Brek is a local favorite and a tourist's dream. Offers great people-watching and cheap, delicious meals served cafeteria-style. Salads and cheeses L3700-4300, pasta L5-6500, enormous pizza L7500-8500. No cover. Open M-Sa 11:30am-3pm and 6:30-10pm.

Bottega del Vino, V. Scudo di Francia, 3 (☎045 800 45 35), off V. Mazzini. Wile away an afternoon sampling the numerous wines of Verona (glasses from L3000). *Panini* from L2000, *primi* from L13,000, *secondi* from L18,000. Cover L7000. Open W-M 10:30am-3pm and 6pm-midnight. Open daily during opera season. V, MC, AmEx.

Caffè Tubino, C. Porta Borsari, 15d (☎045 803 22 96), near the large arch at the intersection of Porta Borsari and V. Fama. Housed in a 17th-century *palazzo,* this tiny cafe has an incredible selection of teas and coffees. Take home a tin of biscuits or caramels along with Turbino's own brand of coffee. 3 tables, so plan to enjoy your caffeine *al fresco.* Open M-Sa 7am-midnight.

Papa & Cicia, V. Seminario, 4a (☎045 800 83 84). From Ponte Nuovo walk down V. Carducci. Look for the giant utensils hanging outside the door. A favorite hangout of students, Papa & Cicia offers good food and great deals. *Primo,* salad, and water or wine for L12,000. *Secondo,* salad, and water or wine for L17,000. Cover L3000. Open M-F noon-2:30pm and 7-10:30pm, Sa 7-10:30pm. V, MC.

SIGHTS

THE ARENA. Serving today as Verona's modern **opera house,** this theater is the physical and emotional heart of Verona. Constructed as a Roman amphitheater in the 1st century, the pink marble arena survived a 12th-century earthquake which toppled much of its outer wall. The view of the staggering 44 tiers of superbly maintained steps is worth the admission fee. For performance listings, see **Entertainment,** below. *(In P. Brà. Visitor info ☎ 045 800 32 04; www.arena.it. Open Tu-Su 9am-7pm; during the opera festival 9am-3pm. L6000, students L4000.)*

PIAZZA DELLA ERBE AND ENVIRONS. Eclectic markets and stunning architecture reminiscent of an earlier empire fill this sprightly square. At the far end, the Baroque sculpture-lined **Palazzo Maffei** overlooks the *piazza.* **Madonna Verona's Fountain** stands in the center of the market. Vendors' awnings nearly hide the four-columned **Berlina,** a platform on which chained convicts were pelted with fruit in medieval days. The winged lion perched above the **Column of St. Mark,** built in 1523, recalls Verona's four centuries of Venetian domination. P. della Erbe lies near **Via Mazzini,** Verona's hippest street, which offers a free window-shopping tour of high Italian fashion.

PIAZZA DEI SIGNORI. The **Arco della Costa** (Arch of the Rib) connects P. Erbe to P. dei Signori. From the arch hangs a whale rib, prophesied to fall on the first passing person who has never told a lie. Somehow the rib has withstood the visits of numerous popes and kings. A severe statue of Dante Alighieri stands in the center of the *piazza.* Though they were brutish warlords, the della Scalas avidly patronized the arts. The **Palazzo degli Scaglieri,** once the main home of the della Scala family, is directly opposite the Arco della Costa. The 15th-century Venetian Renaissance-style **Loggia del Consiglio** also sits in the *piazza.*

Built in 1172 by a noble Veronese family, the *piazza's* **Torre dei Lamberti** offers what may be the most stunning view of Verona. Only an occasional church spire breaks up the sea of red-shingled roofs. An elevator and winding staircase lead 83m to the top. Through the arch in P. dei Signori lie the peculiar outdoor **Tombs of the Scaligeri** and the **Arche Scaligeri.** *(Torre dei Lamberti ☎ 045 803 27 26. Open Tu-Su 9:30am-6pm. Elevator L4000, students L3000; stairs L3000, students L2000.)*

A BALCONY BY ANY OTHER NAME... Perhaps Verona's greatest claim to fame is its role as the setting for Shakespeare's eternally romantic play, *Romeo and Juliet.* The famous **Casa di Giulietta** displays a garden with sprawling ivy and the renowned balcony. Unless you absolutely must stand on the balcony or view the few paintings inside, avoid shelling out your *lire.* Those who stand on the balcony and say "Romeo, Romeo, wherefore art thou Romeo?" are not particularly original or witty. Hundreds of hooting tourists mill around and rub a particular portion of the bronze Juliet's anatomy to shiny brilliance. Modern-day lovers scrawl odes in the entrance. Contrary to propaganda, the dal Capello (Capulet) family never lived here. *(V. Cappello, 23. ☎ 045 803 43 03. Open Tu-Su 9am-7pm. L6000, students L4000.)*

Add insult to injury (or stabbing to poison), and visit **Tomba Di Giulietta** (Juliet's tomb) and the **Museo Degli Affreschi** (Fresco Museum). *(V. del Pontiere, 5. ☎ 045 800 03 61. Open Tu-Su 9am-7pm. Tomb and museum L5000, students L2000.)*

The **Casa di Romeo,** long the home of the Montecchi family, the model for the Bard's Montagues, is around the corner from P. dei Signori at V. Arche Scaligeri, 2. The sight, now private property, offers little more than a plain facade.

BASILICA OF SANT'ANASTASIA AND ENVIRONS. This Gothic church boasts impressive works of art, including Pisanello's *St. George Freeing the Princess* (in the left transept of the Giusti Chapel) and frescoes by Altichiero and Turone. The nearby **duomo** is decorated with medieval sculpture by local carvers. The 1st chapel on the left features Titian's *Assumption of the Virgin. (Basilica at the end of P. delle Erbe, down C. S. Anastasia. Duomo down from the basilica on V. Duomo. Duomo open M-Sa 9:30am-6pm and Su 1-6pm. Single entry L3000. Church aficionados should consider the 5-church ticket, providing entry to the duomo, S. Anastasia, S. Zeno, S. Lorenzo, and S. Permo for L8000, students L7000. Info ☎ 045 59 28 13, or purchase tickets at any of the churches.)*

The nearby **Biblioteca Capitolare,** the oldest library in Europe, maintains a priceless medieval manuscript collection. *(☎ 045 59 65 16. Open M, W, and Sa 9:30am-12:30pm, Tu and F 9:30am-12:30pm and 4-6pm. Free.)*

TEATRO ROMANO AND GIARDINO GIUSTI. A spectacular Roman theater overlooks the city from St. Peter's Hill. Today the theater hosts Shakespeare productions in Italian and houses an **archaeological museum.** *(Rigaste Redentore, 2. Cross the Ponte Pietra from the city center and turn right. ☎045 800 03 60. Open Tu-Su 9am-6:30pm. L5000, students L3000. 1st Su of each month free.)*

Stroll down from the theater to the **Giardino Giusti,** a stunning 16th-century garden complete with a labyrinth of mythological statues. As you ascend, the garden reveals an increasingly breathtaking view of the city. Mozart, Goethe, and Cosimo de' Medici long admired the garden. Add your name to this impressive list and wait for fame to arrive. *(Down V. S. Chiara from Teatro Romano. ☎045 803 40 29. Open daily Apr.-Sept. 9am-8pm; Oct.-Mar. 9am-sunset. L7000, students L3000.)*

CASTELVECCHIO. After being ripped apart in WWII, the della Scala fortress has been lovingly reconstructed. The castle's **museum** features walkways, parapets, and a collection of sculptures and paintings, including Pisanello's *Madonna and Child* and Luca di Leyda's *Crucifixion.* In the courtyard, an equestrian statue of Cangrande I (Big Dog) smiles from its perch above. Be sure to cross the **Ponte Scaligero** to the left of the castle. The steps at the midpoint provide a balcony view of Verona along the river, a sight so romantic that scores of couples have managed to overcome their respect for medieval architecture in order to scrawl their names on the stone of the bridge. *(Down V. Roma from P. Brà. ☎045 59 47 34. Open Tu-Su 9am-7pm. L6000, students L4000. 1st Sunday of each month free.)*

SAN ZENO MAGGIORE. This church is one of Verona's finest examples of Italian Romanesque architecture. The massive brick church, dedicated to Verona's patron saint, surpasses its counterparts in artistic wealth. The 17th-century sculpted bronze doors sparked a craze throughout Italy, and the interior structure is notable for its wooden "ship's keel" ceiling and spacious crypt. The two-story apse contains a Renaissance altarpiece by Mantegna. *(Up from the Castelvecchio. Open daily 8am-noon and 3-7pm.)*

ENTERTAINMENT

Every year, droves of opera lovers flock to Verona to hear the heartwrenching arias of the world famous **Verona Opera Festival.** The festival runs from late June to early August, staging ballet, opera, and jazz shows at the Arena. (☎045 800 51 51; fax 045 801 32 87. General admission seating on the Roman steps Su-Th L38,000, F-Sa L42,000. Reserved seats L110-180,000. Arrive at least an hour before shows if you hold general admission tickets.)

From June to September, the **Teatro Romano** stages dance performances and Shakespeare productions (in Italian). June brings a one-week jazz festival known as **Verona Jazz.** (Theater info ☎045 807 72 19 or 045 807 75 00; Verona Jazz info ☎045 807 72 05 or 045 806 64 85. Tickets for both L20-40,000.) For a free taste of Verona's music scene, check out summer's **Concerti Scaligieri,** a sequence of 40 open-air concerts of jazz, blues, acoustic, and classical music.

Many hostelers in search of more barley-based entertainment pass the night at the **Locos Café,** V. S. Giovanni in Valle, 28, halfway down the hill from the hostel. Locos serves generous beers for L4000, wine for L1800 per glass, and large *bruschette* from L3000. (☎045 59 00 74. Open W-M 9:30am-2pm and 7pm-1am.)

TREVISO ☎0422

Treviso, the provincial capital of the Veneto, has two other names promoted by the tourist industry: *città d'acqua* (City of Water) and *città dipinta* (Painted City). The town's watery name derives from the trickles of the Sile River that flow through the edges of the town. As for its painted character, the frescoed facades of Treviso's buildings hint at former splendor. However, a third aspect of the city's identity needs no promotion from tourist brochures—Treviso rolls in dough. In this birthplace of Benetton, fashion is at the forefront of everyone's life. The people are beautiful and their clothes even more so; even their shoes drop straight from Italian leather heaven. Come to this glitzy spot to browse and window-shop, but bring cash and credit cards at your own risk.

TRANSPORTATION

Trains: P. Duca d'Aosta, at the southern end of town. From the bus station, turn right down P. Roma. To **Venice** (30min., 46 per day 5:09am-11:41pm, L3300) and **Udine** (1¼hr., 25 per day 5:48am-11:10pm, L12,000). To reach **Milan** or **Padua** make a connection in Venice. Station open 4:30am-12:30am. Ticket counter open 7am-7pm.

Buses: Lungosile Mattei, 21 (☎0422 57 73 11), to the left before C. del Popolo crosses the river. Service to Veneto and the villas. To: **Venice** (30min., 36 per day 4:40am-8:10pm, L4200); **Padua** (1hr., 30 per day 6am-7:50pm, L5400); and **Bassano** (1hr., 7am-3:15pm, L6300). Ticket and info office open 6:50am-1pm and 1:30-7:45pm.

ORIENTATION AND PRACTICAL INFORMATION

Treviso lies half an hour inland from Venice. The historical center is within the old city walls, which are bordered alternately on the inside and outside—sometimes both—by flowing water. From the train and bus stations, **Via Roma** leads to the entrance to town. It then becomes **Corso del Popolo** and leads to **Piazza della Borsa.** From there, a short walk up **Via XX Settembre** leads to **Piazza dei Signori,** Treviso's center. Pedestrian-dominated **Via Calmaggiore** leads to the *duomo.*

Tourist Office: P. Monte di Pietà, 8 (☎0422 54 76 32; fax 0422 41 90 92; www.sevenonline.it/tvapt), on the other side of Palazzo dei Trecento from P. dei Signori. Has a map of walking tours. Reserve ahead for a free walking tour of the city (May-Oct. Sa 10am-noon). Open in summer Tu 9:30am-12:30pm, W-Sa 9:30am-12:30pm and 2:30-6:15pm; in winter Tu-Sa 9am-noon and 3-6pm.

Emergencies: ☎113. **Police: Questura,** V. Carlo Alberto, 37 (☎0422 59 91). **Ambulance:** ☎118. **Hospital: Ospedale Civile Ca' Foncello** (☎0422 32 21 11).

Internet Access: Gestioni Televideo and Internet, V. Roma, 39 (☎0422 59 02 47), upstairs from a pricey arcade. Expensive, like the rest of the town. L12,000 per hr. Open daily 10am-1am.

Post Office: P. Vittoria, 1 (☎0422 317 21 11). Open daily 8:10am-7pm. **Postal Code:** 31100.

ACCOMMODATIONS AND FOOD

Treviso's wealthy climate has spawned a number of hotels but few budget accommodations. With singles starting at L85,000, Treviso is best visited as a daytrip. **Da Renzo,** on V. Terragio behind the train station, offers the least expensive rooms in town. All rooms have bath, A/C, phones, and breakfast. (☎0422 40 20 68. Singles L85,000; doubles L130,000.)

The city is famous for its *ciliegie* (cherries), radicchio, and *tiramisù,* a heavenly creation of espresso-and-liquor-soaked cake layered with *mascarpone.* Cherries ripen in June, radicchio peaks in December, and *tiramisù* is always in season. To taste these delights, head to the daily morning **produce market** at the Stiore stop of the #2 or 11 bus. If *primi* and *secondi* seem to be merely an inconvenient delay, begin with dessert at **Nascimben,** V. XX Settembre, 3. (☎0422 59 12 91. *Tiramisù* L2700 per 100g. Open M-Sa 7am-7pm.) For basics, shop at the **PAM supermarket,** P. Borso, 12, behind Banca Nazionale del Lavoro. (☎0422 58 39 13. Open Th-Tu 8:30am-7:30pm.) **All'Oca Bianca,** V. della Torre, 7, on a side street off central V. Calmaggiore, is a casual *trattoria* that serves excellent fish dishes. If you missed cherry season, try the *grappa*-steeped version (*ciliege sotto grappa*). (☎0422 54 18 50. *Primi* L12,000, *secondi* and fish L14-16,000. Cover L3000. Open Tu 9am-3pm, Th-M 9am-3pm and 6pm-midnight. V, MC, AmEx.)

SIGHTS

PALAZZO DEI TRECENTO. Dominating P. dei Signori, this palace proudly recalls Treviso's successful reemergence from a 1944 air raid on Good Friday (and the subsequent Bad Saturday) that demolished half the town. The post-bombing restoration blends perfectly with the original frescoes, though the original position of the stairs and outer wall are clearly labeled. *(☎0422 65 82 50. Open M-Sa 8:30am-12:30pm. Free for groups.)*

DUOMO. V. Calmaggiore's endless *passeggiata* flows beneath the arcades of the *piazza* to this seven-domed church, which displays an unusual classical facade. The *duomo's* **Cappella Malchiostro** dates from 1519 and contains both Titian's *Annunciation* and frescoes by Pordenone, even though the two artists were sworn enemies. *(Open M-Th 9am-noon, Sa-Su 9am-noon and 3-6pm.)*

MUSEO CIVICO. Also called the Museo Bailo, this museum houses Titian's *Sperone Speroni* and Lorenzo Lotto's *Portrait of a Dominican.* The ground floor protects Treviso's archaeological finds, among them 5th-century BC bronze discs from Montebelluna. *(Borgo Cavour, 24. ☎0422 59 13 37. Open Tu-F 9am-12:30pm and 2:30-5pm, Sa-Su 9am-noon and 3-7pm. L3000, students L1000.)*

PALLADIAN VILLAS. Palladio's penchant for villa-building (see **Near Vicenza,** p. 230) spilled into the Treviso area. Among them is **Villa Barbero** (1560) on the Treviso-Bassano line at the small village of Maser. *(☎0423 92 30 04. Open Mar.-Oct. Tu, Sa, Su and holidays 3-6pm; Nov.-Feb. Sa-Su and holidays 2:30-5pm. L9500.)*

The nearby **Villa Elmo** is a bit more difficult to reach, requiring first a bus or train ride from Treviso to Vastelfrance, then a bus ride from there to Fanzolo. The villa is considered to be one of the most characteristic Palladian works, with renowned interior frescoes. *(Open in summer M-Sa 3-7pm, Su 10am-12:30pm and 3-6pm; in winter Sa-Su and holidays 2-6pm. L10,000.)*

BASSANO DEL GRAPPA ☎0422

Bassano del Grappa is a town of scattered orange roofs, a romantic bridge (the Ponte degli Alpini), and a far less gentle namesake: *grappa*, hellfire in a bottle, distilled from the skins and seeds of once-harmless grapes. Originally, *grappa* was used as a medieval elixir—perhaps to cure the problem of having functional vocal chords. Italians have been developing a taste for the wicked stuff ever since. Buckle up; your Italian coming-of-age will not be complete without a sip.

TRANSPORTATION AND PRACTICAL INFORMATION. Bassano's principal *piazze* lie between the train station and the **Fiume Brenta.** The train station is at the end of V. Chilesotti, near the historical center. **Trains** zip to: **Venice** (1hr., 18 per day 5:30am-9:15pm, L6300); **Padua** (1hr., 12 per day 5:35am-6:05pm, L4800); **Trent** (2hr., 9 per day 5:40am-8:46pm, L8200); and **Vicenza** (2hr., 15 per day 7:17am-10:30pm, L4100) via **Cittadella.** The ticket counter is open M-Sa 6:05am-7:30pm, Su 6:30am-8:45pm. The **bus** station is in P. Trento, off V. delle Fosse. **FTV** (☎0424 308 50) serves **Vicenza** (1hr., 24 per day 5:30am-7:50pm, L5100); **La Marca Line** (☎0422 41 22 22) runs to **Treviso** (1hr., 10 per day 7am-7:25pm, L5700). Buy tickets at Bar Trevisani in P. Trento or Bar al Termine, V. Venezia, 45.

From the train station, take **Via Chilesotti** toward **Piazza Trento** and bear right on **Via Museo** to reach the heart of town. At the **tourist office,** Largo Corona d'Italia, 35 (☎0424 52 43 51; fax 0424 52 53 01), the English-speaking staff provides useful pamphlets and a town map. From the station, walk down V. Chilesotti, cross V. delle Fosse, and enter the shopping complex through the gap in the stone wall. Make an immediate right and head to the older, separate building against the wall. (Open M-F 9am-12:30pm and 2-5pm, Sa 9am-12:30pm.)

TRAVELIN' ITALY: LACTOSE-INTOLERANT STYLE Milk, it does a body good. But not yours. Got milk? Got indigestion. You've watched with envy as your friends scarfed down pizza and ice cream. You are lactose intolerant. All your life, you've pondered one question: How can I travel in Italy? Have no fear, gentle traveler. *Let's Go* will show you the way.

Step One: Learn the Early Warning Signs. Study these four critical names: *latte* (milk); *crema* (cream); *formaggio* (cheese); *burro* (butter). Practice these crucial phrases: *"Si potrebbe farlo senza crema?"* (Could you make that without cream?); *"C'è latte?"* (Is that made with milk?); *"Potrei avere una bella, forte pompa stomaco?"* (May I please have a good, hard stomach-pumping?).

Step Two: The Truth About Pizza. Ever taken slack for scraping the cheese off your pizza ("Dude, that's not pizza! That's like...bread with sauce.")? Well in Italy, not only is this acceptable, but it's on the menu. Ask for *pizza marinara:* pizza without cheese, just the way Mother Nature intended it.

Step Three: The Gelato Question. Cities crumble, stomachs growl, but hope survives. Though you can't eat ice cream, you may be able to eat the tastier *gelato.* Fruit flavors, especially lemon and strawberry, have a smaller milk content than flavors like vanilla. Some *gelaterie* even carry soy-based *gelato.*

Step Four: The After-Dinner Coffee. You've long stared longingly at the fluffy sophistication of Italian cappucino, and yet one sip of the lactose-free version (espresso) left you up and shaking half the night. Jitter no more, for in the lovely and culinarily ingenious land of Italia there's *caffè di orto,* a "coffee" made of roasted barley that's caffeine-free and never taken with milk. Who would have thought that a drink made from barley could taste so good—oh, wait.

ACCOMMODATIONS, FOOD, AND DRINK. Consider the **Instituto Cremona,** V. Chini, 6, part hostel, part elementary school, and part residence for migrant workers, although the facilities are kept separate. Walk from P. Libertà down V. Roma and turn right on Salita Brocchi. Turn left onto Vle. Undice Febbraio, pass the post office, and turn right onto V. Chini. The walk is confusing, so try to arrive during the day and grab a map from the tourist office. The low nightly rate includes in-room baths, sheets, bicycle use, basketball, and volleyball. (☎0424 52 20 32; email cremona@nsoft.it. Reception 7-9:30am and 6-10pm. Breakfast L5500. Reservations necessary. Singles L25-28,000; doubles L46,000.)

For the authentic *grappa* experience, buy a bottle at one of the distilleries clustered near Ponte degli Alpini. Some will even provide free tastes upon request. To wash the *grappa* down, try the local favorite **Birreria Ottone,** V. Matteotti, 50. The restaurant has a quirky elegance, with headless busts, opera in the background, and an intricate system of cables suspending a tiny lamp over each table. Try the L16,000 Hungarian *goulash.* (☎0424 222 06. Pasta L9-10,000. Cover L2500. Open M 11:30am-3:30pm, W-Su 11am-3:30pm and 7:30pm-12:30am. Closed Aug. V, MC.) Sample some of Bassano's famed white asparagus and porcini mushrooms at the open-air **market** in P. Garibaldi. (Open Th and Sa 8am-1pm.)

SIGHTS. Wander the streets of Bassano—the best sights are those of the town's daily life. The **Ponte degli Alpini** spans the Brente, with a web of narrow streets linking it to the center. Romantic views of the town and the river (especially during the evening) await. Toward the station and down any one of the twisting medieval streets lies the majestic **Piazza della Libertà.** Its highlight is the imposing statue-topped facade of the **Chiesa di San Giovanni Battista.**

In the adjacent P. Garibaldi, the **Chiesa di San Francesco** sits next door to the **Museo Civico,** a fascinating museum featuring Jacopo da Bassano's paintings of dark worlds split open by divine light. The exhibit includes Bassano's famous

Flight into Egypt and *St. Valentine Baptizing St. Lucilla*, as well as dazzling works by contemporary Italian artists. (☎0424 52 22 35. Open Tu-Sa 9am-6:30pm, Su 3:30-6:30pm. L8000, students and seniors L5000.)

FRIULI-VENEZIA GIULIA

Overshadowed by the touristed cities of the Veneto and the mountains of Trentino-Alto Adige, Friuli-Venezia Giulia traditionally receives less than its fair share of recognition. Trieste, a long-standing exception to this rule, attracts increasing numbers of beach-goers searching for the least expensive resorts on the Adriatic. The area's towns, which owe their charm to their small size, offer an untainted slice of local life and culture absent from Italy's larger cities.

Friuli-Venezia Giulia derives its name from several distinct provinces. Unified by the clergy between the 6th and 15th centuries, the region was appropriated by the Venetian Republic and later swallowed, Venetians and all, by Austria-Hungary. The historical differences within this postwar union and the area's vulnerability to eastern forces combine to give Friuli-Venezia Giulia a hybrid character. The splash of political intrigue and coffee-culture elegance brought by the Austro-Hungarian Empire attracted intellectuals to turn-of-the-century Friuli. James Joyce lived in Trieste for 12 years, during which time he wrote the bulk of *Ulysses*, Ernest Hemingway drew part of his plot for *A Farewell to Arms* from the region's role in World War I, and Freud and Rilke both worked and wrote here.

TRIESTE ☎040

Trieste (pop. 230,000), the unofficial capital of Friuli-Venezia Giulia, lies at the end of a narrow strip of land sandwiched between Slovenia and the Adriatic. From the 9th through 15th centuries, the city was Venice's main rival on the Adriatic. But by the 19th century, Trieste faced a new threat—Austria. In the post-Napoleonic real estate market, the Austrians finally snatched the city, and when they did, they proceeded to rip out its medieval heart, replacing it with Neoclassical bombast. In the years that followed, the Habsburgs' heavy-handed style of government alienated the city's large Italian majority, breeding fervent *irredentisti* who clamored for unification with the new Italian Republic. In 1918, Italian troops finally united Friuli with Italy, but Mussolini's policies of cultural chauvinism equally offended the city's residents. At the end of World War I, when Allied troops liberated the city from Nazi occupiers, the ownership dispute resurfaced, this time between the Yugoslavs and the Italians. Though Trieste finally became part of Italy in 1954, the city still remains divided between its Slavic and Italian origins. Trieste's past lingers in the city's Neoclassical architecture, in the Slavic nuances of local cuisine, and in the Slovenian language that rings through the streets. Modern Trieste is a fast-paced city, where Italians, Croatians, and Slovenians rush among avenues lined with boutiques and department stores, and young Gucci-clad locals gather in sidewalk cafes. While Trieste's center, with its grid-like streets and faded facades, is undeniably urban, the colors of the surrounding hillside and the tranquil Adriatic temper the metropolis with stunning natural beauty.

TRANSPORTATION

Trieste is a direct train ride from both Venice and Udine. Several trains and buses also cross daily to neighboring Slovenia and Croatia. Less-frequent ferries service the Istrian Peninsula as far south as Croatia's Dalmatian Coast.

Flights: Aeroporto Friuli-Venezia Giulia/Ronchi dei Legionari, V. Aquileia, 46 (☎0481 77 32 24/5). Ticket counter (☎0481 77 32 32) open daily 7am-noon and 1-7pm. Daily direct British Airways (☎0652 49 15 71) flights to **London's Gatwick airport.** Open M-F

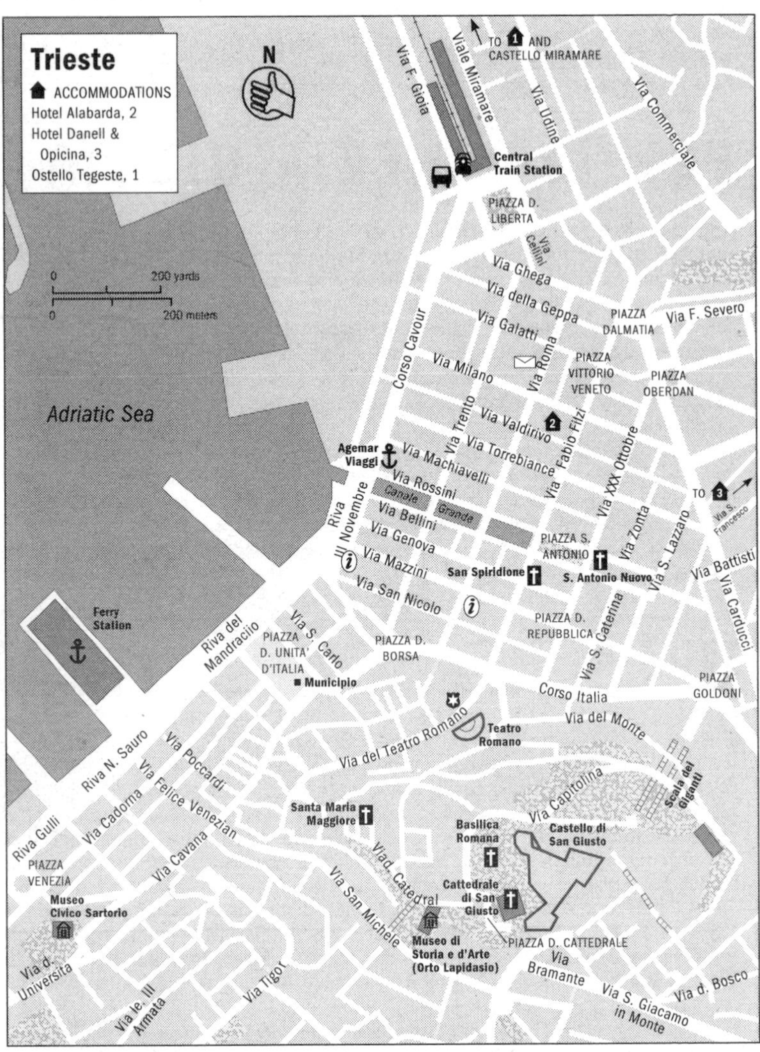

8am-8pm, Sa 9am-5pm. Alitalia (☎1478 656 43) flights to **Milan, Genoa, Rome, and Naples.** To get to the airport, take the public SAITA bus (1hr., M-Sa every hr., L5000) or the private Consorzio Italiano Servizio line (1hr.; M-Sa 8 per day, Su 4 per day; L15,000). Both buses leave from the bus station at P. della Libertà.

Trains: P. della Libertà, 8 (☎040 379 47 37), down C. Cavour from the quays. Ticket counter (☎040 41 86 12) open daily 5:40am-10:15pm. Info office open daily 7am-9pm. To: **Udine** (1½hr., every hr., L9800); **Venice** (2hr., 2 per hr., L14,500); **Ljubljana** (4 per day, L35,100); **Milan** (5hr., 1 per hr., L34,500-50,000); and **Budapest** (11hr., 2 per day, L120,000). **Luggage Storage:** L3-5000 for 6hr. Open daily 6am-10pm.

Buses: (☎040 42 50 01 or 040 42 50 20), in P. della Liberta, next to the train station. From C. Cavour, turn left when the *corso* ends. **SAITA** (☎040 42 50 01) to **Udine** (1½hr., 25 per day, L7700) and **Rijeka/Fiume** (2-2½hr., 2 per day, L13,500). Smaller lines link Trieste to Opicina, Muggia, Miramare, Duino, and other towns. **Luggage Storage:** L2-4000 for 24hr. Open M-F 6:20am-8:20pm, Sa-Su and holidays 6:20am-1pm.

Taxis: Radio Taxi (☎040 30 77 30). Available 24hr.

ORIENTATION AND PRACTICAL INFORMATION

The gray, industrialized quays serving ferries and fishermen taper off into the **Barcola,** Trieste's equivalent of a beach—a stretch of tiered concrete (populated with bronzed bodies) that runs 7km from the edge of town to the castle at Miramare. The center of Trieste is organized as a grid, bounded to the east by **Via Carducci,** which stretches south from **Piazza Oberdan,** and to the west by the shop-lined **Corso Italia,** which runs south from the grandiose **Piazza Unita d'Italia,** overlooking the harbor. The two streets intersect at the busy **Piazza Goldoni.** Steps from P. Unita, along C. Italia, lies the **Piazza della Borsa,** where the cream of the *triestini* crop come to strut their stuff.

TOURIST, FINANCIAL, AND LOCAL SERVICES

Tourist Office: Riva III Novembre, 9 (☎040 347 83 12; fax 040 347 83 20), along the quays, near P. della Unita. Lists of *manifestazioni* (cultural events). Open M-Sa 9am-7pm, Su 10:30am-1pm and 4-7pm. **Tourist administration office,** V. S. Nicolò, 20 (☎040 679 61 11). Open M-F 9am-7pm, Sa 9am-1pm. English spoken at both offices.

Budget Travel: CTS, P. Dalmazia, 3b (☎040 36 18 79; fax 040 36 24 03), just off of P. Oberdan. Agency for air and train tickets and a variety of vacation info. Big discounts for students; also sells ISIC and replaces expired cards. English spoken. Open M-F 9am-1pm and 3:30-7pm. **Aurora Viaggi,** V. Milano, 20 (☎040 63 02 61; fax 040 36 55 87), a block from P. Oberdan. Info on transportation to Croatia and Slovenia. Open M-F 9am-12:30pm and 3:30-6:30pm, Sa 9am-noon.

Consulates: Slovenian Consulate, V. Carducci, 29 (☎040 63 61 61, 040 63 64 88 or 040 63 62 72).

Currency Exchange: Deutsche Bank, V. Roma, 7 (☎040 63 19 25). Cash advances on Visa. Open M-F 8:15am-1pm and 2:35-3:50pm. **Assomar Cambio,** P. della Libertà, 1 (☎040 42 53 07), in the bus station. No commission. Open M-Sa 7:30am-6:30pm.

Car Rental: Maggiore-Budget (☎040 42 13 23), in the train station. Around L150,000 a day. Open M-F 8am-1pm and 3-7pm, Sa 8am-1pm.

English Bookstore: Libreria Cappelli, C. Italia, 12 (☎040 63 04 14). Open Tu-Sa 9am-12:30pm and 4-7:30pm. V, MC, AmEx.

Swimming Pool: Piscina Coperta Bianchi, Riva Gulli, 3 (☎040 30 60 24). Indoor facilities. L6000. Open Oct.-July M-Th noon-3pm, Sa 7am-2pm, Su 7am-1pm.

EMERGENCY AND COMMUNICATIONS

Emergencies: ☎113. **Police:** (☎040 379 01), on V. del Teatro Romano off C. Italia. **Ambulance:** ☎118. **Hospital: Ospedale Maggiore** (☎040 399 11 11), in P. dell'Ospedale, up V. S. Maurizio from V. Carducci.

Late-Night Pharmacy: Farmacia Muggia, V. Mazzini 1/A. 24hr. pharmacies rotate. Check the *farmacia* listings in the local newspaper, *Il Piccolo,* or call the tourist office.

Internet Access: Interl@nd, V. Gallina, 1 (☎040 372 86 35; www.interware.it/interland), on the 2nd floor. A relaxed atmosphere with snack machines and English-speaking staff. L10,000 per hr. Open M-F 10:30am-8:30pm, Sa 2:30-8:30pm.

Post Office: P. V. Veneto, 1 (☎040 36 82 24; fax 040 77 19 72), along V. Roma. From the train station, take the 2nd right off V. Ghega. Fax downstairs. Open M-Sa 8:15am-7pm. **Postal Code:** 34100.

TRIESTE FOR YOU (T FOR YOU)! This card, available free at hotels throughout the city when you stay for two nights or more, entitles visitors to discounts at hotels, restaurants, sights, and stores throughout the city. For more information, contact the local tourist office (see above).

ACCOMMODATIONS AND CAMPING

The prospects are grim for budget travelers seeking a cheap and clean room. Many rooms are geared toward seasonal workers who book them by the month and others are filled with Croatian and Slovenian shoppers.

Hotel Alabarda, V. Valdirivo, 22 (☎040 63 02 69; fax 040 63 92 84; email albergoalabarda@tin.it; www.hotelalabarda.com), near the city center. From P. Oberdan, head down V. XXX Ottobre, near the tram stop, and turn right onto V. Valdirivo. This friendly, family-run hotel in the town center has 18 huge, bright rooms and bathrooms decorated with plants. Singles L50,000; doubles L80,000, with bath L105,000; triples L94,000; quads L120,000. 10% discount with *Let's Go*. V, MC, AmEx.

Ostello Tegeste (HI), V. Miramare, 331 (☎/fax 040 22 41 02), on the seaside, just down from Castle Miramare, 6km from the city center. From the station take bus #36 (L1400), departing from across V. Miramare, the street on the left of the station as you exit. Ask the driver to point out the "ostello" stop. From there, walk back down the road toward Trieste, taking the seaside fork toward the castle. Other hotels in town may be more comfortable, but the view of the Adriatic from the terrace adds enormously to the hostel's charm. Courtyard bar. HI Members only. Breakfast and hot shower included. Dinner up to L14,000. Reception daily 8am-11pm. Bicycles L6-18,000 per day. Check-out 10am. Lockout 10am-1pm. Curfew 11:30pm. Group reservations accepted via fax. Dorms L20,000.

Hotel Daneu, V. Nationale, 194 (☎040 21 42 14; fax 040 21 42 15; email hotel_daneu@libero.it; www.onenet.it/TS/Daneu), in Opicina. A 15min. walk from the tram station–a taxi runs L6000. This 3-star hotel offers 2-star accommodations in the annex across the street. 26 simple rooms with wood furniture. Ground-floor restaurant. Breakfast included. Singles L66,000, with bath L100,000; doubles L116,000, with bath L136,000. V, MC, AmEx, Diners.

Valeria, V. Nazionale, 156 (☎040 21 12 04; fax 040 21 53 97), in Opicina. Take the tram to Opicina from platform #2 in P. Oberdan near Hotel Posta (30min., every 20min., L1400); or take bus #39 to V. Nazionale. Friendly atmosphere and a bar/restaurant filled with spirited locals. The views along the tram ride are far more spectacular than those from the spartan rooms. Singles L35,000; doubles L60,000.

Camping Obelisco, Strada Nuova Opicina, 37 (☎040 21 16 55; fax 040 21 27 44), in Opicina, 7km from Trieste. Take the tram from P. Oberdan (L1400) to the "Obelisco" stop; follow the yellow signs. A tranquil campsite for those not umbilically attached to the beach. Nice facilities with bar. L6500 per person, L4500 per tent, L4000 per car.

NORTHEAST ITALY

FOOD

Although many dishes in Trieste's restaurants have Eastern European overtones, the selection of fresh seafood from the Adriatic rivals that of Venice. The city is renowned for its *frutti del mare*, especially *sardoni in savor* (large sardines marinated in oil and garlic). Another local specialty is *cevap cici* (spicy Serbian influenced sausages infused with garlic) and *jota* (a hearty sauerkraut, bean, and sausage stew). The highlights of Triestine dining are the **osmizze,** informal restaurants dating from 1784 when an imperial decree allowed peasants on the Carso to sell their local produce for 8 days a year. Today, families in the Carso open their backyard terraces to the public for two weeks, serving only produce from their farms and wine from their vineyards. The prices are shockingly low, the food exceedingly fresh, and the views always spectacular.

V. Carducci is home to several **alimentari.** Costumed hero **Supercoop** is on Largo Barriera Vecchia. (Open M and W 8am-1pm, Tu and Th-Sa 8am-1pm and 5-7:30pm.) It wouldn't be Italy without a **STANDA**—Trieste's branch is at V. Battisti, 15. (Open M 3:30-7:30pm, Tu-F 9am-1pm and 3:30-7:30pm, Sa 9am-7:30pm.) Trieste has a **covered market** with fruit, vegetable, meat, and cheese vendors at V. Carducci, 36d, on the corner of V. della Majolica. (Open M 8am-2pm, Tu-Sa 8am-7pm.) Grab a bottle of *Terrano del Carso*, a dry red wine valued for its therapeutic properties. For unadulterated grapes, stroll through the **open-air market** in P. Ponterosso by the canal. (Open Tu-Sa 8am-5:30pm.) Most shops in Trieste close on Mondays.

RESTAURANTS

Pizzeria Barattolo, P. S. Antonio, 2 (☎040 63 14 80), along the canal. Canopied seating with a view of P. S. Antonio's flowers, fountain, and church. A young crowd turns meal-time into party-time. Bar and *tavola calda* offerings. Fresh *insalata barattolo* L10,000. Pizza L7-15,000. *Primi* L8-9000, *secondi* L10-20,000. Cover L2000. Service 15%. Open daily 8:30am-midnight. V, MC, AmEx.

Grapperia Paninoteca Da Livio, V. della Ginnastica, 3 (☎040 63 64 46), inland off V. Carducci and parallel to V. XX Settembre. Real *panini* (L3-4000) and a wide selection of beers (from L3000) in a tiny memorabilia-lined restaurant. Open M-Sa 9:30am-12:30pm and 3:30-11pm.

Buffet Mase, V. Valdirivo, 32 (☎040 63 94 28), near P. Oberdan. Decorated with checkered tablecloths and colorful German ads, locals gather here to watch soccer matches while digging into heaping platefuls of fresh pasta and Bavarian specialties. *Primi* from L7000. Open M-Sa 9am-1am. V, MC, AmEx.

CAFFÈS, GELATERIE, AND PASTICCERIE

Thanks to Viennese influence, coffee is an art form in Trieste. Coffee is usually served on a silver platter with a glass of water and, if you're lucky, a few sweet pastries. Experiment with *resentin*, coffee spruced up with a hint of *grappa*. In spring, look for *presnitz*, a local pastry filled with nuts and raisins.

Caffè Pasticceria Pirona, Largo Barriera Vecchia, 12 (☎040 63 60 46). James Joyce worked on *Ulysses* here. Their thick *cioccolatta calda* (hot chocolate) is by far the best in Trieste (L3600). Open Tu-Sa 7:30am-8pm, Su (in summer) 7:30am-2pm.

Gelateria Zampolli, V. Ghega, 10 (☎040 36 48 68). Follow the crowds of local Triestines that gather here on any warm (or even cold) evening. More than 50 flavors of *gelato*, each one better than the next. Sinfully rich *variegato nutella* consists of warm *nutella* smeared over delicious yogurt gelato. Open Th-Tu 10am-1am.

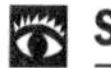

SIGHTS

CITY CENTER

CITTÀ NUOVA. In the 1700s, Empress Maria Theresa of Austria commissioned a "Città Nuova" plan for Trieste, which 19th century Viennese urban planners implemented between the waterfront and the Castello di San Giusto. The resulting grid-like pattern of streets lined with crumbling Neoclassical palaces centers around the **Canale Grande.** Facing the canal from the south is the striking Serbian Orthodox **Chiesa di San Spiridione,** a neo-Byzantine church with distinctive pale blue domes and a lush interior. *(Open Tu-Sa 9am-noon and 5-8pm. Shoulders and knees must be covered.)* The ornate **Municipio** at the head of Piazza dell'Unità d'Italia complements the largest *piazza* in Italy. The *piazza* itself contains beautifully designed buildings and an allegorical fountain with statues representing four continents.

CASTELLO DI SAN GIUSTO. Trieste's Neoclassical architecture gives way to the narrow, twisting alleys recalling its medieval and Roman history. The 15th-century Venetian **Castello di San Giusto** presides over **Capitoline Hill,** the city's historic center. The ramparts of the castle enclose a **museum** that has temporary exhibits in addition to a permanent collection of 13th-century weaponry, furniture, and tapestries. Within the castle walls, a huge outdoor theater holds film festivals in July and August. If you're up for the walk, from P. Goldoni ascend the hill by way of the daunting 265 **Scala dei Giganti** (Steps of the Giants). *(South of P. Unità. Take bus #24 (L1400) from the station to the last stop. ☎040 31 36 36. Castle open daily 9am-sunset. Museum open Tu-Su 9am-1pm. L2000.)*

PIAZZA DELLA CATTEDRALE. This hilltop *piazza* overlooks the sea and downtown Trieste. Enjoy a prime sunset if the *bora* winds don't blow you away. Directly below lie the remains of the old Roman city center, and across the street is the restored **Cattedrale di San Giusto.** The church originally comprised two separate basilicas, one dedicated to S. Giusto, the other to S. Maria Assunta. They were joined in the 14th century, creating the cathedral's irregular plan. Inside, two splendid mosaics decorate the chapels directly to the left and right of the altar.

MUSEO DI STORIA E D'ARTE. This art history museum provides archaeological documentation of the history of Trieste and the Upper Adriatic during and preceding its Roman years. It also holds a growing collection of Egyptian and Greek art and artifacts. The nearby **Orto Lapidario** (Rock Garden) provides...rocks. *(V. Cattedrale, 15. Down the other side of the hill past the duomo, in P. Cattedrale. ☎040 37 05 00 or 040 30 86 86. Open Th-Su 9am-1pm, Tu-W 9am-7pm. L3000.)*

TEATRO ROMANO. The *teatro* was built under the auspices of Trajan in the 1st century AD. Originally, crowds hooted at gladiatorial contests; later spectators wept at passion and blood in the slightly tamer form of Greek tragedy. *(On V. del Teatro, off C. Italia. From the Orto Lapidario, descend the hill and head toward P. Unità.)*

MUSEO REVOLTELLA. This museum brings many temporary modern art exhibits to Trieste. Combining an 18th-century home of Baron Revoltella and the Galleria d'Arte Moderna, the Revoltella also has a permanent collection of art from the Neoclassical period to the present day. *(V. Diaz, 21. ☎040 30 27 42, 040 31 13 61 or 040 30 09 38. Open W-M 10am-7pm.)*

CITY ENVIRONS

CASTELLO MIRAMARE. The *Barcolana* ends at the gorgeous castle of Archduke Maximilian of Austria (brother-in-law of notorious Belgian King Leopold II) who ordered its construction in the mid-19th century. The lavishly decorated apartments feature huge crystal chandeliers, intricately carved furniture, rich tapestries, Asian porcelain, and good explanations of everything in English as you go from room to room. Legend has it that the ghost of Carlotta, Maximilian's wife, still haunts the castle; Carlotta apparently went a bit loopy after losing her husband, the Austrian Ambassador to Mexico, to a Mexican firing squad.

Poised on a high promontory over the gulf, Miramare's white turrets are easily visible from the Capitoline Hill in Trieste or from the trails in the Carso. Its extensive parks and gardens, open to the public at no cost, include a cafe and various ponds housing ducks, swans, turtles, and sunbathing stray cats. In July and August, a series of **sound and light shows** transform Miramare into a high-tech playground. *(To reach Miramare, take bus #36 (20min., L1400) to the hostel (see* ***Accommodations and Camping,*** p. 242*) and walk along the water. ☎040 22 41 43; www.castello-miramare.it. Open daily 9am-7pm, ticket office closes 1hr. earlier. L8000. English tours L4000. English light shows in summer Tu, Th, and Sa at 9:30pm and 10:45pm. L9000. Call the tourist office for info.)*

BARCOLA. West of Trieste (follow Strada Cositiera, to the right facing the train station) you can sunbathe along the cement **Barcola,** the cafe-lined boardwalk that runs along the Adriatic and plays host to rollerbladers, joggers, and *boci* players. Every September Trieste hosts the *Barcolana,* a regatta that attracts sailors from all over the world.

MARINE PARK. Sponsored by the World Wildlife Fund, the marine park conducts several programs throughout the year, including introductions to the coast's marine life. The park is the area marked by buoys surrounding Castle Miramare. Swimming is not allowed without a guide. *(☎040 22 41 47. English snorkeling and scuba tours. You must have a license to scuba dive. Snorkel, fins, and mask included. Scuba L25,000, children L20,000. Must be in groups of 10; ask to be grouped with others if your group is less than 10. Reservations required. Office open M-F 9am-7pm, Sa 9am-5pm.)*

KUGY PATH AND GROTTA GIGANTE. The tram to Opicina, which leaves from P. Oberdan, is one of the longest running funiculars in Europe (25min., every 20min., L1400). After a steep climb, the tram runs past local vineyards and provides breathtaking views of the Adriatic coastline. Hop off at the Obelisk stop to meet up with the Kugy Path, a popular trail that cuts along the sides of the Carso cliffs. There are benches along the path, so stop and admire the views of the Adriatic and the coastline of Slovenia and Croatia. At the end of the tram route, about 15km from Trieste in Opicina, is the cleverly named Grotta Gigante, which is...a damn big cave—the world's largest tourist cave, in fact. (The largest cave in the world is Mammoth Cave in Kentucky, US.) Staircases wind in and around the 107m-high interior. *(V. Machiavelli, 17. In the small parking lot across V. Nazionale from the tram stop is the stop for bus #45 (L1400). ☎040 32 73 12; www.ts.cam.com.it/english/grotta/htm. Open Apr.-Sept. Tu-Sa 10am-6pm, tours every 30min.; Mar. and Oct. Tu-Sa 10am-noon and 1-4pm, every hr.; Nov.-Feb. 10am-noon and 2-4pm, every hr. L13,000.)*

RISIERA DE SAN SABBA. Italy's only WWII concentration camp occupies an abandoned rice factory on the outskirts of Trieste. The *risiera*, Ratto della Pileria, 43, houses a museum detailing Trieste's pivotal role in Hitler's designs on Eastern Europe and the Slovenian-born resistance movement that confronted the Nazis occupying Trieste. *(Take bus #8. ☎040 82 62 02. Open May 16-Mar. Tu-Su 9am-1pm; Apr.-May 15 M-Sa 9am-6pm, Su 9am-1pm. Free.)*

ENTERTAINMENT

The opera season of the **Teatro Verdi** runs November to May, but the theater holds a six-week operetta season in June and July. Buy tickets or make reservations at P. Verdi, 1. (☎040 67 22 500, 040 67 22 298 or 040 67 22 299; www.teatroverdi-trieste.com. Open Tu-Su 9am-noon and 4-7pm. L15-70,000.) The travel agency **UTAT-Galleria Protti** (☎040 63 00 63), has information on dates, times, and prices of all performances. The liveliest *passeggiate* take place along V. XX Settembre, a traffic-free and cafe-lined avenue on the upscale pedestrian shopping street connecting P. della Borsa to P. della Unità. **Bar Unità,** on the southwest corner of P. Unità (upper left if you're facing the sea), sees its outdoor tables packed with university students in warmer weather. (☎040 36 80 63. Open daily 6:30am-3:30am.)

If the weather pushes you indoors, head to **Juice,** V. Madonnina, 10. This trendy restaurant-bar is always packed in winter, with twenty-somethings crowding over menus (written on old vinyl records) listing dishes other than pasta and pizza. Warm up with crêpes filled with nutella (L4000), or try a **scivelo** (literally means a "slide"; L10,000), a local drink made from strawberry Keglevich vodka and lemon soda. (☎040 760 03 41. Open Sept.-June daily 7:30pm-2am.)

AQUILEIA ☎0431

Aquileia was founded in 181 BC on the banks of what was then the Natisone-Torre River. Between AD 200 and 452 it flourished as the Roman capital of the region, serving as the gateway to the Eastern Empire and as the principal trading port of the Adriatic. The Patriarchate of Aquileia was established in AD 313, but when the Huns and Lombards sacked the city in the 5th and 6th centuries, the Patriarch fled to Grado and moved on to Cividale del Friuli. The invaders were finally driven out in 1019 and the city's great basilica was rebuilt in celebration. From then on, the Patriarchate successfully defied the popes until the port silted up and malaria set in. The disgruntled Patriarch moved on to Udine and dwindled into an archbishop, leaving behind in Aquileia an amazing open-air museum of Roman and early Christian art, the most important archaeological remains in northern Italy.

TRANSPORTATION AND PRACTICAL INFORMATION. Aquileia is accessible by **bus** from Udine (1hr., 16 per day, L4600). Local buses travel to Cervignano, a **train** station on the Trieste-Venice line (2 per hr., L1500). For a list of budget accommodations and camping in the surrounding area, including Grado, consult

Aquileia's helpful **tourist office,** a block from the bus stop in P. Capitolo and across the *piazza* from the basilica. (☎0431 910 87 or 0431 91 94 91. Open Apr.-Oct. F-W 8:20am-noon and 1-4pm.)

ACCOMMODATIONS AND FOOD. Aquileia's one affordable hotel, **Albergo Aquila Nera,** P. Garibaldi, 5, by V. Roma, offers pleasant and fresh rooms, some with wood floors. Sparkling bathrooms are down the hall. (☎0431 910 45. Singles L55,000; doubles L90,000. V, MC.) The *albergo*'s **restaurant** serves lunch and dinner at reasonable prices. (*Primi* L9-10,000, *secondi* L10-13,000. Cover L2500. Open F-W noon-2:30pm and 7-11pm.) **Camping Aquileia,** V. Gemina, 10, a shady spot with a swimming pool, lies up the street from the forum. (☎0431 910 42; ☎/fax 0431 91 95 83. L9000 per person, under 12 L6000. Tent sites L15,000. 3-person bungalow L75,000, 4-person bungalow L95,000. Open May 15-Sept. 15.) The **Desparo supermarket** on V. Augusta pleases the tightest of budgets. (Open Tu-Sa 8am-1pm and 3:30-7:30pm, Su 8am-1pm). Upstairs, **Ristorante al Pescatore** specializes in pizza (L6-12,000) and fish. (☎0431 91 95 70. *Primi* L7-20,000, *secondi* L7-20,000. Open Tu-Su 10am-2:30pm and 6pm-midnight.)

SIGHTS. Aquileia's **basilica,** a tribute to the town's artistic heritage, blends artwork spanning many centuries. The floor, a remnant of the original church, is a fantastic mosaic, animating over 700 square meters with geometric designs and realistic bestial depictions. Beneath the altar, the crypt's 12th-century frescoes illustrate the trials of Aquileia's early Christians and scenes from the life of Christ. In the **Cripta degli Scavi,** to the left upon entering, excavations have uncovered three distinct layers of flooring, including mosaics from a 1st century Roman house, vividly illustrating the building's varied history. (Basilica open daily 8:30am-7pm. Crypt open M-Sa 8:30am-7pm, Su 8:30am-7:30pm. L4000.) Beside the basilica, the towering **campanile** offers views of the town and the Roman ruins. (Open daily 9:30am-noon and 3-6pm, Su 9:30am-1pm and 3-6:30pm. L2000.)

The cypress-lined alley behind the basilica, which runs parallel to the once glorious **Roman harbor,** is a pleasant alternative to V. Augusta as a path to the **forum.** From there, continue to the **Museo Paleocristiano,** which displays moss-covered mosaics and explains the transition from classical paganism to Christianity. (☎0431 911 31. Open M 8:30am-1:45pm, Tu-Sa 8:30am-7:30pm. Free.) Artifacts from many excavations reside in the **Museo Archeologico** at the corner of V. Augusta and V. Roma. The ground floor houses Roman statues and portrait busts; upstairs are terra-cotta, glass, and gold pieces. (Open M 8:30am-2pm, Tu-F 8:30am-7:30pm, Sa 8:30am-8pm. L8000.)

UDINE ☎0432

Udine's Piazza della Libertà is a treasure. Tilted and split into elevated levels, with looming statues and Moorish figures that chime the hour, P. della Libertà is 60 square meters of pure Renaissance. At night, the central *piazze* fill with locals, basking in the relaxed ambience. Unfortunately, beyond this small world, little in Udine attracts tourists. Unless you are a fervent Giovanni Battista Tiepolo fan (the Rococo pioneer's works cover the city), the churches and museums remain undistinguished. Conquered by Venice in 1420, appropriated by Austria in the late 18th century, and bombed severely in WWII, Udine has suffered a volatile history. Today, the quiet streets of Udine are unknown to most tourists.

TRANSPORTATION

Trains: On V. Europa Unità. To: **Trieste** (1½hr., 1-3 per hr. 5:12am-11:29pm, L8900); **Venice** (2hr., 1-3 per hr. 5:05am-2:45am, L12,100); **Milan** (4½hr., 2 per day, L31,000); and **Vienna** (7hr., 5 per day 9:52am-1:45am, L86,600). Info office (☎1478 880 88) open 7am-9pm. Tickets and reservations 7am-8:30pm. **Luggage Storage:** L5000 for 12hr. Open daily 7:30am-10:30pm.

Buses: V. Europa Unità. Cross the street from the train station and walk 1 block to the right. **SAF** (☎0432 50 40 12) runs to **Cividale** (every hr. 6:40am-7:15pm, L3100). **Grandese** (☎0432 800 13 28) runs to **Palmanova** (every 2hr. 6:50am-9pm, L3100) and **Aquileia** (every hr. 6:50am-9pm, L4600). **SAITA** (☎0432 63 10 54) runs to **Trieste** (2 per hr. 5:10am-10:55pm, L6900).

Taxi: Radio Taxi (☎0432 50 58 58).

ORIENTATION AND PRACTICAL INFORMATION

Udine's train and bus stations are both on **Via Europa Unità** in the southern part of town. All bus lines pass the train station, but only buses #1, 3, and 8 run from V. Europa Unità to the center by **Piazza della Libertà** and **Castle Hill.** To walk from the station (15min.), go right to P. D'Annunzio then turn left under the arches to V. Aquileia. Continue up V. Veneto to P. della Libertà.

TOURIST, FINANCIAL, AND LOCAL SERVICES

Tourist Office: P. 1° Maggio, 7 (☎0432 29 59 72; fax 0432 50 47 43). From the southern end of P. della Libertà, turn right onto V. Manin and left onto P. 1° Maggio. Look for the pink-arched facade. Otherwise, take bus #2, 7, or 10 to P. 1° Maggio. Itineraries for visiting the town are posted on the town map and in *Udine and its Environs.* English spoken. Open M-F 9am-1pm and 3-6pm.

Mountain Information: The bulletin board of the **Club Alpino Italiano** (☎0432 50 42 90) is at V. Odorico, 3. Info on skiing and mountain excursions. For hikes within Friuli-Venezia Giulia, contact **Società Alpina Friulana,** V. Odorico, 3. Open M-F 5-7:30pm, Sa 9-11pm. Alpine info and excursions.

Currency Exchange: Banco Ambrosiana Veneto, V. V. Veneto, 21 (☎0432 51 74 11), off P. della Libertà. The best rates in town. Open M-F 8:20am-1:20pm and 2:45-4:05pm. Also in the post office, on the left as you enter.

Swimming Pool: Piscina Comunale, V. Ampezzo, 4 (☎0432 269 67 or 0432 269 29), near P. Diacono. Bathing cap required. L6000. Outdoor pool open June-Aug. M-Sa 1-7pm. Indoor pool open Sept.-May.

EMERGENCY AND COMMUNICATIONS

Emergencies: ☎113. **Ambulance:** ☎118. **Hospital: Ospedale Civile** (☎0432 55 21), in P. Santa Maria della Misericordia. Take bus #1 north to the last stop.

Late-Night Pharmacy: Farmacia Beltrame, P. della Libertà, 9 (☎0432 50 28 77). Open M-Sa 8:30am-12:30pm and 3:30-5:30pm. Ring the bell midnight-6am.

Post Office: V. Veneto, 42 (☎0432 50 19 93). Fermo Posta, stamps, and fax. Open M-F 7:20am-7:50pm, Sa 7:30am-1pm. **Branch** at V. Roma, 25, straight ahead from the train station. Open M-F 8:10am-1:15pm, Sa 8:30am-1pm. **Postal Code:** 33100.

ACCOMMODATIONS

The good news is that Udine's hotels are clearly marked on the large map outside the train station. The bad news is that local workers probably snagged the cheapest spots long ago. Reserving ahead may be difficult as many proprietors here do not speak English. Also, the cheaper hotels tend to lie on the outskirts of town.

Hotel Europa, V. L. Europa Unita, 47 (☎0432 50 87 31 or 0432 29 44 46; fax 0432 51 26 54). As you exit the train station, turn right, cross the street, and walk 2 blocks. Small elevator takes you to the bar downstairs. Pristine white halls and grandiose, impeccable rooms, all with baths, TVs, phones, and A/C. Breakfast included. Singles L110,000; doubles L160,000; triples L190,000; quads L200,000. V, MC.

Due Palme, V. L. Da Vinci, 5 (☎0432 48 02 13; fax 0432 48 18 07). Take bus #5 from the station and ask the driver for Hotel Due Palme. Mirrored hallway leads to small, clean rooms with baths, TVs, and telephones. Huge breakfast included. Singles L65,000; doubles L100,000; triples L120,000.

Locanda Da Arturo, V. Pracchiuso, 75 (☎0432 29 90 70). Take bus #4 from the station, get off at P. Oberdan, and walk down V. Pracchiuso on the far side of the *piazza.* Quiet rooms. Restaurant downstairs serves lunch and dinner. Reserve ahead. Closed in either July or Aug. Singles L40,000; doubles L60,000.

FOOD

Udinese cuisine is a mix of Italian, Austrian, and Slovenian fare. A typical regional specialty is *brovada e museto*, a stew made with marinated turnips and boiled sausage. Shop for produce weekday mornings in the **markets** at P. Matteotti near P. della Libertà, or head for V. Redipuglia or P. 1° Maggio. (Open Sa 8am-1pm.) The **Despar supermarket** is at V. Volontari della Libertà, 6, off P. Osoppo. (Open M and W 8:30am-1pm, Tu and Th-F 8:30am-1pm and 4-7pm, Sa 8:30am-7pm.)

Ristorante-Pizzeria Ai Portici, V. Veneto, 8 (☎0432 50 33 22), under the arcade before P. della Libertà. Chic and centrally located, this pizzeria is a local favorite. Pizza L6-14000, *primi* L7-10,000, *secondi* L7-25,000. Cover L2000. Open W-M 9am-midnight or 1am. V, MC.

Ristorante Zenit, V. Prefettura, 15b (☎0432 50 29 80). A reasonable self-service spot. Offers pasta, hot entrees, and salad. Popular with local professionals. *Primi* L4300-6500, *secondi* L6500-7500. Cover L500. Open M-Sa 8am-3pm.

Pizzamania, V. Pracchiuso, 63. Takeout slices L3000. Open Tu-Sa 10am-1:30pm and 4-9pm, Su 4-9pm.

SIGHTS AND ENTERTAINMENT

From July to September, the town celebrates summer with **Udine d'Estate,** a series of concerts, performances, movies, and guided tours of the city.

PIAZZA DELLA LIBERTÀ. This asymmetric, partitioned, and tilting square marks the center of old Udine. Along the raised edge, the **Arcado di San Giovanni** creates a covered walkway overlooking the square. Directly above, the bell tower features automated Moorish figures that swivel to strike the hour. Across from the arcade, the **Loggia del Lionello** (1488), rebuilt after an 1876 fire, serves as a public gathering place with chairs scattered in its shaded opening. Two columns and winged lions recall the Venetian conquest of Udine. In the highest corner of the square, through the **Arco Bollani** designed by Palladio in 1556, a cobblestone road winds ethereally up alongside an archway promenade to the **castello** above. Once home to Venetian governors, the castle today holds the **Museo Civico,** featuring notable but not necessarily exciting works. *(Open Tu-Sa 9:30am-12:30pm and 3-6pm, Su-M 9:30am-12:30pm. L10,000, students and those over 60 L7000.)*

DUOMO. The Roman-Gothic cathedral has several Tiepolos on display in the Baroque interior (the 1st, 2nd, and 4th altars on the right side). The squat, brick **campanile** houses a small **museum** comprised of two chapels with 14th-century frescoes by Vitale da Bologna. *(In P. del Duomo, 50m from P. della Libertà. ☎0432 50 68 30. Open daily 7am-noon and 4-8pm. Free.)*

ORATORIA DELLA PURITÀ. Udine has been called the city of Tiepolo, and some of this Baroque painter's finest works adorn the Oratorio della Purità. The *Assumption* fresco on the ceiling (1759) and the *Immaculate Conception* on the altarpiece represent Tiepolo's fantastic world of light and air. *(Across from the duomo. ☎0432 50 68 30. Ask the cathedral sacristan for admittance. A tip is expected.)*

PALAZZO PATRIARCALE. This *palazzo* contains a sizeable sampling of earlier Tiepolo frescoes. From 1726 to 1730, Tiepolo executed an extensive series of Old Testament scenes here. The museum also displays Romanesque and Baroque wooden sculptures from the Friuli region. *(P. Patriarcato, 1, at the head of V. Ungheria. ☎0432 250 03. Open W-Su 10am-noon and 3:30-6:30pm. L7000.)*

CIVIDALE DEL FRIULI ☎0432

In Cividale, you can wind down serpentine medieval streets, around corners, and through archways only to arrive 5m from where you began. The city hides from tourists at the edge of Italy, a short train ride from Udine. Cividale was founded by Julius Caesar in 50 BC as Forum Iulii, later became the capital of the first Lombard duchy in AD 568, and flourished until the Dark Ages. In 1420, the Friuli hit the fan when Venice conquered the city and stunted its growth, freezing Cividale in its medieval self. Enjoy *cucina friuliani* (regional dishes), a Dark Age spectacle, and a bridge built by the devil himself.

TRANSPORTATION AND PRACTICAL INFORMATION. Cividale is best reached from Udine by **train** (20min., every hr., round-trip L4400). **Buses** from Udine are less frequent (L2400). The train station, which opens onto V. Libertà, is a brief walk from the center of town. (☎0432 73 10 32. Open M-Sa 5:45am-8pm, Su 7am-8pm.) Leave your **luggage** in Udine; Cividale's station has no storage. From the train station head directly onto V. Marconi and turn left through the **Porta Arsenale Veneto** when the street ends. Bear right in P. Dante, then left onto Largo Boiano. The **tourist office,** C. P. d'Aquileia, 10, has a helpful staff. (☎0432 73 14 61; fax 0432 73 13 98. Open M-F 9am-1pm and 3-6pm.) **Banca Antoniana Popolare Veneto,** Largo Boiani, 20, has an **ATM.** In case of **emergency,** dial ☎113, seek out the **police** (☎0432 70 61 11), on P. A. Diaz, or contact the **hospital** (Ospedale Civile), in P. dell'Ospedale (☎0432 73 12 55). The **pharmacy** is at Largo Bioani, 11. (Open Tu-F 8:30am-12:30pm and 3:50-7:30pm, Sa 8:30am-12:30pm.) The **post office,** at Largo Boiani, 31, across from Foro Giulio Cesare, exchanges AmEx traveler's checks. (☎0432 73 11 57. Open M-Sa 8:30am-6pm.) **Postal Code:** 33043.

ACCOMMODATIONS AND FOOD. Budget accommodations are not Cividale's forte. The two-star **Al Pomo d'Oro,** on P. S. Giovanni, is the cheapest game in town, but the stakes have risen. (☎/fax 0432 73 14 89. Breakfast included. Wheelchair accessible. Singles with bath L80,000; doubles with bath L115,000. V, MC, AmEx.) Regional specialties are *picolit* (a pricey dessert wine rarely sold outside of the Natisone Valley), *frico* (a cheese and potato pancake), and *gubana* (a fig-and prune-filled pastry laced with *grappa*). Most bars stock pre-packaged *gubana*, but for mouth-watering sweets, look for the "Gubana Cividalese" sign, C. D'Aquileia, 16, on the right as you near the Ponte del Diavolo. Ask for *Gubana piccola*, unless you want the whole cake. P. Diacono hosts Cividale's open-air **market** every Saturday from 8am to 1pm. For *cucina friuliana*, **Antica Trattoria Dominissini,** Stretta Stellini, 18, creates tasty regional dishes like *frico* and *polenta* in a lively bar setting. The vine-covered terrace has a great view of the church's tower. (☎0432 73 37 63. *Primi* L8-10,000, *secondi* L8-16,000. Cover L2000. Open Tu-Sa 9:30am-3:30pm and 6-11pm, Su 9:30am-3:30pm and 6:30-11pm.) **Bar Al Campanile,** V. Candotti, 4, right off the *duomo*, is a favorite with locals. Specialties include *prosciutto al salto* (cured ham). (☎0432 73 24 67. Open Tu-Su 7:30am-11pm.)

SIGHTS AND ENTERTAINMENT. Built and expanded over the centuries, Cividale's **duomo,** on the left as you exit the tourist office, is an odd melange of architectural styles. Pietro Lombardo completed the bulk of the construction in 1528. The 12th-century silver altarpiece of Pellegrino II features 25 saints and a pair of archangels. The Renaissance sarcophagus of Patriarch Nicolò Donato lies to the left of the entrance. Annexed to the *duomo* is the **Museo Cristiano.** This free display includes the marvelously sculpted **Baptistery of Callisto,** commissioned by the first Aquileian patriarch to move to Cividale, and the **Altar of Ratchis,** a delicately carved work from 740. (Duomo ☎0432 73 11 44. Duomo and museum open Apr.-Oct. M-Sa 9:30am-noon and 3-6pm, Su 3-6pm; Nov.-Mar. M-Sa 9:30am-noon and 3-6pm, Su 3-5:30pm. Both free.)

The greatest Italian work of the 8th century is downhill at the **Tempietto Longobardo,** built on the remains of Roman homes. As you exit the *duomo*, turn right, then head straight through the *piazza* and turn right again onto Riva Pozzo di Callisto. At the bottom of the stairs, turn left and follow the signs. A beautiful sextet of stucco figures lines the wall. (☎0432 70 08 67. Open daily in summer 9am-1pm and 3-6:30pm; in winter 10am-1pm and 3:30-5:30pm. L4000, students L2000.) The lush countryside rolls into the distance, and on a high vista sits **Castelmonte Stara Gora.** For a similarly stunning view, head to the **Ponte del Diavolo,** an impressive 15th-century stone bridge. For a better look at the bridge itself, descend the stairs to the water on the far side. Local legend has it that Lucifer himself, in one of his biblical fits, threw down the great stone on which the bridge rests.

TRENTINO-ALTO ADIGE

At the foot of the Italian Alps, peaks sharpen, rivers run crystalline, and natural blonde becomes the predominant local color. The Mediterranean groove of the southern provinces gradually fades under Austrian influences in Trentino-Alto Adige. In the beginning of the 19th century, Napoleon conquered this integral part of the Holy Roman Empire, only to relinquish it to the Austro-Hungarians. A century later, at the end of World War I, Trentino and the Südtirol fell under Italian rule. Though Germany cut short Mussolini's brutal efforts to Italianize the region, Mussolini had managed to give every German name an Italian equivalent. While southern Trentino is predominantly Italian-speaking, Südtirol (South Tirol), encompassing most of the northern mountain region known as the Dolomites, still resounds with German. Here, street signs, architecture, and even cuisine blend Austrian and Italian traditions. So practice your German—you'll need it to order fine Italian food at one of the region's many *Spaghettihäuser*.

HIGHLIGHTS OF TRENTINO-ALTO ADIGE

GO WILD in the white-peaked **Dolomite** frontier (see below).

AUSTRIA-CIZE YOURSELF in a Habsburg cafe in **Bolzano** (p. 253).

BE AN AMPHIBIAN around **Lake Garda**—explore both land and water (p. 259).

TRENT (TRENTO, TRIENT) ☎0461

When you arrive in Trent, find a cozy *pasticceria* in the center of town and order *Apfel Strudel* and a cappuccino. Before you, you'll find an edible metaphor for the city itself—a harmonious and tasty mix of Germanic and Mediterranean flavors. Located inside the Alpine threshold yet connected to the Veneto by a long, deep valley, Trent became the Romans' strategic gateway to the north. For centuries to follow, fortresses such as the Castello del Buonconsiglio proliferated in the region; armies marched north and south through the great connecting corridor, while the Trentinos, safely behind cattle walls, simply waited for the storm to pass before returning to mountain farms and vineyards. Cultural and political ownership of the city, contested in the 19th century, was settled for good at the end of WWI, when Trent became Italian. Although the city's sights are few and far between, Trent is, nonetheless, worth a stop for its sampling of northern Italian life, superb restaurants, and engaging walks, set against a backdrop of dramatic limestone cliffs.

TRANSPORTATION

Trains: To: **Bolzano** (50min., every hr., L9400); **Verona** (1hr., every hr., L14,200); **Venice** (2½hr., L29,400); and **Bologna** (2½-3hr., 8 per day, L18,600). **Luggage Storage:** L5000 for 12hr. Closed 11:30pm-1am.

Buses: Atesina (☎0461 82 10 00), on V. Pozzo next to the train station. To **Rovereto** (25min., every hr., L4000) and **Riva del Garda** (1hr., every hr., L5500). Also has extensive local service. Schedules at the info booth in the station.

Cableways: Funivia Trento-Sardagna (☎0461 38 10 00), on V. Lung'Adige Monte Grappa. From the bus station, turn right onto V. Pozzo and take the 1st right onto Cavalcavia S. Lorenzo. Cross the bridge over the train tracks and head across the intersection to the unmarked building. To **Sardagna** on Mt. Bondone (every 30min., L1500 for 1hr., L4000 for 24hr.). Open M-F 7am-10pm, Sa 7am-9:25pm, Su 9:30am-7pm.

Taxis: Radio Taxi (☎0461 93 00 02).

ORIENTATION AND PRACTICAL INFORMATION

The bus and train stations are on the same street, between the **Adige River** and the **public gardens.** The center of town lies east of the Adige. From the stations, walk right to the intersection with V. Torre Varga. Continue straight as **Via Pozzo** becomes **Via Orfane** and **Via Cavour** before reaching **Piazza del Duomo** in town's center. To reach the **Castello del Buonconsiglio,** follow V. Roma eastward, away from the river. V. Roma becomes V. Manci, then V. S. Marco.

TOURIST, FINANCIAL, AND LOCAL SERVICES

Tourist Office: Azienda di Promozione Turisitica di Trento (☎0461 98 38 80; fax 0461 23 24 26; email informazioni@apt.trento.it; www.apt.trento.it). Provides info about accommodations in the city and surrounding mountains and offers advice on biking, skiing, and hiking in the Trentino region. English-speaking staff. Open daily 9am-7pm.

Budget Travel: CTS, V. Cavour, 21 (☎/fax 0461 98 15 33), near P. del Duomo. Student IDs, plane and train tickets. English spoken. Open M-F 10am-12:30pm and 4-7:30pm.

Hiking Equipment: Rigoni Sport, Ple. C. Battisti, 30/31 (☎0461 98 12 39). Sells hiking gear; no rentals. Open M 3:30-7:15pm, Tu-Su 9am-noon and 3:30-7:15pm.

Bookstore: Libreria Disertori, V. M. Diaz, 11 (☎0461 98 14 55), near Ple. C. Battisti. Carries literature and romance in English. Open M 3:30-7pm, Tu-Sa 8:30am-noon and 3:30-7pm. V, MC.

EMERGENCY AND COMMUNICATIONS

Emergencies: ☎113. **Police: Questura** (☎0461 89 95 11), on P. Mostra. **Ambulance:** ☎118. **Hospital: Ospedale Santa Chiara,** Largo Medaglie d'Oro, 9 (☎0461 90 31 11), up V. Orsi past the swimming pool. **Alpine Emergency: CAI-SAT** (☎0461 23 31 66).

Pharmacy: Bartolameo, V. Verona, 82 (☎0461 91 35 93).

Internet Access: Call Me, V. Belenzani, 58 (☎0461 98 33 02), near the *duomo.* Open F-W 9am-noon and 2-10:15pm.

Post Office: V. Calepina, 16 (☎0461 98 72 70), at P. Vittoria. Open M-F 8:10am-6:30pm, Sa 8:10am-12:20pm. Another office next to the train station on V. Dogana. Open M-F 8:10am-6:30pm, Sa 8:10am-12:20pm. **Postal Code:** 38100.

ACCOMMODATIONS

Hotel Venezia, P. Duomo, 45 (☎/fax 0461 23 41 14). Large, pleasant rooms, some with a view of the *duomo.* Great location with views, high quality, and fair prices. Breakfast L12,000. Singles L55,000, with bath L65,000; doubles with bath L95,000. V, MC.

Ostello Giovane Europa (HI), V. Manzoni, 17 (☎0461 23 45 67; fax 0451 26 84 34). 10-15min. from the *centro.* From the station, turn right on V. Pozzo then left on V. Torre Vanga, which becomes V. Torre Verde and then V. Manzoni. No-frills dorm rooms with lockers and bathrooms. Bar with TV. Breakfast, showers, and sheets included. Reception 3:30-11pm. Check-out 9:30am. Curfew 11:30pm. Reservations necessary. Dorms L22,000; family rooms L22,000 per person.

Al Cavallino Bianco, V. Cavour, 29 (☎0461 23 15 42), down the street from the *duomo.* Great location, but dim lighting and walls so thin you can hear the action next door. All rooms have showers and bath. Singles L65,000; doubles L92,000; triples L125,000. Closed Dec. and June 16-26. V, MC, AmEx.

FOOD

An open-air **market** with fruits, vegetables, and cheeses spreads out every Thursday 8am-1pm behind P. del Duomo; sharpen your bargaining skills. The **Trentini supermarket,** P. Lodron, 28, lies across P. Pasi from the *duomo.* (☎0461 22 01 96. Open Tu-Sa 8:30am-12:30pm and 3:30-7:30pm.) The **Poli supermarket,** at V. Roma and V. delle Orfane, is near the station. (☎0461 98 50 63. Open M and Sa 8:30am-12:30pm, Tu-F 8:30am-12:30pm and 3:15-7:15pm.)

Patelli, V. Dietro Le Mura A, 1/5 (☎0461 23 52 36), down V. Mazzini from the *duomo,* next to the large stone wall. A restaurant with soul—the owner created Patelli to put sauce on the pasta his brother made from scratch. The lovingly crafted menu features meat from 5 countries and numerous vegetarian options. Pasta remains the house specialty. The prices, starting at L15,000, allow for both low- and high-end dining within the same friendly, welcoming atmosphere. To top off the meal, Patelli boasts potent *grappa* from the Trentino region. Open M noon-2:30pm, Tu-Sa 7-11pm. V, MC, AmEx.

Ristorante Pizzeria Forst, V. Mazzurana, 38 (☎0461 23 55 90), a few steps from P. Duomo. Bavarian in decor, reasonable in price, the Forst delivers typical Germano-Italian cuisine. *Primi* L7-8000, *secondi* L7-16,000. *Menù* L21,000 (includes *primo, secondo,* and one vegetable). Cover L1600. Open Tu-Su 11am-3pm and 5:30-11:30pm. Closed for 3 weeks in July. V, MC, AmEx.

Ristorante Il Capello, P. Anfiteatro, 3 (☎0451 23 58 50), in a courtyard next to Chiesa di San Marco. Flavorful dishes made fresh from seasonal ingredients. Two can eat like kings—fat ones—for less than L50,000. Calm, candlelit dining under the stars. *Primi* L12-14,000. Cover L3000. Open M-Sa noon-2:15pm and 7-10pm. V, MC.

Pasticceria San Vigilio, V. Sigilio, 10 (☎0461 23 00 96), just behind the *duomo.* Bertini Elisio, pastry chef and candy designer, hand-sculpts marzipan into whimsical and tasty animal and fruit shapes. *Mignum* (delectable miniature cakes) and candied fruits L3500 per gram. Go wild (but don't forget to floss). Open daily June and Aug. 7:30am-12:30pm and 3-7:30pm; Sept.-May 7:30am-7:30pm.

SIGHTS AND ENTERTAINMENT

PIAZZA DEL DUOMO. The *piazza,* Trent's center of gravity and social heart, contains the city's best sights. The **Fontana del Nettuno** stands in the center of the *piazza,* trident in hand. Its steps offer a good view of the stretch of frescoes tattooing the **Cazuffi houses.** At night, rippling water makes the spotlights on Neptune flicker as dozens of Trentino locals gather on steps and in the numerous sidewalk cafes. Nearby stands the **Cattedrale di San Vigilio,** named for the patron saint of Trent. The interior is less exciting than the looming outer structure, which wraps partly around the *piazza. (Open daily 6:40am-12:15pm and 2:30-7:30pm.)*

MUSEO DIOCESANO. This museum holds a collection of sacred paintings, altarpieces, and garments related to the cathedral and the famed Council of Trent. *(P. Duomo, 18. ☎0461 23 44 19. Museum open M-Sa 9:30am-12:30pm and 2:30-6pm. L5000, students L1000. Includes access to the archaeological excavations beneath the church.)*

CASTELLO DEL BUONCONSIGLIO. Trent's largest and most characteristic attraction houses everything from woodwork and pottery to local art from the 13th to 17th centuries. The *Locus Reflections* room is where the Austrians captured and condemned to death Cesare Battisti during WWI. The Bolzano Archaeology Museum (see **Sights,** p. 255) may be a worthier place to spend your time, but this well-preserved castle merits a visit. *(Walk down V. Belenzani and head right on V. Roma. ☎0461 23 37 70. Open Apr.-Sept. Tu-Su 9am-noon and 2-5:30pm; Oct.-Mar. Tu-Su 9am-noon and 2-5pm. L9000, students and those under 18 or over 60 L5000.)*

OTHER SIGHTS. Trent expands according to your interests. The hills nearby offer unlimited trails for afternoon strolls; skiing is a bus ride away; wine-tasting and summer music festivals vary every year. If you visit during the summer, try to see a play at one of the private castles. Admission varies from *gratis* to L10,000.

DAYTRIP FROM TRENT: MONTE BONDONE

Monte Bondone rises majestically over Trent and begs for pleasant daytrips and overnight excursions. The tourist office in Trent provides maps and information for skiing, hiking, and daytripping on the mountain. The tourist office in Vaneze can help arrange overnight accommodations. (☎0461 94 71 28; www.montebondone.it. Open Dec.-Easter and June 20-Sept. 20.) Catch the cable car (every 30min.; L1500 ticket valid for 1hr., L4000 ticket valid for the day) from Ponte di San Lorenzo, between the train tracks and the river, to Sardagna, a great picnic spot with good trails. (Open M-F 7am-10pm, Sa 7am-9:25pm, Su 9:30am-7pm.) From there, a 10-12km hike leads to the Mezzavia Campground. (☎0461 94 81 78. Open June-Sept. L6500 per person, L8000 per tent.)

DOLOMITES (DOLOMITI)

Limestone spires shoot skyward from pine forests. These amazing peaks—fantastic for hiking, skiing, and rock climbing—start west of Trent and extend north and east to the Austrian frontier. With their sunny skies and light powdery snow, the Dolomites offer immensely popular downhill skiing. Major ski centers include: Alta Venosta (around Lake Resia) and Colle Isarco near Bolzano; Folgaria, Brentonico, Madonna di Campiglio, and Monte Bondone near Trent; Val d'Isarco, the Zona dello Sciliar, and Val Gardena near Bressanone; and Alta Badia near Corvara. The settimana bianca (white week) package, available at any **CTS** or **CIT** office, affords a convenient, inexpensive way to enjoy a holiday in the Dolomites. If you plan to stay in the region of interlocking trails around the Gruppo Sella, consider purchasing the Superski Dolomiti pass for the Gruppo's 464 cable cars and lifts. Try the **regional tourist office** in Bolzano (☎0471 99 38 08) for additional skiing and hiking info. The **SAD** (Società Automobilistica Dolomiti) deploys **buses** that cover virtually every paved road in the area with surprising frequency.

Alpine huts (*rifugi*) and rooms in private homes (advertised by *Zimmer/camere* signs) litter the trails, easing journeys into the mountains. The *Kompass Wanderkarte* map, available at most newsstands and bookstores, clearly marks all accommodations. Huts operate from late June through early October, but at higher altitudes the season is often shorter. Visit the provincial office in Bolzano and local tourist offices for campground listings.

BOLZANO (BOZEN) ☎0471

In the tug-of-war between Austrian and Italian cultural influences, Bolzano pulls on Austria's side of the rope. The architecture is immediately distinctive—here Italy is dipped in German paint and covered with pointed pastel arches and lacy, white trim-work. The sights in Bolzano are hit or miss—some soar, like the ominous Gothic *duomo;* others flounder, like the diminutive Neptune who leaks an apathetic trickle. Even so, the strange hybrid culture makes Bolzano an intriguing stop, and its prime location beneath vineyard-covered mountains makes it a splendid base for hiking, biking, or skiing forays in the Dolomites.

TRANSPORTATION

Trains: (☎0471 97 42 92), in P. Stazione. To: **Bressanone** (30min., every hr. 6:31am-8:47pm, L4200); **Merano** (45min., every hr. 6:58am-10pm, L6300); **Trent** (1-2hr., 1-2 per hr. 5:22am-9:48pm, L5300); **Verona** (2hr., 1-2 per hr. 5:32am-9:48pm,

L12,500); and **Milan** (3½hr., 3 per day 11:31am-5:31pm, L24,300). More frequent service to Milan via Trent. Info open M-Sa 8am-5:30pm, Su 9am-1pm and 2:30-5:30pm. **Luggage Storage:** L5000 for 12hr. Open 6am-10pm.

Buses: SAD, V. Perathoner, 4 (☎0471 45 01 11; fax 0471 97 98 85), between the train station and P. Walther. To **Merano** (1hr., every hr. 6:50am-8:10pm, L5500) and **Bressanone** (1hr., every hr. 7am-8:15pm, L7200). Less frequent service on weekends. For info call toll-free ☎167 84 60 47.

Public Transportation: ACT (☎0471 45 01 11). Bus service throughout the city. All lines stop in P. Walther.

Cableways: 3 cableways, located at the edges of Bolzano, whisk you up 1000m or more over the city to the nearest trailhead. The **Funivia del Colle** (☎0471 97 85 45), the world's oldest cableway, leads from V. Campiglio (Kampillerstr.) to Colle (Kohlern; 2 per hr. 7am-6pm; round-trip L6000, bike transport L8000). The **Funivia del Renon** heads from V. Renon, a 5min. walk from the train station, to Renon (Ritten; round-trip L7500). The Funivia S. Genesio (Jeneseiner Seilbahn; ☎0471 97 84 36), on V. Sarentino, across the Talvera River near Ponte S. Antonio, goes to Salto's high plateaus (round-trip L6500, bike transport L5000).

ORIENTATION AND PRACTICAL INFORMATION

Bolzano's historic center lies between the train station and the **Talvera River,** with all major *piazze* within walking distance. Street names are listed in Italian and German. Many castles are accessible by bus or bike. A brief walk up **Via Stazione** from the train station, or **Via Alto Adige** from the bus stop, leads to **Piazza Walther.**

TOURIST AND FINANCIAL SERVICES

Tourist Office: P. Walther, 8 (☎0471 30 70 00; fax 0471 98 01 28). Provides lists of accommodations, including hotels, campgrounds, and *agriturismo*. The *Walks and Hikes* brochure suggests nearby hikes of varying lengths and difficulty, and *Manifestazioni* includes several pages of useful phone numbers, excursions, and events. English spoken. Open M-F 9am-6:30pm, Sa 9am-12:30pm.

Budget Travel: CIT, P. Walther, 11 (☎0471 97 61 81). Transalpino tickets. Money exchange services. English spoken. Open M-F 9am-noon and 2:30-6pm. V, MC, AmEx.

Currency Exchange: In the post office or at **Banca Nazionale del Lavoro,** in P. Walther, next door to the Bolzano tourist office. Good rates. Visa services. Open M-F 8:20am-1:20pm and 3-4:30pm.

LOCAL SERVICES

Car Rental: Budget, V. Garibaldi, 32 (☎0471 97 15 31). **Hertz,** V. Garibaldi, 34 (☎0471 98 14 11; fax 0471 30 37 15). From L125,000 per day. Open M-F 8:30am-12:30pm and 2:30-5:30pm, Sa 8:30am-noon.

Public Bikes: V. Stazione, near P. Walther. Borrow a bike for 4hr. by leaving a L10,000 deposit and ID info. City cruisers, not mountain-worthy.

Bike Rental: Sportler Velo, V. Grappoli (Weintraubeng.) 56 (☎0471 97 77 19), near P. Municipale. Mountain bikes L30,000 per day. Big selection of retail bikes and equipment. English spoken. Open M-F 9am-12:30pm and 4:30-7pm, Sa 9am-12:30pm.

Camping Equipment: Sportler Velo (see above). Expensive, extensive selection. Down the street, **Sport Reinstaller,** V. Portici, 23 (☎0471 97 71 90), offers better deals. Open M-F 9am-noon and 3-7pm, Sa 9-12:30pm.

EMERGENCY AND COMMUNICATIONS

Emergencies: ☎112. **Police:** ☎112 or 0471 99 77 88. **First Aid:** ☎118. **White Cross:** ☎0471 24 44 44. **Hospital: Ospedale Regionale San Maurizio** (☎0471 90 81 11), on V. Lorenz Böhler.

Pharmacy: V. Perathoner, 33 (☎0471 97 11 62). Open M-F 8:30am-noon and 3-7pm, Sa 8:30am-noon.

Post Office: V. della Posta, 1 (☎0471 97 94 52), by the *duomo.* Open M-F 8:05am-6:30pm, Sa 8:05am-1pm. **Postal Code:** 39100.

ACCOMMODATIONS AND CAMPING

Bolzano is not a city for the budget-conscious traveler, so consider taking a daytrip from Trent. If you do decide to stay, try the cheaper mountainside options or ask about the *agriturismo* program at the tourist office. Through *agriturismo,* farmers let rooms to travelers, usually for L35-90,000.

Croce Bianca, P. del Grano (Kornpl.) 3 (☎0471 97 75 52). Look for the sign above a bustling outdoor terrace around the corner from P. Walther. Homey rooms with thick mattresses. Breakfast L8000. Reserve in advance. Singles L40,000; doubles L60,000, with bath L78,000; triples with bath L90,000.

Schwarze Katz, Stazione Maddalena di Sotto, 2 (☎0471 97 54 17; fax 32 50 28), near V. Brennero, 15min. from the *centro.* Hotel "Black Cat" is a family-run, friendly place with a garden restaurant popular with locals. All 9 rooms with bath and breakfast. Singles L40,000; doubles L80,000. V, MC, AmEx.

Camping: Moosbauer, V. S. Maurizio, 83 (☎0471 91 84 92; fax 0471 20 48 94). Take the ACT bus to Merano, get off at the Hotel Pircher stop, and walk back 300m toward Bolzano. Showers included. L9500 per person, L8000 per tent, L8000 per car.

FOOD

In Bolzano, pizza and *gelato* take a back seat to *Knödel, Strudel,* and other Austrian fare. *Rindgulasch* is a delicious beef stew; *Speck* is tasty smoked bacon. *Knödel* (dumplings) come in dozens of rib-sticking varieties. The three types of *Strudel—Apfel* (apple), *Topfen* (soft cheese), and *Mohn* (poppyseed)—make delicious snacks. The week-long *Südtiroler Törgelen* tasting spree in the fall is celebrated in the local vineyards. P. delle Erbe (Obstpl.) has an all-day produce **market** with delicious goods from local farms. (M-Sa 6am-7pm.) A **Despar supermarket** is situated at V. della Rena, 40. (☎0471 97 45 37. Open M-F 8:30am-12:30pm and 3-7:30pm, Sa 8am-1pm.) Don't despair, another Despar is at V. dei Bottai, 29. (Open in summer M-F 8:30am-7:30pm.) **Hopfen & Co.,** V. Argentieri, 36, offers a smorgasbord of regional specialties. Try the rich and filling *goulash* (L8000). The restaurant is bright and lively downstairs, dark and drab upstairs—seat yourself wisely. (☎0471 30 07 88. Entrees L5-15,000. V, MC.) At **Bar Imperia,** P. Domenicani, 28 (☎0471 97 52 24), young, chic patrons enjoy a view of the square and tasty *bruschette* with tomatoes, mozzarella, and basil (L5000).

SIGHTS AND ENTERTAINMENT

DUOMO AND CHIESA DEI FRANCESCANI. With its prickly spined tower and a diamond-patterned roof, the Gothic *duomo* is a dark and awesome sight. Inside, the gray walls counteract the numerous frescoes and glass-encased artwork. As a rule, the beauty of Bolzano is in the facades—the best "sights" are found by exploring the winding streets. The immediate exception is Chiesa dei Francescani, where a simple triangular exterior hides a splendid interior. An unusual sight, the church has high, bright white walls with a crucifix suspended by thin wires. At the proper distance, the cross seems to float in front of three dazzling stained-glass windows with devastatingly bright slivers of gold, red, and purple. *(Duomo in P. Walther. Chiesa off P. Erbe from P. Walther. Open M-F 9:45am-noon and 2-5pm, Sa 9:45am-noon. Free.)*

SOUTH TYROL MUSEUM OF ARCHAEOLOGY. For an entirely different experience, visit this fascinating museum, which traces human life in the Alpine region from the Stone Age to the early Middle Ages. Here you can see the actual Ice Man—the prehistoric body discovered by a German couple on vacation—who suffers his embarrassing case of *Decomposus Interuptus* with a quiet dignity. The

L3000 tape-recorded tours in English, filled with fascinating mummy details, are a must. *(V. Museo, 43. ☎0471 98 20 98; fax 0471 98 06 48; email museum@iceman.it; www.iceman.it. Open Tu-W and F-Su 10am-6pm, Th 10am-8pm. L13,000, students L7000.)*

CASTEL RONCOLO. This castle sits on the hills above town. From the bus stop, wind up the path for a spectacular view of the city on the way to see the frescoes in the castle. *(Up V. Weggerstein to V. San Antonio. Take the fresco-covered shuttle bus from P. Walther. ☎0471 32 98 44. Open Mar.-Nov. Tu-Su 10am-6pm. Gates for the frescoes close at 5pm. L2000.)*

DAYTRIP FROM BOLZANO: MERANO (MERAN)

To reach Merano, change at Bolzano for the frequent regional trains (1hr., 1-2 per hr., L6300). Buses leave near the train station for Bolzano (1hr., every hr., L5500) and Bressanone (1hr., every 1-2hr., L5200).

Merano is a decidedly Austrian little town situated one hour north of Bolzano. Houses are painted in shades of pastel, locals greet each other with *"Gruss Gott"* rather than *"buongiorno,"* and *wurst* replaces pasta on local menus. While Russian royal families once frequented the local spa, famous for its rejuvenating therapies, visitors now come to Merano to enjoy the serene atmosphere of the town and to stroll the lengthy walks through the surrounding woodlands.

There are only a few traditional monuments in Merano. From the tourist office, head right along C. Liberta to reach the **Porta Bolzano,** one of the three original medieval town gates still standing, and walk straight ahead toward the 14th-century **Duomo di S. Nicolo.** Behind the *duomo*, the tiny **Cappella di S. Barnaba** holds massive gilded altarpieces and jewel-encrusted skeletons within glass cases. (*Duomo* and chapel open M-Sa 7am-6pm.) To the east of the *duomo*, the arcaded V. Portici offers a picturesque stroll and a number of expensive shops and restaurants. Farther west, follow V. Passiria to the **Porta Passirio,** elaborately carved in bronze, on your left before entering the arch. From here, the dense woods and rushing Passirio rapids offer breathtaking views. The **Passagiata d'Inverno** heads along the east side of the river, while the **Passagiata d'Estate** follows the western bank. Intermittent cafes and shops along the paths provide refreshments, postcards, and vistas. To top off your stroll with a marvelous view, walk 1km along **Passagiata Tappeiner,** behind the *duomo*, to reach the 17th-century **Gun Powder Tower,** with commanding views of the town and surroundings.

The two main arteries of the town are the parallel streets **Via Portici** and **Corso della Liberta,** which both run from the river to the train station. Turn right as you exit the station, follow **Viale Europa** to **Piazza Mazzini Platz,** then take C. della Liberta (Freiheitsstr.) to the center of town. At the **tourist office,** C. della Liberta, 45, pick up a list of accommodations and information on local walks and excursions. (☎0473 23 52 23; fax 23 52 24; email info@meraninfo.it. Open M-F 9am-6:30pm, Sa 9:30am-6pm, Su 10am-12:30pm.) Change money or use the **ATM** at **Cassa Rurale di Merano,** C. Liberta, 23. (Open M-F 8:05am-12:55pm and 2:45-4:45pm.)

Dining in Merano requires at least a gold card. Fortunately, an **A & O Supermarket** is at the corner of V. Portici and V. Cassa di Risparmio. Another option is **Restaurant Sigmund,** C. Liberta, 2, 300m past the tourist office on the left. A friendly staff serves up traditional Tyrolean fare and decent pasta. (☎0473 23 77 49. *Zuppa di gulasch* L9500, spaghetti L9500. Open Th-Tu 11:30am-9pm.)

NEAR BOLZANO: BRESSANONE (BRIXEN) ☎0472

Tyrolean Bressanone is one of the most picturesque towns in Northern Italy. Located in the heart of the Dolomites, Bressanone affords a panoramic vista of the mountains, river, and charming, well-kept pastel houses. In addition, the town's rich medieval heritage has bestowed a number of artistic treasures upon Bressanone, most notably the 14th-century *chiostro*.

TRANSPORTATION AND PRACTICAL INFORMATION. Bressanone is an easy daytrip by train or bus from Bolzano. **Trains** run to: **Bolzano** (30min., every hr. 6:30am-9:15pm, L5200); **Trent** (1-1½hr., every 2hr. 6:30am-9:15pm, L14,200); **Verona** (2hr., 3-4 per day 6:30am-9:15pm); and **Munich** (5hr., 3-4 per day 8:33am-6:57pm). **Buses** run to **Bolzano** (1hr., every hr. 7am-8:15pm, L7200). The center of town is **Piazza del Duomo.** From the train station, follow **Viale Stazione** past the glass-encased **tourist office** (on your right, at the corner of Vle. Stazione and V. Cassiano). At the intersection, take **V. Bastioni Min.** and turn right through the flower-covered arch on your right to enter the courtyard of the Palace. The **tourist office,** Vle. Stazione, 9, provides local information. (☎0472 83 64 01; fax 0472 83 60 67; email info@brixen.org; www.brixen.org. Open M-F 8:30am-12:30pm and 2:30-6pm, Sa 9am-12:30pm.) **ATMs** line V. Bastioni Magg., one block north of P. del Duomo.

ACCOMMODATIONS AND FOOD. **Tallero,** V. Mercato Vecchio, 35, has 12 rooms near P. del Duomo. From the *piazza,* head towards the smaller chapel on your right, turn right and then left onto V. Torre Bianca and continue straight ahead. (☎0472 83 05 77. L50-55,000 per person.) **Cremona,** V. Veneto, 26, offers 12 clean rooms outside the town center. From the station, walk one block down Vle. Mozart to V. Veneto. (☎0472 83 56 02; fax 0472 20 07 94. L50-55,000 per person.)

At the 100 year-old **Restaurant Fink,** Kleine Lauben, 4, with local crafts charmingly displayed in the windows, waitresses in traditional dress serve up Austrian and Italian cuisine. Enjoy comfy couches indoors, or dine *al fresco* beneath the arcades. (☎0472 83 48 83. *Rosti* of potatoes and veggies L13,000, *primi* L10-15,000.) The **STANDA supermarket,** Vle. Stazione, 7, next to the tourist office, offers dining options for more limited budgets. (Open M-F 8:30am-noon and 3-7pm, Sa 8:30am-12:30pm and 3-6pm.)

SIGHTS. Most sights are concentrated around P. del Duomo. A few yards south of the *piazza,* at P. Palazzo, the **Palazzo Vescovile,** originally constructed in 1595, houses the **Museo Diocesano.** The building itself has a stunning interior courtyard, while the museum within describes the development of Western Christianity in relation to evolving European social structures and technological advances such as the printing press. A number of medieval and Renaissance portraits are also on display, including copies of works by Hans Klocker and Albrecht Dürer. Unfortunately, explanatory information is only in Italian and German. (☎0472 83 05 05. Open Mar. 15-Oct. Tu-Su 10am-5pm. L12,000, reduced L9000.)

The **duomo,** in the center of the *piazza,* was originally constructed in 1200 in the Romanesque style, but it acquired Baroque and Neoclassical detailing during renovations in 1595, 1754, and 1790. Today, the elaborately gilded ceiling and pale marble walls are dazzling. The nearby **Chiostro,** to the left as you exit the *duomo,* dates from the 14th century and highlights the evolution of medieval religious painting through a series of well-preserved frescoes. (*Duomo* and *Chiostro* open M-Sa 6am-noon and 3-6pm, Su 3-6pm. Free.)

One of the most enjoyable activities in Bressanone is simply strolling the pleasant streets of the city. From Ponte Aquila behind the *duomo,* cross the bridge to the tiny **Altstadt** (old town), where flowerboxes decorate the windows of pastel houses situated along winding cobblestone lanes. Plaques with the red town seal mark historic buildings and describe their significance in Italian and German.

CORTINA D'AMPEZZO ☎0436

In the heart of the Dolomites, glitzy Cortina draws skiers from across Europe in winter and Italians seeking relief from the heat during the summer. The tempting Tyrolean town makes a wonderful, if expensive, base for skiing and a variety of summer activities. If you're not up for the physical challenges of the mountains, hike the attractive streets of the town and enjoy the many pastel, frescoed facades.

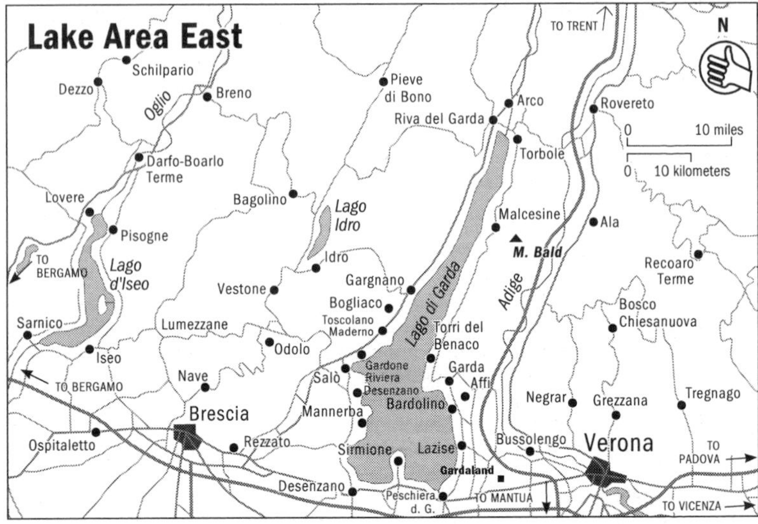

TRANSPORTATION. Cortina D'Ampezzo lies near the Austrian border, east of Bolzano and north of Venice. The nearest **train station** is in **Calazo,** from which local **buses** take a long and winding road to reach **Cortina** (1hr., every hr., L4500). The town is best accessed by car, but if you're relying on public transportation, **trains** run to Calazo from **Venice** (3hr.) and **Milan** (8hr.). **Buses** run directly to Cortina from **Belluno** (2hr., 10 per day); and **Bressanone** (4hr., 1 per day) and **Milan** (6½hr., 1 per day). Contact Dolomiti Bus (☎0436 86 79 21) for more information.

ORIENTATION AND PRACTICAL INFORMATION. The center of town is the pedestrian-only **Corso Italia,** which is lined with expensive shops. From the bus station, take the stairs across the street and follow signs to the *centro.* The **tourist office,** Pitta S. Francesco, 8, lies on the other side of C. Italia from the station. From the *duomo,* take the stairs to your left, turn right at the bottom of the stairs, and cross the street. Turn left, and the office is on your right. (☎0436 32 31; fax 0436 32 35. Open daily 9am-12:30pm and 4-7pm.) **Postal Code:** 32043.

ACCOMMODATIONS AND FOOD. Accommodations are abundant in Cortina, but most are prohibitively expensive. Campsites cost less but are far from the town center. **Hotel Fiames,** Localita Fiames, 13, offers 13 rooms outside of the town center. Take bus #1 (30min.) to the Fiames stop. (☎0436 23 66; fax 0436 57 33. L110,000 per person, L130,000 per person with bath.) **Camping Cortina,** Localita Campo, is a four-star campsite south of town. Take bus #2 and ask for Camping Cortina. (☎0436 86 75 75. L13,000 per person, L17,000 per tent.)

Most restaurants are similarly high-priced, but **Pizzeria Il Ponte,** V. B. Franchetti, 8, has a view of the mountains and delicious pizzas from L6500. Facing the *duomo,* turn left onto C. Italia, then make a left onto V. B. Franchetti. (☎0436 86 76 24. V, MC, AmEx.) Across the street is the even less expensive **supermarket,** V. B. Franchetti, 1. (Open M-Sa 8:30am-12:30pm and 3:30-7:30pm. V, MC.)

SIGHTS. Strolling the streets of Cortina is a pleasure, as the pastel houses are lined with flowerboxes and often have colorful frescoes painted onto the facades. Aside from that, however, there is little to do in town and most visitors take part in activities in the nearby mountains. The tourist office advises and offers a wealth of information on local skiing, hiking, water sports, and nature excursions.

LAKE GARDA (LAGO DI GARDA)

Garda—the ultimate resort destination for many German families—has staggering mountains and breezy summers. Along the lake's shore, Sirmione, with its beautifully situated medieval castle and extensive Roman ruins, can fill a leisurely day or a busy afternoon. The Gardone Riviera prides itself on its must-see sight, the quirky mansion of famous author and lady's man Gabriele D'Annunzio. After dinner the sleepy towns call it a night. Nearby Riva has few sights, but the town is livelier, the crowd younger, and the prices lower. Here, travelers swim, windsurf, hike, and climb in the most visually stunning portion of the lake, where towering Alpine cliffs crash into the water below.

Desenzano, the lake's southern transportation hub, lies on the Milan-Venice train line, 30 minutes from **Verona** and **Brescia,** one hour from **Milan,** and two hours from **Venice.** From Desenzano, the other lake towns are easily accessible by bus, hydrofoil, or ferry. Plan ahead, as buses and ferries often stop running between 8 and 10pm. For shorter trips, take the ferry—it's cheaper than the hydrofoil. Buses cost even less but are less romantic. Though Campgrounds surround the lake, most are between Desenzano and **Salò**. Private residences rent rooms in Lake Garda's larger towns, and tourist offices can provide lists of potential hosts.

SIRMIONE ☎030

Shrewd developers realized the potential of what Catullus once lauded as the "jewel of peninsulas and islands." Sirmione is a bit like Disneyland—flashy, expensive, and quickly exhausted. The neon-lit medieval streets fill with families and retired couples ushering in Sirmione's holy trinity: dinner, shopping, and dessert. Even so, Sirmione can be downright fun. The crowded streets contain a palpable, if aged, electricity. The far northern tip of the peninsula trades this glitz for calm walks, Roman ruins, and stellar views across the lake.

NORTHEAST ITALY

TRANSPORTATION AND PRACTICAL INFORMATION. Sirmione is a thin peninsula at the southern end of the lake. Buses run every hour from **Desenzano** (20min., L2500) which has the closest train station; **Brescia** (1hr., L5800); and **Verona** (1hr., L5000). Buy tickets from the blue machine near the bus stop. **Navigazione Lago Garda** (toll-free ☎800 55 18 01 or 030 914 95 11) provides the easiest way to reach places along and across the lake. Battelli (water steamers) run until 8pm to **Desenzano** (20min., L4500); **Gardone** (1¼hr., L10,000); and **Riva** (4hr., L14,100). For **taxis,** dial ☎030 91 60 82 or 030 91 92 40. The **tourist office,** V. Guglielmo Marconi, 2, is in the disc-shaped building. (☎030 91 61 14. Open Apr.-Oct. daily 9am-9pm; Nov.-Mar. M-F 9am-12:30pm and 3-6pm, Sa 9am-12:30pm.) Sirmione's major attractions are concentrated in the north end of the peninsula, across the bridge from the tourist office. **Via Marconi** leads to **Via Vittorio Emanuele** and Sirmione's historic **castle.** The **Banca Popolare di Verona,** P. Castello, 3-4, across from the castle, has an **ATM**. (Open daily 9am-1:20pm and 2:35-3:35pm.) **Bikes** can be rented at **Adventure Sport,** V. Brescia, 9 (☎030 91 90 00). In **emergencies,** dial ☎113, the **Assistenza Sanitaria Turistica,** V. Alfieri, 6 (☎030 990 91 71), or the **police** (☎030 990 67 77). **Postal Code:** 25019.

ACCOMMODATIONS AND FOOD. Consider touring Sirmione as a daytrip—the hotels are either pricey or remote, and a thorough exploration of the town takes only an afternoon. If you do intend to stay overnight, head to the family-run **Albergo Grifone,** V. Bisse, 5, which has a prime location next to the castle and restaurants and a beach in back. All redwood and frilly curtained rooms offer views of the lake. (☎030 91 60 14; fax 030 91 65 48. Reservations necessary. Wheelchair accessible. Singles with bath L50,000; doubles with bath L88,000. Extra bed L27,000.) Campers should try **Sirmione,** V. Sirmioncino, 9, behind Hotel Benaco, 3km from town. Take the *Servizio Urbano* bus. (☎030 990 46 65; fax 030 91 90 45. Open Mar. 15-Oct. 15. L9-15,000 per person, L15-24,000 per site.)

For eating in Sirmione, the budgeteer has two options: gorge at one of the countless sidewalk pizza and *panino* stands on V. Emanuele or aim high and order creatively. **Pizzeria 4Re,** V. V. Emanuele, 72, is perhaps the cheapest place in swanky Sirmione. (☎030 91 60 24. Pizza L7500-14,000, *primi* L10-L13,000, *secondi* from L13,000. Service 15%. Open Tu-Su noon-2:30pm and 6:30-11pm. V, MC.) The **Ristorante Grifione,** downstairs from the *albergo* of the same name, is by all accounts a fancy restaurant. Nonetheless, you can sidestep the expensive bulk of the menu and enjoy artfully prepared fresh fish, a slice of superb almond cake, and a panoramic view of the lake for L26,000. (☎030 91 60 97. Cover L3500. Open Th-Tu noon-2:15pm and 7-10:15pm. V, MC, AmEx, Diners.) Sirmione's outdoor **market** in P. Montebaldo operates on Fridays from 8am to 1pm.

SIGHTS. The 13th-century **Castello Scaligero** sits in the center of town as a testament to the power of the warlike della Scala family that controlled the Veronese region from 1260-1387. (☎030 91 64 68. Open daily 9am-noon. L8000.) A handful of interesting sights (cannon balls, bricks, and dirt) lie inside, but most of the admission fee pays for the view from the towers. At the far end of the peninsula, the **Grotte di Catullo** houses ruins of a Roman villa. (☎030 91 61 57. Open Mar. to mid-Oct. Tu-Su 8:30am-7:30pm; Nov.-Feb. Tu-Su 9am-5pm. L8000.)

Between the castle and the ruins are two small public beaches and the **Chiesa di San Pietro in Mavino,** Sirmione's oldest church. San Pietro's stone walls and floors enclose a high, chalky-white space. A mix of 8th- and 16th-century frescoes adorn the walls, including a particularly disorienting one above the pulpit. The **Tomelleri Park** at the peninsula's northern tip offers a marvelous view of Sirmione's cliffs.

GARDONE RIVIERA ☎0365

Formerly the playground of the rich and famous, Gardone Riviera is now home to Lake Garda's most famous sight: Il Vittoriale, the villa of 20th-century poet and fanatic nationalist Gabriele D'Annunzio. Since D'Annunzio's death in 1938, Gardone has lost some of its spark. Gone are the days that inspired Casanova the Lover; today, you'll find Casanova the Retired. This new Gardone, however, enchants visitors with its glimpses into the lake's quiet lifestyle.

TRANSPORTATION AND PRACTICAL INFORMATION. Gardone's two main thoroughfares, Gardone Sotto and C. Zanardelli, intersect near the bus stop. **Buses** (☎0365 210 61 or 0365 800 41 25) run to: **Desenzano** (30min., 6 per day, L4100); **Brescia** (1hr., 2 per hr., L5000); and **Milan** (3hr., 2 per day, L15,500). You can purchase bus tickets at the **Molinari Viaggi Travel Agency,** P. Wimmer, 2, near the ferry stop. (☎0365 215 51. Open daily 8:30am-12:30pm and 2:30-7pm.) The **APT tourist office,** V. Repubblica, 8, in the center of Gardone Sotto, provides maps for scenic walks and accommodations information. (☎/fax 0365 203 47. Open July-Aug. 9am-1pm and 4-10pm; Nov.-Mar. M-W and F 9am-12:30pm and 3-6pm, Th 9am-12:30pm.) For **currency exchange,** head to the **Banco di Brescia,** across from the Grand Hotel. From the ferry dock, turn right and climb the stairs. (☎0365 200 81. Open M-F 8:25am-1:25pm and 2:40-3:40pm). In case of an **emergency,** dial ☎113, contact the **police** (☎112 or 0365 54 06 10), or call the **hospital** (☎0365 29 71). For **first aid** at night and on holidays, dial ☎0365 29 71. The **post office,** V. Roma, 8, is next door to the bank. (☎0365 208 62. Open M-F 8:10am-1:30pm, Sa 8:10-11:40am.) **Postal Code:** 25083.

ACCOMMODATIONS AND FOOD. Budget travelers should explore Gardone as a daytrip, since inexpensive accommodations are scarce. The **Hotel Nord,** V. Zanardelli, 18, has clean, dimly lit rooms. If your Italian isn't *abbastanza bene*, it may be difficult to secure one. (☎0365 207 07. Singles L45,000, with bath L65,000; doubles L60,000, with bath L70,000. Full and half-pension available for stays of at least 3 days.) **Pensione Hohl,** V. dei Colli, 4, has a lake view and a charming courtyard with bushes that spell out HOHL. Turn right onto C. Zanardelli from the ferry stop, then turn left onto V. dei Colli. (☎0365 201 60. Breakfast included. Singles L55,000; doubles L98,000.)

Trattoria Ristoro, V. Trieste, 18, serves marvelous, inexpensive food. With pink tablecloths, a motherly owner, and a friendly dog, Ristoro feels like home. From P. Vittoriale near the mansion, take V. Ofi Caduti to V. Carere to V. Trieste. (☎0365 209 86. Open F-W 12:30-3:30pm and 7-10pm.) Down the street from the tourist office towards the ferry stop, **Industria Caffe Regina,** V. S. Pietro, 28, is the perfect place to stop after a hectic day of lakeside relaxation. Indulge in the heavenly Austrian *Sachertorte* for L4500. (☎0376 63 90 79. Open Tu-Su 8:30am-5pm.)

SIGHTS AND ENTERTAINMENT. Above Gardone (off V. Roma and V. dei colli) sprawls **Il Vittoriale,** the estate of Gabriele D'Annunzio, the poet, novelist, and latter-day Casanova (see **Literature,** p. 21). Parked in the garden is the prow of the battleship Puglia, the emblem of D'Annunzio's popularity. His ultra-nationalistic stunts ranged from single-handedly piloting a plane to drop propaganda over Vienna to organizing an army of poetry-lovers to retake Fiume from infant Yugoslavia. Mussolini, who found D'Annunzio's squawking an embarrassment, presented the poet with this lovely rural villa in order to keep him quiet. In the following years, D'Annunzio stuffed his house with expensive and useless bric-à-brac. His bathroom, strewn with 2000 bizarre fragments and fixtures, demonstrates the Fascist rummage-sale effect; the *Sala del Mappamondo* reveals D'Annuzio's fantasies of global conquest, and the *Sala del Lebbroso* houses the cradle/coffin in which D'Annunzio contemplated both the concept of death and the colors of the nearby leopard skins. (☎0365 29 65 11; www.vittoriale.it. Villa open Apr.-Sept. Tu-Su 8:30am-8pm. Gardens open Oct.-Mar. Tu-Su 9am-5pm. Multilingual taped tours available. Visit the house early, before crowds arrive.)

To recover from the perversity, visit the **botanical gardens** on V. Roma. Though seemingly meager, the garden has lush greenery and quirky landscaping. At one point, two sculpted heads spit at each other across a bridge, daring visitors to cross. (Open Mar.-Oct. daily 9am-6:30pm. L9000.) The **Fondazione "al Vittoriale"** sponsors a summer program of plays, concerts, and dance performances in the outdoor **Teatro del Vittoriale.** (☎0365 201 30; ticket info ☎0365 215 51; fax 0365 223 52. Performances mid-July to early Aug. Tickets from L30,000.)

NORTHEAST ITALY

RIVA DEL GARDA ☎0464

You could spend an entire day just basking in the natural spectacle of Riva. The mountains seem to lean toward the city as they plummet to the water below. Even on the clearest of days, clouds cling to their peaks. For some, Riva, with its calm pebble beaches and wide *piazze*, lends a respite from touring and sight-seeing. For others, Riva is an entertainment center, complete with windsurfing, party cruises, archery, and rock climbing. Many visitors dabble in both Rivas.

TRANSPORTATION

Buses: Riva is easily accessible by bus (☎0464 55 23 23) from **Rovereto** (1hr., every hr. 5:05am-7:05pm, L3400); **Trent** (2hr., 6 per day 5:50am-6:15pm, L6000); and **Verona** (2hr., 11 per day 5:05am-8:30pm, L9300). For a train station, try Rovereto.

Ferries: Navigazione Lago di Garda (☎030 914 95 11), in P. Matteotti, services **Sirmione** (L13,900) and **Gardone** (L12,200). Also offers sightseeing tours from L24,000.

ORIENTATION AND PRACTICAL INFORMATION

To reach the town center from the station, walk straight onto Vle. Trento and then take **Via Roma** to **Piazza Cavour.**

Tourist office: Giardini di Porta Orientale, 8 (☎0464 55 44 44; fax 0464 52 03 08), near the water's edge and behind a small playground on V. della Liberazione. Competent and knowledgeable. Lists hotel vacancies and offers a variety of inexpensive tours of the region. Ask for a city map and hiking routes. Open M-Sa 9am-noon and 3-6pm.

Bike Rental: Superbike Girelli, V. Damiano Chiesa, 15/17 (☎0464 55 66 02). Mountain bikes L20,000 per day. Or **Fiori E Bike,** Vle. dei Tigli, 24 (☎0464 55 18 30). L18-25,000 per day. Ask for multiple-day discounts.

Emergencies: First aid: ☎118. **Alpine rescue:** V. Rovereto, 19/21 (☎0464 52 03 33).

Pharmacy: V. Dante Alighieri, 12c (☎0464 55 25 08), and V. Maffei, 8 (☎0464 55 23 02), in P. della Erbe. A doctor is on staff. Both open M-Sa 8:30am-12:30pm and 3:30-7:30pm, Su 9am-12:30pm and 4:30-7pm.

Internet Access: Clem's Bowling Club, Vle. D. Chiesa, 4 (☎0464 55 35 96). L15,000 per hr. Open M-Sa 7pm-1am, Su 3pm-1am.

Post Office: (☎0464 55 23 46), on Largo Bensheim. Issues **traveler's checks** and **changes money.** Open M-Sa 8:10am-6:30pm. **Postal Code:** 38066.

ACCOMMODATIONS AND CAMPING

Riva is one of Lake Garda's few affordable destinations. Although an off-season visit may require little planning, July and August trips demand reservations months in advance.

Ostello Benacus (HI), P. Cavour, 9 (☎0464 55 49 11; fax 0464 55 65 54; www.garda.com/ostelloriva), in the center of town. From the bus station, walk down V. Trento, take V. Roma, turn left under the arch, and follow the signs. The hostel features hot showers, satellite TV, a VCR, old-school toilets, cabinets with locks, and a dining hall. Reception daily 7-9am and 3pm-midnight. Breakfast, sheets, and shower included. Book ahead. 100 beds. Dorms L22,000.

Locanda La Montanara, V. Montanara, 20 (☎/fax 0464 55 48 57). At V. Dante, 47, face the mountains, turn left onto V. Florida, proceed through the arches, and turn right onto V. Montanara. Cozy, bright, and comfortable. Breakfast L8000. Half- and full pension provided in the downstairs *trattoria* for L20-40,000. Reserve a month ahead in summer. Open Easter to mid-Oct. Singles L30,000; doubles with bath L66,000.

Camping: For a complete list of campgrounds, including many year-round options, call ☎0461 91 44 44. **Bavaria,** V. Rovereto, 100 (☎0464 55 25 24; fax 0464 55 91 26), on the road toward Torbole, has an excellent location on the water with a pizzeria on the premises. Filled with die-hard windsurfing families, it has its own windsurfing school and rental, as well as sailing, canoeing, and swimming options. Open Apr.-Oct. L9-11,000 per person, L16,000 per site. Hot showers L1500. **Monte Brione,** V. Brione, 32 (☎0464 52 08 85 or 0464 52 08 90; fax 0464 55 65 48), offers a 1st-rate campground with swimming pool, washing machine, electricity, and free hot showers. L8300-12,500 per person, L20,000 per site.

FOOD

A small **open-air market** sells fruits and vegetables in P. della Erbe. (Open M-Sa mornings.) The Orvea supermarket sells staples on V. S. Francesco, inland from the tourist office. (Open Tu-Sa 8:30am-12:30pm and 2-7pm; Su-M 8:30am-12:30pm.)

Alimar SRL, P. Cavour, 6 (☎0464 55 53 78), next to the hostel, provides the usual *mensa* combo of institutional appearances and prices. Not the tastiest meal around, but *primo, secondo,* and dessert are only L14,000. Open Sa-M 7am-2pm.

Pizzeria alla Rada, V. Fiume, 20 (☎0464 55 73 45). This pizzeria will send your taste buds whirling. The low-arched rooms and kitschy decor provide ample charm. Sample the delicious and affordable local wines. Pizza from L8500, *primi* L10-15,000, *secondi* L15-23,000. *Menù* L19,000; fish *menù* L35,000. Cover L1000. Open Tu-Su 11:30am-2pm and 6-11pm.

Le 4 Stagioni, V. Maffei, 24 (☎0464 55 27 77), just off P. delle Erbe. A delightful respite from harbor-side chic. Outdoor tables and cozy fare weighted on the Mediterranean side. Pizzas L9-12,000. Open Th-Tu noon-3pm and 7:30-11:30pm.

Gelateria Kiosketto, V. Montanara, 52, near V. Fabbri. The best *gelato* in town. Perfectly natural fruit flavors. Cones start at L1500. Open M-Sa 2pm-midnight.

SIGHTS AND ENTERTAINMENT

For fresh-water swimming, pebbly sunbathing, or stunning lake-gazing, follow the lake-side path behind the tourist office and head away from the mountains.

WATERFALL. Outside of Riva, 3km away, the waterfall at **Cascato Varone** has chiseled a huge gorge in the mountain. The falls were once accessible to rock climbers hanging from the mountain peak; visitors now opt for the stairs. *(☎0464 52 14 21. Open May-Aug. daily 9am-7pm; Oct. and Mar. daily 10am-12:30pm and 2-5pm; Apr. and Sept. daily 9am-6pm; Nov.-Feb. Su 10am-12:30pm and 2-5pm. L7000, student groups L3000.)*

FUN FOR THE FAMILY. Seventy kilometers from Riva del Garda is the non-Disney affiliated amusement park called, well, **Gardaland.** Diversions include rollercoasters, a "dolphinarium," and medieval jousts. *(From Riva, hourly APT buses head to Peschiera del Garda, from which a Gardaland-run bus service heads to the park (every hr. 8:50am-10:15pm). There is also a direct bus service from Riva to Gardaland Tu and Th 8:30am and 4:05pm, round-trip L50,000. Gardaland info and buses ☎045 644 97 77. L38,000, children less than 1m tall free. Open late Mar. to late Oct. Hours vary.)*

FUN FOR YOUR LIVER. For nightlife, consider an evening on one of the **party boats** (☎0464 914 95 11) that cruise across the lake to Latin techno beats (cover L22,000, includes one drink; cruises July 27-Aug.). Back on the mainland, the party pumps with a mostly German crowd at **Discoteca Tiffany,** at Giardini di Porta Orientale, across from the tourist office. (☎0464 55 25 12. Disco bar Su-Th; disco dance club F-Sa). Ask at the tourist office for listing of free **concerts.**

HIKING AND OTHER ACTIVITIES. On the other side of town, follow V. Dante up to the mountains and take trail #404 for a steep hike (1½hr.) up to **Chiesetta Santa Barbara** and a breathtaking view of the entire valley. The tourist office dispenses pamphlets on hiking, climbing, canoeing, riding, and golfing opportunities.

WINDSURFING. Two windsurfing schools offer lessons and rent out equipment: **Professional Windsurfing School** (c/o Camping Bavaria; ☎0464 55 60 77; ☎/fax 0464 50 09 63), and **Nautic Club Riva,** V. Rovereto, 44 (☎0464 55 24 53). Expect to pay L70,000 or more for a one-day rental. Ask about hourly or half-day rental or one-week packages that include lessons and equipment.

ROVERETO ☎0464

Rovereto sees tourists in transit from the east and north shores of Lake Garda; its hostel is exceptional as a base for daytrips and athletic excursions into the countryside surroundings. If you're biding time in town, the **Castello di Rovereto,** V. Castelbarco, 7, is Rovereto's most important sight. The **Museo della Guerra** (Museum of War), inside the castle, opened in 1921. (☎0464 43 81 00. Open June-Nov. Tu-Su 8:30am-12:30pm and 2-6pm. Castle L6000; museum L10,000.)

The **tourist office,** V. Dante, 63 (☎0464 43 03 63; www.apt.rovereto.tn.it), next to the public park in the center of town, can fill you in on the latest trekking, biking, rock climbing, and skiing offerings in the area. **Buses** run frequently to **Riva** (1hr., every hr., L3700) and **Trent** (30min., 18 per day, L4200). From the **Stazione,** V. Rosmini, 41-45, **trains** run to **Trent** (15min., 1-2 per hr., L4200); **Verona** (1hr., 1-2 per hr., L6100); **Bolzano** (1hr., 1-2 per hr., L7900); **Milan** (2½hr., 3 per day, L21,000); and **Bologna** (3hr., every hr., L16,100). To get from the bus station to the train station, turn right onto C. Rosmini and walk to the end. Self-service **luggage storage** is at platform #1. (L4000 for 6hr. Open 24hr.)

The **police station** is at Largo Carlo Alberto della Chiesa, 5. Follow the signs directly across the street from the train station. A **pharmacy** lies conveniently between the bus and train station at V. Dante, 3. (☎0464 42 10 30. Open M-F 8:30am-noon and 3-8pm.) An **ATM/change machine** is in the train station. The **post office** is uphill from the bus station. **Postal Code:** 38068.

Although Rovereto's hotels are either high on price or high on industrial atmosphere, the city has an extraordinary hostel, the **Ostello della Gioventù "Città di Rovereto" (HI),** V. delle Scuole, 16/18. Turn right from the bus station onto V.

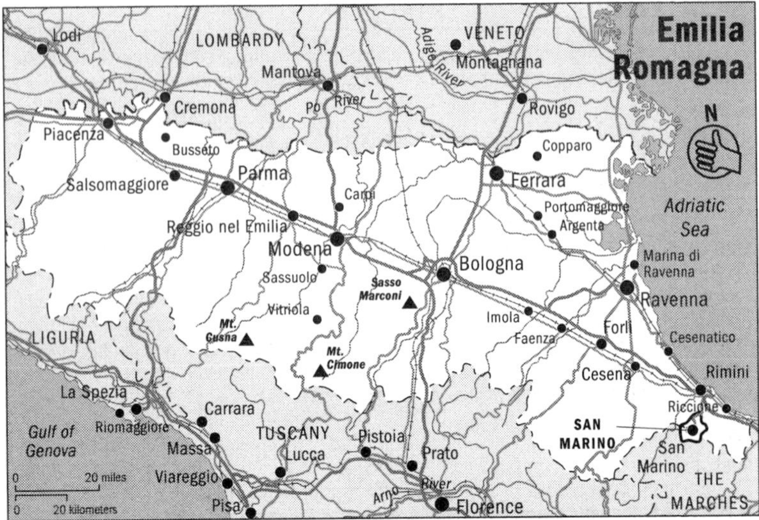

Rosmini and right again onto V. Stoppani. This mom 'n' pop hostel offers a lounge, laundry service, a restaurant that keeps a place set for every guest, and a garden tended by the owners. (☎0464 43 37 07; fax 0464 42 41 37; email youthostrov@tqs.it. Wheelchair accessible. Breakfast and sheets included. Reception 7-10am and 4-11:30pm; in winter 7-9am and 5-10:30pm. Reserve ahead during the summer, Christmas, and Easter seasons. 2- to 6-bed dorms L21,000; family rooms L25,000 per person; singles L25,000.) For groceries, try the **supermarket,** V. Rosmini, 76b. (Open M 3:30-7:30pm; Tu-Sa 8:30am-12:30pm and 3:30-7:30pm.)

EMILIA-ROMAGNA

Go to Florence, Venice, and Rome to sightsee. Come to Emilia-Romagna to eat. Italy's wealthiest wheat- and dairy-producing region covers the fertile plains of the Po River Valley and fosters the finest culinary traditions on the Italian Peninsula. Gorge yourself on Parmesan cheese and *prosciutto*, Bolognese fresh pasta and *mortadella*, and Ferrarese *salama* and *grana* cheese. Complement these dishes with such regional wines as Parma's sparkling red *Lambrusco*.

Although the Romans originally settled this region, most of the visible ruins are remnants of medieval structures. Developed as autonomous *communi*, the towns later fell under the rule of great Renaissance families whose names still adorn every *palazzo* and *piazza* in the region. Outside the towns, the uninterrupted plains seem to stretch forever, and the cold gray fog of winter—replaced in summer by silver haze and stifling heat—magnifies the illusion of distance. Emilia-Romagna, a stronghold of the left since the 19th-century rise of the Italian Socialist movement, looks and feels different from the rest of Italy.

HIGHLIGHTS OF EMILIA-ROMAGNA

SPORT those specs in a dark cafe and eavesdrop on impassioned political arguments among the intellectuals of **Bologna** after a long day of church hopping (see below).

DON'T FALL ASLEEP, because *Nessun' dorme* in **Modena,** where Ferraris rev their engines and Pavarotti serenades (p. 277).

FEAST on **Parma**'s palatable *prosciutto* and *parmigiano* (p. 284).

GO TO PIECES over **Ravenna**'s spectacular golden Byzantine mosaics (p. 286).

SPORTS

See the pride of Bologna play all major Italian soccer teams and join in the celebration when they claim victory at **Stadio Comunale,** V. Andrea Costa, 174 (☎051 24 94 09 or 051 61 45 391). Take bus #21 from the train station or #14 from Porta Isaia. The season runs from September to June, with games on Sunday afternoons. Tickets for games against popular clubs such as Juventus or AC Milan tend to sell fast.

FERRARA ☎0532

Rome has its mopeds, Venice its boats, and Ferrara its bicycles. Old folks, young folks, and babies perched precariously on handlebars whirl by on Ferrara's jumble of major thoroughfares and twisting medieval roads inaccessible to automobiles. Grab a bike yourself and enjoy the pink church or occasional giant castle. Ferrara earned its laurels as the home of the Este dynasty from 1208 to 1598. When they weren't murdering relatives, these sensitive rulers proved to be some of the most enlightened patrons of their age. Their court and university attracted Petrarch, Mantegna, and Titian. Ercole I's early 16th-century city plan broke ground with its open, harmonious design, and the modern theater (with curtains, stage, and seated audience) was invented here. The balding dukes eventually went heirless, and their legacy succumbed to two centuries of neglect. Ferrara has bounced back, however, kept lively by visitors, vendors, and outdoor performances and festivals.

TRANSPORTATION

Trains: Ferrara is on the Bologna-Venice train line. To: **Bologna** (30min., 1-2 per hr. 1:42am-9:38pm, L4900); **Ravenna** (1hr., 1-3 per hr. 6:12am-8:15pm, L6700); **Padua** (1hr., every hr. 3:52am-11:07pm, L7600); **Venice** (2hr., 1-2 per hr. 3:52am-10:11pm, L10,800); and **Rome** (3-4hr., 7 per day 7:47am-7:25pm, L57,200). Ticket office open 7am-9pm. **Luggage Storage:** L3-4000 for 6hr. Open 24hr.

Buses: ACFT (☎0532 59 94 92) and **GGFP.** Main terminal on V. Rampari S. Paolo; most buses also leave from the train station. From the #2 bus stop, turn onto V. S. Paolo and head to the building labeled *biglietteria.* Open 6:15am-8pm. To Ferrara's **beaches** (1hr., 12 per day 7:30am-6:50pm, L7600-8400) and **Bologna** (1½hr.; M-Sa 15 per day 5:20am-7:50pm; Su 10:50am, 1:55, and 6:20pm; L6000). Buses to **Modena** depart from the train station (1½hr.; M-Sa every hr. 6:22am-7:32pm, Su 8:22am and 1:02pm; L8400).

Taxi: Radiotaxi (☎0532 90 09 00). Open 24hr.

NORTHEAST ITALY

ORIENTATION AND PRACTICAL INFORMATION

To get to the center of town, turn left out of the train station and then veer right on **Viale Costituzione.** This road becomes **Viale Cavour** and runs to the **Castello Estense** (1km). Or take bus #2 to the "Castello" stop or bus #1 or 9 to the post office (every 15-20min. 7am-8:20pm, L1400). Past the Castello Estense, V. Cavour changes its name to **Corso Giovecca. Corso Porta Reno,** perpendicular to V. Cavour, heads south to **Piazza Travaglio.**

Tourist Office: (☎0532 20 93 70; www.comune.fe.it), in Castello Estense. Well stocked. Knowledgeable staff discusses everything from local politics to restaurants. Open daily 9am-1pm and 2-6pm.

Currency Exchange: Banca Nazionale de Lavoro, C. Porta Reno, 19, near P. Cattedrale. Open M-F 8:30am-1:30pm and 3:05-4:35pm, Sa 8:30am-noon. A 24hr. **ATM** is in the train station and at V. Garibaldi, #6/a, near the intersection with V. degli Spadari.

Bike Rental: C. Giovecca, 21. L4000 per hr., L20,000 per day. Open daily 9:30am-1pm and 3:30-7pm. Cheaper bikes at P. Stazione (☎0532 77 21 90). L12,000 per day. Open M-F 5:30am-8pm, Sa 6am-2pm; in winter M-F 5:30am-8pm, Sa 6am-6pm.

Emergencies: ☎113. **Ambulance:** ☎118. **Red Cross:** ☎0532 20 94 00. **Hospital: Ospedale Sant'Anna,** C. Giovecca, 203 (☎0532 23 61 11; emergency ☎0532 20 31 31). **Police:** C. Ercole I d'Este, 26 (☎0532 29 43 11), off Largo Castello.

24-Hour Pharmacy: Fides, C. Giovecca, 125 (☎0532 20 25 24). **Comunale no. 1,** C. Porta Mare, 114 (☎0532 75 32 84).

Internet Access: Internet Point, V. S. Romano, 123 (☎0532 76 98 31). L15,000 per hr. Open M-Sa 4-8pm; in winter 3:30-7:30pm. **Centri Servizi Link,** V. Ariosto, 57/a (☎0532 24 15 79). L12,000 per hr. Open daily 9am-1pm and 3-4:30pm.

Post Office: V. Cavour, 29 (☎0532 20 75 12), a block toward the train station from the *castello.* Fermo Posta available. Open M-Sa 8:15am-7pm. **Postal Code:** 44100.

ACCOMMODATIONS AND CAMPING

Ferrara has a few nice budget hotels, but they fill quickly, so reserve ahead. If you choose not to stay in Ferrara, you can visit as a daytrip from Bologna or Modena.

Ostello della Gioventù Estense (HI), C. B. Rossetti, 24 (☎/fax 0532 20 42 27), down C. Ercole I d'Este from the *castello,* or take bus #4c from the station and ask for the *castello* stop. Simple rooms with bunk beds and exposed-beam ceilings only a short walk from the town center. 84 beds. Reception 7-10am and 3:30-11:30pm. Lockout 10am-3:30pm. Curfew 11:40pm. Dorms L23,000; family rooms L23,000.

Casa degli Artisti, V. Vittoria, 66 (☎0532 76 10 38), near P. Lampronti, in the historic center. From the *duomo,* head down C. Porta Reno, turn left on V. Ragno, then left on V. Vittoria. 20 large rooms, some with carpet. Reserve 4 days in advance July-Sept. Singles L34,000; doubles L60,000, with bath L85,000.

Albergo Nazionale, C. Porta Reno, 32 (☎/fax 0532 20 96 04), on a busy street right off the *duomo.* 20 clean, eclectically decorated rooms with telephone and TV. Curfew 12:30am. Singles L65,000, with bath L80,000; doubles with bath L120,000; triples L145,000. V, MC, AmEx.

Albergo San Paolo, V. Baluardi, 9 (☎/fax 0532 76 20 40). Walk down C. Porta Reno from the *duomo.* At P. Travaglio, turn left onto V. Baluardi. 32 new, modern rooms with TV, phone, and bath. Newer section has coveted A/C. Rents bikes and arranges excursions. Singles L90,000; doubles L130,000; triples L160,000. V, MC, AmEx.

Hotel de Prati, V. Padiglioni, 5 (☎0532 24 19 05 or 0532 51 67 38; fax 0532 24 19 66), off L. Ercole I d'Este near Castello Estense. Brand-new 3-star hotel with excellent rates. Yellow hallways are artfully decorated, and a dozen rooms feature red-tiled floors, classy wood-beamed ceilings, A/C, TV, phones, and pre-stocked fridge. Singles L80-125,000; doubles L120-195,000. V, MC, AmEx.

Camping: Estense, V. Gramicia, 76 (☎/fax 0532 75 23 96), 1km from the city center. Take bus #1 to P. S. Giovanni (L1400). From the church next to the bus stop another bus heads straight to the campground (every 20min. 2-8:20pm). Bus route is temporary, so check with the ACFT office in the train station before you head off. Open year-round 8am-10pm. L8000 per person, L12,000 per car.

FOOD

In Ferrara, gorge on *cappelletti,* delicious triangular meat *ravioli* served in a broth, or *cappellacci,* stuffed with pumpkin and served in a light sauce of butter and sage. The gastronomic glory of the city is its robust *salama da sugo,* an aged sausage served cold (with melon) in the summer and hot in the winter. The traditional *Ferrarese* dessert is a chunk of luscious *pampepato,* a chocolate-covered almond and fruit cake. **Negozio Moccia,** V. degli Spadari, 19, sells *pampepato* in various sizes. (☎0532 20 97 72. 750g for L24,000. Open M-Sa 9am-1pm and 3-8:30pm.) For picnic supplies, stop by the **Mercato Comunale,** on V. Mercato, off V. Garibaldi and next to the *duomo.* (Open M-W 7am-1:30pm and 4:30-7:30pm, Th and Sa 7am-1:30pm, F 4:30-7:30pm.) For wine, try the slightly sparkling *Uva D'Oro*

(Golden Grape), compliments of the slightly insane Renata Di Francia, who brought the grapes from France for her 16th-century marriage to Duca D'Ercole II d'Este. All food stores in Ferrara are closed Thursday afternoons.

Osteria Al Brindisi, V. G. degli Adelardi, 9b (☎0532 20 91 42). Today, the oldest *osteria* in Italy grooves to Motown classics, and the young owner's trumpet playing floats from the back room. Hip crowds dine on unbelievably inexpensive traditional dishes. Recently blessed by a full-fledged cardinal, so dig in without fear–Copernicus, Cellini, and Pope John Paul II have all done it. Try delicious *panini* (L5000) paired with one of the 600 varieties of wine (L1000-14,000 per glass). *Menù* L30,000. Open Tu-Su 8:30am-1am. V, MC.

Trattoria Da Noemi, V. Ragno, 31a (☎0532 76 17 15), off C. Porta Reno. The smells of Ferrarese cooking have wafted out of this quiet, traditional *trattoria* for over 30 years. The *salamina* (L10,000) is as succulent as ever, and a plate of the homemade *lasagne* (L10,000) makes for a divine dinner. A veranda stretches out in back. *Secondi* L9-10,000. Cover L2500. Open W-M noon-2:30pm and 7:30-11pm.

SIGHTS

Ferrara is best seen by bicycle. Explore the tranquil wooded concourse that runs along the 9km well-preserved medieval wall of the city, beginning at the far end of C. Giovecca. Alternatively, cruise with locals along the exclusively bicycle and pedestrian V. Garibaldi.

CASTELLO ESTENSE. Towered, turreted, and moated, Castello Estense stands precisely in the center of town. Corso della Giovecca lies along the former route of the moat's feeder canal, separating the medieval section from the part planned by the d'Este's architect, Biagio Rosetti. Marquis Nicholas II built the fortress to protect himself from disgruntled tax-paying masses. The Salone dei Giochi and the surrounding rooms retain rich ceiling frescoes—the best are in the Loggetta degli Aranci. The legendary dungeons below are open for roaming. Parisina, the wife of Duke Nicolò d'Este III, was killed with her lover, the Duke's son Ugolino, in this damp prison. This incestuous tragedy inspired Browning to pen "My Last Duchess." *(☎0532 29 92 33. Open Tu-Su 9:30am-5pm. L8000, reduced L6000.)*

DUOMO. Reshaped by every noble with designs on Ferrara, the cathedral and castle remain the effective center of town. Rosetti designed the tall slender arches and terra-cotta ornamented apse, and Alberti executed the pink campanile. Faux rose windows decorate the facade. Upstairs, the **Museo della Cattedrale** displays Cosmè Tura's 15th-century *San Giorgio* and *Annunciation*, both from the Ferrarese school. *(From the castello, take C. Martiri della Libertà to P. Cattedrale. Cathedral open M-Sa 7:30am-noon and 3-6:30pm, Su 7:30am-12:30pm and 4-7:30pm. Museum ☎0532 20 74 49. Museum open Tu-Sa 10am-noon and 3-5pm, Su and holidays 10am-noon and 4-6pm.)*

PALAZZO DIAMANTI. Built in 1493 by Biagio Rossetti, this palace outshines all other ducal residences. Inside, the **Pinacoteca Nazionale** contains many of the best works of the Ferrarese school. Most impressive are Carpaccio's *Passing of the Virgin* (1508) and Garofalo's incredibly detailed *Massacre of the Innocents*. *(Pinacoteca ☎0532 20 58 44. From Castello Estense, cross Largo Castello to C. Ercole I d'Este and walk to the corner of C. Rossetti. Open Tu-W and F-Sa 9am-2pm, Th 9am-7pm, Su and holidays 9am-1pm. L8000, reduced L4000.)*

PALAZZO MASSARI. Once a 16th-century residence, the palace now houses a museum complex. The **Museo d'Arte Moderna e Contemporanea "Filippo de Pisis"** showcases work by contemporary painters and traces the progression of artist Filippo de Pisis's work. Upstairs, the spectacular **Museo Ferrarese dell'Ottocentro/Museo Giovanni Boldini** has a vast collection of Boldini's work alongside two depictions of Ferrara's native son by Edgar Degas. *(C. Porta Mare, 9. Follow C. Ercole I d'Este behind the castello and turn right on C. Porta Mare. ☎0532 20 69 14. Both museums open daily 9am-1pm and 3-6pm. Pisis L4000; Ottocentro/Boldini L8000; cumulative ticket L10,000.)*

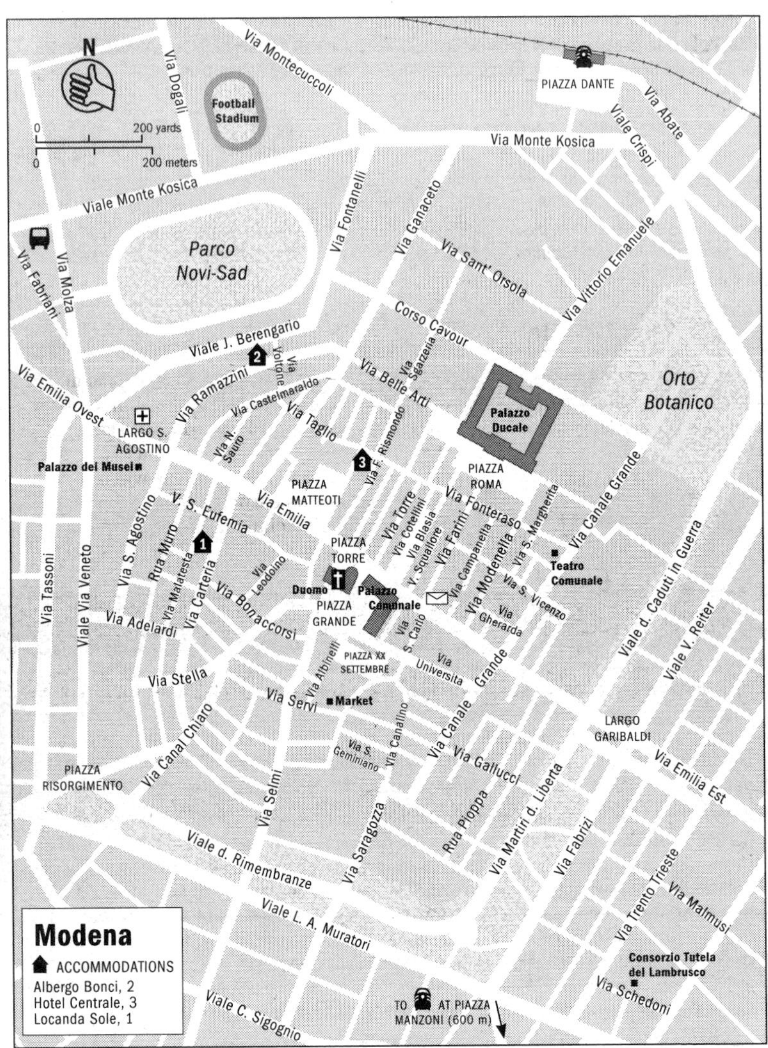

CASA ROMEI. This 15th-century dwelling of a Ferrarese merchant is filled with some of the most richly decorated rooms of the period. The museum displays statues and frescoes salvaged from destroyed churches in Ferrara. *(V. Savonarola, 30. ☎0532 24 03 41. From behind the duomo, turn left and then right on V. Voltapaletto, which becomes V. Savonarola. Open Tu-Sa 8:30am-7:30pm and Su 8:30am-2pm. Hours are flexible, so call ahead. L4000, students L2000.)*

PALAZZO SCHIFANOIA. Only the carved door of the Palazzo Schifanoia hints at the wealth of art inside. The Saloni dei Mesi's magnificent frescoes offer vivid depictions of the 15th-century court. *(V. Scandiana, 23. From P. Cattedrale follow V. Adelardi to V. Voltapaletto and to V. Savonarola. Turn right on V. Madama and left on V. Scandiana. ☎0532 641 78. Open daily 9am-7pm. L8000, students L4000. Cumulative ticket for Palazzo Schifanoia and Palazzina Marfisa L10,000, reduced L5000.)*

PALAZZINA DI MARFISA D'ESTE. Here you'll find a splendid, recently restored, late Renaissance palace in miniature. *(C. Giovecca, 170. Follow C. Gioveca from Largo Castello, or take bus #9 (L1400). ☎0532 20 74 50. Open daily 9:30am-1pm and 3-6pm. L4000, students L3000. 1st Monday of the month free.)*

CIMITERO EBRAICO (JEWISH CEMETARY). Here the Finzi and Contini, the main characters of Bassani's influential *Il Giardino dei Finzi-Contini* (see **The Modern and Postmodern,** p. 23), lie buried along with most of Ferrara's 19th- and 20th-century Jewish community. A monument commemorates Ferrarese Jews murdered at Auschwitz. *(At the end of V. Vigne. From the castello, head down C. Giovecca. Turn left on V. Montebello and continue to V. Vigne. ☎0532 75 13 37. Open Su-F Apr.-Sept. 9am-6pm; Oct.-Mar. 9am-4:30pm.)*

ENTERTAINMENT

Each year on the last Sunday of May, Ferrara recreates the ancient **Palio di San Giorgio** (information ☎0532 75 12 63). This event, dating from the 13th century, begins with a lively procession of delegates from the city's eight *contrade* (districts) followed by a series of four races in P. Ariostea: the boy's race, the girl's race, the donkey race, and, finally, the great horse race. The flag-waving ceremony of the eight *contrade* takes place two weeks earlier in P. del Municipio. During the 3rd or 4th week of August, street musicians and performers from near and far come to display their street music talents in the **Busker's Festival** (☎0532 24 93 37; www.ferrarabuskers.com).

In July and August, a free **Discobus** service runs every Saturday night between Ferrara and the hottest clubs. Call ☎0532 59 94 11 for info, or pick up fliers in the train station. **Pelledoca,** V. Arianuova, 21 (☎0532 24 89 52), just north of the historic center, and **RENFE,** just south at V. Bologne, 17 (☎0532 90 04 57), are the two best clubs in Ferrara proper. (Both open F-Su after 10pm.)

NORTHEAST ITALY

MODENA ☎059

Home to prestigious makers of both music and cars, Modena claims both Luciano Pavarotti and the Ferrari and Maserati factories—and it purrs with prosperity. Conquered by the Romans in the 3rd century BC, the city owed its early prominence to its principal road, Via Emilia, which runs through the heart of town. Modena offers few sights, but with its colorful buildings, tantalizing food, and peaceful atmosphere, the city is among the most livable in Emilia-Romagna.

TRANSPORTATION

Trains: (☎1478 880 88), in P. Dante Alighieri. To: **Bologna** (30min., every hr., L4100); **Parma** (30min., 2 per hr., L5100); and **Milan** (2hr., every hr., L16,000). Train information 8am-7pm. **Luggage Storage:** L3-5000 per 6hr.

Buses: ATCM (☎059 22 22 20), on V. Fabriani, off V. Monte Kosica (to the right from the train station). To **Ferrara** (every hr., L8400) and **Maranello** (every 1-2hr., L3900).

Taxis: V. Viterbo, 82b (☎059 37 42 42).

ORIENTATION AND PRACTICAL INFORMATION

Modena lies roughly midway between Parma and Bologna. From the train station, take bus #7 or 11 (L1700) to **Piazza Grande** and the center of town. Or walk left out of the station on V. Galvini and turn right on V. Monte Kosica. The 2nd left, V. Ganaceto, leads directly to **Via Emilia.** Turn left on V. Emilia and walk several blocks to P. Torre, which opens into **Piazza Grande** on the left. V. Emilia changes names and street numbers from **Via Emilia Ovest** on the west side of the center, to **Via Emilia Centro** in the center, and then to **Via Emilia Est** on the east.

Tourist Office: P. Grande, 17 (email iatmo@comune.modena.it, ☎059 20 66 60; fax 059 20 66 59;), across from the back of the *duomo*. A warehouse of facts and maps available on computers. In the same office as **Informazione Città** (☎059 20 65 80) and **Informagiovani** (☎059 20 65 83), geared specifically to young people. Open M-Tu and Th-Sa 8:30am-1pm and 3-7pm, W 8:30am-1pm.

Currency Exchange: Credito Italiano, V. Emilia Centro, 102 (☎059 41 21 11), across from V. Scudari. Take a ticket at the door. Open M-F 8:20am-1:20pm and 3-4:30pm, Sa 8:20-11:20am. **ATMs:** in the Rolo Banca 1473 building, on P. Grande.

Emergencies: ☎118. **First Aid:** ☎059 36 13 71 or 059 43 72 71. **Ambulance: Blue Cross** (☎059 34 24 24). **Hospital: Ospedale Civile** (☎059 43 51 11), in P. S. Agostino. **Police:** V. Amendola, 152 (☎113 or 059 20 07 00).

Late-Night Pharmacy: Farmacia Comunale, V. Emilia Est, 416 (☎059 36 00 91). Open nightly 8pm-8am.

Internet Access: Informagiovane, at the tourist office in P. Grande. Must have a valid ID. No Hotmail. Registration L2500. L5000 for 2hr., L10,000 for 5hr. Open M-Tu and Th-Sa 8:30am-1pm and 3-7pm, W 8:30am-1pm.

Post Office: V. Emilia Centro, 86 (☎059 24 35 09 or 059 24 21 37). Open M-Sa 8:15am-7:15pm. **Postal Code:** 41100.

ACCOMMODATIONS AND CAMPING

Albergo Bonci, V. Ramazzini, 59 (☎059 22 36 34), a short walk from the center of town. From V. Ganaceto, turn right on V. Cerca, which becomes V. Ramazzini. Dimly lit but clean rooms. No rooms with bath. Singles L50-60,000; doubles L80-90,000. V, MC.

Locanda Sole, V. Malatesta, 45 (☎059 21 42 45), 100m from P. Grande. From the train station on V. Ganaceto, turn right on V. Emilia Centro, and take the 2nd left on V. Malatesta. Clean, cool rooms (none with bath, but some with TV and extra-springy mattresses). English spoken. Reservations recommended. Closed 1st 3 weeks of Aug. Singles L45,000; doubles L80,000.

Hotel Centrale, V. Rismondo, 55 (☎059 21 88 08; fax 059 23 82 01; email info@hotelcentrale.com; www.hotelcentrale.com), just a few blocks from the *duomo*. A modern 3-star hotel with reasonable rates. Comfortable rooms equipped with baths, A/C, TVs, and phones. Breakfast L15,000. Singles L90,000; doubles L140,000. V, MC, AmEx.

Camping: International Camping Modena, V. Cave Ramo, 111 (☎059 33 22 52), in Località Bruciata. Take bus #19 (direction: Rubiera, 6:20am-8:30pm) west from the station for about 10min. Ask the driver and he will let you off within 500m of the site. Open Mar.-Sept. L11,000 per adult, under 9 L8000; L17,000 per tent.

FOOD

The area around Modena has some of the most fertile soil on the Italian peninsula, which results in a bounty of produce. Modena, like nearby Bologna and Parma, produces unsurpassed *prosciutto crudo* and the sparkling *lambrusco* red wine. Modena's own claim to culinary fame derives from the curiously tame but fragrant and full-bodied balsamic vinegar that the Modenese sprinkle liberally over salads, vegetables, and even fruit. Balsamic vinegar is often aged for decades, and a bottle of the finest vinegar can empty your wallet of more than L100,000. Top off a meal with the local *vignola* cherries, considered some of the tastiest in Italy.

Stock picnic baskets at the **Mercato Albinelli,** a few steps down V. Albinelli from P. XX Settembre. Locals come to this food bazaar to haggle over prices for everything from fruit and vegetables to squid and snails. (Open M-Sa 6:30am-2pm; Sept.-May M-F 6:30am-2pm, Sa 6:30am-2pm and 5-7pm.) Sample fresh Modenese cuisine at the weekly **market** in the Parco Novi Sad. (Open M 7:30am-1:30pm.)

Mensa Il Chiostro, V. S. Geminiano, 3 (☎059 23 04 30), in the courtyard of an antique cloister. Turn to the right as you enter the archway. From V. Emilia, turn onto V. San

PIACENZA ☎0523

Recently voted one of Italy's most hospitable cities, Piacenza makes a good stopover on a trip to Parma, Bologna, or Milan. The hamlet abstains from a tourist economy, and though it houses a few noteworthy monuments of the Renaissance and the Middle Ages, there's not enough to see to make it worth an overnight.

GETTING THERE AND GETTING AROUND

Trains: (☎0523 32 12 63 or 0523 39 91 11), in P. Marconi. Piacenza lies on the main line between **Milan** (1hr., every hr., L9500) and **Bologna** (1½hr., every hr., L12,700). A secondary line runs to **Turin** (2½hr., 9 per day, L25,200) via **Alessandria. Luggage storage:** L5000 for 12hr. Open daily 8am-5pm.

Taxis: ☎0523 59 19 19.

ORIENTATION AND PRACTICAL INFORMATION

To reach **Piazza del Duomo** from the train station, walk along the left side of the park on V. dei Mille, and turn right on V. Giulio Alberoni. Bear right onto V. Roma and then turn left onto V. Daveri, which leads to the *piazza*. From there, V. XX Settembre leads straight to **Piazza dei Cavalli.**

Tourist office: IAT, P. Mercanti, 7 (☎/fax 0523 32 93 24; iat@comune.piacenza.it; www.provincia.piacenza.it/turismo), in the Palazzo Farnese. Very friendly English-speaking staff. Open Tu-Sa 9:30am-12:30pm and 3-6pm, Su 9:30am-12:30pm. **Ufficio Relazione con il Pubblico,** P. Cavalli, 7 (tel. 0523 49 22 24). Info on hotels, restaurants, and attractions. Open Tu-W 9am-1pm, M and Th 9am-1pm and 3-6pm, F-Sa 9am-1pm.

Emergency: Ambulances: tel. 118. **Hospital: Ospedale Civile da Piacenza,** V. G. Taverna, 49 (tel. 0523 30 11 11).

Post office: V. Sant'Antonino, 38-40 (tel. 0523 31 64 11). Open M-Sa 8:30am-6pm. **Postal Code:** 29100.

ACCOMMODATIONS AND FOOD

Look for budget accommodations near the train station or in the *centro storico.* Try the **Hotel Astra**, V. R. Boselli, 19. Ten simple, but spotless rooms above a neat street cafe. Open 24hr. Reserve ahead. (tel. 0523 45 43 64. Singles L45,000; doubles L60,000.) **Protezione delle Giovane,** V. Tempio, 26, is close to the *centro.* From P. dei Cavalli, walk left down C. V. Emanuele and take the third right. The nuns keep the 15 rooms immaculate. (tel. 0523 32 38 12. Women only. Curfew 10:30pm. Singles or doubles with full pension L30,000 per person.)

As in any Italian town, specialty shops selling meats, cheeses, bread, and fruit are everywhere. Shop in the markets along V. Calzolai, tucked behind P. Cavalli. An outdoor **market** is held every Wednesday and on Saturday mornings in P. Duomo and P. dei Cavalli. Local specialties include *tortelli*, filled with spinach and ricotta, and *pisarei e fasö*, a hearty mix of beans and small balls of dough. Steer clear of anything containing the word *cavallo*, unless you're hungry enough to eat a horse. **Osteria Del Trentino,** V. del Castello, 71, off P. Borgo, serves delicious meals in a garden as charming as its staff. Try the specialty *tortelli ricotta e spinaci* for L12,000. (*Primi* from L10,000, *secondi* from L12,000. Cover L3000. tel. 0523 32 42 60. Open M-Sa noon-3pm and 8pm-midnight. V, MC, AmEx.) **Trattoria/Pizzeria dell'Orologio,** P. Duomo, 38, serves delicious pizza and traditional *piacentina* cuisine in the shadows of the *duomo.* Pizza from L8000, *primi* from L10,000, *secondi* from L15,000. (tel. 0523 32 46 69, fax 0523 38 41 03. Open F-W 11:15am-3pm and 6-11am. V, MC, AmEx, Diners).

SIGHTS

Though the entire *centro storico* is closed to automobile traffic, bicycles are still a nuisance through the *piazze*.

PIAZZA DEI CAVALLI. This central square is named for the two massive, 17th-century equestrian statues that grace the *piazza*. Although the statues were intended as tributes to the riders, Duke Rannucio I and his father, Duke Alessandro Farnese, the huge horses overpower their masters. The true masterpiece of the *piazza* is the Gothic **Palazzo del Comune,** called **Il Gotico.** The building was constructed in 1280 when Piacenza led the Lombard League, a powerful trading group of city-states in northern Italy. From P. dei Cavalli, follow V. XX Settembre to the **duomo,** constructed between 1122 and 1233 with an unadorned, three-aisle nave. The crypt, a maze of thin columns, is one of the spookiest in Italy—if it's open when you visit, don't go alone. *(Open during exhibitions. Ask the tourist office for details.)*

PALAZZO FARNESE. In P. Cittadella at the opposite end of C. Cavour from P. dei Cavalli, this *palazzo* houses the **Museo Civico,** the **Pinacoteca,** and the **Museo delle Carrozze** (tel. 0523 32 82 70). The most notable work in the Pinacoteca is a Botticelli fresco depicting Christ's birth. *(Open Tu-Th 8:30am-1pm, F-Sa 8:30am-1pm and 3-6:30pm, Su 9:30am-1pm and 3-6:30pm. Admission to the Museo Civico and Pinacoteca L8000; Museo delle Carrozze L4000; to all museums L10,000, students L5000.)* The **Galleria Ricci Oddi,** V. S. Siro, 13, exhibits a collection of modern art, including works by F. Hayez and A. Bocchi. Take C. V. Emanuele from P. dei Cavalli and turn left on V. S. Siro. *(tel. 0523 207 42. Open May-Sept. 10am-noon and 3-6pm; Oct.-Feb. Tu-Su 10am-noon and 2-4pm; Mar.-Apr. 10am-noon and 3-5pm. Recently closed for restoration.)*

RAVENNA ☎0544

Tired of fresco cycles? Come to Ravenna to get byzy…uh, Byzantine and enter a world of golden mosaics. Ravenna's 15 minutes of historical superstardom came and went 14 centuries ago, when Justinian and Theodora, rulers of the Byzantine Empire, made the city headquarters for their campaign to restore order in the anarchic west. Although they were ultimately unsuccessful, the city remained the seat of the Exarchs of Byzantine Italy for two centuries. This period inspired some of the most important works of Byzantine art outside Constantinople. In fact, you haven't really seen *tesserae* (mosaic pieces) until you've visited Ravenna. Today, while art fanatics come to see the mosaics, literary pilgrims come to pay homage at Dante's tomb, guarded from the jealous Florentines, who maintain an empty tomb for their estranged native.

TRANSPORTATION

Trains: (☎0544 21 78 84). To **Rimini** (1hr., every hr. 5am-9:35pm, L3100-4700) and **Bologna** (1hr., every 1-2hr. 5:05am-7:34pm, L7400) with connections to **Florence, Venice,** and **Ferrara** (1hr., every 2hr. 6:20am-9:33pm, L6700). Ticket counter open daily 6am-8pm. Info office in P. Farini open daily 7am-8:30pm. **Luggage Storage:** L3-5000 for 6hr. Open daily 4:45am-11pm.

Buses: ATR (regional) and **ATM** (municipal) buses (☎0544 68 99 00) depart from outside the train station for the coastal towns of **Marina di Ravenna** (L1800) and **Lido di Classe** (L3800). Get info and buy tickets (L1300, 3-day tourist pass L6000) at the ATM booth marked "PUNTO" across the *piazza* from the station. Buy a return ticket too—they're difficult to find in the suburbs. Office open M-Sa 6:30am-8:30pm, Su 7am-8:30pm; in winter M-Sa 6:30am-7:30pm, Su 7:30am-7:30pm.

Taxis: Radio Taxi (☎0544 338 88), P. Farini, across from the train station. Open 24hr.

ORIENTATION AND PRACTICAL INFORMATION

The train station is in **Piazza Farini,** at the east end of town. **Viale Farini** leads from the station to **Via Diaz,** which runs to **Piazza del Popolo,** the center of town.

Tourist Office: V. Salara, 8 (☎0544 354 04; fax 0544 48 26 70), in P. del Popolo. Take V. Muratori to P. XX Settembre and turn right on V. Matteotti. Follow this street to its end, turn left on V. Cavour, and take the 1st right. Useful maps and info. Open M-Sa 8:30am-7pm, Su 10am-4pm; in winter M-Sa 8am-6pm, Su 10am-4pm.

Bike Rental: In P. Farini to the left as you exit the train station. L2000 per hr., L25,000 per day. Mountain bikes L3000 per hr. Open M-Sa 6:15am-8pm.

Gay and Lesbian Resources: ARCIGAY ARCILESBICA"Evoluzione," V. Rasponi, 5 (☎0544 21 97 21).

Emergencies: ☎113. **Questura:** V. Berlinguer, 10 (☎0544 29 91 11). **First Aid:** ☎118. **Hospital: Santa Maria delle Croci,** V. Missiroli, 10 (☎0544 40 91 11). Take bus #2 from the station.

Internet: Biblioteca Oriani, V. C. Ricci, 26, 2nd fl. (☎0544 21 24 37). From P. del Popolo take V. Cairoli and follow it as it becomes V. C. Ricci. L1000 for 15min. Open M, W and F 8:30am-1pm and 2:30-7pm, Tu, Th, Sa 8:30am-1pm. Closed last 2 weeks in Aug. Access also at the hostel.

Post Office: P. Garibaldi, 1 (☎0544 218 67), off V. Diaz before P. del Popolo. Open M-F 8:15am-6pm, Sa 8:15am-1:30pm. Also at V. Carducci, near the station. Open M-Sa 8:15am-7pm. **Postal Code:** 48100.

ACCOMMODATIONS

Ostello Dante (HI), V. Nicolodi, 12 (☎/fax 0544 42 11 64). Take bus #1 or 70 from V. Pallavicini, at the station (every 15min.-1hr. 6:30am-11:30pm, L1300). A clean, simple hostel in the eastern suburbs, offering satellite TV, soda machines, and internet access. Wheelchair accessible. Breakfast included. Reception 7-10am and 5-11:30pm. Lockout noon-3:30pm. Curfew 11:30pm. 140 beds; 4-6 beds per room. Dorms L22,000; L25,000 per person in family rooms. V, MC.

Albergo Al Giaciglio, V. Rocca Brancaleone, 42 (☎0544 394 03). Walk along V. Farini, and turn right across P. Mameli. This recently renovated budget hotel is the best deal in town. 18 carpeted rooms with wood-paneled walls and TVs. Restaurant downstairs. Breakfast L7000. Closed 2 weeks in Dec. or Jan. Singles L45,000, with bath L55,000; doubles L65,000, with bath L85,000; triples L90,000, with bath L100,000. V, MC.

Hotel Ravenna, V. Maroncelli, 12 (☎0544 21 22 04; fax 0544 21 20 77), to the right as you exit the station. 26 neat, clean rooms with tile floors. A classy hotel with polished veneer. Cozy TV room downstairs. Wheelchair accessible. Singles L60,000, with bath L80,000; doubles L70-90,000, with bath L110,000. V, MC.

Camping Piomboni, Vle. Lungomare, 421 (☎0544 53 02 30; fax 0544 53 86 18), in Marina di Ravenna, 8km from Ravenna Centro. Take bus #70 across the street from the train station to stop #34 (15-20min., every 30min. 5:35am-11:30pm, L1300). 3-star camping near the beach. Reception daily 8am-10:30pm. Open May to mid-Sept. L8500 per person, L9800 per tent.

FOOD

Hostelers benefit from the adjacent **Coop Supermarket,** V. Aquileia, 110. (Open M 3:30-8pm, Tu-Sa 8am-8pm.) The busy **Mercato Coperto** occupies P. Andrea Costa, up V. IV Novembre from P. del Popolo. (Open M-Sa 7am-2pm, F 4:30-7:30pm.)

Ristorante-Pizzeria Guidarello, V. Gessi, 9, off P. Arcivescovado beside the *duomo.* A huge *trattoria* with surprisingly good food. Feast on the *Fantasia della Casa* (3 different meats with mixed vegetables; L16,000). *Primi* L6-12,000, *secondi* L10-18,000. Cover

L2500. Open daily noon-2:30pm and 7-9:30pm. Same fare available at the owner's adjoining restaurant, **Ristorante da Renato** (☎0544 21 36 84), around the corner at V. Mentana, 31. Open M-Sa noon-2:15pm and 7-9pm. V, MC.

Bizantino, in P. Andrea Costa, inside the Mercato Coperto. Self-service restaurant with stylish interior and industrial-strength food. *Primi* L4600-7000, *secondi* L6000-8200. Full meal L14,000. Cover L1000. Open M-F 11:45am-2:45pm.

Ristorante San Vitale, V. Salara, 20 (☎0544 353 63). Somewhat expensive, but you can taste the extra *lire*. Sleek black and white interior. Divine and artfully presented seafood, pasta, fish, meat, and vegetable dishes. *Primi* L8-14,000, *secondi* L10-20,000. *Menù* L25,000. Cover L3000. Open W-M noon-2:30pm and 7-10:30pm. V, MC, AmEx.

SIGHTS

MO' MOSAICS. Thanks to a couple of comprehensive tickets, the church, mosaic, and museum rounds in Ravenna are somewhat affordable. The 1st ticket (L10,000, students L8000) is valid at the Basilica di S. Vitale, the Basilica di S. Appolinare, the Mausoleo di Galla Placidia, the Battistero Neoniano, the Museo Arcivescovile, and the Basilica dello Spirito Santo. The 2nd ticket (L12,000) is valid at Chiesa di Sant'Apollinare in Classe, the Mausoleo di Teodorico, and the Museo Nazionale. Buy tickets at participating sights.

BASILICA DI SAN VITALE. Inside and out, the 6th-century Basilica di San Vitale is a jewel. An open courtyard overgrown with greenery leads to the brilliantly glowing mosaics inside. Once known as *biblia pauperum* (the poor man's bible), these mosaics make words unnecessary. The mosaics to the left of the apse portray two events in Abraham's life; one shows him hearing the news of his wife's impending pregnancy and the other depicts God's intervention in his attempt to sacrifice his son Isaac. The right panel illustrates other biblical scenes. The renowned mosaics of the Emperor Justinian and the Empress Theodora adorn the lower left and right panels of the apse, respectively. The work on the apse displays the Byzantine style of portraying human subjects as rigid bodies on a gold backdrop. *(V. S. Vitale, 17. Take V. Argentario from V. Cavour. ☎0544 21 62 92. Open daily Apr.-Sept. 9am-7pm; Oct.-Mar. 9:30am-4:30pm. L6000.)*

NORTHEAST ITALY

The oldest and most interesting mosaics in the city cover the glittering interior of the **Mausoleo di Galla Placidia.** A representation of Jesus as Shepherd, leaning against his cross-shaped staff and caressing a sheep, decorates the upper wall. *(Behind San Vitale. Same hours as basilica. Entrance included with admission to San Vitale.)*

CHIESA DI SANT'APOLLINARE IN CLASSE. Astounding mosaics—including an uninterrupted sheet on the front end—decorate the interior of this 6th-century church. The expressive mosaic of Christ sitting on his throne among angels rivals the stunning gold cross on an azure background in the main apse. St. Apollinare makes his appearance in the lower portion, surrounded by sheepish depictions of the 12 apostles. *(In Classe, south of the city. Take Bus #4 or 44 across the street from the train station (L1300). ☎0544 47 36 43. Open 8:30am-7:30pm, Su 9am-1pm. L4000, Sundays free.)*

DANTE'S TOMB AND THE DANTE MUSEUM. Much to Florence's dismay, Ravenna's most popular monument is the Tomb of Dante Alighieri. The adjoining Dante Museum not only holds 18,000 scholarly volumes, but also displays a number of the poet's old codices. Aficionados of Dante's verse should visit the museum for its collection of old and new interpretations of Dante's *Canti* and its pictures of his smurfy hat. His heaven and hell come alive in etchings, paintings, and sculptures. *(Both on V. Dante Alighieri. From P. del Popolo, cut through P. Garibaldi to V. Alighieri. Tomb open daily 9am-7pm. Free. Museum ☎0544 302 52. Museum open Apr.-Sept. Tu-Su 9am-noon and 3:30-6pm; Oct.-Mar. Tu-Su 9am-noon. L3000.)*

BASILICA DI SANT'APOLLINARE NUOVO. This 6th-century basilica passed into the hands of the Catholics less than 40 years after it was built. Lengthy mosaic strips of saints and prophets detail the sides of the central aisle, and the central apse recounts miracles performed by Jesus. *(On V. di Roma. From the train station follow Vle. Farini and turn left on V. di Roma. Open daily 9am-7pm. L5000.)*

MUSEO NAZIONALE. This collection, housed in the cloister of S. Vitale's former convent, features works from the Roman, early Christian, Byzantine, and medieval periods. Highlights include intricate ivory carvings, ivory inlaid weapons, and recent excavations from a burial ground in Classe. *(On V. Fiandrini. Walk through the gate between S. Vitale and the mausoleum. ☎0544 344 24. Open daily 8:30am-7:30pm. L8000, EU citizens under 18 and over 60 free.)*

BATTISTERO NEONIANO. The baptistery of the *duomo* is thought to have once been a Roman bath. Created in the 5th century, the central dome features Jesus submerged in the Jordan River, with John the Baptist to his right and the personification of the river itself to his left. *(From P. del Popolo follow V. Cairoli, turn right on V. Gessi, and head towards P. Arcivescovado. Open daily 9am-7pm. Admission included with entrance to Museo Arcivescovile.)*

MUSEO ARCIVESCOVILE. The baptistery's adjoining Museo Arcivescovile displays a small but precious collection of mosaics from the *duomo*. Don't miss the lovely mosaic chapel and the Throne of Maximilian, an exemplary piece of ivory carving. *(In P. Duomo. Walk to the right of the Battistero Neoniano. ☎0544 21 99 38. Free. Open daily 9:30am-6:30pm. L5000, includes entrance to Battistero Neoniano.)*

NORTHEAST ITALY

ENTERTAINMENT

Ravenna's recent claim to fame is its internationally renowned **Ravenna Festival.** Some of the most recognized classical performers from around the world, including at least two of the three tenors, gather here each July and August. Tickets start at L20,000. Reservations are essential for popular events. (Info available at V. D. Alighieri, 1. ☎0544 24 92 11; email info@ravennafestival.org; www.ravennafestival.org. Open M-Sa 9am-1pm and 3-6pm. For tickets call ☎0544 325 77; fax 0544 21 58 40.) An annual **Dante Festival,** organized by the Chiesa di S. Francesco (☎0544 302 52), brings the afterlife to Ravenna with exhibits and performances during the 2nd week in September. *Ravenna Oggi*, available in hotels and the tourist office, has listings of local events including concerts, shows, and exhibitions. If looking at mosaics inspires you to try making one, head to **Colori-Belle Arti,** P. Mameli, 16, off of Vle. Farini, where *tesserae* of all shapes and sizes can be purchased. (☎0544 373 87. Open M-Th 8:30am-12:30pm and 4-7:30pm.)

RIMINI ☎0541

Rimini is quickly becoming the party town of choice for young, hip backpackers. Beautiful, well-dressed, hygienic people frolic all day and fondle all night. The main street is everything a boardwalk should be—an infinite psychedelic strip of arcades, discos, pubs, and people. At night the strip lights up as stiletto-heeled mothers push baby strollers past caricature artists, and teens with freshly greased hair frenetically rush from disco to disco. For higher culture, visit the nearly deserted inland historic center, an alluring jumble of medieval streets overshadowed by the Malatesta Temple and crumbling Roman arches. Otherwise, follow the crowds straight to the well-kept beach.

TRANSPORTATION

Flights: Miramare Civil Airport (☎0541 71 57 11), on V. Flaminia. Mostly charter flights. Serves many European cities. Rates vary. Bus #9, across the street from the train station, jets to the airport (every 30min. 5:45am-12:40am).

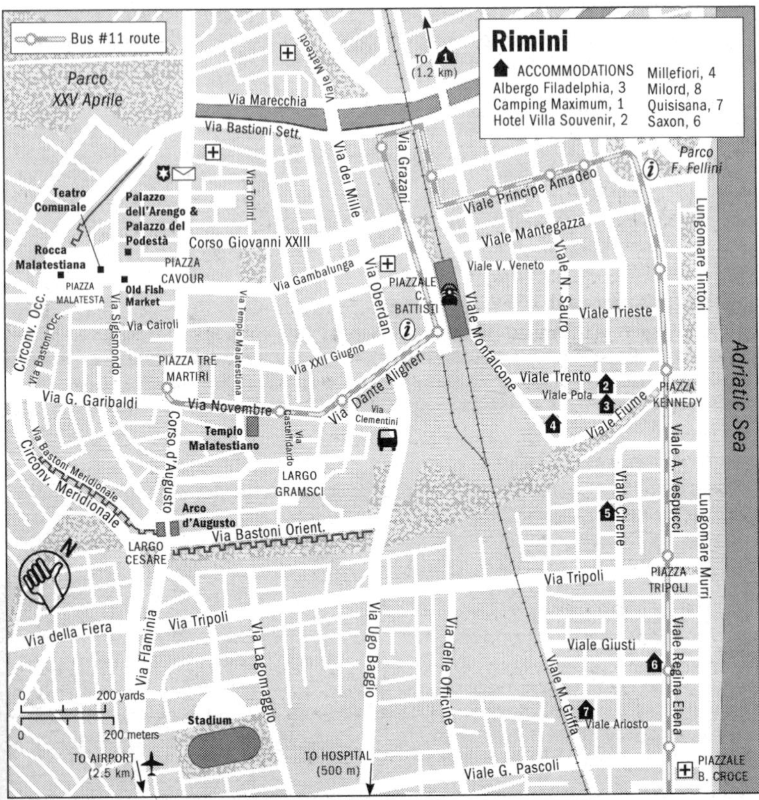

Trains: Ple. C. Battisti and V. Dante. Rimini is a major stop on the Bologna-Lecce train line. To: **Ravenna** (1hr., 1-2 per hr. 1:28am-10:57pm, L5200); **Ancona** (1hr., 1-2 per hr., L8200); **Bologna** (1½hr., 1-3 per hr. 12:38am-10:25pm, L10,100); and **Milan** (3hr., 1-2 per hr. 1:34am-8:23pm, L27,500). **Luggage Storage:** L5000 for 12hr. Open daily 6am-11pm. Self-service for small bags. Open 24hr.

Buses: TRAM intercity bus station (☎0541 245 47), at V. Roma on P. Clementini, near the station. From the train station follow V. Dante Alghieri and take the 1st left. Service to many inland towns. Ticket booth open M-Sa 7:15am-12:30pm and 2:30-6:30pm. **Fratelli Benedettini** (☎0549 90 38 54) and **Bonelli Bus** (☎0541 37 34 32) run the most convenient buses to **San Marino** (50min., 11 per day 7:30am-7pm, L5500). Buses depart from P. Tripoli (bus #11: stop 14) and from the train station. Board at P. Tripoli to avoid the rush for seats at the station.

ORIENTATION AND PRACTICAL INFORMATION

To walk to the beach from the **train station** in **Piazzale Cesare Battisti,** turn right out of the station, take another right into the tunnel at the yellow arrow indicating *al mare*, and follow **Via Principe Amadeo** (15min.). **Via Amerigo Vespucci,** which becomes **Viale Regina Elena,** runs one block inland along the beach and features countless hotels, restaurants, and clubs. Bus #11 (every 15min. 5:30am-2am) runs to the beach from the train station and continues along V. A. Vespucci and V. R. Elena. Bus stops are conveniently numbered. Buy tickets (L1700, full-day L5000) at the kiosk in front of the station or at *tabacchi*. To reach the historic center, take

Via Dante Alighieri from the station (5min.) or bus #11 from the beach. V. Dante Alighieri leads into **Via IV Novembre** which in turn leads to **Piazza Tre Martire. Corso d'Augusto** runs east-west, cutting through the *piazza*.

TOURIST, FINANCIAL AND LOCAL SERVICES

Tourist Offices: IAT, Ple. C. Battisti, 1 (☎0541 513 31; fax 0541 279 27; www.riminiturismo.it), to the left as you exit the train station. Friendly, English-speaking staff. Open M-Sa 8am-7pm, Su 9:30am-12:30pm. **Branch office,** P. Fellini, 3 (☎0541 569 02 or 0541 565 98), near the water at the beginning of V. Vespucci (bus #11: stop 10). Open daily 8am-7pm; in winter 9am-noon and 4-7pm. **Hotel Reservations-Adria** (☎0541 533 99), in the train station, finds rooms for free. Open daily 8:15am-8pm. During the winter, the office is in P. Fellini (bus #11: stop 10). Open M-Sa 8:30am-12:30pm and 3:50-7:30pm.

Budget Travel: CTS, Grantour Viaggi, V. Matteuci, 4 (☎0541 555 25; fax 0541 559 66), off V. Principe Amadeo. Tickets, ISICs, and info on group tours. Open M-F 9am-12:30pm and 3:30-8:30pm, Sa 9:30am-noon.

Car Rental: Hertz, V. Trieste, 16a (☎0541 531 10), near the beach, off V. Vespucci (bus #11: stop 12). L155,000 per day with unlimited mileage, L790,000 per week. Tax included. Open M-Sa 8:30am-1pm and 3-8pm.

Bike Rental: On V. Fiume at V. Vespucci (bus #11: stop 12). L5000 per hr. The amazing *ciclocarrozzelle* goes for L22,000 per hr.

Laundromat: Lavanderia Trieste Exspress, V. Trieste, 16 (☎0541 26 764), off V. Vespucci (bus #11: stop 12). Wash and dry L15,000 per kg. Free speelling lessons. Open M-Sa 8:30am-1pm and 3-8pm.

EMERGENCY AND COMMUNICATIONS

Emergencies: ☎113. **Ambulance:** ☎118 or 0541 70 57 57. Open 24hr. **First Aid:** (☎0541 70 77 04), on the beach at the end of V. Gounod (bus #11: stop 16). Free walk-in clinic for tourists. Open in summer daily 8am-8pm. **Hospital: Ospedale Infermi,** V. Settembrini, 2 (☎0541 70 51 11). English-speaking doctors available. **Police:** C. d'Augusto, 192 (☎0541 353 11 11).

Internet Access: Tourist office, P. Fellini, 3 (see above). L3000 for 30min., L4000 per hr. **Central Park,** V. Vespucci, 21 (☎0541 275 50). L5000 for 30min., L10,000 for 70min.

Post Office: C. d'Augusto, 8 (☎0541 78 16 73), off P. Tre Martiri, near the Arch of Augustus. Open M-F 8:10am-5:30pm, Sa 8:10am-1pm. Also at the beach on V. Mantegazza, 26, at V. Vespucci (bus #11: stop 10). Open M-F 8:10am-1:20pm, Sa 8:10am-12:40pm. **Postal Code:** 47900.

NORTHEAST ITALY

ACCOMMODATIONS AND CAMPING

Reservations are always necessary. The tourist office provides a complete list of hotels and campgrounds. Countless hotels line the smaller streets off V. Vespucci and V. R. Elena, many between stops 12 and 20 of bus #11. Prices peak in August.

Hotel Villa Souvenir, Vle. Trento, 16 (☎/fax 0541 243 65). Bus #11: stop 12. Turn left from the bus and then right onto Vle. Trento. Friendly staff and 16 homey rooms decorated in hues of pink and red. Breakfast included. L30-50,000 per person, with bath L35-60,000. Full pension L48-65,000 per person. Open July to mid-Sept. V, MC, AmEx.

Albergo Filadelphia, V. Pola, 25 (☎0541 236 79). Bus #11: stop 12. 20 clean, spacious rooms at a great price. Glowing owner has a soft spot for *Let's Go* readers. 1st floor rooms decked out with a huge balcony. All rooms with bath. Reservations recommended. Open Apr.-Sept. L30,000 per person.

Quisisana, V. R. Elena, 41 (☎0541 38 13 85; fax 0541 38 78 16). Bus #11: stop 15. Virtual luxury (satellite TV) and choice location—all for near-budget prices. Tear yourself away from the TV—the patio out front provides a safe haven for watching the mayhem on the street below. L45-65,000 per person. Full pension L53-87,000 per person. V, MC.

Saxon, V. Cirene, 36 (☎/fax 0541 39 14 00). Bus #11: stop 13. Exit the bus to the left, turn right on V. Misurata then left on V. Cirene. A small, 3-star hotel on a quiet street. Soothing blue rooms, all 30 with TV, phone, and fridge. Breakfast included. Singles L50-70,000; doubles L80-120,000. V, MC, AmEx.

Milord, V. Ariosto, 19 (☎0541 38 17 66; fax 0541 38 57 62). Bus #11: stop 16. Exit the bus to the right and head left on V. Ariosto. 3-star hotel off the main street. 38 spacious rooms with TV and phone, some with A/C. Restaurant downstairs. L40-70,000 per person. Half- and full pension available. V, MC, AmEx.

Millefiori, V. Pola, 42 (☎0541 256 17; fax 0541 217 08; email hpeonia@libero.it). Bus #11: stop 12. Exit bus to the left, turn right on V. Fiume, and veer right onto V. Pola. It may not have a thousand flowers, but it's charming. A family-oriented *pensione* with large rooms and soft beds. Singles with bath L35-40,000; doubles with bath L50-100,000. Full pension L50-70,000.

Camping: Maximum (☎0541 37 26 02; fax 0541 37 02 71). Bus #11: stop 33. Reception daily 9am-noon and 4-10pm. Open May-mid Sept. L6500-14,700 per adult, L16,300-28,700 per tent. Bungalows from L76,000. Discount for extended stays.

FOOD

Rimini's seaside swarms with sterile eateries, but the resort's delicious snacks are enough to keep you going. Look in the center of town for affordable full meals. Rimini's **covered market,** between V. Castelfidardo and the *Tempio*, provides a wide array of food. (Open M, W, and F-Sa 7:15am-1pm and 5-7:30pm, Tu and Th 7:15am-1pm.) The **rosticceria** in the market has inexpensive seafood. The **STANDA supermarket,** V. Vespucci, 133, close to the beach, offers picnic possibilities. (Open mid-Mar. to Oct. M-Sa 8:30am-11:30pm, Su 9am-11:30pm. V, MC, AmEx.)

NORTHEAST ITALY

Ristorante-Pizzeria Pic Nic, V. Tempio Malatestiano, 30 (☎0541 219 16), off V. IV Novembre at the *tempio.* Local favorite with eclectic decor. Buffet overflows with gourmet specialties. Try the *pizza bianco verde* (a fire-baked cheese and herb delight; L9000). *Primi* L9-12,000, *secondi* from L8000. Cover L2000. Open Tu-Su noon-3pm and 7pm-12:30am. V, MC, AmEx, Diners.

China Town, V. S. Michelino in Foro, 7 (☎0541 254 12). From the train station, take V. Dante Alighieri and follow it as it becomes V. IV Novembre. Turn right on V. S. Michelino in Foro just after the Tempio Malatestiano. Food so good you won't miss the generic fare of nearby Italian restaurants. Try the fried banana (L3000) or, if you're really curious, fried *gelato* (L3000). Entrees from L6000. Wine from L4500. Cover L2000. Open daily noon-2:30pm and 7pm-midnight.

Gelateria Nuovo Fiore, V. Vespucci, 7 (☎0541 236 02), with a 2nd location at V. Vespucci, 85 (☎0541 39 11 22). Endless flavor selection. Cones L3-5000. Sinful specialty concoctions, like *tartufo affogato alla Kalua* (truffle gelato drowned in Kahlua), will run you L13-17,000. Open Mar.-Oct. daily 8am-3am; Jan.-Feb. Sa-Su 8am-3am.

SIGHTS AND BEACHES

THE BEACH. Rimini's most coveted sight is its remarkable beach. The beach itself is free, but settle down a few feet inland to avoid absurdly priced umbrellas. *(Take bus #11 to stops 12 through 18.)*

TEMPIO MALATESTIANO. A tour of the historic center should begin with this Renaissance masterpiece, originally constructed in Franciscan Gothic style. In the 1440s the ruler Sigismondo Malatesta (Sigmund Headache) transformed the church into a classical monument to himself and his fourth wife Isotta. His image remains atop the black elephants in the 1st chapel on the left. Sigismondo Malatesta was the only person in history canonized to hell by the pope, who described him as a guilty heretic. Also a soldier, patriot, and avid patron of the arts, Siggy ruled Rimini at its height (1417-1468) and employed such artists as Piero della Francesca and Leon Battista Alberti. Alberti designed the exterior of the new church, modeling the facade after the Roman **Arch of Augustus,** which still stands at the gates of Rimini (see below). The single-aisled interior and wooden-trussed roof recall the temple's original Franciscan design. *(On V. IV Novembre. Follow V. Dante Alighieri from the train station until it becomes V. IV Novembre (5min.). ☎0541 511 30. Open M-Sa 7:50am-12:30pm and 3:30-6:50pm, Su 9am-1pm and 3:30-7pm.)*

PIAZZA CAVOUR. Rimini's medieval and contemporary center contains one of the oddest ensembles of buildings in Italy. The tall Renaissance arcade of the **Palazzo Garampi** contrasts dramatically with the adjoining fortress-like **Palazzo dell'Arengo** (1207) and the smaller **Palazzo del Podestà** (1334). Between the first two buildings is an Italian version of Brussels's famous *Le Pisseur.* Perpendicular to the municipal building lies the pink brick **Teatro Comunale** (1857), whose auditorium was destroyed by WWII bombs. On the third side, a motley collection of shops, bars, and offices surrounds the Renaissance **fish market** (1747). The four stone dolphins once functioned as fountains, filling the small canals (visible under the benches) with water for fish cleaning. Two statues stand in the center of the *piazza:* an eccentric, mossy fountain (1543) engraved with an inscription about Leonardo da Vinci and a seated Pope Paul V (1614) brandishing ferocious eagles. *(From the train station follow V. D. Alighieri to V. IV Novembre. At P. Tre Martiri turn right on C. d'Augusto. Palazzo del Podestà open for exhibitions; check with the tourist office.)*

ARCH OF AUGUSTUS. This Roman triumphal arch (27 BC) is the most striking vestige of Rimini's past glory, blending the architectural elements of arch, column, and self-promotion. *(Follow V. IV Novembre to P. Tre Martiri and turn left on C. d'Augusto.)*

ENTERTAINMENT

> **PLAYMATE OF THE YEAR.** Don't be flattered by Rimini's roving photographers offering "modeling deals"–attractive as you may be, it's actually a ploy meant to sell photos to tourists. Similarly, the streetside shell games are a great way to lose L100,000 before you can say "one day's room and board."

Rimini is becoming a favorite detour for the roving, international party crowd. The town is notorious for its swinging, sometimes sleazy pick-up scene. *Passeggiata* is a euphemism for the wild cruising that runs nightly along the *lungomare* on **Viale Amerigo Vespucci** and **Viale Regina Elena.** Rimini's hundreds of *discoteche* are among the largest and most dazzling on the continent. But quantity does not breed variety—most of Rimini's *discoteche* are shockingly similar, with multiple floors featuring several types of music, exorbitant cover charges, and a hormonally charged atmosphere. Hang on to the discount passes that you are likely to pick up along V. Vespucci and V. Regina Elena. Ladies often can finagle free admission—but let that be its own warning.

Rimini has instituted a **Blue Line** bus service (L5000 per night) that runs from mid-July to August for disco-goers. Lines originate at the station and travel the bus #11 route up V. Vespucci and Vle. Regina Elena to the nearby beach towns (1hr., every 20min.). Buy tickets on the bus. During the rest of the year, be careful not to miss the last bus; cab rides back to Rimini cost around L50,000.

Cocorico, V. Chietti, 44, in Riccione, accessible by bus #10 or 11 from the Rimini station. One of the area's flashiest discos, Cocorico has 6 bars and 4 dance floors playing underground techno and house. Cover around L50,000. Open Saturday nights.

Walky Cup by Aqua Fan (☎0541 60 30 50; fax 0541 60 64 54), on V. Pistoia in Riccone. Thousands of Rimini residents stand speechless when asked what the hell this name means; then they resume dancing. Take bus #11 to Riccione and then #45 to

Aqua Fan, following the droves of sharply dressed Italians. Complete with outdoor swimming pools and dance floor after dance floor, the club can pack in 4000 people. Call ahead for cover (usually around L50,000) and hours (usually weekends after 11pm).

Carnaby, V. Brindisi, 20. Bus #11: stop 26. Closer to town, this place is a 3-floor dancing bonanza with plenty of room for lounging. Open Mar.-Sept. daily 10pm-4am. Cover L13-15,000, includes one drink.

Cellophane, Vle. Principe di Piemonte, 2 (☎0541 37 21 83). Bus #11: stop 31. Join an alternative crowd and ogle at the work of Rimini's piercing artists. Dance to techno, house, and garage. Open daily midnight-5:30am. Cover varies so call ahead.

Cyber Pub, V. Mantova, 70. Turn left out of the bus, take a right on Vle. Brindisi, and follow the signs. Old-fashioned imbibing meets the information age; internet pictures of the Queen of England look so much better after a brew. Draft beers L5-14,000; mixed drinks L10,000. Internet free with drink purchase. Open M-Sa 8pm-5am. V, MC, AmEx.

SAN MARINO ☎0549

One of the more popular tourist attractions on the Italian Peninsula, San Marino isn't even in Italy. Although it closely resembles the surrounding hill towns, this 26 sq. km patch of turf inhabited by 26,000 people (you do the math) is its own nation, complete with UN recognition and brightly garbed "soldiers." The novelty of the little republic's size is the basis of its wildly profitable tourist industry; cobblestone streets are bloated with trinket stands aimed at those who come just to have their passports stamped. And San Marino shamelessly exploits its status as a tourist spectacle—even the passport stamp will cost you L2000.

San Marino traces its tiny roots to a single man, Marinus the stone-cutter. Marinus left his native land of Dalmatia to help the Emperor Diocletian fortify the city walls of Rimini. Diocletian returned the favor by persecuting Marinus and other Christians, inducing San Marino's patron saint to head for the hills where he could practice his religion in safety. This original community of exiled Christians atop Mount Titano came to be known as the Republic of San Marino, a country that prides itself on its heritage of independence.

Castles balance on the highest peaks of this mountain-top nation, offering panoramas of the patchwork hills, quilted in yellow and green, that roll to the sea. San Marino exists in a world before liability—the castles are yours to explore. Every staircase leads to a higher tower, every precipice to a more dizzying view.

TRANSPORTATION

Trains: The closest station is in Rimini, connected to San Marino by bus.

Buses: Fratelli Benedettini (☎0549 90 38 54) and **Bonelli Bus** (☎0541 37 24 32) run buses from the train station in Rimini to San Marino's historical center (50min., every hr., L5500). Arrive about 15min. before the bus departs; they fill quickly.

Cableways: San Marino's *funivia* runs from Contra Omagnano down to Borgo Maggiore (every 15min. 7:50am-8pm; L4000, round-trip L6000).

Taxis: (☎0549 99 14 41), in P. Lo Stradone.

ORIENTATION AND PRACTICAL INFORMATION

San Marino's streets wind around **Mount Titano,** and helpful signs lead pedestrians from one attraction to the next. From the bus, exit to the left, climb the staircase and pass through the **Porta San Francesco** to start the ascent. From the *porta*, **Via Basilicus** leads up to the **Piazza Titano.** From there, **Contrada del Collegio** leads up through **Piazza Garibaldi** to **Piazza della Libertà,** overlooking the gorgeous hills. The three castles tower above.

Tourist Office: Contra Omagnano, 20 (☎0549 88 24 00 or 0549 88 24 10; fax 0549 88 25 75; email statoturismo@omniway.sm). From P. Garibaldi, follow C. del Collegio to

late. No phone or fax reservations accepted. 96 beds. 4- to 9-bed dorms L23-28,000, with bath L27-35,000. Wheelchair accessible; reserved rooms for handicapped travelers L50,000.

Istituto Gould, V. dei Serragli, 49 (☎055 21 25 76; fax 055 28 02 74), in the Oltrarno. Leave the station by track #16, turn right, and walk to P. della Stazione. Go straight down V. d. Avelli, with the Chiesa di S. Maria Novella on your right. Cross P. S. Maria Novella and continue straight on V. dei Fossi, over the Ponte alla Carraia, and down V. dei Serragli (15min.). Or take bus #36 or 37 from the station to the 2nd stop across the river. One of the best lodgings in Florence, with a welcoming staff and sunny, spotless rooms. Rooms overlooking the street are often noisy. The *palazzo* itself is cool and cavernous, with a large courtyard and plants growing from enormous wine urns. The profits fund social services for local children. Info office open M-F 9am-1pm and 3-7pm, Sa 9am-1pm. Unfortunately, it's impossible to check in or out on Sa afternoons; one may check out on Su, but not check in. No lockout or curfew. 89 beds. Singles L48,000, with bath L55,000; doubles L72,000, with bath L78,000; triples L78,000, with bath L105,000; quads with bath L132,000; quints with bath L142,000.

Ostello Santa Monaca, V. S. Monaca, 6 (☎055 26 83 38; fax 055 28 01 85; email info@ostello.it; www.ostello.it), off V. dei Serragli in the Oltrarno. Crowds up to 10 beds into high-ceilinged rooms. Helpful management and friendly clientele. Kitchen facilities—bring utensils. No meals, but they sell tickets for a nearby self-service restaurant. Sheets and immaculate showers included. Self-service laundry L12,000 per 5kg. 7-night max. stay. Reception 6am-1pm and 2pm-1am. Curfew 1am. Written reservations must arrive at least 3 days in advance. 116 beds. Dorms L25,000. V, MC, AmEx.

Ostello della Gioventù Europa Villa Camerata (HI), V. Augusto Righi, 2-4 (☎055 60 14 51; fax 055 61 03 00), northeast of town. Take bus #17 from outside the train station (near track #5), from P. dell'Unità across from the train station, or from P. del Duomo (20-30min.) and ask the bus driver when to get off. Then walk 8-10 min. from the street entrance past a vineyard on your left. Tidy and popular, in a far-away gorgeous villa with *loggia* and gardens. Manager screens a movie (in English) every night at 9pm. Breakfast and sheets included. Dinner L14,000. Self-service laundry L10,000. Reception daily 1-11pm. Check-out 7-9am or pay for the following night. Rooms open 2pm-midnight. Strict midnight curfew. Reserve in writing. 4, 6, or 8 beds per room. 360 beds. Dorms L25,000. L5000 extra per night without an HI card. When they're full, they rent metal-framed beds (L17,000) in an outdoor tent with wood floors and electricity.

Pensionato Pio X, V. dei Serragli, 106 (☎/fax 055 22 50 44). Follow the directions to the Istituto Gould, and walk a few blocks farther. Usually full in summer. Quiet, with only 3-5 beds per room. Clean rooms and bathrooms. 4 comfortable lounges. Min. 2-night stay. Arrive before 9am. Check-out 9am. Curfew midnight. No reservations. 54 beds. Dorms with shower L25,000, with bath L30,000.

PIAZZA SANTA MARIA NOVELLA AND ENVIRONS

The budget accommodations that cluster around this attractive *piazza* in front of the train station offer a prime location near the *duomo* and the *centro*. Ask for a room overlooking the *piazza*.

Hotel Giappone, V. dei Banchi, 1 (☎055 21 00 90; fax 055 29 28 77). Clean, comfortable rooms and an extremely central location make this one of the best values in Florence. Singles L80,000, with bath L90,000; doubles L110,000, with bath L130,000; triples and quads L45,000 per person, with bath L50,000 per person. V, MC.

Tourist House, V. della Scala, 1 (☎055 26 86 75; fax 055 28 25 52; email management@touristhouse.com; www.touristhouse.com). Extremely friendly proprietors of this modern establishment run Hotel Giappone as well (see above). All rooms include bath, TV, terrace, and breakfast. Singles L100,000; doubles L160,000. V, MC.

Albergo Montreal, V. della Scala, 43 (☎055 238 23 31; fax 055 28 74 91). With fabulously slouchy couch-potato seats, the TV lounge of this cozy hotel is a place of creature comforts. Curfew 1:30am. 14 modern rooms. Singles L70,000; doubles with shower L95,000, with bath L110,000; triples with bath L150,000; quads with bath L185,000.

Hotel Visconti, P. Ottaviani, 1 (☎/fax 055 21 38 77). Neoclassical decor with huge Grecian nudes. Bar, TV lounge, and 10 rooms with carefully planned color schemes. Delicious breakfast included, served by the friendly management on the roof garden (open 24hr.). Singles L65,000, with bath L90,000; doubles L98,000, with bath L140,000.

Hotel Elite, V. della Scala, 12 (☎055 21 53 95; fax 055 21 38 32). When facing the tracks in the station, exit to the left onto V. D. Orti Oricellari, which leads to V. della Scala. Brass accents enhance this 2-star hotel's carefully maintained rooms. Bubbly reception full of good advice about sightseeing, eating, and playing in Florence. Cozy breakfast and sitting room. Breakfast L10,000. Singles with shower L80,000, with bath L110,000; doubles with shower L120,000, with bath L140,000.

Albergo Margaret, V. della Scala, 25 (☎055 21 01 38). Serene, modern decor, kind staff, and 8 beautiful rooms. Curfew midnight. Singles L80,000; doubles L100,00, with bath L120,00. Lower prices Sept.-May and for longer stays.

Soggiorno Abaco, V. dei Banchi, 1 (☎/fax 055 238 19 19; email abacohotel@tin.it). From the station walk straight into P. S. Maria Novella. With the church on the right, V. dei Banchi runs to the left. 7 well-kept rooms with a medieval feel. All rooms have fan, phone, and TV. Laundry washed and dried for L7000 per load. No curfew. Singles L100,000, with bath L120,000; doubles L130,000, with bath L140,000. V, MC.

OLD CITY (NEAR THE DUOMO)

Though flooded by tourists, this area has a surprising array of budget accommodations. Many provide great views of Florence's monuments, while others lie hidden in Renaissance *palazzi*. Follow V. de' Panzani from the train station and take a left on V. de' Cerretani to the reach the *duomo*.

Locanda Orchidea, Borgo degli Albizi, 11 (☎/fax 055 248 03 46; email hotelorchidea@yahoo.it). Take a left off V. Proconsolo from the *duomo*. Dante's wife was born in this 12th-century *palazzo,* built around a still-intact tower. 7 graceful rooms, some of which open onto a garden. Reservations strongly recommended. Singles L70,000; doubles L105,000; triples L150,000.

Albergo Brunetta, Borgo Pinti, 5 (☎055 247 81 34). Upstairs from the Albergo Chiazza, the Brunetta offers an excellent value in this central location. Ask for a room with a view of the *duomo,* and be sure to take advantage of the roof-top terrace that offers a spectacular panorama of Florence and the surrounding hills. All rooms without bath, but showers are free. Singles L65,000; doubles L85,000; triples L120,000. Cash only.

Hotel Il Perseo, V. de Cerretani, 1 (☎055 21 25 04; fax 055 28 83 77; email hotelperseo@dada.it). From the station, walk down V. de' Panzani, which becomes V. de' Cerretani. The hotel is opposite the Feltrinelli bookstore. Enthusiastic Italian-Australian owners welcome travelers to their 19 bright, immaculate rooms. All have fans and many have breathtaking views. Cozy bar and TV lounge. Breakfast included. Internet access L5000 for 30min. Parking L30,000 per day. Pay with cash for a 5% discount. If the hotel is full, the staff will call around to help find you a room. Singles L85,000; doubles L135,000, with bath L155,000; triples L175,000, with bath L210,000. V, MC.

Soggiorno Brunori, V. del Proconsolo, 5 (☎055 28 96 48), off P. del Duomo. 9 simple rooms with parquet floors, art posters, and an occasional balcony. Friendly management speaks English and provides info on the city and excursions in Tuscany. Curfew 12:30am, but you can make arrangements if you're arriving later. Singles (available in winter only) L60,000, with bath L80,000; doubles L96,000, with bath L124,000; triples L130,000, with bath L168,000; quads L164,000, with bath L212,000.

Albergo Firenze, P. dei Donati, 4 (☎055 21 42 03 or 055 26 83 01; fax 055 21 23 70), off V. del Corso, 2 blocks south of the *duomo*. Central and tranquil. Located in a beautiful *palazzo*. 60 modern glossy rooms with tile floors, TV, and bath. Wheelchair accessible. English spoken. Breakfast included. Singles L100,000; doubles L140,000; triples L190,000; quads L240,000. Cash only.

Albergo Costantini, V. dei Calzaiuoli, 13 (☎/fax 055 21 51 28), off P. del Duomo. If you're in the mood to splurge, this 14th-century *palazzo* with elegant frescoes is perfect. 15 large rooms have A/C, TV, and phone. Breakfast L10,000. Singles with bath L120,000; doubles with bath L200,000; triples with bath L300,000; quads L300,000.

Albergo Chiazza, Borgo Pinti, 5 (☎055 248 03 63; fax 055 234 68 88). Exit P. del Duomo on V. dell' Oriuolo behind the *duomo*. Borgo Pinti is on the left. 14 comfortable modern rooms around a bright, quiet courtyard. Most rooms have A/C and satellite TV; all have phone. Cozy bar. Breakfast included. Parking L30-35,000. Singles L100,000, with bath L110,000; doubles L150,000, with bath L170,000. V, MC.

Hotel Maxim, V. dei Calzaiuoli, 11b (☎055 21 74 74; fax 055 28 37 29; email hotmaxim@tin.it; www.firenzealbergo.it/home/hotelmaxim), off P. del Duomo in the city center. Sparkling lobby and 26 pristine rooms with appealing paintings. Luggage room for those arriving early or leaving late. English spoken. Breakfast included. Singles L120,000; doubles L140,000; triples L180,000; quads L220-240,000; quints L260,000. V, MC, AmEx–but you must pay at least one night in cash.

VIA NAZIONALE AND ENVIRONS

From P. della Stazione, V. Nazionale leads to budget hotels that are a short walk from the center, perfect for those who have an early train. The buildings on V. Nazionale, V. Faenza, V. Fiume, and V. Guelfa are filled with inexpensive establishments, but rooms facing the street may be noisy.

Hotel Nazionale, V. Nazionale, 22 (☎055 238 22 03), near P. della Indipendenza. 9 sunny rooms with comfy beds. Breakfast included. Door locks at midnight; social butterflies can request a private key. Singles L90,000, with bath L100,000; doubles L130,000, with bath L150,000; triples L170,000, with bath L200,000. V, MC.

Ausonia e Rimini, V. Nazionale, 24 (☎055 49 65 47; email info@kursonia.com; www.firenze.net/kursonia). 13 spotless, welcoming rooms. Guests have access to many of the services offered at Kursaal (see below). Breakfast included. Laundry L12,000; ironing L2000 per item. No curfew. Singles L90,000; doubles with bath L145,000; triples L165,000, with bath L220,000; quad with bath L280,000. V, MC.

Kursaal, V. Nazionale, 24 (☎055 49 63 24; same email and web address as the Ausonia), downstairs from the Ausonia, with the same charming owners. 9 lovingly decorated 2-star rooms; those with bath have A/C and satellite TV. A modest English library and book exchange; currency exchange with reasonable rates. Wheelchair accessible. Breakfast included. Laundry L15,000. Singles L110,000, with bath L145,000; doubles L160,000, with bath L210,000. V, MC.

Hotel Aline, V. XXVII Aprile, 14 (☎055 48 58 77). Take V. Nazionale from the train station to P. Indipendenza, then turn right on V. XXVII Aprile (10min.). 6 quiet doubles with green doors, fan, shower, and phone. Some with private balconies. Doubles L100,000.

Katti House, V. Faenza, 21 (☎055 21 34 10). Another good option near the train station, with reasonably priced, clean rooms. All bathrooms outside bedrooms. Singles L80,000; doubles L90,000; triples L150,000. Cash only.

VIA FAENZA, 56. This address houses six *pensioni*, among the best budget lodgings in the city. Take V. Nazionale from P. della Stazione and V. Faenza is the 1st intersecting street. The Azzi, Anna, and Paola share the same English-speaking management and prices—listed only in the description of the Azzi.

Pensione Azzi (☎055 21 38 06) styles itself as a *locanda degli artisti* (an artists' inn), but all travelers–not just bohemians–will enjoy the friendly management. 12 large, immaculate rooms, and relaxing terrace. Wheelchair accessible. Breakfast included. No curfew. Singles L70,000; doubles L100,000, with bath L130,000. V, MC, AmEx.

Albergo Anna (☎055 239 83 22). 8 lovely rooms with frescoes for the aesthetes and fans for the physicalists. Singles and doubles available.

Locanda Paola (☎055 21 36 82). 7 minimalist, spotless double rooms, some with views of Fiesole and the surrounding hills. Flexible 2am curfew.

Albergo Merlini (☎055 21 28 48; fax 055 28 39 39). Murals and red geraniums adorn the lounge/solarium. Some rooms offer views of the *duomo*. Breakfast L10,000. Curfew 1:30am. Singles L70,000; doubles L100,000, with bath L120,000. V, MC, AmEx.

Albergo Marini (☎055 28 48 24). A polished wood hallway leads to 10 inviting, spotless rooms. If you're staying in a double, ask for the room with the gargantuan terrace. Breakfast L8000. Flexible 1am curfew. Singles L80,000, with bath L90,000; doubles L110,000, with bath L130,000; triples L130,000, with bath L150,000; quads L140,000, with bath L170,000. Cash only.

Albergo Armonia (☎055 21 11 46). Posters of American films bedeck these 7 clean rooms. The proprietors' interest in movies doesn't stop there; if you share the last name of a movie star (recognized by the management), you get a 5% discount. Singles L70,000; doubles L110,000; triples L135,000; quads L160,000.

VIA FAENZA, 69. This building has four accommodations under the same roof.

Locanda Pina and Albergo Nella, 1st and 2nd fl. (☎055 265 43 46; email hotel.nella@agora.stm.it; www.florence.net/hotelnella). 14 basic rooms, good prices, and friendly proprietors, not to mention free email access. Singles L60,000; doubles L90-110,000. V, MC, AmEx.

Locanda Giovanna (☎055 238 13 53). 7 well-kept rooms, some with garden views. Singles L50,000; doubles L75,000.

NEAR PIAZZA SAN MARCO AND THE UNIVERSITY

This area is considerably calmer and less tourist-ridden than its proximity to the center might suggest. Turn right from the station and left on V. Nazionale. Take a right on V. Guelfa, which intersects V. S. Gallo and V. Cavour.

Hotel Tina, V. S. Gallo, 31 (☎055 48 35 19; fax 055 48 35 93). Small *pensione* with high ceilings, new furniture, and bright bedspreads. Cozy sitting room. Beautiful art prints. Amicable owners will help find a place if the hotel is full. 18 rooms. Singles L80,000; doubles L100,000, with bath L130,000; triples with bath L140,000; quads with bath L160,000.

Albergo Sampaoli, V. S. Gallo, 14 (☎055 28 48 34; fax 055 28 24 28). A peaceful place with a friendly proprietress striving to make her *pensione* a backpacker's "home away from home." Some rooms with balconies, many with antique furniture. Refrigerator available. Accepts reservations only 1-2 weeks before arrival. Singles L90,000, with bath L100,000; doubles L110,000, with bath L160,000; extra bed L56,000.

La Colomba, V. Cavour, 21 (☎055 28 91 39; fax 055 28 43 23; email info@hotelcolomba.it). Friendly Italian-Australian proprietor of this beautifully remodeled 2-star establishment rents 18 immaculate rooms, all with phone, TV, fridge, and A/C. Windows overlook the Florentine roofscape. Continental breakfast included. Negotiable curfew. Singles L110,000; doubles L185,000, with bath L230,000. V, MC.

Hotel Sofia, V. Cavour, 21 (☎/fax 055 28 39 30), upstairs from La Colomba. 8 rooms with floral borders, art prints, new furniture, and bath. Breakfast included. Flexible 1am curfew. Singles L120,000; doubles L180,000; triples L210,000; quads L280,000.

Hotel San Marco, V. Cavour, 50 (☎/fax 055 28 42 35). 3 floors with 15 modern, air rooms. Breakfast included. Key available by request. Curfew 1:30am. Singles L80,000 with bath L100,000; doubles L110,000, with bath L140,000; triples with bath L200,000; quads with bath L260,000. V, MC.

IN THE OLTRARNO

Only a 10-minute walk across the Arno from the *duomo*, this area and its *pensione* offer a respite from Florence's bustling hubs.

Tabasco Gay Club, P. S. Cecilia, 3r (☎055 21 30 00), in a tiny alleyway across P. della Signoria from the Palazzo Vecchio. Spicy! Florence's popular gay disco. Caters primarily to men. Min. age 18. Cover L15-25,000. Open Tu-Su 10pm-4am.

Space Electronic, V. Palazzuolo, 37 (☎055 29 30 82; www.spaceelectronic.com), near S. Maria Novella. A young American crowd multiplied by mirrors and glass floors. Undeniably cheesy. Beer L8000, mixed drinks L10,000. Cover L25,000, includes one drink; with *Let's Go* L15,000. Open Mar.-Aug. daily 10pm-3am; Sept.-Feb. Tu-F and Sa-Su 10pm-3am.

FESTIVALS AND SPORTS

Florence disagrees with England over who invented modern soccer, and every June the various *quartieri* of the city turn out in costume to play their own medieval version of the sport, known as **calcio storico.** Two teams of 27 players face off over a wooden ball in one of the city's *piazze.* These games often blur the line between athletic contest and riot. Check newspapers or the tourist office for the dates and locations of either historic or modern *calcio.* The **stadio,** north of the city center, hosts the real soccer games. Tickets (starting around L20,000) are sold at the **Box Office** (see p. 305) and at the bar across the street from the stadium.

The most important of Florence's traditional festivals, that of **San Giovanni Battista,** on June 24, features a tremendous fireworks display in Ple. Michelangelo (easily visible from the Arno) that starts around 10pm. The summer also swings with music festivals, starting in late April with the classical **Maggio Musicale.** The **Estate Fiesolana** (June-Aug.) fills the Roman theater in Fiesole with concerts, opera, theater, ballet, and film. For ticket info, contact the **Box Office** (p. 305).

In the summer, the **L'Europa dei Sensi** program hosts **Rime Rapanti,** nightly cultural shows with music, poetry, and food from a chosen European country. Call the information office (☎055 263 85 85; www.lapiazzavirtuale.it) for info and reservations. The same company also hosts the more modern and lively **Le Pavoniere,** with live music, pool, bar, and pizzeria, in the Ippodromo delle Caseine (along the river past the train station.) Call the office (☎055 321 75 41) for information and reservations. The city hosts weekly outdoor classical concerts in the **Giardino Botanico Superiore.** (Wednesdays at 6pm. Gardens L4000, concerts free.) In September, Florence hosts the **Festa dell'Unità,** a music and concert series at Campi Bisenzia (take bus #30). The **Festa del Grillo** (Festival of the Cricket) is held the 1st Sunday after Ascension Day—crickets in tiny wooden cages are hawked in the Cascine park to be released into the grass.

SHOPPING

The Florentine flair for design comes through as clearly in window displays as in the wares themselves. V. Tornabuoni's swanky **boutiques** and the well-stocked goldsmiths on the Ponte Vecchio proudly serve a sophisticated clientele. Florence makes its contribution to *alta moda* with a number of fashion shows including the bi-annual **Pitti Uomo show** (in January and July), Europe's most important exhibition of menswear. If you're looking for high-quality used or antique clothing, try **La Belle Epoque,** Volta di S. Piero, 8r (☎055 21 61 69), off P. S. Maggiore, or **Lord Brummel Store,** V. della Vigna Nuova, 79r (☎055 238 23 28), off V. Tornabuoni.

The city's artisan traditions thrive at the open markets. **San Lorenzo,** the largest, cheapest, and most touristed, sprawls for several blocks around P. S. Lorenzo, trafficking in leather, wool, cloth, and gold. High prices are rare, as are quality and honesty. (Open M-Sa 9am-after sunset.) For everything from potholders to parakeets, visit **Parco delle Cascine,** which begins west of the city center at P. V. Veneto and stretches along the Arno River. The market at the Cascine sells used clothing and shoes. At night, commodities of a different sort go up for sale as transvestite prostitutes prowl the *piazza* in search of customers. For a flea market specializing in old furniture, postcards, and bric-a-brac, visit **Piazza Ciompi,** off V. Pietrapiana from Borgo degli Albizi. (Open Tu-Sa.) Even when prices are marked, don't be afraid to haggle (see **Tipping and Bargaining,** p. 49). Generally you should start with half of the price offered, but never ask for a price you're not willing to pay. Often, bargaining is impossible if you are using a credit card.

Books and art reproductions are some of the best Florentine souvenirs. Famed **Alinari,** V. della Vigna Nuova, 46-48r, stocks the world's largest selection of art prints and high-quality photographs from L5000 to L8000. (☎055 21 89 75. Open Tu-Sa 9:30am-1pm and 3:30-7:30pm.) For a wide range of cinematic books, posters, and postcards, head to **Libreria del Cinema dello Spettacolo,** V. Guelfa, 14r (☎055 21 64 16). The tiny **Abacus,** V. de'Ginori, 30r (☎055 21 97 19), sells beautiful photo albums, journals, and address books, all made of fine leather and *carta fiorentina* (paper covered in an intricate floral design). You can even peek in at the artists. Although Florentine **leatherwork** is typically of high quality, it is often affordable. Some of the best leather artisans in the city work around P. S. Croce and V. Porta S. Maria. The **Santa Croce Leather School** in Chiesa di Santa Croce, offers some of the city's best products with prices to match. (On Sunday, enter through V. S. Giuseppe, 5r. ☎055 24 45 33 and 055 247 99 13. Open M-F 9:30am-6:30pm, Sa 9:30am-6pm, Su 10:30am-12:30pm and 3-6pm.)

DAYTRIP FROM FLORENCE: FIESOLE

No trains run to Fiesole, but the town is a 20-minute bus ride away; catch the ATAF city bus #7 from the train station near track #16, P. del Duomo, or P. S. Marco. It runs throughout the day (less frequently at night) and drops passengers at P. Mino da Fiesole in the town center. The tourist office, P. Mino da Fiesole, 37 is nearby at #37. (☎055 59 87 20; fax 055 59 88 22. Open M-Sa 8:30am-1:30pm and 3-6pm.)

Older than Florence itself, Fiesole is the site of the original Etruscan settlement that farmed the rich flood plain below. Florence was actually colonized and settled as an off-shoot of this Etruscan town. Perched atop the majestic hills just 8km from the modern metropolis, Fiesole has long been a welcome escape from the sweltering summer heat of the Arno Valley and a source of inspiration for numerous famous figures—among them Alexander Dumas, Anatole France, Marcel Proust, Gertrude Stein, Frank Lloyd Wright, and Paul Klee. Leonardo da Vinci even used the town as a testing ground for his famed flying machine. Fiesole's location provides incomparable views of both Florence and the rolling countryside to the north—it's a perfect place for a picnic or a day-long *passeggiata*.

Accommodations in Fiesole are prohibitively expensive compared to the profusion of budget options in nearby Florence, but the town is a great place to sit down for a leisurely afternoon lunch. The **Pizzeria Etrusca** in Piazza San Marco has beautiful outdoor seating and reasonable prices. (☎055 59 94 84. Open noon-3pm and 7pm-1am. Pizza L8000-12,000, *primi* from L8000, *secondi* from L14,000.) Up the hill on your left with your back to the train station, you will find the Missionario Francesco, the public gardens, and spectacular views. The **Museo Archeologico,** off P. Mino da Fiesole, has a wonderful Etruscan art collection as well as the ruins of an Etruscan temple, thermal baths, and altar bases. (Open in summer daily 9:30am-7pm; in winter daily 9:30am-5pm. L12,000, students and over 65 L8000.) A **Roman amphitheater** offers incredible views of Florence and the countryside.

CENTRAL ITALY

TUSCANY (TOSCANA)

Tuscany is the stuff of Italian dreams (and more than one Brits-in-Italy movie). With rolling hills covered in olive groves and grapevines, bright yellow fields of sunflowers, and inviting cobblestone streets, it's hard not to wax poetic. Tuscany's Renaissance culture became Italy's heritage, while its regional dialect, the language of Dante, Petrarch, and Machiavelli, developed into today's textbook Italian.

Despite the appearance of eternal eminence, everything of importance in this region occurred within one outstanding half-millennium. After a tumultuous medieval period of strife, Tuscany came under the astute (and despotic) rule of the Medici family, who presided over the nascent philosophy of Humanism and the flourishing of the Renaissance, commissioning huge *palazzi* and incredible art (often just to shame their rivals). In spite of the debauchery and corruption of later Medici heirs, Tuscany struggled to retain wealth and importance, serving briefly as the nation's capital (1865-70). Eventually, the ever-cavalier Tuscans watched their region decline into a cultural and political non-entity. Today, protected by centuries of relative serenity, the cities and towns of Tuscany remain virtually unchanged, but eminence has returned with a thriving tourism industry.

HIGHLIGHTS OF TUSCANY

CHOOSE your own hill-town. You can't go wrong in the **Chianti** region, where blankets of sunflowers give way to medieval skyscrapers and wine tours.

WAIT for hours and hours in the hot sun with the teeming masses only to go wild for 30 seconds during Siena's world-famous **Palio** (p. 337).

STEP into Pisa's **Field of Miracles** and help support that faulty **tower** (p. 366).

CORTONA ☎0575

The ancient town of Cortona regally surveys both Tuscany and Umbria from its graceful mountain peak. Stunning hills and rich farmland punctuated by the shimmering Lake Trasimeno make for spectacular sunsets. Lazy afternoons, hearty meals, and good wine may convince you to linger here. Though currently peaceful, the city once rivaled Perugia, Arezzo, and even Florence in power, belligerence, and tantrum-throwing. When Cortona finally lost its autonomy in 1409, it was auctioned off to the rival Florentines. For all its grumbling, Cortona enjoyed peace and prosperity under Florentine rule. The paintings of Luca Signorelli and Pietro Lorenzetti, signs of this prosperity, are now exhibited in Cortona's Museo Diocesano. Because of its mountain location, Cortona has avoided modern expansion—today, it's not very different from the city that lured and inspired Fra Angelico.

TRANSPORTATION

Trains: Trains from **Rome** (13 per day, L16,000) and **Florence** (8 per day, L12,000) arrive at **Terontola-Cortona** or **Camucia-Cortona** (stations in neighboring valley towns). From either station catch the LFI bus to Cortona's P. Garibaldi (15min. from Carmucia, 30min. from Terontola; L2600). At Terontola, **luggage storage** is available at the *biglietteria* (L5000 for 24hr.). Open daily 6am-8pm.

Buses: Buses run to P. Garibaldi from **Arezzo** (30min., every hr., L4500). Buy LFI bus tickets from the tourist office, a bar, or *tabacchi*. Less hassle than the train.

Taxis: ☎033 58 19 63 13 and 033 87 00 59 99.

ORIENTATION AND PRACTICAL INFORMATION

Buses from neighboring Arezzo, Florence, Siena, Montepulciano, Assisi, Perugia, and Gubbio stop at **Piazza Garibaldi** just outside the city wall. Enter the city by turning left uphill following **Via Nazionale.** Pass the tourist office immediately on the left, and you'll soon reach **Piazza della Repubblica,** the center of town. Diagonally left across the *piazza* lies **Piazza Signorelli,** Cortona's other main square.

Tourist Office: V. Nazionale, 42 (☎0575 63 03 52; fax 0575 63 06 56). Friendly and incredibly helpful English-speaking staff doles out maps and brochures. Also provides rail and bus tickets and schedules. Open June-Sept. M-Sa 8am-1pm and 3-7pm, Su 9am-1pm; Oct.-May M-F 8am-1pm and 3-6pm, Sa 8am-1pm.

Currency Exchange: Banca Populare, V. Guelfa, 4. Open M-F 8:20am-1:20pm. 24hr. **ATM,** V. S. Margherita, 2/3.

Emergency: ☎113. **Police:** V. Dardano, 9 (☎0575 60 30 06). **Medical Emergency:** ☎118. **Hospital:** (☎0575 63 91), on V. Maffei. **Misericordia:** ☎0575 60 30 83.

Pharmacy: Farmacia Centrale, V. Nazionale, 38 (☎0575 60 32 06). Open M-Sa 9am-1pm and 4:30-8pm. When closed it posts a number for filling urgent prescriptions.

Post Office: V. Santucci, 1, 15m uphill from P. della Repubblica. Open M-F 8:15am-7pm, Sa 8:15am-12:30pm. **Postal Code:** 52044.

ACCOMMODATIONS

Ostello San Marco (HI), V. Maffei, 57 (☎0575 60 13 92 or 0575 60 17 65; fax 0575 60 13 92). From the bus stop, walk 5min. up steep V. S. Margarita and follow the signs to the hostel. One of Italy's best hostels, it is a converted, clean, and cozy 13th-century mansion with an exceptionally accommodating management. Cavernous dining room. 8 bunks per high-ceilinged room; some doubles and quads available. Spectacular views. Breakfast (with porcelain plates and a curl of butter), sheets, and showers included. Dinner L14,000. Reception daily 7-10am and 5pm-midnight. Open mid-Mar. to mid-Oct.; open year-round for groups.

Istituto Santa Margherita, V. Cesare Battisti, 15 (☎0575 63 03 36). Walk down V. Severini from P. Garibaldi; the *istituto* is at the corner of V. Battisti, on the left. This nunnery has echoing marble hallways and spacious rooms with baths. Breakfast L5000. Curfew midnight. Dorms L23,000; singles L40,000; doubles (no unmarried couples) L65,000; triples L81,000; quads L100,000.

Albergo Italia, V. Ghibellina, 5 (☎0575 63 02 54 or 0575 63 05 64; fax 0575 60 57 63), off P. Repubblica. This 16th-century *palazzo* offers 3-star rooms, complete with air-conditioning, high ceilings, firm beds, and TVs. Pristine bathrooms, a restaurant downstairs, and a terrace view of Lake Trasimeno. Rooms include bath and breakfast. Singles L110,000; doubles L160,000.

Albergo Athens, V. Antonio, 12 (☎0575 63 05 08). Head up V. Dardano and take a right. In summer, usually filled with University of Georgia students who make it feel like a college dorm. Gold-toned Gothic and faux-Japanese prints, as well as a garden with cats. Singles L40,000; doubles L65,000; triples L80,000; quads L95,000.

FOOD

Cortona's *trattorie* serve scrumptious Tuscan dishes for reasonable prices, and the city is one of the few places where most tourists order the Italian way, enjoying a *primo*, *secondo*, *contorno*, and dessert. Have dinner with a glass of the fine local wine, *bianco vergine di Valdichiana.* Penny-pinchers can pick up a L4000 bottle at the **Despar Market,** P. della Repubblica, 23, which also makes *panini* (L1500-5000) to order. (☎0575 63 06 66. Open Apr.-Oct. daily 7:30am-1:30pm and 4:30-8pm; Nov.-Mar. M-Tu and Th-Sa 7:30am-1:30pm and 4:30-8pm, W 7:30am-1:30pm. V, MC, AmEx.) On Saturday the same *piazza* hosts an **open-air market** with everything from fruits and meats to chainsaws and underwear. (Open 8am-1pm.)

Trattoria La Grotta, P. Baldelli, 3 (☎0575 63 02 71), off P. della Repubblica. Truly delectable fare at outdoor tables in a secluded courtyard. Sample the homemade *gnocchi alla ricotta e spinaci* (ricotta and spinach dumplings in tomato and meat sauce; L10,000). *Primi* L9-11,000, *secondi* from L12,000. Cover L2000. Open W-M noon-3pm and 7:15-10pm. V, MC, AmEx.

Trattoria Etrusca, V. Dardano, 37/39 (☎0575 60 40 88). Specializes in *primi,* offering marvelous, creative, and huge pasta dishes. Don't be misled by the translated menus—this *trattoria* serves excellent food primarily to locals. They specialize in *tagliatelle colle zucchine* (L9000) and *Bistecca "cortonese"* (L5000 per 100g). Open June-Sept. daily 12:30-2:30pm and 7:30-11pm; Oct.-May F-W 12:30-2:30pm and 7:30-11pm. V, MC.

Trattoria Dardano, V. Dardano, 24 (☎0575 60 19 44). A family-run operation that specializes in hearty pasta dishes like *pici contadina* (L8000). The *ribollita* (L8000) is also delicious. *Antipasti* L4-8000, *primi* from L8000, *secondi* from L10,000, *contorni* L4000, fresh fruit or dessert L4000. Open daily noon-2:30pm and 7:30-10pm.

SIGHTS

MUSEO DIOCESANO. The upstairs gallery of the small Renaissance art museum houses the stunning *Annunciation* by Fra Angelico (Room 3). In the same room, Christ's pain-wrenched face looks down from Pietro Lorenzetti's fresco of *The Way to Calvary*. The collection also includes Luca Signorelli's masterpiece, *The Deposition*, a vivid portrayal of Christ's death and resurrection (Room 1). *(Across from the duomo. ☎0575 628 30. Open Tu-Su Apr.-Sept. 9:30am-1pm and 3:30-7pm; Oct. 10am-1pm and 3-6pm; Nov.-Mar. 10am-1pm and 3-5pm. L8000.)*

VAL DI CHIANA. One of the most expansive and beautiful valleys, the fertile Val di Chiana is broken only by the grays of the distant Sienese mountains and the blues of Umbria's Lake Trasimeno. Leaning over the terrace edge in P. Garibaldi and contemplating the valley floor is a sensational way to take in the view. For an even more breathtaking vista, gaze at the Tuscan countryside from the ancient **Fortezza Medicea** on the summit of Cortona's rugged hill, Monte S. Egidio. The fortress also contains several subterranean passages. *(Open July-Oct. Tu-Su 10am-8pm; winter hours severely reduced, if the fortress is open at all. L5000.)*

MUSEO DELL'ACCADEMIA ETRUSCA. While this museum harbors many treasures and artifacts from the Etruscan period, it also possesses an overflow of carvings, coins, paintings, and furniture from the 1st through 18th centuries, not to mention a couple of genuine Egyptian mummies and sarcophagi. In the 1st hall, a 5th-century BC circular bronze chandelier, mounted in a glass case, hangs from the ceiling. With 16 voluminous oil reservoirs, the chandelier weighs 58kg when empty. In the 3rd gallery, you'll find 12th- and 13th-century Tuscan art. The museum ends with the 20th-century lithographs, collages, and the intriguing *Maternità* by Cortona native Gino Severini. *(Inside the courtyard of Palazzo Casali, near P. della Repubblica. ☎0575 63 04 15 or 0575 63 72 35. Open Tu-Su Apr.-Sept. 10am-7pm; Oct.-Mar. 10am-5pm. L8000, children L2000, groups L5000.)*

PALAZZI AND PIAZZE. In P. della Repubblica stands the 13th-century **Palazzo Comunale,** with a clock tower and monumental staircase. **Palazzo Casali,** to the right and behind the Palazzo del Comune, dominates P. Signorelli. Only the courtyard walls, lined with coats of arms, remain from the original structure; the facade and interlocking staircase were added in the 17th century. **Piazza del Duomo** lies to the right and downhill from the Palazzo Casali. Note the original brick entry of the Chiesa di Santa Maria on the facade of the *duomo*. Inside rests an impressive Baroque-canopied high altar, completed in 1664 by Francesco Mattioli.

ENTERTAINMENT AND FESTIVALS

Of the numerous gastronomic festivals throughout the year, the most important is the **Sagra della Bistecca** (Aug. 14-15), when the town fills up the Public Gardens (behind the church of S. Domenico) to feast upon bloody strips of the superb local steak (about L25,000). Following closely on its heels during the 3rd weekend in August is the superb **Festa dei Porcini,** when the Public Gardens fill with funghi-lovers. Tickets are available at the Garden entrance. Various musical and theatrical events take place throughout the year, clustering mainly in July when Cortona absorbs the spillover from the **Perugia Jazz Festival.** On nice days, relax in the Public Gardens or join in the evening *passeggiata* in the park, where Cortona's residents screen Italian **movies** from mid-June through early September. (Films usually start at 9:30pm; buy tickets at the gardens for L8-10,000.) **Route 66,** in P. Garibaldi, is the favorite haunt of American students who drink and dance away their homesickness. (☎0575 627 27. Open Tu-Sa 8pm-3am.)

AREZZO ☎0575

Arezzo's venerable antiquity infuses the city with a grace that blends seamlessly with the city's modern prosperity. The poet Petrarch, the humanist Leonardo Bruni, the artist and historian Giorgio Vasari, the inventor of the musical scale Guido d'Arezzo, and, most recently, Roberto Benigni, who wrote and starred in the award-winning film *Life is Beautiful*, have all found inspiration in Arezzo's streets. Michelangelo, born in the surrounding countryside, attributed his genius to the inspiration he found in Arezzo's hills and valleys, and the poet Carducci once said "Arezzo alone is enough to glorify Italy." That's quite a statement, but the town is indeed a pleasant destination. Arezzo's most famous treasure is Piero della Francesca's *Leggenda della Vera Croce* (Legend of the True Cross), a wonderful fresco cycle housed in the Basilica di Francesco.

TRANSPORTATION

Trains: From P. della Repubblica to **Florence** (1½hr.; 2 per hr. 6am-11:15pm; L8000, InterCity L13,200) and **Rome** (2hr.; every 1-2hr. 4:54am-11:04pm; L20,600, InterCity L33,200). Info open M-F 8am-noon and 3-6pm, Sa 9am-noon. Self-service **luggage storage:** To the left as you exit the tracks. L3-5000 for 6hr.

Buses: (☎0575 38 26 51). **TRA-IN, SITA,** and **LFI** buses stop at P. della Repubblica, to the left from the train station. To: **Siena** (1½hr., 7 per day, L8000) and nearby towns, including **Sansepolcro** (1hr., SITA every hr., L5200) and **Cortona** (1½hr., LFI every hr., L4500). Buy tickets at the ATAM *biglietteria,* across the street from the bus stop. Open daily 6am-7:45pm.

Taxis: Radio Taxi (☎0575 38 26 26). Open 24hr.

ORIENTATION AND PRACTICAL INFORMATION

Arezzo lies on the Florence-Rome train line. **Via Guido Monaco,** which begins directly across from the train station at **Piazza della Republica,** parallels **Corso Italia;** together they form the backbone of Arezzo's commercial district. To get to the city's historic center, follow V. Guido Monaco from the station to the traffic circle at **Piazza Guido Monaco.** Turn right on **Via Roma** and then left onto the pedestrian walkway, C. Italia, which leads to the old city. **Piazza Grande** lies to the right.

TOURIST, FINANCIAL, AND LOCAL SERVICES

Tourist Office: APT, P. della Repubblica, 22 (☎0575 37 76 78; fax 0575 208 39), to the right as you leave the station. English-speaking staff. Free maps. Open Apr.-Sept. M-Sa 9am-1pm and 3-7pm, Su 9am-1pm; Oct.-Mar. M-Sa 9am-1pm and 3-6:30pm.

Budget Travel: CTS, V. V. Veneto, 25 (☎0575 90 78 09 or 0575 90 78 08). Sells Eurail passes and plane tickets. Open M-F 9am-1pm and 4-7:30pm, Sa 9am-1pm.

Currency Exchange: Banca Nazionale del Lavoro, V. G. Monaco, 74, has a 24hr. **ATM.** Open M-F 8:20am-1:35pm and 2:40-4:05pm.

Car Rental: Autonoleggi Ermini, V. Perrenio, 21 (☎0575 35 35 70). Rents cars from L200,000 per day. Min. age 21. Open M-F 8:30am-12:30pm and 3:30-7:30pm, Sa 8:30am-12:30pm. **Avis,** P. della Repubblica, 1a (☎0575 35 42 32). Open M-F 8:30am-1pm and 3-7pm.

EMERGENCY AND COMMUNICATIONS

Emergencies: ☎113. **Police:** V. Dardano, 9 (☎113 or 0575 90 66 67), off V. Fra Guittone by the train station. **Carabinieri:** ☎112. **Medical Emergencies:** ☎118. **Hospital: Ospedale S. Donato,** on V. Fonte Veneziana. **Misericordia:** ☎0575 24 242.

Late-Night Pharmacy: Farmacia Comunale, Campo di Marte, 7 (☎0575 90 24 66). Open 24hr.

Internet Access: Phone Center, P. G. Monaco, 8A (☎0575 37 12 45). L10,000 per hr. Open M-Sa 9am-1pm and 3-8:30pm. Offers discounted international calls.

Post Office: V. G. Monaco, 34, to the left of P. G. Monaco when facing uphill. Open M-F 8:15am-7pm, Sa 8:15am-12:30pm. Exchanges currency (L1000 commission) at *sportello* #1 (same hours). **Postal Code:** 52100.

ACCOMMODATIONS

Hotels fill to capacity during the **Fiera Antiquaria** (Antique Fair) on the 1st weekend of every month. Otherwise, you should have little trouble finding a room.

Ostello Villa Severi, V. Redi, 13 (☎0575 29 90 47), a bit of a hike from town. Take bus #4 (L1200) from P. G. Monaco and disembark 2 stops after the Ospedale Vecchio (about 7min.) when you see the town park on your left. Once a beautiful 16th-century villa, the building has become a bit less elegant. Cattle-sized sinks and suspiciously unorthodox shower facilities aside, the hostel is spacious, with high ceilings and wood-beam detail. Rooms with 4-8 bunks overlook the vineyards and green hills of the suburbs. Breakfast L3000. Lunch or dinner, including several courses and wine, L20,000. Reserve ahead for meals. Reception daily 9am-1pm and 6-11:30pm. Dorms L25,000.

Hotel Astoria, V. G. Monaco, 54 (☎/fax 0575 243 61 or 0575 243 62). From the train station, walk straight up V. G. Monaco, through the *piazza,* and look left. Surprisingly upscale lobby and well-equipped rooms, all with telephones. Combines a friendly proprietor, a great location, a hotel bar, many large rooms, and welcoming hallways. Wheelchair accessible. Sparse breakfast for a whopping L12,000. Singles L50,000, with bath and TV L65,000; doubles L80,000, with bath and TV L105,000. V, MC.

Albergo Cecco, C. Italia, 215 (☎0575 209 86; fax 0575 35 67 30). Follow V. G. Monaco from the train station, take a right on V. Roma and go 2 blocks down the *corso* (5min.). Large, clean rooms trapped in the Age of Formica. Restaurant downstairs. Singles L55,000, with bath L70,000; doubles L80,000, with bath L100,000; triples L110,000, with bath L135,000; quads with bath L160,000. V, MC, AmEx.

FOOD

Arezzo has some wonderful budget restaurants. The large **Despar supermarket,** V. G. Monaco, 84, has supplies for your picnic basket. (☎0575 209 00 16. Open M-Sa 8am-8pm.) An **open-air market** takes place in P. Sant'Agostino on weekdays and on V. Niccolò Aretino on Saturdays. For super cheese, head over to **La Mozzarella,** V. Spinello, 25. (Open M-Sa 8am-1pm and 4:30-8pm.) Enjoy an impressive view of the Tuscan countryside while picnicking in the park behind the *duomo.*

Antica Osteria L'Agania, V. Mazzini, 10 (☎0575 29 53 81), off C. Italia. Locals pack the *osteria* to feast on homemade *gnocchi, ribollita,* and a heavenly *coniglio in porchetta* (roasted rabbit stuffed with wild fennel). Entrees L15,000 or less. Open Tu-Su noon-3pm and 7:30-11:30pm. Reservations suggested for weekends. V, MC, AmEx.

Un Punto Macrobiotico, P. San Gemignano, 1 (☎0575 30 24 20). Turn right on V. Mazzini from C. Italia and take a right on V. Frale Torri to P. di S. Geminiano. Soul-bracing veggie nutrition never tasted so good; try it even if you're a carnivore. A soup and plate of 5 entree selections (L12,000, L4000 for students and pensioners) makes a complete meal. 4-course meal L14,000. Open M-Sa noon-2:15pm and 7:30-9pm.

Trattoria Saraceno, V. Mazzini, 6 (☎/fax 0575 276 44). Pleasant and antique *trattoria.* Wonderful *coniglio* (rabbit) and *cinghiale* (boar). *Tagliatelle con porcini* is particularly good, as is *polenta al cinghiale* (L12,000). For dessert try typically Tuscan *cantuccini* (almond *biscotti*) and *vinsanto* (L7000). Open Th-Tu noon-2pm and 7:30-11pm.

Il Covo Del Pirata, V. Colcitrone, 24 (☎0575 35 11 10). From C. Italia, turn right on V. Mazzini. Follow V. Mazzini as it changes into V. Pesconi and then into V. Colcitrone. A treasure trove of ingredients for the landlubber who needs nutritional strengthening. Elegant atmosphere. Shiver me timbers—deliciously upscale pizzas from L9000, *primi* from L8000, *secondi* from L10,000, and *coperta* L3000. Open W-M for dinner.

Paradiso di Stelle, V. G. Monaco, 58 (☎0575 274 48). Another amazing *gelateria.* Suffice to say, this is some of the best ice cream you'll ever have. Open Mar.-Sept. daily 10:30am-midnight; Oct.-Feb. Tu-Su 10:30am-9pm.

 SIGHTS

BASILICA DI SAN FRANCESCO. A place of silence and serenity, this 14th-century structure houses Piero della Francesca's magnificent and recently restored fresco cycle *Leggenda della Vera Croce* (Legend of the True Cross), portraying the story of the crucifix and its role in the history of the Catholic church. The narrative begins with the death of Adam and proceeds to recount major events involving the crucifix over the next several centuries, including Emperor Constantine's conversion. Rearing horses, vibrant colors, and sculptural figures, all arranged in a decorative rather than narrative order, leap from the panels. The figure kneeling at the foot of the cross is St. Francis, to whom the church is dedicated. *(Up V. G. Monaco from the train station. Basilica open daily 8:30am-noon and 2-7pm. Chapel containing della Francesca's frescoes open M-F 9am-7pm, Sa 9am-6pm, Su 1-6pm. Visitors are admitted in half-hour blocks; the last visit begins 30min. before the chapel closes. Tickets L10,000, EU citizens 18-25 L6000, art students L2000. Admission includes a headset (available in English) that provides a guide to the frescoes. Since space is limited, it is important to make reservations, especially on weekends. Call ☎0575 35 56 68 or visit the office beneath the left side of the church. It is possible to see the upper portion of the fresco cycle without paying to enter the chapel.)*

PIAZZA GRANDE. Lying near the Il Prato garden, the *piazza* contains the **Chiesa di Santa Maria della Pieve,** Arezzo's most important architectural monument. The spectacular Pisan-Romanesque church dates to the 12th century. Its ornate facade and outer apse contrast with an otherwise severe interior. On the elevated presbytery sits Pietro Lorenzetti's brilliantly restored polyptych, depicting the *Annunciation* and *Madonna and Child.* Below are remnants of the 9th-century *chiesa* upon which the Pieve was built. The adjoining tower, pierced by small windows, is known as the "Tower of a Hundred Holes." Surrounding the *chiesa* in P. Grande lies much of Arezzo's best architecture, conveniently organized in chronological order. A reconstruction of the **Petrone,** a column where city leaders displayed criminals, rises at the *piazza's* high point. *(P. Grande is down C. Italia, on the right. Chiesa open M-Sa 8am-noon and 3-7pm, Su 8:30am-noon and 4-7pm.)*

THE DUOMO. The massive cathedral, built in spooky Tuscan Gothic, houses Bishop Guido Tarlati's **tomb.** Carved reliefs relate stories about the iconoclast's unconventional life. To the right of the tomb is Piero della Francesca's fresco of Mary Magdalene. Light filters into the Gothic interior through the series of seven kaleidoscopic 20-foot circular stained glass windows designed by Gugliemo de Marcillat. The *Capella della Madonna del Conforto*, off the severe nave, holds a terra-cotta *Assumption* by Andrea della Robbia. *(Up V. Andrea Cesalpino from P. S. Francesco. Cathedral and tomb open daily 7am-12:30pm and 3-6:30pm. Not "open" as in the "Bishop walks among the living," but open for tourist visits nonetheless.)*

CHIESA DI SAN DOMENICA. As was often the case, the Dominicans built their church on the end of town opposite the Franciscan establishment. The church contains a superb Cimabue crucifix (1265), Spinello Aretino's *Annunciation* in the chapel to the right of the altar, and the Marcillat rose window over the door. *(Take V. Andrea Celaspino from P. S. Francesco, turn left at P. Liberta onto V. Ricasorli and then right onto V. di Sassoverde, which leads to the chiesa. Open daily 8am-noon and 2:30-7:30pm, though hours can be slightly reduced depending on available staff. Closed during mass.)*

Beyond the church lies **Vasari's house.** That selfish historian built it for himself and decorated the walls and ceilings with impressive frescoes of his peers. He even painted himself contemplating the view from one of the windows. *(V. XX Settembre, 55. ☎0575 30 03 01. Open M and W-Sa 8:30am-2pm and 4-7pm, Su 9am-1pm. Free.)*

CENTRAL ITALY

 FESTIVALS

Arezzo's regular **antique fairs** take place in and around P. Grande the 1st Sunday and preceding Saturday of every month, filling the streets with activity. For information, contact the city's tourist office. Beautiful antique furniture and religious

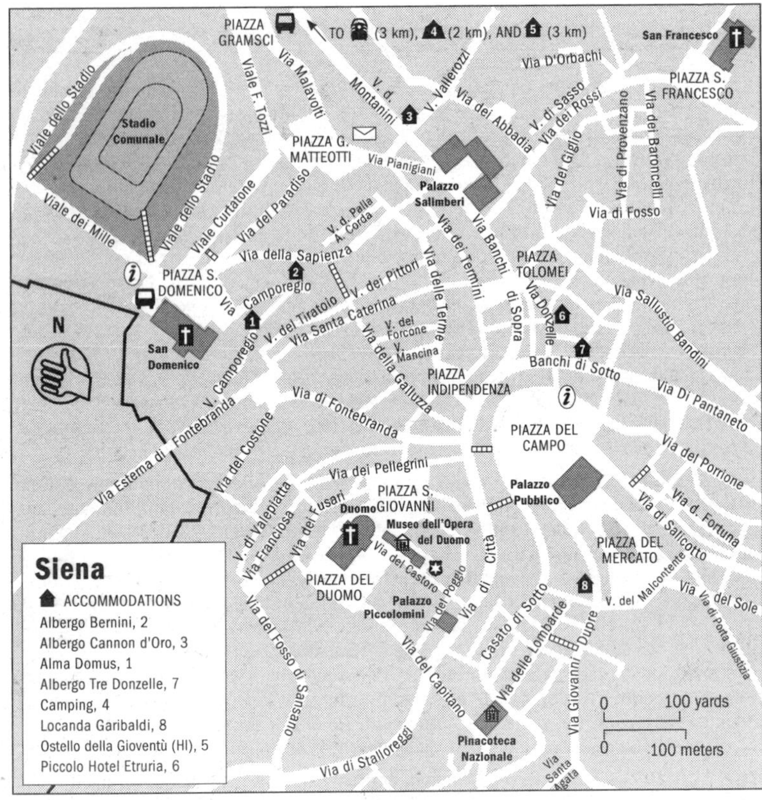

paraphernalia are sold alongside bric-a-brac. If you miss the fair, you can still browse through the innumerable antique shops that dot the old town. The **Giostra del Saraceno,** a medieval joust, is performed on the 3rd Sunday of June and the 1st Sunday of September. In a ritual recalling the Crusades, "knights" representing the four quarters of the town charge with lowered lances at a wooden effigy of a Turk.

CENTRAL ITALY

DAYTRIPS FROM AREZZO

SANSEPOLCRO

Sansepolcro is most easily accessible by the hourly SITA bus from Arezzo (1hr., 8:15pm, L5200; weekend service less frequent). The bus arrives on V. V. Veneto.

A bustling industrial town lost in a valley among Tuscany's densely forested hills, **Sansepolcro's** claim to fame is as the birthplace of painter Piero della Francesca. Sansepolcro's **tourist office,** P. Garibaldi, 2, has maps of the region. Take a left from the bus station and a left at V. Firenzuola. Walk to the street light and pass the Museo Civico on the right. Then take the 1st left onto P. Garibaldi. The tourist office is one block ahead on the left. (☎/fax 0575 74 05 36. Open in summer daily 9:30am-12:30pm and 4-6:30pm; in winter 10am-noon and 3:30-5:30pm.) **Alpes de la Luna Travel** (☎0575 73 63 95) books tours of the area.

Sansepolcro is best seen as a daytrip (unless you visit during the *Palio*), but the comfortable **Albergo Fiorentino,** V. Luca Pacioli, 60 (☎0575 74 03 50; fax 0575 74 03 70), two blocks from the Museo Civico, has well-furnished, welcoming rooms and a beautiful terrace overlooking the city. Aromas waft from the elegant but affordable restaurant downstairs. (Breakfast L10,000. Singles L60,000, with bath and TV L75,000; doubles L80,000, with bath and TV L105,000; triples with bath and TV L140,000; quads L150,000.) **La Cisterna,** V. S. Giuseppe, 27 (☎0575 74 09 38), off V. Matteotti near the *duomo*, offers delicious freshly made fare. (Homemade pasta and *secondi* L10-20,000. Cover L3000. Open Tu-Su 7-9:30pm.)

The **Museo Civico** displays some of della Francesca's finest and most famous works. *The Resurrection* features a triumphant Jesus towering above the sleeping guards and bearing a red and white banner. A muscular Christ rests one foot firmly on his coffin and meets the viewer's eyes with an intense, rather disconcerting gaze. The polyptych *Madonna della Misericordia* depicts a stern Madonna protecting masses of people under her cloak. (V. Aggiunti, 65. ☎0575 73 22 18. Open daily June-Sept. 9am-1:30pm and 2:30-7:30pm; Oct.-May 9:30am-1pm and 2:30-6pm. L10,000, over 65 and groups L7000 per person, students 10-16 L5000.)

MUSEO MADONNA DEL PARTO

To reach Monterchi, take the Arezzo-Sansepolcro bus to Le Ville. Follow the signs to Monterchi and then to the chapel (1hr. walk), or change immediately to another bus to Monterchi. Bus service out of Monterchi (last bus to Sansepolcro 7:57pm, to Arezzo 6:35pm,).

Halfway between Arezzo and Sansepolcro, outside the town of **Monterchi,** lies the **Museo Madonna del Parto.** This tiny chapel, now converted into a two-room museum, displays Piero della Francesca's recently restored *Madonna del Parto*, the sole rendition of a pregnant Madonna in all of Renaissance art. The proud, earthly virgin is flanked by two angels upholding a lavish curtain. Piero's *Madonna* stands in stark contrast to the works of his contemporaries, whose ethereal depictions of Mary skipped this uncomfortable fleshy stage. (Open Tu-Su 9am-1pm and 2-7pm; Oct.-Mar. closes an hour earlier. L5000, students L2500.)

SIENA ☎0571

Many travelers rush directly from Rome to Florence, ignoring gorgeous, medieval Siena. The city is, however, more than Florence and Rome's poor cousin. During the 13th century, Siena's wool trade, crafty bankers, and sophisticated government fashioned the city into a European metropolis. Siena's rise, however, threatened Florence. In 1230, the jealous Florentines catapulted feces over Siena's walls, attempting to trigger a plague. The plot failed, however, and 30 years later Siena routed the mighty Florentines at the Battle of Montaperti. The century of grandiose construction that followed endowed the city with its flamboyant architecture. In the 14th century, Duccio di Buoninsegna, Simone Martini, and the Lorenzetti brothers established the detail-oriented Sienese painting tradition, a style that would later pave the way for 15th-century Realism. Siena lost its prominence in 1348, when the Black Death claimed half of the city's population. But from the destruction, Siena produced St. Catherine (1347-1380), an ecstatic illiterate who brought the papacy back to Italy from Avignon, and St. Bernadino (1487-1564), a wanderer who revived the teachings of St. Francis.

These days, the Sienese proudly celebrate their rich past. One of the richest celebrations in the country is the semiannual Palio, a wild horse race between the city's 17 competing *contrade* (districts). While the Palio, with its intoxicating display of pageantry, is the main attraction of Siena's tourist industry, the event is no mere show. Sienese strongly identify with their local *contrada*, cheering them on to victory regardless of the tourist hordes.

TRANSPORTATION

Trains: in P. Rosselli, several kilometers from the city center. Siena once lay on the main line between Rome and Paris; it now lies on a secondary line to Florence. To get to Siena, change at Chiusi from Rome and points south, at Florence from points north. Hourly departures to **Florence** (1½hr., L8800) and **Rome** (2½hr., L31,400). Ticket office open daily 5:50am-8:25pm. Self-service **luggage storage:** L3-5000 for 6hr. Open 24hr.

Buses: TRA-IN/SITA (☎0577 20 42 45) in P. Gramsci, near the heart of the city; take the stairs that go under the *piazza.* Buses are the easiest and most convenient way to reach Siena. Frequent buses link Siena to Florence and the rest of Tuscany, making Siena an ideal base for exploring the surrounding area. To: **Florence** (express bus every hr., L12,000); **San Gimignano** (every hr., L8600; change at Poggibonsi); **Montalcino** (11 per day, L5500); **Arezzo** (6 per day, L8000); **Volterra** (4 per day, L8400; get off at Colle Val d'Elsa and buy tickets at the newsstand for a **CPT** bus to Volterra); and **Montepulciano** (3 per day, L8000). Open daily 5:45am-8:15pm. **TRA-IN** also runs the bus network within Siena. Buy tickets (L1400 for 1hr.) at the office in P. Gramsci, in bars, *tabacchi,* or any commercial center that displays a TRA-IN sign.

Taxis: Radio Taxi (☎0577 492 22). Open daily 7am-9pm.

ORIENTATION AND PRACTICAL INFORMATION

From the train station, cross the street and take bus #3, 4, 7, 8, 9, 10, 11, 14, 17, or 77 to the center of town. These buses stop in either **Piazza del Sale** or **Piazza Gramsci.** From either *piazza,* follow the numerous signs to **Piazza del Campo** (a.k.a. Il Campo), Siena's historic center. Buy local bus tickets from vending machines by the station entrance or at the *biglietteria* window for bus tickets (L1400). From the bus station in P. S. Domenico, follow the signs to P. del Campo. **Piazza del Duomo** lies 100m west of Il Campo.

TOURIST AND LOCAL SERVICES

Tourist Office: APT, Il Campo, 56 (☎0577 28 05 51; fax 0577 27 06 76), provides local info. Open Mar. 16-Nov. 14 M-Sa 8:30am-7:30pm, Su 8:30am-2pm; Nov. 15-Mar. 15 M-Sa 9am-1pm and 3-7pm, Su 9am-1pm. **Prenotazioni Alberghiere** (☎0577 28 80 84; fax 0577 28 02 90), in P. S. Domenico, finds lodgings for L3000. Open Apr.-Oct. M-Sa 9am-8pm; Nov.-Mar. M-Sa 9am-7pm.

Budget Travel: CTS, V. Sallustio Bandini, 21 (☎0577 28 58 08). Student travel services. Open M-F 9:30am-12:30pm and 4-7pm.

Car Rental: Intercar, V. Mentana, 108 (☎0577 411 48). Suzuki cars available from L156,000 per day. L400 extra for every km over 200. 10% discount for rentals of 3 days or more. Min. age 21. Open M-Sa 9am-1pm and 3:30-8pm. V, MC.

Bike and Moped Rental: DF Bike, V. Massetana Romana, 54 (☎0577 27 19 05). Rents mountain bikes. **Automotocicli Perozzi,** V. del Romitorio, 5 (☎0577 22 31 57). Rents bikes and mopeds. Open M-Sa 8:30am-12:30pm.

Bookstore: Libreria Ticci, V. delle Terme, 5/7 (☎0577 28 00 10). Extensive selection. An array of beautiful art books. Open daily 9am-7:30pm.

Laundromat: Lavorapido, V. di Pantaneto, 38. Wash L5000 per 8kg. Dry L5000. Open daily 8am-10pm. **Onda Blu,** Casato di Sotto, 17 (☎0800 86 13 46). Wash and dry L10,000 per 6½kg. Open daily 8am-10pm. Last wash 9:20pm.

EMERGENCY AND COMMUNICATIONS

Emergencies: ☎113. **Police: Questura** (☎112), on V. del Castoro near the *duomo.* Open 24hr. **Medical Emergencies:** ☎118. **Ambulance: Misericordia,** V. del Porrione, 49 (☎0577 28 00 28). **Hospital:** V. Le Scotte, 14 (bus #77 from P. Gramsci).

Pharmacy: Farmacia del Campo, P. del Campo, 26. Open daily 9am-1pm and 4-8pm; in winter 9am-1pm and 3:30-7:30pm. Late-night pharmacies posted outside.

Internet Access: Internet Train, V. Pantaneto, 54 (☎0577 24 74 60), has lots of computers. Open M-F 10am-11pm, Su 4-9pm. At the **Internet Office Center,** V. Cecco Angiolieri, 51 (☎0577 21 78 30; fax 0577 22 68 11; www.novamedia.it/ioc). L3000 for 20min. Open M-Sa 9am-8pm; in summer M-F 9am-10pm.

Post Office: P. Matteotti, 36. Exchanges currency (L5000 fee for amounts over L10,000). Open M-Sa 8:15am-7pm. **Postal Code:** 53100.

ACCOMMODATIONS AND CAMPING

Finding a room in Siena can be difficult from Easter through October. Book months ahead if coming during *Palio* (see p. 343). For visits of a week or longer, rooms in private homes are an attractive option. The APT and Prenotazioni Alberghiere tourist offices can provide a list of private rooms.

Albergo Tre Donzelle, V. Donzelle, 5 (☎0577 28 03 58; fax 0577 22 39 33). Rooms furnished with tasteful dark wood and speckled tiles. English spoken. Dining area and sitting room. Curfew 1am, or ring porter. Singles L50,000; doubles L80,000, with bath L100,000. Additional bed L30,000 in rooms without bath, L35,000 in those with bath.

Piccolo Hotel Etruria, V. Donzelle, 3 (☎0577 28 80 88 or 0577 28 36 85; fax 0577 28 84 61). Immaculate, modern rooms with floral bedspreads, phones, TVs, and hair dryers. Breakfast L7000. Curfew 12:30am. Singles L65,000, with bath L75,000; doubles with bath L112,000; triples with bath L156,000; quads L192,000. V, MC, AmEx.

Ostello della Gioventù "Guidoriccio" (HI), V. Fiorentina, 89 (☎0577 522 12), in Località Lo Stellino, a 20min. bus ride from the *centro.* Take bus #15, 35, or 36 across from the station at P. Gramsci. Be warned that Sunday evening bus service is infrequent. If coming from Florence by bus, get off at the stop after the large black and white sign announcing Siena. An excellent value, even if the mattresses could be firmer. Small rooms available. Breakfast included. Dinner L16,000. Curfew Apr.-Oct. 1am; Nov.-Mar. 11:30pm. Reservations recommended. L24,000 per person. V, MC.

Santvario S. Caterina Alma Domus, V. Camporegio, 37 (☎0577 441 77; fax 0577 476 01), behind S. Domenico. Spotless and secure rooms offer stunning views of the *duomo.* Curfew 11:30pm. Doubles with bath L100,000; triples with bath L125,000; quads with bath L150,000.

Albergo Bernini, V. della Sapienza, 15 (☎/fax 0577 28 90 47; email bernini@tin.it; www.albergobernini.com). Beautiful rooms have picture windows with incredible views of the *duomo.* Outdoor, canopied breakfast patio lined with plants and full of exotic birds. Breakfast L12,000. Curfew midnight. High-season singles with bath L130,000; doubles L110,000, with bath L130,000; triples L150,000; quads L210,000, with bath L230,000. Off-season prices drop 20%.

Albergo Cannon d'Oro, V. Montanini, 28 (☎0577 443 21), near P. Matteotti. Luxurious rooms with lovely views. All the amenities and an elegant atmosphere. Wheelchair accessible. Breakfast L10,000. With *Let's Go:* singles with bath L120,000; doubles with bath L145,000; triples L175,000; quads with bath L200,000. V, MC, AmEx.

Locanda Garibaldi, V. Giovanni Dupré, 18 (☎0577 28 42 04), behind the Palazzo Pubblico and P. del Campo. Whitewashed walls and dark-ribbed ceilings. Restaurant downstairs. Curfew midnight. Reservations accepted a few days ahead. Doubles L100,000, with bath L120,000; triples with bath L150,000; quads with bath L180,000.

Camping: Colleverde, Strada di Scacciapensieri, 47 (☎0577 28 00 44). Take bus #3 or 8 from town; ask to be sure you are on the right route. Well-kept with nearly flat sleeping space. Grocery store, restaurant, and bar nearby. Open mid-Mar. to mid-Nov. Pool L3000, children L2000. L15,000 (tent included), L8000 per child ages 3-11.

FOOD

Siena specializes in rich pastries. The most famous is *panforte*, a dense concoction of honey, almonds, and citron, first baked as "trail mix" for the Crusaders. For a lighter snack try *ricciarelli*, soft almond cookies with powdered vanilla on top. Sample either one at the **Bar/Pasticceria Nannini,** the oldest *pasticceria* in Siena, with branches at V. Banchi di Sopra, 22-24, and throughout town. **Enoteca Italiana,** in the Fortezza Medicea near the entrance off V. Cesare Maccari, sells the finest Italian wines ranging from *Brunello* to *Barolo* and *Asti Spumante* to *Vernaccia* from L3000 per glass. (☎/fax 0577 22 69 89. Open M-Th, Su 10am-8pm; F-Sa 10am-10pm.) If you're here during the school year, pose as a student for the cheapest of meals at **Mensa Università,** V. Sant'Agata, 1 (☎0577 281 90 85), where you can get a full meal (including *primo, secondo,* dessert, and drink) for L10,000. (Open Oct.-May daily noon-2pm and 6:45-9pm.) Siena's **open-air market** fills P. La Lizza each Wednesday from 8am to 1pm. For groceries, try the **Consortio Agrario supermarket,** V. Pianigiani, 5, off P. Salimberi. (Open M-Sa 8am-7:30pm.) Or head to the **COOP supermarket,** a couple of blocks from the train station—with your back to the station turn left, then left again at the overpass (one block); the supermarket is in the shopping complex immediately to your right. (Open M-Sa 8am-7:30pm.)

Grotta del Gallo Nero, V. del Porrione, 67 (☎0577 28 43 56). A bit touristy, but the food and ambience compensate. Frequented by the university crowd. Pasta L8-12,000, *secondi* L10-20,000. *Menù assaggio* (with an assortment of medieval Tuscan dishes) from L20,000. *Menù turistico* from L22,000. Open Mar.-Oct. daily noon-3:30pm and 7pm-1am; Nov.-Feb. Tu-Su noon-3:30pm and 7pm-1am. V, MC, AmEx.

Osteria il Tamburino, V. Stalloreggi, 11 (☎0577 28 03 06). From P. del Duomo, follow V. del Capitano to P. della Postierla, and turn left on V. di Stalloreggi. No fancy decor, just great Sienese eats. Make reservations–locals fill the place almost as soon as it opens. *Primi* L8-15,000, *secondi* L10-25,000. Wine L8000 per liter. Cover L1000. Open M-Sa noon-2:30pm and 7-9:30pm. V, MC.

Osteria Compagnia San Martino, V. Porrione, 25 (☎0577 493 06). Just off Il Campo, this *osteria* serves delicious Tuscan cuisine. *Primi* L9-12,000, *secondi* from L12,000. Cover L2000, service 10%. Open M-Sa noon-3:30pm and 7-10:30pm. V, MC.

Ristorante Da Renzo, V. delle Terme, 14 (☎/fax 0577 28 92 96). Serves excellent standard Tuscan fare in a lovely setting, with indoor and outdoor seating. Pizza L8500-10,000, *primi* L9500-12,000, *secondi* L14-16,000. Tourist menu includes *antipasto, primo, secondo,* and *contorno,* but not drinks (L29,000); otherwise, cover L2500. Be warned that the service here is authentic Italian–this is not the place to go when you have a train to catch. Open F-W noon-3pm and 7-10pm.

Bibo, V. Banchi di Sotto, 61-63. Come for generous sandwiches (L3500) and beer (L3000). Homemade *gelato* from L2000. Open Tu-Su 7:30pm-2am.

La Costarella Gelateria, V. d. Città, 31 (☎0577 28 80 76), off P. San Domenico. The best *gelato* in Siena. Open daily Mar.-Sept. 8am-midnight; Oct.-Feb. 8am-10pm.

SIGHTS

SIEN-ANY SIGHTS? Siena offers a *biglietto cumulativo,* allowing entry into major monuments and museums. The baptistery, Piccolomini Library, Museo dell'Opera Metropolitana, and the Oratory of St. Bernadino are covered by this cumulative ticket, valid for 3 days (L9500; in winter L8500).

IL CAMPO. Siena radiates from the **Piazza del Campo,** the shell-shaped brick square designed specifically for civic events. The *piazza*'s stones are divided into nine sections representing the city's medieval "Council of Nine." Dante referred to the square in his account of the real-life drama of Provenzan Salvani, the heroic Sienese merchant who panhandled in Il Campo to pay for a friend's ransom. Later, Sienese mystics such as San Bernadino used the *piazza* as a public auditorium. Now it has the dubious honor of entertaining local teenagers, wide-eyed tourists, and souvenir carts by days; in the evening, when the elegant cafes pull back their awnings and the Sienese strut in a ritual *passeggiata,* the *piazza* glitters with leisurely decadence. Twice each summer, the **Palio** reduces the sublimely mellow Il Campo to mayhem as horses race around its outer edge (see p. 343).

At the highest point of Il Campo's sloping plane is the **Fonte Gaia,** surrounded by reproductions of native Jacopo della Quercia's famous carvings (1408-1419). The originals are in the **Spedale di S. Maria della Scala** (see p. 342). The water here courses through the same 25km aqueduct that has refreshed Siena since the 14th century. Closing the bottom of the shell-shaped *piazza* is the graceful Gothic

Palazzo Pubblico. A gluttonous bell-ringer nicknamed "Mangiaguadagni" ("eat the profits") bestowed his moniker on the **Torre del Mangia,** the clock tower that rises to the left. Siena's Council of Nine commissioned the tower to overshadow any other. A pair of Perugian architects produced this 102m tower, the 2nd-tallest in medieval Italy behind only the one in Cremona. *(Tower open July-Aug. daily 10am-11pm; Mar.-June and Sept.-Oct. M-Sa 9am-6pm, Su 9am-1:30pm; Nov.-Feb. daily 10am-6pm. L10,000.)*

In front of the *palazzo* is the **Cappella di Piazza,** built in 1348 at the end of the Black Death epidemic that decimated the population. Siena took 100 years to complete the *cappella*. The transition from Gothic to Renaissance architecture lies where pointed arches give way to gracefully rounded ones.

THE MUSEO CIVICO. The **Palazzo Pubblico (Comunale)** holds masterpieces of Sienese art in its Museo Civico. Although the collection ranges from medieval triptychs to 18th-century landscapes, its greatest treasure is its collection of late medieval to early Renaissance painting in the distinctive Sienese style. The Baroque gallery on the right houses russet-toned boar hunts and the deprecating pouts of large women. The **Sala del Mappamondo,** named for a lost series of astronomical frescoes, displays Simone Martini's overtly religious *Maestà (Enthroned Virgin)*. The religious *Maestà* carries a political undercurrent; the parchment the Christ child holds is inscribed with the city motto of upholding justice, and the steps of the canopied throne are engraved with two stanzas from Dante's *Divina Commedia*. In the next room, the **Sala dei Nove** exhibits Pietro and Ambrogio Lorenzetti's famous frescoes of the *Allegories of Good and Bad Government and their Effects on Town and Country*. On the right side, Good Government creates utopia—people dance in the streets, artisans forge intricate handiwork, and farmers labor on vast stretches of fertile land. On the left side, the Pride, Wrath, and Avarice of Bad Government wield their evil power—here, a gloomy, desolate landscape nurtures only thieves, devils, and lost souls. *The Allegory of Good Government* is remarkably well preserved, while the *Allegory of Bad Government* is flaking its way into oblivion—read into this what you will. Step into the next room to witness Matteo di Giovanni's particularly ghastly rendition of the *Slaughter of the Innocents*. Head back downstairs to the entrance, cross the courtyard, and climb the tower's 500-odd narrow steps for a spectacular view of the *duomo* and the entire city. *(Open July-Aug. daily 10am-11pm; Mar.-June and Sept.-Oct. M-Sa 9am-6pm, Su 9am-1:30pm; Nov.-Feb. daily 10am-6pm. L12,000, students L7000. Combined ticket with Tower L18,000.)*

THE DUOMO. The city's black and white striped *duomo*, atop one of the seven hills, is one of the few full Gothic cathedrals south of the Alps. Civic pride demanded that the 13th-century *duomo* combine enormous scale with a prominent position, but the limited size of the hill posed a design problem. The apse would have hung in mid-air over the edge of the hill had the Sienese not built the **baptistery** below for support (see p. 342). A huge arch, part of a striped wall to your right facing the front of the cathedral, is the sole remnant of Siena's 1339 plan to construct a new nave that would have made this *duomo* the largest church in all of Christendom. That grandiose plan came to an end after the Black Death hit the city, wiping out over half the population. View the unfinished nave from the tower. One of its side aisles has been enclosed and turned into the **Museo dell'Opera del Duomo** (see p. 352). Even though the city's lofty ambitions were humbled, the existing cathedral is one of Italy's finest. Elegant statues of philosophers, sibyls, and prophets, all by Giovanni Pisano, give way to impressive spires that pierce the sky.

The bronze sun symbol on the facade of the *duomo* was the brainchild of St. Bernadino of Siena, who wanted the feuding Sienese to relinquish their loyalty to emblems of nobility and unite under this symbol of the risen Christ. Needless to say, his efforts were futile; the Sienese continue to identify with the animal symbols of their *contrada*. The **marble pavement** on the floor is, like the rest of the *duomo*, extremely ornate, and it depicts intriguing themes from alchemy to the Slaughter of the Innocents. However, to preserve the pieces, the church staff covers them for most of the year. Try to visit between August 31 and October 8 in

2001, when the staff plans to uncover the floor. If you visit during this period, look for the works by the Marchese d'Adamo, perhaps the most spectacular. Halfway up the left aisle is the **Piccolomini altar,** a complete architectural structure designed by Andrea Bregno in 1503. Early in his career, Michelangelo completed the statues of St. Peter and St. Paul. In the neighboring chapel, Donatello's bronze statue of St. John the Baptist, remains graceful in his emaciation. The lavish **Libreria Piccolomini,** commissioned by Pope Pius III, houses the elaborately illustrated books of his uncle Pius II. The library also houses a Roman statue, *The Three Graces*, 15th-century illuminated lyrical scores, and a vibrant fresco cycle by Pinturicchio. *(Duomo open daily Jan.-Mar. 14 and Nov.-Dec. 7:30am-1:30pm and 2:30-5pm; Mar. 15-Oct. 7:30am-7:30pm. Free, except when the floor is uncovered (L5-6,000). Modest dress required. Library open mid-Mar. to Oct. 9am-7:15pm; Nov. to mid-Mar. 10am-1pm and 2:30-5pm. L2000.)*

BAPTISTERY. Lavish and intricate frescoes, mostly of the lives of Christ and St. Anthony, decorate the baptistery. The centerpiece of the baptistery, however, is the hexagonal Renaissance **baptismal font** (1417-30), carved by some of the greatest Italian sculptors. Ghiberti's *Baptism of Christ* and *John in Prison* stand next to Donatello's panel of a carefully composed *Herod's Feast. (Baptistery open daily Mar. 15-Oct. 31 9am-7:30pm; Nov. 1-Mar. 14 10am-1pm and 2:30-5pm. L3000.)*

MUSEO DELL'OPERA METROPOLITANA. The cathedral museum holds all the art that can't fit in the church. The 1st floor contains some of the foremost Gothic statuary in Italy, all by Giovanni Pisano. Upstairs is the magnificent 700-year old *Maestà*, by Duccio di Buoninsegna, originally the screen of the cathedral's altar. Dismembered in 1771 by voracious art collectors, most of the narrative panels have been returned to the Sienese except for a handful held by the National Gallery in London, the Frick Gallery in New York, and the National Gallery of Art in Washington. Other noteworthy works in the museum are the Byzantine *Madonna degli Occhi Coressi* and paintings by Simone Martini and Lorenzetti. Climb the half-hidden **Scala del Falciatore** and walk along the top of the nave of the barely begun cathedral. A smaller staircase at the end of the terrace leads to an exhilarating view. *(Museum is beneath the arches of P. Jacopo della Quercia, off P. del Duomo. Open daily mid-Mar. to Sept. 30 9am-7:30pm; Oct. 9am-6pm; Nov. to mid-Mar. 9am-1:30pm. L6000.)*

PINACOTECA NAZIONALE. Siena's superb art gallery features works by every major artist of the highly stylized Sienese school. The masters represented include the seven magnificent followers of Onccio—Simone Martini, the Lorenzetti brothers, Bartolo di Fredi, Da Domenico, Sano di Pietro, and Il Sodoma—as well as many others. The artists' use of color and ability to display human emotion as early as the 14th century are truly remarkable. Moreover, the museum is refreshingly free of the tourist hordes that can make it difficult to appreciate many of Florence's prime collections. *(V. S. Pietro, 29, in the Palazzo Buonsignori down the street from the cathedral museum. Open Tu-F 8:30am-7:30pm, Sa 8:30am-10:30pm, Su and holidays 8:15am-1:15pm. L8000, EU citizens 18-26 L4000, EU citizens under 18 and over 65 free.)*

HOSPITALS/GALLERIES. The **Spedale di S. Maria della Scala,** which functioned for centuries as an extremely busy hospital, has only recently been opened to the public. Saints Catherine and Bernadino tended the sick here. Now most visitors come for the artistic treasures rather than religious healing. *(Across from the duomo. Open daily Mar.-Nov. 10am-6pm; Dec.-Feb. 10:30am-4:30pm. L10,000, students and seniors L6000.)* The **Sala del Pellegrinaio,** used as a hospital ward until late this century, contains a fresco cycle by Vecchietta often considered to be his masterpiece. In the 1st panel, the pregnant mother of the legendary (probably fictional) founder of the hospital, Beato Sorore, dreams of the future good deeds of her son, and in a panel on the right wall, doctors cure the wounded and examine urine samples. The original della Quercia sculptures from the Fonte Gaia in Il Campo have recently been moved here as well. The most artistically interesting room, the **Sagrestia Vecchia** or **Cappello del Sacro Chiedo,** houses masterful 15th-century Sienese frescoes.

SANTUARIO DI SANTA CATERINA. The sanctuary honors the renowned daughter of Siena, a simple girl who had a vision of herself as Christ's bride. Although she never got down with the godly, she influenced popes, founded a religious order, and in 1939 became patron saint of Italy. The building, converted into a Renaissance *loggia*, opens onto a number of Baroque chapels, some with spectacular frescoes and statues prominently featuring woeful St. Catherines. The **Chiesa del Crosifisso** is especially impressive. *(Entrance on V. S. Caterina, down from P. S. Domenico. Open W-M 8am-2pm and 4-8pm. Free.)*

OTHER SIGHTS. As in other Italian towns, the Franciscans and the Dominicans have rival basilicas at opposite ends of town. The **Chiesa di San Domenico** contains Andrea Vanni's portrait of St. Catherine and a number of other dramatic frescoes which render the saint in a state of religious fervor. The exquisite *cappella* inside, dedicated to St. Catherine, was built in 1460 to store her preserved head. *(P. S. Domenico. Open daily last Su in Oct.-1st Su in Apr. 7am-1pm and 2:30-6pm; rest of the year 9am-1pm and 3-6:30pm.)* The **Chiesa di San Francesco** houses two frescoes by Pietro and Ambrogio Lorenzetti, moved into the church after a fire in the last century. *(Open daily 7:30am-noon and 3:30-7pm.)* The Palio-obsessed may enjoy one of Siena's 17 **contrade museums.** Each neighborhood organization maintains its own collection of costumes, artifacts, banners, and icons, ranging from the eagle and caterpillar to the she-wolf and tortoise. *(Most require an appointment—ask at the tourist office. Schedule visits at least 1 week in advance.)*

ENTERTAINMENT AND FESTIVALS

Siena's **Palio** occurs twice a year, on July 2 and August 16. As the bare-backed horse race approaches, Siena's emotional temperature rises. Ten of the 17 *contrade* (chosen by lot as there's limited space in Il Campo) make elaborate preparations. Young partisans sporting the colors of their *contrada* chant in packs on the street, singing (often obscene) lyrics to the same melody. Five trial races take place over the three days leading up to the race, and a final trial runs the same morning. On the eve of the race revelry concludes around 3am. At 2:30pm on the day of the race, the horses are led into the churches of their respective *contrade* and blessed. A two-hour parade of heralds and flag-bearers prefaces anarchy with regal pomp. The last piece in the procession is the Palio itself, a banner depicting the Madonna and Child, drawn in a cart by white oxen (the race is called *Il Palio* because a *palio*, or banner, is given to the winner). The race begins at 7pm, and it takes the jockeys (usually outsiders from Maremma) about 90 seconds to tear around Il Campo three times. During the race, they have free rein—according to the age-old, almost barbaric set of rules that guide the event (first recorded in 1283), they are allowed (and even encouraged) to whip their opponents. The straps they use are no ordinary pieces of leather; they are made from the skin of a bull's penis, especially durable and said to leave deep welts.

To stay in Siena during the Palio, book rooms at least four months in advance—especially for budget accommodations. Write the APT in March or April for a list of companies and individuals that rent rooms. Also be sure to reserve a seat in the stands. Otherwise, you can stand in the "infield" of the *piazza* for free if you stake out a spot early in the day. From there, you may only be able to see the frenzied sea of fans surrounding you—get to the Campo as early as possible on the morning of the race to avoid this scenario. For information on *Il Palio*, ask at the tourist office and pick up the excellent program (available in English).

In late July, the **Accademia Chigiana** (☎0577 461 52) sponsors an excellent music festival, the **Settimana Musicale Sienese** (Siena's Musical Week). Siena also hosts a jazz festival in July, featuring internationally known musicians. For information, call ☎0577 27 14 01. The town itself is fairly low-key, especially in summer; for a relaxed beer with other travelers, try **The Dublin Post** pub, P. Gramsci, 20. (☎0577 28 90 89. Beers and drinks L7000. Open daily noon-1am.)

DAYTRIPS FROM SIENA

SAN GALGANO

Unfortunately, you'll need a car to reach San Galgano; for more information, contact the tourist office in Siena.

Slightly removed from a winding country pass between Siena and Massa Marittima, the ruined 13th-century **Cistercian abbey of San Galgano** was once one of the richest and most powerful in Tuscany. Its monks served as treasurers and judges for the communes of Siena and Volterra, helped construct the *duomo* in Siena, and became bishops and saints. But by the mid-16th century, widespread corruption spelled the church's decline. The derelict abbey, the foremost specimen of Cistercian Gothic architecture in Italy, lies hidden, but well-preserved, in dense woodland, but it stands without a roof, utterly exposed to the elements. As nature slowly undoes the Gothic church, the absence of vaulted ceilings makes room for blue skies, lazy clouds, and tiny birds that chirp lightly in the stony nooks.

THE CHIANTI REGION

Buses connect Siena to Castellina in Chianti, the nearest major base for exploring the area's vineyards and indulging in wine-tasting (45min., 5 per day, L4700). Three buses a day also connect Radda with Florence (1½hr.; last bus to Florence 6:10pm, last bus to Siena 6:35pm).

Siena also lies within easy reach of the Chianti region, whose wines of the same name have become justifiably famous throughout the world. The private **tourist office,** V. della Rocca, 12, just off the central square **(Piazza del Comune)** in Castellina can help find accommodations and provide information about the town and the area. (☎0577 74 60 20; email info@collinverdi.it. Open M-Sa 9:30am-1pm and 3-7:30pm; reduced hours in winter.) Numerous shops sell the trademark Chianti; one good choice is **Le Volte Enoteca,** V. Ferruccio, 121, a block from P. del Comune, where you can buy a bottle starting at L9000. (☎0577 74 13 54; fax 0577 74 28 91; email rolmast@tin.it. Open Mar.-Oct. daily 9am-7:30pm; Nov.-Jan. Th-Tu 9:30am-12:30pm and 4:30-7:30pm; closed Feb.) For eats head to **Pizza Chiantigiana,** V. Chiantigiana, 7, just off P. Roma. (☎0577 74 12 91. Open M-Sa 11am-10:30pm.)

While Castellina has a few nice blocks in the center of town, it is not nearly as attractive in its entirety as many other Tuscan hill towns. Rather than spend all your time here, consider heading to **Radda in Chianti,** just a few kilometers away, on the same bus from Siena. Radda's **tourist office,** P. Ferrucci, 1, in the town's main square, has an extremely friendly multilingual staff willing to help you find accommodations, either in town or in the surrounding countryside. They will also arrange tours of vineyards and provide you with information about activities that suit your interests. This is *the* place to contact if you are interested in exploring the Chianti region. (☎0577 73 84 94; email proradda@chiantinet.it. Open Apr.-Nov. M-Sa 10am-1pm and 3-7pm, Su 10am-1pm; Dec.-Mar. M-Sa 10am-1pm.) For accommodations, it's hard to beat the clean, modern rooms of **Le Camere di Giovannino,** V. Roma, 6-8, a few meters from the tourist office. All rooms have bath. (☎/fax 0577 73 80 56. Singles L60,000; doubles L80,000.) Like Castellina, Radda is home to numerous *enoteche;* try **Casa Porciatti,** P. IV Novembre, 1-3, within the town's 14th-century walls. Bottles start at L13,000. (☎0577 73 80 55; fax 0577 73 82 34; email casaporciatti@chiantinet.it; www.chiantinet.it/casaporciatti. Open May-Oct. M-Sa 7:45am-1pm and 5-8pm, Su 7:45am-1pm; Nov.-Apr. M-Sa 8am-1pm and 4:30-7:30pm.) The cheapest place to get wine, however, is the **Coop Market,** V. Roma, 26, where bottles start at L6000. (Open M-Tu and Th-Sa 8:30am-1pm and 4:30-8pm, W 8:30am-1pm.) If you don't want to fix your own food, **Ristorante Il Giarrosto,** V. Roma, 41, has a tourist menu for L25,000, including service. (☎0577 73 80 10. Open Th-Tu for lunch and dinner.) A cheaper dining option is **Pizza Pie di Schiano Luigi Ciro,** V. XX Settembre, next to the bus stop, two blocks from P. della Chiesa. (Open daily Apr.-Oct. noon-2:30pm and 4:30-9:30pm; Nov.-Mar. daily 4:30-9:30pm.)

MONTALCINO ☎0577

Montalcino has changed little since medieval times when it was a Sienese stronghold. The foremost activity in this tiny hilltown is its production of the heavenly **Brunello di Montalcino,** a smooth, full-bodied wine widely acknowledged as Italy's finest red. Sample and buy the local Brunello in the numerous wine shops lining the town's quaint streets.

TRANSPORTATION AND PRACTICAL INFORMATION. To reach Montalcino, take one of the daily **TRA-IN buses** from **Siena** (1¼hr., 7 per day, L5500). If coming from **Montepulciano** (1¼hr., L7000), change buses at **Torrenieri.** Contact the **tourist office,** Costa del Municipio, 8, for information about tours of the local vineyards. (☎0577 84 93 21. Open Tu-Su 10am-1pm and 2:30-5pm.)

ACCOMMODATIONS AND FOOD. Rooms are expensive and scarce in Montalcino; try to find a bed in a private home. The tourist office can help find lodgings (for a L2000 fee) and **exchange currency. Albergo Il Giardino,** P. Cavour, 4, offers modern, tasteful rooms. The cozy lounge has leather couches, a stone fireplace, and the friendly proprietor's collection of the finest Italian wines bottled since 1950. Rooms offer beautiful panoramas of the Tuscan hills (over the street) or tranquility (not facing the street). (☎0577 84 82 57. Singles L80,000; doubles L100,000; triples L130,000.) **Affittacamere Casali,** V. Spagni, 3 (☎0577 84 71 50), rents rustic doubles with bath for L80,000.

A **market** on V. della Libertà brims with picnic fare every Friday. (Open 7:30am-1pm.) You'll find the best deals on Brunello at the **COOP supermarket,** on V. Sant'Agostino, off P. del Popolo. (Open M-Tu and Th-Sa 8am-1pm and 5-8pm, W 8am-1pm.) Near the *fortezza*, the **Ostaria di Porta al Cassero,** V. Ricasoli, 32, dishes out *scottiglia di cinghiale* (wild boar stew) for L12,000 and *coniglio arrosto* (roast rabbit) for L11,000. (☎0577 84 71 96. Open Th-Tu noon-3pm and 7-10:30pm.) **Petto's Pizza** off P. del Popolo—walk behind the tower and turn right—serves excellent pizza slices for L1500-3000. (☎0577 84 72 16. Open W-M 8am-2pm and 4-8pm.)

SIGHTS. To appreciate the local vineyards, head 5km away to the **Fattoria dei Barbi in Sant'Antimo** (☎0577 84 82 77). The **Azienda Agricola Greppo,** which produced the first Brunello in 1888, lies 3km away from Montalcino and toward Sant'Antimo. Call ☎0577 84 80 87 to arrange a tour of the cellars. The **Palazzo Comunale** in the P. del Popolo hosts wine exhibitions. Montalcino also produces fabulous honey. **Apicoltura Ciacci,** V. Ricasoli, 26, up the street from the Chiesa di S. Agostino, stocks every honey product imaginable, including honey soap, honey biscuits, honey milk, honey candies, honey *grappa*, and honey clogs. (☎0577 84 80 19. Open Apr.-Mar. daily; Nov.-Mar. weekends. Ring the bell for assistance. V, MC.)

Montalcino's most inspiring sight, the **Abbazia di Sant'Antimo,** lies 9km away down a serpentine road. With its rounded apse and carved alabaster capitals, this early 12th-century abbey, built on the remains of an 8th-century church allegedly founded by Charlemagne, is one of Tuscany's most beautiful Romanesque churches. Moreover, it is surrounded by sloping hills, vineyards, and cypresses—the quintessential Tuscan image beloved of filmmakers. Inside, monks perform mass in Gregorian chant. (☎0577 83 56 69. Open M-Sa 10am-12:30pm and 3-6:30pm, Su 9-10:30am and 3-6pm.) Buses leave from Montalcino for the abbey (M-Sa 6, 7am, 1:40, 4:35pm; return 7:45am, 2:25, 6:45pm; round-trip L4000.) Plan accordingly. If you arrive on the 1:40pm bus, you must run both ways between the stop and the abbey (an 8min. walk) and spend no more than 5 minutes in the cathedral in order to return on the 2:25pm bus. Consider renting a **bike** (L25,000 per day) or **moped** (L50,000 per day) at V. Pietro Strozzi, 25 (☎0577 84 82 82; fax 0577 84 64 07).

Montalcino's 14th-century **fortezza,** which sheltered a band of republicans escaping the Florentine siege of Siena in 1555, still surrounds the city. Composed of the remains of 19 original towers and nearly impregnable walls, the *fortezza* is accessible to the public. Two courtyards beckon inside the fortress,

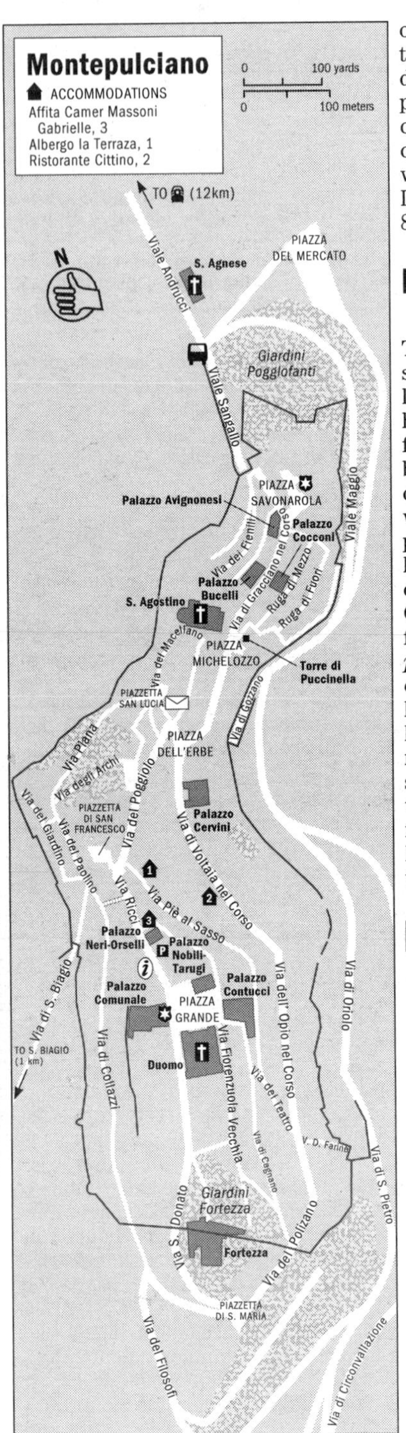

one sunny and cheered by geraniums, the other shaded by foliage. (Open daily 9am-1pm and 2:30-8pm. Ramparts L4000.) The fortezza's sophisticated **Enoteca La Fortezza** offers cheese plates (L12,000) and local wines (L3-8000 per glass; *Brunello* L9000). (Open Apr.-Oct. daily 9am-8pm; Nov.-Mar. Tu-Su 9am-6pm.)

MONTEPULCIANO

☎0578

This small medieval hamlet, stretched along the crest of a narrow limestone ridge, is one of Tuscany's highest hilltop towns and one of the finest locations in which to enjoy the beautiful countryside. Montepulciano is enclosed behind thick stone walls, which were built in four phases, first to protect against belligerent neighbors and later to ward off sickness and noxious pilgrims. Crammed within its impressive fortifications lie many Renaissance-style *palazzi* and churches. Montepulciano is best known, however, for its local Vino Nobile wines. At many local wineries, the traveling epicurean can fully experience the smooth taste of the garnet-colored wine that has earned the town notoriety. Even if you skip the wine, the landscape and museums make Montepulciano an excellent rural refuge.

TRANSPORTATION

Trains: Montepulciano lies on the Florence-Rome line; the station is 12km from the center of town. To **Chiusi** (45min., every hr., L4700). **LFI** buses run to the town from the train station (Sept.-May 6am-9pm, L3500). Summer service is extremely sparse—you will probably have to take a cab (L25,000) to get to the center of town.

Buses: TRA-IN buses run from Siena, Florence, Pienza, and Chiusi. From **Siena** (1½hr., M-Sa 7-8 per day, L8000), some via **Buonconvento.** 2 direct buses also run between Montepulciano and **Florence** (2hr., L14,000). Buy tickets at agencies displaying LFI *Biglietti* and TRA-IN signs.

Taxis: ☎0578 639 89. 24hr. taxi service: ☎0578 71 60 81.

ORIENTATION AND PRACTICAL INFORMATION

Buses stop at the bottom of the hill outside the town. Disembark at the *centro storico*, before the bus begins its descent. A short, steep climb leads to the **Corso,** the main street. Orange ATAF **buses** make the trip easier (L1400). Divided nominally into four parts (V. di Gracciano nel Corso, V. di Voltaia nel Corso, V. dell'Opio nel Corso, and V. del Poliziano), the Corso winds languorously up a precipitous hill. At the end, the street starts to level off; from here, on **Via del Teatro,** another incline on the right leads to **Piazza Grande,** the main square.

Tourist Office: P. Grande, 3 (☎0578 75 86 87). Pick up the helpful booklet *Montepulciano-Perla del Cinquecento,* in English or French, which includes a list of *affittacamere.* Open daily 9am-12:30pm and 3-7pm.

Currency Exchange: Banca Toscana, P. Michelozzo, 2. **ATM** outside. Open M-F 8:20am-1:20pm and 2:45-3:45pm. Currency exchange is also available at the **post office** and the 24hr. exchange machines in P. Savonarola.

Car Rental: Stefano Franco, V. Le Grazie, 1 (☎0578 71 60 81).

Bike Rental: A. S. Cicloposse, V. dell'Opio nel Corso, 18 (☎0578 71 63 92). L7000 per hr., L30,000 per day. Free delivery in Montepulciano and immediate surroundings.

Emergencies: ☎113. **Medical Emergencies:** ☎118. **Police:** P. Savonarola, 16 (☎112).

Pharmacy: Farmacia Franceschi, V. di S. Pietro, 17 (☎0578 71 63 92). Open M-Sa Apr.-Sept. 9am-1pm and 4:30-7:30pm; Oct.-May 9am-1pm and 4-7pm. **Farmacia Sorbini,** V. Calamandrei (☎0578 75 73 52), fills urgent prescriptions at night.

Post Office: V. dell'Erbe, 12, off the Corso. Currency exchange (L1000 commission). Open M-F 8:15am-7pm, Sa 8:15am-12:30pm. **Postal Code:** 53045.

ACCOMMODATIONS

Affittacamere Massoni Gabriella, V. Ricci, 25 (☎0578 75 73 48 or 0578 71 63 41), downhill from the tourist office. Rents small, lovely rooms, some with fantastic views. Must call ahead to reserve a room and get the key. Doubles with bath L80,000.

Albergo La Terazza, V. Piè al Sasso, 16 (☎/fax 0578 75 74 40), off the Corso. Antique-filled rooms and a gregarious proprietor. Watch the sunset from the terrace. Breakfast in the garden downstairs L5000. Reserve ahead. Singles L70,000; doubles with bath L85,000. Apartment for 2 with large kitchen L110,000; apartment for 4 with fireplace, sitting room, and kitchen L170,000. V, MC.

Ristorante Cittino, V. della via Nuova, 2 (☎0578 75 73 35), off V. di Voltaia nel Corso. Popular restaurant with superb food. Full meals L25,000. Closed W and last 2 weeks in June. The smell of mom's cooking wafts from the kitchen downstairs to their 3 clean doubles (L65,000) and 1 triple (L105,000).

FOOD

Minimarkets line the Corso. A **Conad supermarket** is a few blocks down from P. Savonarola, outside the city walls. (Open M-Tu and Th-Sa 8:30am-7pm, W 8:30am-noon.) Thursday brings an **open-air market** to P. Sant'Agnese. (Open 8am-1pm.)

Osteria dell'Acquacheta, V. del Teatro, 22 (☎0578 75 84 43 or 0578 71 70 86), off the Corso. Run by 2 culinary masters. Simple, tasty dishes and great wine. Split the huge and juicy *bistecca alla fiorentina* with a friend. Their cheeses are homemade; try *pecorino miele e noci* (pecorino with honey and nuts) or *pecorino di peinza al tartufo* (pecorino with truffles) for L4000. *Primi* L6-8000. Open W-M noon-4pm and 7pm-1am.

Trattoria Diva e Maceo, V. Gracciano nel Corso, 92 (☎0578 71 69 51). Locals socialize here over *cannelloni* (stuffed with ricotta and spinach) or *ossobuco* (bone marrow). Open W-M noon-4pm and 7-11pm. Closed 1st 2 weeks in July.

Caffè Poliziano, V. del Voltaio nel Corso, 27 (☎0578 75 86 15). This classy cafe bakes wonderful pastries and has a lunch and dinner menu. For the price of an espresso (L2000), you can sit and read one of the free newspapers for as long as you like. Refined and elegant dining downstairs for dinner; romantic candlelit dinners on an outdoor patio decorated with delicate lanterns. Salads L7-12,000. Free tarot readings Thursday beginning at 9:30pm. Open daily 8am-1am.

Pub Grotta del Nano, V. Gracciano del Corso, 11 (☎0578 75 60 23). Inexpensive and quick. Offers sandwiches, pizza by the slice, a *gelato* bar, and a small menu. Wine and *panzanell* L9000. *Crostini* and wine L13,000. Beer L4-6000.

SIGHTS

Montepulciano boasts an impressive assemblage of Renaissance and Baroque *palazzi* dating from the 16th and 17th centuries.

PALAZZI. Noteworthy *palazzi* line the lowest quarter of V. di Gracciano. On the right, **Palazzo Avignonesi** (1507-1575) is attributed to Vignola. The elegant windows of the 2nd floor contrast sharply with the bold protruding windows of the ground floor, displaying the *Palazzo*'s different stages of construction. The lions' heads on either side of the door correspond to those on top of the **Marzocco Column,** in front of the *palazzo*. The lion, the heraldic symbol of Florence, replaced the she-wolf of Siena when Florence took over Montepulciano in 1511. The original statue now rests in the **Museo Civico.** Farther up the street rises the asymmetrical facade of **Palazzo Cocconi,** attributed to Antonio da Sangallo the Elder (1455-1534). Across the street, **Palazzo Bucelli** showcases Roman and Etruscan reliefs, urn slabs, and inscriptions collected by the 18th-century proprietor, Pietro Bucelli.

CHIESA DI SAN BIAGIO. This church, outside the town walls, is Sangallo's masterpiece. The church is a wonder of Renaissance architecture—well-balanced, harmonious from every angle, adorned with restrained yet graceful detail, and gleaming on an emerald green plot of grass overlooking the hills. The cypress-lined V. della Remebranza leads to the church by way of the old cemetery, with its beehive family sepulchres. *(Open daily 9am-1pm and 3:30-7pm.)*

PIAZZA GRANDE. The unfinished *duomo*, the Palazzo Tarugi, the Palazzo Contucci, and the 14th-century Palazzo Comunale all surround this *piazza*. The construction of the *duomo* began in the 16th century when the town council deemed the existing cathedral unworthy. After several years of commissioning and firing architects, the town council settled on Ippolito Scalza, an architect from Orvieto. The product of his painstaking process is an unaccountably stark *duomo* whose rustic, unfinished facade reflects its sparse interior. However unpretentious, the *duomo* does have a poignant *Assumption of the Virgin* by Taddeo di Bartolo in a triptych above the altar; some consider this work the artist's masterpiece. *(In P. Grande, at the top of the hill. Walk up Il Corso. Open daily 9am-1pm and 3:30-7pm.)*

The elegant white facade of **Palazzo de' Nobili-Tarugi** faces the *duomo*. The nearby **Palazzo Contucci** is a graceful, if eccentric, hybrid of architectural styles. The Contucci family has made fine wine within its walls for well over a century and today runs a charming *enoteca* (wine store) on the ground floor. In the mid-1400s Michelozzo completed the austere **Palazzo Comunale,** a smaller version of the Palazzo Vecchio in Florence, which took nearly a century to build. The *palazzo*'s tower offers a view of Siena in the north and the Gran Sasso Massif in the south. *(Tower open M-Sa 8:30am-12:30pm.)*

The **Palazzo Neri-Orselli** houses the **Museo Civico,** one of Montepulciano's foremost attractions. The museum contains a collection of enameled terra-cotta by della Robbia, Etruscan funerary urns, and more than 200 paintings. *(V. Ricci, 10. Open W-Sa 9:30am-1pm and 3-6pm, Su 9:30am-1pm. L8000.)*

FORTEZZA. Now used as a high school, this old fortress was built over an ancient altar to Mercury and houses a natural well. It overlooks a fertile valley, making it a lovely picnic spot. *(Open to the public in Aug.)*

FESTIVALS

Although the artsy **Caffè Poliziano** (see above) hosts a jazz festival in July, it's always a wonderful place for a drink. In the 1st half of August the town fills with musicians who perform at **Cantiere Internazionale d'Arte,** a festival directed by the German composer Hans Werner Henze. At other times, the main form of entertainment for tourists consists of traipsing from one wine store to the next. All offer free samples of the wines they sell; try the one at **Porta di Bacco,** on the left immediately after you enter the city gates. (Open daily 9am-8pm.)

Around August 15, the **Bruscello** (a series of amateur concerts and theatrical productions) occurs on the steps of the *duomo.* (For tickets, around L20,000, contact the tourist office.) Visit Montepulciano the last Sunday in August to see the raucous **Bravio delle Botti** (Barrel Race), held to commemorate the eight neighborhood militias who fended off the Florentines and Sienese. Pairs of youths, dressed in costumes bearing their team markings, roll barrels up the steep incline of the Corso, exchanging insults and blows as they battle their way to the Grande.

DAYTRIP FROM MONTEPULCIANO: SATURNIA

If your legs are feeling the wear from days of hiking around Tuscan hill towns and you're blessed with wheels, head to Saturnia to enjoy free and unrestricted access to **Le Cascatelle,** hot streams of water that bubble to the surface in natural rock pools. The water of the hot springs reflects the intense blue of the skies. Follow the road to Montemerano until the official spa complex of Saturnia appears. About 200m later, the road takes a sharp curve, and a dirt track leads off the highway to the springs. From Montepulciano, Saturnia is about two hours away by car (140km). For more information, contact Saturnia's **tourist office.**

VOLTERRA ☎0588

Atop a huge bluff known as *Le Balze*, the town broods over the surrounding checkerboard of green and yellow. Drawn by the impregnable cliffs, the Etruscans established the town of Velathri here, which by the 4th century BC had become one of the most powerful cities of the Dodecapolis. By the Middle Ages, Volterra had shrunk to one-third its former size—parts of the town even fell off the famous cliffs upon which Volterra was built. Today, Volterra is a popular place to view Etruscan artifacts or to purchase an exquisite alabaster statue carved in one of the many local workshops. The city's medieval architecture and superb views draw tourists, but it is outside the gates, with the semolina fields, distant mountains, and picturesque cliffs, that Volterra reveals its ineffable appeal.

TRANSPORTATION

Trains: (☎0588 861 50), 9km west in **Saline di Volterra.** Take the bus to **Saline** for trains to **Pisa** (L7400) and the **coast.**

Buses: (☎0588 861 50) in P. Martiri della Libertà. To **Florence** (2hr., L12,200). **TRA-IN** connects to **San Gimignano** (2hr., L7500) and **Siena** (2hr., L8400). All 3 require a change at Colle Val d'Elsa; San Gimignano requires a 2nd change at Poggibonsi. Since the services are provided by different companies, navigating the route can be complicated. **CPT** runs between Colle Val D'Elsa and Volterra—buy tickets at a *tabac* or at the vending machines near the bus stop. **TRA-IN** and **SITA** run the buses from Colle Val D'Elsa to Florence, Siena, and elsewhere in Tuscany. Buy tickets at travel agencies or at their offices in those towns. There is one such agency in the square where buses arrive and leave in Colle Val D'Elsa. When buying your 1st ticket, be sure that the connection time at Colle Val D'Elsa is reasonable. **CPT** also runs to **Saline di Volterra** (5 per day, Su and in Aug. 2 per day; L2900) and **Pisa** (2hr., 7 per day, L9500), via **Pontederra.** Buy tickets from vending machines or in the bars down the street.

Taxis: ☎0588 875 17.

ORIENTATION AND PRACTICAL INFORMATION

To get from **Piazza della Libertà** to **Piazza dei Priori,** the town's historic and administrative center, turn left onto **Via Ricciarelli** and walk 40m.

Tourist Office: P. dei Priori, 20 (☎0588 872 57). English spoken. Rents excellent recorded walking tours. (L15,000 per person, L10,000 per person for groups of 2-4, further reductions for larger groups.) Open Apr.-Oct. M-Sa 10am-1pm and 2-8pm, Su 10am-1pm and 2-7pm; Nov.-Mar. daily 10am-1pm and 2-6pm.

Currency Exchange: Cassa di Risparmio di Firenze, V. Matteotti, 1, has a 24hr. exchange machine and an **ATM** outside. Also in P. Martiri della Libertà.

Emergencies: ☎113. **Police:** ☎113. **Medical Emergencies:** ☎118. **Ambulance:** ☎118. **Hospital:** (☎0588 919 11), on P. San Giovanni.

Pharmacy: Farmacia Amidei, V. Ricciarelli, 2 (☎0588 860 60). Open M-Sa 9am-1pm and 4-8pm; they can open Su in emergency situations.

Post Office: P. Priori, 14 (☎0588 869 69). Open M-Sa 8am-7pm. **Postal Code:** 56048.

ACCOMMODATIONS AND CAMPING

Ask at the tourist office for a list of *affittacamere*. Doubles start around L60,000.

Youth Hostel, V. del Poggeto, 3 (☎0588 855 77). From either P. della Libertà or P. dei Priori, take V. Matteotti and turn right at V. Gramsci. Walk through P. XX Settembre and down V. Minzoni—V. del Poggeto is a small street on your left. A squeaky-clean hostel with cheery amateur paintings. Breakfast L4000. Lunch or dinner L17,000. Sheets and shower included. Curfew 11:30pm. Reception Oct.-May 24hr.; June-Sept. noon-3pm and 5:30-11:30pm. Dorms L20,000.

Seminario Sant'Andrea, Vle. V. Veneto, 2 (☎0588 860 28), in P. S. Andrea, next to the church. 5min. outside the Porta A. Marcoli. Quiet, private rooms off frescoed hallways; some have gorgeous views. Dorms L27,000, with bath L34,000.

L'Etrusca, V. Porta all'Arco, 37/41 (☎/fax 0588 840 73). From the bus station, take V. Marchesi about 20m and turn left on V. Porta all'Arco. Clean and modern flats rented by the day, all with bath and kitchen facilities. Reserve ahead. Singles L65,000; doubles L110,000; triples L125,000. L5000 discount for 7 day rental.

Albergo Etruria, V. Matteotti, 32 (☎0588 873 77). Exit P. Libertà and turn right before P. dei Priori; the Etruria is a few blocks down. The best prices in town for a "real" hostel. Large rooms, most with TV. Garden lounge. Breakfast L10,000. Singles L70,000, with bath L90,000; doubles L90,000, with bath L120,000. V, MC.

Camping: Le Balze, V. Mandringa, 15 (☎0588 878 80). Exit through the Porta S. Francesco, and bear right on Strada Provincial Pisana. V. Mandringa veers off to the left. This attractive campground has a pool, a bar, and a small market. The site offers incredible views of Le Balze (the rugged cliffs surrounding Volterra). Showers included. Pool free. Reception 8am-1pm, 2-7pm, and 8-11pm. Cars must be parked by 11pm. Reservations accepted. Open Apr. to late Oct. L9000 per person, L7000 per tent, L3000 per car, L12,000 per camper. V, MC.

FOOD

An excellent selection of game dishes and local cheeses is available at any of the *alimentari* along V. Guarnacci or V. Gramsci. Sample *salsiccia di cinghiale* (wild boar sausage) and *pecorino* (sheep's milk cheese). For a sweet snack, try *ossi di morto* (bones of death), a rock-hard local confection made of egg whites, sugar, hazelnuts, and a hint of lemon, or *pane di pescatore*, dense and delicious sweet bread full of nuts and raisins. Pick up groceries at the **Despar market,** V. Gramsci, 12. (Open M-F 7:30am-1pm and 5-8pm, Sa 7:30am-1pm.)

Il Pozzo degli Etruschi, V. dei Prigioni, 30 (☎0588 80 60 08). Hearty Tuscan fare served in a private garden. Try *risotto ai porcini* (with mushrooms; L10,000) and the *cinghiale alla maremmane* (wild boar; L15,000). *Primi* L3-18,000, *secondi* L7-20,000. Tourist menu L25,000. Cover L2500. Open Su-Th noon-3pm and 6:30-10pm. V, MC, AmEx.

L'Ombra della Sera, V. Gramsci, 70 (☎0588 866 63), off P. XX Settembre. Boars' heads reproachfully watch diners as they feast on homemade pasta and wild game. *Primi* from L8500, *secondi* from L15,000. Cover L2500. Service 10%. Open Tu-Su noon-3pm and 7-10pm. V, MC, AmEx.

Pizzeria/Birreria Ombra della Sera, V. Guarnacci, 16 (☎0588 852 74). Great pizza L7-11,000, big salads L10,000. Open Tu-Su noon-3pm and 7-11pm.

SIGHTS AND ENTERTAINMENT

PIAZZA DEI PRIORI AND FORTEZZA MEDICEA. Volterra revolves around Piazza dei Priori, a medieval center surrounded by sober, dignified *palazzi*. The **Palazzo dei Priori,** the oldest governmental palace in Tuscany (1208-1254), presides over the square. *(Courtyard open 9am-6pm.)* Across the *piazza* sits the **Palazzo Pretorio,** a series of 13th-century buildings and towers that today house municipal offices. Volterra's most prominent structure is the Fortezza Medicea, an elegant remnant of Florentine rule.

DUOMO. Initiated in Pisan-Romanesque style in the 13th century, the *duomo* was never completed (though work continued for three centuries). Inside, on the left, the oratory houses a series of wooden statues depicting the life of Jesus from nativity to crucifixion. The chapel off the transept holds frescoes by Rosselli, including the brilliant *Mission per Damasco*. Amid the ornate ceiling decorations is an intricate alabaster tabernacle with figures of *Faith*, *Hope*, and *Charity* by Mino da Fiesole. Also note the spectacular use of perspective in the *Annunciation* by M. Albertinelli and Fra Bartolomeo on the left wall. *(Down V. Turazza from P. dei Priori to P. S. Giovanni. Open daily mid-Mar. to Oct. 9am-7pm; Nov. to mid-Mar. 9am-2pm.)*

PINACOTECA COMUNALE. A graceful building with a courtyard contains Volterra's best art. Taddeo di Bartolo's elegant *Madonna and Saints* altarpiece will shock anyone who has seen his gruesome *Last Judgement* in San Gimignano. In Rosso Fiorentino's spectacular 1st-floor work, the *Deposition* (1521), Christ's body seems to be painted green (most likely a result of aging and poor restoration). The painting is mesmerizing, in part because Piorentino paints one figure's hair and another's foot slightly onto the frame, thus creating the illusion that his subjects are not confined to a flat surface. A bench is provided for those who are weak in the knees or who just want to take their time. *(V. dei Sartiri, 1. Up V. Buonparenti from P. dei Priori. ☎0588 875 80. Open daily mid-Mar. to Oct. 9am-7pm; Nov. to mid-Mar. 9am-2pm. Cumulative admission includes Pinacoteca, Museo Etrusco, and Museo dell' Opera del Duomo e Arte Sacra for L13,000, students L9000.)*

MUSEO ETRUSCO GUARNACCI. The Etruscan museum displays over 600 finely carved funerary urns from the 8th and 7th centuries BC. A stylized figure representing the deceased tops each urn; below, dramatic bas-reliefs recreate various episodes from classical mythology. The pieces, grouped by story, are not well displayed, and an audio tour will run you an additional L8000 (L10,000 for two). The 1st floor (Room XXII) holds the museum's most famous piece, the oddly elongated bronze figure dubbed *L'Ombra della Sera (Shadow of the Evening)*, which inspired the great modern Italian sculptor Giacommetti. The farmer who unearthed it used it for years as a fireplace poker until a visitor recognized it as an Etruscan votive figure. In Room XX, the museum also contains the famous *Urna* *degli Sposi*, an angry and oddly haggard married couple sculpted together on the same urn. *(V. Minzoni, 15. From P. dei Priori, head down to V. Matteotti, turn right on V. Gramisci, and follow it to V. Minzoni. ☎0588 863 47. Gallery and museum open daily mid-Mar. to Oct. 9am-7pm; Nov. to mid-Mar. 9am-2pm.)*

MUSEO DELL'OPERA DEL DUOMO DI ARTE SACRA. Since it's included in any cumulative ticket, you might consider going to this museum, which holds much of the art originally in the *duomo* as well as pieces from other sources. The objects on display range from liturgical robes to impressive metallic sculptures. *(V. Roma, 1, meters from the duomo. ☎0588 862 90. Open daily mid-Mar. to Oct. 9:30am-1pm and 3-6:30pm; Nov. to mid-Mar. 9am-1pm.)*

ETRUSCAN ARCH. The massive 3rd-century BC Etruscan arch is one of the city's oldest gates. The black lumps of stone on the outside date to the 6th century BC and were once sculpted human heads, symbolizing either Etruscan gods or beheaded enemy prisoners. *(Across the piazza down V. Porta all'Arco to Porta all'Arco.)*

LE BALZE. Exit the city through the **Porta San Francesco** and follow the signs leading to *Le Balze*, where you'll find Volterra's most famous sight, cliffs that tower majestically over the valley floor. These gullies have been growing over the millennia, swallowing churches in the Middle Ages and uncovering an Etruscan necropolis in the 18th century. It takes about 15 minutes to get there (downhill) and 25 minutes to get back; the bulk of the walk is on a shoulderless major road.

SAN GIMIGNANO ☎0577

The hilltop village of San Gimignano looks like an illumination from a medieval manuscript—crushed between clusters of buildings, churches, *palazzi*, and towers bulge out of proportion. The city's famous 14 towers, which are all that survive of the original 72, date from a period when prosperous, warring families fought battles within the city walls, using their towers to store grain for sieges. The towers were also convenient for dumping boiling oil on attacking enemies. Exhausted by war, San Gimignano stagnated in poverty for six centuries. Eventually, its towered horizon (which inspired the city's nickname—"Medieval Manhattan") lured postwar tourists, whose tastes and wallets resuscitated production of the golden Vernaccia wine. With hordes of daytrippers, an infestation of souvenir shops, and countless restaurants, San Gimignano now feels like Disney's MedievalLand. Nevertheless, it's impressive and worth the packed bus rides. Stay overnight to enjoy the city when the streets empty and souvenir shops disappear.

TRANSPORTATION

Trains: The nearest station is in **Poggibonsi;** buses connect the station to the town (M-F every 2hr. 7:20am-8:55pm, Sa-Su every hr. 6:45am-8:55pm).

Buses: TRA-IN buses (☎0577 20 41 11 or 0577 93 72 07) leave from P. Martiri, outside Porta S. Giovanni. Schedules and tickets at **Caffè Combattente,** V. S. Giovanni, 124, to the left as you enter the city gates. Tickets also available from any *tabacchi* in town or at the tourist office in P. del Duomo. Change at **Poggibonsi** (20min., L2600) for **Siena** (1½hr. if you get a good connection, every 1-2hr., L8800) and **Florence** (2hr. with a good connection, every 1-2hr., L10,000).

ORIENTATION AND PRACTICAL INFORMATION

To reach the center of town from the bus station, go through the *porta* and climb the hill, following **Via San Giovanni** to **Piazza della Cisterna** and **Piazza del Duomo.**

Tourist Office: Pro Loco, P. del Duomo, 1 (☎0577 94 00 08; fax 0577 94 09 03; email prolocs@tin.it). Has lists of hotels and rooms for rent. Bus and train schedules. Bus tickets sold. Walking tours of the countryside (2 per day, L20,000). English spoken. Open daily Mar.-Oct. 9am-1pm and 3-7pm; Nov.-Feb. 9am-1pm and 2-6pm.

Accommodations Services: Siena Hotels Promotion, V. S. Giovanni, 125 (☎/fax 0577 94 08 09), on the right as you enter the city gates; look for the *"Cooperativa Alberghi e Ristoranti"* sign. Reserves hotel rooms in San Gimignano and Siena for a L3000 commission. Open M-Sa 9:30am-7pm. **Associazione Strutture Extraberghiere,** P. della Cisterna, 6 (☎/fax 0577 94 31 90). Patient staff makes reservations for private rooms without charge. Doubles with bath L90-100,000. Call a week in advance if you want to stay in the countryside; they can always find a place in the city center. Open Mar.-Nov. daily 9:30am-7:30pm.

Currency Exchange: at the Pro Loco tourist office and the post office. **ATMs** scattered along V. S. Giovanni, V. degli Innocenti, and P. della Cisterna.

Car Rental: Hertz (☎0577 94 22 20), on Vle. dei Fossi.

Bike Rental: Bruno Bellini, V. Roma, 41 (☎0577 94 02 01). Mountain bikes L25,000 per day, L100,00 per week. Includes delivery. Open daily 9am-8pm.

Police: ☎112. **Carabinieri** (☎0577 94 03 13), on P. Martiri. **Medical Emergencies:** ☎118.

Pharmacy: V. S. Matteo, 13 (☎0577 94 03 97). Fills urgent prescriptions all night. Open M-Sa 9am-1pm and 4:30-8pm. Closed late June to mid-July.

Post Office: P. delle Erbe, 8, behind the *duomo.* Open Mar.-Oct. M-F 8:15am-7pm, Sa 8:15am-12:30pm; Nov.-Feb. M-F 8:15am-12:30pm and 2-5pm, Sa 8:15am-12:30pm. Currency exchange available. **Postal Code:** 53037.

ACCOMMODATIONS AND CAMPING

San Gimignano caters to wealthy tourists, and most accommodations are well beyond budget range. *Affittacamere* provide an alternative to overpriced hotels, with doubles around L80,000 (with bath L100,000). The tourist office and the **Associazione Strutture Extralberghiere** (see above) have lists of budget rooms.

Ostello di San Gimignano, V. delle Fonti, 1 (☎0577 94 19 91; reservations ☎055 807 70 09; fax 055 805 01 04). When you call, specify that you want to stay at the hostel in San Gimignano. Turn off V. S. Matteo onto V. XX Settembre and follow the signs. This refreshingly peaceful hostel has great views of the Tuscan countryside. Sheets and buffet breakfast included. Reception daily 7-9am and 5-11:30pm. Curfew 11:30pm. Open Mar.-Oct. Dorms L26,000. Cash only.

Albergo/Ristorante Il Pino, V. S. Matteo, 102 (☎/fax 0577 94 04 15). Rustic simplicity in a quiet quarter of town. Open beamed ceilings, medieval arches, rural bricks, and red bedframes. All rooms with bath and TV. Breakfast L15,000. Reservations recommended. Singles L70,000; doubles L100,000. V, MC, AmEx.

Camere La Stella, V. Dante, 15 (☎/fax 0577 94 04 44). 500m from the town center in an elegant house with a garden and nice views of the countryside. Gregarious manager also runs the excellent restaurant of the same name (see below). All rooms have bath. Free parking. Call for reservations. Doubles L110,000. V, MC, AmEx.

Camere Cennini Gianni, V. S. Giovanni, 21 (☎0577 94 10 51). Reception is at the *pasticceria* at V. S. Giovanni, 88. From the bus stop, enter through the Porta S. Giovanni. Kitchens available for groups of 4. Reserve ahead. Quaint, clean doubles with bath L90,000; can serve as triples for L120,000 and quads for L140,000.

Camping: Il Boschetto (☎0577 94 03 52), at Santa Lucia, 2½km downhill from Porta S. Giovanni. Buses run from P. Martiri (L1500). Ask the driver if the bus is going to the campgrounds; it's also not a bad hike. Bar and market on the premises. Reception daily 8am-1pm, 3-8pm, and 9-11pm. Open Apr.-Oct. 15. L8500 per person, L8500 per small tent. Hot showers included.

FOOD

If you didn't guess from the sad, glass eyes of stuffed tuskers across town, San Gimignano specializes in boar and other wild game. The town also caters to less-daring palates with mainstream Tuscan dishes at fairly high prices. Whether you're looking to save or savor, try the **open-air market** in P. del Duomo on Thursday mornings. (8am to noon.) A small **market** sells cheap, filling sandwiches and take-out pasta, salads, and drinks at V. S. Matteo, 19. (☎0577 94 19 52. Open daily Mar.-Oct. 9am-8pm; Nov.-Feb. F-W 9am-8pm, Th 9am-1pm.) Purchase the famous Vernaccia di San Gimignano, a light white wine with a hint of sweetness, from **La Buca,** V. S. Giovanni, 16 (☎0577 94 04 07). The cooperative also offers terrific sausages and meats, all made on its own farm. The boar sausage *al pignoli* (L3000 per hectogram) and the *salame con mirto* are especially delicious. (Open Apr.-Oct. daily 9am-8pm; Nov.-Mar. F-W 9am-8pm.) To have a drink in the restaurant/hotel featured in *Tea with Mussolini* check out **La Cisterna,** at the top of the hill in the *piazza* of the same name.

La Stella, V. Matteo, 77 (☎0577 94 04 44). This typically rustic Tuscan restaurant offers reasonably priced food made with produce from its own farm. *Cinghiale alla cacciatore* (L13,000) is their specialty. *Gnocchi all'etrusca* (with tomatoes, cream, and cheese) L7000. *Menù* includes *primi,* your choice of a hearty *bistecca di maiale* or a light *pollo arrosto,* potatoes, and dessert for L24,000. Extensive wine list including San Gimignano's famous Vernaccia. Open Th-Tu noon-3pm and 7-11pm. V, MC, AmEx.

Pizzeria Perucà, V. Capassi, 16 (☎0577 94 31 36). Great food, hidden in an alley behind V. Matteo. Try the *maiale Chiantigiato* (boar cooked in Chianti, L13,000). Pizza L8-13,000, *primi* L7-16,000, *secondi* L15-22,000. Cover L3000. Open M-Sa noon-2:30pm and 7-10:30pm. V, MC, AmEx.

La Bettola del Grillo, V. Quercecchio, 33 (☎0577 94 18 44), off V. S. Giovanni, opposite P. della Cisterna. Refreshingly free of bricks and traditional decor. Serves up Tuscan delights. Vegetarian options. Menu L24,000. Open Tu-Su noon-3pm and 6:30-11pm.

Taverna Paradiso, V. S. Giovanni, 6 (☎0577 94 03 02). "Rustic" to the hilt, this taverna offers a solid bet for pranzo: *Menu Veloce* L22,000, with the multi-course works. Friday dinner is a medieval feast with period costumes and music (call for reservations). Open daily noon-3pm and 7-10pm.

SIGHTS AND ENTERTAINMENT

Famous as the *Città delle Belle Torri* (City of Beautiful Towers), San Gimignano has always appealed to artists. During the Renaissance, they came in droves, and the collection of their works complement San Gimignano's cityscape.

MEDIEVAL MANHATTAN. Tickets for the town's museums are available at several different rates. *Biglietti intero* (L18,000) are full-priced adult tickets; *biglietti ridotti* (L14,000) are discounted tickets, available to students under 18 and families with children between the ages of 8 and 18. Children under 7 are allowed *ingresso gratuito* (free entrance) to almost all of the sights. The city treats itself as a unified work of art; one ticket allows entry into nearly all of San Gimignano's sights. Tickets are available at any tourist sight.

PIAZZA DELLA CISTERNA AND PIAZZA DEL DUOMO. Built in 1237, P. Cisterna is surrounded by towers and *palazzi.* It adjoins P. del Duomo, site of the impressive tower of the **Palazzo del Podestà.** To its left, tunnels and intricate *loggie* riddle the **Palazzo del Popolo** (see below). To the right of the *palazzo* rises its **Torre Grossa,** the highest tower in town and the only one visitors can ascend. The 218-step climb offers panoramas of San Gimignano's many towers, the Tuscan landscape, the ancient fortress, and several *piazze.* The tower's huge bell rings every day at noon. Also in the *piazza* stand the twin towers of the Ardinghelli, truncated due to a zoning ordinance that prohibited structures higher than the Torre Grossa. *(Palazzo del Popolo open Tu-Su 9am-7:30pm. Torre Grossa open Mar.-Oct. daily 9:30am-7:20pm; Nov.-Feb. Sa-Th 10:30am-4:20pm. L8000, reduced L6000.)*

PALAZZO DEL POPOLO. Within this palace, the frescoed medieval courtyard leads to the **Sala di Dante.** Dante spoke here on May 8, 1300, as an ambassador from Florence. On the walls, Lippo Memmi's sparkling *Maestà* blesses the accompanying 14th-century scenes of hunting and tournament pageantry. In the **Museo Civico** on the 2nd floor, Taddeo di Bartolo's altarpiece, *The Story of San Gimignano*, teaches proper respect for this bishop of Modena. The small museum has an excellent collection of other Sienese and Florentine works, most notably Filippino Lippi's *Annunciation*, crafted in two circular panels, and Pinturicchio's serene *Madonna in Glory*, one of the last works to be painted by the artist. Fortunately, most tourists seem to skip this attraction, so visitors can enjoy the museum in relative peace. *(Same hours as Torre Grossa. L7000, reduced L5000. Combined tickets with the tower L12,000, reduced L9000.)*

COLLEGIATA. This 12th-century church is covered with a bare facade seemingly unfit to shelter an exceptional frescoed interior. The **Cappella di Santa Fina,** off the right aisle, was designed by Giuliano and Benedetto Maiano. Ghirlandaio's splendid frescoes on the life of Santa Fina, patron saint of San Gimignano, cover the chapel's walls. Santa Fina, though she is said to have saved the village from barbarian hordes, was struck by a fatal illness at age ten. She decided to repent all her sins and give herself to God. Spending the last five agonizing years of her life lying on a plank of wood, she became so weak and paralyzed that she couldn't even scare away the mice that scampered over her body. In the main church, Bartolo di Fredi painted beautiful frescoes of Old Testament scenes along the north aisle, while Barna da Siena provided the extremely impressive, New Testament counterparts along the south aisle. *(In P. del Duomo. Church and chapel open daily Apr.-Oct. 9:30am-7:30pm; Nov.-Mar. 9:30am-5pm; closed late Jan.-Feb. L6000, children 6-15 L3000.)*

MUSEO DI CRIMINOLOGIA MEDIOEVALE. One cheerful addition to the museum scene, this torture museum is home to an inventive collection of over 100 antique instruments of torture. It also outlines the history of human cruelty (starting when Abel used to give Cain noogies). *(On V. del Castello. ☎0577 94 22 43. Open Mar.-July and Sept. 16-Jan. 11 M-F 10am-7pm; July-Sept. 15 daily 10am-midnight; Jan. 12-Feb. M-F 10am-6pm, Sa-Su 10am-7pm. L15,000, individuals in large groups and students L10,000.)*

VINO AND VISTAS. Dinner finishes early in the hills, and the *passeggiata* along V. S. Giovanni and V. S. Matteo provides the principal entertainment. Should you find yourself at V. S. Matteo at sunset, buy a bottle of Vernaccia and enjoy the view from the lookout point outside the city gates. In summer, pass the evening under the stars at the *rocca* (fortress), where movies (L12,000) are shown at San Gimignano's **outdoor theater.** *(Weekly showings July-Aug. Info at the tourist office.)*

PISTOIA ☎0573

In 1177, Pistoia joined several other Italian city-states in declaring itself a free commune. Despite this bold debut, the city was soon surpassed by its neighbors in military, political, and economic sophistication. Pistoia became a murderous backwater, whose inhabitants Michelangelo maligned as the "enemies of heaven." To add to the infamy, the town instigated the bloody division of Guelphs into "Blacks" and "Whites." In 1254, one Pistoian allegedly chopped off a child's hand in retaliation for an injury the boy had caused his son, dragging the entire town into battle. Pistoia lent its bloody name first to an Italian dagger called *pistole* (the favored weapon for Pistoia's routine assassinations) and later to the pistol. Recently, residents have turned their attention to more peaceful endeavors—the city is home to one of the world's leading train manufacturers. Pistoia isn't all steel though; the city sits amid pastures and wildflowers. A handful of interesting monuments, refreshingly few tourists and scooters in the city center, and Pistoia's famous Blues Festival in July make the town a good daytrip from Florence.

TRANSPORTATION

Trains: from P. Dante Alighieri to: **Florence** (40min., every hr., L4200); **Viareggio** (1hr., every 2hr., L6500); **Pisa** (1hr., every 2hr., L6500); and **Rome** (4hr., every hr., L53,500). Info open daily 8:30-11:30am and 2:30-6pm.

Buses: Lazzi buses (☎0573 36 32 43) run from the train station. Buy tickets from the office across from the train station. To: **Florence** (1hr., L5000); **Empoli** (1¼hr., L5000); and **Viareggio** (2hr., L7600). Find additional bus info at V. XX Settembre, 71 (☎0573 36 32 43). Open daily 6:30am-8:15pm.

Taxis: at P. Garibaldi (☎0573 212 37) and at the train station (☎0573 242 91). Night service (☎0573 242 91) available until 1am.

ORIENTATION AND PRACTICAL INFORMATION

From the train station, walk up **Via XX Settembre** and straight onto **Via Vanucci, Via Cino,** and **Via Buozzi.** At the end of V. Buozzi turn right on **Via degli Orai** for the *duomo* (10min.). Local **COPIT buses** (#1 and 3) drop you off at P. Gavinana (L1300); turn right onto **Via Cavour** and left onto V. Roma, which runs into P. del Duomo.

Tourist Office: APT tourist office, P. del Duomo, 4 (☎0573 216 22; fax 0573 343 27), in Palazzo dei Vescovi. Friendly, English-speaking staff. Open in summer M-Sa 9am-1pm and 3-6pm, Su 9am-1pm; in winter M-Sa 9am-1pm and 3-6pm.

Currency exchange: Unless you have traveler's checks, the post office is probably your best option (see below). Traveler's checks and cash can be exchanged next door to the post office at **Cassa di Risparmio di Pistoia e Pescia,** V. Roma, 3 (☎0573 36 90). Open M-F in the mornings and early afternoons. Cash can also be exchanged at **S. Marcello Pistoiese,** V. Roma, 75 (☎0573 622 344). Open M-F 8:15am-1:30pm, Sa 8:30am-12:30pm, last day of the month 8:30am-noon.

Medical Emergencies: ☎118. **Ambulance:** ☎0573 36 36. **Police:** ☎112. **Hospital:** ☎0573 35 21.

24-Hour Pharmacy: Vle. Adua, 101 (☎0573 293 81).

Post Office: V. Roma, 5 (☎0573 99 52 11). Exchanges currency and American Express traveler's checks. Open M-F 8:15am-7pm. **Postal Code:** 51100.

ACCOMMODATIONS AND FOOD

A reasonable room at a reasonable price is a rare find in Pistoia, but **Albergo Firenze,** V. Curtatone e Montanara, 42, provides an excellent mix of comfort and value. From the station walk down V. XX Settembre, cross P. Treviso, and continue straight (the street bends to the left, changing names from V. Vannucci to V. Cino to V. Buozzi to V. Curtatone e Montanara). The hotel is near the end of the street on the right. The friendly American owner offers advice and keeps the place clean. Ask for a room off the courtyard. Rooms have TVs, floral bedspreads, sheer lace curtains, and tile floors. The L10,000 breakfast includes fresh fruit, yogurt, and bread. (☎/fax 0573 231 41. Singles L55,000, with bath L75,000; doubles L90,000, with bath L105,000; triples L120,000, with bath L130,000. V, MC, AmEx.)

Grocery stores and specialty shops line the side streets. Market junkies browse the open-air market in P. della Sala. (Open W and Sa 7:30am-2pm.) There's a daily fruit and vegetable market in P. della Sala, near the *duomo.* (Open 8am-2pm and 5-7pm.) Sample exquisite Italian cuisine and imported wines at **La Botte Gaia,** V. Lastrone, 4, with gourmet cheeses, *antipasti, bruschette, crostini,* and salads. The owner's mother creates divine desserts. Have a glass of wine (L3-8000) at an outdoor table in summer. (☎0573 36 56 02. Reservations recommended. Open Tu-Sa 10:30am-3pm and 6:30pm-1am, Su 6:30pm-1am. V, MC, AmEx.) **Trattoria dell'Abbondanza,** V. dell'Abbondanza, 10, serves excellent meals like *Panzanella di Farro*

Tourist Office: P. Cavour, 6, 3rd fl. (☎0586 89 81 11; email livorno@mail.turismo.toscana.it), up V. Cairoli from P. Grande. Open M and W 8am-1pm and 4-8pm, Tu 8am-1pm and 4-9pm, Th-F 9am-1pm and 3-9pm, Sa-Su 8am-1pm and 3-10pm. Reduced hours Sept.-May. **Branch office** (☎0586 89 53 20), in the Porto Medicino, a 5min. walk from the Stazione Marittima. Same hours as main office.

Currency Exchange: Fair rates at the **train station.** Open daily 8-11:45am and 3-5:45pm. Also at **Stazione Marittima** or one of the many **banks** on V. Cairoli.

Emergencies: ☎113. **Medical Emergencies:** ☎118. **Hospital: Pronto Soccorso,** ☎0586 40 33 51 or 0586 42 13 98.

24-Hour Pharmacy: Farmacia Comunale, V. Fiume, 1, up from P. Grande.

Post Office: V. Cairoli, 12/16 (☎0586 89 76 02). Open M-F 8:15am-7pm, Sa 8:15am-12:30pm. Exchanges currency as well. **Postal Code:** 57100.

ACCOMMODATIONS

Ostello/Albergo Villa Morazzana, V. Collinet, 40 (☎0586 50 00 76; fax 0586 56 24 26), in the countryside, barely within the city limits. Take bus #1 to P. Grande (L1500) and at P. Grande, 25, transfer to bus #3 (20min.). Different #3 buses run different routes on the outskirts of town, so ask at the information booth in P. Grande which one goes directly to the hostel. On weekdays, there is 1 per hr. in each direction. Other #3 buses will drop you off on V. Popogna; from there turn left onto V. S. Martino and follow the signs to the hostel (15min.). Housed in a 17th-century villa, the hostel hosts exhibitions of Livornese artists. The building is decorated with an eccentric mix of statuary, formal gardens, and 20th-century art. Minutes from a quiet beach and lovely Tuscan walks. Breakfast included. Lockout 9:30am-5pm. Curfew 11:30pm. Wheelchair accessible. Call ahead. Dorms L25,000; singles L50,000, with bath L75,000; doubles 105,000, with bath L120,00. V, MC, AmEx.

Pensione Dante, Scali D'Azeglio, 28 (☎0586 89 43 70). Go right as you leave the port and walk straight along the waterfront until you reach a canal on the left. The *pensione* is a few blocks ahead. The friendly proprietor loves hosting travelers from all over the world. Rooms are clean, and many overlook the canal. Singles L45,000; doubles L60,000; triples L80,000; quads L100,000.

Hotel Cremona, C. Mazzini, 24 (☎0586 83 42 78). Take V. Rossi one block out of P. Cavour. Head down V. Enrico Mayer and turn right onto C. Mazzini. Mosaic ceilings, wool-blend furniture, and soft pastel linens. Modern amenities include remote-control TV and alarm clocks. Singles L70,000, with bath L100,000; doubles L100,000, with bath L110,000; triples, one of which is wheelchair accessible, L140,000.

FOOD

Livorno owes its culinary specialties to the sea. The city has its own interpretation of classic *bouillabaise:* a fiery, tomato-based seafood stew called *cacciucco.* An **open-air market** sprawls along V. Buontalenti. (Open M-Sa 8am-1pm.) Fill your brown bag at the **STANDA supermarket,** V. Grande, 174, off P. Grande. (Open daily 8:30am-12:30pm and 4-8pm; in winter M-Sa 8:30am-12:30pm and 3:30-7pm.)

La Cantonata, C. Mazzini, 222 (☎0586 894 04 81). Smiling owner dishes out huge plates of *spaghetti ai frutti di mare* (with seafood; L9000), and brimming glasses of *chianti.* Fabulous *riso nero* (rice turned black from squid ink; L8000), *secondi* L7-20,000. *Menù* L22,000. Cover L2000. Service 10%. Open Tu-Su noon-3pm and 7-10:30pm.

Trattoria Il Sottomarino, V. dei Terrazzini, 48 (☎0586 237 71), off P. della Repubblica at the end of V. Pina d'Oro. Not cheap, but people descend from afar to sample the renowned *cacciucco.* Open Aug.-June F-W 12:30-2:30pm and 7:30-10pm.

Hostaria dell'Eremo, Scali Cialdini, 39 (☎0586 88 14 87; email pual@iol.it). Pink walls, pink tile floors, and little potted plants. Choose from a selection of fresh fish. Try the *cacciucco* (L25,000) or the *cosimo terzo* (house specialty with shrimp and prosciutto; L12,000). Open daily 7:30pm until late, Sa-Su for lunch as well. V, MC, AmEx.

SIGHTS AND ENTERTAINMENT

FORTRESSES. The **Fortezza Nuova,** which is entirely protected by a moat, is in the heart of **Piccola Venezia,** named for the canals that course through the area. The fortress, completed in the early 1600s by the Medici family, now houses a well-maintained public garden and park. From the new fortress, walk to P. Municipio, then down V. S. Giovanni to reach the sprawling **Fortezza Vecchia.** Built by the powerful Marquises of Tuscany in the 9th century, the portly central tower was the first fortification on the site. When Pisans conquered Livorno, they built a fort around the tower (fearful that it would lean over and put them out of business). In the 16th century the Medici family surrounded the ensemble with robust brick walls to consolidate their hold on Livorno, the chief Tuscan port. P. Micheli, across from the port, is home to the **Monumento dei Quattro Mori.** Bandini carved this marble figure of Duke Ferdinand I in 1595. The four manacled bronze slaves, added by Pietro Tacca in 1626, now serve as a pointed reminder of Livorno's participation in the slave market.

MUSEO CIVICO GIOVANNI FATTORI. Livorno made its mark in the wild world of painting with the 19th-century "blotters," *I Macchiaioli* (a movement led by Giovanni Fattori), and the 20th-century portraitist Amadeo Modigliani. Livornese work, both proto-Impressionist and modern, crowds the museum. *(In Villa Mimbelli, at the intersection of V. S. Iacopo and V. Acquaviva. ☎0586 80 80 01. Open daily 10am-1pm and 4-7pm. L12,000, students L6000.)*

FESTIVALS. The **Palio Marinaro,** Livorno's most energetic claim to fame, occurs just off its coast. In mid-July, rowers from the various quarters of the city race traditional crafts toward the old port, spurred on by spectators on the banks.

VIAREGGIO ☎0584

The resort town of Viareggio sits quietly at the foot of the Riviera, tucked between the colorful beach umbrellas of the Versilian coast and the olive and chestnut groves cloaking the foothills of the Apuan Mountains. In the mornings, local trains ferry in beautiful, fluorescent Italian youth intent on soaking up the sun's rays. Each night wealthy European tourists stroll along the shore's wide promenade, distinguished by its grandiose 1920s architecture. Droning away on their cell phones while peering into the windows of glitzy boutiques, they seem unaware of the lapping waves and gentle sea breeze that make these beaches so inviting.

TRANSPORTATION. Viareggio lies on both the Rome-Genoa and the Viareggio-Florence train lines. **Trains** service **Pisa, Livorno, La Spezia, Florence, Genoa,** and **Rome.** Self-service **luggage storage** is available in the train station (L3000 for 6hr., L5000 for a large locker). **Lazzi buses** (☎0584 462 33) connect Viareggio to: **Pisa** (20 per day, L4500); **Lucca** (45min., every hr., L4500); **La Spezia** (2hr., every 2hr., L6200); and **Florence** (2¼hr., 2 per day, L12,600, reservations recommended). All buses stop in P. Mazzini, the town's main square. **Taxis** (☎0584 454 54) are available at the train station.

PRACTICAL INFORMATION. The **tourist office** at the train station has good maps, local bus schedules, and info on hotels, hikes, and car tours. (Open W-M 9:30am-12:30pm and 3:30-5:30pm; reduced hours Oct.-Apr.) From the main exit of the train station, walk directly across the *piazza* and straight down V. XX Settembre to P. Mazzini. Turn right and walk 2½ blocks to the **main tourist office,** V. Carducci, 10. The personable English-speaking staff will give you a decent map and bombard you with brochures. (☎0584 96 22 33; www.versilia.turismo.toscana.it. Open May-Oct. M-Sa 9am-1pm and 3-7pm, Su 9:30am-12:30pm and 4-6pm; Nov.-Apr. daily 9am-1pm; extended hours around Christmas and Easter.) Several of their recommended itineraries necessitate a car—you can rent one at **Avis** (☎0584

456 21), on V. Aurelia Nord in front of the supermarket, only 100m from the station. **Currency exchange** is available at the post office or at any of the banks along V. Garibaldi. In case of **emergency,** dial ☎113; for **first aid,** call ☎118. An all-night **pharmacy** is at V. Mazzini, 14. The **post office** (☎0584 303 45), at the corner of V. Garibaldi and V. Puccini, exchanges currency. **Postal Code:** 55049.

ACCOMMODATIONS AND FOOD. Amid the splendor and pretense of four-stardom hide budget accommodations. Many, however, turn into long-term *pensione* in the summer, catering to Italians on holidays of a week or more. For clean, simple rooms in the center, try the freshly renovated **Hotel Albachiara,** V. Zanardelli, 81. (☎0584 445 41. Sept.-June doubles L140,000; July L160,000; Aug. L170,000.) **Albergo Apuana,** V. S. Martino, 48, two blocks from the beach, has clean rooms and friendly management. (☎0584 96 11 40. Singles L45,000, with bath L50,000; doubles L85,000, with bath L90,000. V, MC.)

Accustomed to catering to a wealthy clientele, Viareggio restaurants are none too cheap. To avoid the ubiquitous L3000 cover and 15% service charge, head to **Pizza al 2000,** V. Battista, 185. Pizza topped with everything from *prosciutto* to nutella costs L7-10,000. At **Lo Zio Pietro,** V. S. Martino, 73, savor *roticceria* fare from *calccio* (fish stew) to vegetables to slow-roasted chicken. (☎0584 96 21 83. Open M-Sa 9am-8pm.) None of the cafes along the promenade are reasonable, so you might as well spend the L5000 enjoying coffee on the ritzy terrace of the **Gran Caffè Margherita** overlooking the sea.

BEACHES AND ENTERTAINMENT. Most of the shoreline has been ungraciously roped off by the owners of Viareggio's private beaches, but you can walk through these areas to the water as long as you've already left your stuff somewhere else. A short walk to the left as you face the water leads to free patches of sandy beach. You can also amble across the canal to the larger free beach *(spiaggia libera)* toward the southern edge of town. Once across the canal, head shorewards and follow Vle. Europa past the port to the *spiaggia libera* (30min. from the train station). Hard-core people watchers should visit the ultra-posh town of **Forte dei Marmi.** Take one of the blue CLAP buses from the station (every hr., L3300). For true Viareggio entertainment, stake out a table at one of the expensive outdoor cafes and watch as Armani-clad locals emerge from their secluded villas to squander fortunes at ritzy boutiques. When night falls, stroll along the promenade, or, if you have access to wheels, head over to **Club La Canniccia,** V. dell'Unita Italia, 1, famous with all European youths.

ELBA

According to legend, the enchanting island of Elba grew from a precious stone that slipped from Venus's neck into the azure waters of the Tyrrhenian Sea. This paradise has drawn the likes of Jason and the Argonauts, Etruscan miners, and Roman patricians. Since Hellenic times, Elba, nicknamed "Sparks" (Aethalia) by the Greeks, has gained renown for its mineral wealth. Of course, the island derives its greatest fame from its association with Napoleon; the Little Emperor was sent into his first exile here in 1814, creating both a temporarily war-free Europe and the famous palindrome: "Able was I ere I saw Elba," supposedly quipped the French-speaking Emperor upon his arrival. All would-be conquerors of Europe should be so lucky: Elba's turquoise waters, dramatic mountains, velvety beaches, and diverse attractions accommodate almost any interest. Each zone of the island attracts a distinct variety of visitors—families lounge in **Marina di Campo** and **Marciana Marina,** party-hard beach fanatics waste away in **Capoliveri,** yacht-club members gallivant in **Porto Azzurro,** and nature-loving recluses gravitate to the mountainous northeast tip of the island between the beachfront **Cavi** and **Rio nell'Elba** in the interior. The southeastern coast is the most commercial and the most welcoming for those looking for sandy beaches and comfortable campgrounds, while the northeastern arm of the island has interior back roads and undisturbed views of the island's desolate desert green. Elba is one of the best places in Italy to bike or scooter, with roads that meander high into the island's mountainous terrain, affording stupendous views of the ocean. Bus rides through the island are therefore also spectacular, if a little harrowing, since the bus frequently seems on the verge of tumbling down the mountainside. Remember that cars drive on the right side of the road in Italy and plan accordingly; if you are going between Portoferraio and Marciana Marina, for instance, you want to sit on the right side of the bus on the way there and on the left side on the way back.

GETTING THERE

Elba's **airport** (☎0565 97 60 11), in Marina di Campo, sends flights to **Rome, Milan, Parma, Bern, Zurich, Munich,** and **Vienna.** The best way to reach Elba is to take a **ferry** from **Piombino Marittima** (also called Piombino Porto) on the mainland to **Portoferraio,** Elba's largest city. Ferries also dock at **Porto Azzuro,** on the opposite side of the island. **Trains** on the Genoa-Rome line sometimes travel straight to Piombino Marittima but usually stop at Campiglia Marittima (from Florence, change at Pisa). From Campiglia Marittima, a *pullman* (intercity bus; 30min., L2500), timed to meet incoming trains, leaves for the ferries in Piombino Marittima. Both **Toremar** (ferry 1hr., L12,000; hydrofoil only in summer 30min., L24,000) and **Moby Lines** (1hr., L12,000) run about 16 trips to Elba per day. The offices of **Toremar** (☎0565 311 00) and **Moby Lines** are located at P. Premuda, 13, in Piombino. You can buy tickets for the next departing ferry at the **FS** booth in the train station in Campiglia Marittima. Should you be stuck in Piombino Marittima, take a train from the port to the city (5min., about every 2hr., L1900). The bus to Campiglia Marittima also stops in the town of Piombino. In town, **Albergo Il Piave,** P. F. Niccolini, 2, across from the train station, provides standard rooms with bath (☎0565 22 60 50. Singles L70,000; doubles L165,000.)

PORTOFERRAIO ☎0565

As the main port of Elba, Portoferraio is part modern, rather unattractive port and part picturesque Tuscan city. It is probably the island's liveliest city and contains most of its essential services. Though low on sights, the old city is charming.

TRANSPORTATION

Buses: ATL, V. Elba, 20 (☎0565 91 43 92), across from the Toremar landing. Hourly service to **Capoliveri, Cavo, Lacona Marciana, Marciana Marina, Marina di Campo, Porto Azzuro, Pomonte,** and **Rio Elba.** Tickets L2500-7000. Schedules, day passes (L11,000) and weekly passes (L30,000). Open June-Sept. daily 8am-8pm; Oct.-May M-Sa 8am-1:20pm and 4-6:30pm, Su 9am-12:30pm and 2-6:30pm. **Luggage Storage:** L2500 per item for the whole day; you must pick it up while they are open.

Ferries: Toremar, Calata Italia, 22 (☎0565 91 80 80). **Moby Lines,** Vle. Elba, 4 (☎0565 91 41 33; fax 0565 91 67 58).

Taxi: ☎0565 91 51 12.

CENTRAL ITALY

ORIENTATION AND PRACTICAL INFORMATION

TOURIST, FINANCIAL, AND LOCAL SERVICES

Tourist Offices: APT, Calata Italia, 26, 1st fl. (☎0565 91 46 71; www.archipelago.turismo.toscana.it), across from the Toremar boat landing. If you have trouble finding it, walk directly next to the water in the port area and look for the huge "Ufficio Turistico" sign. Accommodations info, maps, and bus schedules. Open daily 9am-1pm and 2:30-7:30pm; in winter 9am-1pm and 3-7pm. Open June 15-Sept. 15 M-Sa 8am-8pm. **Associazione Albergatori,** Calata Italia, 21 (☎0565 91 47 54), finds rooms for free. Open M-F 9am-7:30pm, Sa 9am-12:30pm and 3:30-7pm.

Tourist Information for Camping, V. Elba, 7 (☎/fax 0565 93 02 08). Open daily 9am-1pm and 4-8pm.

Currency Exchange: There are countless rip-offs. Be smart and walk up to the banks on V. Manganaro, near Hotel Nobel, including **Banca di Roma,** V. Manganaro, 1 (☎0565 91 90 07), which also has an **ATM.** Open M-F 8:30am-1:30pm and 3:10-4pm.

Boat Excursions: Linee di Navigazione Archipelago Toscano (☎/fax 0565 91 47 97; www.elbacrociere.com) offers tours of Elba's coast as well as excursions to nearby islands (L50-70,000).

Car Rental: Rent Chiappi, Calata Italia, 30 (☎0565 91 66 87). From L75-110,000 per day. Friendly staff helps you get gas and get around. Also mopeds (L45-90,000) and mountain bikes (L20,000). Insurance included.

Bike/Moped Rental: TWN, V. Elba, 32 (☎0565 91 46 66; fax 0565 91 58 99). The best place on the island for most rentals. Provides comprehensive maps. Per day: mopeds from L35,000; two-person scooters L48,000; mountain bikes L25,000; kayaks L28,000; and Fiats from L68,000. Add 20% July-Aug. They have branches around the island (in Marciana Marina, Porto Azzurro, Lacona, Procchio, and Marina di Campo). L10,000 fee for returning rentals to a different branch. 20% discount upon presentation of same-day train ticket going through Piombino. 10% discount for mentioning *Let's Go.* Open 9am-1pm and 3:30-7pm. V, MC, AmEx.

Laundry: Self-service at V. Elba, 61, near the Hotel Nobel; L6000 wash (30min.), L6000 dry (20min.). Open daily 8am-10pm.

EMERGENCY AND COMMUNICATIONS

Emergencies: ☎113. **Ambulance:** P. della Repubblica, 37 (☎0565 91 40 09). **Hospital:** (☎0565 93 85 11), off V. Carducci.

Post Office: in P. Hutre, off P. della Repubblica. Open M-F 8:15am-7pm, Sa 8:15am-12:30pm. There is **another branch** on V. Carducci, closer to the port. Open M-F 8:15am-1:30pm, Sa 8:15am-12:30pm. **Postal Code:** 57037.

ACCOMMODATIONS

Reserve ahead in the summer; the *associazione albergatori* can help.

Ape Elbana, Salita Cosimo de' Medici, 2 (☎/fax 0565 91 42 45), overlooking the main *piazza* of the *centro storico.* A personable, English-speaking staff will show you to cheery, cavernous rooms, all with bath. Singles L90,000; doubles L120,000 (July-Aug. L130,000). In August, half-pension L110,000; full pension L130,000. Roughly L30,000 cheaper in winter. V, MC.

Hotel Nobel, V. Manganaro, 72 (☎0565 91 52 17; fax 0565 91 55 15). Follow V. Elba from the port until it merges with V. Manganaro. The hotel is on the right. Somewhat shabby, but perfect for those on a tight budget. Bar downstairs. Singles L65,000, with bath L80,000; doubles L85,000, with bath L120,000. V, MC, AmEx.

Albergo Le Ghiaie (☎0565 91 51 78), on the pleasant beach of the same name. A labyrinth of white stucco walls cloaked in flowers connects the breezy rooms. All rooms have private bath and many have white balconies with views of the deep blue sea. Singles L120,000; doubles L160,000. Off-season singles L70,000; doubles L120,000.

FOOD

Infested with overpriced tourist restaurants, Portoferraio is not the best place to indulge your appetite. Nonetheless, many cafes and bars offer inexpensive, quick meals. For groceries, head to the centrally located **Conad** supermarket, at P. Pietri, 2-4, off V. Elba and near the Hotel Nobel. (Open M-Sa 7:30am-8:30pm, Su 7:30am-1pm and 4-8pm.) There are a couple of culinary terms worth knowing: *schiaccia* is an Elban bread cooked in olive oil and embedded with either onions or black olives, and *aleatico* is a sweet, full-bodied wine liquor.

Trattoria da Zucchetta, P. della Repubblica, 40 (☎0565 91 53 31), in the historic center. Offers delectable Neapolitan dishes at moderate prices. Pizza L5-14,000, *primi* L8-15,000, *secondi* L10-18,000. Open daily 11:30am-3pm and 6-11:30pm.

Ristorante Frescantico, V. Carducci, 132 (☎0565 918 989). This charming wine bar prepares delicious meals, well worth every *lira*. Fresh homemade pasta, starting at L12,000. Cover L3000. Open May-Nov. daily 12:30-3pm and 7-11pm; Dec.-Apr. W-M 12:30-3pm and 7-11pm. V, MC.

Ristorante Residence (☎0565 91 68 15), on Catala Italia. Affordable dishes, including seafood salad, for takeout or self-service. Open May-Oct. daily 6:30am-11pm; Nov.-Apr. F-W 6:30am-11pm.

SIGHTS

If you're in Portoferraio and aren't in the mood for the beach, stroll along the pleasant, cobblestone streets of the old town; they're lined with pink-, yellow-, and orange-shuttered houses set into the mountainside. Alternatively, head to...

NAPOLEONIC WHATNOTS. The **Napoleon museum** is located at his one-time residence, the **Villa dei Mulini.** The museum features Napoleon's personal library, furniture graced by the imperial *derrière*, a number of letters from exile, and the sovereign Elban flag that he designed and decorated with bees from his own imperial crest. *(☎0565 91 58 46. Open Apr.-Oct. M-F 9am-7:30pm, Sa 9am-10:30pm, Su 9am-1pm; Nov.-Mar. 9am-4pm. L9000.)* For L15,000 you can buy a cumulative ticket that also allows you entry (within three days) to Napoleon's summer residence, the **Villa Napoleonica di San Martino,** located in (who knew?) San Martino. Emblazoned with monogrammatic Ns, you might think that the villa monumentalizes Napoleon's hubris, but they were actually placed there after his death. Note especially the Sala Egizia, with friezes depicting his Egyptian campaign. *(Take bus #1 6km out of Portoferraio. ☎0565 91 46 88. Same hours as Villa dei Mulini.)* A block away from the former museum, you can pay homage to the great man's death mask at the **Chiesa della Misericordia.** *(L1000.)*

NON-NAPOLEONIC WHATNOTS. The **Museo Archeologico** guides you through the history of Elba, with exhibits of archaeological finds from ancient trade boat wrecks. *(Fortezza del Lingrella. ☎0565 91 73 38. Open daily Sept.-June 9:30am-12:30pm and 4-7pm; July-Aug. 9:30am-12:30pm and 6pm-midnight. L4000, children and individuals in large groups L2000.)* The **Medici Fortress** overlooks the port. Cosimo de' Medici, Grand Duke of Tuscany, began the impregnable complex in 1548. So imposing was its structure that back in 1553 the Turkish pirate Dracut declared it invulnerable and called off his planned attack on Portoferraio.

MARINA DI CAMPO ☎0565

Marina di Campo's white beaches wind their way for miles along the coast, attracting masses of vacationing families. Numerous campgrounds around Marina di Campo are popular with a somewhat hipper crowd. Bake in the sun or rent sporting equipment like **sailboards** (L15,000 per hr.) or **paddleboats** (L12,000 per hr.) along the beach. **Biko's Bikes,** in P. Torino—the square a block away from the bus stop towards the beach—rents cycles and mopeds for L20-65,000 per day. (☎0565 97 61 94. Open 8:30am-12:30pm and 2:30-7:30pm.)

The **tourist office,** directly across from the bus stop, offers information on various beaches. (Open F-W 8am-8pm; greatly reduced hours in winter.) In case of an **emergency,** call the **carabinieri** (☎0565 97 69 76) or the **Guardia Medica** (☎118; in summer ☎0565 97 60 61).

The clean and comfortable rooms of **Hotel Lido,** V. Mascagni, 29, near the center of town (turn left from P. Torino), are only a minute from the beach. (☎0565 97 60 40. Breakfast included. Reserve by Easter for July and August. Doubles L100,000, with bath L120,000; triples L135,000, with bath L165,000.) For **camping,** walk straight toward the beach from the bus stop, turn left, and walk the length of V.

degli Etruschi—signs will lead the way. Continue past the sign that marks the end of Marino di Campo and take an immediate right at the "La Foce" sign (20min.). **La Foce** (☎/fax 0565 97 73 85) offers a well-equipped plot directly on the beach. Another camping option is **Del Mare,** which shares the same grounds. (☎0565 97 62 37; fax 0565 97 78 50. Open Apr.-Oct. L11-20,000 per person and L11-15,000 per tent, depending on the season.) The campgrounds also offer two restaurants, a place to rent bikes, and a store with basic goods. In town, the **Minimarket** on V. Bellini, a block away from P. Torino to your left as you come from the bus stop, stocks essentials. (Open Mar.-Oct. daily 7am-10pm.) Contrary to its name, the only things baked at the **Cannabis Restaurant,** V. Roma, 41/43, are the fabulous meals, including crepes stuffed with cheese and *prosciutto* (L7000). A variety of large salads (L8-12,000) and fruit drinks diversify the typically Italian menu. (☎0565 97 75 55. Open June-Sept. daily 6am-1am; Oct.-May M-Sa 6am-1am.) **Trattoria Vecchia Locanda,** V. Garibaldi, 10, offers simple island fare. *Menù* with drinks starts at L20,000. (☎0565 97 80 60. Open daily roughly noon-2pm and 7-10:30pm, but you must call ahead to give the kitchen time to prepare for your particular needs.)

PORTO AZZURRO ☎0565

A favorite sunspot of the ultra-thin and ultra-rich, Porto Azzurro shelters some of the island's finest beaches. But the beauty doesn't come cheap—if you intend to stay in Porto Azzurro, brace yourself for a major financial outlay. Budget travelers should consider staying at the campgrounds at Localita Barbarossa, near the beach. The largest is **Camping Roclan's** (☎0565 95 78 03), followed by **Arrighi** (☎0565 955 68), **Da Mario** (☎0565 95 80 32), and **Il Gabbiano** (☎0565 950 87). **Albergo Barbarossa** at Localita Barbarossa offers charmingly old-fashioned rooms at reasonable prices. (☎0565 950 87. Singles L45,000, with bath L48,000; doubles L70,000, with bath L80,000.) To reach Barbarossa, you can either take the bus headed towards Marina di Campo (but be sure to ask the driver if it stops at Barbarossa) or walk. To do the latter, follow the signs for the *carabinieri* from the main square bordering the ocean, pass the *carabinieri* office, and continue walking until you reach Barbarossa (15min., partially uphill). If you're looking for a quick bite, don't miss **La Friggitoria,** V. Marconi, 4, just off the main square. The *crocchette di patate* (L4000) and the *fritto misto* (mixed fried fish) have put smiles on the faces of many islanders. (☎0338 428 43 10. Closed Jan.-Mar.) **The Grill,** V. Marconi, 26, near the Blumarine Hotel, offers copious portions of *penne* with either tomatoes or clams for L8000. (Open Apr.-Oct. daily 8:30am-2:30pm and 6pm-1am; Nov.-Mar. Tu-Su 8:30am-2:30pm and 6pm-1am.) **Bar Tamata,** V. Cesare Battisti, 3 (☎0347 381 39 86), has a mellow late-night crowd. **Morumbi,** 2km down the road to Capoliveri, is one of the island's hottest discos, offering dance floors, a pizzeria, and a pagoda. (☎0565 92 01 91. Cover L25,000 on weekends. Free passes for women. Open June 30-Sept. 15.) To escape such hedonism, the 1st **bus** leaves at 4:45am and the last at 7:55pm (1hr. to Portoferraio). In **emergencies,** call the **carabinieri** (☎112) or an **ambulance** (☎118).

MARCIANA MARINA ☎0565

The strip of pebbles that borders Marciana Marina's waterfront is just one of countless beaches hiding in isolated coves along the island. Numerous other stretches are accessible only by boat. The lesser known ones lie between Sant'Andrea and Fetovaia, an area rumored to have the island's clearest stretches of water. The coastline here varies from fine white-sand beaches to gentle outcroppings of flat-topped rocks, perfect for sunbathing and diving into the sea.

TRANSPORTATION AND PRACTICAL INFORMATION. Marciana Marina is easy to reach by car, moped, boat, or **bus** (50min. from Portoferraio, L3500). The **tourist office,** V. Scali Mazzini, 13, on P. Vittorio Emanuele, will find you a room for no charge. (☎0565 99 061. Open Th-Tu 8am-8pm, reduced winter hours.) The **post office** is on V. Loyd. (Open M-F 8:15am-1:30pm, Sa 8:15am-12:30pm.) In an **emergency,** contact the **carabinieri** (☎112) or an **ambulance** (☎118).

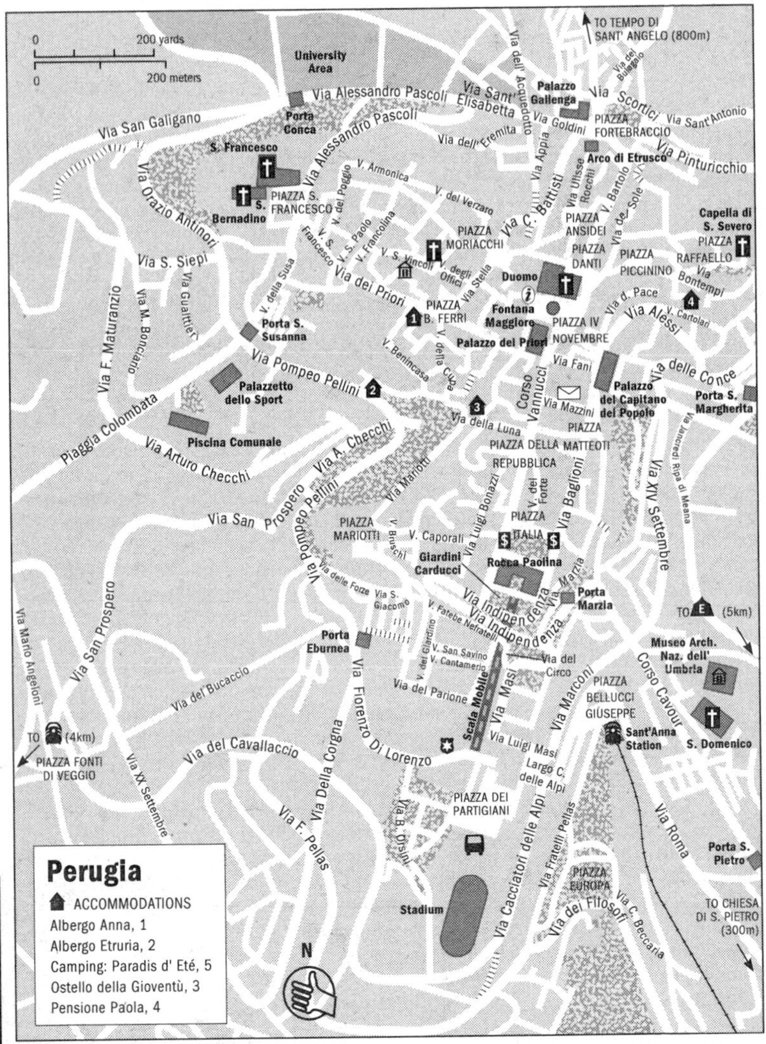

ACCOMMODATIONS, FOOD, AND ENTERTAINMENT. Cheap *affittacamere* are all over; look for signs. In Marciana Marina, **Albergo Imperia,** V. Amedeo, 12, offers comfortable rooms, decorated with sketches of the island. The personable proprietor finagles discounts at local restaurants. All rooms have a TV and refrigerator; some have balconies. (☎0565 990 82; fax 0565 90 42 59; email imperia@elbalink.it. Mid-Sept.-June singles L50-60,000; doubles L70-80,000, with bath L145,000. July-mid-Sept. prices 20-30% higher.) **Casa Lupi,** V. Amedeo, offers clean rooms behind green shutters, all with bath. Just uphill from the beach, its terrace overlooks a vineyard and the sea. (☎0565 991 43. Aug. singles L70,000; doubles L120,000. Off-season singles L50,000; doubles L75,000. Half-pension L95,000.) If finding a room in one of the main centers proves difficult, head to some of the smaller, less-trodden towns, which often prove more charming. **Albergo dei Fiori** in **Chiessi** (30min. from Marciana; 1½hr. from Portoferrario; some buses go directly, others change in Procchio) provides tranquility, great prices, beautiful views of the azure sea, and huge rooms with modern bathrooms. Ask for a balcony or patio facing the ocean. Check in at their family-run restaurant, **L'Olivo,** 20m uphill from the bus stop. (Restaurant and hotel ☎0565 90 60 13. Singles L45,000; doubles L70,000, with bath L80,000.) Back in Marciana, try **Bar L'Onda,** V. Amedeo, 4, for takeout crepes (L6-8000) and *panini* (L6000). At night, partiers head to **Club 64,** in Procchio, for live music. (Cover L20,000.)

SIGHTS. A visit to **Monte Capanne,** Elba's highest peak, provides an uplifting excursion from Marciana Marina. The top of this 1019m mountain offers views of the entire island and Corsica. The strenuous uphill trek takes two hours, but a cable car can take you up. (L12,000, round-trip L18,000. Open 10:30am-12:30pm and 1-5pm.) To reach Monte Capanne, take the bus from Marciana Marina to **Marciana,** a medieval town which clings to the mountainside, and get off at "Monte Capanne" (15min.). Not far from Marciana are the **Romitorio di San Cerbone** and the **Santuario della Madonna del Monte,** two sanctuaries once described as "dense with mysticism." Nearby **Chiessi,** with secluded beaches and rocky coves, may be the perfect place to relax.

UMBRIA

Umbria is known as the "Green Heart of Italy," a land rich in natural beauty, encompassing wild woods and fertile plains, craggy gorges and gentle hills, tiny cobblestoned villages and bustling international educational centers. This irresistible, landlocked region wedged between the Adriatic and Tyrrhenian coasts has long been a cherished and greatly contested prize. Three thousand years ago, Etruscans settled the region, leaving burial grounds, necropoli, tombs, and ruins. Over the years, ravenous barbarian hordes, aggressive neighboring Romans, and the meddlesome papacy have trampled through this land, drenching it in blood and looting its riches. Another conqueror, Christianity, transformed Umbria's architecture and regional identity, turning it into a breeding ground for saints and religious movements. St. Francis shamed the extravagant church with his humility, earning a reputation for pacifism. The region holds some of Giotto's greatest masterpieces and produced medieval masters Perugino and Pinturicchio. Today, Umbria's artistic spirit continues, with the internationally renowned annual Spoleto Festival and Umbria Jazz Festival.

HIGHLIGHTS OF UMBRIA

GRAB HOLD of something sturdy; Assisi's **Basilica di San Francesco** has frescoes so beautiful, they make the earth quake (p. 389).

EXPLORE Orvieto's ancient subterranean **Etruscan city** (p. 402).

GET YOUR GROOVE ON at the world-renowned **Umbria Jazz Festival** (p. 382).

PERUGIA ☎075

Perugians may be the most polite people you'll meet in Italy—an odd fact, considering Perugia's long history as violent and disreputable. An Etruscan *polis* of the 6th century BC, a part of the Roman Empire in the 3rd century BC, and an intact city-state throughout the Middle Ages, Perugia never lost its zest for battle, constantly laying siege to neighboring villages. Even in peacetime, its denizens entertained themselves with the *Battaglia de' Sassi* (Battle of Stones), an annual festival involving two teams that pelted each other with rocks until a sufficient number of casualties or fatalities left a winner. Often considered a city of Christian affinities, Perugia was home to the Order of the Flagellants, whose members wandered Europe publicly whipping themselves for penance. The city, however, quickly displayed its rebellious side, defying papal rule, imprisoning the peace-loving St. Francis of Assisi, and poisoning two popes.

Umbria's present-day capital, while less violent, hasn't lost its energy. Visitors pour in year-round, drawn by Perugia's impressive architecture, steep cobblestone streets, and distinguished universities and art academies—Perugia was home to the great Pietro Vannucci "Perugino," teacher of Raphael, and was a meeting ground for the 13th-15th century Umbrian and Tuscan masters. The enchanting countryside, spirited nightlife, and world-renowned jazz festival in July also draw tourists to the city.

TRANSPORTATION

Trains: Perugia FS, in P. V. Veneto, Fontiveggio. Perugia lies on the Foligno-Terontola line. To: **Assisi** (25min., every hr., L3200); **Passignano sul Trasimeno** (30min., every hr., L4100); **Foligno** (40min., every hr., L3500); **Arezzo** (1½hr., every hr., L7000); **Spoleto** (1½hr., every hr., L6100) via **Foligno; Orvieto** (2hr., 8 per day, L10,500; change at Terontola); **Florence** (2½hr., every hr., from L14,500); **Siena** (every hr., from L14,500; change at **Terontola** and **Chiusi**); and **Rome** (direct 2½hr., from L20,600; via Terontola or Foligno 3hr., from L20,600). Info open daily 6:45am-8pm. Ticket window open daily 6am-9pm. **Luggage Storage:** L5000 for 12hr. Open daily 6:20am-8:20pm.

Buses: P. dei Partigiani, down the *scala mobile* from P. Italia. City bus #6 (L1200) heads to the train station. **ASP** (☎075 573 17 07), in P. dei Partigiani, travels to most Umbrian towns, including **Gubbio** (1¼hr., 8 per day, L7400) and **Todi** (1¼hr., 6 per day, L9200). Additional buses available from the distant **Stazione Fontiveggio.** To get there, take bus #8 from P. dei Partigiani (L1200) to the last stop. Walk down the staircase around the side of the building; the station lies across the street. To **Siena** (every 2hr., L14,000). Tickets available at Radio Taxi Perugia.

Taxis: Radio Taxi Perugia (☎075 500 48 88).

ORIENTATION AND PRACTICAL INFORMATION

From the **Perugia FS train station** in **Piazza V. Veneto,** Fontiveggio, buses # 6, 7, 9, 13d, and 15 go to **Piazza Italia** (L1200). Otherwise, it's a long and ugly 4km uphill trek. To get to P. Italia from the **bus station** in **Piazza dei Partigiani** or from the nearby **Perugia Sant' Anna train station** at **Piazza Giuseppe,** follow the signs to the **escalator** *(scala mobile)* that goes underneath the old city. From P. Italia, **Corso Vannucci,** the main shopping thoroughfare, leads to **Piazza IV Novembre** and the *duomo*. Behind the *duomo* lies the university district. One block off C. Vannucci is **V. Baghoni,** which leads to **Piazza Matteotti,** the municipal center.

TOURIST AND FINANCIAL SERVICES

Tourist Office: P. IV Novembre, 3 (☎075 572 33 27 and 075 573 64 58; fax 075 573 93 86). The friendly, knowledgeable staff provides city maps and info on accommodations and travel. Open M-Sa 8:30am-1:30pm and 3:30-6:30pm, Su 9am-1pm.

Budget Travel: CTS, V. del Roscetto, 21 (☎075 572 02 84), off V. Pinturicchio toward the bottom of the street. Student travel service offers vacation deals to ISIC holders. Open M-F 10am-1pm and 3-6pm. **SESTANTE Travel,** C. Vannucci, 2 (☎075 572 60 61), by the fountain. Makes hotel reservations, sells train tickets, and rents cars. Open M-F 9am-1pm and 3:30-7:30pm, Sa 10am-1pm.

Currency Exchange: Banks have the best rates; those in P. Italia have 24hr. **ATMs.** The Perugia FS train station offers poor rates but charges no commission for exchange of less than L80,000.

LOCAL SERVICES

Bookstore: Libreria, V. Rocchi, 1 (☎075 753 61 64). A variety of classics and a few recent bestsellers and travel guides. English-language books L8-25,000. Open M-Sa 10am-1pm and 3:30-8pm, Su 10:30am-1pm.

Higher Education: Università per gli Stranieri, P. Fortebraccio, 4 (☎075 57 46 1), in Palazzo Gallenga. The university offers courses in Italian language and culture for foreigners. A good place to meet other travelers. Check with the registrar for rooms for rent (only for longer stays). Open daily 7:30am-6:30pm.

Laundromat: Lava e Lava, V. Annibale Vecchi, 5, and V. Mario Angeloni, 32. Wash L6000 per 8kg. Dry L2000 for 15min.

Swimming Pool: Piscina Comunale (☎075 573 51 60), on Vle. P. Pellini near Piaggia Colombata. Open daily 1-7:30pm; off-season M-F 6:30am-8:30pm, Sa 3-8pm. L7000.

EMERGENCY AND COMMUNICATIONS

Medical Emergencies: ☎118. **First Aid:** ☎075 65 84; at night ☎075 40 24. **Hospital:** ☎075 57 81. **Police:** ☎112. **Questura:** V. Cortonese, 157 (☎075 506 21).

24-Hour Pharmacy: Farmacia S. Martino, P. Matteotti, 26 (☎075 572 23 35).

Internet Access: Email and Phones, V. Cartolari, 18 (☎/fax 075 572 27 07). Take V. Calderini from P. IV Novembre. Turn left and take the right fork onto V. Alessi, which then merges left into V. Cartolari. Fax service. L5000 per hr. Open daily 10am-10pm.

Post Office: P. Matteotti. Mail services available M-Sa 8:10am-7:30pm, Su 8:30am-5:30pm. Currency exchange M-F 8:10am-5:30pm, Sa 8:10am-1pm, Su 8:30am-5:30pm. **Postal Code:** 06100.

ACCOMMODATIONS AND CAMPING

Be sure to make reservations during the Umbria Jazz Festival in July.

Ostello della Gioventù/Centro Internazionale di Accoglienza per la Gioventù, V. Bontempi, 13 (☎/fax 075 572 28 80; email ostello@edisons.it; www.ostello.perugia.it). From P. Italia, walk the length of C. Vanucci to P. IV Novembre. Continue past the *duomo* and P. Danti, take the farthest right street through P. Piccinino (basically a parking lot), and turn right onto V. Bontempi; the hostel is a short way down on the right. High, frescoed ceilings and great views add to a pleasant atmosphere. Kitchen, lockers, and TV room. Showers and kitchen use included. Sheets L2000. 2-week max. stay. Lockout 9:30am-4pm. Curfew midnight. Open Jan. 16-Dec. 14. Dorms L18,000.

Albergo Anna, V. dei Priori, 48 (☎/fax 075 573 63 04), off C. Vannucci. Climb 4 floors to clean, cool, and cozy 17th-century rooms. Some boast ceramic fireplaces and great views. White curtains and colorful embroidered bedding. Singles L50,000, with bath L70,000; doubles L80,000, with bath L100,000; triples L95,000, with bath L120,000.

Albergo Etruria, V. della Luna, 21 (☎075 572 37 30), down a narrow passageway off C. Vannucci, 55, in the heart of town. Heavy wooden furniture and antiques fill the pleasant rooms. Rooms are full of light and most have small flower-filled terraces and modern bathrooms. Parakeets preside over an immense 13th-century sitting room. Showers L4000. Singles L48,000; doubles 70,000, with bath L88,000. Cash only.

Pensione Paola, V. della Canapina, 5 (☎075 572 38 16). From the train station, take bus #6 or 7 to V. Pellini, where the bus passes a large parking lot on the left. Walk up the stairs; the *pensione* is on the right. Comfortable rooms with bamboo headboards and patterned tiles. Breakfast L6000. Singles L45,000; doubles L65,000. Cash only.

Camping: Paradis d'Eté (☎075 517 31 21), 8km away in Colle della Trinità. Take a city bus marked "Colle della Trinità" from P. Italia and ask the driver to leave you at the campgrounds. Restaurant nearby. L10,000 per person, L8000 per tent, L5000 per car. Hot showers and pool use included.

FOOD

Though renowned for chocolate, Perugia also serves up a variety of delectable breads and pastries. Both the *torta di formaggio* (cheese bread) and the *mele al cartoccio* (Italian apple pie) are available at **Ceccarani,** P. Matteotti, 16. (☎075 572 19 60. Open M-Sa 7:30am-8pm, Su 9am-1:30pm.) **Co.Fa.Pa.,** P. Matteotti, 12, also carries regional sweets. (Open M-Sa 7:30am-1pm and 5-7:30pm.) **Pasticceria dell'Accademia,** V. dei Priori, 52 (☎0573 43 84), a delectable pastry and coffee shop, is a few doors down from Albergo Anna.

For local confections such as *torciglione* (eel-shaped sweet almond bread) and *baci* (chocolate-hazelnut kisses), nothing beats the old-world elegance of **Pasticceria Sandri,** C. Vannucci, 32. This gorgeous bakery and candy shop doubles as a bar/cafe and is a great place for morning coffee. (Open M-Sa 7:30am-8pm.)

On Tuesday and Saturday mornings you can find delectable meats, mature cheeses, dew-glossed vegetables, and sundries at the **open-air market** in P. Europa. On other days, try the **mercato coperto** (covered market) in P. Matteotti for plenty of fruit, vegetables, and nuts; the entrance is below street level. (Open Tu-Sa 8am-8pm.) On summer nights the market becomes an outdoor cafe. Buy essentials at the small markets in P. Matteotti, such as **COOP,** at P. Matteotti, 15. (Open M-Sa 9am-8pm.) Complement your meal with one of two reasonably priced regional wines: *Sagrantino Secco*, a full-bodied, dry red or *Grechetto*, a light, dry white.

Trattoria Dal Mi Cocco, C. Garibaldi, 12 (☎075 573 25 11), up from the University for Foreigners. Nothing pretentious about this local favorite. The menu, written in the Perugian dialect, is difficult to read. It includes *antipasto,* 2 *primi,* 2 *secondi,* a *contorno,* dessert, wine or water, and a glass of liquor for L25,000–an incredible deal for huge amounts of food. Reservations recommended, especially in the evening and on weekends. Open Tu-Su 1-2:30pm and 8:15-10:30pm.

Ristorante da Giancarlo, V. dei Priori, 36 (☎075 572 43 14). Walk down the stairs from the entrance. Cozy and full of locals dining on delicious food. The *gnocchi* melts in your mouth (L10-13,000). For a special treat, try the lemon *gelato* if available–it's served inside of a carved out lemon. Open Sa-Th 12:30-3pm and 6:30-10pm. V, MC.

L'Era Nuova, V. Baldo, 6 (☎075 573 31 57), off C. Vannucci, just steps away from the *duomo.* Meals are reasonably priced and carefully prepared. Delicious *bruschette* L3-5000. Pizza L6500-10,000, house special *porcaracca* (with truffles and porcini) L11,000, *primi* L9-14,000. Open daily noon-4pm and 6pm-1am.

Brizi, V. Fabretti, 75-79 (☎075 572 13 86), on a side street near the university. Reasonably priced food. *Tagliatelle tartufate* (with truffles) L6500, *primi* L7-10,000, *secondi* L7-13,000. Cover L2500. Open W-M noon-2:30pm and 7pm-midnight.

The Australian Pub, V. de Verzaro, 39. A neighborhood joint for Italians and their English-speaking exchange student friends, this is the place to munch on a burger and drink Peroni. Have an early, quiet dinner on the terrace, or come around 11pm when the lively nightlife picks up. Pizzas and burgers L6-9000. Open daily for meals noon-2pm and 7-11pm, for drinks until 3am.

SIGHTS

PIAZZA IV NOVEMBRE

The city's most visited sights frame Piazza IV Novembre on the north end of the city; most other monuments of distinction lie within a 15-minute walk from there. In the middle of the *piazza* sits the **Fontana Maggiore,** designed by Fra' Bevignate and decorated by Nicola and Giovanni Pisano. The bas-reliefs covering the majestic double basin depict religious and Roman history, allegories of the months and sciences (lower basin), and the saints and other historic figures (upper basin).

PALAZZO DEI PRIORI AND GALLERIA NAZIONALE DELL'UMBRIA. The 13th-century windows and sawtooth turrets of this *palazzo* showcase Perugian war efforts. This building, one of the finest examples of Gothic communal architecture, shelters the impressive **Galleria Nazionale dell'Umbria.** The collection contains magnificent works by Duccio, Fra Angelico, Taddeo di Bartolo, Guido da Siena, and Piero della Francesca. Della Francesca's *polyptych of Saint Anthony* (Room 4) is particularly stunning. Deep and sumptuous colors fill Perugian Pinturicchio's *Miracles of San Bernardino of Siena.* Pinturicchio's rich tones contrast with Perugino's soft, pastel colors. His newly restored *Adoration of the Magi* (Room 10) is the gallery's premier piece. *(In P. IV Novembre at C. Vanucci, 19. Gallery ☎075 574 12 57. Open daily 9am-8pm. Closed Jan. 1, Dec. 25, and the 1st Monday of every month. L8000, EU citizens under 18 or over 65 free.)*

On the right of the Galleria, up the steps across from the fountain and across from the *duomo*, is the **Sala dei Notari,** once the citizens' assembly chamber. Thirteenth-century frescoes portray scenes from the Bible and Aesop's fables. *(Open July-Aug. M-Su 9am-1pm and 3-7pm; Nov.-June Tu-Su 9am-1pm and 3-7pm. Free.)*

DUOMO. Perugia's imposing Gothic *duomo* was begun in the 14th century, but the facade was never finished. Though it lacks the extensive decoration of many other *duomos* in Tuscany and Umbria, the 15th- to 18th-century embellishments are quite beautiful and create a sense of balance and harmony within the church. The town is proudest of the Virgin Mary's wedding ring, a relic they snagged from Chiusi in the Middle Ages. The ring is kept under lock and key. *(At the end of the piazza. Open daily 8am-noon and 4pm-sunset. Mass Sa 6pm, Su 8:30, 10, 11:30am, and 6pm.)*

COLLEGIO DELLA MERCANZIA (MERCHANTS'S GUILD). In this building Perugino suffused his frescoes with the gentleness that he later passed on to his great pupil Raphael. Raphael is said to have collaborated with his teacher on the *Prophets and Sibyls*. *(Next door to the Galleria Nazionale dell'Umbria. ☎075 573 03 66. Open Mar.-Oct. and Dec. 20-Jan. 6 M-Sa 9am-1pm and 2:30-5:30pm, Su and holidays 9am-1pm; Nov.-Dec. 19 and Jan. 7-Feb. 28 Tu-Sa 8am-2pm, Su and holidays 9am-12:30pm. L2000. Cumulative ticket including Collegio Del Cambio L6000, reduced L4000.)*

COLLEGIO DEL CAMBIO (EXCHANGE GUILD). This richly paneled structure is the meeting room for Perugia's merchant guild. The guild's 88 members have met here to debate tax laws and local commerce since 1390. The books in the annexed archive contain the names of all of the guild's members back into the Middle Ages. On the walls of the *Sala dell'Udienza (Audience Chamber)* Perugino's frescoes portray heroes, prophets, sybils, and even himself. Grotesque depictions of personified planets and the decapitation of John the Baptist are equally striking. *(Next to the National Gallery and Merchant's Guild at Corso Vannucci, 25. ☎075 572 85 99. Mar.-Oct. and Dec. 20-Jan. 6 M-Sa 9:30am-12:30pm and 2:30-5:30pm, Su and holidays 9am-12:30pm; Nov.-Dec. 19 and Jan. 7-Feb. Tu-Sa 8am-2pm, Su and holidays 9am-12:30pm. L5000, groups and those over 65 L3000. Combined ticket with Merchant's Guild L6000, reduced L4000.)*

VIA DEI PRIORI

Belying its current calm gray face of *pietra serena*, Via dei Priori was one of the bloodiest and goriest streets of medieval Perugia. Many midnight betrayals occurred here, and the spikes on the lower walls of the street were once used to impale the rotting heads of dead criminals. On the left is the attractive small **Chiesa di Sant'Agata,** with a number of 14th-century frescoes. Two blocks farther, the Baroque **Chiesa di San Filippo Neri** (built in 1627) resides solemnly in P. Ferri; the heart of Santa Maria di Vallicella is kept here. (Both churches open daily 8am-noon and 4pm-sunset.) Around the corner in V. San Francesco, P. S. Francesco al Prato is a rare grassy green square inviting lounging and bare feet. At its edge is the colorful **Oratorio di San Bernardino,** near the end of V. dei Priori. Agostino de Duccio built the building between 1457 and 1461 in the early Renaissance style, embellishing its fanciful facade with finely carved reliefs and sculptures. Inside, a 3rd-century Roman sarcophagus forms the altar.

VIA ROCCHI AND THE NORTHEAST

From behind the *duomo*, medieval Via Ulisse Rocchi, the city's oldest street, winds through the north city gate to the **Arco di Etrusco,** a perfectly preserved Roman arch built on Etruscan pedestals and topped by a 16th-century portico. Walk straight through P. Braccio Fortebraccio and follow C. Guiseppe Garibaldi. Past the newly cleaned **Palazzo Gallenga,** at the end of a little byway off C. Garibaldi, lies the jewel-like **Tempio di Sant'Angelo.** The 5th-century church, constructed with building materials taken from ancient pagan buildings, is the oldest in Perugia. (☎075 572 26 24. Open Tu-Su 9:30am-noon and 3:30pm-sunset.) On your way back, veer to the left of P. B. Fortebraccio to a stairwell that winds up to P. Michelotti. Take V. Aquila on the left of the *piazza* and then take the 1st right into

P. Raffaello. Here you will find the **Capella di San Severo,** home to the *Holy Trinity and Saints,* a fresco painted by both Raphael (who created the upper section) and his teacher Perugino (who painted the lower section). *(☎075 57 38 64. Open Apr.-Sept. daily 10am-1:30pm and 2:30-6:30pm; Oct.-Mar. M-F 10:30am-1:30pm and 2:30-4:30pm, Sa-Su and holidays 10am-1:30pm and 2:30-5:30pm. L3500.)* Follow V. Raffaello down to V. Bontempi to reach the **Pozzo Etrusco** (Etruscan well), P. Danti, 18 (☎075 573 36 69). It was built in the 3rd century BC and was the town's main water reservoir. Make a wish, drop a coin, and listen for it to hit the bottom 36m below.

THE EAST SIDE

At the end of town on C. Cavour, past the Porta S. Pietro, the **Basilica di San Pietro** maintains its original 10th-century basilica layout (a double arcade of closely spaced columns leading to a choir). Inside the *chiesa* are solemn, majestic paintings and frescoes depicting scenes of saints and soldiers. Look for Perugino's *Pietà* along the north aisle. At the far end of the basilica is an exquisitely manicured medieval garden; its lower section offers a must-see view of the surrounding countryside. *(Basilica open daily 8am-noon and 4pm-sunset.)*

Opposite the Parco Sant'Angelo towers the imposing **Chiesa di San Domenico,** the largest church in Umbria. The church's huge Gothic rose window contrasts with the sober, Renaissance interior. The magnificently carved **Tomb of Pope Benedict XI** (1325) rests in the chapel to the right of the high altar. Once kept in a box tied with a red ribbon, the pope's bones were recently placed in an encasement (under glass and wrought iron) inside the tomb's far wall. Near the church in P. Bruno, the **Museo Archeologico Nazionale dell'Umbria** occupies the old Dominican convent and showcases Etruscan and Roman artifacts, including the enormous bronze Statua di Germanico, a reconstruction of a Roman find. *(☎075 572 71 41; email archeopg@iol.it. Open daily 8:30am-7:30pm. L4000, EU citizens under 18 and over 65 free.)*

GIARDINI CARDUCCI

At the far end of C. Vannucci, the main street leading from P. IV Novembre, lie the Giardini Carducci. These well-maintained public gardens are named after the 19th-century poet Giosuè Carducci, who wrote a stirring ode to Italy, inspired by Perugia's historic zeal for independence. From the garden wall, enjoy the panorama of the Umbrian countryside; a castle or an ancient church crowns every hill.

FESTIVALS AND ENTERTAINMENT

Perugia's biggest annual event is the glorious 10-day **Umbria Jazz Festival,** which draws internationally renowned performers in July. (L15-50,000, some events free.) For more information, contact the tourist office or go to www.umbriajazz.com. Summer brings **Teatro è la notte,** a series of musical, cinematic, and dance performances. In September, the **Sagra Musicale Umbra** fills local churches with concerts of religious and classical music. Check Palazzo Gallenga for English film and other event listings. Finally, for 10 days at the end of October, the internationally renowned **Eurochocolate** festival comes to the city. Contact the tourist office or check out www.chocolate.perugia.it for more information.

Perugia has more nightlife options than any other Umbrian city, and its large university population keeps clubs packed nearly every night of the week. Join the nightly bandwagon at **P. Fortebraccio,** where free buses depart (starting at 11pm) for several nearby clubs. Once there, prepare to part with L25-50,000 for the cover charge. The deafening pulse of electronic music and an assortment of scantily clad female dancers welcome you into the Italian club scene. Perugia's three hottest dance clubs are **Domus Delirii,** V. del Naspo, 3, just off P. Morlacchi (open daily midnight-5am); **Subway,** up the hill from P. Danti (follow the road 5min. and down the stairs on the left); and **St. Adams,** in an alley off V. Priori on the left just before #48.

Perugia's many **pubs** allow for much conversation and much ale. **Shamrock Irish** is at P. Danti, 18, on the way to the Pozzo Etrusco. (☎075 573 66 25. Open Tu-Su 6pm-2am.) **Zoologico,** V. Alessi, 64, usually has live music and fills with carousing locals and travelers. (Open Tu-Su 7pm-2am.) Head to **La Terrazza,** in P. Matteotti, on the terrace behind the Mercato Coperto, for cheap drinks (including a variety of ales and beers). It boasts tables with some of the best views in Perugia, open-air movies, cabaret, and book readings by Italian and foreign authors. (Free.) **Zooropa,** down Pozzo Etrusco off P. Danti, has intelligent cocktails (L9000), shots (L4000), and an international crowd. (☎573 23 24. Open 8pm-2:30am.)

DAYTRIPS FROM PERUGIA: LAKE TRASIMENO

This placid and expansive lake, 30km west of Perugia, is a tranquil and refreshing refuge from Umbria's stifling heat and packed tourist centers. While pleasant and peaceful today, Lake Trasimeno once witnessed some violent battles. In 217 BC, during the Second Punic War, Hannibal's elephant-riding army, fresh from the Alps, routed the Romans north of the lake. The names of the lakeside villages, **Ossaia** (place of bones) and **Sanguineto** (bloody), merrily recall the carnage of 16,000 Roman troops. The mass graves of these dead, hastily buried by Hannibal's men, have recently been discovered. If anonymous historical dead people are your thing, take a self-guided walking tour of the site (including the surrounding battlefield in the town of **Tuero**). Tuero is between the two main towns guarding the lake, **Passignano sul Trasimeno** and **Castiglione del Lago,** which are easily accessible by **train** and **bus.** A system of ferries connects Passignano sul Trasimeno, Castiglione del Lago, Tuero, **San Feliciano,** and Lake Trasimeno's two largest islands—**Isola Maggiore** and **Isola Palvese.** Relaxing daytrips are but a ferry ride away.

CASTIGLIONE DEL LAGO

Castiglione del Lago lies on the Florence-Rome train line. To get here from Perugia, change at ***Terontola*** *(1hr.; 10 per day, fewer on Su). The city center is roughly 1½km from the train station and no buses run between the towns.*

The largest resort area around Trasimeno, Castiglione del Lago is a quiet, peaceful town. It stands on a limestone promontory covered with olive groves. Due to its strategic lakeside position and incredibly fertile soil, foreign powers frequently disputed control of the town. Today, it serenely sits within its city walls. The **tourist office,** P. Mazzini, 10, in the old town's single main square, provides boat schedules, exchanges money, and helps find rooms in hotels or in private homes or apartments for L300,000 per week. (☎075 965 82 10. Singles from L60,000; doubles from L80,000. Open Apr.-Oct M-F 8:30am-1pm and 3:30-7pm, Sa 9am-1pm and 3:30-7pm, Su and holidays 9am-1pm; off-season hours reduced significantly.) True budget accommodations are scarce in the immediate vicinity of Castiglione del Lago, but the three-star **La Torre,** V. V. Emanuele, 50, offers clean rooms with bath and other amenities in the heart of the old town. (☎/fax 075 95 16 66. Doubles L100-120,000 depending on the season. V, MC, AmEx.) For food, try the shops lining V. V. Emanuele, or dine at **Paprika,** V. V. Emanuele, 107, which serves local specialties including *spaghetti ai sapori di Trasimeno* (with eel sauce) for L10,000. (Cover L3000. Open F-W noon-2:30pm and 7-10:30pm. V, MC, AmEx.)

ISOLA MAGGIORE

A convenient ***ferry*** *system connects the island to* ***Passignano sul Trasimeno*** *(20-35min.; every 30-60min.; L5000, round-trip L9000) and* ***Castiglione del Lago*** *(30min.; every 1-2hr.; L6000, round-trip L11,000).*

Follow in St. Francis' footsteps and spend a delightful day on Isola Maggiore, Lake Trasimeno's only inhabited island. A **tourist information booth** sits by the dock. (Open daily 10am-noon and 1-6pm.) As you leave the dock, turn right and follow the path to the tip of the island and the ruined **Guglielmi castle.** You may run into the sweet old caretaker who offers less-than-informative tours of the castle all day long (in Italian only). A bit farther on sits a tiny **chapel** enclosing the rock where St. Francis spent 40 days in 1211. From here, hike five minutes up to the **Chiesa di San Michele Arcangelo** for lovely 14th-century frescoes and a wonderful view of the island. (Open Su 10:30am-noon and 3-5pm.) At the side of the island opposite the castle is the island's small private **beach.** Pull up a chair and chat with the friendly, bronzed Hercules who runs the place (chairs L5000, beach umbrellas L25,000).

TODI ☎075

According to legend, an eagle flew here with a tablecloth, leading the founders of Todi to this rocky site. The isolated town long remained untouched by historical change, and it still retains visible traces of its Etruscan, Roman, and medieval past. Though all areas of the modern city seem to have been transformed into parking lots, there's hardly room for cars (or any other 20th-century amenities) in the historic center. An inordinate number of antique shops have nonetheless squeezed their way in, catering to the busloads of daytrippers who unload in P. Jacopone each morning.

TRANSPORTATION AND PRACTICAL INFORMATION. Todi is best reached by **bus** from Perugia. The bus station is in P. Consolazione, a short ride on city bus A or a pleasant 1km walk from the town center. **ASP** (☎075 894 29 39 or toll-free 800 51 21 41) runs buses to and from **Perugia** (1½hr.; 6 per day M-Sa only; last bus from Todi 5pm, last bus from Perugia 6:25pm; L9200). Todi is also accessible by **train** from **Perugia Sant'Anna** (45min., 13 per day, L4700). **Taxis** are available in P. Garibaldi (☎075 894 23 75), P. Jacopone (☎075 894 25 25), or by calling ☎0347 77 48 321. The **Pro-Loco Pro-Todi** tourist office, P. del Popolo, 39, provides maps, transportation schedules, and information about area restaurants and accommodations. (☎075 894 25 26. Open M-Sa 9am-1pm and 4-7pm.) In case of **emergency,** call the **police** (☎112 or 075 895 62 43), an **ambulance** (☎118), the **hospital** (☎075 885 81), or **guardia medica** (☎075 894 24 21). A useful pharmacy is the **Farmacia Dr. Santori** (☎075 39 03), in P. del Popolo. **Postal Code:** 06059.

ACCOMMODATIONS AND FOOD. Unless you've got gold versions of major credit cards, hotels are pretty much out of reach, not to mention out of the way. Todi's most reasonably priced hotel is the three-star **Tuder,** V. Maestà dei Lombardi, 13. (☎075 894 21 84; fax 075 894 39 52. Singles with bath L80-90,000; doubles with bath L130-160,000. V, MC, AmEx.) Pick up provisions at the **alimentari** at V. Cavour, 150. (Open M-Tu and Th-Sa 7:45am-1:30pm and 5:30-8pm, W 7:45am-1:30pm.) Alternatively, **Ristorante Cavour,** V. Cavour, 21/23, offers pizza for around L7500 and filling meals for L22,000. Their specialty is *tortellini al tartufo nero* (with black truffles) for L13,000. Try to find a seat in the medieval dungeon. (☎075 894 37 30. Open Th-Tu noon-3pm and 7:30pm-midnight. V, MC, AmEx.)

SIGHTS. Piazza del Popolo, the town center and Todi's focal point since Roman times, remains the town's high point in altitude and architectural achievement. It is a stately ensemble of glowering *palazzi* and a somber *duomo*. In the *piazza*, the **Palazzo del Capitano,** contains the **Pinacoteca Civica** and the **Museo Archelogico** in its upper floors. Fascinating frescoes in the Sala del Capitano del Popolo lie at the top of the exterior staircase. (Open daily 10:30am-1pm and 2:30-6pm. L6000, ages 15-25 L4500, under 15 L3000.) The stout **duomo** rests solidly atop a flight of broad stone steps. The central rose window and arched doorway command attention with their intricate decoration. The delicate Gothic side arcade, added in the 1300s, shelters an unusual altarpiece—the Madonna's head emerges in high relief from the painting's flat surface. (Across from P. del Popolo. Duomo and crypt open daily 8:30am-12:30pm and 2:30-6:30pm.) Across from the *duomo*, the tower and facade of the **Palazzo dei Priori** (1297-1337) retain vestiges of medieval gloom despite rows of Renaissance windows that were carved in the early 16th century.

Neighboring P. Garibaldi has been reduced to little more than a municipal parking lot, but it still opens onto a superb vista. From the *piazza*, follow the signs leading off C. Cavour to the remaining walls of the **Foro Romano** and the nearby

12th-century **Chiesa di San Ilario.** The **Fonti Scannabecco's** 13th-century porticoes still house a working tap. Return to P. del Popolo and take V. Mazzini to the majestically angular **Tempio di San Fortunato.** Built by the Franciscans between the 13th and 15th centuries, the church features Romanesque portals and a Gothic interior. To the right of S. Fortunato, a path bends uphill toward **La Rocca,** a ruined 14th-century castle. Next to the castle, follow a sinuous path, appropriately named **Viale della Serpentina,** to a breathtaking belvedere constructed on the remains of an old Roman wall. Follow the twisting paths down to the base of the hill and cross Vle. della Consolazione to the Renaissance **Tempio di Santa Maria della Consolazione,** with its elegant domes. Inside are twelve enormous statues of the region's principal saints and a magnificent altar worth the trek.

ASSISI ☎079

For it is in giving that we receive; it is in pardoning that we are pardoned; and it is in dying that we are born to eternal life.

—St. Francis of Assisi

Assisi's serenity originates from the legacy of St. Francis, a 12th-century monk who generated a revolution in the Catholic church. He founded the Franciscan order, devoted to the then unusual combination of asceticism, poverty, and chastity. Young Franciscan nuns and monks still fill the city, dressed in their brown *cappucci* robes, carrying on his legacy with spiritual vigor. Assisi is an important pilgrimage site, especially among Italian youth, who converge here for conferences, festivals, and other religious activities. Nevertheless, fervent religiosity is not a prerequisite for adoring Assisi. Giotto's frescoes adorning the basilica merit a pilgrimage on their own. The Basilica of St. Francis is perhaps the most visited sight in all Umbria, containing the saint's relics and Giotto's renowned fresco series of St. Francis' life, as well as works by Cimabue, Jacopo Torriti, Filipo Rusuti, Simone Martini, and Pietro Lorenzetti. The influence of such masters infuse the streets, *piazze*, and *palazzi* of the town as well as its numerous places of worship. Assisi also has monuments to its Etruscan and Roman roots in the ruins throughout the town. Grand palaces and majestic *rocce* (castles) from a later era tower above the orange roofs. The rose-colored town is beautifully preserved, its accommodations are terrific, and its restaurants are among the best in Umbria. Earthquakes in the fall of 1997 devastated much of the city, but renovations have restored much of the damage.

TRANSPORTATION

Trains: Below the town near the Basilica of Santa Maria degli Angeli. Assisi lies on the Foligno-Terontola line. Trains to: **Perugia** (13 per day, L3200); **Florence** (2 per day, more frequent service via Terontola, L17,000); **Rome** (1 per day, more frequent service via Foligno, L25,500); and **Ancona** (from L20,200). Ticket office open 6am-8pm. **Luggage Storage:** L5000 for 12hr at the newsstand. Open daily 6:30am-6:30pm. **Bike rental** also available at the newsstand (☎033 93 72 45 92).

Buses: ASP buses leave from P. Matteotti. To: **Perugia** (1½hr., 7 per day, L5000); **Foligno** (M-F 5 per day, L6200); **Florence** (2½hr., 1 per day); and **Rome** (3hr., 1 per day). To reach the bus stop from P. del Comune, walk up V. San Rufino to P. San Rufino and take V. del Torrione (to the left of the church) to P. Matteotti.

Public Transportation: Local buses (2 per hr., L1200) run from the train station to the town's bus stop at P. Unità d'Italia (near the basilica), Largo Properzio (near the church of St. Claire), and P. Matteotti (above P. del Comune).

Taxis: In P. del Comune (☎075 81 31 93), in P. San Chiara (☎075 81 26 00), in P. Unità d'Italia (☎075 81 23 78), and at the train station (☎075 804 02 75).

CENTRAL ITALY

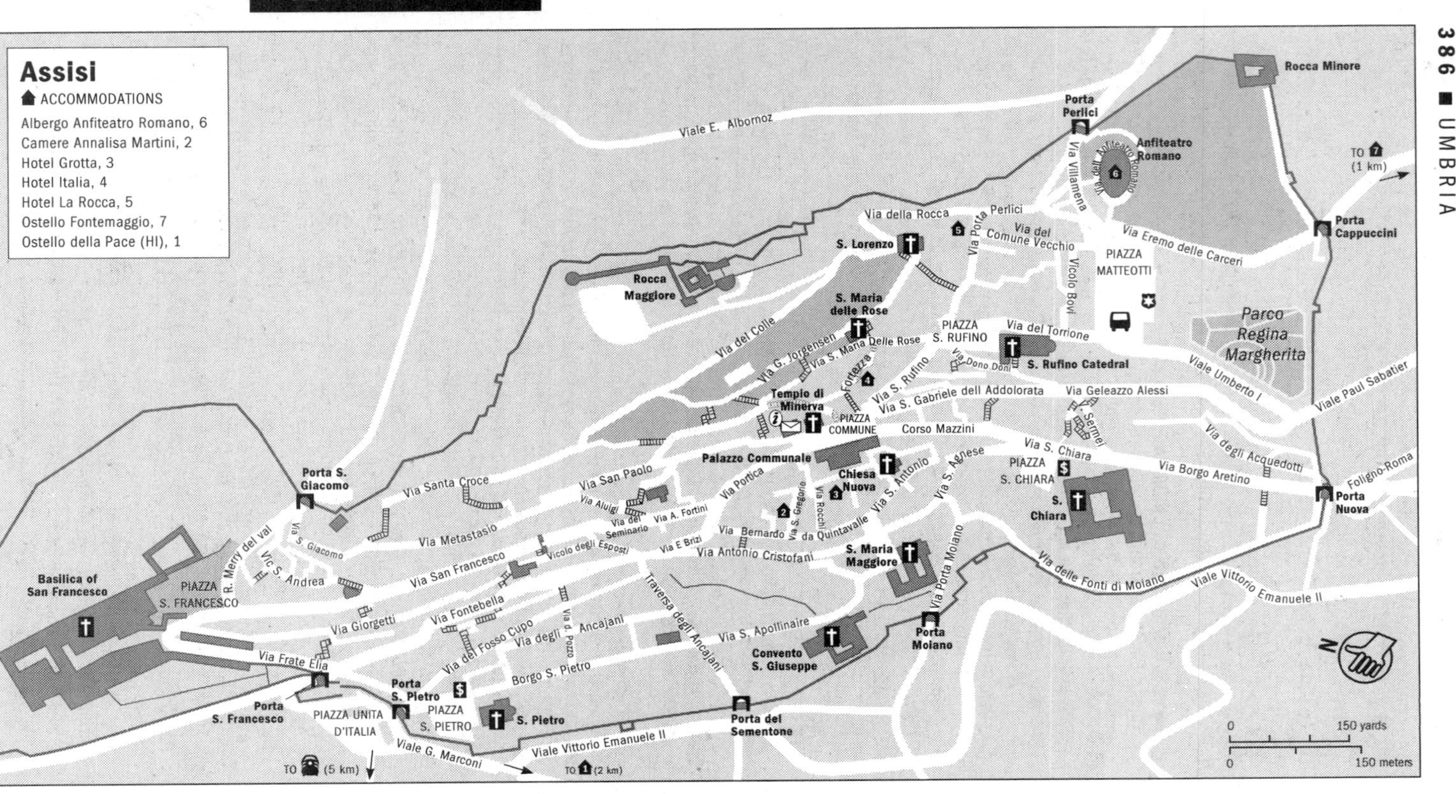

ORIENTATION AND PRACTICAL INFORMATION

Towering above the city to the north, the **Rocca Maggiore** can help you orient yourself should you become lost among Assisi's winding streets. The center of town is **Piazza del Comune.** To reach it from **Piazza Matteotti,** where buses stop, take V. del Torrione to **Piazza San Rufino,** bear left in the *piazza,* and take **Via San Rufino** until it hits the town center. **Via Portica** (which intersects V. Fortini, V. Seminario, and **Via San Francesco**) connects P. del Commune to the **Basilica di San Francesco.** Heading in the opposite direction, **Corso Mazzini** leads to the **Chiesa di Santa Chiara.**

Tourist Office: (☎075 81 25 34; fax 075 81 37 27), in P. del Comune. Head down V. Mazzini and duck through a doorway on the right. Knowledgeable staff provides info and a decent map. Sells the **Assisicard,** good for discounts throughout the city. Train and bus schedules posted outside. Open M-F 8am-2pm and 3:30-6:30pm, Sa 9am-1pm and 3:30-6:30pm, Su and holidays 9am-1pm.

Currency Exchange: Exchange traveler's checks at the post office (L2000 for sums to L100,000; L5000 for larger sums). Otherwise try **Banca Toscana,** on P. S. Pietro; **Cassa di Risparmio di Perugia,** on P. del Comune; and **Banca Popolare di Spoleto,** on P. S. Chiara. Banks open 8:20am-1:20pm and 2:15-3:15pm. **ATMs** are outside.

Car Rental: Agenzia Assisiorganizza, Borgo Aretino, 11a (☎075 81 52 80). Cars from L90,000 per day, L500,000 per week. Min. age 21.

Swimming Pool: Centro Turistico Sportivo (☎075 81 29 91), on V. S. Benedetto. Take the "Linea A" bus from P. del Comune. L7500. Open late July-Aug. daily 9:30am-7pm.

Emergencies: ☎113. **Police: Carabinieri,** P. Matteotti, 3 (☎075 81 22 39). **Hospital: Ospedale di Assisi** (☎075 81 28 24), on the outskirts of town. Take the "Linea A" bus from P. del Comune. **Guardia Medica Turistica:** ☎075 804 36 16.

Internet Access: Agenzia Casciarri, V. Borgo Aretino, 51a (☎075 819 82 31). Open M-F 9am-12:30pm and 4-7pm, Sa 9am-12:30pm.

Post Office: Largo Properzio, 4. Open M-F 8:10am-6:25pm, Sa 8:10am-1pm. **Postal Code:** 06081.

ACCOMMODATIONS

Reservations are crucial around Easter and Christmas and strongly recommended for the Festa di Calendimaggio in early May. Also consider booking ahead of time in August. If you don't mind turning in around 11pm, ask the tourist office for a list of **religious institutions;** these places are peaceful and inexpensive. The tourist office also has a list of *affittacamere* (rooms for rent).

Ostello della Pace (HI), V. di Valecchi, 177 (☎/fax 075 81 67 67). Turn right as you exit the train station and then left at the intersection onto V. di Valecchi (30min.). Or take the bus to P. S. Pietro and walk 50m down the main road to the small path marked by the hostel sign. The hostel is 10min. away. Large, 4-bed rooms and spotless bathrooms. Breakfast included. Generous home-cooked dinner L14,000. Laundry L6500. Reception daily 7-9:15am and 3:30-11:30pm. Check-out 9:30am. Communal areas locked by 11:30pm. Reserve ahead if possible (even if you're just calling from the train station in Assisi). Dorms L22,000, with private bath L27,000. V, MC.

Camere Annalisa Martini, V. S. Gregorio, 6 (☎075 81 35 36). The lovely Annalisa offers *affittacamere* at excellent prices. Located in the medieval core of Assisi, this peaceful refuge is tucked away in a sunny garden. Outdoor picnic seating, washer, telephone, and fax available. Around the corner, off V. dei Macelli Vecchi, is a great little pizzeria. If she doesn't have room, Annalisa can often refer you to one of her friends. Laundry L5-10,000. Singles L38,000, with bath L40,000; doubles L60,000, with bath L65,000; triples L90-100,000. Prices reduced for stays of 3 days or longer.

Ostello Fontemaggio (☎075 81 36 36), on V. per l'Eremo delle Carceri. V. Eremo begins at the top of P. Matteotti and leads through Porta Cappuccini; follow it 1km up the road and then veer right at the sign. 8-bed rooms are a bit crowded but well maintained. Rooms are brightened by a sunny terrace. Delicious, inexpensive home-cooked fare available at the hostel restaurant. Breakfast L7000. Check-out 10am. No curfew. Dorms L18,500. Bungalows available for L3000 more per person. Market and **campground** next door. L8000 per person, L7000 per tent, L4000 per car. Cash only.

Hotel Italia, V. della Fortezza, 2 (☎075 81 26 25), just off P. del Comune. A small, well-kept hotel in the center of town with beautiful views of the *piazza.* Friendly staff speaks some English and welcomes younger guests. Comfortable and spotless rooms, some with more ambience than others. Breakfast L5000. Singles L28,000, with shower L39,000, with full bath L45,000; doubles L55,000, with shower L59,000, with full bath L69,000; triples L66,000, with bath L90,000; quad with bath L100,000. V, MC.

Hotel La Rocca, V. di Porta Perlici, 27 (☎/fax 075 81 22 84). From P. del Comune, follow V. S. Rufino up the hill and cross the *piazza.* Go up V. Porta Perlicia until you hit the old arches; La Rocca is on the left. Attractive rooms all with bath, some with scenic views. Breakfast L7500. Singles L55,000; doubles L75,000. V, MC, AmEx.

Albergo Anfiteatro Romano, V. Anfiteatro Romano, 4 (☎075 81 30 25; fax 075 81 51 10), off P. Matteotti. Built into the Roman amphitheater on the outskirts of town. Enjoyable restaurant downstairs: *primi* L7500-14,000, *secondi* L9500-17,000, *menù turistica* L22,000. Welcoming, quiet rooms filled with antique furniture. Some boast views of the Rocca. Singles L40,000; doubles L60,000, with bath L70,000. V, MC, AmEx.

FOOD

Assisi will tempt you with a sinful array of nut breads and sweets. *Bricciata umbria*, a strudel-like pastry with a hint of cherries, and *brustengolo*, packed with raisins, apples, and walnuts, are divine. **Pasticceria Santa Monica,** at V. Portica, 4, right off P. del Comune, sells these and other treats at low prices with extremely friendly service. (Open daily 9am-8pm.) On Saturday mornings, there's a **market** in P. Matteotti; on weekdays, head to V. S. Gabriele for fresh fruits and vegetables.

Pizzeria Otello, V. San Antonio, 1 (☎075 81 24 15), on a side street off P. del Commune and across from St. Francis's home. No nonsense, family-run pizzeria. Summer dining in the garden. Hearty portions. Pizza L7500-11,000, focaccia sandwiches and large salads L8500-10,000, *primi* L7500-11,000, *secondi* L8500-14,500. Cover L2000. 10% discount with Assisicard. Open for pizza July-Aug. daily 7:30am-noon; Sept.-June M-Sa 7:30am-noon. Main restaurant open July-Aug. daily noon-4pm and 7-11pm; Sept.-June M-Sa noon-4pm. V, MC, AmEx.

Il Duomo Pizzeria, V. Porta Perlici, 11 (☎075 81 63 26). The large pizza oven is the focal point of this medieval lair/pizzeria. In addition to pizza, they offer a diverse and well-priced menu. *Ravioli duomo* L11,000. Open daily noon-2:30pm and 6:30pm-1am.

Trattoria da Ermini, V. Monte Cavallo, 19 (☎075 81 25 06), off V. Porta Perlici. Enjoy *tagliatelle capricciose* for L10,000 or *bistecca di pollo alla brace* (grilled chicken on the bone) for L13,000 while sitting beneath a tremendous vaulted dome. *Menù* L26,000. Open F-W noon-2:30pm and 7-9pm. V, MC.

Hotel Grotta Antica Ristorante Caldrino, V. Macelli Vecchi, 1 (☎075 81 52 20), below P. Commune. Discover this delightful combination of sparkling white tablecloths, friendly waitstaff, and classic Italian fare. *Lasagne carandrino,* the house specialty, can be ordered for large groups (price variable depending on number; L13,000 for one person). *Menù turistica* L20,000. Open daily noon-3pm and 7-10pm.

Trattoria Spadini, V. S. Agnese, 6 (☎075 81 30 05), near P. Santa Chiara. Dine under low, white arches in an elegant antique atmosphere. Specialties include *agnolloti al tartufo* (L15,000) and *penne alla crema di carciafi* (L13,000). *Menù* L22,000. Open Tu-Sa noon-2:30pm and 7-9:30pm.

 SIGHTS

At age 19, St. Francis (b. 1182) abandoned military and social ambitions, rejected his father's wealth, and embraced asceticism. His renouncement of the church's worldliness, his love of nature, and devoted humility earned him a huge European following, posing an unprecedented challenge to the decadent papacy and corrupt monastic orders. St. Francis continued to preach chastity and poverty until his death in 1226, when the order he founded was gradually subsumed into the Catholic hierarchy that it had criticized. Ironically, the Catholic Church has glorified the modest saint through the countless churches it has constructed in his honor.

BASILICA DI SAN FRANCESCO

☎075 819 00 84. Tours 9am-noon and 2-5:30pm. Tours convene outside the basilica; call the basilica's tourist info office to arrange one. Basilica open Easter-Nov. M-Sa 6:30am-7pm; Su and holidays 6:30am-7:30pm (but no tourist visits allowed during the morning, on Su, or on holidays); Dec.-Easter open daily 6:30am-6pm. Closed on holy days. Sala Norsa open M-Sa 9am-12:30pm and 3-6pm, Su 3-6pm. Museo Tesoro della Basilica open M-Sa 9:30am-noon and 2-6pm. Free tours are also given by young, enthusiastic Franciscan monks–usually in perfect English. L3000. Dress codes strictly enforced: no miniskirts, short shorts, revealing shirts, or anything that shows the knees or shoulders. No photography of the interior of the churches permitted.

When construction of the Basilica di San Francesco began in the mid-13th century, the Franciscan order protested—the elaborate church seemed an impious monument to the wealth that St. Francis had scorned. As a solution, Brother Elia, the vicar of the order, insisted that a double church be erected, the lower level to be built around the saint's crypt, the upper level to be used as a church for services. The subdued art in the lower church commemorates Francis's modest life, while the upper church pays tribute to his sainthood and consecration. This twofold structure inspired a new type of Franciscan architecture. Although the basilica was badly damaged by an earthquake in 1997, the furious restoration efforts to prepare for the Jubilee Year of 2000 provided a speedy resurrection.

The walls of the upper church are covered with Giotto's renowned *Life of St. Francis* fresco cycle, dramatically lit from the windows above. A comprehensive introduction to the frescoes is offered in the **Sala Norsa,** across from the basilica. Full appreciation necessitates much neck-craning and creative maneuvering. The story begins on the right wall near the altar and runs clockwise, beginning with teenage Francis in courtly dress surprised by a prophecy of future greatness. The cycle closes with an image of the saint passing through the agony of the "Dark Night." Paralleling St. Francis's pictorial path of holy deeds is the equally linear story of Jesus. Most frescoes and sculptures in the basilica come complete with "History Tell" machines, which charge L1000 for an oral history of each work. They may be suspect: one of them names St. Francis "a sissy," not "of Assisi."

Cimabue's magnificent *Madonna and Child*, *Angels*, and *St. Francis* grace the right transept. Tragically, most of Cimabue's frescoes in the transepts and apse have so deteriorated that they now look like photographic negatives. Pietro Lorenzetti decorated the left transept with his outstanding *Crucifixion*, *Last Supper*, and *Madonna and Saints*. Also stunning are Simone Martini's frescoes in the 1st chapel off the left wall, which revolve around the life of St. Martin. Descend through a door in the right side of the apse to enter the room that houses St. Francis's tunic, sandals, and sundries.

St. Francis's tomb, the inspiration for the entire edifice, lies below the lower church. The coffin itself was hidden in the 15th century, out of fear that the warmongering Perugians would desecrate it. It was not rediscovered until 1818. The original tomb was built in a Neoclassical style, but it was disliked by so many friars that a new, simplified version was constructed in 1935. The stone coffin sits above the altar in the crypt, surrounded by the sarcophagi of four of the saint's dearest friends. The attached library is open to visitors and houses the remarkable **Museo Tesoro della Basilica.** Particularly impressive are the rare illuminated manuscripts, the graceful 13th-century French ivory *Madonna and Child*, 17th-century Murano glass work, and a fragment of the Holy Cross.

OTHER SIGHTS

ROCCA MAGGIORE. The dramatic Rocca Maggiore looms uphill from the *duomo.* Take a dirt path around the periphery of La Rocca, where you'll find a shady perch from which to contemplate the serene panoramic view. *(Uphill on the cobblestone street to the left of the duomo, beyond the steps on the left. ☎ 075 81 52 92. Open daily in summer 9am-sunset; in winter 10am-sunset. Closed in bad weather. L5000, students L3500.)*

BASILICA DI SANTA CHIARA. The pink and white Basilica di Santa Chiara honors Saint Clare. It stands at the opposite end of Assisi on the site where St. Francis attended school. The church shelters not only the tomb (and hair) of St. Clare, but also the tunic and shoes worn by St. Francis and the crucifix that revealed God's message to him. The nuns in this convent are sworn to seclusion. *(☎ 075 81 22 82. Open daily 7am-noon and 2-7pm. Mass 11:30am and 5:30pm.)*

DUOMO. V. S. Rufino climbs steeply up from P. del Comune between closely packed old houses, opening onto P. S. Rufino to reveal the squat *duomo* with its massive bell tower. The restored interior is quite spartan and may come as a disappointment compared to the decorative facade. *(Open daily 10am-noon and 3-6pm.)*

PIAZZA DEL COMUNE AND ENVIRONS. From the Basilica di San Francesco, V. S. Francesco snakes between medieval buildings and their 16th-century additions. The colorfully frescoed **Oratorio del Pelegrino** (Pilgrim Oratory) is especially noteworthy. At the end of the street, P. del Comune sits upon the old **Foro Romano.** Enter from the **crypt of St. Nicholas** on V. Portica and stroll through the historic corridors of the Roman forum. The **Pinacoteca,** which occupies the nearby **Palazzo del Priore,** houses works by important Umbrian artists and a collection of Renaissance frescoes lifted from city gates and various shrines. Rounding out the impressive buildings in the square is the appealing **Chiesa Nuova,** with slightly crumbling exterior columns and a frescoed interior. *(Forum ☎ 075 81 30 53. Pinacoteca ☎ 075 81 52 92. Both open daily Mar. 16-Oct. 15 10am-1pm and 3-7pm; Oct. 16-Mar. 15 10am-1pm and 2-5pm. L4000 for each sight. The biglietto cumulativo allows entry into the forum, La Rocca Maggiore, and the Pinacoteca for L10,000, students L7000. Chiesa Nuova ☎ 075 81 23 39. Open daily 6:30am-noon and 2:30-6pm.)*

FESTIVALS AND ENTERTAINMENT

All of Assisi's religious festivals involve feasts and processions. An especially long, dramatic performance marks **Easter Week.** On Holy Thursday, a mystery play depicts the Deposition from the Cross. Traditional processions trail through town on Good Friday and Easter Sunday. Assisi welcomes spring with the **Festa di Calendimaggio** (the 1st Thursday, Friday, and Saturday of May). A queen is chosen and dubbed *Primavera* (Spring), while the lower and upper quarters of the city compete in a clamorous musical tournament. Ladies and Knights overtake the streets bellowing amorous notes in celebration of the young St. Francis, who wandered the streets of Assisi singing serenades at night. It was on one such night that he encountered a vision of the *Madonna della Povertà* (Lady of Poverty). Classical concerts and organ recitals occur once or twice each week from April to October in the various churches. October 4 marks the **Festival of St. Francis.** Each year a different region of Italy offers oil for the cathedral's votive lamp, and the traditional dances and songs of that region are performed.

On evenings, youth groups flood P. del Comune to croon international folk songs (including "Kumbaya" and "La Macarena") with guitar-strumming monks. There is little late-night carousing in pious Assisi, so don't expect too much Bacchanalian revelry. The most hoppin' bars in P. Commune close around 2am. If you have an itch to disco, head down to **Hermitage,** V. degli Aromatari, 1 (☎ 075 81 66 71; closed Jul.-Aug.), or **Il Tropicana,** V. Madonna delle Grazie, 11 (☎ 075 804 385; closed Th), in nearby S. Maria degli Angeli (the village with the train station).

DAYTRIPS FROM ASSISI

EREMO DELLE CARCERI AND MT. SUBASIO

A pleasant, steep, hour-long hike through the forest above the town leads to the inspiring Eremo delle Carceri (Hermitage of Cells), in the woods of Mt. Subasio. This oasis of peace and tranquility, to which St. Francis used to retreat, conveys the saint's true spirit more successfully than the opulent basilica. At the hermitage, you can view the small cell where St. Francis slept and the altar where he preached. Beyond the hermitage, Mt. Subasio has a number of trails; ask at the tourist office for a map to explore this natural treasure. (Pass through the Porta S. Francesco below the basilica and follow V. Marconi. At the crossroads, take the left road and pass the Seminario Regionale Umbro. Open daily Easter-Oct. 6:30am-7:15pm; Nov.-Easter 6:30am-5:30pm.) On the road up the mountain, the delightful **Le Carcerelle,** V. San Rufino Campagna, 15, has refreshing fruit drinks (L3000), cocktails and beer (L3500-5000), and delicious homemade meals. Feast on *polenta con salcicce* (L8000), *parmigiane con melanzone* (L9000), or *torta al testo* (L4500). (☎075 81 62 86. Open daily 7:30am-11pm.)

CHURCHES

Several churches associated with St. Francis and St. Clare stand in the immediate vicinity of Assisi. A 15-minute stroll down the steep road outside Porta Nuova leads to the **Convent of San Damiano,** where St. Francis received his calling and later wrote the *Canticle of the Creatures.* The chapel contains fine 14th-century frescoes and a riveting woodcarving of Christ. (Open daily 10am-noon and 3-5:30pm.)

The train to Assisi passes the huge **Basilica di Santa Maria degli Angeli,** a church inside a church. The impressive basilica, with its majestic purple dome, shelters the tiny **Porziuncola,** historically the first center of the Franciscan order. Benedictines own the building, and the Franciscans pay them a basket of carp every year as rent. In order to overcome temptation, St. Francis supposedly flung himself on thorny rosebushes in the garden just outside the basilica, thus eternally staining the leaves red. Today, in deference to the saint, the bushes no longer produce thorns. This site gained popularity with St. Francis's institution of the annual **Festa del Perdono** (Aug. 2), during which indulgences were offered to all who visited the church. The adjacent **Cappella del Transito** was the site of St. Francis's death. (Open daily 8am-noon and 2:30-7pm; closes earlier in winter.)

GUBBIO ☎075

Ancient Umbrians founded Gubbio in the 3rd century BC, but a wave of invasions later exhausted the thriving settlement. Its long, tumultuous history has left a rich, if somewhat varied, legacy. The Eugabian Tables (3rd-1st century BC), the fundamental documents of ancient Umbrian language and history, were discovered beneath the city's Roman forum. They bear witness to the town's alliance with the Romans (against the Etruscans). Graceful portals and a well-preserved theater attest to the past grip of Roman emperors, and splendid *palazzi* recall years of subjugation under the powerful Dukes of Urbino. Even without an intriguing past, Gubbio is a very appealing town with its cobblestone streets, lovely vistas, and whimsical chimney-pot skyline. The city also boasts its own school of painting, a distinct ceramic tradition, and Italy's first novelist, Bosone Novello Raffaelli. Still, Gubbio is a bit difficult to reach, and, unless you have a strong interest in the Eugabian Tables, ceramics, or faux medieval weapons, there is little to distinguish Gubbio from the numerous other beautiful hill towns of central Italy.

TRANSPORTATION

Trains: No trains stop in Gubbio; the nearest station is at **Fossato di Vico,** 19km away on the Rome-Ancona line (L7700 from Ancona, L18,6000 from Rome, L6100 from Spoleto). Buses connect Gubbio to Fossato (M-Sa 9 per day, Su 6 per day; L3800). For tickets, go to the newsstand in P. Quaranta Martiri in Perugia (where the bus stops) or to the newsstand in the train station if coming from Fossato. If you are stranded in Fossato without bus service, call ☎075 91 92 02 or 033 53 374 871 for a taxi.

Buses: ASP run to and from **Perugia** (1½hr.; M-F 10 per day, Sa-Su 4 per day; L7400) and are much more convenient than the train.

Taxis: (☎075 927 38 00), in P. Quaranta Martiri.

ORIENTATION AND PRACTICAL INFORMATION

Gubbio is a tangle of twisting streets and medieval alleyways that all lead to sweeping *piazze.* **Piazza della Signoria,** set on the ledge of the hill, remains the civic headquarters. Buses leave you in **Piazza Quaranta Martiri.** A short uphill walk on **Via della Repubblica,** the street directly ahead as you exit the bus, leads to **Corso Garibaldi,** off of which sits the tourist office. Shops on **Via dei Consoli** and the **Piazza Grande** offer some of Gubbio's best ceramic goods.

Tourist Office: P. Oderisi, 6 (☎075 922 06 93), off C. Garibaldi next door to the local Communist Party headquarters. Extremely helpful English-speaking staff. Open Mar.-Sept. M-F 8:15am-1:45pm and 3:30-6:30pm, Sa 9am-1pm and 3:30-6:30pm, Su 8:30am-12:30pm; Oct.-Apr. M-F 8:15am-1:45pm and 3-6pm, Sa 9am-1pm and 3:30-6:30pm, Su 9am-1pm. Also try **Easy Gubbio,** V. della Repubblica, 13 (☎075 922 00 66), on your way up the hill. The English-speaking staff hands out maps, has train info, sells bus tickets, arranges car rentals, and provides telephone and fax service. Open daily Sept.-July 8am-10pm; Aug. 8am-midnight.

Currency Exchange: 24hr. **ATM** at P. Quaranta Martiri, 48.

Emergencies: ☎113. **Police: Carabinieri** (☎075 22 15 42), on V. Leonardo da Vinci. **First Aid/Hospital:** ☎075 23 94 67 or 075 23 94 69.

Pharmacy: C. Garibaldi, 12. Open daily in summer 9am-1pm and 4:30-8pm; in winter 9am-1pm and 4-7:30pm.

Post Office: V. Cairoli, 11 (☎075 927 39 25). Open M-Sa 8:10am-6pm. **Postal Code:** 06024.

ACCOMMODATIONS

Residence di "Via Piccardi," V. Piccardi, 12 (☎075 927 61 08). Large, comfortable rooms overlooking the outdoor breakfast garden. Lovely staff, extremely welcoming to young backpackers. Breakfast included. Singles with bath L50,000; doubles with bath L80,000; triples L100,000.

Albergo dei Consoli, V. dei Consoli, 59 (☎075 927 33 35), 100m from P. della Signoria toward P. Bruno. A fairly luxurious option in the heart of town. Breakfast L5000. Singles L90-130,000; doubles L140-170,000. Closed Jan. V, MC, AmEx.

Locanda del Duca, V. Piccardi, 3 (☎075 927 77 53). Walk across P. Quaranta Martiri (where the bus leaves you) and take a right onto V. Piccardi. A hospitable proprietor rents 7 small rooms on the edge of medieval Gubbio. Includes an outdoor patio with lawn chairs for sunbathing; Restaurant below; breakfast L5000; lunch L25,000; dinner L28,000. Singles L40,000; doubles L70,000, with bath L85,000.

Pensione Grotta dell'Angelo, V. Gioia, 47 (☎075 927 17 47), off V. Cairoli. Tucked away on a quiet road, this *pensione* offers spacious rooms with modern furnishings, TV, and bath. Garden dining offered in attached restaurant of the same name. Breakfast L5000. Singles L55,000; doubles L80,000. V, MC.

FOOD

For a quick bite, try the sandwiches (L2500) at the **salumeria,** P. Quaranta Martiri, 36, across from the bus station. (Open daily 7:15am-1:15pm and 3:15-8pm.) On Tuesday mornings explore the **market** under P. Quaranta Martiri's *loggie.* Local delicacies await you at **Prodotti Tipici e Tartufati Eugubini,** V. Piccardi, 17. Sample *salumi di cinghiale o cervo* (boar or deer sausage) and *pecorino* cheese, or indulge in truffle oil. (Open daily 8:30am-1pm and 3:30-8pm.)

Taverna del Buchetto, V. Dante, 30 (☎075 927 70 34), near the Porta Romana. Enjoy the spicy *pollo alla diavola* (devil's chicken; L13,000) in a cool dining room. Pizza L6-13,000, unless your refined palate demands one with truffles (L15,000). *Primi* L7-13,000. Open Tu-Su noon-2:30pm and 7:30-10pm. V, MC, AmEx.

La Cantina Ristorante/Pizzeria, V. Francesco Piccotti, 3 (☎075 922 05 83), off V. della Repubblica. This pizzeria specializes in *funghi porcini e tartufi* (porcini mushrooms and truffles). Open Tu-Su noon-2:30pm and 7-10pm; 8am-3pm for pizza. V, MC.

San Francesco e il Lupo (☎075 927 23 44), at V. Cairoli and C. Garibaldi. A cozy place with excellent food. Pizza L7-11,000, *primi* L8-18,000, *secondi* L13-25,000. The L20,000 *menù* includes *primo, secondo, contorno,* and fresh fruit; the L24,000 *menù* offers better choices and includes dessert. Open W-M noon-2pm and 7-10pm. V, MC.

SIGHTS

PIAZZA QUARANTA MARTIRI. In the middle of the *piazza* stretches the **Giardino dei Quaranta Martiri** (Garden of the 40 Martyrs), a memorial to those shot by the Nazis in reprisal for the assassination of two German officials. The impressive **Chiesa di San Francesco** stands on one side of the square, one of several places where St. Francis reputedly experienced his powerful conversion. The central apse holds the *Vita della Madonna* (Life of the Madonna), a partially destroyed 15th-century fresco series by Ottaviano Nelli, Gubbio's most famous painter. Across the *piazza* from the church is the **Loggia dei Tiratoi,** where 14th-century weavers stretched their cloth so it would shrink evenly. Today it shades outdoor cafes and a market. V. Matteotti, behind the church, leads to the monumental **Roman theater,** which is well-preserved and still stages classical productions.

PALAZZO DEI CONSOLI. One of Italy's most graceful public buildings, this white stone palace (1332) was built for the high magistrate of Gubbio by local boy Matteo di Giovanello (also known as Gattapone). Within the *palazzo,* on the bottom floor, the **Museo Civico** displays a collection of Eugubine and Roman artifacts. On the top floor, the collection continues with the prized **Tavole Eugubine (Eugabian Tables).** Discovered in 1444 near the Roman theater outside the city walls, these seven bronze tablets (300-100 BC) form one of the few documents in the ancient Umbrian language (although the last two are in Latin). A farmer discovered the tablets, some of the most significant sacred texts from classical antiquity, in an underground chamber of the Roman theater. They earned him two years of grazing rights from the generous city of Gubbio. The ritual texts spell out the social and political organization of early Umbrian society and provide the novice with advice on how to take auguries from animal livers. *(P. della Signoria. Palazzo and Museo open daily mid-Mar. to Sept. 10am-1:30pm and 3-6pm; Oct. to mid-Mar. 10am-1pm and 3-6pm. Both floors of the museum L7000, ages 15-25 L4000, ages 7-14 free.)*

PALAZZO DUCALE AND THE DUOMO. Climb to the pinnacle of the town where the 15th-century Palazzo Ducale and the 13th-century *duomo* face off. Federico da Montefeltro commissioned Luciano Laurana, designer of his larger palace in Urbino, to build this smaller but equally elegant version. The *duomo,* an unassuming pink Gothic building, is complete with 12th-century stained-glass windows, the decaying corpses of several of Gubbio's prominent medieval bishops, and Pinturicchio's *Adoration of the Shepherds. (Palazzo and duomo are a couple of streets north of P. della Signoria. Open M-Sa 9am-1:30pm and 2:30-7pm, Su and holidays 9am-1pm. Ticket office closes 30min. before the museum. L4000, under 18 and over 60 free.)*

MONTE INGINO. When the museums close for lunch, take the seven-minute birdcage chairlift *(funivia)* to the peak of Monte Ingino for a splendid view and prime picnicking. While there, visit the **basilica and monastery of Sant'Ubaldo,** Gubbio's

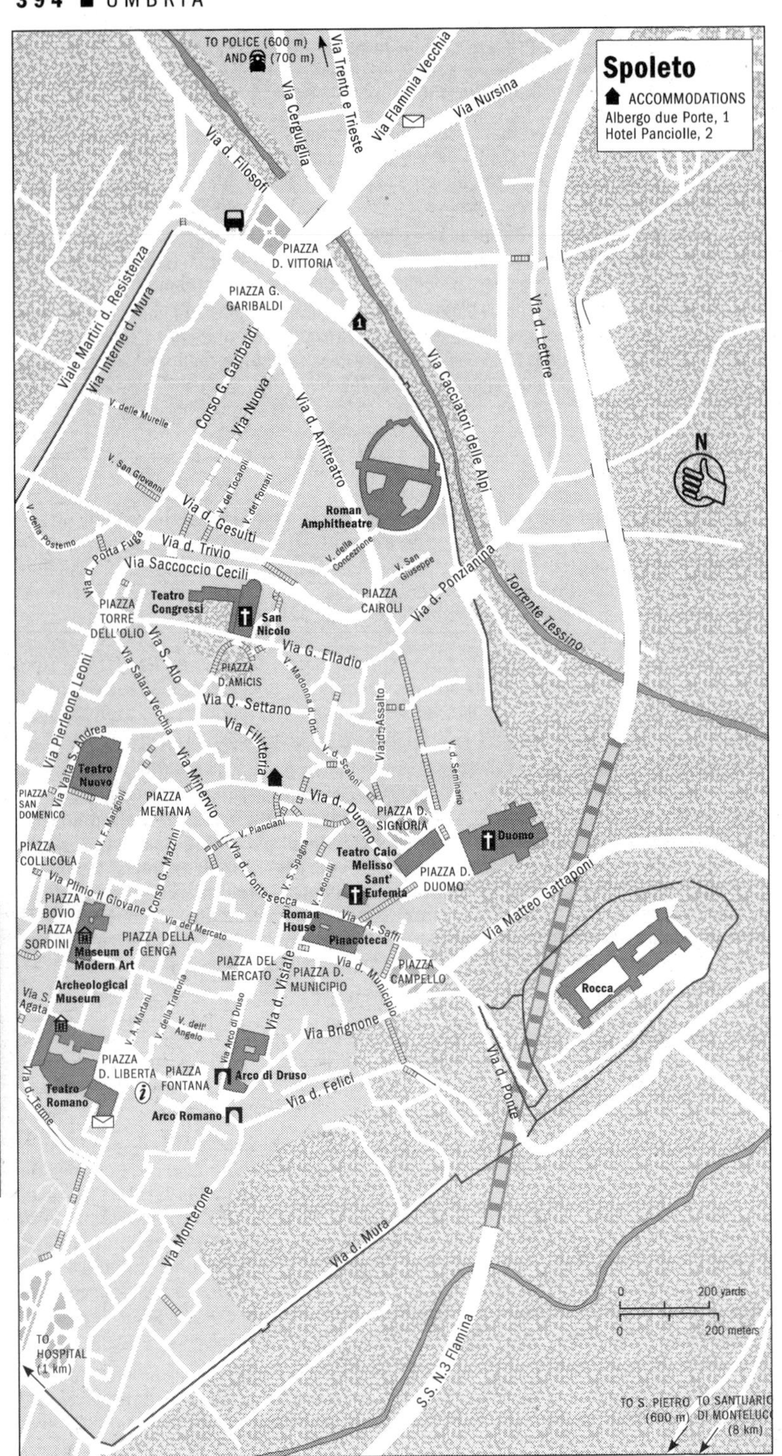

CENTRAL ITALY

patron saint. The basilica houses St. Ubaldo's pickled body (in a glass case) and the three *ceri*, large wooden candles carried in the *Corsa dei Ceri* procession each May (see below). From the uphill entrance to the basilica, veer left and continue upwards on a dirt path to the top of the mountain; here, a ruined lookout tower offers spectacular views of the surrounding countryside. *(Chairlift open June M-Sa 9:30am-1:15pm and 2:30-7pm, Su 9am-7:30pm; July-Aug. M-Sa 8:30am-7:30pm, Su 8:30am-8pm; Sept. M-Sa 9:30am-7pm, Su 9am-7:30pm; Oct. daily 10am-1:15pm and 2:30-5:30pm; Nov.-Feb. daily 10am-1:15pm and 2:30-5pm. One-way L6000, round-trip L8000.)*

ENTERTAINMENT

The **Corsa dei Ceri** (May 15) is a 900-year-old tradition and one of Italy's most noted processions. Intended to represent candles, the three *ceri* are huge wooden blocks carved like hourglasses and topped with little saints. Each one represents a distinct faction of the populace: the masons, the farmers, and the artisans. After 12 hours of furious preparation and frenetic flag-twirling, squads of husky runners *(ceraioli)* clad in Renaissance-style tights heave the heavy objects onto their shoulders and run a wild relay race up Monte Ingino. Making occasional pit stops for alcoholic encouragement, they eventually reach the Basilica of Sant'Ubaldo, where they deposit the *ceri* until the following May. This orgiastic festival meshes the sacred with the profane and turns the quiet medieval streets of Gubbio into clamorous stomping grounds for frenzied locals and entranced visitors.

During the **Palio della Balestra,** held on the last Sunday in May in P. Grande, archers from Gubbio and nearby Sansepolcro gather for the latest rematch of a fierce crossbow contest that dates to 1461. If Gubbio wins, an animated parade ensues. A recent industry in Gubbio is the production of *balestre* (toy crossbows).

SPOLETO ☎0743

A mere 40 years ago, Spoleto, indistinguishable from the other charming towns of central Italy, would have seemed an unlikely mecca for international travelers. Spoleto awoke out of its solemn, medieval past when it introduced its summer arts festival, the *Festival dei Due Mondi* (The Festival of the Two Worlds). The composer Gian Carlo Menotti selected Spoleto in 1958 as the trial site, claiming that art could be a community's bread and butter—his efforts were not misguided. The festival has brought prosperity to the town, making Spoleto an internationally renowned center for the arts. Arts of all sorts, including expressionist pizza parlors and chic boutiques, overtake the town in late June and linger through the summer. Even if you miss the festival, Fra Filippo Lippi's frescoes and the magnificent gorge are well worthwhile.

TRANSPORTATION

Trains: (☎0743 485 16), in P. Polvani. To: **Assisi** (40min., L4900); **Rome** (1½hr., every 1-2hr., from L12,500); **Perugia** (1½hr., every hr., L6100); and **Ancona** (2hr., 8 per day, from L14,500). Ticket window open 6am-8pm. Ask for a free city map at the station's news stand. **Luggage Storage:** L5000 for 12hr. Go to cashier at the bar for luggage service. Open 5am-11pm.

Buses: SSIT (☎0743 21 22 05) departs from P. della Vittoria by P. Garibaldi and connects the town to **Perugia** (L10,400) and **Foligno** (M-F 6 per day, L5000).

Taxis: (☎0743 445 48), in P. della Libertà; (☎0743 499 90) in P. Garibaldi.

ORIENTATION AND PRACTICAL INFORMATION

Have patience with Spoleto's narrow cobblestone streets; they are navigable with the assistance of a map, available from the tourist office in **Piazza della Libertà.** To get there from the train station, walk straight up **Viale Trento e Trieste,** turn right across **Ponte Garibaldi,** walk through **Piazza Garibaldi,** and continue along **Corso Garibaldi.** The road eventually ends at **Corso Mazzini,** which terminates in P. della Libertà (30min., most of which is up a fairly steep hill). You can also take an ATAF bus marked "Centro" from the station (L1200)—buy tickets at the newsstand in the station. From C. Mazzini, turn left up **Via del Mercato** to **Piazza del Mercato,** the bustling center of the city where vendors loudly brag to shoppers about the freshness of their produce. Many shop-lined streets radiate from P. del Mercato. **Via del Municipio** runs to **Piazza del Municipio** and **Piazza Campello,** while **Via Saffi** leads to **Piazza del Duomo.** These three squares contain most of the city's sights.

Tourist Office: P. della Libertà, 7 (☎0743 22 03 11). Offers detailed info and an unwieldy map of the city. Arranges tours, but no hotel or event reservations. Some English spoken. Open Apr.-Sept. M-F 9am-1pm and 4-7pm, Sa-Su 10am-1pm and 4-7:30pm. Off-season hours reduced slightly.

ATM: Cassa di Risparmio di Spoleto, P. Mentana, 3, just off C. Mazzini. Open 24hr. The bank is open M-F 8:20am-1:20pm and 2:50-3:50pm, Sa 8:20-11:50am.

Theater Box Office: Buy advance tickets for events during the Spoleto festival at **Teatro Nuovo** (☎0743 440 97). Open Tu-Su 10am-1pm and 4-7pm.

Emergencies: ☎113. **Police: Carabinieri,** V. dei Filosofi, 57 (☎0743 490 44). English speaker available. **Hospital:** V. Loreto, 3 (☎0743 21 01), outside Porta Loreto.

Late-Night Pharmacy: Farmacia Scoccianti (0743 22 32 42), on V. Marconi. Posts which pharmacy is open for after-hours services.

Post Office: P. della Libertà, 12 (☎0743 403 73). Walk down V. Matteotti from P. della Liberta; the entrance is on your right. Open M-Sa 8:10am-7pm. **Postal Code:** 06049.

ACCOMMODATIONS AND CAMPING

Finding accommodations is almost impossible during the summer music festival (the last week of June through the 1st week of July). If you arrive during the festival, contact **Conspoleto,** P. della Libertà, 7 (☎0743 22 07 73; email info@conspoleto.com; www.conspoleto.com). They will look for rooms and make reservations. The tourist office keeps a list of alternative housing options such as rooms for rent (1-week min.), camping, and *agriturismi.*

Albergo Due Porte, P. della Vittoria, 9 (☎0743 22 36 66), a 5min. walk from the train station, just across Ponte Garibaldi from Vle. Trento e Trieste. Or take the short bus trip (every 10min., L1200) from in front of the station. Huge, spotless bathrooms and nondescript but comfortable rooms with TV and phone. Management also runs the restaurant next door. Breakfast included, served in the lush backyard garden. Cribs available. Wheelchair accessible. With *Let's Go:* singles with bath L45,000; doubles with bath L80,000; triples with bath L100,000; quads with bath L120,000. V.

Hotel Panciolle, V. del Duomo, 3 (☎/fax 0743 456 77), in the *centro storico* near the *duomo.* Bright, airy rooms with modern furnishings and bath. Restaurant downstairs (see **Food,** below). Breakfast L7000. Singles L60,000; doubles L90,000. Cash only.

FOOD

An open-air **market** enlivens P. del Mercato. (Open M-Sa 8:30am-1pm.) The **STANDA supermarket,** in P. Garibaldi, stocks basics. (Open M-Sa 9am-1pm and 4-8pm.)

Trattoria Pecchiarda, V. San Giovanni, 1 (☎0743 22 10 09). Walk up C. Garibaldi and take a right on the tiny V. S. Giovanni. Dine under a large umbrella on a terraced patio brimming with flowers. The *strangozzi ai funghi* (fresh pasta with mushrooms; L11,000) is particularly delightful. L15-20,000 for *primo,* drink, and dessert. No price list, but have no fear. Open daily 7pm-12:30am. V, MC.

Ristorante Il Panciolle, V. degli Eroli (a tiny alley off V. Duomo), 1 (☎0743 455 98 or 0743 22 42 89), below the hotel of the same name. Ample portions of country fare and homemade pasta, exquisitely prepared. Tables on a porch with a panoramic view. Specializes in soups (L13-15,000), *cacciagione allo spiedo* (beef on a skewer), *carni alla brace* (beef on the bone), and *tartufo nero di Norcia* (black truffles). Wide selection of Umbrian wine. *Secondi* L13-25,000. Cover L5000. Reservations suggested during the Spoleto Festival. Open Th-Tu 12:30-2:30pm and 7:45-10:45pm. V, MC, AmEx.

Enoteca Provinciale, V. Saffi, 7 (☎0743 22 04 84), near the *Pinacoteca.* A cozy place to sample local wines and snack on *frittata d'asparaghi* (asparagus omelette; L8000) or sit down for the hearty *strangozzi alla spolentina* (L8000). Open W-M 11am-3pm and 7-11pm. V, MC.

SIGHTS

ROCCA AND PONTE DELLE TORRI. The **papal fortress,** affectionately named **Rocca,** sits on the hillside above Spoleto. This fortress, a prison until 1982, was used during the war to confine Slavic and Italian political prisoners. In 1943, the prisoners staged a dramatic escape to join the partisans in the Umbrian hills. The impressive Rocca is presently closed for renovations, although it opens to host various festival events. Follow the 15-minute walk curving around the fortress for panoramic views of Spoleto and the countryside. Farther on, you'll reach one of the region's most stunning architectural achievements, the 14th-century **Ponte delle Torri.** The 80m bridge and aqueduct span the channel of the river Tessino. On the far bank, the craggy medieval towers for which the bridge was named rise up beyond a small waterfall.

DUOMO. Spoleto's monumental Romanesque cathedral was built in the 12th century and later augmented by a portico (1491) and 17th-century interior redecoration. The soaring bell tower is an amalgam of styles and materials, cobbled together from fragments of Roman structures. Eight rose windows animate the facade, the largest one bearing the symbols of the four evangelists. Did the fun ever stop during the Renaissance? Despite a spartan interior, brilliantly colored scenes by Fra Filippo Lippi fill the domed apse; Lippi died here while working on the frescoes. The Annunciation in the lower left of the fresco cycle is particularly impressive. Lorenzo the Magnificent commissioned Lippi's tomb, which was decorated by the artist's son, Filippino, and now lies in the right transept of the church. In the reliquary there is a consolatory letter written by St. Francis to a fellow brother. *(On a ledge below V. Saffi, between the papal fortress and the Roman Amphitheater. Open daily Mar.-Oct. 7:30am-12:30pm and 3-6:30pm; Nov.-Feb. 8am-12:30pm and 3-6pm.)*

CHIESA DI SANT'EUFEMIA. Situated on the grounds of the bishop's residence, this church is one of Umbria's most significant works of Romanesque art. Constructed in the 1st half of the 12th century, it houses sweeping arches, rhythmic windows, and concentric adornments on the heavy portals. *(Left from P. del Duomo. Open daily 10am-12:30pm and 3:30-7pm. L3000.)*

ROMAN RUINS. Spoleto's many classical ruins testify to the city's prominence in Roman times. The extremely well-preserved **theater** stands just beyond the Roman walls, visible from P. della Libertà. Take V. S. Agata from the *piazza* to reach the entrance of the adjacent **Museo Archeologico,** which houses ceramic and statuary artifacts from the area. *(☎0743 22 32 77. Open daily 9am-7pm. L4000, includes the interior of the theater.)* The **Arco Romano,** at the top of V. Bronzino, once marked the entrance into town. Farther along, the **Arco di Druso** led to the forum (now P. del Mercato). On nearby V. de Visiale you can explore a restored **Roman house** from AD 27 dedicated to the Emperor Caligula. *(Open Tu-Su 10am-1pm and 3-6pm. L5000, under 18 and over 65 L3000; includes the Museum of Modern Art and Pinacoteca.)*

ART MUSEUMS. Spoleto's **La Pinacoteca,** on the 1st floor of the City Hall, houses the work of medieval and modern Umbrian artists. The all-star roster includes Perugino and his student, Lo Spagna. *(Up a flight of stars from P. del Duomo. ☎0743 21 82 70. Open daily 10am-1pm and 3-6pm. L5000, including the Roman House and Museum of Modern Art.)* The same ticket provides admission to the **Museum of Modern Art,** which

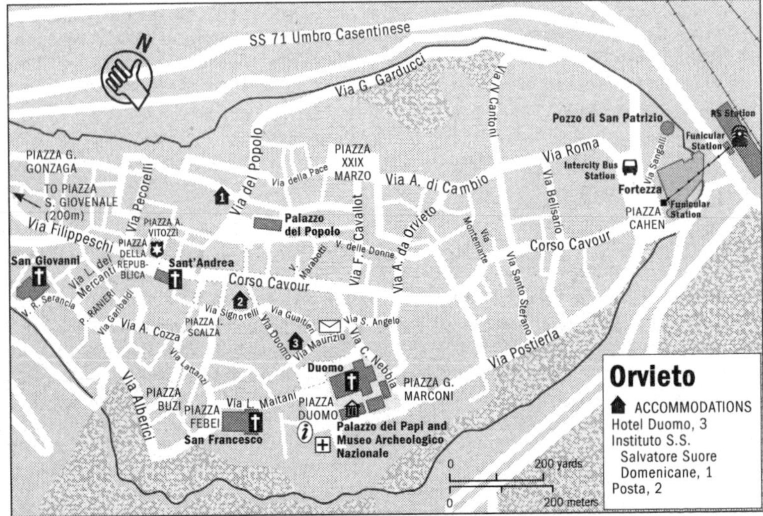

hosts a variety of changing exhibits. *(From C. Mazzini, turn left on V. Sant'Agata then right on V. delle Terme. The museum lies ahead on your right. Open Tu-Su 10am-1pm and 3-6pm. Admission, with ticket from the Roman house and La Pinacoteca, L5000.)*

MONTELUCO. Spoleto's "mountain of the sacred grove" lies an invigorating hour-long climb away, through the forest, past tiny mountain shrines and elegant villa retreats. At the crest of the mountain you'll find a park, several bars, hotels, a skeet-shooting range, and the tiny Franciscan **Santuario di Monteluco,** once the refuge of St. Francis and San Bernadino of Siena. At the base of Monteluco, a five-minute stroll down the right fork of the road brings you to the Romanesque **Chiesa di San Pietro.** Its tan facade is littered with a menagerie of bas-relief beasts cavorting in scenes from popular fables. Note the wolf to the right of the door wearing a monk's cowl and holding a book. *(Cross the Ponte delle Torri and follow the dirt path. Buses leave P. della Libertà for Monteluco approximately every 1½hr. when the sanctuary is open. Sanctuary open daily 9am-5:30pm. Free.)*

ENTERTAINMENT

The **Spoleto Festival** (formerly known as the **Festival dei Due Mondi** or Festival of Two Worlds) is held from the end of June through mid-July and has become not only the pride of Italy but also one of the world's most prestigious international events. The festival features numerous concerts, operas, and ballets, with performances by well-known Italian and international artists. The festival also brings film screenings, modern art shows, and local craft displays to Spoleto. Tickets may be purchased in late April from a ticket office at P. Duomo, 8, and in late May from another ticket office in P. della Libertà (☎0743 44 700; fax 0743 22 03 21). In addition to these offices, during the festival the box offices at **Teatro Nuovo** and **Rocca Albornoziana** are open one hour before the start of most performances. (Email tickets@spoletofestival.net; www.spoletofestival.net. Open Tu-Su 10am-1pm and 4-7pm.) Bookings from abroad are accepted and recommended—send a check plus a 15% pre-sale charge to Associazione Festival dei Due Mondi, Biglietteria Festival dei Due Mondi, 06049 Spoleto (PG), Italia. The box office at the theater opens one hour before the start of the performance. The renowned **Stagione del Teatro Lirico Sperimentale di Spoleto** (Experimental Opera Season) runs from late August to September. The **Istituzione Teatro Lirico Sperimentale di Spoleto "A. Belli,"** P. G. Bovio, 1, 06049 Spoleto provides info. (☎0743 22 16 45; fax 0743 22 29 30; email teatrolirico@caribusiness.it; www.caribusiness.it/lirico.)

Those looking for cultural entertainment of a different sort should be aware that Spoleto has a mild infestation of sexually repressed twenty-something Italian men fulfilling their 10 months of mandatory military service—female travelers who want to sip their beer in peace should start after 11pm (the military curfew). After hitting the pubs, those in the mood to dance can head over to **La Tartaruga,** V. Filitteria, 12 (☎0743 22 32 82), or **La Trottola** (☎0743 22 96 10), in Molinaccio. Though often filled with Spoletan youth, the clubs lack the hype of big city *discoteche.*

DAYTRIP FROM SPOLETO: TREVI

Be warned that Trevi is almost totally inaccessible unless you have a car or really strong legs. The train station is a steep 4km walk from the center of town, and no buses service the town from the station. Moreover, no taxi services exist within the town.

The view of Trevi from the train that passes the small town in the valley below is undeniably appealing. Its ancient pastel buildings, perched jaggedly along almost vertical slopes, form a small island amidst vast silvery-green seas of olive groves. Trevi seems like the perfect spot to take a spontaneous detour from your itinerary and relax in a hill town somewhat off the beaten path. If you want to make the trip, your first step should probably be to contact the Pro-Loco tourist office, in P. del Comune, 5 (☎0742 33 22 22), where you can find out about the town's attractions. **Pinacoteca Rascolta d'Arte di San Francesco** hosts the work of local masters. (Open daily, though hours vary slightly every month—10am-1:30pm and 3-7pm is a good bet.) The **Flash Art Museum,** which hosts changing exhibits of modern and contemporary art. (Hours vary wildly, call ☎0742 38 18 18.) The tourist office can also provide information about the **Illumination Procession,** which takes place every January 27th and is one of the oldest festivals in Umbria. In the same *piazza* as the tourist office note the impressive historic bell tower. Trevi's accommodations are not exactly the haven of budget travelers—if you're set on staying overnight, try **Il Terziere,** Via Salerno, 1, just off P. Garibaldi. Not only is it an elegant hotel with immaculate rooms, it also houses a great restaurant that serves fresh, homemade pasta. Try the *strangozzi al tartufo* (stringy pasta with truffles) for L9000. (☎/fax 0742 783 59. Singles L85,000; doubles L115,000. V, MC, AmEx.)

ORVIETO ☎0763

Orvieto sits, as it has for the past 3000 years, above an incredible volcanic plateau rising from the rolling farmlands of southern Umbria. In the 7th century BC, Etruscans began to burrow under the city for *tufo* (a volcanic stone out of which most of the medieval quarter is built), creating the subterranean companion "city" beneath Orvieto's surface. Five centuries later, the Romans sacked and reoccupied the plateau, calling their "new" city *"urbs ventus"* (old city), from which the name Orvieto is derived. In medieval times the city again became a center of worship. In the 13th century, as Thomas Aquinas lectured in the local academies and fervent Christians planned their crusades, countless churches sprang up along the winding city streets. In the 14th and 15th centuries, the Masters of Orvieto, alongside those of Siena, Assisi, and Perugia, formed a highly influential school of painters. Today, Orvieto is a popular tourist destination; visitors are drawn to the stunning 13th-century *duomo* (and the city's renowned *Orvieto Classico* wine), discovering the city's steeples, streets, and underground chambers.

TRANSPORTATION

Trains: To: **Arezzo** (45min., L10,100); **Rome** (1½hr., every 1-2 hr. 4:25am-10:27pm, L12,500); and **Florence** (2hr., every 1-2hr. 7:29am-11:32pm, L17,700) via **Cortona** (45min.). **Luggage Storage:** L5000 per bag for 12hr. Open 6:30am-8pm.

Buses: COTRAL (☎0761 266 592) runs 1 daily bus from the train station to P. Cahen and to surrounding towns. Buy tickets at the *tabacchi* in the train station. To: **Viterbo** (7 per day 6:25am-3:45pm, L5400). **ATC,** P. della Rivoluzione Francese (☎0763 30 12 24), runs buses to **Perugia** (5:45am, L11,000) and **Todi** (1:55pm, L8000). Buy tickets at the *tabacchi* up C. Cavour or on the bus.

ORIENTATION AND PRACTICAL INFORMATION

Orvieto lies midway along the Rome-Florence train line. From the train station, cross the street and take the funicular (every 15min.; L1300, with shuttle L1600) up the hill to **Piazza Cahen,** where ATC buses stop. A shuttle leads from P. Cahen to **Piazza del Duomo.** If you choose to walk, you can follow **Corso Cavour** to its intersection with **Via Duomo.** The left branch leads to the *duomo* and surrounding museums; the right, to the **Piazza del Popolo.** Sprinkled between V. Duomo and the **Piazza della Repubblica** along Corso Cavour are most of the city's restaurants, hotels, and shops. Past P. della Repubblica is the medieval section of town, housing the city's oldest buildings and roads.

Tourist Office: P. del Duomo, 24 (☎0763 34 17 72; fax 0763 34 44 33). Offers a thorough pamphlet with info on hotels, restaurants, and sights. Also sells special deals on underground tours of Orvieto, as well as the **Orvieto Unica card** (L20,000, students L17,000), which includes an underground tour, a round-trip ticket for the funicular-minibus, and entrance to the Museo "Claudio Faina," the Torre del Moro, and the Cappella della Madonna di San Brizio. Open M-F 8:15am-1:50pm and 4-7pm, Sa 10am-1pm and 4-7pm, Su 10am-noon and 4-6pm. The **Tourist Information Point,** Borgo Largo Barzini, 7 (☎0763 342 297), just off V. Duomo, will help you find a place to stay for free. They also **exchange traveler's checks and currency** for 5% commission. Open M-F 8am-1pm and 4-6pm, Sa 8am-1pm.

Emergencies: ☎113. **Police:** (☎0763 400 88), in P. della Repubblica. **Hospital:** (☎0763 30 91), off P. del Duomo.

Internet Access: See the **Internet@caffe,** (p. 401).

Post Office: (☎0763 412 43), on V. Cesare Nebbia. Stamps are available at *tabacchi* and mailboxes dot the town. Open M-Sa 8am-4:45pm. **Postal Code:** 05018.

ACCOMMODATIONS AND CAMPING

Hotel Duomo, V. Maurizio, 7 (☎0763 34 18 87), off V. Duomo, the 1st right as you leave the *piazza.* Steps away from the cathedral. Light and airy rooms have delicate lace curtains; some have excellent views. Breakfast in the garden L9000. Singles L40,000; doubles L78,000, with bath L85,000; triples L80,000.

Posta, V. Luca Signorelli, 18 (☎076 33 41 909). Halcyon setting. Small *piazza* in back covered by a canopy of grape vines. Beautiful rooms with gilded mirrors, tiled floors, and an occasional Venetian glass chandelier. Breakfast L10,000. Lockout midnight. Singles L60,000, with bath L70,000; doubles L75-80,000, with bath L100,000.

Istituto S.S. Salvatore Suore Domenicane, V. del Popolo, 1 (☎/fax 0763 34 29 10). Extremely friendly nuns to the rescue with reasonably cheap, pleasant accommodations. Ask about free parking, which is sometimes available. Breakfast L5000. 2-night min. stay. Curfew 10:30pm; in winter 9:30pm. Closed July. Singles L50,000; doubles with bath L80,000.

Camping: Scacco Matto (☎0744 95 01 63; fax 0744 95 03 73), on Lake Corbara, 14km from the center of town. From the station, take the local Orvieto-Baschi bus and ask to be dropped off at the site (the stop is 200m from the entrance). Bus service between the campsite and Orvieto's station is extremely infrequent. Private beach and hot showers included. L8000 per person, L9000 per tent, L5000 per car.

FOOD

Amidst a crowd of pricey *ristoranti,* there are reasonable opportunities to treat your stomach well in Orvieto. Track down an Umbrian gem and enjoy all seven courses, or take the lighter road with baked *lumachelle* (snail-shaped buns with ham and cheese), *tortucce* (fried bread dough), aniseed or almond cookies, pizza with pork cracklings, chickpea and chestnut soup, *rigatoni* with nuts and chocolate, and *mazzafegate* (sweet or salty sausages). Tellingly, one of the ancient names of Orvieto was Oinarea (the city where wine flows). Today it still flows (hic!) to the tune of L6-9000 per bottle. Don't leave Orvieto without sampling its world-renowned wine, *Orvieto Classico.* **Alimentari** with local treats dot the city; one is below P. della Repubblica at V. Filippeschi, 29. Bottles of Orvieto Classico start at L5000. (Open M-Tu and Th-Sa 7:30am-noon and 5-8:30pm, W 7:45am-2pm).

Al Pozzo Etrusco Ristorante, Piazza de' Ranieri, 1/A (☎0763 444 56). Follow V. Garibaldi from P. della Repubblica and walk diagonally left across P. de' Ranieri. "*Al Pozzo Etrusco*" means "the Etruscan well," and, believe it or not, they've got one. If you missed the underground city, you can catch up on your studies over delicious regional fare. *Pasta fresco* L7-9000, *secondi* L9-15,000. V, MC, AmEx.

Asino D'oro, Vicolo del Popolo I, 9 (☎0763 34 33 02), in a little *piazza* between C. Cavour and P. del Popolo. At the intersection of V. Duomo and C. Cavour, head towards P. della Repubblica and duck down the 1st alley to your right. Innovative menu changes daily. Casual cafe environment with exquisite and reasonably priced food. *Primi* and *secondi* L6-12,000. Open Tu-Su 12:30pm-midnight. Wheelchair accessible.

Trattoria La Grotta, V. L. Signorelli, 5 (☎/fax 0763 34 13 48), near the *duomo.* Between pouring wine and tending his tantalizing sauces, Franco, the exuberant and garrulous owner, walks from table to table to chew the fat with his customers. Start with *bruschette,* feast on *fettuccine ai carciofi* (artichokes; L12,000), and finish with sublime *tiramisù* (L6500). *Primi* and *secondi* L10-20,000. Open W-M 12:30-3pm and 7:30-11pm. V, MC.

La Volpe è L'Uva, V Ripa Corsica, 1 (☎0763 34 16 12). Follow signs from P. della Repubblica. This vegetarian heaven has an intimate setting with warm lighting, slow dining, and a collection of orgasmic dishes. Summer specialties such as *ombrigelli con la carbonara ai fiori di zucca* (L11,000) and *salsicce e uva* (sausages with grapes; L15,000) will knock your socks off. Open daily 7-11pm; in winter W-Su 7-11pm.

Internet@caffe, V. Cavour, 25 (☎0763 34 12 61). Enjoy delectable pastries that are regional specialties while you check email. Pastries L2-3000. Access L6000 for 30min. Open Oct.-Mar. daily 7am-midnight; Nov.-Apr. Th-Tu 7am-midnight.

SIGHTS

DUOMO. Even a quick glance at Orvieto's pride and joy will shock you. Its fanciful facade, designed around 1290 by Lorenzo Maitani, dazzles the admirer with intertwining spires, mosaics, and sculptures. Initially envisioned as a smaller Romanesque chapel, the *duomo* was later enlarged with a transept and nave. The bottom level features exquisitely carved bas-reliefs of the Creation and Old Testament prophecies as well as the final panel of Maitani's realistic *Last Judgment.* Set in niches surrounding the rose window by Andrea Orcagna (1325-1364), bronze and marble sculptures emphasize the Christian canon. Thirty-three architects, 90 mosaic artisans, 152 sculptors, and 68 painters worked for over 600 years to bring the *duomo* to this point, and the work continues—the bronze doors were only installed in 1970. Visitors in the spring of 2001 should find newly restored frescoes by Ugolino dé Prete Ilario behind the altar.

The **Cappella della Madonna di San Brizio** (sometimes called the **Cappella Nuova**), off the right transept, includes Luca Signorelli's dramatic Apocalypse frescoes, considered to be his finest works. On the right wall, skeletons and muscular humans pull themselves out of the earth while ghoulish apparitions of the damned swarm about in the unsettling *Resurrection of the Dead.* Beside it hangs the *Inferno,* with a depiction of Signorelli (a blue devil) embracing his mistress. Rumor has it that the Whore of Babylon, carried on the back of a devil above the masses, was modeled after an Orvieto woman who rejected Signorelli's advances. Begun by Fra Angelico in 1447, the frescoes were supposed to be completed by Perugino, but the city grew tired of waiting and enlisted Signorelli to finish the

project. His vigorous draftsmanship, mastery of human anatomy, and dramatic compositions were inspirations for Michelangelo. The Cappella also holds the gold-encrusted **Reliquario del Corporale** (chalice-cloth), to which the entire structure is dedicated. The clot inside the box caught Christ's blood, which dripped from a consecrated host in Bolsena in 1263, corroborating the doctrine of transubstantiation. *(Duomo open M-Sa 8:30am-12:45pm and 2:30-7:15pm (though afternoon hours vary monthly), Su and Holidays 2:30-5:45pm. Free. No shorts or short skirts permitted. Capella Nuova L3000, before 10am free. Purchase tickets at the tourist office across the street.)*

PALAZZO DEI PAPI. From this austere, 13th-century "Palace of the Popes" Pope Clement VII rejected King Henry VIII's petition to annul his marriage to Catherine of Aragon, condemning both Catherine and English Catholicism to a bleak fate. Set back in the *palazzo* is the **Museo Archeologico Nazionale,** where you can examine Etruscan artifacts from the area and walk into a full-sized tomb. *(Right of the duomo. Open M-Sa 9am-7pm, Su 9am-1pm. L4000, over 60 and under 18 free.)*

CENTRAL ITALY

UNDERGROUND CITY. For the most complete tour of Etruscan Orvieto, consider the **Underground City Excursions,** which will lead you through the endless dark and twisted bowels of the city. During its 3000 years of history, while the city rose upward, a companion "city" burrowed into the soft *tufa* of the cliff below. Although the ancient Etruscan city of Velzna (which stood where modern Orvieto now sits) was sacked by Romans, its history is still preserved below the earth. Cisterns, underground mills, pottery workshops, quarries, wine cellars, and burial sites weave an impressive web beneath the city. *(☎0763 34 48 91. 1hr. tours leave from the tourist office at 11am and 4pm. L10,000, groups or those with tickets to Pozzo della Cava L8000, students L6000.)*

MUSEO CIVICO AND MUSEO FAINA. These *musei* hold an extensive collection of Etruscan artifacts found in excavations of local necropoli. Its exhibits include coins, bronze urns, red- and black-figure vases from the 6th century BC, and ornaments from Roman times. *(Directly opposite the duomo. Open Apr.-Aug. daily 10am-1pm and 2-6pm; Sept.-Mar. Tu-Su 10am-1pm and 2-6pm. L8000, students and seniors L5000.)*

CHIESA DI SANT'ANDREA. This church marks the beginning of Orvieto's **medieval quarter.** The church, built upon the ruins of an Etruscan temple, served as a meeting place, or *comune*, in medieval Orvieto. Inside, the crypt (at the beginning of the right aisle) contains recently excavated remains from the underground Etruscan temple. *(In P. della Repubblica, 500m down Corso Cavour from P. Cahen.)*

CHIESA DI SAN GIOVENALE. The city's oldest church was dedicated to the first bishop of Orvieto; there's a fresco of him on the left wall as you enter the church. Directly next to the doors on the left is a 14th-century "Tree of Life"—a family tree of the church's founders. The soils of the verdant slope below P. San Giovanni are filled with the graves of thousands who perished in the Black Death of 1348. Walk back from San Giovanni on V. Ripa di Serancia, the city's oldest road. It ends at the **Chiesa di San Giovanni.** Just inside the ancient city walls, this church offers a stunning view of the countryside below. *(From P. della Repubblica, follow V. Filippeschi, which turns into V. Malabranca.)*

ENTERTAINMENT

Orvieto wants to party all the time. In the spring there is the **Palio dell'Oca,** a medieval game of skill on horseback. On Pentecost (49 days after Easter), Orvieto celebrates the **Festa della Palombella.** Small wooden boxes filled with fireworks are set up in front of the *duomo* and the Chiesa di San Francesco. At the stroke of noon, the San Francesco fireworks are set off, and a white metal dove descends across the wire to ignite the explosives. In June, the historic **Procession of Corpus Domini,** marked by pomp and pageantry, celebrates the Miracle of Bolsena. Ladies and flag wavers dance in the streets to period music, followed by medieval banquets. On the feast day itself, a large religious procession galavants through the streets. On August 14, another religious parade makes its way down Orvieto's cobblestone streets, continuing a tradition that dates to the 13th century. From December 29 to January 5, **Umbria Jazz Winter** swings in Orvieto's theaters, churches, and *palazzi* (with the grand finale in the *duomo*). For specific festival information contact **Servizio Turistico Territoriale IAT dell'Orvietano,** P. Duomo, 24 (☎0763 34 19 11 or 0763 34 36 58), or **Informazioni Turistiche** (☎0763 34 17 72; fax 0763 34 44 33) at the same address.

For less formal fun, try **Zeppelin,** V. Garibaldi, 28. This classy old-fashioned bar, with Orvieto's best **nightlife,** is a popular place to enjoy live music and drinks. (☎0763 34 14 47. Open W-M 7:30pm-1am. V, MC.) Otherwise follow signs from P. Duomo for **Engel Keller's Tavern,** on V. Beato Angelico. (Open Th-Tu 7pm-3am.)

THE MARCHES (LE MARCHE)

In the Marches, green foothills separate the gray shores of the Adriatic from the Apennines and the traditional hill-towns from the umbrella-laden beaches. In contrast to overabundant seaside resorts lining the coast, easily-accessible inland towns rely on agricultural production and preserve the region's historical legacy in the architectural and archaeological remains of Gauls, Picenes, and Romans. The region's history is punctuated by such geniuses as Renaissance Urbino's Raphael and Donato Bramante. Yet this history is unassumingly integrated into daily life. Mass is held in Renaissance cathedrals, medieval streets are deftly navigated by aggressive Fiats, and natives converge for the centuries-old truffle festivals. Though, with the exception of Urbino, most travelers will likely find that Le Marche lacks attractions that warrant a major detour, a number of destinations are certainly worthwhile if you happen to be in the area.

HIGHLIGHTS OF LE MARCHE

THROW DOWN your hair from Urbino's steepled **palace on a hill** (p. 408).

LOSE YOUR BACKUP in the small-town gossip of **Ascoli Piceno** and risk falling a rung lower on the social pecking order (p. 411).

ESCAPE the past and idle away an afternoon on San Benedetto's blissful **beaches** without a museum in sight (p. 414).

PESARO ☎0741

Pesaro offers a relaxed alternative to hormone-driven Rimini. The beaches are somewhat less crowded, and the quiet, nearby drag is worlds away from Rimini's orgiastic strip. While surf shops and fast food eateries occupy much of the space along the beach, a number of museums and churches decorate the old quarter, and urban spaces form the heart of town. At night, the very young ride carousels, the still-young flirt cautiously, and the not-so-young trade stories on park benches.

TRANSPORTATION

Trains: At the end of V. Risorgimento and V. della Liberazione. Pesaro lies along the Adriatic coast on the Bologna-Lecce line. To: **Fano** (15min., 1 per hr. 5:44am-11:19pm, L2400); **Rimini** (30min., 2 per hr., L4100); **Ancona** (1hr., 2 per hr., L5700); and **Bologna** (1 per hr., L12,500). Ticket counter open daily 5:45am-9pm. **Luggage Storage:** L5000 for 12hr. Open daily 6am-11pm.

Buses: In Ple. Matteotti, down V. S. Francesco from P. del Popolo. Buses #1, 2, 4, 5, 6, 7, 9, and 11 stop at Ple. Matteotti. Buses to **Fano** (15min., every 30min., L1600) leave from Ple. Matteotti and the train station. **SOBET** runs buses to **Urbino** (1hr.; M-Sa 10 per day 7am-8:05pm, Su 4 per day 8:30am-8:05pm; L3700). Buy tickets on the bus. **Bucci** runs an express bus to Tiburtina station in **Rome** from Ple. Matteotti (4½hr., 6am, L38,000). Buy tickets on the bus.

ORIENTATION AND PRACTICAL INFORMATION

Piazza del Popolo marks the center of the old city. To get to the *piazza* from the train station, head right on V. Risorgimento, and continue as it becomes **Via Branca. Via Rossini** leads north out of P. del Popolo towards the sea, crossing over **Viale della Vittoria,** where it changes names to **Viale Repubblica** and then intersects **Viale Trieste** at **Piazzale della Libertà.** Vle. Trieste runs along the beach. Back in P. del Popolo, **Corso XI Settembre** runs west toward Chiesa di Sant Agostino, while **Via San Francesco** runs east to **Piazzale Matteotti** and the bus station.

Tourist Office: IAT (☎0721 693 41; fax 0721 304 62), at P. della Liberta on the beach. Helpful English-speaking staff. Hours subject to change–call ahead to avoid surprises. Open in summer M-Sa 9am-1pm, 3-7:30pm, and 8-10pm, Su 9am-1pm; in winter M-Tu 9am-1pm, W-Sa 9am-1pm and 3-6pm.

Bicycle Rental: (☎033 088 36 23) in Ple. d'Annunzio, at the intersection of Vle. Trieste and V. Gverdi. L3000 per hr. Open May-Sept. daily 8:30am-midnight.

Emergencies: ☎113. **Police: Questura** (☎0721 618 03), on V. G. Bruno off P. del Popolo. **Ambulance:** ☎118. **Medical Services:** ☎0721 213 44. For late-night and holiday medical care, head to V. Trento, 300 (☎0721 224 05).

Post Office: P. del Popolo, 28 (☎0721 43 22 85). Fermo Posta at *sportello* #1. Open M-Sa 10am-7:15pm. **Postal Code:** 61100.

ACCOMMODATIONS AND CAMPING

Pesaro, with its many reasonably priced accommodations, is a real bargain in the off season. High season runs from mid-June through August.

San Marco, V. XI Febbraio, 32 (☎/fax 0721 313 96). Follow V. Risorgimento from the train station. 3-star hotel at 2-star prices. 40 spacious rooms, all with bath, phones, and TV. 2 are wheelchair accessible. Breakfast L5000. Singles L65,000; doubles L90,000. V, MC, AmEx.

Hotel Athena, V. Pola, 18 (☎0721 301 14; fax 0721 338 78), off Vle. della Vittoria. From the train station, catch the C/B bus, and get off at V. Fiume. Turn right on V. Trento and left on V. Pola. The lobby is overrun by plants. 22 clean rooms are close to the beach. All with bath, phone, and TV. Singles L50,000; doubles L80,000. V, MC.

Pensione Arianna, V. Mascagni, 84 (☎0721 329 19; fax 0721 319 27). From P. del Popolo, follow V. Rossini to the beach. 28 simple rooms, all with bath. English spoken. Singles L45-60,000; doubles L65-80,000. Half-pension L62-77,000 per person. V, MC.

Camping Panorama (☎/fax 0721 20 81 45), on a hillside 7km north of Pesaro on the *strada panoramica* to Gabicce Mare. Bus #13 from Ple. Matteotti will drop you right at the site, but be sure to ask the driver if the bus goes to the campgrounds (20min.; M-Sa 4 per day 6:42am-6:33pm, Su 2:18pm and 6:18pm; L1200). Open May-Sept. L8500-12,000 per person, L19,000 per site. Hot showers and swimming pool free.

FOOD

Pesaro's **public market** is at V. Branca, 5, behind the post office and off P. del Popolo. (Open M-Sa 7:30am-1:30pm.) **Pizzerias** line the beach, and **alimentari** crowd the sidewalks on C. XI Settembre, which runs perpendicular to V. Rossini.

Harnold's, P. Lazzarini, 34 (☎0721 651 55), close to Teatro Rossini. From P. del Popolo, follow V. Branca away from the sea. Outdoor seating in the *piazza*. Fresh, cheap, and delicious, with a wide range of eccentrically named *panini* (L3500-6000). Takeout available. Open daily 8am-3am.

Mensa Volto della Ginevra, V. Mazzolari, 54 (☎0721 343 08), near the Musei Civici, off V. Rossini, in between P. del Popolo and Vle. della Vittoria. A self-service cafeteria with giant portions. Complete meal not including drinks L11,500. Open M-F noon-2pm.

SIGHTS

Pesaro's museums can be accessed with a **cumulative ticket** (L7000), available and valid at the Pinacoteca, Ceramics Museum, Rossini Museum, and Sea Museum.

PIAZZA DEL POPOLO. The robust arcade and *putti*-ful window frames of the 15th-century **Ducal Palace,** home of Pesaro's ruling della Rovere clan, preside over the *piazza,* Pesaro's main square.

MUSEO CIVICO. This museum houses a superb collection of Italian ceramics and primitive artifacts, showcasing specifically the talents of Pesarese potters. *(Toschi Mosca, 27. From P. del Popolo, take V. Rossini toward the sea. Turn left on V. Mazzolari and left again on Toschi Mosca. ☎0721 678 15. Open July-Aug. Tu-Su 5-11pm; hours vary Sept.-June, but roughly Tu-Sa 9:30am-1:30pm and 4-7pm. L5000.)*

ROSSINI BIRTHPLACE AND MUSEUM. Honor Pesaro's prodigal son by pouring over an extensive collection of photographs, portraits, theatrical memorabilia, letters, and scores in this museum. *(V. Rossini, 34. ☎0721 38 73 57. Open July-Aug. Tu-Su 5-11pm; Sept.-June Tu-W 9:30am-12:30pm, Th-Su 9:30am-12:30pm and 4-7pm. L5000.)*

VILLA IMPERIALE AND PARCO ORTIGIULI. Outside town, lavish gardens surround this 16th-century royal "holiday home," open to the public for a short time each year. The grounds are only accessible through tours led by the IAT tourist office. *(☎0721 693 41. Tours leave Ple. della Libertà. June 14-Aug. 23 W 4pm. L10,000.)*

 FESTIVALS AND ENTERTAINMENT

Pesaro hosts the **Mostra Internazionale del Nuovo Cinema,** the International Festival of New Films (☎0644 566 43), during the 2nd and 3rd weeks of June. Movies new and old, commercially and independently produced, are shown in the buildings along V. Rossini and at the **Teatro Comunale Sperimentale** (☎0721 38 75 48), on V. Rossini, just off P. del Popolo. The tourist office has schedules. Native opera composer Rossini founded the **Conservatorio di Musica G. Rossini,** which sponsors events throughout the year. Contact the **Teatro Rossini** (☎0721 331 84), in P. Lazzarini, off V. Branca, for more info. The annual **Rossini Opera Festival** begins in early August, but opera performances and orchestral concerts continue through September. Inquire at the tourist office for exact dates and prices, or reserve tickets through the info office at V. Rossini, 37, 2nd fl. (☎0721 301 61. Open M-F 9am-12:30pm and 3:30-7pm.)

The evening *passeggiata* winds through Ple. della Libertà and P. del Popolo. **Big Ben,** V. Sabbatini, 14, near the Palazzo Ducale, is the closest thing to a bar around. (☎0721 674 60. Open July-Aug. Tu-Su 11am-2am; off-season Sa-Su only.)

DAYTRIP FROM PESARO: FANO

Fano lies south of Pesaro on the Bologna-Lecce line. The ***train*** *station is in Ple. Stazione; trains run to Pesaro (10min., every 30min., L1700). To reach the beach, exit the train station on V. Cavallott, and take a right on V. C. Battisti. City buses also run from Pesaro to Fano (15min., every 30min. M-Sa 6:30am-8:30pm, L1400). Buy tickets on the bus.*

The 12km stretch between Pesaro and Fano is home to the quietest retreats on this side of the Adriatic. The sandy beach on the north side of Fano is a good choice for those seeking seclusion. Even in summer, vacationers are scarce on the beaches north of Fano. To reach the most tranquil spots, walk left along the water. **Viale Adriatico** runs along the coast.

The **tourist office,** V. Battisti, 10, provides a map of the city and a list of local events. (☎0721 80 35 34; fax 0721 82 42 92. Open M-Sa 9am-1pm and 4-7pm, Su and holidays 9am-1pm.)

Although Fano makes a good daytrip from Pesaro, those planning to stay overnight should contact **Associazione Albergatori,** Vle. Adriatico, 132, an organization that helps travelers find lodging free of charge. (☎0721 82 73 76 or 0721 82 57 10. Open M-Sa 9am-12:30pm and 4-7pm, Su 9am-noon.) **Trattoria Quinta,** V. d'Adriatico, 42, at the north edge of town, provides inexpensive home-cooked meals. The menu changes daily. (☎0721 80 80 43. *Primi* L9000, *secondi* L17,000. Cover L1000. Open M-Sa noon-3pm and 7-11pm. V, MC.)

URBINO ☎0722

Urbino's fairytale skyline, scattered with humble stone dwellings and an immense turreted palace, has changed little over the past 500 years. The city is home to many art treasures and Renaissance monuments, including Piero della Francesca's *Ideal City* and Raphael's highly-decorated house. These days, Urbino gains its color from its boisterous university students.

TRANSPORTATION

Buses depart from Borgo Mercatale. Urbino's bus and Pesaro's train timetables are posted at the beginning of C. Garibaldi, at P. della Repubblica, under the portico at the corner bar. Blue **SOBET** (☎0722 223 33) buses run to P. Matteotti and the train station in Pesaro (1hr.; M-Sa 10 per day 6:30am-6:45pm, Su 4 per day 7:10am-5:20pm; L3700; buy tickets on the bus). **Bucci** (☎0721 324 01) runs 1 daily bus to **Rome** (5hr., 4pm, L30,000). **Luggage Storage:** At the car parking office in Borgo Mercatale. L1500 for 12hr. Open daily 7am-midnight.

ORIENTATION AND PRACTICAL INFORMATION

After winding up steep hills, the bus stops at **Borgo Mercatale** below the city center. A short uphill walk on Via Mazzini leads to **Piazza della Repubblica,** the city's hub. **Via Rafaello, Via Cesare Battisti, Via Vittorio Veneto,** and **Corso Garibaldi** branch out in different directions from P. della Repubblica. Another short walk uphill on V. Veneto leads to **Piazza Rinascimento.**

Tourist Office: P. Rinascimento, 1 (☎0722 26 13; fax 0722 24 41; email iat.urbina@regione.marche.it), across from the Palazzo Ducale. Distributes a list of local hotels and a large map. Open mid-June to mid-Sept. M-Sa 9am-1pm and 3-7pm, Su 9am-1pm; in winter 9am-1pm and 3-6pm. There is a small **tourist information booth** at the bus stop in Borgo Mercatale. Open M-Sa 9am-1pm and 3-7pm.

Budget Travel: CTS, V. Mazzini, 60 (☎0722 20 31; fax 0722 32 78 80). Train or plane tickets and student tour info. Open M-F 9am-1pm and 3:30-7:30pm, Sa 9am-1pm.

Laundromat: Self-Service Laundromat, V. Battisti, 35. Open M-Sa 9am-8pm.

Emergencies: ☎113. **Police:** (☎0722 27 25), on Porto Valbona in Borgo Mercatale. Open to public M-F 9am-1pm, Sa-Su 9-11am. **Carabinieri,** V. Comanino, 1 (☎0722 328 82). **Ambulance:** ☎118. **Hospital:** (☎0722 30 11), on V. B. da Montefeltro, off of V. Comandino. Buses #1 and 3 from Borgo Mercatale stop in front.

Internet Access: The tourist office will allow tourists to use their computer for free for up to 10min. **Il Portico,** V. Mazzini, 7 (☎0722 27 22), has 1 computer–be prepared to wait. Open M-Sa 9am-1pm and 4-8pm. L12,000 per hr.

Post Office: V. Bramante, 22 (☎0722 27 78 15), just off V. Raffaello. Traveler's checks available. Financial services open M-Sa 8:15am-6pm. Postal services open M-Sa 8:15am-7pm. **Postal Code:** 61029.

ACCOMMODATIONS AND CAMPING

Cheap lodging is rare in Urbino, and reservations are essential. You might want to consider staying in Pesaro and taking a daytrip to Urbino.

Pensione Fosca, V. Raffaello, 67, top fl. (☎0722 32 96 22 or 0722 25 42). Signora Rosina takes good care of her guests. 9 large, charming rooms without bath have high ceilings but poor lighting. Singles L40,000; doubles L60,000; triples L80,000.

Hotel San Giovanni, V. Barocci, 13 (☎0722 28 27). Modern hotel. Helpful manager. Restaurant downstairs. Open Aug.-June. Singles L35-53,000; doubles L50-80,000.

Piero della Francesca, V. Comandino, 53 (☎0722 32 84 28; fax 0722 32 84 27), in front of the hospital. A 15min. walk from the historic center. Bus #1 from Borgo Mercatale stops in front. A sterile 3-star hotel with 86 fully furnished rooms. Singles L60,000; doubles L100,000. V, MC, AmEx.

Camping: Camping Pineta (☎0722 47 10; fax 0722 47 34), on V. S. Donato in the *località* of Cesane, 2km from the city walls. Take bus #4 or 7 from Borgo Mercatale (L1200); ask to get off at the "camping." Office open daily 9-11am and 3-10pm. Open Apr. to mid-Sept. L10,000 per person, L8000 per child, L20,000 per tent.

FOOD

Many *paninoteche, gelaterie,* and burger joints are around P. della Repubblica. Shop for supplies at **Supermarket Margherita,** V. Raffaello, 37. (Open M-Sa 7:30am-2:30pm and 4-8pm.) The **University MENSA** on V. Budassi offers an incomparable deal—a huge dinner for L6000 with any student ID. (Closed in summer.)

Pizzeria Le Tre Piante, V. Voltaccia della Vecchia, 1 (☎0722 48 63). From P. della Repubblica head up V. Veneto, turn left on V. Nazario Sauro, right on V. Budassi, and left on V. Foro Posterula (5min.). Spectacular view from the outside tables. Good traditional food and friendly service. Very popular. Pizza L7500-9000, *primi* L10,000, *secondi* L10-20,000. Cover L2000. Open Tu-Su noon-3pm and 7-11:30pm.

Un Punto Macrobiotico, V. Pozzo Nuovo, 4 (☎0722 32 97 90), off V. Battisti. Healthy self-serve selections tempt even carnivores. No cell phones are allowed. Daily *menù* of pasta and veggies L4-6000. *Menù* with fish and side dishes L12-22,000. Students get soup and salad for L4000. Open M-Sa noon-2pm and 7:30-9pm.

Bar del Teatro, C. Garibaldi, 88 (☎0722 29 11), at the base of the Palazzo Ducale. Not exactly cheap, but it's got the best view in town, with the Palazzo Ducale on one side and the valley on the other. A cool, shady place to spend the afternoon. Cappuccino or tea outside L2500. Open daily July-Aug. 7:30am-2am; off-season closed Su.

SIGHTS

PALAZZO DUCALE. The Renaissance Palazzo Ducale stands tall in P. Rinascimento. The interior of this palace, designed by Luciano Laurana, is of less interest than Ambrogio Barocchi's facade. Two tall, slender towers enclose three stacked balconies. The central **courtyard** epitomizes Renaissance harmony and proportion.

To the left, a staircase leads to the duke's private apartments, which now house the **National Gallery of the Marches.** The spacious, generally overlooked gallery displays artwork that documents the transition into the age of Humanism. Piero della Francesca's fascinating *Flagellation of Christ* shows a Christ being lightly whipped in the background. Piero's *Ideal City* exhibits the artist's precocious and renowned talent for manipulating perspective. Berruguete's famous portrait of Duke Federico, Raphael's *Portrait of a Lady,* and Paolo Uccello's narrative panel, the *Profanation of the Host* are also here. On the 2nd floor, inlaid-wood panels give the illusion of shelves holding astronomical and musical instruments.

The tour continues down a circular stairway to the **Cappella del Perdono** and the **Tempietto delle Muse,** where the Christian and the pagan mingle. At one time, 11 wooden panels representing Apollo, Minerva, and the nine Muses covered the walls of the temple; these panels have since been removed, and eight are in Florence's Galleria Corsini. *(P. Rinascimento. ☎0722 27 60. Open M 8:30am-2pm, Tu-F 8:30am-7pm, Sa 8:30am-7pm and 8-11pm, Su 9am-8pm. L8000, children and seniors free.)*

ORATORIO DI SAN GIOVANNI BATTISTA. The 14th-century Oratorio di San Giovanni Battista is decorated with brightly colored Gothic frescoes by L. J. Salimbeni (1416) representing events from the life of St. John. If you speak Italian, the custodian will give you an appetizing explanation of how fresco painters drew their sketches with lamb's blood instead of ink. *(At the end of V. Barocci. From P. della Repubblica head down V. Mazzini, turn right on V. Posta Vecchia, and take the 1st left on V. Barocci. ☎0722 32 09 36. Open Sept.-July M-Sa 10am-12:30pm and 3-5:30pm, Su 10am-12:30pm; Aug. M-Sa 10am-12:30pm and 3-6pm, Su afternoon. L3000.)*

CENTRAL ITALY

CASA DI RAFAELE. The site of Raphael's birth in 1483 is now a vast and delightful museum with period furnishings. His earliest work, a fresco entitled *Madonna e Bambino*, hangs in the *sala*. *(V. Raffaello, 57. ☎0722 32 01 05. Open M-Sa 9am-1pm and 3-7pm, Su 10am-1pm. L5000, groups of at least 15 L3000, student groups L2000 per person.)*

FORTEZZA ALBORNOZ. The hike up a hill to this fortress within a fortress ends with an inspiring view of the city. The hill is the perfect spot for a picnic or a picture. *(All the way up V. Raffaello and to the left. Park open daily 10am-4pm.)*

ENTERTAINMENT

Urbino's P. della Repubblica serves as a modeling runway for local youth. Take a walk down this fashion-conscious, people-watching locale and then stroll (or climb) the serpentine streets with the *passeggiata* at dusk. Nightlife picks up in August, when the Italian university summer session convenes. Nobody goes home thirsty from the **Matisse Sound Cafe,** V. Budassi, 14, a university social center. (Beer L5000, cocktails L6000. No cover. Open during school year daily 6pm-2am; in summer Sa-Su 10pm-2am.) By midnight, **The Bosom Pub,** on V. Budassi, next to Skyro, is stacked with drinks and dancers. Keep an eye open for the owner's "Sangria Parties." (☎0722 47 83. No cover. Beer L4-8000, wine L2-4000 a glass. Open during school year daily 10pm-3am; in summer M-Sa 9pm-3am.)

In July, the **Antique Music Festival** holds concerts in churches and theaters around town. Saturday nights are amateur nights—if you have a 3rd-century harp, feel free to jam. August brings the ceremony of the **Revocation of the Duke's Court,** complete with Renaissance costumes.

ANCONA ☎071

Ancona—a major port in a small, whimsical, and largely unexplored city—is the epicenter of Italy's Adriatic coast. Although most Italians know Ancona simply for its port, the city has many personalities. Piazza Roma is light and airy, with pastel buildings and a cartoonish fountain. Piazza Cavour, an expanse of gravel circled in palm trees, is oddly Mediterranean. The shipyard port is rusty and industrial, but from the stunning vista of the hilltop *duomo*, the cranes shimmer like sculptures in the water. If you can see past the grime and chaos and appreciate the city's offerings, you are ready to enjoy just about everything Italy has to offer.

TRANSPORTATION

Trains: (☎0714 24 74), in P. Rosselli. Ancona is an important junction on the Bologna-Lecce train line. To: **Pesaro** (1hr., 1-2 per hr., L5700); **San Benedetto** (1¼hr., 1 per hr., L8500); **Rimini** (1½hr., 1-2 per hr., L8100); **Bologna** (2½hr., 1-2 per hr., from L18,600); **Rome** (3-4hr., 9 per day 2:50am-7:10pm, L24,300-41,000); **Milan** (5hr., 24 per day 12:36am-7:20pm, from L25,600); **Venice** (5hr.; 2:36, 6:20am, and 8:07pm; from L26,300); and **Paris-Lyon** (12-15hr., 7:18pm, L240,000). Ticket office open daily 7am-9pm. **Luggage storage:** L5000 for 12hr. Open 6am-10pm.

Ferries: Ancona offers **ferry service** to **Greece, Croatia,** and **Northern Italy.** Schedules available at **Stazione Marittima,** on the waterfront off P. Kennedy. Reservations necessary July-Aug. Be at the station 2hr. before departure.

Adriatica: (☎071 20 49 15, or 071 20 49 16, or 071 20 49 17; fax 071 20 22 96; email tickets.adn@maritime.it; www.adriatica.it) runs to **Croatia** (from L80,000; July-Aug. L90,000) and **Albania** (from L120,000; July-Aug. L155,000).

ANEK: (☎071 207 23 46; fax 071 207 79 04; email anekit@genan.it; www.anek.gr.) runs to **Greece** (from L94,000; July-Aug. 118,000). Return trips roughly half-price.

Jadrolinija: (☎071 20 71 465; fax 071 207 92 72; www.jadrolinija.tel.hr/jadrolinija) runs to **Croatia** (from L66,000; July-Aug. L80,000).

SEM Maritime Co (SMC): (☎071 20 40 90; fax 071 20 26 18; www.sem.hr) runs to **Split, Croatia** (Sept.-June from L70,000, round-trip L120,000; July-Aug. from L80,000, round-trip L130,000) and **Hvar Island.**

Strintzis: (☎071 207 10 68; fax 071 207 08 74; email sales@strintzis.gr; www.strintzis.gr) runs to **Greece** and **Venice.** Prices start at L62,000; July to early Sept. L82,000 or L94,000.

CENTRAL ITALY

ORIENTATION AND PRACTICAL INFORMATION

From the island directly in front of the entrance to the train station, buses #1, 1/3 and 1/4 (L1300) head along the port past **Stazione Marittima** (☎071 20 11 83) and up **Corso Stamira** to **Piazza Cavour.** Check the posted signs or ask the bus driver before embarking on a bus as routes can always change. For the Stazione Marittima, disembark at P. Kennedy or P. Repubblica and walk straight towards the ocean. C. Stamira, **Corso Garibaldi,** and **Corso Mazzini** run parallel to each other from the western end of P. Cavour, through **Piazza Roma** and **Piazza Kennedy,** and back to the port.

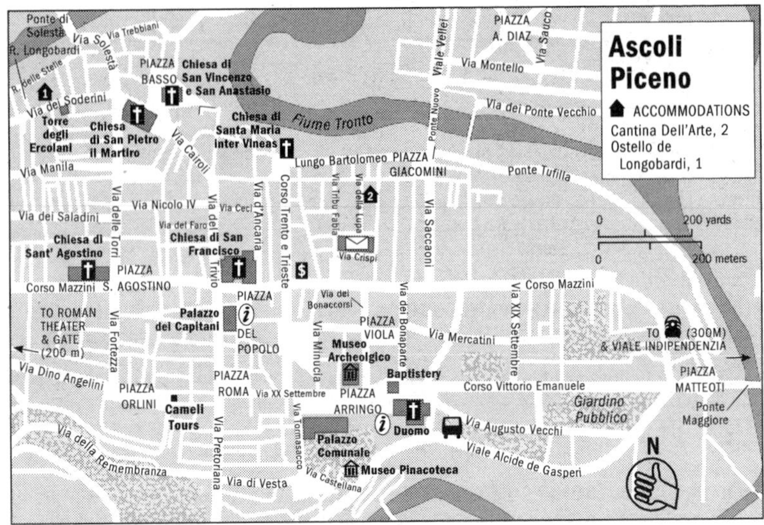

Tourist Office: V. Thaon de Revel, 4 (☎071 332 49; fax 319 66), accessible by bus #1/4 or #1 (L1400) from the canopy outside the train station. Open M-Sa 8am-8pm, Su 8am-2pm. A more accessible **branch** (☎071 20 11 83), which also has ferry info, is in the Stazione Maritima. Open June-Sept. M-Sa 8am-8pm, Su 8am-2pm.

Emergencies: ☎112 or 113. **Ambulance:** ☎118. **Questura:** ☎071 228 81.

Post Office: P. XXIV Maggio, in the center near the port. Open M-Sa 8:10am-6pm. Closed Sa in Aug. **Postal Code:** 60100.

ACCOMMODATIONS AND FOOD

Ancona's recently opened **Ostello della Gioventù,** V. Lamaticci, 7, is clean and perfect for those who just need somewhere to spend the night en route to another destination. Upon exiting the train station, cross the *piazza* and turn left. Take the 1st right, and immediately make a sharp right up the steps behind the newsstand. The hostel is on the right. You must be an HI member and pay with cash. In a restaurant down the street, guests can get a full lunch or dinner, including *primi, secondi, contorno,* and water for L14,000. (☎/fax 071 42 257. Breakfast L2500. Check-out 10am. Dorms L23,000.) Most other budget accommodations and restaurants cluster on or near P. Roma. **Pensione Euro,** C. Mazzini, 142, 2nd fl., is a new addition to Ancona, with nine large, airy rooms and communal baths that you can brave without flip-flops. (☎071 207 22 76. Singles L40,000, with shower L50,000; doubles L70,000, with shower L80,000. Additional person L25,000. Cash only.) **Pensione Centrale,** V. Marsala, 10, 4th fl., off C. Stamira, one block from P. Roma, boasts 10 light, yellow rooms with high ceilings. (☎071 543 88. Shower L2500. Curfew midnight. Singles L38,000; doubles L60,000, with bath L90,000. Cash only.)

Pack a meal for your ferry ride at the old-fashioned **Mercato Pubblico,** P. della Erbe, 130, off C. Mazzini. (Open M-Sa 7:30am-12:45pm and 5-8pm; in winter Su-W and F 4:30-7:30pm, Th and Sa 7:30am-12:45pm and 4:30-7:30pm.) **Supermarket CONAD,** V. Matteotti, 115, offers the best grocery deals. (Open M-W and F 8:15am-1:30pm and 5-7:35pm, Th 8:15am-1:30pm, Sa 8:15am-12:45pm and 5-7:40pm.)

La Dolce Vita, P. Cavour, 31-32, is a family-run restaurant that offers a rotating menu of local favorites. (☎071 20 33 75. Lunch L5-8000. Open M-Sa 6am-8pm.) **Osteria Brillo,** C. Mazzini, 109, offers hearty Italian fare at outstanding prices. Have a taste of three kinds of pasta for lunch (L10,000). (☎071 207 26 29. *Primi* L9-12,000, *secondi* L10-25,000. Open M-Sa 12:30-3pm and 7:30pm-midnight. V, MC.)

SIGHTS

THE OLD CITY. The **Piazzale del Duomo,** atop **Monte Guasco,** offers a fantastic view of the Anconan sea and sky. The *duomo*'s mountaintop position provides just enough altitude to soften the industrial edge of the town below. In Ple. del Duomo stands the **Cattedrale di San Ciriaco,** erected in the 11th century on the site of an early Christian basilica. The basilica in turn had been built upon the ruins of a Roman temple to Venus. *(To reach the duomo from P. Cavour, follow C. Mazzini to the port and turn right on V. Gramsci at P. Repubblica. Follow V. Gramsci into the old city as it becomes V. Ciriaco, V. Pizzecolli, and later V. Ferretti. At P. del Senato, follow the 244 steps up to the duomo. Cathedral open M-Sa 8am-noon and 3-6pm, Su 9-10:30am and noon-9pm.)*

PINACOTECA COMUNALE FRANCESCO PODESTI. Ancona's painting gallery, the Galleria Comunale Francesco Podesti, housed in the 16th-century **Palazzo Bosdari,** has amassed a collection of work by the Camerte school. Carlo Crivelli's flawless *Madonna col Bambino* competes with Titian's *Apparition of the Virgin,* recently restored to its full glory. The endearing curator shares his knowledge (in Italian) as he leads you from room to room. *(V. Pizzecolli, 17. See directions for Museo Archeologico. Open M 9am-1pm, Tu-Sa 9am-7pm, Su 3-7pm. L5000, seniors and children free.)*

MUSEO ARCHEOLOGICO NAZIONALE DELLE MARCHE. Housed in the 16th century Palazzo Ferretti, the foremost archaeological museum of the Marches recently reopened after decades of restoration (to repair damages from WWII bombings and a 1972 earthquake). The impressive collection includes the Ionian *Dinos of Amandola,* Greek vases, and two life-size equestrian bronzes of Roman emperors. *(V. Ferretti, 6. From P. Cavour, take C. Mazzini towards the port, and turn right on V. Gramsci. ☎071 207 53 90. Open Su-F 8:30am-7:30pm, Sa 5-11pm. L8000.)*

RIVIERA DEL CONERO. Smooth pebble **beaches** lie a few kilometers outside of Ancona. Surrounded by towering cliffs, the coastal villages nearby, collectively known as the Riviera del Conero, attract lots of Italian tourists. **Autolinee RENI** runs buses from Ancona's P. Cavour and train station to **Sirolo, Numana,** and **Marcelli** (30min.; M-Sa 1-2 per hr., Su 1 per hr.; L2500). *(Buy tickets at P. Cavour from the "Pink Ladies" bar, at the intersection of P. Cavour and V. Camerini, or from the bar in the train station.)*

ASCOLI PICENO ☎0736

According to one legend, Ascoli was founded by Greeks who had been guided westward by a woodpecker *(picchio)*—this feathered mascot gave the city its name and provided a symbol for the Marches. In another account, Ascoli was the metropolis of the Piceno people, a quiet Latin tribe that controlled much of the coastal Marches and had the woodpecker as its clan totem. Whatever its origins, and despite a number of unfortunate incursions of the modern world, Ascoli Piceno is one of Le Marche's most interesting cities. Tucked among the mountains, the medieval town has escaped the blight of tourism. Reasonable prices and a hostel hidden in a 11th-century castle complete the attractive picture.

TRANSPORTATION

Trains: Ple. della Stazione (☎0736 34 10 14), at the end of V. Marconi. To **San Benedetto** (30min., M-Sa 13 per day 5:30am-8:30pm, L4300). Ticket counter open M 6:20-11:30am and 4-5:30pm, Tu-Sa 8am-noon and 3-5pm.

Buses: Cotravat buses are more crowded than trains and take twice as long. To: **San Benedetto** (1hr., 1-2 per hr. 7am-10:35pm, L3300). Buses leave from the V. Gasperi stop behind the *duomo*. Buy tickets at the *tabacchi* near the stop. **ARPA** runs to **B. Garrufo** and **Giulianova** (1½hr., 15 per day 5:50am-7:10pm, L7200) from the V. Gasperi stop. **Cameli Tours,** V. Dino Angelini, 127 (☎0736 26 11 54; email cametour@tin.it), just off P. Roma, runs to **Rome** (3hr.; M-Sa 4am, 8:45, and 3:30pm, Su 4, 8:45am, and 5:30pm; L21,000). Buses depart from P. Orlini. Office open M-Sa 8am-1pm and 3-7pm, Su 30min. before departures.

ORIENTATION AND PRACTICAL INFORMATION

From the **train station** walk straight for one block to **Viale Indipendenza,** turn right, and walk half a block to the bus stop. Catch buses #1 2, 3, 4a, or 9 (L1200) to the historic center. The **main bus stop** is on V. Gasperi behind the *duomo*, where Cotravat and ARPA buses also stop. Walk between the *duomo* and the small, square baptistery to **Piazza Arringo.** Cross P. Arringo and continue on **Via XX Settembre** to **Piazza Roma.** From there, V. del Trivio leads to **Corso Mazzini** and **Piazza del Popolo.**

Tourist Office: Centro Visitatori (☎0736 29 82 04; fax 0736 29 82 322), in P. Arringo. Open daily Apr.-Oct. 9am-7pm; Nov.-Mar. 9am-5:30pm (summer hours during Carnevale). Another tourist office, the **Ufficio Informazioni,** P. del Popolo, 17 (☎0736 25 30 45; fax 0736 25 23 91; email iat.ascolipiceno@regione.marche.it), has a very helpful staff. Some English spoken. Open M-F 8am-1:30pm and 3-7pm, Sa 9am-1pm and 3-7pm, Su and holidays 9am-1pm.

Currency Exchange: Banca Nazionale del Lavoro, C. Trento e Trieste, 10c (☎0736 29 61). From P. del Popolo turn right on C. Mazzini, which intersects C. Trento e Trieste. Open M-F 8:20am-1:20pm and 3-4:30pm. **ATMs** accept most bank cards.

Emergencies: ☎113. **Police:** (☎112), on V. Indipendenza. **Ambulance:** ☎118.

Pharmacy: Farmacia Sebastiani, P. Roma, 1 (☎0736 25 91 83). Open in summer 9am-1pm and 5-8pm; in winter 9am-1pm and 4:30-7:30pm. The green sign outside indicates which pharmacy is open on the weekend.

Internet Access: Sport Net Centre, P. de Viola, 14 (☎0736 25 54 74). Take V. del Bonaparte from P. Arringo. Painfully slow connection. L4000 for 15min., L7000 for 30min., and L12,000 per hr. Open daily 11am-1pm and 3-8pm.

Post Office: (☎0736 24 22 85), on V. Crispi, off C. Mazzini. Financial services M-F 8:10am-6:15pm and Fermo Posta (open M-F 8:30am-1pm and 4-7:15pm). General postal services available M-F 8:15am-7:15pm. **Postal Code:** 63100.

ACCOMMODATIONS AND FOOD

Rest up and fill up without emptying your pockets. **Ostello de Longobardi,** R. dei Longobardi, 12, is near V. Soderini, close to the historic center. From P. del Popolo take V. del Trivio. Continue straight, turn left on V. Cairoli, and continue to P. S. Pietro il Martiro. Continue left onto V. delle Donne, which becomes V. Soderini. The hostel is on the right, on the street marked V. dei Longobardi. The endearing owner is proud of his 11th-century building with 20th-century plumbing and 16 beds. (☎0736 25 90 07. Showers L1000. Stove L500. Dorms L18,000.) **Cantina dell'Arte,** V. della Lupa, 8, is in the heart of town. Follow C. Mazzini from P. del Popolo, and turn left on V. Tribu Fabia. V. della Lupa runs parallel to V. Fabia from the back of the post office. Gorgeous, modern rooms have marble floors, patios, TV, phone, and bath. (☎0736 25 57 44 or 0736 25 56 20. Singles L50,000; doubles L70,000; triples L90,000; quads L110,000. V, MC.)

Ascoli has an **open-air market** in P. S. Francesco behind P. del Popolo. (Open M-Sa mornings.) **Tigre supermarket** is in P. S. Maria Inter Vineas. Take C. Mazzini from P. del Popolo, turn left on C. Trento e Trieste, and follow it to the *piazza.* (Open M-Sa 8am-1pm and 4:30-8pm.) **Trattoria Lino Cavucci,** P. della Viola, 13, offers delicious home-cooked meals. From P. Arringo, take V. del Bonaparte to P. della Viola. (☎0736 25 93 58. *Primi* L5500-7000, *secondi* L8-10,000. Cover L2500. Open Sa-Th noon-3pm and 7:30-10pm.) **Cantina dell'Arte,** V. della Lupa, 5, across from the hotel of the same name, prepares daily specials, served on communal tables. (☎0736 25 11 35. *Primi* L6-8000, *secondi* L10,000. Generous *menù* only L15,000. Cover included. Open M-Sa noon-2:30pm and 6:30-10pm, Su noon-5pm. V.)

SIGHTS AND FESTIVALS

Practically all the buildings in Ascoli Piceno are made of travertine—a light-colored, porous stone that is actually undeveloped marble. The most spectacular sight in Ascoli is the pink sunset over the hills.

PIAZZA DEL POPOLO. The historic center of town, the *piazza* is a calm oasis in this busy city. The travertine ground, polished by centuries of footsteps, is as smooth as ice. It's easy to while away the day in the 16th-century *portici* lining two sides of the square and their overpriced cafes and *gelateria*. The 3rd side houses the 13th-century **Palazzo dei Capitani del Popolo,** with a massive portal and a statue of Pope Paul III dating from 1548. The building was burned on Christmas Day 1535 in a familial squabble. A decade later the palace was refurbished and dedicated to the Pope, who brought peace to Ascoli. In 1938 the palace was the seat of the principal Fascist party. Works from the Roman Republic and Augustine eras are visible along the serpentine wooden pathway weaving under the structure of the *palazzo*. The *palazzo* currently hosts an array of art exhibits. *(☎0736 27 75 40 or 0736 27 75 52. Open daily 9am-1pm and 3:30-7:30pm.)*

The elegant eastern end of the **Chiesa di San Francesco** (13th-16th centuries) borders the 4th side of P. del Popolo. It contains a 14th-century wooden crucifix, the only art object saved from the 1535 fire. The "singing columns," two sets of five low columns flanking the door on the V. del Trivio side of the church, can be played by drawing your hand quickly across them. *(Open daily 8am-noon and 3-7pm.)*

Abutting the church on the side that faces V. del Trivio, the **Loggia dei Mercanti** (Merchants' Gallery; 1509-1513), is now a favorite meeting place for the town elders. A left on C. Mazzini from the *piazza* leads to the austere 14th-century **Chiesa di Sant'Agostino.** *(Open daily 9am-noon and 3-7pm.)*

PIAZZA ARRINGO. On the other side of town, **Piazza Arringo** (Oration Square) derives its name from its role as a local podium. Join the crowds and try the water straight from the horses' mouths on either fountain—it's the freshest and coolest around. The massive travertine **duomo** is a delicious blend of artistic eras. A Roman basilica forms the transept, topped by an 8th-century octagonal dome. The two towers were built in the 11th and 12th centuries, while the lateral naves and central apse were constructed in the 1400s. Inside, freshly restored frescoes decorate the walls and ceiling. Next to the cathedral stands the compact 12th-century **baptistery,** decorated with a *loggia* of blind arches. *(Open daily 9am-noon and 4-7pm. Mass held M-Sa 7, 8:30, and 9:30am, Su 7, 8:30, 10, and 11:30am.)*

PINACOTECA CIVICA. Works by Crivelli, Titian, van Dyck, and Ribera hang on the pink walls of this museum. Upstairs is a collection of handsome stringed instruments and some Impressionist paintings and sculptures. *(To the left as you exit the duomo in P. Arringo. ☎0736 29 82 13. Open daily 9am-1pm and 3-7:30pm. L6000, seniors and ages 14-18 L3000, children under 13 free.)*

NORTH OF PIAZZA DEL POPOLO. From P. del Popolo turn left on C. Mazzini and right on V. del Trivio. Bear left on V. Cairoli, pass the old stone houses to tiny **Via di Solestà,** which curves to the right as you exit the church. V. di Solestà, one of the oldest streets in the city, leads to the single-arched **Ponte di Solestà,** one of Europe's tallest Roman bridges. Cross this bridge and follow **V. Berardo Tucci** straight ahead for about two blocks to the **Chiesa di Sant'Emidio alle Grotte,** a Baroque facade grafted onto the natural rock wall. Inside are catacombs where the first Ascoli Christians are buried.

FESTIVALS. On the 1st Sunday in August, Ascoli holds the **Tournament of Quintana,** a colorful medieval pageant. The tournament, which features armed (man-on-dummy) jousting and a torchlit procession to P. del Popolo, marks the end of the four-day festival of S. Emidio, the city's patron. Ascoli's **Carnevale** is one of Italy's liveliest. Insanity reigns on the Tuesday, Thursday, and Sunday preceding Ash Wednesday. Residents don costumes and dancers perform in P. del Popolo.

SAN BENEDETTO DEL TRONTO ☎0735

With over 7000 palm trees and as many children playing under their waving fronds, San Benedetto draws summering Italian families and a smattering of foreign tourists. Do not come to San Benedetto expecting to temper your beach time with a little culture—local art appreciation entails checking out art-deco sand castles on the miles of beach. Rest and relaxation are the town's priorities.

TRANSPORTATION

Trains: Vle. Gramsci, 20/A (☎0735 59 21 31). San Benedetto lies on the Bologna-Lecce train line. Trains to: **Ancona** (1½hr., 1-2 per hr. 6am-9:22pm, L8-13,000); **Bologna** (2½-3½hr., every hr., L23,500-36,000); and **Milan** (5hr., 8 per day, 7am-11:30pm, L42-60,000). Ticket counter open daily 6:30am-11:28pm.

Buses: Local lines stop in front of the train station. Bus #2 leaves across the street from the station and travels along the waterfront (every 10min. 6am-midnight, L1200). **Cotravat** buses to Ascoli Piceno leave from the station (1hr., 25 per day 6am-12:02am, L3300). Buy tickets (L3300) in the bar at the train station or at Caffè Blue Express across from the train station.

ORIENTATION AND PRACTICAL INFORMATION

From the train station, cross the street and take bus #2 (L1200) to the *lungomare* (seaside), or turn left on V. Gramsci and left again onto **Via Mazzocchi** toward the beach. A right on **Via delle Palme** leads directly to **Viale Trieste.** The road along the *lungomare* changes names several times as it works its way to the western edge of town, from Vle. Trieste to **Viale Marconi,** to **Viale Europa/Scipioni,** to **Viale Rinascimento,** and finally to **Via San Giacomo.**

Tourist Office: APT, Vle. Marconi, 39 (☎0735 830 36). Take bus #2 across the street from the train station to stop #7. Provides maps and books hotel rooms and campsites. English spoken. Open July daily 8am-8pm; Aug. M-Sa 8am-10pm, Su 8am-8pm; Sept.-June daily 8:30am-12:30pm and 3-7:30pm.

Emergencies: ☎113. **Ambulance:** ☎118. **Hospital: Ospedale Civile,** V. Silvio Pellico, 34 (☎0735 78 13 13). Turn left on V. Gramsci as you exit the train station, head right on V. Montello and then left on V. Silvio Pellico. **Police:** V. Crispi, 51 (☎112).

Post Office: V. Curzi, 26 (☎0735 59 21 57). Head left on V. Gramsci out of the train station, turn right on Vle. Secondo Moretti and left on V. Curzi. Financial services open M-Sa 8am-6:15pm. Postal services open M-Sa 8am-7pm. **Postal Code:** 63039.

ACCOMMODATIONS AND CAMPING

V. A. Volta, parallel to Vle. Marconi, is home to a number of budget accommodations. The tourist office will help you find a place to stay. Most hotels have a private beach, usually included in the price. Countless chalets (little huts) along the waterfront offer storage cabins for L13,000 and umbrellas for L12-L17,000. A public **beach** spreads out from the tourist office.

Albergo Patrizia, V. A. Volta, 170 (☎0735 821 47 or 0735 817 62; fax 0735 817 62). Excellent price, location, and private beach. In-house restaurant serves delicious discounted dinners for guests. Breakfast included. Open June-Sept. 36 rooms. Singles L65,000; doubles L65-90,000. July-Aug. full pension L93,000 per person.

La Playa, V. Cola di Rienzo, 25/A (☎0735 65 99 57), at the end of the *lungomare*. Head straight on V. San Giacomo from Vle. Rinascimento, turn right on V. F. Ferucci, continue for 3 blocks, and turn left on V. Cola di Rienzo. *The* budget locale in pricey San Benedetto. 10 large, spotless rooms with baths and balconies. July-Aug. singles L35,000; doubles L72,000. Sept.-June L35,000/L50,000. Extra bed L10,000.

Hotel Dino, Vle. Europa/Scipioni, 106 (☎0735 821 47; fax 0735 821 75). Take bus #2 to stop #11. From the bus stop, turn right on V. Montessori. Pamper yourself with 33 clean, bright rooms with A/C, patios, TV, phones, and parking. Private beach and bicycles free of charge for guests. Breakfast included. Singles and doubles L75-110,000. Full pension L70-115,000 per person; low season L50-80,000 per person.

Camping Seaside, V. dei Mille, 127 (☎0735 65 95 05). Take bus #2 to stop #11, or from Vle. Rinascimento turn onto V. A. Negri and bear left on V. dei Mille. Rough it San Benedetto style with a pool, supermarket, and restaurant. Open June-Sept. L10,000 per person, L12-20,000 per site. Off-season L6000 per person, L8-12,000 per site.

FOOD

Get some cheap eats at the **Tigre supermarket,** V. Ugo Bassi, 10 (open M-Sa 8:45am-1pm and 4:30-8pm), or near the beach at V. dei Laureati 41/A (open M-Sa 8am-1:30pm and 5-8:30pm, Su 8am-1:30pm). On Tuesday and Friday mornings, head for the **open-air market** in V. Montebello. San Benedetto's specialty is *brodetto alla sambenedettese* (a hodgepodge of fish, green tomatoes, peppers, and vinegar).

Café Fuori Orario, V. C. Colombo, 7 (☎0735 58 37 20). From the train station, turn left on V. Gramsci and take the 1st left on V. Francesco Fiscaletti. The cafe is on the right about 1 block down. Serves coffee, cocktails, food, and late-night snacks on a lovely terrace. *Primi* L9000, *secondi* L10-16,000. Desserts L5000. *Menù* L30,000. Cover and service included. Open daily 7:30pm-2am; in winter Tu-Su 7:30am-2am.

Pub San Michele, V. Piemonte, 111 (☎0735 836 93). From the train station turn left on Vle. Gramsci and follow it as it becomes Ugo Bassi and V. Piemonte. A friendly place for pizza and cold beer. Pizza L4-8000. *Menù* L20,000, includes *primo, secondo,* and *contorno.* Cover L1500. Open daily 12:15-3pm and 7:15pm-2am. V, MC, AmEx.

ABRUZZO AND MOLISE

Clusters of orange thatched roofs, green wooden doors, and the occasional medieval castle lie scattered through the foothills of the Apennine mountains. Remnants of a pristine ancient world relatively untouched by modernity, the artisans, agriculture, and proud regional dialects of Abruzzo and Molise represent the Italy of its ancestors. Only about two hours by train from Rome, but a far cry from the frenzy of tourism, these highlands offer a tranquil retreat. Abruzzo and Molise, a single region until 1963, lie at the junction of north and south. The wealthier of the two, Abruzzo offers the packaged, modern fun of beach and ski resorts, as well as delightful mountain lakes, lush pines, and wild boars in the Abruzzo National Park. Dubbed a religious center by the Samnites, the smaller Molise is home to phenomenal ruins, frequent medieval festivals, and fresh food. Women tote copper pots of fresh water, shirtless men lead donkeys, and youngsters listen to their Discmen.

Having a car in Abruzzo and Molise is advisable, since bus service is often inconsistent. In both regions, however, the **ARPA bus** service is somewhat useful. For information, call their office in L'Aquila (☎0862 41 28 08) or Avezzano (☎0863 265 61). Service is always sharply reduced on Sundays.

HIGHLIGHTS OF ABRUZZO AND MOLISE

KNOW that our coverage of L'Aquila is brought to you by the **number 99** (see below).

FROLIC with wild boars, Apennine wolves, and royal eagles in the **Abruzzo National Park** (p. 420).

L'AQUILA ☎0862

Perched high in the Apennines, L'Aquila (The Eagle) overlooks its subjects with a majestic air. The capital of Abruzzo, L'Aquila was founded in 1254 by 99 lords from 99 nearby castles who celebrated the occasion by building a 99-spout fountain. Local legend claims that there are 99 medieval streets with 99 *piazze* and 99 churches, one of which tolls 99 times at 9:09 each evening.

TRANSPORTATION. L'Aquila has two bus systems: municipal buses and ARPA regional buses. The **yellow municipal buses** (L1500) stop at yellow **ASM** markers and service the surrounding towns and sights (Sunday service is greatly reduced). Tickets are available at *tabacchi*, newsstands, or bars. On Mondays through Saturdays, **blue ARPA buses** connect L'Aquila to **Avezzano** (50min., 32 per day 6am-8:30pm, L8700); **Sulmona** (1hr., 9 per day 6am-7pm, L9800); **Pescara** (1½hr., 9 per day 6am-8:30pm, L14,000); and **Rome** (1¾hr., 16 per day 5am-8pm, L16,900). Sunday service is reduced. Buses depart from the **Fontana Luminosa,** near the *castello.* The **ticket office** (☎0862 412 808) is open M-Sa 5:30am-8:30pm, Su 7:30am-1:15pm and 2:30-8pm. The **train station** (☎0862 419 290) is on the outskirts of town. Take bus #M11, 30, or 79C to the center, or turn right, follow the signs to the Fontana delle 99 Cannelle, and hike 2 ghastly kilometers uphill. Trains head to **Sulmona** (50min.-1hr., 10 per day 6:30am-8pm, L6800) and **Terni** (2hr., 9 per day 6:30am-8:20pm, L10,100).

ORIENTATION AND PRACTICAL INFORMATION. The main street, **Corso Vittorio Emanuele II,** stretches between the **Castello Cinquecentesco** to the north and **Piazza del Duomo,** the heart of the city's historic district, to the south. Beyond P. del Duomo, the street continues as **Corso Federico II** until it reaches the lush gardens of the **Villa Comunale** and **Via XX Settembre,** which separate the southern half of the city. Pick up a map at the tourist office—navigating the small streets is tough.

Pick up the indispensable *Notizie Utili* booklet (which has info for the entire province) at the **EPT Information Office,** V. XX Settembre, 8. (☎0862 223 06. Open M-Sa 9am-1pm and 3:30-6pm, Su 9am-noon.) The office provides everything from maps and taxi services to helicopter rentals. Closer to the *castello* is another office, in P. Maria Paganica. Turn off C. Vittorio Emanuele onto V. Leosini. The office is uphill on the right. (☎0862 41 08 08 or 0862 41 03 40. Open M-F 8am-2pm and 3:30-6pm, Sa 8am-2pm.) **Club Alpino Italiano,** V. Sassa, 34, provides **hiking information.** (☎0862 243 42. Open M-Sa 7-8:15pm.) The **Centro Turistico Aquilano,** C. Vittorio Emanuele, 49, has local bus schedules and info on the Gran Sasso park (☎0862 22 146. Open M-F 9am-1pm and 3:30-7pm, Sa 9am-1pm.) The **police** (☎112 or 113) are at V. del Beato Cesidio. Get naughty on the web at **Gli Internauti,** V. Cimino, 51, opposite the *duomo.* (☎0862 40 43 38; www.internauti.it. L10,000 per hr.. Open Tu-Su 5pm-2am.) The Baroque **post office** is in P. del Duomo, along with currency exchanges. (Open M-F 8:15am-7:40pm.) **Postal Code:** 67100.

ACCOMMODATIONS AND FOOD. There are no convenient budget accommodations in L'Aquila, so try to avoid sleeping here. If you must stay the night, **Il Portichetto,** Strada Statale 80 (☎0862 31 12 18), 5km from town, offers singles for L50,000 and doubles for L100,000, bath and breakfast included). Take bus #15 from the *fontana luminosa.* In town, the expensive **Hotel Duomo,** on V. Dragonetti in the far right corner of P. Duomo as you stand facing away from the *duomo,* has 36 rooms, all with baths, phones, and TVs. (☎0862 41 07 69; fax 0862 41 30 58. Singles L85-90,000; doubles L120-140,000. V, MC, AmEx.)

Torrone, a nougat made of honey and almonds, is to L'Aquila what T'Equila is to Mexico. Manufactured in L'Aquila, *torrone* is available in stores throughout the city. The most established and most popular brand is *Sorelle Nurzia.* Try **Caffè Europa** at C. Emanuele 38. For more substantial fare, **Trattoria Da Lincosta,** P. S. Pietro a Coppito, 19, off V. Roma, offers regional favorites, including *agnello ai ferri* (grilled lamb) for L15,000 and a *menù turistico* for L25,000. (☎0862 286 62. Open Sa-Th noon-3pm and 6pm-midnight. V, MC, AmEx.) Pick up fresh fruit and

smoked meats as well as less edible items like socks and underwear at the **market** in P. Duomo. (Open M-Sa 8am-noon.) The **STANDA supermarket,** C. Federico II, is two blocks up from V. XX Settembre. (Open July-Aug. M 4-8pm, Tu-Sa 9am-1pm and 4-8pm, Su 10am-1pm; Sept.-June M 4-8pm, Tu-Sa 9am-1pm and 4-8pm.)

SIGHTS. Dating from 1292, the **Fontana delle 99 Cannelle** (Fountain of 99 Spouts) is the oldest monument in L'Aquila. Take V. Sallustio from C. Vittorio Emanuele and bear left to V. XX Settembre. Follow the small roads down the hill, staying to the left at the bottom. The fountain is a symbol of the city's historic foundation, when 99 local lords conspired to build a fortress to protect the hill towns. Each spout represents a different town. The source of the water remains unknown, and modern renovations of the fountain have failed to shed any light on the mystery. Those tempted to drink the water should temper their decision based on their ability to fend off water-borne disease.

L'Aquila's **Castello Cinquecentesco** dominates the park at the end of C. V. Emanuele. The Spanish viceroy Don Pedro da Toledo built this fort in the 16th century to defend himself against the rebelling Aquilans, who were forced to pay for its construction. Within the fort's intimidating walls, the **Museo Nazionale di Abruzzo** showcases art and artifacts of Abruzzo's history: sacred paintings, Roman sarcophagi, Renaissance tapestries, and a million-year-old elephant. (☎0862 63 31. Open Tu-F 9am-6:30pm, Sa 9am-7pm and 9pm-midnight, Su 9am-8pm. L8000.)

To reach the **Basilica di Santa Maria di Collemaggio,** take C. Federico I past V. XX Settembre and turn left on V. di Collemaggio after the Villa Comunale. (Open summer 8:30am-12:30pm and 3-7pm). Construction of this church began in 1287 at the urging of local hermit Pietro da Marrone (later Pope Celestine V). The pink-and-white-checked facade with elaborate carvings conceals an austere interior—the Baroque embellishments were stripped away in 1972 to restore a medieval feel.

The majestic **Chiesa di San Bernardino** looks out over the mountains south of L'Aquila. Walk down V. S. Bernardino from C. Vittorio Emanuele. The church was built in the 15th century and heavily restored after an earthquake in 1703. The interior boasts the massive tomb of San Bernardino, covered in fine Renaissance sculpture. (Open daily 7:30am-1pm and 4-7:30pm.)

ENTERTAINMENT. From November through May, the **Società Aquilana dei Concerti** sponsors classical concerts in the *castello* (☎0862 242 62 or 0862 41 41 61), while plays are performed year-round. Students at L'Aquila's **conservatory** V. Gaglioffi, 29, perform free recitals throughout the year.

NEAR L'AQUILA

The forested terrain around L'Aquila conceals isolated medieval towns, abandoned fortresses, ancient churches, and monasteries. Many of the sights remain concealed for those without a car, as buses are generally unreliable and inconvenient. East of L'Aquila lies the 15th-century **Rocca Calascio,** a sophisticated example of military architecture. It is surrounded by the medieval towns of **Santo Stefano di Sessanio** and **Castel del Monte,** as well as the 9th-century **Oratorio di San Pellegrino** in the town of **Bominaco.** To the west of L'Aquila lie the Roman ruins at **Amiternum** and the enormous **Lago di Campotosto,** the largest man-made lake in Italy. **ARPA buses** service these sights from both L'Aquila and Sulmona (1-2hr., 2-3 per day, L5-8000). North of L'Aquila, the town of **Assergi** houses a beautiful 12th-century abbey, **Santa Maria Assunta,** and its well-preserved frescoes. To get there, take municipal bus #6 (20min., 2 per hr., L1500) from the *piazza* near the castle.

The **Grottoes of Stiffe** at **San Demetrio ne' Vestini,** 21km southeast of L'Aquila, afford visitors glimpses of the terrain beneath Abruzzo. An underground river carved striking caves and rock formations that hide lakes and waterfalls. A recent cavern collapse has restricted access, but what remains open is stunning nevertheless. (Open Mar.-Nov.) To get there, take the **Paoli bus** from **Porta Paganica** (25min., 5 per day, L5000). For more information, contact the **EPT** of L'Aquila. For reservations, call or write the **Gruppo Speleologico Aquilano,** Svolte della Misericordia, 2, 67100 L'Aquila (☎/fax 0862 41 42 73).

GRAN SASSO D'ITALIA (BIG ROCK OF ITALY)

Twelve km north of L'Aquila rises the snowcapped **Gran Sasso d'Italia,** the highest ridge contained entirely within Italy's borders and a mountaineer's delight. Midway up the Sasso (and above the treeline) is a large flat plain called Campo Imperatore, home to herds of wild horses, shepherds, and amazing views of the peaks and landscape below. On a clear day, one can see both of Italy's coasts from the range's highest peak, the 2912m **Corno Grande.** Before starting a hike, pick up the Club Alpino Italiano **trail map** in town or at the base of the mountain (L12,000). The *sentieri* (paths) are marked by difficulty—only the more exacting routes reach the top. The peaks are snowed-in from September to July. Both the map and information booklet from L'Aquila's EPT or IAT list overnight *rifugi* (hiker's huts), which cost L9-16,000 per night. Another option is sleeping under the stars at **Camping Funivia del Gran Sasso,** an immaculate patch of grass downhill from the lower cableway. (☎0862 60 61 63. L7-8000 per person; L11-13,000 per large tent.) There is also a youth hostel at **Campo Imperatore**—call from the ropeway station to be picked up. (☎0862 40 00 11. L30,000 per bed.) Always call these lodgings before setting out, and bring food and warm clothing. Its windy and cool at Campo Imperatore even in the summer, and sturdy shoes are essential even for the easier hikes. Prices rise and temperatures drop with altitude.

A **funivia** ascends the 1008m to **Campo Imeratore** (round-trip L18,000, heads up and down every 30min. from 9am-5pm), making the Sasso an easy afternoon excursion from L'Aquila. From L'Aquila, take yellow bus #6 or 6D (30min., 5 per day, L1500) from the *fontana luminosa.* Buy tickets at newsstands and *tabacchi.* The *funivia* is closed during parts of June and October. Many trails start from the upper *funivia* station. Call **Club Alpino Italiano** (☎0862 243 42) for the most current Apennine advice. For information on guides, ask at the tourist office or write to **Collegio Regionale Guide Alpine,** V. Serafino, 2, 66100 Chieti (☎0871 693 38).

In winter, Gran Sasso teems with skiers. The trails around the funicular are among the most difficult, offering several 1000m drops and one of 4000m. Ten trails descend from the funicular and the two lifts. Weekly passes can be purchased at the *biglietteria* at the base of the funicular. **Campo Felice** at nearby Monte Rotondo has 16 lifts, numerous trails of varying difficulty, and a ski school. **Monte Cristo,** near Campo Imeratore, features four lifts and a 2800m trail. Before you bundle up, remember to call (☎0862 42 05 10) for a snow bulletin.

SULMONA ☎0864

Sulmona hides deep within the Abruzzo highlands in the Gizio River Valley. Surrounded on all sides by Abruzzo's extensive national parks, it makes a great base for exploring the outdoors. Its friendliness and hospitality are legendary, its architecture exquisite, and its history rich. Sulmona is known as the homeland of the Latin poet Ovid, who wrote the profound "Sulmo mihi patria est" ("Sulmo is my homeland"). With minimal breaking news in the two millennia since then, Sulmoans continue to litter their town with the acronym "SMPE." Summer after summer the amiable residents satiate their sweet teeth with Sulmona's famous confetti candy (which is made into flowers, sold in Sulmoan shops, and even thrown at weddings). Somehow Sulmona's splendor is forgotten by tourists who crowd Abruzzo's coasts during the summer, leaving the town unspoiled and charming.

TRANSPORTATION. Two kilometers outside of the city center, Sulmona's train station (☎0864 342 93) joins the Rome-Pescara and Carpione-L'Aquila-Terni lines. **Trains** run to: **L'Aquila** (50-60min., 13 per day 6:30am-8:30pm, L6800); **Pescara** (1-1¼hr., 17 per day 5am-9:30pm, L7100-11,400); **Avezzano** (1½hr., 10 per day 5:47am-8:10pm, L7200); **Rome** (1½-2½hr., 6 per day 6am-8pm, L14-23,100); and **Naples** (4hr., 3 per day 6:30am-8:30pm, L17,500). **Bus A** runs from the train station to the town center (5:30am-8pm, L1300); ask to stop at P. XX Settembre.

ORIENTATION AND PRACTICAL INFORMATION. Corso Ovidio runs from the train station west of Sulmona past P. XX Settembre and P. Garibaldi and through Porta Napoli and the eastern wall, changing its name often. There's an English-speaking staff at the **IAT Tourist Information Office,** C. Ovidio, 208. (☎0864 532 76. Open M-Sa 9am-1pm and 3:30-6pm, Su 9am-noon.) A cheery crew mans the **Ufficio Servizi Turistici** office across the street in P. dell'Annunziata. (☎0864 21 02 16. Open daily 9:30am-1:30pm and 4-8pm; in winter 9am-1:30pm and 3:30-7:30pm.) Call the **police** at ☎113. The **post office** is on P. Brigata Maiella, behind P. del Carmine. (Open M-F 8:15am-6:30pm, Sa 8:15am-1pm.) **Postal Code:** 67039.

ACCOMMODATIONS AND FOOD. Reservations are a good idea in summer. The classy **Albergo Stella,** V. Panfilo Mazara, 18/20, off C. Ovidio near the aqueduct, rents out nine well-maintained rooms with bath, phone, and TV. (☎0864 526 53. Small breakfast included. Singles L45-55,000; doubles L80-90,000. V, MC.) Ivy covers the facade of the **Hotel Italia,** P. Tommasi, 3, to the right off P. XX Settembre. Several of its 27 charming rooms overlook the dome of S. Annunziata and the mountains. (☎0864 523 08. Doubles L75,000, with bath L90,000.)

For 40 years, Clemente and his father have served regional favorites at the popular **Ristorante Clemente,** V. del Vecchio, 7, off C. Ovido. As Clemente proudly puts it, "*Si mangia bene, si spende giusto*" (one eats well, spends fairly). (☎0864 522 84. *Primi* from L9000, *secondi* L10-18,000. Cover L3000. Open daily 1-3pm and 7-11pm.) Another local favorite is **Al Quadrivio,** V. Odorisio, 38, off V. Panfila Mazara. The small menu changes daily. Try the *tagliatelle alla crema di carciofi* (with creamy artichoke sauce) if it's available. (☎0864 555 33. *Primi* L12,000, *secondi* L13-15,000. Open Tu-Su 12:30-2:30pm and 8-9:30pm.) Pick up picnic supplies and underwrite Silvo Berlusconi's right-wing agenda at the **STANDA supermarket,** P. Veneto, 2, past the arch at the end of C. Ovidio. (Open M-Sa 9am-1pm and 4-8pm.)

SIGHTS AND ENTERTAINMENT. The Romanesque-Gothic **Cattedrale di San Panfilo** is at one end of C. Ovidio. Its center was built 1000 years ago on the ruins of a temple for Apollo and Vesta. Down C. Ovidio from the gardens stand the **Chiesa and Palazzo di Santissima Annunziata.** The 15th-century Gothic *palazzo* adjacent to the Baroque church houses a small **museum.** If you are fond of Renaissance *sulmonese* gold work, you've stumbled into paradise; there's also a collection of wood statues collected from local churches. (☎0864 21 02 16. Open M-F 9am-1pm, Sa-Su 10am-1pm and 4-7pm. L1000.) Next door, the **Museo in Situ** features the ruins of a Roman house. (Open Tu-Su 10am-1pm. Free.) The colossal **Piazza Garibaldi** surrounds the Renaissance **Fontana del Vecchio,** which gushes clear mountain water from the nearby medieval aqueduct (1256).

Sulmona's prized *confetti* candy is made at, among other places, the Pelino family's **factory,** V. Stazione Introdaqua, 55. Turn right after the arch at the end of C. Ovidio onto V. Trieste, continue 1km up the hill as it becomes V. Stazione Introdaqua, and enter the Pelino building. The Pelinos have been making *confetti* since 1783 without evidence of even one Oompah-Loompah aiding them. The candy is tasty, tooth-decaying goodness. Your personal guide will lead you through candy-coated corridors to the free **confetti museum.** Check out the pictures of past popes and Padre Pio munching on candied religious instruments. (☎0864 21 00 47. Open M-Sa 8am-12:30pm and 3-6:30pm.) Delight in *confetti* flowers, fish, and buildings. Behold the ancient cauldrons, ovens, bottles, and pipes in which the Pelinos have worked their magic for 150 years before Willy Wonka appeared.

During the last week of July, locals celebrate **Giostra Cavalleresca di Sulmona,** a festival in which mounted, beacon-bearing knights run figure eights around P. Garibaldi, celebrating the seven *borghi* (small sections) of medieval Sulmona. You can buy seated tickets (L25-30,000), but it's easy to find a spot to watch for free. In preparation, each *borgo* hosts a public *festa* during a weekend in June. In October, Sulmona waxes cultural, hosting a film and an international opera festival.

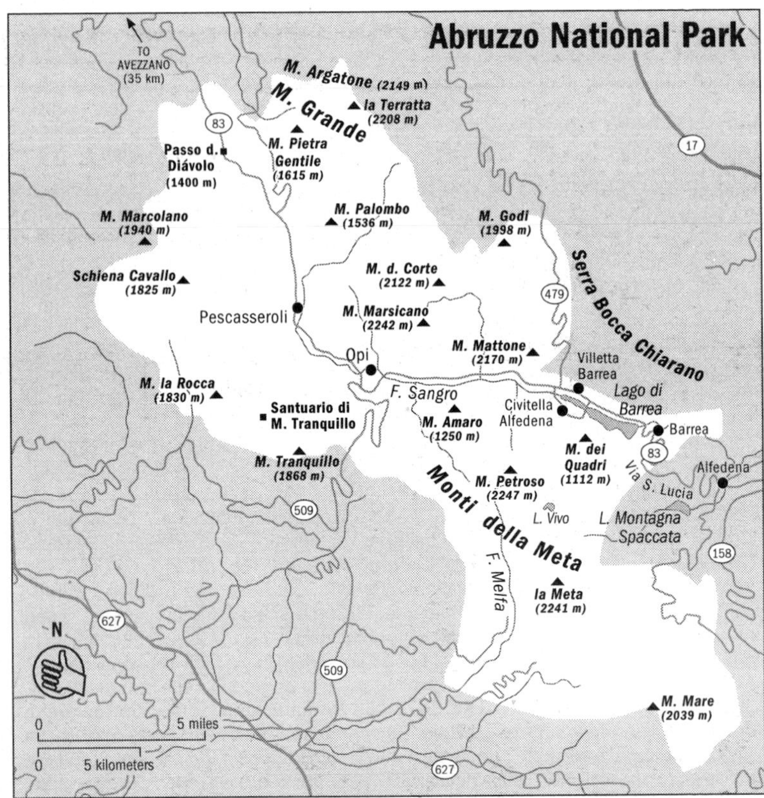

HIKING. Many of the mountains towering over Sulmona are part of the **Majella National Park,** and several trails are easily accessible by foot or bus from the town center. High up on the cliffs perches the mountain retreat of the saintly hermit who became Pope Celestine V—you can see the small cave where he lived. It's a fairly easy 45-minute to one-hour hike each way from the town of **Badia,** a 20-minute bus ride from Sulmona (L1300). If you want to hike other paths, be sure to pick up the **Club Italiano Alpino** map from the tourist office (L12,000). An indispensable guide, these maps describe each hike and the colors of the blazes that mark the trails. Keep in mind that the difficulty level refers to mountaineering experience, not hiking experience, so moderate difficulty hikes may be challenging for those not used to mountain climbing. However, the early sections of almost all trails are manageable. Take the 1st sections of paths 7 and 8 for a hike through the forested hills with some great views (5km one way, starts at the village of Fonte D'Amore and ends at Marane, each around 4km from Sulmona and serviced by local bus). If you use the bus to reach the trailheads, pick up a schedule from the tourist office and watch out for mid-afternoon gaps in service.

ABRUZZO NATIONAL PARK

The Parco Nazionale d'Abruzzo is the region's 4th largest park, protecting 44,000 hectares of mountainous wilderness from the resort hotels so loved by Italians. The mountains provide spectacular views of lush woodlands and crystal-clear lakes. Lynx have recently been reintroduced near Civitella Alfedena, joining Marsican brown bears, Apennine wolves, and Abruzzo Chamois antelopes. Pescasseroli, the park's administrative center, provides the best base for its exploration.

TRANSPORTATION

The best way to get to the park is by taking the **ARPA bus** (☎0863 265 61 or 0863 229 21), which runs from Avezzano through the park to Castel di Sangro (2¾hr.; M-Sa 7 per day, Su reduced service; 6:45am-7:15pm; L7000), making five stops at: **Pescasseroli** (1½hr., L6000); **Opi** (1¾hr., L6200); **Villetta Barrea** (2hr., L6500); **Civitella Alfadena** (2hr., L6600); and **Barrea** (2¼hr., L6800). Each day a bus runs to Pescasseroli from Rome's Tiburtina station at 7:45am and returns in the late afternoon (3hr., 6:15pm, L23,100 one-way). **Trains** run from Avezzano to: **Sulmona** (1-1¼hr., 10 per day 6:30am-8pm, L6800-10,800); **Rome** (1½-2hr., 8 per day 5am-9pm, L10-16,000); and **Pescara** (1¾-2hr., 6 per day 6:30am-8pm, L13,600-19,800).

PRACTICAL INFORMATION

In Pescasseroli, check in at the **Ufficio di Zona,** Vico Consultore, 1, by the P. Antonio bus stop, for hiking information, t-shirts decorated with local animals, and an essential park map. (☎0863 919 55. Map L10,000; profits go to maintaining the park. Open daily 9am-noon and 3-7pm.) For information on accommodations and restaurants, drop by the **IAT Information Office,** V. Piave, 1, off P. Antonio. (☎0863 91 00 97; fax 0863 91 04 61. Open daily 9am-1pm and 4:30-6:30pm.) There are Uffici di Zona throughout the park (get a list in Pescasseroli). They are indispensable information sources on park accommodations, campgrounds, events, and excursions.

ACCOMMODATIONS AND FOOD

PESCASSEROLI. In the middle of the park, alpine Pescasseroli (home to the park's administrative center) is a popular place to stay. Most reasonably priced accommodations in Pescasseroli do not offer single rooms. In the off-season, however, solo travelers can finagle a double or quad for the price of a single. **Pensione Claudia,** V. Tagliamento, 35, 200m across the gravel lot from the main avenue, has 10 quiet rooms with bath. (☎0863 918 37; email m.finamore@ermes.it. Sept.-July doubles L50-60,000. July-Aug. required half-pension L70,000 per person.) **Pensione al Castello,** V. Gabriele d'Annunzio, 7, opposite the park office, has seven beautiful rooms, all with bath, phone, and TV. (☎0863 91 07 57. Breakfast L5000. Doubles L70-85,000. Aug. and Christmas required half-pension L80,000.) Four campgrounds are within 21km of town. The best is **Campeggio dell'Orso,** 1km from Pescasseroli on the main road to Opi. (☎0863 919 55. L6000 per person, L6000 per tent.)

For provisions, the **Delfino A&O** supermarket is on V. S. Lucia, the main highway, past the zoo and park office. (Open daily 8:30am-1pm and 4-7pm. V, MC, AmEx.) For desserts, the **Pasticceria Alpina,** Traversa Sangro, 6, serves an array of award-winning sweets. (☎0863 91 05 61. Open Tu-Su 7am-10pm.)

OPI. ARPA buses follow the winding road through the park to the village of Opi, named for the pagan goddess of abundance, whose temple was located here in ancient times. Two kilometers past the village, on the bus route, lies the campground **Vecchio Mulino.** It's hard to miss the large, multicolored balloon which identifies it. (☎0863 91 22 32. L8000 per person, L9500 per small tent.) In August, Opi hosts the **Sagra degli Gnocchi** (Gnocchifest), a nationally renowned eat-along where thousands converge to consume *gnocchi*, sausages, and cheese.

CIVITELLA ALFEDENA. Ten kilometers past Opi, the bus reaches the village of **Villetta Barrea.** The turn-off to Civitella Alfedena, 200m farther down the road, leads to **Camping Pinus Nigra.** The site, bordered by the River Sangro, is large and pleasant. (☎0864 891 41. L5-6000 per person, L6-7000 per large tent.) In Civitella Alfedena, make yourself at home at one of two adjacent lodgings, **Alberghetto La Torre** or **Albergo Autico Borgo,** V. Castello, 3, both under the same management. (☎0864 89 01 21. Doubles L60,000, with bath L70,000. Extra bed L30,000.) **Museo**

del Lupo has information on the history of the Apennine wolf and the lynx. (☎0864 89 01 41. L5000.) Ice-cold **Barrea Lake** cuts majestically into the mountains, stretching 7km between Villetta Barrea and the neighboring village of **Barrea.**

AVEZZANO. A beautiful city before it was levelled by earthquake in 1915, Avezzano is now notable only as the home of the *telespazio*, a huge satellite transmission system. Because of its location on a rail line from Rome, it is one of the main gateways to the park. Buses into the park leave from the far side of the train station on the left—take the *sottopassagio*. **Hotel Creati,** on V. XX Settembre, offers pleasant, inexpensive rooms. (☎0863 41 33 47. Singles L35,000; doubles L60,000.)

OUTDOORS

You haven't really entered the park until the road begins its scenic ascent from Avezzano to Pescasseroli. Fields of poppies, rocky outcrops, dazzling valleys, and dizzying views will delight you. The twisting bus ride through the park is spectacular. If the wildlife in the park eludes you, compensate in Pescasseroli's **Centro di Visita,** Vle. Colle dell'Orso, 2, off V. S. Lucia as you head towards Opi. The center has a museum and small zoo, displaying indigenous animals, colorful gardens, and exhibits of the park's natural history. (Open daily 10am-1pm and 3-7pm. L8000.)

Purchase the indispensable trail map (L10,000) from the Ufficio di Zona in Pescasseroli. The clear, detailed map indicates prime wildlife viewing (and the locations of other Uffici di Zona throughout the park). You might see brown bears, chamois, deer, wolves, and eagles. The trails are arranged so that all paths that begin with the same letter start from the same point. Some of the best trails lie within walking distance of Pescasseroli. For a short hike, take **trail B1** to the castle ruins at Monte Ceraso (50min. round-trip). To really stretch those legs, brave the beautiful 5hr. round-trip hike on **trail C3** to **Vicolo (Pass) di Monte Tranquillo** (1673m). The trail starts at the southern end of town and leads up through the green Valle Mancina and past the Rifugio Della Difesa. Keep climbing to the pass, with its impressive view of the mountain peaks to the north. True adventurers can take on **Monte Marsicano,** one of the park's highest peaks (2245m). **Trail E6** from Opi (7-8hr. round-trip) is a challenging hike, and the steep path gets arduous.

If you coordinate your hikes with the ARPA bus schedule, you can venture farther afield. From Civitella Alfedena (15km from Pescasseroli) take **trail I1 to K6** through the sublimely beautiful **Valle di Rose** to see the park's largest herd of chamois. From mid-July to early September, this area can be explored only with a guide (L15,000 per person). One day before your excursion, go to an Ufficio di Zona for more information about the trails or to obtain a permit and reserve a guide. From Barrea (20km from Pescasseroli) **trail K5** runs to the refreshing **Lago Vivo** (3½hr. round-trip). However, the lake dries up between June and October.

Mountain bikes are available for L10,000 per day at **Sport House** in Pescasseroli. Turn left from the tourist office, cross the river, turn right, and walk five minutes along the river bank. (☎0863 91 07 96. Open M-Sa 9am-1pm and 4-7pm.) Several paths, including C3, provide good biking. **Ecotur,** P. Vittorio Veneto, 24, in Pescasseroli, offers organized hikes and excursions. (☎0863 91 27 60. Open daily 9am-noon and 4:30-7:30pm.) In winter, this area offers excellent skiing, with challenging slopes and heavy snowfall. Package deals called **settimane bianche** (white weeks) provide accommodations, lift tickets, and half-pension. For a regional snow bulletin, call ☎0862 665 10.

TERMOLI ☎0875

Termoli is the embarkation point for the Tremiti islands, but its beaches are attraction enough for many Italian vacationers. Since most visitors to Termoli are middle-class Italians looking to relax, there are few low-end hotels in town. The large, clean **Hotel Rosary,** Lungomare Colombo, 42, at the intersection with

C. Milano, is a short walk from the station and a stone's throw to the beach. All rooms have bath and TV. (☎0875 84 944. Closed mid-Nov. to mid-Mar. Singles L60,000; doubles L90,000.) Food in Termoli is as unexciting as the beach clubs lining the coast. Stick to the well priced pizzas (L5-10,000) at **La Sacrestia,** V. Ruffini, 48. Turn right from C. Nazionale onto V. Alfano and then right on V. Ruffino. (☎0875 70 56 03. Open daily noon-2pm and 7-11pm.) For fresh bread and other baked goods, stop by **Lineapane,** V. Milano, 18. (Open daily 7am-1:15pm and 4:30-9pm.)

The **FS train** station lies at the west end of the small town. **Corso M. Milano** extends a few hundred meters to **Lungomare Colombo,** the waterfront strip lined with hotels on one side and beaches on the other. **Corso Umberto,** heading from the station to the small old town, is lined with restaurants and shops. To get to the port from C. Umberto, turn left on V. Aubrey to reach **Via del Porto,** which leads to the ferry port. The ferry docks and ticket offices are past the fishing boats on the long breakwater extending into the harbor. The **tourist office** is on Lungomare Colombo, a block to the right of the intersection with C. Milano. (☎0875 70 83 42. Open M-Sa 9am-1pm and 5-7:30pm.)

TREMITI ISLANDS ☎0882

TRANSPORTATION. From **Termoli,** several ferry companies serve the island, including: **Navigargano** (9:15am, return 5:25pm; round-trip L28,000, Aug. 6-21 L32,000); **Navigazione Libera** (☎0875 70 48 59; 8:40am, 11am, and 5:30pm, return 9:45am, 4:20, and 6:40pm; one-way L23,000); and **Adriatica** ferries (daily 9am, return 5pm; L13,600) and hydrofoils (daily 8:35am, return 9:35am; afternoon service varies during the week and monthly). Their ticket windows and docks are all next to each other. Ferry service only operates from June to September. Hydrofoils make the trip in one hour; ferries take about an hour and a half.

PRACTICAL INFORMATION. There are four Tremiti islands—**San Domino, San Nicola, Capraia,** and **Pinosa.** San Domino is the largest and home to the archipelago's pine forests and hotels, while San Nicola is home to an interesting abbey. The last two are small and desolate and of interest only to seagulls. **Motorboats** run throughout the day between San Nicola and San Domino (L2000). A **first aid station** is at the port in San Domenico. (Open 24hr. ☎0882 46 32 34.) The **carabinieri** can be reached at ☎0882 46 30 10. Contact the **Guardia Finanza** (☎0882 46 30 15) to report smugglers and tax evaders. A **pharmacy** is in San Domenico Village, in the middle of San Domino, on V. del Vecchio Forno. Follow the signs from the main square. (☎0882 46 33 27. Open June-Sept. 9am-1pm and 5-9:30pm; Oct.-May 9:30am-12:30pm and 5-7:30pm.)

ACCOMMODATIONS. Hotels are on San Domino, and most offer only doubles and require half or full pension, a mixed blessing considering that there are not many restaurants. Since the islands are a popular vacation spot, be sure to make reservations during the summer. **Hotel La Vela,** on V. San Domino, offers half-pension rooms with bath and fridge—call from the port to be picked up. (☎0882 46 32 54. Aug. L100,000 per person; Sept.-July L75,000 per person.) **Villagio International,** at Punta del Diamente, is another economical choice, with two kinds of housing—prefabricate hut/tent hybrids (external bath) and bungalows with internal bath. (Prefab units L45,000 per person, required half-pension in Aug. L90,000; bungalows L65-75,000 per person, required half-pension in Aug. L120,000; surcharge for singles L30,000.) **Ristorante Diomede** (☎0882 46 34 03) offers a pizza and beer combination for L10,000. At night, it metamorphosizes into a free *discoteca* that gets going daily around 11:30pm.

HIKING, SPEAR FISHING, AND SIGHTS. The **pine forests** that cover much of the island are the highlight of San Domino. Paths snake through the protected forest, alive with the sound of cicadas and the smell of dried, fallen, pine needles. Many paths extend down to small rocky coves along the coast, where vacationers swim in the sapphire waters. Many Italians also live out their *Thunderball*-inspired fantasies and take to the seas with **spear guns,** not to hunt SPECTRE agents, but more edible and less dangerous prey, such as fish. If you'd rather look at moderately interesting religious buildings than shoot fish, then the island of San Nicola, where a **fortified abbey** crowns the cliffs, is the place for you. Accessible by a short path from the harbor, the monastery was founded in the 11th century. Though largely rebuilt over the centuries, portions of the original mosaic pavement survive. The emperor Augustus's adulterous granddaughter Julia was banished here.

ROME

> Italy will return to the splendors of Rome, said the major. I don't like Rome, I said. It is hot and full of fleas. You don't like Rome? Yes, I love Rome. Rome is the mother of nations. I will never forget Romulus suckling the Tiber. What? Nothing. Let's all go to Rome. Let's go to Rome tonight and never come back. Rome is a beautiful city, said the major.
>
> —Ernest Hemingway, *A Farewell to Arms*

Italy's massive capital is an eruption of marble domes, noseless statues, and motorcycle dust. Rome is sensory overload, rushing down the hills of Lazio to knock you flat on your back, leaving you gasping for air and dying for more. The city and those it controlled were responsible for the development of over 2000 years of world history, art, architecture, politics, and literature. Rome has been the capital of kingdoms and republics; from this city, the Roman Empire defined the Western world, and from here, the Catholic Church spread its influence worldwide. For the traveler, there is so much to see, hear, eat, smell, and absorb that the city is both exhilarating and overwhelming, as if it's impossible to experience everything, or even anything. Never fear, however, because in *bella Roma*, everything is beautiful and everything tastes good. Liberate your senses from the pollution eroding the monuments and from the maniacal rush of motorcyclists, and enjoy the dizzying paradox that is the *Caput Mundi*, the Eternal City, Rome.

ORIENTATION

From the train station, **Termini,** the arrival point for most visitors to Rome, **Via Nazionale** is the central artery connecting **Piazza della Repubblica** with **Piazza Venezia,** home to the immense wedding-cake-like **Vittorio Emanuele II monument.** West of P. Venezia, **Largo Argentina** marks the start of C. V. Emanuele, which leads into Centro Storico, the medieval and Renaissance tangle of sights around the **Pantheon, Piazza Navona, Campo dei Fiori,** and **Piazza Farnese.** From P. Venezia, V. dei Fori Imperiale leads southeast to the **Forum** and **Colosseum,** south of which are the ruins of the **Baths of Caracalla** and the **Appian Way** and the neighborhoods of southern Rome, the Aventine, Testaccio, Ostiense, and EUR. **Via del Corso** stretches from P. Venezia north to **Piazza del Popolo.** East of the Corso, fashionable streets border the **Piazza di Spagna** and, to the northeast, the **Villa Borghese.** South and east are the **Fontana di Trevi, Piazza Barberini,** and the **Quirinal Hill.** Across the Tiber to the north are **Vatican City,** and, to the south, **Trastevere,** the best neighborhood for wandering.

Some people say it's impossible to navigate Rome without a map. They are, in fact, correct. Pick up a free map from a tourist office or *Let's Go*'s 30-page **map guide.** The invaluable **Roma Metro-Bus map** (L8000) is available at newsstands.

GETTING THERE AND AWAY

FLIGHTS

Most flights arrive at da Vinci International Airport (☎06 65951), known as **Fiumicino** for the village in which it is located. When you exit customs, follow the signs to your left for **Stazione FS/Railway Station.** Take the elevator or escalators up two floors to the pedestrian bridge to the airport train station. The **Termini line** runs nonstop to Rome's main train station and transportation hub, Termini Station (30min.; 2 per hr. 12 and 37min. past the hr. 7:37am-10:37pm, extra trains 7:37am, 6:37 and 8:37pm; L16,000, L40,000 on board). Buy a ticket at the FS ticket counter, the *tabacchi* on the right, or from one of the machines in the station.

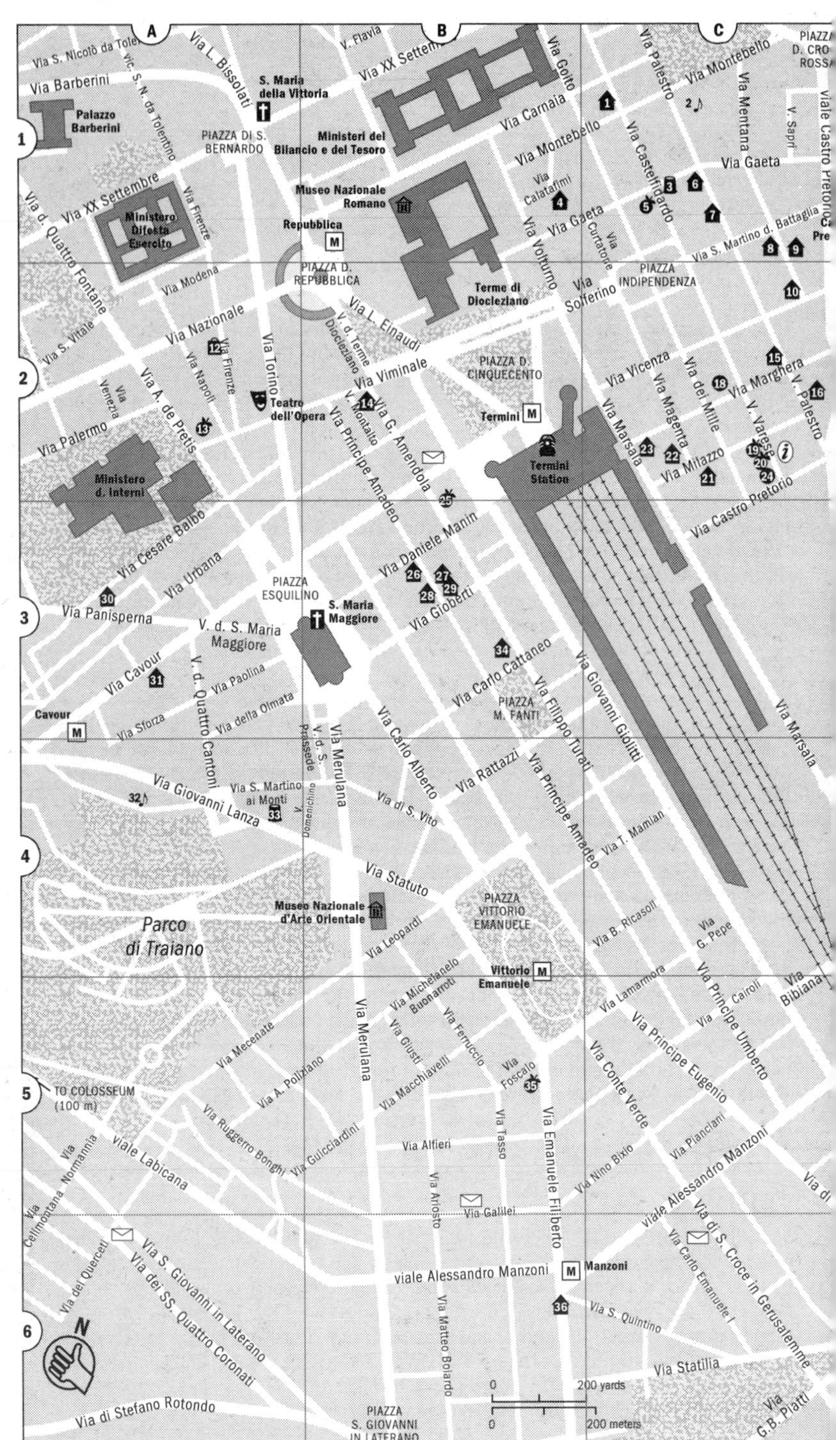

Palazzo Barberini
S. Maria della Vittoria
Ministeri del Bilancio e del Tesoro
Museo Nazionale Romano
Repubblica
Ministero Difesa Esercito
PIAZZA DI S. BERNARDO
PIAZZA D. REPUBBLICA
Terme di Diocleziano
PIAZZA INDIPENDENZA
PIAZZA D. CINQUECENTO
Termini
Teatro dell'Opera
Termini Station
Ministero d. Interni
PIAZZA ESQUILINO
S. Maria Maggiore
Cavour
PIAZZA M. FANTI
Museo Nazionale d'Arte Orientale
Parco di Traiano
PIAZZA VITTORIO EMANUELE
Vittorio Emanuele
TO COLOSSEUM (100 m)
Manzoni
PIAZZA S. GIOVANNI IN LATERANO
Via Barberini
Via XX Settembre
Via L. Bissolati
Via Goito
Via Palestro
Via Montebello
Via Mentana
Via Carnaia
Via Gaeta
Via Castelfidardo
Via Calatafimi
Via Volturno
Via Solferino
Via S. Martino d. Battaglia
Via Nazionale
Via Torino
Via L. Einaudi
Via Viminale
Via Vicenza
Via Magenta
Via dei Mille
Via Marghera
Via Marsala
Via Milazzo
Via Castro Pretorio
Via Palermo
Via A. de Pretis
Via Cesare Balbo
Via Urbana
Via Panisperna
Via Cavour
Via Principe Amadeo
Via G. Amendola
Via Daniele Manin
Via Gioberti
Via Carlo Cattaneo
Via Filippo Turati
Via Giovanni Giolitti
Via Carlo Alberto
Via Rattazzi
Via Merulana
Via Giovanni Lanza
Via Statuto
Via Leopardi
Via Mecenate
Via Labicana
Via Conte Verde
Via Principe Eugenio
Via Principe Umberto
viale Alessandro Manzoni
Via Emanuele Filiberto
Via S. Giovanni in Laterano
Via dei SS. Quattro Coronati
Via di S. Croce in Gerusalemme
Via Statilia
Via di Stefano Rotondo
200 yards
200 meters
N

D
E
F
V. G. B. Morgani
Via Bari
Via Catanzaro
Via Padova
Via Cremona
Bologna
Castro Pretorio
Biblioteca Nazionale
Via G. M. Lancisi
Via Regina Margherita
PIAZZA SASSARI
Policlinico
Via Treviso
Via Chieti
Via Imperia
Via Como
PIAZZA LECCE
Via Catania
Via Pavia
viale delle Province
PIAZZALE DELLE PROVINCE
Viale del Policlinico
viale Regina Elena
Via Borelli
V. Vigevano
LARGO MARCHIAFAVA
viale Ippocrate
Via Antonio Scarpa
V. P. Zacchia
V. Giano della Bella
Via Castro Laurenzia
Min. Difesa Aeronautica
CITTÀ UNIVERSITARIA
Viale delle Scienze
PIAZZA VALERO MASSIMO
Via Tiburtina
Via Piero Gobetti
Via d. Frentani
PIAZZALE ALDO MORO
PIAZZALE S. LORENZO
Cimitero del Verano
Via Cesare de Lollis
Via dei Ramni
Via dei Marrucini
V. dei Dalmati
PIAZZALE DEL VERANO
Via dei Lucani
Via dei Volsci
Via degli Ausoni
LARGO D. OSCHI
SAN LORENZO
Via dei Sabelli
Via dei Marsi
Via dei Sardi
Via degli Enotri
Via degli Apuli
Via di Porta Labicana
Via dei Liguri
LARGO E. TALAMO
Viale dello Scalo di S. Lorenzo
PIAZZA DI PORTA MAGGIORE
Via Prenestina
Via Eleniana
Termini & San Lorenzo
ACCOMMODATIONS
Hotel Adventure, 16 C2
Hotel Canada, 10 C2
Hotel Castelfidardo and Hotel Lazzari, 1 C1
Hotel Cervia, 15 C2
Hotel Des Artistes, 9 C1
Hotel Dolomiti and Hotel Lachea, 8 C1
Hotel Fenicia, 21 C2
Hotel Galli, 21 C2
Hotel Giu' Giu', 14 B2
Hotel Il Castello, 36 B6
Hotel Kennedy, 34 B3
Hotel Magic, 21 C2
Hotel Marini, 7 C1
Hotel Orlanda, 28 B3
Hotel Pensione Stella, 6 C1
Hotel Roxena, 23 C2
Hotel San Paolo, 30 A3
Hotel Selene, 14 B2
Hotel Serena and Pensione delle Rose, 27 B3
Hotel Sweet Home, 26 B3
Hotel Teti, 28 B3
Hotel Ventura, 16 C2
Pensione Cortorillo, 29 B3
Pensione di Rienzo, 26 B3
Pensione Ester, 17 C2
Pensione Fawlty Towers, 22 C2
Pensione Katty, 7 C1
Pensione Papa Germano, 4 B1
Pensione Sandy, 6 C1
SHOPPING
Disfunzioni Musicali, 37, 57 D3, D4
Economy Book and Video Center, 12 A2
SERVICES
Enjoy Rome, 18, 24 C2
FOOD
Africa, 5 C1
Arancia Blu, 50 D5
Armando, 39 D4
Gold Bar, 13 A2
Hostaria Il Varesino, 19 C2
Il Capellaio Matto, 46 D5
Il Pulcino Ballerino, 47 D5
La Pantera Rosa, 38 E4
Osteria da Luciano, 25 B2
Pizzeria Il Maratoneta, 52 D4
Pizzeria l'Economica, 55 D4
Pizzeria la Pappardella, 44 D5
Ristorante da Lisa, 35 B5
Trattoria Colli Emiliani, 56 D4
Trattoria da Bruno, 20 C2
PUBS
Dalhu' Pub, 43 D5
Down Town, 45 D5
Drome, 58 D4
Druid's Den, 33 A4
Julius Caesar, 3 C1
Lancelot, 53 E4
Legend Pub, 58 D4
Lupo Alberto, 41 D4
Nirvana, 48 D5
Pigmalione, 42 D5
Pub Hallo'Ween, 40 D4
Skyline Club, 51 D5
CLUBS
Hangar, 32 A4
Club 52, 2 C1
Il Giardini di Adone, 54 E4

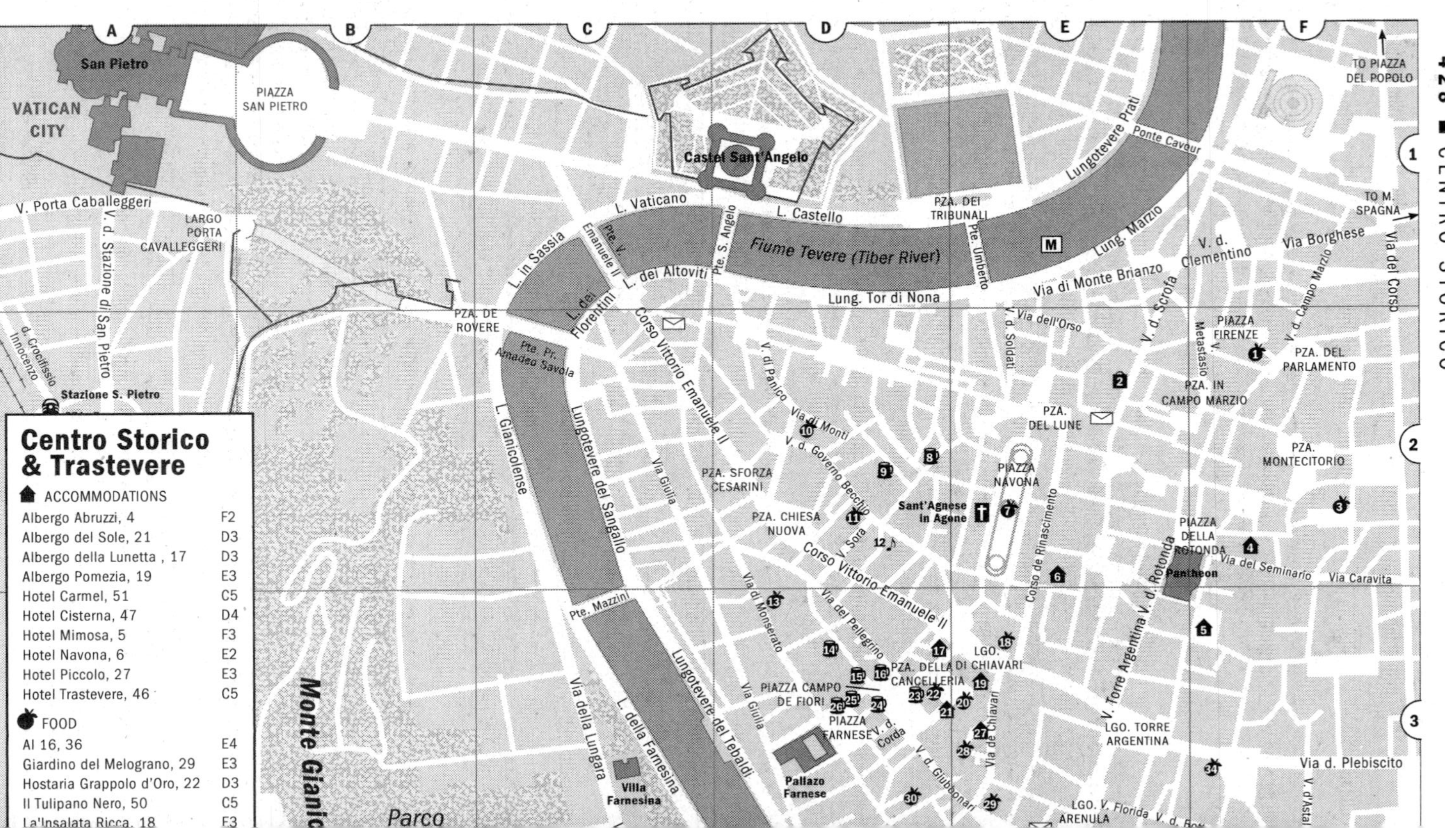
Centro Storico
& Trastevere
ACCOMMODATIONS
Albergo Abruzzi, 4 F2
Albergo del Sole, 21 D3
Albergo della Lunetta , 17 D3
Albergo Pomezia, 19 E3
Hotel Carmel, 51 C5
Hotel Cisterna, 47 D4
Hotel Mimosa, 5 F3
Hotel Navona, 6 E2
Hotel Piccolo, 27 E3
Hotel Trastevere, 46 C5
FOOD
Al 16, 36 E4
Giardino del Melograno, 29 E3
Hostaria Grappolo d'Oro, 22 D3
Il Tulipano Nero, 50 C5
La'Insalata Ricca, 18 E3
VATICAN CITY
San Pietro
PIAZZA SAN PIETRO
Castel Sant'Angelo
Fiume Tevere (Tiber River)
TO PIAZZA DEL POPOLO
TO M. SPAGNA
Via del Corso
Via Borghese
V. d. Campo Marzio
V. d. Clementino
Ponte Cavour
Lungotevere Prati
Lung. Marzio
Via di Monte Brianzo
PZA. DEI TRIBUNALI
Pte. Umberto
L. Castello
L. Vaticano
Pte. S. Angelo
Lung. Tor di Nona
L. dei Altoviti
Pte. V. Emanuele II
L. in Sassia
L. dei Florentini
PZA. DE ROVERE
Pte Pr. Amadeo Savoia
L. Gianicolense
Lungotevere del Sangallo
Pte. Mazzini
Lungotevere del Tebaldi
L. della Farnesina
Via della Lungara
Villa Farnesina
Monte Gianic
Parco
V. Porta Caballeggeri
LARGO PORTA CAVALLEGGERI
V. d. Stazione di San Pietro
d. Crocifissio Innocenzo
Stazione S. Pietro
Corso Vittorio Emanuele II
Via Giulia
PZA. SFORZA CESARINI
V. di Panico
Via di Monti
V. d. Governo Becchio
PZA. CHIESA NUOVA
V. Sora
Sant'Agnese in Agone
PIAZZA NAVONA
PZA. DEL LUNE
Via dell'Orso
V. d. Soldati
V. d. Scrofa
PIAZZA FIRENZE
V. Metastasio
PZA. DEL PARLAMENTO
PZA. IN CAMPO MARZIO
PZA. MONTECITORIO
Corso de Rinascimento
PIAZZA DELLA ROTONDA
Pantheon
Via del Seminario
Via Caravita
V. d. Rotonda
V. Torre Argentina
LGO. TORRE ARGENTINA
Via d. Plebiscito
V. d'Astal
LGO. V. Florida
ARENULA
Via di Monserato
Via del Pellegrino
LGO. DI CHIAVARI
PZA. DELLA CANCELLERIA
PIAZZA CAMPO DE FIORI
PIAZZA FARNESE
V. d. Corda
Pallazo Farnese
Via de Chiavari
V. d. Giubbonari

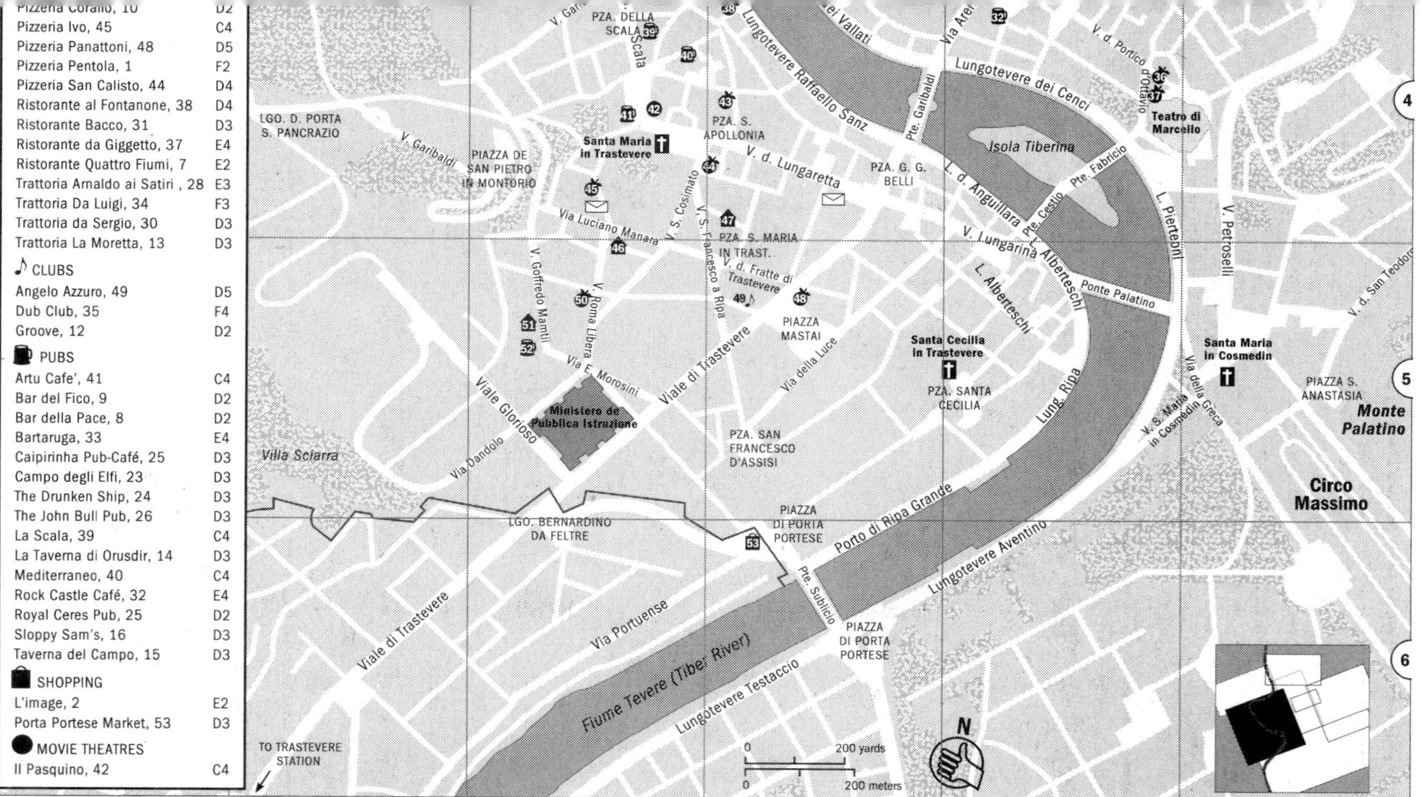
Pizzeria Corallo, 10 D2
Pizzeria Ivo, 45 C4
Pizzeria Panattoni, 48 D5
Pizzeria Pentola, 1 F2
Pizzeria San Calisto, 44 D4
Ristorante al Fontanone, 38 D4
Ristorante Bacco, 31 D3
Ristorante da Giggetto, 37 E4
Ristorante Quattro Fiumi, 7 E2
Trattoria Arnaldo ai Satiri , 28 E3
Trattoria Da Luigi, 34 F3
Trattoria da Sergio, 30 D3
Trattoria La Moretta, 13 D3
CLUBS
Angelo Azzuro, 49 D5
Dub Club, 35 F4
Groove, 12 D2
PUBS
Artu Cafe', 41 C4
Bar del Fico, 9 D2
Bar della Pace, 8 D2
Bartaruga, 33 E4
Caipirinha Pub-Café, 25 D3
Campo degli Elfi, 23 D3
The Drunken Ship, 24 D3
The John Bull Pub, 26 D3
La Scala, 39 C4
La Taverna di Orusdir, 14 D3
Mediterraneo, 40 C4
Rock Castle Café, 32 E4
Royal Ceres Pub, 25 D2
Sloppy Sam's, 16 D3
Taverna del Campo, 15 D3
SHOPPING
L'image, 2 E2
Porta Portese Market, 53 D3
MOVIE THEATRES
Il Pasquino, 42 C4
PZA. DELLA SCALA
Scala
Lungotevere Raffaello Sanz
Lungotevere dei Cenci
V. d. Portico d'Ottavio
Teatro di Marcello
Isola Tiberina
Pte. Garibaldi
Pte. Fabricio
Pte. Cestio
LGO. D. PORTA S. PANCRAZIO
V. Garibaldi
PIAZZA DE SAN PIETRO IN MONTORIO
Santa Maria in Trastevere
PZA. S. APOLLONIA
V. d. Lungaretta
PZA. G. G. BELLI
L. d. Anguillara
L. Pierleoni
V. Petroselli
Via Luciano Manara
V. S. Cosimato
V. S. Francesco a Ripa
PZA. S. MARIA IN TRAST.
V. d. Fratte di Trastevere
V. Lungarina
L. Alberteschi
Ponte Palatino
V. Goffredo Mamtii
V. Roma Libera
PIAZZA MASTAI
Santa Cecilia in Trastevere
Santa Maria in Cosmedin
PIAZZA S. ANASTASIA
Monte Palatino
Via E. Morosini
Viale di Trastevere
Via della Luce
PZA. SANTA CECILIA
Lung. Ripa
Via della Greca
V. S. Maria in Cosmedin
Viale Glorioso
Ministero de Pubblica Istruzione
Villa Sciarra
Via Dandolo
PZA. SAN FRANCESCO D'ASSISI
Circo Massimo
LGO. BERNARDINO DA FELTRE
PIAZZA DI PORTA PORTESE
Porto di Ripa Grande
Lungotevere Aventino
Pte. Sublicio
Viale di Trastevere
Via Portuense
Fiume Tevere (Tiber River)
Lungotevere Testaccio
TO TRASTEVERE STATION
0 200 yards
0 200 meters
N
4
5
6

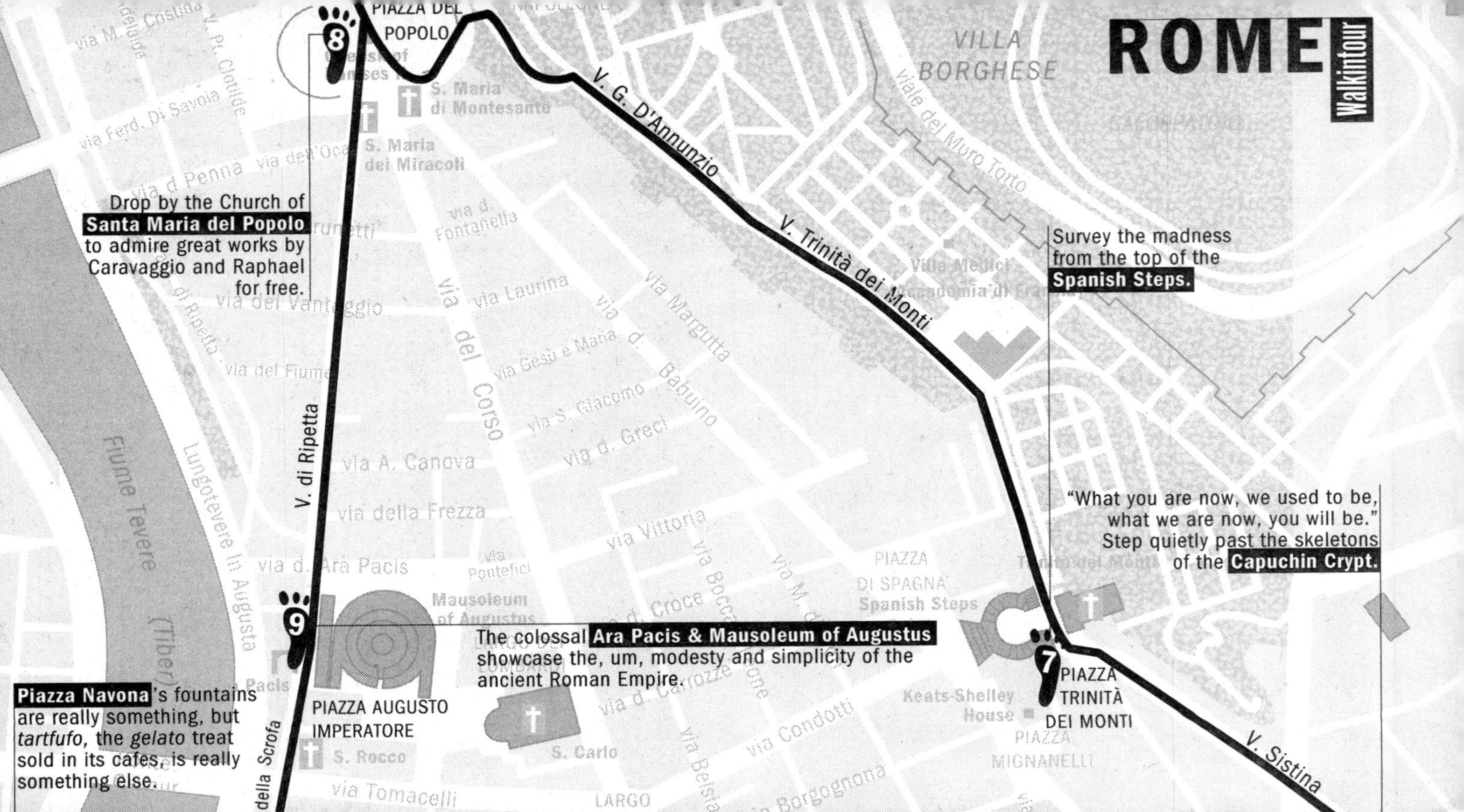
ROME
Walkintour
VILLA BORGHESE
Viale del Muro Torto
PIAZZA DEL POPOLO
8
S. Maria di Montesanto
S. Maria dei Miracoli
V. G. D'Annunzio
V. Trinità dei Monti
Villa Medici
Survey the madness from the top of the **Spanish Steps.**
Drop by the Church of **Santa Maria del Popolo** to admire great works by Caravaggio and Raphael for free.
via d Penna
via dell'Oca
via Ferd. Di Savoia
V. Pr. Clotilde
via d. Fontanella
via del Vantaggio
via Laurina
via del Corso
via Margutta
via d. Babuino
via Gesù e Maria
via S. Giacomo
via d. Greci
via del Fiume
V. di Ripetta
via A. Canova
via della Frezza
Fiume Tevere (Tiber)
Lungotevere In Augusta
via d. Ara Pacis
via Pontefici
via Vittoria
via Bocca di Leone
PIAZZA DI SPAGNA
Spanish Steps
"What you are now, we used to be, what we are now, you will be." Step quietly past the skeletons of the **Capuchin Crypt.**
9
Mausoleum of Augustus
The colossal **Ara Pacis & Mausoleum of Augustus** showcase the, um, modesty and simplicity of the ancient Roman Empire.
7
PIAZZA TRINITÀ DEI MONTI
Keats-Shelley House
PIAZZA MIGNANELLI
V. Sistina
Piazza Navona's fountains are really something, but *tartfufo*, the *gelato* treat sold in its cafes, is really something else.
PIAZZA AUGUSTO IMPERATORE
della Scrofa
S. Rocco
S. Carlo
via d. Carrozze
via Condotti
via Belsiana
via Borgognona
via Tomacelli
LARGO

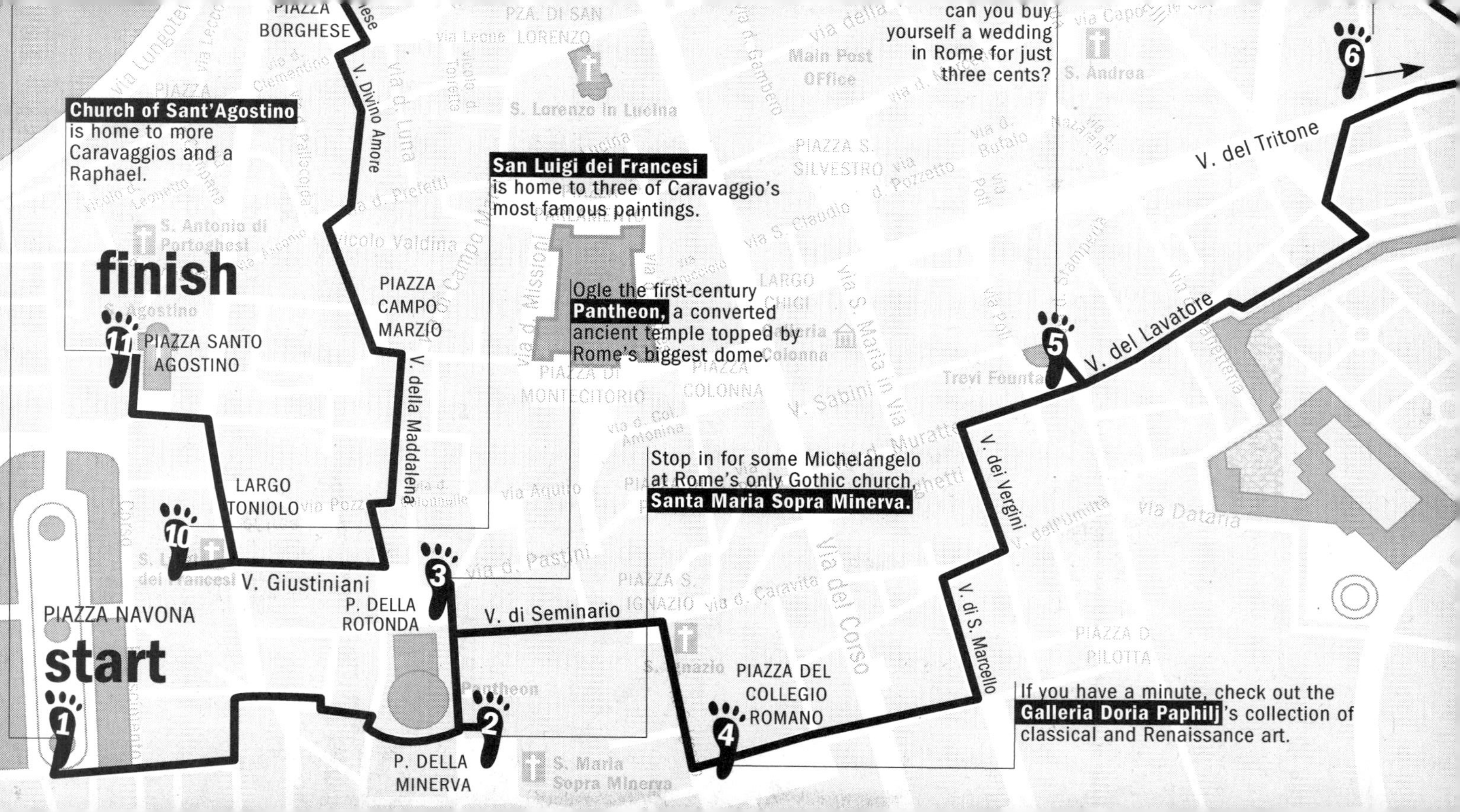
start
finish
1
2
3
4
5
6
10
11
Church of Sant'Agostino is home to more Caravaggios and a Raphael.
San Luigi dei Francesi is home to three of Caravaggio's most famous paintings.
Ogle the first-century Pantheon, a converted ancient temple topped by Rome's biggest dome.
Stop in for some Michelangelo at Rome's only Gothic church, Santa Maria Sopra Minerva.
If you have a minute, check out the Galleria Doria Paphilj's collection of classical and Renaissance art.
can you buy yourself a wedding in Rome for just three cents?
PIAZZA NAVONA
PIAZZA BORGHESE
PIAZZA SANTO AGOSTINO
LARGO TONIOLO
PIAZZA CAMPO MARZIO
P. DELLA ROTONDA
P. DELLA MINERVA
PIAZZA DEL COLLEGIO ROMANO
V. Divino Amore
V. della Maddalena
V. Giustiniani
V. di Seminario
V. di S. Marcello
V. dei Vergini
V. del Lavatore
V. del Tritone
Via del Corso
Via Dataria
PZA. DI SAN LORENZO
S. Lorenzo in Lucina
Main Post Office
S. Andrea
PIAZZA S. SILVESTRO
PIAZZA DI MONTECITORIO
PIAZZA COLONNA
LARGO CHIGI
PIAZZA S. IGNAZIO
PIAZZA D. PILOTTA
Pantheon
S. Maria Sopra Minerva
S. Antonio di Portoghesi
Trevi Fountain

A train leaves Termini for **Fiumicino** from track #22 or 23, which is at the very end of #22 (40min.; every hr. at 20min. past the hr. 7:20am-9:20pm, extra trains 6:50am, 3:50, 5:50, and 7:50pm; L16,000). Buy tickets at the Alitalia office at track #22 at the window marked *"Biglietti Per Fiumicino"* or from machines in the station. Validate (and retain) your ticket before boarding.

To reach Fiumicino from Rome when the train is not running, the most reliable and convenient option is to take a cab. The cheapest option is to take the blue **COTRAL bus** to Tiburtina from the ground floor outside the main exit doors after customs (1:15, 2:15, 3:30, and 5am; L8000, pay on board). From Tiburtina, take bus #40N to Termini. To get to Fiumicino late at night or early in the morning, take bus #40N from Termini to Tiburtina (every 20-30min.), then catch the blue COTRAL bus to Fiumicino outside (12:30, 1:15, 2:30, and 3:45am; L8000, pay on board).

Most charter and a few domestic flights arrive at **Ciampino** airport (☎06 79 49 41). To get to Rome, take the COTRAL bus (every 30min. 6:10am-11pm, L2000) to Anagnina station on Metro Linea A. After 11pm, you'll have to take a cab.

TRAINS

Stazione Termini is the focal point of most train lines and both subway lines. Trains that arrive in Rome between midnight and 5am usually arrive at Stazione Tiburtina or Stazione Ostiense, which are connected to Termini at night by the #40N and 20N-21N buses, respectively. Be wary of pickpockets and con artists around the stations. Services including **hotel reservations** (across from track #20), **ATMs, luggage storage** (at track #1), and **police** (at track #13, or call ☎112) are available in the station. Not to be missed are **Termini's bathrooms,** a black lit wonderland off track #1 (L1000). Be warned, they become a way of life. Trains leave Termini to: **Naples** (2-2½hr., L18,600); **Florence** (2-3hr., L40,900); **Bologna** (2¾-4¼hr., L35,600); **Milan** (4½-8hr., L50,500); and **Venice** (5hr., L66,000).

GETTING AROUND

Tickets for the bus or subway (L1500) can be bought at *tabacchi*, newsstands, some bars, and machines in stations or major bus stops. Each ticket is valid for one ride on the Metro or unlimited bus travel within 1¼hr. of validation. A ticket stamped for bus travel may not be used on the Metro, or vice-versa. A B.I.G. **daily ticket** costs L8000 and allows unlimited bus or train travel everywhere in the *Comune di Roma*, including Ostia but not Fiumicino. A C.I.S. **weekly ticket** costs L32,000. Pickpockets prowl on the jam-packed buses and trains; keep your wits about you, your wallet in your front pocket, and your backpack in front of you.

SUBWAY (METROPOLITANA)

Many sights are far from the subway, but it is good for covering large distances quickly. The two subway lines intersect at Termini. Station entrances are marked with a white "M" on a red square. The Metro runs daily from 5:30am to 11:30pm.

BUSES

Although the network of routes may seem daunting, Rome's buses are an efficient means of getting through the city. The **ATAC** intracity bus company has myriad booths, including one in Termini. (☎800 55 56 66. Open daily 8am-8pm.) Each bus stop *(fermata)* is marked by yellow signs listing all routes that stop there and key streets/stops on those routes. Some buses run only on weekdays *(feriali)* or weekends *(festivi)*, while others have different routes on different days of the week. Most buses begin around 5 or 6am and stop at midnight, when some routes are replaced by the less reliable **night routes** *(notturno)*.

Board through the front or back doors, not through the middle, then immediately stamp the ticket in the orange machine at the back; the ticket is then valid for any number of transfers over the next 1¼hr. Consider buying several tickets at once; at night and on weekends they can be hard to find.

Some useful bus routes are: **46:** Vatican area, C. V. Emanuele, Largo Argentina, P. Venezia; **64:** Termini, V. Nazionale, P. Venezia, Largo Argentina, C. V. Emanuele, Vatican (known as the "wallet-eater"); **81:** P. Malatesta, S. Giovanni, Colosseo, Bocca della Verità, P. Venezia, Vatican; **170:** Termini, V. Nazionale, P. Venezia, Largo Argentina, V. Marmorata, S. Paolo Basilica (service ends at 10pm); and **492:** Tiburtina, Termini, P. Barberini, P. Venezia, C. Rinascimento, P. Risorgimento.

TAXIS

Taxis in Rome are convenient but expensive. You can flag them down in the street, but they are found more easily at stands near Termini and in major *piazze.* Ride only in taxis with meters (if not, settle on a price before you get in the car). The meter starts at L4500. Surcharges are levied at night (L5000), on Sunday (L2000), and for the airports, with a charge per suitcase of L2000. Expect to pay about L15,000 for a ride from Termini to the Vatican. Taxis between the city center and Fiumicino cost around L70,000. **Radio taxis** pick you up at a given location within a few minutes of your call. They start the meter the moment your call is answered. Try **Radio Taxi** (☎06 35 70), **Radiotevere** (☎06 41 57), or **Prontotaxi** (☎06 66 45).

BICYCLES AND MOPEDS

Rome's hilly cobblestone streets and lunatic drivers make the city less than ideal for bikes and mopeds. In summer, there are bike rental stands along V. del Corso at P. S. Lorenzo and V. di Pontifici. (Open daily 10am-7pm.) When in Rome, always wear a helmet. **I Bike Rome,** V. Veneto, 156, in the Villa Borghese parking garage rents bikes (L5-8000 per hr., L10,000 per day, L40,000 per week) and mopeds (L40,000 for 4hr., L60,000 per day, L250,000 per week). (☎06 322 52 40. Open daily 8:30am-7pm.) **Scooters for Rent,** V. della Purificazione, 84, off P. Barberini, has bikes (L20,000 per day, L100,000 per week) and mopeds (L50,000 per day, L250,000 per week). (☎06 488 54 85. Open in summer daily 9am-7pm. V, MC, AmEx.)

PRACTICAL INFORMATION

TOURIST AND FINANCIAL SERVICES

Tourist Agency: **Enjoy Rome,** V. Marghera, 8a (☎06 445 68 90 or 06 445 18 43; fax 06 445 07 34; www.enjoyrome.com). From the middle concourse of Termini (between the trains and the ticket booths), exit right, with the trains behind you. Cross V. Marsala. The office is on the 3rd block down V. Marghera. Owners Fulvia and Pierluigi answer questions and offer useful tidbits about the city free of charge and in perfect English. Enjoy Rome arranges hotels and short-term apartments. Internet and a full-service travel agency, booking transportation worldwide and lodgings throughout Italy. Enjoy Rome also offers 4 3hr. English tours (L30,000, under 26 L25,000), including a superlative stroll through Trastevere and the Jewish Ghetto; a comprehensive **bike tour** (L35,000); a bus tour of Rome's famous cinematic areas (with film clips; L50,000); and Pompeii bus trips (L70,000). Branch office at V. Varese, 39, down V. Marghera another block and then right. Open M-F 8:30am-2pm and 3:30-6:30pm, Sa 8:30am-2pm.

Embassies and Consulates: See **Embassies and Consulates,** p. 41.

Currency Exchange: Banking hours are usually M-F 8:30am-1:30pm. Expect long lines and cranky tellers. **Banca di Roma** and **Banca Nazionale del Lavoro** have good rates, but **ATMs,** scattered all over town and especially near Termini, are the best.

American Express, P. di Spagna, 38 (☎06 67 641; lost or stolen cards and/or checks ☎06 722 81; fax 06 67 64 24 99). Open Sept.-July M-F 9am-7:30pm, Sa 9am-3pm; Aug. M-F 9am-6pm, Sa 9am-12:30pm. Mail: P. di Spagna, 38; 00187 Roma.

Thomas Cook, P. Barberini, 21a (☎06 482 80 82). Open M-Sa 9am-8pm, Su 9:30am-5pm. Other branches: V. della Conciliazione, 23-25 (☎06 68 30 04 35; open M-Sa 8:30am-6pm, Su 9am-5pm); V. del Corso, 23 (☎06 323 00 67; open M-Sa 9am-8pm, Su 9am-1:30pm); P. della Repubblica, 65 (☎06 48 64 95; open M-F 9am-5pm with 1hr. lunch break, Sa 9am-1pm).

LOCAL SERVICES

Lost Property: Oggetti Smarriti, V. Nicolo Bettoni, 1 (☎06 581 60 40; items lost on trains ☎06 47 30 66 82). Open M and W 8:30am-1pm and 2:30-6pm, Tu and F 8:30am-1pm, Th 8:30am-6pm. Also in **Termini,** at the glass booth in the main passageway. Open daily 7am-11pm.

Bookstores: Libreria Feltrinelli International, V. V. E. Orlando, 84-86 (☎06 482 78 78), near P. della Repubblica. Open daily 9am-7:30pm. V, MC, AmEx. **Anglo-American Bookshop,** V. della Vite, 102 (☎06 679 52 22; www.aab.it), south of the Spanish Steps. Open M-F 9am-1pm and 4-8pm, Sa 9am-1pm.

Bisexual, Gay, and Lesbian Resources: The Roman branches of **ARCI-GAY** and **ARCI-Lesbica** share offices at V. Orvinio, 2 (☎06 86 38 51 12) and V. Lariana, 8 (☎06 855 55 22). Both groups hold group discussions, dances, and special events. ARCI-GAY membership card (L20,000 annually) gives admission to gay clubs all over Italy. **Circolo di Cultura Omosessuale Mario Mieli, V. Corinto,** 5 (☎06 541 39 85; fax 06 541 39 71; www.mariomieli.it), provides loads of info about gay life in Rome. Take Metro B to San Paolo, walk 1 block to Largo Beato Placido Riccardi, turn left, and walk 1½ blocks to V. Corinto. Open Sept.-July M-F 9am-1pm and 2-6pm. Rome's only **gay bookstore** is **Libreria Babele** (☎06 687 66 28), on V. dei Banchi Vecchi, across the bridge from Castel Sant'Angelo off V. V. Emanuele. Open M-Sa 10am-7:30pm. During the day, gay and lesbian Romans crowd the **gay beach** Il Buco at Lido di Ostia.

Laundromat: OndaBlu, V. La Mora, 7 (☎800 86 13 46). Many locations in Rome. Wash L6000 per 6½kg load; dry L6000 per 6½kg load. Soap L1500. Open daily 8am-10pm.

EMERGENCY AND COMMUNICATIONS

Emergencies: Police: ☎113 (English interpreter). **Carabinieri:** ☎112. **Ufficio Stranieri (Foreigners' Office):** V. Genova, 2 (☎06 46 86 28 76). Open daily 24hr. **First Aid,** ☎118. **Policlinico Umberto I,** Vle. di Policlinico, 155 (☎06 499 71). M:B-Policlinico. Free first aid. Open 24hr. **Crisis Line: Samaritans,** V. San Giovanni in Laterano, 250 (☎06 70 45 44 44). Native English speakers. Anonymous or face-to-face counseling. Open daily 1-10pm.

24-Hour Pharmacies: Farmacia Internazionale, P. Barberini, 49 (☎06 487 11 95). Open daily 24hr. MC, V. **Farmacia Piram,** V. Nazionale, 228 (☎06 488 07 54). Open daily 24hr. V, MC.

Hospitals: Ospedale San Camillo in Monteverde, Circonvallazione Gianicolense, 87 (☎06 587 01), in Gianicolo. Info open daily 8am-7pm; call for appointment. **Unione Sanitaria Internazionale,** V. Machiavelli, 22 (☎06 70 45 35 44). M:A-Vittorio Emanuele. Info open daily 7am-7pm; tests daily 7-11am.

Internet Services: Internet cafes and kiosks litter the city; these are two of the cheapest and friendliest. **Marco's Bar,** V. Varese, 54 (☎06 44 70 35 91), 3 blocks north of Termini, across the street from Enjoy Rome. Completely renovated for 2001, Marco's boasts a cool, laid-back atmosphere, with music, a well-stocked bar, friendly staff, and cheap internet access (L8000 per hr., with *Let's Go* L5000). Open daily 5:30am-2am. **Trevi Tourist Service: Trevi Internet,** V. dei Lucchesi, 31-32 (☎/fax 06 69 20 07 99). L5000 for 30min., L10,000 for 1½hr. Open daily 9am-10pm.

Post Office: Main office, P. San Silvestro, 19 (☎06 679 84 95), south of P. di Spagna. Come to San Silvestro with especially large packages, or if you need to insure your mail. Stamps at booths #23-25. Currency exchange at booth #19. Fax and telegram service. Open M-F 9am-6pm, Sa 9am-2pm. **Large branch,** V. delle Terme di Diocleziano, 30 (☎06 474 56 02), near Termini. Same hours as San Silvestro branch. **Postal Code:** Rome's postal codes fall between 00100 and 00200.

ACCOMMODATIONS

HOTELS AND PENSIONI

Rome swells with tourists around Easter, from May through July, and in September. Prices vary widely with the time of year, and a proprietor's willingness to negotiate increases in proportion to length of stay, number of vacancies, and group size. Termini is swarming with hotel scouts trying to bring you to their establishments. Many are legitimate and have IDs issued by tourist offices; however, some sneaky imposters have fake badges and direct travelers to rundown locations with exorbitant rates, especially late at night.

CENTRO STORICO

If being a bit closer to the sights is worth it to you, then choosing Rome's medieval center over the area near Termini may be worth the higher prices.

Albergo Pomezia, V. dei Chiavari, 12 (☎/fax 06 686 13 71), off C. V. Emanuele behind Sant'Andrea della Valle. Clean, quiet rooms with phones, fans, and heat in winter. You haven't had too much to drink–the managers are twins. Breakfast in the pleasant dining room included (8-11am). Singles L70-100,000, with bath L100-170,000; doubles L100-170,000, with bath L130-220,000; extra bed 35% surcharge. V, MC, AmEx.

Albergo della Lunetta, P. del Paradiso, 68 (☎06 686 10 80; fax 06 689 20 28). The 1st right off V. Chiavari. Clean rooms with phones, some around a small, fern-filled courtyard. Reserve with credit card or check (at least 2 weeks in advance). Singles L90,000, with bath L110,000; doubles L140,000, with bath L190,000; triples L190,000, with bath L240,000; quads L240,000, with bath 300,000. V, MC.

Albergo Abruzzi, P. della Rotonda, 69 (☎06 679 20 21). 200ft. from the Pantheon, these are indeed rooms with a view. Old-fashioned but clean. Hall bathrooms, but every room has a sink. Singles L75-105,000; doubles L120-150,000; triples L200,000.

Hotel Piccolo, V. dei Chiavari, 32 (☎06 689 23 30). Fans and phones. Breakfast L7000. Curfew 1am. Singles L100,000, with bath L120,000; doubles L120,000, with bath L160,000; triples with bath L170,000; quads with bath L180,000. V, MC, AmEx.

Hotel Navona, V. dei Sediari, 8, 1st fl. (☎06 686 42 03; fax 06 68 21 13 92, call before faxing). Take V. dei Canestrari from P. Navona, cross C. del Rinascimento, and go straight. This 16th-century Borromini building has been a *pensione* for over 150 years, counting among its guests Keats, Shelley, and the University of Alabama chapter of the ΑΠΘ fraternity. Breakfast included. Check-out 10am. Singles L140,000; doubles with bath L190,000, with A/C L220,000; triples with bath L260,000.

Albergo del Sole, V. del Biscione, 76 (☎06 68 80 68 73; fax 06 689 37 87), off Campo dei Fiori. Allegedly the oldest *pensione* in Rome. Modern rooms with phone, fan, TV, and fantastic antique furniture. Parking garage L30-40,000. Singles L110,000, with bath L130-160,000; doubles L150-170,000, with bath L190-230,000.

Hotel Mimosa, V. Santa Chiara, 61, 2nd fl. (☎06 68 80 17 53; fax 06 683 35 57), off P. della Minerva. Spacious rooms and central location offset small bathrooms. No elevator. Curfew 1am, but keys are available. Singles L110,000; doubles L150,000, with bath L170,000. Extra bed L70,000. 10% less in winter.

NEAR PIAZZA DI SPAGNA

These accommodations might run you a few thousand more *lire*, but can you really put a price tag on living but a few steps from Prada? John Keats couldn't.

Pensione Panda, V. della Croce, 35 (☎06 678 01 79; fax 06 69 94 21 51; www.webeco.it/hotelpanda). Lovely rooms, arched ceilings, and neo-Roman reliefs in some of the hallways. Enjoy the painted vaulted ceilings in the bathrooms. Checkout 11am. In high season singles L70,000, with bath L100,000; doubles L120,000, with bath L180,000; triples L180,000, with bath L210,000; quads L240,000, with bath L320,000. V, MC, AmEx.

Pensione Jonella, V. della Croce, 41 (☎06 679 79 66; email jonella@lodgingitaly.com). Quiet, roomy, and cool in summer. No reception: call ahead to arrange for someone to meet you when you arrive. Singles L100,000; doubles L120,000. Cash only.

Hotel Pensione Suisse S.A.S., V. Gregoriana, 54 (☎06 678 36 49; fax 06 678 12 58). Rooms with old-fashioned furniture, comfy beds, phone and fan. Near the wisteria-hung heights of the Steps, but away from the hubbub. In-room breakfast included. Curfew 2am. Singles L135,000, with bath L155,000; doubles L165,000, with bath L225,000; triples L285,000; quads L340,000. Half the bill may be paid by credit card. V, MC.

Hotel Boccaccio, V. del Boccaccio, 25 (☎06 488 59 62). M:A-Barberini. Wood floors, elegant decor and friendly staff. Singles L80,000; doubles L110,000, with bath L150,000; triples L140,000, with bath L180,000. V, MC, AmEx, Diner's.

BORGO AND PRATI (NEAR VATICAN CITY)

Home to lots of priests and nuns, the Vatican and environs are pretty quiet at night.

Colors, V. Boezio, 31 (☎/fax 06 6874 030). M:A-Ottaviano. Take V. Cola di Rienzo to V. Terenzio. Sporting lots of amenities and a super-cool English-speaking staff, Colors offers 20 beds in clean rooms in the elegant Prati area. Kitchen, satellite TV, hair dryers, internet (L2000 per 15min.), laundry service (L8000 per load, the best deal in town). Beautiful terrace open until 11:30pm. Credit card needed for reservations. Dorm beds L30,000; doubles L110-140,000; triples L130-170,000. Cash only.

Pensione Ottaviano, V. Ottaviano, 6 (☎06 39 73 72 53; email gi.costantini@agora.stm.it). Just north of P. del Risorgimento. Dorm rooms hold 3 to 6 beds per room. Amenities include satellite TV, individual lockers, fridges, a microwave, hot showers, free linens, and free email access for guests. Friendly Aussie and British staff and a lively backpacker clientele. Lockout 11am-2pm. No curfew. Dorm-style rooms L30,000, in winter L25,000. Doubles L90,000/L60,000; 1 triple L120,000.

Hotel Pensione Joli, V. Cola di Rienzo, 243, 6th fl. (☎06 324 18 54; fax 06 324 18 93). Winding blue-striped walls and low ceilings make you feel a little like Alice in Wonderland, if Wonderland were a *pensione* with nice beds and gorgeous views of the Vatican. All rooms with bath and phone. Breakfast included. Singles L110,000; doubles L160,000; triples L215,000; quads L270,000. V, MC.

Hotel Florida, V. Cola di Rienzo, 243 (☎06 324 18 72 or 06 324 16 08; fax 06 324 18 57), on the 2nd and 3rd floors. Floral carpets, floral bedspreads, floral wall decorations. If only we could figure out the theme. Fans, TVs, phones, and hair dryers in each room. Singles with sink L120,000, with bath L140,000; doubles with bath L180,000; triples with bath L240,000; quads with bath L280,000. V, MC, AmEx.

Hotel Lady, V. Germanico, 198, 4th fl. (☎06 324 21 12; fax 06 324 34 46). A boisterous, non-English-speaking Roman couple has been running this small *pensione* for 30 years. Phones in rooms. Singles L120,000; doubles L160,000, with bath L180,000.

TRASTEVERE

The streets of this artsy neighborhood come alive at night, and by day they are filled with markets and working-class Romans going about their business.

Hotel Trastevere, V. Luciano Manara, 25 (☎06 581 47 13; fax 06 588 10 16). Take a right off V. di Trastevere onto V. delle Fratte di Trastevere. This homey establishment overlooks colorful P. S. Cosimato in the heart of Trastevere. 9 quiet rooms with graceful furniture, bath, TV, and phone. Breakfast L10,000. Singles L120,000; doubles L150,000; triples L180,000; quads L200,000. V, MC, AmEx, Diner's.

Hotel Carmel, V. G. Mameli, 11 (☎06 580 99 21; fax 06 581 88 53; email hotelcarmel@hotmail.com). Take a right on V. E. Morosini (V. G. Mameli) off V. di Trastevere. 9 no-frills rooms with bath for reasonable prices. Breakfast included. Singles L100,000; doubles L150,000; triples L190,000; quads L220,000.

TERMINI AND SAN LORENZO

Welcome to budget traveler and backpacker central. While Termini is chock full of travelers' services, the area south of Termini is a little sketchy at night.

NORTH OF TERMINI

Pensione Fawlty Towers, V. Magenta, 39 (☎/fax 06 445 03 74; www.enjoyrome.it/ftytwhtl.htm). Exit Termini to the right from the middle concourse, cross V. Marsala onto V. Marghera, and turn right onto V. Magenta. An extremely popular 15-room hotel/hostel, Fawlty Towers never fails to satisfy its customers. The flower-filled communal terrace provides a peaceful respite from the panic of Termini. Common room with satellite TV, library, refrigerator, microwave, and free internet access. Check-out 9am for dorm rooms and 10am for private rooms. Dorm-style quads L30-35,000 per person (no children); singles L70-85,000; doubles L100,000, with shower L110,000, with bath L130,000; triples with shower L140,000, with bath L155,000.

Hotel Des Artistes, V. Villafranca, 20 (☎06 445 43 65; fax 06 446 23 68; email info@hoteldesartistes.com; www.hoteldesartistes.com). From Termini, turn left onto V. Marsala, right onto V. Vicenza, and then left onto the 5th cross-street. 3-star, 40-room hotel with a room for every budget. Clean, elegant rooms with bathrooms, safes, refrigerators, and TVs. 24hr. reception. Check-out 11am. Dorms (in rooms with 4-6 beds) L35,000; singles L70,000; doubles L110,000, with bath L170,000; triples L130,000, with bath L210,000. Winter discounts 20-30%. V, MC, AmEx.

Pensione Papa Germano, V. Calatafimi, 14a (☎06 48 69 19; fax 06 47 88 12 81; www.hotelpapagermano.it). From Termini, turn left onto V. Marsala; V. Calatafimi is the 4th cross-street on your right. 15 clean rooms (all with TV and telephone) and outstanding service. Internet access. Check-out 11am. Singles L45-60,000; doubles L70-100,000, with bath L90-130,000; triples with bath L100-150,000. V, MC.

Hotel Dolomiti and **Hotel Lachea,** V. S. Martino della Battaglia, 11 (☎06 495 72 56; fax 06 445 46 65; email dolomiti@hotel-dolomiti.it; www.hotel-dolomiti.it). From the middle concourse of Termini, exit right, turn left onto V. Marsala and right on V. Solferino (V. S. Martino della Battaglia). Breakfast L10,000. Check-out 11am. **Lachea:** singles L75-85,000; doubles L85-100,000, with bath L110-130,000; triples L110-130,000, with bath L150-170,000; quads L140-160,000, with bath L160-210,000. 5-person rooms available at a negotiable price. **Dolomiti:** singles L90-120,000; doubles L130-180,000; triples L160-210,000; quads L200-230,000. A/C L20,000 per night. V, MC.

Pensione Tizi, V. Collina, 48 (☎06 482 01 28; fax 06 474 32 66), a 10min. walk from the station. From V. XX Settembre, take V. Piave, then go left on V. Flavia. Or take bus #319 or 270 from Termini. Marble floors and inlaid ceilings adorn the spacious rooms. Breakfast L9000. Check-out 11am. Singles L70,000, with bath L90,000; doubles L90,000, with bath L110,000; triples L120,000, with bath L148,000; quads L160,000, with bath L180,000.

Hotel Castelfidardo and **Hotel Lazzari,** V. Castelfidardo, 31 (☎06 446 46 38; fax 06 494 13 78), 2 blocks off V. XX Settembre. Renovated rooms with spanking clean floors, all done up in peach and gray color schemes. Hall bathrooms shared by 3 rooms at most. Check-out 11am. Singles L70,000; doubles L95,000, with bath L120,000; triples L120,000, with bath L150,000; quads available on request. V, MC, AmEx.

Hotel Pensione Cathrine, V. Volturno, 27 (☎06 48 36 34). From Termini, exit right, and turn left onto V. Marsala (V. Volturno). Comfortable *pensione* run by friendly southern Italian woman. 2 uncommonly clean common bathrooms serve the spacious singles and doubles. Breakfast L10,000. Singles L75,000, with bath L100,000; doubles L100,000, with bath L120,000; triples with bath L160,000. *Let's Go* discount L10,000.

Hotel Adventure, V. Palestro, 88 (☎06 446 90 26; fax 06 446 00 84; email hotel.adventure@flashnet.it; www.hoteladventure.com). From Termini, cross V. Marsala onto V. Marghera, and take the 4th right onto V. Palestro. Recently renovated rooms, all with bath, satellite TV, telephone, and safe. Breakfast included. A/C L30,000. Check-out 11am. Doubles L140,000; triples L200,000. Extra bed L35,000. V, MC, AmEx.

Hotel Bolognese, V. Palestro, 15 (☎/fax 06 49 00 45). In a land of run-of-the-mill *pensioni,* this place is spruced up by the artist-owner who provides extra amenities here and there. Check-out 11am. Curfew 2am. Singles L50,000, with bath L70-80,000; doubles L80,000, with bath L120,000; triples L120,000, with bath L150,000.

Hotel Magic, V. Milazzo, 20 (☎/fax 06 495 98 80). Almost all rooms include private baths, TVs, and in-room safes. A/C L20,000. Singles L90,000; doubles L130,000; triples L180,000; quads L200-220,000. V, MC.

Hotel Baltic, V. XX Settembre, 89 (☎06 481 47 75; fax 06 48 55 09), just past the intersection with V. Palestro. 23 modern, comfortable rooms with bath, TV, and telephone. Breakfast L8000. Check-out 11am. Singles L90,000; doubles L120,000; triples L150,000; quads L195,000. Traveler's checks accepted. V, MC, AmEx.

Pensione Monaco, V. Flavia, 84 (☎/fax 06 42 01 41 80). From V. XX Settembre, turn left onto V. Quinto Sellia and right onto V. Flavia. Friendly Italian woman and English-speaking children keep these 11 sunlit rooms clean. Check-out 9am. Student discount prices: singles L55,000, with bath L70,000; doubles L80,000, with bath L100,000; triples and quads L40,000 per person. Prices about 10% lower in winter.

Pensione Piave, V. Piave, 14 (☎06 474 34 47; fax 06 487 33 60), off V. XX Settembre to the left. The cozy bathrooms shouldn't bother anyone who doesn't mind showering less than a foot away from the sink and toilet. Check-in 11:30am. Check-out 11am. Singles L65,000, with bath L95,000; doubles with bath L120,000; triples with bath L150,000; quads with bath L160-180,000. V, MC, AmEx.

Hotel Galli, V. Milazzo, 20 (☎06 445 68 59; fax 06 446 85 01). All rooms have bath, TV, mini-bar, and safe. Breakfast included. A/C L20,000. Singles L100,000; doubles L130,000; triples L180,000; quads L210,000. 10-15% lower in winter. V, MC, AmEx.

Hotel Fenicia, V. Milazzo, 20 (☎/fax 06 49 03 42; email hotel.fenicia@tiscalinet.it; www.fenicia-web-page.net). 11 sparkling, modern rooms close to Termini, all with bath and TV. A/C L20,000. Singles L85,000; doubles L130,000. Extra beds L45,000.

Pensione Ester, V. del Castro Pretorio, 25 (☎06 495 71 23). From Termini, turn right onto V. Marsala and left onto V. del Castro Pretorio. Go through the archway to the courtyard and enter the door on the right marked "C." 5 airy rooms overlooking a courtyard. 10 day max. stay. Check-out 9am. Curfew 1am. Doubles L100,000; triples L135,000.

Hotel Cervia, V. Palestro, 55 (☎06 49 10 57; fax 06 49 10 56; email hotelcervia@wnt.it). Rooms with bath include breakfast; otherwise, it's L5000. 24hr. reception. Check-out noon. Singles L70,000; doubles L90,000, with bath L140,000; triples L135,000/L210,000. V, MC, AmEx.

Hotel Marini, V. Palestro, 35 (☎06 444 00 58). This *pensione* glows with the proprietress's hospitality. All rooms have showers. Check-out 10am. Doubles L80-90,000.

Pensione Katty, V. Palestro, 35 (☎06 444 12 16). The rooms are plain but large, some with beautiful mosaic floors. Check-out 11am. L2000 key deposit. Singles L75,000, with bath L90,000; doubles L90,000, with bath L130,000; triples L120,000, with bath L150,000; quads L140,000, with bath L160,000. Discounts Nov.-Mar. Traveler's checks accepted. V, MC.

Hotel Ventura, V. Palestro, 88 (☎06 445 19 51). In a building with many other hotels, Ventura distinguishes itself through rooms with TVs, telephones, and an inordinate number of pictures. Breakfast L10,000. Doubles L70,000, with bath L80,000; triples L90,000, with bath L105,000. V, MC, AmEx.

Hotel Pensione Stella, V. Castelfidardo, 51 (☎06 444 10 78; fax 06 445 02 70), near the intersection with V. Gaeta. 19 newly renovated rooms have it all: TV, phone, luxurious bathroom, and warm teak furniture. Breakfast L10,000. Check-out 11am. Singles with bath L90,000; doubles L140,000; triples L170,000. V, MC, AmEx.

Hotel Roxena, V. Marghera, 13 (☎06 445 68 23; fax 06 445 26 29). A little drab, but a stone throw from Termini. Breakfast L10,000. Curfew 1am. 12 rooms. Doubles L80,000, with bath L110,000; triples L105,000, with bath L130,000; quads L140,000. V, MC.

SOUTH OF TERMINI (ESQUILINO)

Pensione di Rienzo, V. Principe Amedeo, 79a (☎06 446 71 31 or 06 446 69 80). Large windows overlook a courtyard. It's plain, it's cheap, and it's good. 15 rooms, some with balconies and baths. Breakfast L15,000. Check-out 10am. Singles L35-80,000, with bath up to L90,000; doubles L40-90,000, with bath up to L110,000. V, MC.

Pensione Cortorillo, V. Principe Amedeo, 79a, 5th fl. (☎06 446 69 34; fax 06 445 47 69). TV and bath in all rooms. Breakfast included. Check-out 10am. Singles L100,000; doubles L70-100,000; triples L210,000; quads L280,000. V, MC, AmEx, Diner's.

Hotel Kennedy, V. F. Turati, 62-64 (☎06 446 53 73; fax 06 446 54 17; email hotelkennedy@micanet.it). Ask not what you can do for your hotel, ask what your hotel can do for you. Classical music in the bar, leather couches, a library, and a large color TV in the lounge. Private bath, satellite TV, phone, and A/C. Breakfast included. Check-out 11am. Reservations by fax only. Singles L105,000; doubles L169-179,000; triples L299,000. 10% discount with *Let's Go.* V, MC, AmEx, Diner's.

Hotel Il Castello, V. V. Amedeo II, 9 (☎06 77 20 40 36; fax 06 70 49 00 68; www.ilcastello.com). M:A-Manzoni. Far beyond Termini, but well within the backpacker's budget. Walk down V. S. Quintino and take the 1st left. Housed in a castle with small white rooms and eager serving knaves. Continental breakfast L5000. Check-out 10:30am. Dorms L30,000; singles L50-60,000; doubles L70-80,000, with bath L120-130,000; triples L105,000. V, MC.

Hotel Orlanda, V. Principe Amedeo, 76, 3rd fl. (☎06 488 01 24; fax 06 488 01 83), at V. Gioberti. All 23 rooms have a sink, some hair dryers. Breakfast included. 24hr. reception. Check-out 10am. A/C L20,000. Singles L45-80,000, with bath L50-120,000; doubles L70-120,000, with bath L90-180,000; triples L90-150,000, with bath L120-220,000; quads L120-180,000, with bath L160-280,000. V, MC, AmEx, Diner's.

Hotel Giu' Giu', V. del Viminale, 8 (☎06 482 77 34; fax 06 48 91 26 16), in an elegant but fading *palazzo.* Breakfast L10,000. Check-out 10am. Singles L65,000; doubles L100,000, with bath L110,000; triples with bath L150,000; quads with bath L195,000.

Hotel Selene, V. del Viminale, 8 (☎06 482 44 60; fax 06 47 82 19 77). The parrot behind the reception desk speaks flawless Italian and will continue to do so even if you inform him that you don't understand. 27 clean rooms with bath, TV, and telephone. Renovations planned for winter 2001 may drive prices up—call ahead. Breakfast included. Singles L90,000; doubles L140,000; triples L190,000. V, MC, AmEx.

Hotel Sweet Home, V. Principe Amedeo, 47 (☎/fax 06 488 09 54). At V. D. Manin. Welcome to the Hotel California...oh wait, that's downstairs. Enjoy Home Sweet Home's soothing green decor or watch the goldfish. Such a lovely place... Check-out 11am. Singles L80-100,000, with bath L100-120,000; doubles L120-150,000, with bath L150-180,000; triples L120-150,000, with bath L180-210,000. V, MC, DC, AmEx.

Hotel Teti, V. Principe Amedeo, 76 (☎/fax 06 48 90 40 88; email hotelteti@iol.it). Take the stairs at the end of the courtyard. Spacious rooms, but costly for the neighborhood—all with satellite TV, shower, and telephone. Breakfast L8000. Check-out 11am. Singles L90-140,000; doubles L120-200,000; triples L150-240,000; quads L160-290,000. 10-15% discount for students. V, MC, AmEx, Diner's.

WEST OF TERMINI

Hotel San Paolo, V. Panisperna, 95 (☎06 474 52 13; fax 06 474 52 18; email hsanpaolo@tin.it). Exiting Termini, turn left onto V. Cavour. After you pass Santa Maria Maggiore, bear right onto V. di S. Maria Maggiore (V. Panisperna). 23 tranquil, whimsically decorated rooms in a bright little *palazzo.* Hall baths are clean and private. Breakfast L10,000. Check-out 10:30am. Singles L75,000; doubles L100,000, with bath L140,000; triples L135,000; 6- to 10-person suite L50,000 per person. V, MC, AmEx.

Pensione Sandy, V. Cavour, 136 (☎06 488 45 85; www.sandyhostel.com), past Santa Maria Maggiore. No sign; look for the Hotel Valle next door. On the 4th floor, no elevator (ouch). Under the same ownership as Fawlty Towers and run by Slim, a Roman who is proud to say he learned his English from MTV. Free internet access and individual lockers in each room. Simple, hostel-style rooms, usually for 2-4 people, in a central location. In summer L30,000; in winter L25,000.

ALTERNATIVE ACCOMMODATIONS

INSTITUTIONAL ACCOMMODATIONS

Rome's only HI-affiliated hostel, **Ostello del Foro Italico (HI),** V. delle Olimpiadi, 61 (M:A-Ottaviano), is certainly not the cream of the crop; you should only consider this very, very inconveniently located hostel if central Rome's many hostels are completely full. Exit onto V. Barletta and take bus #32 to Cadorna (get off when you see pink Foro Italico buildings and an obelisk). The hostel has 350 beds in six-to 12-person single-sex rooms. (☎06 323 62 67 or 06 323 62 79; fax 06 324 26 13. Small continental breakfast and hot showers included. Sizeable lunch and dinner available. Reception 2pm-midnight. Check-out 7-9am. Lockout 9am-2pm. Strictly enforced midnight curfew. L25,000 with HI card (buy one at the desk for L30,000); L30,000 without.)

CAMPING

In August, when most Italians go on vacation, arrive early (well before 11am) to secure a spot. Rates average L10,000 per person and another L8000 per car. The **Touring Club Italiano** publishes an annual directory of all camping sites in Italy, *Campeggi in Italia*, available in bookstores throughout Italy. Camping on beaches, roads, and inconspicuous plots is illegal. For legal camping, **Seven Hills Village,** V. Cassia, 1216 is 8km north of Rome. Take bus #907 from M:A-Cipro-Musei Vaticani, or bus #201 from P. Mancini. Ask where to get off—it's 3-4km past the GRA (the big highway that circles the city). From the stop, follow the country road about 1km until you see the sign. Spend a lazy pool side afternoon and dance the night away in the disco. It houses a bar, market, restaurant, and *pizzeria. Lire* are not allowed; buy a Seven Hills card for use all over the campground. There is a doctor on hand during the day. (☎06 303 31 08 26; fax 06 303 31 00 39. Daily Vatican shuttles leave at 8 and 9:30am; round-trip L6000. Check-in 7am-11pm. Open late Mar. to late Oct. L15,000 per person, L9000 per tent, L9000 per car. Camper L16,000; bungalow L90-150,000.)

FOOD

Ancient Roman dinners were lavish 10 hour affairs. Food orgies went on *ad nauseam*, literally—after gorging themselves, guests would retreat to a special room called the *vomitorium*, throw it all up, and return to the party. Meals in Rome are still lengthy affairs, although they generally involve less vomiting. Restaurants tend to close between 3 and 7pm, so plan accordingly.

RESTAURANTS BY LOCATION

ANCIENT CITY

The area around the Forum and the Colosseum is home to some of Italy's finest tourist traps. If you forgot to pack a lunch and the stroll to the Centro Storico seems too long and hot, there are a few places that offer tasty meals at fair prices

Taverna dei Quaranta, V. Claudia, 24 (☎06 700 05 50), off P. del Colosseo. Shaded by the trees of the Celian Park, outdoor dining at this corner *taverna* is a must. The menu changes daily, and in summer it often features delights such as *fiori di zucca* (fried zucchini blossoms; L8500). Half-liter of house wine L5000. Cover L3000. Open daily noon-3:30pm and 7:45pm-midnight. V, MC, AmEx, Diner's.

I Buoni Amici, V. Aleardo Aleardi, 4 (☎06 70 49 19 93). From the Colosseum, take V. Labicana to V. Merulana. Turn right, then left on V. A. Aleardi. The cheap and excellent food is worth the walk. Try the *linguine all'astice* (linguini with crayfish sauce; L10,000). Cover L2500. Open M-Sa noon-3pm and 7-11:30pm. V, MC, AmEx, Diner's.

ROME

CENTRO STORICO

PIAZZA NAVONA

There are plenty of delicious, inexpensive *trattorie* and pizzerias near P. Navona, but it often takes a short stroll to reach them. A walk down V. del Governo Vecchio reveals some of the best restaurants in the city. No matter where you eat, you can expect to be subjected to numerous street performances.

Pizzeria Pentola, V. Metastasio, 21 (☎06 68 80 26 07), off P. di Campo Marzio. Ignore the regular menu: the delicious pizza (L8-16,000) is where it's at. Try the *pizza dello chef* (spinach and parmesan; L13,000). Open daily noon-11pm. V, MC.

Pizzeria Baffetto, V. del Governo Vecchio, 114 (☎06 686 16 17), at V. Sora. Once a meeting place for 60s radicals, Baffetto now overflows with hungry Romans. Always crowded. Pizza L8-14,000. Cover L1000. Open M-F noon-3pm and 7:30pm-1am, Sa-Su noon-3pm and 7:30pm-2am.

Pizzeria Corallo, V. del Corallo 10-11 (☎06 68 30 77 03), off V. del Governo Vecchio near P. del Fico. For those who refuse to eat anywhere that doesn't have outdoor tables with red-checkered tablecloths and a metal palm tree, this local favorite might be the only option. Pizza L8-15,000. Open Tu-Su 7pm-1am. Reservations taken. V, MC, AmEx.

Piedra del Sol, V. Rosini, 6 (☎06 687 36 41), off V. di Campo Marzio. Del Sol offers a distinctly Italian take on Mexican cooking. Decor from Aztec to Zapata. Try *Chimichangas del Sol* (L12,000). Chips and salsa L3000 per person. Margaritas L35,000 per liter. Open Sept.-July daily 12:30-3pm and 7:30pm-2am. V, MC, AmEx.

CAMPO DEI FIORI AND THE JEWISH GHETTO

While you might get yourself horribly lost in the labyrinth of crooked streets and alleyways that surround the Campo, you will certainly find several exceptional *ristoranti* that can provide sustenance until the search party arrives. Across V. Arenula from the Campo, the proud community of the former Jewish Ghetto serves up traditional Roman-Jewish cuisine as it has for hundreds of years.

Trattoria da Sergio, V. delle Grotte, 27 (☎06 654 66 69). Take V. dei Giubbonari and take your 1st right. Just far enough away from the Campo to keep away the tourists, Sergio offers honest-to-God Roman ambience and hearty portions of great food. Open M-Sa 12:30-3pm and 7pm-12:30am.

Trattoria Da Luigi, P. S. Cesarini 24 (☎06 686 59 46), near Chiesa Nuova. Enjoy inventive cuisine such as *tagliolini* with shrimp, asparagus, and tomato (L13,000), as well as simple dishes like *Vitello con funghi* (veal with mushrooms; L15,000). Great *antipasti* buffet. Bread L2000. Open Tu-Su 7pm-midnight.

Ristorante da Giggetto, V. del Portico d'Ottavio, 21-22 (☎06 686 11 05). Rightfully famous but increasingly pricey, Giggetto serves up some of the finest Roman cooking known to man. Be daring and go for the fried brains with mushrooms and zucchini (L20,000). If your food isn't spicy, pepper it with free peppers picked from the potted pepper plants. Cover L3000. Open Tu-Su 12:30-3pm and 7:30-11pm. V, MC, AmEx.

Al 16, V. del Portico d'Ottavio, 16 (☎06 687 47 22), around the corner from the Teatro di Marcello. This neighborhood favorite run by neighborhood guys offers traditional dishes alongside delicious house specialties like *pennette al 16* (with eggplant, sausage, and tomato; L13,000). Be fearless and try the *coda alla vaccinara* (oxtail stew; L16,000). Cover L2500. Open W-M 12:30-3pm and 7:30-11pm. V, MC, AmEx.

La Pollarola, P. Pollarola, 24-25 (☎06 68 80 16 54), off V. del Biscione on the way into Campo dei Fiori. As the Romans say, *"si mangia bene e si spende giusto"* ("one eats well and pays a fair price"). Enjoy typical Roman dishes like *spaghetti alla carbonara* (with egg and *pancetta* ham; L10,000). Open M-Sa noon-3:30pm and 7:30pm-midnight. No service charge. V, MC, AmEx.

L'Insalata Ricca, Largo di Chiavari, 85 (☎06 68 80 36 56). Off C. V. Emanuele II near P. S. Andrea della Valle. You like salads, damn it, so come here. What kind of salad would you like? They have *all* of them (L10-16,000). There are six others around town: P. Pasquino, 72; V. del Gazometro, 62; P. Albania, 3; V. Polesine, 16; P. Risorgimento, 5; and V. F. Grinaldi, 52. Open daily 12:30-3:15pm and 6:45-11:15pm. V, MC.

Giardino del Melograno, V. dei Chiodaroli, 16-18 (☎06 68 80 34 23), off V. dei Chiavari. A renowned Chinese restaurant. The vast menu includes a fine dumpling appetizer (L5000). Tourist *menù* (appetizer, entree, and drink) L13,000. Open Th-Tu noon-3pm and 7-11:30pm. V, MC, AmEx.

Trattoria Arnaldo ai Satiri, V. di Grotta Pinta, 8 (☎06 686 19 15). Take Largo dei Chiavari off C. V. Emanuele and turn right on V. di Grotta Pinta. Try the spicy *Fusili con melanzane* (pasta with eggplant; L12,000). Glowing with red light bulbs and candles, the interior seems like a cross between a bordello and a darkroom. Outdoor dining in summer. Open W-M 12:30-3pm and 7:30pm-1am. V, MC, AmEx.

Trattoria La Moretta, V. Monserrato, 158 (☎06 686 19 00). From Campo dei Fiori, take V. dei Pellegrino to the *piazza* where it turns into V. dei Banchi Vecchi. Offering a lovely view of the river, La Moretta serves pasta and pizza to lost tourists and hungry locals. Open M-Sa noon-3:30pm and 7pm-midnight.

PIAZZA DI SPAGNA

Though the Spanish Steps area may seem very different from the less affluent environs of Termini, there is one big similarity—lots of lousy food. The irony of it all is that while a mediocre meal at Termini might set you back 15,000 *lire*, the same food here will cost twice as much. Here are some exceptions:

Osteria dell'Ingegno, P. di Pietra (☎06 678 06 62), between the Trevi Fountain and the Pantheon. A refreshingly modern take on timeless Italian cuisine in a comfortable, upscale setting. Try the superb *risotto matecato alle punte di asparagi* (risotto with asparagus tips, saffron, and parmesan; L20,000); you also won't regret the daring *crema fredda di melanzane e cerfoglio allo yogurt* (cold eggplant soup with mint and yogurt; L16,000). *Secondi* (L20-30,000) include a delicious *tartara di salmone e spigola* (tartar of fresh salmon and sea bass; L24,000). Huge salads L16-20,000. Service not included. Open M-Sa noon-3pm and 7:30pm-midnight. V, MC, AmEx, Diner's.

Pizza Re, V. di Ripetta, 14 (☎06 321 14 68), a block from P. del Popolo on the left. Even though it's a chain, Pizza Re serves some of the best Neopolitan pizza (L12-18,000) in town. Service is fast and courteous, and the A/C feels so good. Save L3000 if you order in person for take-out. Open M-Sa 12:45-3:30pm and 7:30pm-12:30am, Su 7:30pm-12:30am. Closed for 2 weeks in mid-Aug. V, MC, AmEx, Diner's.

Trattoria da Settimio all'Arancio, V. dell'Arancio, 50-52 (☎06 687 61 19). Take V. dei Condotti from P. di Spagna; take the 1st right after V. del Corso, then the 1st left. Arrive early to avoid the throngs of natives who come for the great service and tasty seafood. Excellent grilled *calamari* L18,000. Fresh fish Tu and F. Cover L2000. Open M-Sa 12:30-3pm and 7:30-11:30pm. Reservations accepted. V, MC, DC, AmEx.

Centro Macrobiotico Italiano-Naturist Club, V. della Vite, 14, 4th fl. (☎06 679 25 09), just off V. del Corso. The Naturist Club offers up extremely fresh, well-seasoned macrobiotic fare at low prices in its breezy attic restaurant. Probably the only restaurant in Rome where they offer ground sesame seeds with salad. Buffet only in the afternoon, but evening brings a full restaurant. Health food store downstairs. *Primi* L10-12,000, *secondi* L12-18,000. Open M-F noon-3:30pm and 7:30-11pm. V, MC.

Birreria Peroni, V. S. Marcello, 19 (☎06 679 53 10), near P. di Trevi. You never thought you'd find an entire shop dedicated to Peroni? Think again. Though the food is nothing to write home about, it is quite inexpensive (*bruschetta* L2500; *wurstel* L8-11,000) and the beer is abundant and cheap (small cups L3500, L12,000 per liter). Cover L2000. Open M-W 12:30-11:30pm, Tu and F 12:30pm-midnight, Sa 7pm-midnight.

Sogo Asahi, V. di Propaganda, 22 (☎06 6786 093). This stylish little Japanese restaurant serves particularly tasty miso soup and surprisingly good sushi. *Nigiri* sushi L4-19,000, 6-piece *maki* plates L12-15,000. Entrees L15-25,000. Open M-Sa noon-2:30pm and 7-10:30pm. V, MC, AmEx.

BORGO AND PRATI (NEAR VATICAN CITY)

The streets near the Vatican are paved with bars and *pizzerie* that serve mediocre sandwiches at hiked-up prices. For far better and much cheaper food, head to the residential district a few blocks north and east of the Vatican Museums.

Franchi, V. Cola di Rienzo, 200-204 (☎06 687 46 51). Franchi ("Frankie") has been serving the happy folks of Prati superb sandwiches and other luxurious picnic supplies for nearly 50 years, and not an unsatisfied customer yet. Open M-Sa 8:15am-9pm.

Pizza Re, V. Oslavia, 39 (☎06 372 11 73). Called by many the best pizza in Rome. Wonderful desserts, from mousse to *tiramisù*. See p. 442. Dinner L7-18,000. Open M-Sa noon-3:30pm, daily 7:30-11pm. V, MC, AmEx.

TRASTEVERE

By day, Trastevere's cobblestone streets rumble only with the sounds of children and Vespas, but when night falls, P. di Santa Maria di Trastevere is packed with expatriate hippies and their dogs, howling along with out-of-tune guitars.

Pizzeria San Calisto, P. S. Calisto, 9a (☎06 581 82 56), off P. S. Maria in Trastevere. Massive pizza (L9-15,000) roams free at this busy neighborhood pizzeria. The *bruschetta* (L3-4000) alone is worth a postcard home. Open Tu-Su 7pm-midnight. V, MC.

Augusto, P. de' Rienzi, 15 (☎06 580 37 98). North of P. S. Maria in Trastevere. Enjoy the daily pasta specials at lunch (around L8000), and the *pollo arrosto con patate* (L10,500). The homemade desserts are out of this world, but you need to be assertive to get service. Open M-F 12:30-3pm and 8-11pm, Sa 12:30-3pm. Closed Aug.

Ristorante al Fontanone, P. Trilussa, 46 (☎06 581 73 12). North of P. S. Maria in Trastevere. Small restaurant with traditional Roman food, including *rigatoni con pajata* (L13,000). Open W-Su noon-2pm and 7-11pm. Closed mid-Aug. to early Sept. V, MC.

Il Tulipano Nero, V. Roma Libera, 15 (☎06 581 83 09). Take V. de Trastevere and turn right on V. E. Morosini. Some of the more innovative pizzas in Rome. Almost removed from the nighttime chaos of P. S. Maria in Trastevere, this pizzeria is smack in the middle of the nighttime chaos of P. Cosimato. Huge portions. Open Tu-Su 6pm-2am.

Osteria der Belli, P. Sant'Apollonia, 11 (☎06 580 37 82), off V. della Lungaretta near P. S. Maria in Trastevere. A bustling *trattoria* specializing in Sardinian cooking, especially seafood. Nice outdoor seating area. Excellent grilled *calamari* L20,000. Cover L2000. Open Tu-Su 11:30am-2:30pm and 7:30-10:30pm.

TERMINI AND SAN LORENZO

You're near the train station, hungry, and in a hurry. This is no reason to subject yourself to the nightmare of a shady tourist trap offering a L10,000 "quick lunch."

La Cantinola da Livio, V. Calabria, 26 (☎06 42 82 05 19). From P. della Repubblica, walk down V. V. E. Orlando, turn right on V. XX Settembre, take the 5th left onto V. Piave, and then the 4th left onto V. Calabria. This lively, pink-walled establishment specializes in seafood: the *spaghetti alla cantinola* (with seafood, caviar, tomato, and cream; L12,000) is transcendent. If it's a special night, one of the nervous-looking live lobsters can be yours for a whopping L120,000. Cover L1500. Open M-Sa 12:30-3pm and 7:20-11:30pm. Closed 1st 3 weeks of Aug. V, MC, AmEx.

Africa, V. Gaeta, 26-28 (☎06 494 10 77), near P. Indipendenza. Decked out in yellow and black, Africa continues its 20-year tradition of serving excellent Ethiopian food. The meat-filled *sambusas* (L4500) are a flavorful starter; both the *zighini beghi* (roasted lamb in a spicy sauce; L12,000) and the *misto vegetariano* (mixed veggie dishes; L11,000) make fantastic entrees. Cover L1500. Open M-Sa 8pm-midnight. V, MC.

Trattoria da Bruno, V. Varese, 29 (☎06 49 04 03). From V. Marsala, next to the train station, walk 3 blocks down V. Milazzo and turn right onto V. Varese. Start with the *tortellini con panna e funghi* (with cream and mushrooms; L10,000) or the tasty homemade *gnocchi* (L10,000) and continue with the delicious *ossobuco* (L13,000). Bruno, the owner, makes créches, and he's very good at what he does: note the picture of him shaking hands with the Pope upon presentation of one of his little masterworks. Open daily noon-3:30pm and 7-10:15pm. Closed Aug. V, AmEx.

Gold Bar, P. del Viminale, 1 (☎06 481 92 27), just off V. A. Depretis. Packed with Romans on lunch breaks, this *tavola calda* serves excellent fare at very reasonable prices. You won't find a seat during peak hours, though, and don't be surprised if the busy staffers get a little surly at your bad Italian. Good *panini* about L3500; entrees around L4-5000 per plate. Open M-F noon-3pm.

Pizzeria da Giggetto, V. Alessandria, 43 (☎06 854 34 90). From Porta Pia, turn right onto C. Italia and right onto V. Alessandria. Popular *bruschetta* with salmon (L6000) and superlative pizza (L8-16,000). Should you have hunger fit for a king, try the *pizze giganti* (L11-30,000). Be sure to give the automatic sliding bathroom door a whirl. Expect a wait on weekends. Open M and W-Sa 7pm-1am. Closed in Aug. V, MC, AmEx.

Ristorante da Lisa, V. Foscolo, 16-18 (☎06 73 00 27), south of P. V. Emanuele II. A homey kosher restaurant with an eclectic selection of the owner's favorite art. The food provides a twist on standard Italian fare and is cooked by the owner and his wife on demand. Try *burik con patate* (potatoes, cinnamon, and parsley wrapped in a crepe; L3000) or *kuskus bianco* (L5000). Open Su-F 1-3pm and 7-11pm.

SAN LORENZO

Though *Let's Go* doesn't recommend Communist-watching, this would be the place to do it if we did (wink wink). San Lorenzo is Rome's university district, and thank god, poor students with discriminating palates have ensured that nearly every eatery here is good and cheap. The walk from Termini may be a little uncomfortable if you're alone at night. From Termini, walk south on V. Pretoriano to P. Tiburtino, or take bus #492 to P. Verano.

Il Pulcino Ballerino, V. degli Equi, 66-68 (☎06 494 12 55), off V. Tiburtina. An artsy atmosphere with cuisine to match. The ever-changing menu includes dishes like *tagliolini al limone* (pasta in a lemon cream sauce; L12,000) and *risotto* (L10-12,000). You also can skip the chef and prepare your own meal on a heated stone. Cover L1000. Open M-Sa 1-3:30pm and 8pm-midnight. Closed 1st week of Aug. V, MC, AmEx.

Arancia Blu, V. dei Latini, 65 (☎06 445 41 05), off V. Tiburtina. This elegant little vegetarian restaurant is technically a cultural association, so you'll have to write out a free membership card. Don't worry, though—once some of the excellent, creative food on the menu arrives, it'll be worth all the paperwork. Enjoy elaborate dishes like *tonnarelli con pecorino romano e tartufo* (pasta with sheep cheese and truffles; L12,000). Extensive wine list. Open M-F noon-3pm and 7-11pm, Sa-Su 7-11pm.

Il Capellaio Matto, V. dei Marsi, 25. From V. Tiburtina, take the 4th right off V. degli Equi. Vegetarians, rejoice! This offbeat place offers pasta and rice dishes like *risotto al pepe verde* (with green peppercorn; L9000), imaginative salads like *insalata di rughetta, pere, e parmigiano* (arugula, pears, and parmesan; L7000), and a variety of crepes (L7-9000). Plenty of meat dishes, too. Cover L1500. Open W-M 8pm-midnight.

Armando, P. Tiburtino, 5 (☎06 4959 270). A great place to go with choosy eaters; the menu contains everything from *fettucine al nero di seppia* (with squid ink; L15,000) to *penne agli asparagi* (with asparagus; L12,000). Bread L4000. Service L1000 per person. Open Th-Tu 12:30-3:30pm and 7:30pm-2am. Reservations accepted.

TESTACCIO

Once home to a giant slaughterhouse, this working-class southern neighborhood is the seat of many excellent restaurants serving traditional Roman fare, as well as the center of Roman nightlife. True to their roots, Testaccio eateries offer food made of just about every animal part imaginable.

Pizzeria Ficini, V. Luca della Robbia, 23 (☎06 574 30 17). Take V. Luigi Vanvitelli off V. Marmorata, then take your 1st left. A no-frills pizzeria befitting this working-class community. They don't even hand you a menu; they just assume you've looked outside and know what you want. Pizzas (L6-8000) are delicious and dirt cheap. *Calzone* L8000. Wine L6000 per liter. Open Sept.-July Tu-Su 6-11:30pm.

Luna Piena, V. Luca della Robbia, 15-17 (☎06 575 02 79). Tastefully decorated with wood paneling and elegant paintings. Savor the stupendous *carpaccio di salmone* appetizer (L10,000) or the excellent *rigatoni con pagliata* (L10,000). Open Th-Tu noon-3pm and 7:30-11:30pm. V, MC, AmEx, Diner's.

Non Solo Pizza, V. Benjamino Franklin, 11 (☎06 568 50 31). Not only pizza, but kebab! Very popular with area students. Open 6:30pm-12:30am; in winter also noon-4:30pm.

Trattoria da Bucatino, V. Luca della Robbia, 84-86 (☎06 574 68 86). Take V. Luigi Vanvitelli off V. Marmorata, then the 1st left. A friendly neighborhood *trattoria* serving a variety of dishes involving animal entrails, as well as pasta (around L8000), pizza (only in the evenings; L7-14,000), and seafood, including *cosse alla marinara* (L10,000), more mussels than anyone in their right mind could hope to eat. Cover L2000. Open Sept.-July Tu-Su 12:30-3:30pm and 6:30-11:30pm. V, MC, DC.

DESSERTS

Cheap *gelato* is as plentiful on Roman streets as pairs of leather pants. Unfortunately, often you get what you pay for. Look for *gelato* with very muted (hence natural) colors, or try some of our favorite *gelaterie* and other sweetshops.

San Crispino, V. della Panetteria, 42 (☎06 679 39 24), near P. di Trevi. Positively the world's best *gelato.* Don't miss the meringue, armagnac, and grapefruit flavors. No cones; the proprietors claim that they "interfere with the purity of the product." Cups L3-10,000. Also at V. Acaia, 56 (☎06 70 45 04 12), south of the center in Appio. Both locations open M and W-Th noon-12:30am, F-Sa noon-1:30am, Su noon-midnight.

Tre Scalini, P. Navona, 30 (☎06 68 80 19 96). This chic, old-fashioned spot is famous for its *tartufo,* a hunk of truffled chocolate ice cream rolled in chocolate shavings (L5000 at the bar, L11,000 sitting). Bar open Th-Tu 9am-1:30am; pricey restaurant open Th-Tu 12:30-3:30pm and 7:30-9pm.

Giolitti, V. degli Uffici del Vicario, 40 (☎06 699 12 43), near the Pantheon. An old-fashioned ice cream shop, Giolitti makes wonderful *gelato* in dozens of flavors. Fashionably no frills staff doesn't have much patience with *turisti;* pay and get a receipt 1st; choose your flavors before you step up to the bar. Very festive and crowded at night. Cones L3-5000. Open May-Oct. daily 9am-1am; Nov.-Apr. Tu-Su 9am-1am. V, MC, AmEx, Diner's.

Forno del Ghetto, V. Portico d'Ottavia, 1 (☎06 687 86 37). This unmarked pastry bakery deep in the Jewish Ghetto serves fabulous blueberry pies, heavy fruitcake-like bars of dough and figs, buttery cookies, and chocolate and pudding concoctions at excellent prices. Takeout only. Open Su-Th 8am-8pm, F 8am-5:30pm. Closed Jewish holidays.

ENOTECHE (WINE BARS)

Roman wine bars, often tucked away in the corners of small *piazze*, range from laid-back and local to chic and international. Have a bite to eat and a delicious glass of wine without dealing with the unrefined drinkers of the pub scene.

Trimani Wine Bar, V. Cernaia, 37b (☎06 446 96 30), near Termini, perpendicular to V. Volturno (V. Marsala). Excellent food at good prices. Pastas (L12,000), filling quiches (try the spiny lobster and leek quiche; L9000), smoked fish, impressive cheese board, and desserts worth writing home about (L9-12,000). The ricotta pie with orange sauce is particularly heavenly (L10,000). Wines from L3500 a glass. Open M-Sa 11am-3:30pm and 6pm-12:30am. Reservations recommended for dinner. V, MC, AmEx.

La Bottega del Vino da Anacleto Bleve, V. S. Maria del Pianto, 9a-11 (☎06 686 59 70). Wonderful light meals of pasta (L9-12,000) and a range of French and Italian cheeses, smoked fish, cured meats, and creative salads. Good wine list. Glasses begin at L4000. Open Tu and Sa 12:45-3pm, W-F 12:45-3pm and 8-10pm. V, MC, DC, AmEx.

Bar Da Benito, V. dei Falegnami, 14 (☎06 686 15 08), off P. Mattei in the Jewish Ghetto. You can't get more authentic than this: a tiny shop lined with bottles and hordes of hungry workmen. One hot pasta is prepared each day (L6000), along with delicious *secondi* like *prosciutto* with vegetables (L8000) or smoked salmon with potatoes and vegetables (L8000). Open Sept.-July M-Sa 6am-8pm. Lunch served noon-3:30pm.

SIGHTS

Rome wasn't built in a day, and it's not likely that you'll see any substantial portion of it in 24 hours either. Ancient temples, medieval churches, Renaissance basilicas, Baroque fountains, and 19th- and 20th-century museums all cluster together in a city bursting with masterpieces from every era of Western civilization. No other city can claim enough nooks and crannies to cram in Rome's 981 churches and 280 fountains. From Etruscan busts to modern canvases, there is more than enough in Rome to captivate visitors for months, even years, on end.

THE ANCIENT CITY

THE ROMAN FORUM

Main entrance: V. dei Fori Imperiali (between P. Venezia and the Colosseum). Other entrances are opposite the Colosseum (from here, you can reach the Palatine Hill, too) and at the Clivus Capitolinus, near P. del Campidoglio. M:B-Colosseo, or bus to P. Venezia. Open in summer M-Sa 9am-7pm, Su 9am-1pm; in winter M-Sa 9am-1hr. before sunset, Su 9am-1hr. before sunset; sometimes closes M-F by 3pm, Su and holidays by noon. Free. Guided tour with archaeologist L6000; audioguide Forum tour L7000 in English. Both available at main entrance.

The Forum was originally a low marshland prone to flooding from the Tiber. Rome's Iron Age inhabitants (1000-900 BC) eschewed its low, unhealthy swampiness in favor of the Palatine Hill, descending here only to bury their dead. In the 7th and 8th centuries BC, Etruscans and Greeks used the Forum as a weekly market. The people who would soon be known as the Romans founded a thatched-hut shantytown on the site of the Forum in 753 BC, when Romulus and Sabine leader Titus Tatius met to end the war triggered by the famous rape of the Sabine women. Now mostly in crumbling ruins, the Forum bears witness to many centuries of civic building, most excavated at random and in a confusing jumble. The entrance ramp to the Forum leads to the **Via Sacra,** the oldest street in Rome, near the area once known as the **Civic Forum.** The other sections of the Ancient Forum are the **Market Square,** the **Lower Forum,** the **Upper Forum,** the **Velia,** and the **Palatine Hill.**

ROME

THE CIVIC FORUM. The **Basilica Aemilia,** built in 179 BC, housed the guild of the *argentarii* (money changers). It was rebuilt several times after fires, particularly the one started by Alaric and his merry band of Goths in AD 410; in the pavement you can still see bronze marks from the melted coins that the *argentarii* lost in these blazes. Next to the Basilica Aemilia stands the **Curia,** or Senate House, one of the oldest buildings in the Forum. It was converted to a church in 630 and restored by Mussolini. The Curia also houses the **Plutei of Trajan,** two parapets that depict the burning of the tax registers and the distribution of food to poor children. The broad space in front of the Curia was the **Comitium,** or assembly place, where male citizens came to vote and representatives of the people gathered for public discussion. This space was also home to the Twelve Tables, bronze tablets upon which the first codified laws of the Republic were inscribed. Bordering the Comitium is the large brick **Rostrum,** or speaker's platform, erected by Julius Caesar just before his death in 44 BC. Augustus's rebellious daughter Julia is said to have voiced her dissenting opinion here by engaging in amorous activities with some of her father's enemies (on the very spot where Augustus had proclaimed his new legislation promoting family values). The hefty **Arch of Septimius Severus,** to the right of the Rostrum, was dedicated in AD 203 to celebrate that emperor's victories in the Middle East. Severus's son and successor, Caracalla, refusing to share power, murdered his brother Geta and scraped his name and portrait off the arch.

THE MARKET SQUARE. A number of shrines and sacred precincts, including the **Lapis Niger** (Black Stone), once graced the square in front of the Curia. It was in this square that a group of senators murdered Julius Caesar. Below the Lapis Niger rest the underground ruins of a 6th-century BC altar, along with a pyramidal pillar where the oldest known Latin inscription in Rome warns the public against defiling the shrine. In the square the **Three Sacred Trees** of Rome—olive, fig, and grape—have been replanted by the Italian state. On the other side, a circular tufa basin recalls the **Lacus Curtius,** the chasm into which the legendary Roman warrior Marcus Curtius threw himself in 362 BC to seal the occult fissure and save the city. The newest part of the Forum (aside from the Neoclassical info booth) is the **Column of Phocas,** erected in 608 for the visiting Byzantine emperor, Phocas.

LOWER FORUM. The three great temples of the lower Forum (to Saturn, the emperor Vespatian, and Concord) have been closed off during excavations and restoration; however, the eight columns of the **Temple of Saturn** have at last shed their scaffolding cloak. Though actually built in the early 5th century BC, Saturn's temple has its mythological origins in the Golden Age of Rome. From these mythological beginnings, the temple became the site of Saturnalia, a raucous Roman winter bash where class and social distinctions were forgotten, masters served slaves, and all was permitted. Around the corner, rows of deserted column bases are all that remain of the **Basilica Julia,** a courthouse, built by Julius Caesar in 54 BC. Look for inscribed grids and circles in the steps where anxious Romans, waiting their turn to go before the judge, played an ancient version of Chutes and Ladders. At the far end of the Basilica Julia, three white marble columns and a shred of architrave mark the massive podium of the recently restored **Temple of Castor and Pollux.** According to legend, the twin gods Castor and Pollux helped the Romans defeat the rival Etruscans at the Battle of Lake Regillus (496 BC). Legend says that immediately after the battle, the twins appeared in the Forum to water their horses at the nearby **Basin of Juturna** *(Lacus Juturnae)*. Down the road from the Temple of Castor and Pollux is the rectangular base of the **Temple of the Deified Julius,** which Augustus built in 29 BC to honor his murdered adoptive father and, incidentally, to proclaim himself the nephew of a god. In his own modest glory, Augustus built the **Arch of Augustus,** which framed the V. Sacra. The circular building behind the Temple of the Deified Julius is the restored **Temple of Vesta,** dating back to the time of the Etruscans. In this temple, the Vestal Virgins tended the city's eternal, sacred fire, keeping it continuously lit for more than a thousand years. Within one of the secret rooms of the temple, where only the Vestal Virgins were permitted to enter, stood the **Palladium,** the small statue of Minerva that Aeneas was said to have taken from Troy to Italy. Across the square from the Temple of Vesta lies the triangular **Regia,** office of the Pontifex Maximus, Rome's high priest and titular ancestor of the Pope.

THE UPPER FORUM. The **House of the Vestal Virgins,** shaded by the Palatine Hill, occupied the sprawling complex of rooms and courtyards behind the Temple of Vesta. For 30 years, the six virgins who officiated over Vesta's rites, each ordained at the age of seven, lived in spacious seclusion here above the din of the Forum. As long as they kept their vows of chastity, the Vestal Virgins were among the most respected people in Ancient Rome. Not only were they the only women allowed to walk unaccompanied in the Forum, they also possessed the right to pardon condemned prisoners. This esteem, however, had its price; a virgin who strayed from celibacy was buried alive with a loaf of bread and a candle—these useless tokens would allow her to survive long enough to contemplate her sins. Statues of the priestesses, including one whose name was scraped away (8th on the left as you enter the courtyard), reside in the central courtyard. The erased priestess is thought to have been Claudia, the Vestal Virgin who, at the end of the 4th century, converted to this new-fangled religion called Christianity. Back on V. Sacra is the **Temple of Antoninus and Faustina** (to the immediate right as you face the entrance ramp), whose strong foundation, columns, and rigid lattice ceiling have preserved it unusually well over the ages. In the 7th and 8th centuries, after numerous unsuccessful attempts to pull the temple down, the **Church of San Lorenzo in Miranda** was built in the interior of the abandoned temple (you can see deep grooves at the top of the eight columns where wire ropes were tied in futile attempts to tear it down). In the shadow of the temple (to the right as you face it) lies the archaic **necropolis.** Excavations earlier this century uncovered Iron Age graves from the 8th century BC, lending credence to the city's legendary founding date of 753 BC. Here V. Sacra runs over the **Cloaca Maxima,** the ancient sewer that still drains water from the valley. The street then passes the **Temple of Romulus** (the round building behind scaffolding), named for the son of Maxentius (not the legendary founder of Rome). Note the original bronze doors, with a working lock from the 4th century AD.

THE VELIA. V. Sacra leads out of the Forum proper to the gargantuan **Basilica of Maxentius** (also known as the Basilica of Constantine). Emperor Maxentius began construction of the basilica in AD 306, building until Constantine deposed him in 312 and completed the project. The middle apse of the basilica once contained a gigantic statue of Constantine—the body was bronze, and the head, legs, and arms were marble. The uncovered remains, including a 6½ ft. long foot, are on exhibit at the **Palazzo dei Conservatori** on the Capitoline Hill. The Baroque facade of the **Church of Santa Francesca Romana** is built over Hadrian's Temple to Venus and Rome—the palindromic *Roma* and *Amor*. It hides the entrance to the **Antiquarium Forense,** a small museum that displays funerary urns and skeletons from the necropolis. *(Open daily 9am-1pm. Free.)* On the summit of the Velia, the road down from the Palatine, is the **Arch of Titus,** built in AD 81 by Domitian to celebrate his brother Titus, who destroyed Jerusalem 11 years earlier. V. Sacra leads to an exit on the other side of the hill, an easy way to get to the Colosseum. The path that crosses in front of the arch climbs up to the Palatine Hill.

THE PALATINE HILL

Open in summer M-Sa 9:30am-7:15pm, Su 9am-1pm; in winter M-Sa 9:30am-1hr. before sunset, Su 9am-1pm; sometimes closes M-F by 3pm, Su and holidays by noon. Last entrance 45min. before closing. L12,000, EU citizens between 18 and 24 L6000, EU citizens under 18 and over 60 free. A 6-day ticket book is good for the 3 Musei Nazionali Romani, the Colosseum, and the Palatine Hill (L30,000).

The best way to attack the **Palatine** is from the access stairs steps away from the Arch of Titus in the Forum, which ascend to the **Farnese Gardens.** The hill, actually a plateau between the Tiber and the Forum, was home to the she-wolf that suckled Romulus and Remus. It was also here that Romulus built the first walls and houses of the city. During the Republic, the Palatine was the city's most fashionable residential quarter, where aristocrats and statesmen, including Cicero and Marc Antony, built their homes. Augustus lived on the hill in a shamefully modest house, but later emperors capitalized on the hill's prestige by building progressively more gargantuan quarters for themselves and their courts. By the end of the 1st century AD, the imperial residence had swallowed up the entire hill, whose Latin name, Palatium, became synonymous with the palace that dominated it. After the fall of Rome, the hill suffered the same fate as the Forum, though Byzantine ambassadors and even popes sometimes set up house in the crumbling palace.

Throughout the garden complex, terraces provide breathtaking views. Lower down, excavations continue on the 9th-century BC village, optimistically labeled the **Casa di Romulo.** To the right of the village is the podium of the **Temple of Cybele,** whose cult statue now sits in an arch in the foundation of Tiberius's palace. The temple was constructed in 191 BC during the Second Punic War, when a Sibylline

Hmm, call home or eat lunch?

Nathan Lane for YOU[SM].

No doubt, traveling on a budget is tough. So tear out this wallet guide and keep it with you during your travels. With YOU, calling home from overseas is affordable and easy.

If the wallet guide is missing, call collect 913-624-5336 or visit www.youcallhome.com for YOU country numbers.

Dialing instructions:
Need help with access numbers while overseas? Call collect, 913-624-5336.

Dial the access number for the country you're in.
Dial 04 or follow the English prompts.
Enter your credit card information to place your call.

Country	Access Number	Country	Access Number	Country	Access Number
Australia v	1-800-551-110	Israel v	1-800-949-4102	Spain v	900-99-0013
Bahamas +	1-800-389-2111	Italy + v	172-1877	Switzerland v	0800-899-777
Brazil v	000-8016	Japan + v	00539-131	Taiwan v	0080-14-0877
China + ▲ v	108-13	Mexico u v	001-800-877-8000	United Kingdom v	0800-890-877
France v	0800-99-0087	Netherlands + v	0800-022-9119		
Germany + v	0800-888-0013	New Zealand ▲ v	000-999		
Hong Kong v	800-96-1877	Philippines T v	105-16		
India v	000-137	Singapore v	8000-177-177		
Ireland v	1-800-552-001	South Korea + v	00729-16		

Service provided by Sprint

v Call answered by automated Voice Response Unit. **+** Public phones may require coin or card.
▲ May not be available from all payphones. **u** Use phones marked with "LADATEL" and no coin or card is required.
T If talk button is available, push it before talking.

Pack the Wallet Guide

and save 25% or more* on calls home to the U.S

It's lightweight and carries heavy savings of 25% or more* over AT&T USA Direct and MCI WorldPhone rates. So take this YOU wallet guide and carry it wherever you go.

To save with YOU:

- Dial the access number of the country you're in (see reverse)
- Dial 04 or follow the English voice prompts
- Enter your credit card info for easy billing

Service provided by Sprint

*Based on AT&T USA Direct rates, Tariff 24.1.3.A, April 8, 2000 and MCI WorldPhone rates, Tariff 3.07341, May 1, 2000. 25% discount applies for calls less then 100 minutes. Promotion subject to change. Restrictions may apply. Copyright ©Sprint 2000. All rights reserved. All trademarks referenced herein are the property of their respective owners.

book commanded one simple order: a temple with the likeness of the Magna Mater Cybele had to be built from a special black stone found only in Pessinus. The stairs slightly to the left lead to the **House of Livia.** As Augustus's wife, Livia was the first Roman empress; Robert Graves's *I, Claudius,* calls her an "abominable grandmother." She had the house, with its vestibule, courtyard, and three vaulted living rooms, connected to the **House of Augustus** next door.

Around the corner, the long, spooky **Cryptoporticus** connected Tiberius' palace with the buildings nearby. Used by slaves and imperial couriers as a secret passage, it may have been built by Nero in one of his more paranoid moments. The short end of the tunnel, the path around the House of Augustus, leads to the vast ruins of a giant palace built by Domitian (AD 81-96) and is divided into two wings. The solemn **Domus Augustana** was the private space for the emperors. The exterior walls that remain are so high that archaeologists are still unsure how they were roofed over. Adjacent to the Domus Augustana lies the other wing of the palace and the sprawling **Domus Flavia,** site of a gigantic octagonal fountain that occupied almost the entire courtyard. Between the Domus Augustana and the Domus Flavia stands the **Palatine Antiquarium,** the museum that houses the major artifacts found during the excavations of the Palatine Hill. *(30 people admitted every 20min starting at 9:10am. Free.)* Outside on the right, the palace's east wing contains the curious **Stadium Palatinum,** or Hippodrome, a sunken oval space once surrounded by a colonnade but now decorated with fragments of porticoes, statues, and fountains. Two theories surround the Stadium. One claims that it was a private racetrack, the other that it was a private botanical garden.

FORI IMPERIALI

Across the street from the Ancient Forum is the Fori Imperiali, a vast conglomeration of temples, basilicas, and public squares constructed in the 1st and 2nd centuries AD. Julius Caesar was the 1st to expand Rome in this direction (most likely he was motivated by a desire to undercut the prestige of the Senate and move the city center away from the Curia). Augustus, Vespatian, Nerva, and Trajan all followed suit, filling the flat space with monuments to their own glory. In the 1930s, Mussolini, with imperial aspirations of his own, cleared the area of medieval constructions and built the V. dei Fori Imperiali through the remains. In late summer of 1999, the city decided to remove V. dei Fori Imperiali and reconnect the forums; however, it's unclear when or how the city will accomplish this task.

FORUM OF TRAJAN. Built between AD 107 and 113, the entire forum celebrated the emperor's victorious Dacian campaign (in modern-day Romania). The complex included a colossal equestrian statue of Trajan and an immense triumphal arch. At one end of the now decimated forum stands the almost perfectly preserved spiral of **Trajan's Column,** one of the greatest specimens of Roman relief-sculpture ever carved. Twenty-five hundred legionnaires have been making their way up the column since AD 113—today's tourist troops may be somewhat disappointed if they ever reach the top; in 1588, a statue of St. Peter replaced Trajan's.

MARKETS OF TRAJAN. This three-floor semi-circular complex provides a glimpse of Rome's first shopping mall and retail warehouses, and it features an impressive, albeit crumbling, display of sculpture from the imperial forums. *(Depending on how excavations proceed, it might be possible to visit them. Enter at V. IV Novembre, 94, up the steps in V. Magnanapoli, to the right of the 2 churches behind Trajan's column. ☎06 679 00 48.)*

FORUMS. Across V. dei Fori Imperiali, in the shade of the Vittorio Emanuele II monument, lie the paltry remains of the **Forum of Caesar,** including the ruins of Julius Caesar's **Temple to Venus Genetrix** (Mother Venus, from whom he claimed descent). Nearby, the gray tufa wall of the **Forum of Augustus** commemorates Augustus' victory over Caesar's murderers at the Battle of Philippi in 42 BC. The aptly named **Forum Transitorium** (also called the **Forum of Nerva**) was a narrow, rectangular space connecting the Forum of Augustus with the Republican Roman Forum. Emperor Nerva inaugurated it in AD 97, dedicating its temple to "Minerva,"

CIAO MEOW Thanks to a bizarre 1988 law, Rome's stray cats have the right to live where they're born. Urban legend has it that Romans care for them in atonement for sins during WWII. When conventional food ran out, the Romans allegedly ate their feline friends. Today, there are 10,000 colonies, hundreds of which are fed by the city. Look for the cats among the ruins, especially near Largo Argentina.

the deity whose name was closest to his own. The nerva of some rulers. The only remnant of **Vespatian's Forum** is the mosaic-filled **Church of Santi Cosma e Damiano** across V. Cavour, near the Roman Forum. *(Open daily 9am-1pm and 3-7pm.)*

OUTSIDE THE FORI

THE COLOSSEUM. The **Colosseum** stands as the enduring symbol of the Eternal City—a hollowed-out ghost of travertine marble that dwarfs every other ruin in Rome; it once held as many as 50,000 crazed spectators. Within 100 days of its AD 80 opening, some 5000 wild beasts perished in the bloody arena (from the Latin word for sand, *harena*, which was put on the floor to absorb blood), and the slaughter went on for three more centuries. The floor (now partially restored and open for various concerts and TV shows) covers a labyrinth of brick cells, ramps, and elevators used to transport wild animals from cages up to arena level. *(M:B-Colosseo. Open daily in summer 9am-6:30pm; in winter 9am-1hr. before sunset. L10,000, EU citizens 18-24 L5000, EU citizens under 18 and over 60 free. 6-day ticket book is good for the 3 Musei Nazionali Romani, the Colosseum, and the Palatine Hill (L30,000). Tours with archaeologist L6000; audioguide in English, French, German, Italian, Japanese, or Spanish L7000.)*

ARCO DI CONSTANTINO. Between the Colosseum and the Palatine Hill lies the Arco di Costantino (Arch of Constantine), one of the latest and best-preserved imperial monuments to grace this area. Constantine built the arch to commemorate his victory over his rival Maxentius at the Battle of the Milvian Bridge in AD 312. He used sculptural fragments from earlier monuments built by the emperors Trajan, Hadrian, and Marcus Aurelius to create the harmonious triple arch.

THE DOMUS AUREA. This park houses a portion of Nero's "Golden House," which once covered a substantial chunk of Rome. Having decided that he was a god, Nero had the architects Severus and Celer make a house to suit divinity. Between the two ends of the palace was an enclosed lake, where the Colosseum now stands, and the Caelian Hill became private gardens. The Forum was reduced to a vestibule of the palace; Nero crowned it with a colossal statue of himself as the sun. Standing 35m tall, it was the largest bronze statue ever made and was justly called the Colossus—this is where the Flavian Amphitheater got its current name. Nero pillaged all of Greece to find works of art worthy of the quarters of an emperor, including the famous *Laocoön*. The grotesques and decorative motifs that cover the walls were a favorite influence for many Renaissance artists—among others, Raphael, Ghirlandaio, Pinturricchio, Perugino, and Filippino Lippi marvelled at the grotesques and some even signed their names on the walls.

The party didn't last long, however. Nero committed suicide only five years after building his gargantuan pleasure garden. Out of civic-mindedness or jealousy the later Flavian emperors tore down his house and replaced all the palace with monuments built for the public good. The Flavian Baths were built on the Caelian Hill, the lake was drained, and the Colosseum was erected. *(On the Oppian Hill, below Trajan's baths. From the Colosseum, walk through the gates up V. della Domus Aurea and take the 1st right. ☎06 39 74 99 07. Open Tu-Su 9am-8pm. Groups of 30 admitted every 15min. L10,000. All visits supervised by a guard who gives a spartan tour in Italian or English for L3000. Audioguide, L3000. Italian tour with archaeologist L6000. Reservations recommended. L2000.)*

THE VELABRUM. The Velabrum lies in a flat flood plain of the Tiber, south of the Jewish Ghetto. At the bend of V. del Portico d'Ottavia, a shattered pediment and a few ivy-covered columns in the shadow of the Teatro di Marcello are all that remain of the once magnificent **Portico d'Ottavia.** The stocky, gray **Teatro di Marcello**

next door bears the name of Augustus' unfortunate nephew, whose early and sudden death remains a mystery. If the theater strikes you as a Colosseum wanna-be, think again—the pattern of arches and pilasters on the exterior, completed in 11 BC, served as a model for the great amphitheater across town. Farther down V. di Teatro di Marcello toward the Tiber, the **Chiesa di San Nicola in Carcere** incorporates three Roman temples originally dedicated to the gods Juno, Janus, and Spes. *(☎06 686 99 72; call to visit the interior. Open Sept.-July M-Sa 7:30am-noon and 4-7pm.)*

One block farther south along V. Luigi Petroselli lies the **Piazza della Bocca della Verità,** the site of the ancient **Foro Boario,** or cattle market. Across the street, the **Chiesa di Santa Maria in Cosmedin** harbors some of Rome's most beautiful medieval decoration. The 12th-century porch and tower welcome busloads of tourists on their way to see the portico's **Bocca della Verità,** which was made famous in the Audrey Hepburn film, *Roman Holiday*. Originally a drain cover carved as a river god's face, the relief was credited with supernatural powers in the Middle Ages. According to legend, the hoary face will chomp on the hand of a liar. *(Portico open daily 9am-7pm. Church open daily 10am-1pm and 3-7pm. Byzantine mass Su 10:30am.)*

THE CAPITOLINE HILL. Home to the original capital, the Monte Capitolino still serves as the seat of the city's government. Michelangelo designed the spacious **Piazza di Campidoglio.** Surrounding the *piazza* are the twin Palazzo dei Conservatori and Palazzo Nuovo, now the home of the **Capitoline Museums** (see **Museums,** p. 462). From the Palazzo Nuovo, stairs lead up to the rear entrance of the **Chiesa di Santa Maria in Aracoeli,** a 7th-century church now filled with a jumble of monuments. Its stunning **Cappella Bufalini** is home to the *Santo Bambino*, a cherubic statue that receives letters from sick children from all over the world. *(Open daily 9am-6pm.)* The gloomy **Mamertine Prison,** consecrated as the **Chiesa di San Pietro in Carcere,** lies down the hill from the back stairs of the Aracoeli. St. Peter, while imprisoned here, baptized his captors with the waters that flooded his cell. *(☎06 679 29 02. Open daily 9am-noon and 2:30-6pm. Donation requested.)*

At the far end of the *piazza*, opposite the stairs, lies the turreted **Palazzo dei Senatori,** which houses Rome's mayor. When Paul III remodeled the top of the hill for Charles V's visit, he not only had Michelangelo fashion the imposing statues of the twin warriors Castor and Pollux, but he also had the famous equestrian **statue of Marcus Aurelius** brought here from the Lateran Palace. Due to air pollution, the statue now resides in climate-controlled comfort in the courtyard of the Palazzo dei Conservatori—a weatherproof copy crowns the *piazza*. *(To get to the Campidoglio, take any bus that goes to P. Venezia. From P. Venezia, face the Vittorio Emanuele II monument, walk around to the right to P. d'Aracoeli, and take the stairs up the hill.)*

CIRCUS MAXIMUS AND BATHS OF CARACALLA. Today's Circus Maximus offers only a grassy shadow of its former glory. After its construction in about 600 BC, the circus drew more than 300,000 Romans, who gathered here to watch as chariots careened around the quarter-mile track. The Baths of Caracalla are the largest and best-preserved baths in the city. Some 1500 muddy Romans could sponge themselves off here. Have a look at the beautiful mosaics that cover the floors in this proto-health club, particularly those in the **Apodyteria** (dressing rooms). *(M:B-Circo Massimo, or walk down V. di San Gregorio from the Colosseum. Circus is always open. To get to the baths, take V. delle Terme di Caracalla from the eastern end of the Circus. ☎06 575 86 26. Baths open in summer daily 9am-6pm; in winter daily 9am-1hr. before sunset. L8000.)*

CENTRO STORICO

PIAZZA VENEZIA AND VIA DEL CORSO

Following the line of the ancient V. Lata, the **Via del Corso** takes its name from its days as Rome's premier racecourse. It runs nearly a mile between P. del Popolo and the rumbling P. Venezia (not much more than a glorified traffic circle dominated by the **Vittorio Emanuele II monument,** or the Vittoriano). The crumbling **Palazzo Venezia,** on the right of the *piazza* as you face the monument, was one of the first Renaissance *palazzi* built in the city. Mussolini used it as office space and delivered some of his most famous speeches from its balcony. The *palazzo* is now home to the **Museo Nazionale del Palazzo Venezia**. The *loggie* of the interior courtyard and of the **Chiesa di San Marco** date from the Renaissance. *(Church open daily 8:30am-noon and 4-7pm. Enter from P. di S. Marco, to the right of the Vittoriano.)*

Off V. del Corso, the picturesque **Piazza Colonna** was named for the colossal **Colonna di Marco Aurelio,** designed in imitation of the emperor Trajan's earlier triumphant column. Sixtus V had the statue of St. Paul added to the top of the column in the 16th century. On the opposite (western) side of the *piazza*, **Palazzo Wedekind,** home to the newspaper *Il Tempo*, was built in 1838 with Roman columns from the Etruscan city of Veio. The northwest corner of the *piazza* flows into **Piazza di Montecitorio,** overseen by Bernini's **Palazzo Montecitorio,** now the seat of the Chamber of Deputies. The obelisk in front of the *palazzo* was once the centerpiece of a giant sundial that was part of Augustus' Ara Pacis complex (see p. 454).

PIAZZA DELLA ROTONDA

THE PANTHEON. With its granite columns and pediment, bronze doors, and soaring domed interior, this famous temple has stood remarkably the same since the day it was put up nearly 2000 years ago. Architects still puzzle over how it was erected—its dome, a perfect half-sphere constructed from poured concrete without the support of vaults, arches, or ribs, is the largest of its kind. The light that enters the roof was used as a sundial to indicate the passing of the hours and the dates of equinoxes and solstices. Across the facade's architrave, an inscription reads "Marcus Agrippa made it in his 3rd consulship." Indeed, Agrippa did build a temple here in 27 BC, dedicated to all the gods. But Hadrian tore it down in AD 119 and started from scratch. To avoid accusations of overbearing pride, he had the old inscription copied here. In AD 606, it was consecrated as the **Church of Santa Maria ad Martyres,** its official name to this day. *(Open June M-Sa 9am-7pm, Su 9am-1pm; July-Aug. M-Sa 9am-7:30pm, Su 9am-1pm; Oct.-May M-Sa 9am-4pm, Su 9am-1pm. Free.)*

OTHER SIGHTS. In front of the temple, the *piazza* centers on Giacomo della Porta's late-Renaissance fountain, which supports an Egyptian **obelisk** added in the 18th century. Around the left side of the Pantheon, another obelisk, supported by Bernini's curious elephant statue, marks the center of tiny **Piazza Minerva.** Behind the obelisk, the **Chiesa di Santa Maria Sopra Minerva** hides some Renaissance masterpieces, including Michelangelo's *Christ Bearing the Cross*, Antoniazzo Romano's *Annunciation*, and a statue of St. Sebastian recently attributed to Michelangelo. The south transept houses the famous **Cappella Carafa,** with a brilliant fresco cycle by Filippino Lippi. *(Open M-Sa 7am-7pm, Su 7am-1pm and 3:30-7pm.)*

From the upper left-hand corner of P. della Rotonda, V. Giustiniani goes north to intersect V. della Scrofa and V. della Dogana Vecchia. Here stands **Chiesa di San Luigi dei Francesi,** the French National Church, home to three of Caravaggio's most famous paintings: *The Calling of St. Matthew, St. Matthew and the Angel*, and *Crucifixion*. *(Open F-W 7:30am-12:30pm and 3:30-7pm, Th 7:30am-12:30pm.)*

PIAZZA NAVONA

Opened as a stadium in AD 86, P. Navona housed wrestling matches, javelin and discus throws, and foot and chariot races. It even hosted mock naval battles, for which the stadium was flooded and filled with fleets skippered by convicts.

Bernini's **Fontana dei Quattro Fiumi** (Fountain of the Four Rivers) commands the center of P. Navona. Each of the river gods represents one of the four continents of the globe (as they were thought of then): the Ganges for Asia, the Danube for Europe, the Nile for Africa (veiled, since the source of the river was unknown), and the Rio de la Plata for the Americas. At the ends of the *piazza* are the **Fontana del Moro** and the **Fontana di Nettuno,** designed by Giacomo della Porta in the 16th century and renovated by Bernini in 1653.

With a (relatively) new Borromini-designed exterior, the **Church of Sant'Agnese** dominates the western side of the *piazza*. Its real attraction is the skull of its namesake saint, who was martyred in Domitian's stadium after refusing an arranged marriage—when stripped naked before her death, her hair grew miraculously to cover her somewhere. *(Open Tu-Sa 4:30-7pm, Su 10am-1pm.)*

West of P. Navona, V. di Tor Millina intersects V. della Pace, steps from the charming semi-circular porch of the **Chiesa di Santa Maria della Pace,** which houses Raphael's gentle *Sibyls* in the Chigi Chapel. On nearby C. del Rinascimento, the **Chiesa di Sant'Ivo**'s corkscrew cupola hovers over the **Palazzo della Sapienza,** the original home of the University of Rome. Continue down this road, turn left on C. V. Emanuele, and walk to P. del Gesù to see the opulent **Il Gesù,** mother church of the Jesuit Order. *(Open daily 6am-12:30pm and 4-7:15pm.)*

CAMPO DEI FIORI

Campo dei Fiori lies across C. V. Emanuele from P. Navona. During papal rule, the area was the site of countless executions. In the middle of the Campo, a statue marks the spot of the death of Giordano Bruno (1548-1600). Philosophically out of sync with his time, Bruno sizzled at the stake in 1600 for taking Copernicus one step further—he argued that the universe had no center at all. Now the only carcasses that litter the *piazza* are of the cod in the colorful produce, fish, and flower **market** that springs up every day except Sunday from 6am to 2pm.

The huge, stately **Palazzo Farnese** dominates P. Farnese, south of the Campo. Alessandro Farnese, the first Counter-Reformation pope (1534-1549), built this, the greatest of Rome's Renaissance *palazzi.* Since 1635 the French Embassy has rented it for one *lira* a year in exchange for office space in Paris's Hôtel Galiffet in Paris, home of the Italian Embassy. To the east of the *palazzo* is the Baroque facade of the **Palazzo Spada** and the collection of the **Galleria Spada** (see p. 463).

As part of his campaign in the early 1500s to clean up Rome after the papacy returned from its "Babylonian Captivity" in Avignon, Julius II commissioned Bramante to construct a road leading directly to the Vatican, giving birth to **Via Giulia,** an elegant, even revolutionary contrast to the narrow, winding medieval streets.

THE JEWISH GHETTO

Across V. Arenula from Campo dei Fiori; take bus #64.

The Jewish community in Rome is the oldest in Europe—Israelites came in 161 BC as ambassadors from Judas Maccabei, asking for Imperial help against invaders. The Ghetto, the tiny area to which Pope Paul IV confined the Jews in 1555, was closed in 1870, but it is still the center of Rome's vibrant Jewish population of 16,000.

PIAZZA MATTEI. This square, centered on Taddeo Landini's 16th-century **Fontana delle Tartarughe,** marks the center of the Ghetto. Nearby is the **Church of Sant'Angelo in Pescheria,** installed inside the Portico d'Ottavia in 755 and named after the fish market that used to flourish here. Jews of the Ghetto were forced to attend mass here every Sunday—an act of forced evangelism that they quietly resisted by stuffing their ears with wax. *(Open for prayer meetings W 5:30pm, Sa 5pm.)*

SINAGOGA ASHKENAZITA. Built between 1874 and 1904 at the corner of Lungotevere dei Cenci and V. Catalan, this temple incorporates Persian and Babylonian architectural devices that consciously differ from Christian elements. Terrorists bombed the building in 1982; guards now search and question all visitors. The synagogue houses the **Jewish Museum,** a collection of ancient torahs, religious wear, and Holocaust artifacts. *(☎06 687 50 51. Open for services or tour through the museum.)*

PIAZZA DI SPAGNA AND ENVIRONS

OFF PIAZZA DI SPAGNA

THE SPANISH STEPS. Designed by an Italian, paid for by the French, named for the Spaniards, occupied by the British, and under the sway of American ambassador-at-large Ronald McDonald, the **Scalinata di Spagna** exude an international air. When the steps were built in 1725, Romans hoping to earn extra *scudi* as artists' models flocked to the steps dressed as the Madonna and Julius Caesar. Nowadays, hordes of adolescent males descend on the *piazza* in order to flirt with foreigners. Equal in number, though less irritating, are the scruffy *artistes* who can write your name on a grain of rice. The pink house to the right of the Steps was the site of John Keats's 1821 death; it's now the **Keats-Shelley Memorial Museum.**

FONTANA DI TREVI. Nicolo Salvi's (1697-1751) extravagant and now sparkling-clean **Fontana di Trevi** emerges from the back wall of **Palazzo Poli,** dwarfing the already-narrow *piazza* and fascinating crowds with the rumble of its cascading waters. The bodacious Anita Ekberg took a dip in the fountain in Fellini's movie *La Dolce Vita*, a stunt most recently replayed by "model" Anna-Nicole Smith (who had to pay a hefty fine). Legend has it that a traveler who throws a coin into the fountain is ensured a speedy return to Rome; a traveler who tosses two coins will also fall in love in Rome. Opposite the fountain is the Baroque **Chiesa dei Santi Vincenzo e Anastasio,** rebuilt in 1630. The **crypt** preserves the hearts and lungs of popes from 1590-1903. *(Open daily 6:45am-noon and 3:30-7:30pm.)*

MAUSOLEUM OF AUGUSTUS AND ARA PACIS. The circular brick mound of the Masoleo d'Agosto once housed the funerary urns of the Imperial Roman family. *(In P. Augusto Imperatore. From P. del Popolo, take V. di Ripetta south toward the Tiber. Open sporadically for tours.)* To the west (the right, coming from the P. del Popolo) of the mausoleum stands the glass-encased Ara Pacis (Altar of Augustan Peace), a piece of propagandic spin-doctoring completed in 9 BC to celebrate Augustus' success in achieving peace after years of civil unrest and war. The reliefs on the front and back of this marble altar depict allegorical figures from Rome's most sacred national myths (a Roman Lupercalia, Aeneas sacrificing a white sow, Tellus the earth goddess, and the goddess Roma) while the side panels show realistic portraits of Augustus, his family, his children, and various statesmen and priests. When discovered, the altar was buried 10m underground and submerged in 3m of water. Mussolini provided the colossal display case. *(Open Tu-Sa 9am-7pm, Su 9am-1pm. L3750.)*

PIAZZA DEL POPOLO

P. del Popolo, once a favorite venue for public executions of heretics, is now the "people's square" and a lively gathering place. In the center is the 3200 year old **Obelisk of Pharaoh Ramses II,** which Augustus brought back as a souvenir from Egypt in the 1st century BC. Behind a simple early Renaissance shell, the **Chiesa di Santa Maria del Popolo** contains several Renaissance and Baroque masterpieces. *(☎06 361 04 87. Open daily 7am-noon and 4-7pm.)* The **Cappella della Rovere** holds Pinturicchio's *Adoration*. Two exquisite Caravaggios, *The Conversion of St. Paul* and *Crucifixion of St. Peter*, are in the **Cappella Cerasi.** Raphael designed the **Cappella Chigi** for the wealthy Sienese banker Agostino Chigi, reputedly once the world's richest man. At the southern end of the *piazza* are the 17th-century **twin churches** of Santa Maria di Montesano, on the left (with a facade by Bernini), and Santa Maria dei Miracoli.

PIAZZA BARBERINI

Rising from the modern hum of a busy traffic circle at the end of V. del Tritone, Bernini's **Fontana del Tritone** spouts a stream of water over the *piazza*, marking the fulcrum of Baroque Rome. Stretching north is **Via Vittorio Veneto,** lined by embassies and airline offices. The *piazza* is home to Bernini's **Fontana delle Api** (Bee Fountain) and the ephemeral Planet Hollywood. Maderno, Borromini, and Bernini all had a hand in the **Palazzo Barberini,** V. delle Quattro Fontane, 13, home to the **Galleria Nazionale d'Arte Antica,** a collection of paintings from the 11th to 18th centuries (see p. 463). A short way up on the right, at V. V. Veneto, 27a, the severe Counter-Reformation **Church of L'Immacolata Concezione** houses the **Capuchin Crypt,** where the artfully arranged bones of 4000 Capuchin friars are displayed. *(Open F-W 9am-noon and 3-6pm. L1000 minimum donation requested.)*

VILLA BORGHESE

In celebration of becoming a cardinal, Scipione Borghese built the **Villa Borghese** north of P. di Spagna and V. V. Veneto. Its park is home to three notable art museums: the world-renowned **Galleria Borghese** (see p. 462), and the intriguing **Museo Nazionale Etrusco di Villa Giulia** (see p. 462). Besides kilometers of fountain-studded paths, the Borghese is home to a second-rate, but fun zoo, the **Bio-Parco.** *(V. del Giardino Zoologico, 3. ☎06 321 65 64. Open daily in summer 9:30am-6pm; in winter 9:30am-5pm. L14,000, ages 4-12 L10,000, under 4 and over 60 free.)* North of Villa Borghese are the **Santa Priscilla catacombs.** The catacombs, along with the gardens of **Villa Ada,** are best reached by bus #57 or 219 from Termini or bus #56 from V. del Tritone. Get off at P. Vescovio and walk down V. di Tor Fiorenza to P. di Priscilla. *(V. Salaria, 430, just before V. Antica crosses V. Ardeatina. ☎06 86 20 62 72. Open Tu-Su 8:30am-noon and 2:30-5pm. L10,000.)*

VATICAN CITY

M: A-Ottaviano or A-Cipro/Musei Vaticani. Alternatively, take bus #64 or 492 from Termini or Largo Argentina, #62 from P. Barberini, or #23 from Testaccio. The official site of the Vatican, www.vatican.va, has info on sights and events. The Pilgrim Tourist Information Office, (☎06 69 88 44 66) P. San Pietro, is to the left as you face the basilica and conducts free English tours of the Basilica daily. Phone to arrange tours of the otherwise inaccessible Vatican Gardens. Tour lasts 2hr.; Mar.-Oct. M-Tu and Th-Sa 10am; Nov.-Feb. Sa 10am; L20,000. Office open M-Sa 8:30am-7pm. Papal Audiences are held every Wednesday, when John Paul II greets up to 3000 pilgrims, usually at 10am behind the colonnade left of the basilica. For free tickets, stop by the Prefettura della Casa Pontificia (☎06 69 88 32 73) the day before you wish to attend. The office is beyond the bronze doors to the right of the basilica. (Open M-Sa 9am-1pm.) To secure tickets in advance, write to the Prefettura della Casa Pontificia, 00120 Città del Vaticano, specifying the number of people and the desired and alternate date. Seating is limited, so arrive early.

Occupying 108½ independent acres entirely within the boundaries of Rome, Vatican City, the foothold of the Catholic Church, once wheeled and dealed as the mightiest power in Europe. The Lateran Treaty of 1929, which allowed the Pope to maintain all legislative, judicial, and executive powers over this tiny theocracy, requires the Church to remain neutral in Italian national politics and Roman municipal affairs. As the spiritual leader for millions of Catholics around the world, however, the Pope's influence extends far beyond the walls of this tiny domain. The nation preserves its independence by minting coins (in Italian *lire* but with the Pope's face), running a separate postal system, maintaining an army of Swiss Guards, and hoarding fine art in the **Vatican Museums** (see p. 461).

BASILICA DI SAN PIETRO (ST. PETER'S)

Open daily Apr.-Sept. 7am-7pm; Oct.-Mar. 7am-6pm. Mass M-Sa at 9, 10, and 11am, noon, and 5pm; Su 9, 10:30, and 11:30am, and 12:10, 1, 4, and 5:45pm. Multilingual confession available. Cover your knees and shoulders. Jeans and t-shirts are acceptable.

PIAZZA AND FACADE. As you enter **Piazza San Pietro,** Bernini's colonnade draws you toward the church. Mussolini's broad V. della Conciliazione, built in the 1930s to connect the Vatican to the rest of the city, opened a wider view of St. Peter's than Bernini had ever intended. The obelisk in the center is framed by two fountains; round porphyry disks set in the pavement between each fountain and the obelisk mark the spots where you should stand so that the quadruple rows of Bernini's colonnades visually resolve into one perfectly aligned row. One hundred and forty statues perch above on the colonnade. Those on the basilica represent Christ (at center), John the Baptist, and the Apostles (except for Peter).

ENTRANCE AND PIETÀ. The pope opens the **Porta Sancta** (Holy Door), the last door on the right side of the entrance porch, every 25 years by knocking in the bricks with a silver hammer. The last opening was in 2000. The basilica itself rests on the reputed site of St. Peter's tomb. A Christian structure has stood here since the Emperor Constantine made Christianity the state religion in the 4th century.

The overwhelming interior of St. Peter's measures 186m by 137m along the transepts. Metal lines on the marble floor mark the puny-by-comparison lengths of other major world churches. To the right, Michelangelo's *Pietà* has been protected by bullet-proof glass since 1972, when an axe-wielding fiend attacked it, smashing Christ's nose and breaking Mary's hand.

INTERIOR. The crossing under the dome is anchored by four niches with statues of saints—Bernini's San Longinus is at the northeast. In the center of the crossing, Bernini's bronze baldacchino rises on spiral columns over the marble altar. The many bronze bees on the canopy are the symbol of the Barberini family, of which Bernini's patron Urban VIII was a member. In the apse is Bernini's Cathedra Petri, a Baroque reliquary housing St. Peter's original throne in a riot of bronze and gold. Below the statue of St. Longinus, steps lead down to the Vatican Grottoes, the final resting place of innumerable popes and saints.

CUPOLA. The entrance to the cupola is near the exit from the grottoes. You can take an elevator to the walkway around the interior of the dome or ascend 350 claustrophobic steps to the outdoor top ledge of the cupola. This ledge offers an excellent view of the basilica's roof, the *piazza*, the Vatican Gardens, and the hazy Roman skyline. *(Cupola closes 75min. earlier than the Basilica, and when the Pope is inside. L7000, elevator—though there's still a climb to the very top—L8000.)*

CASTEL SANT'ANGELO

Walk along the river with St. Peter's behind you, and the castle to your left; follow the signs. ☎06 687 50 36. Open Tu-F and Su 9am-8pm, Sa 9am-midnight; in winter daily 9am-2pm. L10,000, EU citizens under 18 or over 60 free. Audio guide in English L7000.

Built by Hadrian (AD 117-138) as a mausoleum for himself and his family, this hulking mass of brick and stone has served the popes as a fortress, prison, and palace. When the city was wracked with plague in 590, Pope Gregory the Great saw an angel sheathing his sword at the top of the complex; the plague abated soon after, and the edifice was rededicated to the angel. The intriguing fortress now contains a **museum of arms and artillery** and offers an incomparable view of Rome and the Vatican. Outside, the marble **Ponte Sant'Angelo,** lined with statues of angels designed by Bernini, is the starting point for the traditional pilgrimage route from St. Peter's to the **Church of San Giovanni in Laterano** (see p. 459).

TRASTEVERE

Take bus #75 or 170 from Termini to V. Trastevere, or tram #13 from Largo Argentina.

Right off the Ponte Garibaldi stands the statue of the famous dialect poet, G. G. Belli, in the middle of his own *piazza*, which borders the busy P. Sonnino and marks the beginning of V. di Trastevere. On the left is the **Casa di Dante,** where readings of the *Divine Comedy* occur every Sunday from November to March. On V. di Santa Cecilia, behind the cars, through the gate, and beyond the courtyard full of roses, is the **Basilica di Santa Cecilia in Trastevere,** where Stefano Maderno's famous **statue of Santa Cecilia** lies under the altar. *(Open daily 8am-12:30pm and 2:30-7pm. Cloister open Tu and Th 10-11:30am, Su 11:3am-noon. Donation requested. Crypt L4000.)*

From P. Sonnino, V. della Lungaretta leads west to P. di S. Maria in Trastevere, home to numerous stray dogs and expatriates, as well as the **Chiesa di Santa Maria in Trastevere,** built in the 4th century by Pope Julius II. Although the church is being restored, the 12th-century mosaics in the apse and the chancel arch still glimmer in full splendor, depicting Jesus, Mary, and a bevy of saints and popes. *(Open daily 7:30am-7pm.)* North of the *piazza* are the Rococo **Galleria Corsini,** V. della Lungara, 10, (see **Museo Nazionale dell'Arte Antica,** p. 463) and, across the street, the **Villa Farnesina,** the jewel of Trastevere. Baldassare Peruzzi built the suburban villa for banker-philanthropist Agostino Chigi ("il Magnifico") between 1508-1511. The museum has no paintings; its frescoed walls are the main attraction (see p. 463).

ISOLA TIBERINA

According to Roman legend, the Tiber Island shares its birthday with the Roman Republic; after the Etruscan tyrant Tarquin raped the virtuous Lucretia, her outraged family killed him and threw his corpse in the river, where muck and silt collected around it, forming a land mass. Lucretia's family founded a new government, and the Tiber Island transformed into dry land. The island, home to the posh Fatebenefratelli Hospital since AD 154, has been associated with healing. The Greek god Aesclepius appeared to the Romans as a snake and slithered onto the island; his symbol, the caduceus, is visible all over the island.

The 10th-century **Chiesa di San Bartolomeo** has been flooded and rebuilt many times, resulting in the eclectic mix of a Baroque facade, a Romanesque tower, and 14 antique columns. *(Open daily 9am-1pm and 4-6:30pm.)* The bridge leading from Centro Storico, the **Ponte Fabricio,** commonly known as the **Ponte dei Quattro Capi** (Bridge of Four Heads), is the oldest in the city, built by Lucius Fabricius in 62 BC.

GIANICOLO

To reach the summit, take bus #41 from the Vatican, or ascend via the medieval V. Garibaldi from V. della Scala in Trastevere (about a 10min. walk).

At the top of the hill rests the **Chiesa di San Pietro in Montorio,** built on the spot once believed to be the site of St. Peter's upside-down crucifixion. The church contains *Flagellation*, painted by Sebastiano del Piombo from designs by Michelangelo. Next door in a small courtyard is Bramante's tiny **Tempietto.** *(Church and Tempietto open daily 9:30am-12:30pm and 4-6:30pm.)* A combination of Renaissance and ancient architectural elements, it was constructed to commemorate the site of Peter's martyrdom and provided the inspiration for the larger dome of St. Peter's. Rome's **botanical gardens** contain a **garden for the blind** as well as a rose garden that supposedly holds the bush from which all the world's roses are descended. *(Largo Cristina di Svezia, 24, at the end of V. Corsini, off V. della Lungara. Grounds open Apr.-July and Sept. M-Sa 9am-6:30pm; Oct.-Mar. M-Sa 9am-5:30pm. Greenhouse open M-Sa 9am-12:30pm. Closed Aug. L4000, ages 6-11 L2000, under 6 free.)*

NEAR TERMINI

NORTH OF TERMINI

BATHS OF DIOCLETIAN. From AD 298 to 306, 40,000 Christian slaves were kept busy building these public baths, which could serve 3000 people at once. They contained a heated marble public toilet with seats for 30 people, pools of various temperatures, gymnasiums, art galleries, gardens, libraries, and concert halls. In 1561, Michelangelo undertook his last architectural work and converted the ruins into a church, the **Chiesa di Santa Maria degli Angeli.** In the floor leading from the east transept to the altar, a sundial has provided the standard time for Roman clocks for hundreds of years. In the 4th-century rotonda, to the right as you exit the church, statues from the baths are displayed, as well as viewing windows that look down into the excavations. *(Church open daily 7:30am-12:30pm and 4-6:30pm. Rotonda and baths open M-F 9am-2pm, Sa-Su 9am-1pm. Free.)*

PIAZZA DEL QUIRINALE. At the southeast end of V. del Quirinale, this *piazza* occupies the summit of the tallest of Rome's seven hills. The President of the Republic officially resides in the imposing **Palazzo del Quirinale,** a Baroque architectural collaboration by Bernini, Maderno, and Fontana. Down V. del Quirinale, V. Ferrara on the right leads down the steps to V. Milano. At the corner of V. Milano and V. Nazionale towers the **Palazzo delle Espozioni,** home to temporary art exhibitions. Farther along the street lies the marvelous facade of Borromini's **Chiesa di San Carlo alle Quattro Fontane,** often called **San Carlino.**

VIA XX SETTEMBRE. The intersection of V. del Quirinale and V. delle Quattro Fontane showcases one of Pope Sixtus V's more gracious additions to the city. In the corner of each of the four surrounding buildings is a fountain with a reclining figure. V. del Quirinale becomes V. XX Settembre at this intersection and, after a few more blocks, opens into the Baroque P. San Bernardo, site of Domenico Fontana's colossal 1587 **Fontana dell'Acqua Felice.** The beefy statue of Moses is said to have been carved by Prospero Antichi, who nearly died of disappointment after seeing the finished product. Across the way, the **Chiesa di Santa Maria della Vittoria** is named for an icon of Mary that helped the Catholics win a battle near Prague in 1620. Inside, Bernini's fantastic *Ecstasy of St. Theresa of Ávila* (1652) resides in the Cornaro Chapel. *(Open daily 7:30am-12:30pm and 4-6:30pm.)*

VIA NOMENTANA. This road runs northeast from Michelangelo's **Porta Pia** out of the city. Hop on bus #36 in front of Termini, or head back to V. XX Settembre and catch bus #60. A 2km walk from Porta Pia past villas, embassies, and parks brings you to **Chiesa di Sant'Agnese fuori le Mura,** V. Nomentana, 349. Its apse displays an extraordinary Byzantine-style mosaic of St. Agnes with a pair of popes. The nearby **Mausoleum of Constantina** has even more splendid mosaics. The **catacombs** here, contain skeletons of St. Constantina's followers. *(☎06 86 20 54 56. Open Tu-Su 9am-noon and 4-6pm, M 9am-noon. Catacombs L8000 with Italian tour. English guidebook available.)*

SOUTH OF TERMINI

BASILICA DI SANTA MARIA MAGGIORE. As one of the five churches in Rome granted extraterritoriality, this basilica, which crowns the Esquiline Hill, is officially part of Vatican City. In 352, Pope Sixtus III commissioned the basilica when he noticed that Roman women were still visiting a temple to the pagan mother-goddess Juno Lucina. When Sixtus enthusiastically tore down the temple to build his new basilica, he not only substituted a Christian cult for a pagan one, but also celebrated the Council of Ephesus' recent ruling of Mary as the Mother of God. Most of the renowned mosaics inside are designed to commemorate her radiant new status. To the right of the altar, a marble slab marks the **tomba di Bernini** (Bernini's tomb). The 14th-century mosaics in the church's **loggia** recount the story of the miraculous August snowfall that showed the pope where to build the church. *(Four blocks down V. Cavour from Termini. Open daily 7am-7pm. Loggia open daily 9:30am-noon and 2-5:30pm. L5000. Buy tickets in the church souvenir shop.)*

PIAZZA VITTORIO EMANUELE II AND ENVIRONS. From S. Maria Maggiore, take V. C. Alberto south to the shabby P. V. Emanuele, home to one of Rome's largest outdoor markets, selling fresh fish, fruits, clothes, shoes, and luggage. Take V. di S. Croce in Gerusalemme from the eastern end of P. V. Emanuele to see the Rococo facade of the **Church of Santa Croce in Gerusalemme.** Scores of pilgrims come to catch a glimpse of the Fascist-era **Cappella delle Reliquie,** which contains fragments of the "true cross." Perhaps the eeriest of the chapel's relics is the dismembered finger used by doubting St. Thomas to probe Christ's wounds. *(Open M-Sa 9:30am-noon and 3-6pm, Su and holidays 9:30am-noon and 2:30-5:30pm.)*

CHURCH OF SAN PIETRO IN VINCOLI. Dating from the 4th century, San Pietro in Vincoli is so-named after the sacred chains by which St. Peter was supposedly bound after having been imprisoned on the Capitoline. The two chains were separated for more than a century in Rome and Constantinople, brought back together in the 5th century, and now lie beneath the altar. Michelangelo's imposing **statue of Moses** presides regally over the church. *(M:B-Cavour. Alternatively, take bus #75 to Largo V. Venosta. Walk southwest on V. Cavour, down toward the Forum. Take the stairs on your left up to P. S. Pietro in Vincoli. Open daily 7am-12:30pm and 3:30-7pm.)*

THE SOUTH

CAELIAN HILL

Just east of the Colosseum, the Caelian, along with the Esquiline, is the biggest of Rome's seven original hills and home to some of the city's greatest chaos. In ancient times, Nero built his decadent Domus Aurea between these hills (see p. 450). In the wake of its destruction, many of Rome's early churches were constructed at the **church of San Clemente.** Split into three levels, each from a different era, this is one of Rome's most intriguing churches. The complex incorporates centuries of handiwork into three layers: a 12th-century church on top of a 4th-century church, with an ancient **mithraeum** and sewers at the bottom. The upper church holds medieval mosaics of the Crucifixion, saints, and apostles. A fresco cycle by Masolino (possibly executed with help from his pupil Masaccio) dating from the 1420s graces the **Chapel of Santa Caterina.**

The early plan of the sprawling 4th-century lower church has been obscured by piers and walls built to support the upper church. With a little imagination, one can trace the lines of the original nave, aisles, and apse, which retain rare 11th-century frescoes. On this level are a few curiosities, including the tomb of St. Cyril and a series of frescoes depicting Roman generals swearing in Italian, the first written use of the language. Further underground is a creepy 2nd-century **mithraeum.** A little further lies the *insulae*, a warren of brick and stone rooms where Nero is rumored to have played his lyre in AD 64 while the rest of Rome burned. Below this is a still-operative complex of Republican drains and sewers, some 30m down. *(M:B-Colosseo. Turn left out of the station, walk east on V. Fori Imperiali (V. Labicana) away from the Forum, and turn right onto P. S. Clemente. ☎06 70 45 10 18. Open M-Sa 9am-12:30pm and 3-6pm, Su and holidays 10am-12:30pm and 3-6pm. Lower basilica and mithraeum L5000.)*

SAN GIOVANNI

M:A-San Giovanni or bus #16 from Termini.

CHIESA DI SAN GIOVANNI IN LATERANO. This immense church, the cathedral of the diocese of Rome, was the seat of the pope until the 14th century. Founded by Constantine in 314, it's Rome's oldest Christian basilica. The Gothic *baldacchino* over the altar houses two golden reliquaries containing the heads of **St. Peter** and **St. Paul.** *(Open daily 7am-7:30pm. Cloister open daily 9am-6pm. L4000.)*

SCALA SANTA. This chapel houses the so-called *acheropite* image, a depiction of Christ supposedly not created by human hand, and what are believed to be the 28 marble steps used by Jesus outside Pontius Pilate's house in Jerusalem. Pilgrims win indulgence for their sins if they ascend the steps on their knees, reciting prayers on each step. Martin Luther experienced an early break with Catholicism while on pilgrimage here—in the middle of his way up, he realized what he saw as the futility and false piety of what he was doing, stood up, and left. *(Across the street from S. Giovanni. Open daily Apr.-Sept. 6:15am-7:30pm; Oct.-Mar. 6:15am-6:30pm.)*

THE AVENTINE HILL

The easiest approach to the Aventine is from the western end of the Circus Maximus (the end farthest from the Circo Massimo Metro stop) at P. Ugo la Malfa. From here, V. di Valle Murcia climbs past Rome's swankiest homes and a beautiful public rose garden to a park with orange trees and a sweeping view of southern Rome. Across the park, another gate opens onto the courtyard of the **Chiesa di Santa Sabina,** with a porch of ancient columns and a towering campanile. V. di S. Sabina continues along the crest of the hill to **Piazza dei Cavalieri di Malta,** home of the crusading order of the Knights of Malta. Through the **keyhole** in the pale yellow gate on the right, you can see the dome of St. Peter's perfectly framed by hedges.

THE APPIAN WAY

CHIESA DI SANTA MARIA IN PALMIS. In this church, also known as **Domine Quo Vadis,** a fleeing St. Peter had a vision of Christ. When asked *"Domine Quo Vadis?"* ("Lord, where are you going?"), Christ replied that he was going to Rome to be crucified again because Peter had abandoned him. Guilt eventually forced Peter to turn around. *(At the intersection of V. Appia Antica and V. Ardeatina. Take bus #218 from P. di S. Giovanni. Open daily 9am-noon and 4-7pm.)*

CATACOMBS. Since burial inside the city walls was forbidden during ancient times, fashionable Romans made their final resting places along the Appian Way. At the same time, early Christians secretly dug maze-like **catacombs** under the ashes of their persecutors. **San Callisto** is the largest catacomb in Rome, with nearly 22km of subterranean paths. Its four levels once held 16 popes, seven bishops, St. Cecilia, and 500,000 other Christians. **Santa Domitilla** enjoys acclaim for paintings; it houses an intact 3rd-century portrait of Christ and the Apostles. **San Sebastiano** was the temporary home for the bodies of Peter and Paul (or so ancient graffiti on its walls claims). *(M:A-San Giovanni. Take bus #218 from P. di S. Giovanni to the intersection of V. Ardeatina and V. delle Sette Chiese. At least 2 catacombs are open daily 8:30am-5:30pm; in winter 8:30am-5pm. Each catacomb L8000. In all 3, visitors follow a free tour in the language of their choice (every 20min.). S. Calisto: V. Appia Antica, 110. Take the private road that runs northeast to the entrance to the catacombs. ☎ 06 513 01 51. Open Mar.-Jan. Th-Tu, in winter Th-Su only. S. Domitilla: Facing V. Ardeatina from the exit of S. Callisto, cross the street and walk up V. delle Sette Chiese; the catacombs are on your left. ☎ 06 511 03 42. Open Feb.-Dec. W-M. S. Sebastiano: V. Appia Antica, 136. ☎ 06 785 03 50. Open Dec.-Oct. M-Sa.)*

TESTACCIO

M:B-Piramide stop or bus #27 from Termini

South of the Aventine Hill, the working-class district of Testaccio is known for its cheap and delicious *trattorie* and raucous nightclubs. The neighborhood centers on the forbidding, castle-like **Porta San Paolo** (an original remnant of the Aurelian defensive walls) and the colossal **Piramide di Gaius Cestius,** which was built in less than 330 days by the slaves of Gaius, tribune of the plebes under Augustus.

CIMITERO ACATOLICO PER GLI STRANIERI. This peaceful Protestant cemetery, or the "Non-Catholic Cemetery for Foreigners," is the only non-ancient burial space in Rome for those who don't belong to the Catholic Church. Keats, Shelley, and Antonio Gramsci were buried here. *(V. Caio Cestio, 6. From the Piramide station, follow V. R. Persichetti onto V. Marmorata, immediately turning left onto V. Caio Cestio. Ring the bell. Open Tu-Su Apr.-Sept. 9am-5:30pm; Oct.-Mar. 9am-4:30pm. Donation requested.)*

MONTE TESTACCIO. Monte Testaccio began as a dumping ground for terra-cotta pots. The pile grew and grew, and today the ancient garbage heap, with a name derived from *testae*, or pot shards, rises in lush, dark green splendor over the drab surrounding streets. *(At the end of V. Caio Cestio and across V. Nicola Zabaglia.)*

BASILICA DI SAN PAOLO FUORI LE MURA. The Basilica di San Paolo fuori le Mura, another of the churches in Rome with extraterritorial status (along with S. Giovanni in Laterano, S. Maria Maggiore, and St. Peter's), is the largest church in the city after St. Peter's. St. Paul is believed to be buried beneath the altar. Be sure to buy a bottle of monk-made **benedictine** in the gift shop (L13,000). *(M:B-Basilica San Paolo. Alternatively, take bus #23 or 170 from Testaccio. Open daily in summer 7am-6:30pm; in winter 7am-6pm. Cloister open 9am-1pm and 3-6:30pm; in winter 9am-1pm and 3-6pm.)*

EUR

M:B-EUR Fermi or bus #714

South of the city stands a monument to a Roman empire that never was. **EUR** (AY-oor) is an Italian acronym for Universal Exposition of Rome, the 1942 World's Fair that Mussolini intended to be a showcase of Fascist achievements. Apparently, the new, modern Rome was to shock and impress the rest of the world with its futuristic ability to build lots of identical square buildings. **Via Cristoforo Colombo,** EUR's main street, is the first of many internationally ingratiating addresses like "Viale Asia" and "Piazza Kennedy." It runs north from the Metro station to **Piazza Guglielmo Marconi** and its 1959 modernist **obelisk** (see p. 464).

ABBAZIA DELLE TRE FONTANE (ABBEY OF THE THREE FOUNTAINS). According to legend, when St. Paul was beheaded here, his head bounced on the ground three times, creating a fountain at each bounce. The Trappist monks who live here today sell their own potent eucalyptus liquor (L14-27,000), divine chocolate (L9-18,000 for monstrous bars of this wonderful stuff), body cream, and shampoo. *(M:B-Laurentina. Walk 750m north on V. Laurentina and turn right on V. di Acque Salve. The abbey is at the bottom of the hill. Or, take bus #761 north from Laurentina; ask to get off at the intersection of V. Laurentina and V. di Acque Salve. Open M-Sa 11am-5pm, Su noon-5pm.)*

MUSEUMS

Etruscans, emperors, popes, and *condottiere* have been busily stuffing Rome's belly full with artwork for several millennia, leaving behind a city teeming with galleries. Museums are generally closed holidays, Sunday afternoons, and all day Monday.

VATICAN MUSEUMS

10 blocks north of the right-hand side of P. San Pietro along the Vatican wall. From M:A Ottaviano, walk south several blocks to the Vatican wall and turn right. ☎06 69 88 33 33 or 06 69 88 43 41. Info and gift shop (with the official guidebook, L12,000) on the ground level past the entrance. Audio guide L8000. Most collections sport English and Italian labels, although the descriptions are sparse in certain galleries. All major galleries open M-Sa 8:45am-1:45pm; Mar. 16-Oct. 30 M-F 8:45am-4:30pm, Sa 8:45am-1:45pm. Closed on religious holidays. Last entrance 1hr. before closing. L18,000, with ISIC L12,000, children under 1m tall free. Free last Su of the month 8:45am-1:45pm. Most of the museum is wheelchair accessible, though less visited parts, such as the upper level of the Etruscan Museum, are not. Various galleries close without explanation, so call ahead.

The Vatican Museums constitute one of the world's greatest collections of art, a vast storehouse of ancient, Renaissance, and modern statuary, painting, and sundry papal odds and ends. The museum entrance at V. Vaticano leads to the famous bronze double-helix ramp that climbs to the ticket office (near a currency exchange, a first aid station, a post office, and a booth selling guidebooks that are well worth the price). A good place to start your tour is the stellar **Museo Pio-Clementino,** the world's greatest collection of antique sculpture.

Two slobbering Molossian hounds guard the entrance to the **Stanza degli Animali,** a marble menagerie that highlights the importance of brutality in Roman pastimes. Among other gems, it features the **Apollo Belvedere** and the unhappy **Laocoön** family. The last room of the gallery contains the enormous red sarcofago di Sant'Elena, mother of Constantine.

From here, the Simonetti Stairway climbs to the **Museo Etrusco,** filled with artifacts from Tuscany and northern Lazio. Back on the landing of the Simonetti Staircase is the Stanza della Biga (room of an ancient marble chariot) and the Galleria della Candelabra. The long trudge to the Sistine Chapel begins here, passing through the Galleria degli Arazzi (tapestries), the Galleria delle Mappe (maps), the Apartamento di Pio V (where there is a shortcut to *la Sistina,* for all the cheaters out there), the Stanza Sobieski, and the Stanza della Immaculata Concezione.

From the Room of the Immaculate Conception, a door leads into the 1st of the four **Stanze di Rafaele,** the apartments built for Pope Julius II in the 1510s. Raphael painted the astonishing **School of Athens** as a trial piece for Julius, who was so impressed that he fired his other painters, had their frescoes destroyed, and commissioned Raphael to decorate the entire suite. The Stanza della Segnatura features the *School of Athens*, Raphael's masterpiece. From here, there are two paths: a staircase leads to the brilliantly frescoed Borgia Apartments and the **Museum of Modern Religious Art** and another route goes to the Sistine Chapel.

SISTINE CHAPEL. Ever since its completion in the 16th century, the Sistine Chapel (named for its founder, Pope Sixtus IV) has served as the chamber in which the College of Cardinals elects new popes. The ceiling, which is flat but appears vaulted, gleams with the results of its recent restoration. The frescoes on the side walls predate Michelangelo's ceiling. On the right, scenes from the life of

Moses complement parallel scenes of Christ's life on the left. The cycle was completed between 1481 and 1483 under the direction of Perugino by a team of artists including Botticelli, Ghirlandaio, Roselli, Pinturicchio, Signorelli, and della Gatta.

The simple compositions and vibrant colors of Michelangelo's unquestioned masterpiece hover above, each section depicting a story from Genesis. The scenes are framed by the famous *ignudi*, young nude males. Michelangelo painted not flat on his back, but standing up and craning backwards, and he never recovered from the strain to his neck and eyes. Michelangelo's *The Last Judgement* fills the altar wall. The figure of Christ as judge hovers in the upper center, surrounded by his saintly entourage and the supplicant Mary.

PINACOTECA. This is one of the best painting collections in Rome, including Filippo Lippi's *Coronation of the Virgin*, Perugino's *Madonna and Child*, Titian's *Madonna of San Nicoletta dei Frari*, and Raphael's *Transfiguration*. On your way out of the Sistine Chapel, take a look at the **Room of the Aldobrandini Marriage,** which contains a series of rare and famous ancient Roman frescoes.

OTHER PRINCIPAL COLLECTIONS

GALLERIA BORGHESE. This is an exquisite museum, but you'll only have two hours to visit it, so hurry! Room I, on the right, houses Canova's sexy statue of **Paolina Borghese** portrayed as Venus triumphant. The next rooms display the most famous sculptures by Bernini: magnificent **David,** who crouches in controlled aggression with his slingshot; **Apollo and Daphne,** in Room III, which literalizes the twisting form; the weightless body in **Rape of Proserpina;** and weary-looking Aeneas in **Eneo e Anchise.** Don't miss six **Caravaggio** paintings, including the *Self Portrait as Bacchus* and *St. Jerome*, which grace the side walls. The collection continues in the *pinacoteca* upstairs, accessible from the gardens around the back by a winding staircase. Room IX holds Raphael's **Deposition** while Sodoma's *Pietà* graces Room XII. Also look for self portraits by Bernini, del Conte's *Cleopatra* and *Lucrezia*, Rubens's haunting **Pianto sul Cristo Morto,** and Titian's **Amor Sacro e Amor Profano.** *(P. Scipione Borghese, 5. M:A-Spagna. Alternatively, take bus #910 from Termini to V. Pinciana or follow Villa Borghese exit signs and head left up the road to reach V. del Museo Borghese. Helpful brown signs within the park point the way. ☎06 854 85 77. Open Tu-F 9am-7:30pm, Sa 9am-11pm, Su and holidays 9am-8pm. Entrance only on the hr., visits limited to 2hr., last entrance 30min. before closing. A limited number of people are admitted hourly; the gallery does sell out. The basement of the palace contains the ticket office, a bookshop selling a guidebook (L20,000), an info kiosk, a snack bar, and restrooms. L14,000, EU citizens ages 18-25 L8000, EU citizens under 18 and over 60 L2000. Tickets include ground-floor galleries and Pinacoteca. Reserve tickets for L2000 extra.)*

MUSEO NAZIONALE ETRUSCO DI VILLA GIULIA. The villa was built under Pope Julius III, who reigned from 1550 to 1555. Highlights of Rome's Etruscan museum include a graceful sarcophagus of a man and wife in Room 9 and an Etruscan chariot, or *biga*, and the petrified skeletons of two horses found beside it in Room 18. Upstairs, archaeologists have put together the fragments of the entire facade of an Etruscan temple, complete with terra-cotta gargoyles, chips of the original paint, and a relief of the Greek warrior Tydaeus biting into the brain of a wounded but still living adversary. (The goddess Athena, who had been planning on giving Tydaeus immortal life, turns away in disgust.) Don't miss the famous Euphronios vase in a special exhibit near the giftshop. *(In Villa Borghese at P. Villa Giulia, 9. M:A-Flaminio or bus #19 from P. Risorgimento or #52 from P. San Silvestro. ☎06 320 19 51. Open Tu-F, Su, and holidays 8:30am-7:30pm, Sa 9am-8pm; June-Sept. Tu-F, Su, and holidays 8:30am-7:30pm, Sa 9am-11pm. L8000, EU citizens and southern and central Australians under 18 and over 60 free; Canadians under 15 free. Audioguide L8000, guidebook L20,000, at the bookstore.)*

CAPITOLINE MUSEUMS. The collections of ancient sculpture in the Capitoline Museums are among the largest in the world. The frescoes are breathtaking, and the assortment of Italian painting in the *pinoteca* is truly representative of the period. The Palazzo Nuovo contains the original statue of **Marcus Aurelius** that once stood in the center of the *piazza*. The sculpture rooms contain notables like *Dying Gaul*, *Satyr Resting* (the "Marble Faun" that inspired Nathaniel Hawthorne's book), and *Venus Prudens*. The sculpture collections continue across the *piazza* in the Palazzo dei Conservatori. See the fragments of the **Colossus of Constantine** and the famous **Capitoline Wolf,** an Etruscan statue that has symbolized the city of Rome since ancient times. At the top of the stairs, the **pinacoteca** houses an assortment of 16th- and 17th-century Italian paintings. Among the masterpieces not purloined by the Vatican Galleries are Bellini's *Portrait of a Young Man*, Titian's *Baptism of Christ*, and Rubens's *Romulus and Remus Fed by the Wolf*. Also worth seeing are Caravaggio's *St. John the Baptist* and his *Gypsy Fortune-Teller*. *(Atop the Capitoline Hill (behind the Vittorio Emanuele II monument). ☎ 06 39 74 62 21. Open Tu-Su 10am-8pm, holidays 9am-1:30pm. Ticket office closes 30min. before museum. L15,000, with ISIC L11,000, Italian citizens under 18 and over 60 free. Guidebook L30,000; audioguide L7000; daily English tours L6000. Not wheelchair accessible.)*

MUSEO NAZIONALE D'ARTE ANTICA. This collection of 12th- through 18th-century art is split between Palazzo Barberini and Palazzo Corsini. The former houses more masterpieces, but both deserve a visit. **Palazzo Barberini** contains paintings from the medieval through Baroque periods, including works by Lippi, Raphael, El Greco, Carracci, Caravaggio, and Poussin. *(V. delle Quattro Fontane, 13, near P. Barberini. ☎ 06 4814 591. Open Tu-Sa 9am-7pm, Su 9am-8pm. L12000, EU citizens 18-25 L7000, EU citizens under 18 and over 65 and students of art and architecture L2000.)* **Galleria Corsini,** holds a collection of 17th- and 18th-century paintings, from Dutch masters Van Dyck and Rubens to Italians Caravaggio and Carracci. *(V. della Lungara, 10, across Villa Farnesina in Trastevere. ☎ 06 68 80 23 23. Open Tu-Su 9am-6pm. L8000, EU students L2000.)*

VILLA FARNESINA. Thought to be the wealthiest man in Europe, Agostino "il Magnifico" Chigi lived sumptuously and eccentrically in the villa. At one banquet, Chigi had his guests toss his gold and silver dishes into the Tiber River after every course (the shrewd if somewhat prosaic-minded businessman had hidden nets under the water to recover his treasures). To the right of the entrance lies the breathtaking **Sala of Galatea,** mostly painted by the villa's architect, Baldassare Peruzzi, in 1511. The vault displays symbols of astrological signs that add up to a symbolic plan of the stars at 9:30pm on November 29, 1466, the moment of Agostino's birth. The masterpiece of the room is Raphael's **Triumph of Galatea.**

The stucco-ceilinged stairway, with its gorgeous perspective detail, ascends to the **Loggia di Psiche,** for which Raphael received the commission. The **Stanza delle Prospettive,** a fantasy room decorated by Peruzzi, offers views of Rome between *trompe l'oeil* columns. The adjacent bedroom, known as the *Stanza delle Nozze* (Marriage Room), is the real reason for coming here. Il Sodoma, who had previously been busy painting the pope's rooms in the Vatican, frescoed the room until Raphael showed up and stole the job. Il Sodoma bounced back, making this extremely masterful fresco of Alexander the Great's marriage to the beautiful Roxanne. *(V. della Lungara, 230, just across from Palazzo Corsini off Lungotevere Farnesina. Bus #23. ☎ 06 68 80 17 67. Open M-Sa 9am-1pm. L8000, under 18 L6000.)*

GALLERIA SPADA. Seventeenth-century Cardinal Bernardino Spada bought a grandiose assortment of paintings and sculpture and commissioned an even more opulent set of great rooms to house them. Time and good luck have left the palatial apartments nearly intact—a visit to the gallery offers a glimpse of the luxury surrounding Baroque courtly life. In the 1st of the gallery's four rooms, the cardinal hung three portraits of himself by Guercino, Guido Reni, and Cerini. In the portrait-studded Room 2, look for paintings by the Venetians Tintoretto and Titian and a frieze by Vaga, originally intended to be placed in the Sistine Chapel. In Room 4 are three canvases by the father-daughter team of Orazio and Artemisia Gentileschi. *(P. Capo di Ferro, 13, in the elaborate Palazzo Spada. South of Campo dei Fiori. Bus #64. ☎ 06 32 81 01. Open Tu-Sa 9am-7pm, Su 9am-12:30pm. L10,000, EU citizens under 18 and over 60 free. Call for reservations (L2000 extra).)*

MUSEI NAZIONALI ROMANI. The fascinating **Museo Nazionale Romano Palazzo Massimo** is devoted to the history of Roman art during the Empire, including the Lancellotti Discus Thrower, a rare mosaic of Nero's, and ancient coins and jewelry. *(Largo di V. Peretti, 1, in the left-hand corner of P. dei Cinquecento as you stand with your back to Termini. ☎06 481 55 76. Open Tu-Su 9am-7pm. L12,000, EU citizens 18-24 L6000, EU citizens under 18 and over 60 free.)* Nearby, the **Museo Nazionale Romano Terme di Diocleziano,** a beautifully renovated complex partly housed in the huge **Baths of Diocletian** (see p. 457) has exhibits devoted to ancient epigraphy (writing) and Latin history through the 6th century BC. Another wing of the museum is dedicated to exhibits on completely different world cultures. (☎06 39 96 77 00. Open Tu-Su 9am-7pm. L8000, EU citizens 18-24 L4000, EU citizens under 18 and over 60 free. Audioguide L6000; guided tour with archaeologist L10,000.) Across town is the Renaissance man of the trio, **Museo Nazionale Romano Palazzo Altemps,** P. S. Apollinaire, 44, just north of P. Navona. On display is ancient Roman sculpture, including the famous 5th-century *Ludovisi Throne. (P. dei Cinquecento, 78. ☎06 39 08 71. Open Tu-Su 9am-7pm. L10,000, EU citizens 18-24 L5000, EU citizens under 18 and over 60 free. A 6-day ticket book is good for all 3 museums, the Colosseum, and the Palatine Hill (L30,000).)*

EUR MUSEUMS. If anything good came of Mussolini's regime, it just might be the extensive collections in that bastion of fascist organization and architecture, EUR. The expansive **Museo della Civiltà Romana,** contains excellent and comprehensive exhibits on ancient Rome, including vast, incredibly intricate scale models of Trajan's Column (see p. 449) and Republican and Imperial Rome. *(P. Agnelli, 10, M:B-EUR, either stop. North up V. Cristoforo Colombo, or take bus #714 from Termini. ☎06 592 60 41. Open Tu-Sa 9am-7pm, Su 9am-1:30pm. L5000, under 18 and over 60 free.)* The smallest of the museums, the **Museo dell'Alto Medievo,** V. Lincoln, 3, exhibits weapons and other artifacts from the Dark Ages. *(☎06 54 22 81 99. Open M-Sa 9am-2pm, Su 9am-12:30pm. L4000, reduced L2000, under 18 and over 65 free. Wheelchair accessible.)* The **Museo Nazionale delle Arti Tradizioni Popolari** preserves Italian folk art and incredible replicas of traditional attire and farming equipment. *(P. G. Marconi, 8. ☎06 591 07 09; www.ips.it/musis/museo_arti. Open Tu-Su 9am-8pm; closed New Year's, May Day, and Christmas. Call for tours in Italian or braille. L8000, reduced price L4000, under 18 and over 65 free.)* Finally, the **Museo Preistorico ed Etnografico Luigi Pigorini,** contains an impressive collection of ethnographic artifacts, including the skull of the Neanderthal Guattari Man, discovered near Circeo often hosts visiting exhibitions. *(P. G. Marconi, 14. ☎06 549521; for guided tours in Italian ☎06 841 23 12. Open daily 9am-2pm. L8000, under 18 and over 65 free.)*

RECOMMENDED COLLECTIONS

MUSEO CENTRALE TERMOELETTRICA MONTEMARTINI. The building, a turn-of-the-century electrical plant, is a striking contrast to the Classical sculpture on display. Highlights include *Hercules' Presentation at Mount Olympus*, a huge and amazingly well preserved floor-mosaic of a hunting scene. *(V. Ostiense, 106. M:B-Piramide. From P. Ostiense, walk or take bus #702 or 23. ☎06 574 80 30. Open Tu-Su 10am-6pm. L8000, EU citizens18-24 L4000, EU citizens under 18 and over 60 free.)*

GALLERIA COLONNA. Despite its disorganization and inhospitable opening hours, the Galleria Colonna remains an impressive collection of art. The *palazzo* was designed in the 18th century to show off the Colonna family jewels, among them Tintoretto's *Narcissus. (V. della Pilotta, 17, just north of P. Venezia. ☎06 679 43 62. Open Sept.-July Sa 9am-1pm. L10,000, students L8000.)*

GALLERIA DORIA PAMPHILJ. The Doria Pamphilj family, whose illustrious kin included Pope Innocent X, remain in custody of this stunning private collection, on display in their palatial home. The villa's Classical art is quirkily arranged by size and theme. Be sure to seek out the masterpieces, such as Caravaggio's *Rest during the Flight in Egypt* and Raphael's *Double Portrait.* Also catch the preserved corpse (from the catacombs) in the small chapel. *(P.*

del Collegio Romano, 2. From P. Venezia, walk up V. del Corso and take your 2nd left. ☎06 679 73 23. Open F-W 10am-5pm. L14,000, students and seniors L11,000. Audioguide included. Useful catalogue with a L10,000 deposit. Private apartments open 10:30am-12:30pm. L6000.)

MUSEO BARRACCO. This impeccably arranged and labeled collection includes some Greco-Roman art, but its Egyptian and Assyrian holdings are the real attractions. Don't miss the 16th-century BC *Sphynx of Queen Hatshepsut. (C. V. Emanuele, 166. Take bus #64 from Termini to Largo di Torre Argentina. ☎06 68 80 68 48. Open Tu-Sa 9am-7pm, Su 9am-1pm. L3700, with ISIC L2500.)*

MUSEO NAZIONALE D'ARTE ORIENTALE. This museum sports a wide array of artifacts dating from prehistory to the 1800s, divided into six sections: evolution of art in the Near East; Islamic art; Nepalese and Tibetan art; Buddhist art from India; Southeast Asian art; and Chinese history. Highlights include Stone Age fertility dolls and psychedelic paintings of the Buddha. *(V. Merulana, 248, on the Esquiline. ☎06 487 44 15. Open M, W, and F 9am-2pm, Tu and Th 9am-7pm, Su 9am-1pm. Closed 1st and 3rd M of the month. L8000, Italian citizens under 18 and over 60 and humanities students free.)*

MUSEO CRIMINOLOGICO. After overloading on "artwork" and "culture," this crime and punishment museum is the perfect chaser. Torture devices comprise the 1st floor, as well as some old English etchings, among them *A Smith Has His Brains Beaten Out With a Hammer.* On the 2nd floor, learn about criminal phrenology and the secret language of tattoos. The 3rd floor contains terrorist, spy, and drug paraphernalia. *(V. del Gonfalone, 29, near Ponte Mazzini. ☎06 68 30 02 34. Open Tu 9am-1pm and 2:30-6:30pm, W 9am-1pm, Th 2:30-6:30pm, F-Sa 9am-1pm. May be closed in Aug. L4000, under 18 and over 60 L2000.)*

ENTERTAINMENT

Unfortunately, Roman entertainment isn't what it used to be. Back in the day, you could swing by the Colosseum to watch a man mauled by a bear. Today, Romans seeking diversion are more likely to go to a Testaccio nightclub than fight another man to the death. Still, Rome abounds with exciting entertainment options. Check out the weekly *Roma C'è* (with an English-language section) or *Time Out*, available at newsstands, for comprehensive club, movie, and event listings.

PUBS

If you're longing for the days of the organized, indoor drunkenness of your native land, your only recourse might be Rome's countless pubs, many of which have some sort of Irish theme. Drink prices often increase after 9pm.

Jonathan's Angels, V. della Fossa, 16 (☎06 689 34 26), west of P. Navona. Take V. del Governo Vecchio from Campo dei Fiori, turn left onto V. Parione, and take a left toward the lights. Michelangelo's accomplishments pale before the bathroom at Jonathan's Angels, the finest bathroom in Rome, nay, Italy. Medium beer on tap L10,000, cocktails/long drinks L15,000. Open daily 4pm-2am.

Trinity College, V. del Collegio Romano, 6 (☎06 678 64 72), off V. del Corso near P. Venezia. Offers degrees in such curricula as Guinness, Harp, and Heineken. Tuition L6-9000. Pub food served for lunch and dinner. Classes held every day noon-3am.

Pub Hallo'Ween, P. Tiburtino, 31 (☎06 444 07 05). In San Lorenzo, at the corner of V. Tiburtina and V. Marsala. Abandon all hope of not having fun. Plastic skulls, fake spiders, and spiderwebs abound. Enjoy delicious sandwiches such as the Freddy (salami and mozzarella), the Candyman (nutella), or the Frankenstein (double cheeseburger). Draft beer L6-8000, bottles L7-10,000. Cocktails L8-9000. Happy hour (free appetizers) 8:30-10pm. Open Sept.-July daily 8:30pm-2:30am.

Abbey Theatre, V. del Governo Vecchio, 51-53 (☎06 686 13 41). Drop in for a 10am Guinness (L10,000), stay for lunch (a lot of vaguely Irish dishes), watch MTV, and admire the touching painting of a drugged-looking Yeats. Happy hour daily 3-7pm. Open M-Th 10am-2am, F-Sa 10am-3am, Su 2:30pm-2am. V, MC.

The Drunken Ship, Campo dei Fiori, 20-21 (☎06 68 30 05 35). Because you're tired of meeting Italians. Because you want to commune with other hostelers. Because you need an emotion-free fling with a kindred spirit. Beer L8000. Happy hour daily 5-9pm, all night Tu. W 9-10pm is power hour–all the beer you can drink (L10,000). Ask about the student discount on Heineken. Takeout window. Open 5pm-2am.

Caipirinha Pub-Café, V. del Gallo, 10 (☎06 689 25 61), off Campo dei Fiori. This fun Brazilian bar serves up tropical drinks and lots of Latin dancing. *Panini* L4000. Cocktails around L10,000, Bud L4000, Guinness L6000. Open daily 7pm-2am.

Julius Caesar, V. Castelfidardo, 49 (☎06 446 15 65), just north of Termini, on the corner of V. Solferino. Always packed with backpackers and locals here for live music, cheap drinks, and good times. Beer on tap L6-8000, pitchers L15,000, cocktails L10,000, wine L20,000 per bottle. Happy hour (beer and sandwich L10,000) 9-10pm. Inquire about the *Let's Go* discount. Open daily 8:30pm-2am.

CLUBS

Although Italian discos can be a flashy, sweaty good time, you must overcome some obstacles before donning your dancing shoes. First, you won't meet many non-Italians (could be nice for a change). Second, the scene changes as often as Roman phone numbers, and many clubs flee beachward for the steaming summer to **Fregene, Ostia,** or **San Felice Circeo.** Check *Roma C'è* or *Time Out.*

Qube, V. Portonaccio, 212 (☎06 438 10 05). From P. di Porta Maggiore, take V. Prenestina east; turn left on V. Portonaccio. Seedy neighborhood; plan to take a cab home. A warehouse-style disco, and one of Rome's biggest. "Transmania," on Su, is one of Rome's most popular gay nights. Cover L10-20,000. Open Th-Su 11pm-4am.

Radio Londra Caffè, V. di Monte Testaccio, 65b (☎06 575 04 44). Admit it: you've always fantasized about watching Italian bands cover rock classics. Packed with an energetic, good-looking, young crowd. Pizza, *panini,* and hamburgers (L8-12,000). Pint of Carlsberg L7000. Monthly pass L10,000. Open Su-F 9pm-3am, Sa 9pm-4am.

C.S.I.O.A. Villaggio Globale (☎06 57 30 03 29), Lungotevere Testaccio. Take bus #27 from Termini, get off before it crosses the river, and turn left. You may not want to walk alone here at night. Housed in a huge Testaccio slaughterhouse, it hosts all things countercultural: live music, films, art exhibits, and more. Hours and cover vary.

Alien, V. Velletri, 13-19 (☎06 841 22 12), north of Termini. One of the biggest discos in Rome attracts a well-dressed crowd and plays the house you know and love. The comfy chill-out room has not reached 1987. Cover L10-30,000 (includes a drink). Open Tu-Sa 11pm-4am. Moves to Fregene during the summer.

Piper, V. Tagliamento, 9 (☎06 841 44 59), north of Termini. Take bus #319 to Tagliamento. 70s, rock, disco, and the standard house and underground. Very gay friendly. Cover L15-35,000 (includes drink). Open Sa-Su 11pm-3am; in summer Su 11pm-3am.

Alpheus, V. del Commercio, 36 (☎06 574 78 26), off V. Ostiense. 3 huge dance floors and a couple of rooms for relaxing only. Friday is Rome's most popular gay night, "Mucassassina," (literally, cow killer). Other nights feature live jazz, rock, folk, cabaret, and comedy. Cover L10-20,000. Students free Th. Open Tu-Su 10pm-4:30am.

Dub Club, V. dei Funari, 21a (☎06 68 80 50 24), in the Jewish Ghetto. A blue-lit underground, circular disco. Techno, funk, acid jazz, and exotica. Cover L10-20,000. Open Tu-F 11pm-4am, Sa-Su 11pm-6am. Things get rolling at 2am. Closed most of summer.

GAY AND LESBIAN ENTERTAINMENT

Rome has fewer gay establishments than most cities its size, but those it has are solid and keep late hours. Many of the following establishments require an **ARCI-GAY pass** (L20,000 yearly), available from **Circolo di Cultura Omosessuale Mario Mieli** (☎06 541 39 85). Of the above clubs, **Alpheus, Piper,** and **Qube** host gay nights. *Time Out* has good coverage of gay events. For more info on gay life in Rome, see p. 434.

Hangar, V. in Selci, 69 (☎06 488 13 97). M:B-Cavour. Near Termini, off V. Cavour. Friendly John from Philly runs this small bar, once the home of Nero's wife. Hangar is considered the hotspot for gay nightlife in Rome, attracting mostly twenty-something men. Though usually packed, the atmosphere is cool, neon blue, and laid-back. Women are welcome (except M, dirty movie night) but may feel out-of-place. Drinks L3-10,000. Open W-M 10:30pm-2am. Closed 3 weeks in Aug. ARCI-GAY pass required.

L'Alibi, V. Monte di Testaccio, 39-44 (☎06 574 34 48), in Testaccio. Bus #30N. Large, elegant, and diverse, with an expansive rooftop terrace. Especially in summer, this is *the* gay club in Rome. Underground, house, and retro. Mostly gay, though lesbians and straights are welcome. Cover L15-20,000; Th and Su free. Open W-Su 11pm-4:30am.

New Joli Coeur, V. Sirte, 5 (☎06 86 21 58 27), off V. Eritrea. Rome's primary lesbian dance club is a little out of the city center, east of Villa Ada. Kind of seedy neighborhood; women often go together or split the cab fare. Kitsch decor and retro underground music, with the occasional live cabaret show or girl group. Women only. One-drink minimum (L15-20,000). Open Sa 11pm-3am, may be open Su.

LIVE MUSIC

The smaller festivals that run from mid-May to August are just parts of the larger **Roma Estate** (www.romaestate.com). It all starts with the **Festa Europea della Musica,** a weekend of mostly-free concerts at the end of June. In July, the **Accademia Nazionale di Santa Cecilia** (☎06 361 10 64 or 06 361 18 33; credit card reservations ☎06 68 80 10 44) holds concerts in Villa Borghese. The **Theater of Marcellus**, V. del Teatro di Marcello, 44, near P. Venezia, hosts summer evening concerts organized by the **Associazione Il Tempietto.** (☎06 481 4800. L30,000).

Alexanderplatz Jazz Club, V. Ostia, 9 (☎06 39 74 21 71). M:A-Ottaviano. Near Vatican City. From the station, head west on V. G. Cesare, take the 2nd right onto V. Leone IV and the 1st left onto V. Ostia. Known by some as Europe's best jazz club, its stuffy, smoky atmosphere conveys the mythical feeling of the 40s jazz joint, while sparkling walls and a funky bar suggest a modern side. Read messages left on the walls by the greats who have played here, from old pros like Art Farmer and Cedar Walton to young stars like Steve Coleman and Josh Redman. Cocktails L12,000. Two-month pass required (L12,000). Shows start at 10:30pm. Open Sept.-June daily 9pm-2am.

Big Mama, V. S. Francesco a Ripa, 18 (☎06 581 25 51), off V. di Trastevere on the left as you face the river. Blues, blues, and more blues. A L20,000 pass is valid for a year. Occasional L10,000 cover for big-name groups. Open Oct.-June daily 9pm-1:30am; sometimes closed Su and M—call ahead.

Berimbau, V. dei Fienaroli, 30b (☎06 581 32 49). Rome's premier location for Brazilian music. Live music is followed by a raging disco of salsa, merengue, and a variety of other Latin music. Cover L10-25,000, includes a drink. Open W-Su 10:30pm-3:30am.

Testaccio Village, V. di Monte Testaccio, 16 (☎06 57 28 76 61). Live, mostly local rock and pop. Open nightly from mid-June to mid-Sept. around 9pm.

Roma Incontra il Mondo (☎06 418 03 69). A festival of *musica etnica* livens up the lake in Villa Ada at V. di Ponte Salario. Open late June to early Sept. 6pm-late.

THEATER

Roman theaters, though not on par with those in other major European cities, still generate a number of quality productions, ranging from mainstream musicals to black-box experimental theater. Rome's most important theatre, **Teatro Argentina,** V. di Torre Argentina, 52, runs drama and music festivals throughout the year. (☎06 68 80 46 01. Box office open M-F 10am-2pm and 3-7pm, Sa 10am-2pm.) For information on English theater, check the tourist office or the English section of *Roma C'è*. Useful websites include www.musical.it and www.comune.rome.it.

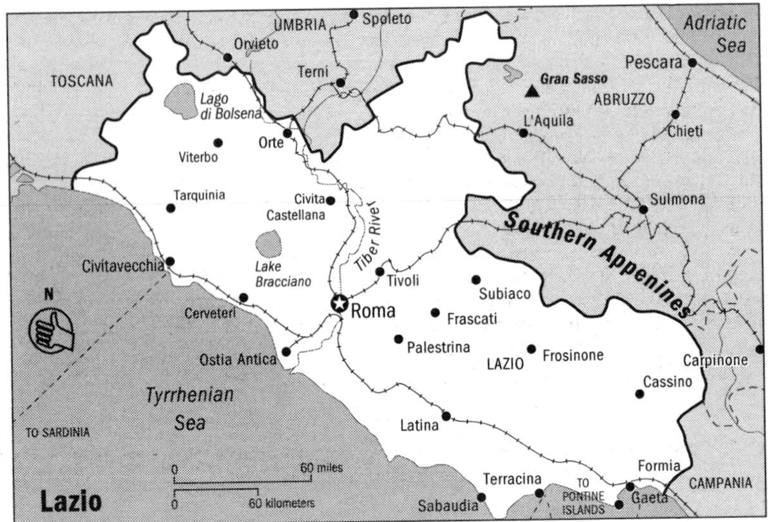

CINEMA

Unfortunately, most theaters in Rome show dubbed movies. Look for a "v.o." or "l.o." in any listing; it means *versione originale* or *lingua originale* (i.e., not dubbed). In summer, especially July, huge screens come up in various *piazze* for **outdoor film festivals.** The **San Lorenzo Sotto le Stelle** film festival occurs at Villa Mercede, V. Tiburtina, 113, with shows at 9am and 11pm. (Tickets L8-10,000.) In addition, films are usually shown outdoors on the southern tip of Tiber Island.

All 1st-run theaters offer lower priced tickets for the first two screenings of the day from Monday to Friday (around 4:30 and 6:30pm), as well as all day Wednesday. One good web resource for cinema in Rome is **I Love Rome,** which has a searchable database of movie theaters and showtimes (www.alfanet.it/welcomeItaly/roma/default.html). **Il Pasquino,** V. del Piede, 19, off P. S. Maria in Trastevere, is Rome's biggest and best English-language movie theater. The program changes daily, so call for the schedule. (☎06 583 33 10 or 06 580 36 22. Tickets L12,000.)

SPECTATOR SPORTS

Though May brings international tennis and equestrian events, sports basically means *calcio*, or soccer. Rome has two teams in Serie A, Italy's prestigious league: the 2000 European champion **A.S. Roma** and **S.S. Lazio.** The wild games at the **Stadio Olimpico,** in Foro Italico are held almost every Sunday (sometimes Saturdays) from September to June, with European cup matches often played mid-week. The can't miss matches of the season are the two Roma-Lazio games, which often prove decisive in the race for the championship. Single-game tickets, typically starting at L30,000, can be bought at the stadium before games (although lines are long and tickets often run out), or at team stores: **A.S. Roma Store,** P. Colonna, 360 (☎06 678 65 14), off V. del Corso, and **Lazio Point,** V. Farini, 24 (☎06 482 66 88). Many sporting events sell tickets at **Orbis Agency,** P. dell'Esquilino, 37 (☎06 482 74 03).

NEAR ROME

Rural Lazio was originally called *Latium*, Latin for "wide land." Lazio stretches from the low Tyrrhenian coastline through volcanic mountains to the foothills of the Abruzzese Apennines. Romans, Etruscans, Latins, and Sabines all settled here, and their contests for supremacy make up some of the first pages of Italy's recorded history. When Rome's mayhem overwhelms you, head for the hills.

BEACHES

A national predilection for tans makes Rome's beaches popular destinations. While most get crowded on weekends, they don't become packed until August.

Bustling **Nettuno** sprawls along the coastline (from Termini: 1hr.; outbound 6:50am-9:30pm, return 5am-9:50pm; L5600). There is a **Pro Loco tourist office** at the marina. (☎06 980 33 35. Open M-F 8am-noon.) Below the gaudy Palazzo Municipale, a busy marina teems with boats; the **public beach** lies to the left. When the beaches near Rome start to feel overcrowded, head south to **Sperlonga** for soft sands, clear blue waves, and plenty of elbow room (direction: Naples; 1¼hr., every 15min.-1hr. 6:10am-10:30pm, L8000). But there's more to Nettuno than just surf, sun, and sand. The little town managed to preserve more of its ancient foundations than Anzio did, including a walled medieval quarter. A few blocks north toward Anzio, at P. S. Francesco, stands the **Fortezza Sangallo,** an early 16th-century fortress that houses the **Museo dello Sbarco Alleato,** devoted to the Allied landing. (Fortress open Tu-Sa 9am-noon and 4-7pm. Museum open M, W, and F 8am-2pm, Tu and Th 8am-7pm. Free.) Nettuno has done its best to forget its war-torn past, but one reminder remains: the **Sicily-Rome American Cemetery** stretches over 77 acres of beautiful parkland donated to the US. Turn right coming out of the train station and then right again onto V. Santa Maria. It holds the graves of 7861 Americans who died during the 1943-44 Italian campaign. (Open daily 8:30am-5:30pm.)

TIVOLI

Metro (B) to Rebibbia, then COTRAL bus to Tivoli (25min., 3-5 per hr., L3000). On the street leading away from P. Garibaldi, a big "I" on a round shack marks the tourist office. (☎07 74 31 12 49. Open M-Sa 9:45am-3pm.)

From P. Garibaldi, sneak your way through the gauntlet of souvenir stands through P. Trento down the path to the **Villa d'Este,** the castle-garden on your left. Villa d'Este was laid out by Cardinal Ercole d'Este (the son of Lucrezia Borgia) and his architect Piero Ligorio in 1550 with the idea of recreating an ancient Roman *nymphaea* and pleasure palaces. Spectacular terraces and fountains abound. (☎07 74 31 20 70. Open daily May-Aug. 9am-6:45pm; Sept.-Apr. 9am-1hr. before sunset. Sa closes 1½hr. earlier. L8000, EU citizens under 18 and over 60 free.)

Follow V. di Sibilla across town to reach the Villa Gregoriana, a park with paths that descend past temples and scattered grottoes carved out by rushing water. The star of the show is the **Great Cascade,** where the river plunges 160m from the opening of Gregory XVI's tunnel. (Open June-Aug. Tu-Su 9:30am-7:30pm; Sept.-May Tu-Su 9:30am-1hr. before sunset. L3500, under 12 L1000.)

From Tivoli proper, it's a 5km trip to the vast remains of the **Villa Adriana.** From P. Garibaldi, take the orange #4x bus from the newsstand (L1400; buy 2 tickets as they're often out at the villa). The villa is the largest and most expensive ever built in the Roman Empire. Emperor Hadrian designed its buildings in the 2nd century in the styles of monuments that he had seen in his travels. Look for the Pecile, built to recall the famous Stoa Poikile (Painted Porch) of Athens, and the Canopus, an expanse of water lined by classical statues that replicates a canal near Alexandria, Egypt. (☎07 74 53 02 03. Open daily 9am-1½hr. before sunset. L8000.)

PONTINE ISLANDS

The Pontine Islands, a stunning archipelago of volcanic mountains 40km off the coast of Anzio, were once a haven for the notorious Saracen and Corsican pirates. The cliff-sheltered beaches, turquoise waters, assorted coves, tunnels, and grottoes provided the pirates a place to unwind after pillaging and plundering.

TRANSPORTATION AND PRACTICAL INFORMATION. From Termini, take the train to **Anzio** (L5100) to catch a **ferry** to the islands. **CAREMAR** has Anzio (☎06 98 60 00 83) and Ponza (☎07 718 05 65; caremar.gestelnet.it.) offices. To **Ponza** (2½hr.; summer only; Th-Tu 8:10am and 2pm, W 8:10am). From Ponza (Th-Tu 11am and 5pm, W 5pm only; L42,200 round-trip). **Linee Vetor** (Anzio ☎06 984 50

83; Ponza ☎ 07 718 05 49; www.vetor.it.) runs speedy *aliscafi* (**hydrofoils**) year-round from Anzio to Ponza and on to Ventotene. To Ponza (75min.; June-Sept. M-F 3 per day, Sa-Su 5 per day 8:30am-5:30pm; L35,000 one-way). **Buses** leave from V. Dante. Follow C. Pisacane until it becomes V. Dante (past the tunnel), and the bus station is to the left. Buses circuit the island every 15-20min. until 1am (buy tickets from the driver, L1750). There are no official stops, so flag down buses along V. Panoramica. There are also scooter rentals near the port.

The **Pro Loco Tourist Office,** in P. Carlo Pisacane off V. Dante at the far left of the port (when facing inland), offers useful brochures with accommodations listings. (☎ 07 718 00 31; email prolocoponza@libero.it. Open daily M-Sa 9am-12:50pm and 4-7:30pm, Su 9am-1pm.) An **ATM** is at **Banca di Napoli,** C. Pisacane, 85. In **emergencies,** dial ☎ 113 or contact **First Aid** (☎ 07 718 06 87), at Località Tre Venti. Three doors to the left of the tourist office, at P. Pisacane, 32, is the **post office.** (☎ 07 71 80 67. Open M-F 8:15am-1:30pm, Sa 8:15am-noon.) **Postal Code:** 04027.

ACCOMMODATIONS AND FOOD. Unfortunately, hotel prices have skyrocketed over the past few years due to increased tourism, and **camping** is illegal. Hotels are spread out across the island and many are atop steep hills; consider a **taxi** (usually L10,000). **Agenzia Immobiliare "Arcipelago Pontino,"** C. Pisacane, 49, can help you find a room in a private home from L45,000 per person per night in July and August and less in the off-season. (☎ 07 718 06 78. Open daily 9am-1pm and 4:30-8:30pm.) Otherwise, try **Pensione-Ristorante "Arcobaleno,"** V. Scotti D. Basso, 6. Go straight up the ramp, follow the street until it ends and veer right until you pass the Bellavista Hotel. Turn left and follow the signs up. It offers great views and clean rooms with TVs. Half-pension is mandatory, but the food is excellent. (☎ 07 718 03 15. L100,000 per person; July-Aug. L120,000. V.)

The Pontine Islands are known and loved for their lentil soup, fish, and lobster. Restaurants and bars line the port, covering the boardwalk with tables and spicing up the nightlife. The best seafood is along the coastal road toward La Forna.

SIGHTS. Grottoes and beaches are hidden throughout Ponza. Explore on foot or try renting a boat (from L80,000). Guided boat tours cost around L45,000 per person. At the port, look for offices offering *una gita* (JEE-tah) *a Palmarola* for a tour of Ponza's coastline and neighboring **Palmarola.** The clear, turquoise water accentuates the white cliffs, tinted red by iron deposits and yellow by sulfur. On the way to Palmarola, you'll pass Dala Brigantina, a natural amphitheater of limestone. Most trips visit the **Pilatus Caves,** a natural breeding ground for fish.

The spectacular beach and surrounding white cliffs at **Chiai di Luna** are a 10-minute walk from the port. Turn left off the main road before the tunnel, and take the road to a path on the left. This descends through ancient tunnels to the beach. Le Forna's **Piscine Naturali** (natural swimming holes) offer views of the burg's whitewashed houses; take the bus to Le Forna and ask to stop at the Piscine.

You can also rent kayaks, paddle-boats, and pontoon boats. Check **Ponza Mare,** on V. Banchina Nuova, for rentals (☎ 07 718 06 79; www.giglio.net/Ponza), and **Scuola Sub "Nautilus"** (☎ 07 71 80 87 01), at Piscine Naturali, for scuba lessons.

ETRURIA

Welcome to Etruscanland, former home of a mythologized tribe that dominated north-central Italy during the 1st millennium BC. Since the Etruscans' buildings were wood, only their carved-out tufa tombs survive. Tomb paintings (at Tarquinia) celebrate life, love, eating, drinking, and sport in the hilly countryside.

TARQUINIA

Trains leave from Termini (1hr., 11 per day, last train leaves Tarquinia at 10:12pm; L10,200). Buses run from the train station to the beach (L1100) and to the city center (L1500) about every 30min. until 9:30pm. Buses also link the town with Viterbo (1hr., L6000). For bus schedules and info on southern Etruria, try the tourist office in P. Cavour, near the medieval walls. (☎ 07 66 85 63 84. Open M-Sa 8am-2pm and 4-7pm.)

When Rome was but a village of mud huts on the Palatine hill, Tarquin kings commanded this fledgling metropolis. Although little remains of the city, a subterranean **necropolis** of tombs lined with vibrant frescoes illustrates Tarquinia's history.

In P. Cavour stands the majestic **Museo Nazionale,** one of the most comprehensive collections of Etruscan art outside Rome. It houses a superb patrimony of Etruscan sarcophagi, some with paintings still visible on the sides, votive statues, and an enormous range of Etruscan and (occasionally sexy) Greek vases. Look for the famous **Winged Horses** upstairs. (☎07 66 85 60 36. Open Tu-Su 9am-7pm. L12000.)

The ticket from the museum will admit you to the **necropolis.** Take the bus marked "Cimitero" from Barriera S. Giusto or walk (15min.) from the museum. Head up C. V. Emanuele from P. Cavour and turn right on V. Porta Tarquinia. Follow this road as it changes its name to V. delle Tombe Etruschi until you reach the necropolis. (☎07 66 85 63 08. Open 9am-1hr. before sunset.)

CERVETERI

Blue COTRAL buses run to Cerveteri from Lepanto (M:A-Lepanto or bus #70) in Rome (every 30min.-1hr., L4900). Last bus to Rome leaves at 8:05pm; ask at the station. Fewer buses run on Sundays. From the village, it's 1½km to the necropolis; follow the signs downhill and then to the right. Whenever you see a fork in the road without a sign to guide you, choose the fork on the right, but don't follow the "Da Paolo Vino" sign at the final fork. The tourist office, V. della Necropoli, 2, will answer any queries. (☎06 995 23 04. Open Tu-Su 9:30am-12:30pm and 6-7:30pm.)

Take a flashlight and duck: the **Etruscan tombs** of Cerveteri's necropolis are a bit awkward to see but every bit worth the trouble. They remain a testament to a people that thought they could take it with them—those crazy Etruscans built a lasting city of stone houses for their dead, with multiple rooms you can now walk into, while their actual houses have decayed into oblivion. (☎06 994 00 01. Open May-Sept. Tu-Su 9am-7:30pm; Oct.-Apr. Tu-Sa 9am-4pm. L8000.)

LAKE BRACCIANO

By train, Anguillara and Bracciano are accessible by the Rome-Viterbo line (every hr.; from Rome's San Pietro station 5:35am-9:45pm, last train to Rome 10:14pm; L5300).

Lake Bracciano provides Rome with its nearest freshwater beach, about an hour away by bus. Despite volcanic, gravelly sand that may hurt your rear, this huge body of water is still well worth a visit. Fresh air, cool water, and a lush and hilly surrounding landscape compensate for its minor flaws. The impressive 15th-century **Orsini-Odescalchi Castle** dominates the town and offers some stunning frescoes and stuffed wild boars. (☎06 99 80 43 48. Open Apr.-Sept. Tu-F 10am-noon and 3-6pm; Oct.-Mar. Tu-F 10am-noon and 3-5pm, Sa 10am-12:30pm and 3-5:30pm, Su 10am-12:40pm and 3-5:40pm. Tours every hr. L11,000, children under 12 and military L9000.) See *Roma C'è* for listings of classical concerts often held here in the summer.

Bracciano's many *trattorie* cook up mounds of fresh lake fish and eel (the local specialty), though siestas often go a little overboard, and hours of operation are inconsistent. Down at the beach, a ferry ride across the lake to nearby **Anguillara** or **Trevignano** offers more spectacular scenery.

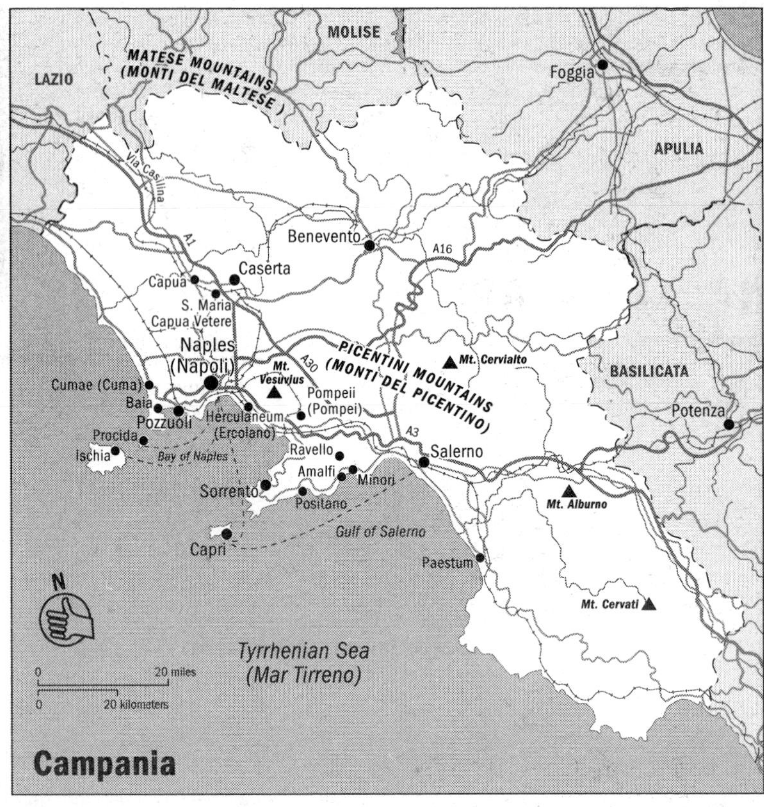

SOUTHERN ITALY

CAMPANIA

Procida and Ischia provide a respite from the hordes of tourists at Capri's luminescent grotto. The intact mosaics and frescoes of Herculaneum supplement those missing from Pompeii. But the intrigue of Campania also lies in the region's mythology. To the north lie the Phlegraean Fields, celebrated by Homer and Virgil and home to Lake Avernus, supposed entrance to Hades. While mermaids bathed in the Bay of Naples, sirens lured sailors to Sorrento. Reality and fantasy combine to provide a variety of attractions. Even in the chaotic capital, magical moments can be found in secret corners of the Museo Archeologico and in the perfect pizza.

HIGHLIGHTS OF CAMPANIA

DELIGHT in the **Farnese Bull,** the largest ancient sculpture, and marvel at the **Alexander mosaic** in Naples's Museo Archeologico Nazionale (p. 483).

CATCH Pompeii in the act and be a volcanic voyeur (p. 501).

DIVE into Capri's glowing **Grotta Azzurra** (p. 492).

RELISH the glorious beaches and stunning seascapes of the **Amalfi Coast** (p. 508).

GO templing in **Paestum,** home to remarkably preserved Greek monuments (p. 519).

NAPLES (NAPOLI)

☎081

Italy's 3rd-largest city is arguably its most colorful and certainly its most chaotic. Underneath Vesuvius the streets of Naples teem with activity, where Italians eat, work, play, and gossip. Here the amazing architectural monuments are not surrounded by tourists in tennis shoes, but are the backdrop to street markets, small shops, and lively neighborhoods. The narrow streets of the old city are home to a treasure trove of churches and *palazzi*, built when the agricultural wealth of Campania and the profits of trade and royal patronage filled the city with the arts.

With rampant poverty and unemployment rates nearing 25%, Naples certainly has its share of problems. But Naples is improving and old stereotypes are less and less applicable. In 1993, the city's former mayor, Antonio Bassolino (now Rome's Minister of Culture), dramatically increased the number of cops on the streets, decreasing crime 25% and increasing tourism 40%. Since the 1984 creation of the *Napoli 99*, a group of citizens determined to maintain Naples's art treasures, the city has aggressively restored monuments and opened them to the public for the first time. Exquisite churches, artisan's workshops, and colorful *trattorie* hide in every narrow alley. However, so do the black market factories that remain eternally hidden from tax collectors and mafia extorters.

GETTING THERE AND AWAY

Flights: Aeroporto Capodichino (☎081 789 61 11) V. Umberto Maddalena, northwest of the city. Connections to all major Italian and European cities. A **CLP bus** (☎081 531 16 46) leaves from P. Municipio (20min., every 50min. 6am-midnight, L3000). The #14 bus runs from P. Garibaldi to the airport (L1500). A **taxi** from the center costs L25,000. **Alitalia,** V. Medina, 41/42 (☎081 542 51 11), off P. Municipio. Open M-F 9am-4:30pm. **TWA,** V. Cervantes, 55 (☎081 551 30 63). Open M-F 9am-5:30pm. **British Airways** (☎081 780 81 30 87), in the airport. Open M-F 8am-8pm, Sa 9am-5pm.

Trains: Naples is served by 3 train companies that each leave from Stazione Centrale.

FS: Frequent connections to: **Salerno** (45min., 8 per day 8am-9pm, L5300); **Rome** (2hr., 38 per day 5am-10:30pm, L18,600); **Brindisi** (5hr., 5 per day 11am-8pm, L35,600); **Milan** (8hr., 13 per day 7:30am-10:30pm, L96,000); and **Syracuse** (10hr., 6 per day 10am-9:30pm, L55,000).

Circumvesuviana: (☎081 772 24 44). From Stazione Centrale (one floor underground) to: **Pompeii** (L3200); **Herculaneum** (L2300); and **Sorrento** (L4800). Trains depart every 30min. from 5am-10pm.

Ferrovia Cumana and Ferrovia Circumflegrea: (☎081 551 33 28). Both run Metro lines from Montesanto station to **Pozzuoli, Baia,** and **Cumae.** Trains depart every 20min. Info booth in Stazione Centrale open daily 7am-9pm. **Luggage Storage:** L5000 for 12hr. Open 24hr.

Ferries: Ferry schedules and prices change constantly; check ahead. *Qui Napoli* (free at the tourist office) and the newspaper *Il Mattino* (L1500) both carry current ferry schedules. Prices listed here are for high season. Weekend prices are often higher. Ferries run less frequently in the off season. Ask about port taxes. **Molo Angioino** and **Molo Beverello,** from which the ferries and hydrofoils depart, are next to each other at the base of P. Municipio. From P. Garibaldi take tram #1; from P. Municipio take the R2 bus.

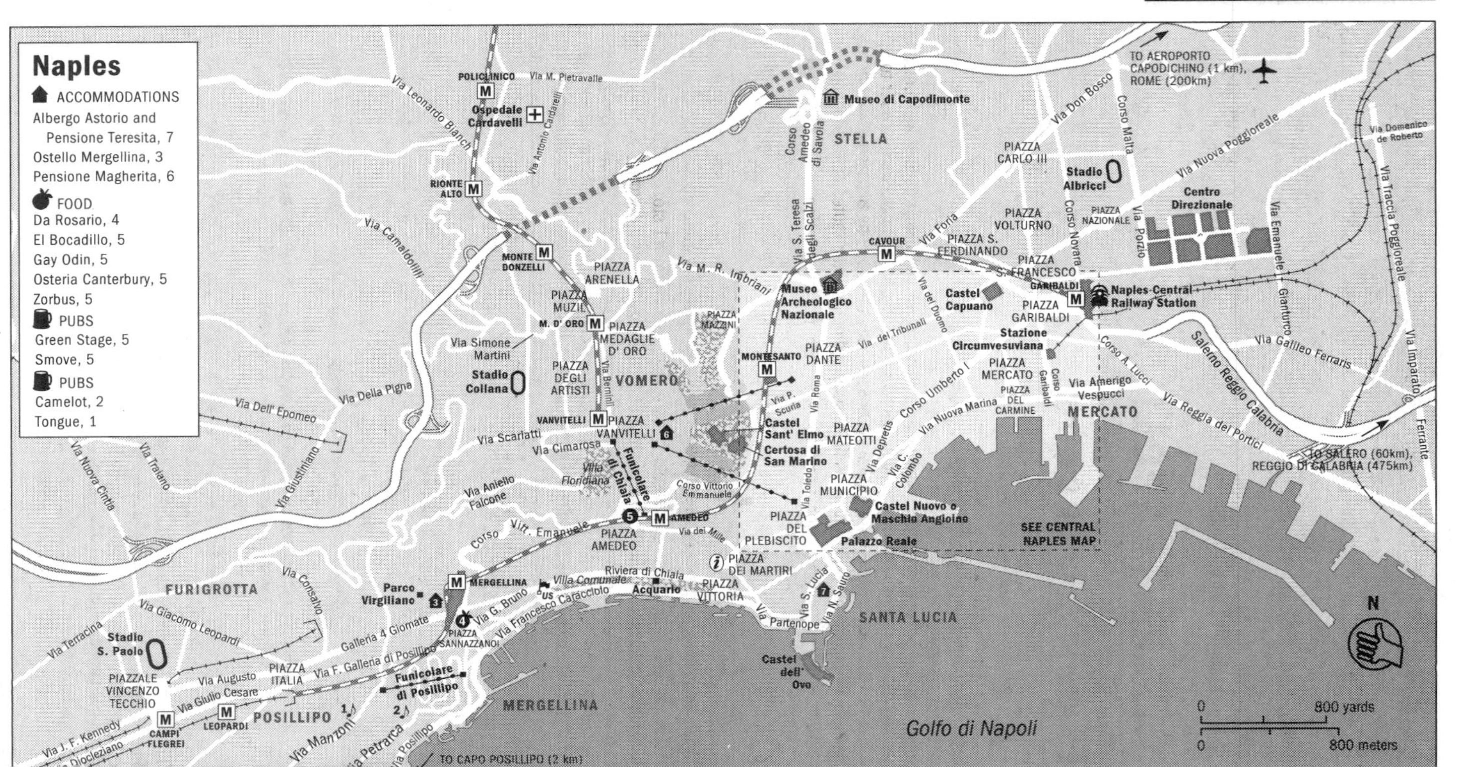

Naples
ACCOMMODATIONS
Albergo Astorio and Pensione Teresita, 7
Ostello Mergellina, 3
Pensione Magherita, 6
FOOD
Da Rosario, 4
El Bocadillo, 5
Gay Odin, 5
Osteria Canterbury, 5
Zorbus, 5
PUBS
Green Stage, 5
Smove, 5
PUBS
Camelot, 2
Tongue, 1
N
0
800 yards
800 meters
TO AEROPORTO CAPODICHINO (1 km), ROME (200km)
TO SALERO (60km), REGGIO DI CALABRIA (475km)
TO CAPO POSILLIPO (2 km)
SEE CENTRAL NAPLES MAP
Golfo di Napoli
SANTA LUCIA
MERGELLINA
POSILLIPO
FURIGROTTA
VOMERO
STELLA
MERCATO
Naples Central Railway Station
Stazione Circumvesuviana
Centro Direzionale
Stadio Albricci
Stadio Collana
Stadio S. Paolo
Museo di Capodimonte
Museo Archeologico Nazionale
Castel Capuano
Castel Nuovo o Maschio Angioino
Palazzo Reale
Castel Sant' Elmo
Certosa di San Marino
Castel dell' Ovo
Funicolare di Chiaia
Funicolare di Posillipo
Acquario
Villa Comunale
Villa Floridiana
Parco Virgiliano
Ospedale Cardavelli
PIAZZA GARIBALDI
PIAZZA MERCATO
PIAZZA DEL CARMINE
PIAZZA CARLO III
PIAZZA VOLTURNO
PIAZZA NAZIONALE
PIAZZA S. FRANCESCO
PIAZZA S. FERDINANDO
PIAZZA DANTE
PIAZZA MATEOTTI
PIAZZA MUNICIPIO
PIAZZA DEL PLEBISCITO
PIAZZA DEI MARTIRI
PIAZZA VITTORIA
PIAZZA AMEDEO
PIAZZA VANVITELLI
PIAZZA MEDAGLIE D' ORO
PIAZZA ARENELLA
PIAZZA MUZII
PIAZZA DEGLI ARTISTI
PIAZZA MAZZINI
PIAZZA SANNAZZARO
PIAZZA ITALIA
PIAZZALE VINCENZO TECCHIO
GARIBALDI
CAVOUR
MONTESANTO
AMEDEO
VANVITELLI
M. D' ORO
MONTE DONZELLI
RIONTE ALTO
POLICLINICO
MERGELLINA
LEOPARDI
CAMPI FLEGREI
Via Imparato
Ferrante
Via Traccia Poggioreale
Via Domenico de Roberto
Via Nuova Poggioreale
Via Emanuele Gianturco
Via Galileo Ferraris
Salerno Reggio Calabria
Via Reggia dei Portici
Corso Malta
Via Porzio
Via Don Bosco
Corso Novara
Corso A. Lucci
Via Amerigo Vespucci
Corso Garibaldi
Via Foria
Via del Duomo
Via dei Tribunali
Corso Umberto I
Via Nuova Marina
Via C. Colombo
Via Depretis
Via Toledo
Via Roma
Via S. Teresa degli Scalzi
Corso Amedeo di Savoia
Via M. R. Imbriani
Via P. Scura
Corso Vittorio Emmanuele
Via dei Mille
Riviera di Chiaia
Via Francesco Caracciolo
Via N. Sauro
Via S. Lucia
Via Partenope
Via Bernini
Via Cimarosa
Via Scarlatti
Via Simone Martini
Via M. Pietravalle
Via Antonio Cardarelli
Via Leonardo Bianchi
Via Camaldolilli
Via Della Pigna
Via Dell' Epomeo
Via Giustiniano
Via Aniello Falcone
Corso Vitt. Emanuele
Via G. Bruno
Galleria di Posillipo
Galleria 4 Giornate
Via F. Galleria
Via Consalvo
Via Augusto
Via Giulio Cesare
Via Giacomo Leopardi
Via Traiano
Via Nuova Cintia
Via Terracina
Via J. F. Kennedy
Via Diocleziano
Via Manzoni
Via Petrarca
Via Posillipo

Caremar: (☎081 551 38 82) has a ticket office on Molo Beverello. Open daily 6am-10pm. Ferries and hydrofoils depart 6:30am-10pm to: **Capri** (ferry: 1½hr., 11 per day, L9800; hydrofoil: 1hr., L18,000); **Ischia** (ferry: 1½hr., 14 per day, L9800; hydrofoil: 1hr, 14 per day, L18,000); and **Procida** (ferry: 1hr., 13 per day 6:30am-10pm, L8000; hydrofoil: 40min., 13 per day, L16,000).

Siremar Lines: (☎081 580 03 40; fax 081 580 03 41). Ticket office at Molo Angioino. Open daily 9am-7pm. 3 ferries per week, 2 per week in summer. To: **Stromboli** (8hr., L30,000); **Lipari** (12hr., L35,000); and **Vulcano** (13hr., L30,400); and intermediate points along the routes.

Tirrenia Lines: (☎081 720 11 11). Ticket office at Molo Angioino. Open daily 8:30am-1:15pm and 2:30-8pm. Ferries to **Palermo** (11hr., 8pm, L85,000) and **Cagliari** (15hr.; 2 per week in summer, 1 per week in winter; L98,000). You must pay an additional L10,000 port tax. Schedules vary—call for more information.

SNAV: (☎081 761 23 48; www.snavali.com). Open 9am-7pm. Runs hydrofoils to **Palermo** (5hr., 5:30pm, L100,200). Apr.-Oct. V, MC, AmEx.

Linee Lauro: (☎081 551 33 52). Ticket office at Molo Angioino. Open daily 9am-7pm. Ferries to **Tunis** (19hr.; 1 per week in winter, 2 per week in summer, L120,000).

GETTING AROUND

One "Giranapoli" ticket is valid for all modes of transport: **bus, Metro, tram,** and **funicular.** Tickets are available in 2 types: 1½hr. for L1500 or a full-day for L4500. Tickets are available at *tabbachi*. Everything stops running around midnight, except for the unreliable *notturno* (night) buses.

Bus: R1, R2, R3, and **R4 city buses** connect the city center (P. Bovio and P. Municipio) to Vomero, P. Garibaldi, Mergellina, and Capodimonte, respectively. Remember to validate your ticket at the yellow boxes. Pick up a copy of *Napoli by Bus*, the essential map to Naples's bus system. All stops have signs indicating their routes and destinations.

Metropolitana: To cover long distances (e.g., from the train station to P. Cavour, Montesanto, P. Amedeo, or Mergellina), use the efficient Metro, convenient for service from the station to points to the west: P. Cavour (Museo Nazionale), Montesanto (Cumana, Circumflegrea, funicular to Vomero), P. Amedeo (funicular to Vomero), Mergellina, and Pozzuoli. Go to platform #4, one floor underground at Stazione Centrale. If you're going to Procida or Ischia, take the Metro to Pozzuoli and depart from there.

Trams: From the station to Mergellina along the coast. Tram #1 stops at the Molo Beverello port. Catch it in front of the Garibaldi statue near Stazione Centrale.

Funiculars: All connect the lower city to the hilltop Vomero: **Centrale,** the most frequently used, runs from P. Fugo on V. Roma/Toledo; **Montesanto** from P. Montesanto; **Chiaia** from P. Amedeo. (M-Sa 4 per hr. 7am-10pm; Su reduced service 8am-7pm).

Taxis: Cotana (☎081 570 70 70), **Napoli** (☎081 556 44 44), or **Partenope** (☎081 556 02 02). Only take taxis with meters. No English spoken. L3000 surcharge 10pm-7am. L5000 surcharge from the airport.

ORIENTATION

DON'T TAKE CANDY FROM STRANGERS AND OTHER GOOD ADVICE. Though personal violence is rare in Naples, theft is common (unless you're in the *Camorra*, the Neapolitan mafia, in which case the opposite is true). Always practice street smarts. Don't carry your money in wallets or purses—keep it inaccessible to pickpockets. Young women will almost definitely be harassed and should travel in mixed company whenever possible. Ignore merchants who call out to you in English; they make it difficult to disentangle from conversation.

The central train station and the major city bus terminal are both in the immense **Piazza Garibaldi,** a crumbling area on the east side of Naples. The broad, commercial **Corso Umberto I** leads southwest from P. Garibaldi, ending at Piazza Bovio. From here **Via De Pretis** branches to the left, leading to **Piazza Municipio,** the financial and administrative center of Naples, and to the nearby Piazza Trieste e Trento

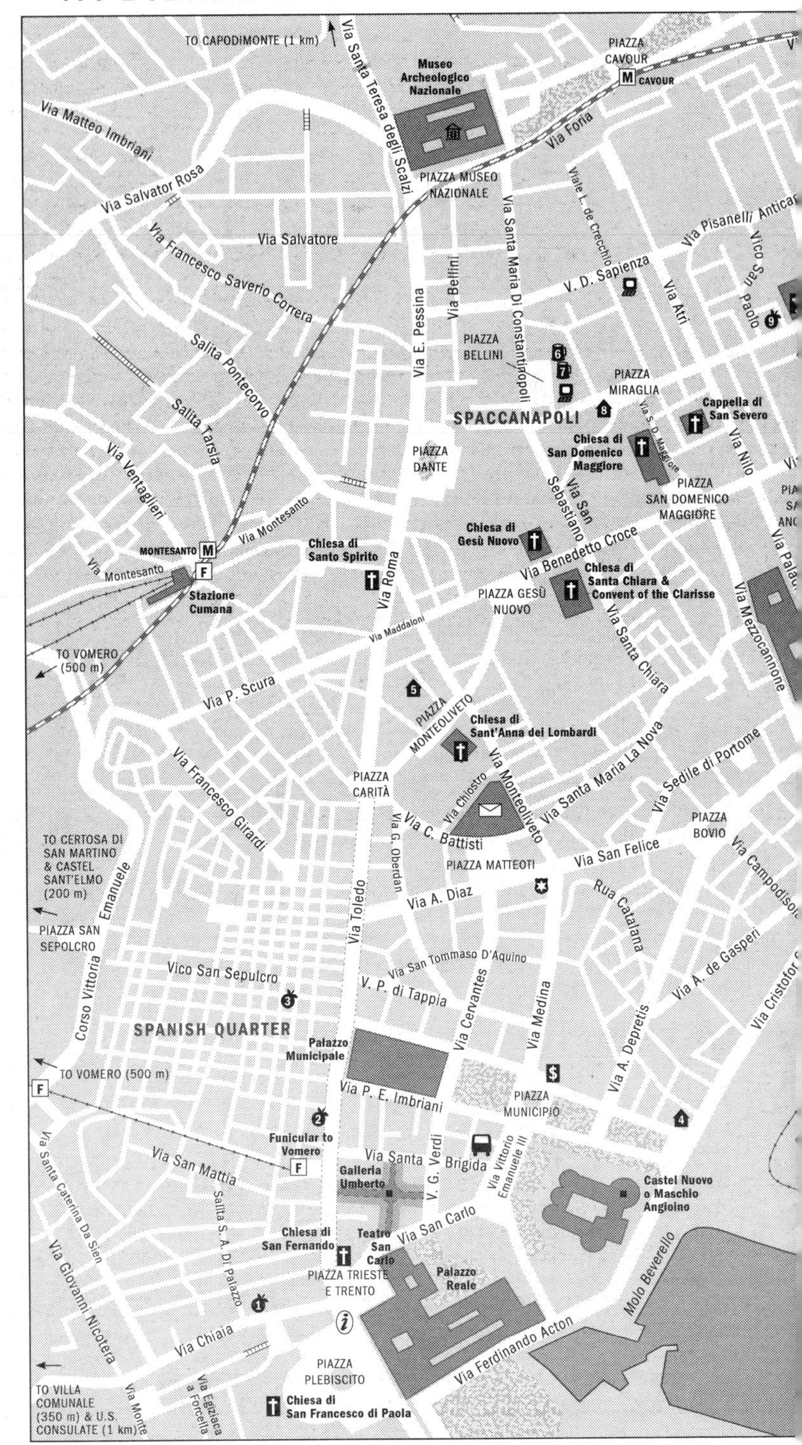
TO CAPODIMONTE (1 km)
Via Santa Teresa degli Scalzi
Museo Archeologico Nazionale
PIAZZA CAVOUR
CAVOUR
Via Foria
Via Matteo Imbriani
Via Salvator Rosa
PIAZZA MUSEO NAZIONALE
Viale L. de Crecchio
Via Pisanelli
Vico San Paolo
Via Salvatore
Via Francesco Saverio Correra
V. D. Sapienza
Via Atri
Via Bellini
Via Santa Maria Di Constantinopoli
Via E. Pessina
Salita Pontecorvo
PIAZZA BELLINI
PIAZZA MIRAGLIA
Salita Tarsia
SPACCANAPOLI
Cappella di San Severo
Chiesa di San Domenico Maggiore
Via S. D. Maggiore
Via Nilo
Via Ventaglieri
PIAZZA DANTE
PIAZZA SAN DOMENICO MAGGIORE
Via San Sebastiano
Via Montesanto
Chiesa di Gesù Nuovo
MONTESANTO
Chiesa di Santo Spirito
Via Benedetto Croce
Via Montesanto
Stazione Cumana
Via Roma
Chiesa di Santa Chiara & Convent of the Clarisse
PIAZZA GESÙ NUOVO
Via Mezzocannone
Via Maddaloni
TO VOMERO (500 m)
Via Santa Chiara
Via P. Scura
PIAZZA MONTEOLIVETO
Chiesa di Sant'Anna dei Lombardi
Via Santa Maria La Nova
Via Francesco Girardi
PIAZZA CARITÀ
Via Chiostro
Via Monteoliveto
Via Sedile di Portome
Via G. Oberdan
Via C. Battisti
PIAZZA BOVIO
TO CERTOSA DI SAN MARTINO & CASTEL SANT'ELMO (200 m)
PIAZZA MATTEOTTI
Via San Felice
Via Campodisola
Corso Vittoria Emanuele
Via A. Diaz
Rua Catalana
Via Toledo
PIAZZA SAN SEPOLCRO
Via San Tommaso D'Aquino
Via A. de Gasperi
Vico San Sepulcro
V. P. di Tappia
Via Cervantes
Via Medina
Via Cristofor
Via A. Depretis
SPANISH QUARTER
Palazzo Municipale
TO VOMERO (500 m)
Via P. E. Imbriani
PIAZZA MUNICIPIO
Funicular to Vomero
Via San Mattia
Via Santa Brigida
V. G. Verdi
Via Vittorio Emanuele III
Galleria Umberto
Castel Nuovo o Maschio Angioino
Via Santa Caterina Da Sien
Salita S. A. Di Palazzo
Chiesa di San Fernando
Teatro San Carlo
Via San Carlo
Via Giovanni Nicotera
PIAZZA TRIESTE E TRENTO
Palazzo Reale
Molo Beverello
Via Chiaia
Via Ferdinando Acton
PIAZZA PLEBISCITO
TO VILLA COMUNALE (350 m) & U.S. CONSULATE (1 km)
Via Monte
Via Egiziaca a Forcella
Chiesa di San Francesco di Paola

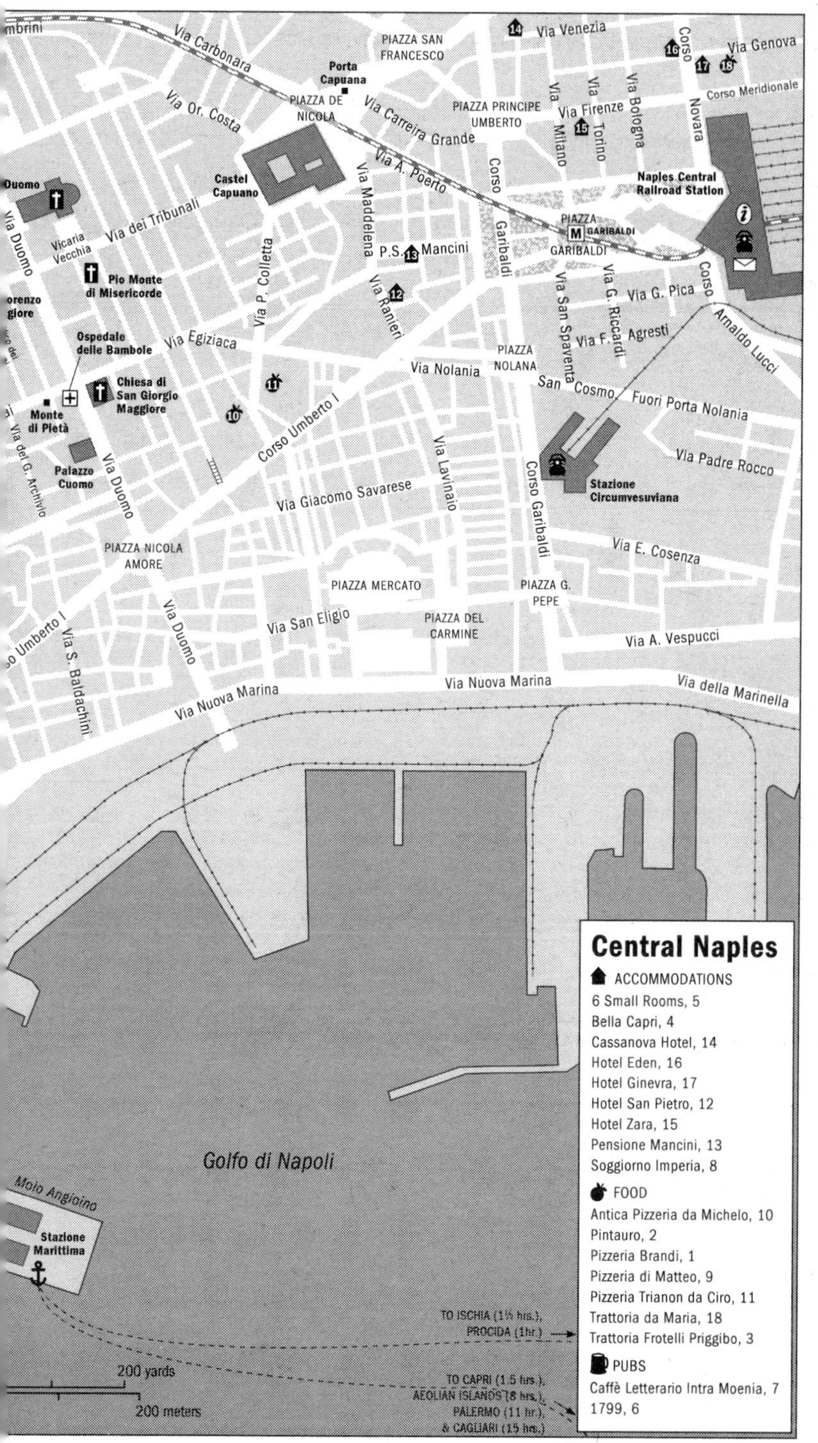
Central Naples
ACCOMMODATIONS
6 Small Rooms, 5
Bella Capri, 4
Cassanova Hotel, 14
Hotel Eden, 16
Hotel Ginevra, 17
Hotel San Pietro, 12
Hotel Zara, 15
Pensione Mancini, 13
Soggiorno Imperia, 8
FOOD
Antica Pizzeria da Michelo, 10
Pintauro, 2
Pizzeria Brandi, 1
Pizzeria di Matteo, 9
Pizzeria Trianon da Ciro, 11
Trattoria da Maria, 18
Trattoria Frotelli Priggibo, 3
PUBS
Caffè Letterario Intra Moenia, 7
1799, 6
Via Carbonara
PIAZZA SAN FRANCESCO
Porta Capuana
Via Venezia
Via Genova
Corso Novara
Corso Meridionale
PIAZZA DE NICOLA
Via Or. Costa
Via Carreira Grande
PIAZZA PRINCIPE UMBERTO
Via Milano
Via Firenze
Via Torino
Via Bologna
Castel Capuano
Via A. Poerto
Via Maddelena
Corso Garibaldi
Naples Central Railroad Station
Duomo
Via dei Tribunali
Vicaria Vecchia
Via Duomo
Via P. Colletta
P.S. Mancini
PIAZZA GARIBALDI
GARIBALDI
Pio Monte di Misericorde
Via Ranieri
Via San Spaventa
Via G. Riccardi
Via G. Pica
Corso Arnaldo Lucci
Ospedale delle Bambole
Via Egiziaca
Via F. Agresti
PIAZZA NOLANA
Via Nolania
Chiesa di San Giorgio Maggiore
San Cosmo
Fuori Porta Nolania
Monte di Pietà
Corso Umberto I
Via Lavinaio
Via del G. Archivio
Palazzo Cuomo
Stazione Circumvesuviana
Via Padre Rocco
Via Giacomo Savarese
Corso Garibaldi
PIAZZA NICOLA AMORE
Via E. Cosenza
PIAZZA MERCATO
PIAZZA G. PEPE
Via San Eligio
PIAZZA DEL CARMINE
Via A. Vespucci
Via S. Baldachini
Via Nuova Marina
Via della Marinella
Golfo di Napoli
Molo Angioino
Stazione Marittima
TO ISCHIA (1½ hrs.), PROCIDA (1hr.)
TO CAPRI (1.5 hrs.), AEOLIAN ISLANDS (8 hrs.), PALERMO (11 hr.), & CAGLIARI (15 hrs.)
200 yards
200 meters

and Piazza Plebiscito. On the water at the foot of P. Municipio lie **Molo Beverello** and the **Stazione Marittima** at **Molo Angioino,** the point of departure for ferries. Turn right from P. Trieste e Trento and go up **Via Toledo** (also called **Via Roma**) and make a right at Piazza Dante to get to Naples's historical district of **Spaccanapoli,** which means "splitting Naples" and is fun to say aloud. Spaccanapoli follows the course of the ancient Roman road, today known as **Via dei Tribunali,** through the middle of town. Be careful not to get yourself split in two by the hordes of youngsters on mopeds using this alley as a racecourse.

If you plan to be in town for a few days, either invest in a detailed city map from a *tabacchi* (L9000) or get one of the two maps at a tourist office. Also pick up the free *Napoli by Bus* brochure to assist you in using the bus system.

PRACTICAL INFORMATION

TOURIST, FINANCIAL, AND LOCAL SERVICES

Tourist Offices: EPT (☎081 26 87 79; fax 081 20 66 66), at Stazione Centrale. Helpful to a fault—you'll have to wait as the staff exhaustively assist those ahead in line. The tourist office will call hotels and ferry companies. Grab a map and the indispensable *Qui Napoli,* a monthly updated tourist information publication full of schedules, events, and listings. English spoken. Office open M-Sa 9am-8pm. **Main office,** P. dei Martiri, 58 (☎081 40 53 11). Open M-Sa 8:30am-3pm. Branch at **Stazione Mergellina** (☎081 761 21 02). Open M-Sa 8:30am-8pm, Su 8am-2pm. **OTC** (☎081 580 82 16; fax 081 41 03 59; email osservatorio@comune.napoli.it; www.comune.napoli.it), at Palazzo Reale in P. Plebiscito, is eager to assist you. Open M-Sa 9am-6:30pm.

Tourist Police: Ufficio Stranieri, at the **Questura,** V. Medina, 75 (☎081 794 11 11), near P. Municipio on the R2 bus line. Assists with passport problems and helps travellers who have been the victims of crime.

Budget Travel: CTS, V. Mezzocannone, 25 (☎081 552 79 60), off C. Umberto on the R2 line. Student travel info, ISIC and FIYTO cards, and booking services. Open M-F 9am-1:30pm and 3:30-7pm, Sa 9am-1pm. **CIT,** P. Municipio, 72 (☎081 552 54 26), is a comprehensive travel agency. Open M-F 9am-1pm and 3-6pm. **Italian Youth Hostel Organization** (☎081 761 23 46), at the hostel in Mergellina (see p. 479). Info on HI and *Transalpino* discounts. HI cards L30,000. Open M-F 9am-1pm and 3-6pm.

Consulates: US (☎081 583 81 11; 24hr. emergency ☎033 794 50 83), P. della Repubblica at the west end of Villa Comunale. Open M-F 8am-5pm. **South Africa,** C. Umberto 1, (☎081 551 75 19). **UK,** V. Crispi, 122 (☎081 66 35 11). Metro to P. Amedeo. Open July-Aug. M-F 8am-1:30pm; Sept.-June M-F 9am-12:30pm and 2:30-4pm.

Currency Exchange: Several large banks operate in P. Municipio and P. Garibaldi. **Thomas Cook,** P. Municipio, 70 (☎081 551 83 99), and at the airport, offers decent rates. Open M-F 9:30am-1pm and 3-6:30pm. **Stazione Centrale** has 24hr. currency exchange but undesirable rates. **ATMs** are in Stazione Centrale and throughout the city.

American Express: Every Tour, P. Municipio, 5 (☎081 551 85 64). Open 9am-1:30pm and 3:30-7pm.

Car Rental: Avis (☎081 554 30 20), at Stazione Centrale. Cars from L160,000 per day; L660,000 per week. Open M-F 8am-7:30pm, Sa 8:30am-1pm and 4-6pm, Su 9am-1pm. Another office in the airport (☎081 780 57 90). Additional 12% tax on cars rented at the airport. Open M-Su 7am-midnight. **Hertz,** P. Garibaldi, 93 (☎081 554 86 57). L121,000 per day; L520,000 per week. Another office near the airport at V. Scarfoglio, 1 (☎081 570 87 01; fax 081 570 78 62). Additional 12% tax applies. Open M-F 9am-1pm and 2-5pm. **Maggiore Budget** (☎081 28 78 58), in Stazione Centrale. From L99,000 per day; L300,000 per week. Open M-F 8am-7pm, Sa 8am-1:30pm.

Bookstore: Feltrinelli, V. S. T. d'Aquino, 70 (☎081 552 14 36). North of Palazzo Municipale turn right off V. Toledo onto V. Ponte di Tappia. The store is 20m ahead on the left. Extensive English selection. Open M-F 9am-8pm, Sa 9am-1:30pm and 4-8pm, Su 9am-1:30pm and 5-8pm. Many used book stalls and new book stores with some English titles can be found in the neighborhood around P. Bellini.

Laundromat: Bolle Blu, C. Novara, 62 (☎033 88 94 27 14 or 033 56 64 30 57), 3 blocks from the train station. Rocket-quick machines (wash and dry in under 1hr.) and a priceless mural of Michael Jackson, Marilyn Monroe, and Elvis, all waiting for their machines to finish. One of the only self-service laundromats in Naples. Wash L6-10,000; dry L6-10,000. Prices depend on load size. Open M-Sa 8:30am-8pm.

EMERGENCY AND COMMUNICATIONS

Emergencies: ☎113. **Police:** ☎113 or 081 794 11 11. **Carabinieri:** ☎112. English spoken. **Ambulance:** ☎081 752 06 96. **Hospital: Cardarelli** (☎081 747 11 11), north of town on the R4 bus line, is the best hospital in Naples.

Late-Night Pharmacy: (☎081 26 88 81), at Stazione Centrale by the FS ticket windows. Open in summer M-F 8pm-9am. On weekends one pharmacy in the area stays open 24hr. *Il Mattino* lists the schedule.

Internet Access: Internetbar, P. Bellini, 74 (☎081 29 52 37). Chic and air-conditioned. Expensive drinks are available to wash down your emails. L5000 for 30min. Open M-F 9am-3am, Sa-Su 9pm-3am. **Internet Multimedia,** V. Sapienza, 43 (☎081 29 84 12; www.viasapienza43.com). From the Museo Archeologico Nazionale head down V. S. Maria di Constaninopoli and turn right on V. Sapienza. You'll have to climb up a flight and buzz to get in. Some of the lowest prices in town, at L3,000 per hr. Scanning and printing also available. Open daily 9:30am-9:30pm. **Livingston,** V. G. Martucci, 8 (☎081 761 88 83; email teo@itb.it). Head out of P. Amedeo on V. G. Martucci. British internet "pub," I presume. L5000 for 30min. Open daily 8pm-2am.

Post Office: (☎081 551 14 56), in P. Matteotti, at V. Diaz. Take the R2 line. Also in Galleria Umberto (☎081 552 34 67) and outside Stazione Centrale. Notoriously unreliable Fermo Posta L1500. All offices open M-F 8:15am-6pm, Sa 8:15am-noon. In summer, Friday afternoons are popular times for strikes. **Postal Code:** 80100.

ACCOMMODATIONS

The gritty area around **P. Garibaldi** is packed with hotels, many of which solicit customers at the station. Avoid them—they will redirect you from your desired hostel to their "hotel" which, while probably safe, may simply be an old *palazzo* divided into rooms with hastily erected partitions. P. Garibaldi has options that are comfortable and inexpensive (though none are really quiet). Further downtown, in the historic district between P. Dante and the *duomo*, lodgings are harder to come by.

Although Naples has some fantastic bargain lodgings, be cautious. Don't surrender your passport before seeing your room, bargain for lower prices, and always agree on the price *before* you unpack your bags. Be alert for shower charges, obligatory breakfasts, and other unexpected costs. When selecting a place to stay, check for double-locked doors and night attendants. The **ACISJF/Centro D'Ascolto,** at Stazione Centrale near the EPT, helps women find safe, inexpensive rooms. (☎081 28 19 93. Open M, T, and Th 3:30-6:30pm.) For **camping,** check out **Pozzuoli** (see p. 488), **Pompeii** (see p. 501), and other small towns in the Bay of Naples.

MERGELLINA

Ostello Mergellina (HI), V. Salita della Grotta, 23 (☎081 761 23 46; fax 081 761 23 91). Metro: Mergellina. From the Metro station, make 2 sharp rights onto V. Piedigrotta and then a left onto V. Salita della Grotta. Turn right on the long driveway after the overpass before the tunnel. Outstanding views of Vesuvius and Capri. 200 beds in 2-, 4-, and 6-person rooms which vary in quality but are well-maintained. Computer, cafeteria, free storage downstairs, and a pleasant lounge. Breakfast, sheets, and shower included, but not towels. Laundry wash and dry L10,000. Lockout 9am-3pm. Curfew 12:30am. Reservations advised July-Aug. Dorms L24,000; doubles L60,000.

PIAZZA GARIBALDI

Casanova Hotel, V. Venezia, 2 (☎/fax 081 26 82 87; email hcasanov@tin.it). From P. Garibaldi, take V. Milano and turn left at its end. On your right, there are 2 entrances. Ivied front, clean, airy rooms, knowledgeable management, and a rooftop terrace with bar. Some rooms with TV, fridge, and telephone. 23 rooms. Breakfast L8000. Reserve ahead. Singles L38,000, with bath L45,000; doubles L65,000, with bath L80,000; triples L100,000; quads L110,000. 10% discount with *Let's Go*. V, MC, AmEx.

Hotel Eden, C. Novara, 9 (☎081 28 53 44). From the station, turn right; the hotel is on the left. Eden boasts a family atmosphere and English-speaking staff. 44 rooms with bath. Breakfast L5000. Free luggage storage. Prices if you flash *Let's Go:* singles L42,000; doubles L66,000; triples L90,000; quads L108,000. V, MC, AmEx.

Pensione Mancini, P. Mancini, 33 (☎081 553 67 31; fax 081 554 66 25; www.mds.it/mancini), off the far end of P. Garibaldi from the station. Knowledgeable owners Alfredo and Margherita will often meet you and escort you to this small, safe *pensione*. More languages spoken than at the United Nations. 6 rooms. Breakfast included. Reservations suggested. Dorms L28,000; singles L40,000; doubles L65,000, with bath L75,000; triples with bath L90,000; quads with bath L110,000.

Hotel Zara, V. Firenze, 81 (☎081 28 71 25; fax 081 26 82 87), from P. Garibaldi, take V. Milano right, then turn right on V. Firenze. Quiet, spacious rooms with telephones. Reservations recommended. With *Let's Go:* singles L40,000; doubles L65,000, with bath L85,000; triples L85,000, with bath L95,000.

Hotel Ginevra, V. Genova, 116 (☎081 28 32 10; fax 081 554 17 57; email hginevra@tin.it; www.mds.it/ginevra). Exit P. Garibaldi on C. Novara, then turn right. A clean, family-run establishment. English spoken. 14 rooms. Singles L45,000; doubles L70,000, with bath L90,000; triples L100,000, with bath L125,000. V, MC, AmEx.

Hotel San Pietro, V. S. Pietro ad Aram, 18 (☎081 28 60 40; fax 081 553 59 14). Exit P. Garibaldi on C. Umberto I, turn right on V. Ranieri, and then make another right. Huge and more professional than most of its neighbors. 50 rooms. Breakfast included. Singles L50,000, with bath L80,000; doubles L80,000, with bath L130,000. V, MC.

HISTORIC DISTRICT

Soggiorno Imperia, P. Miraglia, 386 (☎081 45 93 47). Take the R2 from the train station, walk up V. Mezzocannone through P. S. Domenico Maggiore, and enter the 1st set of green doors to the left on P. Miraglia. Friendly management runs this bright, clean establishment in a refurbished 16th-century *palazzo.* English spoken. 6 rooms. Reservations strongly suggested. Singles L35,000; doubles L55-65,000; triples L80,000.

6 Small Rooms, V. Diodato Lioy, 18 (☎081 790 13 78; email info@6smallrooms.com; www.at6smallrooms.com), half a block north of P. Monteoliveto. Call from Montesanto station for directions. The new hotel, run by an Australian, offers dorms and private rooms, with a large kitchen, pleasant atmosphere, and 2 friendly cats. Breakfast included. No curfew or lockout. Dorms L30,000; private rooms L40,000 per person.

Bella Capri, V. Melisurgo, 4 (☎081 552 94 94; fax 081 552 92 65), at the corner of V. Cristofor Colombo, across the street from the port. Take tram #1 from P. Garibaldi. From the courtyard enter door B and go to the 6th floor. An incredible view of the harbor (although its island namesake is barely visible). Coin-operated elevator? Oh well. All rooms with breakfast, bath, TV, and telephone; some with balcony. Reservations recommended. Singles L90,000; doubles L120,000; triples L150,000. V, MC, AmEx.

SANTA LUCIA

Albergo Teresita, V. S. Lucia, 90 (☎081 764 01 05). Bus R3 or C25. What the? This looks exactly like Albergo Astoria! Cozy, but it's decorated with plaster statuary and heavy yellow drapes. 16 large rooms come with TV, fridge, and phone. Hall baths. Singles L50,000; doubles L75,000; triples L90,000.

Albergo Astoria, V. S. Lucia, 90 (☎081 764 99 03; email astoria1@libero.it). Bus R3 or C25. What the? This looks exactly like Albergo Teresita! 23 rooms come with TV and fridge. Hall showers. Singles L45,000; doubles L70,000; triples L90,000.

VOMERO

Pensione Margherita, V. Cimarosa, 29, 5th fl. (☎081 556 70 44), in the same building as the Centrale funicular station (go outside and around the corner to the right; buzz to get in). 15 spacious rooms, some with terraces. Kind management and the lowest prices available in this posh, peaceful residential area. Bring L50 for the elevator or take the stairs. Curfew midnight. Singles L53,000; doubles L95,000; triples L135,000.

FOOD

PIZZERIAS

Neapolitans invented **pizza** (see **Food and Wine,** p. 30), and they certainly let you know it with their *pizzerie* a plenty. If you come with Pizza Hut preconceptions, you will be blown away; pizza here is completely different—light, flavorful, and good to the last bite. Pizza tried to run for mayor four years ago, but lost in a close vote to a human. It's hard to go astray when choosing a pizzeria, since natural selection and a discriminating local palate have driven out the underachievers.

Pizzeria Di Matteo, V. Tribunali, 94 (☎081 45 52 62), near V. Duomo. Students and pizza connoisseurs crowd this small, preeminent eatery. President Clinton ate here during the G-7 Conference in 1994. He denies having sexual relations with that pizza, *margherita* (L4000). Open M-Sa 9am-midnight.

Pizzeria Trianon da Ciro, V. Pietro Colletta, 42/44/46 (☎081 553 94 26), 1 block off C. Umberto I. *The New York Times* declares this to be the best pizza in Naples. The house speciality is the pizza "*Gran Trianon*" (L12,500), a smorgasbord of 8 different sections. Pizzas L5500-12,500. Service 15%. Open daily 10am-4:30pm and 6:30pm-midnight.

Antica Pizzeria da Michele, V. Cesare Sersale, 1/3 (☎081 553 92 04). From P. Garibaldi, walk up C. Umberto 1 and take the 1st right. Michele makes only the two traditional types, and he makes them right. *Marinara* (tomato, garlic, oregano, and oil) or *margherita* (tomato, mozzarella cheese, and basil) L6000. Open M-Sa 8am-11pm.

Pizzeria Brandi, Salita S. Anna di Palazzo, 1 (☎081 41 69 28), off V. Chiaia. In 1889, Mr. Esposito invented the *margherita* in Brandi's ancient oven. While President Clinton munched at Di Matteo in 1994, his daughter Chelsea ate here. Great atmosphere. *Margherita* L8000. Cover L3000. Open M-Su noon-3pm and 7pm-midnight.

RESTAURANTS AND TRATTORIE

Neapolitans love **seafood,** and they prepare it well. Enjoy fresh *cozze* (mussels) in soup or with lemon. Savor *vongole* (clams) of all varieties and their more expensive 2nd cousin, the *ostrica* (oyster). *Aragosta* (crayfish) is sweeter than lobster, and *polipo* (octopus) is one of the cheapest sources of protein around. **Spaghetti,** an Italian trademark, was reputedly first boiled in the kitchens of Naples—don't mention any nonsense about Marco Polo and China to the Neapolitans if you want to stay on their good side. Today, the city's most famous pasta dishes are *spaghetti alle vongole* (with clams) and *alle cozze* (with mussels); atop pasta, both creatures still reside in their shells. For fresh fruits and seafood, explore Neapolitan **markets.** Try the one on V. Soprammuro, off P. Garibaldi. (Open M-Sa 8am-1:30pm.) Fruit stands, groceries, and pastry shops line V. Tribuali in Spaccanapoli.

PIAZZA AMEDEO AND MERGELLINA

Take the Metro or the C25 bus to **Piazza Amedeo** for a culinary change of pace. Otherwise, take the Metro or tram #4 to **Mergellina,** southwest of P. Amedeo on the waterfront, for informal, hearty Neapolitan dining. **Piazza Sannazzaro,** in the center of Mergellina, has many *trattorie* that serve the beloved local *zuppa di cozze* (mussels in broth with octopus).

El Bocadillo, V. Martucci, 50 (☎081 66 90 30), serves up tasty Spanish and South American dishes with style. Most entrées L10-15,000. Pitchers of *sangría* L10,000. Open Tu-Su 8pm-2am.

Zorbas, V. Martucci, 5 (☎081 66 75 72), 2 blocks off P. Amedeo; enter around the corner (look for the sign). This Greek tavern specializes in *satanas* (devilishly spicy mini sausages) for L10,000. Open Tu-Su 8:30pm-midnight.

Osteria Canterbury, V. Ascensione, 6 (☎081 41 35 84). Take V. Vittoria Colonna from P. Amedeo, take the 1st right down a flight of stairs, then turn right and immediately left. *Secondi* from L7000. Open Tu-Su noon-3:30pm and 6:30pm-2am. V, MC, AmEx.

Da Rosario, P. Sannazzaro, 72 (☎081 570 31 03), in Mergellina, has delicious *frittura* (platters of fried miscellany) for only L5000, wines from L5000, and, of course, *zuppa di cozze* (mussel soup) for L8000. Service 10%. Open Th-Tu 10am-3am.

HISTORIC DISTRICT AND PIAZZA GARIBALDI

The narrow, winding streets around P. Dante shelter the city's most delightful *trattorie* and *pizzerie*. Some of the cheapest, most authentic options lie along V. dei Tribunali in the heart of Spaccanapoli. Tourist-ridden and expensive restaurants dominate P. Garibaldi, but high-quality, low-cost meals hide on the side streets just off the *piazza*. The area around P. Garibaldi becomes seedy at night, so eat early.

Trattoria da Maria, V. Genova, 115 (☎081 28 27 11). From the train station, take a right on C. Novara and then a 2nd right on V. Genova. In a city where tradition, simplicity, and hospitality come first, the Riccio family has kept their small *trattoria* true to Neapolitan style. A favorite is *penne "sciuè sciuè"* (with mozzarella, tomato, and basil) for L6000. Pasta L5-6000. *Secondi* from L6000. Local wines L6-8000. Cover L1000. Open M-Sa noon-3:30pm and 6:30-11pm. Closed mid-Aug. AmEx.

Trattoria Fratelli Prigiobbo, V. Portacarrese, 96. From V. Toledo, turn right across from V. Ponte di Tappia and walk 2 blocks into the Spanish Quarter. Pizza L4-8000. *Primi,* including *gnocchi alla mozzarella,* L4000. Seafood *secondi,* like roasted calamari, are a steal at L6000. Wine L4000 per bottle. Open M-Sa 8am-midnight.

VOMERO

Trattoria da Sica, V. Bernini, 17 (☎081 556 75 20). This family-run *trattoria* serves traditional Neapolitan fare at a traditional Neapolitan pace. *Vermicelli alla puttanesca* (with tomatoes, olives, and capers) for L6000. Excellent wines from L4000 per bottle. Cover L1000. Service 13%. Open Oct.-Aug. Sa-Th noon-3:30pm and 8pm-midnight.

GELATERIE AND PASTICCERIE

Naples's most beloved pastry is *sfogliatella,* filled with sweetened ricotta cheese, orange rind, and candied fruit. It comes in two forms: the popular *riccia,* a flaky-crust variety, and *frolla,* a softer, crumblier counterpart.

Pintauro, V. Toledo, 275 (☎081 41 73 39), near the Centrale funicular station. This tiny bakery has produced the city's foremost *sfogliatella* since 1785. It sells both varieties, piping hot, for L2000 each. Open M-Sa 8am-8pm.

Gay Odin, V. V. Colonna, 15b (☎081 41 82 82), off P. Amedeo. No Norse gods, just the delicious chocolate treats that have been pouring out of their *fabbrica* (factories) on V. Vetriera since 1824. Try their famous *forresta,* a sweet and crumbly chocolate stalk (L4000). Open M-Sa 9:30am-1:30pm and 4:30-8pm.

Scaturchio (☎081 551 69 44), in P. S. Dominico Maggiore. One of the best pastry shops and *gelateria* in the historic district, ideal for a break from church-viewing. Cones L2500. The *ministeriale,* a chocolate and rum pastry, is their specialty. Open M-Sa 8am-11pm.

SIGHTS

FREE RIDE. There is no admission charge to state-sponsored sights and museums for students of Italian art and architecture or for those under 18 or over 60. Some sights are free to EU citizens. Always inquire about discounts!

SPACCANAPOLI

Named because it "splits" the city in two along an east-west axis, Naples's renowned neighborhood is replete with gorgeous architecture and merits at least a half-hour stroll. Don't lose track of yourself while gawking at picturesque churches, *palazzi*, and alleyways, or you'll soon find yourself staring at the wrong end of a **motorino** buzzing toward you at high speed. To get to the neighborhood from P. Dante, walk through **Porta Alba** and **P. Bellini** before turning down **V. dei Tribunali,** which tracks the former route of an old Roman road and now contains some of the city's best **pizzerie** (see **Food,** p. 481).

MUSEO ARCHEOLOGICO NAZIONALE. Situated within a 16th-century *palazzo* and former barracks, one of the world's most important archeological museums houses exquisite treasures from Pompeii and Herculaneum. Unreliable labeling makes the color guidebooks a helpful investment. The ground floor's Farnese Collection displays sculptures snatched from Pompeii and Herculaneum and imperial portraits and colossal statues from Rome's Baths of Caracalla. Highlights include the massive Farnese Hercules, showing the exhausted hero after his last labor, and the **Farnese Bull,** the largest extant ancient sculpture. Carved out of a single piece of marble, the bull was touched up by Michelangelo. The mezzanine contains mosaics taken from Pompeii, ranging from pictures of food to the **Alexander Mosaic,** which shows a young and fearless Alexander the Great routing a Persian army. On the first floor, above the mezzanine, are large murals and domestic items from Pompeii and Herculaneum. The **Secret Collection,** containing erotic paintings and objects from Pompeii, has recently opened. Ranging from images of (ungodly) godly love to phallic good luck charms, the collection shows another side of antiquity. Also of note are the **Jewels,** a collection of ancient trinkets and ornaments which includes the sparkling **Farnese Cup.** In the basement, is a sporadically open Egyptian collection. *(Metro to P. Cavour, turn right as you exit the station, and walk 2 blocks. Otherwise take the #110 bus from P. Garibaldi, or the R4 bus from P. Dante to P. Museo. ☎081 44 01 66. Open M and W-F 9am-7:30pm, Sa-Su 9am-8pm. Guidebook L15-60,000. L12,000. Mandatory tours are conducted every half hour. Ask for a free ticket at the main ticket window.)*

DUOMO. The *duomo* doesn't dazzle at first sight; it lies quietly on a small *piazza*, and a modest facade hides its size. Twice a year throngs of people crowd around it to celebrate the **Festa di San Gennaro** (see **Festivals,** p. 488). The *duomo* has been subject to many additions and renovations since its inauguration in 1315 by Robert of Anjou, and it was endowed with a neo-Gothic facade in the 19th-century. The main attraction is the **Capella del Tesoro di San Gennaro** on the right, decorated with Baroque paintings. A beautiful 17th-century bronze grille protects the high altar, which possesses a reliquary containing the saint's head and two vials of his coagulated blood. According to legend, disaster will strike the city if the blood does not liquefy on the celebration of his *festa;* miraculously, it always does, while thousands of Neapolitans crowd the church and streets (see **Festivals** p. 487). Beneath the main altar of the church is the crypt of the saint, decorated with Renaissance carvings in white marble. The **Chiesa di Santa Restituta,** halfway up the right side of the church, marks the entrance to the excavations of the **Greek and Roman roads** that run beneath the city. *(Walk 3 blocks up V. Duomo from C. Umberto I or take the #42 bus from P. Garibaldi. ☎081 44 90 97. Open M-F 9am-noon and 4:30-7pm, Sa-Su 9am-noon.)*

PIO MONTE D. MISERICORDE. This small chapel was built by a group of nobles who dedicated themselves to charity. They had good taste in art as well as compassion; the main altarpiece is Caravaggio's *Seven Acts of Mercy*. In the *piazza* outside, there's a spire dedicated to San Gennaro for saving the city from the 1656 plague. *(1 block down V. Tribunali after V. Duomo, on a small piazza. Open M-Sa 9am-noon.)*

OSPEDALE DELLE BAMBOLE. Old Naples's most endearing shop, this tiny doll hospital is one-of-a-kind. Its mirthful proprietor reassembles dolls with an unlikely collection of appendages. *(V. S. Biagio Al Librai, 81. Head 2 blocks up V. Duomo from P. N. Amore and take a left. ☎081 20 30 87. Open M-F 10am-2pm and 4-8pm, Sa 10am-2pm.)*

CHIOSTRO DELLE CLARISSE. This tranquil 18th-century garden adjoins **Chiesa di Santa Chiara,** and is surrounded by Gothic walkways and decorated with frescoes and brightly colored tiles. *(Open daily 8:30am-12:30pm and 3:30pm-sunset. L6000.)*

Built in the 1300s by the rulers of the house of Anjou, the neighboring church has been renovated several times, most recently after WWII bombing damage in 1943. The church is littered with sarcophagi and tombs from the Middle Ages. *(From P. Dante, head down V. Toledo and turn left on V. B. Croce. The church sits in P. Gesú Nuovo. ☎081 552 62 09. Open daily 7am-noon and 4-7pm.)*

GESÙ NUOVO. The facade of the church of the Jesuits in Naples consists entirely of raised stone diamonds. The interior is awash in Baroque inlaid marbles, with interesting frescoes adorning the ceiling and chapels. Outside the church is a Baroque spire, or *guglia*, glorifying the lives of Jesuit saints. *(Across from the Chiesa di Santa Chiara, in P. Gesù Nuovo. Open daily 7:15am-12:15pm and 4:15-7:15pm.)*

CHIESA DI MONTEOLIVETO. The highlight of this church is the wealth of Renaissance sculpture that fills the side altars, including eight life-size terra-cotta figures mourning the death of Christ. Vasari's frescoes adorn the sacristy. *(From P. Dante, head down V. Toledo and turn left on V. B. Croce. Cross P. Gesú Nuovo and walk down C. Trinità Maggiore to P. Monteoliveto. Open daily 7:15am-12:15pm and 4:15-7:15pm.)*

SAN LORENZO MAGGIORE. This large church retains a beautiful and striking Gothic simplicity. It was here that medieval writer Boccaccio first met his true love Fiammetta in 1334. (If you think Boccaccio is a flat Italian bread, check out **Into The Light,** p. 22.) Inside lie the tombs of Catherine of Austria and Robert of Arlois. *(P. San Gaetano, 316. 2 blocks down V. dei Tribunali from V. Duomo. ☎081 29 05 80.)*

CORSO UMBERTO I AND PALAZZO REALE

PALAZZO REALE. The exterior facing P. Plebiscito is decorated with huge statues of the various rulers of Naples. Inside the 17th-century *palazzo* is the **Museo di Palazzo Reale,** composed of huge and opulent royal apartments. The *palazzo* is an intellectual mecca even today, housing the 1,500,000-volume **Biblioteca Nazionale,** which contains the carbonized scrolls from the **Villa dei Papiri** in Herculaneum. *(Take the R2 bus from P. Garibaldi to P. Trieste e Trento and walk around the palazzo to the entrance on P. Plebiscito. ☎081 580 81 11. Open M-Tu and Th-F 9am-8pm. L8000. Library ☎081 40 12 73; access to the public varies.)*

Also in the *palazzo* is the famous **Teatro San Carlo,** reputed to have better acoustics than the revered La Scala in Milan (see p. 101). For more information on performances, see **Entertainment,** p. 486. *(The theater's entrance is on P. Trieste e Trento. ☎081 797 21 11. Tours July Sa-Tu and Th 10am; Sept.-June Sa-Su 2pm. Tour L5000.)*

NAPOLI E LA CITTÀ SOTTERANEA. This tour of the subterranean alleys that run beneath the city is fascinating, but not for the claustrophobic: it will have you crawling through narrow underground passageways, grottoes, and catacombs, looking for graffiti from the Mussolini era. *(Office at Vico S. Anna di Palazzo, 52. ☎081 40 02 56. Tours Th 9pm, Sa 10am and 6pm, Su 10, 11am, and 6pm. Tours leave from Café Gambrinus in P. Trieste e Trento. L10,000 per person. Call first.)*

CASTEL NUOVO. It's impossible to miss this huge, five-turreted landmark looking out over the Bay of Naples. Known to friends as the **Maschio Angioino,** the fortress was built in 1286 by Charles II of Anjou to be his royal residence in Naples. Perhaps its most interesting feature is the triumphal double-arched entrance with reliefs commemorating the arrival of Alphonse I of Aragon in 1443. Inside you can see the magnificent cubical "Hall of the Barons," where King Ferdinand once trapped rebellious barons and where Naples's city council holds spirited meetings today. The **Museo Civico** has a collection of 14th- and 15th-century frescoes and a set of bronze doors showing Charles of Aragon defeating rebels. *(P. Municipio. Take the R2 bus from P. Garibaldi. Museum ☎ 081 795 20 03. Open M-Sa 9am-7pm. L10,000.)*

CAPELLA SANSEVERO. The chapel, now a private museum, has several remarkable statues, noteworthy for their amazing bravura realism. *Disillusion* shows a man escaping from a net carved of marble, while *Modesty* and the **Veiled Christ** show bodies covered in thin cloth, all of marble. The crypt houses two grisly 18th-century objects and their story. Legend claims that the alchemist prince Raimondo of the San Severi, who built the chapel, murdered his wife and her lover by injecting them with a poisonous venom that preserved their veins, arteries, and vital organs. *(V. De Sanctis, 19. In the upper corner of P. S. Domenico Maggiore. ☎ 081 551 84 70. Open M and W-F 10am-5pm, Sa-Su 10am-1:30pm. L8000, students L4000.)*

CHIESA DI SAN DOMENICO MAGGIORE. This 14th-century church has a 19th-century, piked Gothic interior. To the right of the altar in the Chapel of the Crucifix hangs the 13th-century painting that allegedly spoke to St. Thomas Aquinas, who lived in the adjoining monastery when Naples was a center of learning in Europe. Fine Renaissance sculptures decorate the side chapels. *(Not surprisingly, in P. S. Domenico Maggiore. ☎ 081 557 31 11. Open daily 7:15am-12:15pm and 4:15-7:15pm.)*

CAPODIMONTE

MUSEO AND GALLERIE DI CAPODIMONTE. Housed in yet another royal **palazzo,** this museum is surrounded by a pastoral park; be careful not to get caught in a soccer game or lovers' tryst—oft-ignored regulations prohibit "misuse" of the grass. The museum includes plush royal apartments and their furnishings. The 2nd floor shows the development of Neapolitan artistic styles. After Caravaggio's visit to Naples (his *Flagellation* is on display), his realistic style and dramatic use of light were adapted by Ribera and Luca Giordano, reinvigorating Neapolitan painting. The **Farnese Collection** on the 1st floor is full of artistic masterpieces, many of them removed from Neapolitan churches for safety's sake. Paintings are the collection's forte; foremost among them are Bellini's *Transfiguration*, Masaccio's *Crucifixion*, and Titian's *Danae*. *(Take the #110 bus from P. Garibaldi or the #24 bus from P. Dante to Parco Capodimonte. The park has 2 entrances, the Porta Piccola and the Porta Grande. ☎ 081 749 91 11. Open Tu-F 10am-7pm, Sa 10am-midnight, Su 9am-8pm. L14,000.)*

CHIESA DI MADONNA DEL BUONCONSIGLIO. Dubbed "Little St. Peter's," this church features copies of Michelangelo's *Pietà* and *Moses*. Outside, the 2nd-century **Catacombe di San Gennaro** are noted for their frescoes. *(Down V. Capodimonte from the museum. ☎ 081 741 10 71. Guided tours of catacombs daily 9:30am-12:30pm. L5000.)*

SANTA LUCIA AND MERGELLINA

CASTEL DELL'OVO (EGG CASTLE). This massive Norman castle of yellow brick and odd angles sits on a rocky island and divides the bay in two. Legend has it that Virgil hid an egg within the castle walls and that with the collapse of the egg would come the collapse of the castle. *(Take bus #1 from P. Garibaldi or P. Municipio to S. Lucia and walk across the jetty. ☎ 081 764 53 43. Only open for special events; call ahead.)*

AQUARIUM. If you're tired of seeing marine life from the Bay of Naples on your dinner plate, try the aquarium in the Villa Comunale. It is Europe's oldest, and it displays a small collection of local species. *(Easily accessible by the #1 tram from P. Garibaldi or P. Municipio. ☎ 081 583 32 63. Open M-Sa 9am-6pm, Su 10am-6pm. L3000.)*

CHE MALE C'È? It's true that the Florentine dialect emerged as Italy's national language through the words of Dante and Petrarch, but it's Neapolitan that's making it on the charts. Naples's Pino Daniele, the 44-year-old, bespectacled, pot-bellied pop star, has been crooning in his native tongue for decades. He continues to infuse Italy with his Neapolitan pride, winning the illustrious Festival Bar in 1997 and topping the charts with his most recent *Dimmi Cosa Succede Sulla Terra.* It's not all praise and glory, however, as the jealous singer Zucchero quipped that Pino is merely an old Joe Cocker wanna-be. But as Pino says: *"Che male c'è?"* (Is it so bad?)

VIRGIL'S TOMB. Anyone who has studied Latin in high school may have at least a passing interest in seeing the poet's resting place at **Salita della Frotta**—if only to shake a fist at the tomb in anger over many frustrating hours spent trying to conjugate the pluperfect. Below the tomb is the entrance to the **Crypta Neapolitana,** a tunnel built during the reign of Augustus, connecting ancient Neapolis to Pozzuoli and Baiae (closed for renovations). *(From the Metro station in Mergellina, take 2 quick rights. The entrance is between the overpass and the tunnel. ☎081 66 93 90. Open Tu-Su 9am-1pm.)*

VOMERO

MUSEO NAZIONALE DI SAN MARTINO. Once a monastery, the massive Certosa di San Martino is now home to an excellent museum of Neapolitan history and culture. In addition to extensive galleries, the monastery includes a chapel lavishly decorated in baroque marbles and statuary, featuring one of Ribera's finest works, *The Deposition of Christ*, and an excellent Nativity by Guido Reni. Numerous balconies and a multilevel garden provide superb views. *(From V. Toledo take the funicular to Vomero, followed by a right on V. Cimarosa. A left on V. Morghen and a right onto V. Angelini lands you in Ple. S. Martino. ☎081 578 17 69. Open daily 9am-6pm. L11500.)*

The massive **Castel Sant'Elmo** next door was built to deter rebellion and hold political prisoners. Ignore the oppressive past; there are great panoramic views from the battlements. *(☎081 578 40 30. Open Tu-Su 9am-2pm. L5000.)*

MUSEO DUCA DI MARLINA. If you're a ceramics fan (and who isn't), then head to this crafts gallery inside the lush gardens of the **Villa Floridiana;** it houses 18th-century porcelain and some Asian items as well. *(The museum is at V. Cimarosa, 77. To get to the entrance, take the funicular to Vomero from V. Toledo, and turn left onto V. Cimarosa as you come out of the station. Enter the gardens and keep walking downhill. ☎081 478 84 18. Visitors admitted at 9am, 10:30am, noon, 3pm, and 4:30pm. L5000, ages 18-25 L2500)*

CENTRO DIREZIONALE

For a glimpse of Italy's most incongruous piece of skyline, head down C. Meridionale (on your right as you exit the train station) to this garishly modern office complex designed by Japanese architect Kenzo Tange. It was supposed to remove Neapolitan business from the chaos and corruption of downtown. Old habits die hard, however, and there have been few takers so far.

ENTERTAINMENT

NIGHTLIFE

Neapolitan nightlife varies widely according to season. While perfectly content to groove at clubs and discos during the winter, Neapolitans instinctively return to the streets in warmer weather. The Sunday evening *passeggiata* floods the Villa Comunale along the bay (#1 tram), and amorous young couples flood picturesque V. Petrarca and V. Posillipo. Most (for obvious reasons) take their cars.

For less exclusive gatherings, everybody heads to the *piazze* to relax and socialize. **P. Vanvitelli** in Vomero (take the funicular from V. Toledo or the C28 bus from P. Vittoria) is where the cool kids go to hit on each other. In **P. Gesu**

Nuovo, near the University of Naples (close to P. Dante), it ain't cigarette smoke you're smelling. Here the sound of bongos resonates as students, tired out from spray-painting surprisingly high-brow graffiti, recuperate and socialize with tourists and drifters. Outdoor bars and cafes are a popular choice, nowhere more so than in **P. Bellini** (a short walk from P. Dante) and **P. San Domenico Maggiore** (a quick walk up V. Mezzocannone from C. Umberto I), where hundreds of people drink, smoke, and chat at sidewalk tables. *Il Mattino* and *Qui Napoli* print decent club listings. There are almost no exclusively gay or lesbian clubs in Naples, but **ARCI-GAY/Lesbica** (☎081 551 82 93) has information on gay and lesbian nights at local clubs.

CAFES, BARS, AND PUBS

Caffè Letterario Intra Moenia, P. Bellini, 66 (☎081 29 07 20), appeals to the intellectuals among its clients by keeping books amidst the wicker furniture in a large outdoor section. *Espresso* L2500. Beer from L5000. Open Tu-Th 10am-1am, F-Su 10am-3am.

Green Stage, P. S. Pasquale, 15 (☎081 245 10 55). Take V. V. Colonna out of P. Amedeo, then turn right on V. S. Pasquale. An extremely popular pub. The Green Stage's crowds often spill out onto the *piazza* on summer nights. It seems like everyone's buying Heineken (L5000), with which this establishment is strongly affiliated, or Budweiser (L6000). Open Tu-Th 7:30pm-3am, F-Su 7:30pm-4am.

1799, P. Bellini, 70 (☎081 29 25 37), appeals to your dark side, opting for black decor and dim lighting. Eerie trance music keeps you from noticing how much that last cocktail was. Beer L5000; cocktails from L9000. Open Tu-Su 10am-1am, F-Su 10am-3am.

S'Move, Vico dei Sospiri, 10 (☎081 764 58 13). Head out of P. dei Martiri on V. C. Poerio, take the 1st right, and then the 1st left. A regular bar from 8am-8pm, this neo-futuristic establishment breaks out the funk from 8pm-midnight, often with a live DJ spinning pop and R&B on weekends. After midnight, it's acid jazz and hip-hop till closing time. "Energy drinks" L6000. Open M-Th 8am-2am, F-Su 8am-4am. Closed Aug.

NIGHTCLUBS AND DISCOTHEQUES

Tongue, V. Manzoni, 207 (☎081 769 08 00), in Posillipo. Take the erratic 404d *notturno* bus from P. Garibaldi. This large discotheque and music hall frequently features visiting DJs. Cover L25,000. Open Oct.-May F-Sa 11pm-4am.

Camelot, V. Petrarca, 101 (☎081 769 25 23), in Posillipo. No round table here. Except for the occasional live performances, they don't stray very far from pop, house, dance, and strict norms of chivalry. Cover L25,000. Open Oct.-May F-Sa midnight-4am.

Madison Street, V. Sgambati, 47 (☎081 546 65 66), in Vomero, features a large dance floor for weekend revelry. Cover L25,000. Open Sept.-May F-Su 10pm-4am.

Riot, V. S. Biagio, 39 (☎081 767 50 54), off C. Umberto I, gives you a chance to hear local artists play jazz and sing the blues. It's not exactly Robert Johnson and the Mississippi Delta, but these folks try hard. Open Th-Su 10:30pm-3am.

CINEMA, THEATER, AND SPORTS

For more passive entertainment, **Cinema Teatro Amedeo,** V. Marcucci, 69 (☎081 68 02 66), four blocks off P. Amedeo, shows films in English once a week during the summer. Call or check *Il Mattino* for more info. **Teatro S. Carlo,** at Palazzo Reale (☎081 797 23 31) hosts performances by the Opera (Oct.-June) and the Symphony Orchestra (Oct.-May). Gallery tickets cost L25,000—buy them well in advance.

For a true picture of Neapolitan life, catch a local soccer game at **Stadio S. Paolo** (☎081 239 56 23), in Fourigrotta. Take the Metro to "Campi Flegrei." **S.S. Napoli,** which recently returned to Serie A and still has a huge nationwide allegiances. Weekly games Sept.-June on Saturday or Sunday. (Tickets L18,000 and up.)

FESTIVALS

Once occasions for famous revelry, Naples's religious festivals have since become excuses for sales and shopping sprees. On the 1st Saturday of May and on September 19, the city celebrates its patron saint with the Festa di San Gennaro. Join the crowd by the *duomo* to see San Gennaro's blood miraculously liquefy in a small vial (see **Duomo,** p. 483). The festival of Madonna del Carmine (July 16) culminates in a fireworks show. In July, free concerts are held in P. S. Domenico Maggiore.

SHOPPING

A thriving black market and low prices make Naples a wonderful, if risky, place to shop. If you choose to buy from street vendors, understand that they are craftier than you. If a transaction seems too good to be true, then it is. Clothing is usually a good deal, though your nifty new shirt may come apart in the washing machine or turn your other clothes a ghastly shade of purple. Never buy electronic products from street vendors—even brand-name boxes have been known to be filled with newspaper and bricks. **V. S. Maria di Constatopoli,** south of the archaeological museum, has old books and antique shops, while the streets south of San Lorenzo Maggiore are home to craftsmen who make the traditional Neapolitan *creches.*

P. Martiri houses a roll call of Italian designers including Gucci, Valentino, Versace, Ferragamo, Armani, and Prada. The most modern and expensive shopping district is in the hills of Vomero along the perpendicular **Via Scarlatti** and **Via Luca Giordano.** If you're looking for jeans, head to the market off Porta Capuana. (Most markets are open M-Sa 9am-5pm, but many close at 2pm.)

DAYTRIPS FROM NAPLES

CAMPI FLEGREI

The earliest Greek inhabitants of Italy once associated Campi Flegrei with the underworld. Hades didn't scare them off, however, and the area is blanketed with their imposing monuments. The volcanic lakes and bubbling mud baths of the Phlegrean (Burning) Fields later became posh spas for the Roman elite. You can still visit the baths at **Baia** or see ruins of Virgilian fame at **Cuma** (Cumae)—although it might be more fun to swim at a beach in **Misena** or cringe at the pungent smell of the smoking Solfatara Crater in **Pozzuoli.** The sights of the fields are spread widely across the area, so allow a full daytrip from Naples to see them.

POZZUOLI

Home to the best camping near Naples and some interesting Roman ruins, **Pozzuoli** is a convenient jumping-off point for the islands of Procida and Ischia (and, incidentally, the birthplace of Sophia Loren). You can get to Pozzuoli from Naples by **Metro** (20min., L1500) or by taking the **Ferrovia Cumana** train from the Montesanto Station (20min., L2200). The Ferrovia station is closer to the port and the Tempio di Serapide, and the Metro station is closer to the Solfatara crater, the Anfiteatro, and campgrounds. To get to the **port** from the subway, take V. Solfatara down a series of hairpin turns, and then turn right on C. della Repubblica and again on V. Cosenza. Ferries run to Procida and Ischia from the port. Buy your tickets at the **Biglietteria Marittima** (☎081 896 03 28). **Traghetti Pozzuoli** (☎081 526 77 36) runs the most frequent ferry to **Ischia** (50min., 16 per day in summer 5:50am-8pm, L8000; ticket office open daily 6am-8pm). **Procida** runs to **Procida** (☎081 897 03 21. 30min., 12 per day in summer 6am-9pm, L4500; ticket office open daily 6am-9pm). Pozzuoli's **tourist office,** P. Matteotti, 1a, at V. Solfatara and C. della Repubblica, can provide a map. Ignore the signs pointing to the administrative office. (☎081 526 66 39. English spoken. Open M-F 9am-2pm and 4:30-7:30pm, Sa 9am-1pm.)

Pozzuoli offers the best **camping** in the area. Large and well run, **Camping Vulcano Solfatara,** V. Solfatara, 161 is part of the Solfatara Crater complex and offers campers free access to the sight. Revel in the swimming pool, sauna, and restaurant.

(☎081 526 23 41; fax 081 526 34 82; www.solfitaro.it; email vulcano.solfatara@iol.it. L15,000 per person; L10,000 per tent; 2-person bungalows L70,000; 4-person L100,000. Laundry L12,000. Lower prices Apr.-May and Sept.-Oct.) If you don't like roughing it, **Albergo Il Capitano,** Lungomare Colombo, 13, right on the port, has 5 pleasant rooms with A/C, TV, and bath. (☎/fax 081 526 22 83. Singles L80,000; doubles L100,000. V, MC, AmEx.)

Grab picnic supplies at the port's plentiful **fruit market.** (Open daily 7am-2pm.) Fish-eating fiends should head for the terrace of **La Trattoria da Gigetta,** Lungomare Colombo, 4/5, on the port. The specialty, *zuppa di pesce*, fish stew (L25,000), is big enough for two. (☎081 526 15 63. Pizza L5-10,000. *Primi* L8-15,000; *secondi* L8-12,000. Cover L2000. Open Th-Tu noon-3pm and 7pm-midnight.)

The imposing **Anfiteatro Flavio,** C. Terracciano, 75, built under the Flavian emperors in the 1st century AD, used to delight citizens with such popular spectacles as "Bear Eats Human." Today, all you'll get to see is the amphitheater itself, as well as the unusually well-preserved underground galleries that held the machinery used to raise and lower the animals' cages. Head down V. Solfatara (on your right as you exit the metro station) and turn right on V. Anfiteatro to get to the entrance. (☎081 52 66 07. Open daily 9am-1hr. before sunset. L4000.) At Piazzetta Serapide, just behind the port, you can peer down at the **Tempio di Serapide,** which wasn't a temple, but rather an ancient market that happened to enclose a statue of the god Serapis. An unusual form of volcanic activity called bradyseism (slow earthquakes that can raise or lower the entire region by several feet over a few months) has intermittently submerged, lifted, and shaken the site. With its pools of water and eerie, half-submerged pillars, the marketplace resembles a little Atlantis rising from the sea. Without a doubt, Pozzuoli's most pungent attraction is the still-active **Solfatara Crater,** V. Solfatara, 161. Sulfurous steam bubbles up from the rocks and boiling mud pits, creating an eerie landscape. From the metro station it is a steep 20-minute walk up V. Solfatara. You can also take one of several buses that go up the street. (☎081 526 74 13. Open daily 8:30am-1hr. before sunset. L8000.)

BAIA

Once the playground of the wild Roman Emperor Caligula, **Baia** had a reputation as a hotbed of hedonism and immorality in antiquity. Now it is a quiet little seaside town with a busy port. Modern Baia is nonetheless interspersed with ancient ruins of varying degrees of accessibility. Though less dramatic than Pompeii, Baia is free of crowds and overpriced tourist stands. Get there by way of the **Ferrovia Cumana** from Naples (30min., L2200), which leaves from near the Mergellina Metro stop, or from Pozzuoli (12min., L1700). The **SEPSA bus** also runs from Pozzuoli (20min., L1700). The most interesting remnants of Baia's libertine past are the ruins of the luxurious **Roman Baths,** one of the few ancient complexes where you can climb stairs to a 3rd and even 4th floor. Don't miss the **Temple of Mercury,** also known as Temple of Echoes, a bath chamber with the oldest dome skylight in the world. A clap of the hands resounds like a gunshot. Coming out of the train station, look for the stairs next to it, climb to the top, and turn left. (☎081 868 75 92. Baths open daily 9am-1hr. before sunset. L4000.) If archaeological treasures are your cup of tea, head to the **Castello Aragonese** and check out the **Museo Archeologico dei Campi Flegrei.** Take a right from the station on V. Roma and prepare for an invigorating walk (1.4km of steep hairpin turns; take the narrow staircase and then follow the signs) or take the infrequent Cuma-Miseno bus one stop towards Miseno (3min., 1 per hr., L1700). The museum has a small collection of sculptures and inscriptions from the area, not to mention an incredible view from a promontory above town. (☎081 523 37 97. Open M-Sa 9am-1hr. before sunset, Su 9am-1pm. L4000.)

CUMAE (CUMA)

Cumae, founded in the 8th century BC, was the earliest Greek colony on the Italian mainland. Mythologically, it was the place where Aeneas, mythical father of Rome, first washed up after being shipwrecked in Virgil's *Aeneid.* The highlight of Cumae's **scavi** (excavations) is the **Antro della Sibilla,** a man-made cave gallery that had been used as a pizza oven until archaeologists realized what it was in 1932. It once sheltered the Sybil, the most famous oracle west of Greece, who counseled countless mythological characters. According to literature, she would get "inspired by the gods" and give advice and predictions in a frenzied rage. "Inspired by the gods" comes from a Latin word that has also been translated as "sloppy drunk." Also worth seeing are the **Temple of Apollo,** up a set of stairs from the cave, and the **Temple of Jupiter** atop the acropolis. The spectacular view of Ischia and the coastline is worth the hike. The sprawling site requires at least an hour's visit. (The *scavi* are open M-Su 9am-1hr. before sunset. L4000.) To get to the site, take a **SEPSA** bus on the Miseno-Cuma line from the train station at Baia to the last stop in Cumae (15min., 1 per hr. L1700), and walk to the end of the V. Cumae. The "Cuma" stop on the **Ferrovia Circumflegrea** is in the modern town, several kilometers away. Take the bus to Cumae from Baia (2 per hr., L1700) on the Napoli-Torregaveta line.

Although you can visit Baia and Cumae as daytrips from Naples, pleasant beachfront hotels abound in **Misena,** a town at the cusp of a nearby peninsula. Take the **SEPSA** bus from the Baia train station to Miseno (10min., 1 per hour, L1700). The **Villa Palma Hotel,** V. Misena, 30, is at the last bus stop in Miseno. This modern and comfortable choice is steps from the beach. (☎081 523 39 44. 15 rooms all with bath. Breakfast included. Singles L50-60,000; doubles L70-80,000. V, MC, AmEx.)

NEAR NAPLES

CASERTA AND CAPUA ☎0823

In Caserta, majestic mountains abruptly appear as you turn around its corners. Once the former spring and autumn court of the House of Bourbon, Caserta is home to the **Palazzo Reale** or Royal Palace, locally called the "Reggia." Capua also boasts an impressive Roman amphitheater.

PRACTICAL INFORMATION. Caserta is easily accessible by train. **Trains** head to and from **Naples** (30-50min., L3900-4300) and **Rome** (2½-3½hr., L18,000). The Caserta station, in the center of town across from the Reggia, is also a major stop for the local **buses** (L1500-1700). Caserta's **EPT tourist offices** are at C. Trieste, 43, and at the corner of P. Dante. (☎0823 32 11 37. Open M-F 8am-4pm.) The **post office** is on V. Ellittico, off P. Carlo III (in front of the train station). **Postal Code:** 81100.

ACCOMODATIONS AND FOOD. Caserta is best visited as a daytrip from Naples. Most of the hotels in Caserta are in the slightly dilapidated area around the train station. If you are too tired to trek elsewhere after touring the Reggia, let **Hotel Baby,** V. G. Verdi, 41, to the right as you exit the station, cradle you with its friendly management and 15 well-furnished rooms. (☎0823 32 83 11. Singles L70,000; doubles L80,000; triples L115,000; quads L140,000.) Caserta's cuisine is simple—the town has numerous **pizzerie** which offer tasty pizza (takeout available). One of the most popular is **Pizzeria La Crociara,** V. Roma, 13, serving up large slices for L2000-L5000. From the train station, walk two blocks towards the Reggia and take a right on V. Roma. (☎0823 32 26 14. Open daily 10am-midnight.) V. Mazzini, running from P. Dante north to P. Vanvitelli, is the social center of town.

SIGHTS AND ENTERTAINMENT. Tourists flock to Caserta for only one reason—to see the magnificent **Reggia.** When Bourbon King Charles III commissioned the palace in 1751, he intended to rival the grandeur of Versailles. The complex was finished in 1775, including the gigantic Royal Palace and the 120-hectare **parco** (palace garden; hectares is metric for "a whole mess of"). Lush lawns, fountains, sculptures, and carefully pruned trees culminate in a 75m man-made waterfall. Sculptural groups at the bottom show Diana transforming the hunter Actaeon into a deer as his hounds pounce on him. To the right are the "English Gardens," complete with fake ruins inspired by Pompeii and Paestum. If you don't feel like attempting the 3km walk, take the bus (L1500) or a romantic horse-and-buggy ride. The **Palazzo** itself boasts 1200 rooms, 1742 windows, and 34 staircases. The main entrance stairway is a highlight of the palace's architecture. Frescoes and intricate marble floors adorn the gaudy royal apartments. (The Reggia is directly opposite the train station, across P. Carlo III. ☎0823 32 14 00. Gardens open daily 9am-1hr. before sunset. L4000. *Palazzo* open M-Sa 9am-1:30pm, Su 9am-5:30pm. L8000.)

One train stop from Caserta lies **Capua** and one of the most impressive **Roman amphitheaters.** Only the contemporaneous Colosseum in Rome rivals this massive structure. You can still see the tunnels where gladiators and beasts were brought into the arena. (Open daily 9am-1hr. before sunset. L5000.) From Caserta, take the **train** to "Santa Maria Capua Vètere" (L2300), walk straight one block, and make the 1st left onto V. G. Avezzana. Take the next left, walk 150m, and turn right onto V. E. Ricciardi, which becomes V. Amphiteatro. If you're not into the train, the blue **bus** from in front of the Caserta train station (L1700) will take you straight to Piazza Adriano. Unlike Spartacus, you don't have to lead a rebellion to leave Capua; Naples buses leave from the intersection a block north of the train station.

BENEVENTO ☎0824

According to legend, this town's original name was *Malaventum* (Bad Wind), but after the Romans defeated Pyrrhus here in 275 BC, they decided it might be a "good wind" *(Benevento)* after all. Even after being bombed during WWII, this peaceful mountain enclave retained its ancient monuments and old-town charm. Benevento is accessible by **train** from Rome (3hr., L22,000), Naples (1½hr., L7500), and Caserta (1hr., L5900). Local **buses** (info ☎0824 210 15) leave from the train station, including bus #1 (L1000) to C. Garibaldi, the center of town. Buses to Naples and local towns leave from the *Terminal Autobus Extraurbani*, several blocks north of the Castel on C. Garibaldi. For **taxis** call 0824 200 00. The **EPT tourist office** in P. Roma (off C. Garibaldi), is an amazing store of info. (☎0824 31 99 38. Open M-F 8am-2pm and 3-6pm.) **Postal Code:** 82100.

Albergo della Corte is in an alley at P. Piano di Corte, 11. Follow the narrow V. Bartolomeo Camerario, off C. Garibaldi. The *albergo* offers newly renovated rooms with TVs. (☎0824 548 19. Singles L55,000; doubles L80,000.) Near Trajan's Arch, **Ristorante e Pizzeria Traiano,** V. Manciotti, 48, serves simple but delectable meals. (☎0824 250 13. Primi L8000, secondi L8000; open W-M noon-4pm and 7pm-midnight.) Though the area is known for its *mozzarella di bufala* cheese, don't leave without falling under the spell of Benevento's *Strega* liqueur, named after the legendary witches of Benevento, or at least the *Strega*-flavored *gelato.*

From the 6th to the 4th century BC, Benevento was the center of the Samnite kingdom. The bell tower in P. Matteotti, off C. Garibaldi, proudly commemorates Benevento's heritage. The **Church of S. Sofia** (762), also in P. Matteotti, has an attached monastery that is now the **Museo del Sannio** (☎0824 218 18), which holds Samnite artifacts, Roman objects, and works by local artists. South of the museum, down Vico Noce, is a sculpture garden with works by Mino Palladino. North of P. Roma is the **Arch of Beneventum** (114-117), depicting the policies of the Emperor **Trajan.** It has the finest and most extensive decoration of any surviving Roman arch. At the other end of town is a huge 2nd-century **Roman theater**—one of Italy's best-preserved, it's still a concert venue (L4000). Every September the town hosts a theater festival; contact the tourist office for details.

The long way back to Naples takes you through the rugged backcountry. Buses stop at the small village of **Montesarchio;** covering a steep hill, its winding streets lead to an Aragonese tower and fabulous views. Talk to the Benevento tourist office to find out the bus schedule. A village stop will take no more than 1½ hours.

BAY OF NAPLES: ISLANDS

The pleasure islands **Capri, Ischia,** and **Procida** beckon the weary traveler with promises of breathtaking natural sights, comfortable accommodations, and gorgeous beaches. The islands can be reached by ferries *(traghetti)* or faster, more expensive hydrofoils *(aliscafi)*. But the tranquility of sun-baked landscapes has its price, and you might end up spending more than you want for accommodations. For jaunts to Ischia and Procida, the route through Pozzuoli is shortest and cheapest; for Capri, Sorrento is the closest starting point. The busiest route to Capri and Ischia is through Naples's Mergellina and Molo Beverello ports. To reach Molo Beverello from Stazione Centrale, take tram #1 from P. Garibaldi to P. Municipio on the waterfront. Ferries and hydrofoils also run between the islands.

CAPRI AND ANACAPRI ☎081

Augustus fell in love with this island's fantastic beauty in 29 BC and swapped it for its more fertile neighbor, Ischia. His successor Tiberius passed his last decade on the island, leaving a dozen scattered villas. Visitors today pay top *lira* to tour the renowned **Blue Grotto** (p. 495) and gawk at the rich and famous. Away from the throngs flitting between Capri's expensive boutiques, Anacapri is home to budget hotels, spectacular vistas, and empty mountain paths. Crowds and prices are high throughout the summer, especially in July and August, so the best times to visit are in the late spring or early fall, though it is well worth the trip at any time of year.

TRANSPORTATION

Ferries: Ticket office, arrivals and departures at **Marina Grande**. For more info about how to get to Capri check out ferries from Naples (p. 473) and Sorrento (p. 505).

Caremar (☎081 837 07 00) runs ferries and hydrofoils. Ferries to **Naples** (1¼hr., 6 per day 7:30am-8pm, L9800) and Sorrento (45min., 3 per day 7am-5pm, L10,000). Hydrofoils to **Naples** (40min., 5 per day 7am-5pm, L18,000). Ticket office open daily 7am-8pm.

SNAV (☎081 837 75 77) runs hydrofoils to **Naples's** Mergellina port (40min., 13 per day 8am-8pm, L16,000). Ticket office open daily 8am-8pm.

Linea Jet (☎081 837 08 19) runs hydrofoils to **Sorrento** (20min., 3 per day 2-4:30pm, L14,000) and **Naples** (40min., 11 per day 8:30am-6pm, L17,000). Office open daily 9am-6pm.

Linee Lauro (☎081 837 69 95), runs hydrofoils to: **Sorrento** (20min., 12 per day 8am-6pm, L14,000); **Ischia** (40min., 4:40pm, L20,000); and **Salerno** (1½hr., 11:40am, L20,000), by way of **Positano** (30min., L19,000) and **Amalfi** (1hr., L19,000). Office open daily 8am-6pm.

Local Transportation: SIPPIC buses (☎081 837 04 20) depart from V. Roma in Capri for Anacapri (every 15min., 6am-1:40am), Marina Piccola, and points in between. In Anacapri, buses depart from P. Barile, off V. Orlandi, for the Grotta Azzurra, the *faro* (lighthouse), and other points nearby. There's also a direct line between Marina Grande and P. Vittoria in Anacapri which only runs on the hour. L1800 per ride.

Taxis: Taxi stands are at the bus stop in Capri (☎081 837 05 43), and at P. Vittoria in Anacapri (☎081 837 11 75).

ORIENTATION AND PRACTICAL INFORMATION

There are two towns on the island of Capri—**Capri proper** above the ports and **Anacapri,** higher up the mountain. Ferries dock at **Marina Grande,** where a **funicular** runs to **P. Umberto** in Capri (every 10min., 6:30am-12:30am in summer, L1700). The alternative is an hour hike up a narrow stairway. Expensive boutiques and bakeries fill the narrow streets radiating off P. Umberto. Windy **V. Roma,** to the right, leads to Anacapri. Buses from Capri to Anacapri run on to the Blue Grotto before reaching the lighthouse across the island. The bus to Anacapri stops in P. Vittoria, Anacapri's center. Villa S. Michele and the Monte Solaro chairlift are nearby. **V. Giuseppe Orlandi,** running from P. Vittoria, leads to the best budget establishments. Save the port road, Capri is comprised of narrow pedestrian paths closed to cars.

TOURIST, FINANCIAL, AND LOCAL SERVICES

Tourist Office: The oft-swamped **AAST information Office** (☎081 837 06 34) lies at the end of the dock at Marina Grande in Capri. There's another branch at P. Umberto, under the clock (☎081 837 06 86). In Anacapri, there's one at V. Orlandi, 59 (☎081 837 15 24), off the main *piazza,* to the right when you get off the bus. Each office offers the yearly handbook *Capri è...* and a detailed map (L1500). Open June-Sept. M-Sa 8:30am-8:30pm; Oct.-May M-Sa 9am-1:30pm and 3:30-6:45pm.

Currency Exchange: Though the post offices have the best rates, there are also official exchange agencies at V. Roma, 33 (☎081 837 07 85), across from the main bus stop, and in P. Umberto. Another agency in P. Vittoria, 2 (☎081 837 31 46), in the center of Anacapri. 3% commission. Open daily 8:30am-7pm, reduced hours in winter.

Luggage Storage: Caremar ticket office (☎081 837 07 00), at Marina Grande Capri's funicular. L3000 per bag. Open daily 8am-9pm, in winter 8am-6pm. Another office in Anacapri's P. Vittoria. L2000 per bag. Open daily in summer 8am-5:30pm.

Public Toilets: At the funicular in Capri (L500) and P. Vittoria, 5, in Anacapri (L500). Open daily 8am-9pm. Not suggested for those weak of heart.

Swimming Pool: Bar Nettuno, V. Grotta Azzurra, 46 (☎081 837 13 62), above the Blue Grotto in Anacapri. Take the bus from Anacapri center. Full use of outdoor pool, ocean access, reclining chairs, shower, and changing room. With *Let's Go* L8000 per day, regular L15,000. *Let's Go* lunch L12,000. Open mid-Mar. to mid-Nov. daily 9am-7pm.

EMERGENCY AND COMMUNICATIONS

Emergencies: ☎113 or 081 838 1205. **Police:** V. Roma, 70 (☎081 837 42 11). **Medical Emergencies: Pronto Soccorso** (☎081 838 12 05) at **Ospedale Capilupi** (☎081 838 11 11) V. Provinciale Anacapri, a few blocks down V. Roma from P. Umberto. **Tourist Medical Emergency Service:** V. Caprile, 30, Anacapri (☎081 838 12 40).

Internet Access: The Newsstand (☎081 837 3283) in P. Vittoria, Anacapri. L10,000 per hr. Open 9am-2pm and 4-9pm. **Capri Graphic,** V. Listrieri, 17 (☎081 837 52 12). Head out of P. Umberto on V. Longano and take a right on V. Listrieri. L5000 per 15min. Open M-Sa 9:30am-1pm and 4-8:30pm.

Post Office: Central office in Capri at V. Roma, 50 (☎081 837 72 40), downhill from P. Umberto. Open M-F 8:30am-7:20pm, Sa 8:30am-1pm. **Currency exchange** with the best rates in town. Commission: L5000 cash, L1000 checks. Open M-Sa 8:10am-6pm. **Anacapri office** at V. de Tommaso, 4 (☎081 837 10 15). Open M-F 8:30am-1:30pm, Sa 8:15am-noon. **Postal Code:** Capri: 80073. Anacapri: 80021.

ACCOMMODATIONS

Lodging in Capri proper is expensive year-round and exorbitant in mid-summer. Try as you might, you will not be able to find a deal in July or August. The lower price ranges listed here usually apply from Oct.-May. Call in advance to reconfirm reservations and prices. It's possible to find impromptu vacancies in June but difficult in July and August. Makeshift camping is illegal and heavily fined.

ANACAPRI

Villa Eva, V. La Fabbrica, 8 (☎081 837 15 49 or 081 837 20 40; www.caprionline.com/villaeva.) Before trying to navigate the 15min. walk through the maze of Anacapri's side streets, call from P. Vittoria and wait to be picked up. Set high among gardens and trees, this is the ideal vacation setting. Vicenzo tends the gardens and built the cozy bungalows and 18 rooms himself. Every night students and backpackers gather at the classy pool and bar area, tended by son Carlo. Near the Blue Grotto. Most rooms with bath. Breakfast included. Reserve early and confirm. Singles L50,000; doubles L80-90,000 and up; triples L105-120,000 and up; quads L140-160,000 and up. V, MC.

Alla Bussola di Hermes, V. Traversa La Vigna, 14 (☎081 838 2010; email bus.hermes@libero.it). Great prices and clean rooms. Free use of kitchen and washing machine. Call from Marina Grande to be picked up. All rooms L35,000 per person.

Hotel Loreley, V. G. Orlandi, 16 (☎081 837 14 40; fax 081 837 13 99), 20m toward Capri from P. Vittoria. Large, bright rooms with baths. With *Let's Go*: doubles L140,000; triples L180,000. Open Apr.-Oct. V, MC, AmEx.

Il Girasole, V. Linciano, 47 (☎081 837 23 51; fax 081 837 38 80; email ilgirasole@capri.it; www.ilgirasole.com). Comfortable terrace, a small pool, and Internet for L10,000 per 30min. Call from Marina Grande to be met (expect to be charged), or walk from the last bus stop and follow the signs up the stairway. Most of the 24 rooms have bath, fridge, and TV. Doubles from L105,000; triples L135-180,000.

CAPRI

Pensione Stella Maris, V. Roma, 27 (☎081 837 04 52; fax 081 837 86 62), across from the bus stop. Capri's cheapest option, near the center of town, with consequent noise. All rooms with bath and TV. Singles L100,000; doubles L120,000. V, MC.

Pensione Quattro Stagioni, V. Marina Piccola, 1 (☎081 837 00 41). From P. Umberto, walk 5min. down V. Roma. Turn left at the 3-pronged fork in the road, and look for the green gate on the left. Though the cheaper rooms do not have the great view of Marina Piccola that the others do, many still open onto the lush garden. Breakfast included. Doubles L140-180,000, with bath L160-200,000.

FOOD

Capri's food is as glorious as its panoramas. Savor the local mozzarella on its own, or with tomatoes, oil, and basil in an *insalata caprese*—many consider it *the* summer meal. The *ravioli alla caprese* are hand-stuffed with tasty local cheeses. Indulge in the *torta di mandorle* (chocolate almond cake). Local red and white wines bear *Tiberio* or *Caprense* labels. A step up (especially price-wise) is the *Capri Blù*. Restaurants often serve *Capri DOC*, a light white. If you want to avoid pricey restaurants, or just grab picnic supplies, head to Capri's **STANDA supermarket.** (Open M-Sa 8:30am-1:30pm and 5-9pm, Su 9am-noon.) Take the right prong of the fork at the end of V. Roma. In Anacapri, try **Alimentaria Russo,** on V. G. Orlandi. (☎081 837 3991. *Panini* L5000. Open 8am-7pm.) Ask at your hotel for budget restaurants, but don't expect to pay less than L25,000 for a full meal.

ANACAPRI

Ristorante Il Cucciolo, V. Fabbrica, 52 (☎081 837 19 17). Dine here on the way from the Blue Grotto (5min.). Follow the signs for Villa Damecuta from the bus stop or call for a free ride from P. Vittoria. The food, served on a terrace with bay views, is fresh and plentiful and the prices low. With *Let's Go*: *primi* L8-10,000, *secondi* L8-16,000. Cover L3000. Open daily Mar.-Oct. noon-2:30pm and 7:30-11pm. July-Aug. 7:30-11pm.

GOOD THING HE DIDN'T CATCH A PORCUPINE By all accounts the Roman Emperor Tiberius was a randy fellow. The two main chroniclers of his life, historians Tacitus and Suetonius, claim that he came to Capri because he was ashamed of his own depravity (he actually had servants whose names were "Sphincter" and "Saddle") and wanted freedom to enjoy his numerous and innovative sexual indulgences away from the eyes of the world. Thinking he was completely isolated in Capri, he was surprised when a fisherman climbed up the rocky shore to present him with a large fish as an offering. Not knowing what to do, Tiberius immediately ordered imperial guards to beat the man with the fish. When the beating ceased, the fisherman thanked the gods that he had not given the emperor the large crab he had also caught. Hearing this, Tiberius ordered his guards to get the crab and beat the fisherman with that too. Today there is a plaque in P. Umberto dedicated to the Emperor that denies this and other tawdry tales about Tiberius.

Il Grottino Ristorante, G. Orlandi, 95 (☎081 837 10 66), a few blocks from P. Vittoria. Munch excellent food in style at Il Grottino's cheery, outdoor tables. Enjoy some of the best *ravioli alla Caprese* (L13,000) in the world while the tourists walking up Anacapri's main drag longingly eye you (or more likely your ravioli). Lunch *menù* L16,500. Cover L2000. Open daily 11am-3:30pm and 7:30-11pm.

Il Ristoro, P. Caprile, 1 (☎081 837 36 71), on the Capri-Anacapri bus line, 5 blocks from P. Vittoria. Mangia, mangia! This family-run establishment will treat you like their own as soon as you step through the doors. *Menù* L20,000 (including service and cover). Pizza and drink combination L12,000. Open daily 8am-midnight. V, MC.

Trattoria Il Solitario, V. Orlandi, 96, falsely marked as #54 (☎081 837 13 82), 5min. from P. Vittoria. Tasty food in an ivy-covered hideaway. Homemade pasta L8000, pizza from L7000. "Light menu" L15,000. Cover L2500. Open daily noon-3pm and 7:30pm-midnight; off-season Th-Su noon-3pm and 7:30pm-midnight.

CAPRI

Longano da Tarantino, V. Longano, 9 (☎081 837 10 87), just off P. Umberto. Possibly the best deal in town, featuring an ocean view and a L26,000 *menù*. Try the *maccheroncelli "Aumm Aumm"* (with eggplant, tomato, and cheese; L9000), so called because that's all your ecstatic mouth will be able to utter. Pizza from L6000. Open Mar.-Nov. Th-Tu noon-3pm and 7:30pm-midnight.

Buca di Bacco, V. Longano, 35 (☎081 837 07 23), off P. Umberto I. Elegant and affordable. Their specialty is the delicious *pennette alla bacco* (with peppers and cheese) for L10,000. Pizza L6-11,000 at night only. Open Dec.-July and Sept.-Oct. Th-Tu noon-2:30pm and 7pm-midnight; Aug. daily noon-2:30pm and 7pm-midnight. V, MC, AmEx.

SIGHTS

GROTTA AZZURRA (BLUE GROTTO). Considered by some to be one of the seven natural wonders of the world, the cavern's shimmering blue hues are a must-see for island visitors. The cliffs do not connect to the sea floor, allowing light to enter the cave from below, making the water shimmer and glow a fantastic neon blue. Although visiting the Grotto is expensive and visits inside are brief, its remarkable beauty is captivating. Despite a recently passed law prohibiting it, many swim at their own peril to the cave after hours. *Let's Go* does not recommend this dangerous activity. The blue light is best seen on a sunny day from 11am to 3pm. *(Reach the grotto by motorboat from Marina Grande (L8000) or take the bus (L1700) from Capri to Anacapri and a 2nd from Anacapri to the Grotto. L8000, with rowboat L8500. Usually open daily 9am-6pm. Closed Nov.-Mar. and in inclement weather. Boat tours can be booked in Capri, L16,000. To find out if the Grotto is open, call ☎081 837 56 46 or 081 837 56 96.)*

CAPRI'S COAST. Every day **boat tours** reveal Capri's coast from Marina Grande, the most impressive vantage point, for L19,000. Two different companies run the tours, which leave on the hour from 9:30am-2:30pm. Many rock and pebble **beaches** surround the island. Take a boat from the port (L9000) or descend between vineyards from P. Umberto to **Bagni di Tiberio,** a bathing area amid the ruins of an imperial villa. A bus or a 10-minute walk down the path (left where V. Roma splits in three) leads to the gorgeous southern stretch of Marina Piccola. *(Buy tickets and get info for all boat tours at the Grotta Azzurra Travel Office, V. Roma, 53, across the street from the bus stop. ☎081 837 07 02; email g.azzurra@capri.it. Open M-Sa 9am-1pm and 3-8pm.)* Cavort in the clear water among immense lava rocks or rent a **kayak** *(L20,000)* or **motor boat** *(L150,000)* from **Banana Sport.** *(Main office on dock at Marina Grande. ☎081 837 51 88. Open daily 9am-6pm.)*

CAPRI'S CLIFFS. If you prefer the mainland to the briny blue, the rugged landscape has many trails to fabulous panoramas—many visitors overlook the island's natural aesthetic beauty in favor of the worldlier urban environment, but some of the best vistas offer solitude and a break from the boutiques. Check out Emperor Tiberius's ruined but magnificent **Villa Jovis,** the largest of his 12 Capri villas.

Always the gracious host, Tiberius tossed those who displeased him over the precipice. The view from the **Cappella di Santa Maria del Soccorso,** built onto the villa, is unrivaled. *(To get to the villa, head out of P. Umberto on V. Longano, which turns into V. Tiberio. Ask directions if the signs confuse you. Open daily 9am-1hr. before sunset. L4000.)*

A path winds along the cliffs, connecting the **Arco Naturale,** a majestic stone arch on the eastern cliffs, and the **Faraglioni,** three massive rocks seen on countless postcards. The path between the two takes about an hour to walk, but there is a magnificent vista around every bend. *(V. Tragara goes from Capri Centro to the Faraglioni, while the path to the Arco Naturale connects to the route to Villa Jovis through V. Matermania.)*

The belvedere (scenic overlook) from **Punta Cannone** foregrounds the dramatic cliffs of the southern coast. The tourist office map has several walking itineraries of the less-touristed parts of the island.

VILLA SAN MICHELE. Henry James once declared that this Anacapri villa was where "the most fantastic beauty, poetry, and inutility [had] ever been clustered together." Built in the early 20th century by Swedish author and physician Axel Munthe on the site of one of Tiberius' villas, the house shelters 17th-century furniture and ancient Roman sculpture. Its gardens boast a remarkable view and free classical concerts on Friday nights, June through August. *(Up the stairs from P. Vittoria and to the left, past Capri's Beauty Farm. Open daily 9:30am-1 hr. before sunset. L8000.)*

OTHER SIGHTS. From P. Vittoria in Anacapri, a 12-minute chairlift climbs to the top of **Monte Solaro.** The ride affords awesome views: on a clear day, you can see the Appennines to the east and the mountains of Calabria to the south. *(Open daily Mar.-Oct. 9:30am-1hr. before sunset. Round-trip L7000.)* A bus from P. Vittoria leads to the **Faro,** Italy's 2nd-tallest lighthouse. Countless Italians snorkel, tan, and dive from its rocks. The yellow-brick paved V. Orlandi, off P. Vittoria in Anacapri, leads to the most inexpensive (but still rather pricey) tourist **shopping** on Capri.

ENTERTAINMENT

Nighttime action carries a hefty pricetag. Anacapri's prices are slightly lower. **Underground,** V. Orlandi, 259, is the town's most popular nightspot. In July and August, the whole club moves outdoors to the Faro (☎081 837 25 23. Live music Tu and F. Cover M-W L7000, Th-Su L10,000. Open daily 10pm-4am.) **Zeus,** V. Orlandi, 103, a few blocks from P. Vittoria, is a cinema most of the time. On Saturdays (and Thursdays in July and August), it morphs into a discotheque. (☎081 83 79 16. Cover L20-35,000, with *Let's Go* L15,000. Open midnight-4pm.)

The Capri scene is classier and much more expensive. Covers are high and gatherings exclusive at the lounges and clubs near P. Umberto. A prime example of the extravagant discos is **Number Two,** V. Camerelle, 1, a popular spot for celebs and affluent twenty-somethings. If you want to try your luck hanging out with crowds of dressed-to-kill Italians, remember that the buses stop running at 1:40am, and a taxi will run you L20,000. (☎081 837 70 78. Open nightly during the summer.)

ISCHIA ☎081

Upon first setting foot on Ischia (EES-kee-yah), you may think you have left Italy entirely, not just because the island is an Edenic vision with luscious beaches, natural hot springs, ruins, forests, vineyards, lemon groves, and a once-active volcano, but also because all the signs, newspapers, and conversations are in German. The island is not the last Axis stronghold in Europe; rather, it is immensely popular with German tourists, who take it over for much of the summer. In August, however, Italians on holiday swarm to Ischia and reclaim it; the population explosion leads to sky-high prices and boisterous crowds. Bargains and breathing room become hard to find, but with good reason: Ischia's beaches are majestic, as are its thermal baths. Its springs, which have been mentioned in such rags as the *Iliad*, the *Aeneid*, and *Let's Go*, have drawn tourists since ancient times. According to mythology, the island is home to the giant Typhoeus, who responded to Jupiter's scorn with the fury of volcanoes. Today the giant seems content to heat the springs of the exclusive spas. There is plenty to see and the crowds often make for a lively atmosphere, even if you don't speak German.

TRANSPORTATION

Ferries: Ischia is best reached by **ferry** or **hydrofoil** from Pozzuoli (see p. 488), though ferries run from Naples as well. Most ferries leave from **Ischia Porto,** where the main ticket offices are. Schedules and prices subject to change. Call for details.

Caremar (☎081 98 48 18) runs ferries to: **Procida** (17min., 11 per day 7am-7pm, L7000); **Pozzuoli** (45min., 3 per day 8am-5pm, L7500); and **Naples** (1½hr., 14 per day 7am-8pm, L9800). Hydrofoils to **Procida** (30min., 11 per day 7am-7pm, L4000) and **Naples** (1hr., 14 per day 7am-8pm, L10,000). Ticket offices open 7am-9pm.

Traghetti Pozzuoli (☎081 526 77 36). To **Pozzuoli** from Casamicciola Terme (50min., 15 per day 7am-7pm, L8000). Ticket offices are in Casamicciola Terme. Open daily 7am-7pm.

Linee Marittime Partenopee (☎081 99 18 88) runs hydrofoils to **Sorrento** (45min., 5 per day 10:30am-5pm, L18,000) and **Amalfi** (1hr., usually at 10:30am, L22,000), via **Positano** (50min., L20,000). Ticket offices open daily 7am-8pm.

Buses: SEPSA buses depart from P. Trieste just off the port. The main lines are **CS, CD,** and **#1.** CS circles the island counter-clockwise, hitting Ischia Porto, Casamicciola Terme, Lacco Ameno, Forio, Panza, Sant'Angelo, Serrara Fontana, and Barano. The CD line follows the same route in a clockwise direction (both every 20 min., every 30min. late at night; 5:45am-1am). The #1 bus follows the CS route as far as Sant'Angelo then comes back (every 20 min. 6am-11:30pm). Other routes are shorter, run less frequently, and stop running earlier. Tickets L1700, full-day pass L5200.

Taxis: Microtaxi (☎081 99 25 50).

ORIENTATION AND PRACTICAL INFORMATION

Ischia's towns and points of interest are almost all on the coast, connected by the main road, which the major bus routes follow. On the east coast, **Ischia Porto,** an almost perfectly circular port formed by the crater of an extinct volcano, is Ischia's largest town. The road continues to **Casamicciola Terme,** on the north coast, with its overcrowded beach and legendary thermal waters, and **Lacco Ameno,** on Ischia's northwest point, the oldest Greek settlement in the western Mediterranean, now known for the island's cleanest boardwalk. The road reaches **Forio,** Ischia's most touristed area, full of restaurants and hotels. In the south, Basano is a good departure point for Mt. Epomeo or the beach at **Maronti.**

Tourist Office: AAST Tourist Office (☎081 507 42 31; fax 081 507 42 30), on Banchina Porto Salvo, next to the ticket offices at the midpoint of the main port. Provides local tour listings and accommodations info. Open in summer daily 8am-2pm and 3-8pm; winter M-Sa 9am-1pm.

Vehicle Rental: Del Franco, V. de Luca, 133 (☎081 98 48 18). Rents cars, bikes, *motorini,* boats, and more. *Motorini* L30-50,000 per day. Open daily 8am-10pm.

Police: Polizio della Stato, V. delle Terme, 80 (☎081 50 74 71 19), 2 blocks up from V. de Luca in Ischia Porto. Helps out with passport problems. Open M, W, F 9am-noon. **Medical Emergency: Pronto Soccorso,** V. Fundera, 1 (☎081 507 92 31), at the **Ospedale Anna Rizzoli,** in Lacco Ameno (accessible by the CS, CD, or #1 bus).

ACCOMMODATIONS AND CAMPING

Despite the island's popularity, Ischia has several budget options amidst the higher priced hotels. Options in Ischia Porto, Casamicciola Terme, and Lacco Ameno tend to be very expensive because many hotels have pools (allegedly) fed by hot springs. Ischia Porto's proximity to nightlife and restaurants is its major draw. Although most tourists flock to Forio, finding a friendly, fair priced accommodation is possible. In early spring, many of the fancier hotels offer rooms at significantly lower rates. In such cases, emissaries are often sent to the docks to solicit newly arrived tourists. Don't count on them, though—be sure to make a reservation, and check to make sure hotels will rent rooms for just one night.

FORIO

Ostello "Il Gabbiano" (HI), Strada Statale Forio-Panza, 162 (☎081 90 94 22), on the main road between Forio and Panza. Accessible by the CS, CD, or #1 bus. Sun-baked white building with bar, pool, a great view of the sea, easy access to the beach at Citara, and an agreement with a swanky nearby restaurant/piano bar that gets HI guests dinner for only L15,000. 100 beds. Breakfast, sheets, and shower included. Lockout 10am-1pm. Curfew 12:30am. Open Apr.-Sept. Dorms L30,000; doubles L60,000.

Hotel Villa Franca and **Baia Verde,** Strada Statale, 270, #183 (☎081 98 74 20; fax 081 98 70 81). Take CS, CD, or #1 bus from Ischia Porto and get off at the "S. Francesco" beach stop. Short walk from the beach. Two hotels with the same prices and management. Patio and 3 swimming pools: 2 cold mineral baths and 1 thermal bath. Breakfast included. 35 rooms. Open Mar.-Oct. With *Let's Go:* singles L50,000; doubles L120,000 with dinner. V, MC, AmEx.

Pensione di Lustro, V. Filippo di Lustro, 9 (☎081 99 71 63), left from the Forio beaches. Its courtyard overflows with tropical plants. Truman Capote slept here in 1968. 10 rooms with TV, bath, A/C, and breakfast. With *Let's Go:* June doubles L100,000; July-Aug. doubles with bath L120,000; Oct.-Mar. doubles L90,000. V, MC, AmEx.

ISCHIA PORTO

Albergo Macri, V. Lasolino, 96 (☎081 99 26 03), along the docks, just off P. Trieste. A tranquil family-run hotel. All 24 rooms have bath. With *Let's Go:* singles L40-55,000; doubles L80-105,000; triples L120-140,000. Higher prices mid-July to mid-Sept.

Pensione Crostolo, V. Cossa, 48 (☎081 99 10 94). From the P. Trieste bus station, ascend the main street and turn right. Perched well above the port, this 3-star hotel boasts terraces and 15 rooms have bath, TV, fridge, and safe. L60-70,000 per person.

CASAMICCIOLA TERME

Pensione Quisisana, P. Bagni, 34 (☎/fax 081 99 45 20). Take bus #3 from Ischia Porto to the *piazza.* Near the beach. Homey establishment with a roof garden. Open May-Oct. Doubles with bath L80,000. Full pension in Aug. L85,000 per person. Extra bed L25,000.

CAMPING

These two delightful campgrounds, the most economical accommodations on the island, lie near Ischia Porto. Prices listed are for August and run L2-5000 less the rest of the year.

Camping Internazionale, V. Foschini, 22 (☎081 99 14 49; fax 081 99 14 72). Take V. Alfredo de Luca from V. del Porto and bear right onto V. Michele Mazzella (*not* V. Leonardo Mazzella) at P. degli Eroi; it's about a 15min. walk from the port. Lushly landscaped. Open Apr. 15-Oct.15. L16,000 per person, L10,000 per tent. Immaculate 2-person bungalows with bath L80,000, L20,000 per additional person.

Eurocamping dei Pini, V. delle Ginestre, 28 (☎081 98 20 69), a 20min. walk from the port. Take V. del Porto to V. de Luca, walk uphill and take a right on V. delle Terme, where you will see the arrow indicating camping. Pleasant campground with friendly management and a mini-soccer field. L15,000 per person, L8000 per tent. 2-person bungalows L65,000, with bath L90,000.

FOOD

While Ischian food, especially the seafood and fruit, is a treat, it is almost impossible to find a local eatery that is not tourist-oriented. Explore side streets in order to escape the L10,000 *pizza margherita* offered up by the cookie-cutter establishments on the main tourist grazing grounds.

Emiddio, V. Porto, 30, at the docks. The jubilant owner will happily feed you. Their *ravioli alla panna* (with *prosciutto* and milk; L7000) reigns supreme. *Primi* L5-10,000. Cover L2000. Open daily noon-3pm and 7pm-midnight. V, MC, AmEx.

Ristorante Zelluso, V. Parodi, 41 (☎081 99 46 27), to the left as you enter Casamicciola. Look for the white sign and walk down the alley. Scrumptious pizza L7000. Cover L2000. Open daily noon-3pm and 7pm-midnight.

SIGHTS

CASTELLO ARAGONESE. Providing some brooding relief to the sun and surf, this castle resides on a small island of its own (Ischia Ponte), connected to the rest of civilization by a 15th-century footbridge. The stronghold, built in 1441, contains both the holy and the macabre. The **cathedral** in the castle, mostly destroyed by WWII bombing, displays a mix of Roman and Baroque styles. Below, the **crypt** houses colorful 14th-century frescoes crafted by the school of Giotto. The **nuns' cemetery** has a ghastly history; when a nun died, the order would prop the decomposing body on a stone throne as a (fragrant) reminder to the other nuns of their mortality. The bodies are no longer visible today. For more family fun, visit the castle's **Museum of Arms and Instruments of Torture,** 200m past the main ticket booth, which contains plenty of nasty things that will make you thankful that you skipped out on the 1500s. *(Buses #7 and 8 run to Ischia Ponte from the port. Castle ☎081 99 28 34. L15,000, includes elevator to the top. Nun's cemetery open daily 10am-7:20pm. L5000. Torture museum ☎081 98 43 46. Open daily 9:30am-1hr. before sunset. A separate ticket of L5,000)*

SANTA RESTITUTA. This *chiesa* in Lacco Ameno holds the ruins of Pithecoussae's ancient villas of the 8th century BC. The island's numerous civilizations can be distinguished in a cross-section of soil. *(Take a CS or CD bus to Lacco Ameno. Walk down V. Roma, towards Ponta Cornacchia. Open daily 9am-noon and 4-6pm. Free.)*

BEACHES, HOT SPRINGS, AND HIKING. Ischia's best and most popular beach is at **Maronti,** on the island's south coast. *(Take the #5 bus from Ischia Porto to get there.)* Another popular choice is the beach at **Citara,** 1km down the coast from Forio. The #1 and #3 buses head there directly from Ischia Porto. For steamier adventures, **Sorgeto**'s (on the far side of the island) hot springs range from tepid to boiling. Somewhat remote, the beach is the perfect spot to lounge and soak aching feet. Locals say that the cleansing lather formed by rubbing the light-green porous rocks together is fantastic for the skin. (Reach the beach by boat-taxi from Sant'Angelo (L5000 per person, ask for a group discount and arrange for pick-up) or walk 20 minutes down from Panza.) **Lacco Ameno** and **Casamicciola Terme** are densely packed with the thermal baths that originally attracted visitors to Ischia.

Hikers should take the CS or CD bus to Fontana, which rests above most towns, making it a good departure point. Head for **Mt. Epomeo** (788m); when not wreathed in clouds, the summit has an incredible view extending from Capri to Terracina.

NIGHTLIFE

Ischia's liveliest nocturnal scene is in Ischia Porto. The best of the bunch is **Valentino,** C. Vittoria Colonna, 97. C. V. Colonna runs parallel to V. de Luca from the port, one block nearer to the sea. A discotheque and piano bar, it's a good place to get down with your bad self. The music varies, so make sure your bad self likes what it hears before paying the cover, which starts at L20,000 and is often much higher. (☎081 98 25 69. Open F-Su midnight-4am.) **Blue Jane** (the disco formerly known as Jane), on V. Iasolino, at Pagoda Beach near the port, advertises on the sides of nearly every bus on the island. The club features a discotheque as well as a smooth hangout called "Lizard Lounge." (☎081 99 32 96. Cover L20-35,000. Open July-Aug. daily 11:30pm-4am; June and Sept. F-Su 11:30pm-4am.)

PROCIDA ☎081

While Capri's beauty is known around the world, and Ischia welcomes countless Germans with open arms, Procida, setting of the film *Il Postino*, remains little touristed. The smallest of the islands, it has neither the amazing vistas of Capri nor the hot springs of Ischia. But unlike its neighbors, Procida has the charm of small towns interspersed with lemon groves and vineyards. Its charming narrow streets hide homes and local shops, rather than boutiques and souvenir stores.

TRANSPORTATION AND PRACTICAL INFORMATION. **Ferries** and **hydrofoils** run to Procida from Naples, Pozzuoli, and Ischia. All boats dock on the east side of the island, at Marina Grande, which is where the ticket offices are located. **Caremar** (☎081 890 72 80. Open daily 6:30am-8pm.) runs hydrofoils to **Ischia** (17min., 13 per day 7am-7:30pm, L7500) and **Naples** (40min., 13 per day 7am-8pm, L17,000). It also runs ferries to Ischia (30min., 13 per day 7am-7:30pm, L4000) and Naples (1hr., 13 per day 7am-8pm, L8000). **Procida Lines** runs ferries to Pozzuoli (30min., 12 per day 5:30am-8:30pm, L4500). (☎081 897 03 21. Open daily 6am-8pm).

A walk across the island takes about an hour, but **buses** (tickets L1500 in *tabacchi*, L1700 on the bus) are regularly available. All four lines leave from the port, though their frequencies vary according to route and season. In summer, **L1,** which covers the middle region and stops at the **Marina Piccola,** runs past the hotels and campgrounds before stopping at the port of **Chiaiolella,** site of the liveliest restaurants and beach (every 20min. 6am-11:30pm). **C1** follows much the same route, but also hits the southwestern part of the island (every 20min. 6:30am-10:30pm, every 30min. 7-10:30pm). **C2** runs to the southeastern part of the island (every 30min. 7am-10pm). **L2** serves the quiet northwestern part of the island (every hr. 7am-9pm). Another means of transportation is the adorable, though cramped, **Microtaxi** (☎081 896 87 85), from the port. The **AAST tourist office,** V. Roma, 92, near the ferry ticket offices to the far right of the main port, has free maps. (☎081 810 19 68. Open daily 9am-1pm and 3:30-6:30pm.) In **medical emergencies,** the **Pronto Soccorso,** V. V. Emanuele, 191 (☎081 896 90 58), accessible by L1 or C1 buses, is open 24hr.

ACCOMMODATIONS AND FOOD. It's hard to find a Procidan hotel not surrounded by lemon groves and private gardens. **Hotel Riviera,** Giovanni da Procida, 36, is no exception. All 22 rooms have bath and phone; most have sea views. (☎/fax 081 896 71 97. Open Mar.-Oct. Singles L55,000; doubles L100,000. Full pension required July-Aug. L100,000.) **Pensione Savoia,** V. Lavadera, 32, is accessible by the L2 bus. The snug hotel has eight rooms, a terrace, and a patio with flowers and lemon trees in back. (☎081 896 17 16. Singles L50,000; doubles L75,000. Extra bed L25,000.) Pitch your tent at the well-maintained **La Caravella,** on V. IV Novembre, accessible by the **L1** or **C1** bus. (☎081 896 92 30. L9000 per person, L9-10,000 per tent. Open June-Oct.) For bungalows, try **Graziella,** V. Salette, 18, on the beach. Take the **L1** or **C1** bus to P. Urno and walk 500m to Spiaggia Ciraccio. It's the last campsite on the left. (☎081 896 77 47. 4-person bungalows L80-110,000.) For tasty wildlife, head to **Da Michele,** V. Marina Chiaiolella, 22/23 (☎081 896 74 22. *Primi* L5-12,000, rabbit L15,000, pizza L4-10,000.) After your meal ask at any bar for the potent *limoncello*, a famous local liqueur made, of course, from Procidan lemons.

SIGHTS

You can walk or take the **C2** to the **Abbazia San Michele Archangelo** (St. Michael's Abbey) on Procida's easternmost and highest hilltop. Its yellow facade, redone in 1890, belies the interior's ornate 15th-century gold frescoes and bleeding Christ figures. Enjoy the outlook from the summit and view the deeds of St. Michael emblazoned on the domes. Take V. V. Emanuele from the left side of the port and turn left on V. Principe Umberto. (☎081 896 76 12. Open daily 9am-1pm and 3-

6:30pm. Free.) The route passes the medieval walls of **Terra Murata** (☎081 896 76 12), the old city below the monastery on V. S. Michele. Procida has several decent **beaches** that are usually uncrowded. The one at **Ciraccio** stretches across the western shore. Its western end, near Chiainella, is accessible by the **L1.** Another popular beach is **Chiaia,** on the southeastern cove, accessible by **L1** and **C1.**

Lemons are ubiquitous in Procida, and the local authorities are hoping that the newly-inaugurated **Festa del Limone,** the 3rd weekend in June, will become a popular tradition. The festival features such disparate events as food tastings, a fashion show, and a debate on the, er, lemon. (Ask tourist office for more info.) From the harbor at **Chiaiolella** on the opposite side of the island, where wealthy Neapolitans dock their boats, you can head across a footbridge to the islet of **Vivara,** where a wildlife sanctuary bristles with furry inhabitants. (Mandatory free guided tours leave from the entrance M-Sa, starting between 9 and 9:30am.)

BAY OF NAPLES: VESUVIUS

POMPEII (POMPEI) ☎081

On August 24, AD 79, life in the prosperous Roman city of Pompeii suddenly halted. A fit of towering flames, suffocating black clouds, and lava from Mt. Vesuvius buried the city—temples, theaters, and all—under more than 7m of volcanic ash. Except for the lucky few who dropped everything and ran at the first tremors, Pompeiians suffered a live burial. Perhaps the most ghastly and evocative relics of the town's demise are the "frozen people," ash casts of the victims' bodies, preserving their last contortions and expressions of horror. These amazing exhibits are visible (in glass cases) all over the ancient site. The excavation is ongoing; from the first unearthings in 1748 through the present, every decade has brought new discoveries to light, providing a vivid picture of daily life in the Roman era.

ORIENTATION AND PRACTICAL INFORMATION

The excavations stretch on an east-west axis, with the modern town clustered around the eastern end. The quickest route to Pompeii (25km south of Naples) is the **Circumvesuviana train** (☎081 772 21 11), which can be boarded at Naples's Stazione Centrale (direction: Sorrento; 2 per hr., L3200), or from Sorrento's station. Get off at the "Pompeii Scavi/Villa dei Misteri" stop; ignore "Pompeii Santuario." Eurailpasses are not valid. The entrance to the ruins is downhill to the left. An alternative is the less frequent **FS train** that leaves from the main track at the Naples station and stops at modern Pompeii en route to Salerno (30min., departs every hr., L3100). The FS train station is a 10-minute walk from the east entrance to the excavations. To get there continue straight on V. Sacra to the end then turn left onto V. Roma. On the way, stop by the **tourist office,** V. Sacra, 1, for a free map. To get to the branch office, P. Porta Marina Inferiore, 12, from the "Pompeii Scavi/Villa dei Misteri" stop, take a right out of the Circumvesuviana station and follow the road to the bottom of the hill. (☎081 850 72 55. Both offices open M-F 8am-3:30pm, Sa 8am-2pm.) Store your pack for free at the entrance to the ruins. There is a **police station** at the entrance to the site, but the main station is at P. Schettini, 1 (☎081 850 61 64), in the modern town, on P. B. Longo, at the end of V. Roma.

ACCOMMODATIONS AND CAMPING

Since most travelers visit the city as a daytrip from Naples, Rome, or Sorrento, Pompeii's hotels and campgrounds are eager for business, and prices can sometimes be bargained down by 15% or more. The tourist office provides a comprehensive list of hotels with prices.

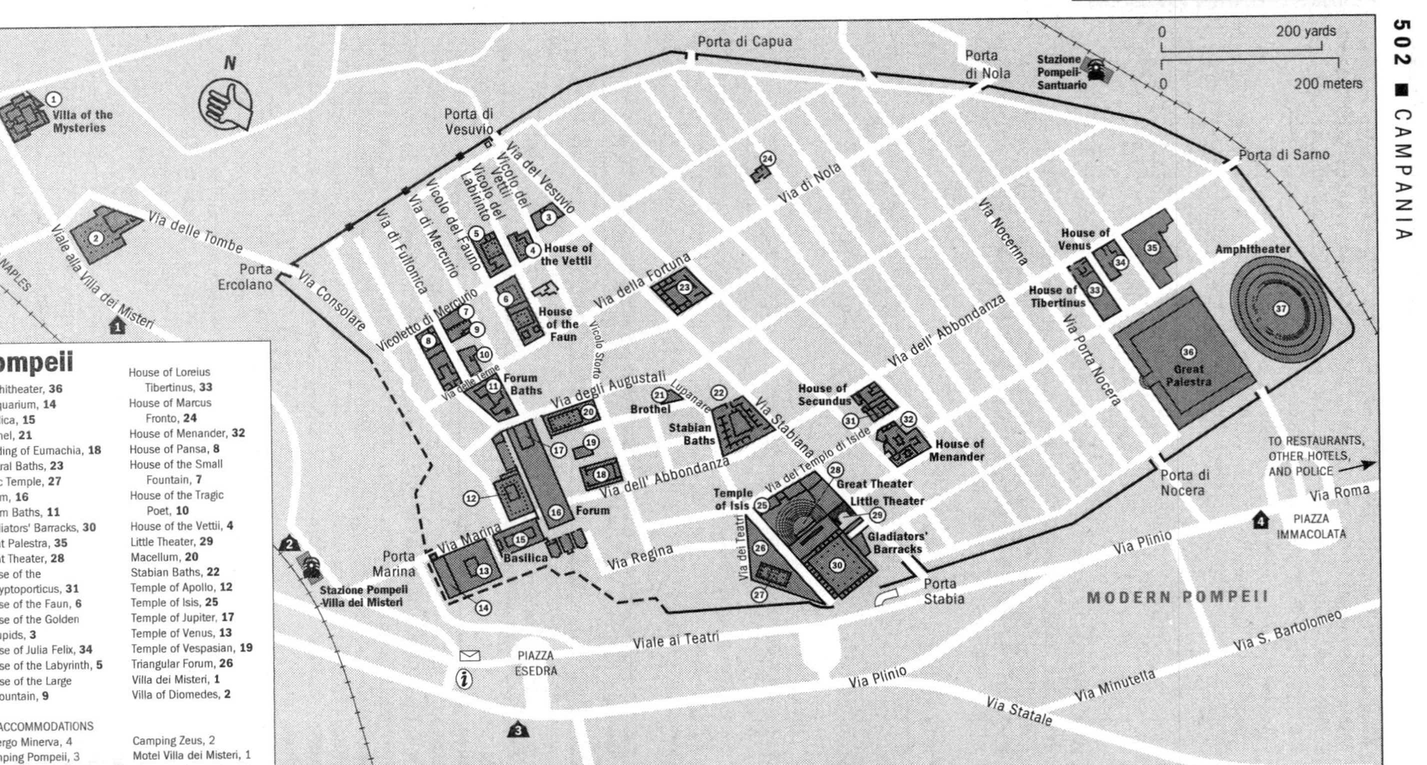
Pompeii
Amphitheater, 36
Antiquarium, 14
Basilica, 15
Brothel, 21
Building of Eumachia, 18
Central Baths, 23
Doric Temple, 27
Forum, 16
Forum Baths, 11
Gladiators' Barracks, 30
Great Palestra, 35
Great Theater, 28
House of the Cryptoporticus, 31
House of the Faun, 6
House of the Golden Cupids, 3
House of Julia Felix, 34
House of the Labyrinth, 5
House of the Large Fountain, 9
House of Loreius Tibertinus, 33
House of Marcus Fronto, 24
House of Menander, 32
House of Pansa, 8
House of the Small Fountain, 7
House of the Tragic Poet, 10
House of the Vettii, 4
Little Theater, 29
Macellum, 20
Stabian Baths, 22
Temple of Apollo, 12
Temple of Isis, 25
Temple of Jupiter, 17
Temple of Venus, 13
Temple of Vespasian, 19
Triangular Forum, 26
Villa dei Misteri, 1
Villa of Diomedes, 2
ACCOMMODATIONS
Albergo Minerva, 4
Camping Pompeii, 3
Camping Zeus, 2
Motel Villa dei Misteri, 1
N
0
200 yards
200 meters
TO NAPLES
Villa of the Mysteries
Viale alla Villa dei Misteri
Via delle Tombe
Porta Ercolano
Via Consolare
Porta di Vesuvio
Via del Vesuvio
Vicolo dei Vettii
Vicolo del Labirinto
Vicolo del Fauno
Via di Mercurio
Via di Fullonica
Vicoletto di Mercurio
Via delle Terme
House of the Vettii
House of the Faun
Forum Baths
Via della Fortuna
Vicolo Storto
Via degli Augustali
Lupanare
Brothel
Stabian Baths
Via dell' Abbondanza
Forum
Basilica
Via Marina
Porta Marina
Stazione Pompeii Villa dei Misteri
PIAZZA ESEDRA
Via Regina
Viale ai Teatri
Temple of Isis
Via dei Teatri
Great Theater
Little Theater
Gladiators' Barracks
Via del Tempio di Iside
Via Stabiana
House of Secundus
House of Menander
Porta Stabia
Via Plinio
Via Statale
Porta di Capua
Via di Nola
Via dell' Abbondanza
Porta di Nola
Via Nocerina
Stazione Pompei-Santuario
House of Venus
House of Tibertinus
Via Porta Nocera
Porta di Sarno
Amphitheater
Great Palestra
Porta di Nocera
Via Plinio
MODERN POMPEII
Via Minutella
Via S. Bartolomeo
PIAZZA IMMACOLATA
Via Roma
TO RESTAURANTS, OTHER HOTELS, AND POLICE

Motel Villa dei Misteri, V. Villa dei Misteri, 11 (☎081 861 35 93; fax 081 862 29 83; www.pt.pandora.it/hmisteri), uphill from the Circumvesuviana station. 41 comfortable, clean rooms, most with balconies overlooking an amphora-shaped pool. A/C available. Breakfast L8000. Doubles with bath L90,000; triples L120,000. V, MC, AmEx.

Albergo Minerva, V. Plinio, 23 (☎081 863 25 87), between Porta di Nocera and P. Immacolata in the modern town, has 10 large, quiet rooms, all with bath. Doubles L70,000; triples L85,000; quads L100,000.

Camping Zeus, V. Villa dei Misteri, 1 (☎081 861 53 20; fax 081 850 87 78; email campingzeus@uniserv.uniplan.it), outside the "Villa dei Misteri" Circumvesuviana stop, is convenient. L7000 per person; L4000 per small tent; L6000 per large tent. Prices L2000 higher Aug.-Sept. Rooms for 2-5 people L50-110,000.

Camping Pompeii, V. Plinio, 121-8 (☎081 862 28 82; fax 081 850 27 72; www.wei.it/cpompei; email campingpompei@uniserv.uniplan.it), located downhill on V. Plinio, the main road from the ruins. 25 bungalows. Singles L40,000; doubles L60,000; triples L80,000; quads L100,000; quints L110,000. If you're desperate, you can sleep on their indoor lobby floor for L7000 per night.

FOOD

Food at the site cafeteria is horribly expensive, so bring a **pre-packed lunch.** A few restaurants and fruit stands cluster outside the excavation entrances. Otherwise, stock up at the **GS supermarket,** V. Statale, on the main road between the entrances to the archaeological site (open M-Sa 8am-8:30pm, Su 9am-1pm).

La Vinicola, V. Roma, 29 (☎081 863 12 44), an alternative to the nearby McDonalds. Tempts visitors with a pleasant outdoor courtyard and abundant *gnocchi con mozzarella* (potato pasta with mozzarella, L6000). Cover L1500. Open daily 9am-11pm.

Empire Pizza Inn, V. Plinio, 71 (☎081 863 23 66). Offers complete meals for L10-20,000. But pizza ain't all, as the Empire strikes back with a music hall/discotheque in the same building. Open Tu-Su 7pm-midnight.

SIGHTS

Entrances to Pompeii open 9am to 1hr. before sunset: in summer around 7pm; in winter around 3pm. L16,000.

A comprehensive exploration will probably take all day. **Guided tours**—which allow you to savor the details of life and death in the 1st century AD—are quite expensive and mostly take groups. Call **GATA Tours** (☎081 861 56 61) or **Assotouring** (☎081 862 25 60) for info. Some of the tour guides are wise to freeloaders, actually yelling at offenders; others remain oblivious. Those with neither the cash nor the savvy to join a tour can buy one of the various guidebooks available outside site entrances (from L8000) or rent the useful audioguide, which follows a numbered route through the site. Despite the hefty admission price, the site is poorly labeled. But it could be worse—you could be trapped under molten lava for 2000 years.

To the right of the Porta Marina entrance, the **basilica** (law court) walls are decorated with stucco made to look like marble. Walk farther down V. D. Marina to reach the **Forum,** which is surrounded by a colonnade. Once dotted with statues of emperors and gods, this site was the commercial, civic, and religious center of the city. Cases along the near-side display some of the gruesome body-casts of Vesuvio's victims. At the upper end rises the **Temple of Jupiter,** mostly destroyed by an earthquake that struck 17 years before the city's bad luck got worse. To the left, the **Temple of Apollo** contains statues of Apollo and Diana (originals in Naples's Museo Archeologico Nazionale, p. 483) and a column topped by a sundial. On the opposite long side of the forum, the **Temple of Vespasian** houses a delicate frieze depicting preparation for a sacrifice. To the right, the **Building of Eumachia** has a carved door frame of animals and insects hiding in acanthus scrolls.

Exit the Forum through the upper end, by the cafeteria, and enter the **Forum Baths** on the left. Here, chipping away parts of the bodycasts has revealed teeth and bones beneath. A right on V. della Fortuna leads to the **House of the Faun,** where a bronze dancing faun and the spectacular Alexander Mosaic (originals in the **Museo Archeologico Nazionale,** p. 483) were found. Before the door, a floor mosaic proclaims *Have* (welcome). The sheer size and opulence of this building lead archaeologists to believe that it was the private dwelling of one of the wealthiest men in town. Continuing on V. della Fortuna and turning left on V. dei Vetti will bring you to the **House of the Vettii,** on the left, decorated with the most vivid frescoes in Pompeii. In the vestibule, a depiction of Priapus, the god of fertility displays his colossal member. In ancient times, phalli were believed to scare off evil spirits; these days they seem only to make tourists titter.

Back down V. dei Vetti, cross V. della Fortuna over to V. Storto, and then turn left on V. degli Augustali, which displays the deep ruts of carriages on either side The Romans who were repaving this worn path when the volcano struck left their task incomplete. A quick right leads to the small **brothel** (the Lupenar) containing several bedstalls. Above each stall, a pornographic painting depicts with unabashed precision the specialty of its occupant. After 2000 years, this is still the most popular place in town; you may have to wait in line. The street continues down to the main avenue, V. dell'Abbondanza. To the left lie the **Stabian Baths** which were privately owned and therefore fancier than the Forum Baths (think ritzy spa vs. YMCA). The separate men's and women's sides each include a dressing room, cold baths *(frigidaria)*, warm baths *(tepidaria)*, and hot steam baths *(caldaria)*. Via dei Teatri, across the street, leads to a huge complex consisting of the **Great Theater,** constructed in the 1st half of the 2nd century BC, and the **Little Theater,** built later for music and dance concerts. North of the theaters stands the **Temple of Isis,** Pompeii's monument to the Egyptian fertility goddess. Through the exit on the right, the road passes two fine houses, the **House of Secundus** and the **House of Menander.** At the end of the street, a left turn will return you to the main road. The Romans believed that crossroads were particularly vulnerable to evil spirits, so they built altars (like the one here) designed to ward them off.

On V. dell'Abbondanza, red writing glares from the walls, expressing everything from political slogans to love declarations. Popular favorites include "Albanus is a bugger," "Restitutus has decieved many girls many times," and the lyrical "Lovers like bees, lead a honey-sweet life"—apparently graffiti hasn't changed much in 2000 years. At the end of the street rest the **House of Tiburtinus** and the **House of Venus,** huge complexes with gardens replanted according to modern knowledge of ancient horticulture. The nearby **amphitheater** (80BC), the oldest standing in the world, held 12,000 spectators. When battles occurred, crowds decided whether a defeated gladiator would live or die with a casual thumbs up or thumbs down.

To reach the **Villa of the Mysteries,** go to the far west end of V. della Fortuna turn right on V. Consolare, and walk all the way up Porta Ercolano. The best preserved of Pompeii's villas, it includes the Dionysiac Frieze, perhaps the largest painting from the ancient world, depicting the initiation of a bride into the cult of Dionysus. Head through the door in the Porta for a great view of the entire city.

DAYTRIPS FROM POMPEII

HERCULANEUM (ERCOLANO)

The archaeological site is open daily 9am to 1hr. before sunset. L16,000. Tours are offered from the tourist office, but are only worth the fees if you are in a large group.

Neatly excavated and impressively intact, the remains of the prosperous Roman town of Herculaneum (modern Ercolano) hardly deserve the term "ruins." Indeed exploring the 2000-year-old houses, complete with frescoes, furniture, mosaics small sculptures, and even wooden doors, feels like an invasion of privacy. To reach Ercolano, take a **Circumvesuviana train** from Naples's central train station to the "Ercolano" stop (direction: Sorrento; 20min., L2300). Walk 500m downhill to the ticket office. The **Municipal Tourist Office**, V. IV Novembre, 84 (☎081 788 12 43) is on the way (open M, W-F 9am-1pm, Tu 4-6:30pm). **Illustrated guidebooks** (L10-15,000) are available at any of the shops flanking the entrance.

Herculaneum does not evoke the tragedy of Pompeii—most of its inhabitants escaped the ravages of Vesuvius. Only a small part of the southeastern quarter of the city has been excavated. Between 15 and 20 houses are open to the public. One of the more alluring is the **House of Deer** (named for the statues of deer in the courtyard), which displays the statue, *Satyr with a Wineskin*, and one of Hercules in a drunken stupor trying to relieve himself. The **baths**, with largely intact warm and hot rooms and a vaulted swimming pool, conjure up images of ancient opulence. The **House of the Mosaic of Neptune and Anfitrite**, which belonged to a rich shop owner, is famous for its namesake mosaic, and the front of the house has a remarkably well preserved wine shop. A mock colonnade of stucco distinguishes the **Samnise House.** Down the street, the **House of the Wooden Partition** still has a door in its elegant courtyard, and an ancient clothes press around the corner. Cardo IV shows you what a Roman street must have looked like. Outside the site, 250m to the left on the main road, lies the **theater,** perfectly preserved underground (occasionally open for visits; call 081 739 09 63 for more info). The **Villa dei Papiri,** 500m west of the site, recently caused a stir when it was thought that a trove of ancient scrolls in the library included works by Cicero, Virgil, and Horace. Unfortunately, neither of these two sites are commonly open to the public.

MT. VESUVIUS

Peer into the only active volcano on mainland Europe. **Trasporti Vesuviani buses** run from Ercolano up to the crater of Vesuvius (L6000 roundtrip, buy tickets on the bus; schedule available at the tourist office or on the bus). It leaves from outside the Ercolano Circumvesuviana station. The bus stop is part way up the crater; it's a 20-30min. walk to the top. Admission to the area around the crater is L9,000. Hikers can take the orange city bus #5 (L1800) from V. IV Novembre to the base of the mountain and climb from there. Bring plenty of water and wear sturdy shoes. Scientists say that on average volcanoes should erupt every 30 years—Vesuvius hasn't since March 31, 1944. Nevertheless, experts say the trip is safe.

SORRENTO ☎081

"Return to Sorrento" is not just the title of a hearty folk song, but the strategy of countless tourists who use the city as a base for their bay explorations. With 20,000 Italians, Sorrento is the largest town in the area, and with 13,000 hotel beds, the most touristed. So popular is the town with British tourists that it is easier to find a cup of tea than a *cappucino*, and prices are often listed in pounds. Still, Sorrento has its charms, including the picturesque streets of the old city and the **Marina Grande.** Frequent ferry connections provide links to the rest of the bay.

TRANSPORTATION

Trains: Circumvesuviana (☎081 772 24 44), just off P. Lauro. 40 trains per day, from 5am-10:30pm to: **Pompeii** (35min., L2300); **Herculaneum** (45min., L4000); and **Naples** (1hr., L4800).

Ferries and **Hydrofoils:** All boats dock at the port, accessible from P. Tassi by bus (L1700). **Linee Marittime Partenopee** (☎081 878 14 30) runs ferries to: **Amalfi** (45min., 2 per day 10:30am-2:30pm, L16,000) via **Positano** (30min., L15,000); and **Capri** (50min., 5 per day 8:30am-4:30pm, L8000). It also runs hydrofoils to: **Capri** (20min., 18 per day 7:30am-5pm, L13,000); **Naples** (40min., 7 per day 7am-6:30pm, L18,000); and **Ischia** (45min., usually at 9:30am, L21,000). Ticket offices open daily 7:30am-7pm. **Caremar** (☎081 807 30 77) runs ferries to **Capri** (50min., 3 per day 7am-5pm, L9000). Ticket offices open daily 7am-5pm.

Buses: SITA buses leave 6:30am-10pm from the Circumvesuviana station for the Amalfi coast. 18 buses per day to: **Positano** (40min., L2200); **Praiano** (1hr., L3100); and **Amalfi** (1¼hr., L3500). Buy your tickets at a bar, *tabacchi,* or hotel in P. Lauro.

ORIENTATION AND PRACTICAL INFORMATION

Most of Sorrento is on a flat shelf with cliffs rapidly descending to the Bay of Naples. **Piazza Tasso,** at the center of town, is connected by a stairway (and roads) to the **Marina Grande** and **Marina Piccola** ports. Corso Italia runs through P. Tasso—facing the sea, the train and bus station are to the right, while the old city is to the left. Via Fuorimura intersects C. Italia and leads away from the cliffs.

TOURIST, FINANCIAL, AND LOCAL SERVICES

Tourist Office: V. de Maio, 35 (☎081 807 40 33). From P. Tasso, take V. de Maio through P. S. Antonio and continue to the right toward the port. The office is to the right in the Circolo dei Forestieri compound. English spoken. Maps and cultural info. Grab a free copy of *Surrentum,* the monthly tourist magazine. Open Apr.-Sept. M-F 8:45am-7:45pm, Sa 8:45am-7:15pm; Oct.-Mar. M-Sa 8:30am-2pm and 4-6:15pm.

Currency Exchange: Exchange offices are more plentiful than tea in Sorrento, but **post office** rates are some of the best in town. Commission L1000. Open 8:15am-6pm.

Car and Scooter Rental: Sorrento Car Service, C. Italia, 210a (☎081 878 13 86). Scooters from L60,000 per day. Helmet and insurance included. Driver's license required. Cars and chauffeurs available. Open daily 8am-1pm and 4-9:30pm.

English Bookstore: Libreria Tasso, V. S. Cesareo, 96 (☎081 807 16 39; email libreriatasso@tin.it), stocks thrillers, including the shocking *Let's Go.* Open M-Sa 9:30am-1:30pm and 5-10:45pm, Su 11am-1:30pm and 7-10:45pm.

Laundromat: Terlizzi, C. Italia, 30 (☎081 878 11 85), in the old quarter. L15,000 per load, L25,000 for 2. Detergent L1000. Dry cleaning as well. Open daily 9am-8:30pm.

EMERGENCY AND COMMUNICATIONS

Emergencies: ☎113. **Police:** (☎081 807 533 11) on Vico 3° Rota. From the station, go right on C. Italia and left after V. Nizza. **Medical Emergencies: Pronto Soccorso** (☎081 533 11 12) at **Ospedale Civile di Sorrento**, C. Italia, 129 (☎081 53 11 11).

Internet Access: Blublu.it, V. Fuorimura, 20 (☎/fax 081 807 48 54; www.blublu.it). Take V. Fuorimura from P. Tasso. English-speaking staff and fast connections. L5000 for 30min. Open M-F 10am-1pm and 4:30-11pm, Sa 3pm-12am.

Post Office: C. Italia, 210 (☎081 878 14 95), near P. Lauro. Open M-Sa 8:15am-7:20pm. **Postal Code:** 80067.

ACCOMMODATIONS AND CAMPING

With so many hotel rooms in Sorrento, the law of averages suggests that some are bound to be inexpensive. Reservations are suggested in July and August. Some hotels allegedly charge more than their established prices. If you feel you're being overcharged, ask to see the official price list; you can then write a letter to the EPT and perhaps eventually get a refund. Prices listed below are for high season.

Hotel Elios, V. Capo, 33 (☎081 878 18 12), halfway to the Punta del Capo. Take bus A from P. Tasso. A friendly couple runs this comfortable hotel with a bay view. Breakfast L10,000. Singles L45,000; doubles L80,000; groups of 3 or 4 L45,000 per person.

Hotel City, C. Italia, 221 (☎081 877 22 10), left on C. Italia from the station. No less a hotel than a city with kind management, currency exchange, local bus tickets, maps, English newspapers and books, and small bar. Breakfast included. Singles L75,000; doubles L120,000. Extra bed L25,000. V, MC, AmEx.

Hotel Savoia, V. Fuorimura, 46 (☎/fax 081 878 25 11), 4 blocks from P. Tazzi. This tranquil hotel has 15 quiet, spacious rooms, all with bath. Singles L85,000; doubles L110,000. V, MC, AmEx.

Pensione Le Sirene, V. Degli Aranci, 160 (☎081 807 29 25). From C. Italia turn right onto V. S. Renato, and take the 1st right. Prepare to wake up to the 1st train or to extra guests crashing your party. Co-ed dorms with bath outside room L25,000, with bath inside room L30,000. Single gender rooms with bath inside L35,000.

Camping: Nube d'Argento, V. del Capo, 21 (☎081 878 13 44; fax 081 807 34 50). Bus A from P. Tasso (L1700). Near the ocean, with a pool, hot showers, market, and a restaurant. L16,000 per person, L8-14,000 per tent. 2-person bungalows L100,000.

FOOD

Delicious local specialties at reasonable prices await in Sorrento's restaurants and *trattorie.* Try to avoid the British food and the most touristed restaurants; there's a reason blood pudding never made it outside of the UK. Sorrento is famous for its *gnocchi alla Sorrentina* (potato pasta smothered in tomato sauce, mozzarella, and basil), its *cannelloni* (pasta tubes stuffed with cheese and herbs), and its *nocillo* (a dark liqueur made from the local walnuts). **Fabbrica Liquori,** V. S. Cesareo, 51, off V. Giuliani, provides free samples, as well as the ubiquitous *limoncello*, a refreshing lemon liqueur found throughout the region. For **market** stands, follow V. S. Cesareo from P. Tasso until it turns into V. Fuoro, where you'll find fresh, ripe, sweet, juicy fruit.

Ristorante e Pizzeria Giardiniello, V. Accademia, 7 (☎081 878 46 16). Take the 2nd left off V. Giuliani, which runs off C. Italia at the cathedral. Mamma Luisa does all the cooking in this family-run establishment set in a peaceful garden. Her *gnocchi* transcend poetry for L7000, and the *spaghetti al carloccio* (with mixed seafood) is a steal at L11,000. Cover L1500. Open June-Sept. daily 11am-2am; Oct.-May F-W 11am-2am.

Il Vicoletto, V. Pietà, 3 (☎081 877 34 42), in the small alley in the corner behind Tasso's cloak in P. Tasso. Stylishly decorated, with Sorrento's most erudite menu, this restaurant offers regional cooking at reasonable prices. Pizza L6-15,000, *primi* L8-12,000. Cover L2000. Open 8pm-1am.

Taverna Azzura, V. Marina Grande, 166 (☎081 877 25 10). From C. Cesareo off P. Tasso, go left on V. Giuliani to the end; Marina Grande is a pleasant 10min. walk to the left on the small road past P. della Vittoria. Fresh seafood and pasta cooked to perfection amidst photographs of Italian celebrities who have dined there. *Primi* from L8000, *secondi* from L9000. Cover L2500. Open noon-3pm and 7pm-midnight.

Gigino Pizza a Metro (Pizza by the Meter), V. Nicotera, 15 (☎081 879 84 26), in Vico Equense, a 10min. train ride. Take the Circumvesuviana to V. Equense, go straight as you exit the station, and follow the winding road uphill to P. Umberto. Take a left on V. Roma and another left on V. Nicotera. Unofficially the world's largest pizzeria, this massive 2-story, 3000-seat facility has monstrous wood-burning ovens that cook 1m-long pizzas. Smaller pizzas L8-12,000. Cover L2000. Service 13%. Open daily noon-1am.

Davide, V. Giuliani, 39 (☎081 878 13 37). Sorrento's best *gelato,* right off C. Italia, 2 blocks from P. Tasso. So much, so tasty, so little time. The watermelon, peach delicate, fig heavenly, and butterscotch savory are irresistible, while the true triumph is the masterful mousse. 55-80 flavors daily. L3500 for 2 scoops. Open daily 10am-midnight.

SIGHTS AND ENTERTAINMENT

Despite the tourism, there is actually very little to see, unless you love t-shirt shops. Away from the crowds of the city center, **Marina Grande** is a traditional fishing harbor and a fine destination for a stroll.

The westerly orientation of the beaches makes sunset swims truly memorable. Take the bus to **Punta del Capo** and walk 10 minutes down the footpath to the right. On the coast stand the remains of the ancient Roman **Villa di Pollio.** A visit to the rather limited ruins is best combined with a dip in the beautiful cove.

The old city and the area around P. Tasso heat up after dark, as locals and tourists stroll the streets, gaze over the bay, and careen about on mopeds. Hands down the most stylish bar in Sorrento, **Gatto Nero,** V. Correale, 21 (☎081 877 36 86), has a gorgeous garden and creatively designed interior—each wall is painted in the style of a modernist painter (among them Picasso and Matisse). Jazz and blues animate the crowd which builds by 11pm. After 10:30pm, a fun-loving crowd gathers in the rooftop lemon grove above **The English Inn,** at C. Italia, 56. Repetitive 80s music gets dancers moving. (☎081 807 43 57. Open daily 9am-1am, much later on weekends.) The **Charley Chaplain Pub**, C. Italia, 18, across the street, usually sees some nighttime action, even if the patrons just come to see the little tramps. (☎081 807 25 51. Open daily 5pm-3am.)

AMALFI COAST

The beauty of the Amalfi coast is one of contrasts and extremes. Immense rugged cliffs plunge downwards into calm azure waters while coastal towns nestle in and climb the sides of narrow ravines. Visitors are drawn by the natural splendor and the unique character of each town. Although some coastal parts may cost you body parts, budget gems exist as well.

The coast is easily accessible from Naples, Sorrento, Salerno, and the islands by ferry or SITA buses. The harrowing bus ride along the Amalfi coast is unforgettable: narrow roads wind along the mountain sides, where spectacular views of the cliffs plummet into the sea. Just remember to sit on the right side of the bus heading south (from Sorrento to Amalfi) and on the left heading back. Those with weaker stomachs should opt for sea service. If you plan to take buses from 2-5pm, buy tickets in advance because *tabacchi* close for the afternoon.

POSITANO ☎089

When John Steinbeck visited Positano in the 50s, he reckoned that its vertical cliffs were already piled so high with homes that no more than 500 visitors could possibly fit, negating the possibility of tourism. He underestimated local ingenuity. After running through a series of industries with variable success (including fashion: the bikini was invented here in 1959), Positano embraced its role as an intellectual and cultural resort. Soon its classy reputation began to draw ordinary millionaires in addition to the writers, painters, actors, and filmmakers, and the *Positanese* squeezed not 500 but over 2000 hotel beds into their town. Today, Positano's most frequent visitors are the wealthy few who can appreciate the beachfront ballet and afford the French chefs in the four-star hotels. There is no denying, however, that Positano has its picturesque charms, and most who come here linger. As Steinbeck rightly observed, "Positano bites deep."

TRANSPORTATION

Buses: 18 blue **SITA** buses, from 7am-9pm, run to: **Praiano** (L1800); **Amalfi** (L2100) and **Sorrento** (L2300). There are 2 main stops in Positano, at the 2 points where the road that runs through town meets the main coastal road. Tickets can be bought at bars or *tabacchi* near the stops.

Ferries and **Hydrofoils:** at the far right of the Spiaggia Grande. **Linee Marittime Partenopee** (☎089 87 50 92) runs **hydrofoils** to: **Capri** (20min., 5 per day 9am- 6pm, L18,000); **Sorrento** (20min., 3 per day 12:30-4pm, L15,000); **Naples's** Mergellina port (45min., 4 per day 10:30am-7:30pm, L26,000); and **Ischia** (1¼hr., 4pm, L28,000). It also runs **ferries** to **Capri** (40min., 4:25pm, L14,000).

ORIENTATION AND PRACTICAL INFORMATION

Positano clings to two cliffs over the Tyrrhenian Sea. The main center of town lies around the large beach of **Spiaggia Grande.** To get there, take **Viale Pasitea** down from the main coastal road between Sorrento and Amalfi at **Chiesa Nuova.** Vle. Pasitea turns into **Corso Colombo** and eventually makes its way up to the main road again at the other end of town. To get over to the quieter **Fornillo** beach, take the footpath from Spiaggia Grande. The orange local bus (every 20min., 7am-midnight) marked "Positano Interno" circles through the town, terminating at **Piazza dei Mulini** downtown.

Tourist Office: V. del Saraceno, 4 (☎089 87 50 67), in the red building below the *duomo* near the beach, provides free maps. Open in summer M-Sa 8:30am-2pm and 3:30-8pm; in winter M-F 8:30am-2pm, Sa 8:30am-noon.

Emergencies: ☎113. **Carabinieri:** (☎089 87 50 11) near the top of the cliffs, down the steps opposite Chiesa Nuova. Nearest **hospital** in Sorrento.

Pharmacy: Vle. Pasitea, 22 (☎089 87 58 63), near P. dei Mulini. Open daily 9am-1pm and 5-9pm.

Internet Access: D.S. Informatica, V. G. Marconi, 188 (☎089 81 19 93; www.positanonline.it), on the main coastal road, accessible by the local bus. L15,000 per hr. Open M-Sa 9:30am-1pm and 3-7:30pm.

ACCOMMODATIONS

Positano has over 70 hotels and residences, and spare rooms are available for rent. Since many hotels are rather expensive, contact the tourist office for help in arranging inexpensive rooms for longer stays.

Ostello Brikette, V. G. Marconi, 358 (☎089 87 58 57; fax 089 812 28 14; email brikette@syrene.it), 100m up the main coastal road to Sorrento from Vle. Pasitea. Friendly staff and incredible views from 2 large terraces. Internet access. 45 beds. Sheets, shower, and breakfast included. Lockout 11:30am-5pm. Curfew midnight. Reservations available. Dorms L35,000; doubles L100,000.

Pensione Maria Luisa, V. Fornillo, 42 (☎/fax 089 87 50 23). Take the local bus down Vle. Pasitea to V. Fornillo. A jolly owner and 12 bright rooms, most with great views from their seaside terraces. All rooms with bath. Breakfast included. Singles L60,000; doubles L100,000. Extra bed L40,000.

Casa Guadagno, V. Fornillo, 22 (☎089 87 50 42; fax 089 81 14 07), next door to Pensione Maria Luisa. Pampers its patrons with 15 spotless rooms, beautifully tiled floors, sublime views, and heating in the winter. Breakfast and bath included. Reserve in advance. With *Let's Go:* doubles L110-120,000; triples L180,000. V, MC.

FOOD

Prices in the town's restaurants reflect the high quality of the food. For a sit-down dinner, thrifty travelers head toward Fornillo.

Il Saraceno D'Oro, Vle. Pasitea, 254 (☎089 81 20 50), on the road to Fornillo. Delicious pizza to go (evenings only) from L6000. The *gnocchi alla Sorrentina* (L12,000) are incredible and one of the better deals. Cover L2000. Open in summer daily 1-3pm and 7pm-midnight; in winter Th-Tu 1-3pm and 7pm-midnight.

Bar-Pasticceria La Zagara, V. dei Mulini, 6 (☎089 87 59 64). Exquisite pastries, tarts, and *limoncello*. The *Forta Afrodisia* (chocolate cake with fruit; L5000) promises to raise your libido. Prices are slightly higher if you choose to eat on the shaded patio, which transforms into a piano bar in the evenings. Open daily 8am-2am.

La Taverna del Leone, V. Laurito, 43 (☎089 87 54 74), on the left side of the main road to Praiano; serviced by infrequent SITA buses. Offers both full meals and snacks. Enjoy frozen strawberries, pears, peaches, and even walnuts filled with sorbet (L3500 per 100g). Cover L3000. Open May-Sept. daily 1-4pm and 7pm-midnight; Oct.-Apr. W-M 1-4pm and 7pm-midnight. V, MC, AmEx.

SIGHTS AND ENTERTAINMENT

For some, Positano's gray beaches are its main attractions. There are two separate beaches, and each has public (free) and private (not so free) sections. The biggest, busiest, and priciest is **Spiaggia Grande,** in the main part of town. To reach the quieter **Spiaggia del Fornillo,** take V. Positanese d'America, a shady footpath that starts above the port and winds past **Torre Trasita.** The three **Isole dei Galli,** poking through the water off Positano's coast, are visible from the sand. Homer's mythical sirens lured unsuspecting victims here with their spellbinding songs. In 1925, the quartet of Stravinsky, Picasso, Hindemith, and Massine bought one of the *isole.* While much of the Fornillo beach is public, you can get your own spot (complete with beach chair, umbrella, shower, and changing room) at the private **Lido L'incanto** (☎089 811 17 77) all day for L15,000. **Noleggio Barche Lucibello** (☎089 87 50 32 or 089 87 53 26), on the beach, rents motorboats from L40,000 per hour and rowboats from L20,000 per hour.

Montepertuso, a high mountain pierced by a large *pertusione* (hole), is one of three perforated mountains in the world (the other two are in India). To get there, hike the 45-minute trail up the hillside or take the bus (every hr. 7am-10pm, L1500) from P. dei Mulini, near the port or from any other bus stop.

Positano offers endless opportunities for spending money. The tragically chic spend afternoons shopping at its exorbitant boutiques. Glass-bottom boats tour offshore shipwrecks and squid-fishing expeditions depart at night. Frequent cruises embark to the Emerald and Blue Grottoes, while ferries daytrip to other destinations along the Amalfi Coast. As numerous boating companies compete for these excursions, the prices can sometimes be reasonable; check the tourist office and booths lining the port area. At night, **Music on the Rocks** (☎089 87 58 74), a fancy piano bar and disco on the far left side of the beach as you face the water, packs in the well-dressed thirty-somethings as tight as sardines. Handfuls of celebrities, from Sharon Stone to Luciano Pavarotti, have been known to stop by. The cover charge, around L35,000, can only get you in if you're wearing fancy threads (collared shirt and tie for men).

NEAR POSITANO: PRAIANO

A winding 6km bus ride down the coast from Positano (15min., L1700), Praiano (pop. 800) lacks a city center by the beach; the town is better described as a loose agglomeration of hotels and restaurants along 10km of coastline. Praiano boasts pleasant accommodations (in case Positano is all booked), good food, and the most popular nightlife on the Amalfi Coast.

ACCOMMODATIONS. Enjoy the panorama from the campground **Villaggio La Tranquillità** and the **Hotel Continental,** V. Roma, 10, which are part of the same complex, located on the road to Amalfi (ask the bus driver to stop at the Ristorante Continental). A long stairway descends to a stone dock and resplendent green water. All rooms include bath and breakfast. (☎089 87 40 84; fax 089 87 47 79; email contraq@contraq-praiano.com. Parking available. Camping L25,000 per site (tent not included), L15,000 per person. Doubles and two-person bungalows L105,000, with terrace L125,000. V, MC.) **La Perla,** V. Miglina, 2 (☎089 87 40 52), 100m toward Amalfi from La Tranquillità on the main road offers rooms with bath and a terrace overlooking the sea. Breakfast is included. (With *Let's Go:* singles L85,000; doubles L140,000. V, MC, AmEx.)

FOOD. Downstairs from Villagio La Tranquillità, **Ristorante Continental** offers *primi* (L12-15,000), *secondi* (L12-15,000), and local wine (L8000). (Cover L3000. 10% discount with *Let's Go*. Open Easter-Nov. daily noon-3pm and 8pm-midnight.) On the road from Positano, next to the San Gennaro Church (the one with the blue and gold domes), **Trattoria San Gennaro,** V. S. Gennaro, 99, lets you choose between their terrace and the garden as the setting for your tasty meal. Enjoy the view and the *spaghetti San Gennaro* (with mushrooms and clams) for only L10,000. (☎089 87 42 93. Pizza in the evenings from L7000. Cover L2500. Open daily noon-4pm and 7pm-midnight.)

SIGHTS AND ENTERTAINMENT. Six kilometers up the road to Positano, descend 400 steps to reach a marvelous beach. Around the bend from Praiano towards Amalfi, V. Terramare, a ramp which starts at **Torre a Mare** (a remarkably well-preserved tower which now serves as an art gallery) leads down to **Marina di Praia,** a 400-year-old fishing village tucked in a tiny ravine. Its pizzerias and restaurants come alive on weekends. Further down the coast **Africana,** on V. Terramare, is the Amalfi Coast's most famous nightclub and has been around since the early 1960s. Fish swim through the grotto under the glass dance floor as the music echoes off the dimly lit cave roof above. The cover charge is L25,000 but free for women on Wednesdays. Lavish shows drive the price up to L30,000 on Saturdays. (☎089 87 40 42. Open mid-June-Sept. daily 11pm-4am.) Down V. Terramare towards Marina di Praia's small beach is Il Piratu, also a discoteque carved into the rock just above the water's edge. The L17,000 cover charge draws a younger crowd and some bluebeards. (☎089 87 43 77. Open July-Sept. daily 10pm-3am.)

A bit farther between Praiano and Amalfi lies the **Grotta Smeralda** (Emerald Grotto). The SITA bus stops at the elevator leading down to the cave. If you didn't make it to the Blue Grotto or haven't had your fill of water-filled caves, the 22m high cavern has green water with a slight glow, walls dripping with stalagtites, and the tours are longer and cheaper. Multilingual guides reveal an underwater nativity scene and a rock formation profile of Lincoln, Napoleon, or Garibaldi (depending on your nationality). (Open daily 10am-4pm. Tour L5000.)

AMALFI ☎089

Between the rugged cliffs of the Sorrentine peninsula and the azure waters of the Adriatic, the narrow streets and historic monuments of Amalfi nestle in incomparable natural beauty. As the 1st Sea Republic of Italy and the preeminent maritime powerhouse of the southern Mediterranean, Amalfi ruled the neighboring coast, no doubt thanks to the compass, invented here by Flavia Gioia. Pisan attacks and Norman conquests hastened Amalfi's decline, but the vigor remains, and the city's past survives in its monuments. Visitors crowd the waterfront and the shops, restaurants, and cafes around the *duomo*. During festivals, music and fireworks echo off the steep mountains around the town.

TRANSPORTATION

Buses: Blue **SITA buses** (☎089 87 10 16) connect Amalfi to **Salerno** (1¼hr., 25 per day 6am-10pm, L3200) and **Sorrento** (1¼hr., 18 per day 6:30am-10pm, L3600), via **Positano** (35min., L2000). Buses arrive at and depart from P. F. Gioia, on the waterfront. Buy tickets at bars and *tabacchi* on the *piazza*.

Ferries and **hydrofoils:** Ticket booths and departures from the dock off P. F. Gioia.

Linee Marittime Partenopee (☎089 87 41 83) runs ferries to **Capri** (1½hr., 3 per day 8:40am-9:10pm, L15,000) and hydrofoils to: **Positano** (20min., 7 per day 8:30am-6pm, L13,000); **Salerno** (30min., 9 per day 8:40am-7pm, L16,000); **Capri** (35min., 4 per day 8:30am-5:30pm, L20,000); and **Ischia** (1½hr., 3:30pm, L30,000).

Travelmar (☎089 847 31 90) runs hydrofoils to: **Positano** (1¼hr., 7 per day 8:40am-6pm, L9000); **Sorrento** (25min., 3 per day 8:30am-3:30pm, L15,000); and **Salerno** (30min., 7 per day 8:40am-7pm, L6000).

Taxis: ☎089 87 22 39.

ORIENTATION AND PRACTICAL INFORMATION

Amalfi's main street is **Via Lorenzo d'Amalfi,** which leads from the port to the hills above. Ferries and buses stop in **Piazza Flavio Gioia** on the waterfront. **Piazza del Duomo** lies up V. d'Amalfi through the white arch. **Piazza Municipio** is 100m up Corso delle Repubbliche Marinare towards **Atrani** from P. Gioia, on the left. Go through the tunnel to reach **Atrani,** 750m up the coast or follow the public path through the restaurant next to the tunnel.

Tourist Office: AAST, C. delle Repubbliche Marinare, 27 (☎089 87 11 07), through a gate on the left as you head up the road. Free maps and brochures. Open May-Oct. daily 8am-2pm and 3-8pm; Nov.-Apr. M-Sa 8am-2pm.

Emergencies: Police: Carabinieri, V. Casamare, 19 (☎089 87 10 22), on the left up V. d'Amalfi. **Medical Emergencies: American Diagnostics Pharmaceutics** (☎0335 45 58 74) is on call 24hr. Clean and modern, they provide blood tests, lab procedures, and excellent, English-speaking doctors.

Post Office: C. delle Repubbliche Marinare, 35 (☎089 87 13 30), next to the tourist office. Offers currency exchange with good rates. Commission L1000, L5000 on checks over L100,000. Open M-F 8:15am-7:20pm. **Postal Code:** 84011.

ACCOMMODATIONS

Staying in Amalfi can be expensive, but you get what you pay for. Accommodations fill up in August, so reserve at least one month in advance.

Hotel Lidomare, V. Piccolomini, 9 (☎089 87 13 32; fax 089 87 13 94), through the alley across from the *duomo.* Take a left up the stairs, then cross the *piazzetta.* Terrific rooms in a 700-year-old church. Local antiques deck the halls and common areas. All 15 rooms with bath, TV, phone, fridge, and A/C. Breakfast included. Singles L70-75,000; doubles L125-160,000. V, MC, AmEx.

A'Scalinatella, P. Umberto, 6 (☎089 87 19 30 or 089 87 14 92), up V. dei Dogi in Atrani. You'll never have trouble finding a place here: genial brothers Filippo and Gabriele have rooms in Atrani, as well as campsites and scenic rooms above Amalfi. Laundry L10,000. Prices vary according to season, and are highest in August. Dorms L20-35,000; doubles L50-70,000, with bath L70-120,000. Camping L15,000 per person.

Pensione Proto, Salita dei Curiali, 4 (☎089 87 10 03). Take V. Lorenzo d'Amalfi from P. del Duomo, and go right into the alley by the sign for the Chiesa di Maria Addolorata. English spoken. 18 rooms. Breakfast in the cavernous dining room L10,000. Doubles L80-100,000, with bath L80-140,000. Extra bed L30-50,000.

Hotel Amalfi, V. dei Pastai, 3 (☎089 87 24 40; fax 089 87 22 50), left off V. Lorenzo onto Salita Truglio, uphill. A 3-star establishment with 42 immaculate rooms, attentive management, terraces, and citrus gardens with bar. Large bathrooms scream "Ajax was here." Bath and TV in all rooms. English spoken. Continental breakfast included. With *Let's Go:* singles L90-140,000; doubles L120-170,000. V, MC.

Villagio Vettica, V. Muista Dei Villaggi, 92 (☎089 87 18 14). Call from the SITA bus stop in Amalfi for directions. Amidst lemon groves in a small village high in the cliffs above nearby Amafli. Rooms offer great panoramas and a quiet retreat. Kitchens available. *Alimentari* nearby. Doubles L50,000, with bath L70,000. Camping L15,000.

FOOD

Food in Amalfi is good but a bit expensive. Indulge in seafood, *scialatelli* (a coarsely cut local pasta), and the pungent lemon liqueur *limoncello*. The town's many **paninoteche** (sandwich shops) are perfect for those on a tight budget.

Trattoria La Perla, Salita Truglio, 5 (☎089 87 14 40), around the corner from the Hotel Amalfi. Elegant and moderately priced. Terrific seafood. Try the bountiful *scialatielli ai frutti di mare* (with seafood; L14,000), or the *bigné al limone* (pastry with lemon cream; L6,000). *Menú turistico* L26,000. Cover L3500. Open Mar.-Nov. daily noon-3:30pm and 7pm-midnight; Dec.-Feb. W-M noon-3:30pm and 7pm-midnight. V, MC, AmEx.

Lo Sputino, Lgo. Scavio, 3, on the left as you walk up C. delle Repubbliche Marinare. Hearty and imaginative *panini* (L3500-6000). Beer from L2000. Open daily noon-1am.

Al Teatro, V. E. Marini, 19 (☎089 87 24 73). From V. d'Amalfi, turn left up the staircase (Salita degli Orafi) with a sign immediately after a shoe store, then follow the signs. Dining is proud to present a pleasant locale, starring authentic atmosphere, and introducing good, cheap food. Try the *scialatelli al Teatro* (with tomato and aubergines) for L11,000. *Primi* and *secondi* from L8000. *Menù* L25,000. Open Th-Tu noon-3pm and 7:30-11:30pm. Closed early Jan. to mid.-Feb. V, MC, AmEx.

Royal, V. Lorenzo d'Amalfi, 10 (☎089 87 19 82), just up from the *duomo*. Quite simply, Amalfi's best ice cream. The *Viagra Naturale* (with hot peppers!) is sure to get you up and at it. The *cioccolato all'arancia* (orange chocolate) is equally delightful. Cones L3-5000. Lip-smacking crêpes with *nutella* L6000. Open June-Sept. daily 7am-2am; Oct.-May Tu-Su 7am-midnight.

Andrea Panza, P. del Duomo, 40 (☎089 87 10 65). This pastry shop has been making local specialties since 1830, and you'll know it with your first bite of their delicious confections. In winter, ask for *sprocollati* (fig with ground almond); all year round the *Baba au limon* (L3000) is delicious. Open 7am-midnight.

SIGHTS

The 9th-century Duomo di Sant'Andrea imparts grace, elegance, and dignity to the P. del Duomo. The *piazza* may need it; the nearby **Fontana di Sant'Andrea** features a marble female nude squeezing her breasts as water spews from her nipples. Those who can put their Freudian complexes behind drink from the fountain. Rebuilt in the 19th century according to the original medieval plan, the cathedral features a facade of varied geometric designs typical of the Arab-Norman style. The **bronze doors,** crafted in Constantinople in 1066, started a bronze door craze that spread through Italy. (Open daily 8:30am-8pm. Appropriate dress required.)

To its left, the **Chiostro del Paradiso** (Cloister of Paradise), a 13th-century cemetery, has become a graveyard for miscellaneous columns, statues, and sarcophagi fragments. The elegant interlaced arches, like the campanile in the square, show the influence of contact with the Middle East. Its museum houses mosaics, sculptures, and the church's treasury. (Open daily June-Sept. 8:30am-8pm. L3000 for cloister, museum, and crypt. Free multilingual guides available.)

The 9th-century **Arsenal** on the waterfront, by the entrance to the city center, contains relics of Amalfi's former maritime glory. Up on V. D'Amalfi, several signs point to a path to the **Valle dei Mulini** (Valley of the Mills). Hike along a stream bed by the old paper mills for a pastoral view of lemon groves and rocky mountains. At the start of the valley is the **Paper Museum,** and its collections of, surprisingly, sundry paper items (open Tu-Su 9am-1pm. L2,000).

BEACHES, HIKING, AND DRAGONS

While there is a small beach in Amalfi itself, a five- to ten-minute trip will bring you to a much better (and free) beach in **Atrani.** A beachside village of 1200 inhabitants just around the bend from Amalfi, Atrani used to be home to the Republic's leaders; today it's a quiet place to escape from Amalfi's crowds. After the tunnel, descend a small winding staircase to the beach and P. Umberto. Atrani's one cobbled road, V. dei Dogi, leads from the beach up past P. Umberto, at which point a white stairway leads to **Chiesa di San Salvatore de Bireto,** with its 11th-century bronze doors from Constantinople. The name refers to the ceremonial hat placed on the Republic's doge when he was inaugurated.

Hikers often tackle paths that head up from Amalfi into the imposing Monti Lattari, winding through lemon groves and mountain streams, suddenly emerging onto beautiful vistas. From Amalfi, you can head up the **Antiche Scale** towards Pogerola. Trek through the **Valley of the Dragons,** named for the torrent of water and mist (like smoke from a dragon) exploding out to sea every winter. Naturally, the hikes are steep, and a good map is essential.

If you just want a short walk, a path leads up through the streets clinging to the cliffs up to the cave where the famous rebel Masaneillo hid from Spanish police. Although the cave is sporadically closed, the view of Atrani alone is worth the hike, which takes about an hour both ways.

DAYTRIPS FROM AMALFI

SITA buses from Amalfi stop on V. G. Capone, which changes its name to V. G. Amendola as it heads north to Minori, 1km away.

MINORI

Although Minori's downtown is better preserved than Maiori's, its main attraction is its beaches. Hotels are more expensive than in Maiori, so it's best to stay there and brave the 1km walk along the coastal road. Unlike Maiori, where only a tiny section of the beach is public, a large swath of Minori's waterfront is free to all. Minori also has the remains of a Roman villa, with monochrome mosaics of a hunt, well-preserved arcades, and a small museum. The site is several blocks up from the beach on V. S. Lucia. (☎089 852 843. Open daily 9am-1hr. before sunset. Free.)

MAIORI

Only a few kilometers from well-known and touristed Amalfi, this beachfront town has few foreign visitors among the many Italians drawn to its shores. Though it lacks either the style of Positano or the history of Amalfi, Maiori has low priced hotels and excellent beaches, as well as several historical sights.

Much of Maiori was damaged in WWII fighting, and what was left was destroyed in a flood several decades ago, so most of its buildings are modern. The pedestrian-only **Corso Regina** intersects **V. G. Capone** by the SITA bus stop. Several blocks up C. Regina, inside a garden on the left, is the **tourist office,** C. Regina, 73. (☎089 877 452; fax 089 853 672. Open M-Sa 8am-2pm.) The nearest medical facilities are in Amalfi; however, there are **carabinieri** (☎089 877 207).

Most visitors come to Maiori to lounge on the beaches. Although much of the beach is privately owned, with a L10-15,000 fee for access with chair and umbrella, there is a small public section near the SITA bus stop. Keep hydrated and score snacks from the nearby stands.

If you'd rather see sights than sun, the town's main attraction is **Chiesa di S. Maria a Mare,** up a flight of stairs in the left side of a mini *piazza* three blocks up C. Regina from the beach. In addition to a great view of the town, it has a beautiful 15th century alabaster altar kept in front of the crypt. Maiori has several inexpensive hotels located conveniently near the beach. **Albergo De Rosa,** V. Orti, 12 (turn left two blocks up C. Regina from the beach), has English speaking management, rooms with bath, and breakfast included. (☎/fax 089 877 031. Singles L55,000; doubles L110,000; triples L140,000.) An inexpensive local restaurant is **Dedalo,** on V. Cerasuoli just off C. Regina one block up from the beach. They serve a L20,000 *menu* and L6-10,000 pizzas in an air-conditioned interior. (☎089 877 084. Open daily noon-3pm and 4:30pm-3am.)

RAVELLO ☎089

Ravello and its lush villas perch 330m atop the cliffs, gazing down on a patchwork of villages and ravines extending to the sea. Settled in AD 500 by Romans fleeing barbarian invasions, it grew to an opulent town of 70,000 during the heyday of the Amalfi Republic and later under Norman rule. Epidemics and raiding Saracens left only 2700 people. Though plague and civil war sapped its strength, the town's natural beauty and romantic decay drew artists and intellectuals. Over the years, its few inhabitants have included an extensive list of writers, musicians, and celebrities. The exquisite gardens of Villa Rufolo inspired Giorgio Boccaccio's literary masterpiece, *The Decameron*, as well as Richard Wagner's opera, *Parsifal.* In fact, Ravello is still known as "*La Città della Musica*" (The City of Music), thanks to the many concert series and performances it hosts throughout the year. For those needing creative inspiration, Ravello is well worth the trip up the mountain.

TRANSPORTATION AND PRACTICAL INFORMATION. Ravello is easily reached by taking the blue SITA bus from Amalfi (20min., 18 per day 6:45am-10pm, L1800). If you're an adventurous scamp, hike the footpaths along the hills and lemon groves from Minori (1hr.), Atrani (2hr. via Scala), or Amalfi (2½hr. via Pontone). The **AAST Information office,** P. Duomo, 10 (☎089 85 70 98), is to the left of the **Piazza Duomo** as you face it. The English-speaking staff provides helpful brochures, event and hotel listings, and a map. More maps are available at magazine or book shops; the best one, published by the *Club Alpino Italiano*, is tough to find. For a **taxi,** call ☎089 85 79 17. If the taxi hits you, the **carabinieri** (☎089 85 71 50) are close by on V. Roma. For pain-killers, a **pharmacy,** P. Duomo, 14, is on the left side of the *piazza* as you face the *duomo.* (☎089 85 71 89. Open in summer daily 9am-1:30pm and 5-8:30pm.) To write home and complain to everyone that your leg is broken, the **post office** is at P. Duomo, 15. (Open M-Sa 8am-1:30pm.) **Postal Code:** 84010.

ACCOMMODATIONS AND FOOD. Ravello offers several affordable options. **Hotel Villa Amore,** V. dei Fusco, 5, on the road to Villa Cimbrone, has 12 cute, tidy rooms and a garden overlooking cliffs and the sea. As their welcome sign says, "A stay at Villa Amore gives peace to the soul and joy to the heart." All rooms have terraces and views; some have bath. (☎/fax 089 85 71 35. Breakfast included. Singles L80,000; doubles L120,000. Off-season L10,000 less. V, MC.) **Albergo Garden,** V. G. Boccaccio, 4, before the tunnel into Ravello, by the SITA bus stop, offers a great view of the cliffs. All 10 rooms have bath and balcony. English is spoken. (☎089 85 72 26; fax 089 85 81 10. Breakfast included. Reservations recommended. Doubles L140,000; low-season L120,000. Extra bed L30,000. V, MC, AmEx.)

Although many wines savored around the globe appear under a Ravello label, actual wine from the area is neither common nor commercially available—make friends in the town if you hope to try some. At **Cumpà Cosimo,** V. Roma, 44/46 (☎089 85 71 56), savor a variety of local specialties with an *assaggio di primi*, a sampler of all the available pasta dishes, for L16,000. **La Colonna,** V. Roma, 20, offers sit-down meals. The affable young owner Alfonso speaks English and is known throughout the town for his delectable fish and homemade pasta. A full meal costs around L35,000. (☎089 85 78 76. Open daily 12:30-3pm and 7pm-midnight.)

SIGHTS AND FESTIVALS. The beautiful churches, ivy-covered walls, and meandering paths of **Villa Rufolo** inspired Wagner's magic garden in the second act of *Parsifal.* In the summer, ugly stages are often erected in the most picturesque spots, spoiling their beauty (but making for great concerts). A medieval **tower** with Norman-Saracen vaulting and statues representing the four seasons serves as the entry to the famous Moorish cloister. Enter through the arch off P. Duomo near the tunnel. (☎089 85 76 57. Open daily 9am-sunset. L5000, under 12 or over 65 L3000, groups of more than 10 L4000 per person.)

In the portal of Ravello's **duomo** you can see the Amalfi Coast's 3rd set of famous bronze doors, cast by Barisano of Trani in 1179. Inside, a group of antique columns sets off two pulpits with elaborate mosaics. To the left of the altar stands the Cappella di S. Pantaleone, the town's patron saint. Behind the painting you can see his blood, preserved in a cracked vessel. Saint Pantaleone was beheaded on July 27 at Nicomedia, AD 290. Every year on this day the city holds a **festival,** when the saint's blood purportedly liquefies. The **museum** within depicts the *duomo*'s history during pagan and Christian eras. (*Duomo* open Mar.-Nov. daily 9:30am-1pm and 3-7pm; Dec.-Feb. Sa-Su 9am-1pm and 2-5pm. Museum L2000.)

Follow Vle. dei Rufo out of P. Duomo to **Villa Cimbrone.** Renovated by Lord Grimmelthorpe in the 19th century in an attempt to draw attention away from his name, the villa sports floral walkways and majestic gardens. Greek temples and statued grottoes hide among Cimbrone's twisty paths, which harbor some of the most magnificent views on the Amalfi coast. A procession of notables made it a retreat; Greta Garbo and Leopold Stokowski had romantic interludes here, and Jackie Kennedy was a town resident in 1962. (Open daily 9am-7:30pm. L6000.)

Ravello deserves its "Città della Musica" moniker. During the year, internationally renowned musicians come to perform at the **classical music festivals** held around New Year's Day, Easter, and throughout the summer. Concerts, most frequent in July and August, are performed in the gardens of the Villa Rufolo (in winter concerts move indoors, into the Villa or the *duomo*). Tickets are usually around L20-35,000, and can be purchased at the AAST Information Office. Call the *Società di Concerti di Ravello* (☎089 85 81 49) for more information.

SALERNO ☎089

The capital of the Norman Empire from 1077 to 1127 and home to Europe's first medical school, Salerno is more recently famous as the site of an Allied landing during World War II. After being blasted to bits, it was rebuilt with a big-city atmosphere: Salerno's urban landscape of postwar buildings may shock those accustomed to the Amalfi Coast's peaceful coastal villages. Though lacking notable sights, Salerno is a cheap base from which to visit the Amalfi coast and Paestum.

TRANSPORTATION

Trains: arrive at and depart from the station in P. Veneto. To: **Paestum** (40min., 9 per day 6am-9:30pm, L4700); **Naples** (45min., 32 per day, L5100-17,100); **Rome** (2½-3hr., 18 per day, L22-45,000); **Reggio Calabria** (3½-5hr., 20 per day, L31-60,000); **Florence** (5½-6½hr., 7 per day, L49-79,500); and **Venice** (9hr., 1am, L64,000). **Luggage Storage:** L5000 for 12hr. Open daily 7:30am-3pm.

Buses: Blue **SITA** buses leave from the train station for **Naples** (1hr., 47 per day 6am-9pm, L5100) and **Amalfi** (1¼hr., 23 per day 6am-10:30pm, L5100). Purchase tickets from a bar or *tabacchi.*

Ferries and **hydrofoils:** One dock is in P. della Concordia, 2 blocks from the train station. Another is in M. Marittimo Manfredi, a 15min. walk up the waterfront. **Linee Marittime Partenopee** (☎089 22 79 79) runs ferries to **Capri** (2hr., 3 per day 7:30am-8:30pm, L15,000) and hydrofoils to **Capri** (1hr., 3 per day 8am-5pm, L26,000) and **Ischia** (1½hr., 7:30am, L34,000). **Travelmar** (☎089 87 31 90) runs ferries to **Amalfi** (1hr., 3 per day 7:30am-8:30pm, L9000) via **Positano** (40min., L7000) and hydrofoils to **Amalfi** (30min., 3 per day 8am-5pm, L6000) via **Positano** (20min., L5000). **Grimaldi Lines** (☎089 25 32 02) ticket office at Salerno Auto Terminal, V. Ligea Porto runs ferries to **Valletta, Malta** (20hr.; every Th noon; single cabins L220-330,000, double cabins L300-500,000).

Local Transportation: The orange **city buses** connect the train station neighborhood to the rest of the city. For routes and schedules, check the ticket booth in P. Veneto. Tickets L1300 for 1hr., L2500 for an all-day pass.

Taxis: ☎089 22 91 71 or 089 22 99 47.

ORIENTATION AND PRACTICAL INFORMATION

From the train station on **Piazza Vittorio Veneto,** the expansive, remarkably clean, pedestrian **Corso Vittorio Emanuele** veers to the right. C. V. Emanuele becomes V. dei Mercanti in the **old quarter,** the most historically interesting and lively part of Salerno. **Via Roma** runs parallel to C. V. Emanuele one block toward the waterfront. Along the waterfront from the train station is P. della Concordia and the **Lungomare Trieste,** which runs to the **Molo Marittimo Manfredi.**

TOURIST, FINANCIAL, AND LOCAL SERVICES

Tourist Office: EPT (☎800 21 32 89 or 089 23 14 32), in P. Veneto to the right as you leave the train station. The *Agenda del Turista* has practical info for Salerno and the Amalfi coast, while the biweekly *MEMO* guide has hotel, restaurant, club, and special events listings. English spoken. Open M-Sa 9am-2pm and 3-8pm.

Car Rental: Hertz, P. Veneto, 33 (☎089 22 21 06; fax 089 22 02 07), L130,000 per day, L300,000 for 3 days. Open M-F 8:30am-1pm and 4-7:30pm, Sa 8:30am-2pm, Su 9am-noon.

English Bookstore: Libreria Leggenda, V. Settimnio Mobilio, 38 (☎089 40 51 59), near the hostel. Classics and new fiction. Open M-Sa 9am-1:30pm and 5-8:30pm.

Laundromat: Onda Blu, V. Mauri, 128 (☎089 33 32 26), in Salerno's Mercatello neighborhood, the city's only self-service laundry. Take the #5, 6, 8, 9, 10, 11n, or 11r bus from C. Garibaldi, opposite the train station, to P. Grasso. Walk 1 block down on V. Mauri. L6000 wash, L6000 dry for up to 7kg. Soap L1000. Open daily 8am-10pm.

EMERGENCY AND COMMUNICATIONS

Emergencies: ☎113. **Police:** ☎113 or 112. **Hospital: S. Leonardo** (☎089 67 11 11). **First Aid:** ☎089 23 33 30.

Internet Access: Mailboxes, Etc., V. Diaz, 19 (☎089 23 12 95), off C. V. Emanuele, 500m from the station. With *Let's Go* L3000 for 30min. Also offers FedEx, UPS, Western Union, and fax service. Open M-F 8:30am-2pm and 4-8:30pm, Sa 8:30am-1pm and 5:30-8:30pm.

Post Office: C. Garibaldi, 203 (☎089 22 99 70). Open M-Sa 8:15am-6:15pm. **Branch office** (☎089 22 99 98) at P. Veneto. Open M-Sa 8:15am-1:30pm. **Currency exchange** only at the main office. **Postal Code:** 84100.

ACCOMMODATIONS

Ostello della Gioventù "Irno" (HI), V. Luigi Guercio, 112 (☎089 79 02 51). Exit the train station and turn left onto V. Torrione and left under the bridge onto V. Mobilio. The hostel is 700m ahead, across from the gas station. Great atmosphere. Free daytrips in the summer to Paestum, Pompeii, and Amalfi. Hot showers, restaurant, TV, spacious rooms, and Internet for L7000 per hr. Breakfast and sheets included. Curfew 2am. Dorms L17,500.

Albergo Santa Rosa, C. V. Emanuele, 14 (☎/fax 089 22 53 46), 1 block from the train station, on the right. 12 clean, comfortable rooms. The helpful proprietors are full of crafty tips that will help you save money and heartache. Singles L45,000, with bath L65,000; doubles L75,000, with bath L95,000.

Hotel Salerno, V. Vicinanza, 42 (☎089 22 42 11; fax 089 22 44 32), the 1st left off C. Emanuele. Close to the train station. Some of the 27 rooms have phone and TV. Singles L50,000, with bath L75,000; doubles L66-75,000, with bath L87,000. V, MC, AmEx.

FOOD

Salerno serves typical Campanian cuisine, including *pasta e fagioli* (pasta and bean soup), as well as unusual specialties of its own, such as *milza* (spleen).

Hosteria Il Brigante, V. F. Linguiti, 4 (☎089 22 65 92). From P. Duomo, head up the ramp and look on the left. Join the locals for a delicious *pasta alla Sangiovannara,* a steal at L6500. Open daily 9pm-midnight.

Taverna del Pozzo, V. Roma, 216 (☎089 25 36 36), serves some of the street's best pizza at truly reasonable prices on a pleasant patio. Pizzas L3-14,000. Cover L2000. Open M-Sa 1-3:30pm and 8pm-2am.

Cueva del Sol, V. Roma, 218 (☎089 23 73 91), serves delicious Mexican food and exotic drinks. Tacos L7000. *Agave spinosa,* tequila, papaya juice, and lime L7000. Open daily 8pm-3am.

SIGHTS AND ENTERTAINMENT

Though most of Salerno is dominated by uninteresting modern buildings, there are a handful of interesting things to see in the old quarter. V. dei Mercanti and its tiny side streets afford a taste of life in the Middle Ages. The city was already considered "ancient" in the 9th century, and this area of Salerno was once the capital of the Norman empire (1077-1127).

Begun in 845 and rebuilt 200 years later by Norman leader Robert Guiscard, **Duomo San Matteo** is decorated in the cosmopolitan style of the Norman regime. The arches of the portico, floor of the apse, and two pulpits in the nave are decorated with beautiful geometric mosaics and patterns influenced by those of the Islamic world. The **crypt,** with vaulted ceiling and beautiful frescoes, houses the **holy tooth** of the city's patron saint, S. Matteo. His holy filling and holy toothbrush are nowhere to be found. (Turn right off V. Mercanti or V. Roma onto V. Duomo and walk uphill. Open daily 10am-noon and 4-6:30pm.) One block down V. Duomo from the *duomo*, the **Museo della Ceramica** exhibits local ceramic art. (☎089 22 77 82. Open M-W and F-Sa 9am-1pm, Th 9am-1pm and 4-7pm. Free.) Climb L. Plebiscito on its far side to reach **Museo Diocesano,** which displays religious paintings and the fine work of medieval ivory-carvers from Amalfi. (Open daily 9am-6:30pm. Free.) Exotic plants grow in the **Parco del Mercatello** east of the city. CTSP bus #6 (L1000) runs to the gardens. If you want to soak up some rays, there is a wide sandy beach after the sailboat harbor (take the bus along Lungomare Trieste).

During the month of July, Salerno hosts the **Salerno Summerfestival,** which includes a concert series (mostly jazz and blues) at the Arena del Mare, near the Molo Marittimo Manfredi. (Concerts usually start at 10pm; prices vary. Call ☎089 66 51 76 for more info.)

At night, the youngest crowd gathers at **Bar-Gelateria Nettuno,** V. Lungomare Trieste, 136-138 (☎089 22 83 75), near the fountain. Discos rock the area around Salerno, but prices are steep without the free passes often dispensed at random. Women can often enter for free, but let that be its own warning. In summer, locals flock to gigantic open-air discos on the western and southern coasts. **Movida, Villaggio del Sole, Morgana,** and **Mermaid's Tavern** along the southern coast are difficult to reach without a car. From June through September, the nighttime hotspot **Fuenti,** in Cetara (4km west of Salerno), has three floors of open-air dancing on the coastal cliffs. (☎089 26 18 00. Cover L20-25,000. Open F-Sa 10:30pm-5am.) **Africana,** the most spectacular club around but far away in Praiano, sometimes charters boats to Salerno and back in the summer (see **Praiano,** p. 510). Check the magazine *MEMO* (at the tourist office or the hostel) for special events and club listings, including those outside Salerno.

Nearby **Vietri sul Mare** is home to hundreds of artisans and a pleasant beach to Salerno. Bus #4 or 9 runs from the station (10min.). Check out the neon-lit **Café degli Artisti,** V. C. Colombo, 35. Live Latin lyrics see salsa swingers swill shameful sums of sangria. (☎089 76 18 42. Open nightly 7:30pm-3am. Cover L15,000.)

DAYTRIPS FROM SALERNO: CERTOSA DI SAN LORENZO

Without a car, the Certosa is best reached from Salerno, and can be seen in an easy daytrip. A bus leaves from Concodia Sq. at 6:25am, 10:30am, noon, and 2:30pm. The last bus returning to Salerno leaves Padula at 5:45pm. (2½hr., L9500 each way.) Buses do not stop at Padula itself, but at the crossroads about 2km away. From the crossroads, follow the signs for 1km to the monastery.

Beneath the small town of **Padula** in the beautiful hilly farmland of southern Campania sits the magnificent Certosa di San Lorenzo, one of the largest monasteries in Europe and a magnificent example of Baroque architecture. The monastery was founded for Carthusian monks in the early 14th century to help the Angevin kings maintain control over routes into Calabria, but it was beautifully redecorated in a lavish Baroque style in the 17th century. Charles V stopped here, and he and his court were served an omelette made from 1,000 eggs; though you won't be able to eat the embryos of 1,000 chickens today, the splendid architecture and beautiful setting of the Certosa make it well worth a visit.

The *certosa* is divided into two sections, "Upper" and "Lower." Lay people could visit the lower section, which is the 1st courtyard through the main gate, but only the monks could pass through the ornate facade into the main body of the monestary. (Open daily 9am-5:30pm. L6000.) The path through the monastery leads through two halves of the chapel, with choir stalls covered in inlaid wood depicting landscapes and Biblical scenes, along with a delicately inlaid marble altar. The path leads through the dining hall and kitchen, decorated in colorful majolica tiles, to the staircase to the library, which winds precariously up, without railings or pillars for support. Pass the staircase into the huge and serenely beautiful **Great Cloister,** decorated with carved miniatures of religious symbols in the entablature. At the far end of the cloister, the Grand Staircase, a wonderfully designed double staircase, curves up to the upper level.

Although you can easily see the *certosa* as a daytrip from Salerno, if you want to relax (or because you missed the last bus), **Albergo La Rosa,** attached to a farm, offers six clean rooms with a kitchen for L25,000 per person. Call to be picked up from anywhere in Padula, or when exiting the *certosa* turn right, take the 1st right, then the 2nd right, then follow the road until the next intersection, turn left, and continue a short way. The *albergo* is on the left. (☎0975 77 81 04.)

PAESTUM ☎082

Not far from the Roman ruins of Pompeii and Herculaneum, the three Greek temples of Paestum are among the best-preserved in the world, even rivaling those of Sicily and Athens. Paestum's perfectly constructed temples remained standing even after the great earthquake of AD 69 reduced Pompeii's to a pile of rubble. Greek colonists from Sybaris founded Paestum as Poseidonia in the 7th century BC, in an attempt to curry favor with the sea god. Apparently it worked, as the city quickly became a flourishing commercial and trade center. After a period of Lucanian (native Italian) control in the 5th and 4th centuries BC, Poseidonia fell to the Romans in 273 BC, was renamed Paestum, and remained a Roman town until the deforestation of nearby hills turned the town into a swampy mush. Plagued by malaria and pirates, Paestum's ruins lay relatively untouched until they were rediscovered in the 18th century. Because Paestum is not urbanized, you may think that you missed your stop as you step off the train and nervously scan the sky for vultures. Fear not the dearth of modern urban squalor; the ruins alone are a must-see, especially when the *Sovrintendenza Archeologica* lets visitors walk around on the temples (sometimes they are fenced off).

TRANSPORTATION AND PRACTICAL INFORMATION. **CTSP buses** from Salerno (1hr., every hr. 7am-7pm, L4700) stop at **Via Magna Graecia,** the main modern road. The tourist office in Salerno provides a helpful list of all return buses from Paestum. **Trains** run from **Naples** (1¼hr., 9 per day 5:30am-10pm, L8200) via **Salerno** (35min., L4700). The **AAST Information Office,** V. Magna Graecia, 155, is next to the museum. (☎082 81 10 16; fax 082 872 23 22. Open July-Sept. 15 M-Sa 8am-2pm and 3:30-7:30pm, Su 9am-noon; Sept. 16-June M-Sa 8am-2pm.)

ACCOMMODATIONS. There is really no reason to stay in Paestum. The "nearby" hotels and restaurants are overpriced, and the site can be visited as a daytrip. However, the pleasant beachside **Ostello "La Lanterna" (HI),** V. Lanterna, 8, in Agropoli, is the nearest budget accommodation. (☎/fax 0974 83 83 64. Sheets and shower included. 56 beds. Dorms L17,000; quads L68,000.) To get to Agropoli take the CTSP buses from Paestum (10min., 1 per hr. 7am-7pm, L2000) or from Salerno (1hr., L4700). Agropoli is also connected by train to Paestum (10min., L2200); Salerno (45min., L4700); and Naples (1½hr., L8200).

SIGHTS. Paestum's three Doric temples rank among the best-preserved in the world. Built without any mortar or cement, the buildings were originally covered by roofs of terra-cotta tiles supported by wooden beams. When excavators first uncovered the three temples, they misidentified (and thus misnamed) them. Although recent scholarship has provided new information about the temples' dedications, the old names have stuck. Sporadic restoration work on the temples occasionally leaves them fenced off or obscured by scaffolding. (Temples open daily 9am-1hr. before sunset. Closed 1st and 3rd Monday of each month. Last admittance 2hr. before sunset. L8000, EU citizens over 60 and under 18 free).

There are three entrances to the ruins. The northernmost entrance leads to the **Temple of Ceres.** Built around 500 BC, this temple became a church in the early Middle Ages but was abandoned in the 9th century. The ancient Greeks built Paestum on a north-south axis, marked by the paved V. Sacra. Farther south on V. Sacra is the Roman **forum,** which is even larger than the one at Pompeii. The Romans leveled most of the older structures in the city's center to build this proto-*piazza,* the commercial and political arena of Paestum. To the left, a shallow pit marks the pool of an ancient **gymnasium.** East of the gymnasium lies the Roman **amphitheater.**

South of the forum lies the 5th-century BC **Temple of Poseidon** (actually dedicated to Hera), which incorporates many of the optical refinements that characterize the Parthenon in Athens. Small lions' heads serve as gargoyles on the temple roof. The southernmost temple, known as the **basilica,** is the oldest, dating to the 6th century BC. Its unusual plan, with a main interior section split by a row of columns down the middle, has inspired the theory that the temple was dedicated to two gods, Zeus and Hera, rather than one. A **museum** on the other side of V. Magna Graecia houses an extraordinary collection of pottery, paintings, and artifacts taken primarily from Paestum's tombs with outstanding bilingual descriptions and essays on site. It also includes samples of 2500-year-old honey and paintings from the famous **Tomb of the Diver,** dating to 475 BC. (Museum open daily 9am-6:30pm. Ticket office open daily 9am-5:30pm. Closed 1st and 3rd Monday of each month. L8000, EU citizens over 60 and under 18 free.)

If visiting the temples puts you in a worshipful mood, bow down on golden sand toward the sun at the **beach** 2km to the west. Unfortunately, much of it is owned by resorts that charge for beach access and chair rental. For a free dip in the Mediterranean, head to a *spiaggia pubblica*—ask for directions.

APULIA (PUGLIA)

Welcome to hard-core Italy, where the sun's scorching rays and the people's intense passions continually threaten to bring things to a boil. Conversations, complete with elaborate hand gestures, quickly progress from pleasant joking to frenzied yelling and then back again. Some travelers interpret the South's mercurial passion as rudeness, but you'll have a better understanding (and a better time) if you try to see it as part of an uninhibited zest for life. Women may find the persisting legacy of *machismo* threatening, especially in large cities.

The heel of Italy's boot, Apulia has been prized throughout the centuries for its fertile plains and numerous natural ports. The Greeks, and later the Romans, controlled the region as a vital stop on the trade route to the East. With the Middle Ages came an onslaught of invaders who shaped the culture. Modern Apulia, having served its time on "skid row," is regaining stature as a wealthy and educated region. Within its borders, remote medieval villages and cone-roofed *trulli* houses dot a cave-ridden plain, and ports have a distinctly Middle Eastern flair.

HIGHLIGHTS OF APULIA

GO BAROQUE in **Lecce's churches** without losing a *lira* (p. 537).

STOP-OVER in **Bari**—it's free (p. 524).

MARVEL at Alberobello's mortarless houses—***trulli*** (p. 529).

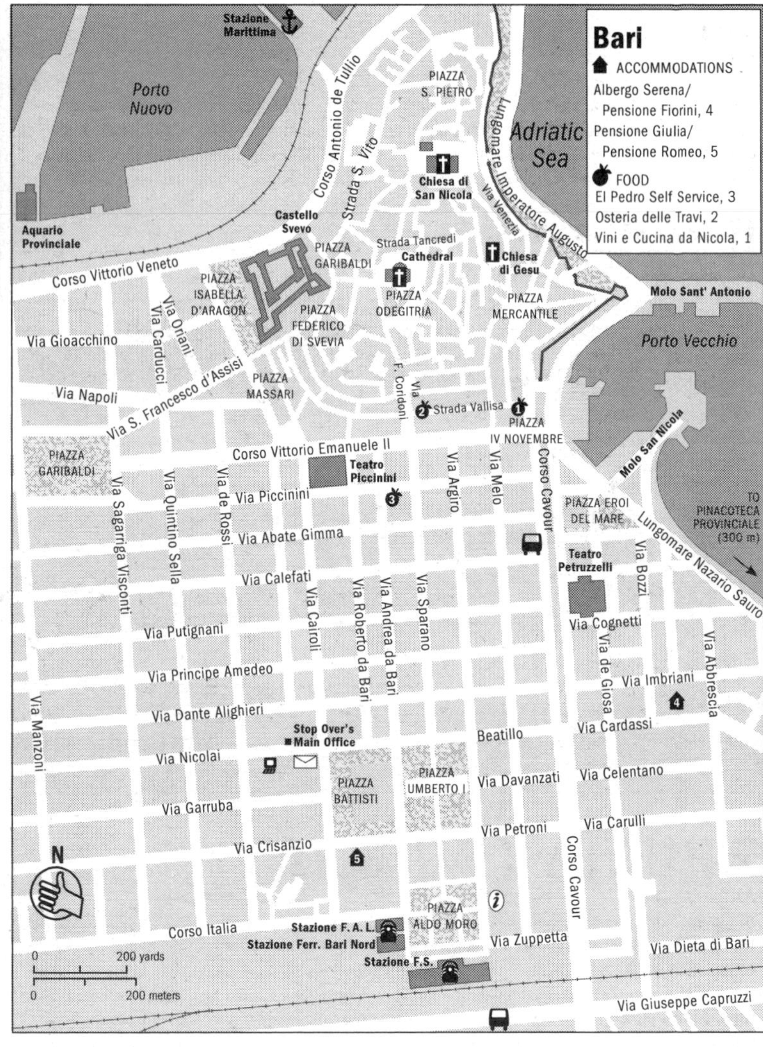

Direct train lines run from Naples to Bari and from Bologna to Lecce, and rail service is supplemented within the region by several private train and bus companies. Eurail pass and *cartaverde* are not valid on these private carriers.

BARI ☎080

Se Parigi ci avesse lo mare, sarebbe una piccola Bari.
(If Paris had the sea, it would be a little Bari.)
— An Italian proverb

Vibrant, modern, and indisputably Italian, Apulia's capital is a chaotic melange of seemingly incompatible ingredients. Begin with a tiny old city, the monuments dating from its days as a Byzantine stronghold. Add a well-organized, modern city grid, a port with ferries to Greece, hip nightlife fueled by a large university population, and vast quantities of delectable Puglian cuisine. Sprinkle in Rome's drivers and Naples's pickpockets, and broil the whole mishmash in some scorching southern Italian weather. The city is often called dirty, violent, and nightmarishly inefficient. And while most tourists stay in Bari only long enough to buy a ferry ticket to Greece, the reputation's bark is worse than Bari's bite. The old city is home to several great monuments and excellent prices. Bari can be a little intimidating and is certainly not for everybody, but the city strives to make tourists feel welcome—you won't regret having given it a taste.

TRANSPORTATION

Trains: Bari is connected to 4 different railways, all of which leave from P. Aldo Moro. The higher prices listed below are for InterCity (IC) or EuroStar (ES) trains.

FS to: **Foggia** (1-1¾hr., 35 per day 4:30am-12:30am, L10,300-25,100); **Brindisi** (1-1¾hr., 26 per day 6am-midnight, L10,100-25,100); **Lecce** (1¾-2¼hr., 26 per day 5am-midnight, L12,100-28,100); **Termoli** (2-3hr., 6 per day 10am-10pm, L19-28,500); **Naples** (4½hr., 8:30am, L25,500); **Rome** (5-7hr., 6 per day 6:30am-11:39pm, L47-65,500); **Reggio Calabria** (7½hr., 3 per day noon-9pm, L45,500-65,000); and **Milan** (9hr., 9 per day 5am-midnight, L67,500-91,000).

FSE (☎080 546 24 44) from the main station to: **Alberobello** (1½hr., 14 per day 5:30am-7:15pm, L5900), sometimes via **Castellana Grotte** (1hr., 3 per day 8:25am-7:15pm, L4700).

Ferrotramviaria Bari Nord (☎080 521 35 77), next to the main station. Trains run to **Andria** (1¼hr., L5100) and **Barletta** (1¼hr., 19 per day 6am-10pm, L5900) via **Bitonto** (30min., L3000) and **Ruvo** (45min., L3900). Su the route is served by a bus leaving from P. Aldo Moro.

FAL (☎080 524 48 81) runs on Su to **Matera** (1½hr., 8 per day 6:30am-9pm, L6700) via **Altamura** (1¼hr., 8 per day, L5700). Across the ATS Viaggi Tours agency on V. Capruzzi, near the tunnel from the station.

Buses: SITA (☎080 556 24 46) usually leaves from V. Capruzzi on the other side of the tracks. Call ahead for fares and schedules. **Marozzi** buses to **Castel del Monte** leave from near the Teatro Petruzzelli on C. Cavour (1hr., M-Sa 2:10pm, L6000).

Public Transportation: Local buses leave from P. Aldo Moro, in front of the train station. Tickets cost L1500.

Taxis: ☎080 55 43 33.

FERRIES

Although there are no discounts for InterRail or Eurail pass holders (as there are in Brindisi), Bari is an important port for ferries to Greece, Turkey, Albania, and Israel. Because Bari's **Stazione Marittima** and the surrounding area can be extremely intimidating, you should take one of the many buses to the port rather than walking the 2km through the old city. **Check in at least two hours before departure.** Many lines offer special student rates and discounts on round-trip tickets (Poseidon discounts 30% on the return-trip). The list of companies below (which is not comprehensive) includes the lowest prices (deck class) for each destination on weekdays. The higher figure denotes high season (July-Aug.) prices, while the lower figure represents low season prices. Call ahead as schedules and prices vary, especially on weekends. Obtain tickets and information at the Stazione Marittima or at the offices listed below.

Poseidon Lines, c/o Morfimare, C. de Tullio, 36/40 (☎080 521 00 22; fax 080 521 12 04). Window #11 at the port. To: **Turkey** and **Israel.**

Ventouris Ferries, c/o P. Lorusso & Co., V. Piccinni, 133 (☎080 521 76 99; fax 080 521 77 34). Windows #7-10. To: **Corfu** (11hr.; June 27-Sept. 29 1 per day; L53-73,000, students L47-67,000); **Igoumenitsa** (13hr.; in summer 1 per day; L53-73,000, students L47-67,000); **Cefalonia** (15hr.; July 26-Aug. 21 every other day; L63-87,000, students L57-77,000); and **Patras** (18hr.; 1 per day; L63-87,000, students L57-77,000).

Marlines (☎080 523 18 24; fax 523 02 87). To: **Igoumenitsa** (13hr.; in summer 4 per week, in winter 2 per week; L50-70,000, return ticket L35-49,000).

ORIENTATION AND PRACTICAL INFORMATION

Via Sparano runs straight from the train station to **Piazza Umberto I,** Bari's main square. Farther along V. Sparano, fancy boutiques line the street and provide some of the city's best window-shopping. The end of V. Sparano intersects **Corso Vittorio Emanuele II** and the edge of the **old city** (Bari Vecchia). Those attempting the long walk to the **port** should skirt the old city's winding streets by turning left on C. V. Emanuele and right at P. della Libertà onto **Via Giuseppe Massari.** Walk around the castle, head right, and follow the coast. Otherwise, take the bus from the station (1 per hr.). For a more leisurely stroll, turn right off V. Sparano onto C. V. Emanuele; this path takes you past **Corso Cavour** to **Piazza Eroi del Mare.**

TOURIST, FINANCIAL, AND LOCAL SERVICES

Stop-Over in Bari: V. Nicolai, 47 (☎080 621 45 38; fax 080 521 18 22; email StopOver@inmedia.it; www.inmedia.it/StopOver). 12 years ago, the local government and several grassroots organizations decided to make Bari an international mecca for backpackers. The result was this comprehensive program for young travelers (only non-residents of Apulia under the age of 30). The program offers free lodgings (including a tent) at a campground outside the city, free bicycle rental (at the campground), free Internet access, and free guided excursions to Alberobello. Stop-Over also organizes free concerts throughout the summer, often featuring "the biggest names" in Eastern European speed-metal. Unfortunately, the program has recently struggled with funding and red tape—check ahead to see which services are available. Main office open M-Sa 8:30am-8:30pm, Su 9am-6pm. The **campground,** Pineta S. Francesco (accessible by the #5, 3, and 3/ buses) is open 24hr. in the summer.

Tourist Office: EPT, P. Aldo Moro, 33a (☎080 524 22 44), to the right as you leave the station, has maps of Apulia. English spoken. Open M-F 9am-1pm.

Currency Exchange: At window #4 in the FS train station. Open daily 7am-9:30pm.

American Express: Morfimare, C. de Tullio, 36/40 (☎080 521 00 22), near the port. Open M-F 9am-1pm and 3:30-7:30pm, Sa 9am-noon.

Laundromat: V. Toma, 35 (☎080 556 70 56). Take the underpass past the last track, turn left on V. Capruzzi and right on C. Croce, continue, then turn left on V. Toma, and walk for 3 blocks. L10,000 per load. Open July-Aug. 21 M-F 9am-1pm and 4-8pm, Sa 9am-1pm; Aug. 22-June M-Sa 9am-1pm and 4-8pm.

EMERGENCY AND COMMUNICATIONS

Emergencies: ☎113. **Police:** ☎113. **Carabinieri:** ☎112.

Pharmacy: Berrino, V. Cavour, 47 (☎080 521 26 15), across from Teatro Petruzzelli. Open M-F 4:30-11pm, Sa-Su 4:30-8pm.

Internet Access: Libreria Palomar, V. Nicolai 8 (☎080 521 28 45). Turn left on the 1st street after P. Umberto. L5000 for 30min., L8000 per hr. Open M-F 8:30am-1:30pm and 4:30-8:30pm, Sa 8:30am-1:30pm. **Bitlandia Club,** V. A. da Bari, 24 (☎080 524 12 23), farther from most accommodations. Cross P. Umberto, go left a block, turn right on V. A. da Bari, and continue until 1 block from the end. L10,000 per hr. Open M-F 9am-1pm and 4-8pm, Sa 9am-1pm.

Post Office: (☎080 521 33 48), in P. Battisti, behind the university. From P. Umberto, turn left on V. Crisanzio, then take the 1st right on V. Cairoli. Recently discovered, to everyone's shock, to be Italy's most efficient. You'd hate to see #2. Open M-F 8:20am-8pm, Sa 8:20am-1pm. **Postal Code:** 70100.

ACCOMMODATIONS

Most travelers don't stay long in Bari, but cheap accommodations are plentiful.

Pensione Fiorini, V. Imbriani, 69 (☎080 554 07 88), a 10min. walk from the station. Walk straight past P. Umberto I and turn right onto V. Dante, which becomes V. Imbriani. A kindly manager. Some of the 6 rooms have balconies, and a few have private baths. Shower L5000. Dorms (limited availability) L19,000; small singles L30,000; doubles L59,000, with bath L69,000.

Pensione Romeo, V. Crisanzio, 12 (☎080 521 63 52; fax 080 523 72 53). Below his star-crossed love, Pensione Giulia. 25 rooms. Singles with bath L65,000; doubles with bath L95,000.

Pensione Giulia, V. Crisanzio, 12 (☎080 521 66 30; fax 080 521 82 71), above her star-crossed love. 13 spacious rooms with balcony (of course). Singles L70,000, with bath L80,000; doubles L90,000, with bath L120,000. V, MC, AmEx.

Albergo Serena, V. Imbriani, 69 (☎080 554 09 80; fax 080 558 66 13). All 14 rooms with shower. Singles L50,000; doubles L80,000; triples L120,000.

FOOD

Bari offers delicious Apulian food at phenomenally low prices. Restaurants in the old town give a taste of old-world style, often providing neither menus nor itemized checks. Purchase food for the ferry ride at **Super CRAI,** V. de Giosa, 97, three streets to the right of P. Umberto I while facing away from the station. (☎080 524 74 85. Open M-Sa 8am-2pm and 5-8:30pm.) There is a daily **vegetable market** in P. del Ferrarese, closer to the port.

Vini e Cucina Da Nicola, Strada Vallisa, 23, in the old city. From P. IV Novembre, enter the old city to the left; the restaurant is on the left. Inexpensive dining at its best. Don't let the no-frills service intimidate you. Dishes change daily. The fried calamari is exquisite. *Menù* L15,000, drinks included. Open M-Sa noon-3pm and 8:30-10pm.

El Pedro Self-Service, V. Piccini, 152 (☎080 521 12 94), off V. Sparano. Turn left (when heading away from the station) a block before C. V. Emanuele. Not a Mexican restaurant, but a busy cafeteria serving authentic Apulian specialties. Complete meal with drink about L14,000. Open M-Sa 11am-3:30pm and 6-10pm.

Osteria delle Travi, Largo Chiurlia, 12 (☎0330 84 04 38), at the end of V. Sparano. Turn left through the arches at the entrance to the old city. True *Mezzogiorno* cuisine including pasta with arugula. Full meal L20,000 with drinks. Open Tu-Sa 12:30-3pm and 7:30-10:30pm, Su 12:30-3pm.

SIGHTS

As a strategic port on the Italian coast, Bari has always been a favorite target for invading armies. To help defend against approaching troops, Bari's citizens built the old city as a labyrinth; residents could hide in the twisting streets or use them to ambush those less familiar with the city. Thieves have learned to use this maze of streets to their advantage, and careless tourists are their favorite victims. **Do not venture alone into the old city, especially at night.** Avoid flashy watches and jewelry, keep valuables inside front pockets, and hold on tightly to purses, bags, and cameras. Stick to the larger streets and use a map (Stop-Over's enlarged map of the old city is great). At the same time, you should not let petty criminals scare you off entirely. The old city is of great historic interest and well worth visiting.

BASILICA DI SAN NICOLA. Yes, Virginia, there is a **Santa Claus,** but he's dead. In 1087, 60 *Baresi* sailors stole St. Nicholas's remains from Demre, Turkey—they don't call Bari *scippolandia* (land of the petty thieves) for nothing. Although the victorious sailors refused to hand over the saint to the local clergy, the Catholic Church built the Chiesa di San Nicola as Santa's final resting place. The church's spartan appearance would be better suited to a fortress—in fact, the tower on the right survives from a Byzantine castle that originally occupied the site. Inside, an 11th-century Episcopal throne hides behind the high altar, and 17th-century paintings with gaudy trim adorn the ceiling. The **crypt,** with its windows of translucent marble, holds the remains of Kris Kringle. To the left of the entrance, a Greek Orthodox shrine welcomes pilgrims visiting from the east. On the back wall several 17th-century paintings commemorate the saint's life, including a scene of the resurrection of three children sliced to bits and plunged into a barrel of brine by a nasty butcher. On a 3rd wall, stockings are hung by the chimney with care. *(Open daily 7am-noon and 4-7:30pm, except during mass.)*

CASTELLO SVEVO. Fortifying the old maze of streets near the port is the colossal Swabian Castle, built in the 13th century by Frederick II on Norman and Byzantine foundations. Isabel of Aragon and Sona Sforza added the bulwarks in the 16th century. Although you can't climb the ramparts, you can see the frequent art exhibits inside the medieval keep. *(Just outside the old city, off C. V. Veneto near the water. ☎080 528 61 11. Open daily 9am-12:30pm and 3:30-6:30pm. L4000, under 18 and over 60 free.)*

DUOMO. Bari's most important monument, this Apulian-Romanesque cathedral was built in the late 12th century, during years of peaceful Norman rule. The *duomo* displays a typically austere tripartite Romanesque facade, augmented by rose windows on the transepts and Baroque decorations around the doors. Its interior, capped by a 36m dome, houses lovely frescoes. *(In the old city at P. Odegitria. Open daily 8am-12:30pm and 7:30pm.)*

OTHER SIGHTS. The 17-room **Pinacoteca Provinciale** displays paintings by Veronese, Tintoretto, Bellini, and the Impressionist Francesco Netti, Bari's most acclaimed artist. The collection of 18th- and 19th-century Apulian landscapes is also refreshing. *(Down Lungomare N. Sauro, past P. A. Diaz. On the 4th floor. ☎080 521 24 22. Open Tu-Sa 9am-1pm and 4-7pm, Su 9am-1pm. L5000, students L2000.)*

The **Acquario Provinciale** sports a large collection of, well, live fish. *(On Molo Pizzoli across P. Garibaldi. ☎080 52 112 00. Open M-Sa 9am-12:30pm. Free.)*

ENTERTAINMENT

Pubs and **clubs** pepper this university town. Most are open daily from around 8pm until 1 or 2am (3am on Saturdays); they are generally closed during the August holidays. Chat with the expatriate owners of **Bohémiene,** V. de Napoli, 17, a popular British pub that features live music every Wednesday and occasional outdoor concerts in the summer. Cross south over the tracks on C. Cavour, turn left after one block on V. Capruzzi, and turn right three blocks later on V. G. David. (Open Tu-Su 7:30pm-2am.) Enjoy cottage pie with your half-pint of Guinness (L3000) at **Joy's Shop,** C. Sonnino, 118, a spirited Irish pub. (☎080 47 44 81. Open nightly 7pm-3am.) On weekends, students cram into Largo Adua and the other *piazze* along the *lungomare* east of the old city, where **Deco,** P. Eroi del Mare, 18 (☎080 524 60 70), serves American food and has live music.

Bari is the cultural nucleus of Apulia, and Stop-Over will help you experience the city to the fullest. **Teatro Piccinni** offers a spring concert season and opera year-round (purchase tickets at the theater). Consult the Stop-Over newsletter or the *Bari Sera* section of *La Gazzetta del Mezzogiorno* (the local newspaper) for the latest info. Stop-Over also organizes concerts in summer, usually held at the Pineta San Francesco, near the train station, or in the park (see **Stop-Over,** p. 524).

Bari's **soccer** team was successful enough in 1997 to move up to Serie A, Italy's most prestigious soccer league; in the past few years, it has done well enough to set its sights on a good finish in the national standings. For true Italian culture, catch a game any Sunday (and often other days of the week) from September to June. Tickets, starting at L18,000, are available at the stadium or in bars.

The great commercial event of the year, the **Levante Fair,** runs for 10 days in mid-September. The largest fair in southern Italy, it displays goods from all over the world in the huge fairgrounds by the municipal stadium. Late April and May bring the **Festival of San Nicola.** Every Sunday *Baresi* carry an image of the saint from church to church.

DAYTRIPS FROM BARI

The numerous train lines that radiate from Bari make daytripping easy and affordable. Nearby towns are arranged in groups along five routes: Barletta, Trani, and Bisceglie to the northwest along the coast; Bitonto, Ruvo di Puglia, and Castel del Monte to the west; Altamura and Gravina in Puglia in the southwest; Castellana Grotte, Alberobello, and Martina Franca to the south; and Polignano a Mare, Monopoli, Egnazia, Fasano, and Ostuni to the southeast.

CASTEL DEL MONTE

In summer, take the Ferrotramviaria Bari Nord train (☎0883 59 26 84) to Andria (1¼hr. from Bari, 19 per day 6am-10pm, L5100) and then take a bus from the station to the castle, 17km away (30min.; leaves Andria 8:30am and 4:40pm, returns 10:50am and 7pm; L3300). Call ☎0883 29 03 29 or contact the Pro Loco tourist office (☎0883 59 22 83) to confirm the schedule. Miccolsi buses from Bari, near the Teatro Petruzzelli, also stop 2km from the castle (1 per day, M-Sa 2:10pm, L6000)

Halfway between the High Murge and the sea, Castel del Monte (1240) sits majestically atop a hill surrounded by rolling farmlands. It is easily the most impressive of the castles of Frederick II, the Swabian king who ruled southern Italy in the 13th century. According to legend, the castle housed the Holy Grail; in reality, it served as a hunting lodge and, later, a prison. Check out the majestic gateway, inspired by a Roman triumphal arch—Frederick tried to revive classical principles of art and good government, and many neoclassical details can be seen throughout the castle. The striking octagonal layout is aligned astronomically, leading scholars to hypothesize that the castle was designed as an observatory rather than a military structure. Atop one of the spiral staircases sits a small room used as a roost for hunting hawks, one of the emperor's hobbies. (☎0883 56 98 48. Open daily Apr.-Sept. 9am-1:30pm and 2:30-7pm; Oct.-Mar. 9am-1pm. L6000.)

CASTELLANA GROTTE

The FSE train from Bari toward Alberobello stops at "Grotte di Castellana Grotte" (1hr., 8 per day 8:30am-7:15pm, L4700). Do not disembark at "Castellana Grotte," the city, which is 2km away down V. Grotte. Check schedules carefully because not all trains stop here. To get to the caves walk across the parking lot and turn left.

The breathtaking, natural caverns of Castellana Grotte, discovered in 1938, are famed for their size, age, and beauty. Stalactites and stalagmites have developed over time into all sorts of whimsical shapes, including a Madonna, a camel, a wolf, an owl, and an ice cream cone. Even if you don't see the resemblances, the various formations invite the imagination to run wild. Those with time to kill can even watch them grow—at the rate of 3cm per century. Visiting the caverns is expensive but worthwhile. To enter, you must join one of two **guided tours.** One is a short 1km jaunt (45min.; every hr. 8:30am-7pm, in winter 8:30am-1pm; L15,000) and the other is a longer 3km trek (2hr.; every hr. 9am-6pm, in winter 9am-noon; L25,000). Both tours start at La Grave, an enormous pit that superstitious locals feared was an entrance to hell. The longer tours culminate in the stunning Grotta Bianca

(White Cave), a giant cavern filled with white stalactites. Tours in English are offered less frequently (in 2000 the long tour left at 11am and 4pm and the short tour at 1pm and 6:30pm—schedules may change. For info, call ☎0167 21 39 76 or 0804 96 55 11, or visit www.grottedicastellana.it. Bring sturdy walking shoes and a jacket (the caves are around 60°F year-round).

THE GARGANO MASSIF

To reach Siponto, take the train to Foggia from Bari (1-1¾hr., 35 per day 4:30am-12:30am, L10,100-25,100) or Termoli (1-1¼hr., 29 per day 4am-2:30am, L7400-12,400). From there, another train will take you to Siponto (20min., 24 per day 5am-10:30pm, L3500). To get to the church, avoid the ugly beach town, and take the path that starts across the tracks next to the small amusement park. To reach Monte Sant'Angelo, take the SITA bus from the train station in Foggia (40min., 9 per day 5:30am-5:30pm, L7000). Ferrovie del Gargano buses (☎167 29 62 47) also run to Vieste (2hr., 8am and 12:30pm, L9000), via Pugnochiuso (1¾hr., L9000). SITA buses also run to San Giovanni Rotondo, home of the famous Padre Pio–his tomb and the church built in his honor draw droves of Italian pilgrims.

The Gargano Massif once ranked among the most popular pilgrimage destinations in Europe. The Archangel Michael was said to have appeared in a cave in **Monte Sant'Angelo** in the 5th century, and in ancient times a respected oracle supposedly occupied the same cavern. Now the peninsula is renowned for its stretches of sand (65km) on the north and east coasts. Popular beach destinations include **Vieste, San Menaio,** and **Pugnochiuso.** Unfortunately, the Gargano is gradually succumbing to the twin blights of the southern coastal areas—smokestacks and beach umbrellas—so visit soon. Inland from the shore is the **Foresta Umbra,** which abruptly gives way to classic Mediterranean terrain in the south.

Residents of **Siponto,** 3km southwest of Manfredonia, abandoned the ancient city after a 12th-century earthquake and plague. The sole remains of Siponto surround the remarkable **Chiesa di Santa Maria di Siponto,** built during the 11th century in the Apulian-Romanesque style. The blind arcade shows strong Pisan influence and the square plan and cupola reveal Byzantine roots. Ask the caretaker to allow you to visit the 7th-century **crypt.** (Open daily 9:30am-12:30pm and 4-7pm.)

RUVO

40min. by train from Bari on the Ferrovie Bari Nord Line, next to the main FS station in P. Aldo Moro (14 per day 6:30am-8pm, reduced service by bus on Su; L3200).

An easy half-day trip from Bari, Ruvo is home to one of the most beautiful Romanesque cathedrals of medieval Puglia. Exit the station, take a right on V. Scarlatti, then a left on V. Fornaci, which turns into C. Cavour; the **cathedral** is to the left when you reach the public gardens. Built in the 13th century, it has one of Puglia's most beautiful doorways, ornamented with a wild assortment of motifs derived from the Saracen, German, and French conquerors who ruled Puglia.

BITONTO

Trains head to Bitonto from Ruvo (20min., L2200) and Bari (30min., L2200).

Midway between Ruvo and Bari on the Ferrovie Bari Nord line, **Bitonto** is home to another impressive Romanesque **cathedral.** From the train station head up V. Matteotti until you reach a squat tower—turn left and continue until you reach the large *piazza* with the church. Modeled after the church of San Nicola in Bari (p. 526), the exterior of the church is decorated with an array of carved details, ranging from geometric designs to ferocious griffins. At the central portal, carved scenes from the life of Christ contrast with abstract patterns. Inside, be sure to check out the beautifully carved pulpit and its reliefs of Frederick II. (Open daily 8am-noon and 4-7pm.)

ALBEROBELLO AND THE TRULLI DISTRICT ☎0804

Hundreds of *trulli*, unusual white stone dwellings with cone-shaped roofs, crowd the **Valley of Itria,** between Bari and Taranto. The first recorded *trulli* were built in the 1400s, but the peculiar buildings did not take their well-known, mortarless form until 1654. Sometime that year, the local court heard of an impending royal inspection and ordered the *trulli*—considered to be substandard peasant housing—razed to the ground in order to avoid fines. After the inspection, the Court had the buildings rebuilt without mortar so that they could be dismantled easily before future royal visits to the farming community. Today, dismantling the *trulli* would be illegal (the ones in Alberobello are a UNESCO World Heritage Site).

The largest, most-celebrated conglomeration of *trulli* is in Alberobello. With more than 1000 dwellings, a *trullo* church, and the two-domed **Trullo Siamese,** the area looks like a scene from a sci-fi movie. It's difficult to escape from Alberobello without buying one of the omnipresent replicas from the gift shops.

TRANSPORTATION AND PRACTICAL INFORMATION. Alberobello lies south of Bari. By **FSE train** from **Bari** (1½hr., 14 per day 5:30am-7:15pm, L5900). To reach the *trulli* masses from the train station (☎080 432 33 08), bear left and take V. Mazzini (which becomes V. Garibaldi) to P. del Popolo. The staff at the **Tourist Information Office** (☎080 432 51 71), in P. Fernando IV, off P. del Popolo, provides helpful maps marked with all the local sights. The **postal code** is 70011.

ACCOMMODATIONS AND FOOD. Eating and sleeping in Alberobello can be expensive; it's less costly to visit the *trulli* as a daytrip. Perhaps the most memorable way to spend the night is to rent a *trullo* from truly terrific **Trullidea,** V. Montenero, 18. As you face the *trulli* district, V. Montenero leads uphill from your left. Spacious *trulli* include kitchen and breakfast. (☎/fax 080 432 38 60; email info@trullidea.com; www.trullidea.com. Singles L80,000; doubles L120,000; triples L150,000. Prices 20% higher in Aug. V, MC.) **Albergo da Miniello,** V. Balenzano, 14, a block down V. Bissolati from P. del Popolo, is one of the only hotels in town without the word *trullo* in its name, and it's also the least expensive. The *albergo* has 15 rooms, all with bath, TV, phone, and fridge, many with great views of the you-know-whats. (☎/fax 080 43 11 88. Singles L50,000; doubles L75,000. V, MC). The local restaurant **L'Olmo Bello,** V. Indipendenza, 33, to the left before entering the *trulli* district, serves local specialties under a century-old *trullo*. Try the *orechiette alla buongustaio*, ear-shaped pasta in a gourmet sauce. (☎080 432 36 07. *Primi* and *secondi* from L8000. Cover L2000. Open W-M noon-3pm and 7-10pm.)

SIGHTS. V. Monte S. Michele leads up the hill to the *trullo* **Church of St. Anthony.** To reach the **Trullo Sovrano** (Sovereign Trullo), take C. V. Emanuele from P. del Popolo and continue past the church at the end. This two-story structure, the largest *trullo* in Alberobello, was built in the 16th century as a seminary. It is decorated to show what the *trulli* were like when farmers inhabited them. (Open M-Sa 10am-1pm and 3-8pm. L2500, includes tour in Italian.) Even if Alberobello isn't the most unique town you've ever visited, perhaps the **Museo del Territorio** will be the strangest museum you've ever seen. Composed of 23 *trulli* linked together, the museum features various temporary exhibits and a permanent display explaining the history and structure of the *trulli*. From P. del Popolo, turn left by the Eritrea store to P. XXVII Maggio. (Open daily 10am-1pm and 4:30-7:30pm. L2500.)

BARLETTA ☎0883

Few tourists visit the several interesting monuments of industrial Barletta. Disdaining the Adriatic muck of Barletta's wide beaches, even its residents skip town on weekends for the Gargano's sand or Trani's nightlife. However, the city is home to Romanesque churches, a castle built by Frederick II, and a 5m statue of a Byzantine emperor. Barletta's claim to fame comes from a battle fought over five centuries ago. On the 1st or 2nd Sunday of September, crowds of tourists fill the city for a reenactment of the *Disfida*, a battle in which 13 Italians fought 13 Frenchmen in defense of their chivalric honor.

TRANSPORTATION. **FS trains** travel from **Bari** (20-65min., 45 per day 4:30am-11:30pm, L5200-17,100) via **Trani** (15min., 28 per day 6am-10:45pm, L2200) to the station (☎088 352 15 62), in P. Conteduca. **Ferrotramviaria Bari Nord trains** head to **Bari** (1¼hr., 19 per day 6am-10pm, L5900) via **Andria** (10min., L1700) and **Ruvo** (35min., L3900) from the other station (☎088 353 10 07), 1km away on V. Andria.

ORIENTATION AND PRACTICAL INFORMATION. Most of Barletta's interesting sights lie along **Corso G. Garibaldi** and **Via Emanuele,** which lead toward the coast and into the old city. From the train station, walk straight ahead on **Via Giannone** and turn right onto **Corso Garibaldi.** The port splits the beaches into a wide stretch on the northwest and a nicer strip, carved into private slices on the other side along the **Litoranea di Levante.** For more information, head to the **IAT Information Office,** V. D'Aragona, 95. From C. Garibaldi, turn right onto the unmarked V. D'Aragona at P. Caduti. (☎0883 33 13 31. Open M-Sa 8am-2pm.)

ACCOMMODATIONS AND FOOD. **Pensione Prezioso,** V. Teatini, 11, off P. del Plebiscito, has 18 small but peaceful rooms, all with bath. From the train station, walk down V. Giannone through P. Aldo Moro, V. da Cordova, and P. del Plebiscito. (☎0883 52 00 46. Singles L30,000; doubles L60,000. V, MC.)

Nearby, **Pizzeria Dai Saraceni,** P. del Plebiscito, 65, makes *pizza ai Saraceni* (with ham, artichokes, olives, and capers; L8000; evening only). Dine indoors or *al fresco* in P. Plebiscito. (☎0883 51 71 00. Cover L2000. Open daily noon-1am.)

SIGHTS AND ENTERTAINMENT. The 12th-century **Chiesa di Santo Sepolcro** graces the center of town at C. Garibaldi and C. V. Emanuele. (Open Apr.-Oct. M-Sa 9:30am-noon and 6:30-9pm; Nov.-Mar. M-Sa 9:30am-noon and 5:30-8:30pm.) Next to the church towers the six-meter-tall **Colosso.** This 4th-century bronze statue is thought to be one of the later Roman emperors (Valentinian I) holding the cross and orb, symbols of the spiritual and temporal realms of his power. As the Venetians were hauling home loot from the Fourth Crusade, a shipwreck sent the Colosso to Barletta's shore, where friars used its bronze limbs to make church bells. New limbs were fashioned in the 15th century—in his new pose, the sporty emperor appears to be practicing his tennis serve. Farther down C. Garibaldi, turn left onto V. Cialdini to find the **Cantina Della Sfida,** the basement of a medieval palace where Barletta's fabled confrontation of the knights occurred. (Open Tu-Su 9am-1pm and 4-7pm. L5000.) V. del Duomo leads to the **Castello,** built by Frederick II and expanded in later centuries. Explore the sub-basements, or climb up to the battlements. Inside is the only surviving portrait of Frederick and a large collection of local impressionist paintings. (Open Oct.-Apr. Tu-Su 9am-1pm and 3-5pm; May-Sept. Tu-Su 9am-1pm and 4-7pm. L5000.) Beyond the *castello*, relax along the beachside **Litoranea di Levante,** a strip of snack bars, pizzerias, and beaches.

At the **Iris Pub,** C. V. Emanuele, 65, the only bar on the block with a frescoed ceiling, a sociable crowd munches Italian pizza and guzzles German beer well into the morning. (Pizza L8000. Open daily 2pm-2am.)

TRANI

☎0883

Trani welcomes visitors with its peaceful gardens, clear water, and scenic old city. The town curls around a picturesque bay, where you can dock your yacht, visit the historic waterfront, stroll through the nearby gardens, or sun yourself Trani style—like a lizard on the rocks off the 12th-century cathedral.

Trani's jewel, a magnificent 12th-century Romanesque **cathedral,** stands tall at the tip of a small promontory. The cathedral has impressive bronze doors and an adjacent **museum.** (Cathedral open daily 8am-noon and 3-7pm. Museum ☎0883 58 46 32. Open in summer M-Sa 9:30am-12:30pm and 4-7pm; in winter M-Sa 9:30am-12:30pm. L4000.) From P. della Repubblica, continue on V. Cavour to P. Plebiscito and the lush seaside **public gardens,** or head left on V. Pagano, walk through P. Mazzini, turn right on V. Beltrani, and continue through the well-kept old city to the **cathedral.** Near the cathedral and along the waterfront is Trani's **castello.** (Open Su-F 10am-1pm and 5-7:30pm, Sa 10am-1pm and 5-10:30pm. L4000, 18-26 L2000, under 18 or over 65 free.) As you walk back to the town center from the cathedral, follow the coast toward the bay, past the 18th-century Baroque **Chiesa di Santa Teresa** and the 12th-century **Chiesa di Ognissanti,** built by the Knights Templar. Trani celebrates the birthday of its patron saint, S. Nicola Pellegrino, with *giochi* (games) at the **festa** on the 1st Sunday in August.

If one day isn't going to cut it, check into **Albergo Lucy,** P. Plebiscito, 11, a 19th-century *palazzo* with huge rooms and balconies overlooking the gardens. All 12 rooms have bath and fridge, and some have kitchens. (☎0883 48 10 22. Doubles L85,000. Extra bed L28,000.) A block off the port, **La Vite,** V. Zanardelli, 17, serves generous portions of Greek and Italian specialties and over 180 varieties of tea. (☎0883 48 12 75. *Menù* L25,000. Open M 4pm-3am, Tu-Su noon-3am.)

The FS train station (☎0883 58 88 01), in P. XX Settembre, connects Trani to **Bari** (40min., 28 per day 6am-10:45pm, L4700) and **Barletta** (15min., 28 per day 6am-10:45pm, L2200). The **IAT Information Office,** V. Cavour, 140 (☎0883 58 88 25), is directly across the *piazza* from the train station. (Open M-F 8am-2pm and 3:30-6:30pm.) **Postal Code:** 70059.

BRINDISI

☎0831

Everyone comes to Brindisi to leave Italy—here Pompey beat a hasty retreat from Caesar's armies, and Crusaders set forth to retake the Holy Land. Today those passing through Brindisi have more peaceful intentions. Backpackers headed for sun-soaked lounging in Greece crowd the town, stopping only to pick up their ferry tickets. Despite the traffic, Brindisi is a safe and pleasant town, and the nearby towns of Ostuni and Lecce amply repay travelers who stop to explore—Corfu will still be there tomorrow.

FERRIES

Brindisi is Italy's major departure point for ferries to Greece. Ferries leave for **Corfu** (8hr.), **Igoumenitsa** (10hr.), **Kephalonia** (16½hr.), and **Patras** (17hr.). Ferries usually follow the Corfu-Igoumenitsa-Patras route, occasionally stopping in Kephalonia. From **Patras,** buses (2½hr., buy tickets at the *stazione marittima*) and trains service **Athens.** Ferries run to **Çesme,** in Turkey (30hr.) and **Durres,** in Albania (9hr.), but there are no InterRail or Eurail discounts to those destinations.

All passengers leaving from Brindisi pay a port tax (usually L10-14,000) in addition to the regular fare. Whether or not you have an InterRail or Eurail pass, any agency in Brindisi can sell you a ticket for any particular ferry, and all charge the same rates. Ask about all options—a store owner who says there is only one way lies like a yellow dog. **Delta Shipping,** Corso Umberto, 116 (☎0831 52 03 67), has a friendly, English-speaking staff. The cheapest option is deck passage *(passagio semplice)*. Most deck passengers are forced to sleep, well, on the deck. Nights at sea are often cold and wet. If you'd rather be inside, a supplemental fee brings comfort. Food and drink are available on board, but stocking up for the ride is cheaper. If you plan to snack at the restaurant or while away the hours at the bar (a surefire recipe for sea-sickness), make sure the boat accepts *lire.*

If you have bought tickets somewhere other than Brindisi, you may lose your reservations if you do not **check in at least two hours before departure.** Allow plenty of time for late trains and for the 1km walk from the train station to the ferry embarkation terminal, and then for a shuttle to the dock. At the port and on the ferries, even the pigeons may steal your belongings. Be sure to take appropriate precautions. Bolt down your bags, sit on your money, sleep with one eye open.

INTERRAIL AND EURAIL TRAVELERS

Some Eurail/InterRail travelers arrive in Brindisi expecting to hop on a free ferry to their destination. Sadly, ferry service is intermittent or interrupted, causing the loss of a day of Eurail travel. Many opt to purchase non-Eurail/Interrail ferry tickets for the sake of convenience, despite cost. Some go directly to Bari to avoid the hassle, even though **no Bari ferries accept Eurail/InterRail passes.** Although the companies that accept Eurail/Interrail are technically supposed to find seats on other lines when their ferries are full, this rarely occurs. Your best bet is to call ahead, arrive early, and be forceful in negotiating.

InterRail and Eurail passes are only valid on Hellenic Mediterranean Lines. Although their tickets can be obtained at any agency, **Hellenic Mediterranean Lines,** C. Garibaldi, 8, has an efficient main office (☎0831 52 85 31; fax 0831 52 68 72; www.hml.it). Eurail pass holders, however, will have to pay a L19,000 fee for travel between June 10 and September 30. InterRail pass holders are exempt from this fee. Your pass will only get you deck passage. A seat inside costs L29,000 extra; cabin places start at L45,000. The port tax is L12,000 on Hellenic Mediterranean Lines. Call ahead to verify departure times. In high season Hellenic Mediterranean ferries leave every other day at 8:30pm.

TRAVELING WITHOUT INTERRAIL OR EURAIL

Traveling to Greece without a pass can easily be faster and only slightly more expensive. Despite signs stating the contrary, **there are no official InterRail or Eurail pass dealers in Brindisi.** Hellenic Mediterranean Lines charges high prices for those who don't have passes (L40-100,000 for deck passage, depending on the season), so you should take some time to explore other options. It is generally possible to get a ticket to Greece for L30-60,000. Prices fluctuate throughout the year, and are highest on weekends in late July and early August. While Eurailers pay a supplement during the entire high season, other companies charge high season prices only on summer weekends. As with Eurail/InterRail tickets, most agencies also sell non-Eurail/InterRail tickets, and all charge the same price. The company offices, as opposed to general agents, will give you info only on their ships, while general agents present a variety of options. Three of the more reliable ferry companies are **Strintzis Lines,** c/o Euroferries, C. Garibaldi, 65 (☎0831 56 22 00); **Fragline,** c/o Discovermare, C. Garibaldi, 88 (☎0831 59 01 96); and **Med Link Lines,** c/o Discovery, C. Garibaldi, 49 (☎0831 52 76 67). At each office, find the total price (including taxes and fees) and the departure point. Ferries leave from various locations—ask where the boat leaves and if there is a **shuttle bus.** Most companies offer a 10-20% discount on round-trip tickets and offer youth/student fares and "bargain" tickets on certain days. A speedier option is **Italian Ferries,** C. Garibaldi, 97 (☎0831 59 03 05; fax 0831 59 01 91; email eta-brindisi@futura.it), which runs a catamaran to **Corfu** (3¼hr., July 24-Aug.15 at 2pm. L100,000, under 26 L60,000).

TRANSPORTATION

Trains: in P. Crispi. Higher prices are for Intercity trains. **FS** to: **Lecce** (20-30min., 28 per day 5:30am-1am, L3900-15,900); **Taranto** (1¼hr., 12 per day 5am-8:30pm, L5900); **Bari** (1¼-1¾hr., 24 per day 4am-11pm, L10,100-25,100); **Rome** (6-9hr., 4 per day 7am-9:45pm, L49-79,500); **Naples** (7hr., 5 per day, L31,000); **Reggio Calabria**

(8¾hr., 9:30pm, L42,000); **Venice** (11hr., 7:50pm, L67,500); **Milan,** (10hr., 6:30 and 9:40pm, L62,000); and **Zurich** (14hr., 8:40pm, L85,000). **Luggage Storage:** L5000 for 12hr. Open daily 6:30am-10:30pm. Also at the port. Open daily 8am-8pm.

Buses: FSE, at the train station, handles buses throughout Apulia. **Marozzi buses** travel to **Rome** (7½-8½hr., 3 per day 11am-10pm, L55-65,000). **Miccolis** runs to **Naples** (5hr., 3 per day 6:35am-6:35pm, L41,000). Buy tickets for both companies at **Grecian Travel,** C. Garibaldi, 75 (☎0831 56 83 33; fax 0831 56 39 67). Open M-F 9am-1pm and 3:30-8pm, Sa 9am-1pm.

Public Transportation: Local city buses (☎0831 54 92 45) run between the train station and the port. Buses also run to various destinations around the city. Buy tickets (L1000) from bars and *tabacchi.*

Taxis: (☎0831 22 29 01). Brindisi's virtually unregulated taxi drivers have a terrible reputation for swindling foreigners. Some say that the only English many of them know is the phrase "queekly, queekly, de boat is leeving." Buses (or feet) are a better option between the train station and port.

ORIENTATION AND PRACTICAL INFORMATION

Corso Umberto runs from the train station, through **Piazza Cairoli,** and to the port. The **stazione marittima** is to the right on **Via Regina Margherita.** Following V. Regina Margherita along the waterfront away from the *stazione* leads past the column that once marked the end of the Appian Way to **Via Flacco** and **Via Revel,** a lively waterfront full of bars, restaurants, food stands, and, in summer, carnival rides.

Tourist Office: APT Information Office, V. Regina Margherita, 5 (☎0831 52 30 72). From C. Garibaldi, turn left on V. Margherita. Pretty useless for ferry info, but the staff does provide a free map and advice about hotels, local services, and sights. Open M-Sa 8am-7pm; in winter M-F 9am-1pm and 4-6pm. Despite the signs, there is no info office at the *stazione marittima.*

Currency Exchange: Banca Nazionale del Lavoro, V. Santi, 11, uphill from P. Vittoria. Open M-F 8:20am-1:35pm and 2:45-4pm. For other exchanges try C. Umberto or C. Garibaldi; all offer dollar-*drachma-lire* conversions.

Emergencies: ☎113. **Municipal Police:** ☎0831 22 95 22. **Carabinieri:** ☎112 or 0831 52 88 48. **Medical Emergencies: Pronto Soccorso** (☎0831 52 14 10) at **Ospedale Di Summa** (☎0831 51 01).

Internet Access: Foto Center, C. Umberto, 114 (☎0831 52 84 25). L12,000 per hr. Open M-F 9am-1pm and 4:45-8:45pm, Sa 9am-1pm. **Jumbo Store,** V. Bastori S. Giorgio, 14/16, the 1st left after the station. Slow connection at peak times. L6000 per 30min. Open 8:30am-8:30pm.

Post Office: P. Vittoria, 10 (☎0831 52 39 56). Open M-F 8:10am-6:30pm, Sa 8:10am-1:30pm. **Postal Code:** 72100.

ACCOMMODATIONS

Ostello della Gioventù, V. Brandi, 2 (☎0831 41 31 23; email hostelbrindisi@hotmail.com), in Casale, 2km from the train station. Exit the station, take the 2nd left, and follow the yellow signs; or catch bus #3 or 4. Better yet, call and have the hostel's free shuttle (which also runs to the port) come pick you up. Recently renovated facilities, lively atmosphere, and fun-loving staff. Shower and sheets included. Laundry L9500. L23,000 per person. Also rents the 80 available beds during the day for L9000.

Hotel Altair, V. Giudea, 4 (☎/fax 0831 56 22 89). From *stazione marittima,* walk up C. Garibaldi and take the 2nd left. Pleasant and near the port. 15 rooms. Singles L25-40,000, with bath L40-60,000; doubles L40-60,000, with bath L50-90,000.

Albergo Venezia, V. Pisanelli, 4 (☎0831 52 75 11). After the fountain, take the 2nd left off C. Umberto onto V. S. Lorenzo da Brindisi, then turn right onto V. Pisanelli. About what you'd expect from Brindisi's cheapest. 12 rooms. Reserve in advance. Singles L25,000; doubles L45,000.

FOOD

An open-air **market,** on V. Fornari off P. Vittoria, sells fresh fruit by the ton. (Open M-Sa 7am-1pm.) Pick up supplies for your ferry ride at the **Maxi Sidis supermarket,** C. Garibaldi, 106, a block from the port. (Open M-Sa 8am-1:15pm and 4:15-8:30pm, Su 9am-1pm and 5:30-8:30pm.) Across the street, **Il Fornaio,** C. Garibaldi, 93, stocks fresh bread and pastries at bargain prices. (Open 7am-10pm.) Avoid the restaurants and cafes on the main strip, where advertised "tourist menus" mean small portions and steep drink prices. Better options lie on nearby side streets. **Black and White,** Corso Umberto, 108, just down from the train station, serves good, inexpensive food while you wait for your ferry. It has superb bathrooms to boot. (☎0831 56 32 18. Pizza L5-9000. *Primi* and *secondi* L5-7000. Breakfast L4500.)

SIGHTS AND ENTERTAINMENT

From the port, V. Regina Margherita leads three blocks to stairs facing the water. The column here marked the end of the **Appian Way.** The marble capital is graced by the figures of Jove, Neptune, Mars, and eight tritons. The column's twin, which once stood on the adjacent base, now resides in Lecce. V. Colonne runs from behind the column to P. Duomo. In the 11th-century **duomo** (rebuilt in the 18th-century) Emperor Frederick II married Jerusalem's Yolande. (Open daily 7am-noon and 4-7pm.) The small **Museo Archeologico** next door traces Brindisi's rich history though pottery, tablets, and other artifacts. (☎0831 22 14 01. Open M-F 9:30am-1:30pm, Tu 9:30am-1:30pm and 3:30-6:30pm, Sa-Su 9:30am-1:30pm; free.)

From the hostel, follow the signs for 15 min. to the pride of Brindisi, the **Chiesa di Santa Maria del Casale.** The interior is decorated with 13th-century frescoes—one of Mary blessing embarking Crusaders. (Open daily 7am-noon and 4-7pm.)

DAYTRIPS FROM BRINDISI: OSTUNI

Ostuni is on the train line between Brindisi (30min., 20 per day 7am-10:30pm, L3900) and Bari (1hr., 20 per day 7am-10:30pm, L6700). From the train station (☎0831 30 12 68), take the city bus to Piazza della Libertà, the center of town (5min.; M-Sa every 30min., Su every hr.; 7am-9:30pm, L1000). Buy tickets at the bar in the train station.

Rising out of a landscape of sea, dark red earth, and olive trees, Ostuni's *città bianca* (white city) appears ethereal. The *centro storico*'s white walls protect the city from the elements and lend a fairy-tale touch to the serpentine streets.

The terrace at the top of C. V. Emanuele boasts a beautiful view of the old city. Just off the *piazza*, the little church of **Santo Spirito** has a doorway with impressive late medieval reliefs. From the *piazza*, V. Cattedrale ascends through the center of the old town. The **Convento delle Monacelle** (Convent of the Little Nuns), V. Cattedrale, 15, has a Baroque facade and a colorful white-tiled dome of Moorish inspiration. (☎0831 33 63 83. Lackluster museum inside open daily 9am-1pm and 4:30-10:30pm. L3000.) Crowning Ostuni's hill, the **duomo** (1437) was the last Byzantine building erected in southern Italy and has a remarkable facade in the Spanish Gothic style. (Open daily 7:30am-12:30pm and 4-7pm.) On August 26 and 27, Ostuni celebrates St. Oronzo with the **Cavalcata,** a parade of costumed horses and riders. Many praise Ostuni's nearby **beach,** accessible by the #47 bus from P. della Libertà (15min., every 30min. 8am-7:30pm, L1500).

Ostuni's **AAST Information Office,** C. Mazzini, 6, just off P. della Libertà, provides both assistance and a booklet entitled *Ostuni, The White Queen of Olive Trees.* (☎0831 30 12 68. Open June-Aug. M-Sa 9:30am-1:30pm and 3-8pm; Sept.-May M-F

9:30am-noon and 4-7pm, Sa 9:30am-noon.) If you choose to stay the night, try the 26 large rooms at **Hotel Orchidea Nera,** C. Mazzini, 118, about half a kilometer from P. della Libertà. (☎0831 30 13 66. Singles L50,000, with bath L60,000; doubles L70,000, with bath L90,000.) There are a great many rustic taverns and *osterie* in the old city. One of the favorites is **Porta Nova,** V. Gaspare Petrolo, 38. Enjoy the panoramic view of the countryside from the pleasant dining room. L25,000 *menu* includes *primi, secondi, contorni,* water, service, and cover. (☎0831 33 89 83. Open Th-Tu 10am-4pm and 7pm-1am.)

LECCE ☎0832

A hidden pearl of Italy, Lecce is where Italians go when foreign tourists invade their country. Once here, they marvel at the city's architecture, a spectacularly ornate style known as Leccese Baroque. Made from *tufigna,* a soft local stone that hardens when exposed to air, most of Lecce's perfectly preserved *palazzi* and elaborate churches are covered with intricate floral carvings, lavishly embellished balconies, and finely decorated portals. Although a succession of conquerors—Cretans, Romans, Saracens, Swabians, and more—passed through here, the Spanish Hapsburgs solidified the old city's current form in the 16th and 17th centuries. Lecce, the "Florence of the Mezzogiorno," is an ideal daytrip from Brindisi, and a great starting point for a tour of the Salento Peninsula, the heel of Italy's boot. Thanks to its university, the city is also home to vibrant nightlife.

TRANSPORTATION

Trains: P. Stazione, 1km from the town center. Buses #24 and 28 run from the train station to the center of town. Lecce is the southeastern terminus of the state railway. **FS** trains (☎0832 30 10 16) to: **Brindisi** (20-40min., 29 per day 5am-10:30pm, L3900-16,000); **Bari** (1½-2hr., 22 per day 5am-10:30pm, L12,100-29,000); **Taranto** (2½hr., 3 per day 1-9:30pm, L10,100); **Rome** (6-9½hr., 5 per day 6:30am-9pm, L67,100-79,500); and **Reggio Calabria** (9hr., 9pm, L45,500). **FSE** trains (☎0832 66 81 11) criss-cross the Salento. To **Otranto** (1¼hr., 9 per day 7am-7:30pm, L4700), via **Maglie;** and **Gallipoli** (1hr., 12 per day 5:30am-8pm, L5100).

Buses: FSE V. Boito (☎0832 34 76 34), easily accessible by bus #4 (L1000) from the train station. To **Gallipoli** (1hr., 5 per day, L4500) and **Taranto** (2hr., 5 per day 7am-2:30pm, L8000). **STP** (☎0832 30 28 73), V. Adua, heads to the smaller towns of the Salento Peninsula. Pick up a helpful schedule at the tourist office.

Taxis: at P. Stazione (☎0832 24 79 78) or P. S. Oronzo (☎0832 30 60 45).

ORIENTATION AND PRACTICAL INFORMATION

Lecce lies 35km south and inland of Brindisi. From the train station, take **Viale Quarta** straight into V. Cairoli, which turns left into **Via Paladini** and winds around the *duomo,* stopping at V. Vittorio. To the left, V. Libertini passes the **Piazza Duomo** and **Chiesa di San Giovanni Battista** and exits the old city walls through Porta Rudiae. To the right lies **Piazza Sant'Oronzo,** Lecce's main square, with the **castello** beyond. Three blocks beyond the castello on V. Trinchese is **Piazza Mazzini.** On the other side of the city, **Via dell'Università** runs parallel to the old city walls from Porta Rudiae to Porta Napoli.

TOURIST, FINANCIAL, AND LOCAL SERVICES

Tourist Office: AAST Information Office, V. V. Emanuele, 24 (☎0832 33 24 63). Maps and info. Open M-F 9am-1pm and 5-7pm, Sa 9am-1pm.

Budget Travel: Centro Turistico Studentesco, V. Palmieri, 91 (☎0832 30 18 62). From P. Sant'Oronzo take V. Emanuele and turn right on V. Palmieri. Provides flight and train info and sells tickets. Open M-F 9am-1pm and 4:30-8pm, Sa 9am-1pm.

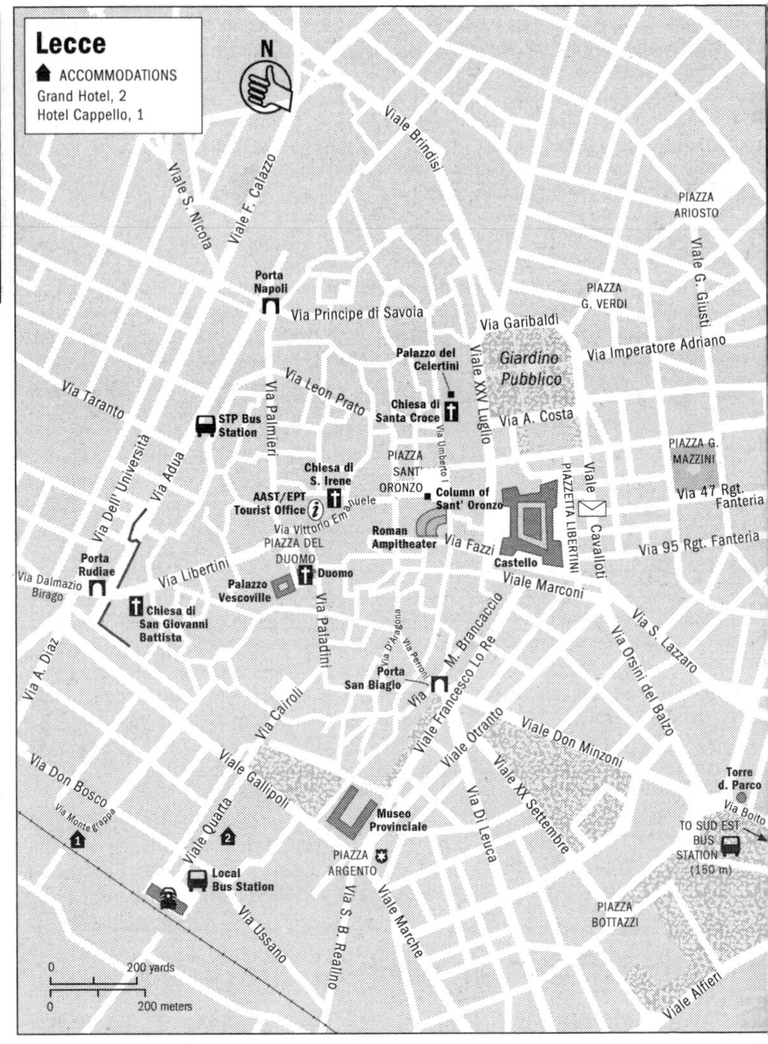

Bike Rental: Giringiro (☎0347 871 07 17), Porta Napoli. L2-3000 per hr. Open M-F 9am-1pm. The store at P. S. Oronzo rents bicycles. L12,000 per hr. Open M-Su 6pm-midnight.

Laundromat: Lavanderia Self-Service, V. dell'Università, 47 (☎0339 683 63 96), halfway between Porta Rudiae and Porta Napoli. L5000 wash, L1000 for 10 min. of drying. Soap L1000. Open M-F 9am-1pm and 5-9pm, Sa 9am-2pm.

EMERGENCY AND COMMUNICATIONS

Emergencies: Police: V. Otranto, 5 (☎113). **Pronto Soccorso** (☎0832 66 14 03), at **Ospedale Vito Fazzi** (☎0832 66 11 11), on V. S. Cesario.

Internet Access: Cliocom, V. 95° Regimento Fanteria, 89 (☎0832 34 40 41; www.clio.it). A 5-minute walk from the castle. L5000 for 30min. Open M-Sa 9am-1pm and 4-8pm. Closed Sa afternoons in July and Aug.

Post Office: (☎0832 30 40 14), in P. Libertini, behind the castle. **Currency exchange** available. Open M-F 8:15am-7:15pm. **Postal Code:** 73100.

ACCOMMODATIONS AND CAMPING

Lecce lacks ultra cheap accommodations. The tourist office lists *affittacamere*.

Hotel Cappello, V. Montegrappa, 4 (☎0832 30 88 81; fax 0832 30 15 35). From the station, take the 1st left off V. Quarta onto V. Don Bosco and follow the signs. Modern, comfortable, and convenient. All 35 rooms with A/C, bath, telephone, TV, and fridge. Singles L53,000; doubles L85,000. V, MC, AmEx.

Grand Hotel, V. Quarta, 28 (☎0832 30 94 05; fax 0832 30 98 91), half a block from the train station. A little faded, but still as elegant as the name suggests. All 70 rooms with phone and TV. Breakfast L10,000. Parking L1500 per day. Singles L55,000, with bath L80,000; doubles L90,000, with bath L140,000. V, MC, AmEx.

Camping: Torre Rinalda (☎0832 38 21 61), on the beach, 15km from town. Bus #32 from P. S. Oronzo. Virtually all the amenities. July 19-Aug. 29 L11,500 per person, L9000 per tent. Off-season L6700 per person, L4700 per tent.

FOOD

Regional specialties range from the hearty *cicerietria* (chickpeas and pasta) and *pucce* (sandwiches made with olive-bread rolls) to *confettoni* (chocolate candies made from a top-secret recipe). Buy picnic supplies at **Salumeria Loiacono,** V. Fazzi, 11, in P. Sant'Oronzo, a century-old cheese store. (Open daily 7am-2pm and 4:20-8:30pm.) The indoor **market** behind the post office provides a chance to haggle over meat and fruit. (Open M-F 4am-2:30pm, Sa 4am-2:30pm and 3:30-9pm.)

Ristorante Re Idomeneo, V. Libertini, 44 (☎0832 30 78 11), just a few blocks from the *duomo*. Reasonably priced, considering the quality of the food and its stylish appearance. Enjoy traditional *cicerietria* for L8000. Pizza L5-15,000, *primi* L8-11,000, *secondi* L9-14,000. Cover L2000. Open W-M noon-3pm and 7pm-midnight.

La Capannina, V. Cairoli, 13 (☎0832 30 41 59), between the train station and P. Duomo. Excellent outdoor dining in the tranquil *piazza* opposite the restaurant. Pizza L4-8000, *primi* L6-10,000, *secondi* L8-12,000. Cover L2500. Service 15%. Open Tu-Su noon-3pm and 7:30pm-midnight.

De Matteis Oronzo, V. Marconi, 51 (☎0832 30 28 00), near the castle. This fantastic candy store sells *confettoni* (L500) and *cotognata leccese* (dried fig candies so delicious they're ordered by the Pope; L500). Open daily 6am-10:30pm.

SIGHTS

Lecce has an endless supply of **churches,** and the best are all within 15 minutes of each other. *(Churches open daily 8-11:30am and 5-7:30pm unless stated otherwise.)*

CHIESA DI SANTA CROCE. The most outstanding of Lecce's churches, this *chiesa* (1549-1695) is the supreme expression of Leccese Baroque. Most of the area's accomplished architects contributed their efforts to this church at some time or another; if you look closely, you can see the profile of Gabriele Riccardi, the original designer, hidden between the upper window and the column to its left. Inside you'll find two rows of massive Corinthian columns. A wonderfully animated altar (1614) by F. A. Zimbalo adorns the chapel to the left of the apse. *(From P. S. Oronzo, head down V. Templari toward the church's extravagant facade.)*

PALAZZO CELESTINI. Giuseppe Zimbalo—nicknamed "Lo Zingarello" (the gypsy) due to his wandering from one church project to another—designed the lower half of the *palazzo's* facade. His pupil, Giuseppe Cino, finished the upper part. Visitors can view the inner courtyard of the building now used for offices. In the summer classical music concerts are held in the courtyard; keep an eye out for posters advertising the concerts or ask at the AAST office for more info. *(Next to the Chiesa di Santa Croce. Concerts L10,000, students L3000.)*

PIAZZA DEL DUOMO. The *duomo* was founded in 1114, and "Zingarelloed" between 1659 and 1670. The interior dates from the 18th century, with the exception of two Leccese altars. The campanile (bell tower, 1682) rises from the left side of the cathedral. Opposite, the *Palazzo Vescovile* (Bishop's Palace) has been remodeled several times since construction in 1632. On the right, with a Baroque well in its center, stands the seminary (1709) designed by Cino. Many of Lecce's churches are illuminated at night; the lighting in P. del Duomo is the most spectacular. *(From P. S. Oronzo, take V. Emanuele. Duomo open daily 8-11am and 4:30-7:30pm.)*

ANCIENT RUINS. Lecce also offers an array of ancient ruins. The **Column of Sant'Oronzo,** one of two that marked the termination of the Appian Way in Brindisi (see p. 534), towers over P. Sant'Oronzo. A statue of the saint now tops the column. Also in P. S. Oronzo lie the ruins of a 2nd-century amphitheater, thought to have held 20,000 spectators (it seems as if at least that many young people gather here on summer nights to check each other out). Half of the structure was filled in to build the nearby church. Near the station, the **Museo Provinciale** is home to Apulian ceramics from the 5th century BC. *(V. Gallipoli, 30. ☎0832 24 70 25. Open M-F 9am-1:30pm and 2:30-7:30pm, Sa-Su 9am-1:30pm. Free. Wheelchair accessible.)*

OTHER SIGHTS. The complex **Chiesa di San Giovanni Battista** (Church of the Rosary) was Lo Zingarello's last work. Here, the artist seems to have surrendered to the Baroque with reckless abandon; finely carved trees, birds, and angels flood the tiny alley where the church stands. *(Take V. Libertini from P. del Duomo).* The **Port Napoli** once stood on the road from Naples. This arch was erected in 1548 in honor of Charles V, whose coat of arms adorns the front. *(From P. del Duomo, take V. Palmieri.)* In a cemetery beyond the arch, Normans founded the **Chiesa di SS. Nicolò e Cataldo** in 1180. Cino modified it in 1716. *(On V. S. Nicola. Closed to the public.)*

ENTERTAINMENT

In 1999, Lecce's soccer team (after one year in Serie B) managed to make it back to Serie A, the country's highest division. (Games are held Sept.-June. Stadium ☎0832 45 38 86. Tickets from L17,000. Buy them at tabacchi and lottery agencies.) The AAST office distributes *Calendario Manifestazioni*, which describes seasonal events of the province and Lecce's annual summer festivals. Every night crowds gather outside the many bars, pseudo-Irish pubs (very popular among Italian university students), and pizzerias along V. V. Emanuele and P. Oronzo. Dancing picks up at **Torre di Merlino,** V. G. Battista del Tufoi, 10, near the Roman Theater (Open Th-Tu 8pm-3am.) Most nightclubs, especially during the summer, are on the coast and are only accessible by car. For current information on nighttime hotspots, ask for the monthly *Balocco* at local bars.

SALENTO PENINSULA

Foreign tourists often overlook Italy's sun-baked high heel, home to beautiful sandy beaches on two seas, hidden grottoes, medieval fortresses, and some of Italy's oldest and best-preserved art and architecture. With cultural roots stretching back to the Greeks, the peninsula is worthy of exploration. Roam an enchantingly varied coastline, or venture to inland villages to sample wine and olives.

OTRANTO

☎0836

Although Otranto is a congested mess in August, its winding streets, crystal-clear waters, and medieval sights make it tranquil and picturesque during the rest of the summer. Once the stage of a famous medieval battle, the town was conquered by Ottoman Turks who killed most of the inhabitants. Rather than convert to Islam, the town's 800 survivors opted to join their fellow Christians in death. The Turkish executioners were so impressed that they too converted to Christianity, at which point they were decapitated. The bones of the *Martiri d'Otranto* ("Martyrs of Otranto"), in glass cases in the *duomo*, are a popular tourist attraction, but most visitors are content to bathe in the warm waters of Otranto's gorgeous beaches.

TRANSPORTATION AND PRACTICAL INFORMATION. Otranto is 40km southeast of Lecce on the Adriatic coast and is downright hard to get to by public transportation. Rustic (read: turn-of-the-century) **FSE trains** run from Lecce (1¼hr., 9 per day 7am-7:30pm, L4700) to Maglie. Get off and take the waiting bus to Otranto. The FSE ticket to Lecce covers both. From the bus stop, turn right at the circle and bear left down the hill on V. Pantaleone. **The AAST Information Office,** V. Pantaleone, 12, is past the stoplight and offers limited information on local transportation, lodgings, and *agriturismo* options. (☎0836 80 14 36. Open M-F 8am-2pm and 5-8pm, Sa 8am-2pm; in winter M-Sa 8am-2pm.) At the end of the hill is the **Lungomare d'Otranto,** with the beach and calm azure water beyond. Three blocks beyond the **public gardens** on V. V. Emanuele is **Piazza de Donno** and the entrance to the *centro storico*. Enter through the city gate and turn right on **Via Basilica** to reach the **duomo.** Past the *duomo*, in the *piazza* in front of the castle, the **APT tourist office** provides advice on lodgings and transportation to smaller towns on the peninsula. (☎0836 80 14 36. Open daily 9:30am-1pm.) The **carabinieri** can be reached at ☎0836 80 10 10. **Pronto Soccorso,** V. Pantaleone, 4 (☎0836 80 16 76), is downhill from the information office. **Pharmacy Ricciardi** is at V. Lungomare, 101. (Open daily 8:30am-1pm and 4:30-9pm.) The **post office** is at the stoplight on V. Pantaleone (☎0836 80 10 02. Open M-F 8:15am-6pm, Sa 8:30am-1:30pm, Su 8:30am-12:30pm; in winter M-F 8:15am-6pm, Sa 8:30am-1:30pm.) **Postal Code:** 73028.

ACCOMMODATIONS AND FOOD. Lodging in Otranto is very expensive from mid-July through August, when most hotels require half-pension. The tourist office can help find rented rooms in local homes. The monolithic **Hotel Miramare,** Lungomare, 55, has 55 well-furnished rooms, some with balconies and TVs. (☎0836 80 10 23; fax 0836 80 10 24. Singles L80,000, doubles L120,000. V, MC, AmEx.) The **Albania Hotel,** with modern rooms and helpful proprietors, is above P. de Donno on V. S. Francesco. All rooms have bath, A/C, phone, and TV. Call ahead to see if renovations are complete. (☎0836 80 11 83. Breakfast included. Singles L50,000; doubles L80,000. Half-pension required in July L75-80,000. V, MC, AmEx.)

The **market** by P. de Donno sells fruit, meat, and fish. (Open daily 8am-1pm and 5-8:30pm.) Across from the public gardens, **Boomerang Self-Service,** V. V. Emanuele, 14, offers tasty dishes served cafeteria-style. (☎0836 80 26 19. Pizza L5-8000. Full meal with drink L22,000. Menu changes daily. Open daily 12:15pm-12:30am.)

SIGHTS AND ENTERTAINMENT. Otranto's picturesque old city is surrounded by fortifications. Lending a majestic air to this enclosed city is the famous **duomo,** paved with a phenomenal 11th-century floor mosaic of the Tree of Life. Visited by Dante as he wrote the *Divine Comedy*, the mosaic extends the entire length of the nave and depicts religious, mythological, and historical figures from Adam to Alexander the Great to King Arthur. And that's just the "A"s. Another section shows the 12 zodiac signs and the farm work done each month. Among the dead bodies and columns pilfered from Greek, Roman, and Arab sites, the crypt also houses the **Capella dei Martiri,** a small chapel with large glass display cases housing the skulls and bones of all 800 who died for their faith. (*Duomo* open daily 8am-noon and 4-6pm. Modest dress required.)

Red, pink, and blue mosaics of the Garden of Eden brighten the intimate interio of 8th-century Byzantine **Chiesa di San Pietro.** (Take C. Garibaldi to P. del Popol and follow the signs up the stairs on the left. Open daily 9:30am-1pm and 3:30 7:30pm.) The 16th-century **Aragonese castle,** with its imposing walls and newl excavated moat, casts a shadow over the town. (Open M-Sa 9am-1pm.) You can' see much of the castle besides the courtyard, but a gate in the ramparts on a sid street leads down to a pier that runs along the small boat harbor, offering views o the old town and anchored sailboats.

In August, Otranto's **beaches** are packed; the fine sand and light-blue waters ar even more enjoyable during the rest of the summer. The public strips along th *lungomare* and farther along on V. degli Haethey are the most popular and acces sible. The beach closest to V. Pantaleone costs L3000, and the beach one bloc down the road is free. Both of these beaches are just as nice as the more crowde ones along the *lungomare*, although some may not enjoy swimming in sight o rusty old freighters belching out smoke as they dock at the port. In the evening nut vendors arrive in droves to feed the crowds—try the delicious *noccioline zuc cherate* (candy coated peanuts). After dark, dance the night away to Europop wit the locals; swoosh over to the beachside **Nike**, 2km from town on V. degli Haethe (☎0836 80 11 96. Cover L25,000. Open F-Sa 10:30pm-4am.) Otranto welcomes tou ists with a feast in honor of the martyrs, the **Festa dei Martiri d'Otranto,** on Augus 13-14. On September 4, the town celebrates again with the **Festa della Madonn dell'Altomare** (Festival of the Virgin of the High Seas).

GALLIPOLI AND BORDERING BEACHES

Electricity nearly killed Gallipoli (*not* the Gallipoli of WWI fame in Turkey) whe the advent of electric light destroyed the town's oil-based economy. But it is mal ing a comeback with its fishing industry and the Italian tourists drawn by its pi turesque location on a small island with winding streets, sea breezes, and beautif beaches. The dilapidated **FSE** trains run to **Lecce** (1hr., 12 per day 5:30am-8pn L5100). **STP buses** roll to **Taranto** (1½hr., 7 per day 7am-6pm, L11,000) and **Brindi** (1½hr., 1 per day, L9000). To reach the old city from the train station, walk on Borvio, turn right on **Corso Roma,** and cross the bridge to a tiny (but beautifu island. The **Kalè Polis tourist office,** P. Imbriani, 5, on the left side after you cross th bridge, has limited information on local accommodations, guides, and boat excu sions. (☎0833 26 40 86. Open daily July-Aug. 8:30am-1:30pm and 4pm-12:30an Sept.-June 10am-noon and 4:30-6:30pm.) On your right after you cross the bridge **Hotel Al Pescatore,** Riviera Colombo, 39. All rooms have bath, phone, TV, A/C, ar views of the commercial park. (☎0833 26 43 34. Singles L65,000, in July L90,00 doubles L110,000, in July L140,000.) **Baia de Gallipoli** is a campsite 3km from tow (☎0833 27 54 05. L11-18,000 per person, tent, and car; L65-130,000 per 2-bed bung low. Open June-Sept.) **Il Giardino Segreto,** V. De Pace, 116, serves gourmet *panir* for L5-8000. (☎0833 26 44 30. Open noon-3pm and 7:30pm-midnight.)

Stop by the **duomo** on V. De Pace, two blocks from Riviera A. Diaz. An elabora Baroque facade and extensive paintings make the trip worthwhile. Many oth churches on the island are decorated with local art. Stretching along Gallipoli northern coast are two beautiful beaches, **Santa Maria al Bagno** and **Santa Caterin** Buses leave from P. Fontana Greca (July-Aug. every 30min., L2500). To the sout take the bus to Lido S. Giovanni and its pebbly sand beach (entrance L2500), continue down Lungomare Galileo Galilei to the free (and far less pleasant) Ba Verde, 15min. from town. A free sandy beach is at the foot of the cliffs near t fishing harbor on the island, but it has no changing facilities. The bars and cafes **C. Roma** stay open well into the night.

TARANTO ☎0994

In ancient times, Taranto was a proud Greek city-state with a navy ruling the seas and 300,000 seafaring citizens prospering on numerous merchant routes. Today Taranto still houses 300,000 citizens, a busy, dirty port, and Italy's fine naval fleet. The downward spiral of high unemployment, government corruption, welfare dependency, and Mafia control has taken its toll. Young, entrepreneurial Tarantinos head to Milan (or Hollywood) to stake their fortunes, as there are few opportunities here. However, Taranto is beginning to experience an urban renewal, and well-to-do young professionals pack trendy downtown cafes and restaurants. Reasonably priced accommodations aren't hard to find, and a world-famous archaeological museum, shady public gardens, wide *piazze*, delicious seafood, and a swinging bridge provide diversion from the more sordid reality.

TRANSPORTATION

Trains: (☎1478 880 88), in P. Liberta, across the old city from the center of town. **FS** to: **Bari** (1¼hr., 16 per day 5am-7pm, L10,100); **Brindisi** (1¼hr., 13 per day 5am-10pm, L5900); **Naples** (4½-5hr., 3 per day 10am-3pm, L25,500); and **Rome** (6-7hr., 3 per day 6am-3pm, L62,500).

Buses: SITA buses run to **Matera** (1¾hr., 5 per day 6am-7pm, L8000). Buses stop at P. Castello (near the swinging bridge); buy tickets at the **Marozzi Ticket Office,** C. Umberto, 67 (☎0994 59 40 89), one block up from P. Garibaldi. **CTP buses** (☎0997 32 42 01) run to **Bari** (1¾hr., 20 per day 5:30am-10pm, L9000) and **Lecce** (1¾hr., 7 per day 6am-6pm, L9000). Buses stop at Discesa Vasto in the old city, downhill from the swinging bridge.

ORIENTATION AND PRACTICAL INFORMATION

Taranto's old city is on a small island between two promontories engulfing a large bay. Bridges join the old city to the new port area and train station. **Be wary of pickpockets during the day, and avoid the old city at night.** From the station, all buses to the new city will take you near **Piazza Garibaldi,** the main square. Tickets on local AMAT buses cost L1000 (L3000 for a full-day pass). On foot, take V. Duca d'Aosta over Ponte Porta Napoli into P. Fontana in the old city. Walk 10min. along the shore to P. Castello and across the swinging bridge to reach the new city; P. Garibaldi is a block ahead.

Tourist office: APT Information Office, C. Umberto, 113 (☎0994 532 43 92), 4 blocks from P. Garibaldi. The staff provides good maps and assistance. Open M-F 9am-1pm and 5-7pm, Sa 9am-noon. The **Info booth** in the station stocks city maps.

Emergencies: ☎113. **Police:** ☎112.

Internet Access: Mare Mare Mare, Voglio Annegare, Lungomare V. Emanuele, 27. Walk up V. d'Aquino from P. Garibaldi, turn right on V. Acclavio, and walk to the waterfront. L10,000 per hr. Open daily 6:30pm-1am.

Post office: (☎0994 359 51), on Lungomare V. Emanuele. Open M-Sa 8:15am-6pm. **Postal Code:** 74100.

ACCOMMODATIONS AND FOOD

Albergo Pisani, V. Cavour, 43, off P. Garibaldi, has tasteful hardwood furniture. (☎0994 53 40 87; fax 0994 70 75 93. Singles with bath L40,000; doubles with bath L88,000.) **Albergo Sorrentino,** P. Fontana, 7, has 13 rooms overlooking the sea. Although cheap and close to the station, it is inconveniently located. The neighborhood doesn't scream "walk through me at 2am." (☎0994 71 83 90. Singles L35,000; doubles L50,000, with bath L60,000.)

Taranto's prosperous fishing industry translates into delicious, plentiful, and inexpensive seafood. Try *cozze* (mussels) in basil and olive oil or spaghetti with *vongole* (clams), but avoid anything raw. Grab your daily bread, sandwiches, and pizza at the **panificio** between P. Garibaldi and the swinging bridge. (Open daily 7am-11pm.) Fruit is available at the **market** in P. Castello. (Open daily 7am-1:30pm). **Queen,** V. de Cesare, 20, offers delectable seafood, local specialties, impeccable service, and affordable prices. The L20,000 full meal lasts the entire next day and includes wine. Menu changes daily. (☎099 459 10 11. *Primi* L4000, *secondi* L6-8000. No cover. Open M-Sa noon-4:30pm and 6:30pm-midnight. V, MC.)

SIGHTS

MUSEO NAZIONALE ARCHEOLOGICO. This museum houses the world's largest terra-cotta figure collection. The museum also has a plethora of ancient pots, marble and bronze sculptures, mosaics, jewelry, and coins. *(C. Umberto, 41, in P. Garibaldi. ☎099 453 21 12. Open M-F 8:30am-1:30pm and 2:30-7:30pm, Sa 9am-midnight. In the summer of 2000, the museum was completely closed for renovations, scheduled to be completed in late spring of 2001. Until then, part of the museum's collection is on display at Palazzo Pantaleone, to the right along C. Emanuele when crossing the bridge from the station. Open daily 8:30am-7:30pm. Free)*

SWINGING BRIDGE. From P. Garibaldi, a bridge built in 1887 hangs over the shipping canal to the *città vecchia*. It was the first of its kind, opening sideways to let ships through. The bridge still swings with the best of 'em, and is fun to watch—check the daily schedule of opening times posted on either side.

ENTERTAINMENT

Every night between 6 and 11pm, **Via d'Aquino** pulses with crowds. On P. Garibaldi, the navy band accompanies the lowering of the flag at sundown. Taranto's **Holy Week Festival** draws hordes from around the country. In a ceremony rooted in medieval Spanish ritual, sheet-covered men carrying papier-maché statues parade to all the churches. Festivities begin the Sunday before Easter.

BASILICATA

Uncovered in Carlo Levi's *Christ Stopped at Eboli* as a land of poverty and pagan mysticism, small, sparsely populated Basilicata is seldom visited. It starts high in the rugged Lucan Apennines and stretches across the Murge to short coastlines on the Ionian and Tyrrhenian seas. Mountainous, almost landlocked, and lacking natural resources, it never attained the strategic importance or historical prominence of neighboring coastal regions. Consequently, and fortunately for travelers, its fascinating prehistoric caves, breathtaking vistas, colorful local culture, and smooth beaches remain unspoiled.

MATERA ☎0835

Matera's claim to fame are the *sassi*, ancient homes carved directly in the rocks of the Materan terrain. Rude teenagers would throw parts of the house at their parents 7000 years ago, prompting the parents to snap "don't give me any of your *sassi*." The settlements remained livable until 1952, when the government deemed the 7000-year-old homes unsafe and unsanitary, displacing the residents. Yuppies and several high-tech firms recently went slumming and restored and occupied several *sassi*. Strikingly beautiful and oddly captivating, the city that calls itself "The Heritage of Humanity" has expanded to become the 2nd-largest in Basilicata, earning it the nickname "Capital of Nowhere." The city is still relatively isolated, but remains the only provincial capital in Italy not connected by FS trains. Nonetheless, its extraordinary sights, inexpensive accommodations, and engaging local culture, including the exhilarating **Festa di Santa Maria della Bruna** (see **Entertainment,** p. 545), make getting to Matera worth the trouble.

TRANSPORTATION

Trains: National railways don't reach Matera, but **FAL** trains (☎0835 33 28 61) do. **FAL** trains run to **Altamura** (30min., 13 per day 6:30am-9pm) and **Bari** (1½hr., 8 per day 6:30am-9pm, L6700). The underground station is at P. Matteotti.

Buses: FAL buses leave from P. Matteotti for **Bari** on Sunday, when train service is suspended (1¾hr., 6 per day 6am-2pm, L6700). Buy tickets at the train station. **SITA buses** leave from the same *piazza;* buy tickets at P. Matteotti, 3 (☎0835 38 50 70). Buses run to: **Altamura** (30min., 4 per day 12:30-6:30pm, L3100); **Gravina** (50min., 3 per day 1-6:30pm, L4700); **Metaponto** (1hr., 5 per day 8:15am-5:30pm, L5100); and **Taranto** (1½hr., 6 per day 6am-5pm, L10,000).

ORIENTATION AND PRACTICAL INFORMATION

Matera's grottoes cut into two small valleys overlooking a deep canyon in the **Parco della Murgia Materana.** From the train and bus stations at **Piazza Matteotti,** head down **Via Roma** to **Piazza V. Veneto,** the heart of the city. The 1st valley, **Sasso Barisano,** is straight ahead; descend through the stairway across from the Banco di Napoli. To reach the nearby **Sasso Caveoso,** continue to the right down V. del Corso, which bears right to V. Ridola, and descend to the left at P. Pascoli. Some of the more important *chiese rupestri* (rock churches) are on the other side of the ridge opposite the Sasso Caveoso. A detailed map of the *sassi* can be found at the tourist office and hotels.

Tourist Office: APT, V. de Viti de Marco, 9 (☎0835 33 19 83; fax 0835 33 34 52). From the station, walk down V. Roma and take the 2nd left. Some English spoken. Open M and Th 8:30am-1:30pm and 4-6pm, Tu-W and F-Sa 8:30am-1:30pm. The city has an **information office** on V. Madonna della Virtu, with better maps of the *sassi.* Open Apr.-Sept. 9:30am-12:30pm and 3:30-6:30pm.

Emergencies: ☎113. **Police:** 0835 37 81. **Ambulance:** ☎0835 24 32 70. **Hospital:** (☎0835 24 31) on V. Lanera.

Internet Access: Internet Café, P. Mulino, 12 (☎0835 34 65 51), one block down V. Minzoni from P. Matteotti and inside the mall on the right. L5000 for 30min. Open M-Sa 7pm-midnight. Some days Internet is unavailable throughout the city.

Post Office: (☎0835 33 25 91), on V. del Corso off P. Veneto. Open M-Sa 8:30am-6pm. **Postal Code:** 75100.

ACCOMMODATIONS

Matera has a great hostel, making it an inexpensive base for regional exploration.

Sassi Hostel (HI), V. S. Giovanni Vecchio, 89 (☎0835 33 10 09). From the station, take V. Roma to P. Veneto and continue on V. S. Biagio to the church, where signs leading to the hostel appear on the right. This hostel, amid the prehistoric caves, will fulfill your troglodyte fantasies. The rooms are renovated *sassi,* each with private bath. Sheets and towels included. Curfew midnight. 22 beds. Dorms L30,000.

Albergo Roma, V. Roma, 62 (☎0835 33 39 12), by the tourist office. 10 rooms. Singles L40,000; doubles L60,000, with bath L65,000.

Hotel De Nicola, V. Nazionale, 158 (☎/fax 0835 38 51 11). Follow V. A. Moro from P. Matteotti to V. Anunziatella on the left, which becomes V. Nazionale, or take orange city bus #7 or 10 from the station (every 10min., L1000). 99 modern rooms, all with bath, TV, and phone. The more expensive ones also have fridge and A/C. Singles L72-94,000; doubles L114-145,000. V, MC, AmEx.

FOOD

Try some of Matera's specialties: *favetta con cicore* (a soup of beans, celery, chicory, and croutons, mixed in olive oil) or *frittata di spaghetti* (pasta with anchovies, eggs, bread crumbs, garlic, and oil). Experience true Materan grit by gnawing on *pane di grano duro*—made of extra-hard wheat, this bread has a shelf-life as long as a Twinkie. Also try the **Divella supermarket,** V. Spine Bianche, 6. (Open M-W and F-Sa 8:30am-1:30pm and 5-8:30pm, Th 8:30am-1:30pm.)

Ristorante Pizzeria La Terrazzina, V. S. Giuseppe, 7 (☎0835 33 25 03), off P. Veneto near Banco di Napoli. Savor immense portions of local delicacies in a cave dug into the cliffs. The cave below doubles as a wine cellar. Try handmade pasta like *cavatelli alla boscaiola* (with a sauce of tomatoes, mushrooms, and *prosciutto*) for L10,000. Pizza L4-10,000. Cover L3000. *Menù* L25,000 Open W-M noon-3:30pm and 7pm-midnight.

Carpe Diem, V. Minzoni, 32/4 (☎0835 24 03 59), between the station and P. Veneto. *Tavola calda,* a stylish interior, and great *foccaccia.* Open daily 7am-9:30pm.

Gran Caffè, P. Veneto, 6. No seating. Grab a sandwich, soda, and *cannoli* for less than L6000 and eat on the pleasant public benches in the *piazza.* Open daily 7am-10pm.

Trattoria Lucana, V. Lucana, 48 (☎0835 33 61 17), off V. Roma. Begin with the *orecchiette alla materana* (ear-shaped pasta with tomatoes and fresh veggies) for L8000 and continue with their specialty, the *bocconcini alla lucana* (thinly sliced veal with mushrooms) for L12,000. Cover L2000. Service 10%. Open M-Sa 12:30-3pm and 8-10:30pm. Closed in early Sept. V, MC, AmEx.

SIGHTS

ALONG THE WAY TO...THE SASSI. The 7000-year old homes lie amid a maze of stone pathways, so you will need a **detailed map** to negotiate them properly. The ones from the information office on V. Madonna della Virtu (or the booth near the train station) are the best. Enter the heart of *sassi* zone from P. Veneto by taking V. del Corso past the Chiesa di S. Francesco d'Assisi to P. Sedile. From there, V. Duomo leads to the Apulian-Romanesque **duomo** in P. del Duomo—check out the beautiful carving on the outside portals. Inside, the 15th-century carved choir stalls compete with the 16th-century **Cappella dell'Annunziata.** *(Open daily 9am-1pm and 4:30-6pm.)* From P. S. Francesco, V. Ridola leads past the creepy **Chiesa del Purgatorio,** with its skeleton and skull-covered facade, to the **Museo Ridola,** which displays the area's archaeological treasures. The museum houses excellent prehistoric and early Classical art in a 17th-century monastery. *(V. Ridola, 24. ☎0835 31 12 39. Open daily 9am-7pm. L4000, but often free.)*

THE SASSI. From P. Sedile, two well-marked paths *(itinerari turistici)* head to the *sassi* in the valleys of **Sasso Caveoso** (through the arch at the left) and **Sasso Barisano** (past the Conservatory at the right). Of obscure origin, the *sassi* are carved from a soft limestone (calcarenite) in several styles. The oldest, inhabited around 7000 years ago, are crumbling structures that line Sasso Barisano along V. Addozio. The second type, dating from 2000BC, includes the carved nooks around Sasso Caveoso in the valley to the east of the *duomo.* The more elaborately carved homes in the rock around V. Buozzi (which stems from V. Madonna delle Virtù near the *duomo*) are about 1000 years old. In addition, most of the 6th-century *chiese rupestri* (rock churches) remain unmodified, and all still display remnants of 12th- through 16th-century frescoes.

As you roam the Sasso Caveoso, you may be approached by children offering "tours;" the organized ones are more valuable. **Tour Service Matera,** P. Veneto, 42 (☎0835 33 46 33), offers 1hr. tours for L10,000 per person. For a comprehensive, self-guided tour, pick up a book at any bookstore or magazine stand.

CHURCHES...WITH SASSI. Churches carved into the rock decorated with centuries old frescoes dot the *sassi*. From the *piazza* past the museum, head down the narrow street to the right of the *palazzo*, continue down Via Buozzi, and follow the signs to reach the **Convicino di S. Antonio,** a large complex of painted rock churches with a great view of the *sassi*. *(Open in summer 8am-7pm; reduced hours in winter. L2000.)* From here follow the path along the cliffs to reach the churches of **San Pietro Caveoso, Santa Maria d'Idris,** and **Santa Lucia alle Malve,** which preserve beautiful 11th-century Byzantine frescoes in their caves. *(Caveoso open daily 9am-noon and 3:30-8pm. Idris closed unless you ask at Malve. Malve open daily in summer 8am-7pm; reduced hours in winter. Tours of Malve L2000.)* A nearby **sasso** is furnished as it was when ten people and two horses shared its two small rooms. *(L2000, includes English tour.)* Further along is the multilevel complex of **Madonna delle Virtu** and **S. Nicola dei Greci,** where the ancient frescoes and rough-hewn houses are juxtaposed against modern sculpture exhibited within. *(Open daily 9am-9pm. L4000, students L2000, includes a guided tour in English.)*

PARCO DELLA MURGIA METERANA. Home to spectacular hiking, this park inhabits the ridge across the canyon from the *sassi*. The entrance to the park is off Strada Statale, 7, a healthy walk down V. Annunziatella and then V. Marconi.

FESTIVALS

Matera celebrates the **Festa di Santa Maria della Bruna** during the last week of June and the 1st week of July. The festival, one of Italy's best, includes numerous musical and cultural events, nightly fireworks displays, and open-air markets where you can buy power tools or have a parakeet predict your future. The culmination of the festival comes on July 2nd during the **Assalto al Carro.**

YOU WANT A PIECE OF ME? The frenzied excitement of the *Festa di Santa Maria della Bruna* reaches its apex during the thrilling *"Assalto al Carro,"* in which a beautiful papier-maché cart is led through the town by people in medieval garb; as it reaches P. V. Veneto, melee sets in, and the cart is destroyed by reveling natives in no longer than ten seconds. Dating back to the Middle Ages, what seems like a simple exercise in mob violence actually possesses an interesting etiquette: the cart is not to be touched until it has made it all the way into P. V. Veneto (a SWAT team of terrified *carabinieri* tries to ensure this), and once the bullies who fought their way to the center of the *piazza* have grabbed themselves a piece of the cart, they run out as quickly as possible, holding the best fragments high over their heads, to the applause of the crowd. Occasionally, though, the first rule is broken, and the cart is attacked before it has quite entered the *piazza*. The first person gets the best piece (actually, the second person usually gets the best piece, while the first person gets trampled), and the *carabinieri*, true to their stereotype, melt away at the first inkling of resistance. When this happens, the people who have gotten chunks of the cart still run out of the *piazza* with their prizes high over their heads and broad smiles on their faces. Scowls and muttered curses, rather than applause, greet the premature evacuators, who have made off with prized cart booty.

DAYTRIPS FROM MATERA

ALTAMURA

The city is on the FAL line between Bari (1¼hr., 8 per day, L5700) and Matera (40min., 8 per day 6:30am-9pm, L4000).

The urban center for the farm country of inland Puglia, Altamura boasts an impressive Romanesque **cathedral,** begun by Frederick II. The beautifully decorated rose window sits above one of the best decorated church portals in Puglia. Scenes from the life of Christ surround the main carving showing the last supper. (Cathedral in P. Duomo, on V. Federico in the old city.) Altamura also has an interesting (and free) museum in P. S. Theresa documenting the life and customs of the Apulian countryside, including more agricultural implements than you can shake a scythe at. (Open M-Sa 8am-2pm. Free.)

Trattoria Federico II di Svevia, V. Luciani, 2, two blocks towards the train station on the left from P. Repubblica, pays tribute to the great Emperor with excellent low priced local specialties. (☎0803 14 56 99. *Primi* from L6000, *secondi* from L8000. Open M-Sa noon-2:30pm and 7:30-10:30pm.)

Viale Regina Margerita runs from the station to the old city, where it becomes **Via Federico di Svevia.** Just after the old city, V. Federico di Svevia splits into **Via Pietro Colletta** and **Via Matera.** A **hospital** is on V. Regina Margerita (☎0803 108 11), and **Guardia Medica** can be reached at ☎080 310 82 01. The **carabinieri** (☎0803 10 29 92) are in P. S. Teresa, down V. N. Melodia from P. Duomo. A chaotic **post office** is in P. Matteotti, just off P. S. Teresa. (☎0803 14 61 72. Open M-F 8:15am-7:20pm, Sa 8:15am-1pm.)

GRAVINA

Gravina is most easily accessible from Altamura by FAL train (15 min., 13 per day 7:15am-9pm, L2200), while FS trains run to Taranto (1½hr., 7per day 6:34am-midnight, L7000); Brindisi (1½hr., 16 per day 7:01am-11:57pm, L7100); and Barletta (1¾hr., 7:50am-10:58pm, L8600).

Gravina is perched along a steep gorge which gives the town its name. The town's highlight is the beautiful view of the city and Apulian countryside from the ravine.

Both train stations are located at the end of **Corso Aldo Moro,** which runs to the old city, becoming **Via V. Veneto** midway down. V. V. Veneto dissolves into a tangled mass of streets in the old city—keep heading downhill to reach P. Notar Domenico and the **Church of the Purgatorio,** decorated with leering statues of reclining skeletons. The bears supporting the columns represent the Roman Orsini family, feudal lords of Gravina. Next to the church in a large *palazzo* is the small **Archaeological Museum.** Free admission includes tours of the collection of Lucanian grave goodies. (☎080 325 10 21. Open Tu-Su 9am-1pm.) Farther downhill sits a small park which leads to the bottom of the ravine and its abandoned caves and rock-carved churches. Locals superstitiously avoid this area, and the gates are often locked. Though you may be able to persuade some local boys to track down someone with a key, sometimes the area is inaccessible. Next to the stations, **Chiesa di Madonna di Grazie** has Italy's largest relief of an eagle spreading its wings across the facade. On C. A. Moro heading away from the stations, turn left down V. Fontana La Stella to the stone bridge leading across the ravine to the cliffs on the other side and a lovely pastoral view of town. Check out the caves dug into the cliffs, used by locals in the 5th century to hide from attacking barbarians.

If Gravina's got your stomach growling, head to the **Old River Pub,** V. S. Giuseppe, 92 (☎080 326 90 23), for pizza and beer (pizza from L6000).

METAPONTO ☎0835/0831

Metaponto consists of a few campsites in a forested band along the beach, some lonely Greek ruins, a museum, and a train station 3km inland. Although the undulating sand along the sparkling Ionian is a beach-lover's delight, it is better enjoyed in early July or September. Metaponto feels like a ghost town for most of the year, but from mid-July through August the campsites burst with hordes of Italians scrambling to the sea.

TRANSPORTATION. Metaponto is most easily reached by train, although both the beach and the ruins are a short bus ride away from the station. **Trains** depart for **Taranto** (30-45min., 25 per day 5am-11pm, L5000); **Bari** (2-2½hr., 4 per day 5:30am-3pm); **Salerno** (3-3½hr., 5 per day 6:30am-midnight, L18,500); **Reggio Calabria** (4½-5½hr., 2 per day 10am-2pm, L36,000); and **Rome** (5½-6hr., 3 per day 6:30am-3:30pm). Blue **SITA buses** run from the train station to **Matera** (1hr., 5 per day 7:05am-4:30pm, L5100).

ORIENTATION AND PRACTICAL INFORMATION. The town can be divided into four areas: **Scalo** (the train station), **Borgo** (the museum), **Lido** (beach and hotels), and the **ruins** of an archaeological park. While Scalo, Borgo, and the ruins are all 1-2km apart, Lido is farther away. Metaponto's best reserved ruin, the **Tavole Palatine,** is 5km from Borgo. Local **Chiruzzi buses** serve the area. Bus #1 runs between the train station, the museum, and Lido (14 per day 7:30am-9:30pm), while the less frequent #2 runs between the train station and the ruins (7 per day 8am-7pm, L1000 tickets on the bus). The Lido district is a small area around P. Nord, where the bus stops and bicycles can be rented. In case of **medical emergency,** contact the **Pronto Soccorso** (☎0835 74 19 97), off the beach. The **post office** is near the Museo Archeologico. (Open M-Sa 8am-1:15pm.) **Postal Code:** 75010.

ACCOMMODATIONS, CAMPING, AND FOOD. Metaponto's many cheap campgrounds host most of its beachgoers. **Camping Magna Grecia,** V. Lido, 1, is on the right of the highway Vle. Jonio towards Lido (connecting Lido to the station). The campground's noisy *discoteca* is a sharp contrast to the quiet national forest next door. There are also tennis courts, game rooms, bars, a swimming pool, and a shuttle to the beach. (☎0831 74 18 55. July 21-Aug. 25 L12,000 per person, L12,000 per tent, L4000 per parking space, L5000 for electricity.) There are no inexpensive hotels near the Lido, and prices rise dramatically in August. The **Hotel Turismo,** in P. Lido, features a penitentiary facade that will bring back your days in Attica. The hotel also showcases authentic 70s furniture, private baths, A/C, and proximity to the beach. (☎0835 74 19 18. Open June-mid-Sept. 50 rooms. Singles L70,000; doubles L110,000. Extra bed L27,000.) Numerous beachside pizzerias and restaurants compete for your tourist dollar—try **Lido self-service restaurant** on P. Lido right by the beach. (Pizza L5-9000. Open daily noon-3pm and 8pm-midnight.) **Maria's** mini-market off P. Nord makes good sandwiches. (Open daily 7am-6pm.)

SIGHTS. Most people go to Metaponto for the beach, and with good reason: the sand is powdery-fine, the water bright turquoise and clean, and large stretches are public. If the sun starts to get to you, catch the #1 bus from the Lido or the train station to the **Museo Archeologico.** The museum displays ancient jewelry, vases, and figurines, most of which are related to the ruins. (☎0831 74 53 27. Open daily 9am-7pm. L5000, ages 18-26 L2500, under 18 and over 60 free.) From the museum head straight through the park, past the post office down a country road to the **ruins** of the Doric **Temple of Apollo Licius** and a **Greek Theater** (6th century BC). It's another 5km to the **Tavole Palatine,** the ruins of a Greek temple of Hera and the best preserved temple in Metaponto. Greek triangle-man Pythagoras taught here until his death in 479 BC. (The #2 bus connects the train station with all the ruins.)

TYRRHENIAN COAST

MARATEA ☎0973

About three hours south of Naples by train, Maratea is the only section of Basilicata to touch the Tyrrhenian Sea. This improbably lush region houses 44 churches and consists of eight coastal and hillside hamlets spanning 30km of rugged, crumbling coastline. Except during high season from mid-July and mid-August, the region's chief pleasures are strolling, swimming, and snoozing; so those in search of landmarks and liveliness should probably go elsewhere.

The most accessible of Maratea's towns are **Fiumicello,** which dissolves into the local beach, as well as visually fascinating (but heavily touristed) **Maratea Centro,** and **Maratea Anziana,** site of the ancient city whose ruins still remain. Maratea Anziana, located atop 'San Baglio,' is protected by the 22m white marble statue of Redentore (Christ the Redeemer). Erected in 1963, the awe-inspiring figure with outspread arms is second in size only to that in Rio de Janeiro—though Marateani usually claim that Rio cheated by placing its statue on a huge pedestal.

TRANSPORTATION. Fiumicello, Maratea Centro, and Maratea Anziana are all accessible by **bus** from Cosenza during the summer (June-Aug. every hr. 9am-midnight; Sept.-May service is more erratic). Though the main bus stop is down the road from the train station, don't hesitate to flag down a bus—they will generally stop anywhere. Trains run from **Maratea Station** to Cosenza, Naples, and Reggio di Calabria. (☎0973 87 69 06. Open 7:30am-noon and 3:30-6pm. V, MC.) If you prefer to walk, **Maratea Porto** (1km) and **Fiumicello** (4km) may be reached on foot from the train station. Exit the station, turn right, and continue down V. Profiti under the bridge. Turn left down the hill to Porto. Fiumicello is farther down the same road. Taxis are available through **Taxi Maratea** (☎0973 87 00 84 or 0337 90 15 79).

PRACTICAL INFORMATION. The peach-colored **AAST tourist office,** 40 V. Santa Venere, on the right at the beginning of Fiumicello's main drag, offers a friendly open door policy, an English-speaking staff, and helpful hotel listings. (☎0973 87 69 08. Open June and Sept. M-Sa 8am-2pm and 4-8pm; July-Aug. M-Su 8am-2pm and 3-9pm; Oct.-May M, W and F-Sa 8am-2pm, Tu and Th 8am-2pm and 3-6pm). From mid-May to October, **Porto Turistico di Maratea** (☎0973 87 73 07), in Maratea's port (2km down the road to the right from Fiumicello) rents out **motorboats** for L150,000. There is a Banca di Napoli with an **ATM** on V. S. Venere, 10m from the tourist office. A **post office** is at the port. (Open M-Sa 8am-1pm.)

ACCOMODATIONS, CAMPING, AND FOOD. Maratea Castrocucco, 8km down the coastal road from Maratea's port, is the site of **Camping Maratea** (☎0973 87 75 80). Because it is close to the sea and usually busy, Camping Maratea requires reservations in the summer. The site is often closed during low season.

In **Fiumicello,** the extra zeros on hotel prices chase visitors all the way to the beach. Look no farther than the sparkling rooms of **Hotel Fiorella,** V. S. Venere, 21, at the village entrance. The bus from the train station drives by the hotel; ask the driver to drop you off. (☎0973 87 69 21; fax 0973 87 73 43. Lockout 2-5pm. Singles with bath L50,000; doubles with bath L80,000. Comparable rooms cost L65-L100,000 during high season from July 25 to Aug. 21. V, MC high season only.)

Locals flow beachward down V. S. Venere onto the wisteria-shaded patio of **Da Felicia,** V. Fiuicello, 13, for *spaghetti*, *insalata*, and fresh seafood dishes. The white linen and attentive service of the chuckling owner is well worth the L2000 cover. The *tagliatelle alla bolognese* will send you home happy. (☎0973 87 68 00. Primi from L7000. Open noon-3pm and 7:30-10:30pm.)

Around the corner from Hotel Fiorella, the friendly pizzeria **Osteria La Bussola,** V. S. Venere, 43, satisfies crowds of friendly locals with generous pizzas from L5000. (☎0973 87 68 63. Open June 10-Sept.; 7pm-1:30am, Oct.-June 9 W and F-Sa 7pm-

1:30am.) Up a well-marked path (keep left on the way down), the more chic **El Sol,** V. S. Venere, 151, serves expensive restaurant fare and cheap pizza (L7-12,000) on its tiled terra-cotta patio. (☎0973 87 69 28. Open mid-Mar.-Oct. until 2am; open only for dinner during low season. V, MC, AmEx.)

Those planning a picnic might try the brand spanking new, well-stocked **Supermarket Velaro,** on V. S. Venere, or stop by Rosario's Mobile **Fruit Stand,** parked outside the tourist office from May to September.

CALABRIA

Calabria tends to get a bad rap. Northern Italy scorns it as part of the "backward" South, Sicilians sneer at its lack of panache, and foreigners tend to avoid it. But two and a half millennia ago Calabria was home to the worlds leading philosophers, artists and athletes while the cities who belittle her were cow towns or backwoods. In this region of contrasts, visitors see oil warehouses marring turquoise seas and the colors of fruit vendors' stands reflected in the windows of Max Mara shops. History in Calabria is quite tangible, its roots easily followed along the rustic shores from Greek temples to Christian domes. Civilizations have coveted Calabria's seaside strongholds, and their eclectic rubbish awaits exploration. Long before the pesky *motorini* came along, ancient Greek traders were littering the streets of Cosenza and merchant ships were fouling the Tyrrhenian with their jars of honey and oil. The World Wars facilitated the formation of organized crime—the *'ndrangheta*—which drove thousands of Calabrians to leave home.

Whatever Calabria lacks in developed tourism, it makes up for in unspoiled landscapes. Trains may cut through mountains and ride over coasts, but they have not tamed the wilderness. Beach paradises line the shore that Calabria shares with Basilicata, and the granite plateau of the Sila Massif offers some of Italy's best hiking and skiing. Near the southern tip of Calabria, orange trees line the lively streets of Reggio Calabria, where a superb archaeological museum houses the famous *Bronze Warriors* from Riace. Many Calabrian towns offer bargains and unmatched beaches unavailable in the tourist traps of Sicily.

HIGHLIGHTS OF CALABRIA

ENCOUNTER wildlife in the parks of the **Sila Massif** (p. 552).

SEE a 2800-year-old novelty sarcophagus and the remarkable Riace Bronzes in Reggio's **National Museum** (p. 556).

LOLL on the beautiful **beaches** of Tropea and Scilla (p. 557 and p. 557).

COSENZA ☎0984

Around AD 410, Cosenza received its first tourist group. Unlike today's well-mannered backpackers, these men were true barbarians—Visigoths actually, ten thousand of them, led by King Alaric I. Upon arriving in Cosenza, the king died of malaria and was buried in the Busento River, along with the treasure he plundered from the Goth sacking of Rome. Today, Cosenza's seven hills make it an ideal base for hiking in the wooded **Sila Massif.** During the winter a half-hour trip inland rewards visitors with excellent ski slopes. In warmer weather, the nearby beaches of **Marina di Belvedere** provide sun and surf.

TRANSPORTATION

Trains: Stazione Cosenza (☎0984 39 47 46), V. Popilia, at the *superstrada.* **FS** (☎1478 880 88; 7am-9pm) handles most of the coastal cities and stations outside Calabria. Trains run to: **Tropea** (3hr., L16,000); **Reggio** (3hr., L20,000); and **Naples** (3½-4hr., L25,500).

Buses: Autostazione (☎0984 41 31 24), on V. Autostazione, off P. Feriale at the end of C. Mazzini. **Ferrovie della Calabria** regional buses for inland destinations leave from both here and the train station; wait at the blue "fermata" sign.

Public Transportation: All orange **buses** stop at P. Matteotti; buy tickets (L1300) at any one of the magazine stands (main stand where V. Trieste crosses C. Mazzini near P. dei Bruzi). Buses #22 and 23 serve the old city, stopping in P. Prefettura (every 30min. 5:20am-11pm). Buses #27 and 28 go between P. Matteotti and the train station (every 7min. 5am-midnight.) For more detailed bus routes look for yellow hanging street signs in P. Matteotti and at all bus stops.

ORIENTATION AND PRACTICAL INFORMATION

The **Busento River** divides the city into two distinct regions: the traffic-plagued "new city," north of the Busento, and the "old city," with its ancient buildings, south of the river. **Corso Mazzini,** the main thoroughfare and shopping center, begins in **Piazza dei Bruzi,** runs perpendicular to the Busento, and ends in **Piazza Feriale.** To get to C. Mazzini, hop on any bus to **Piazza Matteotti,** and then walk a block with your back to the bus stop into **P. dei Bruzi.** From the old city, cross **Ponte Mario Martiri** at C. Telesio and turn left into P. dei Bruzi; C.Mazzini runs to the right. The central bus station is on **Via Autostazione.** V. Autostazione juts to the right off P. Feriale at the end of C. Mazzini, where the *corso* splits seven ways.

The terraced old city is harder to navigate. Its only identifiable street, narrow **Corso Telesio,** begins in the petite **Piazza Valdesi** on the old city side of Ponte Mario Martiri. Slightly to the left with your back to the Mario Martiri Bridge, C. Telesio climbs through the recently revived section of the old city to the statue of the philosopher himself in the well-lit and affluent **Piazza Prefettura.**

TOURIST AND FINANCIAL SERVICES

Tourist Office: APT, C. Mazzini, 92 (☎0984 272 71 or 0984 274 85; fax 0984 273 04), 4 blocks up from P. dei Bruzi. Follow the steps up into the courtyard and take the stairway to your right up 2 flights. Multilingual staff eagerly provides charmingly archaic city maps and loads of info on the surrounding coastal and mountain towns. Open M and W 8:30am-1:30pm and 2-5pm.

Parco Nazionale di Calabria Office: V. della Repubblica, 26 (☎0984 767 60). Provides info on outdoor activities and excursions to the nearby wooded Sila Grande.

Currency Exchange: Several **ATMs** line C. Mazzini. There is also a **Banco di Napoli,** C. Umberto, 17A (☎0984 68 51 00). **Autostop,** V. Monte Santo, 23 (☎0984 229 82), changes money without commission. Open M-F 9am-1pm and 4-7:30pm, Sa 9am-1pm.

EMERGENCY AND COMMUNICATIONS

Emergencies: (☎113). **Police: Municipale** (☎0984 268 02), in P. dei Bruzi, behind the town hall, is open 24hr. **Carabinieri** (☎112). **Ambulance: Croce Bianca,** V. Beato Angelo d'Acri, 29 (☎0984 39 35 28). **Hospital: Ospedale Civile dell'Annunziata** (☎0984 284 09), on V. Felice Migliori. **Red Cross:** V. Popilia, 35 (☎0984 41 11 55).

Late-Night Pharmacy: P. Kennedy, 7 (☎0984 241 55). Open M-Sa 24hr. except 1-2:30pm; Su 10pm-8am. **Farmacia Berardelli,** C. Mazzini, 40. Open 8:30am-1pm and 4:30-10pm.

Internet Access: Casa delle Culture, up C. Telesio near the *duomo,* has 7 terminals with access, but they are always busy. Stop in early and make a reservation.

Post Office: V. V. Veneto, 41, (☎0984 252 84; fax 0984 732 37), at the end of V. Piave, off C. Mazzini. Open M-Sa 8:15am-6pm. **Postal Code:** 87100.

ACCOMMODATIONS

Affordable lodgings cluster at the old city end of C. Mazzini. This quarter is blessed with good *pensioni* and cursed with overpriced craft stores and cafes.

Albergo Bruno, C. Mazzini, 27 (☎0984 738 89), at the end of C. Mazzini closest to the old city. With your back to the *piazza,* look for the wee yellow sign over the door on the left. 1 block from P. dei Bruzzi. Surely Cosenza's best-fortified hostel (or its most hospitable fortress), the family-run establishment is up 4 floors and behind as many locks. A few of its large, tall-windowed rooms have televisions; some have balconies with potted flowers. Free piano practice. Recommended check-in 10pm. Reservations suggested. 9 rooms, 23 beds. Singles L30,000, with bath L50,000; doubles L50,000, with bath L70,000; triples L70,000, with bath L90,000.

Hotel Grisaro, V. Monte Santo, 6 (☎0984 279 52). Take V. Trieste from P. dei Bruzzi. All rooms with TV and phone. Friendly common room downstairs with TV and big comfy armchairs. 6th floor has views of terra-cotta rooftops. Breakfast of coffee and pastry included. Wheelchair accessible. Reservations suggested. Singles L50,000, with bath L60,000; doubles L80,000, with bath L85-90,000; triples with bath L120,000; quads with bath L140,000.

Camping: The best in the area is at the Sila Massif (see p. 552) and in the seaside towns of **Scalea** and **Marina di Belvedere.** Campgrounds are near the beach and draw families, particularly in Aug. **Camping il Gabbiano** (☎0985 205 63), has beach bungalows and free hot showers. Open June to mid-Sept. L8000 per person, L22,000 per tent.

EXTRA, EXTRA! Newspapers cover scandalous events, but in Southern Italy this phrase has literal meaning. The old newspapers that cover the windshields of parked cars often serve not to keep out the sun's heat but to conceal the more torrid heat produced from within. Beware, virgin eyes—it is the age-old art of *l'amore.*

FOOD

Cosenza is a well-fed city. The Sila forests provide rich mushrooms and fresh *prosciutto,* the sparkling waters off the Tyrrhennian coast provide plentiful fish, and Calabria's orchards give the city an excellent fruit supply. For foodstuffs, stop into **Cooper Frutta,** at Vle. di Trieste and V. Trento, a block from C. Mazzini, or acquire the essential victuals from **Cooperatore Alimentare** next door; have yourself a picnic in nearby P. Vittoria—just you, a peach, a loaf, and the old men playing *Gioca Tresete,* a local card game. For artistic fruit handiwork, check out the tiny **Dolcezze di Calabria,** C. Mazzini, 92, underneath the tourist office, which sells candied tangerines and figs cooked in fig honey and wrapped in fig leaves. Figgy fun, indeed.

Gran Caffè Renzelli, C. Telesio, 46 (☎0984 268 14). Run by the same family for over 203 years, this cafe in P. Parrasio behind the *duomo* was once the official confectioner of the king. In the late 19th century, the plush red room in the back was reserved for nobility. The Bandiera brothers, famous patriots of the Risorgimento, stopped by for a cup of Renzelli's excellent coffee; an hour later Bourbon troops caught and executed them beneath the Valle di Rovina aqueduct. Find out if their cappucino is to die for. Nibble on a mini *pizza rustica* (L2000) or the sweet *verchiglie*, from a 700 year-old recipe. Table service L1000. Open M and W-Sa 7:30-1am. V, MC.

Trattoria Tre Lanterne, V. Rivocati, 15 (☎0339 192 67 73). From P. dei Bruzi, go left onto C. Umberto, and take the 1st left onto V. Trento. Head straight down the narrow passage to right onto old V. Rivocati. The yellow *trattoria* is on the left. Dim tavern atmosphere with accompanying red-checked tablecloths. A sprawling Swiss mountainside mural adorns the far wall. Hearty *primi* and *secondi* from L5000. Lunch *menù* (L15,000) includes *primo, secondo,* salad, and a carafe of the house wine. Open daily 1-3pm and 7-10pm.

Da Giocondo, V. Piave, 53 (☎0984 29 81 00). Dine among the business suit-clad Cosenzan elite at prices not so lofty. Sea creatures baked, fried, and roasted, starting at L12,000. "What comes along comes along" is the owner's motto for the menu. The large crowd of animated regulars discuss politics with Cosenzan passion, amplified by house wine. Sample regional specialties including *asciuzzi riciazoni alla silana* and roasted sweet cheese *cacciocavollo* (L8000). Closed Su.

SIGHTS AND ENTERTAINMENT

CHIESA DI SAN FRANCESCO D'ASSISI. The interior of the church houses a number of "slice of life" paintings by the Flemish William Borremons. In the chorus chamber at the church's far end lies the angelic—but shriveled—body of a 400-year-old Franciscan monk. The chambers above (reached by a stairway from the adjoining sacristy) contain astounding views of the city, but are not normally accessible to the public—so ask nicely. Cosenza's greatest treasure lies just below the church. When the *duomo* was reconsecrated in 1222 following an earthquake, Frederick II gave the city a gilt **Byzantine cross** containing a splinter said to come from the True Cross. Whether or not you believe Frederick's drunken ravings, the cross is truly exquisite. Once on public display in the *duomo*, then moved to the Archbishopric, it is now safe and sound in the basement of the Convento di San Francesco d'Assisi. *(Cross the Mario Martiri bridge, turn left up narrow C. Telesio, and climb the old blue-tiled stairway on the right before the duomo. Continue left and into the piazza. For the cross, follow the church's left flank down to the last door and press the buzzer for "Laboratorio di Restauro." Call in advance to see the cross,* ☎ *0984 755 22.)*

DUOMO. On weekend nights, young Cosentini and people from surrounding provinces relax in the *piazza* outside the *duomo*. Inside, a mural of the *La Madonna del Pilerio* (1863), highlighted by Mary's Sicilian features and the infant's crooked halo, adorns the right wall. The next chapel belongs to the *Arciconfraternità della Morte* (Archbrotherhood of Death). Not to be confused with a heavy metal band, the brothers actually belonged to a religious order charged by ancient privilege to aid the condemned. In the chapel are buried many Cosentini executed for their part in the Risorgimento. *(Cross the M. Martini bridge into the old city, and head left up C. Telesio into P. Parrasio. Or take bus #22 or 33 up to P. Preferatura, and with your back to P. del Governo, turn right down C. Telesio.)*

NORMAN CASTLE. Originally built by the Saracens but refurbished by Frederick II after the Cosentini tried to overthrow him, the castle offers impressive views of the surprisingly compact city. In its time, the castle has been a barracks for three different monarchs, a prison, and a seminary. Though three earthquakes have destroyed most of its ornaments, the castle's flowered columns and roofless, open-ended chambers still remain. *(Take bus #22 or 23 to P. Prefettura, and with your back to Rendano Theater, walk up the curved road to the right. Or take bus 4T to the elevated village and follow signs 5min. uphill. Open daily 9am-1:30pm.)*

RENDANO THEATER. Calabria's most prestigious venue, the Rendano Theater was originally constructed in 1895 but was destroyed by WWII bombing. It has since been rebuilt to its former glory. Crimson, white, and gold, its plush interior has hosted the likes of José Carreras. Reservations for non-Calabresi are extremely difficult to get during the opera season (Oct.-Dec.); you might have more luck stopping in during the theater season (Jan.-May). *(☎ 0984 81 32 20. Behind the statue of Telesio in P. Prefettura. For plays, tickets may be available 10am-1pm on the day of the performance. Theater tickets L7-35,000.)*

THE SILA MASSIF AND CAMIGLIATELLO ☎ 0984

The Sila Massif, outside the tiny town of Camigliatello, translates roughly from its ancient Greek and Latin origins to "large, pristine ancient forest (overrun by wild pig aficionados)." And how very true. The national park is *the* spot for Calabria's hikers, campers, and skiers (who converge on the Sila's cross-country trails). Oft-neglected by foreign tourists, the Sila is as worthwhile a destination as the coast.

TRANSPORTATION AND PRACTICAL INFORMATION. Camigliatello is the best base to visit elsewhere in the Sila. Ferrovie della Calabria **trains** travel to Camigliatello from Cosenza, which is served by FS trains (1½hr., 2 per day, L3300) from Reggio as well as points north and by bus (45min., 10 per day, L3400). Service is drastically reduced on Sundays.

Get your bearings with the maps and expertise provided at the **Pro Loco tourist office,** V. Roma, 5 (☎0984 57 80 91), uphill to the right from the train station and bus stop. The friendly Pro Loco staff has (but won't let you keep) a fine map of the park with 10 recommended and worthwhile hikes. Three well-marked trails (2.2km, 3.3km, and 6.5km), leaving the picnic area down V. Roma past Hotel Tassio, make for easier day-hikes.

The **bank,** Banca Carime, is at V. del Turismo, 73. (☎0984 57 80 27. Open M-F 8:30am-1:20pm and 2:35-3:35pm.) For **medical emergencies,** call ☎0984 57 83 28. Camigliatello's **post office,** at the intersection of V. del Turismo and V. Roma, is next to Hotel Tasso; walk uphill on V. Roma and the office is on the left, past the sign for Hotel Tasso. (☎0984 57 80 76. Open M-F 8:15am-1:30pm, Sa 8:15am-noon.)

ACCOMMODATIONS, CAMPING, AND FOOD. Prices for local lodgings are mountainous. Snuggle under a neon bedspread at **La Baita,** V. Roma, 99, 100m from the train station, without worrying about the bill. Each of the small, neat rooms has a bath. (☎0984 57 81 97. Singles L40,000; doubles L70,000. Prices increase in August and during the ski season.) The **La Fattoria** campsite (☎0984 57 82 41), adjoining a vineyard, is a bargain at L8-9000 per person, tent provided. Buses (noon, 2:25pm, and 5:20pm) service La Fattoria from Camigliatello. The **Campeggio Lago Cecita,** just within the Parco Nazionale di Calabria, offers campsites, tents, and hot showers for L10,000 per night.

From the walls embellished with wine bottles and prints to the listings of prices and specialties, the restaurants in Camigliatello vary little. **Le Tre Lanterne,** V. Roma, 142, serves pizza from L6000. (☎0984 57 82 03. Open daily noon-3pm and 7-11:30pm.) **La Stragola,** V. Roma, 160, offers fresh mushroom pasta. (☎0984 57 83 16. *Primi* from L10,000, *secondi* from L12,000. Cover L2000.) For a change of pace, try the *salumerie* (deli-like eateries) that overflow with smoked cheeses, cured meats, and marinated mushrooms. Picnic grounds lie 10 minutes from the *centro*, up V. Tasso past the post office.

SIGHTS AND ENTERTAINMENT. If it's snow you want, you'll get plenty of it at the **Tosso Ski Trail,** on Monte Curcio, about 2km from town up V. Roma and left at Hotel Tosso. In winter, minibuses leave for the trailhead from Camigliatello's bus stop (buy tickets at Bar Pedaggio, next door to the stop). Though Tosso offers 35km of beautiful cross-country skiing, it has only two downhill trails (2km each). (☎0984 57 81 36 or 0984 57 94 00. Lifts run July-Aug. M-F 8:15am-5:20pm, Sa-Su 8:15am-6:20pm; Sept.-June 8:15am-4:20pm; Apr.-June and Sept.-Dec. Sa-Su 8:15am-4:20pm. Round-trip lift ticket L5000, full-day pass L22-30,000.) The slopes are only open for skiing between December and March.)

Getting to the **Parco Nazionale di Calabria** (☎0984 57 97 57), 10km northwest, with its wolves and fleet-footed deer, is not quite so easy. The state bus service sends just one bus a day to the park (leaves bus stop at 2:30pm). **Altrosud** (☎0984 57 81 54) offers guided tours of the park in Italian for L22,000 per person, leaving daily during the summer at 9am and 3:30pm. If you prefer exploring on your own, Altrosud can drop you off and pick you up later in the day for L30,000 per person. During the summer, Altrosud operates out of the Pro Loco tourist office.

If you seek traditional Calabrian culture, ignore the stores filled with knick-knacks. Instead, hop on the bus for **San Giovanni in Fiore** (25km from Camigliatello), where you can view a 12th-century abbey, exhibitions of handicrafts at the museum, and traditional festivals (including the world-renowned **Potato Festival**).

REGGIO DI CALABRIA ☎0965

The devastating earthquake of 1908 left an enduring mark on Reggio's skyline. From the rubble arose a new town, lacking old-world charm but brimming with designer stores and ornate turn-of-the-century *palazzi*. Armadas of watercraft leave Reggio and nearby Villa S. Giovanni for Messina and the Aeolian Islands. Be sure to check out the nearby towns of **Scilla** and **Gerace;** the former has a beach paramount to any in Italy, and the latter is one of the best-preserved medieval towns in the country. In addition to serving as a transportation hub to Sicily, Reggio provides a taste of urban hustle-and-bustle at the tip of Italy's least modernized region. A cool ocean breeze and 300 sunny days a year compete with city smog in this bustling metropolis.

TRANSPORTATION

Flights: Svincolo Aeroporto (☎0965 64 27 22), 5km south of town. To get there catch orange bus #113, 114, 115, 125, or 131 from P. Garibaldi outside Stazione Centrale (L1200). Service to all major cities in Italy.

Trains: Reggio has 2 train stations. All trains stop at the **Stazione Centrale** (☎0965 89 81 23), on P. Garibaldi at the southern end of town. The less-frequented **Stazione Lido** (☎0965 86 36 64) sits at the northern end of town off V. Zerbi, much nearer to the museum, port, and beaches. To: **Scilla** (40min., 8 per day, L3100); **Tropea** (1½hr., 10 per day, L8200); **Cosenza** (3hr., 10 per day, L20,000); **Naples** (5hr., 10 per day, L45,000, *rapido* L55,000); and **Rome** (7hr., 10 per day, L57,000, *rapido* L75,000). The tourist office provides and explains how to use a comprehensive pamphlet for all train schedules in Calabria.

Ferries: From Reggio's port, located at the northernmost end of the city, boats and hydrofoils service Messina as well as the Aeolian Islands. **FS** (☎0965 86 35 45), left and against the water as you enter the port, divides Reggio's hydrofoil service with **SNAV** (☎0965 295 68), located just to the right of FS. FS is open daily 7am-8pm; SNAV's hours are less concrete. **NGI** (☎0335 842 77 84), located beside the "Onda Marina" bar to the right of the port's entrance, runs a ferry service (M-Sa 2:25am-midnight). **Meridiano** (☎0965 81 04 14) lies about a hundred feet away from the water's edge (M-Sa midnight-10pm).

Reggio-Messina: FS: Hydrofoils (25min.; 16 per day, 6 on Su; L5000). **NGI:** Ferries (40min., 12 per day, L1000). **Meridiano:** Ferries (40min.; 12 per day, 7 on Su; L1000).

Reggio-Aeolian Islands: SNAV Hydrofoils: **Lipari** (2-3hr., 5 per day 7:25am-6:50pm, L34,000); **Vulcano** (2hr., 5 per day 7:25am-6:50pm, L34,000); **Stromboli** (2-3hr., 5 per day 7:25am-2:50pm, L36,000); **Panarea** (3hr., 4per day 7:25am-2:50pm, L38,000); **Rinella** (2-3hr., 7:25am-6:50pm, L38,000); **Salina** (2-3hr., 7:25am-6:50pm, L38,000). Also see **Aeolian Islands,** p. 599.

ORIENTATION AND PRACTICAL INFORMATION

Most traffic in Reggio is on **Corso Garibaldi,** which runs along the north/south axis of the town's orderly grid pattern and connects the town's major sights. With your back to **Stazione Centrale,** walk straight through **Piazza Garibaldi** to C. Garibaldi. A left turn leads to the heart of the town. At the end of C. Garibaldi is Reggio's **port,** from which hydrofoils and boats zip off to Messina and the Aeolian Islands. A few blocks to the left of the station, **Corso Vittorio Emanuele III** and **Lungomare Matteotti** run nearly parallel beside the sea. City buses (L800) continuously trace a route along the two roads toward the **Stazione Lido,** 1½km to the north.

TOURIST AND FINANCIAL SERVICES

Tourist Office: APT booth (☎0965 271 20), at the central train station. Beautiful maps and specific directions. Open M-Sa 8am-2pm and 2:30-8pm. Other branches with similar hours at the **airport** (☎0965 64 32 91) and **main office,** V. Roma, 3 (☎0965 211 71). Another **APT office** lies at C. Garibaldi, 329 (☎0965 89 20 12), next to the theater. More English speaking than the aforementioned offices. Open M-F 8am-1:45pm and 2-8pm.

Currency Exchange: Banca Nazionale del Lavoro, C. Garibaldi, 431 (☎0965 805 11). Open M-F 8:20am-1:20pm and 2:45-4pm. The rates at the **FS info booth** in the station are not as good. Open daily 7am-9pm. **ATMs** appear every few blocks on C. Garibaldi.

EMERGENCY AND COMMUNICATIONS

Emergencies: ☎113. **Police:** (☎0965 41 11), on C. Garibaldi near the central station. **Carabinieri:** ☎112. **Hospital: Ospedale Riuniti** (☎0965 39 71 11), on V. Melarino. **First Aid:** ☎0965 34 71 06.

24-Hour Pharmacy: Farmacia Caridi, C. Garibaldi, 327 (☎0965 240 13).

Agen Service (☎0965 81 87 62) At the port, next to the ticket office for ferries to Messina. Internet Access L4,000 for 30 min. Open M-F, 9am-1pm and 4-6pm

Post Office: V. Miraglia, 14 (☎0965 81 21 52), near P. Italia on C. Garibaldi in a gorgeous early 20th-century building. Open M-F 8:15am-7pm, Sa 8:15am-6pm. **Postal Code:** 89100.

ACCOMMODATIONS

Albergo Noel, V. Genoese Zerbi, 13 (☎0965 33 00 44 or 0965 89 09 65), near the port at the opposite end of C. Garibaldi from Stazione Centrale. With the sea behind you, turn left from the station. Convenient location near the port and museum. Flowered bedspreads enliven simply furnished rooms with bath and TV. Reservations recommended July-Sept. Wheelchair accessible. Singles L45-50,000; doubles L70,000.

Hotel Diana, V. Diego Vitrioli, 12 (☎0965 89 15 22), off C. Garibaldi halfway between Stazione Centrale and the museum, past the *duomo*. Look for signs. Chandeliers and marble floors whisper of past grandeur. Rooms with bath and phone. 1-month advance reservation required in Aug. Singles L50,000; doubles L100,000. 25% more for A/C.

FOOD

In Reggio, they like it hot and meaty. Chefs serve *spaghetti alla calabrese* (with pepper sauce), *capocollo* ham (salami spiced with local hot peppers), and *pesce spada* (local harpoon-hunted swordfish). **Dì par Dì supermarket,** across from the train station on C. Garibaldi, is open M-Sa 8am-1:30pm and 5-8:30pm, Tu 8am-2pm.

Pizzeria Rusty, V. Crocefisso, 14 (☎0965 925 30), to the right of the *duomo*. Nothing rusty about this fine eatery. Double-folded Neapolitan slices the size of Fiats come with mushrooms, anchovies, eggplant, prosciutto, or artichokes. Join in a local card game at one of the rustic picnic tables. Another branch located on V. Romeo, next to the museum and near the Antica Gelateria. Both restaurants open daily 3:30-11pm.

Shanghai Ristorante, V. Giulia, 2 (☎0965 33 06 42), off C. Garibaldi. A dynasty of delights and a delicious respite from food *all'italiana*. Vegetarian options from L4000. Pork and chicken dishes from L6000. The spicy dishes will knock your socks off. A/C. Takeout available. Open daily 11am-3pm and 6pm-midnight.

La Pignata, V. Demetrio Tripepi, 122 (☎0965 278 41), up V. Giutecca from C. Garibaldi. Despite the oddly cosmopolitan decor, a good place to try some local specialties. *Primi* from L8000, *secondi* from L13,000. *Menù* L20,000, includes a choice of *primo, secondo,* side dish, and fruit. Cover L3000. Open M-Sa 9:30am-2:45pm and 7:30-11pm. V, MC, AmEx.

SIGHTS

Reggio is not unlike the high-school athlete who gets to college and realizes that the glory days are long gone. Once upon a time, when the ancient Greeks controlled Southern Italy, Reggio was the flower of Magna Graecia, the "greater Greece" of Hellenistic cities. Whatever could be dug or dredged up from ship-

CAN YOU HEAR THE PEOPLE SING? Poor Reggio. First the earthquakes, now this. The Reggesi are fiercely proud of their city—and keenly aware of its millenial decline. In 1971, when Italy's central government decided to move the Calabrian *capoluogo,* or administrative seat, from Reggio to Catanzaro, it was the last straw. The plan was that while Catanzaro got the *capoluogo,* Reggio would get an industrial factory center. But the Reggesi would have none of it. Citizens took to the streets, setting up makeshift barricades and bombarding the nationally-administered carabinieri with stones. After about a year of these shenanigans, the central government got fed up and sent in riot troops, causing a full-scale street war. The ensuing battles, involving everything from sticks to tear gas canisters, created a couple of Reggesi martyrs, though no one is sure how they died or who killed them. One is commemorated by a plaque on the small street leading upwards opposite P. Italia; it reads "Fallen for the Capoluogo." Hardluck Reggio lost the *capoluogo* to Catanzaro anyway, and the promised center of industry never materialized.

wrecks is on display in the most famous of Reggio sights, the **Museo Nazionale.** Scavenger digs in Calabria and underwater hunts off the coast have yielded amazing booty. Amateur archaeologists will giggle with glee at the large display of pottery and Greek sundries on the 1st floor, including an extensive collection of *pinakes*, terracotta votive tablets showing scenes from mythology. The floor above the gallery contains a large coin collection and a 2300-year old novelty sarcophagus shaped like a large, sandaled foot. Those crazy Greeks.

The prize of the museum's collection is downstairs in the **Sezione Subacquea.** Slow down, it's not underwater, but its objects once were. Anchors, amphorae, and pictures of ancient wrecks adorn the cases in the Sezione. Among the underwater booty on show are the famed **Bronze di Riace** (Riace Bronzes), two lifelike bronze statues of muscular bathing beauties, found in 1972 by scuba divers off the coast of Riace, Calabria. Later identified as Greek originals (as opposed to Roman copies), the statues date back to the 5th century BC when the warriors were created to celebrate the victory of Marathon. *(P. de Nave, on C. Garibaldi toward the Stazione Lido. ☎0965 812 55. Open daily in summer 9am-11pm; in winter 9am-7pm. Closed 1st and 3rd Monday of the month. L8000.)*

BEACHES AND ENTERTAINMENT

As the day cools, Reggesi and their *gelato* intermingle along the **lungomare,** a long, narrow botanical garden stretching along the seaside. When they want to make like a nude bronze warrior and take a dip, pale travelers sprawl on the beach near **Lido Communale.** On summer nights, swimsuits are shed for chic club-gear, when the 2nd floor of the **Communale** becomes a groovy *discoteca*. There are more nightlife options outside Reggio, but wheels are a necessity. Calabrians finish the summer with the **Festival of the Madonna della Consolazione.** The four-day festival, celebrated in mid-September, concludes with an astonishing display of fireworks.

DAYTRIPS FROM REGGIO CALABRIA

GERACE

Trains (L9800) run to and from Locri on the coast. From the station, a bus (L1800) runs around every hour up to Gerace and back; check with the driver to find out when he'll stop by again.

Located amidst the rugged and arid beauty of the Calbrian backcountry, some call the well-preserved medieval town of Gerace "peaceful;" others more accurately call it a "ghost town." In an attempt to protect the historical center at the end of the last century, Gerace's regional government did a little spring cleaning; all public offices and agencies were moved to nearby **Locri,** leaving Gerace with nary a whisper of activity. There is a **Banca Carical** with an **ATM** and currency exchange in Largo Barlaam, downhill from the *duomo* on towards P. del Tocco. (Open M-F 8:20am-1:20pm and 2:35-3:35pm, Sa 8:20-11:50am.) The **post office** is in P. del Tocco. In **medical emergencies,** call the **Guardia Medica** (☎0964 39 91 11).

The bus from Locri drops passengers off uphill from the Duomo beside **Largo delle Tre Chiese,** a *piazza* enclosed by three churches. The **Chiesa di San Francesco** (to your left if you stand facing the Largo from the street) has a beautiful portal decorated in the Arabic-Norman style; inside is an elegant wooden altar fully decorated with exquisite black and white marble. Take a short walk up Gerace's pinnacle for the astounding view from **Castello di Roberto il Guiscardo.**

Down V. Caduti sul Lavoro from the bus stop, Gerace's immense **cathedral**—the largest in Calabria—occupies most of P. Duomo. Twenty-six Greek columns pilfered from Locri support the grand Romanesque interior. Highlights of the church are ancient Greek graffiti and Bishop Calceopulo's 16th-century tombstone.

SCILLA

You can access Scilla from Reggio by train (40min., 10 per day, L3100) or by bus (20min., 12 per day, L2500).

The Tyrrhenian coast winds 30km north of Reggio to Scilla, a gorgeous fishing village that doubles as a stunning beach resort. According to Homer, **Scilla** (the massive rock nearby), was the home of a ship-devouring monster with six heads, 12 feet, and an extremely short temper. That nasty beast no longer haunts the caves around Scilla; urban legend has it that she has been elected to the Italian Parliament. The placid blue waters, relaxing beach, and spectacular sunsets from behind the mountain are worth the trip. The Aeolian Islands also cause one of Scilla's meteorological oddities, called *Fata Morgana* by the locals. When the weather is just right (about 10 times a year), the sea air turns into the world's largest magnifying glass, making the Aeolians seem within walking distance.

Instead of trekking back to Reggio, consider spending the night at the seaside **Pensione Le Sirene,** V. Nazionale, 57, across from the train station. A clean, cozy haven with nine rooms, sandwiched between the station and the beach. (Breakfast included in summer. Reservations recommended during the summer. Oct.-May singles L40,000, doubles L70-75,000; June-Sept. singles L46,000, doubles L82,000.)

The cheapest meals around are served at the air-conditioned **Pizzeria San Francesco,** on V. Cristoforo Colombo along the beach near the central train station (pizza L5-10,000). This family-run restaurant has a second location on V. Umberto I, beneath the castle. If your eyes crave the panoramic sea view, dine on the cliff-side terraces of **Vertigine,** P. San Rocco, 14 (☎0965 75 40 15). Devour some specialty seafood as it gazes out to the water for a last glimpse of home. (*Primi* from L8000, *secondi* from L12,000. Drinks from L1500. Cover L3000, service 10%. Open daily noon-3pm and 7:30pm-midnight. V, MC.)

Though Scilla's greatest draw is its irresistable beach, the town itself has a couple of sites of historic interest. The **Castello Ruffo,** overlooking Scilla, has been used for over 25 centuries to govern the Straits of Messina and is now home to a military outpost and the town's lighthouse. Get there by heading downhill from P. San Rocco (or up the beach). Right next to the castello, the **Chiesa di Maria S. S. Immacolata** boasts a huge altar painting and 14 bronze sculptures of Christ.

TROPEA ☎0963

Little Tropea has, hands down, the nicest beach on the Tyrrhenian: turquoise water, a sheltered bay, cool rock formations, and absolutely no sea monsters. Unfortunately, everybody has figured this out, and between mid-July and early September, the town's population swells five-fold. If you want to avoid the dizzying high-season hotel prices, you can easily make Tropea a day trip.

TRANSPORTATION AND PRACTICAL INFORMATION. Trains (station open M-Sa 8:45-11:30am, 1:45-5:30pm) run from Reggio (1½hr., 10 per day 7:45am-11:17pm, L8200) and Cosenza (2.5hr., 5 per day 6:33am-7:06pm). Blue **minivans** *(pullmini)*, destined for 27 different zones around Tropea, pick up passengers on V. Stazione all summer, each van stopping every half-hour or so. The minivans are fantastic (and necessary) for access to the more remote beaches, *agriturismo* sites, or B&Bs. Rides cost L1000 per person. For exact stops, ask the English-speaking staff at the **Pro Loco tourist office** (☎0963 614 75), located down V. Stazione at P. Ercole. It has maps showing historical sites. **Banca Carime,** V. Stazione, has an **ATM.** (Open M-F 8:20am-1:20pm and 2:35-3:35pm.) In an **emergency,** call the **police** (☎0964 612 21) or the **Carabinieri** (☎112). For medical emergencies, call **Pronto Soccorso** (☎113). The **post office** is on C. Rigna. From V. Stagione take the far left street; it is on the corner. (Open M-Sa 8:15am-7pm.) **Postal Code:** 89861.

ACCOMMODATIONS AND FOOD. As long as you call ahead and make reservations, staying in Tropea need not be expensive, even during high season. One of the town's best deals is **Hibiscus Uno,** V. Carmine, 26. To get there, take the 1st paved right after the train station on V. Stazione down to the road out of town. Take that to the right in the Pizzo direction; the unmarked cement entrance is 3km down on the right. Each bungalow in the bird-filled garden is independent, with patio, kitchenette, bathroom (with shower), and airy rooms you could get lost in. (☎0963 60 33 42. Sept.-June L25,000 per person per night; July L40,000 per person; Aug. L50,000 per person. Prices decrease for stays longer than a week.) For camping closer to the sea, try the tree-shaded **Campeggio Marina dell'Isola,** below sandstone cliffs to the left of Santuaria di Santa Maria. (☎0963 619 70. L8,000 per person, L22,000 with car. Hot showers included and tents provided. V, MC.)

Tropea's sweet red onions are reputed to keep eaters thin and healthy. Delight in the delicious aroma of *rigatoni alla Tropea* at **Ristorante Tropea Vecchia,** on Largo Barone, a narrow corridor behind the fountain at the Pro Loco. **Bocconcino,** C. Emanuele, 29, serves tasty Calabrian rice balls for L2000 and calzones for L3000. For a snack on the beach, follow school children to the *alimentare* on V. Stazione in the center of town across from V. V. Veneto.

SIGHTS. The rocky outcropping outside town houses the **Santuaria di Santa Maria.** According to the sanctuary's museum, townsmen take the church's pink-clad *Madonna and Child* out to sea every August 15. (Open daily 2-8pm. Free.) Up the cliff is Tropea's graceful **Norman cathedral.** Besides some nice polychrome marble work and several dead sword-bearing Tropeans, the elegant interior houses two bombs that miraculously failed to destroy Tropea when an American warplane dropped them in 1943. To reach the **beach,** take a winding set of stairs down the cliffs at the end of V. Umberto (turn off V. Stazione to the left).

THE IONIAN COAST

The stupefying beaches that stretch from Reggio Calabria around the cape toward Metaponto in Basilicata are sparsely populated with Italian and German tourists and local Italian children who often make the daytrip to the water. Beaches offer both a cool dip in the Ionian Sea and a contrast to the mountains in the distance. If you desire only a strip of sand, consider taking the train from Reggio or Crotone and climbing off when the scenery becomes enticing. Here, the shores still echo with the names of Greek gods and mythical heroes. **Soverato** (130km from Reggio, L13,600) offers one of the most expansive, scenic, and popular strips, although the beaches at **Bovalino Marina, Palizzi,** and **Brancaleone** are closer and almost as agreeable. Since trains along the Ionian coast often have erratic schedules and multiple connections, allow ample time to reach your destination.

SICILY (SICILIA)

Without Sicily, Italy cannot be fully understood. It is here one finds the key to all things.
—J.W. von Goethe

With a history steeped in chaos, catastrophe, and conquering, it's no wonder that the island of Sicily possesses such passionate volatility. Greek, Roman, Arab, Norman, and Aragonese conquerors have transformed Sicily's landscape but never thwarted its independent spirit. The resulting cultural landscape mimics Sicily's physical extremes—Giuseppe Lampedusa, Sicily's prince-turned-writer, described his land as one "which knows no mean between sensuous sag and hellish drought." Dominated by craggy slopes, the island's few acres of arable land has been planted with olive, citrus, and almond groves. Sicily's position at the edge of the European geologic plate has resulted in a succession of seismic and volcanic catastrophes that have buried entire cities. Those not destroyed seem to have drawn strength from survival; Sicily's artistic and intellectual heritage ranges from Selinunte's stark, ancient grandeur to Noto's Baroque frivolity, from the logic of Pythagoras to the introspection of Pirandello. Sicilian pride is a testament to the city's resilience during centuries of occupation and destruction.

Plagued by the "tradition" of Mafia control, Sicilians are reclaiming their island. Demonstrations against the corruption draw thousands, but Sicilians bear the scars of this history, jealously clinging to *Cosa nostra* (see p. 568). Yet, Sicily speeds into its global future, as locals install condom machines near medieval cathedrals and raise petrochemical refineries next to Greek acropolises. Waves of immigrants arrive from North Africa each year, injecting new variety into an already vivid mosaic. Sicilians are welcoming of foreigners and eager to parade the land they adore. Women, however, should be aware that male attention in Sicily is often aggressive and unceasing, and those unequipped with Sicilian retorts are particularly susceptible. Cases of serious physical harassment are relatively rare, but, unfortunately, petty crime is rampant.

NORTHERN SICILY

PALERMO ☎091

Palermo moves at a speed that dispels any myths of a sleepy Sicily. In a bizarre, almost unholy, compromise, the city presents life as an amalgamation of old customs and modern industry. In the streets, horse-drawn carriages compete with Fiats and Alfa Romeos, and pious nuns hold their own against wantonly robed women. In this vibrant city, purples and crimsons at fruit stands clash with the colors in store fronts, and the blare of street-corner music kiosks drowns out the maniacal screech of scooters. The Phoenicians, Romans, and Byzantines all bedded down in Palermo, but the city didn't blossom until Saracen (831-1071) and Norman (1072-1194) rule. Modern times (and WWII military deals) gave Palermo's reins to the Mafia (see **Organized Crime,** p. 35). The 1993 election of a publicly anti-Mafia mayor, however, brought an end to the mob's knee-breaking control. Graffiti indicates that much of Palermo backs the mayor's efforts, and with political clean-up underway, the city is now restoring its architectural treasures.

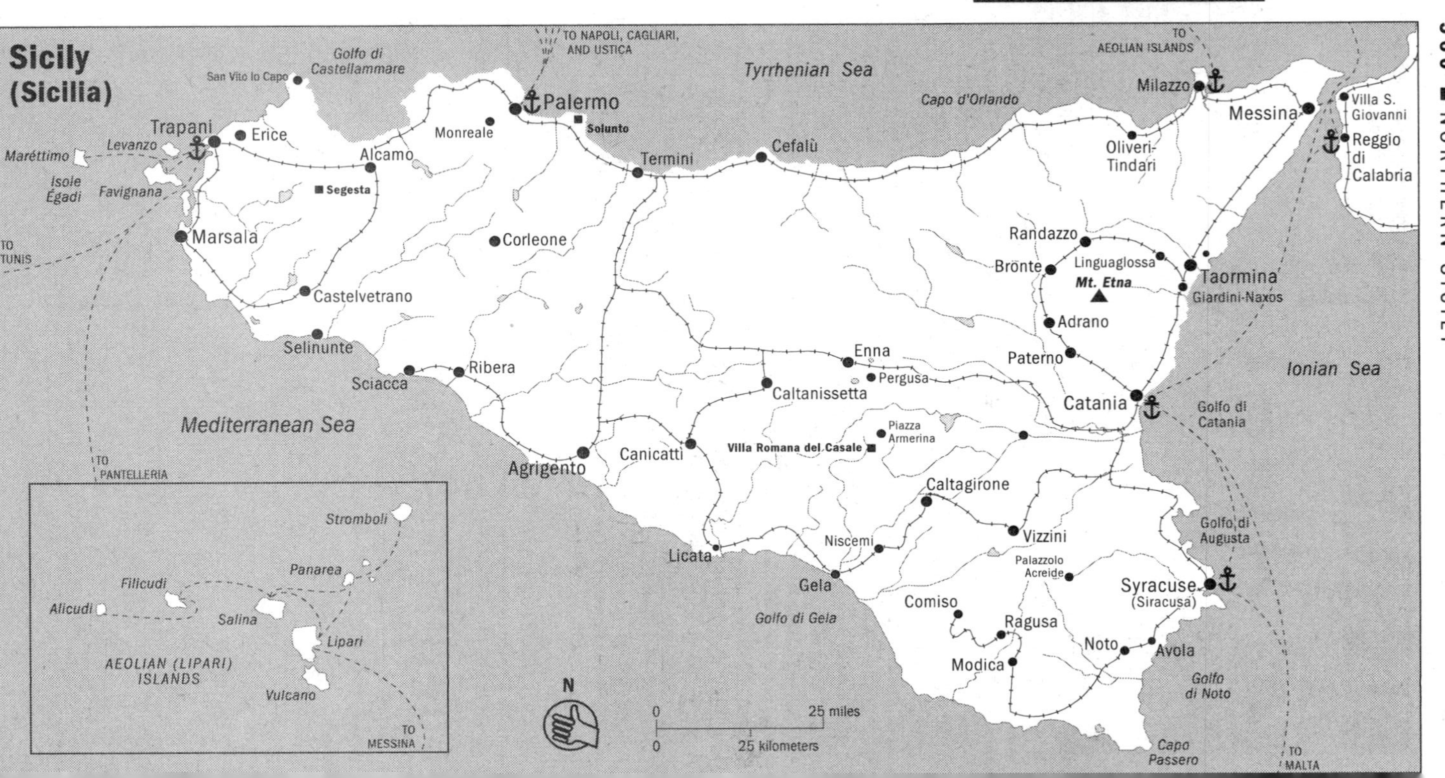
Sicily (Sicilia)
Tyrrhenian Sea
Ionian Sea
Mediterranean Sea
Golfo di Castellammare
Capo d'Orlando
Golfo di Catania
Golfo di Augusta
Golfo di Noto
Capo Passero
Golfo di Gela
TO AEOLIAN ISLANDS
TO NAPOLI, CAGLIARI, AND USTICA
TO MALTA
TO PANTELLERIA
TO TUNIS
Villa S. Giovanni
Reggio di Calabria
Messina
Milazzo
Oliveri-Tindari
Taormina
Giardini-Naxos
Linguaglossa
Mt. Etna
Randazzo
Bronte
Adrano
Paterno
Catania
Syracuse (Siracusa)
Avola
Noto
Palazzolo Acreide
Vizzini
Ragusa
Modica
Comiso
Caltagirone
Piazza Armerina
Villa Romana del Casale
Niscemi
Gela
Enna
Pergusa
Caltanissetta
Licata
Canicatti
Agrigento
Cefalù
Termini
Palermo
Solunto
Monreale
Corleone
Ribera
Sciacca
Alcamo
Segesta
Castelvetrano
Selinunte
San Vito lo Capo
Erice
Trapani
Marsala
Levanzo
Favignana
Marèttimo
Isole Égadi
N
0 25 miles
0 25 kilometers
Stromboli
Panarea
Filicudi
Alicudi
Salina
Lipari
Vulcano
AEOLIAN (LIPARI) ISLANDS
TO MESSINA

HIGHLIGHTS OF SICILY

VISIT Mt. Etna, Europe's tallest volcano, and Taormina, reconstructed from its hardened fury (p. 586).

STROLL on the ebony sands and volcanic leftovers of the **Aeolian Islands** (p. 599).

VENTURE back to BC—Agrigento's **Valle dei Tempii** is home to one of the world's best-preserved Greek temples (p. 615).

HAGGLE in Palermo's **Ballarò Markets** (p. 565), where cow tongue and tripe hang next to fuzzy slippers and gardening tools.

FROLIC in **Pantelleria's** natural saunas, away from tourist throngs (p. 626).

TRANSPORTATION

Flights: Punta Raisi/Falcone & Borsellino airport (domestic info ☎091 601 92 50; international info ☎091 702 01 11), 20min. from central Palermo. **Prestia & Comande** buses (☎091 58 04 57) run from P. Castelnuovo and the central station (every 30min. 5am until the last flight, L6500). Taxis charge at least L65,000.

Trains: Stazione Centrale, in P. Giulio Cesare—a grand old station at the start of Via Roma and V. Maqueda. To: **Termini** (30min., 12 per day 5:45am-5:45pm, L4500); **Cefalù** (1hr., 10 per day 7:05am-8:55pm, L7000); **Trapani** (2hr., 10 per day 7:30am-8:40am, L12,500); **Agrigento** (2hr., 9 per day 7:25am-8:30pm, L12,500); **Milazzo** (2½hr., every hr., L17,000); **Messina** (3hr., 7 per day, L19,500); **Catania** (4hr., 6 per day 5:57am-3:55pm, L20,500); **Rome** (11½hr., 4 per day, L71,000); **Firenze** (15hr., 6:58pm, L89,000); **Milan** (17½hr., 3 per day 11:20am-5pm, L91,600); **Torino** (22hr.; 11:20am, 1:35pm, and 2:33pm; L91,700). Ticket office open 6:45am-8:40pm. **Luggage Storage:** At track #7 on the right. L5000 per bag for 12hr. Open daily 6am-10pm.

Ferries and Hydrofoils:

Tirrenia (☎091 33 33 00), on the waterfront, off V. Francesco Crispi, within the port gates. Ferries to **Naples** (11hr.; 1 per day; armchair "*poltrona*" L68-77,000, cabin L99,000) and **Cagliari, Sardinia** (14hr.; armchair L60,500-78,000, cabin L107,000). Open M-F 8:30am-12:50pm and 2:30-8pm, Sa 2:30-8pm, Su 4:30-8pm.

Siremar, V. Francesco Crispi, 118 (☎091 690 25 55), on the last street before the waterfront, just in front of the port. Ferries to **Ustica** (2½hr., 1 per day, L19,000). From July-Aug. Siremar also runs hydrofoils (1¼hr., 1 per day, L31,000). Open 8:30am-1pm and 4-6:30pm.

SNAV (☎091 33 33 33), off V. Francesco Crispi, inside the port gates; the office is at the far end of Stazione Marittima. Runs hydrofoils twice a day to the Aeolian Islands. All hydrofoils stop in **Lipari** and **Vulcano;** check schedule for other islands. More erratic in winter.

Grimaldi Group (☎091 58 74 04), 100m before Tirrenia with the sea to your left. Ferries to **Livorno** (17hr.; Tu, Th, and Sa 11pm; armchair L103-161,000, June L135,000) and **Genoa** (20hr.; 6 per week M-Sa; armchair L123-181,000, June L155,000). Titanic ships have gyms and discos.

Buses: All 4 lines are along V. Balsamo, adjacent to the train station. With your back to the tracks, turn right; exit with McDonald's on your left, newspaper stands on your right, and unlikely ceiling frescoes above. V. Balsamo and its smorgasbord of bus companies are straight ahead. After purchasing tickets, ask exactly where your bus will be arriving and find out its logo—there is no order in busland.

Cuffaro, V. Balsamo, 13 (☎091 616 15 10), opposite Segesta. To: **Agrigento** (2hr.; M-Sa 7 per day, Su 3 per day; L13,000, round-trip L21,000).

Segesta, V. Balsamo, 14 (☎091 616 79 19), services **Alcamo** (1hr.; M-F 5 per day 11:30am-5pm, Sa 3 per day until 1:50pm; L8000); **Terrasini** (1hr., M-Sa 6 per day 6:30am-8pm, L4500); and **Trapani** (1½hr., M-Sa 18-25 per day 6am-9pm, L12,000). Sometimes uses buses confusingly marked "Sicilbus" or "Interbus."

SAIS Transporti, V. Balsamo, 16 (☎091 617 11 41). To: **Corleone** (1¼hr., 5 per day 6am-6pm, L6550); **Cefalù** (1¼hr., 3 per day 1-6:30pm, L9000); and **Rome** (14hr.; 1 per day 4:15pm; L75,000, students and seniors L65,000).

SAIS, V. Balsamo, 16 (☎091 616 60 28), on the right from the train station and just next door to SAIS Transporti. To: **Piazza Armerina** (1½hr., 6 per day, L18,500); **Pergusa** (2hr., 6 per day,

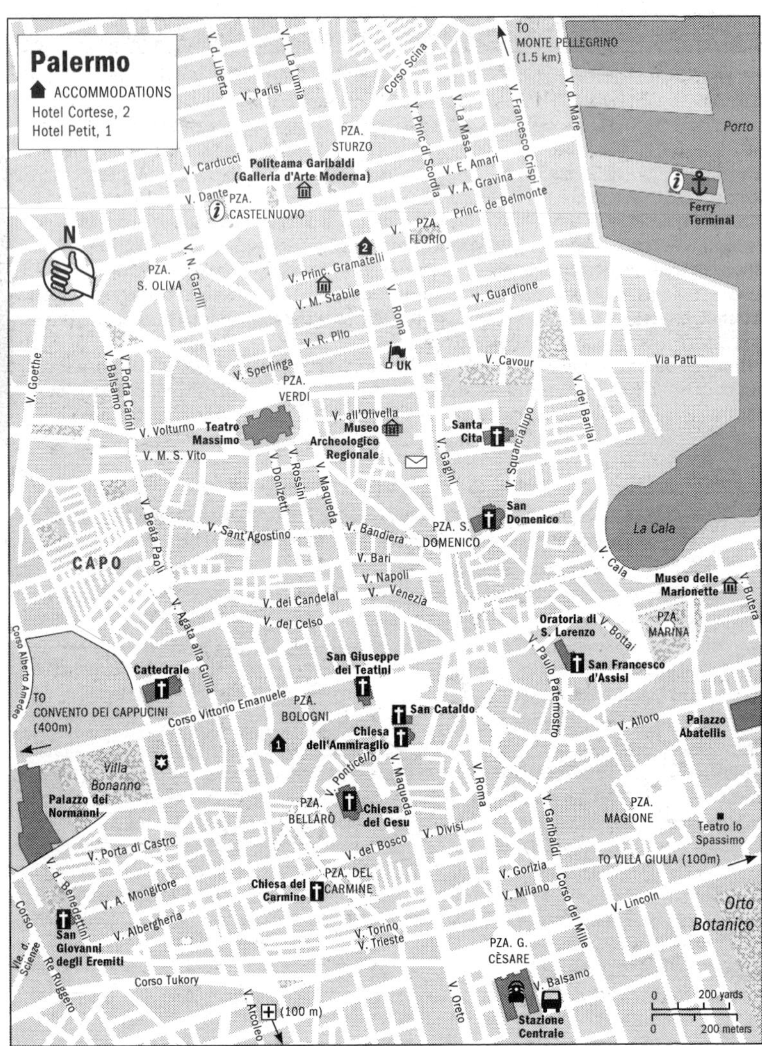

L16,500); **Catania** (2½hr., 17 per day, L22,500); **Messina** (3¼hr., 8 per day, L25,000); and the **Catania airport** (3¼hr., 8 per day, L22,500).

Public Transportation: Orange **city buses (AMAT).** Main terminal in front of the train station, under the dark green overhang. L1500 for 1hr., L5000 for 1 day. Buy tickets from *tabacchi* or the on-site mini offices. 17 **metropolitana** stations around the city are useful for getting to spots north or south of the **centro storico. Metro trains** to suburbs use normal train tracks. Catch trains at the central station. Tickets are the same as those for the bus. Ask at one of the mini offices or information booths for a combined metro and bus map.

Taxis: (☎091 22 54 55), in front of the central station next to the bus stop.

ORIENTATION AND PRACTICAL INFORMATION

'alermo and its crescent-shaped harbor lie at the end of the fertile **Conca d'Oro** Golden Conch) basin. To the north, Monte Pellegrino's 610m limestone mass sep-.rates the city from its beach at **Mondello.** Three major avenues run through cen-ral Palermo. From the station's main exit, **Via Roma** runs straight through the iistoric district to **Piazza Sturzo** at the western side of the city center. Parallel to V. :oma, to the left from the front of the station, **Via Maqueda** runs to the Teatro Aassimo and **Piazza Verdi,** where it becomes **Via Ruggero Settimo.** After 300m, it uns into **Piazza Castelnuovo** (which everyone calls **Politeama**), home to the tourist ffice and the **Politeama Theater.** It then doubles its width through the newer sec-ion of town as **Via della Libertà.** Perpendicular to V. Roma and V. Maqueda, **Corso 'ittorio Emanuele** runs from bus-frequented **Piazza Independenzia** to the sea, dividing he historic district in two equal halves.

Behind the imposing *palazzi* lining the main avenues lies a labyrinth of alleys nd *piazze.* These tiny, winding streets contrast with the grid of the modern quar-er to the west of **Via Cavour** and north of P. Verdi. The historic district is full of pen-air markets, foraging dogs, and streets that change name at will.

A CRASH COURSE IN SICILIAN STREET SMARTS. Palermo shuts down at night and its streets are poorly lit. Knowing where to go and how to get there is essential, especially after dark. When possible, stay on the main streets of V. Roma, V. Maqueda, or C. V. Emanuele—you may feel like the only pedestrian, but the stream of cars and scooters, which continues late into the night, is reassuring. The areas behind the train station and around the port are particularly sketchy after shops close in the evening. Daylight hours are safer, but still be cautious—don't carry cameras around your neck or wear flashy jewelry or watches; women should not carry purses slung sideways across the body.

OURIST, LOCAL, AND FINANCIAL SERVICES

Tourist Office: P. Castelnuovo, 34 (☎091 605 83 51 or 091 605 81 11), underneath the monster high-rise Banco di Sicilia and opposite Teatro Politeama. From the train station, take a bus to P. Politeama at the end of V. Maqueda. Cross the *piazza.* English spoken. Detailed maps and brochures on Palermo, Cefalù, and Monreale. Ask for the monthly *Agenda.* Lends bicycles to tourists for the day. Documents required. Open M-F 8:30am-2pm and 1:30-6pm, Sa 9am-2pm and 4-7pm, Su 9am-1pm. Hours change slightly with season. Two other **branches,** at the train station and at the airport, keep the same hours.

Budget Travel: CTS, V. Garzilli, 28g (☎091 32 57 52). Take V. Maqueda to P. Castelnuovo. From the *piazza,* continue on V. Libertà, and take the 1st right on V. Carducci. V. Garzilli is 2 blocks farther down. Harried but efficient staff. Open M-F 9am-1pm and 3:30-7pm, Sa 9am-1pm.

Consulates: UK, V. C. Cavour, 117 (☎091 32 64 12). **US,** V. Re Federico, 18 (☎091 611 00 20), off Vle. della Libertà. Take bus #28 from V. della Libertà. Emergencies only. Open M-F 8am-12:30pm and 3-5pm.

Currency Exchange: There are *cambios* at the central post office on V. Roma and in the train station. **Banca Nazionale del Lavoro,** V. Roma, 201, and **Banco di Sicilia,** on V. R. Settimo, are open M-F 8:20am-1:20pm. The **ATMs** on V. Roma and V. Maqueda often reject international cards; try for the newer, multicolored *Bankomat 3-plus.* **S. Angelo** (on left when facing the train station) is nice to foreign cards.

American Express Representative: G. Ruggieri and Figli Travel, V. E. Amari, 40 (☎091 58 71 44). From P. Castelnuovo (Politeama), follow V. E. Amari toward the water. Cashes traveler's checks only for card holders. Ask for the red city map "Palermo in your pocket." Open M-F 9am-1pm and 4-7pm, Sa 9am-1pm.

Bookstore: Feltrinelli, V. Maqueda, 395 (☎091 58 77 85), a few blocks before Teatro Massimo from the train station. A selection of classics and mysteries in English occupies two sides of the 2nd floor "foreign titles" island. Open M-Sa 9am-8pm. **Mondadori,** on the corner of V. Roma and P. S. Domenico, adjacent to a department store, offers 3 shelves of mystery, romance, and sci-fi.

Gay and Lesbian Resource Center: ARCI-GAY and **ARCI-Lesbica,** V. Genova, 7 (☎091 33 56 88), off V. Roma. Info on events. Open M, W, and F 5-7:30pm.

EMERGENCY AND COMMUNICATIONS

Emergencies: Carabinieri ☎112. **First Aid:** (☎118 or 091 666 22 07), in Ospedale Civico. **Hospital: Policlinico Universitario,** V. del Vespro (☎091 655 11 11), or **Ospedale Civico** (☎091 666 11 11 or 091 606 11 11), on V. Lazzaro near the train station.

Late-Night Pharmacy: Lo Cascio, V. Roma, 1 (☎091 616 21 17), near the train station; look for the green cross. Open daily 4:30pm until other pharmacies open in the morning. Another branch at the corner of V. Maqueola and V. Stabile at the other end of town. **Di Naro,** V. Roma, 207 (☎091 58 58 69), on the right after C. V. Emanuele. Open M-F 24hr. except from 1-4pm, Sa-Su 8pm-morning.

Internet Access: Informatica Commerciale, V. Notarbartolo, 24 (☎091 34 36 46). Walk down V. Libertà from P. Politeama/Castelnuovo and turn left past the English Gardens. 3 computers with speedy connections. L10,000 per hr. Open M-F 9:30am-1pm and 4-7:30pm, Sa 9:30am-1pm. **Candelai** (see **Entertainment,** p. 569) connects you for L8000 per hr. Open F-Sa 8pm-late.

Post Office: V. Roma, 322 (☎091 160 or 091 695 91 11), at the end of V. Roma closest to Teatro Massimo. From the sidewalk: No, this mammoth-columned monstrosity is *not* a courthouse; it's a post office. Inside: No, this enormous marble half-cylinder is *not* an aircraft hanger; it's a post office. Avoid late afternoon pay check pandemonium and pleas for *"silencio!"* at all costs. Open M-Sa 8:15am-7:30pm. **Postal Code:** 90100.

ACCOMMODATIONS AND CAMPING

Finding a cheap place to stay is a breeze, but among the old *alberghi* lining **V. Roma** and **V. Maqueda,** the quality of accommodations fluctuates with no relation to price. Always ask to see a room before accepting. After dark, women should avoid the eastern part of town by the train station and all streets along the port.

Hotel Regina, C. V. Emanuele, 316 (☎091 611 42 16), in the middle of everything, several meters from Quatrocanti, at the intersection of V. Maqueda and C. V. Emanuele. Carved bureaus, ornate tables, light pine, and a wandering gray kitty make the rooms of this *albergo* feel like home–though your windows at home don't look onto Chiesa dei Teatini. Family-run; English-speaking daughter on morning duty runs an in-house tourist bureau. Small courtyard helps filter out the street noise. Free use of kitchen. 7 singles L30,000, with bath L45,000; doubles L60,000, with bath L80,000.

Petit Hotel, V. Principe di Belmonte, 84 (☎091 32 36 16). From the train station, take V. Roma and keep on truckin' (1½km). Turn left 6 blocks after crossing V. Cavour, or catch any bus from the train station headed for P. Politeama, and jump off a few streets after crossing C. V. Emanuele. A safe, animated neighborhood with Palermo's poshest cafes. The passé wallpaper and paisley sheets make the rooms cozy. Singles (1 available) L35,000; doubles with bath L65,000; triples with bath L90,000. AmEx.

Albergo Piccadilly, V. Roma, 72 (☎091 617 03 76), just 200m from the central station. High class in tonal creams and sunny yellows with snazzy gauze curtains. Is this Paris or Palermo? Stratospheric ceilings with balconies over bustling V. Roma. Singles L45,000, with bath L60,000; doubles L70,000, with bath L85,000.

Hotel Cortese, V. Scarparelli, 16 (☎091 33 17 22; email hotelcortese@Tiscalinet.it; www.paginegialle.it/htcortese). From the train station, walk 10min. down V. Maqueda to V. dell'Università; look for the yellow sign to your left (alternative entrance on Corso V. Emanuele is better for night arrivals; same yellow sign 200m to the left). Direc access to the Ballarò market. Small communal terrace overlooks the city's rooftops. Brady Bunch eating area with flaming orange diner booths on the 2nd floor. 19th-century Parisian scenes decorate the wallpapered rooms, giving the place that certain *je ne sais quoi.* Breakfast L5000. Singles L35,000, with shower L45,000; doubles L60,000, with shower L75,000. V, MC, AmEx.

Hotel Ariston, V. M. Stabile, 139 (☎091 33 24 34). Take V. Roma 4 blocks past V. Cavour, or take bus #122 and get off before V. Amari. Bright, modern rooms recently visited by an Asian minimalist motif fairy. All rooms with bath and TV, 6 floors above a small courtyard. Singles L55,000; doubles L80,000.

Camping: Campeggio dell'Ulivi, V. Pegaso, 25 (☎/fax 091 53 30 21), 35min. outside Palermo. Take bus #101 from Palermo's central station to P. de Gasperi; then take bus #628 to V. Sferracavallo. Walk downhill a block and turn right on V. dei Manderini just after the post office. The campground is on the right. Neurotically clean facilities. L9000 per person, tent included. Bungalows available. Hot showers free.

FOOD

Palermo is famous for its *spaghetti ai broccoli affogati alla palermitana* (with spicy fried broccoli), *pasta con le sarde* (with sardines and fennel), and *rigatoni alla palermitana* (with meat and peas). *Arancini* (fried balls filled with rice, spinach, or meat) and *panini con panelle* (fried balls of chick pea flour sliced and sandwiched) are also rich Sicilian delicacies. Try the popular swordfish *(pesce spada)*. Palermitans claim to have invented their own *cassata* (a sweet ricotta pastry), discovered *paste con gelo di melone* (pastries with watermelon-paste filling), and perfected *gelato.*

STANDA supermarket has outlets at: V. della Libertà, 30 (☎091 33 16 21); in the northern end of town at V. R. Settimo, 18/22 (☎091 58 60 19); and at V. Roma, 59 (☎091 616 90 43). All three are open M 4-8pm, Tu and Th-Su 9am-1pm and 4-8pm, W 9am-1pm. Three huge open-air **markets** provide a taste of daily life in Palermo. With groceries for half the store prices, **Ballarò,** a left off V. Maqueda a few blocks from the train station, **Vucciria,** between P. San Domenico and C. V. Emanuele, and **Capo,** near Teatro Massimo, offer serious budget shopping. (All open M-Sa all day. On Saturday morning the markets are chaotic.) The well-lit streets in the newer part of town near Teatro Politeama are home to the best restaurants.

Lo Sparviero, V. Sperlinga, 23 (☎091 33 11 63), 1 block over towards P. Politeama from the Teatro Massimo. Trust the friendly staff for suggestions on the *pasta del giorno.* The *pesce fumicato miste* (smoked fish appetizer) is a meal in itself. Pizza L6000, *primi* and *secondi* from L10,000. Open F-W 11am-2pm and 7:30-midnight.

Il Mirto e la Rosa, V. Principe di Granatelli, 30 (☎091 32 43 53). Upscale vegetarian fare amid cathedral-like arches and thirty-something Palermitans. The huge *primi* (from L8000) are great bargains. Try *fettuccine al profumo d'estate* (in an aromatic sauce of tomatoes, pine nuts, peppers, garlic, and basil). *Secondi* from L8000. 52 different pizzas from L8000. Lunch *menù* L10-14,000. Open 12:30-3pm and 8-11pm.

Pizzeria Bellini, P. Bellini, 6 (☎091 616 56 91), to the left of P. Pretoria and in the shadow of retired Teatro Bellini. Outdoor umbrella-shaded dining. One of Palermo's more romantic spots. Outstanding brick-oven pizzas from L6000 (take-out for picnics), *primi* from L10,000. Cover L2000. Open Tu-Su 6am-1am. V, MC.

Trattoria da "Massimo," behind Pizzeria Bellini. Rock bottom budget eatin' with *primi* and *secondi* from L2000. Plastic spill protectors cover red tablecloths. Two attentive, scurrying young waiters serve *pane* in silver bread bowls. Easily Palermo's most inexpensive full-blown meal: *primi, secondi, contorno,* and drink for L13,000. Cover L2000.

Hostaria al Duar, V. Ammiraglio Gravina, 31 (☎0347 473 57 44), off V. Roma, 3 blocks north towards the port. Sicilian and North African dishes share the menu. Couscous L8000. Immense *primi* from L8000, *secondi* from L12,000. Cover L2000. Service 10%. Open Tu-Su noon-3:30pm and 7pm-midnight.

Osteria Lo Bianco, V. E. Amari, 104 (☎091 58 58 16), off V. Roma. Delicious food and Sicilian good luck charms keep this 93-year-old restaurant going strong. Calamari L10,000. *Primi* from L6000, *secondi* L9-10,000. Open M-Sa noon-3pm and 7-11pm.

Renna Self-Service, V. Principe di Granatelli, 29 (☎091 58 06 61). Cafeteria-style stainless steel buffet and school-day trays. Fun crayola-green molded plastic seats swing out from under the tables on metal arms. Spotlessly clean, bustling, and popular for its good solid Italian food. Monster salads L4000. *Primi* from L4000, *secondi* from L6000. Open M-Su noon-2:30pm and 7-10pm. V, MC.

SIGHTS

Ancient glory, seven centuries of neglect, and heavy WWII bombing have made Palermo a city of splendor and deterioration, where the beauty of the past hides behind the face of urban blight. The bizarre sight of Palermo's half-crumbled, soot-blackened 16th-century *palazzi* startles visitors accustomed to the cleaner historic districts of northern Italy. For much of the 20th century, corrupt politicians and Mafia activity diverted funds and attention from the dilapidated landmarks. In the past several years, however, cleaning and rebuilding efforts have slowly begun to reopen structures like the magnificent Teatro Massimo.

MONREALE. Palermo's greatest treasure isn't in Palermo at all. Only 8km southwest of the city, **Monreale's cathedral** houses the mother of all mosaics, 6340 square meters of gold and colored glass that draw a hushed "*mamma mia*" from Italians and tourists alike. The massive **Christ Pantocrator** (Ruler of All) presides over 130 panels depicting the Old and New Testaments. To read this visual Bible, start at the logical beginning—Creation—in the upper right corner as you face the altar. The top level of panels shows Genesis—look for Eve rising from Adam's side just left of a window above the great doors in the rear. The middle level shows Old Testament scenes, and the bottom panels deal with the life of Christ. The lava-stone **tesoro** (treasury), off the transept, sits in one of Italy's most raucously Rococo chapels. *(Bus #389 leaves from Palermo's P. Indipendenza for Monreale's P. V. Emanuele (15min., 3 per hr., L1500). To get to P. Indipendenza take bus #109 or 118 from Palermo's Stazione Centrale. Tourist info (☎091 656 45 70) is to the left of the church. Modest dress required. Cathedral open daily 8am-noon and 3:30-6pm. Treasury L4000.)*

Outside, an Arab-style inlay adorns the wall behind the apse and the **Conca d'Oro** lies below. Around the church, the **cloister** is renowned for the 228 unique columns that support the colonnade. Considered the richest collection of Sicilian sculpture in the world, the capitals pack more styles than a Parisian runway, including Greco-Roman, Saracen, Norman, Romanesque, and Gothic. In the corner by the lesser colonnade and its fountain, a capital shows William II offering the Cathedral of Monreale to the Virgin. The **roof** offers a view of the central apse. A sign indicates the access from inside the cathedral. Two doors down from the cloister is the entrance to a series of quiet **gardens** that survey Palermo. *(Cloister open M-Sa 9am-1pm and 3-6:30pm, Su 9am-12:30pm. L4000. Roof access L3000.)*

CAPPELLA PALATINA. Housed in the **Palazzo dei Normanni,** this private chapel of the Norman kings displays their famous tolerance in its fusion of Latin, Byzantine, and Arab styles. Artists summoned from Constantinople created the min[illegible] Monreale, covering every glittering inch with gold and glass. The fantastic carved wooden ceiling (with Arabic words and eight-pointed stars) and the geometric designs along the walls and on the floor are the result of local Arab handiwork. Receive the red-carpet treatment one floor above in the **Sala di Ruggero** (King Roger's Hall). Navy blue suited guards lead small groups through four lavishly decorated rooms, covered with oil portraits (watch for the young woman in the 2nd room), pure glass (and therefore drooping) chandeliers, a domed mosaic hall, and gold, gold, gold. *(Follow C. V. Emanuele all the way up to Palazzo dei Normanni; enter through a small door on the left outside the fence. Palazzo open M and F-Sa 9am-noon except when Parliament is in session. Chapel open M-Sa 9-11:45am and 3-4:45pm.)*

CAPPUCHIN CATACOMBS. These morbid chambers are only for the strong of stomach; they may prove too gruesome for some. The Cappuchin friars propped 8000 bodies against the walls of an underground labyrinth over the course of three and a half centuries. The skeletons range from cleanly-polished bones to decomposing, sneering corpses, but all are dressed in their moth-eaten Sunday best and sorted by sex and profession. The virgins get a room of their own (don't ask how they know). A baby girl still looks alive; she was preserved during WWI by a desperate mother who wanted her soldier-husband to see their only child. Several bishops and the painter Velázquez also inhabit these corridors. *(Take bus #109 or 318 from Stazione Centrale to P. Indipendenza. From there hop on #327 to the catacombs. P. Cappuccini. ☎091 21 21 77. Open M-Su 9am-noon and 3-5:30pm. L2500.)*

THEATERS. Constructed between 1875 and 1897 in a robust Neoclassical style, the **Teatro Massimo** is the largest indoor stage in Europe after the Paris Opera House. After undergoing foot-dragging renovation since 1974, the theater opened in grand Sicilian style with trumpets and confetti for its 100th birthday in 1997. The word on the street is that the 23-year restoration was not a question of artistry but of Mafia feuding. Cleaned, polished, and shined, the columned exterior has now regained its light sand castle-colored appearance, and the interior its former gleam. It was here that Francis Ford Coppola shot the climactic opera scene of The Godfather Part III. Amidst the brilliant gold and rich velvet are the workings of superior acoustic engineering: a whisper from the center of the opulent rotunda echoes loudly. Performances are very accesible and run year-round. *(Across V. Maqueda from the Museo Archeologico, 500m up V. Maqueda from the Quattro Canti intersection with C. V. Emanuele. Toll free ☎800 65 58 58; box office ☎091 605 35 15. Open Tu-Su 10am-4pm for 20min. tours in English, French, and German.)*

A new arrival to Palermo's cultural scene is the **Lo Spasimo theater.** Once a convent and church of the same name, the renovated structure hosts numerous plays, concerts, and art shows. *(Off V. Abramo Lincoln, to the left toward the port, within the walls of the old city. ☎091 616 14 86. Open daily 7am-midnight.)*

PALERMO'S CATHEDRAL. Constructed from the 13th to 18th centuries, the cathedral has a crazed jumble of turrets, domes, arches, and belfries. The cold interior is less spectacular, although the zodiacal signs carved into the floor may strike your astrological fancy. Note the Qu'ranic inscription on the 1st left column before the entrance; in 1185 the Palermitan archbishop chose to plunk his cathedral down on top of a mosque, and this column was part of its stonework. The chapels on the left contain six royal tombs (four canopied and two set in the wall) of Norman kings and Hohenstaufen emperors from the 12th to 14th centuries. The *cattedrale* is connected by flying buttresses to the former archbishop's palace (1460), more massive and opulent than the church itself. *(On C. V. Emanuele. Open M-F 7am-7pm, Sa-Su 4-7pm. Treasury, crypts, and sarcophagi L3000.)*

QUATTRO CANTI AND THE FOUNTAIN OF SHAME. About 630m down V. Maqueda from the train station, the intersection of V. Maqueda and C. V. Emanuele forms the soot-blackened **Quattro Canti** (the four corners). Each sculpted angle of this little 17th-century *piazza* celebrates either a season, a king of once-ruling Spain, or one of the city's patron saints. All appear to look down upon the vehicular chaos with polite disdain. **Piazza Pretoria,** next door, houses the oversized **Fontana della Vergogna** (Fountain of Shame) under **Teatro Bellini.** The statue-bedecked fountain was given its name by irate churchgoers who didn't like staring at mythological monsters and nude figures as they left **Chiesa di San Giuseppe dei Teatini** (1612), across the street (a dismal gray facade disguises a marble-infused Baroque interior). An even more shameful story explains its inappropriate size—the Fountain of Shame was not intended for the small *piazza* it now inhabits. In the early 16th century a rich Florentine commissioned the fountain for his villa, sending a son to the Carrara marble quarries to ensure its safe delivery. The son, in need of some quick cash, shipped it to Palermo and sold the fountain to the city senate. Restoration begun in 1999 is scheduled to finish by 2001.

LA FAMIGLIA Pin-striped suits, machine guns, and *The Godfather* are a far cry from the reality of the **Sicilian Mafia.** The Mafia system has its roots in the *latifondi* (agricultural estates) of rural Sicily, where land managers and salaried militiamen protected their turf and people. Powerful because people owed them favors, strong because they supported one another, and feared because they did not hesitate to kill offenders, they were the founders of a tradition that has dominated Sicilian life since the late 19th century. Since the mid-80s, the Italian government has worked to curtail Mafia influence. Today, Sicilians shy away from any Mafia discussion, referring to the system as *Cosa Nostra* (our thing). For more info see **Organized Crime,** p. 35.

MUSEO ARCHEOLOGICO REGIONALE. The archaeological museum's collection isn't as staggering as others in Sicily and Calabria, but it has two high points: a large section of the Punic Temple of Himera, whose grinning lion heads stick out their tongues in celebration of a victory over Greece, and the Greek *Ram of Syracuse* (3rd century BC), renowned for its realism. *(P. Olivella, 4. Head away from the train station on V. Roma, and turn left on V. Bara all'Olivella. ☎091 662 02 20. Open M, Th, and Sa 9am-1:45pm, Tu-W and F 9am-1:45pm and 3-6:30pm, Su and holidays 9am-1:15pm. L8000.)*

PALAZZO ABATELLIS. Signs in P. Marina point toward this 15th-century *palazzo* (1495), which houses one of Sicily's superb art museums, the **Galleria Regionale della Sicilia.** Upstairs, an entire room is devoted to Sicily's Antonello da Messina (1430-1479). *(V. Alloro, 4. From P. G. Cesare in front of the train station, take V. Abramo Lincoln, then go left for 2 blocks on V. N. Cervello. ☎091 16 50 74. Open M, W, and F-Sa 9am-1:30pm, Tu and Th 9am-1:30pm and 3-5:30pm, Su and holidays 9am-12:30pm. L8000.)*

CHIESA DEL GESÙ (CASA PROFESSA). Via Ponticello winds through a crowded neighborhood to this church colloquially called Il Gesù (1363-1564) and crowned by a green mosaic dome. Stucco conceals a dazzling multicolored marble interior and an almost Surrealist depiction of the Last Judgment. The courtyard shows the effects of WWII bombing. Next to Il Gesù, the **Quartiere dell'Albergheria** droops with shattered buildings and bomb-blackened facades. *(On V. Ponticello, across V. Maqueda. Open daily 7-11:30am.)*

OTHER CHURCHES. The famous **Santa Maria dell'Ammiraglio** ("La Martorana") was built for an admiral of the Norman king Roger II. The Byzantine mosaics inside are the 12th-century equivalent of celebrity photos: Roger I stands with Jesus, and Admiral George admires the Mother of God. *(P. Bellini, a few steps from P. Pretoria. Open M-F 9:30am-1pm, Su 8:30am-1pm.)* Next door lies the **Chiesa di San Cataldo** (1154), whose red domes and arches give it the appearance of a mosque. *(Open M-F 9:30am-1pm, Su 8:30am-1pm.)* Perhaps the most romantic spot in Palermo, the garden and cloister of the **Chiesa di San Giovanni degli Eremiti** (St. John of the Hermits) comes complete with fanciful bulbous pink domes designed by Arab architects. Gazebos and little fountains dot this vine-wreathed paradise. *(V. dei Benedettini, 3. Walk west from the train station on C. Tukory to Porta Montalto, and hang a right. Open M-F 9am-1pm and 3-7pm, Su 9am-12:30pm. L4000.)*

PUPPETS. The **Museo Internazionale delle Marionette** offers a playful glimpse of Sicilian culture. A showcase of Sicilian puppetry is complemented by puppets from India, England, and the Congo; let your inner child free in the Construct Your Own Puppet Room. *(V. Butera, 1. Follow signs from P. Marina. ☎091 32 80 60. Open M-F 9am-1pm. L5000, students L3000. Demonstrations on request.)* Catch an authentic Palermo puppet show at Vincenzo Argenti's **Opera dei Pupi.** Three-foot tall armored puppets wail away at each other, fight dragons, behead saracens and such, re-enacting scenes from the chivalric romance of Orlando Furioso. All in a day's work for a Palermitan puppet. *(V. Pietro Novelli, 1, opposite the duomo. http://digilander.iol.it/aregntopupi. Shows daily at 6pm. Tickets L15,000.)*

ENGLISH GARDENS AND PALERMITAN SHADE. Down wide Vle. Libertà in the new city, **Giardino Inglese,** filled with royal palms, fig trees, banyans, and lots of shade, serves as a daily hangout for newspaper-readers and a nice lunch spot. Toward the sea on C. V. Emanuele, the smaller **Giardino Garibaldi** is similarly woodsy, but not as shady. Along Foro Umberto I, at the portside intersection of V. Abramo Lincoln, lies **Villa Giulia,** with a garden that harbors a little something for everyone, including band shells, playgrounds, sculpture, flower gardens, and monuments. *(Garden open 9am-1pm. Free.)*

ANCIENT ARAB AQUEDUCTS. Cooperative Sociale Solidarietè directs its attention in the opposite direction—downwards. Their guide service leads tours into Palermo's ancient Arab aqueducts, which run beneath the city and around the entire province. All necessary equipment is provided. *(☎091 652 39 19; fax 091 652 00 67. Visits 5 days a week. L15,000, ages 11 and 18 years L10,000. Children under 11 not permitted.)*

SICILY

BEACHES AND ENTERTAINMENT

As part of Palermo's recent tourism push, the city has established **Mondello Lido** as a free tourist-reserved beach. All registered *alberghi* and hotels in the city will be happy to strip a ticket from the thick book and slap on their own special stamp. Tickets are good for the day and must be shown at the beach entrance. From Teatro Politeama, take bus #806 to the beach. The stop is near "Charleston."

Palermo packs buses every weekend to seaside **Mondello,** a long beach by day and a playground of clubs and bars by night. **Addaura** entertains the young jet-set. (To get to Addaura, take bus #833 from P. Castelnuovo. To reach Mondello, take bus #101 or 107 from *stazione centrale* to De Gasperi and then #614, 615, or 677.)

Palermo's nightlife centers around bars that are hard to find and even harder to stagger home from. For more information on cultural events and nightlife, pick up a copy of *Un Mese a Palermo,* a monthly brochure available at any APT office, or the far-from-redundant *News-News.* **Fuso Orario,** in P. Olivella, and **Champagneria,** a block from the Teatro Massimo, form the nucleus of the mob of young Palermitani that floods the street opposite Teatro Massimo every weekend night.

Candelai, V. Candelai, 65, tends to pick up around midnight. It's got one of central Palermo's few dance floors, with live, mainstream rock. The place is usually packed, so arrive early if you want some time on Candelai's three net-connected computers. (☎091 32 71 51. L8000 per hr. Open F-Su 8pm-late.) **Exit** (☎0347 800 74 88 or 0348 781 46 98), in P. San Francesco di Paola up V. Aragona from P. Verdi, has outdoor tables that serve a friendly, exclusively gay clientele.

Finish the night crooning Italian vocals in the quiet *piazza* at **Havana's** outdoor tables (☎091 320 608), in P. S. Onofrio. Follow tiny Vicolo dei Fiovenchi off V. Maqueda, just opposite the intersection of V. Maqueda and V. Bari. The crowd is older and more sedate than those in many of Palermo's other bars.

DAYTRIPS FROM PALERMO

CORLEONE

Bus connections by SAIS Transport (1¼hr., 5 per day 6am-6pm, L6550).

The Godfather anyone? The only tourists making it out this way are on the trail of the Mafia. A hot one-hour bus ride inland from Palermo, sleepy Corleone doesn't let on to be the one-time home of the "boss of all bosses," Salvatore Riina. (Until his 1993 arrest, Riina had been living in the small town for more than 24 years, during which he was the most wanted man in Italy.) With a tiny tourist office in the **public gardens** (open M-Sa 4-8pm) and a few colorful publications, Corleone is still trying to shake its name and its indelible connotations. Although it's out of sight—like anything Mafia related—let your imagination wander. Have a *gelato* and muse about every man you pass in snazzy pants and Italian leather shoes.

OTHER DAYTRIPS

Monte Pellegrino, an isolated mass of limestone rising from the sea, is Palermo's principal natural landmark, separating the city from the beach at Mondello. Near its peak, the **Santuario di Santa Rosalia** marks the site where Rosalia, a young Norman princess, sought ascetic seclusion. When her bones were brought to Palermo in 1624, they ended a raging plague. The present sanctuary stands over the cave where Rosalia performed her ablutions; its trickling waters are said to have miraculous powers. The summit of Monte Pellegrino (a 30min. climb from the sanctuary) offers a gorgeous view of Palermo, Conca d'Oro, the Aeolian Islands, and Mount Etna. *(Take bus #812 from P. Castelnuovo.)*

The volcanic island of **Ustica** lies 36 miles off the coast, within reach of Palermo. Settled first by the Phoenicians, then by pirates and exiled convicts, it features prime snorkeling and grotto exploration. **Siremar** runs ferries and hydrofoils to Ustica (see **Ferries,** p. 563).

CEFALÙ ☎0921

The Sicilian proverb "good wine comes in small bottles" captures the power of Cefalù. Its beaches, pleasant streets, and diverse architecture were featured on screens throughout world in the Academy Award-winning film *Cinema Paradiso.* Unfortunately, hotels fill up during the summer, and the prospects of finding an inexpensive *pensione* are fairly dismal even in the off-season. Don't leave without getting a look at Antonello da Messina's masterpiece, the smug *Portrait of an Unidentified Man.*

TRANSPORTATION

Trains: Station open M-Su 6:45am-8:50pm. From P. Garibaldi and the old city, take V. Matteotti to the V. Roma intersection. Cross straight ahead onto V. A. Moro and turn right to the station at its end. To: **Palermo** (1hr., 32 per day, L7000); **Milazzo** (2hr., 9:57am, L11,500); **Messina** (2½hr., 7 per day, L14,500); and **S. Agata di Militello** (50min., 6 per day, L7000).

Buses: SPISA buses from the train station and from P. Colombo on the waterfront run to all 26 local towns for L2000. Scan the 6-foot yellow monster list on the bar window at the train station or stop by the tourist office to check out destinations.

Taxis: Kefautoservizi (☎0921 42 25 54), in P. Stazione or near P. Colombo.

ORIENTATION AND PRACTICAL INFORMATION

Via Aldo Moro leads to town from the station. At the 1st large intersection, **Via Roma** leads to the left and back into Cefalù's modern quarter. To reach the **old city,** continue on V. A. Moro, which turns first into **Via Matteotti** and then, at **Piazza Garibaldi** (where the old city begins), into **Corso Ruggero.**

Tourist Office: C. Ruggero, 77 (☎0921 42 10 50; fax 0921 42 23 86), in the old city. Well-supplied English-speaking staff in an impressively renovated office with comfy black cushioned chairs. Open M-F 8am-2:30pm and 3:30-7pm, Sa 9am-1pm.

Currency Exchange: Banca S. Angelo (☎0921 42 39 22), near the station at the corner of V. Giglio and V. Roma. Open M-F 8:30am-1:30pm and 2:45-3:45pm. For 24hr. access, try the **ATM** at the **Banca di Sicilia** (☎0921 42 11 03), in P. Garibaldi.

Emergency: Carabinieri: ☎112. **Vigili Urbani:** ☎0921 42 01 04. **Hospital:** V. A. Moro (☎0921 92 01 11), right by the train station in the new city. **First Aid:** ☎0921 42 45 44. **Guardia Medica:** V. Roma, 15 (☎0921 42 36 23), in a modern yellow building in the new city, behind an iron fence. Open M-Su 8pm-8am.

Pharmacies: Dr. V. Battaglia, V. Roma, 13 (☎0921 42 17 89), in the new city. Open M-F 9am-1pm and 4-8pm, Sa-Su 9am-1pm and 4:30-8:30pm. **Cirincione,** C. Ruggero, 144 (☎0921 42 12 09). Open M-F 9am-1pm and 4-8pm, Sa-Su 4:30-11pm. Call ahead in Aug.

Internet Access: Kefaonline, P. S. Francesco, 1 (☎0921 923 09), behind a parking area in P. S. Francesco, where V. Umberto meets V. Mazzini. The local service provider has 3 net-connected computers. L10,000 per hr. Open M-Sa 9:30am-1pm and 3:30-7:30pm. **Bacco On-Line,** C. Ruggero, 36, just up from the tourist office. Would you like red, white, or rosé with your surf time? Deceptively just another well-stocked wine shop, Bacco hides 2 IBM computers in the back. L5000 per 30min. Open 9am-midnight.

Post Office: V. Vazzana, 2 (☎0921 92 17 03), in a modern concrete building on the right off the *lungomare,* 2 long blocks down from P. Colombo. Open M-Sa 8:10am-6:30pm. **Postal Code:** 90015.

SICILY

ACCOMMODATIONS AND CAMPING

Pensione La Giara, V. Veterani, 40 (☎0921 42 15 62; fax 0921 42 25 18), off C. Ruggero, near the *duomo.* Small, quiet rooms with balconies and simple furnishings smack in the center of the old city. Rooftop terrace offers a gorgeous view and peaceful outdoor dining. Good restaurant downstairs. The owner knows all there is to know about Cefalù's history. Half-pension required in Aug. Singles L44-74,000; doubles with breakfast L42-78,000 per person. V, MC, AmEx.

Cangelosi Rosaria, V. Umberto I, 26 (☎0921 42 15 91), up towards the new city from P. Garibaldi. This private home is *the* budget spot. 4 bedrooms branch off grandma's dining room. Separate male/female bathrooms just across the hall. Reserve ahead. Only 1 single available. June-Sept. single L35,000; doubles L70,000. Oct.-May single L25,000; doubles L60,000.

Camping: Costa Ponente (☎0921 42 00 85), 3km west at Contrada Ogliastrillo. It's a 45min. walk or a short ride on the Cefalù-Lascari bus (L2000) from P. Colombo. Swimming pool and tennis court. July-Aug. L9500 per person, L8-10,000 per tent. Sept.-June L8500 per person, L6500-9000 per tent.

FOOD

Affordable restaurants are packed on C. Ruggero and V. V. Emanuele. The views from the *lungomare*'s many *pizzerie* are as stunning as their prices. You can pick up basics at the **STANDA supermarket,** on V. Vazzana near the post office. (☎0921 42 45 00. Open daily 8:30am-1pm and 5-8:30pm.) Cefalù also has a huge **SIGMA supermarket,** at V. Roma, 61. (Open daily 8am-1pm and 4:30-8pm.)

L'Arca di Noé, V. Vazzana, 8 (☎0921 92 18 73), across from the post office under a blue and white striped awning. Twenty-something cell-phone toting, stand-up-cappucino crowd at the bar, with a more sedate crowd in the cluster of stained hardwood booths. Outdoor seating available. Try one of 9 different *risotti* (from L2000) or the spaghetti with mushrooms and saffron. *Primi* from L5000, *secondi* from L8000. Open M-F 6am-5am, Sa-Su 24hr. V, MC, AmEx.

Trattoria la Botte, V. Veterani, 6 (☎0921 42 43 15). Follow C. Ruggero past the *duomo* into the old city. It's the 2nd to the last left, 20m from Pensione La Giara. Ah, romance. The sun sets and the candles come out. Small wooden tables set out on the cobblestones of narrow V. Veterani. Attentive family service. Leather-bound menus. Laundry a flight overhead. *Primi* from L6000. Cover L2000. Open 7-11pm.

L'Antica Corte, Cortele Pepe, 7, or C. Ruggero, 193 (☎0921 42 32 28), 200m past the *duomo.* Dine on seafood dishes in the courtyard or A/C interior. Pizza L6-12,000 in the evening. *Primi* from L8000. Open daily noon-3pm and 7pm-midnight. V, MC, AmEx.

Pasticceria Pietro Serio, V. G. Giglio, 29 (☎0921 42 22 93), the 1st left from the train station, just off V. Roma. This sleek cafe offers a huge assortment of pastries and a freezer with 30 flavors of *gelato*. Their model marzipan *duomo* is an astounding culinary construction. Open Sept.-July Th-Tu 7am-1pm and 3-10pm; Aug. Th-Tu 7am-10pm.

SIGHTS AND BEACHES

Cefalù has always been a defensive city, and its paranoia is visible in its architecture. Invading troops were forced to walk single-file through the narrow alleys that connect courtyard to courtyard.

DUOMO. After building this riot-proof cathedral, King Roger II claimed the most spiritual of motives, calling it the result of an 1131 bargain with God during a shipwreck. Caught in a terrific sea storm while sailing from Salerno to Reggio, he promised to build a temple to his Savior once safely back on land. One can't help thinking that little touches like the crenellated towers or the protected firing positions were not exactly what God had in mind. Cefalù's skilled Arab craftsmen made their mark on the cathedral they helped build, giving its arches an elegant horseshoe shape. Inside, Arab, Norman, and Byzantine artistic cooperation attest to the remarkable religious diversity of the Norman period. The *duomo*'s greatest work, however, is a Byzantine mosaic of **Christ Pantocrator,** or Ruler of All, swimming in the bowl of the apse. *(Open daily 8:30am-noon and 3:30-6:30pm. Modest dress required—a woman's shoulders must be covered, or she'll be handed a shawl.)*

MUSEO MANDRALISCA. No real organizing principle pervades throughout this museum, the private collection of Baron Mandralisca. The good Baron's interests ran from ancient and not-so-ancient coinage to stuffed peacocks with proud plumage. The most famous pieces are a Greek vase showing a tuna vendor and Antonello da Massina's exquisite *Ritratto di un Ignato* (Portait of an Unknown Man). Don't be deceived by the glossy tourist office posters; bring binoculars to see the tiny portrait, roped off in the middle of its own camera-survelienced exhibit room. Pay no mind to its bizarre nouveau-modern wood block presentation either. On the same floor there's an open exhibit "restoration in progress"; sprawling de-framed Renaissance oils lean against the walls, waiting patiently, square by square, to be brought back to life. *(V. Mandralisca, 13, opposite the duomo. ☎0921 42 15 47. Open 9:30am-12:30pm and 4-6pm. L5000, students L2000.)*

ROCCA. According to the house of worship sitting atop this cliff, the town's name derives from the Greek *kephaloidion* (head). For a bird's-eye view, make the half-hour trip by way of the Salita Saraceni, which begins near P. Garibaldi off C. Ruggero. From P. Garibaldi, enter between Banca di Sicilia and the stout fountain. Follow the brown signs for *pedonale Rocca.* The path of slippery volcanic rock is flanked by ping-pong paddle shaped cacti; be careful when it's wet. On the mountain, embattled walls, crumbling cisterns, and a row of ovens from the Middle Ages mark the way to the **Tempio di Diana** (Temple of Diana; 4 BC). The nimble huntress's temple, surrounded by pines and overlooking the city and the sea, was used first as a place of sea worship and later as a defensive outpost. Morning is the best time for pictures, when the direction of the sun does not dull the vivid colors of the city below. Gates close one hour before sunset.

BEACHES. Cefalù's most attractive beaches, **Spiaggia Mazzaforno** and **Spiaggia Settefrati,** lie west of town on SPISA's Cefalù-Lascari bus line. Popular **Spiagga Attrezzata** lies just off the *lungomare.* Crowded for good reason, Attrezzata has white sand, gradual turquoise shallows, and free showers. It's a site of toddler pandemonium on summer Sundays. At the beach in Cefalù, seven stones protrude from the waves. Legend has it that seven brothers died here while trying to save their sister from pirates.

STICKS AND STONES MAY BREAK MY BONES, BUT WHIPS AND CHAINS EXCITE ME As the home of the mythical giant Gargantua, Cefalù has a history of monstrous associations. Perhaps this is why the noted English occultist and sadist Aleister Crowley (rhymes with "holy") chose to found his new "abbey" (nicknamed Thelema) here in 1920. "Do what thou wilt shall be the whole of the law" was the motto of Crowley and his followers. It was in Cefalù that the "magician," or the "Purple Sacerdote," as he liked to be called, practiced his particular flavor of sexual occultism. "All [sexual] acts are allowed, if they injure not others; approved, if they injure not self," he proclaimed from Cefalù.

When one of Crowley's students died in the 1920s, his widow claimed that her husband's death was caused by drinking cat's blood during a Black Mass in Thelema. Suffice it to say, Crowley and his followers were expelled from Italy in 1923. Thelema is known among students of the occult for the grotesque, demonic frescoes that cover its walls. Though the site is closed for the moment, the regional department of Cultural Resources promises to restore and reopen the abbey soon.

DAYTRIP FROM CEFALÙ: THE RUINS OF TYNDARIS

With erratic bus service, Tindari is best reached by train, though even that trip can be difficult on weekends. Take the train to Oliveri-Tindari and hike 40 minutes uphill. Take the 1st right from the station, and bear left under the highway and right past a grove of lemon trees. When you come to a green gate, turn left (following the white arrows). Finally, bear right when the path forks.

Seventy-five kilometers east of Cefalù and 15km west of Milazzo lies **Tindari,** site of the ruins of Tyndaris. Dating from the 4th century BC, the Greek settlement was founded on a hill as a fortification against enemy attacks. Tyndaris chose its allies well, siding with Rome in the Punic Wars and supplying ships for the expedition that razed Carthage in 146 BC. Even a Roman alliance could not save the city from Mother Nature; an earthquake caused massive destruction in AD 365, and the Arabs mopped up the remains in 836. Unearthed in the mid-1900s, the area now offers an archaeological museum, olive groves, and views of the Aeolian Islands.

The first man-made intrusion on the hill to the ancient site is the **Santuario di Tindari,** erected less than 30 years ago for the **Madonna Nera** (Black Madonna). Local legend has it that a statue of this eastern Madonna washed up on the shores of Tindari hundreds of years ago, and the current sanctuary stands on the site where the first church in her name once stood. *(Santuario ☎0941 36 90 03. Open M-F 11am-12:30pm and 2:30-4pm, Su 2:30-4pm.)* Across from the entrance to the sanctuary, a path leads to the heart of the ruins, including the **basilica,** or *ginnasio*, and **agora.** The **theater,** cut into the hill 125m farther down, provides an impressive view of the surrounding seascape. The **tourist office,** P. Marconi, 11, in Patti, has information on performances of **Greek drama** in the ancient theater. (☎0941 24 11 54. Open daily 8:30am-1pm and 4-7pm. The **museum** adjacent to the theater has artifacts from the site and drawings portraying life in the ancient town. In front of the museum lies the main street, the **decumanus.** Follow it to the right as you exit the museum. It curves past the basilica and leads to **Casa Romana,** an old Roman house with intricate mosaics. All around the site are bits of the city's walls, and the original city gate is en route to the *santuario*. *(Ruins open daily 9am-1hr. before sunset.)*

EASTERN SICILY

MESSINA ☎090

Messina is a transportation hub, and its breakneck pace makes it feel like one. Better air-conditioning and a duty-free shop would turn this fast-paced town into an airport. The hubbub lets up only on the weekends, when the Messinese loll on neighboring beaches. Strangely, Messina's history is marked by disaster rather than glorious victory. The Carthaginians first razed the site in the 4th century BC. Thereafter, legions of conquerors, from the Mamertines to the Normans to Richard the Lion-Heart, followed. Under Norman rule, Messina blossomed as a crusader port, and for 600 years it proudly sat as a bastion of civilization. After the 17th century, however, the economy dried up as the gods frowned upon the land: the city was devastated by the plague in 1743, demolished by an earthquake in 1783, bombarded from the sea in 1848, struck with cholera in 1854, slammed with earthquakes again in 1894 and 1908, and flattened by both Allied and Axis bombs during WWII. *Terremotto* (earthquake) is probably the most frequently uttered word within the city's boundaries. The earthquake of 1908 shaped the city skyline with low-to-the-ground buildings. Churches in Messina are the most spectacular structures. The *duomo*, with its gorgeous artwork, is a must-see, while the clock tower, with a gallery of moving figures, may be the world's most allegorical timepiece.

TRANSPORTATION

Trains: Central station (☎090 67 97 95 or info 147 88 80 88), on P. della Repubblica. To: **Taormina** (1hr., 12 per day, L5500); **Palermo** (3½hr., 16 per day, L19,500); **Syracuse** (3hr., 12 per day, L16,000); **Naples** (4½hr., 4 per day, L38,500); and **Rome** (9hr., 4 per day, L53,000; pay a *supplemento rapido* to arrive in 7½hr., 7:20am). Trains to most destinations stop in **Milazzo,** the main port of the Aeolian Islands (45min., L4500). **Luggage Storage:** L5000 for 12hr. Open daily 6am-10pm.

Buses: Messina has 4 parallel and overlapping bus carriers.

SAIS, P. della Repubblica, 6 (☎090 77 19 14). The ticket office is behind the trees, across from the far left tip of the train station. To: **Catania** (1½hr., 10 per day, L12,000); **Palermo** (1½hr., 8 per day, L24,000); the **airport** (3hr., 5 per day, L13,500).

Interbus (☎090 66 17 54), has blue offices left of train station, beyond the line of buses. To **Giardini Naxos** (1½hr., 18 per day, L5000); and **Taormina** (1½hr., 13 per day, L5000).

Giantabus, V. Terranova, 8 (☎090 67 37 82 or 090 67 57 49), in the town center. To **Milazzo:** from their V. Terranova office (45min.; M-Sa 14 per day, Su 1 per day; L5000); from the Catania airport (Apr.-Sept. 4pm, L20,000).

AST (☎090 66 22 44, ask for "informazioni"), is the province's largest carrier; their *biglietteria* is in an orange minibus across P. Duomo from the cathedral. They service all destinations including smaller and less-touristed areas all over Southern Italy and Sicily.

Ferries: NGI (☎0335 842 77 85) and **Meridiano** (☎0347 910 01 19) are under the 1st pair of big yellow cranes on the waterfront, 300m from the FS railroad/hydrofoil station. Both send ferries to **Reggio. NGI:** (40min., 12 per day, L1000). **Meridiano:** (40min.; 12 per day, 7 on Su; L1000).

Hydrofoils: From its waterfront wing of the central rail station, Messina Marittima, **FS** sends hydrofoils to **Reggio** (20min., 14 per day, L5000) and **Villa S. Giovanni** (30min., 3 per hr., L1800). **SNAV** (ticket office ☎0903 640 44; fax 0909 28 76 42), has offices in a squat blue building on the waterfront side of C. V. Emanuele, 2km north of the train station off C. Garibaldi. Hydrofoils to: **Lipari** (40min., 6 per day, L32,000); **Salina** (1¼hr., 4 per day, L37,000); **Panarea** (1¾hr., 3 per day, L37,000); and **Aeolian Islands** (2hr., 3-6 per day for each destination from June-Sept.).

Public Transportation: Orange **ATM** buses leave either from P. della Repubblica or from the bus station, located under a modern gray parking garage on V. Primo Settembre, 2 blocks from the train station. Purchase tickets (L1200, one day pass L3500) at any

tabacchi or newsstand. Detailed bus info on yellow-bordered signs outside the *autostazione*. Note that bus #79, stopping at the *duomo,* museum, and aquarium, can only be taken from P. della Repubblica.

Taxis: Taxi Jolli (☎090 65 05), to the right of the *duomo* when facing its entrance.

ORIENTATION AND PRACTICAL INFORMATION

Messina's transportation center is **Piazza della Repubblica,** in front of the train station, home to the tourist office and headquarters for several bus lines. Along the waterfront perpendicular to the station runs the boat dock. **Via G. la Farina** runs directly in front of the train station; beyond the highrises to the left, **Via Tommaso Cannizzaro** leads to the center of town, meeting palm tree-lined **Viale S. Martino** at **Piazza Cairoli.** Enter P. della Repubblica from the train station and at the far right end begins **Via Primo Settembre,** which intersects **Corso Garibaldi.** Corso Garibaldi runs along the harbor to both the hydrofoil dock and C. Cavour.

> **SAFETY FIRST.** Women should **not** walk alone in Messina at night, and no one should roam the streets near the train station or the harbor after 10pm. Stay near the more populated streets around the *duomo* and the university. Be wary of pickpockets and purse-snatchers, and keep money in a secure place.

TOURIST AND FINANCIAL SERVICES

Tourist Office: Azienda Autonoma Per L'Incremento Turistico (AAPIT), V. Calabria, 301 (☎090 640 22). With your back to central train station, take a left to P. della Repubblica; the office is on the right corner. This well-staffed office offers a deluge of maps and helpful information on Messina, the Aeolian Islands, and even Reggio Calabria. Pick up a map, and ask nicely for a mini Italian grammar guide. Go with questions; leave with answers. English spoken. Open M-Sa 8:30am-6:30pm.

Currency Exchange: Cambio/Ufficio Informazioni (☎090 67 52 34 or 090 67 52 35), just inside the train station. Good rates and information on trains and buses. There are **ATMs** just outside the train station, to the right.

Bookstore: Libreria Nunnari e Sfameri, V. Cannizzaro, 116 (☎090 71 04 69), has 4 shelves of English classics. Open M-Sa 8:30am-1pm and 4pm-8pm.

EMERGENCY AND COMMUNICATIONS

Emergencies: (☎113). **Police:** (☎113). **Carabinieri:** (☎112). **Hospital: Ospedale Policlinico Universitario** (☎090 22 11), V. C. Valeria. **First Aid:** (☎118). **Guardia Medica:** (☎090 22 21).

Late-Night Pharmacy: There is a pharmacy on V. S. Martino; take V. del Vespro 3 blocks up from the station. All pharmacies open M-F 8:30am-1pm and 4:30-8pm. After normal hours, they rotate weekly. Call ☎090 71 75 89 for info. Weekly schedule and late-night locations posted on all pharmacy windows.

Post Office: (☎0906 68 64 15), on P. Antonello, off C. Cavour and across from Galleria. Open M-F 8:10am-5:30pm, Sa 8:30am-1pm. **Postal Code:** 98100.

ACCOMMODATIONS

Messina continues to be a fly-by, and not a stop-over, on the travel itinerary. The handful of hotels the city does possess cater not to cost-minded travelers, but to businessmen with deep pockets. Messina's cheaper hostels tend to be in a shadier neighborhood near the train station; be extremely careful during the evening.

Hotel Mirage, V. N. Scotto, 3 (☎090 293 88 44). Turn left from the train station, pass the buses, and continue under the *autostrata* bridge onto V. Scotto. Mission-style simplicity in tall-windowed, airy rooms. Lockout midnight. Singles L40,000, with bath and TV L65,000; doubles L70,000, with bath and TV L90,000. V, MC.

Hotel Touring, V. N. Scotto, 17 (☎090 293 88 51), near Hotel Mirage. Marxists beware—bourgeois decor and cleanliness rule here. Mirrors and faux marble-lined halls lead to veneered rooms. Midnight curfew. Singles L40,000, with bath and TV L70,000; doubles L70,000, with bath and TV L110,000; triples 90,000, with bath and TV L135,000.

FOOD

Ristorante and *trattorie* cluster in the area around V. Risorgimento, reached by following V. Cannizzaro two blocks past P. Cairoli. Messina is hooked on swordfish, whether baked, fried, or stewed *(pesce stocco)*. Creative chefs stuff eggplants and mix *caponata* (fried eggplant, onion, capers, and olives in a red sauce), producing sensual and nourishing feasts. The sinfully rich *cannoli* and sugary *pignolata* will fix any sweet tooth. The **STANDA supermarket,** P. Cairoli, 222, in the center of town, is a great place to stock up on the basics. (☎090 292 77 38. Open M-Sa 9am-8pm.) Fresh fruit and vegetables are cheaper and readily available on nearly every street. Messina may be large, but restaurants and nightlife are only beginning to flourish, as students continue to flock outside the town for clubbing.

Osteria del Campanile, V. Loggia dei Mercanti, 9 (☎090 71 14 18), behind the *duomo*. Look for the row of street lamps. Locals flock to the elegant old dining room for *linguini all'inferno marina* and a menu that changes daily. Hearty pizzas (from L4000) served at night. *Menù* L22,000. Open noon-2pm and 7pm-midnight. V, MC, AmEx.

Osteria Etnea, V. A. Martino, 38 (☎090 67 29 60), off V. Porta Imperiale and near the university. Always trust the cops to know where to eat. Tapestry tablecloths, signature dishes, brass-knobbed chairs, and all the *carabinieri* in town. Dine inside or streetside under sprawling white umbrellas. Excellent wine selection. *Primi* from L6000. Cover and bread L3000. Open noon-4:00pm and 8:30-midnight.

Pizza e Coca, V. C. Battisti, 45 (☎090 67 36 69). Take V. Primo Settembre 1 block down from the *duomo*. Upscale Italian fast food. The *calamari* (L6000) are especially good and the *bruschetta* (L2000) especially cheap. Open daily 9am-3pm and 5pm-midnight.

SIGHTS

Messina has watched most monuments built over its long history crumble to the ground. It is a city undergoing a constant face-lift; many sights have only recently shed their scaffolding.

PIAZZA DEL DUOMO. Despite the fast-paced life of Messina, the wide-open spaces and large flagstones of the Piazza del Duomo provide much relief. It contains the 12th-century *duomo* and the **Chiesa di SS. Annunziata dei Catalani.** The cathedral's stark exterior features an ornate portal portraying the Archangel Gabriel and Madonna with saints. The interior sports multihued marble layering and Byzantine figures arching over altars. The **clock tower** built in 1933 at the order of Archbishop Paino displays man's arduous ascension from a base being to a noble creature. It also displays the **time of day.** The structure features an astrological wheel, a menagerie of animals, several biblical scenes, and Messina's legendary female heroes. At noon, a grand spectacle takes place as a creaky recording of Schubert's *Ave Maria* booms and the gigantic lion lets out a mechanical roar. Below the clock tower, mythology and local lore meet in stone at the **Fontana di Orione** (1547). Michelangelo was supposed to build the fountain, but 1547 turned out to be a very lazy year for the great master. When he didn't show up in Sicily, his pupil Angelo Montorsoli built the landmark. The **duomo** houses the terrifying *Il Tesoro*. These silver arms and bronze hands once held bits of bones and small bottles of blood from medieval saints and religious figures. *(Duomo open daily 8am-6:30pm. Guided English tours of Il Tesoro L3000.)*

ALPS ASPEN

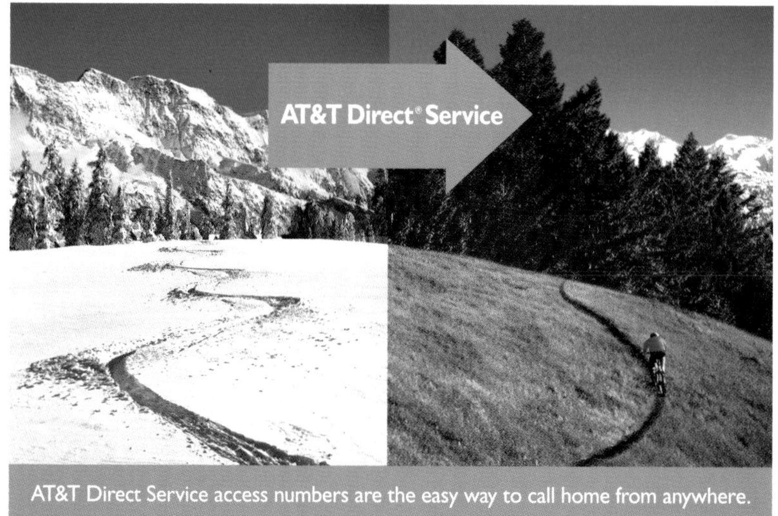

Global connection with the AT&T Network | AT&T direct service

www.att.com/traveler

AT&T Direct® Service

The easy way to call home from anywhere.

AT&T Access Numbers

Austria● 0800-200-288	France........0800-99-00-11
Belarus× ....8◆800-101	Gambia● 00111
Belgium● 0-800-100-10	Germany 0800-2255-288
Bosnia▲ 00-800-0010	Ghana 0191
Bulgaria▲ 00-800-0010	Gibraltar 8800
Cyprus● 080-900-10	Greece● 00-800-1311
Czech Rep. ▲00-42-000-101	Hungary● 06-800-01111
Denmark 8001-0010	Iceland● 800-9001
Egypt●(Cairo)‡....510-0200	Ireland ✓......1-800-550-000
Finland● 0800-110-015	Israel 1-800-94-94-949

AT&T Direct® Service

The easy way to call home from anywhere.

AT&T Access Numbers

Austria● 0800-200-288	France........0800-99-00-11
Belarus× ....8◆800-101	Gambia● 00111
Belgium● 0-800-100-10	Germany 0800-2255-288
Bosnia▲ 00-800-0010	Ghana 0191
Bulgaria▲ 00-800-0010	Gibraltar 8800
Cyprus● 080-900-10	Greece● 00-800-1311
Czech Rep. ▲00-42-000-101	Hungary● 06-800-01111
Denmark 8001-0010	Iceland● 800-9001
Egypt●(Cairo)‡....510-0200	Ireland ✓......1-800-550-000
Finland● 0800-110-015	Israel 1-800-94-94-949

The best way to keep in touch when you're traveling overseas is with **AT&T Direct® Service**. It's the easy way to call your loved ones back home from just about anywhere in the world. Just cut out the wallet guide below and use it wherever your travels take you.

For a list of AT&T Access Numbers, tear out the attached wallet guide.

Italy ● 172-1011	**Russia (Moscow) ◗▲●755-5042**
Luxembourg ✚ ..800-2-0111	**(St. Petersbg.)◗▲● ..325-5042**
Macedonia ● ..99-800-4288	**Slovakia ▲ ..00-42-100-101**
Malta.......... 0800-890-110	**South Africa ..0800-99-0123**
Monaco ● 800-90-288	**Spain 900-99-00-11**
Morocco........002-11-0011	**Sweden 020-799-111**
Netherlands ● ...0800-022-9111	**Switzerland ● 0800-89-0011**
Norway 800-190-11	**Turkey ● 00-800-12277**
Poland ▲● ..00-800-111-1111	**Ukraine ▲ ....8◆100-11**
Portugal ▲ 800-800-128	U.A. Emirates ● 800-121
Romania ●......01-800-4288	**U.K. 0800-89-0011**

FOR EASY CALLING WORLDWIDE

1. Just dial the AT&T Access Number for the country you are calling from. *2.* Dial the phone number you're calling. *3.* Dial your card number.

For access numbers not listed ask any operator for **AT&T Direct®** Service.

In the U.S. call 1-800-331-1140 for a wallet guide listing all worldwide AT&T Access Numbers.

Visit our Web site at: **www.att.com/traveler**

Bold-faced countries permit country-to-country calling outside the U.S.

- ● Public phones require coin or card deposit to place call.
- ▲ May not be available from every phone/payphone.
- ✚ Public phones and select hotels.
- ◆ Await second dial tone.
- ◗ Additional charges apply when calling from outside the city.
- † Outside of Cairo, dial "02" first.
- ✖ Not available from public phones or all areas.
- ✔ Use U.K. access number in N. Ireland.

When placing an international call ***from*** the U.S., dial 1 800 CALL ATT.

EMEA

© 8/00 AT&T

Italy ● 172-1011	**Russia (Moscow) ◗▲●755-5042**
Luxembourg ✚ ..800-2-0111	**(St. Petersbg.)◗▲● ..325-5042**
Macedonia ● ..99-800-4288	**Slovakia ▲ ..00-42-100-101**
Malta.......... 0800-890-110	**South Africa ..0800-99-0123**
Monaco ● 800-90-288	**Spain 900-99-00-11**
Morocco........002-11-0011	**Sweden 020-799-111**
Netherlands ● ...0800-022-9111	**Switzerland ● 0800-89-0011**
Norway 800-190-11	**Turkey ● 00-800-12277**
Poland ▲● ..00-800-111-1111	**Ukraine ▲ ....8◆100-11**
Portugal ▲ 800-800-128	U.A. Emirates ● 800-121
Romania ●......01-800-4288	**U.K. 0800-89-0011**

FOR EASY CALLING WORLDWIDE

1. Just dial the AT&T Access Number for the country you are calling from. *2.* Dial the phone number you're calling. *3.* Dial your card number.

For access numbers not listed ask any operator for **AT&T Direct®** Service.

In the U.S. call 1-800-331-1140 for a wallet guide listing all worldwide AT&T Access Numbers.

Visit our Web site at: **www.att.com/traveler**

Bold-faced countries permit country-to-country calling outside the U.S.

- ● Public phones require coin or card deposit to place call.
- ▲ May not be available from every phone/payphone.
- ✚ Public phones and select hotels.
- ◆ Await second dial tone.
- ◗ Additional charges apply when calling from outside the city.
- † Outside of Cairo, dial "02" first.
- ✖ Not available from public phones or all areas.
- ✔ Use U.K. access number in N. Ireland.

When placing an international call ***from*** the U.S., dial 1 800 CALL ATT.

EMEA

© 8/00 AT&T

MUSEO REGIONALE. Founded in 1806 from five private collections, the Museo Regionale was adopted in 1904 by the state as a repository for the furnishings, valuables, and artwork recovered from various churches and civic buildings after the 1894 earthquake. The museum is crowded with pieces depicting the Madonna and child and houses a collection of Renaissance and Baroque masterpieces. Among the most notable are *The Polyptych of the Rosary* (1473) by local boy-made-good Antonello da Messina, Andrea della Robbia's terra-cotta of the *Virgin and Child*, and Caravaggio's life-size *Adoration of the Shepherds* (1608) and *Resurrection of Lazarus* (1609). *(Just down from the hydrofoil port on V. della Libertà. Take bus #8 from the station or P. Duomo to P. Museo. ☎090 36 12 92. Open Oct.-May M, W, and F 9am-1:30pm, Tu, Th, and Sa 9am-1:30pm and 3-5:30pm, Su 9am-12:30pm; June-Sept. M, W, and F 9am-1:30pm, Tu, Th, and Sa 9am-1:30pm and 4-6:30pm, Su 9am-12:30pm. L8000.)*

LAGE GRANDE AND CAPO PELORO. The route traveled by bus #8 through the ramshackle fishing villages along Messina's periphery provides great scenery at a slower pace. Get off at "Lago Grande," where restaurants and bars surround a long saltwater lake. After Lago Grande, the bus continues seaward to Capo Peloro, which has a spectacular view of the Tyrrhenian and Ionian seas in addition to multiple whirlpools. The bus schedule changes seasonally; check with the driver for return times. *(Buses depart from in front of the train station. L1200, all-day pass L3500.)*

FESTIVALS

Visiting **Montalto,** or other hillside churches, is one way to gain a lovely view of the harbor and mainland. On June 3 the churches flaunt their riches and their religiosity with a **festival** honoring the Madonna della Lettera. Messina fills with sightseers and 150,000 white-robed pilgrims during the nationally-celebrated **Ferragosto Messinese** festival (Aug. 13-15). During the 1st two days of Ferragosto, two huge human effigies—one Arab and one Catholic—and a giant camel are motored around the city in the *Processione dei Gianti* (Procession of the Giants).

TAORMINA ☎0942

According to legend, Neptune wrecked a Greek boat off the eastern coast of Sicily in the 8th century BC, and only one soul survived to climb ashore. He was so inspired by the spectacular scenery that he founded a city. Taormina (Tauromenium, as it was then called) was born. Historians, however, tell a different tale: the Carthaginians founded Tauromenium at the turn of the 4th century BC, only to have it wrested away by the Greek tyrant Dionysius. Regardless of its origin, Taormina is a city of unsurpassed beauty—mansions, pines, and flowers crown a cliff above the sea. Disoriented fanny-packed foreigners, hearty backpackers, and elite VIPs all come for what millions of photographic flashes and hyperbolic statements can't seem to dull: a panorama dizzily sweeping from boiling Etna to the straights of Messina. Through the dense ranks of family *trattorie*, glossy postcard stands, and chic shops, the cliffside tourist destination retains its Sicilian charm.

TRANSPORTATION

Taormina is accessible by **bus** from Messina or Catania. Although **trains** from Catania and Messina are more frequent, the train station lies far from Taormina. Buses run from the station to Taormina (every 20min. 7:35am-11:40pm) and Giardini-Naxos (M-Sa 7:10am-1:10am, Su 9:10am-1:10am).

Trains: (☎0942 510 26 or 0942 515 11), at the bottom of the hill, halfway between Taormina and Giardini-Naxos. To: **Catania** (45min., 29 per day 1:20am-9:36pm, L5500); **Messina** (50min., 35 per day 4am-11:25pm, L5500); and **Syracuse** (2hr., 16 per day 4:12am-9:36pm, L12,500).

Buses: Interbus (☎0942 621 79). To: **Messina** (M-F 13 per day 6:25am-7:30pm, Sa-Su 8:20am, 12:15, and 6pm; L5000); and **Catania** (M-F 15 per day 7am-6pm, Sa-Su 9am, noon, and 6pm; L6000). The same bus runs to **Giardini-Naxos** and the **train station** (direction: Recanti or Catania; M-F every 30min. 7am-4pm, Sa-Su 9am-4pm; L2500). Also to **Isola Bella, Mazzaro, Spisone** (M-F 6:45am-7:30pm, Sa-Su 8:20am, 12:15, 2:15, and 6pm), and **Gole Alcantara** (M-F 9:30am, 1pm, and 4:30pm, Sa-Su 9:30am; return M-F 12:35pm and 2:15pm, Sa-Su 12:35pm.) Ticket office open daily 6am-8:15pm. **CST** (☎0942 233 01) offers *Etna Tramonto,* a sunset trip up the volcano (June-Oct. M-W L80,000).

ORIENTATION AND PRACTICAL INFORMATION

To reach the city from the train station, hop on the blue Interbus that makes the trip uphill (20min., 4 per hr. until 10:20pm, L2000). Taormina's steep and narrow streets are closed to cars; all automobiles are shooed into a small car park at the base of **Via Pirandello.** From the bus depot (200m uphill) the center is only a brief walk left up V. Pirandello to **Corso Umberto I,** which runs the length of the town. Beginning under its stone entrance archway, the *corso* runs left through four principal *piazze.* Small stairways and sidestreets wind downhill to countless restaurants, shops, and bars. **Via Naumachia** leads downhill to **Via Bagnoli Croci,** which continues to the public gardens.

TOURIST, FINANCIAL, AND LOCAL SERVICES

Tourist Office: (☎0942 232 43; fax 0942 249 41), off C. Umberto at P. V. Emanuele, around the corner in castle-like building. Multilingual, well-organized staff. Their usual map is useless; ask instead for the turquoise fold-out "SAT Sicilian Airbus Travel" map. Open M-F 8am-2pm and 4-7pm, Sa 9am-1pm and 4-7pm.

Currency Exchange: Cambio Valuta, C. Umberto, 224, right before P. Sant'Antonio. Open M-Sa 9am-1pm and 4-8pm. **ATM** 3 doors up from Cambio Valuta. Change money at the train station M-F 9am-2pm.

American Express: La Duca Viaggi, V. Don Bosco, 39 (☎0942 62 52 55), on P. IX Aprile. Cash advances and traveler's check refunds. Holds mail 1 month for cardholders. Open M-F 9am-1pm and 4-7:30pm, Sa 9am-noon.

Moped and Car Rental: Autonolo "City," P. Sant'Antonio, 5 (☎0942 231 61), around the corner from the post office at the end of C. Umberto. Scooter L40,000 per day. Vespa L65,000 (must be at least 18 and have a Vespa license). Cars L113-250,000 per day, L529-950,000 per week. Min. age 21. Must have a license for over a year. Open daily May-Sept. 8am-noon and 4-8pm. Call ahead in winter.

EMERGENCY AND COMMUNICATIONS

Emergencies: ☎113 or 0942 537 45. **Police:** ☎112 or 0942 232 32. **First Aid: Guardia Medica** (☎0942 62 54 19). **Hospital: Ospedale San Vincenzo** (☎0942 57 91), in P. San Vincenzo.

Late-Night Pharmacy: Weekly rotation between pharmacies; try **Farmacia Ragusa,** P. Duomo, 9 (☎0942 232 31; at night ☎0942 280 58). Open Th-Tu 8:30am-5pm.

Post Office: (☎0942 230 10), on P. Sant'Antonio at the very top of C. Umberto near the hospital. Cashes traveler's checks. Open M-Sa 7:30am-6:30pm. **Postal Code:** 98039.

ACCOMMODATIONS AND CAMPING

Taormina is a jewel of a city, as reflected in its accommodation prices. Reservations are a must in July and August, but not all *pensioni* accept phone reservations. Additional accommodations are available in the nearby towns of Mazzarò, Spisone, and Giardini-Naxos (p. 580). Either hike down steep trails to Mazzarò and Spisone or take the bus. Bus service to these areas stops around 9pm.

Pensione Svizzera, V. Pirandello, 26 (☎0942 237 90; fax 0942 62 59 06), in a tall, slim building, 100m up from the bus station. A little pricey, but worth every *lira.* Rose-colored building overlooks the magnificent coast. Its neatness would impress even the Swiss. English spoken. All rooms with bath. Full breakfast on a palm-shaded garden terrace. Reservations recommended in Aug. Open Feb.-Nov. and briefly during Christmas. Singles L100,000; doubles L160,000; triples L180,000. V, MC.

Inn Piero, V. Pirandello, 20 (☎0942 231 39), near the base of C. Umberto after the gas station, in 2 buildings overlooking the sea. Sleep snugly in small, colorful rooms. Breakfast included. Reserve months in advance. Singles L90,000; doubles L132,000. Half-pension L93,000, required in peak season. V, MC, AmEx, Diners.

Villa Astoria (☎0942 239 43), in a pink building on V. Pirandello opposite the bus station. Ask Fate to grant you a room with a seaview; the extra L10,000 for bathroom, balcony, and view is worth it. The alternative is early-morning bus station announcements and street noise. Closed Nov.-Feb. Doubles L80,000, with bath L90,000.

Camping: Campeggio San Leo (☎0942 246 58), on V. Nazionale along the cape, 800m up the hill from the train station, in the shadow of the Grand Albergo Capo Taormina. Small campground wrapped around the terraced cliff. Earthen sites and dazzling views. Take any bus from Taormina that passes the station (L2500). Reserve ahead July and Aug. L8000 per person, L12,000 per tent, L5000 per car.

SICILY

FOOD

Even buying bread, cheese, and fruit can be expensive in Taormina. Try **STANDA supermarket,** V. Apollo Arcageta, 49, at the end of C. Umberto, one block up from the post office. (☎0942 237 81. Open M-Sa 8:30am-1pm and 5-9pm.) The narrow streets running down from C. Umberto hold countless hidden *trattorie.*

Trattoria da Nino, V. Pirandello, 37 (☎0942 212 65), between the buses and the town center. Exuberant Nino dishes out fresh pasta and fresh fish, considered by some to be the best in Taormina. Let Nino guide your culinary journey; the best meals come on his recommendations. Try a glass of the *vino al pescola,* a dessert wine. *Contorni* of fruit for 2 or more consists of a monstrous bowl of figs, peaches, plums, and grapes. *Primi* from L6000; *secondi* from L9000. Discounts available for students; lay your *Let's Go* on the table. Open daily noon-3pm and 6pm-midnight. V, MC.

Bella Blu, V. Pirandello, 28 (☎0942 242 39). Descend through a tunnel of purple petunias for huge portions and a stupendous view (interrupted only by cable cars zipping by). Open-air terrace roofed with flowers and delicately wrought iron chairs. *Primi* from L7000, *secondi* from L11,000. L20,000 tourist *menù.* Cover L2000. Open 10am-3:30pm and 6pm until the last person leaves.

San Pancrazio, P. San Pancrazio, 3 (☎0942 231 84), at the end of V. Pirandello. Crowded outdoor tables in this less popular *piazza* attest to the high quality of the food. Pizza L9000, rich *gnocchi* L9000. Cover L1500. Open W-M noon-3pm and 7-11pm. V, MC, AmEx, Diners.

Gastronomia la Fontana, V. Constantino Patricio, 28 (☎0942 234 78), up the hill (middle street, to the right of the archway) from the end of V. Pirandello. A variety of pizzas, *panini,* and savory snacks including *cipolline* and *arancine,* each L2000-2500. Surprisingly good. Stand-up or takeout. Open Tu-Su 9:30am-3:30pm and 6pm-midnight.

SIGHTS

GREEK THEATER. In ancient days, the 3rd-century cliffside arena comfortably seated 5000 spectators; today that number packs in for the annual summer-long festival performances of Taormina Arte. *(Walk up V. Teatro Greco, off C. Umberto at P. V. Emanuele. Open daily 9am-1hr. before sunset. L8000, under 18 or over 60 free.)*

DUOMO. Farther up C. Umberto, at P. del Duomo, the 13th-century cathedral, rebuilt during the Renaissance, takes center stage. The Gothic interior shelters paintings by Messinese artists and a fine alabaster statue of the Virgin. An unusual two-legged female centaur, Taormina's mascot, crowns the nearby fountain.

OTHER SIGHTS. Behind the tourist office, the **Church of Santa Caterina** protects a small theater, the **Roman Odeon.** Slip into the **Church of St. Augustine** in Piazza IX Aprile (now the town library), and read the dailies with men over 60. Descend V. di Giovanni and follow signs to an elegant **English garden,** with sculpted hedges, the Victorian Follies (dollhouses), and views of the sea. A trek to the **piccolo castello** offers an escape from boisterous crowds. V. Circonvallazione, which runs parallel to and above C. Umberto, leads to a small stairway that snakes up the mountainside to the castle, rewarding visitors with cool breezes and incredible views.

ENTERTAINMENT AND FESTIVALS

While the wildest nights are spent below in Giardini-Naxos, Taormina also stays up late. Chic bars line C. Umberto and its tributary side streets. The bar **Mediterraneo,** V. di Giovanni, 6, packs in a lively crowd, alternatively devouring crepes and cocktails. With Arabic tents, treats, and decor, **Cafe Marrakech,** P. Garibaldi, 2 (☎0942 62 56 92), seduces party-goers until 3am. A 30-minute jaunt down the hill leads to **Tout Va,** V. Pirandello, 70 (☎0942 238 24; fax 0942 238 25), an open-air club with good food and great views. **Shateulle** (☎0942 62 61 75), Taormina's most popular gay club, sits directly behind Cafe Marrakech. English, French, and Spanish are spoken here on brightly colored seats.

Every summer from late July to September the city pleases crowds with **Taormina Arte,** an international festival of theater, ballet, music, and film. Performances attracting the likes of Diana Warwick, Kid Creole, and Ray Charles enliven the Greek and Roman theaters. (☎0942 62 87 49. Grandstand L15-70,000.)

Tourists and locals lounge on beach **Lido Mazzarò,** just below town. Shallow sparkling waters flow around the tiny **Isola Bella,** a national nature preserve, 100m off-shore. **Cable cars** (☎0942 236 05) zip from V. Pirandello to Lido (in summer every 13min. 8am-2am; L3000). The island beach is just a 200m walk uphill to the right. The strong-stomached can travel the narrow, winding route to **Castelmola** and other nearby towns on heart-palpitating buses. **Gole Alcantura** is a nearby haven of wonderful waterfalls, gorgeous gorges, and ravishing rapids. The Gole Alcantara office has a monopoly on tours. (☎0942 98 50 10. Entrance L8000; wetsuit L15,000.) Bring a towel, sunscreen, a change of clothes, and a pair of sturdy shoes for climbing the rapids. Restaurants and a bar are on the premises.

GIARDINI-NAXOS ☎0942

Giardini-Naxos was the site of the first Greek colony in Sicily (734 BC). In its heyday, the city (then called Naxos) prospered with 10,000 inhabitants. The region's abundance allowed the Naxians to live the good life, until they fought for the wrong side during the big Athenian-Syracusan conflicts of the late 5th century BC; Syracuse crushed them in 403 BC. Today, the only battles fought in Giardini-Naxos are for the best spot on the beach or for entrance to the swinging *discoteche.*

TRANSPORTATION AND PRACTICAL INFORMATION. Only 5km away from Taormina, the township of Giardini-Naxos shares a train station with its sister city. **Interbus** runs frequently from Giardini to both the train station and Taormina's central bus station (36 per day, last bus 11:30pm, L3000). Signs throughout town point the way to the **AAST tourist office,** V. Tysandros, 54. (☎0942 510 10; fax 0942 528 48. English spoken. Open in summer M-F 8:30am-2pm and 3-7pm, Sa-Su 9:30am-1:30pm; in winter M-F 8:30am-2pm, Sa-Su 9:30am-1:30pm.) In an **emergency,** call the **hospital** (☎0942 537 45) or the **carabinieri** (☎113), near Centro Scavi, to the left along the *lungomare* from the central bus stop. There is a **post office** at V. Erice, 1 (☎0942 510 90).

ACCOMMODATIONS AND FOOD. As in Taormina, hotels in Giardini are often filled in August, but prices are better; make reservations in advance. The **Hotel Villa Mora,** V. Naxos, 47, is set back from the *lungomare* promenade, with direct access to the beach. Antique writing desks and painted trunks give the rooms a luxurious feel. All rooms have TVs. (☎0942 518 39. Singles from L60,000; doubles L95,000. Half-pension L95,000; full pension L110,000. In Aug., half- or full pension required. V, MC.) In the **Pensione Otello,** V. Tysandros, 62, all rooms have seaside balconies to cheer dim interiors. Breakfast is served in the hotel restaurant. (☎0942 510 09. Rooms L55,000 per person. Half-pension L80,000.) Campers head to **Castello San Marco,** where warm showers are included. Ask at the tourist office for directions. (☎095 64 11 81. L9000 per person, L8000 per tent; Aug. L10,000 per person, L8000 per tent.)

Buy staples at **Sigma supermarket,** V. Dalmazia, 31, down the street from the central bus stop. (Open M-Sa 8:30am-1pm and 5-11pm.) **Calypso,** V. IV Novembre, 267, serves alluring Sicilian specialties in a cozy dining room. (☎0942 512 89. Pizza and pasta from L5000. *Menù* L20,000. Open Th-Tu noon-4pm and 6pm-midnight. V, MC, AmEx.) **Angelina,** V. Calcide Eubea, 2, specializes in seafood. (☎0942 514 77. *Primi* from L5000, *secondi* from L9000. Open daily noon-2am. V, MC, AmEx.)

SIGHTS AND ENTERTAINMENT. Excavations in the 1960s unearthed the outlines of the **Greek city,** with walls built of huge blocks of solidified lava. (Open M-Sa 9am-sunset. L4000.) The two-room **museo archeologico** records the city's earliest days, including an inscribed ceramic cup, the earliest writing surviving from the colony. (☎0942 510 01. Open daily 9am-6:30pm. L8000.)

Beach by day, fluorescent-lit pub/promenade strip by night, Giardini-Naxos seems to casually lose the hours in between. Things light up (quite literally) around 11pm, as busloads of glitzed-up revelers descend and disperse among the dense ranks of pubs, restaurants, and flashy *discoteche.* The party starts 20m from the bus stop at bar/pizzeria/karaoke bar **Mister Roll,** V. Jannuzzo, 31. A plaster in-house replica of Michaelangelo's David keeps an eye out for Bathsheba. (☎0942 65 30 87. Open in summer daily 8:30pm-5am; closed Tu in winter.) Disco-happy folk should hang a left down to the famous **Marabu,** Centro Scavi Naxos. Follow back-lit palm trees and the neon blue cursive sign to this red-carpet complex, complete with rotating techno, oldies, Latin, and international pop music. View the mayhem over the paper umbrella of your margherita. (☎0942 540 76. Live piano before 1am. Cover L25,000. Open from 11:30pm until morning.) Just after the bizarre (and permanent) **Fun Land Carnival** (go-carts, bumper cars, and giant trampolines) is **Discoteca Peter Pan,** the smaller and slightly cheaper alternative to Marabu. (Open May-Sept. daily 11pm-4am; Oct.-May Sa-Su 11pm-4am. Cover L20,000.) Farther to the left, a poorly lit but well trafficked road leads down to the all-night party of *lungomare* Via S. Naxos/V. Tysandros. It's an extra-sensory experience with bumping live music, wafting popcorn and cotton candy, whizzing pre-teen in-line skaters, countless free-flowing bars, and people, people, people.

CATANIA ☎095

Catanians claim that their city prepares them for any surprise the world could possibly present. The metropolis is intimidating, with chaotic traffic, collapsing housing projects, and the unfortunate distinction of being Sicily's crime capital. Beneath the squalid veneer of sooty *palazzi,* however, Catania is a surprisingly elegant city. Leveled repeatedly, most often by the nearby volcano, it has been rebuilt again and again since its founding as a Greek colony in 729 BC. Walls of dark volcanic stone lend a characteristic pall to the historic quarter, while Mt. Etna boils furiously above. After the monstrous 1693 earthquake, G. B. Vaccarini recreated and unified the city with his extravagant Baroque *piazze* and *duomo.* The virtuoso composer Vincenzo Bellini brought another type of harmony to Catania: the opera and his eternal arias.

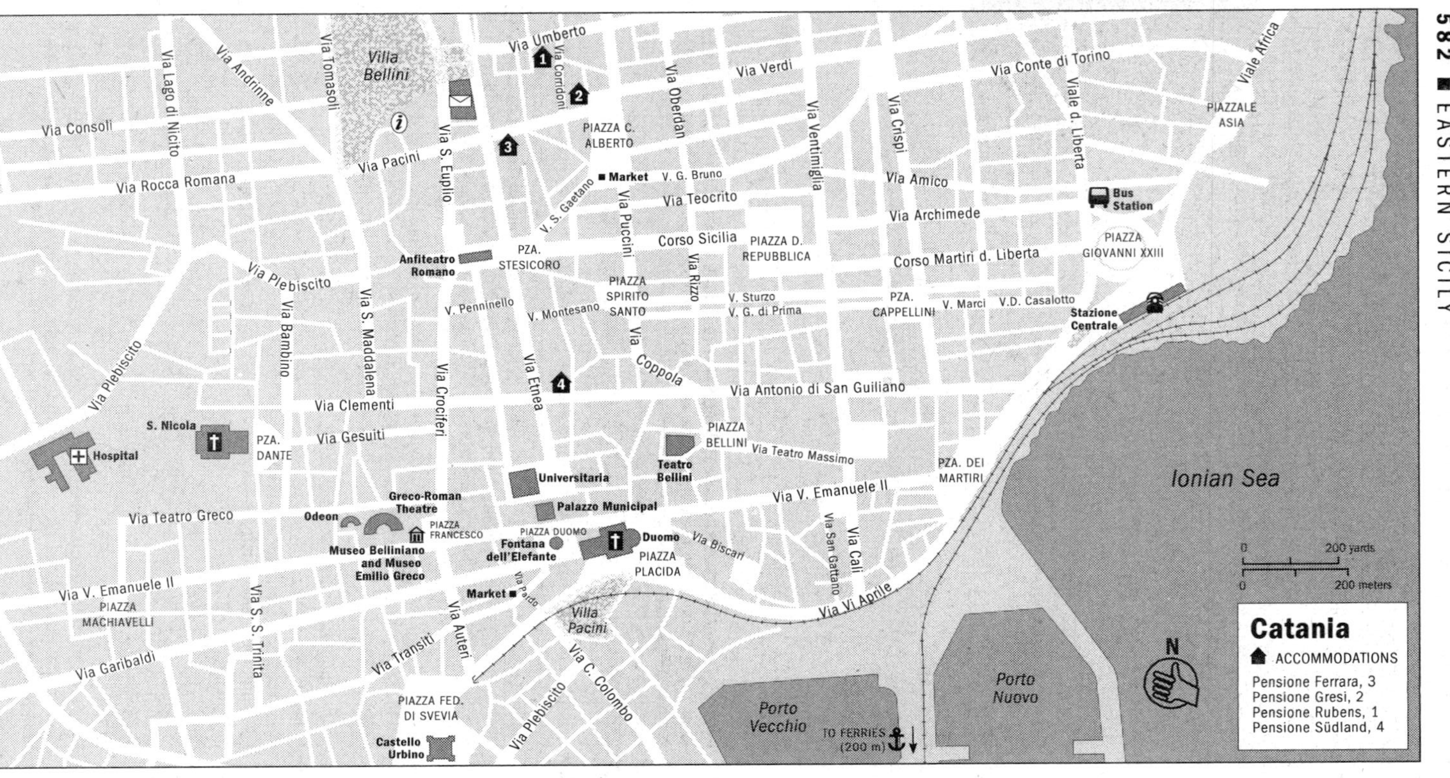
Catania
ACCOMMODATIONS
Pensione Ferrara, 3
Pensione Gresi, 2
Pensione Rubens, 1
Pensione Südland, 4
0
200 yards
0
200 meters
N
Ionian Sea
Porto Nuovo
Porto Vecchio
TO FERRIES (200 m)
Viale Africa
PIAZZALE ASIA
Via Conte di Torino
Viale d. Liberta
Bus Station
PIAZZA GIOVANNI XXIII
Stazione Centrale
Via Crispi
Via Amico
Via Archimede
Corso Martiri d. Liberta
PZA. CAPPELLINI
V. Marci
V.D. Casalotto
Via Verdi
Via Ventimiglia
Via Oberdan
Via Teocrito
Corso Sicilia
PIAZZA D. REPUBBLICA
Via Rizzo
V. Sturzo
V. G. di Prima
Via Umberto
Via Corridoni
PIAZZA C. ALBERTO
Market
V. G. Bruno
Via Puccini
V. S. Gaetano
PIAZZA SPIRITO SANTO
Via Coppola
Via Antonio di San Guiliano
Villa Bellini
Via Consoli
Via Lago di Nicito
Via Andrinne
Via Tomasoli
Via Pacini
Via S. Euplio
Via Rocca Romana
Anfiteatro Romano
PZA. STESICORO
Via Plebiscito
V. Penninello
V. Montesano
Via Etnea
Via S. Maddalena
Via Bambino
Via Crociferi
Via Clementi
Via Gesuiti
S. Nicola
PZA. DANTE
Hospital
Via Plebiscito
PIAZZA BELLINI
Via Teatro Massimo
Teatro Bellini
PZA. DEI MARTIRI
Universitaria
Via V. Emanuele II
Palazzo Municipal
Greco-Roman Theatre
Odeon
Via Teatro Greco
PIAZZA FRANCESCO
Museo Belliniano and Museo Emilio Greco
PIAZZA DUOMO
Fontana dell'Elefante
Duomo
PIAZZA PLACIDA
Via Biscari
Via San Gattano
Via Cali
Via Vi Aprile
Via V. Emanuele II
PIAZZA MACHIAVELLI
Via S. S. Trinita
Market
Via Pardo
Via Auteri
Via Transiti
Villa Pacini
Via Garibaldi
PIAZZA FED. DI SVEVIA
Castello Urbino
Via Plebiscito
Via C. Colombo

TRANSPORTATION

Flights: Fontanarossa (info ☎34 05 05). Take the *alibus* from the front of the train station or pay L35,000 for the 15min. cab ride. Daily flights to Malta with **Air Malta,** V. Libertà, 188 (☎095 31 33 08; fax 095 31 65 58). Open daily 8:30am-1pm and 2:30-7pm. 2 flights per day. Round-trip flights in Aug. from L255,000, plus L40,000 in taxes.

Trains: P. Papa Giovanni XXIII (☎095 730 62 55). To: **Taormina/Giardini-Naxos** (1hr., 4 per day 5:40am-9:40pm, L5500); **Enna** (1½hr.; 5:55, 8:25am, and 1:35pm); **Syracuse** (1¾hr., 13 per day 5:08am-8:10pm, L8500); **Messina** (2hr., 19 per day 5:40am-10:40pm, L9500); **Palermo** (3¼hr. 4 per day 9:45am-6:55pm, L20,500); **Agrigento** (3¼hr., 5:55am and 1:35pm, L16,000); **Ragusa** (4hr., 5:47am, L17,000); **Rome** (10hr., 7 per day 8:27am-10:40pm, L71,800); and **Florence** (12hr., 6 per day 8:27am-8:05pm, L79,400). Info open 7am-9pm. **Luggage Storage:** L5000 for 12hr.

Buses: All companies sit side by side, behind the bus parking lot across from the train station. **SAIS Trasporti** (☎095 53 72 61) to **Agrigento** (3hr., 11 per day, L19,000) and **Rome** (14 hr., 1 per day, L60-70,000). **SAIS Autolinee** (☎095 53 61 68). To: **Enna** (1¼hr., 6 per day, L11,500); **Messina** (1½hr., 30 per day, L12,000); and **Palermo** (2¾hr., 16 per day, L22,500). **Interbus** and **Etna,** under the same roof (☎095 53 27 16), jointly serve: **Taormina** (1hr.; M-F 14 per day 7:30am-6:45pm, Sa 8:15am-9:45pm, Su 8:15am-6:30pm; L6000); **Giardini-Naxos** (same as to Taormina, L4500); **Ragusa** (1¾hr.; 7 per day 6am-7pm, F last bus 8pm; L12,000); **Piazza Armerina** (1¾hr., 4 per day 12:30-7pm, L10,000); **Noto** (3hr.; 5 per day 9:30am-12:40pm, Sa last bus 7pm; L9500); **Brindisi** (6hr., 1pm, L55,000); and **Rome** (14hr.; 9am; L62,000, under 25 L52,000).

Ferries: La Duca Viaggi, V. Etnea, 65 (☎095 31 61 55), sells tickets for ferries to **Malta** (high season: L180,000, under 25 L160,000.) Also to **Venice** (L250,000), **Genoa,** and **Barcelona.** Open M-F 9am-1pm and 4-7:30pm, Sa 9am-noon.

Public Transportation: AMT buses leave from the train station. *Alibus* goes to the airport and bus #27 heads to the beach. Tickets (valid for 1½hr.; L1300, round-trip L2000) sold at *tabacchi* and newsstands.

ORIENTATION AND PRACTICAL INFORMATION

The main street, **Via Etnea,** runs north from P. del Duomo and out of the city center, passing the public gardens at **Villa Bellini.** The bus and train stations are east of the town center at **Piazza Giovanni XXIII,** near the water. With your back to the train station, cross the *piazza* and turn left onto **Corso Martiri della Libertà.** This road travels into P. della Repubblica and becomes the bank-laden **Corso Sicilia,** which crosses V. Etnea at P. Stesicoro and the Bellini monument. Budget accommodations, the public gardens, and chic boutiques await to the right; to the left lie the *duomo*, the small **university,** and the **Teatro Bellini.**

Although notorious for petty thievery, Catania can be conquered by the cautious traveler. Don't let the threat of crime spoil the city for you. Exercise caution when walking and leave expensive watches or jewelry somewhere safe. At night, stick to the well-lit streets around the *duomo* and Bellini theater. Be wary of staged distractions, such as women with babies and children asking for cigarettes. For further information, see **Safety and Security** (p. 50) and **Women Travelers** (p. 79).

Tourist Office: AAPIT (☎095 730 62 33 or 095 730 62 22), on V. Cimarosa. From V. Etnea, turn on V. Pacini and follow signs. Open daily 9am-7pm. **Branches** at the train station (☎095 730 62 55) and airport (☎095 730 62 66). Open M-Sa 9am-7pm.

Budget Travel: CTS, V. Ventimiglia, 153 (☎095 53 02 23), where C. Sicilia becomes C. Martiri della Libertà. Open M-F 9:30am-12:30pm and 4:30-7pm.

American Express: La Duca Viaggi, V. Etnea, 65 (☎095 31 61 55 or 095 31 67 11). Cardholders can get emergency cash and have mail held for 1 month. Open M-F 9am-1pm and 4-7:30pm, Sa 9am-noon.

Emergencies: ☎113. **Police:** ☎112 or 095 736 71 11. **First Aid** (☎095 32 02 29). **Hospital: Garibaldi** (☎095 31 16 66), on P. Santa Maria del Gesù.

Late-Night Pharmacy: Croceverde (☎095 44 16 62), at the intersection of C. Italia and C. della Provincia.

Post Office: V. Etnea, 215 (☎095 715 51 11), in the big building next to the Villa Bellini gardens. Open M-Sa 8:20am-7:40pm. Fax available. **Postal Code:** 95125.

ACCOMMODATIONS

The area between the *duomo* and the post office contains many cheap hotels, mostly in converted family homes. Make reservations for August and September.

Pensione Rubens, V. Etnea, 196 (☎095 31 70 73). Mismatched paintings lend charm to crisply painted, high-ceilinged rooms with TV and phones. A/C in every room makes sticky Catania liveable. Common room with VCR. Singles L39,000, with bath L51,000; doubles L56,000, with bath L73,000. Extra bed L20,000. V, MC, AmEx.

Pensione Gresi, V. Pacini, 28 (☎095 32 27 09; fax 095 715 30 45), off V. Etnea before Villa Bellini and the post office. An old *palazzo* done up like a 19th-century Catanian noble home. Sponge-painted walls, color-by-number ceiling moldings, and pseudo-Baroque frescoes. Even the doorknobs are fancy. All rooms with large bathrooms. Singles L65,000; doubles L90,000. V, MC.

Pensione Ferrara, V. Umberto, 66 (☎095 31 60 00; fax 095 31 30 60), off V. Etnea across from the Bellini gardens. Nothing is impersonal in this high-ceilinged old *palazzo,* where cushioned chairs and matching furniture make you feel at home. Sunlight and minor street noise are part of the package deal with front rooms; more tranquil but dimly lit rooms around the inner courtyard. Singles L44,000, with bath L65,000; doubles L78,000, with bath L85,000. No credit cards.

Pensione Südland, V. Etnea, 270 (☎095 31 24 94 or 095 31 13 43), opposite the post office. Papyrus wall hangings and ancient TVs try to cheer up large rooms. Rooms vary. Singles L36,000, with bath L48,000; doubles L54,000, with bath L69,000; triples L74,000, with bath L92,000; quads L95,000, with bath L115,000.

FOOD

When Catanians ring the dinner bell, they enjoy the famous eggplant- and ricotta-topped *spaghetti alla Norma,* named for one of Bellini's operas. Other local favorites are fresh anchovies known as *masculini.* Vendors at the **market** that extends from the end of V. Pacini (off V. Etnea) to C. Sicilia hawk everything from fist-sized figs to kitschy t-shirts. (Open M-Sa early morning-2pm.) Another market on V. Pardo off P. del Duomo specializes in fish and meat. The **SMA supermarket** is at C. Sicilia, 50. (Open M-Sa 8:30am-10:30pm.) The shiny old-time half-moon countertop of **Bar Savia,** just across from the Bellini Gardens, displays *pizzete* and *arancini* and serves the city's best *granite di Gelsi.* (Open Th-Tu 8am-9pm.) The **Gelateria del Duomo,** across from the elephant fountain, serves a variety of delicious flavors for L2500. The *latte di mandorla* (almond milk) makes a cool treat on a summer evening. (Open daily 5:30pm-midnight.)

Trattoria Via Monte S. Agata (☎095 21 54 53), on V. Monte S. Agata, off V. Etnea. Keep your eyes (and nose) open, lest you miss this tiny extended *piazza.* Peach sun umbrellas outside, aged cheese antipasto tables inside, and extended Catanian families heartily engaged in even more extended meals. Colorful vegetarian *primavera* draws many closed-eyed "mmms." Cover L2000. Open daily noon-3pm and 7-11pm.

Trattoria la Paglia, V. Pardo, 23 (☎095 34 68 38). Lunch in the heart of the bustling market near P. del Duomo. Trade red sauce for black with the *spaghetti nero* (spaghetti with squid ink). *Primi* from L6000, *secondi* L8-12,000. Solo women may be uncomfortable in this area after dark. Open M-Sa 8am-midnight.

Ristorante Rapido, V. F. Corridoni, 17, off V. Umberto about 3 blocks from V. Etnea. The dingy front fades away as colorful and fragrant dishes demand your attention. The *pranzo fisso* is a steal (includes a *primo* and *secondo* for L13,000). Try a Moretti, Italy's most palatable beer. Open M-Sa 9am-3pm and 6:30-10pm.

Nuova Trattoria del Forestiero, V. Coppola, 24/26 (☎095 31 62 83), near the Teatro Bellini. A talkative mamma serves homemade pasta to classy locals at checkered tables. The *boccacina di ricotta* (pastry with ricotta) melts in your mouth. *Primi* and *secondi* from L8000. Open M-Sa 11am-midnight. V, MC, AmEx.

Trattoria Catanese, V. Penninello, 34 (☎095 32 24 61), off V. Etnea near the amphitheater. For 50 years, a native family has been whipping up meals in this *trattoria*. *Menù* L25,000, includes *primo, secondo, contorno,* and a drink. Open M-Sa 9am-10pm.

SIGHTS

PIAZZA DEL DUOMO. In P. del Duomo, Giovan Battista Vaccarini's little lava **Fontana dell'Elefante** (Elephant Fountain; 1736) commands the city's attention. True to anatomical reality, Vaccarini carved his elephant (the symbol of the city) without visible testicles. When the statue was unveiled, horrified Catanian men, who concluded that this omission was an attack on their virility, demanded corrective measures. Vaccarini's acquiescence was, um, monumental. Residents claim that visitors may attain citizenship by smooching the elephant's tush, but the height of the pachyderm's backside precludes such aspirations. The other buildings on the *piazza*, the 18th-century **Palazzo del Municipio** on the left and the former **Seminario dei Chierici** on the right, are striped black and white to mirror the *duomo*'s side.

DUOMO. A 1950s restoration revealed glimpses of the *duomo*'s interior before its Baroque makeover. Restoration teams discovered stumps of old columns and tall, pointed arches of the original three apses. In the Norman **Cappella della Madonna,** on the right, nearly every surface sparkles with precious metals that surround a beautiful Roman sarcophagus and a 15th-century statue of the Virgin. Nine meters from the chapel, the body of Catania's beloved priest, the Beato Cardinal Dusmet, lies with his bronze head and bony (quite literally) fingers protruding from his vestments. To the right as you enter through the main door is **Bellini's tomb,** guarded by a life-size marble angel. The words and music from *Sonnambula*, one of the composer's four principal works, are inscribed above the tomb and translate as "Ah, I didn't think I'd see you wilt so soon, flower." *(Modest dress required.)*

OTHER SIGHTS. Uphill from P. del Duomo lies the entrance to the **Greco-Roman Theater,** built in 415 BC. Behind the theater is the similar but smaller **Odeon,** with an entrance around the back. Mt. Etna's 1669 eruption coated the marble of both theaters in lava. *(V. V. Emanuele, 266. Open daily 9am-1hr. before sunset. Free.)*

From V. V. Emanuele, stroll up V. Etnea to the **Bellini Garden**'s serpentine walkways, mini duck pond, and graceful gazebo. It's the Sunday afternoon refuge for half of Catania's population; children screech and giggle through playground mazes, in-line skaters glide past on shaded walkways, and the elder population complacently occupies winding benches. There's no escape from the Catanian devotion to Bellini; affectionately pruned bushes take the shape of the treble clef and musical notes. A few blocks before the gardens, at the intersection of V. Etnea and C. Sicilia, a 2nd-century **Roman amphitheater** remains a maze of ruins.

BEWARE THE ANIMAL SPIRITS! According to Catanian legend, each of the city's many animal fountains is inhabited by an animal spirit. Anyone who falls asleep by one of these fountains will lose his soul to the resident animal spirit and never wake up. *Let's Go* does not recommend losing your soul to a resident animal spirit, so nap elsewhere.

ENTERTAINMENT AND FESTIVALS

The **Teatro Bellini** (☎095 31 20 20) mesmerizes audiences with opera and concerts. Sink into plush red seats during symphony season (Sept.), or wait for the thrill of the opera (Oct.-June). Student discounts are available for all tickets; contact the tourist office. The AAPIT's free monthly bulletin, *Lapis*, available at bars and the tourist office, details Catania's hot **nightlife,** movies, concerts, and festivals.

Participants in the nightly *passeggiata* promenade around P. del Duomo and swarm near Teatro Bellini. In this area, cafes liven up on weekends, drawing a sometimes raucous crowd. **Mythical Pub,** V. Michele Rapisardi, 8, in the shadow of Teatro Bellini, is where Catania's beautiful people watch one another on weekend nights. The food is more enticing after a few drinks. (Imaginative cocktails L7000. Pub opens at 9pm.) From the *centro*, locals drive to the dance floor of **Banacher,** V. XXI Aprile S.S., 114, a 15-minute taxi ride from Catania. Spectacular lights capture dancing crowds until 5am at what is reputed to be Europe's largest outdoor *discoteca.* Palms and poolside tables provide moments of respite. (☎095 27 12 57. Cover L10,000. Open 10pm-5am.) Weekend summer crowds also scooter 20-minutes away to the north, in the direction of S. Giovani li Cuti, to the nightly destination of *passagiate*, seaside bars, and general mayhem known as **Aci Castello.** This side of Catania's coast may be far from the city chaos, but it isn't out of reach of Etna's fury; huge black boulders thrown from boiling Etna line the jagged shore.

The annual **Feast of St. Agata,** the city's virgin patron, celebrated during 1st five days of February, goes up in "a sparkling explosion of fireworks and wild gaiety." Indeed. The pleasant but crowded beach **La Plaja** has a picturesque view of a nearby power plant (bus #27; June-Sept. #D). Farther from the port is the better **La Scogliera,** with fiery cliffs and a bathing area (30min., bus #34 from P. del Duomo).

DAYTRIP FROM CATANIA: MOUNT ETNA

An AST bus leaves from Catania's central train station at 8:30am for Rifugio Sapienza, making a 10-minute rest stop at Nicolosi (where you can speedily fill up your picnic basket). The bus returns to Catania at 4:45pm (times subject to change; round-trip L6900).

At 3350m, Mt. Etna is one of the world's largest active volcanoes and the tallest in Europe. The Greek poet Hesiod envisioned Etna as the home of Typhon, the last monster conceived by Earth to fight the gods before the dawn of the human race. Apparently Typhon isn't done yet; a 1985 eruption destroyed much of the summit tourist station. Etna blew its top again in 1992, damaging the ski resort on its slopes. Its increasingly frequent activity throughout 1999-2000 has left scientists speculating and visitors worrying.

From Sapienza (1900m), where the AST bus stops, the hike up to **Torre del Filosofo** (Philosopher's Tower, 2920m) and back takes five hours. From here, the looming peaks of Etna's craters and their rising steam stand in full view. The hike is difficult because the ashy, pebbly terrain slips underfoot. Anyone wearing sturdy shoes can freely and safely maneuver around the crater right in front of the parking area for a 30-minute taste of the peaks. Otherwise, an expensive cable-car service runs to 2500m (daily 9am-4pm, last return 4:30pm; L16,000, under 10 L8000). To climb farther (2950m), a jeep and guide are necessary (L62,000).

From the Philosopher's Tower a two-hour hike leads to the **craters** themselves. The return lasts roughly one hour. While the view of the hardened lava, huge boulders, and unearthly craters is incredible, it may not be "to die for"; the trail is so difficult and the volcanic activity so unpredictable that all guided tours have been suspended. Several years ago, 11 tourists died when one of the craters erupted unexpectedly. Those who choose to brave the trip should take precautions; notify someone when you leave, travel with a partner, and carry water. Bring warm clothing as winds are ferocious, and even in mid-July pockets of snow remain. On the return from the tower, you will pass the **Valle de**

Bove, Etna's original crater. For information on tours, call **CIT,** C. Umberto, 101 (☎0942 233 01), or **Gruppo Guide Alpine,** V. Etna, 49 (☎095 53 98 82). In an **emergency,** call ☎0942 53 17 77.

ENNA ☎0935

Rising steeply above the poorest and only landlocked province in Sicily, Enna provides tantalizing glimpses of life in the island's interior. Ennesi are prone to modesty, and coastal Sicilians often view them with a condescending eye. The combination has shut Enna out of the Sicilian tourist industry for years. Regardless, Enna is a breezy city with numerous *piazze* offering panoramas of the lush, golden grain fields. The town has harbored a military base throughout its history, passing through Greek, Roman, Arab, Norman, Lombard, and Bourbon hands. The only vestiges of this past are a huge medieval castle, a Lombard tower, worn cobblestone streets, and a curiously remodeled cathedral.

TRANSPORTATION

Enna, at the center of the island, is known as "the navel of Sicily." It is easily accessible by bus and train. Buses are cheaper and faster, and the bus station is conveniently located. Arriving by bus saves the 8km uphill hike from the train station.

Trains: (☎0935 50 09 10). To: **Catania** (1hr., 9 per day 6:17am-7:55pm, L7200); **Palermo** (2hr.; 11am, 3:58, 5:17, and 8:19pm; L12,700); and **Agrigento** (7:12, 9:50am, and 2:59pm; L9800). Buses connect the station to the center of town (M-Sa 11 per day 6:50am-8:55pm with 2-3hr. gaps after 11am and 6pm, L2500). The schedule is posted in the train station.

Buses: All buses depart from the *autostazione* on V. Diaz, a short walk uphill from P. Matteotti. **Interbus** (☎0935 50 23 90) and **SAIS** (☎0935 50 09 02) are under one roof. To: **Piazza Armerina** (40min., 10 per day 8am-7:05pm, L5000); **Palermo** (1¾hr.; M-F 9 per day 5:45am-5:45pm, Su 6 per day 9:20am-7:10pm; L15,000); **Catania** (2¼hr.; M-Sa 5-7 per day 6:15am-5pm, Su 5 and 6pm; L11,500) continuing to **Ragusa, Syracuse,** and **Noto.**

Taxis: ☎0935 689 50.

ORIENTATION AND PRACTICAL INFORMATION

To reach Enna's center from the bus depot, head downhill on V. V. Emanuele. This road runs directly into **Via Roma,** which branches at P. Matteotti. **Via Roma Alta** leads past **Piazza Vittorio Emanuele** to the **Castello di Lombardia** on the left. To the right, it winds through a residential and shopping district, eventually ending in the vicinity of the **Torre di Federico II.**

Tourist Office: AAPIT, V. Roma, 411 (☎0935 52 82 28). Informed and well-organized. Cubby holes of info line the walls. English spoken. Open M-Sa 9am-1pm and 2-7pm. **Numero Verde Turistico** (☎800 22 11 88). Toll-free tourist info (Italian only).

Currency Exchange: Banks line V. Roma between P. V. Emanuele and P. Umberto I. Exchange currency at the post office. **ATMs:** in P. Umberto on V. Roma.

Emergencies: ☎113. **Police:** ☎0935 50 12 89. **Carabinieri:** (☎112 or 0935 50 13 21), in P. Europa. **Ambulance:** ☎0935 219 33. **Hospital: Ospedale Umberto I** (☎0935 451 11), on V. Trieste. **First Aid/Emergency Room:** ☎0935 50 08 99. **Guardia Medica:** (☎0935 52 04 89 or 0935 50 08 96). Open 8pm-8am.

Post Office: V. Volta, 1 (☎0935 56 23 27). Take a left off V. Roma just before the AAPIT and walk to the right behind the building labeled "Provincia." Open M-Sa 8:10am-7:20pm. **Postal Code:** 94100.

ACCOMMODATIONS AND FOOD

As its owner will inform you, the only hotel in town is **Hotel Sicilia,** P. Colajanni, 7, at V. Roma past AAPIT. Rooms are posher than necessary with antique furniture, phone, TV, hair dryer, and shower. Forgive the art (is that a knight holding an avocado?). (☎0935 50 08 50. Breakfast included. Singles L109,000; doubles L155,000; triples L180,000. V, MC, AmEx, Diners.) If the hotel is full or your wallet isn't, head to the smaller (and cheaper) Pergusa, home to the **Miralogo** ("lake-view," named before Pergusa's lake started drying up), 3km past Pergusa center. Fluffy towels don't really redeem its remote location and the noisy *discoteca* next door. (☎0935 54 12 72. Breakfast L5000. Singles L50,000; doubles L70,000; triples L70,000.) Pergusa can be reached from Enna proper by **bus #5A** (L5000), which makes the 7km trip every hour from Enna's bus station and from in front of Agenzia Viaggi Loppola in the chaotic little *piazza* not far down V. Roma from P. V. Emanuele. In Pergusa, buses normally stop at the town gas station, but drivers will drop you at the hotel if you ask. Another option is continuing to the converted monastery *ostello* in medieval Piazza Armerina (p. 589) and making Enna a daytrip.

The natives sprinkle everything with *piacentino* cheese—sharp, spicy, and available at **Centro Formaggi,** V. Mercato Sant'Antonio, 33, in P. Umberto. (☎0935 50 07 29. Open daily 8am-2pm and 5-9pm.) **Via Mercato Sant'Antonio** is brimming with *alimentari*, fruit stands, and bakeries. The motherly proprietor of **Ristorante La Fontana,** V. Volturo, 6, one block downhill on the right from Hotel Sicilia, off P. Emanuele, concocts scrumptious Sicilian cuisine. The specialty is *risotto all'Ennese* (with tomatoes, mushrooms, and olives; L8000). Snuggle up indoors or dine under an open-air tent. (☎0935 254 65. Cover L2000. Service 15%. Open daily noon-4pm and 7:30pm-midnight. V, MC, AmEx.)

SIGHTS

CASTELLO DI LOMBARDIA AND ENVIRONS. In order to maintain control of the island and repel onslaughts, Frederick II constructed this castle on a 5000-year-old foundation on the mountain peak. Only six of the original 20 towers now stand, and much of the castle is under scaffolding. Frederick, a great huntsman, took shelter in the 24m octagonal **Torre di Federico II** that rises at the opposite edge of the city, surrounded by the city's winding **public gardens.** A secret tunnel once connected the tower with the Castello di Lombardia. *(Walk along V. Roma past the UPIM department store, away from P. V. Emanuele. V. Roma turns into V. Libertà. Castle ☎0935 50 09 62. Open daily 9am-1pm and 3-7pm. Tower closed for restorations. Turn left onto V. IV Novembre for the public gardens. Open daily 9am-8pm. Free.)*

MUSEO ALESSI. Behind the cathedral, this museum holds a surprisingly interesting assortment of objects, including some deranged French engravings of the 18th century (look for the half-jar, half-animals) and the *duomo*'s treasures, among them several fine silver wrists, jeweled crowns, and an incredibly delicate silver cathedral. Look for Paolo Vetri's work (the 1st left on the ground floor): watercolor plans for cathedral frescoes and the exquisite *Portrait of an Elder Man* *(☎0935 50 31 65. Open Tu-Su 9am-1pm and 4-7pm. L5000.)*

While Frederick was off fighting lords and slaying prey, his wife, Queen Eleanor of Aragon, tended souls. At her orders, the **Baroque cathedral** was founded in 1307. In the 16th century the building was expanded. The polygonal transepts, apses, and southern door remain from the original medieval structure. The sacrilegious stretch out on wooden pews to appreciate the marvelous wood-paneled ceiling.

FESTIVALS AND MORE

The **Festa della Madonna,** held on July 2, is marked by incessant popping of firecrackers (*jucu'fuco* in local dialect) and the renowned flavor of *mastazzoli* (apple cookies). Parties also accompany the feasts of **Sant'Anna** on the last Sunday in July and **San Valverde** on the last Sunday in August. Enna's most renowned festivities, however, are at **Easter,** when thousands of hooded figures hit the town.

Processions of a faster sort take place down the hill at the Autodromo di Pergusa (☎0935 256 60; fax 0935 258 25), where the city hosts **Grand Prix auto races** from March to October. The most important are the Formula 3 in July. In other months, you can catch everything from motorcycle races to dog shows there.

PIAZZA ARMERINA ☎0935

The golden city on a hill, Piazza Armerina sits forty-five minutes into the Erei mountains from Enna Proper. Dominated by its green-domed *duomo* and King Martino's *Castello Aragonese*, the medieval Armerina provides buckets of charm and the interior's best budget accommodations. Near Piazza Armerina's rows of golden medieval buildings, the Roman country house, Villa Romana "del Casale," sits bedecked with some of the ancient world's finest mosaics.

TRANSPORTATION AND PRACTICAL INFORMATION. Piazza Armerina is a short bus ride from Enna (45min.; 8 per day; L3700, round-trip L6100). **Buses** arrive at and depart from P. Senatore Marescalchi (formerly P. Stazione), at the city's northern end, up V. Marconi (which becomes V. Mazzini and then V. Chiaranda) from P. Garibaldi. From the bus stop, walk straight ahead into the *piazza*, turning at the 1st right onto V. Roma. One kilometer down on the left, **Via Garibaldi** leads to the historic district, where the **tourist office,** V. Cavour, 15, will do what little it can for you. (☎0935 68 02 01. Open M-Sa 8am-2pm.) The **Quattrino pharmacy,** P. Garibaldi, 31, is on the way to the *duomo*. (☎0935 68 00 44. Open 9am-1pm and 4-8pm.) In **emergencies,** call the **carabinieri** (☎0935 68 20 14).

ACCOMMODATIONS AND FOOD. For the best accommodations in the interior, follow the yellow signs to **Ostello del Borgo,** Largo S. Giovanni, 6, a newly converted monastery in the heart of historic Piazza Armerina. Divine. Sunny yellow and white checker-tiled halls lead to mahogany furniture, TVs, common room, and a courtyard playground. (☎0935 68 70 19. Breakfast included. Singles L55,000; doubles L75,000; triples L100,000; quads L120,000.)

Only a handful of restaurants sprinkle Piazza Amerina's streets; picnicking or a *panino* from **Strazzanti Alimentari,** P. Garibaldi, 15 (☎0935 68 00 84), are possible alternatives. For home style Italian, head for **Pepito,** V. Roma, 140. The large tour groups wolfing down *agnello al forno* (baked lamb) don't know how good they've got it. (☎0935 827 37. *Primi* from L10,000, *secondi* from L18,000. Open W-M noon-4pm and 7-11pm. V, MC, AmEx.)

SIGHTS. **Villa Romana "Del Casale"** lies 5km southwest of town. "I Mosaici," as the locals call it, contains 40 rooms' worth of floor mosaics. Scholars are still debating who owned this villa, complete with sauna and massage rooms. The most probable suggestion is that the villa was the hunting lodge of Maximanius Heraclius, co-emperor with Diocletian at the turn of the 4th century AD. Occupied until the Arab period, sacked in 1160, and buried by a landslide soon after, it remained undiscovered until 1916 when it was excavated by archaeologists Paolo Orsi and Giuseppe Cultrera. It's worth getting a guidebook to discover the villa's smaller treasures. Some of the most unusual attractions are the vestibule (read: bathroom) of Polyphemus, where the emperor could contemplate Odysseus's blinding of the Cyclops while seated on his "other throne;" the Sala delle Deici Ragazze, where muscular bikini-clad women play catch and lift weights; and the famous bare tush of Cubicolo Scena Erotica, near the exit to the villa, where a lot more than a lap

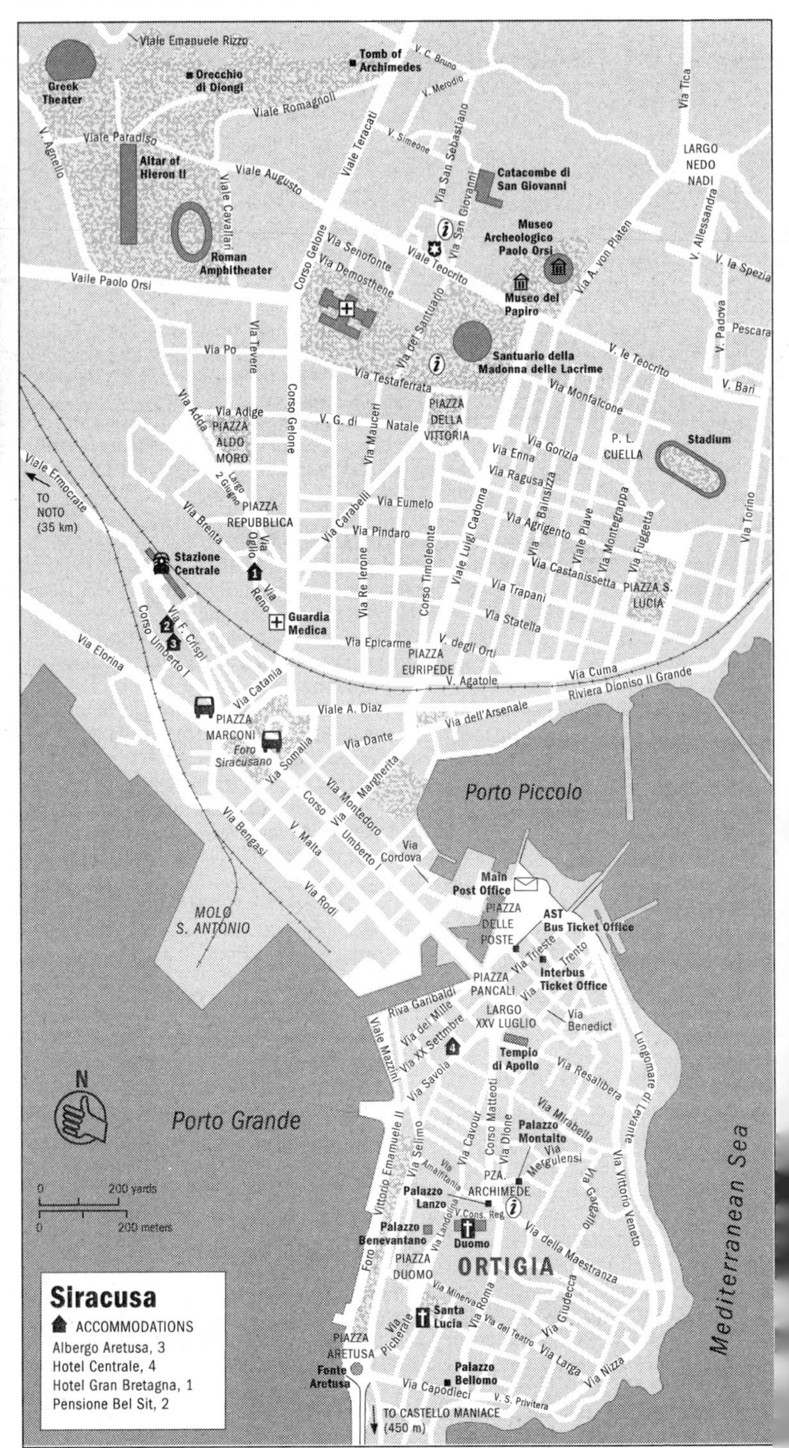
Siracusa
ACCOMMODATIONS
Albergo Aretusa, 3
Hotel Centrale, 4
Hotel Gran Bretagna, 1
Pensione Bel Sit, 2
Greek Theater
Orecchio di Diongi
Tomb of Archimedes
Altar of Hieron II
Roman Amphitheater
Catacombe di San Giovanni
Museo Archeologico Paolo Orsi
Museo del Papiro
Santuario della Madonna delle Lacrime
Stadium
Stazione Centrale
Guardia Medica
Porto Piccolo
Porto Grande
Main Post Office
AST Bus Ticket Office
Interbus Ticket Office
Tempio di Apollo
Palazzo Montalto
Palazzo Lanzo
Palazzo Benevantano
Duomo
ORTIGIA
Santa Lucia
Palazzo Bellomo
Fonte Aretusa
Mediterranean Sea
MOLO S. ANTONIO
TO NOTO (35 km)
TO CASTELLO MANIACE (450 m)
200 yards
200 meters

dance goes on. A sprawling 60x3 meter hallway filled with bounding gazelles, lions, and leopards, and symbolically divided by a great ship, represents the lucrative Roman-era animal trade of India and Africa. Known as The Great Hunt, it provides the strongest evidence for Maximanius's ownership; as an importer of exotic animals himself, he could indeed have privately achieved such enormous wealth (the 8 opening days of the colosseum alone killed over 5000 animals). The incredibly vivid mosaics are the largest and most intact of their kind in the world, and are constructed from naturally colored stones. (From May-Sept. orange ATAN buses (L1200) shuttle between the villa and Piazza Armerina; in fall and winter, you'll have to walk. The bus departs on the hour and returns on the half-hour; beware the 5hr. gap in service between 11:30am and 4:30pm. Catch the orange mini-bus in front of the Hotel Villa Romana on V. Sturze at the base of V. Roma coming from the old city, or from the far end of the bus station *piazza*. The bus directly from Enna stops just outside the *piazza*. Walk towards the line of blue buses ahead on the left; the bus stop is at the far end, with the Agip station on your left. (☎0935 68 00 36. Open daily 9am-1:30pm and 3:30pm-sunset. L8000.)

SOUTHERN SICILY

SYRACUSE (SIRACUSA) ☎0931

The most beautiful and noble of the Greek cities.
—Titus Livius (Livy), on Syracuse

Although Titus's words may seem hyperbolic, modern Syracuse has both subtle charm and style. On the *terra firma*, skyscrapers and supermarkets spring up along speedways, while tiny craft shops and high-fashion boutiques line the narrow roads of Ortigia's island. Ortigia provided the springboard for the city's foundation in 734 BC; from there the Greek settlement prospered and spread onto the mainland. Between the 6th and 3rd centuries BC, Syracuse was arguably the greatest city in the Western world, cultivating such luminaries as Theocritus, Archimedes, and the great Greek lyric poet Pindar. The city boasts the world's largest theater and the first known cookbook. Today Siracusani can only lament their city's millennia-long decline. Some say it began to slide in 211 BC, when it was sacked by the Romans. Others set the fatal date at AD 668, when the bathing emperor Constans was bludgeoned to death with a soap dish. The city's prominence was perhaps most seriously undermined in 879, when Arabs conquered Sicily and established Palermo as the capital of the island. Syracuse is now home to more history than it can handle. Nonetheless, well-organized museums, an archaeological park, and Ortigia's delightful atmosphere continue to attract tourists.

TRANSPORTATION

Trains: V. Francesco Crispi, halfway between Ortigia and the archaeological park. To: **Noto** (35min., 8 per day 5:20am-7:50pm, L4500) via **Modica** and **Gela; Catania** (1½hr., 10 per day 6am-11:05pm, L8500); **Taormina** (2hr., 8:33am, L12,500); **Ragusa** (2¼hr., 5 per day 5:20am-3:22pm, L11,000) via **Gela; Messina** (3hr., 4 per day 4:53am-11:05pm, L16,000); **Rome** (11hr., 7 per day 7:15am-11:05pm, L69,600); **Florence** (13hr., 5 per day 7:15am-5:15pm, L81,900); **Milan** (20hr., 4 per day 3:10-6:25pm, L89,700); and **Turin** (20hr., 1:28pm and 2:30pm, L91,900). Ticket office open daily 7am-9pm.

Buses: AST office (☎0931 46 27), next to the post office on Ortigia, to the left after the stone bridge. While construction continues, blue buses leave from Bar Alta Marea, C. Umberto, 6, on the mainland side of the stone bridge. To: **Ragusa** (3hr., 6 per day, L10,500); **Piazza Armerina** (3hr., 1 per day, L14,000); and **Gela** (4hr., 2 per day, L14,000). **Interbus,** V. Trieste, 28 (☎0931 66 710), 1 or 2 blocks from P. delle Poste toward the center of Ortigia, the 2nd street to the left after the stone bridge. To: **Noto** (1hr., 11 per day, L4500); **Catania** (1¼hr.; M-F 17 per day 5:45am-6:30pm, Sa-Su 8 per day 6:45am-6:30pm; L8000); **Giardini-Naxos** (2hr., 1 per day, L12,500); **Taormina** (2hr., 1 per day, L12,500); **Palermo** (3¼hr.; M-F 14 per day 7:25am-3:20pm, Sa-Su 4 per day 9:45am-12:45pm; L21,500); and **Rome** (12hr., 1 per day, L67,000).

Local Transportation: Orange **AST** buses depart from P. delle Poste. Bus #21, 22, and 24 run past Fontane Bianche. #23 to Aranella. Tickets (L1000) in *tabacchi.*

Taxis: (☎0931 697 22 or 0931 609 80). From the train station to Ortigia about L5000.

ORIENTATION AND PRACTICAL INFORMATION

A bridge joins the island of **Ortigia** to mainland Syracuse. This bridge becomes **Corso Umberto I,** leading to **Foro Siracusano** at the base of the town. As you stand on C. Umberto I in the Foro, the city's main artery, **Corso Gelone,** is to the right, accessible through a gap in some unused railway tracks. C. Umberto continues past Foro Siracusano to the train station.

Tourist Office: APT, V. S. Sebastiano, 43 (☎0931 67 710). From P. delle Poste, follow busy C. Gelone past the hospital to the 2nd set of lights. Turn right onto Vle. Teocrito, then left onto V. S. Sebastiano before the giant cone-shaped sanctuary. The tourist office is on the left, just after the police station. Offers a necessary map (but few pamphlets). **Ortigia Office** (historic district), on V. Maestranza. After crossing this stone Umbertino Bridge, turn right through P. Pancali to uphill C. Matteotti. Turn left onto V. Maestranza at the fountain in P. Archimede; the office is unmarked. On the 1st floor of an impressive Renaissance *palazzo,* 100m down on the left, after V. Coronati. Plenty of pamphlets. English spoken. Open M-Sa 8:30am-1:45pm and 3:30-6:30pm, Su 9am-1pm; in winter M-Sa 8:30am-2pm and 3:30-6:30pm, Su 8:30am-2pm.

Emergencies: ☎113. **Police:** (☎0931 46 35 66), on V. S. Sebastiano. **Guardia Medica:** ☎0931 48 46 39. From P. Archimede on Ortigia, turn down V. Maestranza, and take your 1st left onto V. S. Coronati. Open M-F 8pm-8am, Sa-Su 8am-8pm. **Hospital: Ospedale Generale Provinciale** (☎0931 72 41 11), a beige brick monstrosity on V. Testaferrata, off C. Gelone towards the *corso*'s end.

Pharmacy: La Madonnina, C. Gelone, 1 (☎0931 664 28), just off P. delle Poste. Open M-F 8:30am-1pm and 4:30-8pm.

Internet Access: Unnamed, on V. Salvatore Chindevi. Just after the replacement Ortigia Bridge, up the 1st throughway beginning to the left. Enter the 5th door on the right, with fluorescent computer jargon stickers splashed over windows. 6 new stations. L10,000 per hr. Open M-F 9am-1pm and 4-8pm, Su 9am-1pm. 24hr. access expected in 2001. **Libreria Gabò,** C. Matteotti, 38 (☎0931 662 55), on Ortigia. 1 computer half-hidden by piles of books. Connection operated by a hamster in a wheel–surf *slowly.* Open M-Sa 9am-1pm and 4:30-8:30pm, Su 4:30-8:30pm.

Post Office: P. delle Poste, 15 (☎0931 684 16). Turn left after crossing the bridge to Ortigia. The larger office (☎0931 669 95) has Fermo Posta. Open M-Sa 8:15am-7:40pm. The smaller office across the street (☎0931 689 73) exchanges currency M-F 8:30am-5:30pm, Sa 8:30am-1pm. **Postal Code:** 96100.

ACCOMMODATIONS AND CAMPING

The area between the train station and the bridge to Ortigia offers many budget options. Ortigia proper offers more luxury, with prices to match. The area immediately around the train station can be dangerous at night.

Albergo Aretusa, V. Francesco Crispi, 75 (☎/fax 0931 242 11), down the street from the train station. A well-maintained old *palazzo* whose owners have kept the original marble floor tiling. High-ceilinged rooms, half with slick, new dark wood furniture. Rooms vary considerably in size, shape, and lighting; don't be afraid to view a few. Common room with TV and cushy green dormitory chairs. English spoken. Breakfast

L5000. Reserve in August. 50 rooms. Singles L40,000, with bath L50,000; doubles L70,000, with bath and breakfast L90,000; triples L90,000, with bath L105,000.

Hotel Centrale, C. Umberto I, 141 (☎0931 60 528), near the train station. Large, simple rooms with peeling metal furniture. Low prices and stupendous sea views have made this hotel popular with Anglo-American backpackers. Spartan decor and exposed pipes, but clean, well-lit rooms. Best views: single: #18, 20 and doubles: #19, 21. Singles L30,000; other rooms L25,000 per person, L30,000 with bath. No credit cards.

Pensione Bel Sit, V. Oglio, 5 (☎0931 602 45). Follow signs from C. Gelone, close to the train station. Upstairs rooms with fluorescent lighting. Downstairs rooms let in sunlight. Huge, sparkling white-tiled bathrooms. Reserve a week ahead for July-Aug. Singles with shower L40,000; doubles L50,000, with bath L65,000; triples L80,000; quads L90,000. No credit cards.

Hotel Gran Bretagna, V. Savoia, 21 (☎/fax 0931 687 65). The only budget option on Ortigia. A *palazzo* full of character with luxurious carpeting and pillows and a sunny, lush courtyard. Upper rooms are far superior. Ask for room #47, where frescoed angels watch over you while you slumber. Renovations are expected to be completed by January 2001. Breakfast in downstairs restaurant included. Call ahead: prices will vary depending on the cost of the renovations. Singles L53,000, with bath L63,000; doubles L87,000, with bath L99,000. V, MC, AmEx.

Camping: Fontane Bianche, V. dei Lidi, 476 (☎0931 79 03 33), 30km from Syracuse, near the beach of the same name. Take bus #21 or 22 (L1000) from the post office. Open May-Sept. L11,000 per person, L8-11,000 per tent.

FOOD

Budget restaurants dot the area between the train tracks, the archaeological park, and Ortigia's V. Cavour. An open-air **market** sets up on V. Trento, off P. Pancali in Ortigia (open M-Sa 8am-1pm). A **FAMILA supermarket,** V. Teracati, 34, recalls good old Western consumerism. (Open M-Tu and Th-Sa 8:30am-1:45pm and 4:30-8:15pm, W 8:30am-1:45pm. V, MC.)

La Siciliana, V. Savoia, 17 (☎0931 689 44), in Ortigia, next door to Hotel Gran Bretagna. Cheerful brothers in matching "La Siciliana" t-shirts whisk Papa's tasty thin-crust pizzas to your table. Indoor and outdoor seating among chattering local crowd. *Primi* and 53 varieties of pizza from L6000. Open Tu-Su 10am-4pm and 6pm-midnight.

Spaghetteria do Scugghiu, V. D. Scinà, 11, a tiny street off P. Archimede, on Ortigia. A known and respected culinary landmark, this tiny spaghetti eatery boasts 18 different types of spaghetti (most L7000). Lots of vegetarian options. Wine L6000 per liter. Open Tu-Su noon-3pm and 5pm-midnight.

Al Ficodindia, V. Arezzo, 7/9 (☎0931 46 28 38), off V. Cavour in Ortigia. This *trattoria* popular with the summer tourist crowd, smacks faintly of mass production. But the price is right, and it's got more character than a "self-service" joint. L10,000 *menù* includes pizza, water, wine, and *gelato.* L15,000 *menù* includes *bruschetta, antipasto,* mussel soup, and *gelato.* Open daily noon-3:30pm and 7:30pm-midnight. V, MC, AmEx.

Pizzeria Trattoria Del Forestiero, C. Timoleonte, 2 (☎0931 46 12 45), on the mainland between the Sanctuary and the Foro Siracusano. Under the train tracks at the bridge; the restaurant is opposite P. Euripide. Large portions and premium quality. Wide range of pizza for takeout in the evenings (L4-8000). Cover L2000. No credit cards.

SIGHTS

MAINLAND SYRACUSE

ARCHAEOLOGICAL PARK. Syracuse's three centuries as the most important city on the Mediterranean left behind a collection of immense monuments. Two theaters, an ancient quarry, and the world's largest altar share a fenced compound and can be visited with a single ticket. Take a deep breath before plowing through the paper fan- and bead-hawking tourist tunnel. *(Follow C. Gelone to V. Teocrito; the park entrance is down V. Augusto to the left. Open daily 9am-2hr. before sunset. L8000, EU residents under 18 or over 60 L4000.)*

GREEK THEATER. This theater, where Aeschylus produced his *Persians*, was scooped out of solid rock in 475 BC. Much of it is still recognizable, including the lowered, semi-circular pit where the chorus performed, the stage, cluttered with the remains of a two-story permanent set, and the track circling the stage, which guided the *deus ex machina*, a sort-of divine jack-in-the-box that routinely rescued characters from certain catastrophe or death. More than 15,000 spectators sat comfortably in the theater to watch these spectacles. Classical Greek plays are now staged in the theater every year (see **Entertainment,** p. 595).

PARADISE QUARRY. This flowered area borders two large grottoes of the chalk cliffs: the **Orecchio di Dionigi** (Ear of Dionysius) and the **Grotta dei Cordari** (Rope-makers' Cave). The latter is closed to the public for safety reasons, but visitors can still see the former, an artificial grotto with cathedral proportions (65m long, 11m wide, and 23m high). The name was derived from its resemblance to a giant ear-lobe, while its exceptional acoustics spawned the later legend that the tyrant Dionysius placed his prisoners here in order to eavesdrop on their conversations.

Outside this area lies **Ara di Ierone II,** the altar of Heiron II (241-215 BC), once used for public sacrifices. It would have been hard to keep them private; at 198m by 23m, this is the world's largest altar. Walk up the hill and through the other gate to reach the **Roman amphitheater.** Constructed in the 2nd century AD, the theater is stunningly well-preserved. Visitors can see the tunnels through which gladiators and wild animals entered.

CATACOMBE DI SAN GIOVANNI. The extensive catacombs (AD 315-360), a few blocks away down V. Teocrito across from the main APT office, were once the site of Bacchus's temples. Guided tours are mandatory. Outside the catacombs lie the ruins of the (alleged) first Christian church in Sicily. The 4th-century **Cripta di San Marziano** (the first bishop of Syracuse), containing some faded yet haunting frescoes and Latin inscriptions, lies below the ruins. *(Open Mar. 15-Nov. 14 Th-Tu 9am-12:30pm and 2-5pm; Nov. 15-Mar. 14 Th-Tu 9am-1pm. L4000, under 10 L1000.)*

MUSEO ARCHEOLOGICO PAOLO ORSI. Down from the park, this new museum has a huge collection of Greek artifacts, but unfortunately lacks any English explanations or clear organizing principles. Nevertheless, it's fun to wander among the bawdily decorated Greek vases, huge terracotta Gorgon masks with protruding tongues, a sexually aroused dwarf clutching chickens, and the skeletons of two pygmy elephants. *(V. Teocrito. ☎0931 46 40 22. Open Tu-Sa 9am-1pm and 3:30-7:30pm. Ticket office closes 1hr. before museum. L8000.)*

SANTUARIO DELLA MADONNA DELLE LACRINE. French architects Michel Arnault and Pierre Parat, winners of a 1957 international competition, built the sanctuary to commemorate four miraculous days in 1953 when a mass-produced statuette of the Madonna cried continuously. It appears that they may have commemorated the wrong Madonna, however, as the building bears an uncanny resemblance to a cone-shaped bra. *(☎0931 214 46. Open daily 7am-noon and 4-7pm.)*

MUSEO DEL PAPIRO. Up the narrow street from the Orsi museum, this tiny collection of papyrus texts and woven objects (sandals, boats, ropes, etc.) displays four or five pages from the ancient Egyptian Book of the Dead, containing invocations (translated into Italian) to the Eater of Souls and the Snake-that-Rises. *(☎0931 221 00. Open Tu-Su 9am-2pm. Free.)*

ORTIGIA

Cross the bridge from C. Umberto, the main approach to the island. This road splits off in a handful of directions, weaving in and about the small village, around the ruins of two Greek temples and several Gothic and Renaissance churches. Past the bridge and across **Piazza Pancali** stand the remnants of the **Tempio di Apollo,** the oldest peripteral (columns on all sides) Doric temple in Sicily (built in 575 BC). Only two columns supporting a piece of entablature and parts of the *cella* wall remain. To the right, up **Corso G. Matteotti,** lies **Piazza Archimede,** the principal square of the old city, centered on the corpulent **Fontana di Diana. Via Maestranzo** is home to the **Pallazzo Impellizzeri (#22),** with its crumbling stone animal heads.

DUOMO AND TEMPLE. More than 2300 years separate the 18th-century Baroque facade of Syracuse's *duomo* from the attached 5th-century BC Tempio di Athena. The temple was famous for its opulence; the Roman Senate had difficulty preventing local governors from stealing the facade's ostentatious trinkets. The looting ceased with the arrival of St. Paul and Christianity, when the Temple of Athena became—or so the Siracusani like to claim—the Western Empire's first church. The crazed facade is the result of several centuries of alterations, one of them overseen by a drunken sculptor who is responsible for the engraving of Saint Lucia's name beneath a bearded man. *(Down V. Minerva from P. Archimede. Open daily 8am-noon and 4-7pm. Modest dress required.)*

FONTE ARETUSA. This small, ancient pond fed by a "miraculous" fresh-water spring near the sea overlooks Porta Grande. Siracusani believe that the nymph Arethusa escaped the enamored river god Alpheus by diving into the ocean and that the goddess Diana rescued her by transforming her into this fountain. Alpheus, pining for his lost love, transformed himself into a subterranean river, so their waters could mingle eternally. The river surfaces here at the Fonte Aretusa. When an animal was sacrificed in Corinth, Syracusans believed the blood from its ritual washing traveled underground to this fountain—another good reason not to drink Italian fountain water. *(P. Aretusa. From P. Duomo, walk down V. Picherale.)*

ENTERTAINMENT

Siracusani, like all Italians, fall prey in summer to powerful ancestral instincts that force them to leave the cities and head for the beach. For most nightlife, you'll have to follow them seaward. **Fontane Bianche** is a glitzy, fleshy beach with many discos by night; staying at the *campeggio* there ensures you a place to sleep when the buses stop. Take bus #21, 22, or 24 (30min., L1000). **Malibu,** a packed outdoor dance club, is 15 minutes away by taxi or an unpleasant 1½hr. walk past the end of C. Gelone and out of town. (Cover L10,000.) On Ortigia, the summer nightlife isn't as bad as locals claim, but it still leaves something to be desired; if you're around in winter, check out the trendy after work spot **Troubador,** off P. S. Rocco. In summer, the Ortigia hotspot is **Nonsolobar Bar,** or "Not Just-A-Bar Bar," behind the Fonte Aretusa. Patrons drink in a mossy natural grotto below street level. (Open W-M 7am-2am; cave open only after 6pm.)

The prime place to promenade is along the port in the **Foro Vittorio Emanuele.** After 8pm, a sea of Siracusani and their rambunctious children flood the area by the water, taking breaks in cafes, admiring the trinkets for sale, playing passionate foosball (L500), and gawking at the foreign luxury yachts docked nearby.

Every even-numbered year the city stages **Greek classical drama** in the spectacular Greek theater. The APT office has all the details. Tickets for **Istituto Nazionale del Dramma Antico** (INDA; ☎0931 674 15 and 0931 653 73) are available at the theater box office daily 10am-1pm and 6-9:30pm. Tickets are also available on Ortigia in the Palazzo Greco daily 9am-1pm. General admission is L15,000; reserved seats start at L30,000. Performances begin at 9pm.

DAYTRIP FROM SYRACUSE: NOTO

SAIS and AST buses head from Syracuse in a steady stream (40min.; 12 per day, return at 5:20, 5:45, and 6:50pm; L5000, round-trip L8000). The ticket office is opposite the bus stop in the Bar Efirmmedio. You can also reach Noto by train (30min., 9 per day, L3200), but the station is 20min. uphill from town.

After the 1693 earthquake shook Sicily's shore, the filthy-rich Laudlino family made Noto, 32km southwest of Syracuse, their favorite renovation project. Its architecture epitomizes Baroque elegance, with monumental staircases, chubby cupid moldings, and pot-belly balconies.

Toward the city center from C. V. Emanuele stands the immense **Chiesa di San Francesco all'Immacolata,** built in 1704. (Open daily 7:30am-noon and 4-8pm.) From C. V. Emanuele turn right on V. Niccolaci, and pause to gawk at the balconies of the **Palazzo Niccolaci,** supported by cherubs, griffins, and sirens. The noteworthy *duomo* contains captivating frescoes, currently under renovation. Nonetheless, the facade is worth a peek, if merely for the "SPQN" (Noto's adaptation of the ubiquitous imperial stamp "SPQR"—*senatus populusque romanus*) written above the bronze door. Fine **beaches** are 7km away at **Noto Marina.** Buses depart from the **Giardini Pubblici** (July-Aug. M-Sa 4 per day, Sept.-June 2 per day; L1200).

From the bus stop at **Giardini Pubblici** (Public Gardens), cross the empty green and head left under the **Porta Reale** (built in 1838) onto **Corso Vittorio Emanuele.** The **APT tourist office,** in P. XVI Maggio, is 500m ahead, to the right behind the octagonal red wall of Fontana d'Encole. (☎0931 57 37 79. English spoken. Free map. Open in summer M-Sa 8am-2pm and 4-7pm, Su 9am-1pm.) To reach the town center from the train station, follow the road leading uphill and to the right; at the 2nd traffic light, turn right, and then right again.

Trattoria al Buco, V. Zanardelli, 1, provides *affittacamere* of varying quality, most in the historic district. All units have kitchen, bath, eccentric furnishings, and mohair bedspreads. (☎0931 83 81 42. Singles L30,000; doubles L60,000. Rates may be negotiable for longer stays. The *trattoria* serves excellent homemade pasta, accompanied by infamous local wine. Feast on *tagliatelle alle melanzane* (egg noodles with eggplant) for L5000. (*Menù* L15,000. Cover L1000. Open daily 10am-3pm and 7pm-midnight.) Though it shares a building with the basilica, **Pasticceria La Vecchia Fontana,** C. V. Emanuele, 150, scoops sinfully good *gelato* (L2000). We're talking immaculate confection. (☎83 94 12. Open Tu-Su 7am-3pm and 5pm-midnight; no closing hour in Aug. AmEx.)

RAGUSA ☎0932

Hot Ragusa's frustratingly lethargic pace contrasts with the frantic modernity of other Sicilian cities. The language cascading off the Baroque buildings has very little to do with Italian, and it is rare that a tourist tongue is heard. A 200m cleft, remarkably lush and free of construction, splits the older section of **Ragusa Ibla** from its younger mate, **Ragusa Superiore.** Its views of the lush surrounding countryside, ornate *palazzi*, and secluded, contemplative atmosphere provide an escape into the Sicily of legends.

TRANSPORTATION

Trains: At the new town end of V. Roma, off P. della Libertà behind the bus stop. To: **Gela** (1½hr., 7 per day 4:08am-8:20pm, L8000); **Syracuse** (2hr., 13 per day 6:05am-6:32pm, L11,000); **Caltanissetta** (2¼hr., 6 per day 6:08am-5:20pm, L17,000); and **Palermo** (5¼hr., 3 per day 10:50am-4:17pm, L25,000).

Buses: Buses pull up beside the train station, just above P. della Libertà, at the new town end of V. Roma. To: **Noto** (1½hr.; M-F 7 per day 6:50am-7pm, Su 11am and 2:05pm; L7500); **Gela** (1½hr., M-F 9:45am and 4:15pm, L6500); **Catania** (2hr.; M-F 11 per day 5:45-7pm, Sa 8, 11am, and 2:30pm, Su 5 and 6pm; L12,500); **Syracuse** (2hr., M-F 7 per day 6:50am-7pm, L10,500); and **Palermo** (4hr.; M-F 4 per day 5:30am-5:30pm, Sa-Su 2:15 and 5:30pm; L22,500). Connections to **Agrigento** and **Enna** via Gela. Tickets at **Bar Puglisi,** across the street. Open daily 5am-10pm.

ORIENTATION AND PRACTICAL INFORMATION

The train and bus stations are in P. del Popolo and neighboring P. Gramsci. To reach the center from either of these adjacent *piazze*, turn left on **Viale Tenente Lena,** walk through P. Libertà on **Via Roma** and over the Ponte Senatore F. Pennavaria, the northernmost of three bridges crossing the Vallata Santa. **Corso Italia,** off V. Roma, leads downhill for several blocks, becomes **Via XXIV Maggio,** and ends at the Chiesa di Santa Maria della Scala. Here stairs and roads wind down to **Ragusa Ibla.** In Ibla, **Via Tenente di Stefano** leads past the AAPIT to the **Piazza del Duomo.**

Tourist Office: AAPIT, V. Capitano Bocchieri, 33 (☎0932 62 14 21 or 0932 65 48 23), in lower Ragusa Ibla beyond the *duomo* from the new city; look for signs in P. del Duomo. Red-carpet treatment accompanies brochures, maps, and info on nearby beaches and sights. English spoken. Open M-Sa 9am-1pm.

Emergencies: ☎113. **Police:** ☎112. **Medical emergency:** ☎118. **First Aid:** ☎0932 60 02 69. **Guarda Medica:** (☎0932 62 39 46), in P. Igea. **Hospital: Ospedale Civile** (☎0932 60 01 11), in a peach building on V. da Vinci.

Post Office: (☎0932 62 40 43), in P. Matteotti, 2 blocks down C. Italia from V. Roma. Open Oct.-June M-Sa 8:15am-6:30pm, last day of the month 8:15am-noon. **Postal Code:** 97100.

ACCOMMODATIONS AND CAMPING

Hotel San Giovanni, V. Transpontino, 3 (☎/fax 0932 62 10 13). With your back to the bus station, turn left down V. Transpontino, beyond V. Roma; the hotel is before Cappuccini Bridge. Great location, convenient to both stations, overlooking a cleft dividing the old and new towns. Quiet, with marble bathrooms and ceiling fans. Singles L40,000, with bath L60,000; doubles L60,000, with bath L90,000. V, MC, AmEx.

Hotel Jonio, V. Risorgimento, 49 (☎0932 62 43 22). Facing away from the train station entrance, walk across the *piazza* to V. Sicilia. Turn right, and walk past the gas station. Strong, hot showers. Singles L35,000, with bath L45,000; doubles L60,000, with bath L80,000; triples with bath L100,000. V, MC, AmEx.

Camping: Marina, 20km south of Ragusa. Tumino buses (☎0932 62 31 84) run from P. Gramsci in Ragusa to P. Duca degli Abruzzi in Marina (30min.; every hr.; L4000, round-trip L6500). L6000 per person, L6-10,000 per tent. **Baia del Sole** (☎0932 23 98 44), a nauseatingly well-organized "tourist village" near the beach, 1km down from the main *piazza* (with the water to your right) on Lungomare Andrea Doria. L6-10,000 per tent; L6000 supplement covers showers, although hot water usually shuts off after 6pm.

FOOD

While in Ragusa, try some *panatigghie* (thin pastries filled with the unholy trio of cocoa, cinnamon, and ground meat). Unfortunately, they aren't cheap, and neither are the meals at the quality *trattorie* where they're sold. The immense **SMA/UPIM supermarket** on V. Sicilia, to the right from the train station, provides another option. (Open M-Tu and Th-Sa 8:30am-8pm, W 8:30am-1pm.)

Pizzeria La Grotta (☎0932 22 73 70), on V. G. Cartia, the 2nd right off V. Roma with your back to the bridge. Backstreet pizzeria. The usual *tavola calda* standards with a twist: get the only eggplant *arancine* you'll find in Sicily, or chomp down on a venison sandwich. Open Th-Tu 5:30pm-midnight.

La Valle, V. Risorgimento, 70 (☎0932 22 93 41), downhill from Hotel Jonio. Waiters in Art Deco vests and bowties whisk bread to your table, popping tops off fizzy water. Peppermint green and curious pastel interior. Vegetarian-friendly pizza served. *Primi* from L7500-9500, *secondi* from L12,000. Cover L2500. Open Tu-Su 9am-3pm and 7pm-midnight.

La Rusticana, V. Venticinque Aprile, 68 (☎0932 22 79 81), in Ibla, 1 block from the public gardens. Exquisitely prepared dishes, and a plush-lined interior with velvet wallpaper. The desserts are brought in daily from Modica, Italy's pastry capital. *Primi* L7-8000, *secondi* from L17,000. Open W-M 11am-2:30pm and 8pm-late.

New Mexico, V. Risorgimento, 30 (☎0932 65 11 99). Near Hotel Jonio. Spaghetti Western revisited—cowboys, covered wagons, and John Wayne decor attempt to convince you that the Duke ate ricotta-filled *cavatelli* and *ravioli*. Pizza L4500. Open M-Sa 11am-3pm and 7pm-midnight. *Primi* from L7000, *secondi* L8-11,000. V, MC, AmEx.

SIGHTS AND ENTERTAINMENT

RAGUSA IBLA. The most interesting section of Ragusa is a steep and lovely 10-minute climb down from the church at the very bottom of C. Italia (a.k.a. V. XXIV Maggio). The stairs at S. Maria offer a stellar view of Ragusa Ibla, crowned by a monastery and the 18th-century dome of San Giorgio, which glows an unearthly turquoise at night. (Modest dress required in the church.) Walk down 200m of tricky steps to P. Repubblica. The road to the left circumscribes the town, passing abandoned monasteries and lush farmland. P. del Duomo di San Giorgio sits at the top of the city. C. XXV Aprile runs downhill from the *piazza* and ends at the **Giardino Ibleo,** whose shaded walks pass two churches and end in wide views of the surrounding countryside. *(Take the #3 city bus (L1000), departing every hr. from the station at P. del Popolo, and from C. Italia, next to the duomo.)*

MUSEO ARCHEOLOGICO. A daunting collection of broken jars from the nearby Syracusan colony of Camarina graces this gallery. *(Go down the stairs behind the STANDA off V. Roma. Turn right under the bridge, walk up the road, and take another right. ☎0932 62 29 63. Open M-Sa 9am-1:30pm and 3-5:30pm, Su 9am-1:30pm. L8000.)*

MARINA DI RAGUSA. In summer, any citizen with a swimsuit spends the weekend at this bikini-packing, Vespa-roaring, booty-shaking stretch of sand. The surprisingly clean beach is a madhouse. **Autolinee Tumino** (☎0932 62 31 84) runs buses to Marina from P. Gramsci (40min.; 14 per day; L3500, round-trip L6500). A schedule is posted in Polleria Giarrosto in Marina's P. Duca degli Abruzzi. In the same *piazza*, savor Marina's best *gelato* at **Delle Rose** (L2400 per scoop). Every year since 1990, Ragusa has hosted an **International piano/voice/composition** competition from late June to early July. Organized by a Sicilian-American professor at NYU, performances are held in the theater of Palazzo Comunale in Ragusa Ibla.

MILAZZO ☎090

Ready, set, hydrofoil. Milazzo is touted as the transportation bridge to the Aeolian Islands, the one-stop drop off point from Messina. If time is of the essence, you can be bused from the train station, dropped at the docks, packed onto a sprightly young hydrofoil, and skipping your way over waves to the archipelago in just over an hour. If the islands' easy going pace has already charmed you from across the bay, more infrequent (and inexpensive) ferries might grant an opportunity to take a load off and leave fresh in the morning.

TRANSPORTATION AND PRACTICAL INFORMATION. Trains: To: **Messina** (45min., every hr. 5:15am-9:07pm, L4500); **Taormina** (2hr., 10:32am, L8500); **Palermo** (2½hr., L23,000); and **Siracusa** (4¼hr., L18,000). Milazzo's center is a harrowing 10-minute orange bus ride from the train station. Whether arriving by train or bus, you will most likely be dropped in **Piazza Della Repubblica.** With your back to the water, the happening **Lungomare Garibaldi** curves around to the right. A left down Via Crispi and right into Piazza Caio Duilio, following the yellow signs, leads directly to the **tourist office,** P. C. Duillo, 20. The English-speaking staff hands out fold-out maps of town and armfuls of information on the islands. (☎090 922 28 65. Open July-Aug. M-F 8am-2:30pm and 3-6:30pm.) Milazzo's **castello** in the old center is considered one of Sicily's best: hourly guided tours run from 9am-8pm in summer. Call the tourist office for a monthly schedule.

ACCOMMODATIONS AND FOOD. At **Hotel Capitol,** V. G. Rizzo, 91, all 23 rooms have unusually comfortable beds; some have bathrooms nice enough to spend the day in. From the hydrofoil dock, take the first left off V. Manzoni onto V. G. Rizzo. (☎090 928 32 89. Singles L40,000, with bath L100,000; doubles L80,000, with bath L100,000.) To reach **Hotel Central,** V. del Sole, 8, turn right with your back to the water and take V. del Sole at the Agip station intersection. The owner parks a smart baby-blue, classic VW bug out front. All 12 rooms have a cheery yellow ambiance. (☎090 928 10 43. Singles L40,000; doubles with bath L80,000. **Pensione Cosenz,** V. E. Cosenz, 5 (☎090 928 2996), has amiable management. All rooms have bath. Head down V. del Sole and take the fourth left onto V. E. Cosenz. Call ahead June-Sept. If the Central doesn't suit you, **Hotel California,** V. del Sole, 9 (☎090 922 23 89), is just across the street. A few lumpy pillows never hurt anyone. Hardwood and pane glass doors open onto personal people-watching terraces, and the sixth-floor has great views. **Campground: Villaggio Turistico Cirucco** (☎090 928 46 46; open mid-June to mid-Oct.) and **Riva Smerelda** (☎090 928 29 80) are both located out on Capo Milazzo, 6km out of town (take the bus from P. della Repubblica).

For self-caterers, the well-stocked **Punto Convenienza Supermerkato** is at V. del Sole, 34, just 20m from neighboring Hotels California and Central. (Open Th-Tu 8:30am-1pm and 5-8:30pm.) **Fruit vendors** siesta under umbrellas at the corner of V. del Sole and V. M. Regis. *Pane, pane;* get your carbohydrates: the fresh bread fairy visits **Biscotti Focacce Panificio,** V. Umberto, 41, throughout the morning, and again around 4:30pm, in time for dinner. Take a right at the supermarket from V. del Sole, and left at the *piazza;* there's a yellow sign 200m down on the left. Enjoy homemade feasts of *bruscetta,* nectarines, and peach juice in the palm shaded **Piazza Natasi,** off V. Regis. If self-service is just too much of an effort, run on over to the air-conditioned **Pizzeria Da Tonino,** V. Manzoni, 4. The turquoise interior was designed by a New Mexican emigrant. Silverware comes tucked into funny paper envelopes. (Pizzas from L4000. Open daily 11:30am-2:25pm and 6:30pm-midnight.)

AEOLIAN ISLANDS (ISOLE EOLIE)

Set in the sparkling Mediterranean, the **Aeolian** (or **Lipari**) **Islands** promise visitors a chance to savor *la dolce vita*. The archipelago comprises one of Italy's last unspoiled seashores, glorified by Homer as the second home of the gods; only recently has it become a tourist spot. Incomparable vistas, fiery volcanoes, and rock beaches all contribute to the area's remarkable beauty. Although pleasantly affordable in the off-season, the islands suffer an exponential rise in prices at the end of July and August. Those planning a summer excursion should make reservations no later than May. Fortunately, Lipari does have a youth hostel; but if even this shelter's rates seem daunting, whipping out a sleeping bag on Aeolian beaches is a pleasant (though risky) alternative to shelling out hard-earned *lire*.

Although often called sisters, each of the seven isles possesses a distinct character. Visit **Lipari** for a helpful tourist center, a castle, and easily navigable natural splendor; **Vulcano** for bubbling mud baths and a sulfurous crater; **Stromboli** for spectacular colors and a restless volcano; **Panarea** for inlets and an elite clientele; and **Salina** for grottoes and luxurious vegetation.

Before traveling to any of the other islands, buy food at the **UPIM supermarket** on C. V. Emanuele in Lipari (see p. 603) in order to avoid dishing out L1000 for a roll in the meagerly stocked *alimentari* or L30,000 for dinner at a *pensione*. Bargaining is always helpful. Though Aeolian residents are charged three times less than tourists when buying hydrofoil tickets, *Let's Go* does not recommend asking a friendly local to purchase them for you. That would be breaking the law.

FERRY SCHEDULE

DESTINATION	DURATION	OFF-SEASON	HIGH-SEASON
Vulcano	1½hr.	5 per day, L10,000	3-5 per day, L12,000
Lipari	2hr.	8 per day, L10,500	3-6 per day, L12,500
Salina	3hr.	5 per day, L13,000	2-4 per day, L16,000
Panarea	3½hr.	3 per week, L12,300	1-2 per day, L15,000
Alicudi	4hr.	6 per week, L22,000	W-M 1 per day, L24,000
Filicudi	4½hr.	6 per week, L18,000	W-M 1 per day, L21,300
Stromboli	5hr.	3 per week, L16,500	M-Tu and Th-Sa 1-2 per day, L20,000

HYDROFOIL SCHEDULE

DESTINATION	DURATION	OFF-SEASON	HIGH-SEASON
Vulcano	40min.	8-9 per day, L18,000	15 per day, L20,000
Panarea	40min.	6-8 per day, L23,500	7 per day, L25,000
Lipari	50min.	9-11 per day, L19,500	15 per day, L21,500
Salina	1½hr.	8-9 per day, L24,000	8 per day, L24,500
Stromboli	2hr.	7-8 per day, L30,000	7 per day, L31,000
Filicudi	2hr.	4 per day, L31,500	2-3 per day, L33,500
Alicudi	3½hr.	4-5 per day, L40,000	2-3 per day, L41,000

GETTING THERE

The archipelago lies off Sicily, north of **Milazzo,** the principal and least expensiv embarkation point. **Trains** run to Milazzo from **Messina** (40min., 18 per day, L4500 and **Palermo** (3hr., L15,500). **Giuntabus,** V. Terranova, 8 (☎090 67 37 82 or 090 67 5 49), brings you directly to Milazzo's port from: **Messina** (45min.; M-Sa 14 per day Su 1 per day; L5000) and from the **Catania airport** (Apr.-Sept. daily 4pm, L16,000 From the Milazzo train station, you can buy a ticket for the orange **AST bus** to th seaport (10min., every hr., L600). **Ferries** leave less frequently from **Naples's** Mol Beverello. **Hydrofoils** *(aliscafi)* run regularly in late July and August from **Messina** **Naples, Cefalù, Palermo,** and **Reggio Calabria** for a bit more than a ferry.

Three companies operate from Milazzo; fortunately, all have their ticket offices on V. dei Mille. Hydrofoils run twice as often as ferries for twice the price and half the time. Off-season runs from Sept.-June 30. High-season is July-Aug. 31.

Navigazione Generale Italiana (NGI): V. dei Mille, 26 (☎090 928 40 91; fax 090 928 34 15), in Milazzo; V. Ten. Mariano Amendola, 14 (☎090 981 19 55), in Lipari; Molo di Levante (☎090 985 24 01), in Vulcano; and P. Santa Marina (☎090 984 30 03), in Salina. Sends ferries to the islands.

SNAV: (☎090 928 45 09), V. dei Mille, sends hydrofoils to the islands.

Siremar: (☎090 928 32 42; fax 090 928 32 43), V. dei Mille, sends both ferries and hydrofoils to the islands. Also has offices in Lipari (☎090 981 22 00) and in Naples (☎081 551 21 12) from which it services the Aeolian islands (see Naples, p. 473).

LIPARI ☎090

...a floating island, a wall of bronze and splendid smooth sheer cliffs.
—Homer

Centuries ago, wild-eyed pirates ravaged Lipari's shores. Today, boats and hydrofoils let loose swarms of equally ravenous visitors. Lipari is, and has always been, the most developed of the islands off the coast of Sicily. Because it is the largest of the Aeolians, it was always the first to get burned, razed, sacked, and depopulated through 2000 years of invasions. You can hear the influence of the raiding civilizations in the local dialect, which is interspersed with French adjectives, Arabic nouns, and Spanish verbs. In the town, pastel colored houses and bright shops surround the base of a medieval *castello*, the site of an ancient Greek acropolis. Although superficially serene, Lipari bustles with summer activities from folk festivals to discos. From the busy port, crowds move to Spiaggia Bianca and Spiaggia Porticello, the most popular beaches, to splash idly in the waves and bask in luxurious sunshine. For those who prefer the colors of the surrounding sea and mountains to neon umbrellas and swimsuits, short hikes often lead to private beaches. Inexpensive hotels, luscious beaches, and one of Italy's best museums have made Lipari the ideal launching point for daytrips to the six neighboring islands.

TRANSPORTATION

Public Transportation: Autobus Urso Guglielmo (☎090 981 12 62 or 090 981 10 26), on V. Cappuccini. Ticket office open daily 9am-1pm; tickets also available on the bus. Hits most spots on the island (see **Sights,** p. 604, for specific stops).

Taxis: on C. V. Emanuele (☎090 981 11 10) or at Marina Corta (☎090 981 11 95). You can also hail one at either port.

ORIENTATION AND PRACTICAL INFORMATION

The looming *castello* sits at the center of the town's shoreline, separating the ferry dock on the right from the hydrofoil landing on the left as you approach by sea. The most vital services lie between the borders of the two ports and **Corso Vittorio Emanuele II,** Lipari's main drag, which runs parallel to the harbor. From the front of the hydrofoil dock, **Via Garibaldi** runs around the base of the *castello* to the ferry dock. A rock stairway leads up to the castle and hostel halfway along this street.

TOURIST, FINANCIAL, AND LOCAL SERVICES

Tourist Office: AAST delle Isole Eolie, C. V. Emanuele, 202 (☎090 988 00 95; fax 090 98 11 190; email infocast@netnet.it; www.netnet.it/aasteolie). From the ferry docks, take a right up V. Garibaldi for 200m, then turn left on V. XXIV Maggio, following the traffic. Turn right onto C. V. Emanuele—the office is 100m down on the right. The information hub for all 7 islands. Offices elsewhere are nonexistent, or they perform a disappearing act at the end of August. English-speaking staff proffers a comprehensive color-coded booklet, *Ospitalita in blu* (even published in Japanese). Pick up a map at any *tabacchi*. Open July-Aug. M-Sa 8am-2pm and 4-10pm, Su 8am-2pm; Sept.-June M-F 8am-2pm and 4:30-7:30pm, Sa 8am-2pm.

Currency Exchange: Banca del Sud (☎090 981 13 47) and **BAE** (☎090 981 21 18) are on C. V. Emanuele. Both change AmEx traveler's checks. Open M-F 8:30am-1:30pm and 2:40-4:30pm. The post office offers comparable rates (cash only). Lipari is the only island with plentiful exchanges (and ATMs), so fill your wallet here.

Bike/Moped Rental: De. Sco., V. Stradale Pianoconto, 5 (☎090 981 32 88), at the end of C. V. Emanuele closest to the hydrofoil docks. Flamenco music and shiny scooters lined up showroom-style. 24hr. rental includes gas. Helmets provided. Open 8:30am-8pm. June-Aug. L35-50,000. Nov.-Mar. L25,000; Apr.-May L30,000; V, MC. **Carbonara** (☎090 981 19 94), on C. V. Emanuele just a few steps away from De. Sco., offers 12hr. rental. July-Aug. L45,000. Sept-June L30,000.

EMERGENCY AND COMMUNICATIONS

Emergencies: ☎113. **Carabinieri:** ☎112 or 090 981 13 33 in emergencies. **Hospital:** (☎090 988 51), on V. Santana, off the southern end of C. V. Emanuele. At end of C. V. Emanuele, descend the sidestreet between scooter rentals and take a right up V. Roma. V. Santana turns upward at the 2nd left. **First Aid:** ☎090 988 52 67. **Night Doctor: Guardia Medica** (☎090 988 52 26), office 50m up V. Garibaldi from the waterfront, on the left under the Italian flag.

Pharmacy: Farmacia Internazionale, C. V. Emanuele, 128 (☎090 981 15 83). Open M-F 9am-1pm and 5-9pm. **Farmacia Cincotta,** V. Garibaldi, 60 (☎090 981 14 72). Open M-F 9am-1pm and 5-9pm. Mini computer screen on storefront window of every pharmacy list the pharmacist on call 24hr.

Internet Access: NetNet, V. Mare, 3 (☎090 981 24 62; www.net.net.it). With your back to water, turn left off the port, cross the bridge, and continue up to the church. Turn right on V. Mare. It's the 2nd door on the left. The Internet service provider to the islands has 9 computers. L5000 for 30min. Open 4-8pm. **Centro Telefonia** and **S.I.E.L.** on the *lungomare* in Canneto also provide Internet connections at L10,000 per hr.

Post Office: C. V. Emanuele, 207 (☎090 981 13 79). From the tourist office, 40m up C. V. Emanuele to the left, in the building that looks like 2 stacked steam-pipes. Open M-F 8:30am-1pm and 1:30-6pm, Sa 8:30am-1pm. Fax available. **Postal Code:** Lipari 98055; Canneto-Lipari: 98052; the rest of the islands: 98050.

ACCOMMODATIONS AND CAMPING

Three steps down the swaying hydrofoil exit ramp and you will be swamped with offers for *affittacamere* (private rooms for rent). If you have not yet booked a room, especially in July-Aug., these are often worth checking out. Ask to see the room before accepting, and don't be afraid to show a bit of hesitation, as prices tend to drop a few thousand *lire*. Because many private rooms are not registered (and thus are technically illegal), it is always a good idea to politely ask for your price quote in writing. As the summer progresses, Lipari is increasingly invaded by tourists, and the island reaches its saturation point in August. Hotels fill almost instantaneously and owners raise their prices by as much as 25%. Make reservations far in advance, even for early July.

Casa Vittorio, Vico Sparviero, 15 (☎/fax 090 981 15 23). Head up V. Garibaldi from the dock. Turn left down 1st side street and right down Vico Sparviero. The *casa* is the yellow building halfway down on left. If door is locked, continue to the end of the street and turn right. At the red iron gate ring the top white button on the left for the owner. Mama, Papa, and baby bear sized rooms and apartments from well-furnished singles to 5-person penthouses. Top-floor communal kitchen and open terrace with an ocean view. May-July singles L30-40,000; doubles L60-70,000, with kitchen L80,000.

Pensione Enso il Negro, V. Garibaldi, 29 (☎090 981 31 63), 20m up V. Garibaldi and up 3 flights. Terracotta-tiled rooftop terrace has tiptoe edge over others. White-washed archways, blond wood furnishings, and flourishing internal courtyard. 24 beds. Nov.-Mar. L40,000 per person; June L60,000; July L75,000; Aug. L100,000.

Tivoli (Quatropani) (☎/fax 090 988 60 31 or 0339 263 08 76). Ask at tourist office for directions to this former newly-wed getaway. Quatropani sits on the northwest cliffs of the Lipari island, 500 sheer meters down to the sea. Sailboats look like toys and waves like tiny rivulets. Family-run, with a terrace placed by the hand of God. 5 double rooms, 3 separate apartments. June L30,000. July L35,000; half-pension L75,000. Aug. L40,000, half-pension L80,000. Discounts for children.

Hotel Europeo, C. V. Emanuele, 98 (☎090 981 15 89). Great location. Rooms are bright and monkishly bare. L10,000 less if you use the bright purple common bathroom. Mmmm, grapey. Sept.-June singles L40,000; doubles L80,000. July-Aug. singles L55,000; doubles L110,000.

Camping: Baia Unci, V. Marina Garibaldi, 2 (☎090 981 19 09 or 090 981 25 27 in low season; fax 090 981 17 15), 2km from Lipari at the entrance to the hamlet of the beachfront town Canneto. When the islanders emigrated to Australia, the gum trees immigrated here. No koala bears. 10m from the beach. Amiable management and an inexpensive self-service restaurant (open daily noon-2pm and 7pm-midnight). Reserve for Aug. Open Mar. 15-Oct. 15. June-Aug. L15-19,000 per person with tent.

SICILY

FOOD

Legions of lovers have sprinkled sauces, garnished salads, and spiced meats with the island's *capperi* (capers), renowned for their aphrodisiac powers. The extremely sweet local Malvasia dessert wine perfectly complements dinner. Unfortunately, eating cheaply on Lipari is something of a challenge. Anieri Bartolo's **UPIM supermarket,** C. V. Emanuele, 212, stocks the basics. (☎090 981 15 87. Open M-Sa 8am-3:20pm and 4-11pm. V, MC, AmEx.) The *alimentari* lining C. V. Emanuele are open daily and sell cheap fruit.

Da Gilberto, V. Garibaldi, 22-24 (☎090 981 27 56), has become famous nationwide for what may well be Italy's best sandwiches. Into the hot *panini* go any of the ingredients on Gilberto's shelves: prosciutto, capers, fresh and dried tomatoes, olives, garlic, mint, the kitchen sink, etc. Construct whatever you want, starting from L5000. 7pm-2am, 7am-10pm in low season.

La Cambusa, V. Garibaldi, 72. Checkered tablecloths spill out into the street. This tiny *trattoria* is attended by one owner/waiter and his wonder-wife. Exceptionally tasty *pasta normale* (plain ol' spaghetti) with nothing normal about it. *Primi* from L8000. Cover L2000. Open daily 7-11pm.

Il Galeone, C. V. Emanuele, 220 (☎090 981 14 63 or 090 981 26 35), close to the ferry dock. Lipari's best spot for people-watching. The bar, with its hundred bottles of liquor on the wall, is quite a sight (and makes for a catchy song). Pizza, including *eoliana* (with basil, capers, tomatoes, and onions) from L7000, *primi* from L7000, *secondi* from L10,000. Cover L3000. Open June-Sept. daily 8am-midnight; Oct.-May Th-Tu 8pm-midnight. V, MC.

Kasbah, V. Maurolico, 25 (☎090 981 10 75), on a sidestreet connecting C. V. Emanuele and V. Garibaldi. Arabic archways, Eolian pizzas, thick Irish bread, and a backyard jungle garden—cobalt tile mosaic and wrought-iron tables, oh-so-sexy jazz music, wind chimes, and smartly dressed (and handsome) waiters scurrying about. Come, if only for the ambiance and a bit of Malvasia. Pizza from L8000, stylishly presented salads L4000.

Pasticceria Subba, C. V. Emanuele, 92 (☎090 981 13 52). The archipelago's oldest *pasticceria* is considered one of Italy's best. Indulge in the heavenly *paradiso,* a lemon-stuffed dumpling topped with almonds. Pastries from L1500. Open in high season Th-Tu 7am-3am; off-season Th-Tu 7am-midnight.

SIGHTS AND ENTERTAINMENT

A splendidly rebuilt medieval fortress dwarfs the surrounding town. It shares the hill with an archaeological park, the **San Bartolo church**, and the **Museo Eoliano.**

MUSEO ARCHEOLOGICO EOLIANO. Aside from the beaches, this archaeological gallery is definitely the best sight Lipari has to offer. English captions explain a dizzying parade of artifacts from prehistoric Lipari, including many of the huge urns into which Liparites were placed for burial. The collection also contains numerous painted Greek jars and *kratere.* Check out the outrageous funerary jars which display the raucous hedonism the deceased were expected to engage in upon arrival in the underworld. Lava-lovers should check out the **Serione Geologico-Vulcanologica,** showcasing the rich history of volcanic islands. *(☎090 988 01 74. Up the stone steps off V. Garibaldi. Turn left at the church. Open May-Oct. M-Su 9am-1:30pm and 4-7pm; Nov.-Apr. M-Su 9am-1:30pm and 3-6pm. L8000.)*

CHURCH AND ARCHEOLOGICAL PARK. San Bartolo is currently undergoing violent restoration, but you can still look at the marble mosaics in the vestry. Originally constructed in the 12th century, the abbey was rebuilt after a 16th-century pirate raid burned it to the ground. Across the way from the church is Lipari's archeological park, where 3500-year-old buildings have been excavated. *(Both sites are across from the museum. Church L1000.)*

BEACHES, BATHING, AND BUMMING AROUND

Lipari is known for its beaches and its hillside views. Take the Lipari-Cavedi bus to Canneto, a couple of kilometers north, for the popular beaches at **Spiaggia Bianca** (White Beach) and **Porticello.** Spiaggia Bianca is *the* spot for topless (and sometimes bottomless) sunbathing. Protect your flesh—the pebbles are sharp and the sun is hot. From Canneto center the secluded, sandy coves flanking Spiaggia Bianca can be explored by renting one of the rafts, kayaks, or canoes that line the beach at V. M. Garibaldi (L6-8000 per hr.; L25-35,000 per day). The sand isn't as white anymore, now that environmentalists have stopped the dumping of pumice into the sea. Just a few kilometers north of Canneto lies **Pomiciazzo,** where white pumice mines line the road. On clear days, spectacular views of Salina, Panarea and Stromboli adorn the horizon. A few kilometers north at **Porticello,** you can bathe at the foot of the mines while small flecks of stone float on the sea's surface. As you dive beneath the waves for polished obsidian, notice the red and black veins that stretch from the beach into the seabed. For the island's finest view, take the Lipari-Quattropani bus to the Pianoconte stop, and head over to **Monte S Angelo.** The path to Monte S. Angelo is tiny and hidden; ask or you'll never find it.

From July to September, **"Bus Tours of the Isle of Lipari"** (L5000) run from **Autobu Urso Guglielmo** (☎090 981 12 62) on V. Cappuccini. But the best way to see th island's many tiny beaches is a leisurely day aboard a rented **boat** from the hydro foil port in Lipari. **Menalda Tours,** V. V. Emanuele, 247 (☎090 988 05 73; fax 090 98 01 59), runs excursions to Salina, Lipari, and Panarea (L45,000), Strombo (L45,000), and Vulcano (L20,000). Times and frequency vary through the summe For lower prices, try privately contracting a fishing boat. Bargain for a dece price—L15,000 per person per hour is reasonable.

ENTERTAINMENT

Two cups of disco fever, one midnight pirate boat ride, and a twist of lemon i your rum and Coke. A lamp-lit pirate ship leaves for Vulcano's **Euro-disco** from th Lipari docks. Good-size crowds of all ages hop on board every Saturday night bounce around until the early morning hours. Swarthy captain warns that ar sober return passengers will have to swim to Alicudi. Tickets may be purchased Salvatore's shorefront stand. (L20,000 for star-lit voyage and ticket. No matt what anyone says, the boat will leave an hour late and return at 5am.)

FESTIVALS

Religious fervor and summer joy combine celebrating the patron St. Bartholomew. Lipari hosts a vibrant procession, fireworks, and other **festivities** on **August 24.** Watch a donkey race, stomp on grapes, learn to weave a basket, or drink a lot of wine. The Pianoconte district **Wine and Bread** festival kicks off in mid-November.

VULCANO ☎090

Stretch out and immerse yourself; the hand of the god Vulcan will hold you gently, transforming thoughts into bubbles of music and culture.

—A signpost in Vulcano

Although the psychedelic sensations promised by the words of signposts may elude you, the bright yellow streaks of rock and the funky fragrance of rotten egg is sure to stir some passionate exclamations. Vulcano's nature must be seen (and smelled) to be believed. Frolic on unique black beaches, climb up the sulfurous crater, dip your feet into the bubbling sea, or sink into therapeutic mud. Beware—some geologists think the gurgling volcano will burst its top within the next 20 years. For now, the great furnace lies dormant at the island's center. Its proximity to Lipari and pervading sulfur perfume make a day in Vulcano time enough.

The legends surrounding Vulcano have, not surprisingly, always been tied to the volcano. Sages, from Aristotle to Thucydides to Homer, called the island home to Hephaestus (Vulcan), god of fire and blacksmiths. Medieval lore regarded the deep crater as the gate to Hell. And much like Hell, Vulcano is a summer island; before June and after September, most hostels and restaurants close down, making it hard to find a place to curl up for the night.

TRANSPORTATION

Ferries: N.G.I. Biglietteria (☎090 985 24 01), under a blue awning on V. Provinciale, just off P. Levante. To **Lipari** (30min., 3-4 per day, L2500) and **Milazzo** (1½hr.; 4 per day; Sept.-June L11,000, July-Aug. L12,000).

Hydrofoils: SNAV (☎090 985 22 30), in a tiny cranny directly off the port between a yellow bar and big white hotel; **Siremar** (☎090 985 21 49), at the top of an elevated stone walkway at the Porto Levante intersection. Both run to **Lipari** (7min., 22 per day, L4500); **Milazzo** (40min., 14 per day, L20,000). SNAV makes the hike to **Palermo** (4hr., 7:45am-4:30pm, L60,000).

Buses: Scaffidi Tindaro (☎090 985 30 47), in front of the Ritrovo Remigio bar, just off the port on V. Provinciale. Buses run from the port to Vulcano Piano (L3000).

Taxis: (☎090 985 24 04), or at the stand in the port. Call **Centro Nautico Baia di Levante** (see **boat rental,** below) for 24hr. watertaxi service.

ORIENTATION AND PRACTICAL INFORMATION

Undomesticated Vulcano refuses to mark its streets or number its buildings, but with a dash of directions and a sprinkling of specificity, any traveler can cope. Ferries and hydrofoils dock at **Porto di Levante,** on the eastern side of the isthmus. With your back to the dock, **Via Provinciale** curves to the left (toward the volcano), and **Via Porto Levante** all the way to the right leads into the center of town. As you walk down **Via Porto Levante,** the road curving back and right leads past **Spiaggia Sabbie Nere** (Black Sands Beach) to the Vulcanello peninsula. Farther down, V. Porto Levante splits three ways at the squat stone statue of "Aeolus at Rest." To the left on a little spur that rejoins **V. Provinciale** are most of Vulcano's shops and boutiques; ahead is a less crowded road leading to the island's western coast, and to the right is a little *piazzetta* with a pharmacy at its far end. Vulcano has no street signs; don't be afraid to ask for directions even if you don't know Italian.

TOURIST, FINANCIAL, AND LOCAL SERVICES

Tourist Office: AAST, V. Provinciale, 41 (☎090 985 20 28). Open July-Aug. daily 8am-1:30pm and 3-5pm. For info on **rented rooms** *(affittacamere)*, call ☎090 985 21 42. Otherwise, get info from the Lipari tourist office (see p. 601).

Bank: Banca de Sicilia, 5min. down from the port on V. Provinciale, has an **ATM.**

Currency Exchange: SNAV Office (☎090 985 22 30), at Porto di Levante.

Boat Rental: Centro Nautico Baia di Levante (☎090 982 21 97 or 0339 337 27 95) under a canopy on the beach behind the Ritrovio Remigio bar, near the hydrofoil dock. 4-person motorboats (L150,000 plus gas) 8am-8pm. Larger boats available.

Scooter and Bicycle Rentals: The loud yellow sign of **Noleggio da Paolo** (☎090 985 21 12) greets travelers right off the dock. Luigi at **Noleggio Sprint** (☎0347 760 02 75) is located down the middle extension of V. Provinciale. Paolo and Luigi duke it out in price wars each year; make a quick rate comparison. May L30,000; June L40,000; July-Aug. L60-75,000. Bicycles L3-10,000. Open 8am-8pm.

EMERGENCY AND COMMUNICATIONS

Police: ☎090 985 21 10. **First Aid:** ☎090 985 22 20.

Pharmacy: Farmacia Bonarrigo (☎090 985 22 44), straight ahead from the port, at the far end of the *piazzetta,* off the town center. Open M-F 9am-1pm and 5-9pm, Sa 9am-1pm. V, MC.

Post Office: down V. Provinciale; do *not* turn right at the arrow saying "posta." Open M-F 8:30am-1pm, Sa 8:30am-12:30pm. **Postal Code:** 98050.

ACCOMMODATIONS AND CAMPING

Reasonable rooms are easy to find in winter, but spring and summer can be challenging. Call ahead in July and August.

Hotel Agostino (☎/fax 090 985 23 42). Convenience, convenience. From your terrace, observe the market below, pharmacy to the left, and the slip of bubbling *Aquacalda* just beyond. Double and triple rooms with sky-lit baths open onto terraces big enough to cook dinner, sleep, and even throw a party. All 8 rooms with TV, mini-stove, fridge, and A/C. Cribs available. All terraces are not created equal; ask for room #19 if you wanna party. Extra person costs 35% more. Doubles Jan.-May L70,000; June L80-100,000; Aug. L140,000. Solo travelers should seek discounts of up to L20,000 in off season.

Pensione La Giara (☎090 985 22 29), down V. Provinciale, on the way to the crater from the hydrofoils. Aqua-trimmed rooms with fridge, A/C, bathroom, and candy-cane striped bedcovers. 2nd floor rooms let in more sunlight. Rooftop terrace. Breakfast included during summer. Apr.-May L43,000; June L50,000; July L59,000; Aug. L72-95,000; Sept. L43-59,000.

Camping: Campeggio Togo Togo (☎090 985 23 03), at Porto Ponente on the opposite side of Vulcanello's isthmus neck, 1½km from the hydrofoil dock and adjacent to *Sabbie Nere* (black beach). Showers and hot water included. Pizzeria and Internet point in Aug. Open Apr.-Sept., reserve in Aug. L15,000 per person. 15 quad bungalows with TV, fridge, and kitchenette L35,000 per person.

FOOD

The **Tridial Market** (☎090 985 22 22) in the little white *piazza* off the Aeolus center, has all the basics, including an inexpensive sandwich counter. (Open 8:30am-1pm and 4-8pm.) For fruit and vegetables, there is an *alimentari* on V. Provinciale, toward the crater from the port. *Granitas* (crushed ice drinks) and *gelato* are in abundance at the port, but take a plunge off the main roads for a good full meal. The long and winding road past the crater to isolated Gelso ends in two family-run restaurants (15km to work up an appetite).

Il Sestante-Ritrovo Remigio (☎090 985 20 85), near the port. Hot and cold sandwiches, *gelato*, and probably the widest selection of desserts on the isles. *Tiramisu* (L3000), *cassata* (L4000), *cannoli* (L2500), and an awesome selection of marzipan fruits. Terrace for people-watching. Piano bar and dancing July 10-Sept. 10. Open daily Sept.-July 6am-1am; Aug. 6am-3:30am.

Don Piricuddu (☎090 985 24 24), 5min. down the middle fork of V. P. Levante. Chic open-air establishment with periwinkle tablecloths; far enough away from the port to be authentic (not distant enough to be cheap). Excellent seafood salad (L11,000) and traditional catch-of-the-day fish. Cover L3000. Open noon-2:30pm and 7:30pm-2am.

Ristorante Il Castello (☎090 985 21 17), on Vulcano Porto, has Sicilian specialties served cafeteria-style. Pizza from L6000. Self-service lunch L15,000. Open July-Aug. daily noon-2:30pm and 8-10pm.

Faraglione Hotel (☎090 985 20 54). Ever longed for an onion *granita*? Crazy Guiseppe whips up 20 fresh flavors of icy goodness each morning. Swizzle traditional nectarine, strawberry, and grape, or go wild with outrageous cucumber, carrot, or rose petal.

SIGHTS

GRAN CRATERE. Anyone visiting Vulcano for more than a day should tackle the one hour hike to the inactive crater, up a snaking footpath along the mountainside. Visible from the base, the path begins as a well-worn ash sand trail before slashing across the top through more difficult orange rock formations, powdered with moon dust (watch the puffs that appear as you step). At the topmost ridge, you'll begin to pass the crater's bright yellow fumaroles, fissures in the mountain from which noxious smoke pours. The smoke is perfectly safe to breathe (though unpleasantly hot) and supposedly good for your lungs. Between 11am and 3pm the sun transforms the volcano into a furnace, so head out in the early morning or late afternoon. Bring sunscreen, a hat, plenty of water, and sturdy climbing shoes. Obey the signs, and don't sit or lie down as poisonous gases are heavy and tend to accumulate close to the ground. Though you risk taking an unpleasant spill, sprinting straight down the side of the volcano shaves a good 30 minutes off the time required for descent (and is quite a rush to boot). *(With your back to the water at the port turn left onto V. Provinciale, and follow it until you reach a path with "Cratere" signs. The notices point the way to a dirt turn-off 300m down on the left.)*

ACQUACALDA. Near Porto Levante, underwater volcanic outlets make the sea percolate like a jacuzzi. You'll get used to the heat, but not to the sulfurous holes in your bathing suit; wear something you don't mind destroying. **Ugly bathing suits** (L20,000) are available nearby. (*Directly behind the mud baths. From the port, walk up Porto Levante to the town center and turn right at the statue of Aeolus.)*

LAGHETTO DI FANGHI. Get back to childish roots, and jump into this famous mud pool, a bubbling pit frequented by hundreds of zealots who spread the allegedly therapeutic glop all over their bodies. Not only is the stuff green and stanky, it's also high in **sulfuric acid** and quite **radioactive.** Remove all silver and leather accessories, and keep it away from your eyes. If some should happen to get in, *immediately* rinse them with running water and a few drops of lemon juice from a nearby restaurant. *(Up V. Provinciale and to the right from the port.)*

BEACHES AND BOATING

Sunbathers under bright striped umbrellas line the crescent shore of **Sabbie Nere** (Black Sand), Vulcano's best and most-frequented beach. The water is clear and the sand is jet black. To enjoy yourself a bit farther out to sea, hire **boats** from C. La Cava (☎090 981 33 00), on V. Porto Levante across from the *tabacchi*. (From the port, turn left at the town center—past Aquacalda and the mudbaths.)

OTHER ISLANDS

STROMBOLI ☎090

The billowing clouds and bubbling lava that plume from the island of Stromboli (pop. 370) give credence to the ancient wisdom "where there is smoke, there is fire." Stromboli is still an active volcano; the town, however, lies dormant until the summer tourist season. From the coal-black beach, virgin-white houses climb the rich green slope. Only the yuppie boutiques, brimming with china and handpainted t-shirts, hint that tourists flood the island. The deluge is at its height from mid-June to September, making cheap accommodations almost impossible to find. In the off-season, many *pensioni* are closed and owners are reluctant to rent rooms for fewer than three nights at a time. Ferries are rare, so it is worthwhile to call ahead.

TRANSPORTATION. Along the shorefront, **Siremar** (☎090 98 60 11; open 2:30-6pm), **SNAV** (☎090 98 60 03), and **N.G.I.** (☎090 98 30 03) run comparatively infrequent ferries and hydrofoils to the islands. Boat rentals are available at the port from the **Società Navigazione Pippo.** (☎090 98 61 35. Open 9am-noon and 2-10pm. L70-130,000 per 4hr. rental, 10am-2pm or 2-6pm, gas not included.)

ORIENTATION AND PRACTICAL INFORMATION. On the calmer slopes of smoking Stromboli, the three towns of Scari, Ficogrande, and Piscita have melded into one continuation of whitewash known as the town of Stromboli.

From the ferry docks, the wide *lungomare* is on the right, while the narrow **Via Roma** heads toward the center of town. Twisting uphill to the left, the hike up V. Roma passes the following: the **carabinieri** station (☎090 98 60 21), the **post office** (☎090 98 60 27; open M-Sa 8:10-1:20pm with **currency exchange**), the island's **only ATM,** and the **pharmacy** (☎090 98 67 13; open June-Aug. 8:30am-1pm and 4-9pm; Sept.-May 8:30am-1pm and 4-7:30pm; V, MC, AmEx), and finally reaches **Piazza San Vincenzo.** V. Roma then dips downhill becoming **Via Vittorio Emanuele,** running past the **Guardia Medica** (☎090 98 60 97) to the end of town.

ACCOMMODATIONS. Stromboli's hotels are booked solid in August, and your best bet may be one of the un-reservable affittacamere. You should expect to pay between L30,000 and L50,000 for your room. Ask to see the room before paying, and don't be afraid to check for hot water and good beds. As for hotels, the best value is **Casa del Sole** V. Giuseppe Cincotta, off of V. Regina at the end of town. The hostel-style rooms have cathedral ceilings and tall antique oriental beds. Enclosed gardens, large communal kitchen, and rooftop terrace with an ocean view. Private doubles painted in sea colors upstairs. Four separate bathrooms downstairs. (☎/fax 090 98 60 17. Apr.-May and Oct. singles L25,000; June and Sept. L30,000 downstairs, L35,000 upstairs; July L35,000; Aug. L40,000.) Another option is **Locanda Stella,** V. F. Filzi, 14, on the left off C. V. Emanuele as you descend from the piazza. Large whitewashed rooms with blue doors look onto a communal, reed-roofed terrazza with a sea view. (☎0338 827 22 03 or 090 198 67 22; www.netnet.it/locandastella/index.html. Mar. 30-June 15 and Aug. 16-Oct. 30 L35,000 per person, with bath L40,000; June 16-Aug. 15 doubles L130,000, with bath L150,000.) More rudimentary is the **Pensione Roma** which shares an address with Da Luciano restaurant. Rooms have excellent sea views but tiny bathrooms. Some rooms have exterior bathrooms. There is only one single. (☎090 98 60 88. June-Sept. L35-50,000 per person; Oct.-May L30,000 per person, with bath L40,000. L50,000 for single person in double room; June-Sept. L40,000 per person.)

FOOD. Stuff your pack at the **Duval Market,** on V. Roma just before the church. (☎090 98 60 52. Open daily 8am-1pm and 4-9pm. V, MC, AmEx.) **La Lampara,** V. V. Emanuele, 27, serves Stromboli's most creative dinners. Try the stella di mare (ravioli stuffed with fish and topped with shrimp) or the linguini al cartoccio (fish cooked in a pot and then seared in brandy). (☎090 98 64 09. *Primi* from L12,000, *secondi* from L15,000. 10% discount with *Let's Go.* Open daily 7pm-1am.) **Ristorante da Luciano,** V. Roma, 15, offers the delicious caper-spiced pasta strombolana. The terrace offers a tremendous view of the sea and the hulking Strombolicchio. (☎090 98 60 88. Pizza from L8000, *primi* from L12,000, *secondi* from L20,000. Open daily noon-2pm and 6-11:30pm.) At the rosticceria **La Trattola,** V. Roma, 34, delve into the pizza Stromboli, a cone-shaped creation bursting with mozzarella, tomatoes, and olives. (☎090 98 60 46. Pizza from L7000. Open daily 8:30am-2:30pm and 4-11pm.)

The plateau of **Piazza San Vincenzo** is Stromboli's geographic center, its highest point and its most happening 500 square feet (besides the crater itself). Each night around 10pm, islanders flock to **Bar Ingrid** for drinks, a bit o' *gelato*, and animated conversation. The *piazza* is abuzz with voices, occasional singing, and a jolly good time. The moon rising directly over the *piazza* is quite a sight, and from behind the church there's a great view of the *volcano*.

SIGHTS. At the **volcano** each evening, orange cascades of lava and molten rock spill over the slope, lighting the **Sciara del Fuoco** (trail of fire) at 10-minute intervals. The **Società Navigazione Pippo** (☎090 98 61 35), at the port next to the Guide Alpine, runs an evening boat trip to view the bursts (1hr., 10pm, L25,000).

! STOP IN THE NAME OF LAVA. *Let's Go* does not recommend, advocate, or take responsibility for anyone hiking Stromboli's volcano, with or without a guide. A red triangle with a black, vertical bar means "danger."

An ordinance passed in 1990 made hiking the volcano without a guide officially illegal, and with good reason: not long ago a photographer was burnt to death after getting too close to the volcanic opening; in 1998, a Czech diplomat, lost in the fog, walked off the cliff's edge. So if such criminality is not your cup of lava, look into a trip with the island's authorized guides through the **Guide Alpine Autorizzate** (☎090 98 62 11), down a flight of steps across from the P. Vincenzo church. The hike (L35,000) leaves from P. Vincenzo on M, W, Sa, and Su and by request at 5:30pm with a midnight return. Those who choose to ignore the law (feigning ignorance of the four languages on the warning signs) and head up alone can arrange to do the more dangerous descent with a returning GAA group. Hikers should take sturdy shoes, a flashlight, extra batteries, snacks, lots of water, and warm clothes for the exposed summit. Don't wear contact lenses, as the wind sweeps ash and dust everywhere. Excess weight can make for an unpleasant three-hour hike. During the day only smoke is visible, so plan to reach the summit around dusk to snuggle into a rock dugout and watch the brilliant lava bursts. Climbing shoes, daypacks, flashlights, and walking sticks can be rented at the GAA office. Helmets are also available; every two years someone gets hit by a piece of flying rock.

To reach the volcano, follow C. V. Emanuele from P. Vincenzo for a kilometer until you reach a large warning sign; bear right at the fork in the road. The path turns upward when a secluded stretch of beach comes into view and (after 400m) cuts between two white houses. Smart hikers take only the well-trodden shortcuts—anything else will lead to a maze of thick brambles and reeds. Halfway up the slope the trail degenerates into a scramble of volcanic rock and ash; follow the striped red, orange, and white rock markings. Follow markings very carefully or you'll end up stranded in a landslide of loose volcanic ash, sand, and soil. The warning signs at the top ridge are sincere. At all costs, avoid climbing with heavy loads or in the dark. The risk of walking off the edge is greater during the spring and fall fogs. The most important rule of all: **when hiking down the volcano at night, use the same path you took up.** The professional guides' shortcuts are tempting but infinitely easier to get lost on. For an overnight trip (which *Let's Go* does *not* recommend), bring a sturdy food bag, plastic to place on the wet sand, warm clothing, and foul-weather gear for the frigid fogs that can envelop the peak.

Strombolicchio, a gigantic rock with a small lighthouse, rises 2km in the distance from the black beach at **Ficogrande.** The ravages of the sea have eroded the rock from 56m to a mere 42m in the past 100 years.

PANAREA ☎090

Panarea, smallest of the Aeolian islands, has a reputation as an elite playground for celebrities. It definitely has wealthy residents—this is the only island where you can get groceries home delivered—but they've come to flee the North's noise and glitz, not to seek it. Panarea's reputed snobbishness keeps many budget travelers away from the archipelago's best beaches and quiet sheltered coves. It's a manageable daytrip from Lipari.

ORIENTATION AND PRACTICAL INFORMATION. Panarea is accessible by ferry or hydrofoil (See **Getting There,** p. 600). All directional signs are listed not in km or miles, but in minutes buy foot. Street signs are nowhere to be found. But for the sake of formality, **V. San Pietro** runs past Chiesa San Pietro, and along an undulating stone path to the **Punta Milazzese.** Panarea remains an almost completely pedestrian island. The handful of residential scooters have a limited zooming time of 8-11am, after which the monopolized golf carts of the elite zip hotel-dwellers to and from the beach. (At night, the especially posh "taxis" are decorated with *bauganvillia.*) **Banca Antonveneta** (head up V. S. Pietro from the port and continue left at pedestrian intersection—after yellow building on right) proudly sports a brand-spanking new **ATM.** The **post office,** on V. S. Pietro, past the bank and on the right, changes cash and AmEx traveler's checks, with more reliable service in high season. (☎090 98 32 83. Open 8am-1:30pm.) In an **emergency** call the **Guardia Medica** (☎090 98 30 40) or the **carabinieri** (July-Aug. in Panarea ☎090 31 81; Sept.-June in Lipari ☎090 981 13 33).

ACCOMMODATIONS AND FOOD. Though expensive year-round, hotel prices skyrocket in August when rooms are solidly booked. In other months, try **Pensione Pasqualino** (☎090 98 30 23), which shares space and management with **Trattoria da Francesco,** up a flight of steps from the port (fight the current; the steps are to the right). The spacious rooms have more light above the ground floor; sunlight filters in from the communal terrace. (June-Aug. breakfast included. Apr.-May L40-50,000; June L75,000; July-Aug. L100,000.) **Hotel Tesoriero,** on V. S. Pietro just up from the port, has big whitewashed rooms with vibrant tiled floors, each connected to a bamboo-shaded communal terrace with an ocean view. (☎090 98 30 98; fax 090 98 30 07; email hoteltesoriero@ctonline.it. Breakfast included. Mar. 15-June 15 and Oct. 15-30 L70,000 per person; singles L90,000. June 16-July 15 and Oct. 1-15 L90,000; singles L135,000. July 16-Aug. L130,000; singles L230,000. V, MC.)

The **Da Bruno supermarket** is up the street on V. S. Pietro. (☎090 98 30 02. Open daily 8am-9pm; off-season 8am-1pm and 4:30-9pm). Fruit-stocked **Supermercato Crai** lies just up V. Communale Iditella, two uphill rights after the 1st intersection from the docks. At the *panificio* next door to Da Bruno, locals line up for baked goods including *biscotti*, *foccacia*, and pizza slices. (Open daily Sept.-July 7am-1:30pm and 5-8pm; Aug. 7am-8pm.) Hold out for a filling *panino* (L3500-5000) at **Ritrovo da Tindero,** on V. Comunale Iditella, near tiny Piazza Lauricella. Huge green salads (L8000) and *cannolis* that ooze with fresh *ricotta* (L4000). (☎090 98 30 27. *Primi* from L11,000, *secondi* L15-18,000. Open Apr.-Oct. daily 8am-1am.)

SIGHTS AND ENTERTAINMENT. From Punta Milazzese, Panarea's three famous beaches cut into the coastline; their rocks tend more towards sand the farther you go. Taking two rights from the center of town to Calcara (also known as **"Spiaggia Fumarole"**), you'll reach a beach near the thermal springs at **Acquacalda.**

Panarea lights up at night during summer, when pricey Bohemian cafes spill out onto the shorefront, with clientele lazing on oversized pillows and drinking champagne. Up the short *lungomare* past the bars, the Raya discoteca sits right smack in the middle of Panarea's most drippingly posh hotel. The disco fevered come from as far away as Milan to party in the glass-walled, ceiling-less laser-beam paradise under the stars. (Open mid-July to Aug. circa 1-6am.)

SALINA ☎090

Some consider Salina the archipelago's most beautiful island; if nothing else, it is certainly the most verdant. Next in size to Lipari, Salina is renowned for the astounding rock formations at **Semaforo di Pollara** and for the region's best Malvasia wine. Hotel prices might make Salina a better daytrip than an overnight destination, but the island is still captivating, uncorrupted by tourism, with uncrowded beaches and a sleepy, welcoming character.

TRANSPORTATION. From Lipari, Salina is accessible by **hydrofoil** (20min., 15 per day, L10,000) and **ferry** (4 per day, L5500). Salina's main port is the **Porto Santa Marina. SNAV** (☎090 984 30 03) and **Siremar** (☎090 984 30 04) share a blue-trimmed building at the port. The island's blue **buses** stop in front of the hydrofoil offices (monthly schedules posted at SNAV office), with 13 daily runs to Levi, Valdichiesa, Malfa, Pollara, Gramignazzi, Rinella, and Lingua (approx. L2000 per town).

ORIENTATION AND PRACTICAL INFORMATION. Scooter rentals are available at **Bongiorno Antonio,** V. Risorgimento, 240. Take a left with your back to the docks and a rainbow of scooters will greet you. (Scooters L35-40,000 per day; mountain bikes L15-20,000. Open 8:30am-8pm.) In case of emergency, call the **police** (☎090 984 30 19). The **Farmacia Comunale,** V. Risorgimento, 111, is at the bottom of the street. (☎090 984 30 98. Open M 5:30-8:30pm, Tu-F 9am-1pm and 5:30-8:30pm, Sa 9am-1pm.) There is a **post office,** at V. Risorgimento, 13, which changes AmEx travelers checks. (☎090 984 30 28. Open 8am-1:20pm.) **Postal Code:** 98050.

ACCOMMODATIONS AND FOOD. Most food and accommodations are located in the small settlement that rises above Santa Marina's docks. Outside of July and August, try **Il Delfino** in Lingua, boasting handpainted tiles, breezy upstairs rooms, and many, many shades of blue. All rooms have bath. (☎090 984 30 24. May-June L35,000 per person; July-Aug. mezza-pensione L90-110,000. V, MC.) A few steps up the price ladder, **Pensione Mamma Santina,** V. Sanità, 40, offers first-rate rooms painted in traditional Aeolian colors. Guests mingle on the melon-colored terrace, and the enthusiastic owner makes everyone feel at home. Think of the obligatory half-pension as a blessing—the owner and chef has been featured in Cucina Italiana. (☎090 984 30 54; fax 090 984 30 51. *Primi* from L8000, *secondi* from L12,000. Off-season L90,000 per person. V, MC.) Take the bus or aliscafo to Rinella for Salina's only true budget accommodations. Camping Tre Pini, Via Rotabize, 1, has a market, bar, and restaurant. Terraced sites drop down to the sea. (☎090 980 91 55. Reserve in July and Aug. L12,000 per person, L14,000 per tent.)

Ristorante da Franco is far from the port, but there's no better view in Salina. Follow signs from the top of V. Risorgimento (right, with your back to the docks). *Antipasti* and *primi* (L8-12,000) overflow with home-grown vegetables. (☎090 984 32 87. Open daily July-Aug. 8pm-midnight; Sept.-June noon-3pm and 8pm-midnight.) At night, **Lausta,** V. Risorgimento, 188, fills with tourists nibbling on crepes (L8000), and banging away on the piano in the funky room upstairs. (Open daily 8am-midnight.) As always, the cheapest way to eat is the cold lunch route; assemble a beach picnic at any *alimentari* on V. Risorgimento.

SIGHTS. At the end of the devilishly twisting road to Malfa is **Pollara,** famous as the setting for Massimo Troisi's *Il Postino.* Pollara itself is a geological wonder, the sight of an eruption 13,000 years ago. Resting in the collapsed palm of a half-submerged crater, its raked sandstone cliffs fall 100m down to the most dramatic **beach** in the Aeolians. Someone tossed a handful of veridian into the sea. Black sand wraps around the crescent shore and a natural rock archway towers to the

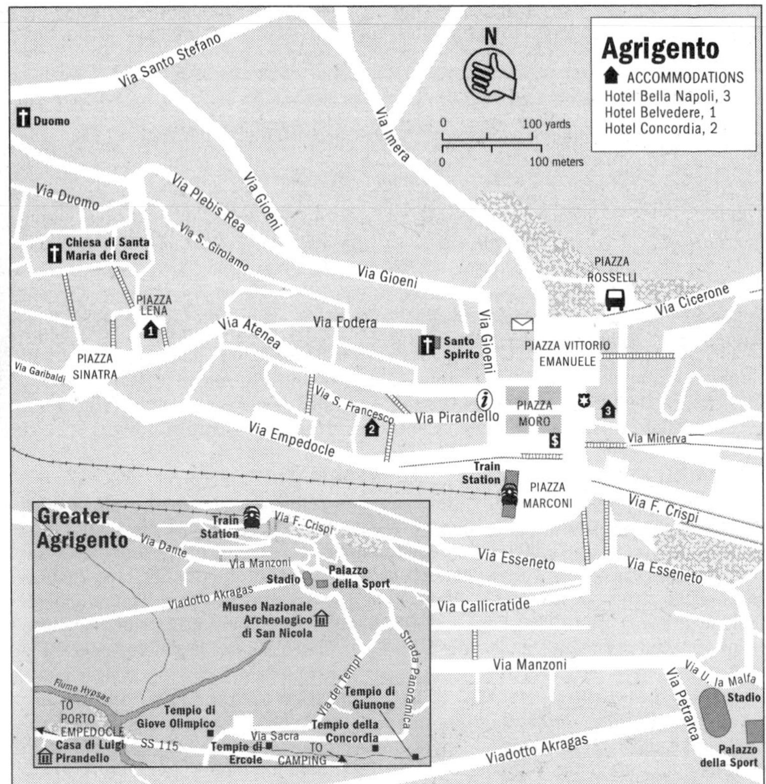

right. From Malfa, a road cuts through the center of the island via **Valdichiesa** and down the slopes of **Rinella,** another port village and the sight of the island's only campground. Paths from Valdichiesa lead up the green peak of **Monte Fossa delle Felci.** The 962m trek through the nature preserve is superb. From the Rinella beach, you can watch the sconcassi on calm days. The sea floor burps these giant sulfur bubbles, killing the occasional fish.

FILICUDI AND ALICUDI ☎090

Arrive in Filicudi before the summer tourism rush, and the bakery shelves and *gelato* bins will be empty. At any time of year, however, Filicudi captures the imagination with an array of volcanic rock formations and the enchanting **Grotta del Bue Marino** (Grotto of the Monk Seal). **La Canna,** an impressive rock spike (71m high, 9m wide), towers from the sea from Filicudi's west coast. Foot paths around the rocky terraces of **Fossa Felci** (774m) lend views of the rock. A boat tour (L25,000 per person) visits the grotto and provides views of the spike. *Motorini* are available to rent beside the steps of the mountain to the right as you stand with your back to the water. Ask at the bar if no one's there. (☎090 988 99 84. Must be 18 to rent; no license required. L35,000 per day.) A jaunt up Filicudi's only paved road leads to a small stretch of stone beach, and 3km of rock-scrambling good times. With many a private cove, this is a favorite spot for nude bathing; be alert for passing boats with binoculars. Start up the road and around the bend—do not turn off onto the dirt path, but wait for the stone walkway.

Filicudi's most soul-nourishing accommodations are at the **Hotel La Canna**, V. Rossa, 43, a 20-minute lactic acid-producing climb up the steps to the right from the port. Pull a chair on the long terra-cotta *terrazza* and look pensively out to sea. Watch out; the sea is so blue, it might swallow your thoughts. (☎090 988 99 56. Sept.-June L32-56,000 per person; July 17-Aug. 31 obligatory half-pension L120,000.) Just down from La Canna is the orange local hangout/market/bakery/restaurant/game hall/*pensione*, **Villa La Rosa.** At any time of day, Villa Rosa's foosball and ping-pong tables are filled with well-tanned Filicudari. On summer nights, their *terrazza* and sleek adjoining bar turn into a *discoteca*. Villa Rosa also has 18 eccentrically decorated bungalows. The rooms vary nicely in character and shape; #13, for example, has a bathroom carved out of rock, reached by a winding internal stairway (☎090 988 99 65; June-Sept. up to L110,000; Oct.-May L70,000.) In case of **emergency** call the **carabinieri** (☎090 988 99 42). The **post office** (☎090 98 80 53) is uphill to the right of the port. Filicudi does not have an **ATM.**

WESTERN SICILY

AGRIGENTO ☎0922

Aisles of skyscrapers rise above the famous Valley of the Temples, setting the pace of modern Agrigento. The city was founded by Greek colonists in the 6th century BC, but the tree-lined avenues and squares have a certain Parisian flair. In the *centro storico*, pricey boutiques and animated *gelaterie* line cobblestone streets, while honking cars battle leisurely pedestrians for the road. The father of modern Italian literature, Luigi Pirandello, was born here—something no Agrigentan will let you forget. With its ancient streets, some of the most impressive Greek architecture in the world, stretches of golden beach, and cheap lodgings, Agrigento is one of Sicily's most worthwhile destinations.

TRANSPORTATION

Trains: In P. Marconi, below P. Moro. To **Palermo** (2hr., 11 per day 4:50am-8pm, L12,500) and **Catania** (3hr., 2 per day 12:15-6pm, L17,000) via **Enna** (2¼hr., 12:15 and 6pm, L10,000). Ticket office open M-Sa 5:45am-8pm, Su 7am-8pm. **Luggage Storage:** L5000 per bag for 12hr. Open daily 8am-9pm

Buses: From P. Vittorio, buses are to the left in P. Roselli. The ticket booth (☎0922 596 490), is in the back right corner of the parking lot. Office open M-Sa 5:30am-6:10pm. Buses to: **Sciacca** (1¾hr.; M-F 12 per day 7:55am-8:40pm, Su 9:40am, 5, and 6pm; L9000); **Palermo** (2hr.; M-Sa 4 per day 5:45am-2:30pm, Su 7am and 5pm; L13,000); **Trapani** (4hr.; M-Sa 6:20, 8:30am, and 1:55pm, Su 9:40am, 5, and 6pm; L18,000); and **Syracuse** (5hr.; daily 8, 11am, 5, and 5:45pm, M also 8:30am; L27,000). **SAIS Trasporti,** V. Ragazzi, 99 (☎0922 59 59 33), behind the ticket office. To: **Caltanissetta** (1hr., 9 per day, L9000); **Catania** (2¾hr., 11 per day, L19,000); and the airport. Also indirectly to **Rome** and **Messina.**

Public Transportation: Orange **TUA city buses** depart from the train station. Ticket (L1500) valid for 1½hr. Buses #2 and 2/ run to the beach at San Leone; #1, 2, and 2/ run to the Valley of Temples; #1/ runs to Pirandello's house. Alternatively, take the bus to **Porto Empedocle** (L2000) and get off at "La Casa di Pirandello." Tickets available at the ramshackle cream-colored bar cart in the parking lot. Ask for schedules on board.

ORIENTATION AND PRACTICAL INFORMATION

Via Imera connects the train station in **Piazza Marconi** to the bus terminal. To reach V. Imera, take your 1st left uphill off P. Marconi, passing through **Piazza Moro** and then **Piazza Vittorio Emanuele.** The central street of the historic district, **Via Atenea,** leads up from the gardens at P. Moro. The temples are a short bus ride (#1, 2, or 2/) or a long walk below the town.

Tourist Office: Ufficio Informazioni Assistenza Turisti (AAST), V. Battista, 13 (☎0922 204 54), the 1st left off V. Atenea. Staff will outfit you with maps and brochures. Open in summer M-F 9am-2pm and 4:30-7pm, Sa 9am-2pm. Another summer office in **Valle dei Templi,** adjacent to car park and bar. English spoken. Open daily 8am-7:30pm.

Emergencies: ☎113. **Carabinieri:** (☎0922 59 63 22), in P. Moro opposite V. Atenea. **Hospital: Ospedale Civile** (☎0922 49 21 11), on S. Giovanni XXII.

Late-Night Pharmacy: BATO Fontanelle, V. Atenea, 285.

Internet Access: Libreria Multimediale, V. Cellauro, 7 (☎0922 40 85 62), off V. Atenea, 2 blocks down from P. Moro. L9000 per hr. Open M-Sa 9am-1pm and 4-8:30pm.

Post Office: P. V. Emanuele. Space-capsule interior designed by Mike Brady on a UFO trip. Open M-F 8:10am-6pm, Sa 8:10am-1:20pm. **Postal Code:** 92100.

ACCOMMODATIONS AND CAMPING

Agrigento's hotels are central and cheap, but so are many park benches; in this case, "low price" and "good value" are not synonymous. Consider spending a little more or heading to one of the easily accessible campgrounds.

Hotel Belvedere, V. S. Vito, 20 (☎/fax 0922 200 51). Follow the hotel signs in front of the train station left to P. Moro. With Banco di Siclia behind you and the stand of trees to your left, look for a yellow sign on the right pointing up a flight of stone steps. Agrigento's nicest 2-star, with sleek, colorful, eccentrically painted rooms, funky antique furniture, and a garden overlooking P. Moro and the valley. Ask for a room with a view. Breakfast L4000. Singles L55,000, with bath L75,000; doubles L70,000, with bath L105,000; triples with bath L157,000.

Hotel Concordia, V. S. Francesco, 11 (☎0922 59 62 66). At the lower end of P. Moro (downhill from the bus station and uphill from the train station) follow V. Pirandello into the historic district. V. Pirandello turns into V. S. Francesco. Pygmy-sized singles. Late risers may not appreciate the early-morning shouting from the street market below. Rooms on the far side have less noise and more light. Without bath means without access to a shower. Spend L5000 for cleanliness. Singles L30,000, with bath L35,000; doubles L60,000, with bath L80,000; triples with bath L90,000.

Hotel Bella Napoli, P. Lena, 6 (☎/fax 0922 204 35), off V. Bac Bac. Take V. Atenea 1km uphill and turn right after you pass the Justice Building. Beds as firm as soggy bread. Institutional hallways, mismatched wood furniture, and large bare bathrooms. Rooftop terrace overlooks the valley. 20 rooms, all with bath. Singles L40,000; doubles L85,000; triples L100,000.

Camping: 2 campgrounds lie on the beach, 3km from San Leone in **Le Dune.** Buses #2 and 2/ go to the campsites from the train station. **Camping Nettuno** (☎0922 41 62 68), on V. L'Acquameno at the bus stop. Reasonable market, restaurant, bar, and pizzeria. L9000 per person, L9000 per tent. Showers L1000. Up the road, the shaded and better-equipped **Camping Internazionale San Leone,** V. Alessandro Giuliana Alaimo, 2 (☎/fax 0922 41 61 21), is run by a family of extroverts. July-Aug. L10,000 per person, L8-12,000 per tent (depending on size), L4000 per car. Sept.-June L9000 per person.

FOOD

The small fruit and vegetable stands in front of the Hotel Concordia are open Monday through Saturday mornings. Agrigento's **STANDA** doesn't stock food, so your best bet is one of the small *alimentari* that line V. Pirandello or V. Atenea. Indulge a sweet tooth at the candy stalls along V. della Vittoria. The local specialty is *torrone*, a nut-filled nougat. Authentic, inexpensive *trattorie* lie off V. Atenea.

Trattoria Atenea, V. Ficani, 32 (☎0922 202 47), the 4th right off V. Atenea from P. Moro, just beyond the Stefanel store. Like grandma's kitchen: huge portions on no-fuss flowered paper tablecloths. Extensive seafood offerings. *Calamari* (squid) and *gamberi* (shrimp) for L10,000. The house specialty is *grigliata mista di pesce* (mixed grilled fish; L9000). Smooth local wine L4000 per liter. Open M-Sa noon-3pm and 7pm-midnight.

Manhattan Trattoria/Pizzeria, Salita M. degli Angeli, 9 (☎0922 209 11), up the steps to the right off V. Atenea near P. Moro. A rather expensive little *trattoria* with an inventive menu. Try the spiral pasta with swordfish, eggplant, and tomato (L12,000). *Primi* from L8000, *secondi* from L10,000. Cover L2000. Open M-Sa 11am-4pm and 7pm-1am.

Trattoria de Paris, P. Lena, 7 (☎0922 254 13), next to Hotel Bella Napoli. It's like France, only in Italy. Sit with locals for home-cooked fare. Tasty *rigatoni alla Pirandello* (with tomatoes, *prosciutto*, mushrooms, and cream). *Primi* L8000, *secondi* from L10,000. *Menù* L20,000. Open M-Sa 12:30-3pm and 7:30-10:30pm. V, MC, AmEx.

Pizzeria Tavola Calda F. Ursu (☎0922 228 28), on V. Pirandello, down the street from the tourist office and before Hotel Concordia. This is real budget eating. Eggplant parmigian L3000, octopus salad L5000, huge swordfish L7000. Open M-Sa 8am-10pm.

SIGHTS

VALLE DEI TEMPII

Valle dei Tempii is several kilometers from the city. Starting on V. F. Crispi, it's a 30-minute walk from the train station to the entrance, following signs downhill and left at the lower intersection. Or, take bus #1, 2, or 2/ from the train station; it stops in a dirt lot with a snack bar and many tour buses. Tempii di Giove open 8:30am-sunset. L4000; all other temples free. Museum open M-Sa 8am-12:30pm. L8000.

A golden swoop of hills, feather-puff clouds, and wafting breezes fill the Valle degli Dei (Valley of the Gods). The Hellenistic temples that fill Agrigento's Valle dei Tempii were mostly divine thank-you gifts, the Agrigentan way of expressing gratitude to their deities for victories over the Carthaginians. Nonetheless, the Punic Wars brought many of them down, and most of the rest were destroyed by earthquakes and early Christians. Come after sundown, when the temples are lit.

Start at the **Tempio di Ercole** (Hercules), the oldest, dating from the 6th century BC and now little more than a forlorn line of replaced columns. Uphill, the **Tempio della Concordia,** complete with 34 columns, is one of the best-preserved Greek temples in the world. Erected in the mid-5th century BC from limestone and now weathered to a golden hue, it owes its remarkable state to an early exorcism of demons and sanctification as a Christian church by the bishop of Agrigento, San Gregorio delle Rape (St. Gregory of the Turnips). The niches in the interior walls, carved for Christian worship, remain visible. The half-standing **Tempio di Giunone** (Juno) dates from the 5th century BC. To your left during the ascent, holes in the ground mark an early Christian burial ground.

Across the street lies the entrance to the **Tempio di Giove Olimpico,** still patiently waiting to be completed. Had its construction not been interrupted by Carthaginian troops in 406-405 BC, it would have been one of the largest Greek temples ever built. The temple's many 18m columns were supported by 8m *telamones* (sculpted male figures that slightly resemble muscular snowmen). A reconstructed *telamon* lies face-up among the ruins, deepening his bronze tan, while his companions' snowball appendages lie strewn about. Farther along in the same area, four columns and an entablature represent the piecemeal effort to rebuild the 5th-century BC **Tempio di Castore e Polluce** (Castor and Pollux).

SICILY

The excellent **Museo Nazionale Archeologico di San Nicola,** 1km uphill from the parking lot, contains Greek statuary and vases from Agrigento, as well as a reconstructed upright *telamon* from the temple sight.

CHIESA DI SANTA MARIA DEI GRECI. Built atop a 5th-century BC Greek temple, this church is the most interesting building in medieval Agrigento. The interior contains a Norman wooden ceiling, original Doric columns, and 14th-century frescoes of a strangely wizened Christ child. *(Follow the signs up the hill from V. Bac Bac off V. Atenea. Open 9:30am-1pm and from 3pm until the curator leaves. Donation expected.)*

CHIESA DEL PURGATORIO. The legendary Serpotta employed all of his wizardry in making this church's stucco doodads look like marble. The statues of the "Virtues" are meant to help you stay out of purgatory, but most of the imagery reminds you how imminent purgatory actually is—note the unusual skull and crossbones on the confessional and the countless depictions of roasted sinners. To the left of the church, below a sleeping lion, lies a 5th-century BC Greek entrance to a network of underground channels.

SIX TOURISTS IN SEARCH OF AN AUTHOR. Literature aficionados will want to visit the birthplace of playwright **Luigi Pirandello** (see **The Modern and Postmodern,** p. 23), now a small museum of books, notes, and family photographs. Pirandello's ashes are buried "in a rough stone" under his favorite (now denuded) pine tree, a few hundred meters from the house. Though currently undergoing restoration, the museum will reopen in spring 2001. *(Take the Lumia bus #1 to P. Kaos. ☎ 0922 51 11 02. Open daily 8am-1:30pm. L4000.)* The **Settimana Pirandelliana,** a week-long outdoor festival of plays, operas, and ballets in P. Kaos, occurs in late July and early August. *(Info ☎ 0922 235 61. Tickets L15-30,000.)* The **Teatro Pirandello** recently reopened inside the town hall. Built in 1870, the interior was created by G. Battista Basile, who also designed the decor for La Fenice in Venice.

FESTIVALS

The 1st Sunday in February brings the **Almond Blossom Festival,** an international folk-dancing fest, to the Valle dei Tempii. In early July, town folk throw bread to the effigy of St. Calogero, thanking him for having spared them from food poisoning during the plague. During summer months, Agrigentans move to the splendid beach and packed nightlife strip at **San Leone,** 4km from Agrigento by bus #2 or 2/.

SCIACCA ☎ 0925

Known as *Thermae Selinuntinae* in the Greek age, Sciacca was famous as "the thermal town" for its natural vapor and sweat grottoes. Steamy situations continued into the 15th century, with the "Caso di Sciacca" *(Sciacca's tragedy)*, the violent and vengeful quarreling of the mighty *Perollo* (Sicilian) and *De Luna* (Spanish) families over their divorced and discontented Romeo and Juliet (Margherita Peralta and Giovanni Perollo). The feuding simmered on for over half a century, resulting in the deaths of many locals. All has cooled down in the last few hundred years: streets are free of sword fights, all the Mercutios have gone home, and constant breezes waft in off the sea. Sheer cliffs assure sweeping views throughout the terraced historic city, and all recent passions have been poured into the more demure art of pottery making. The port jostles noisily below, a vibrant, chaotic, brightly painted counterpart to its cliffside city.

TRANSPORTATION AND PRACTICAL INFORMATION. The thermal city is accessible by air conditioned Lumina **buses** from Trapani and Agrigento, which stop on **Via Agatocle,** next to the lush Villa Comunale (the town gardens). A white case on the stone wall near the top of the street displays departure schedules. Bus tickets are available in Bar Lorenzo, on Vle. della Vittoria, at the top of V. Agatocle and across the street. Orange **city buses** stop at the entrance to the town gardens, just left from the top of V. Agatocle. Meticulous bus drivers check every *tabacchi-*

purchased (L1500) ticket. Heading off to the left, **Corso Vittorio Emanuele** runs through the center of town to the **tourist office,** C. V. Emanuele, 94, and to Piazza Scandalito. (☎0925 86 247. Open M-Sa 8am-2pm and 3-10pm.) In an **emergency**, call the **carabinieri** (☎112), **police** (☎113), **hospital** (☎0925 96 21 11), or **first aid** (☎0925 231 66). The **post office** is in P. M. Rossi, beyond P. Scandaliato on C. V. Emanuele. (☎0925 858 78. Open M-Sa 8:10am-1:30pm.)

ACCOMMODATIONS AND FOOD. **Paloma Blanca,** V. Valverde, 2, the only budget option in town, rises above its own *gelato* bar off of Vle. della Vittoria. Upper-level streetside rooms are brighter, with garden views. (☎0925 262 99. Reservations recommended in summer. Singles L55,000; doubles L95,000.) If you feel like splurging, head downhill to the plush **Grand Hotel delle Terme, Lungomare delle Terme,** on sweeping cliffs at Sciacca's southeastern tip. With luxurious silver teapot breakfasts, thermal baths, and other in-house frivolities, expect to spend. (☎0925 870 02. Singles L96-137,000; doubles L166-248,000.) For campers, **Campeggio Mimose** is right on the sea, 5km west of town at Contrada Foggia. Take bus #3 from V. Agatocle. (☎0925 99 11 67. L9000 per person, L8-11,000 per tent.)

Below the town, **Porto San Paolo**'s 2nd-floor terrace takes in the jostling port and summer seaside sunsets. Descend the stairs from P. Scandaliato, off C. V. Emanuele. Facing the water, turn left down the *lungomare* at the end of the port. San Paolo's is up the last set of stairs on the left, sporting a classy dining room with sweeping views. (☎0925 27 982. Pizzas from L7000, *primi* from L8000.)

SIGHTS. Buses #1 and 4 run 3km outside of town to the olive-grove-shaded **Il Castello Incantato** (The Enchanted Castle) and its startling sea of stone heads. Jaded, bitter, and lovesick from a sour experience in the US, Sciacca native *Filuppu di Testi* (Philip of the heads) returned home to spend the rest of his life painting and chiseling surrounding trees and stones. Giving each of his carvings an imaginative name, he added them to his fanciful community of "subjects," over which he reigned as "king." Back in town, Philip preferred to be addressed as "Your Excellency." (Open Tu-Sa 10am-noon and 4-8pm. Ask about return times, lest you be stranded among the sculptures.)

SELINUNTE ☎0924

During the First Punic War, Selinunte decided to side with Rome. After Carthage was trounced all over the Mediterranean, the retreating African power sent troops to Selinunte to kill the inhabitants and smash the enormous temple complex. The heaps of columns and cornices, many bearing reddish burn marks from the bitter destruction, now await exploration. As Guy de Maupassant once quipped during an unrelated dinner party conversation, Selinunte's splendid jumble of ruins is "an immense heap of fallen columns, now aligned and placed side by side on the ground like dead soldiers, having fallen in a chaotic manner." His guests rewarded this statement with blank stares. Nonetheless, the **ruins** are perfect for a sunset stroll. (Open daily 9am-1hr. before sunset. L8000, under 18 and over 65 L4000.)

Getting to Selinunte requires some planning. From **Palermo, Trapani,** or **Marsala,** take the bus or train to last stop, **Castelvetrano.** The blue **Lumina bus** to and from **Sciacca** and **Agrigento** (the only transportation from Castelvetrano) also stops uptown at Bar Selinus, where you can wait at the AST bus stop for a connection to Selinunte. Orange **AST buses** run to Selinunte from Castelvetrano's Bar Selinus, the train station (times listed on wall), and P. Margherita (3-5 per day; L2500, round-trip L4800). The AST bus careens to a stop at the main S. S. 115 intersection at the entrance to Selinunte. With your back to the bar, take a left; the park entrance is up on the right. Those who show up at Selinunte in the afternoon will have to deal with a 7-hour gap in service (5hr. gap on Su) after the 1:30pm bus. One bus leaves from P. San Giovanni at 7:45pm.

Mamma Maria and her family run the wonderful **Il Pescatore,** V. Castore e Polluce, 31 (☎/fax 0924 463 03. L30-L40,000 per person; singles L5000 extra. Mattress on 4th-floor terrace L10,000.) The *lungomare* is lined with touristy, moderately overpriced eateries that even the locals frequent. For a table with a view, have a seaside seat on the terrace of **Baffo's Ristorante-Pizzeria.** Try the *Siciliana* (capers, eggplant, onions, and sardines) for a taste of the west coast. (Tasty pizza from L7000, *primi* from L9000, *secondi* from L8000. Cover L2000. Service 10%. Open noon-3pm and from 7pm until the food runs out. V, MC.)

MARSALA ☎0923

When Garibaldi and his thousand red-shirted devotees landed at Marsala, the city loaded them with men and means, making itself the *Risorgimento*'s proud launchpad (see **Unification,** p. 13). Outside Italy, the city is best known for its exquisite Marsala wine, which gained fame thanks to the business skills of Englishman John Woodhouse. Despite its small size, the city has several worthwhile sights, including a famed Carthaginian warship.

TRANSPORTATION AND PRACTICAL INFORMATION. **Trains** service the town from **Trapani** (20min., 13 per day, L4500), as do **buses** (30min., 4 per day, L4600). **Taxis** answer to ☎0923 71 29 92. With your back to the train station, a 1st right facing V. A. Fazio and another slight right through the intersection onto **Via Roma** leads straight into Marsala's historic center. V. Roma turns into **Via XI Maggio** and then **Via Veneto.** The **Pro Loco tourist office** is at V. XI Maggio, 1000, in the old city, just before Palazzo Comunale and the *duomo*. The staff checks bus schedules and suggests housing but doesn't speak English. (☎0923 71 40 97. Open M-Sa 8am-8pm, Su 9am-noon.) In an **emergency,** call the **carabinieri** (☎0923 95 10 10 or 112), **first aid** (☎0923 95 14 10), or **Guardia Medica** (☎0923 78 23 43). **Pharmacies,** like the old-time **Farmacia Calcagno** (no sign outside), V. XI Maggio, 80, all have the rotating nocturnal schedule posted in their windows. (☎0923 95 32 54 or 0923 95 30 38. Open M-Sa 9am-1:30pm and 4:30-8pm.)

ACCOMMODATIONS AND FOOD. For Marsala's best stab at a cheap hotel, head to **Pensione Garden,** V. Gambini, 36, just a hop and skip away from the train station. The gritty station neighborhood and drab exterior hides a sparkling interior with marble, mirrors, and shiny communal bathrooms. The tidy rooms have TV, standup fan, and woven rugs. (☎0923 98 23 20. Singles L55,000, with bath L65,000; doubles L75,000, with bath L90,000.) Those planning to spend a few days wine tasting might check out **Andrea's affittacamere.** Though quite a distance from the center, the series of rooms (100 spots in all) scattered about the countryside near the old salt mills and the lagoon can be great values. Call ahead for free pickup at the bus or train station. (☎0923 74 57 47; ring the tourist office if there's no answer. Rooms: Aug. L50,000 per person; Sept.-July L25,000.)

With its snails, roasted eggplant, and octopi, the *antipasto* table at **Trattoria da Pino,** V. San Lorenzo, 27, is Marsala's most biodiverse eatery. Facing the cathedral's main door, head left through the Porta Nuova arch into P. Garibaldi. Take your 1st right and look for a sign several blocks down. (☎0923 71 56 52. *Primi* from L8000, *secondi* from L8000. Open M-Sa 12:30-3pm and 7pm-late. AmEx.) For scrumptious *cannolo di ricotta* stop by streetside **E & N Cafe,** V. XI Maggio, 130. The bustling morning crowd downs espresso served from sparkling gold and glass countertops, wiping powdered sugar from their mouths as they hurry to work. Self-caterers should head to the **STANDA supermarket,** V. Cammareti Scurtil, 10. (☎0923 71 54 76. Open M 4-7:30pm, Tu-Sa 9am-1pm and 4-7:30pm.)

SIGHTS AND ENTERTAINMENT. The **Museo Baglio Anselmi** contains the blackened skeletal remains of a **Carthaginian warship.** The skeletal vessel sank in the devastating final battle (241 BC) of the First Punic War, in which Rome defeated Carthage and established its permanent naval supremacy. Though only

25% of the original remains, a new wrought-iron skeleton hints at its once elegant and powerful lines. (Follow V. XI Maggio through its portal end to P. della Libertà. Facing the bright pink cinema, take the flower-filled road slightly to its left, continuing right at its end. (☎0923 95 25 35. Open Su-Tu and Th-F 9am-1pm, W and Sa 4-7pm. L4000, EU residents free.)

Also down V. XI Maggio and left down V. Sauro, the **Chiesa di San Giovanni** conceals the **Groita della Sibilla** (reached via a trapdoor), where an ancient oracle spent 28 years preaching to believers through a hole in the ceiling. Early Christians took over the cave in the 4th centuy AD (hence the frescoes of fish and doves); St. Paul is said to have baptized converts in the pool here, and a statue of St. John covers the reclusive sibyl's grave. (Open daily but with fluctuating hours.)

Just behind the *duomo* (virtually attached) at V. Garraffa, 57, the **Museo degli Arazzi** contains eight violent 16th-century Flemish tapestries illustrating Titus' war against the Jews. (☎0923 71 29 03. Open Tu-Su 9am-1pm and 4-6pm. L2000.) A few steps down from P. Reppubblica and the *duomo*, the **Museo Civico** houses several of the thousand red shirts, as well as Garibaldi's own rather snazzy uniform. (Open Tu-Su 9am-1pm and 4-8pm.)

Visitors can watch the Marsala grapes be crushed during a free tour (with free samples) of the monstrous **Cantina Florio** facilities, still distilling on Lungomare V. Florio. Take V. Francesco Crispi toward the water from the main intersection of V. Roma next to the train station. At the end, follow Lungomare Mediterraneo until the wall-painted Florio sign. (☎0923 78 11 11. Open Sept.-July M-Th 3-6pm, F 11am-1pm. Call ahead for monthly tour times.) On the way back, stop by the **Fontana del Vino** (Fountain of Wine), where a wine-loving lady drinks gustily with a barrel-bearing donkey. The *piazza* surrounding the fountain, with a brick pattern that mimics the Union Jack, is a subtle poke at the British presence in Marsala.

The **Marsala DOC Jazz Festival** whips it up in the last two weeks of July, attracting the greats of the international jazz scene. The festival emblem colorfully depicts a mellowed-out bass player strumming his six-foot wooden stained bottle of Marsala (apparently, he's already been sampling).

SICILY

TRAPANI ☎0924

Situated on a peninsula on the northwestern tip of Sicily, Trapani juts into the sea, making it seem like every street reaches the water. The winds that sweep across this tiny peninsula are the scorching *scirocco* from North Africa rather than the cooling ocean breezes in other towns. Easy transportation and solid lodgings make Trapani, with its exceptional location, a desirable launching point for adventures to Segesta's ancient ruins, medieval Erice, the lush Lo Zingaro nature reserve, the islands of Sicily's western coast, and even Sardinia or Tunisia.

TRANSPORTATION

Flights: V. Florio Airport, in Birgi en route to Marsala. 16km outside the city. Buses from P. Malta are timed to coincide with flights. Not a heavily used airport.

Trains: P. Stazione (☎0924 280 71). To: **Marsala** (20min., 13 per day, L4500; not specifically listed, but via other destinations); **Castelvetrano** (45min., 6 per day 6:55am-10:47pm, L8000); and **Palermo** (2hr., 15 per day 4:40am-10pm, L11,500). Office open M-Sa 5:40am-7:50pm, Su 5:45am-7:50pm. **Luggage Storage:** L5000 per piece for 12hr. Open 8am-9:30pm.

Buses: AST (☎092 32 10 21). Main bus station at P. Malta. Weekday buses are fairly punctual, but Sunday schedules are as sure as pigs in flight. Buses to: **Erice** (45min.; M-Sa 10 per day 6:40am-7:30pm, Su 5 per day 9am-7pm; L3500, round-trip L5500); **San Vito Lo Capo** (1½hr.; M-Sa 7 per day 7am-8:30pm, Su 2 per day 9am-3pm; L5000, round-trip L8500); **Segesta** (M-Sa 6 per day 8am-6pm, Su 2 per day; L5000, round-trip L8000; buy tickets on the bus).

Ferries: Ferries and *aliscafi* (hydrofoils) leave Trapani for the **Egadi Islands** (Levanzo, Favignana, and Marettimo), **Ustica, Pantelleria** (an Italian island 20min. off the Tunisian coast), and **Tunisia.** All boats leave from the docks across from P. Garibaldi by V. A. Staiti, which runs the length of the southern side of the peninsula. 4 companies operate ticket offices in front of the hydrofoil/ferry dock: **Ustica** (☎0923 222 00), in a yellow booth on the waterfront; **Siremar** (☎0923 54 54 55), with ticket offices both at a blue and white striped waterfront booth and in Stazione Marettima; **Tirrenia** (☎0923 52 18 96; www.tirrenia.com), in Stazione Marettima; and **Lauro** (☎092 392 40 73), at the Stazione Marettima. (Ustica, Siremar, and Tirrenia open by 6:30am; V, MC. Lauro open W-M 9am-1pm and 4-7pm, Tu from 7am.) You can also purchase tickets for these lines from the travel agents along V. A. Staiti. Keep in mind that the schedules for inter-island ferries can be unreliable. Off-season frequency and prices may fluctuate from those in the chart.

DESTINATION	COMPANY	DURATION	FREQUENCY	PRICE
Favignana (Egadi Islands)	Siremar (ferry)	1hr.	3 per day	L6000
Favignana (E.I.)	Ustica (hydrofoil)	25min.	7 per day	L9500
Favignana (E.I.)	Siremar (hydrofoil)	25min.	3 per day	L10,000
Levanzo (E.I)	Siremar (ferry)	1¾hr.	3 per day	L6000
Levanzo (E.I.)	Siremar (hydrofoil)	15min.	10 per day	L10,000
Levanzo (E.I.)	Ustica (hydrofoil)	15min.	6 per day	L9500
Marettimo (E.I.)	Siremar (ferry)	3hr.	1 per day	L12,500
Marettimo (E.I.)	Siremar (hydrofoil)	1hr.	3 per day	L22,500
Marettimo (E.I.)	Ustica (hydrofoil)	1hr.	1 per day	L21,000
Pantelleria	Siremar (ferry)	6hr.	1 per day	L42,500
Pantelleria	Ustica (hydrofoil)	2¼hr.	4 per week	L59,000
Ustica via Favignana	Ustica (hydrofoil)	2¼hr.	3 per week	L32,500
Cagliari (Sardinia)	Tirrenia (ferry)	11½hr.	1 per week	L76,000
Tunis	Tirrenia (ferry)	10½hr.	1 per week	L95,000
Tunis	Linee Lauro (ferry)	12hr.	2 per week	L80,000

Public Transportation: SAU, the orange city bus, has its main terminal at P. V. Veneto, down V. Osorio from the station right on V. XXX Gennaio and straight ahead all the way to the water. Tickets sold at most *tabacchi* (L1100).

Taxis: ☎0923 232 33 or 0923 228 08. Often in P. Umberto, outside the train station.

ORIENTATION AND PRACTICAL INFORMATION

Trapani sits on a scythe-shaped peninsula two hours west of Palermo by bus or train. The old city began at the outer tip of the hook, growing in cautious backward steps until it tripped and spilled new wide streets and cement high-rises onto the mainland. The **train** and both regional and local **bus stations** run a jagged line across the peninsula, separating the old and new districts. Crossing **Piazza Umberto** in front of the train station, take **Via Osorio** on the left of the stand of trees. Follow V. Osorio past the park and take the 2nd left onto **Via XXX Gennaio,** the unofficial border between the old and new towns. Across from the heavily guarded **Justice Building,** make a right onto **Corso Italia,** which runs into the historic district. Once in **Piazza Sant'Agostino,** with C. Italia behind you, the tourist office is straight ahead and the port is to the left.

Tourist Office: Ufficio Informazioni Turistiche (☎0923 290 00; fax 0923 240 04), at P. Saturno, up V. Torrearsa from the port. Omniscient English-speaking tourist gods dispense train and bus schedules, a map of Trapani, and armfuls of info on cultural events and surrounding towns. Open M-Sa 8am-8pm, Su 9am-noon.

Currency Exchange: Banks on C. Italia have better rates than the train station. Open daily 8:10am-1pm. For larger amounts, head for the post office (see below). **ATMs** are at Stazione Marettima in the old city and along V. M. V. Scontrino in front of the train station. Withdrawal in L50,000 increments.

Police: (☎113), in P. V. Veneto. **Carabinieri:** V. Orlandini, 19 (☎0923 271 22).

Hospital: Ospedale Sant'Antonio Abate (☎0924 80 91 11), on V. Cosenza far northeast of the city center.

Late-Night Pharmacy: Check the rotating schedule on the door of any pharmacy. A good bet is **Bianchi,** V. Torrearsa, 25, near the tourist office.

Post Office: P. V. Veneto (☎0923 219 96). With your back to the train station, turn right down V. M. V. Scontrino and left through the small fountain park. Continue left down V. Fardella, with iron fenced public gardens on the left. The post office is on the left after the Palazzo del Governo. Stare at the impressive stained glass ceiling as you wait. Cambio is booth number 18. Open M-F 8am-7pm. **Postal Code:** 91100.

ACCOMMODATIONS AND CAMPING

Pensione Messina, C. V. Emanuele, 71 (☎0923 211 98), through a musty Renaissance courtyard and up 4 flights of worn stone steps. Welcome to grandma's house, complete with the complacent ticking of a baby grandfather clock, eclectic bric-a-brac, garden statues, and familial vibes. 3 communal bathrooms. July-Aug. singles L25,000; doubles L50,000. Sept.-June singles L20,000; doubles L40,000.

Ostello per la Gioventù (HI) (☎0923 55 29 64), Strada Proviniciale, Trapani-Erice. The hostel is a hike from the train station. If possible, call ahead to arrange pickup; otherwise, head toward the AST regional bus station. The AST bus to Erice via "V. Martogna" stops at the front door (4 per day, round-trip L4000). Do not take the Erice bus via "Valderice." This hostel's distance from Trapani is both its greatest selling point and its worst feature. A peaceful, wooded setting with cheery red bunk beds, the scent of evergreen, and cappuccino. Many English-speaking travelers. HI members only. Meals L14,000. Showers and sheets included. Lockout 10am-4pm, even for check-in. Curfew midnight (keys otherwise available). 6-bed dorms L18,000, with breakfast, L21,000. Free camping space available; shower and bathroom use L5000 per person.

Albergo Maccotta, V. degli Argentieri, 4 (☎0923 284 18), behind the tourist office. Soft beds in cool, tiled, bright white, and impeccably modern rooms with A/C. July 15-Aug. 31 singles L40,000; doubles L80,000. Sept. 1-July 14 singles L35,000, with bath L45,000; doubles L60,000, with bath L80,000. V, MC, AmEx, Diners.

Albergo Moderno, V. Genovese, 20 (☎0923 212 47). From P. S. Agostino on C. V. Emanuele, go left on V. Roma, then right on V. Genovese after Cafe Moderno. Institutional, linoleum hallways, but nicely renovated rooms with framed pictures, TVs, and diamond tiled bathrooms. Singles L45,000; doubles L70,000; triples L94,000. V, MC.

Camping: Campeggio Lido Valderice (☎0923 57 30 86), on V. del Detince, in the seaside town of the same name. Take the bus for Bonegia or San Vito La Capo (L5000) and tell the driver your destination. Follow the flower-lined road opposite the bus stop and perpendicular to the highway, and turn right at its end. Well-shaded campground near a couple of clean beaches. Gravel flooring for mobile campers and packed earth sites for tents. L6500 per person, L5-15,000 per tent. Hot showers L1000.

FOOD

In Trapani, couscous is actually touted as a Sicilian dish, with local fish added to the North African favorite. Bakeries carry *biscotti con fichi*, the Italian Fig Newton, for about L400 each. Unlike hotels, food in Trapani leans toward the expensive side; dinner can cost as much as your bed. Pick up essentials at supermarket **Margherita,** V. S. Domenico, 32, between the port and the train station. (Open M-Sa 8am-1:30pm and 5-8pm.) A daily fish and fruit market springs up each morning along the northern *lungomare*, at the intersection of V. Maggio and V. Garibaldi in the old city. Almost everything in Trapani closes on Sunday.

Pizzeria Calvino, V. N. Nasi, 79, 1 street portside behind C. V. Emanuele. By 8pm lines form at this neatly tiled backstreet favorite (for good reason). Towering stacks of multi-sized pizza boxes await speedy takeout service. Duck into the back room and devour personal pizzas (only for dinner) from L3000. Cold beers available. Open W-M noon-3pm for lunch and 7pm-late.

Trattoria da Salvatore, V. N. Nasi, 19 (☎0923 54 65 30), 1 street toward the port from C. V. Emanuele. Single old-timers with tables to themselves can't decide which to concentrate on: perfect spaghetti in front of them or the tiny TV in the corner. Overhead fan does its best to swirl about rather warm air. Couscous or *busiate alla Trapanese* (oil, garlic, and almonds over house pasta) for L7000. Cover L2000. The house wine may clean your teeth, but it's only L3000 for a generous half liter. Open Sept.-June M-Sa noon-3:30pm and 7-11pm; July-Aug. daily noon-3:30pm and 7-11pm. AmEx.

Trattoria Minamare (☎0923 200 11), on the port side *lungomare*, at the end of V. Torrearsa. Tiny *trattoria* sports white stucco walls, stout rush wooden chairs, and a disproportionately large wine shelf. Couscous is their specialty, in a fish sauce so spicy that they won't serve it to foreigners unless prodded. Locals dive right in without preliminaries. *Tortellini con panna* (with cream) L10,000. *Primi* from L8000. Cover L2000. A non-smoking Italian anomaly. Open daily 7am-4pm and 7pm-midnight.

Pizza Sport, V. Libertà, 16 (☎0923 87 37 51). Come watch the pies fly at this hyper but friendly takeout parlor. Wide selection of pizzas. Small from L6000, medium from L8500, large from L15,000. The *trapanese* (with anchovies, eggplant, and sausage) is particularly memorable. Open M-Sa 7pm-late.

SIGHTS

MUSEO NAZIONALE PEPOLI. This museum's magnificent Baroque staircase leads to a collection of local sculptures and paintings, coral carvings, and folk-art figurines, including a frighteningly violent collection portraying the biblical Herod's baby hunt. Call to make sure it's open. *(Take SAU buses #24, 25, or 30 from P. V. Emanuele, 2 blocks to the right of the train station (L1100). ☎0923 55 32 69. Open Tu and Th-F 9am-1pm and 3-6pm, W and Sa 9am-1pm, Su 9am-12:30pm. L8000.)*

OTHER SIGHTS. Those ambitious enough to rise before dawn and trek down C. V. Emanuele and up and to the right, can watch the fishing boats set out from the **Torre di Ligny.** About three hours after sunrise, this tower turns back into a pumpk—er, into the **Museo di Preistoria.** The museum is built on the tip of a jetty, and the view from the roof encompasses the entire coastline and Isole Equle. The museum houses an odd collection of shells, prehistoric artifacts, and underwater excavation pieces. *(☎0923 223 00. Open daily 9:30am-12:30pm and 4-7:30pm. L3000.)*

A LITTLE SONG AND DANCE. "Honey, haven't we seen this poster before?" Poster-sized performance schedules plastered over every town in the province advertise Trapani's **Luglio Musicale Trapanese,** an annually sponsored festival of opera, operetta, ballet, cabaret, and dance. Classy posters advertise classy acts—the month-long festival attracts many well-known local and foreign artists. Performances occur in the open-air theater at Villa Margherita in the city park (next to the post office) throughout July and early August. *(☎0923 214 54; fax 0923 229 34. Shows at 9pm. Tickets from L25,000. Info booth just inside park gates has programs.)*

DAYTRIPS FROM TRAPANI

SAN VITO LO CAPO

Buses to San Vito Lo Capo, the closest town to the reserve, leave from Trapani at P. Malta (1¼hr.; 7 per day 7am-8:30pm, Su 3 per day 9am-3pm; L5000, round-trip L8500).

This is beach bumming at its best. Heavily touristed by the Italian population on vacation, it's also the favorite destination of local Sunday *festivo* sun bathers. San Vito prides itself on having one of the best beaches in Sicily, an arc of smooth white sand with bundles of bright colored beach umbrellas and nice gradual shallows. Make sure to bring or rent an umbrella, as shade is at a minimum.

Pensione Costa Gaia, V. Savoia, 123-125, on the main street four blocks from the beach, has rooms with A/C and bath. (☎0923 97 22 68 or 0923 97 23 75. July-Oct. half-pension L95,000; full pension L110,000. Nov.-June singles L45,000; doubles with breakfast L90,000; half-pension L85,000; full pension L95,000.) For camping, try **Campeggio La Pineta,** V. del Secco, 88. (☎0923 97 28 18. Reservations recommended in Aug. L10,000 per person, L9600 per tent in Aug. V, MC, AmEx, Diners.) Central **Camping La Fata,** on V. P. Matarella with bar and disco, is two streets from the beach and has an interestingly blocked-off bamboo-shaded rectangle for tenting. Take one of nine daily buses from Trapani (7am-7pm; L5000, round-trip L8500). (☎0923 97 21 33. Open June-Sept. Reservations recommended. L7-10,000 per person; L6-13,000 per tent; cars L4-6000. V, MC, AmEx.) Reach the **Guardia Medica** at ☎0923 97 20 91 and the **beach police** at ☎0923 97 43 71.

RISERVA DELLO ZINGARO

Inquire at Mare Monti, V. Amadeo, 15 (☎0923 97 22 31), for bus service to the reserve (L15,000). Scooter rental from San Vito is a viable option.

For shade and seclusion, drive 10km outside of San Vito to the green mountains of Riserva dello Zingaro. One unfinished half mile of four-lane highway hangs perilously close to the pristine reserve. A 1981 environmentalist rally march halted the highway in its tracks, sending jackhammering workers on a permanent lunch break and leaving the province of Trapani holding Sicily's (and Italy's) first nature reserve, complete with Bonelli's eagles, mountain trails, prehistoric caves, and almost alpine scenery. Follow the yellow brick road (umber dirt for fairy dust-lacking grown-ups) to a succession of secluded pebble beaches. With entrances on both sides of the coast, the middle two are most private. Camping is officially illegal, and motor vehicles are prohibited, but hiking is encouraged and superb. Entrance is free and English trail guidebooks are available.

SEGESTA

Buses run to Segesta from Trapani (M-Sa 6 per day 8am-5pm, Su 2 per day; L4500-5000, round-trip L8000.) Be sure to confirm the times of return journeys, lest you be stranded.

Segesta's rough, wild hills and cliffs are a perfect backdrop for its impressive ruins. Not a town in any respect, Segesta for the last millennium has remained purely an archaeological sight. The monumental, roofless **Doric temple,** dating to the 5th century BC, provides a rare glimpse of an ancient work-in-progress, offering hints to archaeologists about how ancient temples were constructed. Though perfectly preserved, it was mysteriously never completed (a cellar was never built and the rough columns never grooved). Visitors are free to venture into the skeleton of the temple and chase its resident lizards. Others may prefer to don togas and take up residence; vineyards and brown fields roll as far as the eye can see. One lone bench under one lone olive tree comprise all of the existing on-site shade. No half-naked leaf-fanning attendants or succulent grapes are available; avoid perspiring like the gods with an early morning or late afternoon visit. Purchase tickets (L8000, students L4000) at the window adjacent to the cafe. Down below the car park, raffia-shaded picnic tables beckon imported picnics (*panini* from L4000). Segesta's **amphitheater,** high above the temple, once packed in crowds of 4000 spectators. A row of trees and low bushes lined the walls, from which Latin comedians gleefully jumped out to frighten inattentive audiences. To avoid hiking to the theater, take the bus to the top (2 per hr., round-trip L2000).

NEAR TRAPANI: ERICE ☎0923

Perched 750 meters above the coast, tiny medieval Erice confidently presides over its own lofty mountain-let. On overcast days, a rising sea of clouds isolates the hilltops and gives a fluffy illusion of coastal proximity. Daily buses huff and puff up the ear-popping switchbacks of mountain road, beeping at sharp corners. In 415 BC, Erice was so wealthy that Segesta borrowed its gold and silver cups to court Athens. As the mythical home of several fertility goddesses, Erice attracted sailors and pilgrims searching for different types of abundance. The cult of the Elyman Astarte, the Greek Aphrodite, and the Roman Venus all spread their influence here. Today, budget-minded Vespa-riding Ericians coast down the steep paved descent. Stubbornly sheer cliffs have prevented any structural expansion from medieval to modern. Yet, here at the relative top of the world, little Erice is now bearing the disproportionate radio tower burden of modern telecommunication. Steep and narrow cobblestone streets strike up and downhill through one of Sicily's most charmingly unchanged villages.

TRANSPORTATION AND PRACTICAL INFORMATION. The **AAST** tourist office is a tiny, easily missed stone cottage at V. C. A. Pepoli, 11, a few meters uphill on the left from the 1st bus stop. (☎0923 86 93 88. Open M-Sa 8am-2pm, Su 9am-1pm.) The bus from Trapani departs from P. Malta to **Montalto** (45min.; M-Sa 11 per day, Su 5 per day; L3000, round-trip L5000).

ACCOMMODATIONS AND FOOD. Lofty hotel prices make Erice more affordable as a daytrip. If you're still enamored with Erice's medieval streets, try the small and white, clean and bright accommodations at **Edelweiss,** Cortile P. Vincenzo, 9. (☎0923 86 91 58. Breakfast included. Singles with bath L100,000; doubles L130,000.) You can also try the **private hostel** on V. delle Pinete between July 15 and August 30 or the HI youth hostel in Trapani (see **Accommodations,** p. 621).

Although dinner is no longer served on plates of gold and silver, local prices seem to suggest that it is. Do the Greek thing at **Pizzeria Ristorante Ulisse,** Vico S. Rocco. Head off the main road at Cafe Maria, down through a stone tunnel, and up onto the shaded, flowered terrace. (☎0923 86 93 33. Thick, excellent pizzas from L7000. Cover L3000. Open daily from 12:30-3pm and 7:30-midnight, closed Th in winter. V, MC, AmEx, Diners.) At **La Vettu,** V. G. Fontana, 5, *primi* and *secondi* start at L10,000. Decent pizzas run from L6000. (☎0923 86 94 04. Open daily 11:30am-3pm and 7pm-midnight.) Otherwise, Erice's Balio Gardens provide shady **park bench picnic perfection;** a Norman castle, sweeping views, your own personalized *panino*...it just doesn't get any better than this. Down the street, the **Antica Pasticceria del Convento,** V. Guarnotta, 1, concocts wonderful sweets for L20,000 per kg. Despite their name, the *bellibrutti* (pretty-ugly) almond paste cookies are pretty good. (☎0923 86 90 05. Open in summer daily 9am-midnight.)

SIGHTS. Visitors must content themselves with delights less carnal than those of yesteryear. Past the gardens, broadcast aerials adorn the medieval towers of a **Norman castle,** which was built on the site of the ancient fertility temple. The area is enchanting, with lush **Balio gardens** where cicadas sing and a sweeping coastal vista from which one can see all the way to Tunisia. On the other side of town near the bus stop lies Erice's 14th-century pastry-like *duomo*. Nearby, a 13th-century **bell tower,** which once served as a watchtower, then a prison, and now a watchtower again, can be climbed (L2000). From the *duomo*, wander up V. Rabata and follow the **Elym Punic walls** (6th-7th century BC) that guard the city. In P. Museo, the **Museo Comunale di Erice** houses a small but interesting collection of treasures and trinkets from Erice's illustrious history as a city sacred to fertility goddesses. (Open M-Sa 8:30am-7:30pm, Su 9am-1pm. Free.)

EGADI ISLANDS (ISOLE EGADI)

The summer sun is far kinder to the Egadi Islands than to scorched Sicily. The *scirocco* wind from North Africa loses its biting vengeance and warmly fans white-washed houses. You might want to skip Favignana, a hackneyed tourist trap that profitably exploits the archipelago's tuna trade, and head instead for the smaller, outlying islands of Marettimo and Levanzo (see **Trapani: Ferries,** p. 619). Unknown to mass tourism, these rough and rugged islands, speckled with cacti and grazing sheep, offer archaeological marvels, sea grottoes, hiking trails, and dizzying views. The best way to see the islands is to choose one and spend an entire day, as the finest beaches and most intriguing discoveries lie far from the ports. Stop by the **bankomat** before leaving; Levanzo and Marretimo have no banks or ATMs.

LEVANZO

Ustica hydrofoils skip across to the first of the Egadi islands, Levanzo (25min., 7 per day, L9500). Ferries stop at **Favinginana** first and take 1½ hours. The **Albergo Paradiso** has newly renovated rooms that overlook the sea. (☎0923 92 40 80. Booked solid for August by mid-March; reservations are crucial. July-Aug. singles L45,000; doubles L85,000; *mezza-pensione* L100,000. Sept.-June singles L35,000; doubles L70,000. V, MC, AmEx, Diners.) Levanzo's main attraction is the **Grotta del Genovese** cave, where Paleolithic incisions and ochre-grease paintings depict the early fishing trade and its attendant rituals (the figures resembling bugs are actually dancing women). The prehistoric cave art is guarded by gate and padlock, guaranteeing the grotto's preservation and a monopoly to the Italian guides. Ask at V. Calvario, 27 (☎0923 92 40 32), down the street from the Siremar ticket office, to reserve a place on one of the small boats (1½hr., L20,000) or body-bumping jeeps (2hr., L20,000) that make the trip during bad weather. The motors are usually ready for passengers at 10am, with a 2nd trip around 2pm. From the port, walking 20min. to the left (with your back to the port) through town and up the island's main coastal road reveals a secluded beach and shallow grotto for swimming. The crystal-clear water between the rounded rock beach and the neighboring island has a ripping current when the winds pick up; snorkel carefully.

MARETTIMO

The most physically remote of the Egadi Islands, Marettimo is equally distant in spirit. The town itself is actually larger than Levanzo and has a few *piazze.* **Siremar** runs to Marettimo from Levanzo (2 per day, L22,000), and **Ustica** sends one hydrofoil daily. Ask at **Il Pirate** about renting a room for L20-35,000 per night, and be ready to haggle. Because there are few roads, paved or otherwise, you'll need a boat to see the island's most intriguing little caves. Beyond the port and the village, the most recent interruption to its rustic environment is an outstanding new set of stone/earth hiking trails crossing the island. The two-hour hike (71 min., 32 seconds if you run) to **Pizzo Falcone** (884m), the highest point on any of the islands, is worth every minute. The trailhead is on the sea road, past the Siremar office and Il Pirate. An ascent around 6pm is prime time, and it makes for one helluva *passeggiata.* Sunset from the peak over the wild and uninhabited far side of the island is unforgettable. Along the way, snuggled between dramatic cliffs and lush greenery, stand the **Case Romane,** domestic and sacred ruins dating back to Roman domination. To the right of the little village and past an arc of beach sand at **Punta Traia,** a 17th-century Spanish castle tops the cliff.

PANTELLERIA ☎0923

Seven thousand years ago, this island of thickly wooded mountains, terraced hillsides, and jagged rock was inhabited by Neolithic people in search of **obsidian,** black, petrified lava that was once as valuable as gold. Today the volcanic island is home to many dazzling natural phenomena, including a natural sauna, myriad hot springs, and the best capers in the Mediterranean. Attracted by its isolation and natural beauty, several celebrities, including Giorgio Armani and Sting, have set up camp on the island. Although Pantelleria lies six hours off the coast from Trapani, it's just five hours from Kelibia, Tunisia; the island is closer to the Arab world than Italy in other ways as well. If you come to Pantelleria, expect to linger; many of the best accommodations require a minimum stay of several days, and the sleepless, nighttime ferry ride means you'll spend much of your first day face down. Once you get behind the wheel of your moped, you may never want to leave.

TRANSPORTATION

Unless you don't mind spending your first day sleeping, dish out the hydrofoil cash for the first leg and save your pennies on the afternoon return ferry.

Hydrofoils: Ustica Lines (☎0923 91 10 78) has a mini ticket office at #66 on the *lungomare*. Open M-Sa 9am-noon and 7-10:45pm. Tickets are also available at **La Cossica travel agency,** left of Khamma Hotel, where V. Catania meets the *lungomare*. (Open daily 9am-1pm and 5-7pm.) To: **Trapani** (3hr., 4:40pm, L65,000).

Ferries: Siremar, on the waterfront, runs to **Trapani** (6hr.; noon; Mar.-June L39,500, July-Aug. L42,500). The return journey is a bit more practical than its nocturnal counterpart—it arrives in Trapani at 6pm.

Island Buses: Catch the few and far between *Panteschi pullmen* at the yellow bus stop sign in the middle of P. Cavour.

ORIENTATION AND PRACTICAL INFORMATION

The island of Pantelleria is shaped something like a large keyhole, tilted counterclockwise so that the smaller upper bulb points northwest toward Sardinia. Bombed and flattened by eruptions, the metropolis of Pantelleria town still bears the charcoal scars of WWII. Most essential services are up in elevated **Piazza Cavour,** off the **lungomare.** Paved roads lead right, left, and inland around the lower and larger bulb of the keyhole from Pantelleria town. Facing the water, the right sea highway leads to **Bue Marino, Gadir, Lago Specchio di Venere,** and **Arco dell'Elefante.** The lower left sea road runs to the **Sesi, Scauri town,** and **Rekhale.** An inland road (above and to the right of the southwest sea highway, past the dockside Agip station) leads to the **airport, Sibà,** and **Montagna Grande.**

Tourist Office: Pro Loco (☎0923 91 18 38), in P. Cavour. Tiny, visually unmarked office on the far left corner (closest to Banco di Sicilia) of the municipal building. Stop by for a handful of brochures and an indispensable road map. Open M-Th 8am-2pm and 4-6pm; hours subject to change Aug.-May.

Currency Exchange: Banco di Sicilia, in P. Cavour across from the municipal building.

Scooter and Car Rental: Autonoleggio Policardo, V. Messina, 31 (☎0923 91 28 44). Just off the port, up the small street to the right after giant fenced-in scooter lot. Gianni and Maria at your service. Scooters Sept.-June L20,000 per day, L100,000 per week; July. L35,000 per day; Aug. L50,000 per day. Small cars L210,000 per day; "big" cars L280,000 per day.

Emergencies: Carabinieri (☎0923 91 11 09), on V. Trieste. **Guardia Medica:** (0923 91 04 21), in P. Cavour, on the far right side of the Municipal building (opposite Banco di Sicilia). Separate tourist and resident services. English-speaker available. Open M-F 8pm-8am, Sa 10am-8pm, Su 8am-8pm. **Hospital:** (☎0923 91 18 44), on V. Almanza.

Pharmacy: Farmacia Greco (☎0923 91 13 10), in P. Cavour. Large green sign is on the side farthest from the water. Open 8:30am-1pm and 5-8:30pm.

Internet Access: Cossyra Computer Center/Meditel, V. Salibi, 5 (☎0923 91 31 11). As you face the water, the inconspicuously marked pink building is on the right, 600m up the road to the left of the coastal highway. Come in the morning around 9 or 10am and the proprietor may provide use of the front room computer for free. Open M-Sa 9am-1pm and 5-7:30pm. At the **Taurus Pub** (see **Nightlife** below), Internet access available on 2 new computers for L8000 per hr. Open daily from 7pm to early morning.

Post Office: (☎0923 91 13 34), on V. de Amicis, adjacent to the municipal building and across from Banco di Sicilia (off P. Cavour). Changes cash and traveler's checks. Open M-Sa 8am-1:20pm. **Postal Code:** 91017.

ACCOMMODATIONS

Dammusi, the square-shaped, domed dwellings of Arab descent unique to this island, are one of the most interesting sleeping options available. Their one meter-thick black lava stone walls keep the interior cool, and water is drawn from a cistern filled by tubes running from the rain-trapping roof. The classic *dammuso* is whitewashed inside and simply furnished, with a sleeping alcove or two and several niches for storage. There are over 3000 *dammusi* on Pantelleria, and nearly every resident rents one out or knows someone who does.

There are also some very reasonable *affitacamere* options available in Pantelleria town (many are full-fledged furnished apartments). Room quality varies considerably and landing a pad often requires some patient perseverance. For both *dammusi* and *affitacamere* options, the best places to start are the bars lining the *lungomare*. Walk up to the counter and state your situation and price—singles L30-50,000, doubles L60-80,000 is reasonable.

La Vela (☎0923 91 18 00), on Scauri Scalo. Follow the sea road 9km west from Pantelleria town to these 14 luxurious *dammusi,* with kitchen, bath, and terrace. Black volcanic stone, startlingly white domed roofs, brilliant purple bougainvillea, and bamboo-shaded porches. Small beach and sea-view restaurant just below. Reserve 3 months in advance for July and Aug. July and Sept. L35,000 per person; Aug. L40,000 per person; Oct.-June L30,000 per person.

Hotel Khamma (☎0923 91 25 70), on the *lungomare* to the far left as you face the sea. No budget accommodations here. Dark red wood and muted purple bedspreads. If you're paying this price, secure a room with a sea view. Flashy black-and-white tiled, top floor breakfast expanse with wrap-around windows. 7-day min. stay in Aug. Reserve far ahead. Aug. singles L90,000; doubles L80,000 per person; triples L70,000. Sept.-July singles L70,000; doubles L65,000 per person; triples L55,000. V, AmEx.

FOOD

Arab domination in the 8th century AD turned Pantelleria away from fishing to the cultivation of its rich volcanic soil. A local specialty, *pesto pantesco*, is a sauce of tomato, capers, basil, and garlic, eaten with pasta or *bruschetta*. The local variety of *zibbibi* grape yields the island's yellowish grape jelly and the sweet amber *passito* or *muscato* dessert wine (delicious Pantelleria gold). The **SISA supermarket** in Pantelleria town sits above the *lungomare*. Hike up two flights of stairs at the 90 degree bend of the *lungomare*, passing Banco de Popolo on the right. (Open M-Tu and Th-F 8am-1pm and 5:30-8:30pm, W 8am-1pm. V, MC.)

Ristorante/Pizzeria Il Cappero, V. Roma, 31 (☎0923 91 26 01). At the right end of the *lungomare,* just after the Agip station, when facing the water. Open-air and overlooking the port bay, this Arab gone Italian eatery has polished, ergonomic dark wood chairs, wrought lanterns and plump, sparkling Arab glass decanters. Try the aromatic island improvisation of classic *insalata mista*: fragrant tomatoes, potatoes, olives, mozzarella, capers, and a dash of olive oil and oregano. Excellent pizzas from L7000, *primi* L9000, *secondi* L12-16,000. Open daily noon-3:30pm and 7pm-midnight.

Ristorante Il Dammuso (☎0923 91 14 22), on the waterfront before Banco del Popolo, at the 90 degree turn in the port-facing *lungomare*. Petite *trattoria* serves fish. Pasta with *pesto pantesco* (L9000). *Primi* from L9000, *secondi* from L10,000. Fills up by 8pm on weekends. Open noon-3pm and 7pm-midnight.

SIGHTS

Most of Pantelleria's sights are of the spend-an-afternoon-here-with-a-book kind, rather than the peek-in-and-move-on variety, so don't plan to hit more than two of them in a single day. The island is deceptively large, and if you crave liberation from the tyranny of Pantelleria's bus system (which may leave you waiting in the sun for up to five hours), a colorful portside line of free-flying mopeds await your motor-revving inner speed demon. Motorized transportation is an absolute necessity for most destinations inland and to the south; even some coastal spots are a good hour's walk from the scattered bus stops.

BAGNO ASCIUTTO AND MONTAGNA GRANDE. Far away from the port near the inland town of Sibà, a natural rock sauna and the summit of Pantelleria's highest mountain await. Signs guide you through and beyond Sibà town to the sauna; the last 10 minutes or so must be traveled on foot. Inside, Panteschi lie face down in a deep, low cave. Bring water and a towel; the oven-like heat is hard to stand, and it's normal to leave and re-enter several times. Farther along the sauna path, at the foot of Monte Gibole, the **Favara Grande** is a fumarole that still emits clouds of hot smoke. Many trails, most pretty but short, lead off the asphalt road, and a shady picnic area in a pine grove near the summit is the perfect place to relax after a *bagno asciutto*. Even if the midday heat is already steamy enough, head to Montangna Grande just for the view. The mountain road past Sibà leads almost to the top, with fantastic views of the 2nd half of the lush *Piano di Ghirlanda*. *(To get to Sibà, either take the marked bus from P. Cavour (6:40am, 12:40, 2, and 7:40pm) or turn left at the beginning of Sibà following signs for Montagna Grande.)*

THE SESI AND PUNTO DI SATARIA. The Neolithic people that inhabited Pantelleria have left behind the **sesi,** dome-shaped funerary monuments built without mortar. Tunnels in the *sesi* gave access to the womb-shaped chambers where kneeling corpses were placed. The largest remaining *sese* (many have been torn down for building material) contains 12 chambers. *(Take a left off the western sea road, when you see a yellow sign past the posh Mursia Hotel.)*

Past the prehistoric village is **Punto di Sataria,** where stairs lead down to the cement-lined Cave of Calypso. A bath in the thermal pools (37° C) is relaxing. From the pools, you can hop directly into the sea two feet away.

LO SPECCHIO DI VENERE (THE MIRROR OF VENUS). Legend has it that Venus used this lake as a mirror before her dates with Bacchus, a frequenter of Pantelleria for its superb (and powerful) *zabbibo* wine. Even those without a drunken date will be unable to resist a long look down into this startlingly aquamarine pool, fringed with firm white mud and surrounded by its bowl of green hillsides. Sulfur springs warm the water and enrich the mud. According to local practice, you're supposed to let the sun dry the therapeutic mud to a white cake on your skin.

THE NORTHEAST COAST AND THE ARCO DELL'ELEFANTE. There's prime swimming in three little inlets along the right side of the bulb of Pantelleria's keyhole. All three are on the Pantelleria-Tracino bus line, or an easy drive down the eastern sea road. **Cala di Tramontana** and **Cala di Levante** are a short walk from Tracino. The 1st inlet, **Gadir,** is popular for its outdoor *acquacalda*, a cement-encased thermal pool. The swimming is all right here, too, although if you like your ocean natural, you should head down the shore to Cala di Tramontana and Cala di Levante, where the local government apparently forgot to cover everything in concrete.

These two rocky coves, perfect for sunbathing, are really one cave split by a small point. Just visible to the right of Cala di Levante, the rock **Arco dell'Elefante** looks like a huge stone elephant slurping up sea water. It is Pantelleria's most photographed sight and an emblem of the island.

IL PIANO DI GHIRLANDA. Surrounded by its own crumbled lip, this fertile crater makes a perfect two-hour hike from Tracino. The area is one of Pantelleria's prettiest, and a reminder that the island makes its living by farming. Here, terraced hills and caper fields are tended by peasants working out of small, utilitarian *dammusi*. To explore this region, take the road that leads out of Tracino's P. Perugio.

BEACHES AND BOAT TOURS

After being mesmerized by turquoise sea from the hydrofoil window, your first inclination on arrival may well be to drop your bag and jump in the water. Do know, however, that the classic definition of a "beach" is not to be found on Pantelleria. Swimming areas around the coast are rated 1-3 on maps by difficulty of access. Rocky coves and swimming grottoes abound, but require some seeking out. The closest swimming to Pantelleria town can be found at **Grotta del Bue Marino,** just 2km to the east (to the right when facing the water) along the *lungomare.* Snorkelers prowl the coast, sunbathers perch on volcanic rock, and maniacal young boys hurl themselves off cliffs into the deep waters below. Exercise caution, wear water shoes, and jump *only* where they jump.

If you want to give each grotto equal amounts of love take a boat tour of the hidden grottoes, tiny caves, colorful fishes, and spectacularly sheer cliffs, all with a sea which resembles undulating turquoise glass. The coastline layers of leaning lava formations would bring a gleam to any geologist's eye. Gilligan and the Captain stop at all grotto-snorkeling hot spots. Passengers slip demurely in with mask and flippers or dive recklessly off top decks for an unrivaled *bagno dolce* ("sweet swim"). View some of Pantelleria's greatest (and otherwise inaccessible) delights: *Cinderella's slippers*, *L'Arco dell' Elefante*, and *I cinque diente* (before cosmetic dentistry). The colorful portside line of boats offer various advantages; while smaller boats actually make it into a few grottoes, their larger cousins provide bamboo shade, napping cushions, and room for young ones to play. One of the larger boats is the **Esperanza.** (Tours generally leave the port at 10am and return at 5pm. Reserve early in the morning or a day in advance. Groups of 5+ should haggle. June-Aug. with or without spaghetti lunch L40-50,000.)

ENTERTAINMENT

The **Taurus Pub,** V. Borio, 7, in Pantelleria town, is the island's most happening *dammuso*. With your back to the water, walk left along the *lungomare* to the rowdy, fishermen-crowded Pub Spinnaker. Turn right onto V. Borio just before the Spinnaker; the green-painted entranceway to Taurus is on the right. Look for the phosphorescent orange "tutto" sign on the door. Whitewashed, air-conditioned, and with a striped floor cushion, Taurus has a Bohemian flavor with live music most nights. (☎0923 91 34 12. No cover or drink minimum. Use of two Internet connected computers L8000 per hr.) Pantelleria's most obvious nightlife is at the port, where Panteschi take 24-hour *passagiate* at either of two nearly interchangeable bars: **Tikirikki** (open 5am-4am) and **Il Goloso** (open 5am-3am). Twelve kilometers away in the small town of Scauri is the sleek, clubbish **U Frisco** (☎0923 91 60 52), on the western seaside road from Pantelleria.

The one *discoteca* open on Pantelleria during the summer is **Oxidana,** on the western seaside road near Hotel Mursía-Cossira; look for a huge electronic scrolling banner that reads "Tutte le Sere." Come midsummer, tourists pack the protozoan seating pods and multi-level outdoor dance floor. (☎0923 91 82 98. Open July-Sept. 15. Cover L10,000; L10,000 drink minimum.)

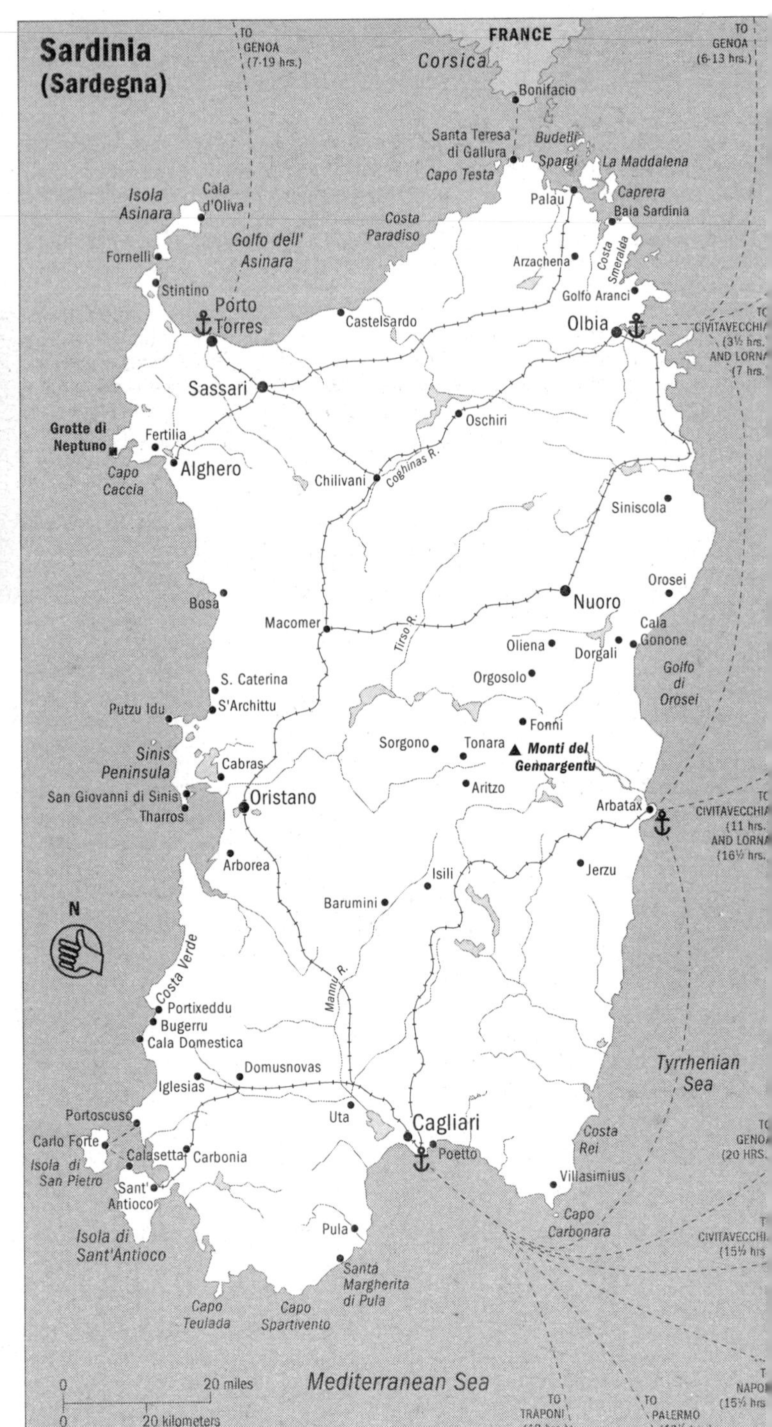
Sardinia
(Sardegna)
FRANCE
Corsica
TO GENOA (7-19 hrs.)
TO GENOA (6-13 hrs.)
Bonifacio
Santa Teresa di Gallura
Budelli
Spargi
La Maddalena
Capo Testa
Caprera
Palau
Baia Sardinia
Isola Asinara
Cala d'Oliva
Costa Paradiso
Golfo dell' Asinara
Costa Smeralda
Arzachena
Fornelli
Stintino
Golfo Aranci
Porto Torres
Castelsardo
Olbia
Sassari
Oschiri
Grotte di Neptuno
Fertilia
Alghero
Capo Caccia
Chilivani
Coghinas R.
Siniscola
Orosei
Bosa
Nuoro
Macomer
Tirso R.
Cala Gonone
Oliena
Dorgali
Orgosolo
Golfo di Orosei
S. Caterina
S'Archittu
Putzu Idu
Fonni
Sorgono
Tonara
Monti del Gennargentu
Sinis Peninsula
Cabras
Aritzo
San Giovanni di Sinis
Oristano
Tharros
Arbatax
Arborea
Jerzu
Isili
Barumini
N
Costa Verde
Mannu R.
Portixeddu
Bugerru
Cala Domestica
Domusnovas
Iglesias
Tyrrhenian Sea
Uta
Portoscuso
Cagliari
Carlo Forte
Calasetta
Carbonia
Poetto
Costa Rei
Isola di San Pietro
Sant' Antioco
Villasimius
Capo Carbonara
Isola di Sant'Antioco
Pula
Santa Margherita di Pula
Capo Teulada
Capo Spartivento
Mediterranean Sea
0
20 miles
0
20 kilometers
TO TRAPONI (12 hrs.)
TO PALERMO (13½ hrs.)

SARDINIA (SARDEGNA)

Vhen the boyish vanity of over cultivated mainland Italians starts to wear thin, vhen one more church interior will send you into the path of the nearest speeding 'iat, Sardinia's savage coastline and rugged people are bound to soothe your soul.). H. Lawrence sought respite from the "deadly net of European civilization" that lagued him even in the outermost reaches of Sicily, and he found his escape mong the wild horses, wind-carved rock formations, and pink flamingos of this emote island. An old Sardinian legend says that when God finished making the vorld, he had a handful of dirt left over, which he threw into the Mediterranean nd stepped on, creating Sardinia. The contours of that divine foot formed some of he world's most spectacular landscapes. The haphazard rough-hewn coastlines, iny rivers, rolling hills, and mighty mountain ranges today support about a million ardinians, a people some describe as too sturdy and manly to be Italians.

The ancient feudal civilizations of warring shepherd-kings that settled in Sarinia some 3500 years ago left 7-8000 scattered *nuraghe* ruins, gutted cone-shaped ɔwer-houses built of stone blocks and assembled without mortar. The first ecorded invaders of this land were the seafaring Phoenicians, followed by the qually belligerent Carthaginians. Sardinia finally settled down when the Romans acified the island and made it an agricultural colony. In the 13th century, Sardinia ecame a stomping ground for the Pisans, the Aragonese, the newly united Spanh, and the Piemontese. From this exploited island, Vittorio Emanuele, Italy's first ing, began his campaign to unify Italy in 1861. In 1948, the island regained some utonomy, establishing an autonomous administration. Only decades ago, *padɔni* (landlords) still held Sardinia's land, and farmers toiled under a system akin) serfdom. Italian Communism leapt to the rescue, and today much of the land is wned by those who till it. But even here, capitalism has infiltrated the coastline, 'here tourists relax in resorts, lounge on the beaches, and sip fruity drinks.

Sardinia's cuisine, like its terrain, is rustic and rugged. Hearty dishes like *sa fregula* (pasta in broth with saffron), *malloreddus* (shell-shaped pasta), *culurgiones* (ravioli stuffed with cheese, beets, tomato sauce, lamb, and sausage), and *pane frattau* (thin bread covered with eggs, cheese, and tomato sauce) frequent the island's menus. Celebrated dishes include *cardo* (lamb entrails), pork cooked in lamb's stomach, and grilled pig, horse, donkey, and goat. The infamous product of Sardinian shepherds, *casu fatizzu* (cheese with worms) and savory *pecorino* (sheep's milk cheese) are considered delicacies. Local wines are often sweet and strong. Try *vernaccia d'uva* (for its almond after-taste) with fish or the robust *cannonau di Sardegna* with red meat.

Sardinians are rightfully possessive of what is theirs. Mainland politicians parcel ıt the pristine coastline for NATO bases, and tourism brings overdevelopment. ne of Sardinia's defense mechanisms may be a train system that renders railısses all but useless. Don't fret; like love, Sardinia is well worth the trouble. After o much time on the continent grappling with the "deadly net," where is there to ? Let it be Sardinia. *Eia*, Mr. Lawrence (Sardo for yes). And now, *Aio* (Let's go).

HIGHLIGHTS OF SARDINIA

WADE with the **pink flamingos** along Cagliari's darling beaches (p. 637).

SAVOR mountain views and Picasso-esque graffiti in **Orgosolo** (p. 646).

EXPLORE the living rock of the divine **Grotto di Nettuno** (p. 655).

BEHOLD breathtaking views of Corsica while lounging in the rock-cut caves of **Santa Teresa di Gallura** (p. 662).

GETTING THERE

FLIGHTS

Flights link Olbia, Alghero, and Cagliari to major Italian cities. Airlines also fly t Paris, Geneva, Zurich, Munich, and Frankfurt. Flights are faster than water travel but the chaos of an Italian airport and exorbitant fares discourage most travelers.

FERRIES

The cheapest way to get to Sardinia is by ferry to Olbia from Civitavecchia, Genoa or Livorno; expect to pay around L35,000 and as much as L80,000 depending o season, speed of the boat, and departure time (night trips cost more). The cheap est tickets are for daytime *posta ponte* (deck class) slots on the slow-movin boats, but most ferry companies require that the slightly more expensive *poltron* (reserved armchairs) be sold to capacity before they open *posta ponte* for sale. I the price ranges in the table below, the low number is the low-season *poste pont* fare, and the high number is the high-season *poltrone* fare. Expect to pay an addi tional L10-60,000, depending on the season, duration, and compartment size. Tour ist rushes in July and August and the possibility of a strike make advance plannin advisable. Travelers with cars, mopeds, animals, or children should arrive one t two hours before departure; everyone else should arrive 45 to 90 minutes early Allow more time if departing after the maritime station has closed, as finding th exact departure point of the ferry can be quite nerve-wracking.

Tirrenia (info and booking ☎1478 990 00 or (toll-free) 800 82 40 79; www.tirrenia.it. runs the most ferries to and from Sardinia, has the most offices, and almost alway costs the least. *Bravo,* Tirrenia. Offices are in the *stazione marittima* in most cities including **Cagliari** (☎070 66 60 65), **Civitavecchia** (☎0766 217 03), **Genoa** (☎01 269 82 28), and **Olbia**. There are also Tirrenia offices in **Livorno** (☎0586 42 47 30 Calata Addis Abeba–Varco Galvani; **Palermo** (☎091 33 33 00), Calata Marinai d'Italia **Porto Torres,** V. Mare, 38; and **Rome,** V. Bissolati, 41 (☎06 474 20 41).

Sardinia Ferries (☎019 21 55 11; fax 019 215 53 00; www.sardiniaferries.com Offices in **Livorno,** at the *stazione marittima* (☎0586 881 380; fax 0586 89 61 03 and in **Civitavecchia** (☎0766 50 07 14; fax 0766 50 07 18), at Calata Laurenti.

Moby Lines has offices in **Olbia**'s *stazione marittima* (☎0789 279 27) and in **Livorn** (☎0586 42 67 88; fax 0586 44 39 40), at Varco Galvani.

Grand Navi Veloci (www.grimaldi.it) has offices in **Genoa,** V. Fieschi, 17 (☎010 58 9 31), and in **Porto Torres** (☎0795 160 34), in the *Porto Industriale.*

Tris (www.tris.it) has offices in **Genoa,** at P. della Vittoria, 12/14 (☎010 576 24 11; fa 010 576 24 02), in **Porto Torres** (☎079 51 26 34) and in **Palau** (☎0789 70 86 31 at the port terminal.

ROUTE	COMPANY	DURATION	FREQUENCY	PRICE
Civitavecchia-Olbia	Tirrenia (Rapido)	4hr.	2-4 per day	L46-61,500
Civitavecchia-Olbia	Tirrenia (Traditional)	8hr.	1 per day	L28-44,500
Civitavecchia-Cagliari	Tirrenia (Traditional)	15-18hr.	2 per day	L48-77,000
Genoa-Olbia	Tirrenia (Rapido)	6hr.	5-7 per week	L87-137,500
Genoa-Olbia	Tirrenia (Traditional)	13½hr.	July-Sept. 1 per day	L50-83,000
Genoa-Porto Torres	Tirrenia (Rapido)	6hr.	June 23-Sept. 1-2 per day	L87-137,500

ROUTE	COMPANY	DURATION	FREQUENCY	PRICE
Genoa-Porto Torres	Tirrenia (Traditional)	13hr.	5-7 per week	L50-83,000
Genoa-Cagliari	Tirrenia (Traditional)	20hr.	July-Sept. 2 per week	L86-102,000
Naples-Cagliari	Tirrenia (Traditional)	16hr.	Jan.-Sept. 1 per week	L48-78,000
Palermo-Cagliari	Tirrenia (Traditional)	13½hr.	1 per week	L45-73,000
La Spezia-Golfo Aranci	Tirrenia (Rapido)	5½hr.	June 23-Sept. 10, 1 per day	L119,000
Trapani-Cagliari	Tirrenia (Traditional)	11hr.	1 per week	L45-73,000
Civitavecchia-G. Aranci	Sardinia Ferries	3½-7hr.	1-3 per day in summer	L32-95,000
Livorno-Golfo Aranci	Sardinia Ferries	10hr.	2 per day in summer	L40-86,000
Olbia-Livorno	Moby Lines	10hr.	2 per day	L54-106,000
S. Teresa-Bonifacio	Moby Lines	1hr.	10 per day in summer	L14-18,000
Genoa-Palau	Tris	12hr.	1-2 per day	L52-84,000
Genoa-Olbia	Grand Navi Veloci	10hr.	1 per day	L79-133,000
Genoa-Port Torres	Grand Navi Veloci	10hr.	1 per day	L79-133,000

CAGLIARI PROVINCE

CAGLIARI ☎070

Sardinia's capital peeks out from the southern coast of the island as a polished gemstone from a land of raw earth. Regal tree-lined streets run past rows of tiny boutiques and stately *piazzas*, lorded over by the hilltop 13th-century Castello district. Medieval Pisan towers dragoon bewildered map-clutching tourists, and an ancient Roman amphitheater welcomes modern-day opera-lovers to performances of *Carmen*. With a port that never sleeps and sweeping beaches perfect for a day of hard-earned respite in the sun, it's little wonder that the devil chose to ride Cagliari's mountains and that the Savoy king (briefly) made the city his home.

TRANSPORTATION

Flights: (☎070 24 02 00), in the village of **Elmas.** ARST buses run from the airport to the city terminal at P. Matteotti (30min., 23 per day 6:15am-midnight, L1300).

Trains: FS (☎070 65 62 93), in P. Matteotti. To: **Oristano** (1½hr., 20 per day 5:42am-10:20pm, L8500); **Sassari** (4hr., 4 per day, L22,700); **Olbia** (4hr., 3 per day noon-6:20pm, L24,300); and **Porto Torres** (4hr., 6:45am-2:25pm, L24,300). Open daily 6am-8:30pm. 24hr. ticket machines. **Ferrovie della Sardegna** (☎070 49 13 04), in P. della Repubblica. Private railroad with supplementary services to **Arbatax** (6:45am and 1:45pm, L33,100). Info open daily 7:30am-8:45pm.

Buses: PANI, ticket booth in Stazione Marittima; buses depart outside. To: **Oristano** (1½hr., 5 per day 5:30am-6:15pm, L11,300); **Sassari** (3hr., 7 per day 5:30am-7pm, L26,000); and **Nuoro** (3½hr., 4 per day 5:30am-6:15pm, L21,900). Open M-F 8-8:30am, 9am-2:15pm, and 5:30-7pm; Sa-Su 1:30-2:15pm and 5:30-7pm. When the office is closed, buy tickets on the bus. **ARST,** P. Matteotti, 6 (☎070 40 98 324), serves local towns, including **Pula** (direction: Anna Azzesi; 18 per day 5:25am-8:35pm; L3900, round-trip L7400); **Uta** (11 per day 6:15am-8:30pm, L2800); **Barumini** (3 per day 2-7pm, L8600); **Arbat** (10:25am-3pm, L14,800); and the **airport** (10min.; 23 per day 5:45am-9:45pm, return 6:15am-midnight; L1300). Open daily 6am-9pm. **FMS** (toll-free ☎8000 445 53) runs to **Bugerru** (3 hr., 5 per day 5:40am-5:50pm, L10,400). Buy tickets at the newsstand across from Farmacia Spanno on V. Roma.

Ferries: Tirrenia (☎167 82 40 79), in Stazione Marittima. Free **luggage storage** 7am-7pm. Open M-F 8:30am-8pm, Sa 8:30am-6pm, Su 4-7pm. For details, see p. 632.

Local Transportation: Orange **CTM** buses run from P. Matteotti. Buy tickets at the ARST station's newsstand. L1500 for 90min., L2500 for 120min., L4000 for 24hr., L15,000 for a pack of 12 tickets. Buses **P, PQ,** and **PF** go to the beach at **Il Poetto.**

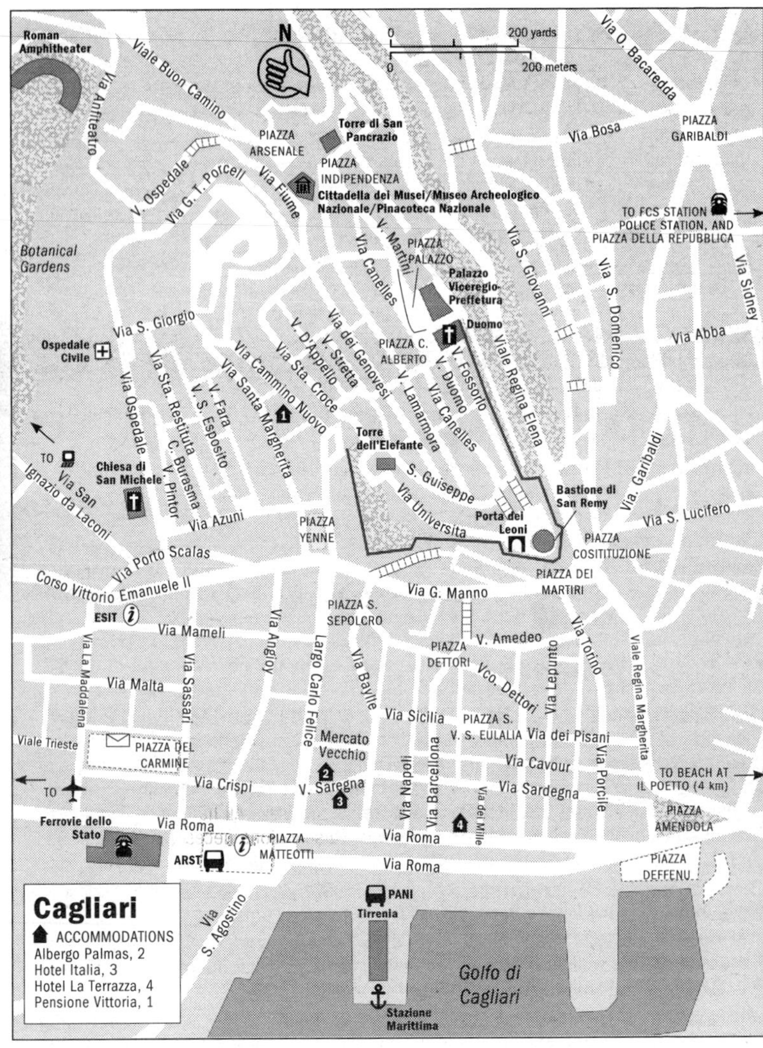

ORIENTATION AND PRACTICAL INFORMATION

Sandwiched by the harbor, Stazione Marittima, and the PANI bus stop on one side and outdoor cafes on the other, **Via Roma** stretches before those arriving by train, boat, or bus. At one end of V. Roma, **Piazza Matteotti** houses the train station, the ARST station, and the tourist office. Across from P. Matteotti, broad **Largo Carlo Felice** climbs the steep hill leading to the *castello* and the historic center of town.

TOURIST, FINANCIAL, AND LOCAL SERVICES

Tourist Office: (☎070 66 92 55), in P. Matteotti, in the park across from the train and bus stations. This oddly-shaped wooden cabin has a multilingual staff and offers substantial info on local sights. Open in summer M-Sa 8am-8pm; in winter M-Sa 8am-1:30pm. If you can't get the answers (or the maps) you need, ask the extremely accommodating and cheerful staff at the **Stazione Marittima branch,** open daily 8am-7pm.

Budget Travel: CTS, V. Cesare Balbo, 12 (☎070 48 82 60). Info on student discounts and packages. Open M-F 9am-1pm and 4-7:30pm, Sa 9am-1pm. **Memo Travel,** V. Pitzolo, 1a (☎070 40 09 07). Open M-F 9am-1pm and 4-8pm, Sa 9am-1pm.

Car Rental: Ruvioli, V. dei Mille, 11 (☎070 65 89 55). All cars with A/C. Insurance included. You can make reservations here, but you have to pick up the car at the **airport branch** (☎070 24 03 23), where the friendly staff speaks English. Min. age 21. Major credit card required. L90,000 per day. Both open M-Sa 9am-9pm. V, MC, AmEx.

Laundry: Lavanderia Self-Service, V. Sicilia, 20, off V. Bayle. 6kg wash L6000; 20min. dry L5000. Happy hour 8-10am and 2-4pm. Open daily 8am-10pm.

Bookstore: Cocco, V. Roma, 65 (☎070 65 02 56). Well-stocked in classics and current best-sellers. Open M-Sa June-Aug. 9am-midnight; Sept.-May 9am-9pm. V, MC.

MERGENCY AND COMMUNICATIONS

Emergencies: ☎113. **Police:** V. Amat, 9 (☎070 602 71). **First Aid/Ambulance:** ☎118 **Hospital:** V. Ospedale, 46 (☎070 66 57 55), by Chiesa di S. Michele.

Pharmacy: Farmacia Dr. Spano, V. Roma, 99 (☎070 65 56 83). Open M-Sa 9am-1pm and 4:50-8:10pm.

Internet Access: V@ssel, V. Tigellio, 22A/B (☎070 67 20 20). From V. Porto Scalas, turn right on V. San Ignazio da Laconi and take the 2nd left onto V. Tigellio. Take the right fork and V@ssel is on the right at the end. Internet access L6000 for 30min., L10,000 per hr. Open M-F 10am-1pm and 4-9pm.

Post Office: (☎070 65 82 57), in P. del Carmine. Take V. Sassari from P. Matteotti. Fermo Posta, telephone cards, and **currency exchange.** Open M-F 8am-6pm, Sa 8am-1:20pm. **Postal Code:** 09100.

ACCOMMODATIONS

Pensione Vittoria, V. Roma, 75 (☎070 65 79 70). Cross V. Roma from the train station or ARST station and turn right. Check in on the 3rd floor. With 14 majestic rooms, refined Venetian chandeliers, and sparkling bathrooms, this family-run *pensione* is quite possibly the nicest in Cagliari, and it ranks among the top budget accommodations in Sardinia, if not Italy. Ask for a room with a sea view. All have A/C, phone, and radio. Breakfast L9000. Wheelchair accessible. Reservations necessary. Singles L55-60,000, with bath L65-70,000; doubles L85-90,000, with bath L100-108,000.

Hotel La Terrazza, V. S. Margherita, 21 (☎070 66 86 52; fax 070 66 08 63), close to the *centro storico.* Walk right about 20m on V. Roma and turn left on Largo Carlo Felice. At P. Yenne, turn left on V. S. Margherita. Friendly staff and 14 clean, remodeled rooms with huge beds, TV, and telephone. Most with A/C and fridge. Singles L50,000, with bath L75,000; doubles L75,000, with bath L100,000. V, MC, AmEx.

Albergo Palmas, V. Sardegna, 14 (☎070 65 16 79). Cross V. Roma and turn right. Take the 1st left on Largo Carlo Felice and the 1st right on V. Sardegna. Excellent location and accommodating management. 14 rooms have chair, sink, and bed. Lounge with fish tank, TV, and stereo. Singles L35,000; doubles L50,000, with shower L60,000.

FOOD

long V. Sardegna, many small shops provide fruit, cheese, and bread. Try **Panette-a Mura,** V. Sardegna, 40 (☎070 66 38 64), a small market and a heavenly bakery at carries soy milk and other hard-to-find protein products. (Open M-Sa 7:30am-30pm and 4:30-8:30pm.) The colossal **Iper Pan La Plaia,** V. la Plaia, 15, sells grocer-s. (Open daily 9am-9pm.) On Sundays, explore the **market** on the far side of the adium in Borgo S. Elia for fresh fruit and seafood.

Trattoria Lilicu, V. Sardegna, 78 (☎070 65 29 70). Established 80 years ago and sti run by the same family, this simple *trattoria* serves traditional Sardi dishes like *lacet di agnelle* (lamb; L10,000) and expertly prepared seafood (L15-20,000) at clamorou communal tables. The menu changes daily. Full meal L35-40,000. Cover L3000. Ope M-Sa 12:30-3pm and 9-11pm. Reservations recommended. V, MC, AmEx.

Antica Hostaria, V. Cavour, 60 (☎070 66 58 70; fax 070 66 58 78). Reputedly one c Cagliari's best restaurants but still not entirely out of the budget traveler's reach Founded in 1852, this beautiful restaurant maintains an art nouveau decor. Tasty *ma loreddus gnocchetti* (L51,000) are far from malodorous. Veal in *vernaccia* sauc L18,000. Cover L4000. Open M-Sa 1-3pm and 8-11pm. Closed Aug. V, MC, AmEx.

Trattoria Gennargentu, V. Sardegna, 60 (☎070 65 82 47). Join the locals in th *salumeria* and restaurant for a Sardinian feast of *spaghetti alle arselle e bottarg* (loaded with baby clams and seasoned with ground fish eggs) for L12,000 and a zest *salsiccia arrosto* for L7000. The wine list is as long as the menu. Cover L2500. Open M Sa 12:30-3pm and 8-11pm. V, MC, AmEx.

Ristorante Pizzeria Downtown, P. Jenne, 18, at the top of Largo Carlo Felice. Fill up aft the climb down from the *castello*. Lunch *menù* (L18,000) includes a starter, mai course, and dessert—perhaps *riso nero,* shrimp, and *tiramisù*. The *pizza alla downtow* (L14,000) is loaded with every topping imaginable. Cover L3000. Open daily 1-2:30p and 8pm-midnight. V, MC, AmEx.

Antico Caffè, P. Costituzione, 10/11 (☎070 65 82 04). The haunt of Nobel Prize wi ners, Italian presidents, and flashy Italian TV stars; this elegant, snobbish cafe has ov 150 years of history. Reserve a table outside. Delicious crepes (L5500-10,000), dec dent ice cream sundaes (L8-10,000), and bountiful salads (L6-9000). Breakfast L 13,000, *primi* L7-9000. 20% service charge. Open daily 7am-2am. V, MC, AmEx.

SIGHTS

ROMAN AMPHITHEATER. Sardinia's most significant Roman ruin, this 2nd-ce tury theater was constructed after the Carthaginians succumbed to the Roman ju gernaut in 238 BC. Built into a rocky hillside, the amphitheater conform beautifully to the natural slope. Underground cages once hosted ferocious an mals, and the arena itself was used for gladiatorial combat. Today summer perfo mances in the temporarily refurbished theater are a little more civilized. From Jul to September, the city hosts an **arts festival,** bringing the ancient ruins into th present. The amphitheater comes alive with concerts, operas, and classic plays.

BASTIONE DI SAN REMY. Climb up the graceful (though graffiti-covered) doubl stairway at **Piazza Costituzione** and through the archway to the terraces of the 19t century *bastione* for a spectacular view of the Golfo degli Angeli, the pink flami gos, and the **Sella del Diavolo** (Devil's Saddle), a rock formation within the mou tains surrounding Cagliari (you'll see the saddle on the inner right side). He young Rasta-types come together to play bongos during the day, and a chic neig boring bar organizes tango dancing at night. Named after a viceroy, the *bastion* was destroyed during a World War II bombing but was rebuilt to continue its fun tion as a divide between the modern city and the *castello;* in medieval Cagliari na row streets wind past Aragonese churches and Piedmontese royal palaces, comir to a halt only at the Pisan wall around the hill.

DUOMO. This stunning cathedral was modeled after the one in Pisa (see p. 363 Dazzling gold mosaics sit atop each entryway. The pulpits on either side of the ma entrance and the four wrestling lions at the base of the 12th-century altar are th works of Guglielmo Pisano. The ornate wooden balcony to the left of the altar serv as the seat of the Piedmontese king—he refused to sit among the people for fear regicide. The **sanctuary** below the *duomo* was carved into the rock in 1618. Colo ful marble inlays cover the 292 niches that contain the relics of early Christi martyrs. *(P. Palazzo, 3. ☎070 66 38 37. Open 8am-12:30pm and 4-8pm.)*

MUSEUMS. Although the menacing spear above the entrance recalls the building's original purpose, today the Arsenale houses a modern complex of research museums that includes the vaguely inspiring **Museo Archeologico Nazionale.** Among the Phoenician statuettes and Roman glass works are impressive armies of tiny, 1000 year-old bronze figurines. *(Take V. Buoncammino to P. Arsenale and pass under the Torre di S. Pancrazio to the Arsenale. ☎070 65 59 11. Open May-Aug. Tu-Su 9am-8pm; Sept.-Apr. 9am-1:30pm and 3-7:30pm. L5000, over 65 and under 18 free. Wheelchair accessible.)*

The **Pinacoteca Nazionale,** in the same complex as the archaeological museum, displays medieval and Baroque religious paintings. The labyrinthine museum is built around the remains of a 16th-century city fortification, visible on the ground floor. Works include portraits by the most influential Sardinian painter of the 19th century, Giovanni Marghinotti. *(☎070 66 24 96. Open Tu-Su 8:30am-7:30pm. L4000, ages 18-25 L2000, over 60 and under 18 free. Wheelchair accessible.)*

BOTANICAL GARDENS. A perfect spot for a picnic, the university gardens protect over 500 species of plants, many of which are unique to Sardinia. *(V. Fra Ignazio, 11. Head down V. S. Ignazio da Laconi to the university. ☎070 675 35 22. Open daily Apr.-Oct. 24 3-8pm; Oct. 25-Mar. 8am-1:30pm. L1000, under 6 and over 60 free.)*

BEACHES. **Il Poetto,** Cagliari's most popular stretch of pure white sand and emerald-sapphire water spans 10km from the massive Devil's Saddle to the Margine Rosso (Red Bluff). Locals claim it's ugly, but only because the nearby treasures of **Villasimus** and **Chia** put most beaches in Sardinia to shame. Behind Il Poetto, the salt-water **Stagno di Molentargius** (Pond of Molentargius) provides habitat for pink flamingos and their fair-skinned admirers. City buses P, PQ, and PF run to the beaches (20min., L1500). Get tickets at the green kiosk in P. Matteotti. To avoid the most crowded areas, hold off for a few stops once you see the beach. For more private sunning and swimming head to the less crowded **Cala Mosca,** a smaller beach surrounded by dirt paths leading to isolated coves. Take city bus #5 to Stadio Amsicora and then city bus #11 to the beach.

ENTERTAINMENT

Most bars and clubs in the city are open 9pm-5am. They shut down in August, when dancing moves outdoors. All bars are members-only digs—you'll have to shell out a one-time L10-25,000 fee for a nifty AICS card. Good choices include: **Red Fox,** V. S. Giovanni, 400 (☎070 40 16 14), a small, dark pub-style bar that also serves cheap food; **De Candia,** V. De Candia, 1, which serves expensive drinks to an older crowd, but also sponsors tango dancing on the Bastione di San Remy during the week and live jazz on Friday nights (☎070 65 58 84; open 8am-3am during the summer); **Fuori Orario,** V. Forlianini, 12 (☎070 30 39 99), a bar/pizzeria popular among the locals; and **Doctor Blues,** V. Monastir, 210 (☎070 54 25 42; open after 10pm and requires a round-trip L15,000 cab ride).

Fortunately, discos don't require AICS cards, and they generally have a more happenin' scene anyway. If you have a car or moped at your disposal and appreciate big pick-up scenes, you'll definitely enjoy a night at the beach with the young local crowd. If you don't have a car, take the PQ bus before 10:30pm to Il Poetto and return by cab. Bronzed Italians fill **Pandemonium** (the last stop on Il Poetto) on weekends. Nearby **Assemini** is home to several clubs that are open only during the winter, including **Citta Global** on V. Sardegna, and the gargantuan **Eurogarden,** V. Trieste, 125 (☎070 94 00 09). Bus #9 from P. Matteotti goes to Assemini, but you'll need a taxi to return. (Both open Tu-Su at 11:30pm. Cover L20-30,000.)

Outdoor movies are shown without subtitles in July and August (around 9pm) at the Marina Piccola off Spiaggia del Poetto. Buy tickets (L5-10,000) at the Marina. Merchants converge on the terraces of the Bastione di S. Remy for a **flea market** on Sunday mornings and a smaller daily flea market in P. del Carmine.

On the 1st of May, Sardinians flock to Cagliari for the **Festival of Sant'Efisio,** honoring a deserter from Diocletian's army who saved the island from the plague but couldn't save himself from a beheading. A costumed procession escorts his effigy from the capital down the coast to the small church that bears his name.

DAYTRIPS FROM CAGLIARI

BARUMINI. An agricultural village in the rolling countryside 60km north of Cagliari, Barumini is 1km west of Sardinia's most complex set of *nuraghi* ruins at **Su Nuraxi.** Construction of the 1st of five towers next to a natural spring began in 1500 BC; this central tower grew to 14m over the course of several centuries, reflecting the amplifying power of the prehistoric fortress's rulers. Correspondingly, the surrounding village huts multiplied, and their walls, hearths, and mortar stones remain. In AD 238, well after the decline of *nuraghi* civilization, Romans built over the silt-covered village. Their usurpation altered little, and superstitious farmers left the mound of earth-covered ruins untouched (except for use as a burial pit) through 1851, when archaeologists excavated them. *(Site open daily 9am-sunset. L8000. Free tours every half hour in Italian.)*

Horse lovers should watch for *cavallini di Giara*—a small, sleek breed unique to Sardinia—galloping wildly across the plateau of nearby **Gestiu** (2km away, follow the signs, or keep your eyes peeled on the bus ride to San Luri).

The only direct service from Cagliari to Barumini is the **ARST bus** (1½hr., 2pm and 5pm, L7200). Buses return to Cagliari in the morning. If you want to return in the evening, take the ARST bus (40min., 6:05pm, L3500) to San Luri. Once in San Luri, you should have just enough time to catch the commuter train to Cagliari (50 min.; 7:04pm; L4200, L10,000 if purchased on the train). If the bus is running late, the next train is at 9:01pm.

NORA. The city of Nora, reputedly the oldest city in Sardinia, was settled by Phoenicians (c. 850 BC) who coveted its strategic location. The prosperous town, which passed through the hands of the Carthaginians and the Romans, was finally abandoned in the 8th century after too many pirate raids. Today Nora is one of the most tranquil spots in southern Sardinia. Explore the remains of Punic temples, patrician homes, and a well-preserved Roman theater, or take a short walk to the watchtower for an awe-inspiring view of the site and coastline. Free tours in Italian provide historical background. *(Site open daily May-Sept. 9am-8pm; Sept.-Apr. 9am-sunset. L5000, ages 6-14 L2000. English guidebooks L10,000. Call far in advance (☎070 920 91 38) to arrange tours in English.)* Nora is accessible via tiny local buses from the town center in Pula (10min., 8 per day 7am-11:30pm, L1100).

NEAR CAGLIARI

SANT'ANTIOCO ☎0781

This island off the southwestern coast of Sardinia is the region's biggest, ranking in Italy's top four. Of volcanic origins, it now oozes little lava and lots of lore; a history-lover's haven, the city of Sant'Antioco is built where the Punic city of Sulci once stood and is surrounded by 27 Nuraghic villages. The population of this former Mediterranean trade hub was diminished by Arab raids. Today, descendants of those who stuck it out stroll along Sant'Antioco's main strip, V. Nazionale/C. V. Emanuele, and on warm evenings the crowd spills into P. Umberto.

FMS buses (toll-free ☎8000 445 53) run from V. Nazionale to **Cagliari** (2hr., 5 per day 5:23am-6:08pm, L9500-11,300) and **Calasetta** (20min., 11 per day 7:36am-9:13pm, L1300). Buy tickets at the newsstand at V. Nazionale, 23. **Euromoto,** V. Nazionale, 57, rents bikes (L20,000 per day) and scooters (L50-90,000). (☎0781 84 09 07. Open Tu-F 9am-1pm and 4-8:30pm, M and Sa 9am-1pm. Cash only.)

Services include: the **Pro Loco Tourist Office,** P. Repubblica, 41 (☎0781 84 05 92; open in summer M-F 10am-12:30pm and 5-9pm, in winter 10am-12:30pm and 4-8pm); a **Banco di Sardegna,** V. Nazionale, 2, with **currency exchange** and a 24hr. **ATM** (open M-F 8:20am-1:20pm and 2:35-4:05pm); the **carabinieri,** V. della Rinascita, 14 (☎0781 831 22); **Guardia Medica** (☎0781 835 91); a **pharmacy,** P. Umberto, 9 (☎0781 830 31; open M-F 9am-1pm and 5:10pm-8:30pm); and a **hospital** (☎0781 66 83 44).

Albergo Moderno, V. Moderno, 82, boasts a restaurant with quiet, shaded outdoor seating and ten warm, comfortable, pastel rooms. (☎0781 831 95. Singles L65,000, with bath L70,000; doubles with bath L105,000. V, MC, AmEx.) For supplies, stock up at the **Italcoop Supermarket,** V. Roma, 31. (☎0781 820 83. Open M-Sa 8am-1pm and 5:15-8:30pm.)

CALASETTA ☎0781

On the northwestern tip of Sant'Antioco Island, Calasetta has Nuraghic, Punic, and Roman roots. Over the course of Tabarcan, Piemontese, French, and Spanish occupation, these roots have long withered away, and nothing but a small, nondescript, quiet Sardinian town remains, with a simple grid of streets centered around **Via Roma** (the main thoroughfare), a few beaches, and port access to **Carloforte.**

Saremar Ferries (☎0781 884 30) has a ticket office on the port open 15 minutes before each departing ferry and runs boats to **Carloforte** (30min.; 13-17 per day; 7:35am-11:50pm; L3-4000, children L1500-2000, cars L8600-21,700). Buy **FMS** (☎0781 882 91) tickets at the *tabacchi* on the corner of V. Roma and V. Sicilia. **Buses** leave from the port to **Sant'Antioco** (30min., 12 per day 4:54am-10:10pm, L1300-3800) and **Cagliari** (3hr., 9 per day 4:54am-5:45pm, L10,400).

The **Pro Loco Tourist Office** on V. Lungomare Colombo, in the same building as the *biblioteca*, has lots of historical information and a pittance of maps. In case of an **emergency,** call the **police** (☎113), **carabinieri** (☎0781 884 22), **medical emergency hotline** (☎0781 884 40), or the **hospital** (☎0781 66 83 44). For **Internet access,** try the *Biblioteca Comunale* (Community Library) on V. Lungomare Colombo below the tourist office. If you assure the librarian you only need access a few times, there should be no charge. (☎0781 883 78. Library open M and W-F 4:30-6:30pm.) There's also a **post office** at V. R. Margherita, 53. (☎0781 884 24. Open M-Sa 9am-1pm.)

The sheets at **Hotel Cala di Seta,** V. R. Margherita, 61, may not be silk, but the bedspreads sure are pink. Twenty-one feminine rooms, all with bath and telephone. (☎0781 883 04. Singles L50-60,000; doubles 80-85,000. Half-pension L75-120,000; full pension L90-140,000. Half-pension required in Aug. V, MC, AmEx.) The **Nonna Isa Supermarket,** at the corner of Lungomare Colombo and V. Barcelona, is just the place to restock. (Open M-Sa 8am-1pm and 5-8pm, Su 9am-noon.) **FMS buses** leave from the port to Spiaggia Grande, Calasetta's biggest and most appealing beach (10min.; 7 per day 10:15am-7pm; L1300, round-trip L2400).

CARLOFORTE ☎0781

On the eastern coast of the Isola San Pietro, Carloforte was founded by Ligurians but is named after one strong Piedmontese king. Massive salt ponds support flocks of pink flamingos, and fields of grass littered with crumbling towers and lighthouses lead to several lovely beaches, including **La Caletta.**

Saremar Ferries (☎0781 85 40 05) runs boats to **Carloforte** (30min.;13-17 per day; 6:55am-11:10pm; L3-4000, children L1500-2000, cars L8600-21,700). **Marinatour Noleggio,** V. Porcile, 12 (☎0330 44 29 41 or 0781 854 11), offers bike and scooter rentals and organizes diving excursions.

Services include: the **Pro Loco Tourist Office** in P. Carlo Emanuele (☎0781 85 40 09; open M-Sa 9:30am-12:30pm and 4-8pm); a **Banca Commerciale Italiana,** C. Cavour, 1, with **currency exchange** and a 24hr. **ATM** (open M-F 8:20am-1:40pm and 2:50-4:15pm, Sa 8:20am-11:50pm; the **carabinieri** (☎0781 85 58 21); **Guardia Medica** (☎0781 85 62 28); an **ambulance** (☎ 0781 85 52 70); and a **post office,** on Porto Paglia off P. dei Galanzieri (☎0781 85 40 38; open M-F 9am-1pm and Sa 9am-12:30pm).

Located in a refurbished old town home right on the water, the **Hieracon Hotel,** C. Cavour, 63, caters to a mature clientele that appreciates the quiet backyard garden, dignified interior, and reasonable prices. (☎0781 85 40 28. Singles L55,000-80,000; doubles L90-140,000. Half-pension L80-120,000; full pension 100-150,000. Mini-apartments for 4 L90-200,000. V, MC, AmEx.) On the other end of C. Cavour, the **Hotel Riviera** is far more modern and can be far more expensive. All 28 rooms have TV, telephone, and bathroom. (☎0781 85 40 04. Breakfast included. Singles L50-110,000; doubles L100-220,000. V, MC, AmEx.) For **camping,** catch the bus toward La Caletta and ask to be let off at the **Campeggio "La Caletta."** (☎0781 85 21 12. Open June 15-Sept. 15. L21-23,000 per person, children L12-15,000.)

Beaches line the shores south of Carloforte, but a 15-minute bus ride (11 per day 9:25am-7:14pm; L1300, round-trip L2400; buy tickets from the Saremar office in P. Carlo Emanuele) takes you past the *Saline di Carloforte* (salt ponds awash with pink flamingos) to La Caletta, on the western side of the island. Here papery strands of seaweed touch toes dangling off rocky waterside outcroppings. Dark cliffs enclose a mini-bay, underpopulated compared to the island's other beaches.

SARDINIA

BUGERRU ☎0781

Once a mining town, Bugerru's only feature of note today is its small port, surrounded by slag-ridden cliffs and abandoned mining edifices. Though the town has its own beach, it is best used as a base for excursions to nearby beaches, which make the long, winding bus ride from Cagliari worth your while.

The bus drive from Bugerru provides breathtaking views of rolling, rock-strewn hillsides falling into the sea. At **Cala Domestica,** campers park near the slightly dirty beach, which opens into a bay sheltered by clay-colored cliffs. Tents appear sporadically among the rocks; the occasional wild boar fails to scare the avid camper/hiker/beach-bum away. Any good Sardinian surfer will tell you **Portixeddu** is the place to go to catch the island's best waves. A grassy sand knoll flattens into expansive stretches of sand refreshingly clear of beach umbrellas. Largely untouched by seaside capitalism (due to its remote location and the wall of mountains that separate the coast from the rest of the island), the beach provides respite from tourists and plenty of water space in which to hang *dieci.*

FMS buses (toll-free ☎8000 445 53) leave from V. Roma for **Portixeddu** (10min.; 3 per day 8:20am-3:25pm, return 3:09pm; L1300); **Cala Domestica** (30min.; Sa-Su only, return 5:04pm; L6700); and **Cagliari** (3hr., 4 per day 5:38am-3:25pm, L10,400). Buy tickets from *tabaccheria.*

The **Pro Loco Tourist Office,** V. Roma, 41 (☎0781 545 22), is open only sporadically. If you're in a bind, call the **carabinieri,** V. Roma, 35 (☎112), or the **Guardia Medica Turistica,** P. del Minatore, 7 (☎0781 54 04 2). The **pharmacy** is at V. Uffici, 25. (☎070 66 28 66. Open M-F 9am-1pm and 5-8pm.) There is a **post office** at P. del Minatore, 7. (☎0781 54 06 2; fax 0781 54 03 1. Open M-F 7:50am-1pm, Sa 8:10am-12:30pm.)

You can camp at Cala Domestica or ask at the tourist office or the bar on V. Roma about renting a private room. The town's sole restaurant is **Il Nido di Natalino,** V. Diaz, 36. Be wary of the *Specialita della Casa*; although delicious and filling, it'll run you L45,000. It includes wine, pasta, fish, and dessert. *Pasta al Carbon Sulcis* (L15,000) is a meal in itself, smothered in a delicious black sauce of octopus, lobster, and shrimp. (*Primi* from L7000, fish *secondi* from L6000 per *etto* (330 grams). (☎0338 139 61 82. Open daily 9am-5pm and 7pm-1am.)

ORISTANO PROVINCE

ORISTANO ☎0783

In the 7th century, the stoic inhabitants of Tharros repelled invasion after invasion until a band of merciless Moorish pirates finally forced them to abandon their homes. With nowhere else to go, they set up camp around Oristano. Today, as in the 7th century, it would take nothing less than an angry mob of Moorish pirates to convince you to stay here, were it not for the enticing nearby Phoenician ruins in Tharros, S'Archittu's awe-inspiring arch, and the spectacular beaches of Is Arutas.

TRANSPORTATION

Trains: (☎0783 722 70), on P. Ungheria, 1km from the center of town. To **Cagliari** (1-2hr., 25 per day 4:52am-9:22pm, L8500), **Olbia** (2½hr., 6 per day 4:52am-9:22pm, L16,500) via **Ozieri Chilvani**, and **Sassari** (3hr., 6 per day 5:36am-7:29pm, L14,500).

Buses: PANI, V. Lombardia, 30 (☎0783 21 22 68), inside Bar Blu. Open daily 7am-10pm. To: **Cagliari** (1½hr., 4 per day 8:50am-9:30pm, L11,300); **Nuoro** (2hr., 4 per day 7am-7:50pm, L11,300); and **Sassari** (2¼hr., 4 per day 7am-7:45pm, L13,900). **ARST,** on V. Cagliari, runs local routes (☎0783 71 185). Ticket office open daily 7:30am-1pm and 4-6pm. To: **Santa Caterina** (direction Porto Alabe; 40 min., 7 per day 7:10am-7:10pm, L3400); **San Giovanni di Sinis** (July-Aug., direction Is Arutas; 40min., 4 per day 8:25am-5:30pm, L2800); and **Putzu Idu** (direction Su Pallosu; 50min., 2 per day 8:15am-12:30pm, L3300). ARST also runs slower buses to **Cagliari** (2hr., 2 per day 6:15am-2:10pm, L11,700). **Luggage storage:** same hours as ticket office, L1000.

Taxis: (☎0783 35 93 26) at P. Roma, (☎0783 743 28) the train station, and (☎0330 43 04 98) from PANI.

SARDINIA

ORIENTATION

To get to the city center from the ARST bus station, take the back exit and turn left. Continue past the *duomo* and head straight onto V. De Castro, which spills into **Piazza Roma,** the heart of the city. From the train station, follow **Via Vittorio Veneto,** the street farthest to the right, to **Piazza Mariano.** Then take **Via Mazzini** to P. Roma (25min.). From the PANI station on V. Lombardia on the other side of town, face the Blu Bar and turn right. At the end of the street, turn right onto **Via Tirso,** left onto **Via Cagliari,** and left on **Via Tharros,** which leads directly into the P. Roma.

PRACTICAL INFORMATION

TOURIST, FINANCIAL AND LOCAL SERVICES

Tourist Office: Pro Loco, V. V. Emanuele, 8 (☎0783 706 21). Maps and info on local festivals. Conveniently located. Open M-Sa 9am-12:30pm and 5-8:30pm. Mobile tourist info booth in P. Roma. Open July 15-Sept., open daily same hours. **Branch office,** V. Cagliari, 278, 46th fl. (☎0783 731 91 or 0783 741 91), across from the ARST station and near P. Mannu. English-speaking, well-informed staff has regional and local info. Open M and Th-F 8am-2pm, Tu-W 8am-2pm and 4-7pm.

Currency Exchange: Banca Nazionale del Lavoro, Banca di Napoli, and **Credito Italiano** are in P. Roma. All open M-Sa 8:30am-1:20pm and 3-4:30pm, Su 8:20-11:50am.

Car Rental: Avis, V. Liguria, 17 (☎0783 31 06 38), near the post office. Cars from L127,000 per day. Min. age 21. Open Su-F 9am-1pm and 4-7:30pm, Sa 9am-1pm.

Scooter Rental: Marco Moto, V. Cagliari, 99/101. Scooters L50,000 per day. Tandems L75,000 per day. 5-day rental specials. Min. age 18. Open M-F 8:30am-1pm and 4-8pm. V, MC, AmEx.

EMERGENCY AND COMMUNICATIONS

Emergencies: ☎113. **First Aid:** ☎0783 743 33. **Ambulance:** ☎0783 782 22. **Hospital:** (☎0783 31 71), on V. Fondazione Rockefeller.

Pharmacy, C. Umberto 49/51 (☎0783 05 07 00). Open M-F 9am-1pm and 5:30-8:20pm, Sa 9am-1pm.

Internet Access: Center for Cultural Services at the **Community Library,** V. Carpaccio, 9 (☎0783 21 16 56). Free internet access. Technically only available M-F 4:30-7pm, although the library is also open in the mornings 9am-1pm.

Post Office: V. Liguria, 60 (☎0783 21 17 78), near the PANI station. Open M-Sa 8:15am-6:40pm. **Postal Code:** 09170.

ACCOMMODATIONS AND CAMPING

Oristano caters primarily to travelers on their way to the beaches, and low competition maintains high prices. For *agriturismo* options, ask at the tourist office or **Consorzio Agriturismo di Sardegna,** P. Cattedrale, 17. (☎0783 739 54; fax 0783 739 24; email cas.agriturismo@tiscali.net. Open Apr.-Oct. M-F 9am-1pm and 4-7pm, Sa 9am-noon; Nov.-Mar. M-F 9am-1pm.)

ISA, P. Mariano, 50 (☎/fax 0783 36 01 01). Exit from the back of the ARST station, turn left, and turn right on V. V. Emanuele. Walk through P. Martini and continue to the end of V. Lamarmora. Turn right, then immediately left. Take the 1st right down V. Mazzini to P. Mariano. Half of the 47 rooms have been newly remodeled; the rest have immaculate baths, baby-blue decor, telephones, TV, and A/C. Breakfast included in high season. Reservations recommended July-Aug. Singles L55-78,000; doubles L80-125,000. Extra bed L20,000. Half-pension L90,000. V, MC, AmEx.

Piccolo Hotel, V. Martignano, 19 (☎0783 715 00). From the ARST station take the back exit, turn right, and continue across P. Mannu. Head down the street slightly to the left and take the 1st left. Turn right at the end of this street. From the PANI station, call a cab. The town's best budget option, with a friendly owner, clean rooms, and firm beds. Mosquitoes are everywhere–close your windows or lather on plenty of repellent. All 10 rooms with bath, many with balconies. Singles L50,000; doubles L100,000.

Camping: Marina di Torregrande (☎/fax 0783 222 28), on V. Stella Maris, near the beach and 100m out of Torre Grande towards Oristano (7km). Orange local buses leave from V. Cagliari in front of the ARST station (10 min., 2 per hr. 7:30am-12:30am, L1500). The site has clean bathrooms, hot showers, a restaurant/pizzeria, a bar, and a small market with fresh produce. Unpleasant fumes may waft over from the nearby tar plant. Packed during the summer. 400 lots. Check-in 8am-1pm and 4-9pm. Open May-Sept. L9000 per person, L9-12,000 per tent. Tent rental L55,000 for 4-person capacity. 5-person bungalows L90-125,000; off-season L50-65,000. No credit cards.

FOOD

The **Euro-Drink market,** P. Roma, 22, sells inexpensive basics and special *Sarde* products. (Open M-Sa 8am-1:30pm and 5-8pm. V, MC.) A **STANDA supermarket,** V. Diaz, 53, is at the corner of V. XX Settembre. (Open daily 8:30am-9pm. V, MC, AmEx.) A **SiSA supermarket** is at V. Ansicora, 26. (Open M-Sa 8am-8pm.)

Ristorante Craf da Banana, V. De Castro, 34 (☎0783 706 69). Slightly more expensive than other restaurants near the town center, but far more elegant. Low arched brick ceilings, earthy lighting, and fine cuisine. *Primi* L13,000, *pesce* from L8000 per *etto* (330 grams). Open M-Sa noon-4:30pm and 7:30-11:30pm. V, MC, AmEx.

La Torre, P. Roma, 52 (☎0783 707 84). This local favorite serves traditional Sardinian fare. Pizza L6500-11,000, *gnocchetti all'orgosolese* (pasta with tomato meat sauce; L10,000), *gamberoni alla vernaccia* (shrimp in wine sauce; L10,000). Cover L2000. Restaurant open daily noon-3pm and 7-11pm. Pizzeria open daily 6:30-11pm. V, MC.

Trattoria del Teatro, V. Parpaglia, 13 (☎0783 716 72), off P. Roma. The basics–done well. The best deal is a pizza/appetizer combo (L20,000). 4-course fish *menù* L40,000. Cover L3000. Open M-Sa noon-3:30pm and 8-11pm. V, MC, AmEx.

THE LORD IS MY SHEPHERDESS Unlike most Italian cities, Oristano is heir to a matriarchal, even feminist, tradition, with roots in the 14th-century reign of Eleonora d'Arborea. Not only did Eleonora develop the progressive *Carta de Logu* legal code, but she also paved the way for future female leaders. In contrast to other cities, dotted with marble Vittorio Emanueles and Gramscis, Oristano's *piazze* are guarded by statues of powerful *donne*. This estrogen-rich tradition still continues—every 2nd Saturday of September, crowds of women don yellow flowers and march on Oristano's streets, celebrating this legacy.

SIGHTS AND HIKING

CHIESA DI SAN FRANCESCO. This pastel church was heavily reconstructed in Neoclassical fashion during the 19th century, leaving little of the original interior intact. A notable remnant is the gruesome wooden crucifix draped with the emaciated and tortured body of Christ. Though the artist was actually a 16th-century teacher of Catalán culture, the townspeople originally attributed the cross to Nicodemus—they felt that such a vivid image could only have been captured by an actual eyewitness to the Crucifixion. The sacristy houses a 16th-century polyptych of *St. Francis Receiving the Stigmata* and Nino Pisano's 14th-century marble statuette of San Basilio. *(In P. E. d'Arborea at the end of V. de Castro. Open daily 7:30-11:30am and 4:30-8pm. Free)*

TOWER OF SAN MARIANO II. Once a fortified entrance to the medieval city, this 13th-century tower dominates P. Roma. On summer evenings, young *oristanesi* gather in this *piazza* and the adjoining C. Umberto.

ANTIQUARIUM ARBORENSE. This museum shelters a small but engrossing collection of Nuraghic, Punic, Phoenician, and Roman artifacts unearthed at Tharros. On display are urns, cups, containers, and earthenware of all shapes and sizes. The museum also showcases a tabletop model of ancient Tharros. *(In P. Corrias, near P. E. d'Aborea. ☎ 0783 744 33. Open daily 9:30am-1pm and 5-7:30pm. L4000, students L2000, over 65 L1000. Wheelchair accessible.)*

BASILICA OF SANTA GIUSTA. In its synthesis of Lombard and Pisan influences, this 12th-century basilica is typically Sardinian. Far from inspiring pious tranquility, the sculpted facade depicts two tiny lions dismembering and devouring a deer. *(V. Manzoni, 2, on the road to Cagliari, 3km out of town. Take the ARST pullman (☎ 0783 35 92 05) towards "Arborea" and get off at the 1st stop (5min., every hr. 6:15am-8:05pm, L1300). Basilica open daily 7:30am-1pm and 2:15-7pm.)*

OUTDOOR ACTIVITIES. Based in Cuglieri, 45km from Oristano, the **Malu Entu Adventure Team** offers scuba diving classes and expeditions, rents canoes and sailboats, and leads hikes and mountain bike tours. (☎ 0785 383 52.) **Naure Ventura** in nearby Lungomare Mandriola offers outdoor tours. (☎ 0785 521 97. Mountain bike tours L35,000; hiking tours L180,000 for 10 people all day; boat tours L25,000 per day. Open M-Sa 8:30am-12:30pm and 5-7pm.) **Maneggio Ippocamo** in Rimedio, leads full-day horseback tours. (☎ 0783 330 02. Open M-Sa 9am-5:30pm. Tours including lunch L100,000. Lessons L20,000 per hr. Discounts for groups of 5 or more.)

FESTIVALS

On the last Sunday of Carnevale and the following Tuesday (usually in March), the **Sartiglia** occurs. Inhabitants of Oristano don traditional finery and ride on horseback through the streets. *Falegnami* (wood workers) and *contadini* (farmers) gallop down the street and try to pierce their swords through six-inch metal stars. The more stars pierced, the better the upcoming harvest will be.

DAYTRIPS FROM ORISTANO: SINIS PENINSULA

The Sinis Peninsula is home to tranquil beaches, stark-white cliffs, and ancient ruins. Public transportation is poor, so consider renting a moped or a car.

THARROS. The peninsula's southernmost tip, a narrow finger of land rising into a hill 17km west of Oristano, holds the ruins of the ancient Phoenician port of Tharros. Much of the city remains submerged, but excavations have revealed Punic fortifications, a Roman temple dedicated to Demeter, an adapted Christian baptistery, and a Phoenician shrine. A medieval Spanish watchtower crowns the hill, offering a comprehensive view and a good starting point for your hike through the ruins. (☎0783 37 00 19. Open daily 9am-7:30pm. L8000.) To reach Tharros from Oristano, take the ARST bus to **San Giovanni di Sinis** (July-Aug. direction Is Aruttas; 40min., 4 per day 8:25am-5:30pm, last return 6:05pm; L2800).

S'ARCHITTU. Gracing the coast slightly to the north of the peninsula proper (off the road to Cuglieri) is S'Archittu, where throngs of young locals lounge on and leap 15m from a massive naturally formed limestone arch into the waters of a breathtakingly beautiful rocky inlet. (Take the ARST bus to S'Archittu: 1hr., 6 per day 7:10am-7:10pm, L2800.)

SARDINIA

IS ARUTAS. Also well-worth the trip is the secluded (but well-exploited) beach of Is Arutas, on the coast north of San Giovanni di Sinis. With white quartz sand the texture of fine caviar, this is the place to go for a relaxing day amidst glimmering opal opulence. The ARST bus to Is Arutas runs only during July and August (50 min.; 4 per day 8:25am-5:30pm, last returning bus 6:30pm; L3200).

PUTZU IDU. The shallow-sloping waters of **Putzu Idu** are dotted with bobbing fishing boats, seaweed, and sun-worshippers. The beach is on the northern tip of the peninsula, accessible by car or bus. ARST buses run to Putzu Idu in July and August (direction: Su Pallosu; 1hr., 2 per day 8:15am-12:30pm, last returning bus 6:45pm, L3200). September through June, take the local orange bus and follow the Italians to **Torregrande's** coarser sands (15-20min., 2 per hr., L1200).

NUORO PROVINCE

Of all the provinces in Sardinia, Nuoro is by far the least frequented by tourists. Most vacationers head to the Costa Smeralda in the north or the beautiful beaches near Cagliari in the south. Few tourists realize that as the heart of Sardinia, Nuoro contains some of the most spectacular terrain in the country. Nuoro spans from Bosa on the west coast to the Golfo di Orosei on the east. Between these two towns lie smooth plateaus, rolling hills, and the island's highest mountain.

NUORO ☎0784

With its solid, pastoral buildings, this provincial capital betrays its agricultural heritage. Relatively small, Nuoro offers little but a few decent museums. The real attractions are in the surrounding countryside, so plan on a lot of daytrips.

TRANSPORTATION

Trains: on V. Lamarmora at V. Stazione (☎0784 301 15). To **Cagliari** (3½-5hr., 6 per day 6:15am-6:37pm, L20,400). Buy tickets M-Sa 7:30am-7pm. No trains on Sundays.

Buses: The following bus companies serve the island.

ARST (☎0784 322 01), on the corner of V. Sardegna. Tickets also available at the bar next door or at the corner of V. Lamarmora and V. Stazione. To: **Orgosolo** (30min., 8 per day 5:50am-6:30pm, L2800); **Oliena** (30min., 12 per day 6:53am-7:20pm, L1700); **Dorgali** (1hr., 6 per day 6:53am-7pm, L3900); **Olbia** (7 per day 5:30am-8:50pm, L12,200); and **Cagliari** (2 per day 2:10pm-7:10am, L18,400). Ticket office open M-F 6:30am-8pm, Sa-Su 6:30am-2pm. **F. Deplanu** (☎0784 20 15 18) runs buses from the ARST station to the **Olbia airport** (1½hr., 5 per day 5:45am-5pm, L18,000). **Redentours** offers the same service to the **Alghero airport** (2¾hr., 2 per day, L24,000).

PANI, V. B. Sassari, 15 (☎0784 368 56). Walk up V. Stazione and follow it to the right. Buses to: **Oristano** (2hr., 4 per day 6:52am-7:31pm, L11,300); **Sassari** (2½hr., 6 per day 5:52am-7:31pm, L13,100); and **Cagliari** (3½hr., 4 per day 6:52am-7:31pm, L21,900). Ticket office open 9am-noon, 5-7:30pm, and 30min. before each departure.

Local Transportation: Buy tickets (L1100) for the local buses at a *tabaccheria.* **Bus #4** runs from P. V. Emanuele to the train station (3 per hr.), **bus #3** to V. Sardegna.

ORIENTATION AND PRACTICAL INFORMATION

Facing the PANI bus stop, turn left and take V. B. Sassari directly into **Piazza Italia,** where you'll find the friendly tourist office and a pleasant park. As you exit the ARST bus stop, turn right onto V. Lamarmora and follow it to **Piazza delle Grazie.** Turn left and follow V. IV Novembre uphill to P. Italia. V. Roma leads from P. Italia to P. San Giovanni and the town's social hub, **Piazza Vittorio Emanuele,** known to the locals simply as "**Giardini.**"

SARDINIA

Tourist Office: EPT, P. Italia, 7 (☎0784 300 83), on street level in summer and on the 4th floor in winter. Well-stocked with booklets and brochures, the office is overseen by an enthusiastic and helpful multilingual staff eager to offer hiking and historical info. Open Th-Su 8:30am-1:30pm and 2:30-8pm, Tu-W 9am-1pm and 3-8pm.

Punto Informa, C. Garibaldi, 155 (☎/fax 0784 387 77), is a private tourist office with extensive brochures and published guides. Sympathetic staff will help sort through Sardinia's transportation system. Open June-Sept. M-Sa 10am-1pm and 4-7pm.

Car Rental: Autonoleggio Maggiore, V. Convento, 32 (☎0784 304 61). L135,000 per day. Min. age 21. Open M-F 8am-1pm and 3:30-7:30pm, Sa 8am-1pm. V, MC, AmEx.

Emergency: ☎113. **Medical Emergency:** ☎118. **Red Cross:** ☎0784 312 50.

Internet Access: Rigenera Toner Internet Service, C. Garibaldi, 156 (☎0784 372 89). L15,000 per hr. Open M-F 9am-1pm and 4:30-8pm, Sa 9am-1pm.

Post Office: P. Crispi, 8 (☎0784 302 78), off V. Dante. Open M-F 8:15am-6:30pm, Sa 8:15am-12:45pm. **Currency exchange** L5000. **Postal Code:** 08100.

ACCOMMODATIONS

Inexpensive hotels are rare in Nuoro, and campgrounds are in distant towns. Nearby *agriturismo* options include **Testone,** to the northeast of the city. The owner can be reached at V. Verdi, 8100 (☎0784 23 05 39), which offers hiking, nature excursions, and other services.

Mini Hotel, V. Brofferio, 13 (☎0784 331 59), off V. Roma. Firm beds and embroidered sheets. Some rooms are cramped, others cavernous. 7 rooms with bath. Breakfast L9000. Curfew midnight. Singles L60,000; doubles L80,000; triples L108,000.

Il Portico, V. M. Bua, 15 (☎0784 25 50 62; fax 0784 37 50 35), off the north end of P. V. Emanuele. Reception same hours as the pleasing restaurant (see below). Friendly staff, 10 clean rooms, great location. Breakfast L5000. Singles L50,000; doubles L70,000. Half-pension L70,000; full pension L100,000. V, MC, AmEx.

FOOD

For provisions head to the **Comprabene supermarket** in P. Mameli. (Open M-F 8:30am-1:30pm and 5-8pm, Sa 5-8pm.) **Mercato Civico,** P. Mameli, 20, off V. Manzoni and across from Comprabene, is the place to look for fresh fruit, cheese, and meat. (Open M-Tu and Th-Sa 8am-1pm and 4:30-7pm, W 8am-1pm.) An old-fashioned, wood-oven **bakery,** V. Ferraccio, 71, off P. delle Grazie, sells hot, fresh rolls, the Sardinian bread *pane caratau*, and scrumptious *panzerotti* (filled with cheese, tomato, and your choice of eggplant, mushroom, or ham; L3000). (Open M-F 9am-3pm and 6-9pm, Sa 9am-3pm.)

Il Portico, V. M. Bua, 15, underneath the hotel of the same name. Excellent rustic cuisine in one of Sardinia's few smoke-free restaurants. Try the L18,000 *menù*, including *primo, secondo, contorno,* fruit, and drink. Or sample the house specialty, *ravioli di ricotta alla crema di carciofi* (ricotta-stuffed pasta in a cream of artichoke sauce; L10,000). *Secondi* from L15,000, excellent fish L6000 per *etto* (330 grams). Cover L2500. Open Tu-Su 12:30-2:30pm and 8-10:30pm. V, MC, AmEx.

Canne Al Vento, V. Repubblica, 66 (☎0784 20 17 62), a 15min. walk down V. Lamarmora from P. delle Grazie. Handsome decor, livened by bright flowers. Generous servings of classic Sardinian *pane frattau* (cheese, egg, and tomato sauce on a bed of thin, crisp bread; L9000), or the house specialty *porcetto* (chicken-based staple; L17,000). Cover L2500. Open M-Sa 12:30-3pm and 8-10:30pm. V, MC, AmEx.

Pizzalandia, V. Repubblica, 2 (☎0784 20 36 24). The name of this takeout pizza joint may be more fantastic than the food. Quick service makes a journey to this land worthwhile if you happen to be near the train station (L5-9000). Open daily 7-11:30pm.

SARDINIA

SIGHTS AND FESTIVALS

The cement P. V. Emanuele—*Giardini* for short—is the hangout spot of choice for locals who come to sit, talk, and smoke in the evenings.

MUSEUM OF THE ART OF THE PROVINCE OF NUORO. The striking white building that houses the MAN contrasts with its surroundings, as does the local contemporary art found inside; this is as about as cutting-edge as the Sardinian museum scene gets. *(V. Manara, 1. ☎0784 25 21 10. Open in summer 10am-1pm and 4:30-8:30pm; in winter 10am-1pm and 4-8pm. L5000, students L3000.*

MUSEO DELLA VITA E DELLE TRADIZIONI POPOLARI SARDE. If the MAN is cutting-edge, this place is in serious need of a grindstone. It showcases masks, ceremonial costumes, and a lot of wool that hearkens back to the days when men, sheep, and culture weren't afraid to get intimate. *(V. Mereu, 56. ☎0789 24 29 00. Open daily June 15-Sept. 9am-8pm; Oct.-June 14 9am-1pm and 3-7pm. L5000.)*

MONTE ORTOBENE. A mind-blowing view, a bronze statue of Christ the Redeemer, and a shady park overlooking the neighboring hamlets await at the peak of this hill. From the bus stop on Monte Ortobene, walk 20m down the road for a view of colossal Monte Corrasi, dwarfing neighboring Oliena. *(To reach the summit, take the orange ATP bus #8 from P. V. Emanuele (3 per day 8:15am-8pm, last return 8:15pm; L1100) or hike about 6km up the hillside. Beware: Cinghiali (wild boar) haunt the hills.)*

SAGRA DEL REDENTORE. Nuoro celebrates The Feast of the Redeemer in the last week of August. A spartan religious procession during which the townfolk ruminate upon that whole dying-for-your-sins thing takes place on August 29. A colorful parade of revelers dressed in traditional Sardinian garb and lively productions of traditional folk dances and choral performances precede it.

DAYTRIP FROM NUORO: ORGOSOLO

Entrust your life to an ARST driver (40min.; 8 per day 5:50am-6:30pm, last return 7:05pm; L2800).

The bus ride alone merits a trip to sleepy **Orgosolo,** the definitive Sardinian mountain town. The twisting tour will leave you slack-jawed at the radiance of the verdant hills below. Once in the town proper, you'll be rewarded with tremendous mountain vistas and Picasso-esque murals dotting the buildings. Francesco del Casino, a local teacher, initiated this ongoing outdoor art project in the 60s after finding inspiration during his studies in Latin America. His work focuses on society's woes from imperialism to fascism to commercialism. Del Casino drew inspiration from the 1963 film *The Bandits of Orgosolo*, which immortalized the bloody *banditismo* in the south of Oliena. Schoolchildren from as far away as Russia have come to make contributions to this truly incredible outdoor museum.

Exit the bus at the 3rd stop and follow the signs to the **Hotel Sa'e Jana,** V. E. Lussu, 17 (☎0784 40 24 37), a family-run hotel offering attractive, spacious rooms with bath. Even the room numbers, true to the town's artistic bent, are painted with colorful designs. The restauraunt downstairs serves solid *Sarde* food with *primi* (L6-8000) and *secondi* (L12-13,000). (Breakfast L7000. Singles L57,000; doubles L80,000. Half-pension L75,000; full pension L85,000.) More del Casino artwork decorates the **Petit Hotel,** V. Mannu, 9 (☎0784 40 20 09), off C. Repubblica. Backtrack (keeping the police station on your right) from the bus at the small park with the murals, then head up the incline on the left and follow the signs. (Breakfast L5000. Singles L40,000; doubles L60,000. Half-pension L55,000. V, MC, AmEx.)

SARDINIA

DORGALI ☎0784

Placed on a sloping hillside and buttressed by an agrarian-based economy, Dorgali locals supplement their incomes with a fervent craft trade. Stores hawk huge wooden tribal masks, woven rugs, baskets, and tons of tacky t-shirts that'll let your friends at home know that, yes, Sardinians Do It Better. One art they've unquestionably mastered is hitting the beach, and Dorgali's two budget hotels will put you a short bus ride away from the *mare* maven's workshop: Cala Gonone.

TRANSPORTATION AND PRACTICAL INFORMATION. ARST buses run to **Cala Gonone** (20min., 10 per day 6:20am-7:50pm, L1300); **Nuoro** (50min., 9 per day 7am-7:50pm, L3900) via **Oliena** (30min.); and **Olbia** (3hr., 2 per day 6:35am-5:25pm, L12,200). Buy tickets at the **Blues Bar,** V. La Marmora, 154. (Open daily 8am-10pm.) Buses stop at the corner of V. La Marmora and C. Umberto.

The main commercial street (with a hotel, grocery store, and several tourist shops) is **Via La Marmora,** which winds along the hillside and hosts ARST bus stops. Running perpendicular to V. La Marmora is **Corso Umberto,** your best bet for a cold drink or *gelato*. Services include: the **Pro Loco tourist office,** V. La Marmora, 108B, with maps and limited info on hotels, *agriturismo*, and rooms for rent (☎0784 962 43; open M-F 9am-1pm and 4-8pm, Sa-Su 9:30am-1pm and 4:30-8pm); a **Banco di Sardegna,** V. La Marmora, 152, with **currency exchange** and an **ATM** (open M-F 8:20am-1:20pm and 3:05-4:05 pm); **carabinieri** (☎112 or 0784 961 14); an **ambulance** (☎0337 81 81 80); the **Farmacia Mundula,** V. Mannu, 1, off V. La Marmora (open M-Tu and Th-Sa 8:30am-1pm and 4:30-8pm); and a **post office** at the corner of V. La Marmora and V. Ciusa (☎0784 974 24; open M-F 8am-1pm). **Postal Code:** 08022.

ACCOMMODATIONS AND FOOD. Albergo San Pietro, V. La Marmora, 124 (and its lovably loquacious proprietress), have been here for 50 years. The well-tended, dark wood interior and central location make the San Pietro the best bargain in town. (☎0784 961 42. 20 rooms. Singles L30,000; doubles L60,000, with bath L65,000.) The **Sarde Hotel,** V. Concordat, 38, has spacious rooms with pine furniture, bathroom, A/C, TV, and telephone. At the intersection of C. Umberto and V. La Marmora, take V. Mare and follow the signs. The hotel runs a shuttle to Cala Gonone (1 per day, L10,000) and organizes excursions to *nuraghe* ruins and archaeological sights. (☎0784 944 12; fax 0784 944 12. Breakfast L10,000. 30 rooms. Singles L60-80,000; doubles L100-120,000. Bars and *gelaterie* line C. Umberto; for a solid meal, try **Ristorante S'Udulu,** C. Umberto, 20. (☎0784 952 39. Pizza from L6500. *Primi* from L9000, *secondi* from L12,000. Cover L3000, L2500 downstairs. Open 12:30-3pm and 7:30-11:30pm. V.)

SIGHTS. The **Museo Arceologico,** V. La Marmora, past the post office and next to the elementary school houses some provocative pottery shards discovered in and around Dorgali and Cala Gonone, including items from 70 or so surrounding *nuraghe* village sites dating from the Neolithic Age to High Medieval times. (Open daily in summer 9:30am-1pm and 4-7pm; in winter 9:30am-1pm and 3-5pm. L4000, under 12 L2000. L7000 for both the museum and Serra Orrios, a nuragic village 10km away by car.

DAYTRIP FROM DORGALI: CALA GONONE. The gateway to several spectacular beaches and caves, Cala Gonone has sands that are pebbly and crowded. Boats (5 per day 10am-3pm, L20,000) travel to the stunning **Grotta del Bue Marino** (Cave of the Monk Seal), one of the last haunts of the elusive creature. The seals rarely appear during the day, and stampeding crowds and a locked gate mar the experience. Just down the coast lies the vast beach of **Cala Luna.** Encircled by marshes and caverns, the beach is accessible only by boat (L19,000, combined ticket for cave and beach L32,000). Boats also run to the more remote beaches of **Cala Sisina** (L23,000) and **Cala Mariolu** (L32,000).

Cala Gonone lies just over an hour east of Nuoro by **ARST bus** (7 per day 6:53am-7pm, L5000) and 20 minutes from **Dorgali** (11 per day 6:40am-8:10pm, L1300). Buy ARST tickets at **Bar Fronte del Porto,** V. Acquadolce, 5. **Consorzio Marittimo Transport** (☎0784 933 05) has monopolized the boat market for beach access. Charter boats from **Boat Marine Charter** (☎0784 935 46) start at L75,000 per person and rentals from **Noleggio Gommoni** (☎0368 388 70 15) begin at L100,000.

Surf the net at **New Age Internet Point,** V. Colombo, 5. (☎0784 92 00 15. L13,000 per hr. Open M-Sa 9:30am-1pm, 5-8pm, and 9pm-midnight.) The **post office,** P. Giovanni da Verrazzano, 7, offers **currency exchange,** but not traveler's checks. (☎0784 932 78. Open M-F 8:10am-1:15pm, Sa 8am-12:45pm.) **Postal Code:** 08020.

SASSARI PROVINCE

SASSARI ☎079

Founded as the first free commune of Sardinia in 1294, Sassari held onto its medieval walled-town layout until the late 1800s. In the last 100 years, it has become an important petrochemical center and Sardinia's second largest city. The city continues to have a strong youth presence. Congregating along the wide boulevards and the refurbished 18th-century **Piazza d'Italia,** pink-haired rebels roll their eyes at grim religious processions where participants carry Christ's instruments of passion closer to their heart than their cell phones. When the preaching's done, the kids switch their phones back on and city-dwellers again say "Pronto" to the highest standard of living on the island.

TRANSPORTATION

Flights: (☎079 93 50 33), near **Fertilia,** 35km south of Sassari. Allow about 1 hr. to get there from the bus station (see **ARST** below). Domestic flights year-round, charter flights to European destinations only in summer.

Trains: (☎079 26 03 62), in P. Stazione, 1 block from P. Sant'Antonio. To: **Porto Torres** (20min., 9 per day 6am-6:40pm, L2300); **Alghero** (40min., 11 per day 6:09am-8:55pm, L3200); **Olbia** (2hr., 4 per day 8:02am-8:40pm, L10,500); and **Cagliari** (3½hr., 6 per day 7:04am-6:45pm, L22,700). Take the #8 bus from P. d'Italia. Tickets (L1100) available at newsstands. **Luggage Storage:** (☎079 26 03 62). L5000 for 12hr. Open 7am-8:30pm.

Buses:

ARST (info ☎079 26 39 200). Buy tickets at Tonni's Bar, C. M. Savoia, 11. Buses depart from V. Italia in the public gardens to **Porto Torres** (35min., 1-2 per hr. 5:20am-9:15pm, L2300) and **Nuoro** (2hr., 2 per day 9:35am and 2:50pm, L12,200-14,800). Buses to **Fertilia Airport** (40min.; 5-6 per day 5:10am-4:55pm, last return 10:55pm; L3400) and **Castelsardo** (1hr.; 11 per day 7:20am-7:45pm; L3900, round-trip L7400) leave from in front of Tonni's bar.

FDS (☎079 24 13 03), with buses leaving from Emiciclo Garibaldi, serves the local area. Tickets are sold at Bar Garibaldi, Emiciclo Garibaldi, 26. Destinations include **Alghero** (1½hr., 13 per day 5:50am-8:15pm, L4500-5000).

PANI, V. Bellieni, 25 (☎079 23 69 83; fax 079 26 00 66), 1 block from P. d'Italia. Buses leave from P. Italia to: **Torralba** (40-60min., 6 per day 6:36am-7:15pm, L4500); **Nuoro** (2½hr., 6 per day 6:36am-7:15pm, L13,100); and **Cagliari** (3-4hr., 7 per day 6am-7:15pm, L26,000) via **Oristano** (2¼hr., 4 per day 6:36am-7:15pm, L13,900). Office open M-F 5:30-6:35am, 8:30am-2:15pm, and 5-7:15pm, Sa-Su 5:30-6:35am, 9-9:30am, noon-2:15pm, and 5-7:15pm.

Taxis: Radiotaxi (☎079 26 00 60). Open 24hr.

SARDINIA

ORIENTATION AND PRACTICAL INFORMATION

All buses into town stop in the *Giardini Publici* (the town park) before heading to the bus station. Since these gardens are much closer to Sassari's attractions, get off at **Via Italia** in the park (unless you've made reservations at a hotel near the station). The semicircular **Emiciclo Garibaldi** lies ahead, past **Via Margherita di Savoia.** To reach the town center, head straight through Emiciclo Garibaldi onto **Via Carlo Alberto,** which spills into **Piazza Italia.** The majestic Provincial Administration building is straight ahead. To the right, **Via Roma** runs to the tourist office and the Museo Sana. To the left lies **Piazza Castello,** an eatery-packed, people-watching playground, 200m from **Corso Vittorio Emanuele,** a major thoroughfare.

TOURIST, FINANCIAL, AND LOCAL SERVICES

Tourist Office: V. Roma, 62 (☎079 23 17 77), a few blocks to the right of P. d'Italia when facing the Provincial Administration building. The English-speaking staff provides a great indexed map and bus and train schedules. Open M-F 9am-1pm and 4-6pm.

Budget Travel: CTS, V. Manno, 35 (☎079 20 04 40). Open M-F 9am-1pm and 4-7pm.

Ferry Tickets: Ajo Viaggi, P. Fiume, 1 (☎079 20 02 22). **Agitour,** P. Italia, 13 (☎0792 317 67).

Currency Exchange: Banca Commerciale D'Italia, in P. D'Italia, has an **ATM** outside. Open M-F 8:20am-1:20pm and 3-4:45pm, Sa 8:20-11:50am.

Car Rental: Avis, V. Mazzini, 2 (☎/fax 079 23 55 47). From L124,000 per day. Min. age 25. Open M-Sa 8:30am-12:30pm and 4-7:30pm. V, MC. **Eurorent,** V. Roma, 56 (☎079 23 23 35). Fiats L140,000 per day, L900,000 per week. Min. age 21. Open M-Sa 8:30am-1pm and 3:30-7pm.

English Bookstore: Gulliver Librerie, V. Portici Crispo, 4 (☎079 23 44 75). Open M-Sa 9am-9pm, Su 9am-1pm and 5-9pm.

EMERGENCY AND COMMUNICATIONS

Emergencies: ☎113. **Police:** V. Coppino, 1 (☎079 28 35 500). **Ambulance: Red Cross,** C. Vico, 4 (☎079 29 22 23). **First Aid: Ospedale Civile** (☎079 206 16 21 or 079 20 61 000), on V. Italia and V. Nicola.

Late-Night Pharmacy: Simon, V. Brigata Sassari, 2 (☎079 23 32 38). Open M-F 9am-1pm and 4:30pm-9am, Su 8:30pm-9am. Posts list of 24hr. pharmacies.

Internet Access: Buffetti (☎079 215 10 55), at V. Italia and P. Maria. L10,000 for 30min. Open daily 9am-1pm and 4:30-8pm. **PCMainia,** V. Cavour, 71A (☎079 23 49 71), offers intermittent access. L12,000 per hr. Open 9am-1pm and 4:30-8pm.

Post Office: V. Brigata Sassari, 13 (☎079 23 21 78), off P. Castello. Open M-F 8:15am-6:15pm. Currency exchange, phone cards, Fermo Posta. **Postal Code:** 07100.

ACCOMMODATIONS

Sassari Hotel, V. Umberto, 65 (☎079 23 95 43). Face the Provincial Administration building in P. Italia and turn right. Walk straight onto V. Roma and take the 1st left and then the 1st right onto V. Umberto. The hotel is 1 block down on the right. 40 large rooms with antique doors and wrought-iron balconies. Keep windows closed during the day, otherwise you're liable to return to a swirl of insects. Clean common bathrooms and friendly management. Ask for a room on the quiet side, away from V. Umberto. Reservations recommended July-Aug. Singles L30,000; doubles L40,000.

Hotel Giusy, P. Sant'Antonio, 21 (☎079 23 33 27; fax 079 23 94 90), near the train station. Though the hotel can be noisy, it's modern. All 39 rooms with bath, some with balcony. Breakfast included. Singles L55,000; doubles L75,000.

FOOD

A wide selection of pizzerias line **Corso Emanuele.** Any college ID and a ticket affords a meal at the **University Mensa,** V. Manzella, 2. A ticket costs L4800. Meals include *primo*, *secondo*, *contorno*, and fruit. (☎079 21 64 83 or 079 25 82 11. Open M-Sa 12:15-2:30pm and 7:30-9pm. Closed the last week of July-Aug.) Another *mensa* is located on V. dei Mille, but is only open for lunch in the summer. A large, enclosed **market** occupies P. Mercato, down V. Rosello from V. V. Emanuele. (Open M-F 8am-1pm and 5-8pm, Sa 8am-1pm.) **Multimarkets supermarket** is on the corner of V. Cavour and V. Manno. (☎079 23 72 78. Open M-Sa 8am-8:30pm.) Dining in Sassari is not credit card-friendly, so bring plenty of cash.

Trattoria Da Antonio, V. Arborea, 2B (☎079 23 42 97), behind the post office. The wood-paneled, arched interior and the subdued ambience is a refreshing alternative to P. Castello. No menus, just amazing food. Serves the best of local cuisine to the best of locals. If there's one place to be adventuresome in what you order, it's here. Expect the waitstaff to recommend horse, donkey, and tentacled creatures. A full meal runs around L25,000 (including L2000 cover). Open daily 1-3pm and 8:30-11pm.

Trattoria Da Peppina, V. Pigozzi, 1 (☎079 23 61 46), off C. Emanuele. The *menù* is delicious but unfriendly to vegetarians (with everything from horse to tripe). *Primi* L5-9000, *secondi* L9-15,000. Open M-Sa 12:30-2:30pm and 7:30-10:30pm.

Pronto Pronto, P. Castello, 4 (☎079 23 86 42). Thin, crispy pizza (L5,500-10,500) made with fresh toppings right before your very eyes. Delivery service available. Open M-Sa 9:30am-2:30pm and 6-11:30pm, Su 6-11:30pm.

SIGHTS

MUSEO GIOVANNI ANTONIO SANNA. This museum houses models portraying *nuraghi* dating from 1500 BC, Sardinian paintings, petrified tree stumps, and skulls with drilled holes (remnants of attempted ritualistic curing). *(V. Roma, 64. ☎079 27 22 03. Open Oct.-May Tu-Su 9am-8pm; June-Sept. Tu-F and Su 9am-11:30pm. L4000, ages 18-25 L2000. EU citizens, under 18, and over 60 free.)*

CATTEDRALE DI SAN NICOLÒ. Sassari's *duomo*, dubbed "an immense flower of stone" by Elio Vittorini, is a 13th-century Romanesque structure with a 17th-century Spanish colonial facade. Renovations have uncovered vibrant, early frescoes sunk into the church walls. For those looking for 16 men on a dead man's chest, the reliquary of St. Benedetta masquerades as a skull-and-crossbones. *(Walk down C. Emanuele from P. Castello and turn left on V. al Duomo to P. Duomo.)*

FESTIVALS AND ENTERTAINMENT

The lavish **Sardinian Cavalcade,** held on the 2nd to last weekend in May, is Sardinia's most notable folk festival. Festivities include a procession of costumed emissaries from Sardinian villages, a *palio* (horse race), singing, and dancing. **I Candelieri,** the festival of the candlesticks, takes place on the Day of Assumption (Aug. 14). The *Gremi*, or farmers' guilds, sport traditional Spanish dress and carry huge wooden columns (in the shape of enormous tapers) through the streets.

If it weren't for the **University Pub,** V. Amendola, 49/A, Sassari would be devoid of a hip youth scene. A favorite among locals, the subdued pub offers dirt-cheap drinks (beer from L2500) and overflows with jovial students when school's in session. Request (but don't inhale) the Cannabis beer (L7000) or the super-secret Sardinia Island mixed drink (L10,000), whose recipe is more closely guarded than Coca Cola's. (☎079 20 04 23. Open W-M 10am-2pm; closed Aug.)

DAYTRIP FROM SASSARI: CASTELSARDO

To reach Castelsardo, take the ARST bus from Sassari (last return 8:50pm). (From P. Pianedda, face uphill and walk up the stairs. Open M-Sa 9:30am-1pm and 2:30-9pm. Castle and museum L3000.)

Castelsardo's striking location atop a lofty crest and its proximity to sandy beaches make it a popular stop along Costa Paradiso. Renowned across the island for its enchanting beauty, the town was once described by a Sardinian poet as a "flower of light that smiles from the top of a sharp promontory upon the glimmering sea." A large, well-preserved and well-situated castle (containing a dull wickerwork museum) crowns the village.

SARDINIA

PORTO TORRES ☎079

Founded in 27 BC, the village of Turris Libissonis on the mouth of the river Mannu was the first Sardinian outcropping of the Roman Empire, serving as one of Rome's principal ports along the corn-trading routes between Sicily and Africa. Today the town's ancient spice can be savored in its Roman ruins and Romanesque 12th-century church—but good luck getting rid of the outlying industrial zones' bitter aftertaste. This modern port town is best sampled as a stop-over and as a point of access to luscious Stintino.

TRANSPORTATION. Trains, synchronized with ferries, leave from the port to **Sassari** (20min., 8 per day 5:50am-8:10pm, L2300), continuing on to **Olbia. ARST** buses (toll-free ☎800 86 50 42) run from the ferry port in Porto Torres to **Cagliari** (4¼ hr., 4 per day 6:30am-6:08pm, L24,300); **Sassari** (35min., 1-2 per hr. 5:20am-10pm, L2300); **Stintino** (40min.; 6 per day 5:55am-7:20pm, last return 8:20 pm; L3400); and the **Alghero Fertilla Airport** (40min., 5 per day 8:15am-8:30pm, L2800).

ORIENTATION AND PRACTICAL INFORMATION. Porto Torres has one major thoroughfare, **Corso Vittorio Emanuele,** which runs perpendicular to the ocean from the port. The 1st stop you should make in Porto Torres is the **Pro Loco Tourist Office,** P. XX Settembre, 2, about 20m up on the right. The multilingual staff will provides bus schedules and info on local sights, beaches, and mountain biking. (☎/fax 079 51 50 00. Open July-Sept. M-Sa 8:30am-12:30pm and 3:30-7:30pm, Su 8:30am-12:30pm; Oct.-June M-Sa 8:30am-12:30pm.) Farther up the street, the bank **BNL,** C. V. Emanuele, 18, has an **ATM** outside. (Open M-F 8:30am-1:30pm and 2:15-2:45pm.) In case of **emergency,** call the **police** (☎112 or 079 50 24 32 or 070 51 01 19), **Guardia Medica** (☎079 51 03 92), or an **ambulance** (☎079 51 60 68). The town's **pharmacy,** C. V. Emanuele, 76, is down the block. (☎079 51 40 88. Open daily 9am-1pm and 5-8pm.) The **post office** is at V. Sachi, 113. (☎079 51 49 05. Open M-F 8:15am-6:15pm, Sa 8:15am-noon.) **Postal Code:** 07046.

ACCOMMODATIONS AND FOOD. **Albergo Royal,** V. S. Satta, 8, has 20 beds in rooms with comfortable decor, TV, and private bathrooms. From the port or bus stop, walk up C. V. Emanuele away from the water until you reach a yellow "Albergo Royal" sign hanging overhead. Turn left and walk about 200m along V. Petronia and follow the signs. (☎079 50 22 78. 20 beds. Singles L40-80,000; doubles L80-110,000.) The lodging closest to the ferry port is the **Hotel Elisa,** V. Mare, 2. A bland exterior masks what is in fact one lovely lady. This three-star joint is all class. 27 rooms all have private baths and mint green bedspreads. They are a bit pricier than the average budget digs, but it's worth it. Ask the amicable Alessandro about the local beaches and nightlife. (☎079 51 32 60; fax 079 51 37 68. Breakfast included. Singles L75-85,000; doubles L120-130,000. Half-pension L95,000.)

In the mornings, an **outdoor market** is at the intersection of V. Delle Vigne and V. Sacchi. Fun, young waitstaff and good, fast food await at **Poldiavolo,** in P. Settembre XX. Ask the energetic cook to make you a fresh *poldiavolo panino* (eggplant, ham, tuna, cheese, and veggies; L6000). Sandwiches and pizza start at L5000, pasta from L6000. (Open daily noon-3pm and 6pm-1:30am.) The **Self-Service Restaurant,** downstairs from the Hotel Elisa, offers cheap, edible food, with a complete meal from L19,000 and *primi* from L6000. (Open noon-midnight.)

SARDINIA

SIGHTS AND BEACHES. The 11th-century **Basilica di San Gavino,** up the stairs in P. Marconi at the end of C. V. Emanuele, houses the crypt of local Saints Gavino, Proto, and Gianuario. Proto and Gianuario were Christians persecuted by the Romans around AD 300; Gavino was a Roman soldier who, while holding the Christians captive, was converted and set them free. All three were eventually captured and beheaded. The holy bones of murdered martyrs aren't the church's only Roman remnant—the mismatched columns supporting the church were salvaged from nearby Roman ruins. (Open 7am-noon and 4-7:30pm.) The ruins of the **Roman Thermal Baths,** along V. Ponte Romane, five minutes from the center of town, were ravaged in the 19th century by dynamite-wielding quasi-archaeologists searching for the site of the martyrs' decapitation. (Open 9am-8pm. Free.)

Take in some suds at the two beaches along Porto Torres's shore. **Scoglio Lungho Spiaggia,** a sandy beach 250m from the port, is family-friendly, complete with rock-diving and plastic-dolphins. **Acquedolci,** right down the road, is more picturesque with craggy coral and emerald waters.

DAYTRIP FROM PORTO TORRES: STINTINO. Northwest of Porto Torres on the Capo del Falcone, Stintino was once a legitimate fishing village; then came the Eurotourist deluge. The winter population of fewer than 1000 swells to almost 20,000 in summer. Exploitation of the captivating **Spiaggia di Pelosa,** a beach 4km outside town, spawned Stintino's transformation. Here children fondle captured baby octopi along the rocky shore, and sparkling waters glisten against the bone-dry Isola Piana. On the other side of Piana lies Isola Asinara, which until recent years was an island penal colony. To reach a slightly more accessible miniature version on the far end of shore, either tackle the 500m swim from the beach or strap on sandals and make a wet scramble 50m over the rocks. Octopi aren't the beach's only marine life; be wary of sea urchins lurking within small crevices along the way (forget your shoes and you'll feel like a captive once you get to the other side). Whichever way you go, the reward is a close look at the marooned 18th-century Aragonese tower.

Orange line **A buses** run from the beach back to Stintino (every hr. 8am-12:30am, L1100). Six **buses** run daily from Pelosa to **Sassari** (1¼hr., 6:45am-8:15pm, L5400) via **Porto Torres** (40min., L3700). In Stintino you can catch the bus in P. Municipio (6:50am-8:20pm). If you get stuck waiting for a bus, head to **Lu Funali,** Lungomare C. Colombo, 89 (☎079 52 30 54), along the water. Admire the tiny port's collection of sailboats, have a drink to the sounds of Bob Marley, and feel all right.

ALGHERO ☎079

Salty sea breezes flatten oceanfront sand dunes into fabulous beaches for sun-filled serenity during the day. After dark the same breezes whip through the twisting medieval streets and Gothic arches of the *centro storico*, grazing its three surrounding towers, cooling the passions of *lungomare* lovers, and swirling the sounds of live music through the night air. Equally melodious is the town's Catalán dialect, left by Pere I of Aragon after his 14th-century conquest.

TRANSPORTATION

Trains: (☎079 95 07 85), on V. Don Minzoni, in the northern part of the city. Take the AP or AF bus from in front of the Casa del Caffe in the park (3 per hr.), or walk 1km along the port. Open daily 5:45am-9pm. If you buy your ticket at the FS stand in the park, you can ride the city bus to the station for free. To **Sassari** (40min.; 11 per day 6:09am-8:55pm; L3500, round-trip L6000). **Luggage Storage:** L1500 per item.

Buses:

ARST (☎079 95 01 79) blue buses depart from V. Catalogna next to the park. Buy tickets at the tiny stand in the park. To: **Sassari** (1hr., 18 per day 5:35am-7pm, L5000); **Porto Torres** (1hr., 7 per day 6:40am-8:50pm, L5000); and **Bosa** (1½hr., 4 per day 6:35am-6:35pm, L5600-7300).

FS orange city buses (info ☎079 95 04 58 or 079 95 01 79). Buy tickets (L1100) at a *tabaccheria*. Book of 12 tickets L11,000. Buses run from V. Cagliari in front of the Casa del Caffè bar to the **airport** (20min.; 6 per day 5:45am-8:30pm, last return from airport 11:45pm). **Line AF** travels between **Fertilia** and V. Cagliari, with a stop at the port (every 40min.; 7:10am-9:30pm, return from Fertilia 7:50am-9:50pm). **AP** (from P. Della Mercede) runs to the train station (3 per hr. 6:20am-9pm). **AO** (from V. Cagliari) heads to the *lido* (beach) and the hospital (2 per hr. 7:15am-8:45pm). **AC** (from V.Liguria) runs to Carmine (2 per hr. 7:30am-8pm).

Taxis: (☎079 97 53 96) in Alghero, can be caught on V. V. Emanuele across from the (BNL) bank. And (☎079 9350 35) at the airport.

ORIENTATION AND PRACTICAL INFORMATION

ARST buses stop at the corner of **Via Catalogna** and **Via Cagliari,** on the waterfront one block from the port. The tourist office, in **Piazza Porta Terra,** lies diagonally across the small park, on the right beyond the easily visible towers of the *centro storico*. The train station is a hike from the town center, but is accessible by local orange buses (lines AF and AP). If you'd rather walk from the station, follow **Via Don Minzoni** until it turns into **Via Garibaldi** along the waterfront.

TOURIST, FINANCIAL, AND LOCAL SERVICES

Tourist Office: P. Porta Terra, 9 (☎079 97 90 54; fax 079 97 48 81), on the right from the bus stop (towards the old city). The most organized office in Sardinia. Cheerful, multilingual staff offers an indexed street map, tours of the city, and daytrips to local villages. Open May-Sept. M-Sa 8am-8pm, Su 9am-1pm; Oct.-Apr. M-Sa 8am-2pm.

Tours: Il Cocchio (☎0338 37 29 973) offers 20-30min. tours of the old city in horse-drawn coaches. Tours depart from the port. Adults L8000, children over 3 L5000, groups L7000. Taxi service to and from hotels L5-15,000. Tours daily Easter-June 10am-8pm; July-Aug. 10am-midnight.

Horseback Riding: Club Ippico Capuano (☎079 97 81 98), 3km from Alghero on Strada Villanova. Afternoon guided excursions. They will pick you up in Alghero for L15,000 per carload. Reserve 2-3 days in advance. L30,000 per hr.

Currency Exchange: Banca Nazionale del Lavoro, V. Emanuele, 5, across from the tourist office, has a 24hr. **ATM.** Open M-F 8:20am-1pm and 3-4:30pm. Exchange also at the **post office** for L5000.

Car Rental: Autonolotaxi Farris Carlo, V. Mazzini, 44 (☎079 97 85 51 or 079 97 41 07). From L140,000 per day. Min. age 25. Open M-Sa 8:30am-1pm and 4-8pm; Su 8:30am-1pm. V, MC, AmEx. **Europcar** (☎079 93 50 32), at the airport. From L150,000 per day, including insurance. 150km per day limit. Open daily 8am-11pm.

Bike/Moped Rental: Cycloexpress di Tomaso Tilocca (☎/fax 079 98 69 50), at the harbor near the intersection of V. Garibaldi and V. La Marmora. Prices per day: bikes L15,000; mountain bikes L20-25,000; tandem bikes L25,000; scooters L50,000. Bring your credit card–L300,000 security deposit required for scooters. Insurance included. Open M-Sa 9am-1pm and 4-8:30pm. V, MC, AmEx.

English Bookstore: Libreria Labadinto, V. Carlo Alberto, 119 (☎079 93 04 96). Open daily in summer 9am-1pm and 4pm-midnight; in winter 9am-1pm and 4-8pm. **Internet access** L10,000 per hr. V, MC, AmEx.

EMERGENCY AND COMMUNICATIONS

Emergencies: ☎113. **Police:** P. della Mercede, 4 (☎113). **Carabinieri:** ☎112. **Ambulance:** ☎118 or 079 97 66 34 or 079 98 05 87. **First Aid:** ☎079 99 62 33. **Hospital: Ospedale Civile** (☎079 99 62 00), Regione la Pietraia, V. Don Minzoni.

Pharmacy: All pharmacies, including **Farmacia Puliga di Mugoni,** V. Sassari, 8 (☎079 97 90 26), across from the market, open M-Sa 9am-1pm and 4:30-8:30pm.

Internet Access: Soft, V. Tarragona, 22 (☎079 97 99 57). L15,000 per hr. Open M-Sa 9am-1pm and 3-9pm. See Caffe Teatro, Libreria Labadinto.

Post Office: V. XX Settembre, 112 (☎079 97 93 09; fax 079 98 10 29). Fermo Posta M-F 9:30am-1:30pm and 2:30-6:15pm. **Currency exchange** M-F 8:15am-5pm, Sa 8:15am-1pm. Open M-F 8:15am-6:15pm, Sa 8:15am-1pm. **Postal Code:** 07041.

ACCOMMODATIONS AND CAMPING

Prices escalate and rooms vanish in July and August. Unless you've made a reservation far in advance or are willing to pay for half-pension, consider staying at the youth hostel in Fertilia or redirecting your search to the hotels along the beach.

Ostello dei Giuliani (HI), V. Zara, 3 (☎/fax 079 93 03 53), 6km from Alghero in Fertilia. Take the orange AF city bus from V. Cagliari outside the Nuova Case bar in the park or from V. La Marmora next to the train station (25min., every 40min. 7:10am-9:30pm, L1100). ARST pullman buses bound for Sassari and Porto Conte also stop in Fertilia (last bus 7pm, L1300). From the bus stop in Fertilia, face the church (with your back to the water), and take the street on the left out of the *piazza*. Take the 1st right onto V. Zara, and the hostel is on the left. Walk through the small rose garden and up the steps into the loving arms of Mamma Margherita, the embodiment of genuine hospitality. 70 beds are a short walk from a small, odoriferous beach and 4km from the fabulous Spiaggia Bombarda–a beach with emerald waters. Breakfast L2500. Delicious and filling lunch or dinner L14,000. Showers L2000. Curfew 11:30pm, not strictly enforced. Reserve ahead July-Aug. Dorms L14,000.

Hotel San Francesco, V. Machin, 2 (☎/fax 079 98 03 30). Walk straight from the tourist office and take the 3rd right. 21 comfortable rooms in the church cloister, all with bath, telephone, and a prayer to St. Francis for sweet dreams. Breakfast included. Must reserve ahead June-Aug. Singles L60-85,000; doubles L100-130,000. V, MC.

Hotel San Guian, V. G. M. Angioy, 2 (☎079 95 12 22; fax 079 95 10 73), 1 block east from the beach. Firm beds and immaculate bathrooms. Breakfast included. Reserve June-Aug. 22 rooms. Singles L60-75,000; doubles L100-130,000. V, MC.

Camping: La Mariposa (☎079 95 03 60), on V. Lido, near the beach and 3km away on the Alghero-Fertilia road. Reservations suggested in summer. Open Apr.-Oct. L13-21,000 per person, L6000 per tent, L3400 per car. Apr.-June. tents and cars free. Bungalows L70-105,000.

FOOD

On V. Sassari, two blocks from the tourist office, a **market** offers fresh Sardinian produce every morning. On Wednesdays, the **open-air market** on V. de Gasperi floods with crowds. Take the *linea mercato* bus from V. Cagliari. Be sure to stop by the **Antiche Cantine del Vino Sfuso,** C. V. Emanuele, 80, a *cantina sociale* that shoots inexpensive (but decent) table wine from giant space-age machines for a piddly L2100 per liter. (Open M-Sa 8am-1pm and 4:30-8pm.) Beware of the *algherese menù;* most cost upwards of L30,000 and consist of little more than spaghetti with tomato sauce and the unavoidable fried calamari.

Ristorante La Muraglia, Bastioni Marco Polo, 7 (☎079 97 55 77), offers a soaring view of the sea from its upstairs balcony. Outdoor dining is slightly more grounded. Rather touristy, but the food is excellent. Curry *penne* with mixed seafood L15,000. Finish off the meal with *seadas,* a Sardinian cheese pastry doused in honey. Cover L3000. Open Th-Tu noon-3:30pm and 7pm-2am. V, MC, AmEx.

Ristorante La Piconia, V. Principe Umberto, 27 (☎079 97 80 01). Low stone-vaulted ceilings and walls hung with poppies and garlic make for pleasant dining. *Spaghetti al nero* L12,000, pizzas L7-13,000. Cover L2000. Open Tu-Su noon-3pm and 7pm-midnight. V, MC, AmEx.

Rhapsody in Blues, V. Garibaldi, 53 (☎079 98 45 22), serves delectable crepes (L5-10,000) on the waterfront. *Primi* L10-15,000, *secondi* L13-17,000. Open daily 7pm-3am, until dawn in August. V, MC, AmEx.

De Gustibus Gelateria, P. Ginnasio, 76. A wide range of *gelato* flavors, thoughtfully translated into Latin. Cones L2500. Open daily 10am-4am.

SIGHTS

A leisurely walk through the *centro storico* reveals tiny alleyways, half-hidden churches, and the ancient town walls. The old city is intricate and hard to navigate without a map, so stop by the tourist office before heading inside.

CHIESA DI SAN FRANCESCO. The heavy Neoclassical facade of this church conceals a graceful Gothic presbytery. Originally erected in the 14th century, the church was partially rebuilt in the 16th century—the colored stones mark where the original ends and the reconstruction begins. *(From P. Sulis, take V. Carlo Alberto to the intersection with V. Machin. Open 7:30am-noon and 5-8pm. Free.)*

DUOMO. Begun in 1552, this cathedral took 178 years to construct, resulting in a motley Gothic-Catalán-Renaissance facade. Rebuilt in the 19th century, the cathedral retains its striking Gothic choirs and a mosaic of John the Baptist. *(On V. Roma.)*

ENTERTAINMENT

Alghero truly comes alive at night—revelers stream through the cramped streets of the *centro storico* and pour out onto the promenade along the water until the early hours of the morning (be wary of indulging in the late-night scene if you're staying at the hostel; the last bus to Fertilia is at 11:30pm). Lungomare Dante is lined with open-air bars that attract thirsty locals in search of warm evening breezes and decent cover bands. Even closer to the water, **Bar del Trò,** Lungomare Valencia, 3, at a picturesque bend in the bay, offers live music after 11:30pm. (Open nightly 9pm-6am; in winter 7:30pm-3am.) To find escape from the nighttime stampede in P. del Teatro, duck into the cool, tunnel-like confines of **Caffe Teatro,** V. Principe Umberto, 23, where buying a drink is your ticket to free internet access. (☎079 97 32 119. Open daily 5am-3am.) In July and August, the town screens **outdoor movies** in Forte della Maddalena. Call ☎079 97 63 44 for info.

DAYTRIP FROM ALGHERO: GROTTE DI NETTUNO

ARST buses run to Capo Caccia and Porto Conte (50min., 3 per day 9:15am-5:10pm, last return 6:05pm, L2400). Or take the more frequent and more pleasant Navisarda Grotte di Nettuno boat tour. Boats (☎079 62 02 or 079 95 06 03) leave Alghero's Bastione della Maddalena hourly (round-trip 2½hr.; 8 per day 9am-5pm; L17,000, under 13 L10,000).

The Duke of Buckingham dubbed the **Grotte di Nettuno** "the miracle of the gods." And while he may have had horrible teeth, he was dead-on. The majestic caves have been around for 60-70 million years and are today one of Sardinia's most coveted tourist attractions. Respect your elders and watch where you bump your head—one cubic centimeter of stalactite took 100 years of dripping rain water to form. Well-run tours are conducted in just about any language. The caves are in **Capo Caccia,** a steep promontory that juts out from **Porto Conte.** Once there, descend the 632 steps that plunge to the sea between massive white cliffs. (☎079 94 65 40. Open daily Apr.-Sept. 9am-7pm; Oct. 10am-5pm; Nov.-Mar. 9am-2pm. Groups admitted hourly. L15,000, under 12 L8000.)

ARST buses to Capo Caccia stop along the way at the **nuraghe of Palmavera** (☎079 95 32 00), where a central tower surrounded by several huts forms a limestone complex dating from 1500 BC. (Ruins open daily Apr.-Oct. 9am-7pm; Nov.-Mar. 9:30am-4:30pm. L4000, with guided tour L5000.)

BOSA ☎0785

It's strange how a town with a 12th-century castle, perched atop a hill overlooking lush valleys and emerald waters, could remain relatively under-touristed, but Bosa pulls it off. Bosa has a peculiar, sleepy feel. Sardinia's only navigable river winds through the town, running near one of the island's few hostels and a sizable public beach. The view alone may be enough to put Bosa on your itinerary, but even an expansive panorama isn't likely to eradicate the eeriness of the place.

TRANSPORTATION. Bosa is actually two cities. **Bosa,** the larger of the two, is about 3km inland from the ocean, while **Bosa Marina** is across the **River Temo,** right on the beach. Buses stop in Bosa's **Piazza Angelico Zanetti.** Buses run from Bosa to **Piazza Palmiro Togliatti** in Bosa Marina (5min., 22 per day, L1300). Additionally, Pullman buses from **Alghero** or **Oristano** often continue to Bosa Marina. **ARST** buses run from Bosa to **Oristano** (1½hr., 6 per day 5:10am-4:20pm, L7400) and **Sassari** (2hr., 4 per day, L8600-10,400). Tickets are available in the *tabacherria* at V. Alghero, 7A. **FDS buses** run to **Alghero** (4 per day; *linea mare* 55min., L5600; *linae montagna* 1½hr., L7200) and **Nuoro** (1¾hr., 2 per day 6:09am-7:31pm). Tickets can be bought at the FDS office in P. Zanetti. (Open in summer 5:30-8:30am, 9:30am-3:20pm, and 4:10pm-8:25pm; in winter 5:30-8:30am and 9:30am-7:35pm.)

PRACTICAL INFORMATION. The **Pro Loco tourist office,** V. Zuni, 5, at the intersection of V. Francesco Romagna and V. Azuni, has a good map of the city (L1000). Pick one up for free at the hostel (☎0785 37 61 07. Open M-Sa 10am-1pm and 6-9pm.) For **currency exchange** head to **Credito Italiano,** C. V. Emanuele, 62, or at its 24hr. **ATM.** (Bank open M-F 8:20am-1:20pm and 2:35-4pm, Sa 8:20-11:50am.) In case of **emergency,** dial ☎113 or call **Croce Rosa** (☎0785 37 38 18) or **carabinieri** (☎0785 37 31 36). Get some **internet access** with all the toppings at **Al Gambero Rosso,** V. Nazionale, 12, in Bosa on the Bosa Marina side of the river. This cyber-pizzeria charges L10,000 per hr. (☎0785 37 41 50. Access available 12:45-3pm and 7:30pm-1am.) The **post office,** V. Pischetta, 1, offers fax service and currency exchange. (☎0785 37 31 39. Open M-F 8:30am-6:30pm, Sa 8:15am-12:45pm.) **Postal Code:** 08013.

ACCOMMODATIONS AND FOOD. Bosa Marina is home to a well-run **Youth Hostel** at V. Sardegna, 1. Ask the bus driver to let you off near the hostel. From P. Palmiero Togliatti, take V. Sassari to V. Grazia Deledda and turn right. After two blocks, turn left and look for the hostel at the end of the street. Fifty meters from the beach, this hostel has a restaurant, a bar that's open until midnight, and an amicable staff. (☎0785 375 009. Lockout Sept.-June noon-3pm. Midnight curfew. 50 beds. 6- to 8-bed dorms L18,000; doubles available seasonally if reserved. Half-pension L40,000; full pension L55,000.) If you're looking for something classier, try **Albergo Perry Clan,** V. Alghero, 3, in Bosa. From the bus stop, walk along V. D. Manin and turn right. The hotel is on the left after P. Dante Alighieri.

(☎0785 37 30 74. 32 beds. Singles L30-50,000; doubles L70-100,000.) If you can shell out the clams, **Tattore,** in P. Monumento, sates the appetite with savory, fresh seafood. (☎0785 37 31 04. Open Tu-Sa noon-3pm and 8pm-midnight.)

SIGHTS AND OUTDOORS. Walk around the town's historic area, **Quartiere Sa Costa,** and inhale the history. One of the largest in Sardinia, it has serpentine alleys and small squares. A large, free **beach** awaits in Bosa Marina, with its very own **Aragonese Tower.** (Open daily 10am-1pm and 4-7pm, L2000.) The **Bosa Diving Center,** V. Colombo, 2 (☎0785 37 56 49; fax 0785 37 56 33), in Bosa Marina, offers snorkeling (L30,000) and scuba excursions (L50-95,000 per dive plus accessory costs), 4km river boat trips with exceptional views of the city (L15,000), and ocean sightseeing boat trips to nearby grottoes and a white sand beach (2hr., L25,000).

OLBIA

☎0789

Most visitors stop in Olbia only en route to other Sardinian destinations. With a single, unremarkable medieval church and nary a beach in sight, the city offers little more than convenient ferry connections to Corsica and the rest of Italy.

SARDINIA

TRANSPORTATION

Flights: A few km southeast of the town. Check-in terminal at the corner of C. Umberto and V. XX Settembre. Buses #2 and 8 shuttle to and from the airport (L1100).

Trains: (☎0789 224 77), on V. Pala. Turn off C. Umberto, pass through the bus station to the tracks, and turn right. Trains run to the port to meet departing ferries. To: **Golfo Aranci** (20min., 7 per day 7:03am-8:04pm, L3200); **Sassari** (2hr., 4 per day 6:43am-8:22pm, L10,500); and **Cagliari** (4hr., 4 per day 6:43am-6:17pm, L24,300). Ticket office open M-Sa 6am-12:40pm and 1:50-8:30pm. **Luggage Storage:** L5000 for 12hr.

Busses: ARST, C. Umberto, 168 (☎0789 211 97). To: **Arzachena** (30min., 13 per day 6:25am-11:15pm, L2400); **Palau** (1hr., 13 per day 4:20am-11:15pm, L4500); **Santa Teresa di Gallura** (2½hr., 7 per day 6:40am-8:15pm, L7200); **Nuoro** (2½hr., 7 per day 6:40am-7:20pm, L12,200); and **Dorgali** (3hr.; 2 per day 8am-12:40pm, fewer buses on Sundays, frequency increases Sept.-May). Schedule posted in the station. Waiting room open daily 7am-8pm. Tickets at the train station ticket window.

Ferries: Tirrenia, C. Umberto, 17/19 (☎0789 285 33 or 0789 286 33). To **Civitavecchia** (4-8hr., L28,500-61,500) and **Genoa** (6-13½hr., L28,500-137,500). Open M-Sa 9am-1pm and 5-8pm. **Port office** open when ferries are running. Check-in 1½hr. before departure. **Grand Navi Veloci,** in *stazione marittima,* also has a ferry to Genoa.

ORIENTATION AND PRACTICAL INFORMATION

Blue intercity **ARST buses** and a train timed to meet incoming passengers greet **ferries** arriving at the port. To reach Olbia's *centro*, take the waiting train to the 1st stop. To find the tourist office, walk directly from the train station up **Via Pala** until it intersects **Corso Umberto;** the ARST bus station is 200m to the right. Turn left and continue past **Piazza Margherita** until you reach **Via Catello Piro.**

TOURIST, FINANCIAL, AND LOCAL SERVICES

Tourist Office: V. Catello Piro, 1 (☎0789 214 53; fax 0789 222 21), off C. Umberto. Look for the modern white building. Ask for *Annuario Hotels and Camping*. Open in summer M-Sa 8:30am-1pm and 4-7pm; in winter M-F 8am-2pm and 3:30-6:30pm, Sa-Su 9am-noon. Hours vary with staff availability.

Currency Exchange: Credito Italiano, C. Umberto, 165. Open M-F 8:20am-1:20pm and 2:50-4:20pm. **ATM** outside. **Banco di Sardegna,** C. Umberto, 142, off P. Margherita and **Banca Popolare di Sassari,** C. Umberto, 3, have **ATMs** outside.

American Express: Avitur, C. Umberto, 142B (☎0789 243 27), will cash checks (9am-1pm) and hold mail for AmEx cardholders. Also books ferry and plane tickets. Friendly, English-speaking staff. Open M-F 9am-1pm and 4-7pm, Sa 9am-12:30pm.

Car and Moped Rental: Avis (☎0789 695 40), in the airport or in town at V. Genova, 67 (☎0789 224 20). V, MC. **Gallura** (☎0789 275 70), on V. Aldo Moro. Cars from L90,000 per day plus VAT and insurance. Mopeds from L55,000.

EMERGENCY AND COMMUNICATIONS

Emergencies: ☎113. **First Aid: Guarda Medica** (☎0789 55 24 31), on V. Canova, facing the hospital. **Hospital: Ospedale Civile** (☎0789 55 22 00), V. Aldo Moro.

Pharmacy: Farmacia Lupacciolu, C. Umberto, 134 (☎0789 213 10), at the corner of V. Porto Romano. Open M-Sa 9am-1pm and 5-8:20pm. Local papers, *La Nuova Sardegna* and *L'Unione Sarda,* list pharmacies open on Sunday.

Internet: Mailboxes, Etc., V. R. Elena, 24 (☎0789 260 00). There's only 1 computer, so you may be in for a wait. L12,000 per hr. Also offers Western Union, UPS, and FedEx services. Open M-F 9:30am-1pm and 4:30-8pm, Sa 9:30am-1pm.

Post Office: V. Acquedotto (☎0789 222 51), 2 blocks from P. Matteotti. Open M-F 8:15am-6:15pm, Sa 8:15am-1pm. **Postal Code:** 07026.

SARDINIA

ACCOMMODATIONS

Albergo Terranova, V. Garibaldi, 3 (☎0789 223 95; fax 0789 272 55), off P. Margherita. This labor of love has been run by the same family for 40 years. Recent renovations make it the best option in the city for the financially secure budget traveler. All 21 rooms with bathroom, TV, and A/C. Some doubles have balconies. Breakfast L8000. Singles L70-105,000; doubles L95-190,000. Half-pension L85-105,000. V, MC, AmEx.

Hotel Minerva, V. Mazzini, 6 (☎/fax 0789 211 90). From P. Margherita, take C. Umberto toward the water and take the 1st right. The management is friendly, the rooms bright, and the lobby amusingly eclectic. Pets allowed (within reason). Breakfast L6000. Singles L45-50,000, with bath L60-65,000; doubles L65-70,000, with bath L80-L90,000.

FOOD

For bargains, shop at **Mercato Civico,** on V. Acquedotto (open M-Sa 7:30am-1pm and 4:30-8pm), or **Superpan,** P. Crispi, 2, off V. R. Elena (open daily 8:30am-9pm).

Ristorante da Paolo, V. Garibaldi, 18 (☎0789 216 75). The combination of rugged brown stone, soft pastel tablecloths, and pleasantly kitschy wall murals creates a soft and self-indulgent air. Try the house specialty *porcetta* (L13,000). *Secondi* L12-20,000. Cover L3000. Open daily noon-2:30pm and 7-10:30pm. V, MC.

Pizzeria al Ciclope, V. Dettori, 5. You don't have to blind the eye of the Cyclops, just eat them. Sliced black olives are the only toppings you'll find on pizza here—but it's fast, cheap, and piping hot. L1700 per slice. Open daily 6pm-midnight.

SIGHTS AND DAYTRIPS FROM OLBIA

A walk along the water in Olbia leads through an industrial area, sadly obscuring Sardinia's peaks and blue coasts. Nearly all traces of Olbia's Greek, Roman, and medieval past have disappeared. The sole exception is the relatively boring 12th-century **Chiesa di San Simplicio,** behind the train station. Built in the Pisan-Romanesque style, the imposing facade is etched in off-white granite.

If you have a car or feel up to a bike ride, think about taking an excursion from Olbia to **S'Abe,** an archaeological site 6km away, or to the **Giants' Tombs** (prehistoric burial grounds with giant megaliths emerging from the ground) of **Su Monte.** The bus to Nuoro passes the surreal Isola Tavolara, an immense prism of rock protruding 450m out of the sea.

ARST buses run to **San Teodoro** (1hr.; 5 per day 6:40am-7:25pm, last return 8:15pm; L3400), where a long, luxurious beach eases into ultramarine water. **Hotel La Palma,** on V. del Tirreno, offers 18 budget rooms. (☎0784 86 59 62. Doubles L90-180,000. Half-pension L75-135,000; full pension L95-155,000. V, MC, AmEx.) One kilometer from San Teodoro, the **Cala d'Ambra campground** has satisfactory facilities and 100 lots 250m from the beach. (☎0784 86 56 50. Open Apr.-Oct. L11-20,000 per person, up to L8000 per tent.)

PALAU ☎0789

Come to Palau to see a rock. Sculpted by the cutting Mistral wind into the shape of a bear, the *roccia dell'orsù* appears in many a brochure on Sardinia. It was an object of intrigue as far back as Homer, who immortalized it in the *Odyssey* (Tenth Chant) by warning of the ferocious *Lestrigoni* people that once lived around it. The locals have mellowed a bit since then, and Palau is now a sleepy coastal town. Those who seek more than sunbathing and swimming can kayak, sail, windsurf, dive, and hike. Perhaps more than anything else, convenient ferry shuttles that transport passengers across the bay to the islands of La Maddalena and Caprera attract visitors; it was as a transfer point to La Maddalena that Palau was developed during the 18th century.

TRANSPORTATION AND PRACTICAL INFORMATION. The port-end of **Via Nazionale**—Palau's single thoroughfare—contains a white building that houses a bar, several ferry ticket offices, and a newsstand that also sells ARST bus tickets (the buses stop outside). **ARST buses** head to **Santa Teresa di Gallura** (6 per day 7:15am-9:25pm, L3400) and **Olbia** (16 per day; L4500 to the *centro*, L5000 to the port). The **Trenino Verde** (little green train) provides a slow, indirect, and expensive means of transportation to Sassari—the train goes to Tempio in July and August (2 hr., 2 per day 9:50am-7pm, L18,000) and on Thursdays a train runs from Tempio to Sassari (2hr., 4:54pm, L20,000). **TRIS** (☎0789 70 86 31) and **Saremar Ferries** (☎0789 70 92 70) serve the island of **La Maddalena** (15min.; 1-3 per hr. 7:15am-11:50pm; round-trip L8000, under 12 L4000, locals L3000; cars L7600-15,700; moped/motorcycle L3-7500; bicycles free). For **car rental** head to **Centro Servizio Autonoleggio,** P. Chiesa, 2. (☎0789 70 85 65. From L80,000 per day, including insurance and unlimited mileage. Min. age 20. Open daily 9am-1pm and 5-7:30pm. V, MC, AmEx.)

Palau's **tourist office,** V. Nazionale, 94, slightly uphill in the center of town, offers info on nearby beaches, outdoor activities, and tours of neighboring islands. (☎/fax 0789 70 95 70. Open M-Sa 8am-1pm and 4-7:30pm; off-season 8am-1pm and 3-6pm.) **Banca di Sassari,** V. Roma, 9, has **currency exchange** and **ATMs** in front. (Open M-F 8:20am-1:20pm and 2:30-3:30pm, Sa 8:20-11:20am.) In an **emergency,** dial ☎113, contact the **carabinieri** (☎0789 70 95 03), call the **Guarda Medica** (☎0789 70 60 38), or ring the **hospital** (☎0789 73 77 51). The **pharmacy** (☎0789 70 95 16) is at V. Delle Ginestre, 19. (Open M-Sa 9am-1pm and 5-8:30pm. V, MC, AmEx.) The **post office** is at the intersection of V. Garibaldi and V. La Maddalena. (☎0789 70 85 27. Open M-F 8:15am-1:15pm, Sa 8:15am-12:45pm.)

ACCOMMODATIONS. Accommodations in Palau may be prohibitively expensive. The best of the lot is **Hotel Serra,** V. Nazionale, 17, close to the port. The hotel provides 20 simple, clean rooms, all with bath. (☎0789 70 95 19; fax 0789 70 97 13. Singles L55,000; doubles L75,000; triples L90,000. V, MC, AmEx.) **Hotel La Roccia,** V. dei Mille, 15, is not owned by a WWF wrestler. The Rock simply affords refuge. Renovations are set for completion in spring/summer of 2001. All 20 rooms have bathrooms; some have balconies. (☎0789 70 95 19; fax 0789 70 97 13. Call ahead. Singles L70,000; doubles L120,000. V, MC, AmEx.) For **camping** try **Acapulco,** Loc. Punta Palau. The facility has a private beach, picturesque setting, nightly piano music (live singer in August), and a bar and restaurant. Bring your own tent. (☎0789 70 94 97. Open May-Sept. 30. Reservations necessary in the summer for bungalows. L12-25,000 per adult, L10-16,000 per child. Bungalows L25-45,000 per person. 3-person caravans L65-95,000. V, MC, AmEx.)

KILLER CLOWNS FROM OUTER SPACE

Ancient Sardinian lore, spun from the mouths of fishermen's wives along the northern coast, warns of the dangers that lurk in the waters between Sardinia and Corsica. Just as mainland Italians look down upon native Sardinians as a bit brutish, Sardinians consider all Corsicans to be descended from fools. It is said that after God spread mankind throughout the world, the island of Corsica remained empty and uninhabited, because all right-minded folk headed to Sardinia first and found no reason to leave. Only the fishermen of the clan *Shearer* ventured to the shores of the island to the North, in search of the legendary *Matt Ben,* the waters of plenty. According to legend, one particularly foolish fisherman cast his net too high and brought a star crashing down into his boat. He managed to paddle to shore before the boat collapsed and sank. There, the star—which had been part of a constellation known to Sardinians as 'The Idiot Jester'—spawned the first Corsicans. A band of celestial clowns followed, descending from the sky to take their revenge on the poor fisherman for unbalancing the heavens. After dispatching the poor sap, they submerged themselves in the waters between the two islands, becoming deadly enforcers waiting patiently for the next foolish fisherman to cast his net too high.

FOOD. Numerous **bakeries** and **alimentari** line V. Nazionale. The friendly, attentive waitstaff of **L'Uva Fragola,** P. V. Emanuele, 2, serves a variety of crisp, refreshing salads (L10-12,000), pizzas (L6-12,000), and desserts in a relaxed, shaded outdoor setting. (☎0789 70 87 65. Cover L2000. Open daily noon-3pm and 7pm-2am.) **Ristorante Robertino,** V. Nazionale, 20, dishes out flavorful spaghetti with scallops or *zuppa marinara* for around L20,000. (☎078 970 96 10. Cover L3000. Open Tu-Su 12:30-2:30pm and 8-11:30pm. V, MC.)

SIGHTS. Tiny **Spiaggia Palau Vecchia** is the beach to the left of the port when facing the water. Palau's main draw and its only sight of merit is the bear-like *roccia dell'orsù.* **Caramelli buses** (15min.; 30 per day 7:30am-6:19pm, last return 6:39pm; L1200) run to the rock at **Capo d'Orso** from the port. Caramelli also runs to **Porto Pollo,** a beautiful beach brimming with big-bottomed tourists and baby-blue water (30min.; 45 per day 8:15am-7:20pm, last return 7:55pm; L2300). An **antique steam-engine tour** departs in July and August for Tempio (9:50am, return 5pm; round-trip L23,000). Several private boat companies run all-day tours of the archipelago, including the islands of **Budelli** and **Spargi** (see below).

LA MADDALENA ARCHIPELAGO ☎0789

Corsica and Sardinia were once joined by a massive land bridge; La Maddalena and Caprera and the 50-plus smaller islands that surround them are its fragmented remains. The islands today are still a point of conjunction; one-fifth of La Maddalena's inhabitants are members of the Italian or US Navy. The Americans have a base here, as well as a battleship. Though US tourists are still a rarity, plenty of real American heroes jog through the streets, kayak through the waters, and enjoy drinks at the bars of La Maddalena. Italian patriots mob La Maddalena to fawn over national hero Giuseppe Garibaldi's island home of Caprera as well as the now-deserted Savoia and Fascist military fortifications that dot the archipelago.

TRANSPORTATION AND PRACTICAL INFORMATION. Tris (☎0789 73 54 68) runs ferries between Palau and La Maddalena (15min., 2-3 per hr. 7:15am-11:20pm, L8000), as does **Saremar** (☎0789 73 76 60; 1-2 per hr. 4:30am-11:45pm, L8000). For a **taxi,** call ☎0789 73 65 00. For **scooter rental,** the people at **Nicol Sport** (☎0789 73 54 00), on V. Amendola, will hook you up for L40,000 per day

Services include: a **tourist office** in P. Barone de Geneys (☎0789 73 63 21; open in summer M-Sa 9am-1pm and 5-8pm, Su 9:30am-12:30pm and 5-8pm); a **Banco di Sardegna,** on V. Amendola off P. XXIV Febbraio, with **currency exchange** and a 24hr.

ATM (open M-F 8:45am-1:30pm and 2:45-6pm); **carabinieri** (☎0789 73 69 43); **Pronto Soccorso** (☎0789 79 12 18); a **hospital** (☎0789 79 12 00); a **pharmacy,** V. Garibaldi, 5 (☎0789 73 73 90; open M-Sa 9am-1pm and 5-8:30pm); **internet** access at **Sotta Sopra Internet Cafe,** V. Garibaldi, 48 (☎0789 73 50 07; L12,000 per hr.; open daily noon-3:30pm and 6pm-1am); and a **post office,** in P. Umberto (☎0789 73 73 95; open M-F 8:15am-6:15pm, Sa 8:15am-noon).

ACCOMMODATIONS AND FOOD. **Hotel Arcipelago,** V. Indepedenza, 2 is the best deal for an island brimming with four-star hotels. From P. Umberto, follow V. Mirabello along the water until you reach the intersection with the stoplight. Take a left here and then a right at the Ristorante Sottovento. Continue uphill to the sign directing you to your left; then take a left at the grocery store. The brown stucco hotel is on your right. Or catch the bus to Caprera from the Garibaldi column and ask to be let off at the *semaforo* (stoplight). All 12 rooms have bath and TV; some have balconies. (☎0789 72 73 28. Breakfast included. Reservations necessary in July and August. Singles L70-90,000; doubles L100-135,000.)

Pick up the basics at the **Dimeglio Supermarket,** V. Amendola, 6. (☎0789 73 90 05. Open M-Sa 8am-1pm and 5-9pm, Su 8:30am-1pm. V, MC.) The **Gastronomia Terra Mare,** V. Amendola, 35 (☎0789 73 10 25), offers a taste of both sea and land-dwelling creatures, from octopus *(polpa)* to horse *(cavallo)* measured out by the kilogram. A full meal can be devoured here for under L15,000.

SIGHTS. The islands of **Spargi, Razzoli, Budelli,** and **Santa Maria** compose a paradise of uninhabited natural beauty. Some time ago, National Park status was conferred upon the islands to protect them from development and to curb the throngs of tourists. Some spots, including the infamous **Spiaggia Rosa,** have been closed-off all together. Boatloads of swimsuit-wearing sightseers still pack large tour ships to make all-day cruises of the archipelago, stopping along the way at Spargi's **Cala Connari** and Budelli's **Spiaggia Cavaliere.** To avoid the crowds, you have to hike along the thorny, glittering granite cliffsides that cascade down to the beaches. Even then, you're bound to share the crystalline waters with swimmers diving off anchored yachts and tiny power boats. Take a short swim, prop yourself up on your own private island, and experience sultry solitude above whirling waters. Ticket sellers clamor along the docks of both La Maddalena and Palau every morning until the boats begin to depart (10-10:30am). The tour should include an on-board lunch of pasta and two or three two-hour stops at beaches along the way. Most boats return around 6:30pm. Though rather expensive (L45-50,000), the tour is the most affordable way to reach the islands.

Pine groves shade picnic tables on the quiet island nature reserve of **Caprera.** With few inhabitants, the calm is interrupted only by carloads of tourists coming for a stay at Caprera's Club Med or for a visit to the much-adored **House of Garibaldi** (☎0789 72 71 62). **Buses** run from the Garibaldi column in P. XXIIII Febbraio in La Maddalena to Caprera (13 per day 8:45am-6:45pm, last return 7:15pm; one-way L1300). During his *Risorgimento* efforts to unite Italy, Garibaldi was forced into exile in Tunisia, the US, and finally Caprera in 1854. Two years later he bought a parcel of land and constructed a home, destined to spend the rest of his life commuting back and forth between Caprera (which he eventually bought) and the mainland to continue his patriotic endeavours. Here he raised eight children, married his 2nd and 3rd wives (sequentially), and died facing his cherished sea in 1882. The house contains much of Garibaldi's original furniture and possessions, including the notorious red and white cape which he wore to meet King Vittorio Emanuele II. Outside are the graves of Garibaldi and most of his family. (L4000, ages 18-25 L2000, under 18 and over 65 free. Tours in Italian every 10min.)

SANTA TERESA DI GALLURA ☎0789

If you can bear the throngs of tourists swooping about like vultures, Santa Teresa di Gallura makes a lovely launching point for exploring coves, inlets, and the Capo Testa, a rocky plain with magnificent beaches looking out to the sea. The town boasts its own small beach, Rena Bianca, from which the hazy shores of Corsica are visible. If Sardinia's most breathtaking views don't put you under a spell, then the gentle sound of waves lapping at cliffs will.

TRANSPORTATION

Buses: ARST (☎0789 211 97) buses depart from V. Eleonora d'Arborea, adjacent to the post office off V. Nazionale. Buy tickets at Baby Bar on V. Nazionale, 100m to the left from the bus stop. To: **Palau** (40min., 6 per day 6:10am-8:50pm, L3400); **Tempio** (1½hr., 3 per day, L6700); **Olbia** (2hr., 6 per day, L7200); and **Sassari** (2½hr., 5 per day 5:15am-7:15pm, L11,300).

Ferries: Moby Lines (☎0789 75 14 49) runs to **Bonifacio, Corsica** (1hr.; 10 per day 7am-9:10pm, last return 10pm; L14-18,000 plus additional L4000 port tax for entrance into Corsica). Tickets can be purchased at the office on V. del Porto. Open daily 6:30am-10pm. For ferry details, see p. 632.

Taxis: (☎0789 75 42 86), on V. Cavour. Open 6am-midnight.

SARDINIA

ORIENTATION AND PRACTICAL INFORMATION

The ARST bus stops in front of the post office. Facing the post office, turn right, head to the intersection, and turn right onto **Via Nazionale.** Head for the church at the end of the street in **Piazza San Vittorio,** and turn right again to reach **Piazza Vittorio Emanuele.** The tourist office is on the opposite side of the *piazza.*

TOURIST, FINANCIAL, AND LOCAL SERVICES

Tourist Office: The Consorzio Operatori Turistici, P. V. Emanuele, 24 (☎0789 75 41 27). List of rooms for rent. Ask about horse, moped, and boat rental. Open June-Sept. daily 8:30am-1pm and 3:30-8pm; Oct.-May M-Sa 8am-1pm and 3:30-6:30pm.

Boat Tours: Consorzio delle Bocche, P. V. Emanuele, 16 (☎0789 75 51 12), tours the islands of the archipelago. Daily tours lasting from 9:30am until 5pm with lunch (L55-60,000 per person, ages 3-10 L30-35,000). Alternative itineraries can be requested. Office open daily 10am-noon and 6pm-midnight.

Horseback Riding: Scuola di Turismo Equestre/Caddhos Club (☎0789 75 16 40), in nearby Marazzino (4km away), conducts guided excursions for L35,000 per hr.

Scuba Diving: No Limits Diving Center, V. del Porto, 16 (☎/fax 0789 75 90 26), offers a 7-day course for PADI and SSI certification (L550,000), guided excursions (L60-90,000), and package deals (accommodations, meals, and a dive for L90-150,000 per day per person). V, MC, AmEx.

Car Rental: Avis, V. Maria Teresa, 41 (☎0789 75 49 06). Min. age 23. From L153,000 per day, which includes some insurance and unlimited mileage. Open M-F 9am-12:30pm and 4:30-7pm, Sa 9am-12:30pm. V, MC, AmEx.

Scooter/Moped Rental: GULP, V. Nazionale, 58 (☎0789 75 56 89), rents cars from L126,000 per day, insurance included. Min. age 21. Mopeds L32-60,000 per day. Scooters L40-60,000 per day.

EMERGENCY AND COMMUNICATIONS

Emergencies: ☎113. **Carabinieri** (☎0789 75 41 22), V. Nazionale. **Medical Emergencies:** ☎118. **First Aid: Guarda Medica** (☎0789 75 40 79), V. Carlo Felice. Open 24hr.

Pharmacy: P. S. Vittorio, 2 (☎0789 75 43 65). Open daily 9am-1pm and 5-8:30pm.

Internet Access: Infocell (☎/fax 0789 75 54 48), V. Nazionale near the Black and White bar, off V. D'Arborea. L10,000 per hr. Open M-Tu and Th-Sa 9am-1pm and 4:30-8pm, W 9am-1pm.

Post Office: (☎0789 73 53 24), on V. Eleonora D'Arborea, across from the bus stop. Open M-F 8:05am-12:45pm, Sa 8:05am-12:30pm. **Postal Code:** 07028.

ACCOMMODATIONS AND CAMPING

Hotel Moderno, V. Umberto, 39 (☎0789 75 42 33), off V. Nazionale. True to its name, Moderno is in the midst of renovations—A/C is slated for all rooms by summer 2001. Central location, 16 white rooms, and big, bright bathrooms. Breakfast included. Reservations required. Singles with bath L60-90,000; doubles L100-150,000. V, MC, AmEx.

Hotel Bellavista, V. Sonnino, 8 (☎/fax 0789 75 41 62), 2 blocks past P. V. Emanuele. Incredible views of the sea. 16 bright, airy rooms with balconies and baths. Singles L45-50,000; doubles L75-85,000. Half-pension L70-98,000; full pension L98-115,000.

Hotel del Porto, V. del Porto, 20 (☎0789 75 41 54). From the ARST stop on V. Nazionale, face the post office and go left. At the intersection, take another left and then a right. Follow V. del Porto down the hill. A walk from the town center, but likely to have vacancies. 20 large rooms, some with bathrooms and views of the nearby rocks, all close to the ferry horns. Breakfast L10,000. Singles, L40-55,000; doubles L60-100,000. Half-pension L100,000; full pension L110,000 only in Aug. V, MC, AmEx.

SARDINIA

FOOD

Alimentari scattered along V. Aniscara, off P. V. Emanuele, sell inexpensive basics. A fruit and clothing **market** by the bus station opens on Thursday mornings.

Papé Satan, V. Lamarmora, 22 (☎0789 75 50 48). Look for the sign off V. Nazionale. You wouldn't think the Prince of Darkness would be such a good cook, but this home of Lucifer is ranked among the top 100 Neapolitan pizzerias in all of Italy and among the top 4 in Sardinia. White stucco booths on the back patio place you in view of the wood-burning ovens—sinners beware. Try the devilishly rich *pizza alla Papé Satan* (L12,500). Open daily noon-2:30pm and 7pm-midnight.

Gastronomia Artigiane del Corso, V. XX Settembre, 15 (☎0338 283 22 33). *Menù* includes tasty *primo, secondo,* and *contorno* for L15,000, possibly the cheapest full meal on the entire coast. For a picnic, pick up fresh and creatively prepared food like salmon lasagna or eggplant parmesan. Open daily noon-3pm and 7-11:30pm.

BEACHES AND HIKING

V. XX Settembre leads towards the sea. As the road forks, veer left and continue past Hotel Miramar to reach **Piazza Libertà.** Words cannot do justice to the perfect **Aragonese Tower** framed by the deep blue of the wide ocean, with the shores of Corsica just barely visible through the mist across the sea. After wiping the drool from your chin, take a walk down the stairs in the *piazza* to reach **Spiaggia Rena Bianca,** a crowded beach. Those seeking a more peaceful, off-the-beaten-path sunbathing experience must sacrifice sand for rock. Above the beach, an unkempt trail winds up and around the rocks along the coast, giving the more adventurous traveler access to the coves and lagoons below. The trek is thorny and overgrown, so proper footwear is a must. The path rewards hikers with excellent views of **Isola Municca,** a stadium-like islet with high rocks encircling a field of grass. Farther up, the path offers glimpses of the impressive beaches of **Capo Testa.** If you prefer flip-flops to hiking boots but still want to get to the beach, either take the **Sardabus** from the post office to Capo Testa (10min.; 5 per day; L1300, round-trip L2400) or brave the traffic and walk the 3km along **V. Capo Testa** from V. Nazionale.

ENTERTAINMENT

Groove's Cafe (☎0789 75 45 19), V. XX Settembre, 2, offers a limited pub menu, cushioned booths, and outdoor balcony seating where you can nod your head to acid jazz and deep house after 11pm. **Conti** (☎0789 75 42 71), on the other side of the *piazza*, has similar music with an upstairs dance floor and loft beds where you can nod your bod to the sounds of a live DJ. (Both open 7am-late)

MALTA

US$1 = 0.44 LIRE (LM)	LM1 = US$2.26
CDN$1 = LM0.30	LM1 = CDN$3.35
EUR€1 = LM0.40	LM1 = EUR€2.49
UK£1 = LM0.67	LM1 = UK£1.50
IR£1 = LM0.51	LM1 = IR£1.96
AUS$1 = LM0.26	LM1 = AUS$3.86
NZ$1 = LM0.20	LM1 = NZ$5.01
SAR1=LM0.06	LM1 = SAR15.60
IT L1000 = LM0.21	LM1 = L4818

DENOMINATIONS. The Maltese lira (Lm) is divided into 100 **cents** (¢); each cent is divided into 10 **mils.**

alta's beauty and strategic location have lured visitors from all corners of the editerranean over the last three centuries. Prehistoric farmers, Phoenician trads, Roman governors, monastic knights, and British admirals have all been drawn these small islands, and all have contributed to the rich and fascinating montage attractions that cover them. The lavish Baroque churches and palaces of the ights of Malta are only a short bus ride away from austere neolithic temples, easant beaches, and hopping nightlife. Malta becomes an international melting t during the summer, with two foreign visitors for every local.

The Maltese archipelago is composed of the islands of Malta, Gozo, and Comino, well as the tiny uninhabited islets of Cominotto and Fifla. Valletta, the capital, is cated on a narrow finger of land on Malta's southeast side. Malta's official lanages are **Maltese,** a language derived from ancient Phoenician that sounds like a avily Italian-accented version of Arabic, and the Queen's own **English.**

COUNTRY CODE Malta's country code is 356. There are no city codes.

GETTING THERE

r more info about getting to Malta, check out www.maltayellowpages.com.

Flights: Air Malta (Malta office: ☎69 08 90, 23 43 97, or 22 12 07; London office: ☎+44 (020) 87 85 31 99; fax +44 (020) 87 85 74 68) and **Alitalia** (☎24 67 82) land at Malta's **International Airport** (☎24 96 00), which has flights to **Rome** and **London.** Bus #8 runs to the airport from Valletta (3 per hr. 6am-8pm, 11¢). Malta's **NSTS travel service** (☎24 49 83; fax 23 03 30) has discount fares to **Rome** (Lm35 without tax) and **London** (Lm68 without tax).

Ferries: Two ferry companies serve Malta from Italy. **Island Seaway,** c/o S. Mifsud and Sons, 311 Republic St., Valletta (☎32 06 55), runs to **Catania** (Lm20) and **Reggio Calabria** (Lm25). Reserve cabins in advance. **Virtu Rapid Ferries,** 3 Princess Elizabeth Terrace, Ta'xbiex (☎31 70 88), send nauseating **catamarans** to **Catania, Syracuse, Pozzallo,** and **Licata** (summer 3 per week, winter 1 per week). These destinations are popular, so reserve well ahead. Boats depart from the Grand Harbor. For early morning departures, make taxi reservations in advance. **S. Mifsud and Sons,** 311 Republic St., Valletta (☎32 06 55); **S. Nicotra Bertuccio,** V. Dusmet, 131, Catania (☎095 32 50 81); and **Giovanni Boccadifuoco,** V. Mazzini, 8, Syracuse (☎0931 46 38 66), sell ferry tickets. To see the world's only Socialist

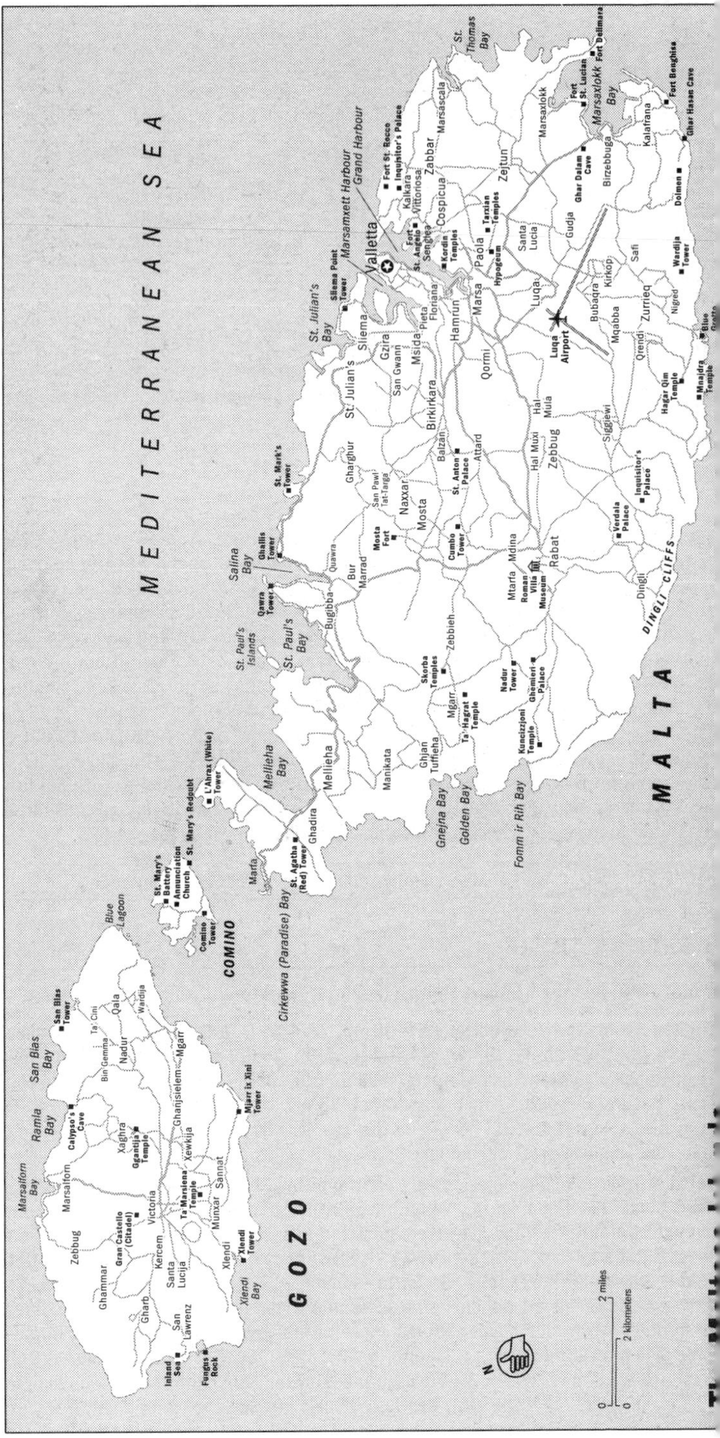

MEDITERRANEAN SEA

MALTA

GOZO

COMINO

Valletta
Sliema
St. Julian's
Gzira
Msida
Pieta
Floriana
Senglea
Vittoriosa
Cospicua
Kalkara
Zabbar
Marsascala
Marsaxlokk
Zejtun
Paola
Marsa
Hamrun
Qormi
Birkirkara
San Gwann
Balzan
Attard
Naxxar
Mosta
Mdina
Rabat
Mtarfa
Zebbug
Siggiewi
Luqa
Gudja
Santa Lucia
Birzebbuga
Kalafrana
Safi
Kirkop
Mqabba
Zurrieq
Qrendi
Bubaqra
Nigred
Dingli
Gharghur
San Pawl Tat-Targa
Bur Marrad
Bugibba
Qawra
Mellieha
Manikata
Ghadira
Marfa
Mgarr
Zebbieh
Ghajn Tuffieha
Hal Mula
Hal Muxi

Grand Harbour
Marsamxett Harbour
St. Julian's Bay
Salina Bay
St. Paul's Bay
St. Paul's Islands
Mellieha Bay
Gnejna Bay
Golden Bay
Fomm ir Rih Bay
St. Thomas Bay
Marsaxlokk Bay
Cirkewwa (Paradise) Bay
Blue Lagoon
DINGLI CLIFFS

Luqa Airport
Fort St. Elmo
Fort St. Rocco
Inquisitor's Palace
Fort St. Angelo
Kordin Temples
Tarxien Temples
Hypogeum
Fort St. Lucian
Fort Delimara
Fort Benghisa
Ghar Hasan Cave
Ghar Dalam Cave
Dolmen
Wardija Tower
Blue Grotto
Mnajdra Temple
Hagar Qim Temple
Inquisitor's Palace
Verdala Palace
St. Anton Palace
Cumbo Tower
Mosta Fort
Roman Villa Museum
Sliema Point Tower
St. Mark's Tower
Ghallis Tower
Qawra Tower
Skorba Temples
Ta' Hagrat Temple
Nadur Tower
Ghemieri Palace
Kuncizzjoni Temple
L'Ahrax (White) Tower
St. Agatha (Red) Tower
St. Mary's Redoubt
St. Mary's Battery
Annunciation Church
Comino Tower

Victoria
Marsalforn
Xaghra
Qala
Nadur
Ghajnsielem
Mgarr
Xewkija
Sannat
Munxar
Xlendi
Kercem
Santa Lucija
Gharb
San Lawrenz
Ghammar
Zebbug
Wardija
Ta' Cini
Bin Gemma
Marsalforn Bay
Ramla Bay
San Blas Bay
Xlendi Bay
San Blas Tower
Calypso's Cave
Ggantija Temple
Ta' Marsiena Temple
Gran Castello (Citadel)
Xlendi Tower
Mgarr ix Xini Tower
Inland Sea
Fungus Rock

N
0 2 miles
0 2 kilometers

Valletta

ACCOMMODATIONS
- Asti Guest House, 3
- Bonheur Guest House, 1
- Coronation Guest House, 2

Abercrombie's Bastion
Ball's Bastion
Fort St. Elmo
War Museum
St. Gregory Bastion
St. Lazarus Bastion
The Malta Experience
Grand Harbour
Spur St.
Fountain St.
St. Joseph St.
North St.
Old Hospital St.
Old Wells St.
Mediterranean Congress Centre
Lower Barracca Gardens
St. Nicholas St.
Sebastian St.
St. Sebastian Bastion
St. Dominic St.
Casa Rocca Piccola
Republic St.
St. Frederick St.
Merchants St.
St. Paul St.
St. Ursula St.
Mediterranean St.
Bull St.
St. Charles St.
St. Christopher St.
Bounty St.
St. Paul's Anglican Cathedral
Archbishop St.
REPUBLIC SQ.
Grandmaster's Palace
St. Barbara Bastion
East Street
Marsamxett St.
West St.
Carmelite Church
Old Mint St.
Manoel Theatre
Old Bakery St.
Old Theatre St.
QUEEN'S SQ.
St. Paul's Shipwreck Church
St. Lucia St.
Strait St.
GREAT SIEGE SQ.
St. John's Co-Cathedral
Auberge d'Italie
St. John St.
St. Patrick St.
St. Salvatore Bastion
Auberge de Castille & Leon
Battery St.
St. Anthony St.
St. Mark St.
Auberge de Provence (Nat'l Archaeological Museum)
St. Zachary St.
St. Barbara
Melita St.
National Museum of Fine Arts
South St.
Republic St.
Victory St.
Church of Our Lady of Victories
Upper Barracca Gardens
St. Andrew's Bastion
Marsamxett Harbour
Vassalli St.
Windmill St.
St. John's Cavalier
Ordnance St.
FREEDOM SQUARE
St. James Cavalier
Lascaris War Rooms
Pope Pius V St.
St. James Bastion
St. Michael's Bastion
Hastings Garden
Triton's Fountain
TO US & UK EMBASSIES (200m)
FLORIANA
Triq L'Assedju L-Kbir
N
0 100 yards
0 100 meters

MALTA

Arab *Jamahiryah*, or just find out what a *jamahiryah* is, **Libya Sea Malta Co.** rur several ferries a week to **Tripoli.** Their office is located inside the Sea Passeng Terminal (☎259 42 61).

VALLETTA

Capital of the nation and city of 10,000 steps, Valletta was one of the first centrall planned European cities, and its streets make a neat grid. The city teems with tou ists during the day but falls silent at night. Across Marsamxett Harbor to the wes Sliema, St. Julians, and Paceville are crowded with resort hotels, souvenir shop and the island's best nightlife.

TRANSPORTATION

Buses: (☎37 32 82). Malta's bright yellow and orange buses are cheap, convenier reliable, and decorated with everything from stuffed animals to votive statues. From t fountain outside City Gate and the Sliema ferry stop, buses run to: the **Gozo Ferry Bo Terminal** (#45, 48, and 645; 4 per hr. 5:35am-9pm, 30¢); **Mdeina/Rabat** (#80 a 81; 4 per hr. 5:50am-8:30pm, 11¢); and the **airport** (#8; 3 per hr. 6am-8pm, 11¢). summer, buses from Paceville have extended hours on weekend nights. At the touri office, grab a helpful map with every bus route on the islands.

Ferries: A ferry service (☎33 89 81) runs from Marsamxett Harbor in Valletta to the Stra in **Sliema** (10min.; 2 per hr. M-Sa 7:30am-6pm, Su 7:30am-4pm; 35¢).

Taxis: Radio cabs or "black cabs" are often cheaper than the metered white cabs. **We bley's Garage** (☎37 41 41 or 37 42 42), in St. Julian's, is one of the least expensiv Taxis to Sliema cost about Lm2.50, to the airport Lm4. Reserve ahead. Open 24hr.

Car Rental: Hertz (☎23 28 11), at the Preluna Hotel on Tower Road in Sliema, or on Tr Elija Zamit (☎37 80 79), in Paceville. Economy model with unlimited mileage Lm15. per day, Lm81.00 per week. Valid driver's license required. Min. age 21. Under 25 Ln surcharge per day. Open daily 8am-noon and 5-8pm.

Moped Rental: Rent through your hotel, travel agency, or NSTS. Or try **Albert's,** 2(Upper Saint Albert St. (☎34 01 49), in Gzira. 3-day min. rental. Lm6 per day.

ORIENTATION AND PRACTICAL INFORMATION

Buses arrive in Valletta at the rotary outside City Gate. Inside, **Republic Street** lea to the tip of the peninsula at **Fort Saint Elmo,** running parallel to **Merchant's Stree** site of the daily morning market. To reach the suburbs of Sliema, St. Julian's, Paceville, jump on bus #62, 64, 67, 68, 667, 662, or 671 (6 per hr. 5:30am-11pm) the fountain in Valletta. **The Strand,** Sliema's waterfront street, becomes **Tower Ro** across the peninsula, **Main Street (Triq Il-Kbira)** along Balluta Bay in St. Julian's, a **Saint George Street** as it climbs the hill to Paceville and St. George's Bay.

TOURIST, FINANCIAL, AND LOCAL SERVICES

Tourist Office: (☎23 77 47), on Pope Pius V St., just inside the city gate and to the rig from the bus terminal. Offers bus schedules and lists of accommodations in Malta a Gozo. Open Apr.-Oct. M-Sa 8:30am-6:30pm, Su 8:30am-1pm; Nov.-Mar. M-Sa 8:30a 6pm, Su 8:30am-1pm. **Branch office** (☎69 99 61 74) at the airport.

Budget Travel: National Student Travel Service (NSTS), 220 St. Paul's St. (☎24 49 8 fax 23 03 30). From City Gate, turn right on South St. and left onto St. Paul's St. Castille Sq. Offers excellent maps, info on ISIC discounts, and a budget travel a accommodations service. Open May-Sept. M-F 9am-1pm and 3-6pm, Sa 9am-1p Oct.-Apr. M-F 9am-12:30pm and 2:30-5pm, Sa 9am-12:30pm. V, MC.

Embassies and Consulates: Australia (☎33 82 01; fax 34 40 59), in Villa Fiorentina Ta'xbiex Terrace, in Ta'xbiex, between Valletta and Sliema. Take the Sliema bus **Canadian** citizens should report to either the UK or the US embassy. **European Uni** 51 Villa "The Vines" (☎34 51 11; fax 34 48 97), on the Ta'xbiex Sea Front, in Ta'xbi

Italy, 5 Vilhenast St. (☎23 31 57; fax 23 53 39), in Floriana. **South Africa** (☎38 08 32), the Palmi, Coast Rd., in Baharic-Caghac. **UK,** 7 St. Anne St. (☎23 31 34; fax 24 40 01), in Floriana, across from the US Embassy. **US** (☎23 59 60; fax 24 32 29), in Development House, on St. Anne St. in Floriana.

American Express: A&V von Brockdorff Ltd., 14 St. Zachary St. (☎23 21 41), and in Sliema (☎33 40 51), off St. John's Sq. The Sliema branch will hold mail. Open M-F 8:30am-12:30pm and 2:30-5:30pm, Sa 8:30am-12:30pm.

Laundromat: Square-Deal (☎33 00 71), on the Strand in Sliema. Wash Lm2.50; dry Lm0.40 per 10min. Dry cleaning available. Open M-F 9:30am-1pm and 4-7:30pm, Sa 9am-1pm and 4-8pm.

EMERGENCY AND COMMUNICATIONS

Emergency: Police: (☎191 or 22 40 01), on St. Lucia St. Turn left off Republic St. from the city gate. **Ambulance:** ☎196. **Hospital: St. Luke's** (☎23 41 01), in Guardamangia, on the Valletta-Sliema bus line. Bus #75 runs from Valletta (every 30min. 8am-6pm).

Telephones: Assistance is available from either an overseas (☎194) or local (☎190) operator. An AT&T operator can be reached at ☎0800 89 01 10.

Internet Access: Internet Café, 178 Merchant St. (☎24 06 80), in Valetta. It's fun to check email at the Y-M-C-A! No construction workers, policemen, or sailors, but 75¢ for 30min., 60¢ with ISIC. Open M-Sa 10am-10pm. **Waves Internet Café,** 139 Tower Rd. (☎34 22 42; fax 33 59 33). Lm1 for 30min. Open noon-4am.

Post Office: (☎22 62 24), on Victory St., Castille Sq., in Valletta. **Poste Restante** (☎22 07 93) is on West St. in a small building beside the Auberge d'Aragon. Both open mid-June to Oct. M-Sa 7:30am-6pm; Nov.-June M-Sa 8am-6:30pm.

ACCOMMODATIONS

Valletta's **guest houses,** close to the city's monuments, burst with Old World charm, while establishments in Sliema, St. Julian's, and Paceville provide better nighttime offerings and access to the beach. By July and August, every mattress on the island is occupied, and reservations are a must.

VALLETTA

Coronation Guest House, 10 E. M. A. Vassalli St. (☎23 76 52). Turn left on South St. at the City Gate and descend the steps near the Osborne Hotel. 15 clean, spacious rooms in quirky pastel shades. One of Malta's trademark balconies graces each chamber. Toilets and showers in the hall. Super-friendly manager. Breakfast included. June-Aug. Lm5 per person; Oct.-Mar. Lm4 per person.

Valletta Asti Guest House, 18 S. Ursula St. (☎23 95 06), near the Upper Barracca Gardens. A gleaming lobby and breakfast room, small inner garden, comfortable beds, and new bathrooms down the hall. 10 rooms. Breakfast included. Lm5.50 per person.

Bonheur Guest House, 18 Sappers St. (☎23 84 33). From the City Gate, turn left on South St., and take the 3rd left onto Sappers St. 12 tidy, tiled bedrooms. Showers in room; toilets down the hall. Breakfast included. Lm5.50 per person.

SLIEMA, ST. JULIAN'S, AND PACEVILLE

Hacienda Guest House, 35 Wilga Street (☎31 96 29; fax 37 65 05; email hacienda@mail.link.net.mt), in Paceville, crawling distance from the discos. Clean and pleasantly run. 15 rooms. Breakfast included. Lm6 per person.

Hibernia House (HI) (☎33 38 59), on Depiro St. in Sliema. Take the St. Julian's bus, get off near the Snoopy's Bar sign, walk up St. Francis St., and turn right at the Depiro St. intersection. The hostel is just ahead. Made-for-students suites have multi-bed bedrooms, lounge, bathroom, and kitchenette. Perhaps the hostel's biggest perk are the ISIC card keys, good for free admission to the NSTS Aqua Center and the majority of sights on the island. 120 beds. Reserve through the NSTS office (see **Budget Travel,** p. 668). HI members Lm3, non-members Lm3.70.

FOOD

On Malta you can eat an English breakfast, a spicy Arabic lunch, and an Italian d ner. But be sure to try traditional Maltese fare at least once. Seafood dish include *torta tal-lampuki*, a fish pie made from the cod-like *lampuka* fish. *Fen* (rabbit), is the national dish. *Qaqà-tal-ghasel* (pastry filled with molasses) a *pastizzi* (tart pea and cheese cakes) are delightful. Try the *kinnie*, a citrus a herb soda. Hop Leaf, Cisk Lager, and Shandy are the Maltese beers. Cheap, loca produced wines include the potent *Marsovin* and *Lachryma Vitis*.

VALLETTA

A variety of options line Republic St. Many are packed with tourists during lun Grab a sandwich or basic foods at the **Wembley Store,** 305 Republic St., just insi the city gate. (Open M-F 8am-7pm, Sa 8am-1:30pm.)

Labour Party Club, 42 Republic St. (☎24 25 92), across from the "King's Own Ba Club" sign, 2 blocks from the City Gate. Enjoy delicious fish and chips (Lm1.25) un the stern glare of portraits of past party leaders. Open daily 8am-10pm.

King's Own, 274 Republic St. (☎23 02 81). Look for the tiny "King's Own Band Cl sign 2 blocks from the City Gate. Pictures of former band club members grace the p tic table-clothed, marble-floored dining room. Large breakfast Lm1. Dinner menu Lm1.99. Breakfast served daily until noon. Open daily 8am-11pm.

Trattoria Palazz, 43 Old Theatre St. (☎22 66 11), just off Republic Sq., to the right co ing from the City Gate. Pasta dinners from Lm2.95. Open M-Th noon-3pm and 6: 10pm, F-Sa noon-3pm and 6:30-11pm. V, MC, AmEx.

SLIEMA, ST. JULIAN'S, AND PACEVILLE

An endless array of rather pricey pizza and pasta restaurants pack the waterfr along the Strand in Sliema and Main St. in St. Julian's. Cheap, diner-style fare available uphill on Church St. and Gort St. in Paceville. For provisions, head to **supermarket,** on Triq Wilga in Paceville. (Open M-Sa 8am-8pm, Su 8am-1pm.) F more substantial fare, try **Ta' Kolina Restaurant,** 151 Tower Rd., in Sliema. Excell Maltese dishes are served in a homey dining room overlooking the ocean. (☎33 06. *Lampuki* Lm3.95. *Escargot alla Kolina* Lm1.95. Reservations recommend Open M-Sa 6-10pm, Su noon-2pm and 6-10pm. V, MC, AmEx.)

SIGHTS

ST. JOHN'S CO-CATHEDRAL. Valletta's most spectacular architectural sho piece, this Cathedral (1573-1577) was designed by Gerolamo Cassa in a lav Baroque style, with ceiling paintings by Maria Pretti. The floor is paved with inlaid marble tombs of the knights, while the side chapels are reserved for the v ious nationalities that made up the order. Inside, the **oratory** and **museum** cont a stunning collection of manuscripts, more ecclesiastical robes than you c shake a bishops staff at, tapestries by Mattia Preti, Caravaggio's *Beheading of John*, and his portrait of St. Jerome. (*Walk 3 blocks down Republic St. from the City G and turn right on St. John's St. The church is on your left. Church and museum open M-F 9:30 12:45pm and 1:30-5:15pm, Sa 9:30am-12:45pm and 4-5pm. Museum Lm1, under 15 and dents with ISIC free. Donation requested.*)

LASCARIS WAR ROOMS. These well-hidden underground headquarters w used by Winston Churchill, Dwight Eisenhower, and other Allied military gre for strategic planning operations during WWII. An excellent audio tour (free w admission) provides a detailed history of the chambers and Malta's role in the fi against the Axis powers. (*Turn onto S. Ursula St. from Republic St. and follow signs thro subterranean passages. ☎23 49 36. Open M-F 9:30am-4pm, Sa-Su 9:30am-12:30pm. Lm1. students and children 85¢.*)

CASA ROCCA PICCOLA. Inhabited for the past 400 years by Maltese aristocrats, this house is full of fascinating art and artifacts from the centuries when the knights ruled the island. Guided tours highlight facets of the island's history. *(74 Republic Street. ☎23 17 96; www.vol.net.mt/casarocca. Tours M-F every hr. 11am-4pm. Lm1, students 65¢.)*

NATIONAL ART MUSEUM. Housed in yet another former palace, this museum has an excellent collection of Baroque religious paintings, especially by Maria Pretti, decorator of the Co-Cathedral. *(On South St., 4 blocks to the left of Republic Street with your back to Freedom Square. ☎23 95 45. Open mid-June to Sept. daily 7:45am-2pm; Oct. to mid-June M-Sa 8:15am-5pm, Su 8:15am-4:15pm. Lm1, students, seniors, and children free.)*

NATIONAL MUSEUM OF ARCHEOLOGY. This museum, with clear explanations of Maltese excavations and a small but well-presented collection of prehistorical relics, provides an excellent introduction to the temple sites scattered across the islands. *(On Republic St., in the charming Auberge de Provence. ☎23 95 45. Open daily mid-June to Sept. 7:45am-2pm; Oct. to mid-June M-Sa 8:15am-5pm, Su 8:15am-4:15pm. Lm1; students, seniors, and children free.)*

FORT ST. ELMO AND THE WAR MUSEUM. Constructed by Maltese hero Grandmaster LaVallette (older brother of Grandmaster Flash), this fort has withstood attacks by Ottoman Turks and Nazis. It now houses the country's War Museum, which showcases the coveted **George Cross,** England's highest honor. For gallantry and endurance during the bombings, King George VI awarded this honor to the Island of Malta in 1942. The museum documents Malta's massive WWII losses, serving as a moving reminder of the damage and pain wrought on one of the worst-bombed populations in history. *(From the City Gate, walk down Republic St. Fort St. Elmo's entrance is just to the right, and the War Museum is just to the left. Fort open Sa 1-5pm, Su 9-5pm. Lm1.80. Museum open daily 8am-1:30pm; in winter M-Sa 8:30am-4:30pm, Su 8:30am-3:30pm. Lm1, students with ISIC, seniors, and children free.)*

GRANDMASTER'S PALACE. This opulent home of Malta's rulers since 1575 is today the President's official residence. The adjacent armory houses 16th- to 18th-century armor that reflects the martial prowess of the Knights of St. John. *(3 blocks down Republic St. from Fort St. Elmo on the right. Open usually a few times a week, depending on when Parliament is in session. Stop by the tourist office in the morning to find out. Lm1 for state room, Lm1 for armory room; students with ISIC, seniors, and children free.)*

BEACHES. Though you'll be disappointed if sand is your thing, Tower Rd. in Sliema's rock-slab coast provides carved out, sea-filled swimming alcoves. For water sports, head over to the NSTS Aquacenter (☎33 84 68), on Tigne Point in Sliema. Ask them about beach parties. *(Entry free with ISIC card. Waterskiing Lm5 for 10min.)*

SHOPPING

Along with the souvenir dishtowels and sundry gimmicks sold in Freedom Sq. Malta is known for its high-quality lace and delicate silver filigree jewelry, characterized by an elaborate pattern of thin strands of metal. A good place to pick up both at a reasonable price (Lm2.50 for a silver ring or pin) is **Joesph Busuttil's shop,** 222 Merchant St. in Valetta. (☎24 32 41. Open M-F 9:30am-1:30pm and 4-7pm, Sa 9:30am-1:30pm.) For more mundane items like bootleg CDs, frying pans, and clothes, a *souk* (street market) fills Merchant St. weekdays 9am-noon.

ENTERTAINMENT

While people-watching along the waterfront in Sliema and St. Julian provides hours of entertainment, the real scene is up the hill in **Paceville,** where bars and discos rock until the clock chimes 4am.

CARAVAGGIO THE FOUL OF TEMPER Like many *Let's Go: Italy* users, the Baroque painter Caravaggio traveled extensively throughout Italy and Malta, making his travel plans on the spur of the moment. Unlike most *Let's Go: Italy* users, his itinerary was not determined by famous sights or great hostels, but the more pressing need to escape criminal prosecution in a remarkable number of cities. After a couple of run-ins with Roman authorities (one involving a ballistic collision between a plate of badly cooked artichokes and the face of a waiter, another the killing of his opponent in a dispute over the score of a tennis match), he was finally forced to flee the country. He then traveled down through Naples and Sicily to Malta, hoping to be made a knight, an honor he received after painting several excellent works for the knights. But true to form, things went awry when he insulted the Grandmaster of the Knights and was locked in prison. Caravaggio made a remarkable escape from jail and headed back to Naples, where trouble befell him once again during a harborside tavern brawl. He never fully recovered from his wounds and died soon after.

Misfits, in the White House Hotel. From the Burger King, head 2 blocks down Triq Il-Wilga, and turn right on Triq Paceville; Misfits is on the left. A constant techno beat, a picnic-table-strewn deck, a tapestry-draped ceiling, and the city's best DJs grace the place. Open daily 8pm-4am.

Axis (☎34 47 42), on Triq St. George, about a block from Burger King. Look what happens—you bomb the crap out of Malta and get a club named after you. Filled with ecstatic locals and gyrating tourists. The 3 soundproof rooms start bumping around midnight. Cover Lm2.50, Lm1 ISIC discount. Open Su-F 9:30-4am, Sa 8pm-4am.

Lady Godiva (☎38 10 58), Triq Il-Wilga, a few doors down from Burger King. Look what happens—you ride naked through an English suburb and get a club in Malta named after you. The country's hippest place for gay events. Comic-book-style pictures line the walls. Open daily 9pm-4am.

The Alley (☎37 22 46), on Triq Il-Wilga, half a block from Burger King. Look what happens—oh, never mind. Half-bar, half-club, the Alley is a nice breather from the furious dancing at Axis. Open daily 9pm-4am.

Rock Café, on Triq Santa Rita, across the street from Burger King. Relive your headbanging days and bite the head off a live bat for old times' sake. Open daily 9:30pm-4am.

Simon's, at the corner of Triq Depiro and Triq Dimech in Sliema. Simon says this is a relaxed, family-style local pub, complete with a grapevined terrace. Open W-Su noon-4am.

DAYTRIPS FROM VALLETTA

MDINA AND RABAT

Buses #80 and 81 run from Valetta, and the same stop serves both Mdina and Rabat (20min., 4 per hr. 5:50am-8:30pm, 11¢).

Mdina and Rabat were the capitals of the island before the arrival of the knights, and both boast sights dating from the Roman Empire. Mdina is a small town in desperate need of a vowel, contained within a fort. Follow the signs from the bus station. Vilegaignon St. runs down the middle of Mdina, and a **cathedral** sits in a small *piazza* 250m from the main gate. (Open daily 8:30am-noon and 3:30-5pm. Modest dress required.) More interesting is the cathedral **museum** next door, which houses lavish ecclesiastical vestments, local paintings, and such a large collection of Durer woodcuts that Kaiser Wilhelm II tried (and failed) to persuade the Maltese to let him take them back to Germany. (Open M-Sa 8:30am-4:30pm, Su 10am-1pm. Lm1, free with ISIC.) The bastions surrounding the town provide a great view of the countryside.

St. Paul's Church, in the nearby town of Rabat, houses a **grotto** that sheltered Paul from the Romans. (Church and grotto open M-Sa 9am-5pm. Free guided tour. Donation requested.) Down St. Agatha's Rd. lie **Saint Paul's Catacombs,** 200m of early Christian burial chambers carved from local stone. (Open M-Sa 8:15am-5pm, Su 8:15am-4:15pm. Lm1, free for students with ISIC and seniors.)

BLUE GROTTO

Take bus #38 or 138 (30min., 2 per hr. 9:45am-3:45pm, 40¢) from Valletta and get off with the other camera-toting folk.

On Malta's southeastern coast, the dazzling and heavily touristed **Blue Grotto** hides near the village of **Wied Iz Zurrieq.** From the village, follow the sign-posted path to the harbor. **Boat tours** offer a closer look at the blue waters of the Blue Grotto and its five sister caves. (☎64 99 28. 15-20min.; 9am-5pm; Lm2.50, children Lm1.25.)

HAGAR QIM AND MNAJDRA

Take bus #38 to the end of the route, or walk 20 minutes from the Blue Grotto.

Constructed in limestone, **Hagar Qim** (hah-jahr-EEM) and **Mnajdra** (im-NYE-drah), haunting megalithic temples, overlook the southern coast and the desolate island of **Filfla.** At Hagar Qim, **giant phalli,** up to 7m high, were erected as a masculine balance to the sight's fertility temple. The **Mnajdra Temples** are located downhill. Like all temples on the islands, they are arranged in the form of a central chamber flanked by small rounded rooms; archaeologists are unsure of what each room was used for. If you look closely you can still see the repetitive spiral patterns used as decoration. As the temples are in a desolate area, women should visit them in groups. (All temples open daily mid-June to Sept. 8am-2pm; Oct. to mid-June M-Sa 8:15am-5pm, Su 8:15am-4:15pm. Lm1, students 50¢.)

MALTA

BEACHES AND BAYS

The Maltese coastline has a few sandy **beaches.** The crowded **Golden Bay** (bus #47 from Valletta, #652 from Sliema) and quieter **Gnejna Bay,** 1km to the south, lie along the western coast. On the eastern coast, **Pretty Bay** (bus #11) draws a pretty big crowd, as do the beaches of the **Marfa Peninsula** in the northwest (bus #50).

GOZO

History and tourism have tread more lightly on Gozo than the rest of Malta, and life takes a slower pace on this largely agricultural island. The capital, Victoria, has a fortress and cathedral, while the surrounding farmland and coast are dotted with unusual geologic formations and neolithic remains. Gozo's kitchens are an attraction in themselves, turning the island's fresh produce and the daily catch of her fishermen into hearty Maltese cooking.

TRANSPORTATION AND PRACTICAL INFORMATION. The trip to **Victoria,** Gozo's capital, requires a couple of transfers; take **bus** #45 from Valletta to **Cirkewwa** (35min., 3 per hr. 5:35am-9pm, 11¢), on Malta's northwest tip. **Ferry** service, provided by **Gozo Channel Company** (☎58 04 35 on Malta; 55 61 14 on Gozo), runs from Cirkewwa to Gozo's main port of **Mgarr** (30min., 30 per day in summer, round-trip Lm1.70). From the Mgarr port, bus #25 runs to **Victoria** (15min., 5:30am-8:45pm, 9¢). **Buses** leave Victoria for the port at Mgarr 30 minutes before each ferry departs (5:30am-8pm).

From the Victoria bus station, turn right on **Main Gate Street** and then left on **Republic Street** to reach Gozo's **tourist office** in **Independence Square,** Victoria's largest plaza. The helpful staff can find rooms and provide a map. (☎56 14 19. Open M-Sa 9am-12:30pm and 1-5pm, Su and holidays 9am-12:30pm.) **Bike** and **scooter rental** is available at **Victoria Garage,** across from the bus station on Main Gate St. (☎55 64 14. Bicycles Lm2 per day; scooters Lm13.50 for 3 days.) In an **emergency** dial ☎196 or call the **police** (☎56 20 40). On Republic St., Gozo's **hospital** (☎56 16 00) is just outside of Victoria. **Internet access** is available at **ICS** on President JFK Sq., opposite McDonald's. (☎55 87 83. Open M-F 9am-noon and 4-7pm, Sa 9am-3pm.) The

post office is located a block down Republic St., off Independence Square. (☎55 15 28. Open M-Sa 7:30am-5:15pm.) To **telephone** off the island, dial 08 first.

ACCOMMODATIONS AND FOOD. In Victoria, **Casalgo House at the Gardens,** on Kercem Rd., provides a decent place to relax. From Independence Sq., continue away from the bus station to Sabina Sq. and bear left. The hotel is opposite the public park. Charming arches and a garden seduce Odyssean travelers. (☎55 37 23. 6 rooms. Breakfast included. Lm4 per person in high season.) **Marsalforn,** Gozo's most popular resort town, has inexpensive lodging seconds from a sandy beach. From Victoria, take bus #21 (9¢). **Lantern Guest House,** on Qbajjar Rd. a block from the bus stop in Marsalforn in a more touristed area near the beach, is a pleasant bed and breakfast. (☎55 62 85. 10 rooms. July-Aug. Lm6 per person; May-June and Sept. Lm5 per person; Oct.-Apr. Lm4.50 per person.)

For the freshest lunch on the island, take bus #64 or 65 (every hr. 7am-7pm) to Xaghra and the popular **Gesther Restaurant,** on VIII September Ave. The menu includes such Maltese specialties as rabbit casserole (Lm2.90) and beef olives (Lm3.10). (☎55 66 21. Open M-Sa 11:30am-1:30pm.) **Ta' Giannina,** on Republic St. just downhill from Main Gate St., has a three-course Maltese meal for Lm2.50. (☎55 60 26. Open daily 7:30am-3pm and 6:30-11pm.)

MALTA

SIGHTS AND ENTERTAINMENT. An elaborate **citadel** and the **Gozo Cathedral** crown Victoria, the island's capital. To reach the fortified complex, follow Republic St. to Independence Sq. and climb Castle Hill Rd. to the entrance. The Gozans ran a bit low on cash and painted the ceiling of the church to look like the dome they could not afford. (Cathedral open daily 6am-8pm. Donation requested.) To the right of the cathedral an old home houses an extensive collection of folk items from Gozo, ranging from folk art to more agricultural implements than you can shake a threshing rake at. To the left at the bottom of the cathedral stairs lies the informative **Archeological Museum,** a complement to the island's historic temples. (Both museums open M-Sa 8:30am-4:30pm, Su 8:30am-3pm. Lm1, students with ISIC and children free.)

North of Victoria, **Xaghra** (SHAH-rah), at the end of bus #64's route (every hr. 7am-7pm, 9¢) hosts the **Ggantija Temples** (jig-AHN-tee-ha), dating from 3600 BC and named for the legendary giants who constructed them. Legend has it that a giant woman walked from the valley below, carrying the temple's giant stones on her head. The fertility temples predate Egypt's Great Pyramids by 800 years. The same ticket includes a nearby windmill and a small folk and agriculture museum. (Open M-Sa 8:30am-4:15pm, Su 8:30am-3pm. Lm1; seniors, students, and children free.)

Dwejra Bay is home to the **Inland Sea,** a clear salt-water pool. If you're a fun guy, check out the **Fungus Rock**—it's covered with lichens with supposedly curative powers. Nearby is the **Azure Window,** a beautiful sea-carved arch. Buses #1 and 2 run to Dwerja from Victoria (9 per day 7am-5:30pm, 9¢). On a hilltop above the beautiful orange sands of Ramla Bay, **Calypso's Cave,** legendary brothel of Odysseus, is always open and free. Sadly, sea nymphs no longer frolic there. Take bus #64 or 65 to Xaghra, and follow the signs.

Liberty, Justice, and Globe-trotting for all.

Sip espresso in Paris. Cheer the bulls in Barcelona. Learn the waltz in Saltzburg. 85 years after the Wright brothers discovered flying was easier than walking, wings are available to all. When you Name Your Own Price℠ on airline tickets at priceline.com, the world becomes your playground, the skies your road-less-traveled. You can save up to 40% or more, and you'll fly on top-quality, time-trusted airlines to the destinations of your dreams. You no longer need a trust fund to travel the globe, just a passion for adventure! So next time you need an escape, log onto priceline.com for your passport to the skies.

INDEX

APPENDIX

INDEX

H

INDEX

N

INDEX

ABOUT LET'S GO

FORTY-ONE YEARS OF WISDOM

As a new millennium arrives, *Let's Go: Europe*, now in its 41st edition and translated into seven languages, reigns as the world's bestselling international travel guide. For over four decades, travelers criss-crossing the Continent have relied on *Let's Go* for inside information on the hippest backstreet cafes, the most pristine secluded beaches, and the best routes from border to border. In the last 20 years, our rugged researchers have stretched the frontiers of backpacking and expanded our coverage into Asia, Africa, Australia, and the Americas. This year, we've introduced a new city guide series with titles to San Francisco and our hometown, Boston. Now, our seven city guides feature sharp photos, more maps, and an overall more user-friendly design. We've also returned to our roots with the inaugural edition of *Let's Go: Western Europe.*

It all started in 1960 when a handful of well-traveled students at Harvard University handed out a 20-page mimeographed pamphlet offering a collection of their tips on budget travel to passengers on student charter flights to Europe. The following year, in response to the instant popularity of the first volume, students traveling to Europe researched the first full-fledged edition of *Let's Go: Europe*, a pocket-sized book featuring honest, practical advice, witty writing, and a decidedly youthful slant on the world. Throughout the 60s and 70s, our guides reflected the times. In 1969 we taught travelers how to get from Paris to Prague on "no dollars a day" by singing in the street. In the 80s and 90s, we looked beyond Europe and North America and set off to all corners of the earth. Meanwhile, we focused in on the world's most exciting urban areas to produce in-depth, fold-out map guides. Our new guides bring the total number of titles to 51, each infused with the spirit of adventure and voice of opinion that travelers around the world have come to count on. But some things never change: our guides are still researched, written, and produced entirely by students who know first-hand how to see the world on the cheap.

HOW WE DO IT

Each guide is completely revised and thoroughly updated every year by a well-traveled set of nearly 300 students. Every spring, we recruit over 200 researchers and 90 editors to overhaul every book. After several months of training, researcher-writers hit the road for seven weeks of exploration, from Anchorage to Adelaide, Estonia to El Salvador, Iceland to Indonesia. Hired for their rare combination of budget travel sense, writing ability, stamina, and courage, these adventurous travelers know that train strikes, stolen luggage, food poisoning, and marriage proposals are all part of a day's work. Back at our offices, editors work from spring to fall, massaging copy written on Himalayan bus rides into witty, informative prose. A student staff of typesetters, cartographers, publicists, and managers keeps our lively team together. In September, the collected efforts of the summer are delivered to our printer, who turns them into books in record time, so that you have the most up-to-date information available for your vacation. Even as you read this, work on next year's editions is well underway.

WHY WE DO IT

We don't think of budget travel as the last recourse of the destitute; we believe that it's the only way to travel. Living cheaply and simply brings you closer to the people and places you've been saving up to visit. Our books will ease your anxieties and answer your questions about the basics—so you can get off the beaten track and explore. Once you learn the ropes, we encourage you to put *Let's Go* down now and then to strike out on your own. You know as well as we that the best discoveries are often those you make yourself. When you find something worth sharing, please drop us a line. We're Let's Go Publications, 67 Mount Auburn St., Cambridge, MA 02138, USA (email: feedback@letsgo.com). For more info, visit our website, www.letsgo.com.

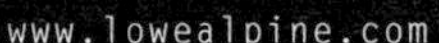

If I had my life
to live over again,

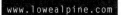

I would relax. I would limber up. I would take more chances.

I would take more trips.

I would climb more mountains, swim more rivers, and watch more sunsets.

I would go places and do things and travel lighter than I have.

I would ride more
merry-go-rounds.

Excerpt from Nadine Stair, 85 years old / photo> John Norris

technical packs & apparel

Find Yourself. Somewhere Else.

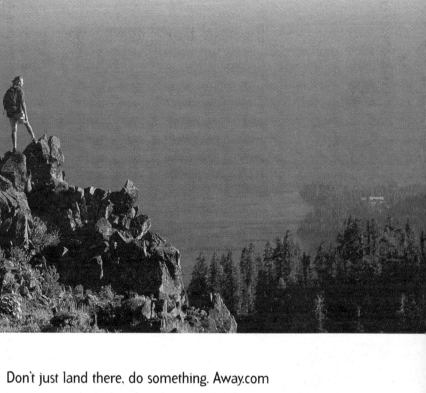

Don't just land there, do something. Away.com is the Internet's preferred address for those who like their travel with a little something extra. Our team of travel enthusiasts and experts can help you design your ultimate adventure, nature or cultural escape. Make Away.com your destination for extraordinary travel. Then find yourself. Somewhere else.

Will you have enough stories to tell your grandchildren?

Yahoo! Travel

Do You Yahoo!?™

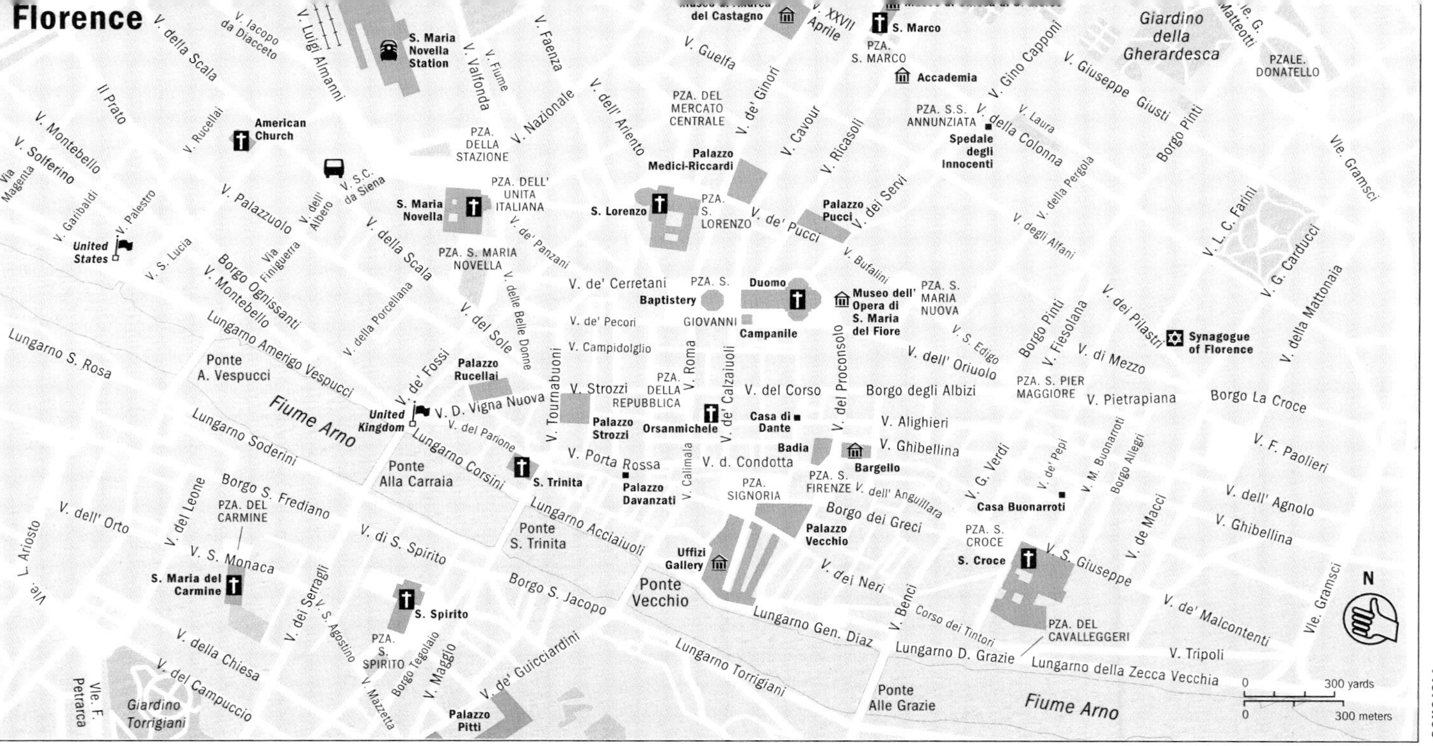

Florence
V. della Scala
V. Iacopo da Diacceto
V. Luigi Almanni
S. Maria Novella Station
V. Valfonda
V. Fiume
V. Faenza
del Castagno
V. XXVII Aprile
S. Marco
PZA. S. MARCO
Accademia
V. Gino Capponi
Giardino della Gherardesca
Vle. G. Matteotti
PZALE. DONATELLO
Il Prato
V. Montebello
V. Solferino
Via Magenta
V. Rucellai
American Church
PZA. DELLA STAZIONE
V. Nazionale
V. dell' Ariento
V. Guelfa
PZA. DEL MERCATO CENTRALE
V. de' Ginori
V. Cavour
V. Ricasoli
PZA. S.S. ANNUNZIATA
V. della Colonna
V. Laura
Spedale degli Innocenti
V. Giuseppe Giusti
Borgo Pinti
Vle. Gramsci
V. Garibaldi
V. Palestro
United States
V. Palazzuolo
V. dell' Albero
V. S.C. da Siena
S. Maria Novella
PZA. DELL' UNITA ITALIANA
Palazzo Medici-Riccardi
S. Lorenzo
PZA. S. LORENZO
V. de' Pucci
Palazzo Pucci
V. dei Servi
V. della Pergola
V. degli Alfani
V. L. C. Farini
V. G. Carducci
V. della Mattonaia
V. S. Lucia
Via Finiguerra
Borgo Ognissanti
V. Montebello
V. della Scala
PZA. S. MARIA NOVELLA
V. de' Panzani
V. della Porcellana
V. delle Belle Donne
V. de' Cerretani
PZA. S. GIOVANNI
Baptistery
Duomo
Campanile
Museo dell' Opera di S. Maria del Fiore
V. Bufalini
PZA. S. MARIA NUOVA
V. S. Egidio
V. dell' Oriuolo
Borgo Pinti
V. Fiesolana
V. dei Pilastri
V. di Mezzo
Synagogue of Florence
Lungarno S. Rosa
Lungarno Amerigo Vespucci
Ponte A. Vespucci
V. del Sole
V. de' Pecori
V. Campidolglio
V. de' Fossi
Palazzo Rucellai
V. Tornabuoni
V. Strozzi
PZA. DELLA REPUBBLICA
V. Roma
V. de' Calzaiuoli
V. del Corso
V. del Proconsolo
Borgo degli Albizi
PZA. S. PIER MAGGIORE
V. Pietrapiana
Borgo La Croce
Fiume Arno
United Kingdom
V. D. Vigna Nuova
V. del Parione
Palazzo Strozzi
Orsanmichele
Casa di Dante
V. Alighieri
V. Ghibellina
Badia
Bargello
Lungarno Soderini
Lungarno Corsini
Ponte Alla Carraia
S. Trinita
V. Porta Rossa
Palazzo Davanzati
V. Calimala
V. d. Condotta
PZA. SIGNORIA
PZA. S. FIRENZE
V. dell' Anguillara
V. G. Verdi
V. de' Pepi
V. M. Buonarroti
Borgo Allegri
Casa Buonarroti
V. F. Paolieri
V. dell' Agnolo
Borgo S. Frediano
PZA. DEL CARMINE
V. dell' Orto
V. del Leone
V. di S. Spirito
Ponte S. Trinita
Lungarno Acciaiuoli
Borgo dei Greci
Palazzo Vecchio
PZA. S. CROCE
S. Croce
V. de Macci
V. Ghibellina
Vle. L. Ariosto
V. S. Monaca
S. Maria del Carmine
V. dei Serragli
V. S. Agostino
S. Spirito
Borgo S. Jacopo
Uffizi Gallery
Ponte Vecchio
V. dei Neri
V. Benci
Corso dei Tintori
V. S. Giuseppe
V. de' Malcontenti
Vle. Gramsci
N
V. della Chiesa
V. del Campuccio
Vle. F. Petrarca
Giardino Torrigiani
PZA. S. SPIRITO
Borgo Tegolaio
V. Mazzetta
V. Maggio
Palazzo Pitti
V. de' Guicciardini
Lungarno Gen. Diaz
Lungarno Torrigiani
Lungarno D. Grazie
PZA. DEL CAVALLEGGERI
V. Tripoli
Lungarno della Zecca Vecchia
Ponte Alle Grazie
Fiume Arno
0
300 yards
300 meters

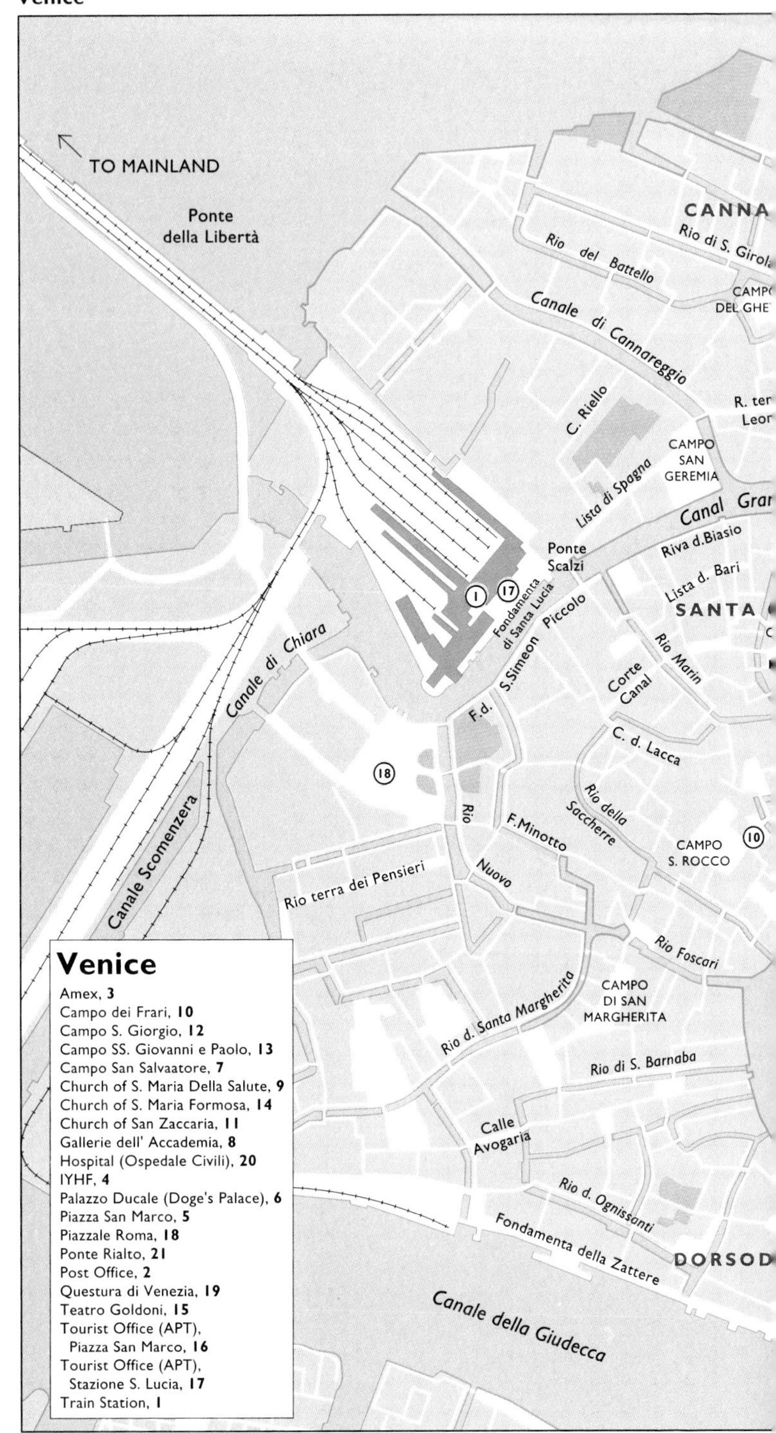
TO MAINLAND
Ponte
della Libertà
CANNA
Rio di S. Girol
Rio del Battello
Canale di Cannareggio
CAMP
DEL GHE
C. Riello
R. ter
Leor
CAMPO
SAN
GEREMIA
Lista di Spagna
Canal Gran
Ponte
Scalzi
Riva d.Biasio
Lista d. Bari
SANTA
Fondamenta di Santa Lucia
F.d. S.Simeon Piccolo
Canale di Chiara
Rio Marin
Corte Canal
C. d. Lacca
Rio della Saccherre
Rio
F.Minotto
Nuovo
CAMPO
S. ROCCO
Canale Scomenzera
Rio terra dei Pensieri
Rio Foscari
CAMPO
DI SAN
MARGHERITA
Rio d. Santa Margherita
Rio di S. Barnaba
Calle
Avogaria
Rio d. Ognissanti
Fondamenta della Zattere
DORSOD
Canale della Giudecca
Venice
Amex, 3
Campo dei Frari, 10
Campo S. Giorgio, 12
Campo SS. Giovanni e Paolo, 13
Campo San Salvaatore, 7
Church of S. Maria Della Salute, 9
Church of S. Maria Formosa, 14
Church of San Zaccaria, 11
Gallerie dell' Accademia, 8
Hospital (Ospedale Civili), 20
IYHF, 4
Palazzo Ducale (Doge's Palace), 6
Piazza San Marco, 5
Piazzale Roma, 18
Ponte Rialto, 21
Post Office, 2
Questura di Venezia, 19
Teatro Goldoni, 15
Tourist Office (APT), Piazza San Marco, 16
Tourist Office (APT), Stazione S. Lucia, 17
Train Station, 1

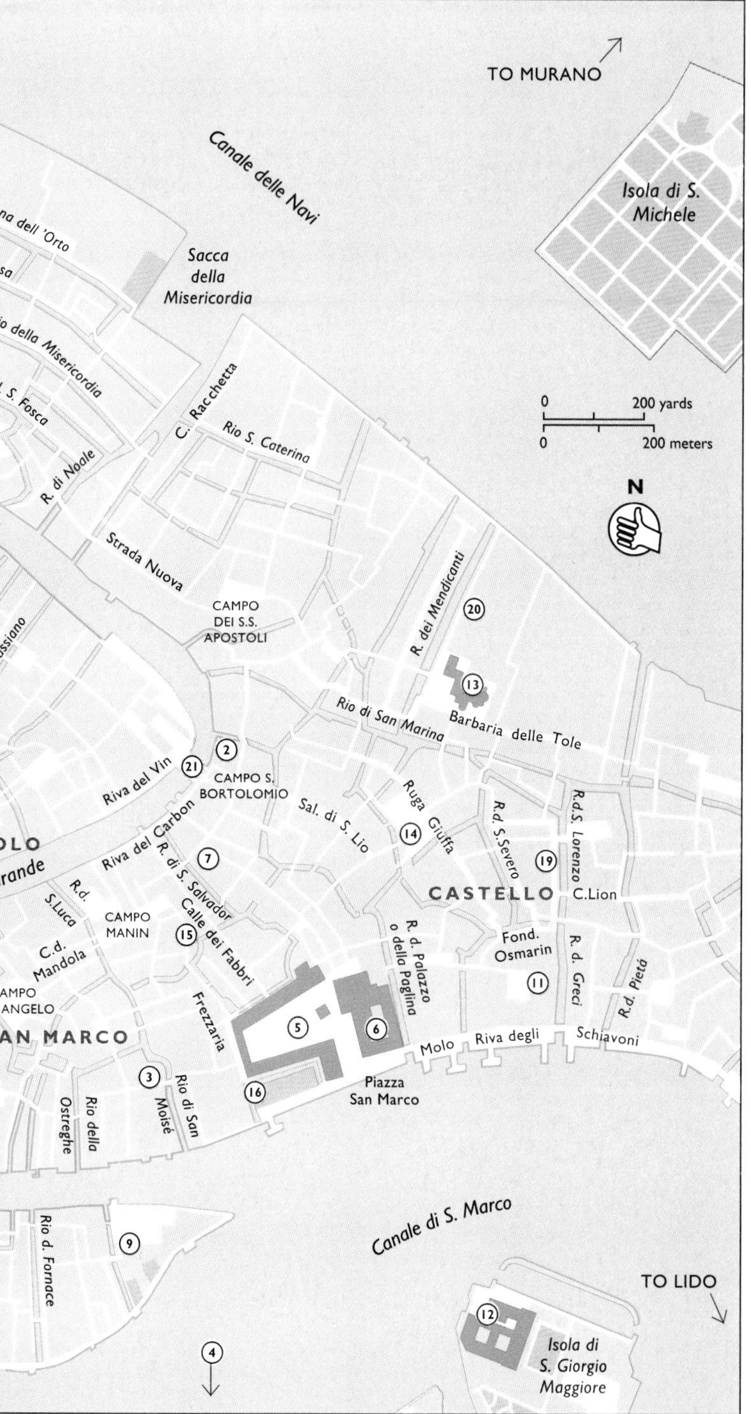
TO MURANO
Canale delle Navi
Isola di S. Michele
Sacca della Misericordia
Rio della Misericordia
C. Racchetta
Rio S. Caterina
R. di Noale
Strada Nuova
CAMPO DEI S.S. APOSTOLI
R. dei Mendicanti
Rio di San Marina
Barbaria delle Tole
Riva del Vin
CAMPO S. BORTOLOMIO
Ruga Giuffa
Sal. di S. Lio
R.d. S.Severo
R.d.S. Lorenzo
Riva del Carbon
R. di S. Salvador
Calle dei Fabbri
CASTELLO
C.Lion
CAMPO MANIN
C.d. Mandola
Fond. Osmarin
R. d. Palazzo o della Paglina
R. d. Greci
R.d. Pietà
CAMPO ANGELO
Frezzaria
Molo
Riva degli Schiavoni
Piazza San Marco
Rio di San Moisé
Rio della Ostreghe
Canale di S. Marco
Rio d. Fornace
TO LIDO
Isola di S. Giorgio Maggiore
0 200 yards
0 200 meters
N

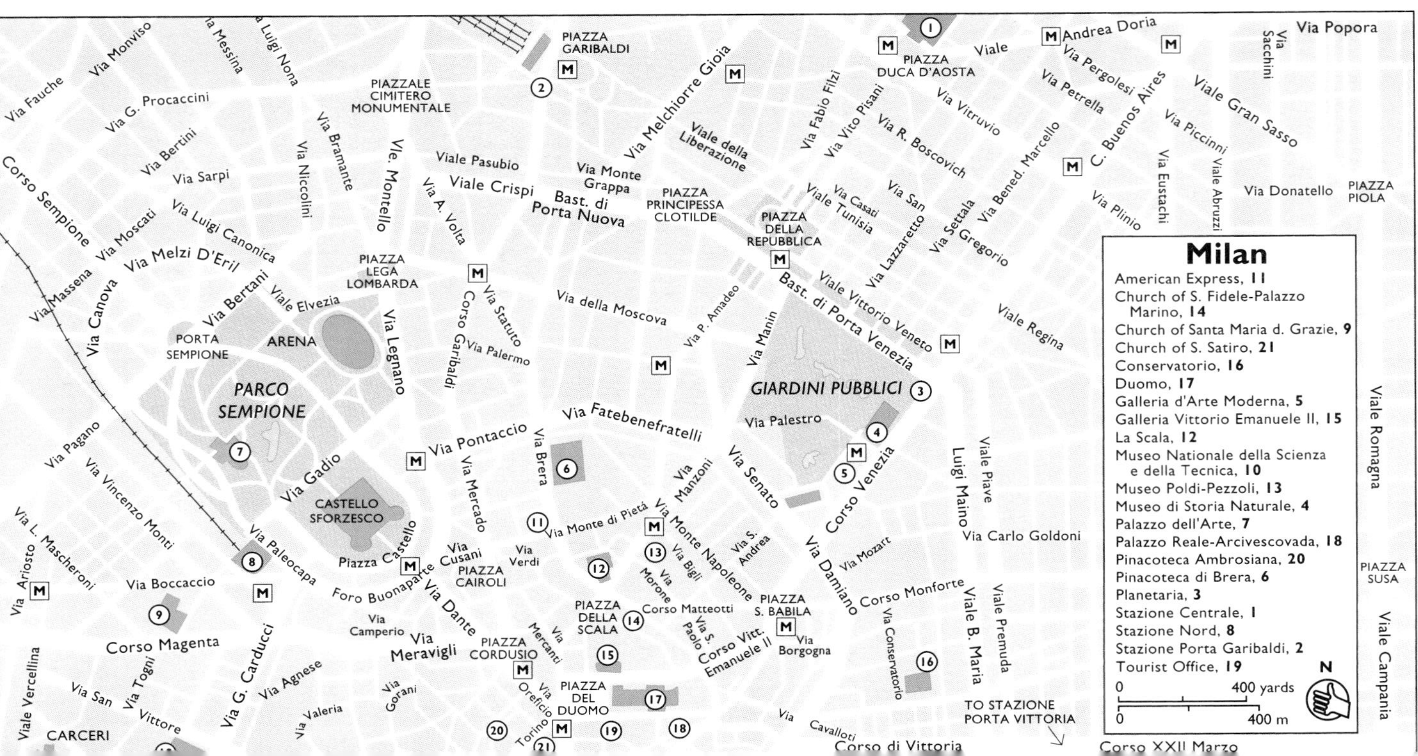
Milan
American Express, 11
Church of S. Fidele-Palazzo Marino, 14
Church of Santa Maria d. Grazie, 9
Church of S. Satiro, 21
Conservatorio, 16
Duomo, 17
Galleria d'Arte Moderna, 5
Galleria Vittorio Emanuele II, 15
La Scala, 12
Museo Nationale della Scienza e della Tecnica, 10
Museo Poldi-Pezzoli, 13
Museo di Storia Naturale, 4
Palazzo dell'Arte, 7
Palazzo Reale-Arcivescovada, 18
Pinacoteca Ambrosiana, 20
Pinacoteca di Brera, 6
Planetaria, 3
Stazione Centrale, 1
Stazione Nord, 8
Stazione Porta Garibaldi, 2
Tourist Office, 19
N
0 400 yards
0 400 m
GIARDINI PUBBLICI
PARCO SEMPIONE
CASTELLO SFORZESCO
ARENA
PORTA SEMPIONE
PIAZZA DEL DUOMO
PIAZZA DELLA SCALA
PIAZZA DELLA REPUBBLICA
PIAZZA GARIBALDI
PIAZZA DUCA D'AOSTA
PIAZZALE CIMITERO MONUMENTALE
PIAZZA LEGA LOMBARDA
PIAZZA PRINCIPESSA CLOTILDE
PIAZZA CAIROLI
PIAZZA CORDUSIO
PIAZZA S. BABILA
PIAZZA PIOLA
PIAZZA SUSA
TO STAZIONE PORTA VITTORIA
CARCERI
Corso Sempione
Corso Magenta
Corso Venezia
Corso Monforte
Corso di Vittoria
Corso XXII Marzo
Viale Romagna
Viale Campania
Via Manzoni
Via Dante
Via Brera

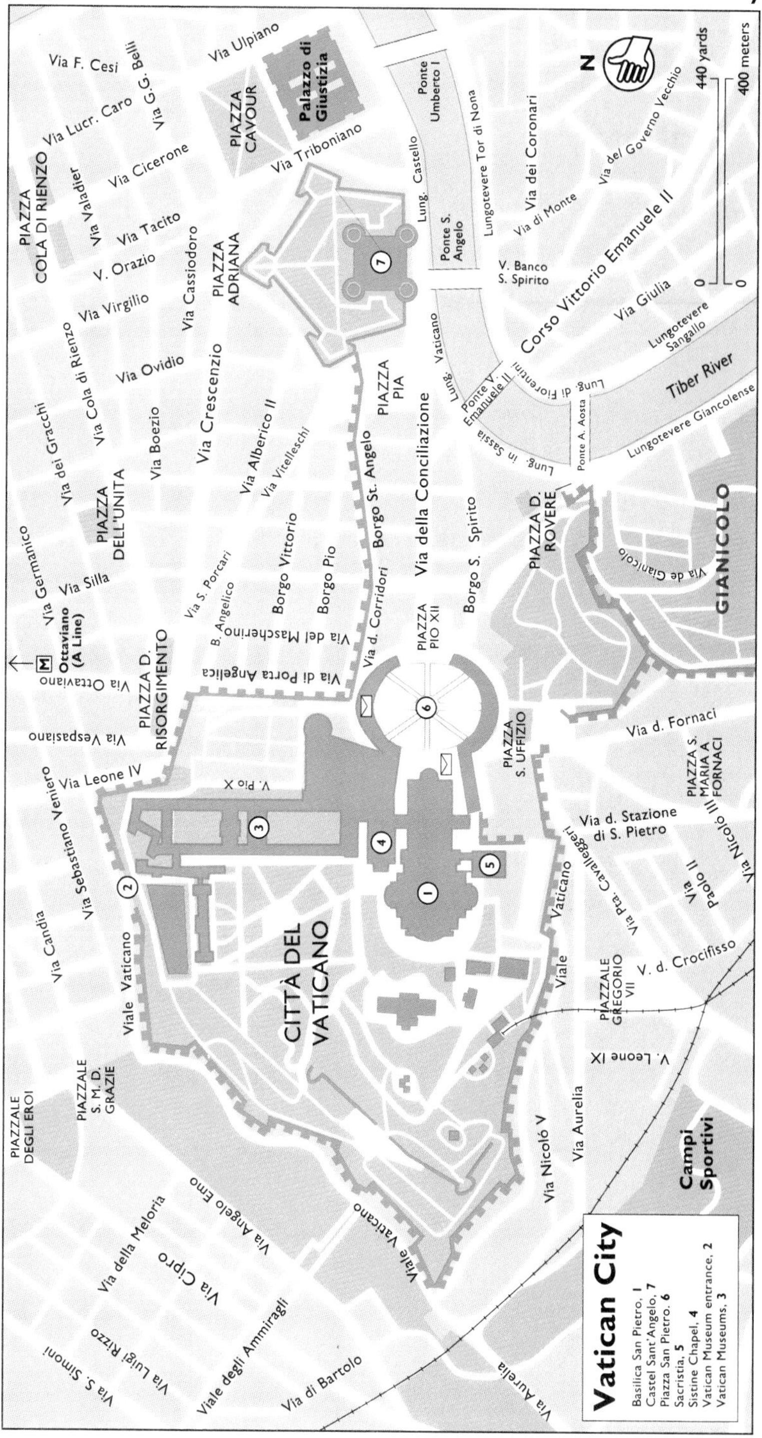
Vatican City
Basilica San Pietro, 1
Castel Sant'Angelo, 7
Piazza San Pietro, 6
Sacristia, 5
Sistine Chapel, 4
Vatican Museum entrance, 2
Vatican Museums, 3
N
0
440 yards
0
400 meters
CITTÀ DEL VATICANO
GIANICOLO
Campi Sportivi
Tiber River
Palazzo di Giustizia
PIAZZA CAVOUR
PIAZZA COLA DI RIENZO
PIAZZA ADRIANA
PIAZZA DELL'UNITÀ
PIAZZA D. RISORGIMENTO
PIAZZA PIA
PIAZZA PIO XII
PIAZZA S. UFFIZIO
PIAZZA D. ROVERE
PIAZZA S. MARIA A FORNACI
PIAZZALE GREGORIO VII
PIAZZALE S. M. D. GRAZIE
PIAZZALE DEGLI EROI
Ottaviano (A Line)
Via Ulpiano
Via F. Cesi
Via G.G. Belli
Via Lucr. Caro
Via Cicerone
Via Tribonano
Via Valadier
Via Tacito
V. Orazio
Via Cassiodoro
Via Virgilio
Via Cola di Rienzo
Via Ovidio
Via Crescenzio
Via dei Gracchi
Via Boezio
Via Alberico II
Via Vitelleschi
Via Germanico
Via Silla
Via S. Porcari
B. Angelico
Borgo Vittorio
Borgo Pio
Via del Mascherino
Via d. Corridori
Borgo St. Angelo
Via della Conciliazione
Borgo S. Spirito
Via di Porta Angelica
Via Ottaviano
Via Vespasiano
Via Leone IV
V. Pio X
Via Sebastiano Veniero
Via Candia
Viale Vaticano
Ponte Umberto I
Lung. Castello
Lungotevere Tor di Nona
Ponte S. Angelo
Via dei Coronari
Via del Governo Vecchio
Via di Monte
V. Banco S. Spirito
Corso Vittorio Emanuele II
Via Giulia
Lungotevere Sangallo
Lung. Vaticano
Ponte V. Emanuele II
Lung. di Fiorentini
Ponte A. Aosta
Lungotevere Giancolense
Lung. in Sassia
Via de Gianicolo
Via d. Fornaci
Via d. Stazione di S. Pietro
Via Pta. Cavalleggeri
Via Paolo II
Via Nicolò III
V. d. Crocifisso
V. Leone IX
Via Aurelia
Via Nicolò V
Via Angelo Emo
Via della Meloria
Via Cipro
Via S. Simoni
Via Luigi Rizzo
Viale degli Ammiragli
Via di Bartolo

Rome: Overview

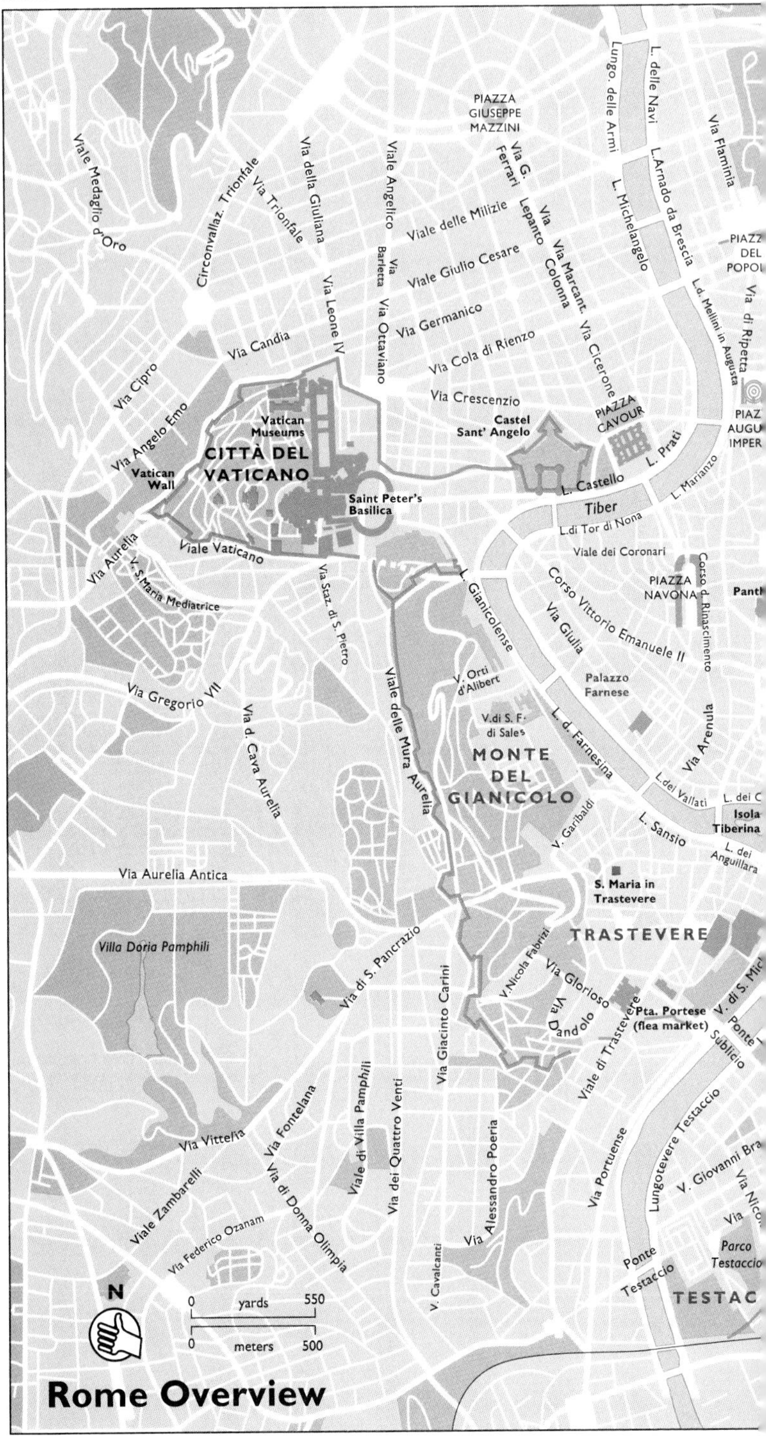

Rome Overview

PIAZZA GIUSEPPE MAZZINI
Lungo. delle Armi
L. delle Navi
Via Flaminia
Viale Medaglio d'Oro
Circonvallaz. Trionfale
Via Trionfale
Via della Giuliana
Viale Angelico
Via G. Ferrari
Viale delle Milizie
Via Lepanto
L. Michelangelo
L.Arnado da Brescia
PIAZZ DEL POPOL
Via Barletta
Viale Giulio Cesare
Via Marcant. Colonna
L.d. Mellini in Augusta
Via di Ripetta
Via Leone IV
Via Ottaviano
Via Germanico
Via Cicerone
Via Candia
Via Cola di Rienzo
Via Cipro
Via Crescenzio
PIAZZA CAVOUR
PIAZ AUGU IMPER
Via Angelo Emo
Vatican Museums
Castel Sant' Angelo
CITTÀ DEL VATICANO
Vatican Wall
L. Prati
L. Castello
L. Marianzo
Saint Peter's Basilica
Tiber
L.di Tor di Nona
Via Aurelia
Viale Vaticano
Viale dei Coronari
V. S.Maria Mediatrice
Via Staz. di S. Pietro
L. Gianicolense
Corso Vittorio Emanuele II
PIAZZA NAVONA
Corso d. Rinascimento
Panth
Via Giulia
V. Orti d'Alibert
Palazzo Farnese
Via Gregorio VII
Via d. Cava Aurelia
Viale delle Mura Aurelia
V.di S. F. di Sales
L. d. Farnesina
Via Arenula
MONTE DEL GIANICOLO
L.dei Vallati
L. dei C
Isola Tiberina
V. Garibaldi
L. Sansio
L. dei Anguillara
Via Aurelia Antica
S. Maria in Trastevere
TRASTEVERE
Villa Doria Pamphili
Via di S. Pancrazio
V.Nicola Fabrizi
Via Glorioso
Via Dandolo
Pta. Portese (flea market)
V. di S. Mic
Ponte Sublicio
Via Giacinto Carini
Viale di Trastevere
Viale di Villa Pamphili
Via dei Quattro Venti
Via Vitellia
Via Fontelana
Via Alessandro Poeria
Via Portuense
Lungotevere Testaccio
V. Giovanni Bra
Via Nico
Viale Zambarelli
Via di Donna Olimpia
Via Federico Ozanam
V. Cavalcanti
Via
Ponte Testaccio
Parco Testaccio
TESTAC
N
0 yards 550
0 meters 500

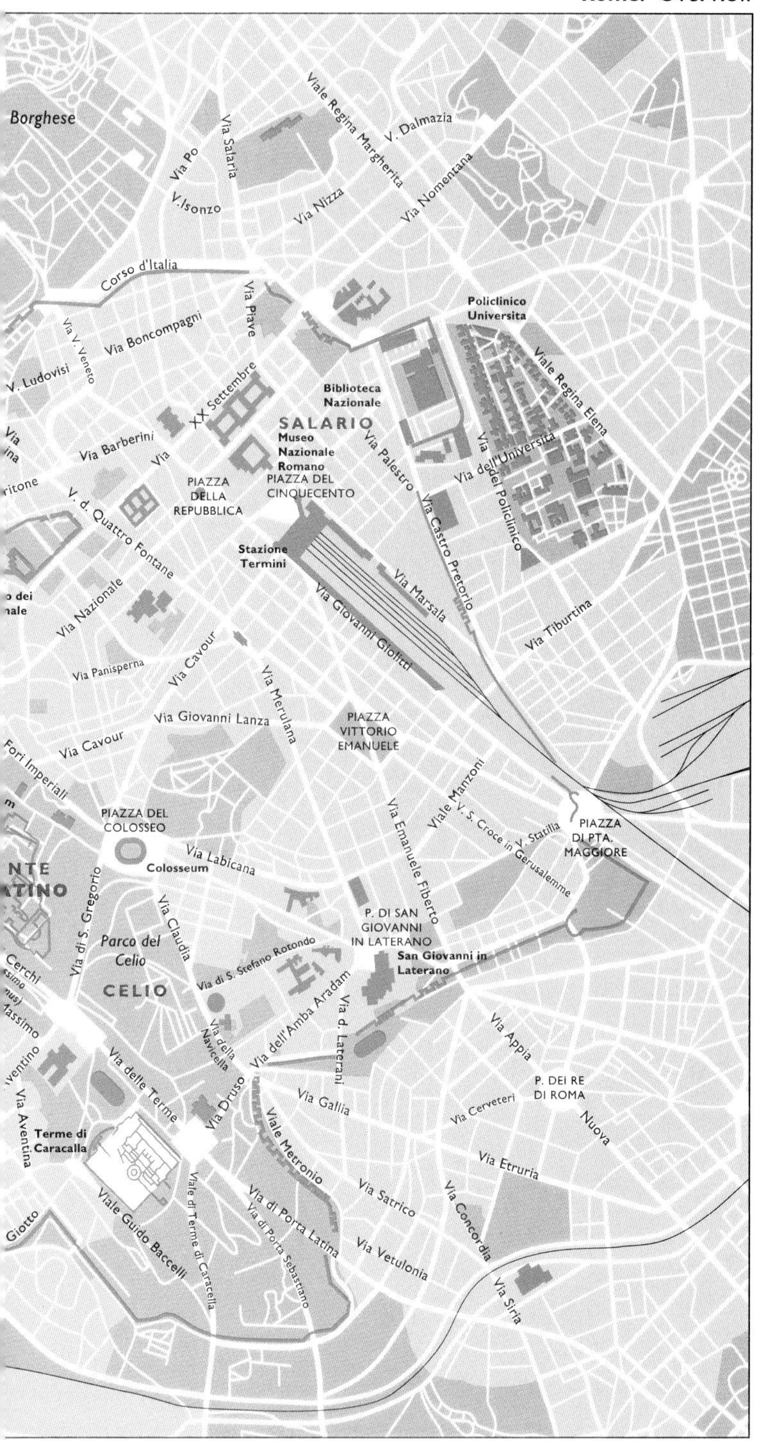
Borghese
Via Po
Via Salaria
Viale Regina Margherita
V. Dalmazia
V. Isonzo
Via Nizza
Via Nomentana
Corso d'Italia
Via Piave
Via V. Veneto
Via Boncompagni
V. Ludovisi
Policlinico Universita
Viale Regina Elena
Biblioteca Nazionale
XX Settembre
SALARIO
Museo Nazionale Romano
Via Palestro
Via dell'Università
Via del Policlinico
Via Barberini
PIAZZA DELLA REPUBBLICA
PIAZZA DEL CINQUECENTO
V. d. Quattro Fontane
Via Castro Pretorio
Stazione Termini
Via Marsala
Via Nazionale
Via Giovanni Giolitti
Via Tiburtina
Via Panisperna
Via Cavour
Via Merulana
Via Giovanni Lanza
PIAZZA VITTORIO EMANUELE
Fori Imperiali
Viale Manzoni
PIAZZA DEL COLOSSEO
V. S. Croce in Gerusalemme
V. Statilia
PIAZZA DI PTA. MAGGIORE
Via Labicana
Colosseum
Via Emanuele Filiberto
Via di S. Gregorio
Via Claudia
P. DI SAN GIOVANNI IN LATERANO
Parco del Celio
Via di S. Stefano Rotondo
San Giovanni in Laterano
CELIO
Via dell'Amba Aradam
Via d. Laterani
Via della Navicella
Via Appia
Via delle Terme
Via Druso
P. DEI RE DI ROMA
Via Gallia
Via Cerveteri
Nuova
Terme di Caracalla
Via Aventina
Viale Metronio
Via Etruria
Viale di Terme di Caracalla
Via di Porta Latina
Via Satrico
Via Concordia
Viale Guido Baccelli
Via di Porta Sebastiano
Via Vetulonia
Via Siria
Giotto

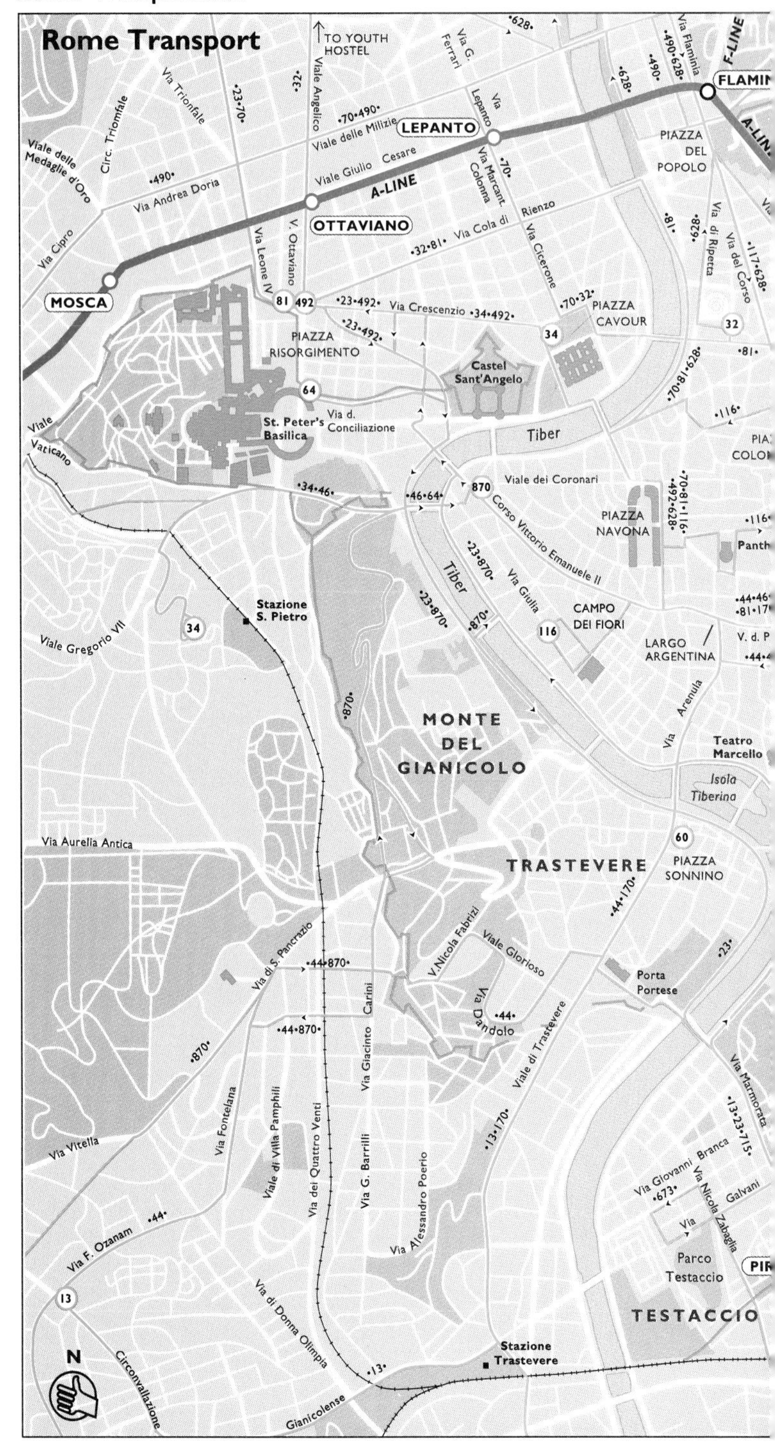
Rome Transport
TO YOUTH HOSTEL
LEPANTO
FLAMINIO
OTTAVIANO
MOSCA
A-LINE
F-LINE
PIAZZA DEL POPOLO
PIAZZA RISORGIMENTO
PIAZZA CAVOUR
Castel Sant'Angelo
St. Peter's Basilica
Tiber
PIAZZA NAVONA
CAMPO DEI FIORI
LARGO ARGENTINA
Stazione S. Pietro
MONTE DEL GIANICOLO
Teatro Marcello
Isola Tiberina
TRASTEVERE
PIAZZA SONNINO
Porta Portese
Parco Testaccio
TESTACCIO
Stazione Trastevere
Viale delle Milizie
Viale Giulio Cesare
Via Andrea Doria
Via Cola di Rienzo
Via Crescenzio
Via d. Conciliazione
Viale dei Coronari
Corso Vittorio Emanuele II
Via Giulia
Viale Gregorio VII
Via Aurelia Antica
Viale Trastevere
Via F. Ozanam
Circonvallazione Gianicolense
N

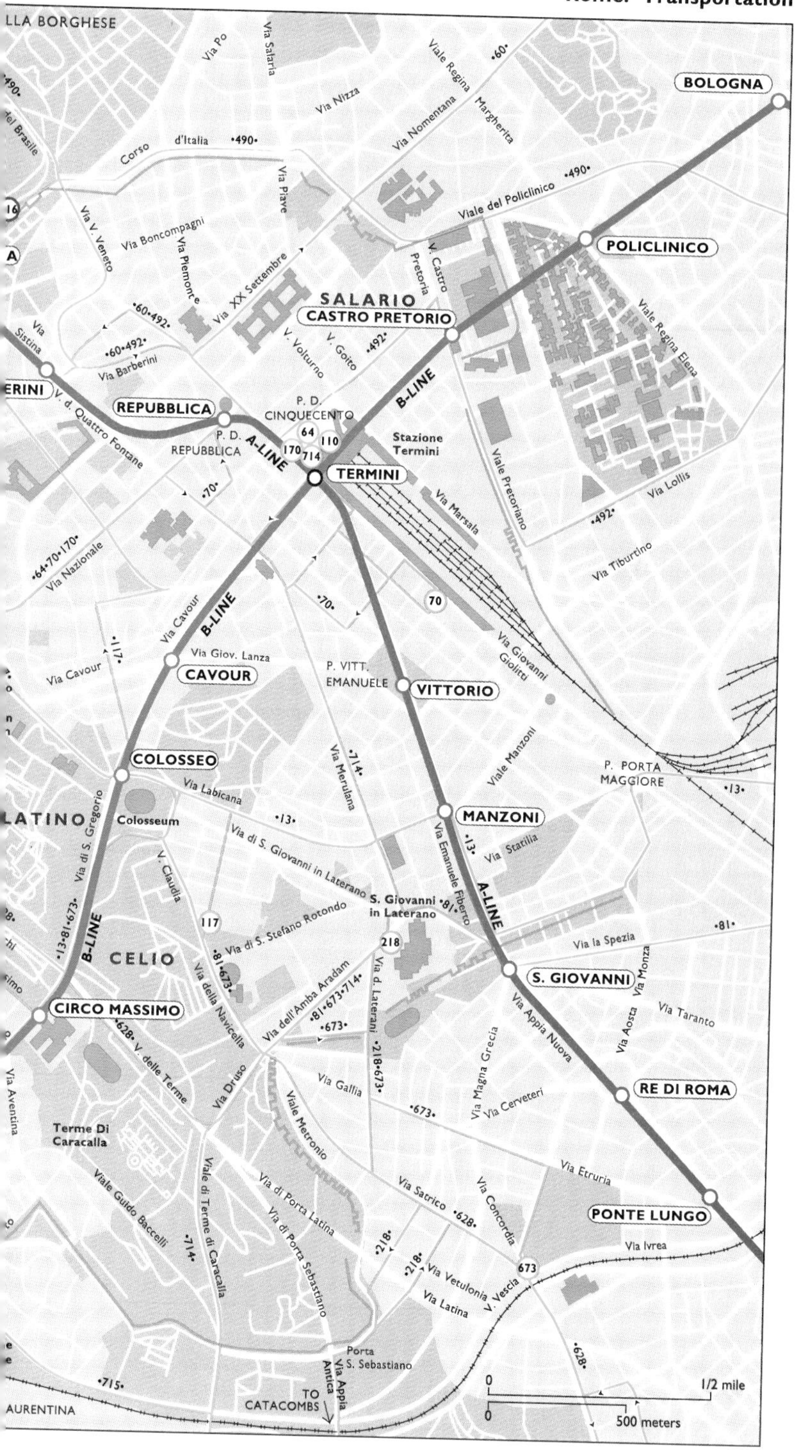

BOLOGNA
POLICLINICO
SALARIO
CASTRO PRETORIO
REPUBBLICA
TERMINI
CAVOUR
VITTORIO
COLOSSEO
MANZONI
S. GIOVANNI
CIRCO MASSIMO
RE DI ROMA
PONTE LUNGO
A-LINE
B-LINE
Stazione Termini
P. D. CINQUECENTO
P. D. REPUBBLICA
P. VITT. EMANUELE
P. PORTA MAGGIORE
S. Giovanni in Laterano
Colosseum
Terme Di Caracalla
Porta S. Sebastiano
TO CATACOMBS
CELIO
LATINO
Via Po
Via Salaria
Via Nizza
Via Nomentana
Viale Regina Margherita
Corso d'Italia
Via Piave
Viale del Policlinico
Via V. Veneto
Via Boncompagni
Via Piemonte
Via XX Settembre
V. Castro Pretoria
V. Volturno
V. Goito
Viale Regina Elena
Via Sistina
Via Barberini
V. d. Quattro Fontane
Via Marsala
Viale Pretoriano
Via Lollis
Via Tiburtino
Via Nazionale
Via Cavour
Via Giov. Lanza
Via Giovanni Giolitti
Via Merulana
Viale Manzoni
Via Labicana
Via di S. Giovanni in Laterano
Via di S. Gregorio
V. Claudia
Via Emanuele Filiberto
Via Statilia
Via la Spezia
Via Monza
Via Taranto
Via Aosta
Via Appia Nuova
Via di S. Stefano Rotondo
Via della Navicella
Via dell'Amba Aradam
Via d. Laterani
Via Gallia
Via Magna Grecia
Via Cerveteri
V. delle Terme
Via Druso
Viale Metronio
Via Etruria
Via Satrico
Via Concordia
Via Ivrea
Via Aventina
Viale Guido Baccelli
Viale di Terme di Caracalla
Via di Porta Latina
Via di Porta Sebastiano
Via Vetulonia
Via Latina
V. Vescia
Via Appia Antica
LLA BORGHESE
del Brasile
AURENTINA
0
1/2 mile
500 meters

Central Rome

Ara Pacis, 3
Campo dei Fiori, 27
Captioline Hill and Museums, 22
Castel Sant'Angelo, 9
Chiesa Nuova, 10
Il Gesù, 23
Galleria Corsini, 31
Galleria Doria Pamphilij, 19
Galleria Spada, 28
Mausoleum of Augustus, 4
Museo Barrocco, 26
Museo Mario Praz, 7
Museo Napoleonico, 7
Museo di Palazzo Venezia, 18
Palazzo di Giustizia, 8
Pantheon, 13
P. Farnese, 29
P. Navona, 11
P. del Popolo, 2
P. della Rotonda, 13
P. di Spagna, 5
P. Venezia, 20
Sant'Agnese in Agone, 11
Sant'Andrea delle valle, 25
Sant'Antonio dei Portoghesi, 6
Santi Apostoli, 17
Sant'Ignazio, 15
San Luigi dei Francesi, 12
San Marcello, 16
Santa Maria sopra Minerva, 14
Santa Maria del Popolo, 1
Spanish Steps, 5
Theater of Marcellus, 24
Trevi Fountain, 16
Villa Farnesina, 30
Vittorio Emanuele II Monument, 21

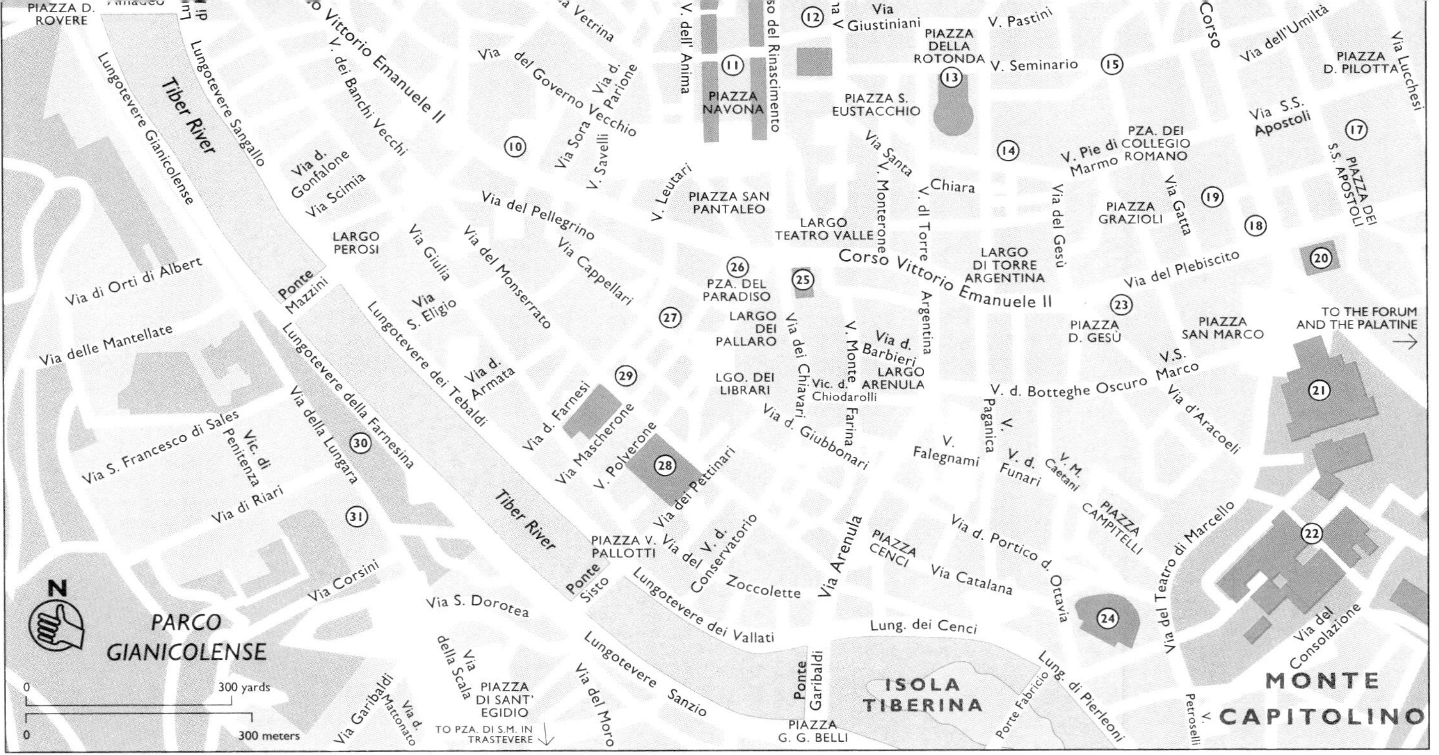
MONTE CAPITOLINO
TO THE FORUM AND THE PALATINE
Via Lucchesi
PIAZZA D. PILOTTA
PIAZZA DEI S.S. APOSTOLI
Via dell'Umiltà
Via S.S. Apostoli
Corso
PIAZZA SAN MARCO
Via del Plebiscito
Via Gatta
PZA. DEI COLLEGIO ROMANO
PIAZZA GRAZIOLI
V.S. Marco
Via d'Aracoeli
Via del Consolazione
Via del Teatro di Marcello
V. Petroselli
V. Pastini
V. Seminario
V. Pie di Marmo
Via del Gesù
PIAZZA D. GESÙ
V. d. Botteghe Oscuro
PIAZZA CAMPITELLI
V. M. Caetani
V. d. Funari
V. Paganica
LARGO DI TORRE ARGENTINA
Corso Vittorio Emanuele II
PIAZZA DELLA ROTONDA
Chiara
V. dl Torre
Argentina
Via Giustiniani
PIAZZA S. EUSTACCHIO
Via Santa
V. Monterone
LARGO TEATRO VALLE
Via d. Barbieri
LARGO ARENULA
V. Falegnami
Via d. Portico d. Ottavia
Via Catalana
PIAZZA CENCI
Lung. dei Cenci
Lung. di Pierleoni
Ponte Fabricio
ISOLA TIBERINA
V. Monte
Farina
Vic. d. Chiodarolli
Via d. Giubbonari
Via Arenula
Ponte Garibaldi
PIAZZA G. G. BELLI
so del Rinascimento
PIAZZA NAVONA
PIAZZA SAN PANTALEO
Via dei Chiavari
PZA. DEL PARADISO
LARGO DEI PALLARO
LGO. DEI LIBRARI
Via dei Pettinari
V. d. Conservatorio
Zoccolette
Lungotevere dei Vallati
V. dell' Anima
V. Leutari
Via Sora
Via d. Parione
V. Savelli
Via del Governo Vecchio
Via Vetrina
Via del Pellegrino
Via Cappellari
V. Polverone
Via Mascherone
Via d. Farnesi
PIAZZA V. PALLOTTI
Via del
Ponte Sisto
Lungotevere Sanzio
Via del Moro
Tiber River
Via del Monserrato
Via d. Armata
Via Giulia
Via S. Eligio
Lungotevere dei Tebaldi
Via S. Dorotea
Via della Scala
PIAZZA DI SANT' EGIDIO
TO PZA. DI S.M. IN TRASTEVERE
Vittorio Emanuele II
V. dei Banchi Vecchi
Via d. Gonfalone
Via Scimia
LARGO PEROSI
Ponte Mazzini
Lungotevere della Farnesina
Via della Lungara
Via Corsini
Via d. Mattonato
Via Garibaldi
Lungotevere Sangallo
Lungotevere Gianicolense
PIAZZA D. ROVERE
Via di Orti di Albert
Via delle Mantellate
Via S. Francesco di Sales
Vic. di Penitenza
Via di Riari
PARCO GIANICOLENSE
N
0
300 yards
300 meters

Rome: Villa Borghese

Villa Borghese
VILLA BORGHESE
GIARDINO ZOOLOGICO
Zoologico
Galleria Borghese
PIAZZALE DEI RAIMONDI
Galleria Naz. d'Arte Moderne
Museo Naz. di Villa Giulia
VILLA STROHL FERN
VILLA RUFFO
VILLA MEDICI
GALOPPATOIO
PIAZZA DI SIENA
PIAZZALE PAOLA BORGHESE
PIAZZALE DEL FIOCCO
PIAZZALE D. CANESTRE
PIAZZALE DEI MARTIRI
PIAZZALE BRASILE
PIAZZA E. SIENKIEWICZ
Porta Pinciana
PIAZZALE FLAMINIO
PIAZZA DEL POPOLO
PIAZZA AUGUSTO IMPERATORE
PIAZZA DELLA MARINA
PIAZZA DELLE CINQUE GIORNATE
PIAZZA MONTE GRAPPA
PIAZZA D. LIBERTA
PIAZZA COLA DI RIENZO
Fiume Tevere
Ponte d. Risorg
Ponte G. Matteotti
Ponte Nenni
Ponte Margherita
Flaminio
Spagna
Lepanto
A LINE
Corso d'Italia
V. Giovannelli
Giovanni Paisiello
Via Po
Via di S. Teresa
V. Puglia
V. Romagna
Via Boncompagni
Via Quintina
Via Piemonte
Via Sardegna
Via Sicilia
Via Toscana
Via Marche
Via Vittorio Veneto
Via Emilia
Via Aurora
Via Liguria
Via Ludovisi
Via Porta Pinciana
Via Pinciana
Viale Museo Borghese
V. Pupazzi
Viale dei Cavalli Marini
V. d. Pineta
Viale Goethe
V. di S. Paolo del Brasile
Viale Casina di Raffaello
Viale P. Canonica
Via S. Mercadante
Via P. Raimondi
Via dei Daini
Viale dell'Uccelliera
Viale del Giardino
Via Ulisse Aldrovandi
V. dell'Aranciera
V. F. Laguardia
Via d. Magnolie
Viale Galoppatoio
V. del Muro Torto
Via del Babuino
Via Omero
Via Bernadotte
Viale Madama
Viale delle Belle Arti
V. Washington
Viale Valadier
Viale d. Belvedere
Viale Trinità dei Monti
Via del Babuino
Via Vittoria
Via della Croce
Via del Corso
V. A. Canova
Via Ripetta
Via Brunetti
Via del Vantaggio
V. di S. Eugenio
Via di Villa Giulia
Via Flaminia
V. D. A. Azuni
V. G. Pisanelli
V. Romanosi
V. Disavoia
Via Savoia
Lungo. in Augusta
Lungo. d. Mellini
Lungo. Arnaldo da Brescia
Lungotevere delle Navi
Lungo. Michelangelo
Lungotevere delle Armi
Via Fed. Cesi
Via G. Belli
Via E. Q. Visconte
Via Valadier
Via dei Gracchi
Via Pompeo Magno
Via degli Scipioni
Via Giulio Cesare
Viale della Milizie
Via Settembrini
Viale Giuseppe Mazzini
Via Marc. Colonna
Via Boezio
Via Ezio
N
0 200 yards
0 200 meters